REDISCOVERING
JAPANESE SPACE

Redis

covering Japanese Space

by Kisho Kurokawa

New York • WEATHERHILL • *Tokyo*

*The publication of this book was assisted
by a grant from the Japan Foundation.*

First Edition, 1988

*Published by John Weatherhill, Inc., of New York and Tokyo, with editorial offices at 8–3
Nibancho, Chiyoda-ku, Tokyo 102, Japan. Copyright © 1988, by Kisho Kurokawa; all
rights reserved. Printed in Japan.*

Library of Congress Cataloging in Publication Data: Kurokawa, Kisho, 1934–   / Redis-
covering Japanese space. / Includes bibliography. / 1. Architecture—Japan—Aesthetics.
2. Architecture and society—Japan.   3. Metabolism in architecture (Movement)   4. Architecture, Modern—20th century—Japan.   5. Architecture—Philosophy. / I. Title. /
NA1550.K87   1988   720'.1   / 88–20523 / ISBN 0–8348–0224–4

Contents

Foreword

A great many critics and writers have recognized the complexity of the Japanese way of architecture. They have recorded the eclectic and hybrid nature of it and consistently reflected upon its richness and distinctive qualities. Even in its most Western-influenced moments it has, by some special chemistry, remained essentially different. Some would say it remains essentially and uniquely Japanese, Regrettably, I am not an expert on this phenomenon. I have never visited Japan and cannot read or write Japanese. Clearly I am at a disadvantage. However, I have ventured to write occasionally on Japanese architecture; I read and contribute to Japanese magazines. My own books have been published in Japan and I have also organized architectural and photographic exhibitions on Japanese topics. I have had the privilege of introducing Japanese speakers to British audiences, seen Japanese films, listened to Japanese music, worn Japanese clothes, drunk sake, eaten and admired Japanese food. I have also visited the work of Japanese architects and designers in the West. In the company of my late friend and colleague the architect and writer Chris Fawcett (d. Osaka 1986)—who shared my office at the *AA Quarterly* for four years—I helped originate and supervise a major study on *The New Japanese House* (London 1980) and together we prepared special features on Japanese architecture, rituals, and culture.

I record all the personal details not for mere curricula validation but because it reflects my own complex interest in and admiration for things Japanese. While I have not seen the buildings of some of the architects and designers I admire at first hand, I have spoken to them and corresponded with them about their projects over many years. It also puts my interest in and meager knowledge of Kisho Kurokawa's work into context. My "absentee" process of assimilating facts about Japanese personalities, buildings, projects, and movements has been consistently extended to Kisho Kurokawa's work. Like vessels in the night we have passed each other on foreign seas, briefly spoken together, lectured at the same forums, and communicated. Indeed, it is one of the most pleasant aspects of our great and profound profession that wherever architects go they acknowledge their debts to each other and to those places they visit, admire, and explore. Architects are part, in this sense, of a very special brotherhood; they enjoy a symbiotic relationship.

My comments, in introducing this collection of writings by Kurokawa, have to be tempered by the knowledge that they are written by an outsider looking in, by an admirer who looks on but who remains somewhat like a chef who is unable to taste the dish he is about to concoct!

Clearly, Japan has been—as the editors of a broad survey in a recent issue of *Time* magazine have indicated—experiencing a new golden age in architecture and design. This golden period comes at the end of another lengthy transitional phase. Like an earlier transitional period which was referred to by Frank Lloyd Wright as so fundamental that it influenced the whole of Japanese life, technology, and art, the new phase has been universally recognized. One of the important aspects of the transition in architecture of the 1920s which Wright isolated was concerned with the change from "wood to masonry": "I believe", he wrote, "I could show them how to build an earthquake-proof-masonry." He did. In so doing he invented the "waiters tray" form of construction at the center of which was a basic cantilever principle. It was consolidated as a means of both expression and construction in his famous Imperial Hotel in Tokyo.

Notwithstanding the accumulation of interest in the work of Le Corbusier in Japan in the period after World War II and also in the growing regard for Louis Kahn's buildings the legacy of Frank Lloyd Wright has remained clear. Although block masonry was superseded by an adventurous use of reinforced concrete, Wright's influence was much wider in substance than a contribution to the use of building materials. His work was received as a way to a new architecture and as a means of architectural expression. It was confident, clear in its conception, and thoroughly innovative. It is surprising that it has not been much more imitated. One must therefore conclude that, along with the work of Wright's brilliant assistant Antonin Raymond, its influence was more theoretical than imitative.

Perhaps people of my generation in Britain who had recognized the importance of the Wright association with Japan and had also observed the beginnings of a new and possibly even more fruitful bond with Le Corbusier and Kahn had also felt that the new Japanese work had found a way of creating a new round of International Architecture. The early work of Kenzo Tange justified this confidence. It was widely reported and admired. We watched eagerly as this reawakening of Modern Architecture (we dared not at that time refer to it as Modernism) took hold in Japan. But I should add that this was not a kind of colonial paternalism— nor a regional bias, for that matter—that applauded the Japanese for adopting Western ways and ideas. Rather, it was seen as a vindication of the universalist zeal we all shared for a modern attitude to architecture. It was stimulated by the "Group" discussions of the period which themselves reflected a youthful, intellectually based internationalism. It also, in my view, took the searchlight beam away from Europe and the United States and swung it onto Japanese art and culture, which had been veiled for so many of us for years by both the noble mysteries of Zen and the filters of war. The aperture was widening. Of course, Japanese architecture had never been entirely isolated, although it had been obscured for many by its Zen bases. However, besides the things that Wright had written about it there were other books by Cram and Harada and statements by Bruno Taut, who had spoken and written (in English) with great reverence of the inspiration of Japanese architectural culture. Antonin Raymond's work also gave it a special relevance to my generation—an issue of the *AA Journal* was published on his work, edited by one of my own *AA* tutors, John Killick, in the early 1960s. All of this was played off against a background of the rapidly growing importance of Japanese consumer goods in the European market place and the increasing relevance of Japanese film, art, and architectural publications as the country's growing economic supremacy became apparent.

Charles Jencks, in his introduction to Kurokawa's earlier book *Metabolism in Architecture* (1977), paid tribute to the growth of the new Japanese architecture movements and to their theoretical background. I am tempted to outline my own received knowledge of that history but that would seem unnecessarily repetitive. Perhaps I should dwell on what has happened since that book was published and on the more recent changes that now appear to have taken place.

Both in Japan and in the Western countries there has been an unmistakeable shift in architectural attitudes and values. While many of us still advocate the tenets of the so-called Modern Movement there could be no doubt that these have now to be tempered by new attitudes. The speculative nature of Postmodernism (or *Past*-modernism, as it is now rapidly becoming known) and the influence of conservation and preservation are of great significance, as are reflections on ancient and traditional forms, reinterpreted through modern methods and materials. Whereas, "Concrete, Le Corbusier plus Modernism" may have been a reasonable argument in earlier decades, when there was a demand for more sculptural buildings and a natural development in the refinement of an elegant International Style, the new condition has brought us abruptly back to the problem of urban context and to the condition of the city. In the wider landscape, the relationship of what there is to "what there will be," and indeed to the whole patchwork or collaging process that gives comprehensibility to the urban scene, is now within the purview of the architect. Vision has been taken over by practical need. For some architects this has weakened the innovative drive but to others it has opened up daring possibilities. On the one hand it has led to the development of irregular and ambiguous forms of expression and to the dissolution of the plan; on the other, to technical virtuosity. There is some evidence that architects have found in their new love for rhetoric and wry humour—even for ironic statements—a fondness too for the more traditional visual and tactile qualities of handicraft buildings.

In the heyday of the Neomodern there was, both in Japan and in the West, a kind of counterpoint between the new and the old. Now we can detect a notable respect for the past and a desire to harmonize with it more closely and less con-

trapuntally. Although there is now still a shifting focus which allows a wide variation of architectural attitudes—to theory, style, and expression—a much closer
dialogue between users, designers, and the physical environment is possible. Nowhere is this multivalent, symbiotic attitude more apparent than in Kisho Kurokawa's more recent work. Perhaps that searchlight beam I spoke of earlier should
be held on his more recent writings as they clearly indicate the shift in attitudes
I also spoke about, They possess a sharpness of detail that we have now come to
expect in Japanese theory. In pursuing an architecture of symbiosis it soon becomes
clear that culture and artefact, site, symbols, meaning, learning, and the latitude
afforded by today's expressive freedoms provide a stronger basis for ideas and
their practical demonstration than the cult of personalities or such stylistic pretensions as Postmodernism or High Tech. Through this more intelligent and re-
spectably intellectual endeavour the poetics of our great art can more comfortably
cohabit not only with techniques but with form and empathetic feelings as well.
Materials, as Kurokawa himself insists, can then be seen to be a potent force in
the presentation of a building's envelope—not monolithic as the Modern masters
decreed—and can amiably coexist and contribute to the three-dimensional whole.
An understanding of, as well as an interpretative desire for, history to invade the
present and to offer up its own traditional values and means of expression is of
course behind such views.

Other views expressed in this book of original and perceptive essays reflect upon
the unique circumstances of the vast contemporary urban conglomerates, particularly Tokyo. When the now famous Tokyo Bay scheme was published in the West
it was welcomed as another master key to urban renewal, a concept capable of
interpretation and a strong and perfect symbiosis of past and future. Inspired by
this project and such important historical precedents as the inhabited and highly
built-up London Bridge (finally removed from its original site in 1825) and the
great MARS Plan for London (1938) by Korn and Samuely, a group of Liverpool
architects, including myself, designed an island city on the nearby Dee estuary;
other schemes appeared for the Ribble and the Wash. When Tokyo Bay appeared
it offered us the reassurance that we had not produced work of a deliberately sen-
sationalist or controversial kind, as the British press claimed, but were sharing
contemporaneous ideas. This was the beginning of the high regard I now feel for
Japanese ideas and designs, particularly those that have stressed a desire for ex-
perimentation and the welfare of people. Thus, it is immensely gratifying to see
Kurokawa again absorbed in a long-term discussion on the symbiotic nature of
urban philosophy with the New Tokyo Plan 2025. Not, as he says, to make some
new "city of symbiosis," but to draw out rich, deep, organic, and inorganic human
physiological and psychological qualities.

With these facts, the reconsideration of the city as an ambiguous, (dis)ordered,
naturally grown, labyrinthine organism becomes a tenable proposition. Architecture then finds its place within that context completing a greater symbiotic relationship with urban needs. As the new challenges of city planning move from the

core and the special suburb to the new development locations—the bay, the water-front, the motorway corridor—it is this kind of thinking and the way he and his colleagues design that will set new precedents and give new meanings to the rich ambiguities Kisho Kurokawa desires.

DENNIS SHARP

REDISCOVERING
JAPANESE SPACE

Introduction

M y THINKING has been shaped in many ways by the course of my personal development. Looking back as far as early childhood, I recognize certain influences, and in some cases, the very prime matter of ideas that have occupied me throughout my career.

My own family background is a good place to start. First of all, my father was an architect. Upon graduation from the architecture curriculum of Nagoya Vocational Academy (present-day Nagoya Technical University), he entered the employ of the architectural section of the Aichi prefectural government, where he continued working up until the end of the war. Though an official by profession, he also displayed talent in oil painting, and, judging from a recent retrospective held in Nagoya, he was a fairly accomplished artist. My mother belonged to the Saiga family. Her elder brother, my uncle, was a literary scholar specializing in *waka* poetry. His lifework, a source book on *waka* called *Saiga Bunko,* was recently granted a cultural award by the city of Nagoya.

My earliest memories are of the neighborhood in Nagoya's Showa ward where I was born. At the time, Nagoya still bore traces of the original city plan of the Edo period (1600–1868), which resembled that of Edo (now Tokyo) itself, particularly in the Buddhist temple district just east of the center of town. In both cities, streets were the seat of civic life. Neighborhoods were defined not by block, but by street; the households facing each other on either side of the street made up one neighborhood. In Edo, core back-lot areas not facing onto the street were called *kaisho,* or "meeting places." In Nagoya, such vacant spaces behind the street fronts were initially conceived as sites for temples, and the narrow passageways leading into the temples were called *kansho,* meaning idle or median places. Gradually, however, this scheme spread to the planning of most residential areas. A blind passageway ran up the middle of the block, and houses faced in toward the passageway as well as out onto the main streets. These passageways also came to be called *kansho.*

3

The house we lived in around the time I was born, if I remember correctly, was at the dead end of one such *kansho,* on the left side. That blind passageway was where I played. Even now I can picture that open space very clearly. Somehow the image of that *kansho* seems tied in with my interest in urban space; that, and what I recall of my grandfather's tearoom where I did my schoolwork when we took refuge in the country during the worst part of the war. Nagoya was bombed rather heavily by B-29s. I must have been in the third grade when we started having air-raid drills. Eventually it was decided that the family should move out to the town of Kaniecho, where my grandfather lived. My grandfather's house was fairly old, parts dating back to the mid-Edo period. He himself was town landlord, and owned river-front property where he had a tearoom and a pavilion for receiving guests. Indeed, after the war, my grandfather's house became the scene of many a social gathering, a salon for literati as it were. My grandfather, it seems, was a cultivated gentleman, and writers and poets the likes of Kan Kikuchi and Eiji Yoshikawa, not to mention the tea master Sogo Matsuo, frequented the place year round. Furthermore, my grandfather had responsibilities as lay parish leader for the local temple, so there were always Buddhist clergy about.

It was Sogo Matsuo who designed the tearoom on the property, Mushin'an, which means Hut of No-Mind. In addition, Yoshitsuan, the Hut of Accommodating Knees, an especially fine example of a mid-Edo-period tearoom, was built directly onto the main house. Yoshitsuan became my study and bedroom from middle school on, thanks to which every architectural detail, the very scale of tearoom space, is ingrained into my being.

Immediately after the war, my father established an architectural office in Nagoya's Showa ward. The smoke was still rising from the rubble when we returned, so we had to prepare the site for the building ourselves, my brother and I pitching in. My father then commuted back and forth to the new office while the family stayed in Kaniecho. Those were demanding times for architects, and my father, who was perhaps forty at the time, was driven by the realization that it was up to him to see the city rebuilt. Young as I was, I could not help but be impressed with his enthusiasm and commitment. I remember thinking how important architects were, and I'd made up my mind, without a doubt, to become an architect myself. Of course, since I was a small child I'd always liked drawing pictures and building things.

Meanwhile, my schooling proceeded. I attended Tokai Middle School, a private boys' school run by the Pure Land sect of Buddhism—the same school from which my father had graduated. It was an interesting and unique school, with a long history dating back to the late Edo period. Almost all the teachers were priests and the rules were very strict: unless your grades were good, you couldn't wear *geta* clogs or grow your hair long, two privileges much coveted by us all. Nonetheless, the atmosphere was nothing like the intensely conformist prep schools of today. The school prided itself on its easy-going pace and there were many individualists, real characters, among my classmates. There was plenty of time for extracurricular activities; I myself was in the debate society and even went in for drama.

When I entered my first year of high school, the renowned mathematician of prime and periodic number theory, Goro Azumaya, then assistant professor at Nagoya University—since become a professor at Princeton University—taught at our school. I had the greatest admiration for him and almost "apprenticed" myself to him, not only taking his theoretical mathematics classes for three years running, but even going to his house for a tutorial three times a week. All this had absolutely no bearing on the university entrance examinations awaiting me; theoretical mathematics seemed a kind of aesthetic to me. I was fascinated that such beauty could come of so purely theoretical bases. This has stayed with me: even today I have a certain infatuation with mathematics. I truly enjoy working with numbers, making calculations, and computer programming.

When it came time to think about higher education, a number of things steered me toward Kyoto University. Prominent on my father's bookshelves were works by John Ruskin and William Morris, collected volumes on art, and art magazines, as well as books and magazines related to architecture. But the book that really caught my eye was a book by Uzo Nishiyama entitled *The Dwelling of the Future* (*Kore kara no Sumai*), which sported a promotional cover wrap-around proclaiming it winner of the Mainichi Publishing Award. Up to that point, the only background in architecture I'd received from my father was some training in drawing and sketching. I saw architecture as art, so my image of becoming an architect meant first becoming accomplished at rendering. My encounter with Nishiyama's book was a shock. It awakened me to the social role of architecture. Based mainly on surveys he'd conducted of farming and fishing villages, Nishiyama advocated an approach to architecture with social consciousness. This called my attention to the problems in my own thinking up to then, yet at the same time it also confirmed my belief in the importance of the architect. I knew I would have to learn about the structure of society and its discrepancies and contradictions. I was an impressionable youth, to say the least, and I absorbed Nishiyama's ideas right down to the paper they were printed on. In any case, my mind was made up that I wanted to study under him at Kyoto University.

My father was not entirely in favor of my selection. Tokyo University and Tokyo Technical University were better known for architecture. I also remember him recommending Waseda University. But my heart was set on Kyoto University and Nishiyama. In retrospect, I think I made the right choice. I already enjoyed drawing and sketching, and left on my own I might have been creative enough, but my study under Nishiyama at Kyoto University gave me much more stringent training, because I had to assimilate things that were entirely new to me. From the time I was still in freshman general education I was reading every architecture book I could get my hands on, frequenting Nishiyama's office, and helping out with survey research. I still remember that when we were conducting a study toward bettering living conditions in the residential area in front of Kyoto Station, we actually took up living there to better grasp the realities of the situation.

At the time, Kyoto University was a hotbed of student activism, and I was a member of the steering committee for the engineering department. Through Professor Nishiyama's seminar I came in contact with student movements and future participants in the Japan Architecture Students Congress. We were all very occupied with social concerns. Being in Kyoto, we also tended to observe the goings-on in Tokyo with a certain measure of objectivity and oblique curiosity, out of a combination of a sense of detached superiority and the inferiority complex we had toward the debates and movements in Tokyo. This was around the time Kenzo Tange, Kunio Maekawa, and the MIDO Group were making a splash with their bold projects and competitions and international works. It was an extremely dramatic period and I seemed to be watching it from the sidelines. Despite Nishiyama's criticisms of these rising star "artist" architects, I found myself secretly attracted to the artist's role, and I struggled to resolve this dichotomy within me.

Ultimately, however, the deciding factor for me was that I began to take a good look at Nishiyama's works. He was quite active with numerous projects, hardly covered in the media, yet I was hard pressed to see any real connection between his ideological populism and his actual works. He was a leader of one trend of postwar Japanese architectural thought, but my realization that he was not a creator led me more and more toward Tokyo. For although Tange's work had been the prime target of Nishiyama's criticisms, all along I had kept one eye on Tange. I read everything Tange wrote from cover to cover, studied photographs of his buildings and him at work, and acquired an admiration for him as a creator. My observations combined with Nishiyama's criticisms and made me want to go to Tange and to see for myself, to check out firsthand the criticisms Nishiyama leveled against him. Thus my leap from Kyoto University to graduate work at Tokyo University.

My first responsibilities there were doing furniture layout toward the final stages of the Tokyo Metropolitan Government Building. The sculptor Taro Okamoto had designed some impossible chairs for the lobby, and I executed life-size drawings and a plan for their placement. Next, I helped out at Tange's office with drafting the plans for Isamu Noguchi's garden for UNESCO in Paris. And after that, I worked on several more comprehensive projects together with Arata Isozaki, who was also a graduate student under Tange. There was the overall plan for the Tokyo Metropolitan Government Building, followed by the Tokyo Project 1960 and the Floating City Project, both of which were relatively far removed from actual planning. Isozaki's presence in Tange's seminar was very stimulating for me. I'm sure we were both difficult students.

The so-called G Group formed around this time. The seven young architects in it—Mera Koichi, Nobuhiro Nogami, Hidehiko Saito, Kazue Matsuno, Kiyoshi Nishimura, Tomoko Nishino, and myself—were mainly friends from the Architecture Students Congress I'd chaired back in my Kyoto University days. We entered competitions as a team. Our first entry was in an asphalt-slate housing competition, and we won an honorable mention. The following year we monopolized first and second prizes and honorable mention. We then went on to participate in the design competition for the Toronto City Hall. Fully licensed first-class architects were competing, so I used my father's name in applying. Fifteen proposals made it to the final judging, the only two from Japan being those of the G Group and Kunio

Maekawa. Thus, without actually belonging to any professional planning team, there we were in Tange's seminar, Isozaki and I, actively at work in the world outside.

In 1958, exactly two years after my arrival in Tokyo, the Fifth World Architecture Students Congress was held in Moscow. Thanks to the backing I received from Ikuzo Kitano, my senior at the Japan Students Congress, from the president of the Shimizu Construction Company, and from contributions by members of the Japan Students Congress, I was able to attend. This was my first trip overseas, so of course it was an extremely stimulating experience. Back in the 1950s, it was almost unheard of for anyone to go abroad, except, perhaps, for university professors attending conferences or government officials on diplomatic missions; overseas vacations were simply out of the question. To have been able to travel—and to Moscow no less—had a great impact on me.

As the name suggests, the World Architecture Students Congress was a fullfledged international conference. Even so, few countries sent formal representatives. I remember being overwhelmed at the reception I got for representing the Japan Architecture Students Congress, then being really astounded when they selected me of all people to chair the Congress. It was my first experience to even participate in an international function, and here I was expected to attend to each and every country's participants. It was a trying but eye-opening experience. There were students from Syria, Egypt, China, West Germany, France—twenty-seven countries in all.

I was involved with the Congress for about a month, and on the way back to Japan I spent another month or so traveling through Northern Europe—a very rewarding experience. But before that, I stayed on a while in the Soviet Union to learn what I could about the advanced practical research on the prefab architecture of large factory-produced panels. Upon returning to Japan I assembled the materials I had gathered to publish my first book, *Prefab Housing* (*Purehabu Jutaku*, Jutaku Kenkyusha, 1958). Despite my youth, I was later able to make repeated trips to the Soviet Union, attending both the World Architecture Students Congress in Leningrad and the General Assembly of the UIA (Union Internationale des Architectes) held in Moscow. Again, upon my return I published translations of reports from each attending country as a series of articles in *International Architecture* (*Kokusai Kenchiku*) entitled "The Present State of Urban Planning Around the World" (*"Sekai Shokoku no Toshi Keikaku no Genjo"*), as well as writing essays for other architectural magazines.

These activities came to the attention of Noboru Kawazoe, then chief editor of *The Japan Architect (Shinkenchiku)*, and I began helping him with preparations for the World Design Conference held in Japan in 1960. Through this connection I came in contact with architects Masato Otaka, Fumihiko Maki, Kiyonori Kikutake, graphic designer Kiyoshi Awazu, industrial designer Kenji Ekuan, and photographer Shomei Tono, and together we founded the Metabolist Group. This was at a point when I was trying to decide whether to go ahead with doctoral studies. As it turned out, however, I was granted a scholarship to continue under Tange at the doctoral level, though in fact I was to find myself more involved with Metabolist Group endeavors than with actual drafting work.

Then in 1961 I received an invitation from the Team Ten group of Peter and Alison Smithson, Jacob B. Bakema, and Georges Candilis, upcoming leaders—a generation apart from the likes of Tange, Louis Kahn, Gio Ponti, and Ernesto Rogers—who were drawing young architects around them with their bold, new stance. James Stirling, Hans Hollein, Christopher Alexander, and Charles Jencks had already been invited to join their circle. And when Team Ten held a conference in 1962 at Royaumont Convent on the outskirts of Paris, I made a presentation on the Kyoto Nishijin Labor project and inclusive Nishijin district redevelopment plan I was working on at the time. I also presented a paper entitled "The Architecture of the Street" (*Michi no Kenchiku*), written in conjunction with the Nishijin Labor Center article I published in *The Japan Architect*. In it I argued that the Western concept of the public square would inevitably be superseded by the Eastern concept of street space.

The Royaumont Conference proved instrumental in steering me in my own direction, because I was able to confirm that my ideas were communicable to other architects around the world and I could go on to pursue my own special interests in the area of comparative culture and Oriental spatial concepts.

Furthermore, the acquaintances I made then were a compass to guide me through the world. At that time, no one in Japan except Tange had such international ties. Thereafter, whenever I traveled abroad I tried to keep in touch with my Western colleagues and stay abreast of their efforts. And in 1960, at the New York Museum of Modern Art's exhibition of unrealized "Visionary Architecture" by twenty-five world architects, Kikutake's City Over the Sea Project and my own grid-plan Agricultural City Project rubbed shoulders with works by such major international figures as Sant'Elia, Le Corbusier, and Frank Lloyd Wright.

Soon the time arrived for me to stand on my own feet, and I decided to establish my own office. In 1962 I submitted an official business registration, but of course no work came my way at first, so it was by no means a functioning office. There was no staff; in fact, all I had was an office on paper. After a brief stint shuffling from place to place among quarters loaned to me by senior architect friends, I converted one room of my apartment in Sendagaya into a studio of sorts, but it was so cramped that I had no space for a chair or drafting table. I would sit on my bed with a drawing on my lap. With no work coming in, I gave myself a project to work on each month—let's say this month I'd been commissioned to do the Tokyo Metropolitan Government Building within certain parameters—and I'd actually work it up.

How, then, did I manage to support myself? I still had my scholarship, for one thing, and then there were commissions for translating German architectural papers or writing newspaper and magazine columns—much of which went to paying the architecture students who helped me. In an article I wrote for *The Japan Architect*, I was already speaking of "information," "entropy," "energy savings" and "intermediate spaces," key terms that were to become catchwords from the latter half of the 1960s into the 1970s. I still had no realized projects, but since I was actively writing and producing plans, I was becoming known. I was even written up in the series "This Year's Hope" in the *Asahi Shimbun* newspaper as an architect to watch. The article touted me as an internationally renowned young architect without, as yet, any actual works—which won me some sympathy, it seems, because not much later the president of Nitto Foods came to ask me to do a project for them. Thus, my very first work after becoming an independent architect was the design for the Nitto Foods cannery at Sagae in northern Yamagata Prefecture.

Somewhere around that time I completed plans for the Nishijin Labor Center, as well as the Shiga Residence, a private home. Then, thanks to my work on the Nitto Foods plant, I was given an additional commission to do the Sagae City Hall. Strangely enough, absolutely no work came my way via either my father's architectural office or that of my teacher, Tange. Still, I went on to draft plans for the Lake Ira Public Rest Village and Yamagata Resort Center, while even popular periodicals such as *Asahi Journal* were beginning to write up my works.

By the Tokyo Olympics in 1964, I had become particularly prophetic in my own writings. My book *Urban Design (Toshi Dezain)* came out around that time, as did my articles "The Architecture of the Street—On Street Space" (*"Michi no Kenchiku—Michi Kukanron"*) in *Architectural Culture (Kenchiku Bunka)* and "An Oriental Homeopathic Scheme of Urban Planning" (*"Kampo Chiryoteki Toshi Keikaku"*) serialized in the journal *Science Asahi (Kagaku Asahi)*. Predictions I made then have generally all come to pass.

It was already the latter half of the 1960s when I wrote *Homo Movens,* and by then my horizons had expanded to fields beyond architecture. I was involved with Tadao Umesao and other Kyoto University scholars, not to mention such pioneering futurologists as professor of social engineering Yujiro Hayashi, columnist Junnosuke Kishida, and scientist Noboru Makino. I believe we were the first to even use the word "futurology" in Japan. In this futurologists' group, I was always the one to raise general issues—"information society," "entropy," "post-industrial society," and the like—for the notion of "information-space" seemed crucial in defining the invisible dimensions of the city and of society at large. These discussions with specialists outside of the field of architecture had a great influence on me, and the Institute for Social Engineering (Shakai Kogaku Kenkyujo), which I head, also had its origins among these contacts.

On into the 1970s, I began to sense the limitations of studio architecture, and at the same time I feared for the survival of the studio architect in the new information-age society. The situation called for casting off the role of studio architect and establishing a new type of planning workshop, and for a five-year period from 1970 on I put all my energies toward this reorganization. Once again, I entered a period where my contacts outside the world of architecture expanded dramatically. One after another I met with talented persons in diverse fields through participation on such panels as the National Railway Advisory Board (1970), Ministry of Construction Housing Committee (1970), Bureau of Science and Technology

Review Board (1971), Ministry of Education Metropolitan School Architecture Study Group (1971), Tokyo Metropolitan Government Main Building Construction Commission (1971), Japan Foundation Administrative Commission (1972), Policy Science Study Group (1972), and Ministry of Welfare Social Security Long-term Planning Discussion Group (1973). Even today, I continue this line of cross-disciplinary activity.

Still, after five years, I felt a renewed pull toward architecture. I began to reflect that my contacts within architecture were becoming all too few. It was time for me to make a more concerted effort in my own field. Around 1975 I made a strong renewal of my commitment to architecture. I cut back sharply on publications and concentrated all my energies on architecture—as I continue to do today. The Japan Red Cross Headquarters, Ishikawa Welfare Annuity Hall, and Head Offices of the Fukuoka Bank were all projects I undertook at the time. With the completion of these new works on into the latter half of the 1970s, I once again became involved with overseas exhibitions and speeches, although I had actively participated and won prizes in competitions abroad from the beginning of the 1970s: Peru (1969), Centre Pompidou (1971), Tanzania (1972), and Abu Dhabi (1975). It was around then that I attended the Aspen International Design Conference.

Meanwhile, from 1968 or so, I'd also started having opportunities to realize urban planning projects. The first of these was the Hishino New Town Project in Aichi Prefecture, followed by the Shonan Life Town Project in Fujisawa, Kanagawa Prefecture. Back in the days of my Sendagaya office, I had a staff of ten to fifteen people—small enough that we could all pile into a microbus and head out to construction sites—but by the time of Expo 70 in Osaka, that number had reached close to fifty. Toward the late 1970s, our number was up to one hundred, and we were doing the basic concept and design for such large contracts as the Sapporo, Karuizawa, Shimoda, and Akasaka Prince Hotels, the Takadanobaba Big Box athletic center, and, occasionally, comprehensive redevelopment projects such as the one for the area in front of Kawasaki Station.

For a while, many of the ties I had made with figures in the fields of graphic design and architecture through international conferences during the 1960s seemed to fall by the wayside, victims, perhaps, of the shifts in values that occurred during the years of rapid economic growth in the early 1970s. But by the late 1970s, when I decided to make a return to architecture, I realized that even relations that seemed to be dormant were easily reactivated, and also that one of the major effects of those international activities was to reinforce ties across an entire generation between persons in a variety of disciplines. For me, the most important achievement of the 1960s and 1970s was the creation of very human channels of interdisciplinary communication between professionals in the more "intangible" fields of endeavor, from politicians, writers, and philosophers to architects working in form and environment. New things, new ideas and creative activity occur when people from different backgrounds come together. Looking back on the cultural movements of the turn of the century and the 1920s, we can see that it was the gathering in the salons and cafes of people from different backgrounds that gave birth to the Art Nouveau and Jungendstil movements. This is true in every age. If the 1980s bring forth something new, I believe it will have again sprung from interdisciplinary contacts first established in preceding decades.

When I am overworked, the very first place I turn to recharge my energies is contact with persons of other disciplines. My second source of renewal is reading. I make a conscious, concentrated effort to gather information, taking notes as I go. The stimulation from working outside Japan is also a major source of rejuvenating energy. But it is impossible to overlook one other activity as a major organizing and clarifying principle in my life and my work, and that is writing.

I often wonder what kind of building Aristotle might have designed, if he had been so inclined. Or Descartes, or Sartre. It may be impossible to communicate the entirety of their philosophies through architecture, but there can be no denying that architecture can express, at least in part, a philosophy, a way of thinking.

The same can be said of literature. For writers and for readers, whether consciously or unconsciously, the city, the town, is an indispensable setting, without which literature would be impossible. To put it another way, philosophy and literature are clearly both architectures, but invisible architectures, invisible spaces.

My aim to create an architecture that is philosophy, is literature, is not unrelated to the Japanese cultural tradition, which has always valued the invisible, the imagination. From that point of view, I do not regard the design of architecture—the realization of material objects—as my sole task. Writing is also an extremely important part of my work.

Very few works of the Italian Futurists were ever realized. Most exist only in the form of the Futurists's manifestos or as sketches. Yet the impact of the unrealized works has been so great that it is difficult to measure. My own writings have spanned a wide variety of subjects, including philosophy, urban planning, culture, art, and history (especially the Edo period of Japanese history). These writings cannot be separated from my architectural works.

My architectural designs from the 1960s to the beginning of the 1970s were closely linked to the philosophy of the Metabolist movement. From the late 1970s to the late 1980s, they have been intimately connected to the philosophy of symbiosis. I believe that there is a philosophical link between those two periods and the ideas that dominated them, though the emphasis is different. My architectural works from those two periods—from 1960 to the late 1970s and from then to now—show a definite evolution. What I have set down in the present book is the thought, the philosophy, that is an integral, inseparable part of my work, especially in the last decade.

It will be helpful, I believe, to provide readers with an overview of my thought as an introduction to this book. I will take up again many of the topics I briefly touch on here, and at the same time, for those familiar with my writings at various stages in the development of my thoughts on architecture, I offer an interpretation, from my present vantage point—the philosophy of symbiosis—of that evolution.

I first began to use the phrase "the concept of symbiosis" (*kyosei no shiso*) in 1980. My interest in the idea began when I was serving as the chairman of the Yokohama Design Conference, the main theme of which was "Toward the Era of Symbiosis." But as early as the 1960s I had been using the words "the concept of coexistence" (*kyoson no shiso*). One of the chapters in a book I published in the Kinokuniya Shoten Shinsho series in the early 1960s, *Urban Design (Toshi Dezain)*, was titled "The Philosophy of Coexistence." The idea of symbiosis, in one form or another, has been my most basic conviction over the years since that time.

The early sixties were also marked by my involvement with the Metabolist movement, and I will discuss the relationship between symbiosis and Metabolism soon, but let me say here that as I interpret it, Metabolism is an Eastern, primarily Buddhist concept. At its base is the philosophy of symbiosis. I remember reading with great interest around the time we launched the Metabolist movement *The Way of Thinking of Eastern Peoples* by Hajime Nakamura of Tokyo University. Nakamura's work, which is well known in its English translation, traces the evolution of Buddhism as it was transmitted from India, its land of origin, to Tibet, Thailand, China, Korea, and finally Japan. He investigates the way in which the Buddhist scriptures were translated from Sanskrit and Pali into other Asian languages and explores the changes that took place in Buddhism as it encountered other peoples and cultures. The purpose of Nakamura's study was to illuminate the various Buddhist-influenced civilizations of Asia. His book had a very great influence on me, and through it I was directed to other sources of stimulation: the Edo-period Japanese philosopher Miura Baien (1723–89), for example, and the Consciousness Only current of Buddhist thought that is one of the bases of Mahayana Buddhism. These are subjects I will explore at greater length in chapter 1. At any rate, the book made me aware of the rich and unique traditional cultures of India, Tibet, Thailand, China, Korea, and Japan, about which I had had no clear idea until then. For me, Nakamura's work was a catalyst. After reading it, the Buddhist way of thinking that I had unconsciously absorbed in my secondary school education took root as a conscious part of my personal beliefs.

The 1960s were the years when the Metabolist movement got underway, and they were also a decade when I debated at length with Noboru Kawazoe about the relationship between Eastern philosophy and Metabolism. I remember trying to establish a connection between Metabolism and such Buddhist concepts as reincarnation, transmigration, and impermanence. Because the presentation of the theory of Metabolism devoted a great deal of energy to the subject of technology and human beings, the movement is often mistakenly thought of in retrospect as a technological movement, but I recall that the fundamental concept of Metabolism was, in fact, symbiosis.

For that reason, a general overview of my work from the 1960s to the present can justifiably be built around the theme of the philosophy of symbiosis. Over the years, I have articulated this philosophy in many different ways. From my first encounter with Buddhism through the Metabolist movement in the 1960s I called it the philosophy of coexistence; later I used a variety of terms, but behind them all has been the philosophy of symbiosis.

Metabolism and Symbiosis

To put it in its simplest form, the theory of Metabolism was based on two principles. The first was the symbiosis of different time periods, or diachronicity. The term "metabolism" was borrowed from the science of biology, where it refers to the processes and changes that a creature undergoes as it lives. The first principle of the Metabolist movement was to introduce this regenerating, metabolizing process into architecture and city planning. The name "metabolism" was chosen for the movement to express the conviction that a work of architecture should not be frozen and unchanging once it is completed but should be apprehended instead as a thing—or as a process—that evolves from past to present and from present to future. Another way to express this process of evolution from past to present to future is to call it a symbiosis of the three time periods.

A work of Modern Architecture is designed under present conditions. As much as possible, anticipated future conditions are transposed into the present work, but that work is given a particular form within the context of the present. Traditionally, then, Modern Architecture has been regarded as entirely restricted to the present, and it is in that sense that Modern Architecture is "an architecture of the present." But historically speaking, architecture has not always restricted itself to expressing the present. At times, architecture has found its present in the past or has enclosed the present in an image of the future.

In, for example, Giambattista Piranesi's *Prisons* (*Carceri d'Invenzione;* ca. 1745), there is neither present nor future. All is expressed in terms of the past. The *New City* (*Città Nuova*; 1914) drawings by the Futurist Antonio Sant'Elia lack both past and present—all existence is enfolded in an image of the future. Modern Architecture in turn rejected history and tradition, particularly as symbolized by "nonfunctional" decoration; at the same time, it refused to predict any future—the future having effectively been reduced to a mere extension of the past. The Metabolist movement, however, sought not to exclude any particular time period but to express the past, present, and future and the objects that existed in them in a single architectural space. In other words, it regarded every point in time as equidistant from the human observer. Metabolist time is neither linear nor heaped in a pyramidal hierarchy. It is complexly interwoven, like a net of rhizomes. This is the symbiosis of time, or diachronicity, from the Metabolist perspective.

If we adopt this way of thinking, we need no longer discard, as Modern Architecture starting with Le Corbusier has done, symbols and *simulacres* representing history, tradition, and the past as they take form in the decorative elements of architecture. Since we feel an almost equal distance from past, present, and future, we are free to incorporate and synthesize symbols of the past (which have naturally accumulated in the process of architectural evolution), the present, and the future (which will inevitably become the present) into our architecture, producing diachronicity in the work. This clearly represents a major challenge to the dogma of Modern Architecture, as well as providing the architect a great new freedom in using at the same time the symbols and *simulacres* of past, present, and future. In particular, diachronicity allows us to actively introduce concepts and images of the future into our architecture. Architecture comes to express the idea that it is something that does not yet exist, on the same level as the conceptual.

The principle of diachronicity can be detected in the themes and ideas I was concerned with in the early sixties. On the one hand, I was convinced of the importance of the Katsura Detached Palace, an Edo-period structure; at the same time, I emphasized the economic and technological factors that we were facing in the present; and I was also greatly concerned with creating the city of the future. My triple stance in past, present, and future has not changed to this day. If anything, the validity of the principle of diachronicity has come to be more widely recognized in this Postmodern period.

During that period I designed several capsule buildings, one of which was called the Capsule Summer House K. Capsule K incorporated a quotation of a classical Japanese tearoom designed by the great medieval master of the tea ceremony, Kobori Enshu (1579–1647), within a high-technology capsular superstructure. In the central patio of the National Ethnological Museum in Osaka I have placed what I call "a relic of the future." It takes the form of a capsule that, appropriately enough, conceals the end of the information-access computer for the video system called the videotape capsule. The very core of the building, the patio, is already a relic at the time of its construction. This implies that the building is without a center; instead, it extends in defined units for infinity, evolving and metamorphosing as it goes. At the same time, it expresses the Metabolist position of diachronicity—that the future is already a relic.

The equal distance placed between the human observer and past, present, and future provides architecture with a wide variety of motifs but it also presents certain problems. One is the role of the architect: How is he to attain autonomy as the creator? If a work of architecture is frozen into a definite form in the present, the total autonomy of the architect is assured. But if the assumption is that the work will continue to grow and change after its initial construction, what should be the source and impetus for that change? Of course, the architect himself can take a positive role in the process. But the life of the architect is inevitably shorter than the life of his work. As a result, the work cannot avoid entering into a discourse with society and being modified at the hands of the people who live in it or use it. I thought at that time that the distinction between Modernism and Postmodernism could be drawn according to whether this change was actively welcomed or not. The diachronicity of Metabolism clearly assents to the participation of those who use the work. This concept of participation, or a "self-aid system," was an important current in my work from the late sixties through the early seventies.

Three members of the Metabolist group, Fumihiko Maki, Kiyonori Kikutake, and myself, joined forces to enter a design competition for low-cost housing in Peru. Our design objective was to produce a self-aid system by applying the principles of Metabolism. Of course, architecture everywhere changes, grows, regenerates, and reproduces itself due to changes in the society or economy that supports it. But we were seeking a kind of architecture that would grow, change, and regenerate by stimulating the people living in it to participate, to create a self-aid system. This led us to pursue new technological possibilities. Kikutake's Movement Kitchenette and Sky House were great stimuli to the Metabolist group. Louis Kahn's concept of master space / servant space was another.

In the early 1960s I spent a considerable amount of time in the development of the technology for realizing this concept, and the capsule architecture I produced at that time was the result of those efforts. The three Osaka Expo pavilions—the Toshiba IHI Pavilion, the Takara Beautilion, and the Capsule House in the Theme Pavilion at Festival Plaza—can be considered the final presentation of that phase of my work. Next I tried to realize this concept within the confines of commercial architecture; the Nakagin Capsule Tower resulted from that challenge. It was a symbol for me because in the process of realizing the work, many issues, technical and economic, that are a part of commercial architecture were raised and brought into relief. It represents the idea that architecture is a conglomeration of units and by rearranging the units the expressive quality of the work can be freely changed. Two principles are at work here: that architecture has the capability of changing and regenerating in response to the future and that architectural form can be modified depending upon the way the space is used, or the principle of participation.

The second principle of Metabolism is the synchronicity of space. Before the advent of Claude Lévi-Strauss and his Structuralism, the various cultures of the world were regarded as occupying different levels of development, with European—in particular, French—culture at the highest level, followed by the Anglo-Saxon and Germanic cultures, then Chinese and Japanese civilization, then the cultures of the less-developed and developing nations of the Middle East, Africa, and Southeast Asia. The American economist Walt Whitman Rostow's theory of the stages of economic development offered seemingly objective support for this view of the world. Rostow's premise that developing countries pass through a "take-off" stage to a stage of maturity, and then to a stage of highly developed consumer culture, was an influence on many, including Tange in the 1960s. If culture is viewed in a similar fashion, gradually developing until it approaches that of the West, modernization must be interpreted by the developing nations as Westernization, or adopting the culture of the West, and this is in fact the route that many developing countries, including Japan, began to march along.

Immediately after the Meiji Restoration in 1868, Japan sought to modernize by Westernizing. These efforts spanned all fields, including industry, education, law,

and architecture. Western-style buildings, in particular, were symbols of modernization. The style of syncretic late-Edo-period architecture that I have been urging a
reevaluation of, architecture with "Japanese spirit and Western invention," was
deplored by the Meiji government for its lack of modernity, and today it has largely
ceased to exist.

According to this scheme of things, it is only natural that the entire world will
gradually be Westernized and homogenized. The ideal touted by this school of
thought is a unified, one-dimensional world culture created according to the values
and standards of Western civilization. A single icon was to exist for the entire world.
The weapons for realizing this icon were, in language, Esperanto; in architecture,
the International Style. The International Style was an icon that was the product
of Western civilization, and it was also Architecture with a capital *A*—to borrow
the terminology of Jacques Lacan. The Modern movement in architecture was an
affirmation of the theory of stages of development, the conclusion of which is that
all architectures of the world should eventually be homogenized into a single, one-
dimensional, International Style. This system of values still prevails quite strongly
in the world. It is the mainstream. The same glass boxes that rise in Manhattan are
being constructed in the world's deserts, the humid forests of Southeast Asia, and
the loess plains of North China.

Synchronicity, the second principle of Metabolism, offers a challenge to the
dogma of Modernism on this score. Synchronicity begins by affirming the structuralism of Lévi-Strauss. Lévi-Strauss claimed that it is wrong to envision the cultures of the world as occupying levels in a uniform progress toward civilization;
it was his discovery that each culture has its own distinct character that can at the
same time be linked to every other culture in the world. In other words, all the
cultures of the world existed in a single global structure, and Western culture could
not be considered at the forefront of some one-dimensional evolutionary progress
but instead had to be considered in relation to all other cultures of the world. Lévi-
Strauss relativized "superior" Western civilization and recognized that each culture
of the world occupied its unique niche within a multidimensional world culture.
We live in a time when the gaps that separate Japan, for example, from Islamic
civilization, from the rest of Asia, from Africa, or from Europe, are all felt as equal.
Synchronicity is another way of describing the feeling of equal distance (or equal
closeness) to all of these different cultures. The universal icon that supported the
superstructure of Modernism has passed out of existence, and now we are free to
create an architecture that can employ the contexts of many different civilizations.
The syncretism I speak of is in this respect essentially different from syncretism in
the past. The new syncretism must be based on the principle of equal distance between each culture of the world. I regard this second principle of Metabolism as
the main philosophic base for the move from internationalism to interculturalism.
We are already on the path to an intercultural style; the origins of that development were present already in the early 1960s—synchronicity of space, the second
principle of the Metabolist movement.

The Symbiosis of the Part and the Whole

There are several requirements to be fulfilled before architecture can incorporate the principles of the symbiosis of space and time, or, in Metabolist language, diachronicity and synchronicity. The first is that time and space must be deconstructed. The members of the Metabolist group set themselves to this task in the early 1960s. In order to create architecture that would change, grow, and metabolize to create a new form that would encourage the participation of those who used its products, architectural space and time had to be deconstructed and articulated. The linear concept of time as a progression from past to present to future had to be abandoned and a new concept of time as independent moments or discrete, suspended particles considered. Time came to be seen like a pearl necklace, or like the DNA helix, like something that could be altered in shape or arrangement to fit the vessel that held it or the situation that surrounded it.

There was a need to deconstruct time in order to reconstruct it in a new way that permitted the symbiosis of history with the present and future: in the same way, space had to be deconstructed, too. When the pyramid that placed Western civilization at the top was dismantled, the cultures of different locales became free-floating units or particles that possessed their own independent values. Once this was achieved, it became possible to assemble or group the many different cultures of the world in any variety of forms. In addition to the key words growth, change, accretion, metabolization, and exchange, I used the terms asymmetry, "group form," karma (*en*), the Oriental Individuum, syncretism, coexistence, and symbiosis. Underlying all of these terms is the assumption of the necessity to deconstruct and articulate space.

Within Metabolist thought, the problem arose how to reconstruct articulated space and time. It was not simply a matter of assembling prefabricated parts, as one might of an automobile or other machine, for architecture, while possessing a material unity on the one hand, must also have a nonmaterial unity of space and information, a unity that can only be achieved by an intellectual or creative synthesis. Through this process, articulated space can once again become a unified work of architecture. Our Metabolist group published *Metabolism 1960: Toshi e no Teian,* and for two years following I was intensively occupied with the problem of part and whole. Though unfortunately the follow-up volume to *Metabolism 1960,* which was to be titled *Metamorphosis 1962,* did not see publication, the theme of part and whole continued to play a major part in my thinking, and I pursued it in subsequent publications such as the aforementioned "Architecture of the Street" and *Urban Design,* and later, in the 1970s, expressed the same ideas with such concepts as the art of ambiguity, mediating bodies, zones of emptiness, warmth, *ma* (interval), *en* (karmic) affinity, and Rikyu gray.

In *Action Architecture: the Aesthetics of Metabolism (Kodo Kenchiku Ron: Metabolism no Bigaku,* Shokokusha, 1968), I emphasized that architecture must possess both metabolism and metamorphosis. For me, these are two aspects of the same reality, and they hold the key to overcoming the fatal dualism that Modern Architecture stands on and has failed to breach.

The problem of part and whole has occupied others as well, and there have been many different approaches to it, especially with regard to urban planning. At the 1962 Team Ten Conference, three presentations caused quite a sensation. One was Kenzo Tange's Tokyo Plan 1960; the second was the Toulouse-le-Mirail New Town Plan of Georges Candilis, Shadrach Woods, and Alexis Josic; the third was Piet Blom's plan for the rebuilding of Amsterdam, presented by Aldo Van Eyck. The most controversial point at issue among these three plans was whether an urban infrastructure was necessary in architecture and city planning. Tokyo Plan 1960 was a plan for the central city, mainly concerned with the hardware of the area, transportation routes. This approach was based on the hierarchical logic that had prevailed up to that time. In other words, the basic elements of the city are its infrastructure—the roads, public buildings, and transportation facilities. On top of these gradually rise, in a pyramidal hierarchy, the city's districts, its buildings, and finally its residents' homes. At the base of modern thought is the presupposition that the whole comes before the part, and this supposition has resulted in the construction of metropolises and metropolitan networks as well as the enormous superstructures that comprise them. Concentrating the main functions of the city in a central hub was thought to be the most efficient means to establish the whole.

In contrast to Tange's approach, the Toulouse-le-Mirail New Town Plan presented a city without a center or an infrastructure. Through the city's center flowed a river with a path along its banks. This was quite simply what already existed, a gesture to the city's natural and historical setting. This approach suggested that in city planning, "software"—nature and the daily activities of the residents—were of fundamental importance. The parking lots, public facilities, and roads that occupied the center of the Tokyo Plan 1960 were here located in cul-de-sacs approaching the city from the outskirts.

The central idea of the Amsterdam reconstruction was that by adding more and more housing, the city could be enlarged infinitely. All the necessary conveniences of city life were to be included in dwellings. These facilities would connect the housing and bind it into a city network. Based on the principle of building the whole from its parts, it was a far more radical proposal than the Toulouse-le-Mirail New Town plan.

The presentation I made at Team Ten was a plan to revitalize the Nishijin district of Kyoto, centered around a new Nishijin Labor Center. The idea was to give form to the architecture of the district by making the narrow streets (*roji*) between buildings the central focus. The goal of the plan was to create a system of roads and a network for daily activities that was completely separate from automotive traffic. This was to be done by creating architecture that gave first priority to urban software and then by extending that type of architecture in links. Within this approach can be seen the concept of building the whole from the parts. The Team Ten Conference way the first of many to emphasize, in defiance of the dogmas of Modern

Architecture, the importance of the part, a theme that continues to live in my own work.

The Nakagin Capsule Tower was the culmination of my work with the concept of the symbiosis of part and whole. Until that time, Modern Architecture had been represented by the so-called Harvard Box, a rectangle of glass and steel; there was no way to tell how its interior space might be divided from its expressionless, non-articulated exterior. The Nakagin Capsule Tower, in contrast, was an attempt to represent in spatial terms the role of the individual in society. The Sony Tower Osaka and the National Ethnological Museum shared that same inspiration. The National Ethnological Museum, in particular, was a realization of the first principle of Metabolism. It has been added to several times until at present it is roughly twice its original size. The basic units, consisting of an exhibition space with a central courtyard, are each individually expressive while existing in symbiosis with the whole. These parts are not only suggestive of exhibition units but also of the auto-nomy of the different regions whose cultural artifacts they house. While each reflects specific internal and external conditions, each also contributes to the formation of the harmonious whole.

The Symbiosis of Interior and Exterior

The term intermediary zone is useful when considering the symbiosis of interior and exterior space.

In Western culture, particularly in the currents of modern thought that are based on rationalism, it is considered important to clearly differentiate between any two distinct phenomena. But by dividing all of existence into either yes or no, interior or exterior, mind or body, the warmth that lies at the border between the two ex-tremes is lost, sacrificed to rationality. The basic principle of democracy is based on this way of thinking. The yeses and nos are tallied, and whichever is greater, if even by one, determines the course taken. This is the principle of majority rule. But the doubt must crop up whether this method, which ignores the reality of existence as something that is not simply black or white, yes or no, is really a proper one. It was because I felt strongly that it was important to value a less clearcut but warmer and richer zone of reality, one that could not be apprehended through dualistic thinking, that I have come to place great importance on the ideas of intermediary zones and intermediary nature.

I first began to speak of architecture of the street in 1962; I developed this idea as an alternative to the Western concept of the plaza. Whether it be the Grecian agora or the Renaissance piazza, in the primary Western models of city space we find an open central area surrounded by public facilities, the church, and the market. All daily activities take place there. In contrast, the street has no easily demarcated boundaries. The street, in constant dialogue with the buildings that face it on both sides, is an unlimited zone that unfolds in time as it progresses. The face of the street changes with time, throughout the day, following the pace of human activity. In the morning, there is a bustle around the milk stand and the newspaper kiosk. During the day, little local parks become the gathering places of housewives and children. In the evening, restaurants are a focus of activity, and late at night the bars suddenly grow lively. It is appropriate to describe the activities that take place along the street as warm activities. The street serves sometimes as a transportation space, other times as an extension of private space, and still other times it is a community space. The street exists as a space with a variety of contents, a plural nature and a plural meaning.

In other words, it is an intermediary zone where the private interior space of the individual dwelling meets the public exterior space of the road. These two natures interpenetrate, exist in symbiosis, and stimulate each other, creating a zone that can be described as extremely warm and suggestive. This symbiosis of interior and exterior represents a typically Asian attitude toward space. There is some truth in the statement that while the West is a culture of stone, Japan is a culture of wood. At the very least, European architecture since Rome has been built mainly from stone, brick, or earth. European buildings were constructed to provide greater protection from cold than heat. The demarcation of inside from outside is quite clear, with well-developed walls. Windows for ventilation and light were reduced in size as much as possible, as walls were designed to protect interior space against the elements that threatened from outside. If we look at the medieval Italian *commune,* we see that every town no matter how small possessed a protective castle wall. Inside the wall was the town; outside were the fields. Interior and exterior are two different worlds in European architecture, and the wall is regarded as a form that protects one from the destructive powers of nature. City walls existed to protect the city in wars with other cities. Outside the walls were the enemy; inside were the citizens. The wall, then, was looked on as an absolutely necessity for the survival of the community. This clearcut distinction between interior and exterior had the effect of raising civic consciousness and at the same time creating solidarity against outsiders. The existence of the city wall also increased the density of the population living inside it. Though the Italian *communi* existed long before the age of elevators, we find many multistory dwellings within them.

In contrast, the concept of a clearcut division between interior and exterior does not seem to have existed in the East. According to descriptions of the ideal city in the Vedic literature of India, a bodhi tree should occupy the center of the city to provide a place to commune with buddhas and gods. The streets should be divided into breezy streets and sunny streets; during the rainy season, the sunny streets will be community gathering places and during the hot dry season the cool and breezy streets will serve as the common space. Thus one of the major components of the ideal city is the street, treated as an extension of living space. This way of thinking can be seen in the traditional Japanese view of city space, too. In Kyoto, from the start of the feudal period, the facing sides of a street became a unit of urban organization. Toyotomi Hideyoshi (1536–98), the great warlord, declared that the streets of Kyoto belonged to its residents for eternity, and from that time the central street has been lent to the residents on both sides as a community space; its function as a transportation route is secondary. Today streets and alleyways in residential areas of Japan serve the function of community spaces and are also regarded as extensions of private space.

The symbiosis of interior and exterior space is evidenced in the Japanese treatment of space in a variety of ways. The lattice doors of the urban houses of Kyoto, for example, create an intermediary space between street and home, as do the frequently employed hedges, which, while marking the boundaries of personal property, do not shut it off completely from the outside, but allow inside and outside to interpenetrate. The open corridors (*en*) of *sukiya*-style architecture are another example. Though they may superficially resemble the Western veranda, they are actually quite distinct in content. The Japanese open corridor, which was widely incorporated into the houses of the common people, farmers, and city people alike in the Edo period, is a multivalent intermediary zone for entertaining guests, enjoying the flowers and the sunshine—in short, for making contact with the outside world.

As cities were eventually modernized, a division between private property and public property came to be regarded with increasing importance and with that division the common space within our cities began to disappear. The communal property that had existed at the village level—communal forests, communal land, and communal water rights—was all divided into either private or public property. Communal city space—roads and streets, lavatories and wells, and meeting places—were similarly divided. As a result, the city lost a space that enveloped its residents. We step directly from the public road through the door into a private home; the city has lost the quintessentially human intermediary space it once had.

Intermediary zones have come to be regarded as an important means for reducing the feeling of alienation that has been created by modern architecture's rejection of exterior space and the complete separation of urban space into public and private. The modern city's lack of continuity can also be ameliorated by reintroducing such multivalent space. The large corridorlike area beneath the eaves of the Head Offices of the Fukuoka Bank was designed as this sort of intermediary zone, and it is being actively used by the city's residents. The area inside the entrance way of the Japan Headquarters of the Red Cross Society fills the space between the two wings of the building, one the main office of the society and the other a rental property. It serves as a connecting, interiorlike space for the the two parts of the building while at the same time suggesting the exterior. The lattice structures in the Museum of Modern Art, Saitama, and the Shoto Club were designed with the same purpose in mind.

My aim has been to create the conditions for a new multivalence and warmth that has been lacking in Modern Architecture by achieving a symbiosis of exterior and interior. This I have tried to do by bringing the feeling of the exterior into the interior or by raising the exterior to the same level of architectural importance as the interior. Modern Architecture, with its emphasis on function, has until now had a far simpler meaning, but in following that course has lost its narrative quality.

Interior space completely cut off from exterior space creates a feeling of alienation. The role that intermediary space can play to supplement this failing of Modern Architecture is a very important one.

The symbiosis of interior and exterior can also be formulated as the symbiosis of architecture and environment, the symbiosis of nature and architecture, and the symbiosis of nature and humankind.

Western architecture is founded on a confrontation with nature. In individual homes, walls are a means to sharply separate exterior and interior; the walls of a castle separate the city from nature. Japanese architecture, on the other hand, existed within nature. Partly, this difference, again, is the difference between a stone culture and a wood culture. The basic structural unit of a wood culture is not the wall but the pillar, and as a result, the placement of walls is free and flexible.

Aside from this, in the traditional Japanese pattern of life, influenced by Buddhist thought, humankind, their dwellings, and their cities are all regarded as a part of nature. The Japanese city is not surrounded by a protective castle wall. Even the so-called castle towns were not surrounded by walls. The castle was ringed only by outer and inner moats and the town was located outside the perimeter of the outer moat. In this type of city, nature and human dwellings intermingle in a symbiotic relationship between man and nature, interior and exterior. The works mentioned above—the Fukuoka Bank, the Red Cross Headquarters, and all my other designs which incorporate intermediary space—were all planned with the idea of recreating the symbiosis of environment and architecture that is so typically Asian and Japanese.

The Symbiosis of History and the Present

Modern Architecture was established by freeing itself from history and the styles of the past. The leaders of Modern Architecture such as Gropius and Le Corbusier regarded this severance from the past as important for two reasons.

The first reason for denying the past was that they felt it necessary to free themselves from the the authority of the academicism represented by the École des Beaux-Arts, the formalism and formalistic architecture that reigned unchallenged in the West. The second reason was that Modern Architecture was to be divorced from the traditional handwork and craftsmanship of architecture in the past; in its stead, the works of Modern Architecture would be constructed with the products of modern industry.

As I have discussed at length above, the concept of Metabolism is based on the principles of synchronicity and diachronicity. Diachronicity is, of course, the symbiosis of past, present, and future. One of the basic methods of Metabolism is to overlap and overlay time that is quite clearly and definitely past with the present and the future. The fundamental ideal of the symbiosis of past and present was inherent in the very concept of Metabolism. Afterward, I came to strongly advocate the need for Modern Architecture to make contact with the culture and history of its region. In other words, our identity would be obtained not by creating a false, Western-skewed "International Style" but by incorporating our history—and our respective histories—into the most advanced contemporary technology, into life in modern society. In contrast to universalism, this approach valued and preserved individuality and uniqueness. The goal of achieving a new interculturalism by those means is an important part of the view of history within the philosophy of symbiosis. But there are two ways of thinking about history and tradition. One is the history that we can see: architectural forms, decorative elements, and symbols that have come down to us. Then there is the history that cannot be seen: attitudes, ideas, philosophies, religions, sensibilities, aesthetics, and patterns of living.

When history is considered in the West, great importance is given to evaluating the visible relics of the past. It is my opinion that in Japan we more frequently consider the invisible sensibilities that have been transmitted through the years. This is strongly reflected in the great shrines at Izumo and Ise. Ise Shrine continues to be rebuilt every twenty years, as it has for centuries. Thought the intent is to recreate the shrine exactly upon each reconstruction, there are gradual, unavoidable changes in details and in hardware, for example, and we cannot regard the present shrine as an exact copy of some original. Yet the aesthetic principles of the shrine are passed down through generation after generation of the shrine carpenters and survive after well over a thousand years. In contrast, the construction materials of the Parthenon are those of ancient times; it has never been rebuilt and survives to this day—in ruins. Materially, it is today as it originally was. That is its great difference from Ise Shrine: in the West, history is preserved as matter; in Japan, it is preserved as a spiritual heritage, as part of a genetic code. When creating a work of architecture, both of these approaches must be borne in mind. During the Second World War, Japanese architects capped concrete buildings with traditional Japanese tile roofs as an architectural style of the Greater East Asia Co-Prosperity Sphere: the present was made to wear a historical hat. This was, however, a distinctly European approach. In Modern Architecture as well we can find examples of attempts to express locality or history by recreating exactly the styles of the past. But except for rare instances, this does not succeed. When attempting to transmit history through material objects, a more oblique approach is likely to be successful. First history must be deconstructed into symbols and signs, and these fragments, endowed with a new meaning, must be incorporated into the work as bits of memory.

I have used this method in the National Bunraku Theater. Selecting Edo-period fragments such as the *yagura* watchtower, *kura* storehouse-style windows, and the moon-shaped door handles of the Katsura Detached Palace, I deconstructed historical elements into fragments and incorporated them into the modern work in sophisticated forms. By this method the visible symbols of history can be incorporated into Modern Architecture.

The other method of achieving symbiosis between past and present is to incorporate the atmosphere or mood of the past—Japanese Buddhist thought or traditional Japanese aesthetics, or philosophy, or patterns of living, or arrangements of space—into Modern Architecture. In this case, the past that we are trying to incorporate is invisible, a spiritual legacy, and our intellectual task is to discover a way to make this spirit come alive in Modern Architecture in a sophisticated form. The evaluation of that intellectual task becomes an important element in the symbiosis of history and Modern Architecture.

The Symbiosis of Man and Technology

Another point at which Metabolism and symbiosis touch is the way in which they regard the relationship between humanity and technology. Metabolism is a philosophy of symbiosis between humankind and technology. In Western philosophy, which is the base on which Modern Architecture is built, humanity and technology, religion and technology, art and science are regarded as fundamentally opposed to each other. An extension of this dualism is the belief that the human being is composed of body and spirit, two opposing and mutually exclusive entities. This is the fundamental dualism of Western culture, from which the dialectic, Western philosophy, and the principles of majority rule were born. This dualism produces the art of *simulation* by means of the dilemma. By the endless repetition of the choice between yes and no an extremely practical scientific method is born, the purpose of which is to reach the truth, if in a gradual, piecemeal fashion. Rationalism is firmly based on this fundamental dualism. The philosophy of Metabolism, in contrast, sought to transcend the Western opposition between man and technology and to do that began from the assumption that man and machine could live in symbiosis.

The design for the Toshiba IHI Pavilion is a concrete example of the search for symbiosis between man and technology. The pavilion is built of tetrahedron-shaped units called tetraunits, made of welded steel. A computer was used to select from five different types of tetraunits to meet various different functional requirements, and these were combined to create a three-dimensional spaceframe. The method of design was clearly patterned after industrial and scientific principles, as was the actual construction. My idea was to see if this quintessentially technological approach could be pushed to the point where it became antitechnological, suprarational, and close to the quality of human emotion. If I could achieve this, I felt, I would have made an important contribution to discovering a form of symbiosis between science and art and science and humanity. Would the computer-designed steel tetra framework finally be transformed into a Baroque structure that expressed human feeling? That was my concern. It seems to have been a success, since the completed work is far more than an image of rationality, science, and technology; rather, it calls forth an emotional response from a level deep inside the viewer.

Visitors to the pavilions remarked that the three works gave them strong impressions of the themes "forest," "monster," and "Baroque," respectively. I interpret this public reaction as proof of the success of my aims. It signifies to me that because man is a creative being the methods of high technology have the potential to become another and important means of expressing his creativity.

The Wacoal Kojimachi Building represents a more symbolist approach to the dichotomy of man and technology. To put it another way, this building is a metaphor for "a sentient machine," a demechanized, convivial machine along the lines of the *machine* described by Gilles Deleuze and Felix Guattari. They have termed human society, as a complex interweaving of a wide plurality of desires produced by the efforts and activities of each individual, *les machines desirantes*; the structures that strive to stabilize society in the face of those sometimes conflicting desires they call *les machines sociales*. A convivial machine, then—a *machine plaisante*—is one that in its constant motion produces schisms as well as countless new relationships.

Deleuze and Guattari's concepts of man and machine, society and technology, are not as two essentially opposed entities but as two states of existence that are intimately interwoven in a rhizomelike web. The symbiosis of man and machine as interpreted from a symbolist framework is clearly evident here. Quotations from the Edo period exist side by side with UFOs in the Wacoal Kojimachi Building. The pleasing machine is not only a symbiosis of man and technology but also of the diachronicity of past and future.

After the period of high economic growth in the 1960s, an antitechnological philosophy was popularly voiced in Japan as a means to restore a human scale to life. I was opposed to this. Since the Industrial Revolution, the world has always threaded a path between technology and humanity. In the West, reality is always thus divided into two polar extremes between which we bounce like the arm of a metronome as history pursues a course that dances between the poles of technology and art. William Morris initiated the Arts and Crafts Movement in an effort to restore humanity in the face of technology's ascendancy during the Industrial Revolution; in architecture, there has been the unending debate between rationalism and nonrationalism. But can we today attain humanity simply by denying technology? Technology has already been incorporated into our daily lives in various forms as a means of expanding and extending our humanity. Those who suggest that we must find the essence of what we seek in either technology or the arts will, I believe, never find that essence, for it is to be discovered in the undifferentiated symbiosis of the two in reality.

The Eastern concept of technology is represented by the *karakuri,* or automata. In the *Illustrated Collection of Automata* (*Karakuri Zui*) by Hosokawa Yorinao (three volumes, published in 1796) there are drawings and explanations of many different automata, but perhaps the most representative is *chakumi ningyo,* or tea-carrying doll, the world's first robot. This doll has a simple self-governing mechanism that allows it to move forward, stop, and move specific distances forward and backward in a prescribed order. It also has a governor that keeps it running at a set speed and springs and cams that allow it to move backwards without a bevel gear. What I wish to emphasize is that this tea-carrying automaton, with its very advanced premodern robotics, does not look mechanical, like the Western vision of a robot. In fact, it looks like a finely made doll, a handcrafted masterpiece, and in its appearance the Japanese concept of *karakuri* can be discerned. Behind the achievements in the realm of *karakuri* was the craftsman and his art (both referred to by the single word *takumi*), his practice of putting his heart into the technology he worked with. The tea-carrying doll was a machine for representing a human being. For the Japanese, a machine is necessarily a representation of a human being, his extension and expansion. Why do children love steam locomotives? Why is a sewing machine a nostalgic thing for us? As they do our work for us, giving the appearance of "trying" their best, they take on a symbolic import. A sewing machine has a poetic feeling about it because it recalls a mother's kindness. These kinds of machines have transcended their purely mechanical functions and serve in addition a symbolic function, and such "symbolic machines" are an important point of contact between human beings and technology.

The architecture that is now being called High Tech does not really function as a high technology machine but—the Norman Foster Hong Kong Shanghai Bank is a good example—is a machine as symbol. My own works, the Nakagin Capsule Tower, Sony Tower Osaka, and the Wacoal Kojimachi Building, are not only meant to represent rationality and functionalism; their symbolic nature as dramatic machines is also crucial. This is the kernel of thought—the symbiosis of man and machine—that lies at the heart of the Japanese *karakuri*.

As we approach the twenty-first century, the most advanced technologies of computers and communications are coming to play a greater part in our daily lives. Information-processing machines are becoming a part of human existence. For that very reason, it is important that these machines should partake of the philosophy of the *karakuri,* the philosophy of the symbiosis of man and machine.

With this brief overview of several of the themes that are occupying me now, I direct the reader to the body of this work. In this Postmodern age, some might think that criticizing Modern Architecture is like flogging a dead horse. I am convinced, however, that the methods and aesthetic of Modern Architecture survive in the Postmodern age. The truth of this claim is hinted at by the term Postmodern itself—how it preserves, builds on, and qualifies the Modern. In addition, my critique of Modern Architecture is not simply as an artistic style but as symbol of Western cultural dominance of non-Western societies, and this fact deserves repeating, for it can be said to apply to much of Postmodernism as well. After having said farewell to Modern Architecture and the West, I would like to explore traditional Japanese sources, both architectural models and ideas and broader cultural motifs as well. These I encompass with the idea of Rikyu Gray, the title of the second chapter. Finally, in the last chapter, I will recap my most recent thoughts on the core of my thought and my work, the philosophy of symbiosis.

CHAPTER ONE

Beyond Modernism,
Farewell to the West

A T THE RISK OF oversimplification, it probably suffices to say that from the outset of the century up until 1958 we are looking at the Modern Period in architecture. Or in a narrower sense, we can trace the first decisive steps toward Modernism to the 1929 founding of CIAM (Congres Internationaux d'Architecture Moderne) and the La Sarraz Declaration. From the twenty-sixth to the twenty-eighth of June 1928, architects from many countries convened at Chateau de la Sarraz in Switzerland. There the keynote position and methodology statements by Le Corbusier and Siegfried Giedion were condensed into the central ideas that were to characterize the Modernist movement from then on. The CIAM movement was founded on the idea of rationally reconstructing the city out of single-purpose spaces functionally articulated for working, dwelling, and recreation. Up through the nineteenth century, cities and societies were characterized by a haphazard inter-mingling of natural functions, an oppressive awareness of the cumulative dictates of history, unsanitary living conditions, inefficient manual industries, feudalistic social and political hierarchies, and conservative and authoritarian academicism centered in the universities. Small wonder that the steady achievements of the In-dustrial Revolution and the general image of industrialization shone in the eyes of architects as a heroic goal. They saw industrialization as the weapon with which to revolutionize archaic class structures, smash the confines of academicism, and open up new social and artistic possibilities.

Altogether, three basic underlying directives of Modern Architecture can be summed up as follows: 1) rational restructuring to break up the sediment of his-torical precedents and the natural confluence of activities and needs, all under the banner of functionalism and the division of labor; 2) the promotion of standardiza-tion over individualistic handcrafting so as to facilitate industrial growth and efficiency; and 3) rejection of the traditional, regional, and ethnic, replacing these with so-called international or universal principles supposed to be applicable the world over.

The backbone of Modern Architecture, of course, turned out to be the Western spirit and philosophy of rationalism, the very same ethos that paved the way for the industrialization and economic expansion of Western society, which eventually came to dominate every corner of the globe. From the beginning, then, the ideals of Modern Architecture went hand in hand with industrial development—and we must not forget that, historically, that has meant Western industrial development first. The system of zoning separate residential districts, business districts, industrial districts, and parks as a means of modernizing cities spread worldwide. Over the next half of the century, the Modernist philosophy and methodology rapidly reached out to conquer the world, and the vision of the future outlined in the La Sarraz Declaration was fulfilled. As industrial society became a reality, architecture found itself tied fast to economic dictates, firmly enmeshed in the workings of economics itself. Efficient, systematized production and standardization found their way into not only industrial architecture, but all fields of architecture, effectively rendering hand-finished architecture a status symbol of the privileged classes.

Land-use planning and zoning attained universal acceptance in country after country as the functionalist vision in urban planning became the order of the day, giving rise to those red-, yellow-, and green-blocked city plans we all know so well. All around the globe, "sensible," hygienic (aseptic), practical, concrete boxes appeared. They soon began to thwart the natural human desire for sunshine, so that for the first time in the history of the world it became necessary to explicitly formulate the legalities of "sunlight rights." Meanwhile, the authority of the academies tottered, having been insistently undermined by an avant garde that depreciated tradition and regionalism as retrogressive and provincial and instead actively campaigned for universals in the name of internationalism—the International Style.

Yet as much as these three directives proved the success of Modern Architecture, they likewise accounted for its shortcomings. It is precisely the functionalist scheme of subdivision that has done away with the complexities and interfused qualities that were the very life of the city. Zoning the city into residential areas, commercial areas, industrial areas, and park areas may have done much to facilitate urban planning by providing each city district with a single function, but by the same token it drove amusements, businesses, and cottage industries out of residential areas, where they originally had formed an integral part of urban life. Gone was the round-the-clock, bustling, neighborhood activity. Residential areas have been so thoroughly reduced to serving solely for dwelling that they have effectively sacrificed the intensely intermingled and diversified use of space that historically characterized the heart of the city. Now they are populated solely by housewives, old people, and children by day, and they revert to a lifeless, silent fringe where no one dares venture out alone at night. Crime rates have never been higher than they are now in these "uninhabited" residential districts. Conversely, city center business districts have become the exclusive domain of office workers during the day and deserted wastelands when night falls. Retail districts are gradually becoming areas of store fronts only, while in recent years the owners of small local shops serving residential areas have begun to sell out, and their stores are now staffed and run by commuters from outside the district.

Separatism by race is a given in many big cities, and this separatism serves only to decrease mutual understanding and increase racial friction. In big American cities, the idea of maximum efficiency in urban management has led to relegating the elderly off to old folks' "homes" in the suburbs, a step which will only further estrange the younger generation from their elders. Policies have even been proposed to promote separate living quarters for each generation within the nuclear family. Multigenerational households and neighborhoods are replaced by retirement villages, singles' apartment complexes, and standardized housing tracts for standardized families who live in constant pursuit of distinction from their neighbors. All of this separation breeds an isolating, competitive mentality in place of a sense of community.

Modern Architecture and urban planning ended up exchanging success in achieving a certain type of industrial and administrative efficiency by isolating the various sectors of society according to function for a critical loss of organic integrity and humanity. Peripheral areas and intermediating zones, places where no clear divisions can be drawn between opposing elements or distinct functions—such ambiguous spaces are ultimately the most human. Sometimes such spaces may act as catalysts to meld and harmonize opposites, whether personal, social, or economic. Modern architecture gives them no importance; in fact, they are anathema to its fundamental principles of function and efficiency.

Granted, the shift from handcrafting to industrial production brought formerly unattainable luxury goods and materials within the reach of the general public, and it was no mean achievement. Product standardization and factory quality controls likewise aided in bringing Modern Architecture to the level of the people. Yet this inevitably meant that the element of spatial creativity, which in essence had been tantamount to *quality* in the vision of architecture as culture, was now straitjacketed within the limits dictated by the workings of the construction industry. Traditional Japanese architecture in particular, with its richly detailed expression, was rejected as a premodern throwback to handcrafting. Soon whole cities were covered in a bland, featureless monotone of steel, glass, and concrete. Not only that, but the indigenous industries and traditional crafts of the local society, local skills, even the traditional aesthetics of the local residents—things that had interrelated in so many ways through the creative presence of architecture—all fell silently by the wayside. What greater irony, that Modern Architecture, supposedly the harbinger of culture, should have wrought such havoc on the traditions and cultures of regional societies.

Though ironic, this is no surprise. From the start, Modern Architecture was touted as a rejection of tradition and regionalism. In the nineteenth century, multifarious regional cultures, each with its own tradition and history, prevailed; this was to the founders of Modern Architecture an obstacle, a deeply entrenched authority preventing creative exploration of new possibilities in both art and social organization. Their rejection of tradition and regionalism may have been justified at the time, but it meant a loss of diversity that was later to be so sorely missed.

Separatism and subdivision as means to functionalist, rationalist ends have clearly reached a turning point. From here on urban space will strive for greater complexity and multivalence through the compounding of functions and transfusing of purposes. We may even see this as a sign of the coming new symbiotic age in urban planning. And cannot the same be said of the world of architecture? Functionalist architecture's achievement has been to functionally articulate spaces, to organize them along "lines of movement" in accord with the principle of efficiency. Or, more simply put, functionalist architecture has had us eat in the dining room and sleep in the bedroom. This scheme is the very stuff of Le Corbusier's proclamation that the "house is a machine for living." On the other hand, Ludwig Mies van der Rohe also championed a functionally undefined "universal space" that would adapt to various functions. Either way, Modern Architecture was constructed on the paradigm of clear divisions of space—interior from exterior, environment from building, private from public, historic from contemporary—a strict order based on dichotomy. Yet what was lost to such dualistic articulation were the "in-between" multivalent ambiguities, that is to say, the human qualities harbored in fringe and median environments. I seek a new symbiotic architectural space, to reintroduce symbiotic spaces *between* exterior and interior, symbiotic ambivalences *between* nature and architecture, symbiotic multivalences *between* contradictory elements.

Functional Modern Architecture was not only technocentric by definition, but it cut itself off from history in the abstract pursuit of universality. This inevitably meant the exclusion of vernacular popular culture, and ultimately reduced it to an architecture of a cultural abstraction less than the sum of the various cultural realities it assembled as its parts. Modern Architecture's mission was to provide the most rational accommodation of the *exclusively* present-day functions and wants of human society. Le Corbusier's Unites d'Habitation and Mies van der Rohe's Lake Shore Drive Apartments thus stood at the vanguard of then-contemporary architecture as eternally frozen icons to an idealized, static image of society. All was a series of largely identical present moments, built up one on another, like a pyramid.

The poverty of this abstraction has been felt even in its cradle, the industrialized West. Today's Postmodern architecture is inclusive: it takes in diverse unique cultural histories, utilizing their vernacular texts as is, within a contemporary syntax. Nonetheless, the decorativism of Robert Venturi's style or of Philip Johnson's New York AT&T Building come from a vantage point utterly removed from the classicism or traditionalism of times past. Theirs is a reinclusion of historical, decorative, popular rhetorics formerly excluded from Modern Architecture. In other words, they both make it their thematic challenge to combine the most disparate, most marginal, most manifold elements in their architectural creations.

Modern Architecture is a product of the West, closely linked not only to the process of its evolving philosophical ideals and social ethos but to its economic expansion as well. It is no coincidence that Modern Architecture's "universalized" International Style was, first, structured on the scale of a global economy far outstripping that of local, regional economies; and second, propagated a uniform package of Western values and standards worldwide.

In Japan, as in many other non-Western nations, modernization unfolded in the form of industrialization—which is another way of saying Westernization. Modern Architecture's pretensions to universality were little more than a global scheme of Western cultural conquest in disguise. And with what thoroughness was that success achieved in Japan! Even today, these assumptions unconsciously color the vision of Japanese architects young and old, so much that their own tradition of architecture has faded, grown obscure and even opaque to them.

Western-style buildings erected in Japan in the late nineteenth and early twentieth centuries are highly regarded. Architecture of the middle nineteenth century—of the late Edo period (which ended in 1867), a time when Western influences were just beginning to be felt strongly—is, however, generally despised. Partly because very few examples have survived, no satisfactory study has ever been made of it.

Personally, I find late-Edo buildings much more interesting than the more celebrated, later, "pure" copies of Western architecture. Some examples of late-Edo buildings include the Tsukiji Hotel, the Great Lantern of the Shokonsha Shrine, the Tokyo First National Bank, the Nihombashi Mitsuigumi House, the shops along the shore at Yokohama, the Yokohama Court House, the residences for foreigners in Yokohama, and school buildings in various outlying regions.

The majority of these buildings were designed and built by master carpenters who, though ardently incorporating Western details, lacked the skill to copy exactly and produced an arresting eclectic combination of the familiar and the alien. In the foreigners' residences in Yokohama the gates were arches. The outer walls were of a traditional Japanese construction in which gray tiles are set into white mortar, which rises in mounds in the interstices among the tiles. The buildings were topped with Western-style hipped roofs, but the windows are often either round, as is the case in some examples of old-fashioned Japanese architecture, or of the roughly ogival form called *kato* seen in some Japanese temple buildings. Wooden window sashes were painted red to simulate traditional vermilion lacquer, and overall compositions were a startlingly bold blend of Japanese and Western elements. As architectural works, these buildings are far superior to later copies in purely Western styles. The secret of their vigor is the way they represent the collision and combination of two heterogenous cultures before integration on the basis of Western values had occurred.

I do not champion traditionalism or ethnicism in contrast to the universalism of Modern Architecture. But I do believe that the time has come for the creation of a new internationalism in which regional cultures, while preserving their identities, collide with value systems of different cultures and mutually influence each other for the production of new, distinctive, individual cultures. In other words, it is possible to engage in international dialogues through the media of local cultural identities. Pluralistic cultural criteria are actually being worked out today.

In the modernization-cum-Westernization scheme of things, in which the standard conception of Westernization was universal industrialization, technological and economic assistance to developing countries were build-in adjuncts to industrialization. From the very outset, Western cultural values stood matter-of-factly as the only valid paradigm for modernization. If all outside Western culture is dualistically conceived as barbarian, then the unification of the world under Western values must seem indeed to constitute a liberating, humanist effort. Western colonialism and the continuing interventions of the Western powers in the affairs of other, always smaller, and usually non-Western nations bears witness to this one-dimensional system of Western thought.

Nonetheless, times do change and the world is moving into a new age of multidimensional perspectives. The Islamic world of the Middle East; the Third World nations of Africa and Latin America; China, Japan, and the rest of Asia—all are asserting their own value systems. And by no means only in narrow ethnocentric or traditional terms, but rather as component elements in an emerging new world order, a value system of multidimensional, multilayered structure. This new world order will not obtain through abstract universals, but amass from beneath regional cultures, supporting and underwriting their diversity.

In much of my writing I have advocated the reexamination of Japanese culture from the fourteenth to the eighteenth century. In doing this, I have lavished praise on the communal spaces—or street spaces—found in Kyoto before the middle nineteenth century. My reason for investigating these spaces was to seek the cultural identity lacking in the universalist approach of Modern Architecture and to discover intermediary spaces, vagueness, ambiguity, and diversity from the encounter between traditional Japan and contemporary architecture. It is from this vantage point that I continue in my search for points of connection between contemporary architecture and Japanese culture.

The Death of Architecture with a Capital A

Kafka's works are neither separate, partial objects nor firm totality; it is rather reference itself that emerges where any polarity is avoided. This also shows where the viewpoint is situated in the minor literature that is used to define objectively Kafka's literature.

Minor literature as "literature created by minor peoples adopting a language widely used" partly assimilates itself into Literature, with a capital *L* (i.e., established literature), while obstinately refusing various kinds of codes prevalent in the whole. If we think of "Literature" and "literature" as lying at opposite poles, one being the "whole," the other being the "part," minor literature, which intersects the two territories, goes beyond its own part, but also refuses to be totally assimilated. The language of "literature," which is of such an intermediary existence, must necessarily be exposed to decoding and extraterritorialization. But when it attains a certain intensity through *agence-*

ment, something that deserves to be called "being minor, that is, being revolutionary," emerges. Such is the form of literature that Deleuze and Guattari read in Kafka's works in their *Kafka pour une littèrature mineur.*

—Takao Tomiyama

Literature is an evocation of the Other (*Autre*) as defined by Jacques Lacan. The absolute Other stands at a transcendental height, gazing down on the plane of relativity. It is the monarch or the state itself that holds power over the realm of symbols as the order in the age of supercodes. In the modern world, with the passing away of kings and states, the center is relativized, and the subject lies in each separate individual, with no absolute Other standing high above it. A good metaphor for this decoded modern world is the ideal prison, the Panopticon, conceived by the philosopher Jeremy Bentham, with its watchtower in a central rotunda surrounded by a ring of cells. Each prisoner is watched over by an guard invisible to him, hidden in the central tower. In time, the guard's eyes are internalized, so that, in effect, each individual is under his own surveillance.

To contain in the self the absolute Other that has hitherto ruled it—this is the beginning of the decoded age and the end of that Modernism in which the Other of Western values, dualism and rationalism, stood high above the world looking down upon the interrelationships of the world. Modern Architecture, established under the dogma that modernization equals Westernization, was put on a pedestal. Architecture presented the International Style, which was to be spread to every corner of the world. That is the power of absolute Architecture, the absolute Other. Even in an age when sovereigns are powerless, Architecture wielded the power to force architects to conform to its will. The history of Modern Architecture in Japan is due witness to that power. The modernization of Japan since the beginning of the Meiji period (1868–1912) was, as I have said before, equivalent to Westernization. Japanese traditional culture as it had developed before that time was considered antithetical to Modernism. The modernization of architecture in Japan was, in fact, identical with its Westernization. Since that time, save for the period of architecture of imperial Japan's Greater East Asia Co-Prosperity Sphere, Western-cum-Modern Architecture has been the style of architecture presented as the face of the modern Japanese state. Even today, Westernization seems to have permeated not only the field of architecture, but also, as pointed out by Tomiyama Takao, every aspect of social institutions and culture.

But with the establishment of Structuralism by Claude Lévi-Strauss, the Western world was brought down to the relative plane. It became no more than one region of the world. At the height of the West's cultural hubris, some dreamed that Esperanto, an artificial language fabricated semiotically from Western languages, would become the universal language of the world. The dream was never more than that. Language with a capital *L* had collapsed. French, English, German, Hebrew, Japanese—all are languages emerging from distinct cultural contexts, and it finally came to be recognized that the deepening of cultural uniqueness could lie in their symbiotic relation to dialogue with the world. It is not that the center has shifted from the West to the East, but that an age of symbiosis among heterogeneous cultures has begun in which diverse values horizontally coexist.

With this the death of *A*rchitecture is confirmed. Minor literature, i.e., *l*iterature, and minor architecture, *a*rchitecture, are arising. Minor architecture—the heterogeneous, the sacred, the violent, and noise—is introduced into *A*rchitecture, which previously controlled the whole and the center. In his *La violence et le sacre* and *To Double Business Bound,* René Girard, Post-Structuralist, criticizes Lévi-Strauss, saying that the Lévi-Straussian mythology retains a system without any self-destructive factor; that the very concept of structure contains something static that refuses and negates intervention from outside. He then defines the true intention of mythology as a series of crises or events that create—or recreate—a cultural order. Such a crisis, event, sacred thing, or instance of violence, which Girard calls the "theatrical factor," has something in common with the intervention of "contingency" and "order from noise" as repeatedly emphasized in the numerous writings of Edgar Morin. Callard emphasizes, too, in his *Exploration of Signs,* synchronic "happenings" and the intervention of the diachronic noise of tradition and past as opposed to "static" structure, system, and form. This is also related to Masao Yamaguchi's ideas concerning the center versus the periphery.

The effort to explore uniquely Japanese space or to discover the meeting points between Modern Architecture and Japanese culture, the importance of which I have asserted for decades, means, in this context, to contrast the Other, the Architecture, and the whole system of Western values with Japanese culture as theatrical "event" and as "noise."

The advent of *a*rchitecture announces the death of *A*rchitecture.

Structuralism as Method

People harshly harshly ridiculed my warning quoted in an essay in the *Mercure de France,* "The artist must swallow locomotives and spit out pipes." What I meant by this phrase was that in order to mechanize their art, painter and musician alike should make use of the orderly excitation called forth by the appearances of machines.

—Jean Cocteau, *Le coq et l'arlequin*

In contrast to the atomistic thesis to simply equate a sum entity (composite) with an inventory of disparate sub-elements (components), structuralism searches out those relationships that situate value or advantage at particular loci within that unified total body (system) organized of bonding correlations between referent elements, and further, it consists in grasping these whole systems as replenished with signs through the action of articulated interplay between wholes. Accordingly, structuralism involves two notions: the one being integral continuity, and the other mutual irreducibility.

—Jean Pouillon, editor, *Problémes du structurisme*

Modern Architecture stands, in many ways, directly opposed to structuralism. First, functionalism as a direction in modern architecture assumed an atomistic approach in regarding any given architectural entity as nothing more than the sum of its parts, an articulated assemblage of various component spaces for different functions. Second, as a product of the West, and, particularly, the economic expansion of the West in the form of industrialization, and not just a product, but a harbinger and evangelist as well, Modern Architecture assumed the hierarchy of civilizations, with the West at its spex, that we have discussed earlier; and it carried this gospel with it as it spread, and was spread, from the West across the globe during the industrializing boom of the nineteenth and the first half of the twentieth century.

This relentlessly expansionist period has been aptly characterized by Lévi-Strauss as an "age of violence." One after another Asian, Islamic, and African cultures were marginalized, the diversity and integrity of their unique spatial configurations supplanted by a unilateral time scale under the nineteenth-century historical imperative to developmental progress. Lévi-Strauss challenged the "old line" through rediscovery of yet older values. His structuralist investigations into the processes by which these "minor" cultures diversified in concert with their respective historical circumstances effectively reintroduced the qualities of relativity and mutuality to the Westernized world.

But when we consider carefully, is not the triumph of Modern Architecture as an extension of the nineteenth-century historical imperative continuing to this very day? Wherever we go throughout the Islamic, African, or Asian world we encounter the same modern structures of steel, glass, and concrete, and, more recently, mirror-glass. Everywhere the same line of thought, the same none-too-subliminal message—"Thou shalt assimilate Western cultural values. Thou shalt partake of the joys of Western living"—in utter disregard of a broad spectrum of equally valid world views. It has been the Structuralism of Lévi-Strauss that has raised a critical dissenting voice to the violent displacement of these unique cultural spaces in irreversibly uniform time. Specifically, his panchronic survey of the sheer range of cultures as simultaneously inhabitable parallel spaces may be said, as a method, to have laid the foundations for the Postmodern sensibility.

The Structuralist method so widely applied in cultural anthropology articulates matters at the smallest objective unit—for instance, at the level of family or totem—and proceeds to correlate these elements by tracing the thread of their own inherent logic to arrive at mutual relationships on a higher order of abstraction; then on to build up a network of relationships among relationships. The result is a conceptual model constructed and proven operational by purely Structural means. Such Structuralist models have not, however, escaped their share of criticism. For no matter how systematic these structures, their diverse bases are bound to incorporate certain potential contradictions in order to achieve even temporary stability. Furthermore, these models structured of admissible "signal" information invariably exclude a vast background of unrecognized "noise" non-information, with no allowance for their integration.

Clearly, to the degree Postmodern society continues to move in the direction of a "hot society," its structure will remain in a dynamic state. The inherent inconsistencies between multiple determinant parameters as reflected in tensions across a plurality of mutually exclusive social standards will cause the system to undergo ceaseless change.

Pleasing Machines

Once we posit a structure abstracted via some conceptual model of reality, we must come to terms with that residual quantum of "non-information" we have failed to incorporate in our structuralized reality. We must invoke dualistic notions of internal structure and exterior areas, order and chaos, center and periphery.

In order to overcome the obvious limitations of such thinking, Deleuze and Guattari introduced a provocative new concept: *la machine*. Not to be confused with machinery in the sense of physical mechanics, this *machine* finds its metaphor in the rhizomelike convolutions of organic physiology by which it embraces reality as is, intact in all its life and activity. "A machine far removed from so-called machines," it goes against our customary associations with the word. So it is when speaking of those uniquely human mechanics, the multifarious configurations of enmeshing desires through which we give rise to human society, Deleuze and Guattari refer to *les machines désirantes*; while the workings which counterbalance these toward some measure of stability they label *la machine sociale*. An indiscriminately unraveling fabric of desire laid out with no particular area more central than any other, there is much here on common ground with Barthes's *texte*. Perpetually in flux, always generating schisms, a living machine bearing forth a rich cross-fertilization of relationships.

Now what is architecture if not one class among the more basic in that seemingly endless list of desire-force interweavings to human society? Whether through the characterization, articulation, arrangement, or structuring of space, the real structural model here is nothing other than society itself. Cast amidst the "noise" or not, this interpenetrating body of relationships we know as society cannot help but enjoy a compounded share of ambiguities and multivalences. A dining room is not just "a space for dining," any more than a bedroom is merely "a space for bedding down." To take them at face value would be to misread the abstract and altogether provisional nature of such model structures.

Nonetheless, a structure that subsumes its own externalized "noise" has already ceased to be a defined structure. For once released from interior-exterior, order-chaos dichotomies, that which was structure itself becomes infused with "other-than-structure." A happy "confusion," as it turns out, precipitating entrance into an unrestricted diversity as divertissement; a play world in every sense of the word, where to see is simultaneously to be seen to appear, where to observe is at once to be observed in action. And architecture sets the double stage, replete with signs as visible emblems to the world outside in the same instant it provides opera glasses through which to look out on that world as an "open object." This again concurs with Barthes: in *le plaisir du texte,* pleasure derives from and indeed is identified with total immersion in the textual object.

Not actually partaking as such, but rather taking the external world and actions of others as "open objects" freely available for viewing, listening, enjoying—so that these pursuits become wholly absorbing acts of scrutiny. Once this level of play is achieved, all is equally fascinating. And much as there are no such things as localized erogenous zones, contrary to what we have been led to believe, we soon discover that any apparent "central" concern or object to *les machines plaisantes* just disappears. The center is everywhere and nowhere. This phenomenon resists explanation by either structural or functional approaches. An atmosphere of pleasure intensifies over the entire machine like a charged field.

The fervor of the 1920s, especially in the sudden enervation of Modern Architecture, turned excited eyes toward machines. And what machines were these back in the twenties? When Le Corbusier made his famous statement, "Houses are machines for living," the image of the machine was on the order of a 1921 Delage sports car or a grain silo. They were looking to mechanistic machinery, but even so the focus was not on its mechanical junctioning. Rather the machine was taken up as a symbol, the machine at work in our sensibilities.

If the *machine* of Deleuze and Guattari is a machine in the philosophical sense, then that of Le Corbusier and company ranged over the artistic awareness of the times. The inner workings were never so much in question as the symbolic values projected by the sleek surfaces of machines.

The artists, architects, and designers of de Stijl saw machines separating humanity from base nature, working to promote the spiritualization of life. In an unfinished paper, Theo van Doesburg held that "The machine is a superlative manifestation of spiritual refinement. Materialism in life and art exalts it as direct psychological expression. The new spiritually aesthetic sensibilities of the twentieth century do not merely respond to the beauty of the machine, but recognize in the machine infinite possibilities of expression unheard of in the plastic arts. Every machine is a spiritualized organism." The machine thus stood as a perishable spiritual essence of organic existence, a symbol.

Unfortunately, the path taken thereafter by Modern Architecture was that of functionalism, in analogy with the mechanical workings of the machine. The very principle of linearity governing mechanized motion was uncritically adopted as the guiding principle for Modern Architecture. The modern world was launched on the road to ruin the moment Le Corbusier attacked Camillo Sitte's city planning as "disorderly thinking." He blasted meandering streets, calling them "donkey paths," and claimed straight thoroughfares alone to be fit for "human streets." He even went so far as to declare, "People have purpose, therefore they head straight" (*Vers une architecture,* 1923), when in fact it was the precision of mechanized motion that proceeded straight ahead, faithful to orders. Does not our very humanity consist in the ability to veer, zigzag, detour, go any which way to attain our purposes?

The great error of Modern Architecture was to forget that initial vision of the machine as a "spiritualized organism," to forcibly constrain our search to the straight and narrow path of the machine-as-mechanism analogy. It was only logical, then, to reduce the surface aspect to pure abstraction and concentrate on the structure in order to clarify the workings of the mechanism. So all traditional, historical signifiers were fated to be swept aside.

But times have changed. Have we not reached the point of return to the ideals of Modern Architecture of the twenties? Have we not come the full circle back to reviving the machines of spiritualization? Architecture now demands something beyond functionalism, beyond structuralism, beyond semiotics.

What this something might be is difficult indeed to pinpoint, for if anything the aim is to realize an enjoyable atmosphere, *une architecture plaisante.* We seek a concretized poetic that transcends both linearity and literalism. People do not proceed in straight lines because they have purpose; they wander through complex mazes, digress down meandering rhizomelike passageways in order to discover their purposes. Function enters into the picture, of course, but that is only one consideration. Desire, excitement, expectation, disappointment, supposition, fear, all the shades of our humanity play in the general amazement. Seeing and being seen, centricity and periphery, ostentation and understatement, vulgarity and sanctity, seriousness and frivolity, the past and the future—all dichotomies arise simultaneously to coexist in the rhizome mazeway. This mutuality, above all else, is what sets our sights toward architecture as *machines plaisantes.* The philosophy of symbiosis is, in a word, an attempt to give conceptual and architectural form to this atmosphere, this ambiguity, this rhizome mazeway. It was the search for ways to imbue architectural and urban space with the qualities of diachronicity and synchronicity.

The exaltation of the West, which reigned unchecked in Modern Architecture, is dead. We are now able to easily move across diverse cultural contexts and combine elements of different backgrounds in the creation of a synchronic architecture. The international age of Modern Architecture and the International Style is over; let us usher in the intercultural age of a truly Intercultural Style.

The dualism that shaped Modern Architecture is fundamental to Western culture, and the source of the analytical approach taken by functionalism is not, strictly speaking, modern. It can be seen at the very basis of Western rationalism. Traced to its origin, it can be found in the architectural thought of the ancient Greeks. In the *Metaphysics,* Aristotle says that the forms of the major elements of beauty are *taxis, symmetria,* and *horismenon,* which are especially clearly revealed in mathematics. *Taxis* means order. *Symmetria* means measured together, indicating total division of the whole on the basis of a fixed dimension or volume. *Horismenon* means restriction. The ancient Greeks interpreted philosophy to mean first separating things from chaos and then ordering and restricting them by means of rational operations. The principle of rational selection and division has been the dominant current in Western thought in all ages. This has led to a strong reliance on thinking in terms of dualities: good and bad gods, gods of light and the dark world of matter, the mythoreligious duality between god as creator and his created beings. Descartes evolved a duality between the physical being and the spirit, which, as a finite entity, must rely on God. Kant's philosophy of matter and phenomena or of freedom and predestination is a further development of the same dualism. Today the analytical approach and dualism dominate architectural, urban, and social structures in all industrialized nations.

In his book *Culture and Ambiguity (Bunka to Ryogisei)*, anthropologist Masao Yamaguchi says, "It is possible to assume from the ambiguous communal relation between ancient peoples and their gods that human culture has produced, reproduced, and maintained its peripheral surroundings in many different forms. Interestingly, the closer things are to the center of a culture, the more primary they are; and the more strongly and clearly we discriminate among them. In contrast, we are much less clearly aware of things on the periphery. For this reason, such things are imbued with vagueness, which is the same thing as polysemy. Polysemy works, not for analytical separation, but for synthesis and the formation of new connections. This can be illustrated from semantics. A word that has many meanings (polysemy) is discriminated from all other words by its most surface meaning and connected with them by its latent meanings."

The longer Modern Architecture occupies a central place in Western culture, the more evident it becomes that the only way to revitalize it is through invigorating contacts with the heterogenous cultures now forced to the periphery of things. And a philosophical means for doing this is also required, a way of thinking that allows apparently disparate elements to coexist without undermining the uniqueness and value of either. This is, I believe, to be found in the idea of coexistence or symbiosis.

Transcending the Modern Dualism: The Mediating, Third Element

The idea of coexistence is easy to discover in many stages of the lineage of Oriental philosophy. For instance, the Indian Vedantas put forth a principle of absolute nondivisibility, according to which the individual, fundamental self includes many other mutually opposing entities, which are, however, fused. The Indian religious philosopher Nagarjuna (second and third centuries), founder of the Madhyamika School of Mahayana Buddhism, insisted that we are neither existent nor nonexistent and that we can attain enlightenment by rejecting such dualisms as existence and nonexistence. Interestingly, the Buddhist concept of *sunyata* (often, though not entirely accurately, translated as void) assumes a third viewpoint between existence and nonexistence. The Buddhist idea of *sunyata* can be contrasted with the idea of nothingness (*xuwu*) of Laozi or the idea of mystery (*xuan*) of Zhuangzi. The yin-yang philosophy, an important cornerstone of ancient Chinese culture, posits not a duality but a triad including the heavens (*yang* element), earth (*yin* element), and man. Although the concepts of nothingness, void, and humanity differ from each other, they are all basically third (intermediate) concepts making possible the coexistence of opposites.

Since human beings live in contradictory ways, it is only natural that society and cities too should contain mutually contradictory, opposing elements. As might be expected, however, the analytical approach strives to eliminate from architecture and cities the intermediate spaces and vagueness that formerly existed harmoniously there. In doing away with these things, they decrease ambiguity and diversity in human beings as well.

I must make it perfectly clear that I do not consider functionalism inefficacious. But I do think we should glean and pick up again the things—intermediary zones and vagueness—that the functionalists have cast away. Oriental philosophy and Japanese culture provide an excellent groundwork on which to do this gleaning. As I mentioned above, the view of existence held by the great Buddhist thinker Nagarjuna contrasts sharply with both materialistic and scientific interpretations. In his verses collected in the *Mula-madhyamika-sastra,* Nagarjuna explains the nature of *sunyata* and, in doing so, comments that truth is not found in the rejection of all things as illusory. Instead, ultimate truth is to be found in an understanding of all things in their true states—an understanding that all things, though nonexistent, mysteriously exist. The Madhyamika school of Buddhist thought, based largely on the interpretation of *sunyata* in the *Prajñaparamita,* or Wisdom, sutras, advocated the rejection of the existence of all things and phenomena According to this teaching, all phenomena that we conceive as such are no more than conceptual names (*namadheya*) and are lacking in true existence. Nagarjuna rectified, organized, and systematized this philosophy of *sunyata,* which tends to lapse into nihilism. Some years after Nagarjuna's death, the *Samdhinirmocana-sutra,* the first classic of the Consciousness Only school of Buddhist thought, was compiled, and it shows evidence of influence from and development of Nagarjuna's thought. This new school of Buddhist thought was further developed and elaborated by three great teachers: Maitreya (c. 270 to c. 350), Asanga (310–90), and Vasubandhu (fifth century). To clarify my own theory of intermediary zones and vagueness, I shall discuss the teachings of the Consciousness Only School here briefly.

The pre-Buddhist Upanishads, philosophical and devotional texts of the Indian Brahmanic tradition, held that the ultimate aspect of the human individual is the self (*atman*), which is one with the greater universal self (*Brahman*). Shakyamuni, the historical Buddha, rejected this theory and explained that there is no such thing as an eternally persisting, indestructible, unified self. All that does exist is a succession of selves instantaneously coming into existence and undergoing destruction. This is called the nonself (*anatman*). Side by side with the *atman* in traditional Indian thought was the concept of *samsara* (transmigration) and of karmic law, according to which good or bad acts in one life account for births in good or bad states in numerous other lives. Transmigration and the *anatman* (nonself) of the Buddhist teaching are clearly contradictory. This contradiction was resolved, however, by the Yogacara school of Mahayana Buddhism, which evolved the idea of the storehouse consciousness (*alaya-vijnana*) containing potentials (seeds) for the generation of all kinds of existences. Given the right opportunity and contributory cause, the storehouse consciousness manifests itself in concrete phenomena, the effects of which it receives in turn. According to this doctrine, the ultimate self is not the *atman* but consciousness, or the storehouse consciousness, which can be subject to transmigration. In other words, the concept of the storehouse consciousness reconciles the difference between the Buddhist teaching of nonself (*anatman*) and the older tradition of transmigration, both of which are assimilated within the Consciousness Only school of Mahayana Buddhism.

Descartes interpreted matter and spirit as two absolute entities. A believer in the Consciousness Only school of Buddhist thought, on the other hand, would say that both matter and spirit are manifestations of something more fundamental than either. This more fundamental something is the storehouse consciousness. (I cannot say whether Louis Kahn ever studied this school of Buddhist philosophy, but his general approach resembles it.)

Early Buddhism and Japanese aesthetic awareness after the medieval period are strongly colored by spiritualism. Both give the spirit precedence over matter and devote much attention to the transience of the world and the pathos of that transience. In contrast, the Consciousness Only Buddhist approach views both matter and spirit as no more than manifestations in code of the fundamental storehouse consciousness. They are only forms of existence. In architectural terms, this approach does not emphasize the duality between beauty and function—function is beauty; only the beautiful is functional—but insists that both beauty and function are only coded manifestations of awareness or consciousness. This seems an excellent hint for the reconstitution of architecture on the basis of semiology or semantics.

Early Buddhism explains all things, including essential being and phenomena, in terms of what is called the five aggregates—form, perception, mental concepts, volition, and self-consciousness. The Consciousness Only school, however, employs a different classification of five aggregates: form, mind, emotion, a category including things that are neither mental nor physical but that partake of both, and nonaction. The category of things neither mental nor physical but that partake of both represents what I call an intermediate zone and is a characteristic of the Consciousness Only philosophy. This idea is most clearly set forth in fascicle three of the Chinese Consciousness Only School work entitled *Cheng Weishi Lun,* which is a theoretical analysis of the storehouse consciousness. In that work, the storehouse consciousness is described as "unimpeding moral neutrality"; that is, it consists of those acts that are neither morally good nor morally bad but neutral, and that do not impede a person on the way to enlightenment. This is another intermediate zone quite unlike the clear Christian dichotomy between good and evil. The division made is not bipartite but tripartite: good, evil, and neutral. Neutral is neither good nor bad, and the fundamental entity, the storehouse consciousness, is neutral in this respect.

The Mahayana view of Consciousness Only left deep impressions on the neutral zones and ambiguity of Japanese culture. In the following chapter, I will point out many examples of this kind of thing in the past: the moment of silent pause in the Noh drama that Zeami calls *senuhima*; the neutral grays associated with the seventeenth-century tea master Sen no Rikyu; the eternal flow mentioned by the haiku poet Basho; the juxtaposition of two alien images to generate neutrality in the work of the poet Fujiwara no Teika; the blend of *shoin* and *sukiya* architectural styles in what is called *hana suki*; the street as communal space; Daisetz Suzuki's teaching of nondifferentiation and nonuniformity; the widespread use of the word *ma,* or interval, in Japanese aesthetics; and so on. All these things represent intermediate zones, ambiguity, and vagueness that, arising in part from the philosophy of Consciousness Only, flow throughout Japanese culture.

The highly original Japanese natural philosopher Miura Baien (1723–89) represents an attempt to organize the thought manifest in these cultural traits. The foundation of his trilogy *Discourse on Metaphysics, Discourse on Corollaries,* and *Discourse on Morality,* is the idea that mankind must set aside all preconceived views and examine the universe as an endless unity. He advocates what he called the logic of things (*jori*) that finds unity in contradiction and that, in mathematical terms, is illustrated by the idea that one remains one whether divided by itself or multiplied by itself. Though some scholars have interpreted Miura's thought as a dialectic born a half century before Hegel, I prefer to view it as derived from the Consciousness Only school of Buddhist thought and from a rejection of dualities. In these respects, his is an extremely typical Oriental philosophy.

Miura interprets space not as a container but as something that fills bodies. In part of his *Discourse on Metaphysics,* he says that place includes interior (*naka*). This interior is the skeleton or framework of place. Time opens the present. The present vitalizes time. Nothing exists without form. Consequently, place and things are able to come into being. Place exists in containers. As soon as something is, it is capable of being a vehicle. As soon as something is contained, it is being borne as if in a vehicle. The interior partakes of the natures of both the bearer and the borne. By *interior* Miura means something that is not physical in nature and that is neither area nor volume. In a letter, Miura wrote: "Considering the theory of the division of one makes it apparent that all things in the universe contend with each other. But, though they are different in quality, in the total view, they are all one. They are all, therefore, compounded of the same divinity. It is important to see unity transcending difference."

In a recent work on this important thinker, Masakazu Takahashi said that Miura Baien's approach is incompatible with the dialectical method. He finds more pertinent sources for Miura's thought in Chinese writings: the Book of Changes and the ancient classics *Laozi, Zhuangzi, Huainanzi, Fangzhi,* and a work on physics called the *Wuli Xiao Lun.* It is not certain that Miura ever studied the Consciousness Only Buddhist doctrine, but I see similarity between its view of *sunyata* and his theory of space. His concept of interior is very much like the *alaya-vijnana* storehouse consciousness of this school of Buddhist thought.

In short, Miura Baien is an illustration substantiating my belief that the Japanese cultural context and research into it can contribute to the construction of a new paradigm for contemporary architecture that can overcome the analytic, dualistic approach—interior and exterior, architecture and nature, residence and city, technology and humanity, part and whole, detail and structure, private ownership and public ownership, function and beauty, material and spiritual—and help restore intermediate zones, ambiguity, and vagueness.

Another important inspiration for my thought over the years has been the words of the Zen philosopher Daisetz Suzuki. In particular, Suzuki's discussion of the "logic of identity and nonidentity" (*sokuhi no ronri*) has played a major part in my thinking. The logic of identity and nonidentity is summed up by the statement "A is non-A; therefore it is called A." "A" refers, in the Buddhist context, to "the perfection of wisdom" (in Sanskrit, *prajnaparamita*), or enlightenment; "non-A" is ignorance, or this karmic realm (*samsara*). The Diamond Sutra, a classic of Buddhist literature, is Suzuki's source for this discovery. Though Suzuki uses the English phrase "logic of identity and nonidentity," another, perhaps more accessible way to translate *sokuhi no ronri* is "the principle of the dynamic identity of opposites," for the identity A and non-A is not just a linguistic trick. We do not simply choose to call contradictory opposites one. They are *actually* the same, since they are dynamically interrelated and in fact each is the sine qua non, and, in a soteriological sense, the *cause* of the other. In other words, what seem to be contradictions turn out in the end to be identities, which is why Suzuki calls the mutually inclusive relation of part and whole a logic of identity and nonidentity. In Zen Buddhism one frequently encounters the teaching that while the human being is only a part of the universe, since the entire universe is embraced within his consciousness, the universe and the individual are mutually embracing.

With the crisis of modern Western philosophy and the new interest in the concept of coexistence, or symbiosis, worldwide, these nondual philosophies are attracting the attention of many.

One is Arthur Koestler (1905–85). In such works as *Transcending Reductionism, The Holon Revolution,* and *Beyond Atomism and Holism: Concept Holon* (original title, *Janus*), he explains that he has coined the term *holon* by combining the greek root *holos,* meaning the whole, and the suffix *on,* for "part" or "particle." Thus the word *holon* simultaneously signifies the part and the whole. Koestler is a critic of reductionism, which reduces a phenomenon to its parts for analysis. In that process, he insists, the essence of the phenomenon, which is what it is because of the harmonious sum of its parts, is inevitably lost and the thing itself falsified. Koestler contributed an essay entitled "The Tree and the Candle" to *Unity Through Diversity,* a collection of papers published to commemorate the seventieth anniversary of the birth of Ludwig von Bertalanffy, the originator of general systems theory. In his essay, Koestler describes the properties of the *holon* with two examples. He uses a burning candle as a metaphor for the concept of an open system, since the candle, while retaining its own basic form, takes oxygen from the atmosphere around it and in turn releases moisture, carbon dioxide, water, and heat. He cites a tree as a living example of levels of hierarchy. The tree is an intermediate structure, because it represents the whole system for all units smaller than it, but at the same time it is only another unit in an even larger system, the forest.

According to Koestler, biological and social structures as well as human activities and linguistic systems all exhibit these two properties of openness and hierarchy. He calls this the open hierarchy, which he regards as the fundamental characteristic of the *holon*. The original title *Janus* refers to the two-faced god of Roman mythology who on the one hand forces humanity into the various levels of the hierarchy but on the other hand urges them on to a transcendent and whole reality. For in Koestler's part and whole there is the drive toward the symbiosis of man and God. Koestler also postulates three levels of reality: sensual awareness is the first level, followed by conceptual awareness, and finally the mystical awareness of "oceanic feeling," a world that transcends both sense perceptions and concepts. Koestler claims that this oceanic feeling is similar to the synchronicity that was described by Carl Jung and Wolfgang Pauli. I have interpreted the idea of synchronicity to mean the symbiosis of past, present, and future. Koestler, however, while referring to Jung and Pauli's synchronicity, enlarges it to mean the symbiosis of body and spirit, consciousness and the unconsciousness, and man and god. As Koestler formulates it, synchronicity is not simply a symbiosis of different time periods, but approaches the concept of a metamorphosis of consciousness.

The Dutch architect Aldo van Eyck's Twin Phenomena Paradigm has caused a restructuring within the existing hierarchy of Western thought, shattering the barrier of dualism with the two-sided declaration, "The city is a big house and the house is a small city." Impressive as this concept is for the major influence it exerted on world architecture, I personally find more of interest in the "I and Thou" philosophy of Martin Buber, upon which it is based. Unlike the one-sided "I" of one's space-time existence measured against the "it" of things, the "I" one becomes through engaging in a relationship with an identical-yet-different "Thou" exists outside space-time, beyond Western logical order. That Buber has taken a step toward Buddhist philosophy becomes self-evident when we count up how often he quotes from the Buddhist canon. Even Van Eyck's paradigm can be said to have brought an element of non-Western Buddhist philosophy to contemporary architecture. And as Charles Jencks stressed in his *Modern Movements in Architecture,* the issue of ambivalence or multiple meaning is the key to the most important happenings in all that is current in art, architecture, and culture.

Functionalism as a direction in Modern Architecture assumed an atomistic approach in regarding any given architectural entity as nothing more than the sum of its parts, an articulated assemblage of various component spaces for different functions. At the same time, the whole of Modern Architecture itself, having first broken ground within the rather special context of the post-industrial revolution West, should rightfully be considered an outgrowth of that culture. In its spread worldwide, the so-called International Style thus hallmarked the all-encompassing sweep of Westernization. We must deconstruct the linear, dualistic models of time and space that are the legacy of the Western rational tradition and the Modern

Architecture born from it. And, of course, the destructuring of space-time is pre-requisite to the establishment of the two principles of diachronicity and synchron-icity. Not only does time have to be dismantled from the constraints of linear con-tinuity, but each point in time has to achieve a free-floating autonomy. Time now becomes like a pearl necklace or DNA double helix, assuming whatever configura-tion the situation demands. Moreover, just as time has to come apart at its under-pinnings in order for history to symbiotically coalesce with the present and with the future, space also has to be deconstructed to collapse the Western-dominated cultural pyramid and allow each particular culture an autonomy of values. Only in such a destructured world could the various different cultures freely permute recombinations.

The breaking down of space-time came as an inevitable step toward reversing the worldwide onslaught of Western values and modern uniformity, but that alone is not enough. The destructuring of one architecture does not instantaneously bring forth the next. Nor will the analytical recombination of bits of particulate space-time make for effective creation. We must plumb deeper, to the nondual core of being and knowing. Even Western science has come to realize that the phenomenon of light can only be properly understood as a "wavicle"—both wave and particle. No matter how it is divided up into function-specific units, architec-tural space begins to fuse back together in interpenetrations of meanings, an ongo-ing functional articulation that at the same time links up information. This mutually inclusive symbiotic relationship between part and whole, between function and meaning is the metamorphosis which we must seek.

The dismantling of conventional architecture afforded the opportunity to analyt-ically dissect the signs embedded in architectural space. It was discovered that the "parts" did not necessarily have to correspond to functions. No, each differentiated space corresponded to something utterly inexplicable in terms of function: semiotic meaning. In the semiology of Ferdinand de Saussure and Roland Barthes, the "signified" (*signfiié*) and "signifier" (*significant*) stand in one-to-one correlation to one another. But does this necessarily still hold true in today's society? The surface of urban life, replete with an overabundance of signs, seems to utterly disavow any such correspondence. In Japan, it is said, at least half those who buy pianos today see their purchase as a status symbol or piece of interior decor. The sign has come to yield meanings wholly removed from what it originally signified.

Architecture and urban planning must serve to facilitate not only function, but meaning, too. We sense this already in the newer writings of Gilles Deleuze, Felix Guattari, Julia Kristeva, and others, in Jean Baudrillard's *l'échange symbolique*—a shift from sign to *simulacre*. Clusters of signifiers divorced from meaning now produce *simulacres* of meaning or pseudomeanings, which color and humanize spaces with humor, wit, speculation, and conviviality. The metamorphosis of free-floating signifiers and *simulacres* creates realms of "atmosphere" or "mood." These poetic spaces open up not through the recombination of signs, but in stretching ambiguities to the very periphery of sign systems, to the ambivalent interplay of diverse *simulacres*.

Even such a Postmodern sensibility as Camp may be seen as a sophisticated form of recognizing the multiple meanings of things. Turning its back on accepted aesthetic judgments of good and bad, Camp and similar bad-is-good movements afford a new perspective on staid standards and issue a strong warning against the decay that comes from following the rules of the past too literally. They seek to acknowledge and accept the complications of human existence. Jean Genet remarked in *Notre Dame des Fleurs* that, in order to find a sense of multiple meaning within culture, good taste must not only be good taste but an awareness of what is bad taste as well. Camp achieves this, for it manages to interpret things in two ways and on two levels at the same time.

Our contemporary age has been characterized by the functionalist trend to minimalize inconsistencies and increase efficiency and rational planning. This has been the driving force behind modernization worldwide, as testified by the birth of the International Style in architecture and international standards of good design. We have achieved our initial ends; is it not time we returned to the starting point, to the actual ambivalent quality of the life we humans live? Admittedly, the acceptance of seemingly chaotic ambiguity may be hard to come to terms with, yet do we not all feel the need for a rehumanization of our living environment? Should we not broaden our perspectives outward to the peripheries of possibility, and inward to the profundities of the human spirit, a spirit that in its original nature is indivisible, rich with ambiguities, and harmoniously balanced—a world of Rikyu gray?

CHAPTER TWO

Rikyu Gray:
An Open-Ended Aesthetic

I N THIS CHAPTER I would like to explore the Japanese sources, both architectural and those of broader cultural scope, to which we may turn in search of
Japanese space. I will begin with a brief introduction of the Edo period, which I
believe is little understood and appreciated in comparison with earlier periods of
Japanese history. Following that, I would like to outline some general concepts of
Japanese aesthetics by discussing selected terms that I think are suggestive of the
principles behind the Japanese aesthetic sensitivity. Then I will proceed to what
is one of the primary models of Japanese space, the tea room, and the aesthetic
ideal of *wabi* associated with the way of tea and usually regarded as the main or,
indeed, sole lineage of Japanese aesthetics. I believe that many in West and East
have misunderstood the tea aesthetic, and I would like to present what may be a
controversial interpretation but is to me a valid reevaluation of it, while looking
in detail at classic historical tea rooms and those of my own design.

From there I will pull back and widen the scale of my discussion, from the minimal
space of the tea room to the Japanese village and city: urban space, a subject which
has occupied me at all stages of my career from the earliest beginnings to the present.
I would like to explore a variety of models, including those of ancient Indian cities;
Buddhist mandalas as a depiction of the city; Kyoto, where the street is the unit of
urban life; and a theory of urban revitalization based on stimulus of critical points,
after the model of traditional Chinese healing practices.

Reappraising the Edo Period

Japan was a blank space to the rest of the world during the more than two hundred
sixty years between 1600 and 1868, a time known in Japan as the Edo period. At

the start of the period, the rulers of Japan adopted an isolationist policy, effectively withdrawing from international affairs. They preserved that stance with remarkable success until the end, when Commodore Perry's "black ships" arrived and forced Japan's doors open. The Edo period is named after the city of Edo, which was the capital of the Tokugawa shoguns, Japan's military rulers. The period is also called the Tokugawa period. Their capital was renamed Tokyo in 1868. The Edo period also represents the last historical period before the opening of Japan to the flood of Westernization that began in the following era, the Meiji, or "Luminous Reign," which lasted from 1868 to 1912. Thus the Edo period—or more broadly, the three-century span of purely Japanese culture from the mid-sixteenth to the mid-nineteenth century—holds the roots of all that is Japan today.

The major Japanese art traditions that survive today—the way of tea (*sado*), flower arrangement (*ikebana*), the Noh and Kabuki dramas, *sukiya* architecture—all can be traced back to the latter half of the sixteenth century and all gained popular acceptance in the Edo period. They flourished until the "reforms" of the Meiji era brought on a wholesale rejection of everything associated with the past. Certainly the new government, but also the populace, sought to disassociate itself from the feudal past in the push toward Westernization, even if that meant depreciating "premodern" life and culture.

With the opening to the West, architecture in Japan suddenly started copying Western architecture outright. Japanese took to wearing Western clothes. This seems to support the dogma that modern Japan began from the Meiji era. We often hear that Japan rose from a backward country to an advanced industrial state in a little over a hundred years, and that the leaders of developing nations should look to Japan as a model for their next hundred years of growth. Such explanations, however, overlook a number of important facts.

As is gradually becoming clear, the Edo period saw grand achievements in mass culture and was far more "modern" than previously thought. Ronald Dore notes in his *Education in Tokugawa Japan* that by the end of the Edo period (1868), forty-three percent of boys and ten percent of girls between the ages of six and thirteen attended school—higher percentages than in England at the time. Edo was the largest city in the world, with a population of well over a million. In scholarship, Yamagata Banto (1746–1821) proposed a steady-state theory of the solar system in his *Instead of Dreams* (*Yume no Shiro,* 1801), while Newton's leading pupil John Keill's early seventeenth-century commentary on his master's *Principia* was translated into Japanese by Shizuki Tadao (1760–1806) only very shortly after the work had reached France. By the early nineteenth century, cartographer Ino Tadataka (1745–1818) had drawn accurate maps of the Japanese islands. Moreover, in the 1770s, philosopher Miura Baien had set forth his dialectical system, predating Hegel's dialectic by half a century. Most important, however, Edo society had already attained its own unique modernity, quite distinct from Europe. No doubt the speed with which Japan was able to assimilate Western ideas and practices in the Meiji era, like a blotter absorbs ink, was in no small part due to the basically modern character of mature Edo society.

Yet further aspects of the Edo period have failed to receive the appreciation they deserve. Except for a few isolated "symbolic" buildings of particular acclaim—Katsura Detached Palace, Shugakuin Detached Palace, Toshogu Shrine—Edo-period architecture as a whole has resisted proper evaluation even to the present day. There are reasons for this. No one dominant architectural style emerges, as in the *shoin*-style castles, palaces, and samurai villas of the late sixteenth to early seventeenth-century Azuchi-Momoyama period. Many of the Nara, Heian, and Kamakura-period shrines and temples that for a thousand years had stood as the heart of Japanese architecture were destroyed by warlords Oda Nobunaga and Toyotomi Hideyoshi in their opposition to the Shinto and Buddhist backing of the old regimes immediately preceding the Edo period. Recovery was slow and did not result in the appearance of a dominant new style of temple architecture.

Another reason Edo architecture has suffered lack of recognition is its supposed "sameness." While carpenters' trade secrets had previously been discreetly passed down through the apprentice system, the publication of such manuals as the *Master's Revelations* (*Shomyo*) of the Heinouchi lineage or the *Kenninji School Transmission* (*Kenninjiha Kadensho*) of the Kora lineage of carpenters gave access to the carpentry trade, eventually leading to the conformity of methods and standardization of measures that can be seen in the 1655 *New Edition Pattern Book* (*Shimpen Hinagata*).

Standard proportions greatly contributed to the modernization and cumulative specialization of building, but they also created the impression that Edo architecture is undistinguished. Furthermore, in 1633 the shogunate instituted an Office of Carpentry (*sakujikata*), which was followed in turn by similar offices throughout the provinces. This no doubt infringed upon the creative liberties of the carpenter families, who up to then had served Shinto shrines and Buddhist temples generation after generation. Officialdom enforced increasing specialization and division of labor among the trades of chief carpenters, woodcarvers, painters, blacksmiths, plasterers, decorative artists, roofers, and wall builders. It also established the *kiwari* system through which all architectural details, materials, and measures were exhaustively stipulated and rigorously standardized. Anyone could understand and apply these standards, which meant considerable loss of individuality in works of architecture. In addition, it became difficult for any one creative architectural vision to prevail under such bureaucratized conditions. Large-scale projects presented less and less opportunity for the expression of the vision of an individual architect or master carpenter.

Edo painting and craft are similarly said to lack the originality of medieval Japanese art. Yet despite these partially justified criticisms, I believe that Edo architecture clearly embodied the leading features of the times as admirably as the architecture of any other historical period. What were, then, the features of Edo-period culture?

First, Edo Japan was a predominantly popular culture. In the eighth century, the total population of Japan was five million, and even a thousand years later, immediately prior to the Edo period, that figure had only just reached ten million.

One hundred years into the Edo period, however, the population had tripled, so that by the time of shogun Tokugawa Yoshimune (1716–45) it had reached thirty-one million. This in itself made for accelerated urbanization.

The city of Edo, as we have seen, was the world's largest metropolis, with upwards of a million inhabitants. Here flourished the world's first mass popular culture. The vast shrine and temple complexes of earlier ages gave way to the popular architecture of *sukiya*-style tea rooms, Kabuki, Noh, and Joruri theaters, as well as vernacular masterpieces in the forms of farmhouses and merchant townhouses. As papermaking and woodblock printmaking techniques developed, an incredible amount of popular literature burst forth in the forms of romances, humor, erotica, and several varieties of picture books—"blue books," folios, and "yellow covers" for adults, and "red books" and "black books" for children. Book stores sprang up all over Edo.

Architecture, too, became popularized, as we have seen above. Its secret traditions were made public, and its aristocratic, master-architect system was replaced with a code of methods and standards that could be applied freely by all.

The second great characteristic of Edo culture was its eclecticism. Of course, Japanese culture as a whole has always been an admixture of new stylistic features layered over earlier styles. Edo culture was more than a mere extension of this basic tendency, though; it carried this age-old process to a new zenith. The *gongen* architectural style, ranging from shogun Tokugawa Ieyasu's Toshogu shrine in Nikko to the Kanda Myojin, Yushima Tenjin, and Kameido Temmangu shrines of Edo, exemplifies this eclecticism. Named for the *gongen,* or "avatar," doctrine of Japanese Buddhism that taught that Shinto deities were local, Japanese manifestations of cosmic Buddhas, the *gongen* style freely blended elements from both Shinto and Buddhist architecture. The early Edo-period Hiunkaku, or "Flying Cloud Pavilion," of Nishi Honganji temple in Kyoto is likewise a masterpiece of eclectic styling, combining the aristocratic *shoin* style with the "rustic" thatched-hut (*soan*) style to create the *sukiya* style. In the late Edo period, as seen in woodblock prints, unique buildings blending newly imported Western-style architecture with traditional domestic architecture began to appear. The Yokohama Ijinkan, or "Foreigners' Hall," built late in the Edo period when Western influences were already being felt, especially in the port city of Yokohama, presents a unique example of mixed Japanese and Western styles.

The third characteristic of note in Edo culture were trends to compression and detail. The city of Edo was not only the largest but probably also the most densely populated metropolis in the world. In the rowhouse merchant quarters lived an estimated 675 persons per hectare, over four times the present-day 150 persons per hectare for the twenty-three wards of central Tokyo. Japanese residential architecture was keyed to the extended family, and individuals rarely had rooms of their own. Crowded into constant and intimate contact, people developed a sensitivity to subtle shifts of feeling, to changes in expression, gestures, and attitudes. Such interpersonal "fine tuning" enhanced a psychological appreciation of the introspective, emotional aspect of things. Etiquette demanded that one read the situation before acting. Words were shunned, and one attempted to reveal one's thoughts and feelings in unspoken ways. It was this densely peopled, compressed society that gave rise to the subtle, humanistic "daily life" (*sewamono*) dramas of Kabuki and the puppet theater.

Meticulous detailing was also evident in Edo-period crafts, including architecture. Handcrafted miniatures such as a writing box of millimeter dimensions decorated in *maki-e* lacquer exemplify the Edo mania for compression and detail. The typical Edo "pinpoint" (*komon*) kimono patterns, miniature books, and Buddhist altars for home use that reproduced temple altars in miniature all reveal this concern with miniaturizing. In architecture, more attention went to decorative detailing than ever before, as can be seen in the decorative carvings of Toshogu Shrine and the ornately ornamented Himeji Castle. *Sukiya* architecture, though less decorated than works of the *shoin* style, was more exacting in its array of natural materials, precise proportions, and finishing detail. Even crooked natural timbers were carefully selected, one from among hundreds, to consciously achieve just the right degree of artless appearance.

The complexity of human relations and social ties and the forced intimacy of the extended family and urban life in general led to an internalization of a whole spectrum of shades and nuances of feeling. At the same time, the closed, parochial society of isolationist Japan, steeped in centuries of its own tradition of nature appreciation, was conducive to reinforcing and refining a sensitivity toward the seasonal changes in nature. A fourth characteristic of Edo culture is the sophistication of its fictions. For a city mostly lacking in parks and plazas, Edo was uncommonly endowed with flowers and greenery. The doorways and inner courtyards of houses in the merchant quarters were lined with rows of potted bonsai, and in summer, morning glory and gourd vines climbed the facades. The villas of the samurai elite and wealthy entrepreneurs invariably encompassed large gardens in emulation of mountain retreats. Just as they invested years of patient pruning into shaping the branches of their bonsai, these city dwellers contrived fictitious "natural" settings that were amalgamations of many famous scenes, unlike any single real natural setting. The *sukiya*-style landscape gardens were fictions in miniature. People devoted much time and effort to creating artifices to inspire the imagination, and these artifices came to be more highly appreciated than the real thing.

This fictional quality was present in all the arts of the Edo period. The wood, paper, and mud of *sukiya*-style buildings and tea rooms were illusory evocations of a sense of naturalness. The Rimpa-school paintings of the brothers Ogata Korin (1658–1716) and Kenzan (1663–1743) are renowned for their striking compositional artifice, while the androgynous beauties of the mid-Edo period ukiyo-e artist Suzuki Harunobu (1725–70) achieved overwhelming popularity among the common classes for their idealized unreality. The typical Edo-period kimono patterns *benkei goshi* and *bojima* stripes further exemplify a sublimation of illusion into an abstraction close to that of contemporary art and design. The *onnagata* actors of Kabuki—males playing female roles—were widely believed to display a more heightened femininity than real women, and the puppets of the Joruri theater were thought more human than living actors. The same fictional inversion was adopted by popular courtesans of the Fukugawa brothel district, who affected male names. Such fictions and ambiguities were the hallmark of the sophisticated sensibility of Edoites.

A fifth characteristic of Edo culture was what can be called a humanized Asian rationality. The Tokugawa government's policy of isolationism notwithstanding, Western science and technology had in fact filtered into Japan by the mid-Edo period, spurring such developments as Nagasaki *bidoro* (*vidro*) blown glass, Satsuma *kiriko* cut glass, firearms, astronomy, geographical studies, and painting in perspective. With these had come a measure of rationalist thinking. Soon enough, however, this imported rationalism was deftly grafted onto Japanese traditions, yielding a tempered rationality peculiarly suited to Asian civilization and completely different from the direct copying of the West that was to take place after the Meiji Restoration of 1868. Gone was any divisive sense of dichotomy. Technology and humanity may have been at odds in the West, but in Japan technology became an extension of humanity to be integrated and internalized, just as material things were considered extensions of the spirit and part of the same undifferentiated existence. In Edo-period Japan, the "workings" (*karakuri*) of technology were not set apart from humanity, but rather humanized as something intrinsically mystical.

The idea of *karakuri* mechanized "works," as in the 1720 *Educational Catalogue of Automata* (*Karakuri Kummo Kagamigusa*) and the 1796 *Illustrated Collection of Automata* (*Karakuri Zui*), is representative of this approach. The mechanical puppet theater of Takeda Konoe Shojo was once the rage of Osaka, while the carpenter Hasegawa Kambei invented mechanized stage equipment that enabled the staging of even greater spectacle in Kabuki.

Karakuri devices in Edo architecture include the floating central columns of the 1793 five-story pagoda of Kanoji temple in Yanaka and the 1818 pagoda in Nikko. These columns are suspended from above and cut off just above ground level, lending no structural support. Yet in the event of an earthquake, their downward inertia served to increase the stability of the pagoda. Other examples of architectural *karakuri* can be found in the 1780 Sansodo, or "Three-turn Hall," of Rakanji temple and the 1796 Sazaedo, or "Spiral-shell Hall," of Shosoji temple in Aizu Wakamatsu. Integrated into the structure of the buildings, wholly invisible from the exterior, spiral staircases conveyed worshippers first upward along an outer spiral course, then downward via yet another inner course, giving them a symbolic experience of karmic transmigration. Here again, the Edo approach to rationalist technology was not to expose the workings, but to create a sense of mystery and wonder by concealing, and thus humanizing the mechanisms.

Even after Japan began to emerge from isolation and Western influences grew ever stronger in the late Edo period, the trend of cultural syncretism did not abate. Witness the Yokohama prints of Yoshitora (active 1830–80) and Hiroshige III (1843–94), or the Yokohama Courthouse, the various foreign trade offices of Yokohama, the Tsukiji Hotel, and other buildings introducing Western trusses and other structural innovations into traditional Japanese wood-frame construction.

1. This interior of a Kabuki theater, from a 1743 print by Torii Kiyotada, shows the eclectic, popular nature of Edo-period architecture and, especially, the creative use of intermediary space: the actor's passageway *(hanamichi)* through the audience, the projecting stage apron, and the raised divisions between the seats, which also serve as paths for the audience and for food and souvenir vendors. Note also the fictitious roof over the stage, a standard architectural feature of Kabuki theaters of this age.

2. The roof lines of the Hiunkaku—Flying Cloud Pavilion—of the Nishi Honganji in Kyoto are one of the best examples of the bold eclecticism of Japanese architecture of the Edo period.

3. Himeji Castle, in Hyogo Prefecture, shows the compression of detail that is a characteristic of Edo-period culture.

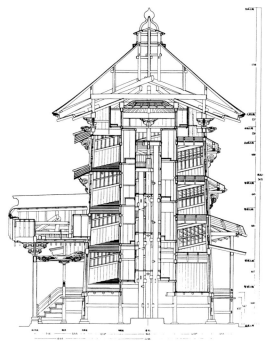

4. A cross section of Sazaedo—Conch Hall. A delight in invention, *trompe l'oeil,* and a belief in technology put to entertaining and aesthetically pleasing purposes are other traits of the Edo period.

5. Intermediary space in the *shoin,* or aristocratic residential, style of architecture: the moon-viewing platform *(tsukimidai)* projects into the garden of the Katsura Detached Palace in Kyoto.

6. The lattice doors of many traditional buildings in Kyoto are an ingenious combination of funcion and beauty, creating a warm intermediary space that marks the boundary between interior and exterior without insisting on it.

7. The "baroque" aesthetic of Rikyu gray: a symbiotic combination of floating and grounded spaces, curving and straight lines in the Yodomiseki tea room of the Saioin subtemple in Kyoto.

8. *(below)* A masterpiece of *hanasuki,* Furoan of the Garyu Sanso Villa in Ehime Prefecture. The vaulted ceiling is made of woven bamboo and is angled precisely to reflect the light of the moon riding over nearby Tomosuyama and shining on the Hiji River.

9. The exterior of Garyuin at Garyu Sanso Villa, seen from the garden. ▷

10. The very deep eaves shading the twisting *engawa of* Kyojuso, Apricot Tree Lodge, in Hachioji, Tokyo, are meant to pull the garden into the architecture. (Designed by Kisho Kurokawa)

11. The interior of the north wall of Ritsumeian, Chestnut Light Hut, the tea room on the grounds of Kyojuso, showing the interior eaves and the crawl-in entrance.

12. The interior of Chokaso, Morning Mist Lodge, Tokyo. A variety of graceful traditional forms adorns the tea room and provides dramatic interest: flower-shaped windows above the shoji doors at right, the gently cut arched transom after Katsura, and the cut-out wall to the left of the tokonoma. (Designed by Kisho Kurokawa)

13. The hearth area of Yuishikian, modeled after Kobori Enshu's Shosuitei by way of Shokado Shojo's Kan'unken. (Designed by Kisho Kurokawa)

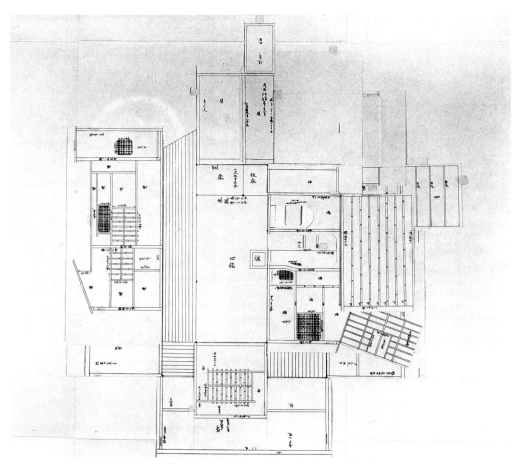

14. The folding paper plan for Shokado Shojo's Takimotobo residence at Hachimangu shrine, which included Kan'unken.

These five characteristics of Edo-period culture—its popularity, eclecticism, compression and detail, illusionism, and Asian humanism—served the Japanese very well and contributed to creating a remarkably rich, sophisticated, and truly modern culture, but with the advent of the Meiji Restoration and the overturning of the Edo regime, everything associated with it was swept aside, and for the last eleven decades up to the present Japan has followed a path of modernization—that is to say, Westernization. Yet it is now, at this turning point, when Modernism has met with setbacks on all fronts, that we should look again at Edo-period models of modernization and the special Japanese cultural characteristics these roots possess. I am convinced that Edo-period architecture can be an important guide toward the future of contemporary architecture. Next I would like to explore several key concepts of Japanese culture, particularly the Japanese spatial sensitivity, which I believe can best be summed up by the theme of Japan as a culture of grays.

A Culture of Grays

The spacial character of Japanese culture can perhaps best be described by its multiplicity of "grays." At the risk of oversimplifying, let me explain this by saying that Western societies have two-dimensional cultures, while Japanese society has a three- or multidimensional culture. The word *en,* which means "bond," "relationship," or "affinity," illustrates this point. *En* becomes a kind of prefix for other words such as *endan,* which refers to the negotiations (*dan*) involved in locating a marriage partner; marriage, of course, involves forming a long-lasting personal bond (*en*). *Engi,* the occurrence (*gi*) of a bond, is a Buddhist term that means "fortune" or "fate" or "destiny." The expression *engi ga yoi*—auspicious, lucky—thus describes many things, such as the Chinese character for eight, because the strokes of this character flare out at the base, suggesting prosperity and expansion, and such a motif clearly signifies good fortune. Certain days in the traditional calendar are designated as days of good fortune or "good *engi.*" Days that fall in the category of *taian* (great peace) are the most auspicious, and on those days wedding halls continue to be booked solid and airliners are full of honeymooning couples on their way to Hawaii or Guam.

Another term prefixed with *en* is *engawa,* or veranda, the special feature of domestic architectural styles that first appeared in the medieval period. The three major historical architectural styles in Japan, starting with the *jiin-zukuri,* or temple style, and evolving into the *shoin-zukuri,* or palace style, and finally the *sukiya-zukuri,* or residential style, are all distinguished by the employment of *engawa.* An *engawa* is built around the core structure as a continuous veranda under extended eaves. Its function is distinct from the Western porch or terrace. The *engawa* is multipurpose, serving simultaneously as an external corridor connecting all the rooms of the house, a sheltering structure against rain, wind, and summer heat, an area for greeting or entertaining guests, and as the passageway to the garden, among many other miscellaneous functions. The *engawa* represents a handy resolution to the complex design problem of providing corridors connecting the rooms in a house.

Perhaps the most important role of the *engawa* is as an intervening space between the inside and the outside—a sort of third world between interior and exterior. Insofar as it sits in the shelter of the eaves, it may be considered interior space, but since it is open to the outside, it is also part of exterior space. The *engawa* is an outstanding architectural example of what I call "gray space," or the intervening area between inside and outside. But the special significance of the *engawa* gray space is that it is not cut off or independent from either the interior or the exterior. It is a realm where they both merge.

Traditionally, Japanese cities do not have public squares or plazas, but in their place the residential street or *roji* has served the same purpose. The sixteenth-century ruler Toyotomi Hideyoshi (1536–98), who united Japan after a long period of civil strife, organized the city of Kyoto into units, all the houses in each being built to face upon one street. This development coincided with the burgeoning of Japan's urban culture, and streets lined with homes, shops, and workshops began to function, like the architectural *engawa,* as multipurpose, semipublic space. Windows with wooden parallel batons (*renji*), built-in bench-like porches (*age-dana*), and the cloth curtains (*noren*), which became standard in the design of such urban dwellings, were facades that grew out of a pattern of life whose focus was the street itself. These three types of facades are all very different, but they all function to blur the boundary between interior and exterior, constituting only a transparent barrier between the private and public worlds. Streets thus played a dual role, at times becoming extensions of private living and at others providing a forum for public activities.

Since the war, the type of streets I am referring to have been rapidly disappearing from Japan's major cities, where the automobile now dominates the landscape and new building styles have gradually eased out the old. On the other hand, the so-called pedestrian paradises created by prohibiting all automobile traffic from major shopping streets on holidays, or the thoroughfares set aside for students going to and from school, as well as the popular mall design for shopping areas, all seem to suggest a restoration of the function of the *roji* in modern cities. For Japanese, the revival of the street can make the metropolis more livable and bring about a rebirth of traditional elements in the Japanese urban environment.

To return to the idea of gray, in the West the color gray is considered to be the result of mixing black and white. The new hue is neither black or white, but a distinct color somewhere in between. Later I will discuss at length the Japanese idea of gray in terms of the concept Rikyu gray. For now suffice it to say that this hue represents not only Japanese taste in color but also the multidimensional cultural essence that we have described as a "synthesis of contradictions." The gray space which is the *engawa* is also a "synthesis of contradictions," for it is not independent of either the interior or exterior of the building but incorporates both, an in-between space or transitional space that shifts between both.

It is difficult to discuss the aesthetics of Rikyu gray or the grays of Japanese culture without bringing in another key word, *ku*. This character can also be read *sora*. In the former reading it means "emptiness" or "void"; in the latter, it means "sky." The idea of *ku* goes back to the concept of absolute emptiness, or *sunyata*, that I discussed in the first chapter. It is, as we have seen, one of the core concepts of Mahayana Buddhism and Japanese Buddhist thought. To recap briefly, the doctrine denies any distinction between existence and nonexistence, but posits that they both exist simultaneously in the state of *ku*. This concept demonstrates the multidimensional quality of Japanese culture, so different from the dualism of Western thinking in which everything is divided into absolute and distinct categories of man versus technology, man versus nature, spirit versus body, black versus white, and so on.

The second reading of the character *sora,* meaning "sky," implies the universe and the infinite. Therefore *ku* represents a view of the universe which embraces all contradictions and paradoxes. In Japanese the word for space is *kukan,* composed of *ku* and the character for *kan* (interval, space). The character *kan* can also be read *ma,* which is also a key word providing important clues to the nature of Japanese culture. *Ma* and *en* and *ku* are all interrelated concepts. *Ma* is the temporal interval between two different phenomena or between two contradictory elements or between dimensions of varying natures. Spatially, one might call *ma* the "buffer zone."

Zeami Motokiyo (1364?–1443), who developed the art of Noh drama into one of Japan's great dramatic forms, wrote in *Kakyo* (The Mirror of the Flower), his discourse on the Noh, of a concept called *senuhima. Senuhima* are the moments in which the music stops and the actor arrests all perceptible movement; yet in this moment of suspended action and sound the actor can express the spirit of his role more movingly than through all his other modes of performance. Even today Japanese respect the ability to communicate with others wordlessly, and they admire the person who is reserved in manner and speech more than one who is flamboyant and voluble in expressing himself. In interpersonal relations the technique of feeling out and intuitively grasping the feelings and thoughts of another person without recourse to words has become a refined art in Japan that is known as *haragei,* a nonverbal form of communication whose roots lie in the tradition of *senuhima* as Zeami explained it centuries ago. *Senuhima,* then, describes the role of *ma* on the Noh stage, but there it does not mean "interval" as of time between events, but a moment of silent fullness that contains profound meaning. In this, *senuhima* also bespeaks the idea of *ku*. We may describe it as the "gray zone" in time.

Japanese ink painting consists of simple lines drawn in black india ink, the background largely empty, untouched paper. This space is the *ma* of painting and the leftover space sometimes represents the sky, sometimes mountains, or even ocean. In any case it is a technique which stimulates and stirs the imagination of the viewer. In calligraphy as well, both as an art and as a means of personal expression, spaces possess the same fullness of meaning.

From ancient times *ma* has also been a consistently important feature of Japanese music, whether in the refined music of the imperial court or in traditional folk music. In the moments between beats, for example, a musician or singer is free to embroider an original melody of his own devising into the song. *Ma* allows the performer a space to improvise according to his own individual mode of expression.

In contemporary architectural language, a floor plan is called a *madori*. One of the features of Japanese architecture is the way the layout of rooms in a building is designed not only to be functional, but also to accommodate aesthetic factors that cannot be explained in functional terms. This involves nonfunctional, "silent" spaces—spaces of withdrawal or detachment such as a corridor, a veranda, a tokonoma alcove, or a study (*shoin*). This is the *ma* of architectural design, and the skill in placing these *ma* where they will achieve the best balance with the overall design is called "inserting the *ma*," or *madori*. In Japan these *ma* are spaces of spiritual or philosophical significance that respond to the need for mental repose and detachment. The importance of detachment and calm is also emphasized in personal character, and a person who lacks those qualities is said to be a person without *ma*. He is scorned as a *manuke*—a stupid fellow.

One of the major trends in modern Japanese architecture is to discover, through the concept of *ma*, where the unique qualities of Japanese culture can be blended into modern architecture. Architects hope to develop this concept by creating a fluid, vague, intervening space which is neither inside nor outside, and to provide the experience of spatial continuity between the public space of the streets outside and the private space inside buildings and residences. This *ma*, or gray zone, recognition of which is now being restored in contemporary architecture, could not be created on the basis of functionalism and rationalism alone. The awareness of *ma* opens new frontiers in symbolism and pluralism for architecture. *En, ku,* and *ma* are all key words which express the intervening territory between spaces, temporal, physical, or spiritual, and in this they all share the "gray" quality of Japanese culture.

Throughout its history Japan has received strong influences from many other cultures. One of Japan's strengths was the capacity for self-preservation by passively receiving cultural invasions from outside and adopting as many characteristics as possible of those cultures; to assimilate them as quickly as possible was the expedient thing to do. The indigenous system of religious beliefs called Shinto developed long before any continental imports, but when Japanese adopted Buddhism, they placed it right alongside Shinto in popular belief. Buddhism was only one of many exogenous cultural elements which, passing through the civilization of China, were absorbed from other peoples and incorporated into the fabric of a unique Japanese culture. Among the treasures of the Shosoin, the storehouse where the seventh-century emperors kept their valuable possessions, are not only refined pieces of art but artifacts of daily life which found their way through China from Greece, Persia, and many other countries to the west and south.

A small island country, Japan found it expedient to withdraw into its natural fortress and take advantage of the surrounding ocean to discourage invasion. It secluded itself as much as possible from the outside world, yet did not cut itself off completely. Japanese ships ranged widely, bringing back trade and new goods, ideas, arts, and techniques from many countries. Thus, while Japan remained as closed as possible to other countries, it maintained continuous and active contact with the outside. This semiseclusionism is part and parcel of Japan's culture of grays. During the two hundred and sixty-odd years of the Edo period, the Tokugawa government institutionalized this expedient in the official policy of a closed nation (*sakoku*). As a measure of self-defense, all diplomatic relations and trade were prohibited. But the seclusion was not complete, and a significant volume of trade and intellectual discourse was maintained with the Netherlands through the port of Nagasaki. While officially closed, Japan still actively absorbed influence through this channel, keeping the nation open to goods and ideas advantageous to itself. In this sense, the Edo-period policy of a closed nation is also an example of semiseclusionism. Semiseclusionism made it possible for heterogeneous elements to be absorbed and incorporated into Japanese culture without seriously threatening the core of its identity.

In view of this long tradition, it is no wonder that the changes brought on by the revolution known as the Meiji Restoration, which threw open the doors to the world, heralded a period of considerable confusion. When Japan learned to cope with the problems of the modern age, it did so in a very traditional manner. Postrestoration Japan took up the Prussian model for its constitution, people began to wear shoes with their kimono, and in their traditional tatami-floored homes, they built Western-style parlors. They borrowed European culture piecemeal, tacking it on or building it in where most advantageous or appealing.

The continuous absorption of foreign cultures which had been going on since the seventh century made it possible for Western and traditional Japanese culture to mix without creating outright chaos. Depending on how one looks at it, Japan's immense megalopolises and the confusion of modern and traditional throughout the country may suggest the breakdown of tradition, or they may give an impression of stubborn conservatism and attachment to indigenous tradition. Yet this mixture is an essential part of Japan's special character.

There have been no violent revolutions in Japanese history, and Japanese have little liking for sudden or abrupt change. Although conservatism might not always provide clear-cut solutions, they prefer to uphold tradition and precedent, while they are perfectly willing to absorb whatever is necessary to preserve their country and culture. Preserving continuity within the course of change is a typically Japanese pattern. Experience has taught that results transcending mere invention can be obtained by absorbing existing cultural or technological achievements and combining and improving upon them. This is a method of creating something new and superior through synthesis and adaptation. Japanese developments in electronics, motorcycles, TV, and architecture since the end of World War II amply demonstrate this technology of assimilation and adjustment. Perhaps it is possible to explain the special place of change within continuity in Japanese thinking by its relation to the uninterrupted, subtle cycle of seasonal change, which has deeply affected the Japanese consciousness.

The Buddhist concept of impermanence or transience teaches that man's life, all natural phenomena, and all aspects of the universe are constantly changing. Man must be aware how ephemeral is life. All existence—human beings, animals, plants, and all natural phenomena, even buddhas—belong to a great stream of life that is in a process of perpetual creation and regeneration. Man's existence within this cycle of transmigration is a central teaching of Buddhism. In this context, man does not seek to subjugate nature, to do battle with or hunt animals, or to live in conflict with nature. He exists and lives as part of nature. It is an ancient Japanese belief that a house is only a temporary abode. If it burns down it can easily be rebuilt. This attitude was widely accepted in Japan as natural and is a direct result of the philosophy of impermanence.

Japanese gardens are often built to incorporate the landscape lying beyond into the total garden design. This practice, known as "borrowing scenery" (*shakkei*), is another expression of the sense of man's oneness with nature. As illustrated in *sukiya*-style design, a premise of traditional Japanese architecture is the unity and continuity of buildings with garden and landscape, the assumption that buildings, too, are a part of nature. The *engawa* described above is one technique of creating that continuity between nature and buildings.

Among the many types of enclosures around Japanese houses is the hedge. Trees or shrubs are planted to form a fence or enclosure, but most hedges are not intended to shut off all visibility to the outside; they make it possible to see outside and protect the privacy of the home, and at the same time to maintain continuity with the surrounding landscape. In this sense, the hedge demonstrates the same semiseclusionist approach as the Edo-period policy of closing the country.

I mentioned earlier the *renji* used on windows in both rural and urban buildings in Japan. This grill-like device is another type of incomplete, semienclosure between private space and the public space of the street, which does not entirely shut off one from the other. It allows continuity without resistance or antagonism against outside elements. It functions much the same as the hedge enclosure.

Another term that helps describe the continuity of man and nature in *ne*, sound or tone. In Japanese the word music is written with two characters meaning "to enjoy sounds." *Neiro*, or sound color, refers to tone quality. *Ne o ageru*, to let out a sound, is used when things go badly or circumstances press upon a person; it means to admit defeat or to give in. In Japan, it is still common to keep caged insects at home and in some restaurants, where the sounds of the insects give pleasure by evoking the mood of the season. To Japanese, the singing of insects is not noise but a kind of music. Their sounds are also called *ne*. *Ne*, therefore, is a word which refers to musical sounds created both by man and in nature. It stands midway between sound and music—representing the gray space between these two realms. Again, the concept of *ne* embodies the Japanese inclination to recognize, live with, and preserve continuity with nature.

Another aspect of continuity in Japanese tradition is the relationship between man and technology. Tools are regarded as extensions of the human body, and even when technology develops beyond the level of simple tools, it is still considered an integral part of daily life and its artifacts are treated with affection. The word *takumi*—skill or ingenuity—refers both to technical skill and the person who possesses that skill. It also expresses the achievement of mastery in a certain craft or skill. For Japanese, technology, man, and daily life are all in the same dimension. Think of the Japanese attitude toward their cars or motorcycles, for example. These are first and foremost vehicles of transportation, but as substitutes for walking, they have a significance greater than their performance, design, or the technology that went into them. People in Japan treat their cars with the same fastidiousness with which they bathe themselves, washing them almost as often and keeping them polished to a sparkling glow. A dirty car is thought to reflect a person's personality the same way an unclean physical appearance does. A car is often considered an extension of the home as well and becomes an integral part of daily activity. Japan is perhaps one of the few countries where curtains, a vase for flowers, clothes hangers, and sometimes even a television set are not extraordinary furnishings in the ordinary family car. For a people whose houses are generally small and cramped, the car has become another home. A drive in the family car is now a common and central weekend activity, for the car or motorcycle is, for those who own one, an expression of their way of life and their dreams.

The gray zones of which I have been speaking exist in various forms within the structure of Japanese society. In the Edo period there emerged associations called *ko,* originally established to provide a forum to discuss the meaning of Buddhist scriptures. These sessions have their roots in Buddhist rites, but they spread, especially during the Edo period, throughout the general populace. Under the feudal government, the *ko* was the only completely voluntary organization open to anyone. There were *cha ko* (tea associations) and *shiru ko* ("potluck" associations), which formed units of social interaction in villages; there were religious associations like the Ise *ko* and the Minobu *ko,* affiliated respectively with Ise Shrine and the mountain headquarters of the Nichiren sect of Buddhism; associations for women such as the *koyasu ko,* occupational associations such as the Ebisu *ko,* and associations for mutual financial assistance like the *tanomoshi ko.* These associations allowed opportunities to cultivate free, creative human relationships independent of feudal loyalties or family ties.

The *ko* stood between the feudal, parochial villages of local areas and the state, forming a gray zone of fluid human interaction. In the case of the Ise *ko,* the parish register at Ise Shrine for the year 1756 shows that 4,390,000 households, or sixty percent of all registered households in Japan, were participants in the Ise *ko.* The *ko* in those days provided a place to spend leisure time and to exchange information with other members. The *ko* organized pilgrimages, primarily to visit religious sites, and also provided opportunities for sightseeing, shopping, or just plain uninhibited fun while traveling in a group. This tradition is more alive than ever today, as the world is all too aware: the Japanese penchant for package group tours at home and abroad has become notorious, but it is certainly not new.

The Japanese company of today is a kind of community group—perhaps it is a modern version of the *ko.* Even though Japanese companies are gradually adopting some Western features, they still possess a different character from companies in Europe or the United States. Japanese do not approve of switching jobs— or loyalties—and the lifetime employment system is still firmly entrenched. Even persons who retire at the standard retirement age of fifty-five, if they have been working in a large enterprise, usually take up a post in one of its subsidiary companies, so that ultimately their entire working lives are spent in the context of that group of companies. Most companies provide housing and recreation facilities for their employees, and often cooperative day-care centers and training facilities which are used by all in the company "family." The company tries to reinforce a familial closeness among all its staff by holding year-end parties, New Year's parties, and regular organized company trips and athletic meets. Loyalty to the company among employees is so strong that it often exceeds loyalty to the local community or even the country. The company is an organization devoted to enterprise, but like its predecessor, the *ko,* it serves as a social group which mediates between local society and the state.

Japanese design can hardly be discussed without reference to the word *kata.* Anyone familiar with judo is aware that its basic techniques are taught through prescribed exercises called *kata.* In actual competition these *kata* are appropriately employed by the individual competitor in overcoming his opponent. Flower arrangement and the tea ceremony also have established *kata,* or prescribed forms, and the student of these arts seeks mastery of the form so that he can freely apply them to any given season or occasion. In Japan, it is believed to be far more important to inculcate these fundamental forms than merely to teach technique and its application. Perhaps the reason this pattern has become so strongly rooted in Japanese thinking can be found in its relationship to traditional Japanese aesthetics.

In earliest times, beauty, and therefore meaning, was found in concrete things, *mono,* which were visible to the eye. Truth or genuineness (*makoto*) was the core of that ancient aesthetic and there was a certain fetishism in the belief that particular things such as rocks, trees, and other natural phenomena were divine. By the medieval period, this basic aesthetic attitude was supplemented with an emphasis on spiritual qualities that could not be detected with the eye, and this sentiment, sensitivity to things (*mono no aware*), became the central aesthetic concept. Slowly, however, as the medieval age gave way to early modern times, things began to fade from aesthetic consciousness until sensitivity alone remained. The major aesthetic concepts that developed thereafter—mystery (*yugen*) and flower (*hana*) of the Noh theater; *wabi* and *sabi* (two words that defy brief translations) of the tea ceremony; and *iki* (style or chic), the aesthetic ideal of the Edo period—all attempt to express a condition, atmosphere, or spiritual quality rather than a material or concrete quality.

With the period of "civilization and enlightenment" and subsequent modernization after the Meiji Restoration, Japanese discovered materialism and its aesthetic. Yet even today, in the final design or shape of a creation, the fundamental principle of *kata* and the philosophy behind it are still of great importance in Japan. When we add to *kata* the syllable *chi,* it forms the word expressing the final form or design of a thing—its *katachi*. One meaning of the syllable *chi* is "blood" and, although it may not be etymologically sound, it is still true that a design's final form is achieved by adding *chi,* or the lifeblood of individuality brought through the unique talent of a creative person, to *kata.*

Another word which tells much about the world of Japanese design is *ke,* also read *ki.* It is an element of words like *fun'iki* (atmosphere, ambience), *kehai* (sign, signal), and *mono no ke* (specter). *Ke* suggests the essential nature of things that cannot be explained by demonstration, form, or design; it denotes the atmosphere or ambience that accompanies concrete things and the destiny embracing them. In design, *ke* represents the intermediary spaces; the sense of suspension between interpenetrating spaces is the feeling described by *ke.* In design, then, *ke* is a gray zone of sensation.

Now it is time to look more closely at the gray I have invoked with such insistence, and the aesthetic that produced it.

Rikyu Gray: An Open-ended Aesthetic

Rikyu gray (Rikyu *nezumi*) more nearly names the qualities of ambiguity or multiple meaning in the arts than any other expression that I know of; it has become my personal symbol and label for the multiple meanings and simultaneous possibilities of things.

The earliest reference to Rikyu gray is thought to be the following passage from *Choando Ki,* the tea writings of Kubo Gondayu (also known as Choando, 1571–1640), head priest of Kasuga Shrine in Nara:

> From the time that he came to serve as tea master to Lord Hideyoshi, everyone began to learn Soeki's [Sen no Rikyu, 1522–91] way of tea. Thus did Soeki's distaste for colorful show achieve a widespread following, as did his verses advocating *wabi* austerity. [Practitioners were instructed to] change the color of the collar of their underkimono, to wear cotton kimono dyed with ash to a neutral hue, and to outfit themselves with new sashes, footwear, and fans. Hosts were advised that it was befitting to serve simple dishes such as bean broth and vinegared shrimp and vegetables. From then on, the color gray enjoyed great popularity, and large quantities of gray cotton twill and broadcloth were imported from China.

It was this "ash-dyed neutral hue" that came to be known as Rikyu gray. It is actually somewhat surprising that a shade of gray should have become as popular as it did, because the cultural associations in Japan with this "rat color" or "ash color" had never been very pleasant. Nonetheless, from the latter part of the Edo period, when it assumed the stamp of approval as Rikyu's color, gray was much favored by aesthetes, along with sombre blues and browns. As the art of tea gained ground, people showed an increasing fondness for gray. Their tastes ran to such esoteric blends as silver gray, indigo gray, scarlet-tinged gray, lavender gray, grape gray, brown gray, dove gray, and, lastly, plain gray—that color devoid of color, born of all saturation, permitting the enjoyment of subtle variations in tonality and color balance. These grays were the hallmark of aesthetic sensibility from the Genroku era (1688–1704) on through to the Temmei era (1781–89).

Toru Haga, a specialist in comparative literature, has made studies on the An'ei (1772–81) and Temmei eras and states that "women of the period favored kimono fabrics known as *kabe shijira* and *akebono shibori*. The latter was a pale periwinkle lavender material tie-dyed in morning glory patterns, while the 'whitewashed-wall weave' of *kabe shijira* bespoke the most delicate refinement of taste, a pure white silk of the finest texture which, in certain lights, revealed woven patterns." Gen Itasaka, a specialist in Edo-period literature, speaks of an aesthetic shift in the ukiyoe prints of two artists who were very much of their times, "the change from the Genroku ideal of Hishikawa Moronobu (ca. 1618–94) to the An'ei-Temmei ideal of Suzuki Harunobu (1724–70)." Whereas the beauties depicted by Moronobu were full-figured, voluptuous women, Harunobu depicted willowy courtesans with slender features and swanlike necks. The contrast is most instructive; if we may think of Moronobu's women as symbolic of the boom in population, the economy, urbanization, and material prosperity up through the Genroku era, then the rejection of this in favor of a nonsensual, almost other-worldly aesthetic represents a shift to a higher plane, to the sophisticated rhetoric of ambiguity characteristic of the age. This idea is echoed by Masayoshi Nishida, a specialist in Japanese literature, in his *Nihon no Bi* (Japanese Beauty): "The nonsensual aesthetic sense finds expression in that colorless color of numerous hues which completely cancel each other out—Rikyu gray." Specifically, it was a dark grayish green which came into fashion as Rikyu's color during the late Edo period.

I myself am interested in Rikyu gray because its contradictory elements collide with and neutralize each other, producing a state of continuity in discontinuity, a contrapuntal coexistence that disallows sensual appreciation. It is as if this blend temporarily freezes time-space, through the medium of color perception, into a two-dimensional world. Rikyu gray works to transform volumetric, sculptural, physical space into planar, pictorial space.

The streets of Kyoto, and indeed of all traditional Japanese towns in general, take on a special beauty in the graying light of dusk. There is a fusing of perspectives as the slate-colored tiles and white plaster walls dissolve into gray, flattening all sense of distance and volume; a drama of transition from three-dimensions down to two which is not often seen in Western cities. Based on the premise that traditional Japanese streets represent the essence of Japanese urban space, I began to develop a practical theory that I could put to use in architecture. In further analyzing the qualities of these streets, I saw that they were passages of house fronts in rows that unroll like handscrolls before a moving viewpoint. This is comparable to the grounds of the Katsura Detached Palace, which are laid out in the manner of a succession of views to be appreciated while strolling, views that present glimpse after glimpse of the garden and the structures but that never allow a view of the entire garden or main building all at once. The palace rejects a fixed, single perspective. Instead, space is broken down into a series of picture planes that are accessible only from a moving viewpoint. In the gray of twilight, the planar pictorial effect is enhanced.

Once again we discover an aesthetic sensibility common to all the Japanese arts. At the heart of all creative manifestations of traditional Japanese culture there is a sense of two-dimensionality or frontality, an attempt to crystallize awareness out of the sensual in frozen instants of stopped time. The denial of the sensual seen in the reduction of tangible, three-dimensional space to intangible, two-dimensional space; continuums crossing whole spectrums of values, allowing the coexistence of opposites; blurred boundaries between dimensions; and the acceptance of interchangeable or reversible interpretations—all these resolve into that conceptual gray zone reached through the medium of Rikyu gray.

Here we are bound to recognize a certain underlying Buddhist attitude. Buddhist philosophy made indispensable contributions to the shaping of Japanese culture. Let us examine a passage from the *Nambo Roku* compendium of tea teachings in which Rikyu's disciple Nambo Sokei (dates unknown) is said to have recorded his master's thoughts on the essential unity of the art of tea and Buddhist training:

Rikyu said, "Tea of the small room is foremost a matter of practice and attainment in accord with the Buddha-dharma. To take pleasure in the grandeur of one's dwelling or in culinary delicacies are marks of worldliness. Shelter suffices if the roof does not leak, and food if it fends off starvation. This is the teaching of the Buddha and the basic intent of tea. Fetching water, gathering firewood, boiling the water, and making tea, one offers it to Buddha, serves it to others, and also partakes of it oneself. One arranges flowers and burns incense, in all activities learning from the example of the Buddha and patriarchs. Further details are left to the trainee's own clarification."

In the same work, Rikyu's teacher Takeno Joo (1502–55) is quoted as having said:

The spirit of *wabi* is entirely in keeping with the vision of this poem by Lord Fujiwara Teika from the *Shin Kokin Shu* poetry anthology:

> Casting wide my gaze,
> Neither blossoms
> Nor scarlet leaves;
> From the rush-thatched seaside hut,
> Only the autumn dusk.

The cherry blossoms and autumn leaves here might well refer to the splendor of the formal tea in the *shoin* room, using the *daisu* utensil stand. For it is only after one has gazed long and deep at those blossoms and autumn colors that one may attain the realm of primal nonbeing, the rush-thatched hut on the beach. One ignorant of the blossoms and scarlet leaves will be unable to dwell in such a hut from the very outset. Yet, after viewing them time and time again, one gains perspective on the solitude to be found in such a hut as nowhere else. This is the true mind of tea.

Teika's verse is at one with the ultimate objectives of the art of tea, and it expresses the same transfixing vision which leads us down back streets as evening settles on the old houses of Kyoto. Elsewhere in *Nambo Roku,* we read of Rikyu's thoughts on set forms and standards of measurement:

Over and over again it must be stressed that the profound meaning of tea is to be found in the informal thatched hut. While the procedures in [the formal tea in] the *shoin* using the *daisu* must conform strictly to prescribed form, the arrangements for both the informal small tearoom and for the garden path that leads to it, although based on the original standards of measurement used in the formal tea, ultimately depart from such standards, forget about technique, and return to the mind of emptiness beyond the doings of this world.

The very notion of departing from standards, forgetting technique, and returning to the mind of spiritual emptiness is completely at odds with the systems of standardized measurement that have formed the very basis of Western architecture from the classical orders of Greece and Rome to contemporary modular concepts. Rikyu's pursuit of his spiritual ideal ultimately led him to challenge all preconceived limits to physical space and to compress the four and three-quarter-mat tearoom to an unheard of one and three-quarter mats. Rikyu's tearoom refuses to submit to our everyday sense of scale or cater to our sensual desire for creature comforts, yet far from giving the expected feeling of being cramped, once inside we experience an amazing spiritual space.

By Western standards the height of the ceiling is so low and the windows and entrance are so small as to seem almost inhuman. Moreover, the Western sense of order would be hard pressed to make sense of the clashing combination of diverse design elements—for instance, a round window next to the rough-hewn post of the tokonoma, a variety of ceiling materials, and openings in the walls of all different sizes and shapes—which coexist peacefully in such tea rooms. Indeed, in all of traditional Japanese architecture, ceilings, floors, and walls are each conceived of as independent design elements—two-dimensional panel surfaces or flats—each independently designed. Two separate walls, as vertical surfaces, might easily boast windows bearing no relation to one another either in size or placement. It is this approach to design that steers our attention away from the three-dimensional, acting as a means of "down shifting" to two dimensions.

I have already spoken several times of the Buddhist concept of emptiness, and said that if it had a color, it would surely be Rikyu gray. Nagarjuna, the south Indian Mahayana master active some six hundred years after Shakyamuni who first propounded this idea in one of his major writings, the *Mula-madhyamaka-sastra,* states, "We are not nihilists; through rejecting views both of being and nonbeing, we clarify the path to attainment of nirvana," and he sets forth the "middle path of eightfold negation," or the "middle path in which nothing is grasped." Vasubandhu, as we have seen, developed Nagarjuna's teaching, claiming claiming that absolute emptiness is wondrous existence. His teachings resemble the philosophy of "formless emptiness" in the Diamond Sutra, which states: "Transcending the transient things of the visible world, concentrate on the emptiness of things. Knowing that the formless is the infinite, free of all samsaric discrimination, live unattached to anything." Emptiness is not the opposite of matter or being; rather, it is a nondiscriminative and nonperceptual concept of existence that signifies neither being nor nothingness. Hence, it is possible to say that it suggests the spacial dimension of the twilight color of Rikyu gray.

Western block and brick architecture, as I mentioned earlier, builds a hard, physical reality of three dimensions, space being created as hollows are carved out or holes cut through solid forms. This gouging cannot help but sharpen the sense of volume, perspective, and contrast between light and shadow in buildings. Traditional, wood-frame Japanese architecture, on the other hand, in most cases does not give such feelings of physical solidity. This is especially noticeable in the *shoin* tradition of the Katsura Detached Palace and in *sukiya*-style tea rooms, where we sense that each section of the construction exists in relation to a distinct viewpoint, similar to a theatrical stage set. Each section is transformed from physical reality into mental image, and so stands *sunyata*-like between the substantial and the nonsubstantial. It cannot be a coincidence that traditional Japanese architecture is an architecture of two-dimensional sections connected one to the other, nor can it be a coincidence that Rikyu gray—in that it neutralizes opposing colors—mirrors the simultaneity of being and nonbeing in *sunyata*.

In Japanese architecture, it has only been within the last century that there has been felt to be a need to draft architectural blueprints with any accuracy. Before this, plans and thumbnail sketches were simply roughed out on boards at the construction site. Japanese master carpenters relied solely on exterior or sectional elevations and on floor plans, without any need for the bird's-eye-view or perspective drawings that Western architects required to render intelligible the volumetric organization of their buildings. In this sense, architecture proves to be a microcosm of the whole of Japanese culture. The fact that architecture and building construction was a process of extending elevations into a continuity, without total resolution or synthesis of differences, is exemplary of a culture of coexistence on all levels. It is interesting to look at Japanese handscrolls in contrast to Western paintings: to eyes accustomed to Western perspective, the simultaneous presence in a single picture plane of representation and pattern, of subjects drawn to different scales, from different angles, at irreconcilable distances, and of events occurring at diverse points in time, may be quite jarring.

Continuums linking apparently disparate elements into an intermediary state appear over and over again throughout various fields of Japanese art and culture.

In *waka* (Japanese verse of thirty-one syllables), for instance, we observe this in "unrelated verses" as explained in the *Guhi Sho* collection of poetic extracts, attributed to Fujiwara Teika (1162–1241):

> Excellent poetry is not to be found among "related verses," or only rarely if at all. It is precisely because these verses are all too predictable, each phrase taking up so surely after the previous one—roots connecting to the branches in turn connecting to the leaves and so on—that there are no surprises. Everything is only too plain and ordinary, with hardly ever anything unusual. In "unrelated verses," however, each phrase stands apart from the next, the better for the unexpected to come about.

An example of this is the following unrelated verse by Teika's father, Fujiwara Shunzei (1114–1204):

> With the passing of evening,
> The autumn wind sweeps across the fields,
> Piercing to the bone.
> Even the quails cry—
> At Fukakusa, village deep in the grass.

The poetic effect here does not come from self-explanatory links between images, but rather from the way the dissimilar images are juxtaposed. As with Rikyu gray, the space between the images gives the impression of nonsensual ambiguity and multiple images.

This intermediating technique, in the context of Noh, was what the Noh actor and theorist Zeami referred to as the "undone interval" (*senuhima*) of pause, mentioned in the discussion of *ma* earlier:

> Often, critical acclaim rests on the idea that "parts left undone stimulate interest." This is a secret point of assurance for the performer. Say that there are two measures of music for which he must assume the proper stances and all the various body postures. The parts left undone, then, refer to the interval of pause. But what is it about this undone interval that should be regarded as so interesting? It is the underlying, unbroken train of thought. In that interval when the dancing stops, the music stops, and furthermore all speech, role-playing, everything stops, the actor does not simply cast aside all thought but maintains an inward state of mindfulness. It is this sense of inward awareness hinting through that provides interest. Even so, it is no good for this inner awareness to visibly show, for were it to show anywhere it would become a mannerism and so cease to be "undone." In this artless balance, in this peace of mind when one's thoughts are lost even to oneself, the undone interval links that which came before and that which is to follow. This in itself is the sensitivity which unites the whole of art.

The pause and silence between one action and the next is of utmost importance to the Noh performer, because it is the moment for the expression of his inward sense of mindfulness. This same thing can also be found in *sunyata* and in Rikyu gray: the gap left unfilled and undone becomes a transitional, complex, silent, multivalent space.

My original idea of bridging spaces of different qualities was a fundamental first step in the direction of a consciously Buddhist attitude of *sunyata* for architecture, albeit the intermediary body I had in mind at the time was still the physical. The full realization of a *sunyata*-like "body" of transitional space did not come home to me until my discovery of the public-private ambiguity of traditional Japanese urban street space, with its interpenetration of meanings far exceeding the uniformity of use of the Western plaza. Twenty-four hours a day, the traditional Japanese street is open to any spatial function for which one cares to use it, public or private. Its very ambiguous character makes for an intensification of its value as various demands and applications overlap. Street space—like *sunyata*—is not visible, but has a great variety of possible meanings.

In my own architectural designs, I began to utilize covered plazas and the like as intermediary "peripheral spaces" where interior and exterior were allowed to overlap and interpenetrate each other. Paradoxically, however, at first I encountered more resistance in Japan than abroad. It seems that in our rush to assimilate the lessons of the West, we had hastily settled on a rigid yet superficial legal formula for dividing space. Postwar city planning simplistically declared all street space to be public thoroughfare, while limiting private property to the narrow confines of buildings and their immediate sites. The concept of the street as ambivalent living space was simply ignored, and as automobile traffic took over, this zone, once intensely alive, turned into a deadly stream moving at an inhuman pace. I tried to find ways to revitalize the appreciation of intermediary zones and to revise the associated legal precedents.

Toward this end I found reinforcement in the writings of Daisetz T. Suzuki on the idea of identity-in-difference, mentioned in the first chapter. His argument, based on the concept in the Diamond Sutra that "A is non-A, therefore is it called A," was that the "Oriental Individuum" is not the "independent individual" of the West. The Oriental Individuum does not seek the basis of his existence within himself, but in the meta-individual of *sunyata*. The "individual" and the "meta-individual" exist in a state of contradiction, without any loss of self-identity. In other words, identity means that the two are not separate, and difference means that the two are not one and the same. This has become a fundamental philosophy for me in explaining the relationship of part to whole and of mutually contradictory elements. It is a theory in which identity means nondisparity and difference means nonuniformity, bringing an airy, floating sense of ambiguity to our perception of the world, much as a Rikyu gray zone does on the conceptual plane.

Westerners need not travel all the way to the East, however, to transcend the dichotomy of affirmation and denial; they have only to witness the ongoing process of society's own self-reassessment, a uniquely twentieth-century phenomenon spurred by Western theoreticians. From 1900 to 1930, the conceptual firmament was rocked by Planck's theory of quantum mechanics, Heisenburg's uncertainty principle, Bergson's creative evolution, and Einstein's theory of relativity. In the 1930s, rational foundations started to crumble with the publication of Crémieux's *Inquietude et reconstruction,* Ortega y Gasset's *La rebelión de las masas,* and Freud's *Das Unbehagen in der Kultur.* Up until the twentieth century, Western thought had been solidly based on the idea of the community, that is, on a social whole composed of individuals. But with the questioning of the social hierarchy the pendulum is swinging back. It is becoming possible to see the part and the whole as inseparable and equal in value; to subsume the individual and the meta-individual into a new sense of self-identity that can live with apparent contradictions and inconsistencies, as the Oriental Individuum already does.

Thus far I have painted the West as completely black and white, but any knowledgeable cultural anthropologist or historian can surely come up with a multitude of Western shades of Rikyu gray. Improbable as it may sound, I have found close parallels in Baroque and even Camp aesthetics.

In his book entitled *Lo Barócco,* Eugenio Dorus says that whenever two conflicting intentions are conveyed in one act, it belongs in the category of Baroque. Simply put, Baroque means not knowing what one wants to do: asking for approval and rejection at the same time. It is attempting to fly while being dragged down by gravity. The spirit of Baroque tries to raise the arm while lowering the hand.

Dorus uses Correggio's *Noli me tangere* in the Prado as an example of what he means. The painting shows Mary Magdalene at Christ's feet, Christ outstretching his arms toward her. Dorus detects a note of Baroque irony in the choice of this theme: Christ may well be showing her the way to Heaven, but leaves her on the ground in tears of desperation all the same. She, too, is pure Baroque, because for all her intent of repentance she still is portrayed as a coquette, trying to turn his head. She is willing to follow her Lord anywhere, but remains kneeling. This picture shows the Baroque sensibility as basically fickle.

There is a conceptual affinity between the continuity-in-polarity of the Baroque and Rikyu gray. In architecture, the Toshogu shrine in Nikko is often cited as an example of "Japanese Baroque," but not in the same sense as the parallel I wish to draw in defining Rikyu gray as Baroque. Far from mere eclecticism, there must be an interactive coexistence of motion and suspended stillness, straight lines and curves, not a haphazard or muddy admixture but an intricate balance. A better example of "Japanese Baroque," then, may be found in the Hiunkaku Pavilion, formerly of Hideyoshi's Jurakudai palace but now located within the Nishi Honganji temple compound in Kyoto. A curious blend of diverse arcs and lines, this asymmetrical three-storied structure somehow achieves an atmosphere of quietude and repose. Here we discover the Rikyu gray sensibility coupled with early Baroque aesthetics.

Closer still to Rikyu's own world and the tradition of tea-inspired architecture, there is the interior space of the Yodomi tea room in the Saioin subtemple of Konkai Komyoji temple. The arched doorway leading from the preparation room to the host's mat in the tearoom cuts a white curve across the line of vision, an off-register yet not inharmonious note that conveys a dynamic stillness. Evident here is a sense of design which corresponds to the use, in Western Baroque, of such dramatic elements as sweeping curves to break up the classic order. I see this tea-room as truly Baroque. Another example of Baroque sensitivity is the outdoor seating arbor located on the grounds of the Katsura Detached Palace. It features a post and beam construction of naturally bent tree trunks embedded in earth-plastered walls. Each element is autonomous, with no attempt to adapt or recon-cile them to one another, yet these typically unrelated materials contribute to the dramatically contrapuntal whole.

If, as I suggest, the Rikyu gray aesthetic may be seen in terms of the Baroque, then perhaps we may conversely color certain characteristics of the Baroque sen-sibility in Rikyu gray. The Baroque period was scientifically and technologically more advanced than the Renaissance, yet probably at no other time in Western history were greater efforts made to give full expression to human sentiments and spirituality. This was the one time in the West when the rational and irrational were allowed to coexist, and when religion took a turn toward nondualism.

Admittedly, my usage of the word "Baroque" focuses on one narrow aspect of the range of styles in Baroque art and architecture; in the strictest sense, I am talk-ing about the original idea behind early Baroque. Just as the term "Mannerism" originally was simply a derogatory label that seventeenth-century critics applied to the "mere mannered semblance of art" produced by painters of the late sixteenth century, I see Baroque art as mainly a departure from the exacting rules of the Greco-Roman tradition. It is that nonsensual ambiguity, that tenuous balance between the rational and irrational, the desire to fly in spite of being pulled down by gravity, that is sensed in Bernini's *Ecstasy of Saint Teresa*, El Greco's *Adoration of the Shepherds*, Tintoretto's *Goddess of Good Fortune Banishing Vices*, and the Sagrada Familia Church by Gaudí.

The point I wish to make here is that just as Rikyu gray embodies a fully devel-oped philosophy, ambiguity is by no means a vague concept. William Empson probed deeper into the subject in his Seven Types of Ambiguity. Quoting from Shakespeare, Chaucer, and Milton, he posited that poetic ambiguity—the versa-tility or possibility of accommodating multiple explications—depends on the choice of particular words or grammatical constructions capable of simultaneously func-tioning in several different ways depending on the context. His seven types of am-biguity may be outlined as follows:

1. One detail achieves a number of effects at one time.
2. One meaning combines two or more alternative meanings.
3. Two unrelated or non sequitur meanings are juxtaposed.
4. Several alternative meanings combine to shed light on the writer's complex mental state.

5. The writer is attempting to discover new ideas while in the middle of the creative process.
6. The expressed ideas themselves are inconsistent and require interpretation by the reader.
7. Utterly contradictory elements express the writer's own fragmented mental state.

Ambiguity generated in any of these ways is not, of course, limited to literature, but also characterizes ambivalence or multiple meaning throughout the arts and culture in general. Even so, certain areas of the arts and culture are more apt to engender ambivalence than others.

As Masao Yamaguchi points out in *Culture and Ambiguity,* cited earlier, a sensitivity to boundaries—one sign of cultural or artistic ambivalence—itself constitutes a receptivity to images that can only arise away from the constraints of everyday life in peripheral areas of overlapping meanings. There it becomes possible for two contradictory phenomena to appear simultaneously, for the peripheries are where preverbal images and symbols always emerge, cross-fertilize, and unite to bear new meaning. Such sensitivity cannot arise within conventional logical order.

To be sure, it was probably only with the utmost difficulty that in Europe a culture of ambivalence and ambiguity managed to flourish as much as it did in the overwhelmingly rational climate of Western logical order. The Baroque period and other eras of creative ambivalence are all too rare in the history of Western culture. Yet, if ideas of identity-in-difference are but minor tributaries in the West, in Japan such receptivity and aesthetic sensibility, transcending conventional logic, form the main undercurrent.

According to Yamaguchi, the discovery of ambivalent boundaries as the fundamental leitmotif repeated throughout Japanese culture is the main thrust of Kunio Yanagita's ethnological research. The sexual ambivalence of the paired roadside deities known as *dosojin,* or "guardian ancestors; the ancient grave sites which were treated as transitional space lying between arable farmland and wilderness; folktales such as that of the Janus-faced bridgekeeper maiden who would take people's lives if angered or bestow rare treasures upon them if pleased—Yanagita's literature is so full of examples of cultural ambivalence that they form the rule rather than the exception. In the West such elements do exist, as we have noted in the Baroque, and in Empson's citations from Shakespeare and Chaucer, but they only bear discussion in the limited terms of some particular historical age or school of art.

From *Wabi* to *Sabi* to *Hana*

My advocacy of Rikyu gray as a dynamic for understanding Japanese culture and, in particular, Japanese space, carries with it, I know, the possibility of furthering a misunderstanding about Japanese culture. Though I have said time and again that the gray I speak of is not a rejection of color, as gray is often perceived in the West, but a "mediating" color in which contradictory hues are simultaneously resolved and allowed to exist, for many, Rikyu gray, with its associations to the way of tea and its aesthetic, will call up visions of the spare, minimalist, supposedly "Zen" aesthetic stereotype that is so often thought of as the quintessential Japanese aesthetic. This widely accepted view of traditional Japanese aesthetics is, however, long overdue for reexamination. I must argue iconoclastically against the orthodoxy: the Japanese sense of beauty is not essentially one of negation or dying away; not an appreciation of emptiness, nothingness, and nonbeing. The time has come to amend the historic charter that established the aesthetic of *wabi* and *sabi,* the antidecorative "less is more" aesthetic, as the mainstream of Japanese culture and architecture.

When we consider Japanese culture and the aesthetics of Japanese architecture, we encounter a rich, highly expressive decorative aesthetic running through Azuchi-Momoyama and Edo-period castles, through the *shoin* style and the paintings of Ogata Korin, to the extravagances of Kabuki theater and the lavish Toshogu mausoleum in Nikko. These hallmarks of decorativism are not anomalies, idiosyncratic flashes of color against a monochrome ground. In fact, when one looks for this decorative aesthetic in Katsura and Ise, it is there to be found—if we have eyes to see it. Have not Japanese aesthetics always been characterized by a tension, a conscious balancing of abstinence from display and the urge to create ever richer decorative expression? It is this contrapuntal, symbiotic aesthetic of being and nonbeing, the plain and the sumptuous, silence and eloquence, that I call the aesthetic of *hana* (*hana suki*).

The ideal of *wabi* has generally been considered the epitome of Japan's aesthetic sensibility. *Wabi* means solitude; as an aesthetic, it has taken the form of a spare, even severe style of design with a strong emphasis on common and rough materials and objects. It is usually associated with poverty, a poverty not of real need but of renunciation of luxury and display. In this usage, and for the historical reason that the aesthetic was largely developed by Zen monks and lay practitioners, it has taken on an aura of spiritual discipline. Furthermore, through the way of tea it became identified with a sere, dematerialized beauty that eschewed all ostentation. A whole tradition in tea connoisseurship developed around the figures of Murata Shuko (1423–1502), who first advocated the practice that was to be known variously as *shimojimo no chanoyu, wabi cha,* and *cha suki,* followed by Takeno Joo, and his leading disciple Sen no Rikyu.

The architectural expression of this *wabi* sensibility emerged in the *sukiya* style. The very spatial design of the tea room came to reflect the tenets of elemental simplicity and plainness. Rikyu in particular advanced this line of thought, claiming the rustic thatched hut (*soan*) as the primary inspiration for tea architecture. In the *Nampo Roku* we read: "It must be repeated over and over again that the deep significance of tea is to be found in the thatched hut."

From Japan's middle ages on, certain lineages of aesthetic sensibility, epitomized by the terms *aware, yugen, hie* (chill), and *kare* (sere), were characterized by an idealist trend, in marked opposition to the materialist appreciation of the beauty of things. *Wabi* was, in fact, an extension of these older ideals. But it was by no means the only true Japanese aesthetic, as has often been suggested. Too many sweeping generalizations are made to support the supremacy conferred upon *wabi*.

I cannot, for instance, accept the unconditional praise Bruno Taut and Walter Gropius heaped upon the Great Shrine at Ise and the Katsura Detached Palace as exemplars of Japan's austere, undecorated *sukiya* architecture, when in the same breath they utterly dismissed Toshogu Shrine in Nikko as a brazen flaunting of the Tokugawa shogun's bad taste. It seems that for Taut and Gropius, not only *sukiya* architecture but also provincial farmhouses and simple folkcrafts stood as icons marking the ideal point toward which Modern Architecture aspired to return. And indeed, the quietist refinement of *wabi*-inspired arts proved a most convenient *texte* for these leaders of the Modern movement, especially at a time when they sought to establish the International Style. Still, in a very real sense, they consciously ignored an even greater current in the Japanese tradition—the symbiotic aesthetic of nondualistic mutuality.

As the painter and sculptor Taro Okamoto has pointed out, the simple, non-decorative, and ineffably subtle has always coexisted with the bold and colorful from the very beginnings of the Japanese tradition, as seen in the distinct Yayoi and Jomon prehistoric cultures respectively. It is then in no way paradoxical or contradictory that the very same Edo period should have produced both the Katsura Detached Palace and the Toshogu Shrine. Nor can the lavish decoration of the latter be ascribed solely to the excesses of the ruling class. My challenge to the orthodoxy is deeper than just dethroning *wabi*. I contend that that very concept is multivalent. *Wabi* is not, in other words, what we have been led to believe it is.

From the novelist Jun'ichiro Tanizaki's classic 1934 essay *In Praise of Shadows (In'ei Raisan)* comes the following passage, often quoted but still very much worthy of note:

> People commonly find those gaudy *maki-e* decorated lacquer letter boxes and writing desks all waxed bright and shiny most uncomfortably jarring, even distasteful to look at. Yet envelope these furnishings in pitch blackness, then substitute a single lamp or candle for the rays of the sun or electric lights, and suddenly that brashness is plunged to the depths of a solemn, astringent subtlety. The craftsmen of old surely always kept in mind such dark interiors, and sought the effects of faint light playing over surfaces when they applied lacquer and drew *maki-e* designs on their wares. Hence their extravagant use of gold evidences consideration of how to bring just the right qualities up out of the darkness by reflected lantern flame.

Tanizaki speaks of an aesthetic of symbiotic coexistence between the two diametric codes of shadow and gold decoration. In the same essay, Tanizaki's striking turn of phrase, "the *maki-e* decor of the night itself" reveals the delineations of the *wabi* aesthetic beyond mere negation and nonsubstantiality.

The ambiguities encountered in *wabi* become all the more pronounced when we arrive at the *sabi* aesthetic of the poet Matsuo Basho (1644–94). *Sabi* is often defined as loneliness, sadness, or a sort of elevated melancholy. But these are flat and lifeless, one-dimensional renderings of the aesthetic of *sabi*. One of Basho's principal disciples, Mukai Kyorai (1651–1704) used the words "unchanging flux" *(fueki ryuko)* to explain his master's verse. That state in which ceaseless change coexists with ageless constancy is, according to Kyorai, the very heart of Basho's *sabi*. In *Kyorai Extracts (Kyorai Sho),* he went on to state:

> *Sabi* is found in verse of a certain color, but not in resignedly quietist verse. It is, for instance, like the figure of an old man who dons armor to go into battle, or adorns himself with brocades to attend a banquet. It is the fortuitous bringing together of a flower bearer and a white-haired crone.

It was through the symbiosis of such contradictory elements as showy brocades and wizened age that the poet was to create a sense of *sabi*.

By now, it should be clear that the accepted view of the traditional Japanese aesthetics of *wabi* and *sabi* as unequivocally simple, understated, and nondecorative misses the mark considerably. Returning to the world of the Noh theater, we find Zeami writing in his *Flower Transmission of Grace (Fushi Kaden)* and *Flower Mirror* of *hana,* the "flower" that is the life of performance. This *hana* aesthetic was seen to arise in the symbiotic interplay of incommensurable objects and diverse feelings. In *Flower Transmission,* Zeami advises the performer to maintain a supple, giving tenderness in the heart while playing a demon, and to be youthful in acting the role of an old man. Or again, he recommends that when the staging falls during daylight hours, one should draw the shadowy specter of night into the performance, and vice versa.

If we trace the *wabi* aesthetic back to the thatched hut and farm house of the common people, we must surely recognize that this same popular culture simultaneously enjoyed the pageantry and color of Kabuki theater and woodblock prints. Even within the Katsura Detached Palace, so long upheld as the quintessence of the plain, non-decorative aesthetic, we find a surprising wealth of decorative detailing. It includes the sculptural metal fittings on the *chigaidana* shelf in the main room of the Chushoin wing, the bold checkerboard pattern of the tokonoma in the Shokintei tea house, the round windows of the tokonoma of the second room of the Shinshoin, the transom of the Shoiken retainers' quarters, and the velvet *koshibari* "baseboard" wall covering and elegant doorpulls of those same quarters. No, there is something amiss, something narrow and distorted, about the way the *wabi* aesthetic has been represented.

The more we look into the subject of *wabi,* the more we see its larger implications. We discover a whole aesthetic tradition of substance coexisting with nonsubstantiality, undecorated simplicity alongside flamboyant embellishment, darkness in symbiotic union with light. Let us turn again to the poem by Fujiwara Teika quoted by Nambo in the *Nambo Roku* as he describes the *wabi* tea of Takeno Joo:

Casting wide my gaze,
Neither blossoms
Nor scarlet leaves;
From the rush-thatched seaside hut,
Only the autumn dusk.

The hidden lesson here is that only those who are already well acquainted with the splendor of cherry blossoms and crimson-tinged maples can truly appreciate the *wabi* of a stark, weather-beaten thatched hut. The aesthetic here is not one of unmitigated barrenness and negation. Rather, the very idea of gazing out from an age-worn hovel while bearing in mind the beauty of blossoms and autumn leaves constitutes a layering or double encoding of sensibilities. This coexistence of flamboyance and simplicity assumes the ambivalence of a fully symbiotic aesthetic.

We learn that even with Murata Shuko, known for the severity of his Zen-influenced tea practice, this awareness of covalences ran deep. In the *Yamanoue Soji Ki,* the writings of Sen no Rikyu's disciple Yamanoue Soji (1544–90), it is recorded that "Shuko often said there is excellence in tying a prized horse up to a thatched hut." For Shuko, the poverty of spirit embodied in the thatched hut alone was not *wabi.* Only when the atmosphere was charged by the commanding presence of a splendid steed could one speak of *wabi* beauty. Once again, our understanding must embrace two levels simultaneously; we must take in the seemingly conflicting codes signified in this ambiguous paradigm by the humble dwelling on the one hand and the majestic thoroughbred on the other.

Rikyu, too, it seems, though he spoke of tea of the thatched hut, had not rejected all display. The interpretation of the *wabi* aesthetic as a rejection of vain decoration for the beauty of nothingness has been said to correspond to Rikyu's elevating his way of tea from an art into a spiritual discipline, an interpretation of Rikyu's vision in *sukiya* tearoom architecture. Clearly, Rikyu took the existing connoisseurship of tea and Chinese art treasures in formal *shoin*-style drawing rooms and transformed it into his own way of tea after the spirit of the thatched hut, characterized by a spare and disciplined aesthetic. Nonetheless, what he sought was not simplicity of the thatched hut in itself; it was, rather, a simultaneous invocation of the *shoin* aesthetic and the thatched-hut aesthetic. For did he not conceive of the thatched hut as the ideal place in which to express the beauty of a single flower? Did not Rikyu's *wabi* already embrace a latent aesthetic of *hana*?

Similarly, Sen no Rikyu's disciples Furuta Oribe (1543–1615) and Oda Uraku (1547–1621), as well as the later tea connoisseur Kobori Enshu (1579–1647) strove to open up tea house interiors by cutting more windows in dramatic new spatial compositions. Moreover, they actively endeavored to bring special views in through those highly decorative windows and to achieve imaginative new combinations of materials. While Rikyu's ideal tea house was shaped by the *wabi* aesthetic of the thatched hut, that of his followers sought a double-encoded ambiguity of understatement and pageant, silence and eloquence, introspection and extroversion. Their vision of the tea house thus might well be called *hana suki* architecture.

With the addition of but one extra tatami mat to the long three-and-three-quarter-mat plan, Oribe's En'an, Swallow Hut—itself a variation upon Rikyu's own three-and-one-half mat Taian, the Hut of Waiting—becomes virtually identical in layout with Enshu's long four-and-three-quarter-mat tearoom. The deep eaves over the earthen area by the corner entrance, the displaced external post construction, the abundance of windows including a small floor-level latticework portal staggered with another higher portal and a flower-viewing window—there is a wealth of detailing that evidences sensibilities attuned to the symbiotic interplay of simplicity and grandeur, silence and eloquence. And drama: a skylight is cut through the roof of the entrance eaves to permit a view of nearby Mount Atago.

Oda Uraku's Joan, the Hut of Thusness, is likewise a classic example of inventive and original *hana suki*: a round window is boldly cut through the sleeve-wall at the left end of the main facade, a triangular floorboard inset beside the display alcove brings a fresh new touch to the three-and-three-quarter-mat plan, not to mention the decorativeness of the arched cut-out wooden hearth-partition, old calendar pages pasted around the base of the walls, and the bright atmosphere created by the row of waist-high windows.

Kobori Enshu, being a disciple of Uraku, further refined this taste in tea architecture into what became known as the "Enshu style," particularly associated with his preference for long four-and-three-quarter-mat layouts. The Enshu-style Shosuitei of his Fushimi estate was evidently just such a tearoom; there exists a 1641 entry in the *Matsuya Family Records* (*Matsuya Kaiki*) a "Diagram of Four-and-three-quarter-mat Tearoom of the Fushimi Estate." There is also a 1715 *okoshiezu* folding paper "Plan of Lord Soho's [Enshu's] Fushimi Tearoom" by one Yoshida Dosaku. These records reveal Shosuitei to have been identical with the priest-poet Shokado Shojo's Kan'unken—which, of course, is logical, since Enshu was Shokado's tea teacher. The *Otokoyama Antiquarian Register* (*Otokoyama Koko Roku*) tells us that "This was the tearoom where Shokado Shojo and Kobori Masakazu [Enshu] liked to talk and hold functions throughout the Kan'ei era [1624–44]." Or again, we find written on a floor plan in a certain tearoom anthology in the collection of Sutemi Horiguchi that "The Hachiman Takimotobo room is like the Fushimi Enshu chamber, a four-and-three-quarter-mat room."

The hallmark of the Enshu style, however, is his inclusion of many view windows, as seen in the eight-window tearoom of *Tsukiyama Gardening Tracts* (*Tsukiyama Teizo Den*). In this sense, Kan'unken is a typical Enshu-style tearoom. It has eleven windows and two skylights, the second one an exterior skylight through the entrance area eaves. Everything focuses on the brightly illuminated host's mat, giving it a dramatic onstage feeling. And although Furuta Oribe, as recorded in *Transcriptions from His Lordship Furuta Oribe* (*Furuta Oribe Shoden Monsho*), specifically warns against cutting a skylight directly above the host's three-quarter mat, Enshu went ahead and did just that to bring in more light.

The host's mat occupies a very nearly central position with the four guest mats facing it in one straight row, for a bold, clean-lined plan reminiscent of the stage and seats of a theater. This dramatic potential is further heightened by the eleven windows, which can be opened and closed according to the season and weather. Kan'unken is truly a classic in the lineage of *hana suki*.

We can cite any number of examples of this "other tradition" in Japanese culture. Among the many masterworks of symbiotic architecture, we find—aside from the Katsura Detached Palace—the Toshintei arbor at Minase Shrine and the Hiunkaku Flying Cloud pavilion. And on into the very late Edo period, there were the Tsukiji Hotel, Mitsui House, and Yokohama Trading House in that characteristic blend of Eastern and Western architectural styles, which unfortunately was to disappear as the post-1868 Meiji government pressed ahead with relentless Westernization in the name of modernization.

What followed was a protracted debate whether Japan was to take up predominantly Renaissance or Baroque styles; meanwhile Western architecture spread throughout Japan. Paradoxically, Japanese architects only took note of their own traditions again when Taut and Gropius "discovered" the Katsura Detached Palace and Great Shrine at Ise. But, as we have observed, they misconstrued these *textes*, seeing only what served their Modernist ideology. Theirs was a projection of Western rationalism upon the Japanese tradition. It is harder to comprehend what happened afterward. Amazing as it may seem, soon Japanese architects themselves were spouting this very Western conception of Japanese aesthetics as elemental, subdued, reticent, and self-effacing, and from the 1950s on, were designing pseudo-Japanese-influenced Modernist structures.

This thinking may have had its redeeming values—the Ludwig Mies van der Rohe aphorism, "Less is more," for example—but ultimately such minimalism was not the end-all of Japanese aesthetics. I have attempted to tap this "forgotten" lineage of *hana suki* in several of my own works, including traditional tea rooms and houses. My rooftop tearoom Yuishikian, the Hut of Consciousness Only, is a re-creation of the Kan'unken, Shokado Shojo's Restive Cloud Shelter, mentioned in passing above. Kan'unken was once part of Shokado's quarters, the Takimotobo, or Hermitage at the Foot of the Waterfall, on the grounds of Hachimangu shrine at Otokoyama near Yamasaki, south of Kyoto. Kan'unken was built in the 1620s, but it burned to the ground in 1773. There exists, however, a 1757 folding paper plan of the tearoom, which is reproduced in Sutemi Horiguchi's *Folding Paper Tearoom Plans, Volume 4* (*Chashitsu Okoshiezu Shu Daiyonshu,* Bokusui Shobo). Kan'unken, in turn, is known to have been identical in every measurement with the tearoom Shosuitei, Pine-green Arbor, built by Kobori Enshu. In effect, then, my Yuishikian is a recreation of Enshu's Shosuitei by way of Kan'unken.

I have tried to faithfully reconstruct the tearoom according to the materials and dimensions noted in the folding paper plan, but of course there were points left unclarified. Terminology often differed from that of the present day; certain measurements conflicted. In these cases, I had to "borrow" from other sources. I based my design for the *roji* tea garden on a diagram of the Fushimi estate gardens found in *Secret Tea Extracts* (*Chanoyu Hissho*), utilizing a Kenninji-style bamboo fence and Rikyu-style swinging gate to separate it from the Western-style garden on the rest of the roof.

The name Yuishikian, Hut of Consciousness Only, refers to the Indian Buddhist philosophy of that name. And as master of this Hut of Consciousness Only—a tearoom built in a garden in mid-air, atop an eleven-story condominium—I was given the honorary tea name Kuchu, meaning both "Mid-air" and "In Emptiness," by Michitaka Kondo, the tea master and president of Hakuhodo, one day at a tea gathering. Actually, as it turns out, Shokado Shojo's tea name was Kushiki, or Consciousness of Emptiness. Could this be sheer coincidence?

Sukiya Architecture in the Light of the Aesthetic of *Hana Suki*

I have been insisting that ambiguity, the quality of intermediacy, constitutes a distinctly Japanese cultural trait. By trial and error, I have approached this quality through discussions of mediating spaces, street space, the *engawa,* a culture of grays, and the idea of Rikyu gray. My vision of these things may well, as I have suggested in my introduction to this work, have something to do with my childhood experience of the urban space in Nagoya and the years I spent in my grandfather's tea room while we were evacuated from the city during the war. I am quite sure, in fact, that *sukiya*-style tea rooms can serve as models for contemporary architecture. The covered area in the Head Offices of the Fukuoka Bank relates to the earthen-floored area under the eaves at En'an, the huge square pillar corresponding to its freestanding entryway post. Likewise, the mediating spaces in the Japan Red Cross Headquarters or the Daido Insurance Company's Tokyo Office correspond to the area under the eaves of Joan or Teigyokuken. It is in just such interiorization of exteriors and exteriorization of interiors, the creative vision of intermediate zones, that the properties of *sukiya* space may allow us valuable points of reference as contemporary architecture tends toward introspection and closed spatial self-regulation.

My recollections of the city of Nagoya up to my third year of primary school are of an urban environment devoid of nature. Among these rather gray impressions one very human element stands out: *kansho,* "idle" or "median places." These were back-lot passages through the dense residential areas. Some had trees, but most were simply unpaved blind alleys. Occasionally one *kansho* opened up into a neighboring *kansho,* or there might be half-meter passages barely wide enough for a person to squeeze through. Add a few holes through walls and I had my my own maze! Playing in these spaces provided me with a lasting mental store of prototypes for discovering a Japanese vision of mediating spaces in streets, passageways, undereaves, and *engawa* sheltered verandas. These *kansho* were, nonetheless, man-made urban mediating spaces.

It was not until my third year of primary school, when Nagoya was bombed and my family took refuge at my grandfather's house in rural Kaniecho that I was able to experience the interpenetration of nature and architecture, mediating spaces of nature and architecture. Kaniecho is about twenty minutes west of Nagoya by train, where even now the sprawl of the city has not reached. In those days it was a typical farming community. Rice paddies, the Kanie and Saya rivers, and their tributaries made this an area abounding in water. Kashima Shrine was a local landmark, next to which, seen from a distance, you could make out the stand of camphor trees that surrounded my grandfather's house.

The main house, built seven generations before, had a thatched *yose-mune* hipped roof, a large earthen-floored entry, guest room, and banquet room on the south side, and the kitchen, dining room, family room, Buddhist altar chamber, and storage room on the north—a classic farmhouse for that area. The place had been repeatedly enlarged over the years each time it was repaired following an earthquake, and if I remember correctly, it was again damaged in the Nagoya Earthquake and Ise Typhoon of the postwar era. Nonetheless, the basic frame of the house still retains the original mid-Edo timbers. The tearoom Yoshitsuan is recorded as dating from the initial construction, when it was connected to the south side banquet room. The original one-and-three-quarter-mat tearoom featured a one-quarter-mat floorboard inset with hearth, papered sliding doors to the banquet room, a small portal on the south wall, two papered window panels on the east, and a hanging flower-vase peg in the middle of the north wall. This flower-display wall was later remodeled by my grandfather and father, who turned it into a recessed tokonoma display alcove.

The original form of the tearoom before the addition of the tokonoma alcove seems to have been based on the Urasenke tearoom Konnichian, or Hut of This Day, built by the grand master Sen Sotan (1578–1658). Konnichian, as it still stands, likewise consists of one-and-three-quarter mats with a board insert and features a peg in the north wall and a sleeve wall adjacent to the floorboard inset in the host's mat. The only difference is that where Konnichian has a utensil cabinet built into the wall, Yoshitsuan has sliding doors. No records remain to tell who built Yoshitsuan back in the mid-Edo period, or under what circumstances it was constructed. The name Hut of Accommodating Knees (a reference to the difficulty of sitting on the floor for the length of a formal tea service) came later, bestowed by Sogo Matsuo, tenth-generation grand master of the Nagoya-based Matsuo school of tea.

To the east of the main house stood the family storehouse, which as I remember served not only for safekeeping valuables but also for drying reeds for thatching the main house. Then to the north of the main house was a building called the back house, which was linked to the Buddhist altar chamber via a covered stairway passage. This back house stood some one and one-half meters higher than the main house on a rise terraced with a stone wall. A *roji* tea garden ran along the west side of the tearoom, extending up the rise to join up with a narrow lot along the west side of the back house and, in between the main and back houses, a small terraced garden. This combination of a back house along with a main house is not uncommon in central Japan; here it seems to have been a post-Meiji addition, built in event of floods that often swept through this river country. Lastly, to the south of the storehouse stood another building, the so-called Hermitage, while on the western edge of the yard space to the south of the banquet room was another freestanding thatched-hut-style tearoom known as Mushin'an, the Hut of No-mind.

The small portal in Yoshitsuan was carefully placed to afford a view to the southwest of Mushin'an and a picturesque "sleeve-draping" pine, which was very reminiscent of the gnarled old pine at Rikyu's Taian, the Hut of Waiting, in Yamasaki, Kyoto. Unfortunately, the old tree rotted as a result of the one-meter flood that came in the wake of the Ise Typhoon, and so a new tree has since been planted in its place.

During the six-year period from middle school through graduation from high school, Yoshitsuan was my study and living space. The contrast to living completely oblivious to nature in the heart of Nagoya couldn't have been greater; there was an abundance of so many stimulating things that struck me as fresh and new. All the dreams and ambitions of youth naturally coalesced with the spatial experience of Yoshitsuan and that view of the gardens.

My grandfather was a noted tea practitioner and a man of taste. It was he who after the war asked his good friend Sogo Matsuo to design Mushin'an. The result was a three-and-one-half-mat tearoom similar to the Gensosho, or Vestibule of the Original Elder, of sixth-generation Omotesenke grand master Sen Kakukakusai Genso (1678–1730). The preparation room is situated on the north side with the host's entrance from the west; the host's mat has a latticework portal; the guests' entrance is on the east side. The slanted *kakekomi* ceiling, a stylistic extension of the eaves into the interior, over the guests' entrance contrasts with the skylight over the host's mat.

Mushin'an was blessed with many gorgeous views of the changing seasons: to the west were magnificent hedges, and beyond them the fields and rice paddies of the surrounding countryside; through the row of eastern windows could be seen the *roji* tea garden, middle gate, and sleeve-draping pine; through the nobleman's entrance there was the hand-washing basin in the garden; and a close-up view of the old pine was to be had through the skylight.

Given the deep impression life in Mushin'an made on me in my youth, my increasing interest in *sukiya*-style architecture over the years is in some ways a coming home. That interest has taken shape in my own tea room designs as well as study of classical tea rooms and tea houses. One which holds special fascination for me is Shishobo, a tea room, no longer extant, that was once a part of Todaiji temple in Nara. From the end of Japan's middle ages through the beginning of the Edo period, the Shishobo tearoom of Todaiji temple was the center of the tea practice in Nara. The Shishobo originally comprised the easternmost chambers of the northern section of a three-wing monks' quarters that had burned down. Later it was reconstructed on a different site as a separate subtemple. According to records in the collection of Sutemi Horiguchi, the Shishobo in the Jizoin subtemple of Todaiji housed both a tearoom after the style of Murata Shuko and a four-and-three-quarter-mat tearoom by Hosokawa Sansai (1563–1646). Yet there also exists a folding-paper plan, formerly in the collection of the Tokugawa family, which is inscribed with the legend "Reverse [-layout] Rikyu [-style] four-and-one-half-mat [tearoom], in Shishobo, Todaiji temple." If indeed this were a Rikyu-style four-

and-one-half-mat tearoom, then it would have to have been close to the style of his teacher Takeno Joo, and it would have predated Rikyu's mature taste for the "thatched hut" tea house.

A point of note in the four-and-three-quarter-mat tearoom attributed to Hosokawa Sansai is that upon crossing the "crawl-through" portal (*nijiriguchi*), guests first entered into a small earthen-floored area before stepping up to the *tatami*-floored area through a pair of low translucent papered doors. Interestingly enough, this "buffer zone" recalls Takeno Joo's preference for four-and-one-half-mat tea rooms with *engawa* sheltered verandas. It was Joo's disciple Rikyu who, in adding his own touches, replaced the *engawa* with an earthen-floored area and turned the entrance into a *nijiriguchi*.

The three-and-three-quarter-mat En'an, or Swallow Hut, of Rikyu's disciple Furuta Oribe furthered this trend by turning one corner of the layout into an earthen-floored deep undereaves area, its roof supported by a free-standing entryway post and pentrated by a skylight. The skylight was so situated as to offer a view of nearby Mount Atago. Likewise, Oda Uraku, another of Rikyu's disciples, designed his Joan, the Hut of Thusness, with an earthen-floored area under the eaves behind a sleeve wall at the far left of the main facade so that the guest entrance would not be directly exposed. Later, Kanamori Sowa (1584–1656) went beyond the idea of the simple earthen-floored area under the eaves in his Teigyokuken, or Garden Jewel Shelter. By bringing the middle garden gate closer to the tearoom, he was able to turn the inner *roji* garden into a covered courtyard known as an *uchi tsukubai* or interior washbasin area, an innovation that supposedly came to him from having lived in the cold north. Whatever the case, this gradual transition from *engawa* to earthen-floored undereaves to courtyard is particularly interesting in terms of how interior and exterior spaces came to be interrelated in tearoom architecture. On the one hand, there was a reversal on the originally centripetal pull of interior spaces, an opening up, as Furuta Oribe had it, to include scenery. On the other, paving stones, washbasins, middle gates, stepping stones, and other features of the *roji* garden merged more and more into the architecture, becoming interiorized.

Plans to reconstruct the Shishobo have yet to be realized, and surely it would be difficult to isolate as a separate structure a tea room that was once architecturally incorporated in the larger monks' quarters. Still, I feel the effort would prove worthwhile, considering the room's value as an example both of an early Rikyu four-and-one-half-mat tearoom and a Sansai four-and-three-quarter-mat tearoom. Another *sukiya*-style structure of great interest is Garyu Sanso, or Reclining Dragon Villa, which I came to know when I was working on a project in the Hiji River basin in Ehime Prefecture. Located at the eastern edge of Ozu City by the Hiji River, overlooking the scenic Reclining Dragon Canyon, the garden of some three thousand *tsubo* (nearly ten thousand square meters) takes in views of the Kagurayama, Tomisuyama, Yanaseyama, and Kameyama mountains, the Hiji River and plains, and Myohoji temple, in the Japanese landscaping tradition of borrowed scenery. This particular location is said to have been the site where Todo Kambei—

a direct relation of Todo Takatora—had a garden at the very end of the sixteenth century. Successive generations of the family eventually let the garden fall into ruin.

The property was then purchased by the wealthy wax merchant Torajiro Kochi, who in 1907 constructed Garyu Sanso, a compound comprised of the tearoom Furoan, or Hut of Perennial Youth; Garyuin, or Reclining Dragon Retreat; Chishian, or Hut of Knowing Finality; Garyu Horaisan, or Mount Penglai of the Reclining Dragon; and the garden. The Kyoto *sukiya* architect Yagi reportedly spent ten years in the compound's design, while craftsmen employed in its decoration included lacquerer Sotetsu Nakamura, metalworker Joeki Nakagawa, woodworker Risai Komazawa, and screen mounter Kichibei Okumura, all among the so-called Ten Craftsmen of the Kyoto Sen Family (*Senke jushoku*).

Garyuin is a thatched hipped-roof *sukiya* building, with proportions reminiscent of Saigyoan, or Saigyo's Hut, named after the medieval priest-poet, at Makuzugahara as well as Toshintei, or Illumined Mind Arbor, of retired Emperor Gomizunoo (r. 1611–29) at Minase Shrine southwest of Kyoto. It is a classic example of a lineage of Japanese architecture not to be found in either the Katsura or Shugakuin detached palaces, for it draws upon the solid strength of the farmhouse, or *minka* tradition. Here, then, is a truly masterful symbiosis of *shoin, sukiya,* and *minka* styles.

Inside are various rooms: Geirei no Ma, or Reception Chamber; Kagetsu no Ma, or Misty Moon Chamber; Seisui no Ma; Isshi no Ma; Saya no Ma, or Attendants' Chamber; and a Buddhist altar room, library, dining hall, and kitchen. The earthen-floored entryway before Geirei no Ma is modeled after the typical farmhouse entryway yet has all the grace of the covered courtyard of Teigyokuken. The model for Kagetsu no Ma is said to have been seventh-generation Omotesenke grand master Joshinsai's (1705–51) Kashoseki, or Misty Recess, tearoom in Gyokurin'in subtemple of the Daitokuji temple complex. A four-and-one-half-mat hybrid of *shoin* and thatched-hut styles with a one *ken-* (approximately 1.8 meter) wide tokonoma, *koshibari* papered wallbases, and a grid-and-panel ceiling, Kashoseki contrasts markedly with the other tea room within Gyokurin'in, the three-mat-plus-board-inset Saan, or Straw Raincoat Hut, to which it is linked through the Nammeian, or Southern Light Hall, mortuary tablet reliquary. As in the Kashoseki, the grand tokonoma of Kagetsu no Ma features an ink-wash mural of Mount Fuji spanned by staggered shelves for displaying art objects. But while Kashoseki is situated next to the Nammeian reliquary, next to Kagetsu no Ma is the Buddhist altar room, its lamplight illuminating a round window in the tokonoma wall above Mount Fuji. There is also a reproduction of the rain-pattern openwork clerestory window from Shugakuin Detached Palace, while the Rikyu-gray paper of the *fusuma* sliding panels with their bat-shaped door-pulls reads as the darkening evening sky.

Sen Sotan's *Chafu* (Tea Tracts) relates that "The coloring of all posts and the ceiling in Rikyu-school [tea] rooms is to be dark. . . . Thin [woven] ceilings in the Rikyu manner are to be roughly plaited and soot-darkened for color." Walls were to be plastered with a mixture of rice-paddy mud and rust from old nails to achieve a dark rust color. Moreover, *Koshin Gegaki* (Summer Writings of Koshin) by the fourth-generation Omotesenke grand master Sen Koshin Sosa (1613–72) holds that in the four-and-one-half-mat Fushin'an, or Hut of Uncertainty, which Rikyu built in his villa opposite the gate of Daitokuji, "Light gray [Rikyu gray] paper was pasted everywhere" as an expression of the *wabi* aesthetic of his new thatched-hut ideal.

Ichize no Ma is flanked on the south and east by the twelve-*daime* (three-quarter-size mat) Saya no Ma, a layout common to Toshintei of Minase Shrine. Beneath the floorboards, large Bizen ceramic jars are embedded in earth—three on each of the four sides—for improved acoustics, as is done beneath the floor of a Noh stage, and the hallway is copied from Katsura Detached Palace, exact to the details of the *shoji* translucent-paper doors, ceiling boards, and windows. An exercise in contrasts, the fence outside is decorated with the Urasenke *tsubo-tsubo* toy pattern, while the openwork transom reproduces the *odori kiri,* or dancing paulownia, pattern from the transom of Zangetsutei, or Waning Moon Arbor, of Omotesenke. The combination of so many disparate elements into one symbiotic whole that seems neither strained nor unnatural is no mean feat.

Furoan, which stands at the edge of the property, situated in magnificent view of the Hiji River below, is another masterpiece of *sukiya* architecture. Half leaning out over a roughly stacked stone wall, a tree growing right beside Furoan acts as a living external post with branches supporting the eaves. The interior is just as unique: a vaulted ceiling surfaced with bamboo strips is precisely angled so that when the moon rises from behind Tomosuyama across the river, the light reflected off the river will bounce off the ceiling arc and illuminate the room. One entire wall is given over to a *kekomidoko,* or stepped tokonoma, with a gently curving bamboo crossbeam (*otoshigeka*) above, a theme reiterated by the elliptical shape of a clerestory window—touches that transcend the *wabi* aesthetic of Rikyu's thatched-hut style. Here, then, is another masterpiece of what I term *hana suki,* the aesthetic of the flower, as opposed to *wabi suki,* the aesthetic of poverty. In this context, Garyu Sanso stands as an important resource for further study.

As we have seen above, Zeami posited *hana,* the "flower" of art, as the life of the Noh stage. *Hana* could be of various kinds, but essentially he conceived it as the creation of a richly profound quality through the symbiosis of disparate aesthetics or simultaneous coexistence of distinct moods. He described it, as we have seen, as bearing gentleness in mind when playing the role of a demon; bringing a sense of darkness into the bright atmosphere of a daytime performance, so that opposites interpenetrate to create a wholly other beauty. Rikyu's way of tea, including his preferences in teahouses, was in marked contrast to the earlier *shoin*-style tea centered on the appreciation of rare artifacts from China and Korea on the continent. For although *shoin*-style tea had been "all flowers," it lacked the spiritual flower that Rikyu sought in the tranquility, simplicity, discipline, and control of the more rustic thatched-hut-style tea. For him, the sight of a single flower by the roadside at dusk was far more striking than viewing a whole field full of flowers. By an extension of this metaphor, combined with Zeami's idea of a shimmering coexistence of opposites, I selected the term *hana suki* aesthetic to contrast with Rikyu's *wabi* aesthetic.

Rikyu had seven famous disciples. His two leading disciples were Hosokawa Sansai and Furuta Oribe. They are often contrasted in the following manner: Hosokawa Sansai was the orthodox traditionalist who remained true to Rikyu's *wabi* aesthetic, while Furuta Oribe veered away from *wabi* in the demonstration of his own exceptional creative energies. Sansai himself was highly critical of Oribe, and in *Tea Discourses of Hosokawa Sansai (Sansai Chanoyu Kogi)* he remarks: "The sad truth that what in past tea practice was considered inept is now considered skillful is to be understood first and foremost from the example of Furuta Oribe. . . . For although Oribe lacked a discerning eye and all claimed him poor at tea, after the skilled few died off, Oribe came to be the high priest of tea. Oribe's lack of distinction is demonstrated by the very fact that none of his followers surpassed even his [meagre] example."

I see Oribe's vision in tea architecture, as evidenced in his En'an tea room, as an attempt to achieve more *hana* than Rikyu. His insistence on visual effects (*kei*) heightened the spatial density of the tearoom. And his refusal to cling to traditional forms liberated his creative potential, perhaps not so very unlike Rikyu's original achievement in creating his distinctive style of tea room. Clearly, Oribe's achievements were a definite step in the advance of the aesthetic of *hana*.

The floor plan of my Kyojuso, or Apricot Tree Lodge, is composed of an eight-mat room, a ten-mat room, and a three-mat entryway offset in a diagonally staggered layout. On the north side, a hallway links these rooms to a bathroom and kitchen. That is to say, the hallway as a diagonal central axis connects utility spaces at the northern end and living spaces at the southern end. Very deep eaves cover both the chestnut wood wraparound eaves (*kure en*) and attached bamboo slat-flooring (*sunoko*) in an effort to bring the garden a little further into the architecture. The angled offset of the eight-mat room was likewise intended to free the rectilinear structure from the usual compass-point directionality. Originally I had thought to thatch the roof, but instead achieved something of the soft feeling of the thatched-hut style by a subtly convex rounding (*mukuri*) of all rooflines. Lathe-grid frame standing screens (*tateshitomi*) hint at the *kekkai* partitions of classical Japanese architecture, while the shoji translucent paper panels of the ten-mat room extend only partway down between to floor level, allowing a view out across the veranda as in Kobori Enshu's Bosen, or Forgotten Net, tearoom in Kohoan subtemple of Daitokuji.

My second tea room, Ritsumeian, or Chestnut Light Hut, is a four-and-one-half-mat tearoom with a three-quarter host's mat plus tokonoma. A preparation room is located behind the host's mat to which there is a service entrance. This tearoom has nearly the same layout as the three-and-three-quarter-mat tearoom of Rikyu's Osaka estate. In the Rikyu tearoom, one enters through the crawl-in entrance facing the host's mat with a noble's mat on the right in front of the tokonoma and the service entrance in between. A similar floor plan is also seen in Sen Sotan's three-mat tearoom diagrammed in *Matsuya Kaiki* (Matsuya Family

Record of Tea Gatherings), as well as in Kobori Enshu's Tengoan, now in the collection of the Tokyo National Museum.

The placement of the noble's mat and crawl-in entrance in Ritsumeian is calculated for an expansive visual effect, bringing a generous view of the *roji* garden into the room. Further attention was given to creating a mediating space interpenetrated by garden space by attaching a waiting arbor under the deep eaves on the *roji* side. The tokonoma has a tatami-mat floor, the decorative tokonoma post is of camellia, and the tokonoma threshold timber is a cryptomeria log. The ceiling is of basket-woven cryptomeria lathing and bamboo poles, and there is a drop-ceiling above the noble's mat. The central post is modeled after that in Joshinsai's Saan.

A stream pebbled with rust-colored stones from the Sakura River runs through the *roji* garden. An expansive "mountain" landscape has been fashioned in the main garden, while in the back a pond "seascape" has been created out of tide-worn stones.

An experimental "practice" attempt at *sukiya* architecture, I doubt Kyojuso and Ritsumeian yet qualify as *hana suki,* though for me they represent an important first step on the quest to achieving what I believe is one of Japan's main aesthetic ideals. At this point I would like to turn my attention away from Japanese architectural styles and aesthetics and move on to another, though related subject. Up to now I have been discussing Japanese space from a comfortable seat inside the room, looking from one room to the next, and out from my seat to the garden near at hand, or the view of the moon or the mountain through a tea house window; now I would like to rise from those "accommodating knees" and walk outside, to climb a nearby rise and look down on the Japanese village, town, and city and discuss not only Japanese space as it takes shape in individual works of architecture but in the broader designs of works of architecture together: Japanese urban patterns, their design and planning.

The Essential Japanese Landscape:
Hill, Village, Network

Tadahiko Higuchi, professor of architecture at Niigata has posited a provocative thesis: that the essential Japanese landscape is to be found "near the water's edge, on a mountainside." He describes the village site conceived of as ideal by the Japanese from ancient times as being perched on a mountainside or in a valley. The vista is open to the south, and a river flows past the village down the mountain or valley slope into a broad, open plain. Tracing the river back upstream brings us to a basin of rice fields nestled in among hills to the east, west, and north. Further up there is the local shrine of the watercourse, and on the slopes even further up lie villages, hermits' retreats, and sacred places where the exalted dwell. This is the classic depiction of agrarian Japan: the flat belt of rice fields with settlements spreading out before it, while behind to the north lies the austere forest. Even today we often encounter this pattern of a village open to the south with mountains to the north.

Analyzing the component elements to this archetypal landscape reveals three basic elements: mountains (or forests) as the seat of the gods, rice fields as the locus of endeavor, and the river (or stream) as the symbol of life. From ancient times, Japan's mountains and forests were sacred environs, a wholly other dimension, distinct from living space, a metaphor for the gods, ancestral spirits, and the dead. The foothills—the locus of the ideal Japanese village—can be seen variously as a middle ground between the divine and secular realms, an overlap where nature meets the human domain, or an interface between the sloping hills and the level fields. It is a landscape of periphery, of edges, that is equally a landscape of intermediation. And considering that historically Japanese settlements were without walls, fringe areas always meant an ambiguity, an interfusing of natural and urban spaces. Even today's suburban sprawl seems to carry on this time-honored Japanese tradition. The problem with our contemporary fringes is that they have lost many of the rich ambiguities and multivalences they once had as mediating spaces; now they are merely chaotic conglomerations of disparate elements.

The mound, hill, or mountain as a sacred site is a hallowed anthropological theme with special importance in East Asia. Once when discussing the semiotics of the square-front, round-aft "keyhole" shape of ancient Japanese imperial tumuli, I suggested a connection with the "heaven is round and earth is square" (*tian yuan di fang*) thesis of *Huainanzi,* a Chinese philosophical text dating from the second century B.C., during the Later Han dynasty. This metaphor of long standing in East Asia has established the rounded shapes of the hills as symbols of the sacred in the Oriental mind. The theory that the "keyhole" tumulus shape is related to this primal intuition is my own; however, it is worth noting that in Buddhist iconography, too, the Buddha realm is round while our world, known as Jambudvipa, is represented as a flat, nearly rectangular platform. In India, the mountains represented are the Himalayas, and the platform the Indian subcontinent (the shape of which, incidentally, is engraved on the base platform of the statue of the Great Buddha of Todaiji temple in Nara). But whichever source we favor, the fact remains that the physical environs of Asuka and Nara, seat of the earliest imperial capitals of Japan, conform very strongly to this archetypal "foothill landscape" still visible in Japanese farming villages today.

Contemporary cities have lost sight of the essential Japanese landscape of the sacred hill. I have taken on as my own personal task the reinstatement of the essential Japanese "mountain village" into the city. Already more than ten years ago, the runner-up entry I submitted to the Centre Pompidou design competition I'd called the "Urban Hill Proposal." This idea of constructing hills in the city, of introducing slopes into the urban environment, traces back to "Metamorphosis 1962," the second manifesto of the Metabolist Group. This publication, subtitled the "Helix Plan," aimed at introducing a mediating tertiary order of diagonals into the Western rationalist vertical-horizontal scheme of things, then to take it one step further to discover helical structures therein. My Centre

Pompidou "Urban Hill Proposal" sprang from a notion to insert an artificial hill into the Parisian cityscape. The idea was not so much tied to the significance of hills in the Japanese landscape archetype as to the effect of creating a "peripheral zone" right in the center of the level city—a second Montmartre as it were. I followed up on this "Urban Hill" idea through several successive projects, realizing one such plan in the Suzuya Aoyama Bell Commons building, with its low, stepped structure around the base. Actually, until the last minute, the project still went under two names: Suzuya Urban Hill and Aoyama Bell Commons.

The history of urban development in Japan is a history of leveling. Countless physical features within the city—hills, rises, rivers, and their dikes—all but disappeared in short order. And in each case, no sooner had everything been reduced to a featureless expanse than it was replanted with artificial woods and forests— "landscaping" on the Western model. Not only that, but where once the city had known a marvelous coexistence of garden and architecture, of river and street, a symbiosis of street and river, of hill and flatland, now there was nothing. After the leveling and Western-style relandscaping, nothing remained of the multivalent mediating and peripheral spaces the Japanese city once had.

In 1979 I designed a proposal that I called Urban Hill Matsudo to put these ideas into concrete form. The site conditions for my Urban Hill Matsudo were a prime example of the depressing state of the contemporary Japanese city. It is no easy thing to return what has been utterly and devastatingly lost. Still, it was my earnest desire to reclaim the essential Japanese landscape from out the collective mindscape and to revive it. In this sense, Urban Hill Matsudo has to be seen as a village in the city. A village is not a scaled-up version of a single building. It ought to be a random collection of individual structures; it ought to have its own sacred woods, its own locally enshrined patron deity. There ought to be scenic metaphors for the village well, the village fire watchtower.

While it proved impossible to intermix housing with other facilities at every level from top to bottom, Urban Hill Matsudo does have the rudiments of a local community core: a small theater, a cultural school, and a workshop. The sloping hillside presents a face heretofore unseen in the physical features of the area—a distinctive "peripheral zone" amidst an otherwise characterless expanse—though undoubtedly not enough to create on its own enough of a sense of "neighborhood." While I envisioned open-air markets and community celebrations taking place several times a month, these plans remain unrealized. Nor has a plan to provide a network of paths in the vicinity of the railway station been carried to fruition, although that was to have been implemented along with the Urban Hill plan itself. Nonetheless, even under these less-than-perfect conditions, I am optimistic about the future of this little "hill village."

The primordial image of the Japanese village likewise relates to the essential Japanese image of the city. The geomancy of these spaces has much to do with traditional Chinese beliefs: mountains to the north, east, and west, and an open area from the foothills to the south, echoing the idea that "the Son of Heaven (the emperor) faces south" and is to be approached from the south. This directionality is clearly seen in the layout of cities and orientation of temples and shrines. Another way in which the Japanese village relates to the Japanese image of the city was brought home to me, though certainly not for the first time, by Sir James Richards. He sat next to me once at a gathering in London, speaking with an effusion that belied his eighty years: "How does it feel to have come all the way from great rural Tokyo to great rural London?" he asked. He referred to the reputation of Tokyo, even today, as the conglomerate of countless settlements it had been as the city of Edo, a situation not far removed from that of London, composed as it is of countless "picturesque" little subunits. I was caught slightly off guard at the incisive observation of this similarity between Tokyo and London, but I had to admit that Tokyo—or at least Tokyo up through the Taisho era—was surely just such a conglomerate of settlements. Noboru Kawazoe in his book *The Essential Tokyo Cityscape* (*Tokyo no Genfukei*) refers to Tokyo as a "flower patch city" (*hana no toshi*), a garden-mosaic of a city. By extension, I might qualify Tokyo as a village-mosaic of a city.

After the Great Fire of the Meireki Era (1655–58), the Tokugawa shogunate ordered Hojo Masabusa and Watanabe Tsunasada to draw up a city plan of Edo. Orders also went out for the branches of the Tokugawa clan to move out of the city limits of Edo. As many as 1,324 samurai households were relocated, along with members of their entourages and the fellow provincials who dwelled around each lord's estate. Whole temples moved. These were truly "settlements," now allotted a measure of empty land around them to check the spread of future fires. The entire scene was composed of autonomous "village" units.

In my *Introduction to Urban Studies* (*Toshigaku Nyumon*, Shodensha, 1972), I proposed that Tokyo ought to be broken up. What does that amount to if not the rediscovery of "villages," autonomous cities within the greater metropolis? In order for a city to exist as an administrative unit, it must be seen as a homogeneous unity. The search for settlements within the city thus means recreating small "unit-size" landscapes from scratch. We must cast aside our futile dichotomization of "city" and "village" and create villages in the city. The cumulative mass of these villages, embracing all manner of diversity and multivalence, would then become a driving force toward qualitative change in the urban environment.

The idea of the city as a collection of villages led me to an approach to urban renewal and revitalization based on that model and incorporating another portion of the heritage of East Asia: the theories of Chinese medicine. The most characteristic technique of Western-derived urban revitalization has been the creation of superblocks. This involves combining smaller areas into one large sector. It has the advantage that it increases the efficiency of land use by centralizing public spaces and facilities and reducing duplication, and it has been widely employed in Japanese urban redevelopment as well as that of Western cities. I have strong reservations about this tactic, however.

A visit to New York City or any other major urban center where redevelopment has been carried out implementing the urban superblock plan, or to Brasilia, which was designed from the start as a group of superblocks, reveals the shortcomings of this approach. Though these cities are indeed filled with the sun, space, and greenery that Le Corbusier invoked, their superhuman scale makes them extremely alienating places. And when these superblocks are surrounded by other, ordinary urban spaces, the gap in scale and in the quality of the two types of space serves to isolate the superblocks from the remainder of the city.

To me, this method of redevelopment suggests a similarity to surgery in the modern Western medical tradition. When a kidney fails, it is cut out and replaced with an artificial kidney; when a heart falters, it is replaced with a manmade heart. The methods of traditional Chinese medicine are different. Using such techniques as acupuncture, moxibustion, and massage, human organs that are not performing well are stimulated and encouraged to make their own recoveries. They are not removed. This approach can be adapted as a highly suggestive method of urban redevelopment. Cities are no different from living beings in at least this respect: they cannot survive when severed from their past.

A look at the sections of cities that are said to be deteriorating is revealing. Though their public facilities may have become obsolescent, in many cases they still provide rich living environments. Greenwich Village in New York some twenty years ago and the Nishijin District of Kyoto are examples. Instead of bulldozing the aging sections of our cities and rebuilding them from scratch, might not it be more effective to preserve the rich urban environment they provide and at the same time introduce new and efficient facilities at certain strategic points, stimulating these urban areas so that they redevelop themselves?

Such areas can also be made to "heal themselves" by judiciously introducing or increasing pedestrian thoroughfares and open public spaces. My 1962 Nishijin redevelopment plan called for inserting a new pedestrian thoroughfare at a right angle to the existing streets and alleyways so characteristic of the district. I am not alone in advocating this sort of approach. Aldo Van Eyck has offered a redevelopment plan for Amsterdam that begins by creating children's parks at many locations and then gradually connecting these in an expanding network. Both plans adopt the approach of traditional Chinese medicine, applying stimulus at crucial points to encourage healing and growth and strengthening the organism's own networks.

A second advantage of this approach is that it invites private financial participation in urban redevelopment. In an age when there is less and less public money available for such projects, the involvement of the private sector has at last gained the acceptance it has long deserved. Public finance still has a role to play, much like the herbal potions of Chinese medicine. It can act as a trigger, a small "seed" of stimulus that provokes a much larger positive reaction—in this case, vigorous private investment.

In place of the superblock, redevelopment of networks or crucial points must be explored. As was proposed in the plan to redevelop Tokyo's core business district, Marunouchi, in the early 1960s, government could encourage this redevelopment by constructing crucial points, or "vertical streets"—and by this I mean such facilities as multistory parking spaces, water treatment facilities, heating and cooling facilities, and elevators and stairways. Private firms would then be encouraged to construct their own buildings connected to these public facilities. The area would take on organic life as a network of private spaces and public, mediating spaces, or urban connectors. It would also be possible for the common spaces to be developed from the start by private enterprises, in a consortium fashion. The same stimulus treatment can be applied to the problem of traffic-congested roads and streets. Where traffic is heavy, there are alternatives to simply bulldozing street-front homes and shops and widening the road. A new street level can be added piggyback to the first, for example, and the original street-front community preserved. Where there are problems of mixed pedestrian and automobile traffic, a pedestrian walkway can be built above the roadway, encouraging private development of shops and homes along the walkway, one story up from ground level.

What all of these suggestions have in common is a concentration on an organic approach to the challenges of urban redevelopment and urban planning based on the model offered by Chinese medicine that the best solutions to the body's problems are to be found in the body's own restorative powers, its crucial points and networks, when properly supplemented and stimulated.

In addition to the sacred hill and the urban village, I also find another essential Japanese landscape in the mindscape of wayfaring, of the journey: the views along the road. This idea proved the starting point for my 1960 urban architectural thesis "The Architecture of the Street," which grew out of a comparative study of Oriental and Occidental city planning. My thesis in "Architecture of the Street" was that cities in the East do not have plazas, while cities in the West do not have streets. Although Eastern cities lack spaces formally set aside as plazas, their streets function as gathering places. The Oriental conception of the city is one in which street space is conceived of as something between public and private space, as both urban thoroughfare and residential space. Having neither any clear-cut indicators limiting spatial boundaries nor any constrictions placed on the range of space-time applications, the Eastern street struck me as differing markedly in concept from European plaza space, which is explicitly articulated in both space and function.

It is interesting that a common element among the utopian cities of Dendaka, Nandyavarta, Padmaka, and Swastika, described in the Vedic literature of ancient India, is that they were laid out in grids, which—despite the absence of any public plazas—were oriented with a sun axis and a wind axis, the *rajapata* and *mahakala*. That orientation was probably designed so that after the long monsoon season, people could throng to the "sun streets" to sunbathe, and on sweltering nights they could haul their bedding out into the "wind streets" to sleep in the cool under the stars. Public facilities and religious establishments were situated along both axes, so that the street space assumed the character of both thoroughfare and living area. Ancient Kyoto was similarly without any plazas, though temples, shrines, and public facilities dotted the sides of the streets. Having no specially distinguished urban commons or city core, it became a capital of multiple city cores. When Toyotomi Hideyoshi—the brilliant sixteenth-century ruler who initiated many changes in the structure of the capital—was in power, he restructured the local divisions within the city grid. Where city districts of *machi* had been bounded by streets, he quartered these blocks into core quadrant neighborhoods, called *cho,* which he then reassembled in fours around intersecting streets to form new districts, again termed *machi.* The change was by no means trivial, for in the new scheme the *machi,* which were the formal units of residential areas, were no longer enclosed by streets but now incorporated street space. Seen in the context of urbanization, the growth of commerce and subsequent rise of the merchant class, and other changes characteristic of the times, Hideyoshi's restructuring of the residential areas in this way brought an additional measure of social cohesion, which consequently encouraged an architecture of town houses facing each other across the new community cores, the streets. These wood-frame town houses were not only more open toward the communal street space, but actually came to incorporate a number of technical innovations to mediate between the demands of the street and the home. For example, such architectural details as wooden window slatting (*koshi*); hinged, fold-down, exterior benches (*agedana*); and low fencing to keep horses from approaching too closely (*komayose*) were common features of these town houses. Street space came to link private areas to the city at large, and to serve as a center of domestic activities that spilled out from the houses. It had become both an extension of the home and the scene of civic functions.

The lack of total privacy within the home was more than made up for by the number of possible domestic and community uses to which the street space could be put. In European functionalist city planning, instead of this versatility of street space, there is the sunlight, greenery, and the expansive grandeur of the plaza. Although I recognize the positive aspects of both conceptions, I feel that there is a need to recover the lost qualities of ambiguous, diversified space characterized by the urban ideal of the East.

The strongest statement I can make about the differences between Japan and the West in this regard, without fear of being misconstrued, would be to say that Western space is divisive while space in Japan is cohesive. The European architectural tradition assails nature, and so establishes itself in divisive opposition to it. Walls take on an extreme importance in the West, severing one interior space from another, and interior from exterior spaces. This dualism does not arise in the Japanese concept of space, which, rather, embraces nature, bringing the "outside" in and diffusing any "inside" outward. Everything forms a part of the totality that is nature; architecture is harmonized and indeed merged with the surroundings. Walls designed to sever the exterior from the interior did not develop in Japan. This was due, in part, to the material and structural differences inherent in wood-frame construction as opposed to stone-block construction, but was more importantly a result of a conscious decision not to obstruct the interpenetration of different spaces.

Hence, many details of traditional Japanese architecture—for example, the extended space beneath the roof overhang and the peripheral *engawa* veranda—should rightly be considered intermediate zones. From this realization began my endeavors to rediscover the ambiguity and multiple meaning that is possible within bounded areas, a pursuit that has become, evolving through many phases and bearing many names, the central concern of my thought and my work: the philosophy of symbiosis.

CHAPTER THREE

An Architecture of
Symbiosis

IT HAS GRADUALLY BECOME CLEAR that the mere replacement of the words "Modern Architecture" with "Postmodern Architecture" is a largely sterile and meaningless effort.

Recent editions of the magazine *Art and Design* have introduced criticisms of the exhibition entitled The Revision of Modernism: Postmodern Architecture, organized by Heinrich Klotz, the director of the Frankfurt Museum. The exhibition is centered around well-known Postmodern architects such as Robert Venturi and Michael Graves and features the work of some thirty-five architects, including Richard Meier and Jean Nouvel. As would be expected, the discussions touch on such questions as the definition of Postmodern Architecture and whether, for example, Norman Foster is a Modern or Postmodern architect. As if in reply to the critical appraisals of the first exhibit, Klotz is now preparing a second, The Modern Vision. It is to include the work of figures ranging from Theo van Doesburg, Konrad Wachsmann, R. Buckminister Fuller, and Norman Foster to Frank Gehry and Rem Koolhaas. Some architects, such as Helmut Jahn and J. Paul Kleihues, are included in both exhibits. It is unthinkable that the thoughtful Klotz has selected the architects he features in these exhibitions in a cavalier manner. Clearly his aim is to interpret the category Postmodern Architecture in an extremely broad fashion in order to dissect and analyze the boundary between Modernism and Postmodernism.

In 1985 I made a presentation at the AIKA Modern Architecture Seminar in Sapporo which I called "What's Wrong with Modern Architecture?" I intentionally gave my talk this ambiguous title, which can be interpreted as either a positive reevaluation or a criticism of Modern Architecture. I am convinced that the double-edged thrust of this question, or the direction toward symbiosis, is, in fact, the road we must take.

The Symbiosis of History and the Present

In remarks made at the completion ceremony of the Koshi Kaikan in Toyama, the prefectural governor and several of the guests noted that the roof of the building symbolized the Tateyama mountain range and the lobby suggested Toyama Bay. The attempt to incorporate historical signs into the shape of a roof (to give just one example) has marked my work for some time, beginning with the Children's Land Central Lodge 1962 and continuing through the National Bunraku Theater, the Institute for Japanese Studies of Thammasat University, the Yoshiundo building, the Nittokuno Research Center, and the Hiroshima Municipal Museum of Modern Art.

The National Bunraku Theater, for example, quotes the roof of the Flying Cloud Pavilion of the Nishi Honganji temple, while the Institute for Japanese Studies of Thammasat University, Yoshiundo, and the Koshi Kaikan quote either the roofs of the classical Japanese architectural style known as *shinden-zukuri* or those of Japanese folk architecture. The Nittokuno Research Center is a joint project partly funded by the German conglomerate Bayer, and in a gesture of tribute to Bayer, that work quotes a European historical sign, the vaulted roof.

In order to create the atmosphere of the Edo period in the National Bunraku Theater, fragmentary signs of that period were incorporated here and there in the work. The roof of the Flying Cloud Pavilion is one of those. The Institute for Japanese Studies of Thammasat University is on one level a parody of Kenzo Tange's award-winning plan for the Japanese Culture Center in Bangkok. Tange's plan was an attempt to symbolize the Greater East Asia Co-Prosperity Sphere by reproducing the layout of *shinden-zukuri* architecture as is; the fundamental difference of my plan is that it subjects the signs that it incorporates to an intellectual process of transformation and sophistication rather than using them as they are. During the Second World War, many Japanese offices and halls were built throughout Asia by setting a traditional Japanese tile roof on top of a concrete box. The aim in this type of building was to symbolize the tradition of the Japanese people, but, much like Tange's Japanese Culture Center in Bangkok, these attempts were totally lacking in intelligence. The symbolization was a mere copying of a form, a direct quote. Such a quote is unambiguous. It conveys a single simple message: the tradition of the Japanese race. It allows for no other, more personal, individual, or pluralistic interpretation.

The Postmodern Architecture of Michael Graves is mainly characterized, as everyone knows, by the incorporation of historical signs into the work. In his recent works such as the La Jolla University Center in California these historical quotations have grown increasingly direct, even approaching Neoclassicism. The delightful transformations of such quotations that can be found in his early works have disappeared; at the same time, the number of his supporters has quickly dwindled. By comparison, though the layout of my Institute for Japanese Studies of Thammasat University is designed as a quotation of *shinden-zukuri,* I have transformed the roof by giving it a pitch of nearly forty-five degrees. This transformation provides room for a plurality of interpretations. Some who see it will associate it with traditional Thai architecture; others will recall Japanese folk houses or Shinto shrines. The methods of transforming historical signs used in this work are, first, the abstraction of forms—in this case, the creation of triangular roofs with a sharp, nearly forty-five-degree angle—and, second, the commitment to making the widest use possible of modern materials in the roof and the building exterior. By means of these transformations, this sophistication, the regionalism of the building is subtly transformed into internationalism (or nonregionalism).

The Tateyama mountain range is clearly visible from the restaurant on the top floor of the Koshi Kaikan. For the people of Toyama Prefecture, the mountain range is a local symbol, one that they encounter every day of their lives. I was greatly pleased that the form of the Koshi Kaikan roof, which was in fact a quotation from the context of traditional Japanese architecture, should be interpreted by the people of Toyama as representing the landscape so symbolic of the region, the Tateyama mountain range. The interpretation of the main lobby as a symbol of Toyama Bay grew up gradually and was passed on through word of mouth during and after the building's construction (as was the interpretation of the roof as a representation of Tateyama). From the planning stages, I had conceived of the image of water as appropriate for this space. I made the stairway to the second floor in the open lobby the central focus and designed the flooring in a pattern suggesting an ever-spreading ripple. To underline the image, the floors of the hallways were done in a wave pattern. With various functional areas such as a gallery, coffee shop, a Japanese restaurant, and the main desk anchored in the surrounding space around the main lobby, it takes on the further dimension of a harbor, a haven for travelers.

Symbiosis of Part and Whole

Needless to say, the principle of order in classical architecture, especially the classical architecture of the West, is expressed through symmetry and frontality. The gods (or as Jacques Lacan puts it, "the absolute subject") who ruled the ancient world always made their appearance in the world of human beings through the principles of symmetry and frontality, symbolic of the divine order. The architecture of Karl Friedrich von Schinkel, which harkens to the authority of classical architecture, and neoclassicist architecture, which in modern times has been widely used in public and official architecture to symbolize authority, are also characterized by symmetry and frontality.

Incidentally, my criticism of the Tange plan for the new Tokyo Municipal Building in Nishi Shinjuku as an anachronism is partly because Tange has chosen to resort once more to symmetry and frontality in a design that is sure to be interpreted by the masses as a Notre Dame-like symbol of the age when God still ruled the world. No matter how the exterior of the building is decorated, it is impossible for the new municipal building to serve as a symbol of a new age, of technology and democracy; there is no way it can relate to the dynamic, free-floating sensibility of our time. Although Tange has clearly tried to break clear of the dead end of Postmodernism, he has ended up by reversing modern architectural history and wandering back into our neoclassical past.

Modern Architecture began as a movement that rejected the neoclassicism that had dominated architecture from the second half of the nineteenth century through the early years of the twentieth century. Its aims were to gain freedom from the shackles of symmetry and frontality, in other words, to remove the bonds of classical order and liberate space itself. But in its rejection of the domination of the part by the whole in neoclassicism, Modern Architecture did not completely liberate the part. Rather, it created a new hierarchy. Le Corbusier's module, based on the dimensions of the human body, and his hierarchy of intercity transport from V_1 to V_7 are examples of the new order created by Modern Architecture.

The reevaluation of Modern Architecture must be based on a reform of its hierarchy of part and whole. I have often referred to Daisetz Suzuki's logic of identity and difference and emphasized the mutually embracing relationship of part and whole in what is nothing less than a revolution against the Western concept of hierarchy. In the Western world, change comes about through a dualistic process. Rationalism is opposed by Expressionism, high tech by high touch, totalitarianism and centralization are opposed by grass-roots democracy and small government. Corporate architecture stands opposed to atelier or studio architecture, and industrial and mass-produced architecture is opposed by craftsmanship and handmade architecture.

History clearly shows that this dualistic, pendulum-swing type of evolution is fruitless in the extreme. The revolutionary nature of Daisetz Suzuki's concept of the mutually embracing relationship of part and whole is in its power to transcend such dualistic traps. Attempts by the most advanced Western thinkers to escape this well-worn dualistic track have attracted worldwide attention in recent years. One of these intellectuals was Arthur Koestler, who contributed the concept of the holon. Koestler identifies the most disturbing symptoms of the human race as first, the desire to devote one's life to some transcendent being or cause such as God or nation, and second, the chronic split between our intellectual and emotional natures. In his book *Janus,* Koestler explains the derivation of his coined word, *holon.* It is a combination of *holos,* which is Greek for "whole," and the suffix *on,* which means "part." Koestler means to say that the whole always exists as a harmonious combination of parts. When a complex whole is broken into its parts and analyzed, something crucial is always lost. He criticizes this dissecting method as falsifying reality. The open hierarchic system based on the concept of holon is what he offers in its place. In another work, *The Act of Creation* (1964), he describes the essence of the creative act as the merging on a new plane of two previously totally unrelated frames of awareness. He calls this phenomenon "bisociation."

Two other Western thinkers who have contributed new concepts of the relation between part and whole are the theoretical physicist David Bohm and the fractal geometer Benoit Mandelbrot. Bohm presents a metaphysical theory of logical development from awareness to insight. His concept of implicate order is that all movement of the whole is inherent within each part, and part and whole are joined like the two-faced god Janus. Starting from this premise, he unfolds a new theoretical physics that does not mark a separation between mind and matter. Mandelbrot's geometry opened a new horizon in the consideration of the relationship between part and whole, as Mandelbrot pursued the "soft" structure that is to be found in the midst of chaos and explained the natural "Chinese box" order of the universe. Ilya Prigogine's dispersal theory of structure and Hermann Haken's synergetics are concepts that can also be counted as belonging to the Western rethinking of part and whole and the principle of hierarchy in general.

In short, the age—and its architecture—is changing from one dominated by Newtonian physics, or the systematic, axiomatic mathematics of the pseudonymous Nicolas Bourbaki, to a new plane. That new world is characterized by a shift from the theoromatic to the problematic; from a closed order to one that permits chaos; and from this acceptance of movement and change a new, flexible, changing order is developing. Leibniz's conception of the world, which recognized the whole within each part, will no doubt be reappraised now and seen for its true worth.

This symbiotic relationship between part and whole is created in the Koshi Kaikan by a coexistence of circle and rectangle, by off-centeredness, by the contrast between above and below, and a balance between large and small spaces.

The Aesthetic of Symbiosis: Simulacres

In the previous chapter I have expressed my strong reservations about the thesis that the traditional Japanese aesthetic is one of *wabi* and *sabi,* of discipline, simplicity, and unornamented stillness. I wrote that the designation of Katsura Detached Palace and Ise Shrine as the paradigms of Japanese architecture, and the denigration of Toshogu Shrine at Nikko and the Flying Cloud Pavilion of the Nishi Honganji as well as the hybrid architecture of the late Edo period as "in bad taste," were the plot of Bruno Taut and Gropius, who saw Japanese architecture as nothing more than fuel for the debate to justify the principles of Modernism and Modern Architecture. It was my aim to expose their prejudice and correct this widely held but mistaken view.

I arrived at the conclusion that the traditional Japanese aesthetic was in fact one of symbiosis, in which the aesthetic of *wabi* and *sabi* existed symbiotically with their counterparts. Nonbeing and being, simplicity and extravagance, shadow and light, reason and the nonrational coexist in an aesthetic I called the aesthetic of *hana* (the flower), or *hana suki.* The aesthetic of symbiosis, with its ambiguity of form or expression and its plurality of implication, is an aesthetic that is more complex in its appeal to the sensibilities than a simpler, monistic aesthetic, for it requires (and creates) a sophistication and transformation within those sensibilities.

I named this aesthetic the aesthetic of *hana* in reference to the concept of *hana* developed by the medieval Noh playwright, aesthetician, and actor Zeami. Zeami's instructions for performing the role of an old person—"Perform the role of an elderly person with gentle grace"—represent a unique sort of symbiosis. Western acting methods tell the actor to portray age by striving to actually "become" elderly, in a monistic method of expression. Zeami's acting method, in contrast, is to present a different reality, a symbolization or transformation of reality, by incorporating a certain spirit within the actor or by layering different levels of feeling on top of one another. Because what Zeami's actor creates is "only" a simulation, it contains the possibility of actually transcending the reality it is meant to simulate. This aesthetic is what makes it possible for the portrayal of a woman by the well-known Kabuki female impersonator Tamasaburo to transcend the portrayal of a woman by a female actress.

At the core of such simulation is Jean Baudrillard's concept of the *simulacre*. In his work, *L'échange symbolique et la mort,* Baudrillard writes: "Today all systems are trembling within uncertainty, as reality has been swallowed by a hyper-reality of codes and simulations. Now the law of simulation rules us as reality once did. All connectivity has dissolved and we are now born from models. There are no longer any ideologies, only *simulacres*." A *simulacre* can be described as a sign without a predetermined meaning. To put it another way, it is a sign that offers the reader the freedom to interpret it in a variety of ways, a pluralistic sign, a free-floating linkage of signs that says "this sort of thing." The philosopher of aesthetics Susanne K. Langer has said, "It is out of fashion to find beauty at the core of art. Today, meaning occupies the central place that beauty once held." Nevertheless, it is impossible to create an architecture that is an assemblage of of symbols that will be read by all in only one way.

There is no guarantee that the revival of decoration in architecture will result in making it more readable, that is, in increasing its literary quality. To return to the principles of classical Western architecture, frontality and symmetry, is anachronistic in a double sense. That option is not available to us, but perhaps there is another: through the incorporation of linked *simulacres,* a chain of meaning (literariness) and feeling (poesy) can be created. The sudden connection and disconnection of meaning creates atmosphere (feeling), and meaning, in turn, invades the structure of a monovalent atmosphere (feeling) as noise. The interaction of these two creates, through transformation and sophistication, a cluster of warm, pluralistic *simulacres*. I would like to explore this subject at length below.

Le Poétique in Architecture: Beyond Semiotics

A total spectacle but a divided one, Bunraku of course excludes Improvisation; to return to spontaneity would be to return to the stereotypes which constitute our "depth." As Brecht had seen, here citation rules, the sliver of writing; the fragment of code, for none of the action's promoters can account in his own person for what he is never alone to write. As in the modern text, the interweaving of codes, references, discrete assertions, anthological gestures multiplies the written line, not by virtue of some metaphysical appeal, but by the interaction of a *combinatoire* which opens out into the entire space of the theater: what is begun by one is continued by the next, without interval.

—Roland Barthes

Roland Barthes separates Bunraku into three types of *écriture*—the puppets, the puppeteers, and the narrator(s) (the *gidayu* or *joruri* singers)—each expressed independently but integrated into an art. One can well imagine why, in our modern, centerless, mass-consumer society, in which all things are consumed as mere signs, the theatrical order of the three *écritures* comprising Bunraku should have struck Barthes as distinctively semiotic. In fact, the narration of the *gidayu* singer, the music of the shamisen, the puppeteers, and the puppets themselves are each an art in and of themselves. The movements of the three men—the main puppeteer and two assistants (*kuroko*)—and the puppet are a boisterous dance of signs, or, one might say, *simulacres*.

The facial expression of the puppeteer is impassive, and the movements of the puppets are not completely faithful to those of human beings; the puppets can perform feats of which human actors or actresses are incapable. They can fly through the air, and if beheaded, a head will fly off in one stroke. In Kabuki the male performers of female roles, known as *onnagata* ("the form of a woman") enact an essential femininity that goes beyond true femininity: it is woman as *simulacre* rather than sign, and in that sense it may be called the performance of a fiction. Bunraku, on the other hand, is a form of semiotic expression, a *simulacre* realized on a level of fictitiousness that goes beyond the fiction of the *onnagata*. The forms of the Bunraku puppet heads, which became fixed in the early nineteenth century, very successfully convert human character into signs: the Bunshichi head is a tragic protagonist who patiently endures his fate. It is masculine with regular and bold features and a tragic expression of suppressed grief. The Kodanshichi head typifies the ironic role of the rogue who turns to good (*modori*) in the end. The Genta head is the sensuous young lover; Komei is a thoughtful, refined face with a touch of sorrow. Other types include the solidly built, rounded face of the stubborn and aging warrior Masamune and the cheerful face of the comic young woman, Ofuku, with drooping eyes and fat, cherry-red dimpled cheeks. There are heads with fixed expressions and others in which the eyebrows or eyes are moveable, but in every case they maintain the purity of the sign, free of that element of obnoxious empathy bestowed by the too complacent actor.

Then how are the three separately expressed types of *écriture* described by Barthes integrated into one dramatic form? Does the "integration" take place on a different plane from mere drifting signs and separately produced *écritures*? Herein lies the problem that involves not only theatrical space but also architectural space.

Ferdinand de Saussure regarded linguistic activity as emerging from *langue* and *parole,* and he defined *langue* as the system of agreed-upon symbols necessary for communication, in other words, the collective sum of individual linguistic marks, the "sociolect" or group language, that embraces both social institutions and values. *Parole* is to *langue* as words are to language. Is it possible for sociolect or language to be a key term for integration? But we should beware of regarding drifting signs as "parts" and integration as the "whole." No integration is possible if there is intention to identify the total, for the system that may integrate fragmental signs. It may be that the word "integration" is itself misused, for what Barthes meant was integration without integration. Rather, we ought to say that Bunraku is separated into three different *écritures*—the puppets, the puppeteer, and the narrator—*in which there exists a system in constant flux with chains or transverse lines that reveal the relationship.*

The italicized portion above, of course, is borrowed from Gilles Deleuze. There is something very appealing about this image of movement along a transverse line that is ever relating to, while at the same time rejecting, the whole. One might call it *le poétique,* or poetical practice, to dip into the structure of atmospheres that emerge beyond the transverse line.

The structure of the atmospheres that drift in the theatrical space of Bunraku cannot be detected by means of the body of Western dramaturgy. It possesses something that cannot be explicated through the semiotic analysis of, for instance, the performer and the performed, the *signifiant* and the *signifié,* or sign and content. The theatrical space of Bunraku throws into clear relief many of the things cast aside by Modernism as well as the problem inherent in Postmodernism.

Jean Baudrillard writes of *le poétique*:

> In the field of language, too, exists the model of symbolic exchange, something like the nucleus of an anti-economic politic, where value and law have been eliminated; it is poetic language. In this area of the anti-discursive, beyond the economic politics of language, Saussure's *Les anagrammes* offers fundamental discoveries.

Saussure left 146 notebooks of anagrams explaining the mysteries and unconscious techniques found in the poetry of ancient Greece and Rome and the Vedas. He arrived at an interest in anagrams, after completing his theories of general linguistics, as things that are not graspable by analytical or digital ways of thinking, and his theories on anagrams in folklore, mythology, and poetical language were the fruit of thirteen years of study between the turn of the century and his death.

It is thought that Saussure's theory of anagrams may be a semiotic clue to the structure of the unconscious and such problems of intertextuality as polyphony, *bricolage,* dialogue between texts, and linkage between *écriture* and *lecture.* Baudrillard goes on to say:

> It must be said that *le poétique* is, on the contrary, a process of *extermination of value* [linguistic value]. The law of poetry is in effect to produce, according

to a rigorous process, something *of which nothing remains*. It is in this respect that poetry is opposed to linguistic discourse; it is a process of the accumulation, production, and distribution of the language as value. *Le poétique* is not reducible to a mode of meaning that is nothing more than the mode of production of values of the language. Therefore it is not reducible to linguistics, which is the science of this mode of production. *Le poétique* is the insurrection of language against its proper laws.

And:

Le poétique as the symbolic exchange makes use of the strictly limited and distributed corpus, but is charged with the duty to use it *to the ultimate*. . . . Over our language an economy of profusion and wastefulness reigns—a utopia of abundance. . . . The utopia of an unlimited capital of language for value of usage and exchange. Each, for signification, proceeds by accumulation and cumulative exchange of signs. . . . This wasteful manipulation, sustained by the imagination of profusion, results in a prodigious inflation, leaving, to the image of our societies of uncontrolled growth, a refuse that is also too prodigious, and the waste cannot be reduced from signs consumed incompletely, for the words that have served do not fade away, but are accumulated as refuse—a pollution—of signs as fantastic, and contemporary, as industrial pollution.

And:

Le poétique—it is the restitution of symbolic language at the very heart of words. Whereas in a discourse on the signification of words, all bound to finality by sense, do not respond or refer to one another . . . in *le poétique,* on the contrary, once the action of the sense is destroyed, all the constituting elements begin to interact with and respond to each other.

Baudrillard goes on to discuss the utopia of language versus the argument of discourse, and the cycle of literature versus the order of discourse.

If the poem refers to anything, it always refers to *nothing,* to the term of nothingness, to zero content (*signifié zéro*). . . . what characterizes *le poétique* and distinguishes it from discourse is ambiguity: "The machinations of ambiguity are at the very base of poesy," says Empson. . . . the ambiguity, polysemy, polyvalence, polyphony of the senses—it is always a matter of an irradiation of the *signifié,* and the simultaneity of significations.

Here is a pointed critique of semiotic finality, a pronouncement of death on discourses on semiotic signification produced by the economy in its new phase and by mass consumer society.

If the Metabolist movement was mistaken at any point, it may have been that

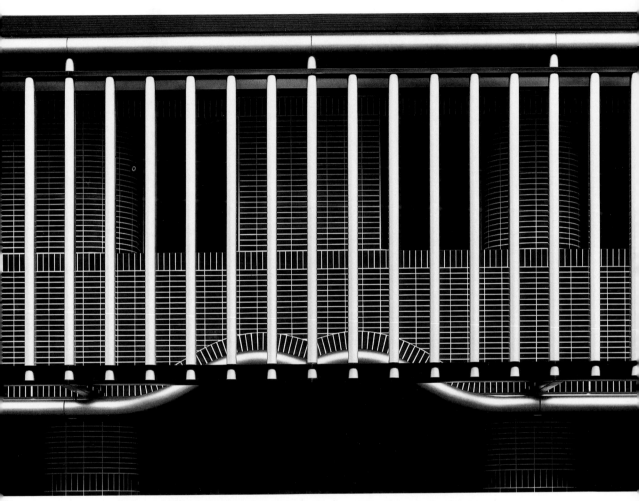

15. Incorporating *hana* into today's architecture as *simulacres:* lattice, plaster-and-lathe walls, and Edo roof lines suggested in the exterior of the National Bunraku Theater in Osaka.

16. *Simulacres* must be used with sophistication: a *shinden*-style roof transformed for the Japanese Studies Institute at Thammasat University, Pathumthani, Thailand.

17. The Tateyama mountain range and the nearby sea brought into the Koshi Kaikan Center, Toyama Prefecture, in a symbiosis of nature and architecture.

18. A Shinto torii gate is incorporated into the entrance to the Nagoya City Museum of Modern Art, as part of a lattice-pillar structure of intermediary space. (Design by Kisho Kurokawa)

19. Bird's-eye view of the Nagoya City Museum of Modern Art. In the garden at the rear of the museum, the middle gate *(chumon)* of the tea garden, the staggered stepping stones of the garden of Katsura Detached Palace, and other signs of traditional Japanese architecture are quoted.

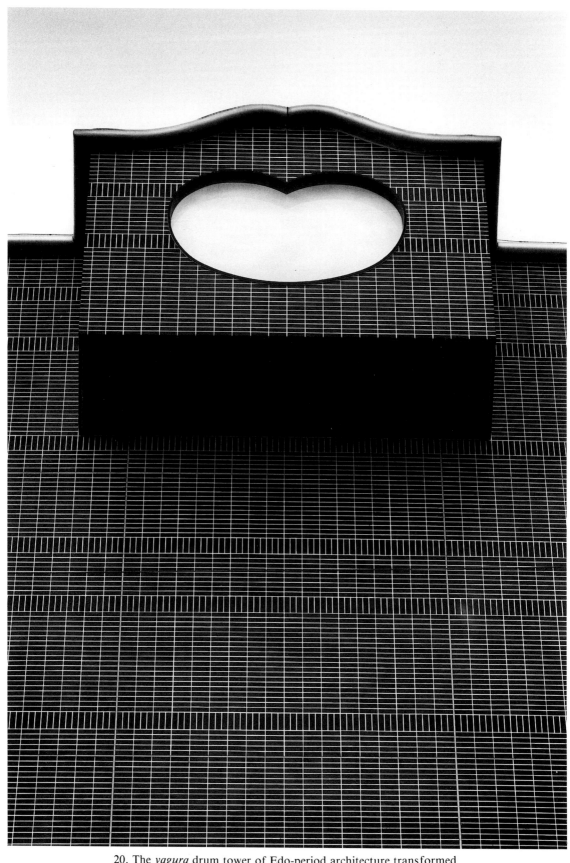

20. The *yagura* drum tower of Edo-period architecture transformed for the roof of the National Bunraku Theater in Osaka.

21. The *yagura* in its original form in Joruri puppet theaters of the Edo period.

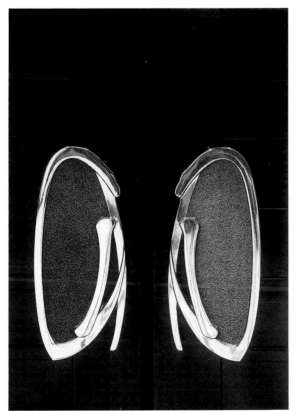

22. *(left)* The moon-shaped door pulls of Katsura Detached Palace quoted in the National Bunraku Theater. 23. *(right)* Windows in the style of the traditional Japanese storehouse *(kura)* are set in the walls of the National Bunraku Theater.

24. The roof of the Sarnath Yoshiundo Building, in Shirone, Niigata, slants as steeply as those of the traditional Japanese farmhouses *(minka)* of the snow country. (Design by Kisho Kurokawa)

25. Urban planning that integrates urban dwellers with their city center, in the Redevelopment Project for South Friedrichstadt. (Design by Kisho Kurokawa)

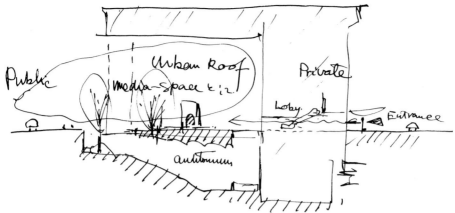

26. Cross section for the Head Offices of the Fukuoka Bank, an example of the symbiosis of interior and exterior, public and private space.

27. The Head Offices of the Fukuoka bank provides an immense *engawa* as an intermediate space for new kinds of urban life.

28. *Simulacres* of the machine as *texte* in the exterior
of the Wacoal Kojimachi Building, Tokyo.

29. The Royal Reception Room of the Wacoal Kojimachi Building
with floating illumination pillar and radiated windows.

its attempt to break down architecture led to the discourse of semiotic signification, namely, to architectural semiotics. There is no denying that consciously or unconsciously, the methodology of Metabolism was absorbed in the economic mechanism. We sought to secure our identity by manipulating architecture with our own hands in the tide of rapid economic growth, to establish a system for men to control technology, but our efforts themselves were relativized by a drastic change of a more essential nature, of the perspective itself. The economy itself had shifted from an age of production by technological operations to an age of mass consumer society based on the production and consumption of signs. Our reorientation from Metabolism to metamorphosis was an intuitive effort to cope with landslidelike change.

In fact, I had begun the work of extracting methodology from the context of Japanese culture at an earlier stage of Metabolism. The discovery of street space vis-à-vis the public space of the square, city planning on the principle of Chinese herbal medicine, the philosophy of symbiosis as against Western dualism, the emphasis on intermediate space—these are examples of my work along these lines in the early 1960s.

As stated earlier, the viewpoint on Japanese culture and the historical context was as intervention—"noise"—in *A*rchitecture, in Western culture, but in another way it was a process for taking off from that stage of Metabolism to accelerate the production and consumption of signs.

The architectural utopia contained in the concept of metamorphosis was an attempt at finding a process of poetic language that would render architectural codes ambiguous and polysemous. The issues I raised from the latter half of the 1960s—intermediary space, *en* space, Rikyu gray space, the art of ambivalence, intermediate zones, ambiguity, *hana suki,* Early Baroque, Camp, the culture of grays, spiritualism, the philosophy of symbiosis—these were tests for the poetic language that was extracted from the Japanese cultural context.

In *Poésie et negativité*, Julia Kristeva says of the ambivalence of poetic *signifié*:

It is at once concrete and universal; it contains both affirmation and rejection; and it reveals the simultaneity of possibility and impossibility. Poetic *signifié* is a space in which existence and nonexistence are intertwined in a very extraordinary way.

The rhizome that intertwines opposites—the Klein bottle—is the epitome of what I call the philosophy of symbiosis. The only way out is to fly, taking off from the short runway provided by the discourse of significations and poetic language.

The "Flower" as Simulacre: The Structure of "Atmosphere"

Why should we bother with Japanese culture now? It is not because the pendulum is swinging toward the Eastern pole in the trite dualism of East and West. It is the intervention of "noise" in the overwhelming rhetoric of Western culture and Modern Architecture. The Japanese historical and cultural texts are *lignes de fuite* from the present of the economy of production and consumption of signs. I believe they can be found from the mid-fourteenth through the mid-eighteenth century, for this limited span of time offers useful key terms for exploring Postmodernism, ideas such as the qualities of mediating space, fictionalism, massification, high density, ambiguity, ambivalence, and polysemy.

The National Bunraku Theater takes Edo-period culture as its pretext in a dual sense: first, as a place for discovering abundant key terms for the revolt against Modernism—in other words, "noise" or *lignes de fuite* for metamorphosing Modern Architecture; and second, as the native soil out of which Bunraku was born and nurtured.

Jean Baudrillard states in his *Le système des objets* that while arrangement is manneristic and technical injunction, atmosphere is created by cultural injunction. What transforms everyday atmosphere is not an object itself (a natural object) but a concept of a *simulacre* of nature that is identical with nature, and the structure of atmosphere is organized through cultural signs. The idea of this atmospheric structure is to be developed into *le poétique,* as we have seen earlier.

A *simulacre* as a conceived object—something more than a mere sign of signification, something that may subvert semiotics based upon the major presupposition that one reality corresponds to one sign, one *signifié* with one *signifiant*. A *simulacre,* by its absence of reference, ambiguity, obscurity, and polysemy, absorbs the impurities of signs. A *simulacre,* by the transverse line formed by "noise" and traces of *lignes de fuite,* creates the structure of atmosphere. As Baudrillard says, such "discourses of atmosphere" as colors, objects, sizes, and spaces are abstracted and become objects of mental operation. A *simulacre* is to use a *comme.*

To create the atmosphere of the Edo period in the National Bunraku Theater, therefore, I gave it *simulacres* of the Edo period: bamboo lattice fences, Chinese-style gabled turrets, black exterior walls, a "flying roof line" in the style of the Flying Cloud Pavilion of Nishi Honganji temple, lattice textured ceilings, red-and-black entrance doors, *tsuiji*-style screen panels, door knobs copied from the sliding *fusuma* doors of Katsura Detached Palace, chic black skirt walls around the interior of the theater, *kura*-style windows in the stair landings, Chinese-style gables on the entrance vestibule, hand fans in the lattice of the main stairway—all *simulacres* of objects and motifs from the Edo period. They have no actual referents, drifting without any fixed contextual signification. They exist as "noise" that intervenes in the overwhelmingly Westernized life of the present age, and at the same time they are an "injunction" to create the "structure of atmosphere" with a compositional traversing line. As Julia Kristeva says in *La révolution du langage poétique,* it is the pleasure of poetic language to discover the vocalized place where fusion and separation take place synchronically, the *chora* (of Plato's *Timaeus*), a vague, undefined, chaotic space as a process of generating meaning, or the "abject" as the pleasure of the fusion of the subject and object—these define the cultural domain of the space.

Already in Zeami's fifteenth-century *Fushi Kaden* the idea of *simulacre* as activating the structure of atmosphere was advocated in the form of the "flower." Zeami explains that the "flower" is a metaphorical expression for the charm of Noh or the emotion that the Noh players transmit to the audience. And in the seventh of his secret instructions he says that it is synonymous with uniqueness and amusement. It is noteworthy that concerning "maskless" acting he states that manner and atmosphere should be modeled on the thing represented. Facial expressions should be modeled on the thing represented. Facial expression should be held exactly as it is without any affection of imitation. In other words, Zeami is recommending a *simulacre* of a thing with the face undisguised and its manner and atmosphere incorporated into the act. This is in fact in sharp contrast to the Western dramaturgy that demands that the actors should be affected identically as the character. It has something in common with the separately issued *écritures* in Bunraku.

Concerning the performance of a character of an old man, he writes:

Without the flower there is nothing that may amuse us. If the action and manner of an old man were performed with the back and knees bent and the whole body shrunk as a real old man would be, then the flower would be gone and the performance would appear antiquated and musty; there would be, therefore, hardly any enjoyment in it. Instead, the role of an old man should be played simply, vaguely, and with a serene gracefulness. Especially the dance of an old man requires extreme delicacy and profound realization. The art of appearing to be an old man with the flower in full bloom should be learned well. It is as if an ancient tree bears exquisite flowers.

This marvelously represents the idea of the ambiguous *simulacre*. Zeami's advice is to explore the flower in the *simulacre* of an old man instead of imitating oldness in reality.

The domain of poetic language is not realized by the mechanical combination of signs but emerges epiphanically beyond the traversing line that momentarily runs through obscure and ambiguous *simulacres,* between signs, in the peripheral region of the system of signs.

The atmosphere of Japanese culture or Edo-period culture is created not so much by visible semiotic expressions and decorative, morphological expressions as by consuming them and rendering the condition of *le degré zéro* without any residue, by the structure of the invisible organization of ambiguity—the structure of invisible atmospheres such as stillness to repress the explosion of the senses or the polysemous intermediating zone that allows contradictions to fuse.

Rather than to the new Kabuki Theater or the National Theater, which has attempted to wholly imitate the traditional style, or to the Esperanto architecture constructed semiotically solely from Western languages, much less to the nonsensical "tofu" buildings of mirror glass, my way leads to *le poétique* through a limited, intermediary horizon, precarious and ambiguous.

The Techniques of Symbiosis

Next I would like to turn to several specific examples of the philosophy of symbiosis (and its corollary, coexistence) in my work, beginning with the design for the Headquarters of the Japan Red Cross. The design for the former main building of the Japan Red Cross began from discussions between Tsunetami Sano (1822–1902), who is called the father of the Japan Red Cross, and Raio Tsumaki, the designer of the building that this new one has replaced. The Red Cross itself began in 1863 with the formation of a committee of five people, which was the forerunner of what is now the Red Cross International Committee. In June 1859, the Swiss Jean Henri Dunant (1828–1910), one of the main members of this group, passed through Solferino, in northern Italy, where he was deeply impressed by the sufferings of people caught up in the war for Italian unification. He later wrote about what he saw in a book called *Un souvenir de Solferino*. His call to the wounded and ill to separate themselves from the field of battle and, without distinction between enemy and ally, to help each other in a humane way found great support throughout the world. With the backing of the Welfare Committee of Geneva, the five-man group of which I spoke earlier was formed.

In October 1863, this group and a total of thirty-six representatives from fourteen European countries met for the first time in Geneva and drew up the ten articles of the Red Cross agreement. The Geneva Convention, which insures the neutrality of the Red Cross, was signed in August 1864. The Japan Red Cross, the fourteenth such organization to be formed in the world, was officially recognized by the international committee in 1887, fourteen years after the establishment of the five-man committee in Geneva.

Tsunetami Sano, the first director of the Japan Red Cross, was a politician who maintained an international viewpoint throughout the dramatic changes that took place in Japan in the late nineteenth century. In addition, he was a physician, an engineer, a scholar of Western learning—then called Rangaku, or Dutch studies—and a connoisseur of art. It was with his cooperation that the relief organization Hakuaisha was formed in 1877 to provide aid to people who had suffered in the Satsuma Rebellion, one of the most important disturbances following the restoration of imperial power after the fall of the Tokugawa shogunate in 1868. When the name of the group was changed to the Japan Red Cross, its headquarters were moved to Iida-machi, Kojimachi Ward (a place that is now called Iida-machi, Chiyoda Ward). The headquarters building, designed by Raio Tsumaki, was not completed until 1912, ten years after the death of Tsunetami Sano.

Perhaps Tsumaki and Sano never met; we cannot know now. Still, since Sano had traveled abroad, had a deep understanding of Western technology and art, and, in 1877, had established the Ryuchi Kai (the forerunner of the present Japan Fine

Arts Association), it is by no means unthinkable that he and Tsumaki had come into contact with each other. Even if they never met, the spirit of Sano was alive in the officers of the Japan Red Cross and without doubt found expression in Raio's design of the old headquarters building.

At the time of the building of the headquarters, the defeat of the English-oriented faction within the Japanese government, headed by Shigenobu Okuma, by the Prussian-oriented faction, headed by Hirobumi Ito, had resulted in the adoption of a Prussian scheme for the new constitution of the nation and the modernization of Japan. In the field of architecture, however, the English style, represented by the work of Josiah Conder (1852–1920) was beginning to take root. In 1886, for the sake of the concentration of facilities for the national assembly and other government organs, a temporary building bureau, headed by Ende Beckmann, an architect from Berlin, was established. Conder and his students worked in the bureau. During this work, Tsumaki, who had been one of the first students in the Engineering Institute but had left before graduation, went to study in Germany with a group of Japanese artisans. Unlike some of the leading architects in Japan of his day—notably Kingo Tatsuno (1854–1919) and Tatsuzo Sone (1852–1937)—Tsumaki was fond of German architecture and had great interest in technique, structure, and the rational use of materials. His most important extant building, the Yokohama Shokin Bank (1904), which has been declared an important cultural property, is in a classic, massive, stern German style. In contrast, his Japan Red Cross building shows the influence of some of the buildings he worked on while studying in the Ende Beckmann office—the Ministry of Justice (1896) and the Tokyo Court (Supreme Court). It is true that the facade of the Ministry of Justice has a look of simplicity that seems to have been the outcome of calculated reduction. The facade of the Red Cross building was much richer, but I suspect that Tsumaki may have revised an earlier design as severe as that of the Ministry of Justice and that the Red Cross building facade was the result.

In the course of time, the Red Cross building suffered twice from fire. The original interior, roof, and structure were destroyed. In reconstructions the very pitch of the roof was altered. The original granite frames of the windows were patched and repaired, imperfectly, with terrazzo. When it became necessary to decide what to do with the old building, we were faced with the conclusion that a perfect restoration and conservation of the old building would be impossible. In addition, for the sake of raising funds for construction, it was decided to cut the site in two and sell half. Even if the old building were to be preserved, it would have to be moved to a different site.

After my final judgment on the subject, which was to recommend preservation of the building in the form of a thorough architectural record of it, gained the approval of the Japan Cultural Agency and the headquarters of the Japan Red Cross, we set about assembling the available data. Fortunately we found a large number of written works on the designs, the measurements, and construction bids. Before the building was dismantled, photographs were taken. Part of the dismantled building will be reconstructed at Meiji Village, a fairly extensive settlement of old Japanese buildings that, for various reasons, have been demolished but have been totally or partly rebuilt there because of their cultural value. Other parts of the old building have been incorporated in the new one. The documentary material that we have compiled will be published as a record of the old Japan Red Cross headquarters.

Although when the old building was torn down I was in anything but a cheerful frame of mind, I was totally absorbed with and enthusiastic about compiling the most perfect records possible and about designing a building that would be even better than the old one. If a piece of architecture is a landmark and a historic witness in a given cityscape, it must be preserved in its original position if at all possible. Still, moving buildings to places like Meiji Village to serve as scholarly records is not without significance. In this instance, the vast sums of money needed to move the entire building to Meiji Village were not forthcoming; and we had to be content largely with documentary records. To prevent this kind of thing in the future, I strongly urge the establishment of a national architectural museum-village for the transferral of valuable works.

The dramatic life of Tsunetami Sano and the personality of Raio Tsumaki never left my mind throughout the design process. But I cannot say for certain how well I have succeeded in carrying on the forward-looking spirit of these two men.

An Intermediary and
the Space-Time Continuum

The tower is an indispensable landmark in the European city. I first began thinking that it would be possible to identify the characteristic space of a Japanese city by turning San Gimignano upside down when I made my initial trip to Italy about twenty years ago. After investigating the compositions of Japanese towns, I came to the conclusion that it is the presence of openings of various dimensions that takes the place of the European tower and characterizes our urban spaces.

In stone or brick architecture, it is possible to use party walls between two houses. In the kind of wooden architecture widely used in Japan, such a system makes it difficult to deal with rainwater and creates problems when it becomes necessary to dismantle one of the buildings sharing the party wall. This is one of the advantages of the open space or crevice found among many Japanese buildings. But it is not the only one.

Such crevices provide the psychological pleasure of the sudden view of a different, unexpected world or of a patch of blue sky among the town houses. If the tower in Western cities can be described as an actual symbol of presence, the crevicelike open space in Japanese cities can be called a psychological symbol of absence.

The modern city, since the advent of wide-scale use of reinforced concrete structures, has done away with the crevicelike open space. Designers cannot be said to have devised adequate methods for dealing with the open zones among buildings or for reducing the sense of oppression produced by vast wall surfaces. I believe that one way to achieve this end is to reevaluate the passageway, zone under the eaves, cut-through passage, space open to the sky, and breezeway. This belief led me to use a central crevice space in the Japan Red Cross building.

A functional consideration, too, played a part in my decision. We were required to provide two blocks with separate entrances, cores, and lobbies to meet the needs of the Red Cross facilities and those of the rental office space. The twin towers are joined structurally by the seventh floor, which acts as a bridge between them, and by the connected single block of basement levels that house parking space, machinery rooms, and storage space. The open crevice space serves as a vague connector between two blocks that, though separate, are not completely unrelated. It further acts as a main lobby linking the two blocks.

I have long been inclined to believe that a method for developing continuity from the external spatial experience to the internal spatial experience characterizes both Japanese architectural space and Buddhist culture. My inclination has taken the form of interest in a third, vague region called the intermediary zone. In the Red Cross building, too, I have been strongly influenced by the desire to make the crevicelike space more psychologically and rationally important as an intermediary.

In the Head Offices of the Fukuoka Bank, the intermediary zone was an under-eaves space, or covered exterior zone. We felt that the introduction of natural elements and the employment of the qualities of street furniture would imbue the space with the characters of both interior and exterior. But it seems that the heat-absorbent glass used in the curtain wall to produce something like the feeling of semipenetration created by the lattices of Kyoto townhouses has the effect of spoiling the sense of vague boundary and mutual penetration between the interior and the intermediary zone.

The intermediary in the Red Cross building does not have the semipublic significance of the covered exterior zone in the Fukuoka Bank. In this instance, we have carried the exterior cladding material—jet-burner-finished, Brazilian red granite—into the interior, where it has the effect of producing a reverberation of the mood of the outside. The same thing is true of the beams supporting the glass roof of the carport. These beams, too, penetrate the interior as both materials and design details. For the sake of producing a psychological reversal of awareness of interior and exterior, glass shielding is used at the main entrance. Led inward by a continuity of materials, the visitor is unaware of the boundary separating interior from exterior. Once inside the entrance, which is clearly interior, he has a topological experience caused by the reverberation of the exterior in the form of light flooding inward through the glass of the vaulted roof.

On the granite-clad walls facing the crevice space are two granite window frames in the style of the former building, whose window frames had been so coated and patched with terrazzo that they could not be preserved. The ones installed in the walls of the new building have been reconstructed from Tsumaki's original detail drawings.

The significance of the intermediary space surpasses a mere reversal of the continuity of interior and exterior to become a reversal of continuity between the past and the present. We have used a reflection method to impart something of both significances to the materials. The same red granite employed on the exterior walls is introduced into the entranceway in three stages of finishing: jet-burner finish, ordinary polish, and water polish. This has been done to provide a way of manipulating the light flooding in from the glass vault. The decorative ends of the beams projecting into the entrance from the elevator halls are clad with a curved covering of water-polished red granite, as are the large round sunken floor area in the center of the room and its barrier walls. Lighting fixtures are built into the projecting, rounded beam ends. The round sunken part of the floor was to have been a pond, but objections to the use of running water in this part of the building led us to treat it as a variation of the dry stone and sand gardens (*kare sansui*) used in Zen temples as symbolic evocations of water. The exterior, passing through the glass vault, reflects and reverberates from the polished stone of this symbolic dry pond.

The incorporation of reconstructions of Tsumaki's window frames is an attempt to create a symbolic historical testimony and thus to establish temporal continuity between the old and new buildings. We tried to use as many of the other elements of the old building—lighting fixtures, chandeliers, doors and door frames, and mantelpieces—as we could in this symbolic way.

The bronze lamps on the granite barrier walls of the round sunken floor in the entrance originally stood on the newel posts of the main staircase in the old building. They are employed in the new building to evoke something of the impression once produced by the older entrance hall. The sculpture on the lamps, which were produced by a now unknown craftsman, is of a fairly high level. Takejiro Sato of Tokyo University of Fine Arts repaired the lamps and told me that the bronze in them is quite different from the metal used today.

The interiors of the old building had been repaired so many times that it was impossible to recover their original appearances. But from drawings and plans we reconstructed the ceremonial lounge. Nevertheless, the drawings did not reveal the color schemes. We have used pure white throughout to produce what amounts to an abstract reconstruction of the appearance as it once was. The door frames are from the old building. They have been painted white to inspire them with symbolic life in their new setting. The result is that these frames act as a psychological time tunnel for the sake of coexistence and continuity with history.

The master carpenters and craftsmen of Japan of the past skillfully incorporated older elements in new buildings. The inclusion of structural parts, transom ornaments, painted sliding panels, or any other similar element is not merely a matter of spatial treatment and details; a temporal continuity with the technical skills of the artisans and of the people who produced the building materials is necessary. In this case, achieving such continuity was the most serious cause of trouble. Historical conservation of monuments entails preservation of the production techniques and craft skills that supported the historical period in which the monuments were produced. This is not easy to do.

The Shosoin depository at the Todaiji, in Nara, and the many treasures it contains became the basis of much of the interior design of the new Red Cross building. In 756, on the forty-ninth day after the death of Emperor Shomu, his empress,

Komyo, donated a collection of the emperor's personal belongings and Buddhist dedicatory texts to the Todaiji temple. These treasures were stored for centuries, under official imperial seal, in a log-structure building called the Shosoin. Though the collection includes objects from China, India, Assyria, Persia, Turkey, Afghanistan, and Rome, the choice exercised in their selection clearly represents Japanese taste and aesthetic sensibilities.

For the past ten years, I have entertained the ambitious wish of interpreting those sensibilities by selecting for myself objects that I consider representative from the imported cultural treasures in the Shosoin. I made some attempts at this in the design of the Fukuoka Bank and the New Otani Hotel in Tottori City. But with official permission, I delved much more deeply into the material for the designs used in the cloth wall coverings and carpets for parts of the new Red Cross building.

The interiors of the two rooms for special guests are based on the themes of spring and fall, and the patterns are taken from a lacquered and painted box stored in the central section of the three-section Shosoin. On the black lacquered box, in white, yellow, red, purple, blue-green, ultramarine, and cut gilt are phoenixes, flowers, clouds, flying birds, flowering branches, and other patterns. These were copied as accurately as possible, rearranged to suit our needs, and worked into patterns for textiles for the walls and for carpets, which were especially woven and sculpted at the famous ancient carpet factories of Tientsin. The colors of the originals were not reproduced, however. After test productions, we decided to use vague, non-primary shades and transparent colors that return light.

I am fond of designing so that different materials can coexist. Stone and brass in the benches, leather and brass in the reception room, and cloth and wooden frames are some examples from the Fukuoka Bank. In the Red Cross building, too, there are numerous instances of this technique. For instance, in the facade, granite-clad columns seem to cut into the mirror surfaces of the glass wall. In the reception rooms, wood, metal, and cloth are combined in details. And strips of marble mediate between the carpeting and the wall surfaces. Furnishings made of leather on brass frames are used in the special-guest reception rooms and executive rooms. My approach to the development of such details can be expressed in this way: I allow two materials to collide and use a third material—or an open space—to modulate and to enable the two conflicting elements to coexist.

I first became aware of my feelings in connection with this issue when I realized that no such textual modulation or sense of materials is to be found in the works of Le Corbusier. No matter whether it is the Ronchamp Church or the Marseilles Habitation, his details are always one-dimensional. The unfinished-concrete walls rise directly from the earth. They are rain spattered at their bases, where weeds often grow. The interiors are composed of nothing but intersecting geometrical planes of posts, walls, ceilings, and floors. The collision between the curtain wall and the plaza of the Fukuoka Bank was a problem on which I worked with great enthusiasm. In the Red Cross building, at the junction between the paving stones of the court and the granite cladding of the posts and walls, I have inserted a third zone of granite that is polished to reflect things and, in this way, to eliminate a sense of its own actual existence. In these ways, I am developing the theory of the intermediary on the level of details.

Among the treasures of the Shosoin there are many articles of daily use, clothing, musical instruments, and writing appurtenances that show surprising ideas about detail with different materials. Lacquered areas are surrounded with ivory borders; weathered wood is enclosed in frames of hard wood, and metal forms the boundary between them. The eighth century, when many of these things were produced, witnessed the dramatic clash between the spheres of influence of Tang China and the Saracen empire. It was against this background that Japanese artists and artisans naturalized imported cultural elements. They were able to do this because they raised the symbiosis of conflicting elements to a high qualitative level. Nationalized foreign artisans transferred cultural elements to Japan. In order to allow these elements to take root, Japanese artisans must have constantly striven to uncover details that would make symbiosis possible.

Though centuries separate their times of production, there is not much aesthetic distance between the tortoiseshell and pearl-inlaid octagonal box in the Shosoin and the pearl-inlaid inkstone boxes—one showing a peasant carrying firewood, another showing a boat among reeds—designed and made by the great Japanese artist Hon'ami Koetsu (1558–1637). The use of various methods—inlay, bordering, overlapping, and so on—to combine traditional and modern materials in continuous details is a classic example of cultural symbiosis brought about by the conjunction of alien elements. This approach embraced such relations as those of intermediaries, vague zones, polysemy, and ambivalence.

But in all cultures at all times, conflicting, heterogenous elements come together to produce a multiplicity of meaning and ambivalence. My concept of the intermediary is of a thing that, standing between two spaces—interior and exterior—partakes of both. In this sense, I believe that the pursuit of details in architectural design is a way of discovering a point of juncture, of symbiosis, between the structure and the materials, between technology and sensual perception.

Karakuri *as Philosophy*

I have mentioned many times the positive Japanese attitude toward technology and in passing pointed out that this is not a recent phenomenon but can be traced back to the *karakuri,* or automatons, that were so much the rage in the Edo period. A three-volume work entitled *Karakuri Zui* (Pictorial Register of Mechanical Devices) was published in Japan in 1796 by Hosokawa Hanzo Yorinao. The first volume was devoted to various types of clocks—wall clocks, freestanding clocks, "pillow" clocks, and "footruler" clocks—while the second and third volumes presented mechanical assembly drawings and explanations of a number of automated devices, largely amusements—the *chakumi ningyo,* or tea-bearing doll; the *godan gaeshi,* a doll that did backflips down and back up five steps; the *ryumon taki,* a waterfall toy with leaping carp; mechanical fife-and-drum boys, the "swaying sake cup," fighting cocks, fisherman dolls, courtesan dolls, and others. Among these, perhaps the most exemplary piece of Edo-period robotics was the *chakumi ningyo*. According to the text, one had only to "Set a teacup on the tray borne by the doll, and it moves forward; take the teacup away, and it comes to a stop; then return the teacup to the tray, and the doll withdraws to its original position, all on account of its internal mechanical devices." Here was a simple robot outfitted with a rudimentarily ordered servomechanism that permitted it to initiate forward motion, stop, proceed some set distance, and back up as a fixed command routine. It also incorporated a governor to maintain a constant speed in its motions, as well as a cam and spring to allow a change of direction even without a bevel gear.

All this is interesting enough, but what really calls my attention to these devices is their outward appearance. Of those still existing today, Tachikawa Shoji's reconstruction of the *chakumi ningyo,* or that in the collection of Shirota Masaharu, the sake-cup-bearing doll in the Nishizawa Toy Culture Research Center collection—all are made to resemble traditional Kyoto-style dolls, which were fine works of craftsmanship and sculptural beauty, clothed in fabrics of exquisite design. This proves a fundamental difference from today's robots, whose apparatuses are permitted to show undisguised.

The heart of the matter seems to be that *karakuri* devices incorporate more than a little of the tradition of the master craftsperson's loving dedication, a technology that fairly breathes with its creator's humanity. In giving material form to this human spirit, the *chakumi ningyo* was a machine playing at being human. Moreover, this sort of *simulacre* or performing machine represents a certain way of thinking, a native philosophical attitude I find particularly Japanese. That is, the context of Japanese culture seems somehow peculiarly suited to the development of *karakuri* as human-machine interfaces, machines capable of coexisting, and more, of communicating with people.

We see a steam locomotive puffing clouds of white smoke as it races up an incline, and we find ourselves involved with the efforts of that machine. It is not the internal steam-powered workings of that locomotive that arouse our empathy, however, not the functioning, but those billows of smoke that show how hard it is working—a "performance" as it were. This is not to say there is any exact one-to-one correspondence between the outward appearance of that steam locomotive as sign and the import of its contents as signifier. There is only a vague, ambiguous, or, at best, multivalent semblance of meaning to it all. But is that not the very stuff of performance, and as such a point of continuity with the traditional idea of *karakuri* as performing machines?

Modern society would have machines go unseen. We treat them as eyesores. Our society and certainly our architecture presumes to closet them within a system or structure. These "invisible" machines no longer communicate with anyone. They are grouped and set apart in opposition to people as an infrastructure that threatens to dominate humanity. All the talk of technological advancement, from new information media networks to genetic engineering of human life itself, merely skirts the issue. It still equates technology with "invisible" machines that realize their functions by heading straight on at given purposes, machines that constitute a wholly inhospitable and impenetrable "other world." A philosophy based on the *karakuri* idea, on the other hand, would stress the process of valuation through communication across an open human-machine interface as a natural by-product of the purposes of living itself.

Let us have an architecture that performs as a machine. We must return to architecture that displays a sensitivity toward machines which makes a place for the discovery of real living pleasure, not escapist fancies.

> —Like my feet?
> —Mmm, sure I do . . .
> —I like them, too.
> —And my thighs?
> —Mmm, them too . . .

The conversation above, quoted from the dialogue during a bedroom scene in Godard's *Le mépris* (Contempt), goes on to cover the entire body, the woman's nudity divided up into some ten piecemeal elements or visible signs. No longer a whole embodiment of an individual personality, nor even the object of desire, she is scanned in discontinuity. Hair, head, eyes, nose, lips, ears, neck, chest, breasts, waist, buttocks, legs, feet—the paradigm shifts through a succession of seemingly random body parts, creating an atmosphere of perversion. The naked body becomes a fabric or *texte* as the viewer moves bit by bit across its surface.

The Wacoal Company, a lingerie manufacturer, may well be said to have taken this approach to the naked body as *texte*. To each part of the body as a paradigm unto itself, they present a unique "solution" in the form of pantygirdles, brassieres, and panty hose. The female body of Wacoal's vision is not a tract for desire's partaking that can be possessed, nor is it parceled off into isolated erogenous zones. It is a multivalent two-dimensional nude form observed as "open object." Likewise, when Wacoal presented a list of requirements for its new Tokyo headquarters, it became clear that it had to be multivalent space to simultaneously fulfill a wide variety of functions as the company's creative atelier, business offices, display areas, and new product warehouse—and all this not only for Wacoal's original lingerie concerns but also for the planning and production of other product lines such as nightgowns and outer apparel. The new Wacoal Kojimachi Building, completely designed as of 1976 ago but temporarily delayed due to changes in the economic climate, was thus planned to accommodate a multiplicity of uses over the entire space of each floor. It is markedly different from other examples of corporate architecture; in it functions and meanings overlap and intermingle: storerooms serve as is for display areas, display areas for atelier space, and atelier space for offices. In other words, the whole of the Wacoal Kojimachi Building exists as a signifier, an open-ended multivalent space that is at once the company studio, warenow-empty house, guesthouse, and display facility.

As a creative center for the fashion industry, it stands as an observatory to peer into the future of haute couture. This role is underscored by the incorporation of numerous "stimuli" attending the penetrating vision of what lies ahead. Among the more prominent signs, the white wall backdrop to the main facade showcase shapes itself around Issey Miyake Body Works, striking *simulacres* of the naked human form. The eave-awning extending over the main entranceway calls down a flying saucer, a brief visitor from the world of the future, while on the wall immediately before us as we enter, a mirrored stainless steel sculpture by Tada Minami casts a distorted reflection from the past. Then on into the elevator hall, the floor depicts an age-old geomantic symbol in a mosaic of marble gathered from the countries along the Silk Road. Up on the ninth floor, the guesthouse reception room overlooking the imperial palace is a Japanese-decor space shuttle whose guiding telescope-window is a traditional astrological chart taken from *Ensai Kansho Zusetsu* (Maps of the Firmament Gazing West) published in 1826 by Yoshio Shunzo (also known as Nanso). Ceiling lighting elements repeat the auspicious geomantic sign of the eight directions, and Japanesque fusuma sliding doors and decorative bracketing turn our thoughts to Kyoto. We exit this timeless setting through a juxtaposed "Della Porta" facade which lends a surprisingly smooth note of counterpoint. Proceeding down to the seventh-floor meeting room, we find a smaller telescope-window patterned after the *Botai Hampi Zu* (Chart of Divisions and Opposites) by the Edo-period philosopher Miura Baien.

These and other signs—some from the future, some from the recent past, some from as far back as the Edo period—bring together elements of "noise" from the farthest flung contexts of Japanese culture to play into a vast diachronic performance, a synchronic *plaisir du texte*.

The City of Symbiosis

Another arena in which the philosophy of symbiosis has taken shape in my work is in the New Tokyo Plan 2025. This is a plan that was conceived by a group of specialists—including architects, economists, civil engineers, urban planners, systems engineers, social engineers, and transportation systems specialists—to solve the urgent problem of lack of reasonably priced housing in Tokyo.

One of the unfortunate phenomena of the 1980s was a renewed rush to Tokyo from other regions of Japan and from abroad as well. Until then, the government's regionalization policy had met with relative success, and a halt had been brought to the unhealthy concentration of industry and population in Tokyo. But in the 1980s, the heavy industries that the government had worked to regionalize two decades earlier—steel, shipbuilding, and the petroleum industry—fell into a slump and regional economies were suffering. At the same time, the thrust of the Japanese economy switched to the service and high-tech sectors—finance, communications, publishing, education, and computer hardware and software. These industries were intimately linked to the highly urbanized environment of Tokyo, and their growth meant Tokyo's economic growth. Internationally, in the 1980s Tokyo became a major world financial market. The enormous surplus of money, domestic and foreign, floating through the city's economy encouraged land speculation. Land in central Tokyo increased from three to ten times in value in the period from 1980 to 1987.

This tremendous leap has made it impossible for a working man to own a home in Tokyo. The 2025 group was formed with the goal of mapping out a strategy to lower these unrealistic land prices and to provide a large amount of housing for ordinary working families. After studying the problem from many angles, we came to the conclusion that the solution was to construct an artificial island of 30,000 hectares in Tokyo Bay. Why an island? With the present high demand for space and the limited area of Tokyo, the redevelopment of the present city can only result in the exclusive construction of high-cost homes, offering ordinary workers no alternative but to desert the city. We decided that the use of Tokyo Bay, which is located nearby the already developed urban infrastructure of central Tokyo, was the fastest way to provide a large amount of housing in as short a time as possible; it was in fact the most feasible solution to the problem. In addition, the construction of a new island in Tokyo Bay is a promising commercial venture that would attract private interests. Not only would this relieve government of an enormous financial burden, but it would put the excess capital of the city to economically sound and productive use. It would also increase Japan's domestic demand and help to redress Japan's international trade unbalance. Finally, as a concept, the island in Tokyo Bay is the ultimate realization of the philosophy of symbiosis, since it aims to preserve the present Tokyo as much as possible and create at the same time an island that is equipped with the latest in twenty-first-century high technology: a perfect symbiosis of past and future.

One of the main pillars of the New Tokyo Plan 2025 is the concept of relocating the capital. But the "relocation" we propose is not a relocation in the usual or the historical sense; we do not propose to actually change the capital's locale or to create a new capital. Rather, we propose the removal of the capital's functions to a new island to be built in Tokyo Bay, and the creation of a completely new, twenty-first-century-style capital that will extend from the present Tokyo for a radius of 500 kilometers and include the cities of Nagoya, Osaka, and Kyoto.

We have dubbed that conception the Metropolitan Corridor, and the concept is an important one with many reverberations. To realize this Metropolitan Corridor, the implementation of two recent technological advances will be necessary. The first is the Linear Motor Car, which rides on an invisible magnetic cushion produced by superconducting magnets and can traverse a 500-kilometer distance in an hour. The second is a fiberoptical communication network that will facilitate communication between the decentralized functions of the capital which will be spread out through the Metropolitan Corridor. Government agencies and ministries will be distributed among the new island in Tokyo Bay, Nagoya, Osaka, and Kyoto. To commemorate the 1,200-year anniversary of the establishment of Kyoto as Japan's capital, a new imperial palace will be built in that city and the imperial family will return to Kyoto. This will strengthen the old capital's role as a symbol of Japan's history and traditions. The new Tokyo and Nagoya international airports, presently in the planning stages, and the new airport in Osaka that is presently under construction will all be part of an air network that will accommodate the new SST—the Orient Express—which will place Japan within three hours of the major capitals of the world.

In the twentieth century, relocating a nation's capital meant building a new city in an ideal image in a new place. Brasília, Canberra, and Islamabad are typical examples of this twentieth-century vision. But all of these attempts to relocate or reestablish the capital city ended in failure. These failures cannot be accounted for by any simple or single reason, but we can identify three problems with this approach: first, the functions of the capital were completely extracted from their context and transferred as an isolated unit; second, the move represented a complete break with history and tradition; and third, these new capitals were designed from start to finish as a symbol of the nation.

The capital of the twenty-first century will be an invisible one. It will not take the shape of an entire city designed as a symbol and then concretely realized. Rather, it will be found in the relationships created between various urban centers as they are linked to each other and, together, as a whole, carry out the functions of a capital. The task of planning the twenty-first-century capital is to design those invisible links and relations. We speak of Washington, D.C. as the capital of the United States. That is where the White House and the Congress are, to be sure. But in fact the functions of America's capital cannot be carried out by Washington, D.C. alone. It is far more accurate to describe America's capital as the metropolitan corridor that links and includes Washington and New York City. Washington is nothing more than the door to the corridor, a window to the capital.

The tragic failure of Brasília is the failure to create a metropolitan corridor connecting the city to Rio de Janeiro, and the failures of Canberra and Bonn can be ascribed to the same failing.

The Metropolitan Corridor is created by exploiting and incorporating history—in the form of the already existing city, which is an historical accumulation. It is a network, a city in which history and advanced technology exist symbiotically.

The failed relocations of national capitals in the twentieth century have conclusively demonstrated that a capital metropolis cannot successfully exist when it is exclusively a political center. Political and economic activities became in this century an inseparable complex. No doubt the twenty-first century will further prove that a capital metropolis cannot survive when it is only a political and economic center. The metropolis of the next century will be a complex of political, economic, and cultural activities. This is nothing other than the rhizome described by Deleuze and Guattari.

The Metropolitan Corridor will be a conglomeration of cities. It will lack a center. In the twentieth century, the capital was the most classical of all cities. It was a symbol of authority, and within it, the national legislature and the prime minister or political leader's residence served as a symbol of the capital. The Plaza of the

Three Powers in Brasília and the grand and imposing parliament house in Canberra are examples of this. Does contemporary society require a center? Will the capital of the twenty-first century require a symbol of authority? The White House in Washington does not serve any longer as a symbol of authority. What towers above our heads now, challenging the heavens, are skyscrapers. Do the buildings that house the French Parliament or the Palais de l'Elysee really qualify as monuments of Paris? They stand quietly and inconspicuously among a flock of imposing and gorgeous cultural facilities. Even in Tokyo, the National Diet Building and the prime minister's residence are not symbols of the city's authority. Tange Kenzo's new Metropolitan Office Building to be built in Shinjuku is an attempt to restore order to the city by introducing a symbol of authority, but this is nothing more than an effort to turn back the wheels of history. It is clearly a mistake. The capital city of the twenty-first century will be a capital without a center.

The Metropolitan Corridor we propose will be made up of a network of several independent cities, each with its own character, which divide the activities and functions of the capital among themselves. With a network of that sort there is no longer any need to construct buildings that symbolize a metropolitan center.

The idea of building an island in Tokyo Bay can be traced back to the Edo period. The first plan in the modern period was presented in 1959, by an industrial planning commission made up of economic leaders of the time. That plan called for a manmade island of some twenty thousand hectares, to be created from landfill. After that first proposal, the Tange Research Group produced its Tokyo Plan 1960; the Ministry of Industry proposed creating a ten-thousand-hectare island; and many other similar plans were also considered. Yet none of those plans were very realistic. There are four great obstacles to creating a manmade island in Tokyo Bay. The first is the fact that creating a manmade island out of landfill is likely to harm the water quality of the bay. The second is that the creation of an island would put an end to navigational use of the bay, which services some 330,000 vessels annually. The third is the difficulty in finding a source for enough landfill to create an island without causing harm to the environment. And the fourth is a lack of sufficient energy sources, electricity in particular, to make the new island livable.

The proposals to construct an island in Tokyo Bay that have been presented so far were little more than abstract ideas or architectural visions. There have been no proposals that included solutions to these four practical problems. Our research took as its starting place the solution to these four obstacles to creating an island in the bay. To solve the first problem, we propose the construction of a Boso Canal that will cut across the Boso Peninsula of Chiba Prefecture. Taking advantage of the two- to seven-meter difference in the tides of Tokyo Bay and the Pacific coast off Chiba, sea water from the Pacific Ocean could be drawn into Tokyo Bay, which would flush and circulate the water in the bay. It is thought that this would result in an increase in the number of varieties of fish living in the bay from fifty-three to seventy. According to a computer simulation we carried out, this linkage of the bay to the Pacific would purify the bay's water, lowering its chemical oxygen demand

(COD) from the present 7.5–9.5 to 2.5. (The dredging of the bay, discussed later, would also contribute to its purification.)

To tackle the second obstacle—the obstruction that an island in the bay would present to shipping and other commercial vessels—we propose the construction of a tunnel seventy meters below ground along the bay's shoreline. (A tunnel at that depth would sidestep the problems of land rights and compensation costs entailed in shallower construction work.) Pipelines for oil and natural gas, fiberoptical, telex, and telephone cables, and computer-controlled container cars would be installed inside these tunnels. The six docks in the present Tokyo Bay would become harbors for pleasure crafts—privately owned boats, tour vessels, and leisure fishing crafts. New commercial ports would be constructed in two locations: one at the mouth of the bay and one at the Pacific mouth of the Boso Canal. Foreign cargo vessels and tankers would dock at these new ports and unload their shipments, which would then be sent to their destinations through the underground tunnel described earlier. This new system would eliminate the need for commercial shipping traffic in Tokyo Bay and make the construction of the island in the bay feasible.

The third problem with the construction of an island in the bay is to find a source of landfill that can be obtained without environmental destruction. We have calculated that for the thirty-thousand-hectare island we propose, 840 million cubic meters of landfill is required. A major portion of that—450 million cubic meters— can be obtained by dredging Tokyo Bay to a depth of twenty meters. Another 280 million cubic meters can be obtained from excavations related to the construction of new cities on the Boso Peninsula, and sixty million cubic meters will be produced in the excavation of the Boso Canal. The last fifty million cubic meters needed will come from the amount of refuse suitable for recycling as landfill that the city of Tokyo will produce by the year 2000. All of these sources are near at hand and none of them will cause destruction of the natural environment.

The solution to the fourth difficulty has been made possible by a surprising discovery. Tokyo Electric is gradually moving from steam-generated power plants to nuclear facilities. There are twelve steam-generated plants along the rim of the bay that are scheduled for shutdown in the future. An investigation shows that these plants release a total of five million kilowatts of energy into Tokyo Bay in the form of heat loss from their gas turbines. If these plants were kept in operation in the future and their heat loss could be recouped and used, a ready source of energy— enough to supply the annual energy needs of a city of five million—would become immediately available.

With the investigations reviewed above, our group has for the first time demonstrated that it is possible to construct an island thirty thousand hectares in area in Tokyo Bay. We estimate that the cost of this project, including all public facilities such as bridges, subways, and energy facilities, plus the Boso Canal and the new airport and harbors, would be approximately seventy-seven trillion yen. This can be translated into a land cost of one million yen per *tsubo,* or 3.3 square meters. The present cost of land in central Tokyo is fifty million yen per 3.3 square meters—fifty times our estimated cost. In other words, at one-fiftieth the cost of land in Tokyo, we are able to produce at central Tokyo's doorstep a thirty-thousand-hectare area of land. At a land area to land use ratio of four hundred percent (taking into account, of course, that almost all structures will be multistory), this area could support a population of five million.

Tokyo's skyrocketing land values have pushed the price of a condominium of one hundred square meters to one hundred million yen, and the average citizen can no longer afford to buy a home or an apartment in the city. The new island in the bay that we propose will provide the average citizen with that home—with a yacht harbor attached. In addition, there is a strong possibility that the availability of this large amount of land will result in a drop in demand that will reduce the price of land in mainland Tokyo.

This new island in Tokyo Bay will serve yet another important function. It will provide the "elbow room" that is necessary for the redevelopment of Tokyo itself. With the present cost of land in the city it is almost impossible to acquire the land needed for redevelopment. But as many facilities are transferred to the new island in the bay, plans for mainland Tokyo's redevelopment, including making it more secure from earthquakes and fires, can be pursued. The space made available in Tokyo by the opening of the new island can also be used for the canals and "pocket forests," discussed below, that we propose to build in the city.

The land of the new island will be employed for certain facilities of the new capital, for industry and business, for foreign embassies and consulates, for leisure facilities, and for housing. The island will be administered as a separate municipality, but no attempt will be made to make it an independent self-supporting city; rather, it will remain a part of the network of cities located along the bay, including Tokyo, Yokohama, and Chiba, and it will serve as a part of the larger Metropolitan Corridor discussed earlier.

The new island is an urban loop. Its outer edges will form a loop-shaped city center, without a core. The city with a market in its center is the ancient Greek vision of the city. The center of a Renaissance city was occupied by a public square, on which faced the two symbols of secular and divine authority: the palace and the church. Modern Western cities are heirs to this tradition of urban planning. The city hall or the parliament and government ministries formed the city's center. The city core (2P) was an important theme of CIAM. Even now, when the city's center is dominated by economic functions taking architectural form as office and industrial space, we have not been able to escape the concept of the city's center, its core. The creation of subcenters is nothing but an extension of the concept of the center, as is the idea of the "linear core," which proposes stretching these central points into a line.

But in the twenty-first century, the focus will switch from the core to the edges, and the city, too, will move from the age of the center to the age of the city's edges. The concept of the urban loop is in opposition to the idea of the center. It will be the form that the city takes in the age of the edges.

On an international scale, the city is evolving from the continental city to the seaport. In America, a chain of new "rim cities" and waterfront cities will spring up along both coasts. In China, too, the twenty-first century will be the era of coastal cities. The center of Manhattan is Central Park; the face of the city looks down on the park. But in the twenty-first century, Manhattan will lose its core and gain an interesting new face as it turns toward the waterfront; this is already underway, with the redevelopment of the southern tip of the island. Japan will be no exception to this new trend. Tokyo's waterfront, which has been defaced by heavy industrial development, will be reborn and come to form the new urban loop of Tokyo.

The new island is an island and, at the same time, not an island. A series of concentric, loop-shaped canals will make it a grouping of loops of land. In its very center will be an artificial lake, which will strengthen the image of a city without a core. This city made up of loops of canals is a quotation of Venice and Amsterdam. At the same time, it recalls and revives Tokyo's earlier incarnation as Edo, a city that was looped and crisscrossed by canals. Our proposal represents a new lifestyle, a symbiosis of the city and nature, the city and the country, the city and the fishing village (that Edo once was).

The concept of the loop city can actually be traced back to 1962, when the Tange Research Group, of which I was a member, presented as part of its Tokyo Plan 1960 a loop-shaped transportation network, which was termed the cyclic transportation network. After that, as a member of the Metabolism movement, I declared in our plan for the city of the future, the "Metamorphosis Plan 1962," that the age of the center had come to an end. I rejected neighborhood planning, which makes schools and commercial facilities the core of an area, and I proposed at that early date a plan of locating the functions of the city center on the city's outskirts. I realized my concept of the urban loop in later projects such as the Fujisawa Shonan Life Town and Hishino New Town.

If there is a need to redevelop the present Tokyo, it is a need to make the city safer in the case of earthquakes and other natural disasters. By parasimulation, we have calculated that if an earthquake of the magnitude of the Great Kanto Earthquake of 1923 were to take place in Tokyo today, between five hundred thousand and one million people would die. The main cause of these fatalities, it is thought, would not be collapsing buildings but the fires that would break out and raze from sixty to seventy percent of the city.

There are three steps that can be taken to protect Tokyo from fires in the aftermath of an earthquake. One is to build canals that will act as firebreaks. Another is to create pocket forests—small areas of greenery—throughout the city. The third is to create an architectural firebreak with a belt of fire-resistant buildings. The numerous urban fires in Japan's past have clearly testified to the importance of canals and areas of greenery in stopping the spread of conflagrations.

Within the earlier estimate of 5 million inhabitants for the new island in Tokyo Bay, we expect that from 1.5 to 2 million will move there from mainland Tokyo. That is, the island's population will not represent an increase in Tokyo's population, but in fact a significant decrease in that of mainland Tokyo. This decrease, we calculate, will provide the space to construct canals and small forests in Tokyo.

The two canals that we propose for Tokyo will each create a loop city with a width of 1.5 kilometers. These loop cities will be futuristic, high-tech belts made of fire-resistant building materials. The French philosopher of semiotics Roland Barthes discusses Tokyo in his book *The Empire of Signs*. There he declares that Tokyo has no center, that the imperial palace in its geographical center is a forest, an open space, an absence of a core. This metaphorical suggestion is interesting as an interpretation of Japanese culture, but we cannot escape the fact that Tokyo clearly and definitely follows the Western pattern of city planning, and its central organs are grouped around the imperial palace.

This intense concentration of capital and transportation facilities in this core area make the redevelopment of the city very difficult. Tokyo, too, very much needs to undergo a great transformation that brings the center to the edges. Our proposal to construct loop-shaped belts bordering two canals is a proposal to transform the city from a radial city to a loop city.

Yet our plan to redevelop Tokyo does not entail redevelopment of the entire city. Rather, we propose that most of the city be left precisely as it is. Aside from the two canals and the loop cities that will be constructed on both banks of each of them, the rest of the city will be left to its natural processes of metabolism and evolution. The philosophy that led the twentieth century was a philosophy of ruling the world according to an ideal. City planning that regarded the natural growth and development of a city as bad or disorganized was held to be the triumph of reason and the ideal. Le Corbusier's image of "the shining city" testifies to this belief. There is no room in this vision for the kind of urban labyrinth that arises naturally and organically.

The Modernism of the twentieth century took humankind as its ideal. Human beings were regarded as being composed of spirit and flesh. The goal of this Modernism has been to promote mental and physical health. This ideal represents the orthodox line of Western thought, traced back to ancient Rome and Greece. According to this way of thinking, for example, illness arises when a virus or bacteria invades our bodies from without; by extension, health is achieved when all other living things are attacked and either killed or driven out of our bodies. In the same pattern, a wise (that is, healthy) philosophy drives out any other way of thinking or any other way of living (culture) in order to preserve its purity and rationality. According to this way of thinking, ambiguity and nonrationality threaten the integrity of the spirit and are to be avoided. By their very nature, compromise and eclecticism are to be rejected as defiled, and all middle ground is eliminated. The modern city, too, has incorporated this concept of health.

The failures of Brasília and Canberra are the failure of this ideal vision of the city based on the Modernist vision of humanity. It is a vision that allows no room for the growth of the labyrinth.

The reason that I make no proposals regarding the redevelopment of Tokyo other than the two canal loops is that it is not my intention to create some new

"City of Symbiosis." A city has charm and life precisely because it contains anomalies, oddities, impurities, and irrationalities (or nonrationalities). The city of the twenty-first century must be a labyrinth.

The traditional Western view that human beings are composed of body and spirit is no longer useful. Human beings are a symbiotic existence made up not only of body and spirit but other living things and inorganic substances as well. If the viruses inhabiting our bodies (in the intestine, for example) were all eliminated, we would die. If the inorganic substances and minerals in our bodies were all expelled, we would perish. The new concept of the human being must include both other living things and inorganic substances as well as body and spirit. This new definition of a human being is at the root of my concept of symbiosis.

The abstract conception of health that derives from the two-dimensional idea of humanity composed of spirit and flesh and the resulting philosophy of Humanism are fraudulent notions. This type of health is nowhere to be seen in this world, nor is the humanity that is the very subject of such Humanism. If a human being exists in symbiosis with other things, organic and inorganic, the city, too, can only preserve its life by including in itself different things and different forms. The eminently natural conclusion is that there is a purpose in a city being a labyrinth and in its symbiosis with the past as well as with other types of cultural standards.

The period when opposing dualisms—sacred and profane, high technology and tradition, macro and micro, whole and part, city and farm, technology and nature, economics and culture, development and preservation—reigned supreme has come to an end. Opposing value systems and diverse elements stand in relationship to each other and, while opposing on one level, form the rhizome spoken of by Deleuze and Guattari. This is not to say that harmony has been achieved between opposing forces, as in the dialectic, nor is it a philosophy of anarchy or laissez-faire. A dynamic city where different currents flow together in new relationships and at the same time exist in symbiosis will mark the beginning of the age of the city of symbiosis.

In Conclusion

Though I still believe that the binomial opposition of Modern Architecture versus Postmodern Architecture was to a certain extent an effective weapon in exposing the shortcomings of the former, devoting too much time to this exercise in dichotomizing is counterproductive. It also undermines my own most basic position. Binomial opposition is an outgrowth of the Cartesian and Judaeo-Christian dualism that lies at the base of Western culture, and it can be detected in the rationalism of Modern Architecture as well. The concept of Modernism itself, in all its aspects, is built on the various binomial oppositions that grow from the fundamental dualism of the Western tradition. Those dichotomies range from the philosophical opposition between freedom and necessity and spirit and flesh, through the religious dichotomies of good and evil deities and God and his creation, and on to many other opposing pairs: tradition and the future, man and nature, interior and exterior, opposing cultures, science and religion, the part and the whole, chaos and order.

Thus it is that to attempt to transcend Modernism by opposing it with Postmodernism is to fall victim to the same practice of dichotomizing, is self-contradictory, and, in the end, self-defeating. We must instead escape Modernism while walking arm-in-arm with it; we must embrace it as we reject it. This is the only way to avoid binomialism ourselves. In my recently published *Philosophy of Symbiosis (Kyosei no Shiso),* my insistence on moving from Postmodernism to a philosophy of symbiosis is an alternative way of articulating the escape from binomialism.

The tactic of rejecting while affirming, rejecting while embracing, is not, as I have stated above, a method of harmonizing opposites. Nor is it the conventional dialectical method of opposition followed by resolution on a higher plane. It is, instead, a method of creating *relationships* between opposites. I call this method of escape from binomialism the philosophy of symbiosis.

The issue of ambiguity, which has long occupied me and which I have articulated in the form of such concepts as mediating spaces, *ma, Rikyu gray,* and *senuhima,* is related to my search for a method to escape binomialism. Within the very philosophy of symbiosis, which in its dynamism swallows binomialism by rejecting it and affirming it at the same time, lies an ambiguous region where meaning is indeterminate, divisions are blurred, and the unknown, the chaotic, the maze reside. This ambiguous zone is what has been lacking in the architecture and the cities of Modernism up to now. The architecture of symbiosis, which possesses this ambiguity, will appear at times to resemble Modern Architecture and, at other times, Postmodern Architecture.

The philosophy of Maurice Merleau-Ponti, which has often been described as a philosophy of ambiguity or multivalency, seeks a unifying principle to transcend binomial opposition. In Alphonse De Waelhens's foreword to Merleau-Ponti's book *La structure du comportement,* he remarks that Merleau-Ponti was constantly preoccupied with the subtle connections between mind and body. By way of example, Merleau-Ponti considered the case of a man in a cell, and the dramatic way in which his perception of food placed beyond the cell bars changes depending upon whether he can slip through the cell's steel bars and reach the food. In other words, the state of the body is intimately linked to the state of the mind; at the same time, the mind is an external projection of the body, slightly out of synch with it. Merleau-Ponti's philosophy of ambiguity was an attempt to find a unifying principle that transcended the binomial opposition of mind and body. But Jacques Lacan criticizes Merleau-Ponti, pointing out that as long as one dichotomizes mind and body it is impossible to escape the Cartesian dualism.

My adoption of the ideas of the Consciousness Only school of Buddhist philosophy was because of its teaching regarding the binomial opposition of being and nonbeing. According to Consciousness Only thought, these two apparent opposites are only that: appearances. This is not a philosophy of being but a philosophy of relationship—not "In the beginning there was creation," but "In the beginning there were relations." Relation is a source of dynamic creation, from which a manifold variety of "existences" rise, appear, and take shape. This dynamic, varied, plural state is nothing other than the state of symbiosis. When we interpret this sort of symbiotic space, we can read it binomially as internal space or external space; but we can also read it as internal space, intermediary space, and external space. We can go further, too, and see a plurality and variety of degrees, including completely internal space, slightly internal space, largely internal space, space resembling internal space, slightly external space, space resembling external space, and so forth. The internal and the external do not exist from the start as self-defined entities. I continue to be interested in the dynamic relationships produced by heterogenous elements, whether they be cultural symbols, physical elements, or moods and atmospheres.

The concept of the rhizome as explained by Deleuze and Guattari in *Rhizome, extrait de Mille Plateaux* is a dynamic, varied, and plural form. They liken modern society to a tree. A tree has roots, a trunk, branches, and leaves; each part has an unchanging function, and each exists in a hierarchy within the whole. This they offer as a symbol for modern society, modern cities, and Modern Architecture. In contrast, a rhizome is an interlocking web. It is a conjunction of dynamic relations—producing bulbs here and there, interweaving with great complexity, reaching outward in its continuing growth. It represents the principle of dynamic, varied pluralism that absorbs the hierarchical structure of the tree.

How is this principle expressed in architecture? In the unclear, the inexact, the ambiguous; in things that feel as if they are in motion; in a sensation of drifting or floating; in a sense of liberation created by many entrances (many exits) and the constant search for relationship with other worlds; in space that makes us feel disjointed or out of synch; in space that seems to move away from us as it approaches us; in a relationship not so much of different units of space but of many different dimensions altogether. Deleuze and Guattari call this symbiosis of order and chaos the "chaosmos." They characterize modern society and Modern Architecture with the model of the tree rather than the rhizome because these modern phenomena have sought to realize the human ideal of universal order—the cosmos—in this world. The Modern Movement has marched forward under the banner of Truth, with its emphasis on humanity and human scale. It has placed its belief in human ideals and icons, and it has defined the Truth as the realization of those ideals. Further, this ideal, which was born from the value system of Western culture, was held to be equally applicable to other cultural contexts, such as the Islamic and Asian worlds. According to this way of thinking, behind all plural and varied appearances there lies a single, universal Truth. This was first of all a philosophical position that affirmed a single concrete reality; it was also a bid to sell the Western value system to the rest of the world. In the so-called Good Design movement, there was obviously a preconceived notion of just what constituted design excellence, a model or an idea (an icon). The aim of those who wished to create good architecture was to try to approach that ideal image, which was assumed to actually exist.

But just what is good design, what is "good architecture"? What is a good person, and where in actual existence do we find the human ideal? Were the good design of the Bauhaus and the International Style of CIAM that sort of model, that sort of ideal? The concept of progress can be apprehended as the approach toward these goals. Based on this model of the hierarchy of the tree, Western culture is at the peak of world civilization and all other cultures are in the midst of a progression to that goal. The efforts of Japanese architects since the Meiji Restoration in 1868 have been of just this sort. All their labors were based on the equation of modernization with Westernization. The architecture designed in the era following the Second World War, Postmodern Architecture, and all contemporary architecture, built in the idiom of the West, are attempts to approach this idea, this icon, and spread it to the rest of the world in an ideological campaign of Truth.

But in fact aren't we living at the start of the era that has seen the death of God, the crumbling of the icon, and the extermination of the Western-style ideal? It is not Truth's mandate to conquer the world and spread the values of a single culture. We are living in an age when we must recognize that each of the many and varied cultures of the world has its own independent system of values, and that meaning is produced by the dynamic interactions of these different cultures and values. From that recognition will come a new architecture, an architecture of the rhizome.

In a discussion with Arata Isozaki, I repeated my cry of "Death to Esperanto!" Isozaki responded with a reference to Noam Chomsky's concept of the deep structure of language, suggesting that there is a sort of natural Esperanto at the base of all languages. According to Chomsky, though every language has its own identity, at the bottom of the individual words of each language is a deep structure common to them all. Yet this transformational grammar (or productive grammar) is the linguistic version of the tree model attacked by Deleuze and Guattari. They have shown that Chomsky's linguistic tree begins from point S and works from there by dichotomizing and that Chomsky's "grammar," the categoric, symbolic capital S that rules all sentences, is a sign of authority before it is a sign of syntax.

And what of the human ideal? What is the reality behind the abstract notion of the human being that has become an icon of Modernism? In our world exist men and women; elderly people, young people, and children; fathers and mothers; Mister A and Mister B; but nowhere do we encounter this abstract human being. We have been taught that this nonexistent, ideal model or icon of a human being is composed of pure flesh and pure spirit. Earlier I pointed out what I believe are the limits of this view, and the limits of the medical corollary of health as an absolute "integrity" of the human system, free of all "intruding" organisms and elements. Is it right, then, to try to achieve an absolutely pure state of humanity? Or is it right to live in symbiosis with other existences, sentient and otherwise? I believe that symbiosis is the right path to walk. Can modern medical science conceive of no other means of handling the virus called cancer than to attack and try to eliminate it completely? For me there is no doubt that a new medical science will be born, a holistic medical science, that will allow us to live, *with* cancer, to the age of one hundred years.

In like manner, there exists no ideal model of good architecture. We must search out an architecture that transcends the binomialism of good and bad. We will put behind us the binomial method of evaluating and judging, discard the false opposition between beauty and ugliness, good and bad, skill and lack of it, and we will discover beauty amidst ugliness, skill in clumsiness, and good architecture that seems bad. Our new standard will be the pleasure architecture provides us. Pleasure is different in nature from the abstract concepts good and bad; behind it there is no ideal model or icon of good architecture. Pleasure is something that each person discovers for himself, and it differs from person to person, depending on the individual's values. The architect's task, as a result, will be to create an architecture that many different people can read in many different ways, and architecture that provides not Pleasure but many different pleasures.

The concept of the rhizome is a productive one, giving birth to many different meanings and rich ambiguities.

"Less is more." There is no need to mention the source of this famous maxim. Modern Architecture seems to believe that it is in the absolute minimum of expression that the greatest spiritual force and the most profound meaning are conveyed. But it is important to see the assumption that lies behind this belief. It is that before any relationships exist, there is a universal ideal, an invisible, potential structure to existence. Art, and the art of architecture, is the process of revealing that hidden reality with the absolute minimum of expression. This belief in a substratum of true reality (or an ideal) has been at the root of Western culture since the time of Plato. In that sense, American structural linguistics, the work of Leonard Bloomfield and of Chomsky—all of these currents of thought are faithful to the ancient Western paradigm of the preeminent existence of an ideal or a substratum of existence. In contrast to this, when we think of ourselves as "animals possessed by chaos," or when we regard the essentially human as "joy, anger, sadness, and pleasure," we find no need to cling to a prescriptive ideal or a universal notion of what architecture is. We can create an architecture that is a collection of devices for producing pleasure.

This pleasure is not that which is to be had by fulfilling biological desires, but a cultural pleasure. By converting the biological desire for the opposite sex to pleasure in the clothing of the opposite sex, sexual desire is transformed into cultural desire, that is, cultural pleasure—the delight in dress and fashion. Architecture is a cultural activity as well, and one that requires a theory of relations to be understood, for just as we read sexual desire in the *simulacre* of dress, we can read divinity in the *simulacre* of architecture. The cultural symbols distributed throughout architectural space create a maze, create chaos, and the opportunity for *l'échange symbolique* described by Baudrillard.

Saussure criticized the traditional view of language as an expression of a preexisting substratum of reality. The writer does not merely record a preexisting *texte*; the very act of writing is the creation of the *texte*. The reader, likewise, whether confronting music, painting, or architecture, not only receives meaning from the object (the *texte*), but also gives his own meaning to the text in the act of reading. His act is a participative, mutual one. Just as the architect creates an architecture that provides meaning, the one who experiences the architecture creates a way of reading it.

Quite aside from its practical functions, architecture as a *texte* is constantly read and transformed from moment to moment, place to place, through the cultural symbols that are incorporated in it. Julia Kristeva calls the interlocking nature of architecture as a *texte* that becomes a locus for the event of producing other *textes* the pleasure of experiencing *intertextualité*. If we regard architecture as no different from an aircraft, it will only be desired for its usefulness. If we regard architecture as no different from Lenin's statue, the univocal realization of a preexisting notion (ideology), it will have no use for ambiguity or plurality of meaning. If we regard architecture as a sign, however, there is no need to suppose a preexisting concept (or reality). All we need is a code (a grammar) that tells us red is stop.

In all of these examples, the author conveys no message (he has no meaning to give) and the reader creates no meaning (he has no meaning to make). But if we regard architecture as akin to literature, if, in other words, it is a *texte,* it becomes a place for reading meanings, a place for creating meanings, a pleasurable place to be and act.

Editorial Note

The present book was adapted from the author's *Kenchiku Ron: Nihonteki Kukan E,* a collection of essays published by Kajima Shuppan, Tokyo, in 1984. Additional and more recent writings are incorporated in the English book, in particular essays concerning the 2025 plan for Tokyo's redevelopment and the author's autobiographical essay, appearing as the introduction of the present book, as well as later developments of his philosophy of symbiosis.

The essays that comprise this book were written for a wide variety of audiences over several years, and inevitably there is much repetition within them. One of the editorial aims in adapting them for the English book was to eliminate as much of this as possible; the attempt can be only partly successful, however, because of the very nature not only of the author's style but of his argument and his method. It was Nakamura Hajime, the Buddhist scholar whom the author invokes in his Introduction, who characterized the Asian method of reasoning as nonlinear. Instead of proceeding from *A* to *B*, the head-on, direct view of Western logic, the great thinkers of Asia, he wrote, have preferred to circle their target, reasoning around it and pointing to it again and again until it is clarified from all perspectives and seems, often suddenly, to be eminently right and reasonable in its unique totality. Each repetition is in fact a slight variation, a slight shift in angle, focus, or balance that adds a new dimension to the argument. This method the author not only shares but consciously advocates, and to attempt to eliminate it from his writings is not only impossible, it is wrong-headed.

Following the author's preference, the names of contemporary Japanese figures are given in Western order, first name followed by surname, though this is contrary to the Japanese practice. The names of historical figures are usually familiar to readers in their Japanese form, and they have been given that way. The rough dividing line for reversing name order has been the start of the Meiji period, 1868. Japanese and Sanskrit words have been romanized without diacritical marks and, following the author's preference, certain terms and titles of works in European languages have been left in the original, even though equivalents are in use in English. Whenever possible, titles of the author's writings have been given in English translation with the original Japanese following in parentheses.

KISHO KUROKAWA
A Concise Biography

Born in Nagoya in 1934, Kisho Kurokawa received his degree in architecture from Kyoto University. In 1960, while doing postgraduate work for his doctoral course at Tokyo University, he formed with several others the Metabolist Group. Based on Buddhist philosophy, they advocated that the city and architecture are organisms capable of growth and change. Kurokawa's early important works such as the capsule pavilions at the international Expo 1970 (Osaka), Nakagin Capsule Tower (Tokyo, 1972), and Sony Tower (Osaka, 1976) are illustrations of the Metabolist concept.

From Metabolism, Kurokawa developed his Philosophy of Symbiosis, which, again influenced by Buddhism and other aspects of traditional Japanese culture, probes the interrelationship between time and space, man and technology. Expanding the concept of symbiosis to include the interrelationships of the past and future, man and nature, and one culture and another, Kurokawa has employed it as his main theme in numerous major architectural and urban planning projects. Among these are the Head Offices of the Fukuoka Bank (1975), National Ethnological Museum (Osaka, 1977), Headquarters of the Japanese Red Cross Society (Tokyo, 1977), Saitama Prefectural Museum of Modern Art (Urawa, 1982), National Bunraku Theater (Osaka, 1983), Wacoal Kojimachi Building (Tokyo, 1984), Roppongi Prince Hotel (Tokyo, 1984), a series of furniture designs entitled *Edo* (1982), The Japanese Studies Institute, Thammasat University, Thailand (1985), Koshi Kaikan Center (Toyama, 1986), Nagoya City Museum of Modern Art (Nagoya, 1987), and the Japanese-German Center of Berlin (West Berlin, 1988).

He is currently engaged in a number of projects around the world—in the United States, Southeast Asia, Western and Eastern Europe, Australia, Korea, and China. These projects include Bayer A.G.'s Plant Protection Research Headquarters in Monheim, West Germany; Haskovo Opera House, Bulgaria; high-rise commercial complexes and a leisure and shopping center, both in Seoul; high-rise office buildings in Melbourne and Brisbane; the Chinese-Japanese Youth Center in Beijing; a sports center in Chicago; Ville de Nimes ZAC in Rond Point Nord, Nimes, France; Republic Plaza in Singapore; and many others.

He has received seventeen major design awards and won many international competitions, including his work for the Bayer A.G.'s Research Headquarters in West Germany; the second prize for the new Centre Georges Pompidou; first prize for the New TANU Headquarters and the Parliament in Tanzania; and first prize for Conference City in Abu Dhabi as well as first prize for the U.A.E. University Town in Al Ain, both in the United Arab Emirates.

He has published over thirty books, in France, Italy, England, and the United States. A collection of his design works, ranging from architectural drawings to Japanese woodcut prints and furniture, was exhibited at major galleries in London, Paris, Rome, Moscow, Budapest, Pistoia, Dublin, Sofia, Helsinki, Bucharest, Buenos Aires, Sarajevo, Wroclaw, Warsaw, and Los Angeles. An active lecturer, he has addressed numerous institutions and organizations, both in Japan and abroad.

Kisho Kurokawa is now an analyst with the Japan Broadcasting Corporation (NHK), honorary professor at the University of Buenos Aires, visiting professor at Tsinghua University in Beijing, adviser of the International Design Conference in Aspen, Colorado (of which he was co-chairman in 1979), and a member of the executive board of the International Conference of Design and Culture, which he initiated and founded in Japan in 1980. He has also been active on many Japanese government committes.

In 1981, Kisho Kurokawa became an honorary fellow member of The American Institute of Architects, and of the Royal Institute of British Architects in 1986. The same year he was awarded the 1986 Gold Medal from the Academy of Architecture in France, and in 1988, the 1988 Richard Neutra Award from California State Polytechnic Institute in Pomona, California. In 1979 Bulgaria decorated him with "Madara," First Order, and in 1985 Finland presented him with the "Commandeur de l'Ordre du Lion." In 1988, he was made Doctor Honoris Causa by Sophia University, Bulgaria.

The "weathermark" identifies this book as a production of John Weatherhill, Inc., publishers of fine books on Asia and the Pacific. Editorial supervision: Jeffrey Hunter. Book design and typography: Miriam F. Yamaguchi. Layout of photographs: Yutaka Shimoji. Production supervision: Mitsuo Okado. Composition: Korea Textbook, Seoul. Printing: Shobundo Printing, Tokyo. Binding: Makoto Binderies, Tokyo. The typeface used is Monotype Times New Roman.

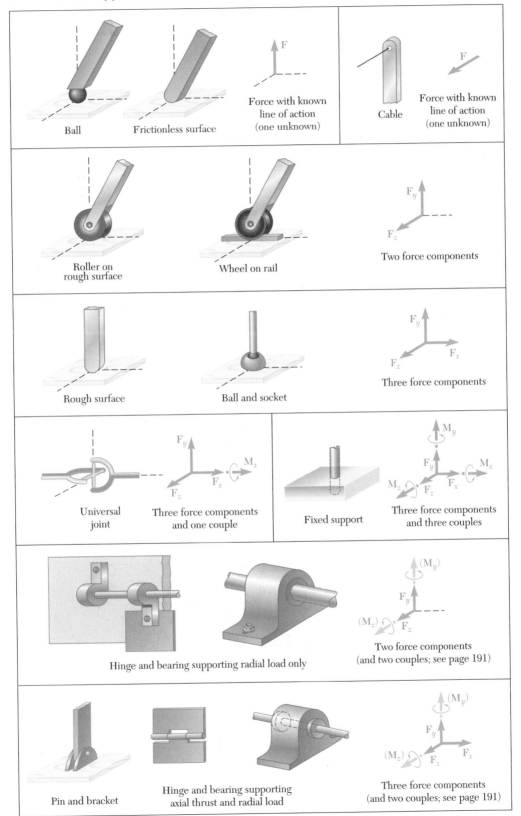

Ball   Frictionless surface   Force with known line of action (one unknown)

Cable   Force with known line of action (one unknown)

Roller on rough surface   Wheel on rail   Two force components

Rough surface   Ball and socket   Three force components

Universal joint   Three force components and one couple

Fixed support   Three force components and three couples

Hinge and bearing supporting radial load only   Two force components (and two couples; see page 191)

Pin and bracket   Hinge and bearing supporting axial thrust and radial load   Three force components (and two couples; see page 191)

VECTOR MECHANICS FOR ENGINEERS
Statics

NINTH EDITION

VECTOR MECHANICS FOR ENGINEERS
Statics

Ferdinand P. Beer
Late of Lehigh University

E. Russell Johnston, Jr.
University of Connecticut

David F. Mazurek
U.S. Coast Guard Academy

Elliot R. Eisenberg
The Pennsylvania State University

 Higher Education

Boston   Burr Ridge, IL   Dubuque, IA   New York   San Francisco   St. Louis
Bangkok   Bogotá   Caracas   Kuala Lumpur   Lisbon   London   Madrid   Mexico City
Milan   Montreal   New Delhi   Santiago   Seoul   Singapore   Sydney   Taipei   Toronto

Higher Education

VECTOR MECHANICS FOR ENGINEERS: STATICS, NINTH EDITION

Published by McGraw-Hill, a business unit of The McGraw-Hill Companies, Inc., 1221 Avenue of the Americas, New York, NY 10020. Copyright © 2010 by The McGraw-Hill Companies, Inc. All rights reserved. Previous editions © 2007, 2004, and 1997. No part of this publication may be reproduced or distributed in any form or by any means, or stored in a database or retrieval system, without the prior written consent of The McGraw-Hill Companies, Inc., including, but not limited to, in any network or other electronic storage or transmission, or broadcast for distance learning.

Some ancillaries, including electronic and print components, may not be available to customers outside the United States.

This book is printed on acid-free paper.

2 3 4 5 6 7 8 9 0 VNH/VNH 0

ISBN 978–0–07–352923–3
MHID 0–07–352923–0

Global Publisher: *Raghothaman Srinivasan*
Senior Sponsoring Editor: *Bill Stenquist*
Director of Development: *Kristine Tibbetts*
Developmental Editor: *Lora Neyens*
Senior Marketing Manager: *Curt Reynolds*
Senior Project Manager: *Sheila M. Frank*
Senior Production Supervisor: *Sherry L. Kane*
Senior Media Project Manager: *Tammy Juran*
Designer: *Laurie B. Janssen*
Cover/Interior Designer: *Ron Bissell*
(USE) Cover Image: *©John Peter Photography/Alamy*
Lead Photo Research Coordinator: *Carrie K. Burger*
Photo Research: *Sabina Dowell*
Supplement Producer: *Mary Jane Lampe*
Compositor: *Aptara®, Inc.*
Typeface: *10.5/12 New Caledonia*
Printer: *RR Donnelley*

The credits section for this book begins on page 603 and is considered an extension of the copyright page.

Library of Congress Cataloging-in-Publication Data

Vector mechanics for engineers. Statics and dynamics / Ferdinand Beer . . . [et al.]. — 9th ed.
 p. cm.
  Includes index.
   ISBN 978–0–07–352940–0 (combined vol. : hc : alk. paper) — ISBN 978–0–07–352923–3
  (v. 1 — "Statics" : hc : alk. paper) — ISBN 978–0–07–724916–8 (v. 2 — "Dynamics" : hc : alk. paper)
    1. Mechanics, Applied. 2. Vector analysis. 3. Statics. 4. Dynamics. I. Beer, Ferdinand Pierre, 1915–

TA350.B3552 2009
620.1'05—dc22

2008047184

www.mhhe.com

About the Authors

As publishers of the books by Ferd Beer and Russ Johnston, we are often asked how they happened to write their books together with one of them at Lehigh and the other at the University of Connecticut.

The answer to this question is simple. Russ Johnston's first teaching appointment was in the Department of Civil Engineering and Mechanics at Lehigh University. There he met Ferd Beer, who had joined that department two years earlier and was in charge of the courses in mechanics.

Ferd was delighted to discover that the young man who had been hired chiefly to teach graduate structural engineering courses was not only willing but eager to help him reorganize the mechanics courses. Both believed that these courses should be taught from a few basic principles and that the various concepts involved would be best understood and remembered by the students if they were presented to them in a graphic way. Together they wrote lecture notes in statics and dynamics, to which they later added problems they felt would appeal to future engineers, and soon they produced the manuscript of the first edition of *Mechanics for Engineers* that was published in June 1956.

The second edition of *Mechanics for Engineers* and the first edition of *Vector Mechanics for Engineers* found Russ Johnston at Worcester Polytechnic Institute and the next editions at the University of Connecticut. In the meantime, both Ferd and Russ assumed administrative responsibilities in their departments, and both were involved in research, consulting, and supervising graduate students—Ferd in the area of stochastic processes and random vibrations and Russ in the area of elastic stability and structural analysis and design. However, their interest in improving the teaching of the basic mechanics courses had not subsided, and they both taught sections of these courses as they kept revising their texts and began writing the manuscript of the first edition of their *Mechanics of Materials* text.

Their collaboration spanned more than half a century and many successful revisions of all of their textbooks, and Ferd's and Russ's contributions to engineering education have earned them a number of honors and awards. They were presented with the Western Electric Fund Award for excellence in the instruction of engineering students by their respective regional sections of the American Society for Engineering Education, and they both received the Distinguished Educator Award from the Mechanics Division of the same society. Starting in 2001, the New Mechanics Educator Award of the Mechanics Division has been named in honor of the Beer and Johnston author team.

Ferdinand P. Beer. Born in France and educated in France and Switzerland, Ferd received an M.S. degree from the Sorbonne and an Sc.D. degree in theoretical mechanics from the University of Geneva.

He came to the United States after serving in the French army during the early part of World War II and taught for four years at Williams College in the Williams-MIT joint arts and engineering program. Following his service at Williams College, Ferd joined the faculty of Lehigh University where he taught for thirty-seven years. He held several positions, including University Distinguished Professor and chairman of the Department of Mechanical Engineering and Mechanics, and in 1995 Ferd was awarded an honorary Doctor of Engineering degree by Lehigh University.

E. Russell Johnston, Jr. Born in Philadelphia, Russ holds a B.S. degree in civil engineering from the University of Delaware and an Sc.D. degree in the field of structural engineering from the Massachusetts Institute of Technology. He taught at Lehigh University and Worcester Polytechnic Institute before joining the faculty of the University of Connecticut where he held the position of chairman of the Department of Civil Engineering and taught for twenty-six years. In 1991 Russ received the Outstanding Civil Engineer Award from the Connecticut Section of the American Society of Civil Engineers.

David F. Mazurek. David holds a B.S. degree in ocean engineering and an M.S. degree in civil engineering from the Florida Institute of Technology and a Ph.D. degree in civil engineering from the University of Connecticut. He was employed by the Electric Boat Division of General Dynamics Corporation and taught at Lafayette College prior to joining the U.S. Coast Guard Academy, where he has been since 1990. He has served on the American Railway Engineering and Maintenance of Way Association's Committee 15—Steel Structures for the past eighteen years. His professional interests include bridge engineering, tall towers, structural forensics, and blast-resistant design.

Elliot R. Eisenberg. Elliot holds a B.S. degree in engineering and an M.E. degree, both from Cornell University. He has focused his scholarly activities on professional service and teaching, and he was recognized for this work in 1992 when the American Society of Mechanical Engineers awarded him the Ben C. Sparks Medal for his contributions to mechanical engineering and mechanical engineering technology education and for service to the American Society for Engineering Education. Elliot taught for thirty-two years, including twenty-nine years at Penn State where he was recognized with awards for both teaching and advising.

Contents

3 Rigid Bodies: Equivalent Systems of Forces 72

4 Equilibrium of Rigid Bodies   156

5 Distributed Forces: Centroids and Centers of Gravity   218

6 Analysis of Structures   284

7 Forces in Beams and Cables   352

8 Friction   410

10 Method of Virtual Work 556

Preface

OBJECTIVES

The main objective of a first course in mechanics should be to develop in the engineering student the ability to analyze any problem in a simple and logical manner and to apply to its solution a few, well-understood, basic principles. It is hoped that this text, designed for the first course in statics offered in the sophomore year, and the volume that follows, *Vector Mechanics for Engineers: Dynamics*, will help the instructor achieve this goal.†

GENERAL APPROACH

Vector analysis is introduced early in the text and is used in the presentation and discussion of the fundamental principles of mechanics. Vector methods are also used to solve many problems, particularly three-dimensional problems where these techniques result in a simpler and more concise solution. The emphasis in this text, however, remains on the correct understanding of the principles of mechanics and on their application to the solution of engineering problems, and vector analysis is presented chiefly as a convenient tool.‡

Practical Applications Are Introduced Early. One of the characteristics of the approach used in these volumes is that mechanics of *particles* is clearly separated from the mechanics of *rigid bodies*. This approach makes it possible to consider simple practical applications at an early stage and to postpone the introduction of the more difficult concepts. For example:

- In *Statics*, statics of particles is treated first (Chap. 2); after the rules of addition and subtraction of vectors are introduced, the principle of equilibrium of a particle is immediately applied to practical situations involving only concurrent forces. The statics of rigid bodies is considered in Chaps. 3 and 4. In Chap. 3, the vector and scalar products of two vectors are introduced and used to define the moment of a force about a point and about an axis. The presentation of these new concepts is followed by a thorough and rigorous discussion of equivalent systems of forces leading, in Chap. 4, to many practical applications involving the equilibrium of rigid bodies under general force systems.
- In *Dynamics*, the same division is observed. The basic concepts of force, mass, and acceleration, of work and energy, and

†This text is available in a single volume, *Vector Mechanics for Engineers: Statics and Dynamics*, ninth edition.

‡In a parallel text, *Mechanics for Engineers: Statics*, fifth edition, the use of vector algebra is limited to the addition and subtraction of vectors.

of impulse and momentum are introduced and first applied to problems involving only particles. Thus, students can familiarize themselves with the three basic methods used in dynamics and learn their respective advantages before facing the difficulties associated with the motion of rigid bodies.

New Concepts Are Introduced in Simple Terms. Since this text is designed for the first course in statics, new concepts are presented in simple terms and every step is explained in detail. On the other hand, by discussing the broader aspects of the problems considered, and by stressing methods of general applicability, a definite maturity of approach is achieved. For example, the concepts of partial constraints and statical indeterminacy are introduced early and are used throughout.

Fundamental Principles Are Placed in the Context of Simple Applications. The fact that mechanics is essentially a *deductive* science based on a few fundamental principles is stressed. Derivations have been presented in their logical sequence and with all the rigor warranted at this level. However, the learning process being largely *inductive*, simple applications are considered first. For example:

- The statics of particles precedes the statics of rigid bodies, and problems involving internal forces are postponed until Chap. 6.
- In Chap. 4, equilibrium problems involving only coplanar forces are considered first and solved by ordinary algebra, while problems involving three-dimensional forces and requiring the full use of vector algebra are discussed in the second part of the chapter.

Free-Body Diagrams Are Used Both to Solve Equilibrium Problems and to Express the Equivalence of Force Systems. Free-body diagrams are introduced early, and their importance is emphasized throughout the text. They are used not only to solve equilibrium problems but also to express the equivalence of two systems of forces or, more generally, of two systems of vectors. The advantage of this approach becomes apparent in the study of the dynamics of rigid bodies, where it is used to solve three-dimensional as well as two-dimensional problems. By placing the emphasis on "free-body-diagram equations" rather than on the standard algebraic equations of motion, a more intuitive and more complete understanding of the fundamental principles of dynamics can be achieved. This approach, which was first introduced in 1962 in the first edition of *Vector Mechanics for Engineers*, has now gained wide acceptance among mechanics teachers in this country. It is, therefore, used in preference to the method of dynamic equilibrium and to the equations of motion in the solution of all sample problems in this book.

A Four-Color Presentation Uses Color to Distinguish Vectors. Color has been used, not only to enhance the quality of the illustrations, but also to help students distinguish among the various types of vectors they will encounter. While there was no intention to "color code" this text, the same color is used in any given chapter to represent vectors of the same type. Throughout *Statics*, for example, red is used exclusively to represent forces and couples, while position vectors are shown in blue and dimensions in black. This makes it easier for the students to identify the forces acting on a given particle or rigid body and to follow the discussion of sample problems and other examples given in the text.

A Careful Balance Between SI and U.S. Customary Units Is Consistently Maintained.

Because of the current trend in the American government and industry to adopt the international system of units (SI metric units), the SI units most frequently used in mechanics are introduced in Chap. 1 and are used throughout the text. Approximately half of the sample problems and 60 percent of the homework problems are stated in these units, while the remainder are in U.S. customary units. The authors believe that this approach will best serve the need of students, who, as engineers, will have to be conversant with both systems of units.

It also should be recognized that using both SI and U.S. customary units entails more than the use of conversion factors. Since the SI system of units is an absolute system based on the units of time, length, and mass, whereas the U.S. customary system is a gravitational system based on the units of time, length, and force, different approaches are required for the solution of many problems. For example, when SI units are used, a body is generally specified by its mass expressed in kilograms; in most problems of statics it will be necessary to determine the weight of the body in newtons, and an additional calculation will be required for this purpose. On the other hand, when U.S. customary units are used, a body is specified by its weight in pounds and, in dynamics problems, an additional calculation will be required to determine its mass in slugs (or $lb \cdot s^2/ft$). The authors, therefore, believe that problem assignments should include both systems of units.

The *Instructor's and Solutions Manual* provides six different lists of assignments so that an equal number of problems stated in SI units and in U.S. customary units can be selected. If so desired, two complete lists of assignments can also be selected with up to 75 percent of the problems stated in SI units.

Optional Sections Offer Advanced or Specialty Topics.

A large number of optional sections have been included. These sections are indicated by asterisks and thus are easily distinguished from those which form the core of the basic statics course. They may be omitted without prejudice to the understanding of the rest of the text.

Among the topics covered in these additional sections are the reduction of a system of forces to a wrench, applications to hydrostatics, shear and bending-moment diagrams for beams, equilibrium of cables, products of inertia and Mohr's circle, the determination of the principal axes and the mass moments of inertia of a body of arbitrary shape, and the method of virtual work. The sections on beams are especially useful when the course in statics is immediately followed by a course in mechanics of materials, while the sections on the inertia properties of three-dimensional bodies are primarily intended for students who will later study in dynamics the three-dimensional motion of rigid bodies.

The material presented in the text and most of the problems require no previous mathematical knowledge beyond algebra, trigonometry, and elementary calculus; all the elements of vector algebra necessary to the understanding of the text are carefully presented in Chaps. 2 and 3. In general, a greater emphasis is placed on the correct understanding of the basic mathematical concepts involved than on the nimble manipulation of mathematical formulas. In this connection, it should be mentioned that the determination of the centroids of composite areas precedes the calculation of centroids by integration, thus making it possible to establish the concept of the moment of an area firmly before introducing the use of integration.

CHAPTER ORGANIZATION AND PEDAGOGICAL FEATURES

Chapter Introduction. Each chapter begins with an introductory section setting the purpose and goals of the chapter and describing in simple terms the material to be covered and its application to the solution of engineering problems. Chapter outlines provide students with a preview of chapter topics.

Chapter Lessons. The body of the text is divided into units, each consisting of one or several theory sections, one or several sample problems, and a large number of problems to be assigned. Each unit corresponds to a well-defined topic and generally can be covered in one lesson. In a number of cases, however, the instructor will find it desirable to devote more than one lesson to a given topic. The *Instructor's and Solutions Manual* contains suggestions on the coverage of each lesson.

Sample Problems. The sample problems are set up in much the same form that students will use when solving the assigned problems. They thus serve the double purpose of amplifying the text and demonstrating the type of neat, orderly work that students should cultivate in their own solutions.

Solving Problems on Your Own. A section entitled *Solving Problems on Your Own* is included for each lesson, between the sample problems and the problems to be assigned. The purpose of these sections is to help students organize in their own minds the preceding theory of the text and the solution methods of the sample problems, so that they can more successfully solve the homework problems. Also included in these sections are specific suggestions and strategies that will enable students to more efficiently attack any assigned problems.

Homework Problem Sets. Most of the problems are of a practical nature and should appeal to engineering students. They are primarily designed, however, to illustrate the material presented in the text and to help students understand the principles of mechanics. The problems are grouped according to the portions of material they illustrate and are arranged in order of increasing difficulty. Problems requiring special attention are indicated by asterisks. Answers to 70 percent of the problems are given at the end of the book. Problems for which the answers are given are set in straight type in the text, while problems for which no answer is given are set in italic.

Chapter Review and Summary. Each chapter ends with a review and summary of the material covered in that chapter. Marginal notes are used to help students organize their review work, and cross-references have been included to help them find the portions of material requiring their special attention.

Review Problems. A set of review problems is included at the end of each chapter. These problems provide students further opportunity to apply the most important concepts introduced in the chapter.

Computer Problems. Each chapter includes a set of problems designed to be solved with computational software. Many of these problems are relevant to the design process. In statics, for example, they may involve the analysis of a structure for various configurations and loadings of the structure or the determination of the equilibrium positions of a mechanism which may require an iterative method of solution. Developing the algorithm required to solve a given mechanics problem will benefit students in two different ways: (1) it will help them gain a better understanding of the mechanics principles involved; (2) it will provide them with an opportunity to apply their computer skills to the solution of a meaningful engineering problem.

SUPPLEMENTS

An extensive supplements package for both instructors and students is available with the text.

Instructor's and Solutions Manual. The *Instructor's and Solutions Manual* that accompanies the ninth edition features typeset, one-per-page solutions to the homework problems. This manual also features a number of tables designed to assist instructors in creating a schedule of assignments for their courses. The various topics covered in the text are listed in Table I, and a suggested number of periods to be spent on each topic is indicated. Table II provides a brief description of all groups of problems and a classification of the problems in each group according to the units used. Sample lesson schedules are shown in Tables III, IV, and V.

McGRAW-HILL CONNECT ENGINEERING

McGraw-Hill Connect Engineering is a web-based assignment and assessment platform that gives students the means to better connect with their coursework, their instructors, and the important concepts that they will need to know for success now and in the future. With Connect Engineering, instructors can deliver assignments, quizzes, and tests easily online. Students can practice important skills at their own pace and on their own schedule.

Connect Engineering for *Vector Mechanics for Engineers* is available at **www.mhhe.com/beerjohnston** and includes algorithmic problems from the text, Lecture PowerPoints, an image bank, and animations.

Hands-on Mechanics. Hands-on Mechanics is a website designed for instructors who are interested in incorporating three-dimensional, hands-on teaching aids into their lectures. Developed through a partnership between the McGraw-Hill Engineering Team and the Department of Civil and Mechanical Engineering at the United States Military Academy at West Point, this website not only provides detailed instructions for how to build 3-D teaching tools using materials found in any lab or local hardware store but also provides a community where educators can share ideas, trade best practices, and submit their own demonstrations for posting on the site. Visit **www.handsonmechanics.com**.

ELECTRONIC TEXTBOOK OPTIONS

Ebooks are an innovative way for students to save money and create a greener environment at the same time. An ebook can save students about half the cost of a traditional textbook and offers unique features like a powerful search engine, highlighting, and the ability to share notes with classmates using ebooks.

McGraw-Hill offers two ebook options: purchasing a downloadable book from VitalSource or a subscription to the book from CourseSmart. To talk about the ebook options, contact your McGraw-Hill sales rep or visit the sites directly at **www.vitalsource.com** and **www.coursesmart.com**.

ACKNOWLEDGMENTS

A special thanks go to Amy Mazurek of Williams Memorial Institute who thoroughly checked the solutions and answers of all problems in this edition and then prepared the solutions for the accompanying *Instructor's and Solution Manual;* Yohannes Ketema of University of Minnesota; David Oglesby of University of Missouri-Rolla; and Daniel W. Yannitell of Louisiana State University.

We are pleased to recognize Dennis Ormond of Fine Line Illustrations for the artful illustrations which contribute so much to the effectiveness of the text.

The authors thank the many companies that provided photographs for this edition. We also wish to recognize the determined efforts and patience of our photo researcher, Sabina Dowell.

The authors also thank the members of the staff at McGraw-Hill for their support and dedication during the preparation of this new edition. We particularly wish to acknowledge the contributions of Senior Sponsoring Editor Bill Stenquist, Developmental Editor Lora Neyens, and Senior Project Manager Sheila Frank.

Finally, the authors gratefully acknowledge the many helpful comments and suggestions offered by users of the previous editions of *Vector Mechanics for Engineers*.

E. Russell Johnston, Jr.
David F. Mazurek
Elliot R. Eisenberg

List of Symbols

a	Constant; radius; distance
$\mathbf{A}, \mathbf{B}, \mathbf{C}, \ldots$	Reactions at supports and connections
$A, B, C, \ldots$	Points
A	Area
b	Width; distance
c	Constant
C	Centroid
d	Distance
e	Base of natural logarithms
$\mathbf{F}$	Force; friction force
g	Acceleration of gravity
G	Center of gravity; constant of gravitation
h	Height; sag of cable
$\mathbf{i}, \mathbf{j}, \mathbf{k}$	Unit vectors along coordinate axes
$I, I_x, \ldots$	Moments of inertia
$\bar{I}$	Centroidal moment of inertia
$I_{xy}, \ldots$	Products of inertia
J	Polar moment of inertia
k	Spring constant
k_x, k_y, k_O	Radii of gyration
$\bar{k}$	Centroidal radius of gyration
l	Length
L	Length; span
m	Mass
$\mathbf{M}$	Couple; moment
$\mathbf{M}_O$	Moment about point O
$\mathbf{M}_O^R$	Moment resultant about point O
M	Magnitude of couple or moment; mass of earth
M_{OL}	Moment about axis OL
$\mathbf{N}$	Normal component of reaction
O	Origin of coordinates
p	Pressure
$\mathbf{P}$	Force; vector
$\mathbf{Q}$	Force; vector
$\mathbf{r}$	Position vector
r	Radius; distance; polar coordinate
$\mathbf{R}$	Resultant force; resultant vector; reaction
R	Radius of earth
$\mathbf{s}$	Position vector
s	Length of arc; length of cable
$\mathbf{S}$	Force; vector
t	Thickness
$\mathbf{T}$	Force
T	Tension
U	Work

V	Vector product; shearing force
V	Volume; potential energy; shear
w	Load per unit length
W, W	Weight; load
x, y, z	Rectangular coordinates; distances
$\bar{x}, \bar{y}, \bar{z}$	Rectangular coordinates of centroid or center of gravity
α, β, γ	Angles
γ	Specific weight
δ	Elongation
$\delta\mathbf{r}$	Virtual displacement
δU	Virtual work
$\boldsymbol{\lambda}$	Unit vector along a line
η	Efficiency
θ	Angular coordinate; angle; polar coordinate
μ	Coefficient of friction
ρ	Density
ϕ	Angle of friction; angle

VECTOR MECHANICS FOR ENGINEERS
Statics

In the latter part of the seventeenth century, Sir Isaac Newton stated the fundamental principles of mechanics, which are the foundation of much of today's engineering.

Introduction

1.1 WHAT IS MECHANICS?

Mechanics can be defined as that science which describes and predicts the conditions of rest or motion of bodies under the action of forces. It is divided into three parts: mechanics of *rigid bodies,* mechanics of *deformable bodies,* and mechanics of *fluids.*

The mechanics of rigid bodies is subdivided into *statics* and *dynamics,* the former dealing with bodies at rest, the latter with bodies in motion. In this part of the study of mechanics, bodies are assumed to be perfectly rigid. Actual structures and machines, however, are never absolutely rigid and deform under the loads to which they are subjected. But these deformations are usually small and do not appreciably affect the conditions of equilibrium or motion of the structure under consideration. They are important, though, as far as the resistance of the structure to failure is concerned and are studied in mechanics of materials, which is a part of the mechanics of deformable bodies. The third division of mechanics, the mechanics of fluids, is subdivided into the study of *incompressible fluids* and of *compressible fluids.* An important subdivision of the study of incompressible fluids is *hydraulics,* which deals with problems involving water.

Mechanics is a physical science, since it deals with the study of physical phenomena. However, some associate mechanics with mathematics, while many consider it as an engineering subject. Both these views are justified in part. Mechanics is the foundation of most engineering sciences and is an indispensable prerequisite to their study. However, it does not have the *empiricism* found in some engineering sciences, i.e., it does not rely on experience or observation alone; by its rigor and the emphasis it places on deductive reasoning it resembles mathematics. But, again, it is not an *abstract* or even a *pure* science; mechanics is an *applied* science. The purpose of mechanics is to explain and predict physical phenomena and thus to lay the foundations for engineering applications.

1.2 FUNDAMENTAL CONCEPTS AND PRINCIPLES

Although the study of mechanics goes back to the time of Aristotle (384–322 B.C.) and Archimedes (287–212 B.C.), one has to wait until Newton (1642–1727) to find a satisfactory formulation of its fundamental principles. These principles were later expressed in a modified form by d'Alembert, Lagrange, and Hamilton. Their validity remained unchallenged, however, until Einstein formulated his *theory of relativity* (1905). While its limitations have now been recognized, *newtonian mechanics* still remains the basis of today's engineering sciences.

The basic concepts used in mechanics are *space, time, mass,* and *force.* These concepts cannot be truly defined; they should be accepted on the basis of our intuition and experience and used as a mental frame of reference for our study of mechanics.

The concept of *space* is associated with the notion of the position of a point P. The position of P can be defined by three lengths measured from a certain reference point, or *origin,* in three given directions. These lengths are known as the *coordinates* of P.

To define an event, it is not sufficient to indicate its position in space. The *time* of the event should also be given.

The concept of *mass* is used to characterize and compare bodies on the basis of certain fundamental mechanical experiments. Two bodies of the same mass, for example, will be attracted by the earth in the same manner; they will also offer the same resistance to a change in translational motion.

A *force* represents the action of one body on another. It can be exerted by actual contact or at a distance, as in the case of gravitational forces and magnetic forces. A force is characterized by its *point of application,* its *magnitude,* and its *direction;* a force is represented by a *vector* (Sec. 2.3).

In newtonian mechanics, space, time, and mass are absolute concepts, independent of each other. (This is not true in *relativistic mechanics,* where the time of an event depends upon its position, and where the mass of a body varies with its velocity.) On the other hand, the concept of force is not independent of the other three. Indeed, one of the fundamental principles of newtonian mechanics listed below indicates that the resultant force acting on a body is related to the mass of the body and to the manner in which its velocity varies with time.

You will study the conditions of rest or motion of particles and rigid bodies in terms of the four basic concepts we have introduced. By *particle* we mean a very small amount of matter which may be assumed to occupy a single point in space. A *rigid body* is a combination of a large number of particles occupying fixed positions with respect to each other. The study of the mechanics of particles is obviously a prerequisite to that of rigid bodies. Besides, the results obtained for a particle can be used directly in a large number of problems dealing with the conditions of rest or motion of actual bodies.

The study of elementary mechanics rests on six fundamental principles based on experimental evidence.

The Parallelogram Law for the Addition of Forces.
This states that two forces acting on a particle may be replaced by a single force, called their *resultant,* obtained by drawing the diagonal of the parallelogram which has sides equal to the given forces (Sec. 2.2).

The Principle of Transmissibility.
This states that the conditions of equilibrium or of motion of a rigid body will remain unchanged if a force acting at a given point of the rigid body is replaced by a force of the same magnitude and same direction, but acting at a different point, provided that the two forces have the same line of action (Sec. 3.3).

Newton's Three Fundamental Laws.
Formulated by Sir Isaac Newton in the latter part of the seventeenth century, these laws can be stated as follows:

FIRST LAW. If the resultant force acting on a particle is zero, the particle will remain at rest (if originally at rest) or will move with constant speed in a straight line (if originally in motion) (Sec. 2.10).

SECOND LAW. If the resultant force acting on a particle is not zero, the particle will have an acceleration proportional to the magnitude of the resultant and in the direction of this resultant force.

As you will see in Sec. 12.2, this law can be stated as

$$\mathbf{F} = m\mathbf{a} \tag{1.1}$$

where $\mathbf{F}$, m, and $\mathbf{a}$ represent, respectively, the resultant force acting on the particle, the mass of the particle, and the acceleration of the particle, expressed in a consistent system of units.

THIRD LAW. The forces of action and reaction between bodies in contact have the same magnitude, same line of action, and opposite sense (Sec. 6.1).

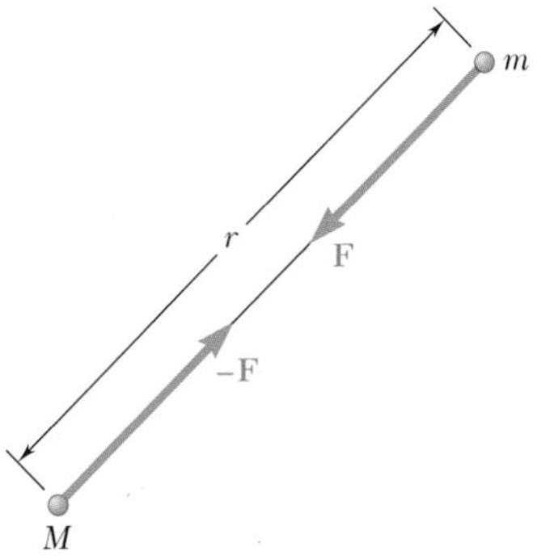

Newton's Law of Gravitation. This states that two particles of mass M and m are mutually attracted with equal and opposite forces $\mathbf{F}$ and $-\mathbf{F}$ (Fig. 1.1) of magnitude F given by the formula

$$F = G\frac{Mm}{r^2} \tag{1.2}$$

where r = distance between the two particles
$\quad\ G$ = universal constant called the *constant of gravitation*

Newton's law of gravitation introduces the idea of an action exerted at a distance and extends the range of application of Newton's third law: the action $\mathbf{F}$ and the reaction $-\mathbf{F}$ in Fig. 1.1 are equal and opposite, and they have the same line of action.

A particular case of great importance is that of the attraction of the earth on a particle located on its surface. The force $\mathbf{F}$ exerted by the earth on the particle is then defined as the *weight* $\mathbf{W}$ of the particle. Taking M equal to the mass of the earth, m equal to the mass of the particle, and r equal to the radius R of the earth, and introducing the constant

$$g = \frac{GM}{R^2} \tag{1.3}$$

the magnitude W of the weight of a particle of mass m may be expressed as†

$$W = mg \tag{1.4}$$

The value of R in formula (1.3) depends upon the elevation of the point considered; it also depends upon its latitude, since the earth is not truly spherical. The value of g therefore varies with the position of the point considered. As long as the point actually remains on the surface of the earth, it is sufficiently accurate in most engineering computations to assume that g equals 9.81 m/s^2 or 32.2 ft/s^2.

Fig. 1.1

Photo 1.1 When in earth orbit, people and objects are said to be *weightless* even though the gravitational force acting is approximately 90% of that experienced on the surface of the earth. This apparent contradiction will be resolved in Chapter 12 when we apply Newton's second law to the motion of particles.

†A more accurate definition of the weight $\mathbf{W}$ should take into account the rotation of the earth.

The principles we have just listed will be introduced in the course of our study of mechanics as they are needed. The study of the statics of particles carried out in Chap. 2, will be based on the parallelogram law of addition and on Newton's first law alone. The principle of transmissibility will be introduced in Chap. 3 as we begin the study of the statics of rigid bodies, and Newton's third law in Chap. 6 as we analyze the forces exerted on each other by the various members forming a structure. In the study of dynamics, Newton's second law and Newton's law of gravitation will be introduced. It will then be shown that Newton's first law is a particular case of Newton's second law (Sec. 12.2) and that the principle of transmissibility could be derived from the other principles and thus eliminated (Sec. 16.5). In the meantime, however, Newton's first and third laws, the parallelogram law of addition, and the principle of transmissibility will provide us with the necessary and sufficient foundation for the entire study of the statics of particles, rigid bodies, and systems of rigid bodies.

As noted earlier, the six fundamental principles listed above are based on experimental evidence. Except for Newton's first law and the principle of transmissibility, they are independent principles which cannot be derived mathematically from each other or from any other elementary physical principle. On these principles rests most of the intricate structure of newtonian mechanics. For more than two centuries a tremendous number of problems dealing with the conditions of rest and motion of rigid bodies, deformable bodies, and fluids have been solved by applying these fundamental principles. Many of the solutions obtained could be checked experimentally, thus providing a further verification of the principles from which they were derived. It is only in the twentieth century that Newton's mechanics was found at fault, in the study of the motion of atoms and in the study of the motion of certain planets, where it must be supplemented by the theory of relativity. But on the human or engineering scale, where velocities are small compared with the speed of light, Newton's mechanics has yet to be disproved.

1.3 SYSTEMS OF UNITS

With the four fundamental concepts introduced in the preceding section are associated the so-called *kinetic units*, i.e., the units of *length, time, mass,* and *force*. These units cannot be chosen independently if Eq. (1.1) is to be satisfied. Three of the units may be defined arbitrarily; they are then referred to as *basic units*. The fourth unit, however, must be chosen in accordance with Eq. (1.1) and is referred to as a *derived unit*. Kinetic units selected in this way are said to form a *consistent system of units*.

International System of Units (SI Units†). In this system, which will be in universal use after the United States has completed its conversion to SI units, the base units are the units of length, mass, and time, and they are called, respectively, the *meter* (m), the *kilogram* (kg), and the *second* (s). All three are arbitrarily defined. The second,

---

†SI stands for *Système International d'Unités* (French).

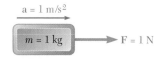

a = 1 m/s²

m = 1 kg → F = 1 N

Fig. 1.2

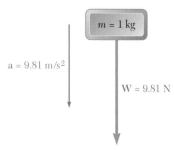

m = 1 kg

a = 9.81 m/s²

W = 9.81 N

Fig. 1.3

which was originally chosen to represent 1/86 400 of the mean solar day, is now defined as the duration of 9 192 631 770 cycles of the radiation corresponding to the transition between two levels of the fundamental state of the cesium-133 atom. The meter, originally defined as one ten-millionth of the distance from the equator to either pole, is now defined as 1 650 763.73 wavelengths of the orange-red light corresponding to a certain transition in an atom of krypton-86. The kilogram, which is approximately equal to the mass of 0.001 m³ of water, is defined as the mass of a platinum-iridium standard kept at the International Bureau of Weights and Measures at Sèvres, near Paris, France. The unit of force is a derived unit. It is called the *newton* (N) and is defined as the force which gives an acceleration of 1 m/s² to a mass of 1 kg (Fig. 1.2). From Eq. (1.1) we write

$$1 \text{ N} = (1 \text{ kg})(1 \text{ m/s}^2) = 1 \text{ kg} \cdot \text{m/s}^2 \qquad (1.5)$$

The SI units are said to form an *absolute* system of units. This means that the three base units chosen are independent of the location where measurements are made. The meter, the kilogram, and the second may be used anywhere on the earth; they may even be used on another planet. They will always have the same significance.

The *weight* of a body, or the *force of gravity* exerted on that body, should, like any other force, be expressed in newtons. From Eq. (1.4) it follows that the weight of a body of mass 1 kg (Fig. 1.3) is

$$\begin{aligned} W &= mg \\ &= (1 \text{ kg})(9.81 \text{ m/s}^2) \\ &= 9.81 \text{ N} \end{aligned}$$

Multiples and submultiples of the fundamental SI units may be obtained through the use of the prefixes defined in Table 1.1. The multiples and submultiples of the units of length, mass, and force most frequently used in engineering are, respectively, the *kilometer* (km) and the *millimeter* (mm); the *megagram*† (Mg) and the *gram* (g); and the *kilonewton* (kN). According to Table 1.1, we have

$$\begin{aligned} 1 \text{ km} &= 1000 \text{ m} & 1 \text{ mm} &= 0.001 \text{ m} \\ 1 \text{ Mg} &= 1000 \text{ kg} & 1 \text{ g} &= 0.001 \text{ kg} \\ 1 \text{ kN} &= 1000 \text{ N} \end{aligned}$$

The conversion of these units into meters, kilograms, and newtons, respectively, can be effected by simply moving the decimal point three places to the right or to the left. For example, to convert 3.82 km into meters, one moves the decimal point three places to the right:

$$3.82 \text{ km} = 3820 \text{ m}$$

Similarly, 47.2 mm is converted into meters by moving the decimal point three places to the left:

$$47.2 \text{ mm} = 0.0472 \text{ m}$$

†Also known as a *metric ton*.

TABLE 1.1   SI Prefixes

Multiplication Factor	Prefix†	Symbol
$1\ 000\ 000\ 000\ 000 = 10^{12}$	tera	T
$1\ 000\ 000\ 000 = 10^{9}$	giga	G
$1\ 000\ 000 = 10^{6}$	mega	M
$1\ 000 = 10^{3}$	kilo	k
$100 = 10^{2}$	hecto‡	h
$10 = 10^{1}$	deka‡	da
$0.1 = 10^{-1}$	deci‡	d
$0.01 = 10^{-2}$	centi‡	c
$0.001 = 10^{-3}$	milli	m
$0.000\ 001 = 10^{-6}$	micro	μ
$0.000\ 000\ 001 = 10^{-9}$	nano	n
$0.000\ 000\ 000\ 001 = 10^{-12}$	pico	p
$0.000\ 000\ 000\ 000\ 001 = 10^{-15}$	femto	f
$0.000\ 000\ 000\ 000\ 000\ 001 = 10^{-18}$	atto	a

†The first syllable of every prefix is accented so that the prefix will retain its identity. Thus, the preferred pronunciation of kilometer places the accent on the first syllable, not the second.

‡The use of these prefixes should be avoided, except for the measurement of areas and volumes and for the nontechnical use of centimeter, as for body and clothing measurements.

Using scientific notation, one may also write

$$3.82 \text{ km} = 3.82 \times 10^{3} \text{ m}$$
$$47.2 \text{ mm} = 47.2 \times 10^{-3} \text{ m}$$

The multiples of the unit of time are the *minute* (min) and the *hour* (h). Since 1 min = 60 s and 1 h = 60 min = 3600 s, these multiples cannot be converted as readily as the others.

By using the appropriate multiple or submultiple of a given unit, one can avoid writing very large or very small numbers. For example, one usually writes 427.2 km rather than 427 200 m, and 2.16 mm rather than 0.002 16 m.†

Units of Area and Volume.   The unit of area is the *square meter* (m^2), which represents the area of a square of side 1 m; the unit of volume is the *cubic meter* (m^3), equal to the volume of a cube of side 1 m. In order to avoid exceedingly small or large numerical values in the computation of areas and volumes, one uses systems of subunits obtained by respectively squaring and cubing not only the millimeter but also two intermediate submultiples of the meter, namely, the *decimeter* (dm) and the *centimeter* (cm). Since, by definition,

$$1 \text{ dm} = 0.1 \text{ m} = 10^{-1} \text{ m}$$
$$1 \text{ cm} = 0.01 \text{ m} = 10^{-2} \text{ m}$$
$$1 \text{ mm} = 0.001 \text{ m} = 10^{-3} \text{ m}$$

†It should be noted that when more than four digits are used on either side of the decimal point to express a quantity in SI units—as in 427 200 m or 0.002 16 m—spaces, never commas, should be used to separate the digits into groups of three. This is to avoid confusion with the comma used in place of a decimal point, which is the convention in many countries.

the submultiples of the unit of area are

$$1 \, \text{dm}^2 = (1 \, \text{dm})^2 = (10^{-1} \, \text{m})^2 = 10^{-2} \, \text{m}^2$$
$$1 \, \text{cm}^2 = (1 \, \text{cm})^2 = (10^{-2} \, \text{m})^2 = 10^{-4} \, \text{m}^2$$
$$1 \, \text{mm}^2 = (1 \, \text{mm})^2 = (10^{-3} \, \text{m})^2 = 10^{-6} \, \text{m}^2$$

and the submultiples of the unit of volume are

$$1 \, \text{dm}^3 = (1 \, \text{dm})^3 = (10^{-1} \, \text{m})^3 = 10^{-3} \, \text{m}^3$$
$$1 \, \text{cm}^3 = (1 \, \text{cm})^3 = (10^{-2} \, \text{m})^3 = 10^{-6} \, \text{m}^3$$
$$1 \, \text{mm}^3 = (1 \, \text{mm})^3 = (10^{-3} \, \text{m})^3 = 10^{-9} \, \text{m}^3$$

It should be noted that when the volume of a liquid is being measured, the cubic decimeter (dm^3) is usually referred to as a *liter* (L).

Other derived SI units used to measure the moment of a force, the work of a force, etc., are shown in Table 1.2. While these units will be introduced in later chapters as they are needed, we should note an important rule at this time: When a derived unit is obtained by dividing a base unit by another base unit, a prefix may be used in the numerator of the derived unit but not in its denominator. For example, the constant k of a spring which stretches 20 mm under a load of 100 N will be expressed as

$$k = \frac{100 \, \text{N}}{20 \, \text{mm}} = \frac{100 \, \text{N}}{0.020 \, \text{m}} = 5000 \, \text{N/m} \qquad \text{or} \qquad k = 5 \, \text{kN/m}$$

but never as $k = 5 \, \text{N/mm}$.

TABLE 1.2   Principal SI Units Used in Mechanics

Quantity	Unit	Symbol	Formula
Acceleration	Meter per second squared	. . .	m/s^2
Angle	Radian	rad	†
Angular acceleration	Radian per second squared	. . .	rad/s^2
Angular velocity	Radian per second	. . .	rad/s
Area	Square meter	. . .	m^2
Density	Kilogram per cubic meter	. . .	kg/m^3
Energy	Joule	J	$\text{N} \cdot \text{m}$
Force	Newton	N	$\text{kg} \cdot \text{m/s}^2$
Frequency	Hertz	Hz	s^{-1}
Impulse	Newton-second	. . .	$\text{kg} \cdot \text{m/s}$
Length	Meter	m	‡
Mass	Kilogram	kg	‡
Moment of a force	Newton-meter	. . .	$\text{N} \cdot \text{m}$
Power	Watt	W	J/s
Pressure	Pascal	Pa	N/m^2
Stress	Pascal	Pa	N/m^2
Time	Second	s	‡
Velocity	Meter per second	. . .	m/s
Volume			
Solids	Cubic meter	. . .	m^3
Liquids	Liter	L	10^{-3}m^3
Work	Joule	J	$\text{N} \cdot \text{m}$

†Supplementary unit (1 revolution $= 2\pi$ rad $= 360°$).
‡Base unit.

U.S. Customary Units. Most practicing American engineers still commonly use a system in which the base units are the units of length, force, and time. These units are, respectively, the *foot* (ft), the *pound* (lb), and the *second* (s). The second is the same as the corresponding SI unit. The foot is defined as 0.3048 m. The pound is defined as the *weight* of a platinum standard, called the *standard pound*, which is kept at the National Institute of Standards and Technology outside Washington, the mass of which is 0.453 592 43 kg. Since the weight of a body depends upon the earth's gravitational attraction, which varies with location, it is specified that the standard pound should be placed at sea level and at a latitude of 45° to properly define a force of 1 lb. Clearly the U.S. customary units do not form an absolute system of units. Because of their dependence upon the gravitational attraction of the earth, they form a *gravitational* system of units.

While the standard pound also serves as the unit of mass in commercial transactions in the United States, it cannot be so used in engineering computations, since such a unit would not be consistent with the base units defined in the preceding paragraph. Indeed, when acted upon by a force of 1 lb, that is, when subjected to the force of gravity, the standard pound receives the acceleration of gravity, $g = 32.2$ ft/s² (Fig. 1.4), not the unit acceleration required by Eq. (1.1). The unit of mass consistent with the foot, the pound, and the second is the mass which receives an acceleration of 1 ft/s² when a force of 1 lb is applied to it (Fig. 1.5). This unit, sometimes called a *slug*, can be derived from the equation $F = ma$ after substituting 1 lb and 1 ft/s² for F and a, respectively. We write

$$F = ma \qquad 1 \text{ lb} = (1 \text{ slug})(1 \text{ ft/s}^2)$$

and obtain

$$1 \text{ slug} = \frac{1 \text{ lb}}{1 \text{ ft/s}^2} = 1 \text{ lb} \cdot \text{s}^2/\text{ft} \tag{1.6}$$

Comparing Figs. 1.4 and 1.5, we conclude that the slug is a mass 32.2 times larger than the mass of the standard pound.

The fact that in the U.S. customary system of units bodies are characterized by their weight in pounds rather than by their mass in slugs will be a convenience in the study of statics, where one constantly deals with weights and other forces and only seldom with masses. However, in the study of dynamics, where forces, masses, and accelerations are involved, the mass m of a body will be expressed in slugs when its weight W is given in pounds. Recalling Eq. (1.4), we write

$$m = \frac{W}{g} \tag{1.7}$$

where g is the acceleration of gravity ($g = 32.2$ ft/s²).

Other U.S. customary units frequently encountered in engineering problems are the *mile* (mi), equal to 5280 ft; the *inch* (in.), equal to $\frac{1}{12}$ ft; and the *kilopound* (kip), equal to a force of 1000 lb. The *ton* is often used to represent a mass of 2000 lb but, like the pound, must be converted into slugs in engineering computations.

The conversion into feet, pounds, and seconds of quantities expressed in other U.S. customary units is generally more involved and

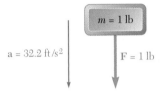

$a = 32.2$ ft/s²

Fig. 1.4

Fig. 1.5

requires greater attention than the corresponding operation in SI units. If, for example, the magnitude of a velocity is given as $v = 30$ mi/h, we convert it to ft/s as follows. First we write

$$v = 30 \ \frac{\text{mi}}{\text{h}}$$

Since we want to get rid of the unit miles and introduce instead the unit feet, we should multiply the right-hand member of the equation by an expression containing miles in the denominator and feet in the numerator. But, since we do not want to change the value of the right-hand member, the expression used should have a value equal to unity. The quotient (5280 ft)/(1 mi) is such an expression. Operating in a similar way to transform the unit hour into seconds, we write

$$v = \left(30 \frac{\text{mi}}{\text{h}}\right)\left(\frac{5280 \text{ ft}}{1 \text{ mi}}\right)\left(\frac{1 \text{ h}}{3600 \text{ s}}\right)$$

Carrying out the numerical computations and canceling out units which appear in both the numerator and the denominator, we obtain

$$v = 44 \ \frac{\text{ft}}{\text{s}} = 44 \text{ ft/s}$$

1.4 CONVERSION FROM ONE SYSTEM OF UNITS TO ANOTHER

There are many instances when an engineer wishes to convert into SI units a numerical result obtained in U.S. customary units or vice versa. Because the unit of time is the same in both systems, only two kinetic base units need be converted. Thus, since all other kinetic units can be derived from these base units, only two conversion factors need be remembered.

Units of Length. By definition the U.S. customary unit of length is

$$1 \text{ ft} = 0.3048 \text{ m} \tag{1.8}$$

It follows that

$$1 \text{ mi} = 5280 \text{ ft} = 5280(0.3048 \text{ m}) = 1609 \text{ m}$$

or

$$1 \text{ mi} = 1.609 \text{ km} \tag{1.9}$$

Also

$$1 \text{ in.} = \tfrac{1}{12} \text{ ft} = \tfrac{1}{12}(0.3048 \text{ m}) = 0.0254 \text{ m}$$

or

$$1 \text{ in.} = 25.4 \text{ mm} \tag{1.10}$$

Units of Force. Recalling that the U.S. customary unit of force (pound) is defined as the weight of the standard pound (of mass 0.4536 kg) at sea level and at a latitude of 45° (where $g = 9.807$ m/s^2) and using Eq. (1.4), we write

$$W = mg$$
$$1 \text{ lb} = (0.4536 \text{ kg})(9.807 \text{ m/s}^2) = 4.448 \text{ kg} \cdot \text{m/s}^2$$

or, recalling Eq. (1.5),

$$1 \text{ lb} = 4.448 \text{ N} \tag{1.11}$$

Units of Mass. The U.S. customary unit of mass (slug) is a derived unit. Thus, using Eqs. (1.6), (1.8), and (1.11), we write

$$1 \text{ slug} = 1 \text{ lb} \cdot \text{s}^2/\text{ft} = \frac{1 \text{ lb}}{1 \text{ ft/s}^2} = \frac{4.448 \text{ N}}{0.3048 \text{ m/s}^2} = 14.59 \text{ N} \cdot \text{s}^2/\text{m}$$

and, recalling Eq. (1.5),

$$1 \text{ slug} = 1 \text{ lb} \cdot \text{s}^2/\text{ft} = 14.59 \text{ kg} \tag{1.12}$$

Although it cannot be used as a consistent unit of mass, we recall that the mass of the standard pound is, by definition,

$$1 \text{ pound mass} = 0.4536 \text{ kg} \tag{1.13}$$

This constant may be used to determine the *mass* in SI units (kilograms) of a body which has been characterized by its *weight* in U.S. customary units (pounds).

To convert a derived U.S. customary unit into SI units, one simply multiplies or divides by the appropriate conversion factors. For example, to convert the moment of a force which was found to be $M = 47 \text{ lb} \cdot \text{in.}$ into SI units, we use formulas (1.10) and (1.11) and write

$$M = 47 \text{ lb} \cdot \text{in.} = 47(4.448 \text{ N})(25.4 \text{ mm})$$
$$= 5310 \text{ N} \cdot \text{mm} = 5.31 \text{ N} \cdot \text{m}$$

The conversion factors given in this section may also be used to convert a numerical result obtained in SI units into U.S. customary units. For example, if the moment of a force was found to be $M = 40 \text{ N} \cdot \text{m}$, we write, following the procedure used in the last paragraph of Sec. 1.3,

$$M = 40 \text{ N} \cdot \text{m} = (40 \text{ N} \cdot \text{m})\left(\frac{1 \text{ lb}}{4.448 \text{ N}}\right)\left(\frac{1 \text{ ft}}{0.3048 \text{ m}}\right)$$

Carrying out the numerical computations and canceling out units which appear in both the numerator and the denominator, we obtain

$$M = 29.5 \text{ lb} \cdot \text{ft}$$

The U.S. customary units most frequently used in mechanics are listed in Table 1.3 with their SI equivalents.

1.5 METHOD OF PROBLEM SOLUTION

You should approach a problem in mechanics as you would approach an actual engineering situation. By drawing on your own experience and intuition, you will find it easier to understand and formulate the problem. Once the problem has been clearly stated, however, there is

TABLE 1.3 U.S. Customary Units and Their SI Equivalents

Quantity	U.S. Customary Unit	SI Equivalent
Acceleration	ft/s^2	0.3048 m/s^2
	$in./s^2$	0.0254 m/s^2
Area	ft^2	0.0929 m^2
	in^2	645.2 mm^2
Energy	$ft \cdot lb$	1.356 J
Force	kip	4.448 kN
	lb	4.448 N
	oz	0.2780 N
Impulse	$lb \cdot s$	$4.448 \text{ N} \cdot s$
Length	ft	0.3048 m
	in.	25.40 mm
	mi	1.609 km
Mass	oz mass	28.35 g
	lb mass	0.4536 kg
	slug	14.59 kg
	ton	907.2 kg
Moment of a force	$lb \cdot ft$	$1.356 \text{ N} \cdot m$
	$lb \cdot in.$	$0.1130 \text{ N} \cdot m$
Moment of inertia		
Of an area	in^4	$0.4162 \times 10^6 \text{ mm}^4$
Of a mass	$lb \cdot ft \cdot s^2$	$1.356 \text{ kg} \cdot m^2$
Momentum	$lb \cdot s$	$4.448 \text{ kg} \cdot \text{m/s}$
Power	$ft \cdot lb/s$	1.356 W
	hp	745.7 W
Pressure or stress	lb/ft^2	47.88 Pa
	lb/in^2 (psi)	6.895 kPa
Velocity	ft/s	0.3048 m/s
	in./s	0.0254 m/s
	mi/h (mph)	0.4470 m/s
	mi/h (mph)	1.609 km/h
Volume	ft^3	0.02832 m^3
	in^3	16.39 cm^3
Liquids	gal	3.785 L
	qt	0.9464 L
Work	$ft \cdot lb$	1.356 J

no place in its solution for your particular fancy. *The solution must be based on the six fundamental principles stated in Sec. 1.2 or on theorems derived from them.* Every step taken must be justified on that basis. Strict rules must be followed, which lead to the solution in an almost automatic fashion, leaving no room for your intuition or "feeling." After an answer has been obtained, it should be checked. Here again, you may call upon your common sense and personal experience. If not completely satisfied with the result obtained, you should carefully check your formulation of the problem, the validity of the methods used for its solution, and the accuracy of your computations.

The *statement* of a problem should be clear and precise. It should contain the given data and indicate what information is required. A neat drawing showing all quantities involved should be included. Separate diagrams should be drawn for all bodies involved, indicating clearly the forces acting on each body. These diagrams are known as *free-body diagrams* and are described in detail in Secs. 2.11 and 4.2.

The *fundamental principles* of mechanics listed in Sec. 1.2 *will be used to write equations* expressing the conditions of rest or motion of the bodies considered. Each equation should be clearly related to one of the free-body diagrams. You will then proceed to solve the problem, observing strictly the usual rules of algebra and recording neatly the various steps taken.

After the answer has been obtained, it should be *carefully checked*. Mistakes in *reasoning* can often be detected by checking the units. For example, to determine the moment of a force of 50 N about a point 0.60 m from its line of action, we would have written (Sec. 3.12)

$$M = Fd = (50 \text{ N})(0.60 \text{ m}) = 30 \text{ N} \cdot \text{m}$$

The unit $N \cdot m$ obtained by multiplying newtons by meters is the correct unit for the moment of a force; if another unit had been obtained, we would have known that some mistake had been made.

Errors in *computation* will usually be found by substituting the numerical values obtained into an equation which has not yet been used and verifying that the equation is satisfied. The importance of correct computations in engineering cannot be overemphasized.

1.6 NUMERICAL ACCURACY

The accuracy of the solution of a problem depends upon two items: (1) the accuracy of the given data and (2) the accuracy of the computations performed.

The solution cannot be more accurate than the less accurate of these two items. For example, if the loading of a bridge is known to be 75,000 lb with a possible error of 100 lb either way, the relative error which measures the degree of accuracy of the data is

$$\frac{100 \text{ lb}}{75,000 \text{ lb}} = 0.0013 = 0.13 \text{ percent}$$

In computing the reaction at one of the bridge supports, it would then be meaningless to record it as 14,322 lb. The accuracy of the solution cannot be greater than 0.13 percent, no matter how accurate the computations are, and the possible error in the answer may be as large as $(0.13/100)(14,322 \text{ lb}) \approx 20 \text{ lb}$. The answer should be properly recorded as $14,320 \pm 20$ lb.

In engineering problems, the data are seldom known with an accuracy greater than 0.2 percent. It is therefore seldom justified to write the answers to such problems with an accuracy greater than 0.2 percent. A practical rule is to use 4 figures to record numbers beginning with a "1" and 3 figures in all other cases. Unless otherwise indicated, the data given in a problem should be assumed known with a comparable degree of accuracy. A force of 40 lb, for example, should be read 40.0 lb, and a force of 15 lb should be read 15.00 lb.

Pocket electronic calculators are widely used by practicing engineers and engineering students. The speed and accuracy of these calculators facilitate the numerical computations in the solution of many problems. However, students should not record more significant figures than can be justified merely because they are easily obtained. As noted above, an accuracy greater than 0.2 percent is seldom necessary or meaningful in the solution of practical engineering problems.

Many engineering problems can be solved by considering the equilibrium of a "particle." In the case of this excavator, which is being loaded onto a ship, a relation between the tensions in the various cables involved can be obtained by considering the equilibrium of the hook to which the cables are attached.

Statics of Particles

2.1 INTRODUCTION

In this chapter you will study the effect of forces acting on particles. First you will learn how to replace two or more forces acting on a given particle by a single force having the same effect as the original forces. This single equivalent force is the *resultant* of the original forces acting on the particle. Later the relations which exist among the various forces acting on a particle in a state of *equilibrium* will be derived and used to determine some of the forces acting on the particle.

The use of the word "particle" does not imply that our study will be limited to that of small corpuscles. What it means is that the size and shape of the bodies under consideration will not significantly affect the solution of the problems treated in this chapter and that all the forces acting on a given body will be assumed to be applied at the same point. Since such an assumption is verified in many practical applications, you will be able to solve a number of engineering problems in this chapter.

The first part of the chapter is devoted to the study of forces contained in a single plane, and the second part to the analysis of forces in three-dimensional space.

FORCES IN A PLANE

2.2 FORCE ON A PARTICLE. RESULTANT OF TWO FORCES

A force represents the action of one body on another and is generally characterized by its *point of application*, its *magnitude*, and its *direction*. Forces acting on a given particle, however, have the same point of application. Each force considered in this chapter will thus be completely defined by its magnitude and direction.

The magnitude of a force is characterized by a certain number of units. As indicated in Chap. 1, the SI units used by engineers to measure the magnitude of a force are the newton (N) and its multiple the kilonewton (kN), equal to 1000 N, while the U.S. customary units used for the same purpose are the pound (lb) and its multiple the kilopound (kip), equal to 1000 lb. The direction of a force is defined by the *line of action* and the *sense* of the force. The line of action is the infinite straight line along which the force acts; it is characterized by the angle it forms with some fixed axis (Fig. 2.1). The force itself is represented by a segment of

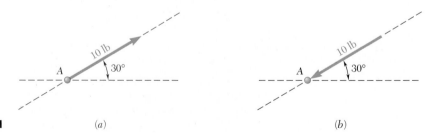

Fig. 2.1   (a)   (b)

that line; through the use of an appropriate scale, the length of this segment may be chosen to represent the magnitude of the force. Finally, the sense of the force should be indicated by an arrowhead. It is important in defining a force to indicate its sense. Two forces having the same magnitude and the same line of action but different sense, such as the forces shown in Fig. 2.1*a* and *b*, will have directly opposite effects on a particle.

Experimental evidence shows that two forces **P** and **Q** acting on a particle *A* (Fig. 2.2*a*) can be replaced by a single force **R** which has the same effect on the particle (Fig. 2.2*c*). This force is called the *resultant* of the forces **P** and **Q** and can be obtained, as shown in Fig. 2.2*b*, by constructing a parallelogram, using **P** and **Q** as two adjacent sides of the parallelogram. *The diagonal that passes through A represents the resultant.* This method for finding the resultant is known as the *parallelogram law* for the addition of two forces. This law is based on experimental evidence; it cannot be proved or derived mathematically.

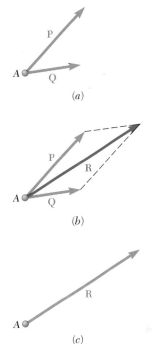

Fig. 2.2

2.3 VECTORS

It appears from the above that forces do not obey the rules of addition defined in ordinary arithmetic or algebra. For example, two forces acting at a right angle to each other, one of 4 lb and the other of 3 lb, add up to a force of 5 lb, *not* to a force of 7 lb. Forces are not the only quantities which follow the parallelogram law of addition. As you will see later, *displacements, velocities, accelerations,* and *momenta* are other examples of physical quantities possessing magnitude and direction that are added according to the parallelogram law. All these quantities can be represented mathematically by *vectors,* while those physical quantities which have magnitude but not direction, such as *volume, mass,* or *energy,* are represented by plain numbers or *scalars.*

Vectors are defined as *mathematical expressions possessing magnitude and direction, which add according to the parallelogram law.* Vectors are represented by arrows in the illustrations and will be distinguished from scalar quantities in this text through the use of boldface type (**P**). In longhand writing, a vector may be denoted by drawing a short arrow above the letter used to represent it ($\vec{P}$) or by underlining the letter (*P*). The last method may be preferred since underlining can also be used on a typewriter or computer. The magnitude of a vector defines the length of the arrow used to represent the vector. In this text, italic type will be used to denote the magnitude of a vector. Thus, the magnitude of the vector **P** will be denoted by *P.*

A vector used to represent a force acting on a given particle has a well-defined point of application, namely, the particle itself. Such a vector is said to be a *fixed,* or *bound,* vector and cannot be moved without modifying the conditions of the problem. Other physical quantities, however, such as couples (see Chap. 3), are represented by vectors which may be freely moved in space; these

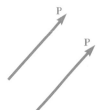

Fig. 2.4

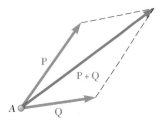

Fig. 2.5

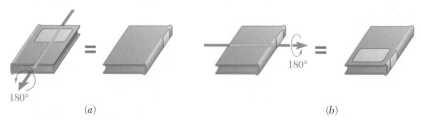

Fig. 2.6

vectors are called *free* vectors. Still other physical quantities, such as forces acting on a rigid body (see Chap. 3), are represented by vectors which can be moved, or slid, along their lines of action; they are known as *sliding* vectors.†

Two vectors which have the same magnitude and the same direction are said to be *equal*, whether or not they also have the same point of application (Fig. 2.4); equal vectors may be denoted by the same letter.

The *negative vector* of a given vector **P** is defined as a vector having the same magnitude as **P** and a direction opposite to that of **P** (Fig. 2.5); the negative of the vector **P** is denoted by $-\mathbf{P}$. The vectors **P** and $-\mathbf{P}$ are commonly referred to as *equal and opposite* vectors. Clearly, we have

$$\mathbf{P} + (-\mathbf{P}) = 0$$

2.4 ADDITION OF VECTORS

We saw in the preceding section that, by definition, vectors add according to the parallelogram law. Thus, the sum of two vectors **P** and **Q** is obtained by attaching the two vectors to the same point A and constructing a parallelogram, using **P** and **Q** as two sides of the parallelogram (Fig. 2.6). The diagonal that passes through A represents the sum of the vectors **P** and **Q**, and this sum is denoted by **P** + **Q**. The fact that the sign + is used to denote both vector and scalar addition should not cause any confusion if vector and scalar quantities are always carefully distinguished. Thus, we should note that the magnitude of the vector **P** + **Q** is *not*, in general, equal to the sum $P + Q$ of the magnitudes of the vectors **P** and **Q**.

Since the parallelogram constructed on the vectors **P** and **Q** does not depend upon the order in which **P** and **Q** are selected, we conclude that the addition of two vectors is *commutative*, and we write

$$\mathbf{P} + \mathbf{Q} = \mathbf{Q} + \mathbf{P} \tag{2.1}$$

---

†Some expressions have magnitude and direction, but do not add according to the parallelogram law. While these expressions may be represented by arrows, they *cannot* be considered as vectors.

A group of such expressions is the finite rotations of a rigid body. Place a closed book on a table in front of you, so that it lies in the usual fashion, with its front cover up and its binding to the left. Now rotate it through 180° about an axis parallel to the binding (Fig. 2.3a); this rotation may be represented by an arrow of length equal to 180 units and oriented as shown. Picking up the book as it lies in its new position, rotate

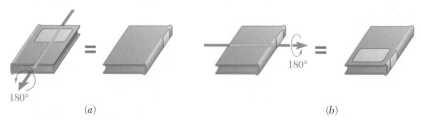

Fig. 2.3 Finite rotations of a rigid body

From the parallelogram law, we can derive an alternative method for determining the sum of two vectors. This method, known as the *triangle rule,* is derived as follows. Consider Fig. 2.6, where the sum of the vectors **P** and **Q** has been determined by the parallelogram law. Since the side of the parallelogram opposite **Q** is equal to **Q** in magnitude and direction, we could draw only half of the parallelogram (Fig. 2.7*a*). The sum of the two vectors can thus be found by *arranging* **P** *and* **Q** *in tip-to-tail fashion and then connecting the tail of* **P** *with the tip of* **Q**. In Fig. 2.7*b*, the other half of the parallelogram is considered, and the same result is obtained. This confirms the fact that vector addition is commutative.

The *subtraction* of a vector is defined as the addition of the corresponding negative vector. Thus, the vector **P** − **Q** representing the difference between the vectors **P** and **Q** is obtained by adding to **P** the negative vector −**Q** (Fig. 2.8). We write

$$\mathbf{P} - \mathbf{Q} = \mathbf{P} + (-\mathbf{Q}) \tag{2.2}$$

Here again we should observe that, while the same sign is used to denote both vector and scalar subtraction, confusion will be avoided if care is taken to distinguish between vector and scalar quantities.

We will now consider the *sum of three or more vectors.* The sum of three vectors **P**, **Q**, and **S** will, *by definition*, be obtained by first adding the vectors **P** and **Q** and then adding the vector **S** to the vector **P** + **Q**. We thus write

$$\mathbf{P} + \mathbf{Q} + \mathbf{S} = (\mathbf{P} + \mathbf{Q}) + \mathbf{S} \tag{2.3}$$

Similarly, the sum of four vectors will be obtained by adding the fourth vector to the sum of the first three. It follows that the sum of any number of vectors can be obtained by applying repeatedly the parallelogram law to successive pairs of vectors until all the given vectors are replaced by a single vector.

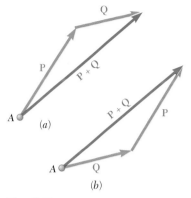

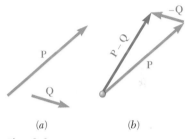

Fig. 2.7

Fig. 2.8

it now through 180° about a horizontal axis perpendicular to the binding (Fig. 2.3*b*); this second rotation may be represented by an arrow 180 units long and oriented as shown. But the book could have been placed in this final position through a single 180° rotation about a vertical axis (Fig. 2.3*c*). We conclude that the sum of the two 180° rotations represented by arrows directed respectively along the *z* and *x* axes is a 180° rotation represented by an arrow directed along the *y* axis (Fig. 2.3*d*). Clearly, the finite rotations of a rigid body *do not* obey the parallelogram law of addition; therefore, they *cannot* be represented by vectors.

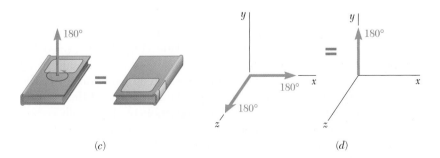

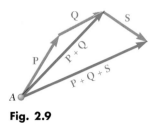

Fig. 2.9

Fig. 2.10

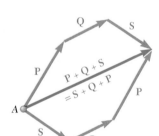

Fig. 2.11

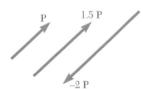

Fig. 2.12

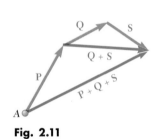

Fig. 2.13

If the given vectors are *coplanar*, i.e., if they are contained in the same plane, their sum can be easily obtained graphically. For this case, the repeated application of the triangle rule is preferred to the application of the parallelogram law. In Fig. 2.9 the sum of three vectors **P**, **Q**, and **S** was obtained in that manner. The triangle rule was first applied to obtain the sum **P** + **Q** of the vectors **P** and **Q**; it was applied again to obtain the sum of the vectors **P** + **Q** and **S**. The determination of the vector **P** + **Q**, however, could have been omitted and the sum of the three vectors could have been obtained directly, as shown in Fig. 2.10, by *arranging the given vectors in tip-to-tail fashion and connecting the tail of the first vector with the tip of the last one.* This is known as the *polygon rule* for the addition of vectors.

We observe that the result obtained would have been unchanged if, as shown in Fig. 2.11, the vectors **Q** and **S** had been replaced by their sum **Q** + **S**. We may thus write

$$\mathbf{P} + \mathbf{Q} + \mathbf{S} = (\mathbf{P} + \mathbf{Q}) + \mathbf{S} = \mathbf{P} + (\mathbf{Q} + \mathbf{S}) \qquad (2.4)$$

which expresses the fact that vector addition is *associative*. Recalling that vector addition has also been shown, in the case of two vectors, to be commutative, we write

$$\begin{aligned}
\mathbf{P} + \mathbf{Q} + \mathbf{S} &= (\mathbf{P} + \mathbf{Q}) + \mathbf{S} = \mathbf{S} + (\mathbf{P} + \mathbf{Q}) \\
&= \mathbf{S} + (\mathbf{Q} + \mathbf{P}) = \mathbf{S} + \mathbf{Q} + \mathbf{P}
\end{aligned} \qquad (2.5)$$

This expression, as well as others which may be obtained in the same way, shows that the order in which several vectors are added together is immaterial (Fig. 2.12).

Product of a Scalar and a Vector. Since it is convenient to denote the sum **P** + **P** by 2**P**, the sum **P** + **P** + **P** by 3**P**, and, in general, the sum of n equal vectors **P** by the product $n\mathbf{P}$, we will define the product $n\mathbf{P}$ of a positive integer n and a vector **P** as a vector having the same direction as **P** and the magnitude nP. Extending this definition to include all scalars, and recalling the definition of a negative vector given in Sec. 2.3, we define the product $k\mathbf{P}$ of a scalar k and a vector **P** as a vector having the same direction as **P** (if k is positive), or a direction opposite to that of **P** (if k is negative), and a magnitude equal to the product of P and of the absolute value of k (Fig. 2.13).

2.5 RESULTANT OF SEVERAL CONCURRENT FORCES

Consider a particle A acted upon by several coplanar forces, i.e., by several forces contained in the same plane (Fig. 2.14*a*). Since the forces considered here all pass through A, they are also said to be *concurrent*. The vectors representing the forces acting on A may be added by the polygon rule (Fig. 2.14*b*). Since the use of the polygon rule is equivalent to the repeated application of the parallelogram law, the vector **R** thus obtained represents the resultant of the given concurrent forces, i.e., the single force which has the same effect on

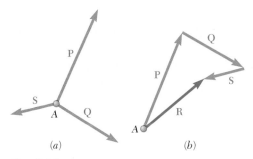

Fig. 2.14

the particle A as the given forces. As indicated above, the order in which the vectors $\mathbf{P}$, $\mathbf{Q}$, and $\mathbf{S}$ representing the given forces are added together is immaterial.

2.6 RESOLUTION OF A FORCE INTO COMPONENTS

We have seen that two or more forces acting on a particle may be replaced by a single force which has the same effect on the particle. Conversely, a single force $\mathbf{F}$ acting on a particle may be replaced by two or more forces which, together, have the same effect on the particle. These forces are called the *components* of the original force $\mathbf{F}$, and the process of substituting them for $\mathbf{F}$ is called *resolving the force $\mathbf{F}$ into components*.

Clearly, for each force $\mathbf{F}$ there exist an infinite number of possible sets of components. Sets of *two components $\mathbf{P}$ and $\mathbf{Q}$* are the most important as far as practical applications are concerned. But, even then, the number of ways in which a given force $\mathbf{F}$ may be resolved into two components is unlimited (Fig. 2.15). Two cases are of particular interest:

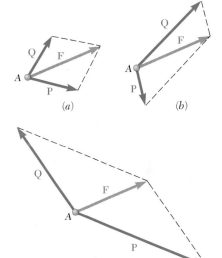

Fig. 2.15

1. *One of the Two Components, $\mathbf{P}$, Is Known.* The second component, $\mathbf{Q}$, is obtained by applying the triangle rule and joining the tip of $\mathbf{P}$ to the tip of $\mathbf{F}$ (Fig. 2.16); the magnitude and direction of $\mathbf{Q}$ are determined graphically or by trigonometry. Once $\mathbf{Q}$ has been determined, both components $\mathbf{P}$ and $\mathbf{Q}$ should be applied at A.

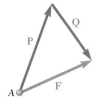

Fig. 2.16

2. *The Line of Action of Each Component Is Known.* The magnitude and sense of the components are obtained by applying the parallelogram law and drawing lines, through the tip of $\mathbf{F}$, parallel to the given lines of action (Fig. 2.17). This process leads to two well-defined components, $\mathbf{P}$ and $\mathbf{Q}$, which can be determined graphically or computed trigonometrically by applying the law of sines.

Many other cases can be encountered; for example, the direction of one component may be known, while the magnitude of the other component is to be as small as possible (see Sample Prob. 2.2). In all cases the appropriate triangle or parallelogram which satisfies the given conditions is drawn.

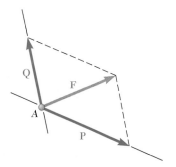

Fig. 2.17

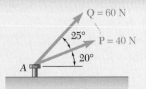

SAMPLE PROBLEM 2.1

The two forces **P** and **Q** act on a bolt A. Determine their resultant.

SOLUTION

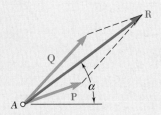

Graphical Solution. A parallelogram with sides equal to **P** and **Q** is drawn to scale. The magnitude and direction of the resultant are measured and found to be

$$R = 98 \text{ N} \qquad \alpha = 35° \qquad \mathbf{R} = 98 \text{ N} \measuredangle 35° \ \blacktriangleleft$$

The triangle rule may also be used. Forces **P** and **Q** are drawn in tip-to-tail fashion. Again the magnitude and direction of the resultant are measured.

$$R = 98 \text{ N} \qquad \alpha = 35° \qquad \mathbf{R} = 98 \text{ N} \measuredangle 35° \ \blacktriangleleft$$

Trigonometric Solution. The triangle rule is again used; two sides and the included angle are known. We apply the law of cosines.

$$R^2 = P^2 + Q^2 - 2PQ \cos B$$
$$R^2 = (40 \text{ N})^2 + (60 \text{ N})^2 - 2(40 \text{ N})(60 \text{ N}) \cos 155°$$
$$R = 97.73 \text{ N}$$

Now, applying the law of sines, we write

$$\frac{\sin A}{Q} = \frac{\sin B}{R} \qquad \frac{\sin A}{60 \text{ N}} = \frac{\sin 155°}{97.73 \text{ N}} \tag{1}$$

Solving Eq. (1) for sin A, we have

$$\sin A = \frac{(60 \text{ N}) \sin 155°}{97.73 \text{ N}}$$

Using a calculator, we first compute the quotient, then its arc sine, and obtain

$$A = 15.04° \qquad \alpha = 20° + A = 35.04°$$

We use 3 significant figures to record the answer (cf. Sec. 1.6):

$$\mathbf{R} = 97.7 \text{ N} \measuredangle 35.0° \ \blacktriangleleft$$

Alternative Trigonometric Solution. We construct the right triangle BCD and compute

$$CD = (60 \text{ N}) \sin 25° = 25.36 \text{ N}$$
$$BD = (60 \text{ N}) \cos 25° = 54.38 \text{ N}$$

Then, using triangle ACD, we obtain

$$\tan A = \frac{25.36 \text{ N}}{94.38 \text{ N}} \qquad A = 15.04°$$

$$R = \frac{25.36}{\sin A} \qquad R = 97.73 \text{ N}$$

Again,

$$\alpha = 20° + A = 35.04° \qquad \mathbf{R} = 97.7 \text{ N} \measuredangle 35.0° \ \blacktriangleleft$$

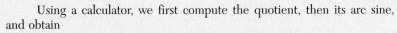

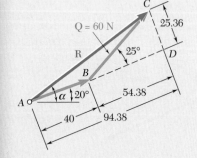

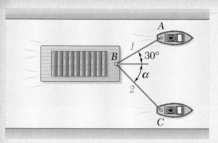

SAMPLE PROBLEM 2.2

A barge is pulled by two tugboats. If the resultant of the forces exerted by the tugboats is a 5000-lb force directed along the axis of the barge, determine (*a*) the tension in each of the ropes knowing that $\alpha = 45°$, (*b*) the value of α for which the tension in rope 2 is minimum.

SOLUTION

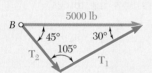

a. Tension for $\alpha = 45°$. *Graphical Solution.* The parallelogram law is used; the diagonal (resultant) is known to be equal to 5000 lb and to be directed to the right. The sides are drawn parallel to the ropes. If the drawing is done to scale, we measure

$$T_1 = 3700 \text{ lb} \qquad T_2 = 2600 \text{ lb} \quad \blacktriangleleft$$

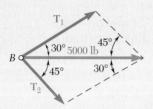

Trigonometric Solution. The triangle rule can be used. We note that the triangle shown represents half of the parallelogram shown above. Using the law of sines, we write

$$\frac{T_1}{\sin 45°} = \frac{T_2}{\sin 30°} = \frac{5000 \text{ lb}}{\sin 105°}$$

With a calculator, we first compute and store the value of the last quotient. Multiplying this value successively by sin 45° and sin 30°, we obtain

$$T_1 = 3660 \text{ lb} \qquad T_2 = 2590 \text{ lb} \quad \blacktriangleleft$$

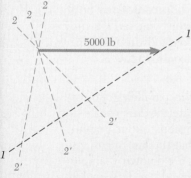

b. Value of α for Minimum T_2. To determine the value of α for which the tension in rope 2 is minimum, the triangle rule is again used. In the sketch shown, line *1-1'* is the known direction of $\mathbf{T}_1$. Several possible directions of $\mathbf{T}_2$ are shown by the lines *2-2'*. We note that the minimum value of T_2 occurs when $\mathbf{T}_1$ and $\mathbf{T}_2$ are perpendicular. The minimum value of T_2 is

$$T_2 = (5000 \text{ lb}) \sin 30° = 2500 \text{ lb}$$

Corresponding values of T_1 and α are

$$T_1 = (5000 \text{ lb}) \cos 30° = 4330 \text{ lb}$$
$$\alpha = 90° - 30° \qquad\qquad \alpha = 60° \quad \blacktriangleleft$$

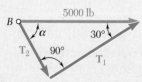

SOLVING PROBLEMS
ON YOUR OWN

The preceding sections were devoted to the *parallelogram law* for the addition of vectors and to its applications.

Two sample problems were presented. In Sample Prob. 2.1, the parallelogram law was used to determine the resultant of two forces of known magnitude and direction. In Sample Prob. 2.2, it was used to resolve a given force into two components of known direction.

You will now be asked to solve problems on your own. Some may resemble one of the sample problems; others may not. What all problems and sample problems in this section have in common is that they can be solved by the direct application of the parallelogram law.

Your solution of a given problem should consist of the following steps:

1. Identify which of the forces are the applied forces and which is the resultant. It is often helpful to write the vector equation which shows how the forces are related. For example, in Sample Prob. 2.1 we would have

$$\mathbf{R} = \mathbf{P} + \mathbf{Q}$$

You may want to keep that relation in mind as you formulate the next part of your solution.

2. Draw a parallelogram with the applied forces as two adjacent sides and the resultant as the included diagonal (Fig. 2.2). Alternatively, you can *use the triangle rule*, with the applied forces drawn in tip-to-tail fashion and the resultant extending from the tail of the first vector to the tip of the second (Fig. 2.7).

3. Indicate all dimensions. Using one of the triangles of the parallelogram, or the triangle constructed according to the triangle rule, indicate all dimensions— whether sides or angles—and determine the unknown dimensions either graphically or by trigonometry. If you use trigonometry, remember that the law of cosines should be applied first if two sides and the included angle are known [Sample Prob. 2.1], and the law of sines should be applied first if one side and all angles are known [Sample Prob. 2.2].

If you have had prior exposure to mechanics, you might be tempted to ignore the solution techniques of this lesson in favor of resolving the forces into rectangular components. While this latter method is important and will be considered in the next section, use of the parallelogram law simplifies the solution of many problems and should be mastered at this time.

PROBLEMS†

2.1 Two forces **P** and **Q** are applied as shown at point A of a hook support. Knowing that P = 75 N and Q = 125 N, determine graphically the magnitude and direction of their resultant using (a) the parallelogram law, (b) the triangle rule.

2.2 Two forces **P** and **Q** are applied as shown at point A of a hook support. Knowing that P = 60 lb and Q = 25 lb, determine graphically the magnitude and direction of their resultant using (a) the parallelogram law, (b) the triangle rule.

2.3 The cable stays AB and AD help support pole AC. Knowing that the tension is 120 lb in AB and 40 lb in AD, determine graphically the magnitude and direction of the resultant of the forces exerted by the stays at A using (a) the parallelogram law, (b) the triangle rule.

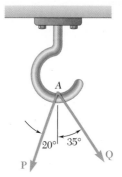

Fig. P2.1 and P2.2

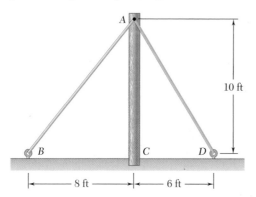

Fig. P2.3

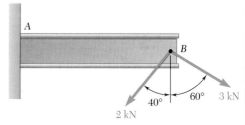

Fig. P2.4

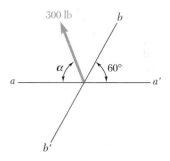

Fig. P2.5 and P2.6

2.4 Two forces are applied at point B of beam AB. Determine graphically the magnitude and direction of their resultant using (a) the parallelogram law, (b) the triangle rule.

2.5 The 300-lb force is to be resolved into components along lines a-a' and b-b'. (a) Determine the angle α by trigonometry knowing that the component along line a-a' is to be 240 lb. (b) What is the corresponding value of the component along b-b'?

2.6 The 300-lb force is to be resolved into components along lines a-a' and b-b'. (a) Determine the angle α by trigonometry knowing that the component along line b-b' is to be 120 lb. (b) What is the corresponding value of the component along a-a'?

2.7 Two forces are applied as shown to a hook support. Knowing that the magnitude of **P** is 35 N, determine by trigonometry (a) the required angle α if the resultant **R** of the two forces applied to the support is to be horizontal, (b) the corresponding magnitude of **R**.

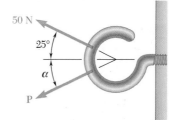

Fig. P2.7

†Answers to all problems set in straight type (such as **2.1**) are given at the end of the book. Answers to problems with a number set in italic type (such as **2.4**) are not given.

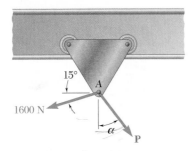

Fig. P2.9 and P2.10

2.8 For the hook support of Prob. 2.1, knowing that the magnitude of **P** is 75 N, determine by trigonometry (*a*) the required magnitude of the force **Q** if the resultant **R** of the two forces applied at *A* is to be vertical, (*b*) the corresponding magnitude of **R**.

2.9 A trolley that moves along a horizontal beam is acted upon by two forces as shown. (*a*) Knowing that α = 25°, determine by trigonometry the magnitude of the force **P** so that the resultant force exerted on the trolley is vertical. (*b*) What is the corresponding magnitude of the resultant?

2.10 A trolley that moves along a horizontal beam is acted upon by two forces as shown. Determine by trigonometry the magnitude and direction of the force **P** so that the resultant is a vertical force of 2500 N.

2.11 A steel tank is to be positioned in an excavation. Knowing that α = 20°, determine by trigonometry (*a*) the required magnitude of the force **P** if the resultant **R** of the two forces applied at *A* is to be vertical, (*b*) the corresponding magnitude of **R**.

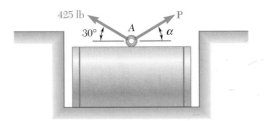

Fig. P2.11 and *P2.12*

2.12 A steel tank is to be positioned in an excavation. Knowing that the magnitude of **P** is 500 lb, determine by trigonometry (*a*) the required angle α if the resultant **R** of the two forces applied at *A* is to be vertical, (*b*) the corresponding magnitude of **R**.

2.13 For the hook support of Prob. 2.7, determine by trigonometry (*a*) the magnitude and direction of the smallest force **P** for which the resultant **R** of the two forces applied to the support is horizontal, (*b*) the corresponding magnitude of **R**.

2.14 For the steel tank of Prob. 2.11, determine by trigonometry (*a*) the magnitude and direction of the smallest force **P** for which the resultant **R** of the two forces applied at *A* is vertical, (*b*) the corresponding magnitude of **R**.

2.15 Solve Prob. 2.2 by trigonometry.

2.16 Solve Prob. 2.3 by trigonometry.

2.17 Solve Prob. 2.4 by trigonometry.

2.18 Two structural members A and B are bolted to a bracket as shown. Knowing that both members are in compression and that the force is 15 kN in member A and 10 kN in member B, determine by trigonometry the magnitude and direction of the resultant of the forces applied to the bracket by members A and B.

2.19 Two structural members A and B are bolted to a bracket as shown. Knowing that both members are in compression and that the force is 10 kN in member A and 15 kN in member B, determine by trigonometry the magnitude and direction of the resultant of the forces applied to the bracket by members A and B.

2.20 For the hook support of Prob. 2.7, knowing that $P = 75$ N and $\alpha = 50°$, determine by trigonometry the magnitude and direction of the resultant of the two forces applied to the support.

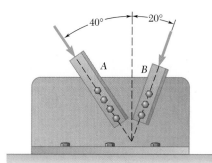

Fig. *P2.18* and *P2.19*

2.7 RECTANGULAR COMPONENTS OF A FORCE. UNIT VECTORS†

In many problems it will be found desirable to resolve a force into two components which are perpendicular to each other. In Fig. 2.18, the force **F** has been resolved into a component **F**$_x$ along the x axis and a component **F**$_y$ along the y axis. The parallelogram drawn to obtain the two components is a *rectangle*, and **F**$_x$ and **F**$_y$ are called *rectangular components*.

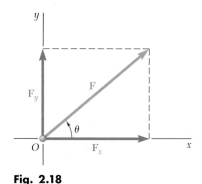

Fig. 2.18

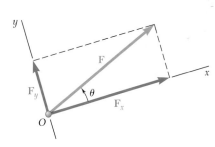

Fig. 2.19

The x and y axes are usually chosen horizontal and vertical, respectively, as in Fig. 2.18; they may, however, be chosen in any two perpendicular directions, as shown in Fig. 2.19. In determining the rectangular components of a force, the student should think of the construction lines shown in Figs. 2.18 and 2.19 as being *parallel* to the x and y axes, rather than *perpendicular* to these axes. This practice will help avoid mistakes in determining *oblique* components as in Sec. 2.6.

†The properties established in Secs. 2.7 and 2.8 may be readily extended to the rectangular components of any vector quantity.

Two vectors of unit magnitude, directed respectively along the positive x and y axes, will be introduced at this point. These vectors are called *unit vectors* and are denoted by $\mathbf{i}$ and $\mathbf{j}$, respectively (Fig. 2.20). Recalling the definition of the product of a scalar and a vector given in Sec. 2.4, we note that the rectangular components $\mathbf{F}_x$ and $\mathbf{F}_y$ of a force $\mathbf{F}$ may be obtained by multiplying respectively the unit vectors $\mathbf{i}$ and $\mathbf{j}$ by appropriate scalars (Fig. 2.21). We write

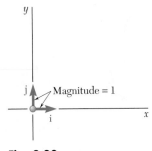

Fig. 2.20

$$\mathbf{F}_x = F_x\mathbf{i} \qquad \mathbf{F}_y = F_y\mathbf{j} \tag{2.6}$$

and

$$\mathbf{F} = F_x\mathbf{i} + F_y\mathbf{j} \tag{2.7}$$

While the scalars F_x and F_y may be positive or negative, depending upon the sense of $\mathbf{F}_x$ and of $\mathbf{F}_y$, their absolute values are respectively equal to the magnitudes of the component forces $\mathbf{F}_x$ and $\mathbf{F}_y$. The scalars F_x and F_y are called the *scalar components* of the force $\mathbf{F}$, while the actual component forces $\mathbf{F}_x$ and $\mathbf{F}_y$ should be referred to as the *vector components* of $\mathbf{F}$. However, when there exists no possibility of confusion, the vector as well as the scalar components of $\mathbf{F}$ may be referred to simply as the *components* of $\mathbf{F}$. We note that the scalar component F_x is positive when the vector component $\mathbf{F}_x$ has the same sense as the unit vector $\mathbf{i}$ (i.e., the same sense as the positive x axis) and is negative when $\mathbf{F}_x$ has the opposite sense. A similar conclusion may be drawn regarding the sign of the scalar component F_y.

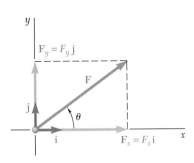

Fig. 2.21

Denoting by F the magnitude of the force $\mathbf{F}$ and by θ the angle between $\mathbf{F}$ and the x axis, measured counterclockwise from the positive x axis (Fig. 2.21), we may express the scalar components of $\mathbf{F}$ as follows:

$$F_x = F \cos \theta \qquad F_y = F \sin \theta \tag{2.8}$$

We note that the relations obtained hold for any value of the angle θ from 0° to 360° and that they define the signs as well as the absolute values of the scalar components F_x and F_y.

EXAMPLE 1. A force of 800 N is exerted on a bolt A as shown in Fig. 2.22a. Determine the horizontal and vertical components of the force.

In order to obtain the correct sign for the scalar components F_x and F_y, the value $180° - 35° = 145°$ should be substituted for θ in Eqs. (2.8). However, it will be found more practical to determine by inspection the signs of F_x and F_y (Fig. 2.22b) and to use the trigonometric functions of the angle $\alpha = 35°$. We write, therefore,

$$F_x = -F \cos \alpha = -(800 \text{ N}) \cos 35° = -655 \text{ N}$$
$$F_y = +F \sin \alpha = +(800 \text{ N}) \sin 35° = +459 \text{ N}$$

The vector components of $\mathbf{F}$ are thus

$$\mathbf{F}_x = -(655 \text{ N})\mathbf{i} \qquad \mathbf{F}_y = +(459 \text{ N})\mathbf{j}$$

and we may write $\mathbf{F}$ in the form

$$\mathbf{F} = -(655 \text{ N})\mathbf{i} + (459 \text{ N})\mathbf{j} \quad \blacksquare$$

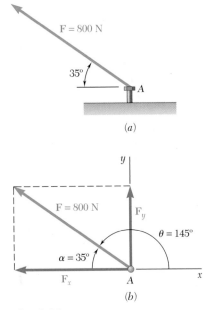

Fig. 2.22

EXAMPLE 2. A man pulls with a force of 300 N on a rope attached to a building, as shown in Fig. 2.23a. What are the horizontal and vertical components of the force exerted by the rope at point A?

It is seen from Fig. 2.23b that

$$F_x = +(300 \text{ N}) \cos\alpha \qquad F_y = -(300 \text{ N}) \sin\alpha$$

Observing that $AB = 10$ m, we find from Fig. 2.23a

$$\cos\alpha = \frac{8 \text{ m}}{AB} = \frac{8 \text{ m}}{10 \text{ m}} = \frac{4}{5} \qquad \sin\alpha = \frac{6 \text{ m}}{AB} = \frac{6 \text{ m}}{10 \text{ m}} = \frac{3}{5}$$

We thus obtain

$$F_x = +(300 \text{ N})\tfrac{4}{5} = +240 \text{ N} \qquad F_y = -(300 \text{ N})\tfrac{3}{5} = -180 \text{ N}$$

and write

$$\mathbf{F} = (240 \text{ N})\mathbf{i} - (180 \text{ N})\mathbf{j} \quad\blacksquare$$

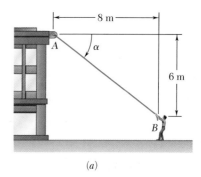

(a)

When a force $\mathbf{F}$ is defined by its rectangular components F_x and F_y (see Fig. 2.21), the angle θ defining its direction can be obtained by writing

$$\tan\theta = \frac{F_y}{F_x} \tag{2.9}$$

The magnitude F of the force can be obtained by applying the Pythagorean theorem and writing

$$F = \sqrt{F_x^2 + F_y^2} \tag{2.10}$$

or by solving for F one of the Eqs. (2.8).

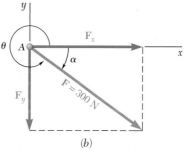

(b)

Fig. 2.23

EXAMPLE 3. A force $\mathbf{F} = (700 \text{ lb})\mathbf{i} + (1500 \text{ lb})\mathbf{j}$ is applied to a bolt A. Determine the magnitude of the force and the angle θ it forms with the horizontal.

First we draw a diagram showing the two rectangular components of the force and the angle θ (Fig. 2.24). From Eq. (2.9), we write

$$\tan\theta = \frac{F_y}{F_x} = \frac{1500 \text{ lb}}{700 \text{ lb}}$$

Using a calculator,† we enter 1500 lb and divide by 700 lb; computing the arc tangent of the quotient, we obtain $\theta = 65.0°$. Solving the second of Eqs. (2.8) for F, we have

$$F = \frac{F_y}{\sin\theta} = \frac{1500 \text{ lb}}{\sin 65.0°} = 1655 \text{ lb}$$

The last calculation is facilitated if the value of F_y is stored when originally entered; it may then be recalled to be divided by $\sin\theta$. $\blacksquare$

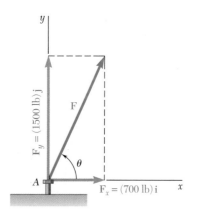

Fig. 2.24

---

†It is assumed that the calculator used has keys for the computation of trigonometric and inverse trigonometric functions. Some calculators also have keys for the direct conversion of rectangular coordinates into polar coordinates, and vice versa. Such calculators eliminate the need for the computation of trigonometric functions in Examples 1, 2, and 3 and in problems of the same type.

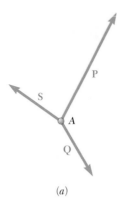

(a)

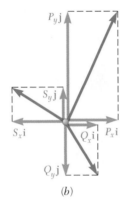

(b)

(c)

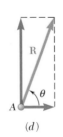

(d)

Fig. 2.25

2.8   ADDITION OF FORCES BY SUMMING X AND Y COMPONENTS

It was seen in Sec. 2.2 that forces should be added according to the parallelogram law. From this law, two other methods, more readily applicable to the *graphical* solution of problems, were derived in Secs. 2.4 and 2.5: the triangle rule for the addition of two forces and the polygon rule for the addition of three or more forces. It was also seen that the force triangle used to define the resultant of two forces could be used to obtain a *trigonometric* solution.

When three or more forces are to be added, no practical trigonometric solution can be obtained from the force polygon which defines the resultant of the forces. In this case, an *analytic* solution of the problem can be obtained by resolving each force into two rectangular components. Consider, for instance, three forces **P**, **Q**, and **S** acting on a particle A (Fig. 2.25*a*). Their resultant **R** is defined by the relation

$$\mathbf{R} = \mathbf{P} + \mathbf{Q} + \mathbf{S} \tag{2.11}$$

Resolving each force into its rectangular components, we write

$$\begin{aligned} R_x\mathbf{i} + R_y\mathbf{j} &= P_x\mathbf{i} + P_y\mathbf{j} + Q_x\mathbf{i} + Q_y\mathbf{j} + S_x\mathbf{i} + S_y\mathbf{j} \\ &= (P_x + Q_x + S_x)\mathbf{i} + (P_y + Q_y + S_y)\mathbf{j} \end{aligned}$$

from which it follows that

$$R_x = P_x + Q_x + S_x \qquad R_y = P_y + Q_y + S_y \tag{2.12}$$

or, for short,

$$R_x = \Sigma F_x \qquad R_y = \Sigma F_y \tag{2.13}$$

We thus conclude that *the scalar components R_x and R_y of the resultant **R** of several forces acting on a particle are obtained by adding algebraically the corresponding scalar components of the given forces.*†

In practice, the determination of the resultant **R** is carried out in three steps as illustrated in Fig. 2.25. First the given forces shown in Fig. 2.25*a* are resolved into their x and y components (Fig. 2.25*b*). Adding these components, we obtain the x and y components of **R** (Fig. 2.25*c*). Finally, the resultant $\mathbf{R} = R_x\mathbf{i} + R_y\mathbf{j}$ is determined by applying the parallelogram law (Fig. 2.25*d*). The procedure just described will be carried out most efficiently if the computations are arranged in a table. While it is the only practical analytic method for adding three or more forces, it is also often preferred to the trigonometric solution in the case of the addition of two forces.

---

†Clearly, this result also applies to the addition of other vector quantities, such as velocities, accelerations, or momenta.

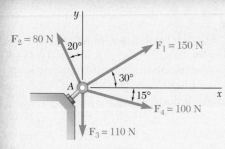

SAMPLE PROBLEM 2.3

Four forces act on bolt A as shown. Determine the resultant of the forces on the bolt.

SOLUTION

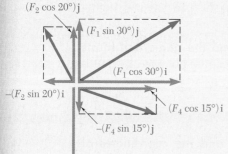

The x and y components of each force are determined by trigonometry as shown and are entered in the table below. According to the convention adopted in Sec. 2.7, the scalar number representing a force component is positive if the force component has the same sense as the corresponding coordinate axis. Thus, x components acting to the right and y components acting upward are represented by positive numbers.

Force	Magnitude, N	x Component, N	y Component, N
$\mathbf{F}_1$	150	+129.9	+75.0
$\mathbf{F}_2$	80	−27.4	+75.2
$\mathbf{F}_3$	110	0	−110.0
$\mathbf{F}_4$	100	+96.6	−25.9
		$R_x = +199.1$	$R_y = +14.3$

Thus, the resultant $\mathbf{R}$ of the four forces is

$$\mathbf{R} = R_x\mathbf{i} + R_y\mathbf{j} \qquad \mathbf{R} = (199.1 \text{ N})\mathbf{i} + (14.3 \text{ N})\mathbf{j} \blacktriangleleft$$

The magnitude and direction of the resultant may now be determined. From the triangle shown, we have

$$\tan \alpha = \frac{R_y}{R_x} = \frac{14.3 \text{ N}}{199.1 \text{ N}} \qquad \alpha = 4.1°$$

$$R = \frac{14.3 \text{ N}}{\sin \alpha} = 199.6 \text{ N} \qquad \mathbf{R} = 199.6 \text{ N} \measuredangle 4.1° \blacktriangleleft$$

With a calculator, the last computation may be facilitated if the value of R_y is stored when originally entered; it may then be recalled to be divided by $\sin \alpha$. (Also see the footnote on p. 29.)

SOLVING PROBLEMS ON YOUR OWN

You saw in the preceding lesson that the resultant of two forces may be determined either graphically or from the trigonometry of an oblique triangle.

A. When three or more forces are involved, the determination of their resultant **R** is best carried out by first resolving each force into *rectangular components*. Two cases may be encountered, depending upon the way in which each of the given forces is defined:

Case 1. The force F is defined by its magnitude F and the angle α it forms with the x axis. The x and y components of the force can be obtained by multiplying F by $\cos \alpha$ and $\sin \alpha$, respectively [Example 1].

Case 2. The force F is defined by its magnitude F and the coordinates of two points A and B on its line of action (Fig. 2.23). The angle α that **F** forms with the x axis may first be determined by trigonometry. However, the components of **F** may also be obtained directly from proportions among the various dimensions involved, without actually determining α [Example 2].

B. Rectangular components of the resultant. The components R_x and R_y of the resultant can be obtained by adding algebraically the corresponding components of the given forces [Sample Prob. 2.3].

You can express the resultant in *vectorial form* using the unit vectors **i** and **j**, which are directed along the x and y axes, respectively:

$$\mathbf{R} = R_x\mathbf{i} + R_y\mathbf{j}$$

Alternatively, you can determine the *magnitude and direction* of the resultant by solving the right triangle of sides R_x and R_y for R and for the angle that **R** forms with the x axis.

PROBLEMS

2.21 and 2.22 Determine the x and y components of each of the forces shown.

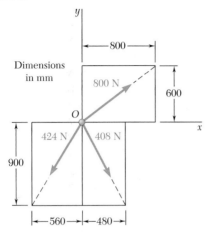

Fig. P2.21

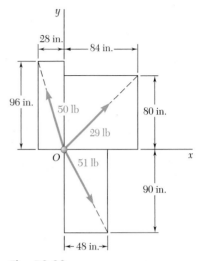

Fig. P2.22

2.23 and 2.24 Determine the x and y components of each of the forces shown.

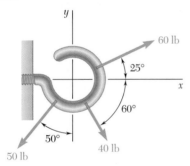

Fig. P2.23

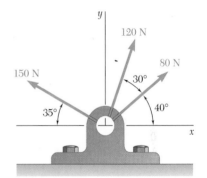

Fig. *P2.24*

2.25 Member *BD* exerts on member *ABC* a force **P** directed along line *BD*. Knowing that **P** must have a 300-lb horizontal component, determine (*a*) the magnitude of the force **P**, (*b*) its vertical component.

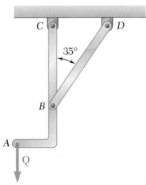

Fig. P2.25

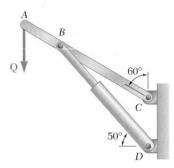

Fig. P2.26

2.26 The hydraulic cylinder *BD* exerts on member *ABC* a force **P** directed along line *BD*. Knowing that **P** must have a 750-N component perpendicular to member *ABC*, determine (*a*) the magnitude of the force **P**, (*b*) its component parallel to *ABC*.

2.27 The guy wire *BD* exerts on the telephone pole *AC* a force **P** directed along *BD*. Knowing that **P** must have a 120-N component perpendicular to the pole *AC*, determine (*a*) the magnitude of the force **P**, (*b*) its component along line *AC*.

2.28 The guy wire *BD* exerts on the telephone pole *AC* a force **P** directed along *BD*. Knowing that **P** has a 180-N component along line *AC*, determine (*a*) the magnitude of the force **P**, (*b*) its component in a direction perpendicular to *AC*.

2.29 Member *CB* of the vise shown exerts on block *B* a force **P** directed along line *CB*. Knowing that **P** must have a 1200-N horizontal component, determine (*a*) the magnitude of the force **P**, (*b*) its vertical component.

2.30 Cable *AC* exerts on beam *AB* a force **P** directed along line *AC*. Knowing that **P** must have a 350-lb vertical component, determine (*a*) the magnitude of the force **P**, (*b*) its horizontal component.

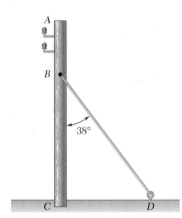

Fig. P2.27 and P2.28

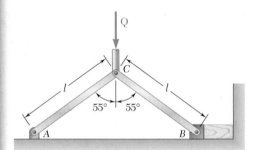

Fig. P2.29

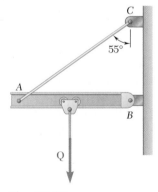

Fig. P2.30

2.31 Determine the resultant of the three forces of Prob. 2.22.

2.32 Determine the resultant of the three forces of Prob. 2.24.

2.33 Determine the resultant of the three forces of Prob. 2.23.

2.34 Determine the resultant of the three forces of Prob. 2.21.

2.35 Knowing that $\alpha = 35°$, determine the resultant of the three forces shown.

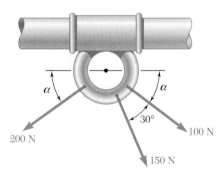

Fig. P2.35

2.36 Knowing that the tension in cable BC is 725 N, determine the resultant of the three forces exerted at point B of beam AB.

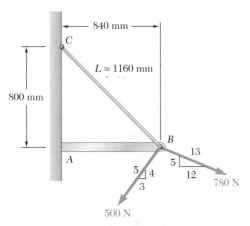

Fig. P2.36

2.37 Knowing that $\alpha = 40°$, determine the resultant of the three forces shown.

2.38 Knowing that $\alpha = 75°$, determine the resultant of the three forces shown.

2.39 For the collar of Prob. 2.35, determine (*a*) the required value of α if the resultant of the three forces shown is to be vertical, (*b*) the corresponding magnitude of the resultant.

2.40 For the beam of Prob. 2.36, determine (*a*) the required tension in cable BC if the resultant of the three forces exerted at point B is to be vertical, (*b*) the corresponding magnitude of the resultant.

2.41 Determine (*a*) the required tension in cable AC, knowing that the resultant of the three forces exerted at point C of boom BC must be directed along BC, (*b*) the corresponding magnitude of the resultant.

2.42 For the block of Probs. 2.37 and 2.38, determine (*a*) the required value of α if the resultant of the three forces shown is to be parallel to the incline, (*b*) the corresponding magnitude of the resultant.

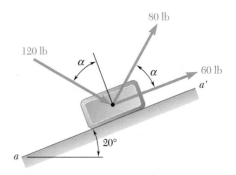

Fig. P2.37 and P2.38

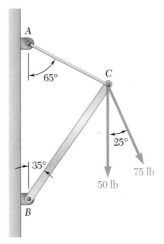

Fig. P2.41

2.9 EQUILIBRIUM OF A PARTICLE

In the preceding sections, we discussed the methods for determining the resultant of several forces acting on a particle. Although it has not occurred in any of the problems considered so far, it is quite possible for the resultant to be zero. In such a case, the net effect of the given forces is zero, and the particle is said to be in equilibrium. We thus have the following definition: *When the resultant of all the forces acting on a particle is zero, the particle is in equilibrium.*

A particle which is acted upon by two forces will be in equilibrium if the two forces have the same magnitude and the same line of action but opposite sense. The resultant of the two forces is then zero. Such a case is shown in Fig. 2.26.

Fig. 2.26

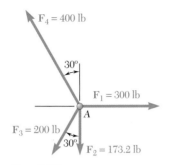

Fig. 2.27

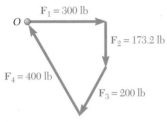

Fig. 2.28

Another case of equilibrium of a particle is represented in Fig. 2.27, where four forces are shown acting on A. In Fig. 2.28, the resultant of the given forces is determined by the polygon rule. Starting from point O with $\mathbf{F}_1$ and arranging the forces in tip-to-tail fashion, we find that the tip of $\mathbf{F}_4$ coincides with the starting point O. Thus the resultant $\mathbf{R}$ of the given system of forces is zero, and the particle is in equilibrium.

The closed polygon drawn in Fig. 2.28 provides a *graphical* expression of the equilibrium of A. To express *algebraically* the conditions for the equilibrium of a particle, we write

$$\mathbf{R} = \Sigma\mathbf{F} = 0 \tag{2.14}$$

Resolving each force $\mathbf{F}$ into rectangular components, we have

$$\Sigma(F_x\mathbf{i} + F_y\mathbf{j}) = 0 \qquad \text{or} \qquad (\Sigma F_x)\mathbf{i} + (\Sigma F_y)\mathbf{j} = 0$$

We conclude that the necessary and sufficient conditions for the equilibrium of a particle are

$$\Sigma F_x = 0 \qquad \Sigma F_y = 0 \tag{2.15}$$

Returning to the particle shown in Fig. 2.27, we check that the equilibrium conditions are satisfied. We write

$$\Sigma F_x = 300 \text{ lb} - (200 \text{ lb}) \sin 30° - (400 \text{ lb}) \sin 30°$$
$$= 300 \text{ lb} - 100 \text{ lb} - 200 \text{ lb} = 0$$
$$\Sigma F_y = -173.2 \text{ lb} - (200 \text{ lb}) \cos 30° + (400 \text{ lb}) \cos 30°$$
$$= -173.2 \text{ lb} - 173.2 \text{ lb} + 346.4 \text{ lb} = 0$$

2.10 NEWTON'S FIRST LAW OF MOTION

In the latter part of the seventeenth century, Sir Isaac Newton formulated three fundamental laws upon which the science of mechanics is based. The first of these laws can be stated as follows:

If the resultant force acting on a particle is zero, the particle will remain at rest (if originally at rest) or will move with constant speed in a straight line (if originally in motion).

From this law and from the definition of equilibrium given in Sec. 2.9, it is seen that a particle in equilibrium either is at rest or is moving in a straight line with constant speed. In the following section, various problems concerning the equilibrium of a particle will be considered.

2.11 PROBLEMS INVOLVING THE EQUILIBRIUM OF A PARTICLE. FREE-BODY DIAGRAMS

In practice, a problem in engineering mechanics is derived from an actual physical situation. A sketch showing the physical conditions of the problem is known as a *space diagram.*

The methods of analysis discussed in the preceding sections apply to a system of forces acting on a particle. A large number of problems involving actual structures, however, can be reduced to problems concerning the equilibrium of a particle. This is done by choosing a significant particle and drawing a separate diagram show-ing this particle and all the forces acting on it. Such a diagram is called a *free-body diagram.*

As an example, consider the 75-kg crate shown in the space diagram of Fig. 2.29*a*. This crate was lying between two buildings, and it is now being lifted onto a truck, which will remove it. The crate is supported by a vertical cable, which is joined at *A* to two ropes which pass over pulleys attached to the buildings at *B* and *C*. It is desired to determine the tension in each of the ropes *AB* and *AC*.

In order to solve this problem, a free-body diagram showing a particle in equilibrium must be drawn. Since we are interested in the rope tensions, the free-body diagram should include at least one of these tensions or, if possible, both tensions. Point *A* is seen to be a good free body for this problem. The free-body diagram of point *A* is shown in Fig. 2.29*b*. It shows point *A* and the forces exerted on *A* by the vertical cable and the two ropes. The force exerted by the cable is directed downward, and its magnitude is equal to the weight *W* of the crate. Recalling Eq. (1.4), we write

$$W = mg = (75 \text{ kg})(9.81 \text{ m/s}^2) = 736 \text{ N}$$

and indicate this value in the free-body diagram. The forces exerted by the two ropes are not known. Since they are respectively equal in magnitude to the tensions in rope *AB* and rope *AC*, we denote them by $\mathbf{T}_{AB}$ and $\mathbf{T}_{AC}$ and draw them away from *A* in the directions shown in the space diagram. No other detail is included in the free-body diagram.

Since point *A* is in equilibrium, the three forces acting on it must form a closed triangle when drawn in tip-to-tail fashion. This *force triangle* has been drawn in Fig. 2.29*c*. The values T_{AB} and T_{AC} of the tension in the ropes may be found graphically if the triangle is drawn to scale, or they may be found by trigonometry. If the latter method of solution is chosen, we use the law of sines and write

$$\frac{T_{AB}}{\sin 60°} = \frac{T_{AC}}{\sin 40°} = \frac{736 \text{ N}}{\sin 80°}$$

$$T_{AB} = 647 \text{ N} \qquad T_{AC} = 480 \text{ N}$$

When a particle is in *equilibrium under three forces*, the problem can be solved by drawing a force triangle. When a particle is in *equilibrium under more than three forces*, the problem can be solved graphically by drawing a force polygon. If an analytic solution is desired, the *equations of equilibrium* given in Sec. 2.9 should be solved:

$$\Sigma F_x = 0 \qquad \Sigma F_y = 0 \qquad (2.15)$$

These equations can be solved for no more than *two unknowns*; similarly, the force triangle used in the case of equilibrium under three forces can be solved for two unknowns.

The more common types of problems are those in which the two unknowns represent (1) the two components (or the magnitude and direction) of a single force, (2) the magnitudes of two forces, each of known direction. Problems involving the determination of the maximum or minimum value of the magnitude of a force are also encountered (see Probs. 2.57 through 2.61).

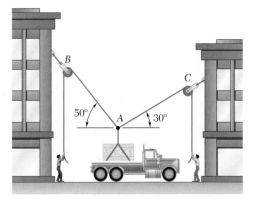

(*a*) Space diagram

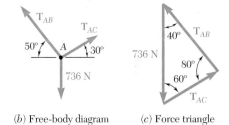

(*b*) Free-body diagram   (*c*) Force triangle

Fig. 2.29

Photo 2.1 As illustrated in the above example, it is possible to determine the tensions in the cables supporting the shaft shown by treating the hook as a particle and then applying the equations of equilibrium to the forces acting on the hook.

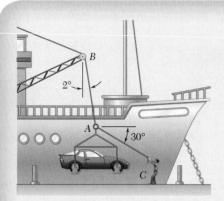

SAMPLE PROBLEM 2.4

In a ship-unloading operation, a 3500-lb automobile is supported by a cable. A rope is tied to the cable at A and pulled in order to center the automobile over its intended position. The angle between the cable and the vertical is 2°, while the angle between the rope and the horizontal is 30°. What is the tension in the rope?

SOLUTION

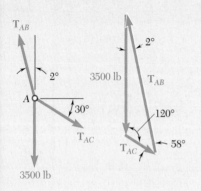

Free-Body Diagram. Point A is chosen as a free body, and the complete free-body diagram is drawn. T_{AB} is the tension in the cable AB, and T_{AC} is the tension in the rope.

Equilibrium Condition. Since only three forces act on the free body, we draw a force triangle to express that it is in equilibrium. Using the law of sines, we write

$$\frac{T_{AB}}{\sin 120°} = \frac{T_{AC}}{\sin 2°} = \frac{3500 \text{ lb}}{\sin 58°}$$

With a calculator, we first compute and store the value of the last quotient. Multiplying this value successively by sin 120° and sin 2°, we obtain

$$T_{AB} = 3570 \text{ lb} \qquad T_{AC} = 144 \text{ lb} \quad \blacktriangleleft$$

SAMPLE PROBLEM 2.5

Determine the magnitude and direction of the smallest force $\mathbf{F}$ which will maintain the package shown in equilibrium. Note that the force exerted by the rollers on the package is perpendicular to the incline.

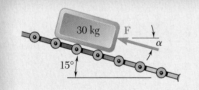

SOLUTION

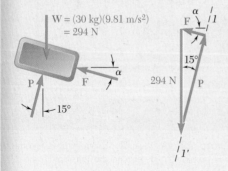

Free-Body Diagram. We choose the package as a free body, assuming that it can be treated as a particle. We draw the corresponding free-body diagram.

Equilibrium Condition. Since only three forces act on the free body, we draw a force triangle to express that it is in equilibrium. Line *1-1'* represents the known direction of $\mathbf{P}$. In order to obtain the minimum value of the force $\mathbf{F}$, we choose the direction of $\mathbf{F}$ perpendicular to that of $\mathbf{P}$. From the geometry of the triangle obtained, we find

$$F = (294 \text{ N}) \sin 15° = 76.1 \text{ N} \qquad \alpha = 15°$$
$$\mathbf{F} = 76.1 \text{ N} \; \searrow 15° \quad \blacktriangleleft$$

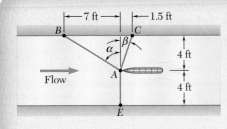

SAMPLE PROBLEM 2.6

As part of the design of a new sailboat, it is desired to determine the drag force which may be expected at a given speed. To do so, a model of the proposed hull is placed in a test channel and three cables are used to keep its bow on the centerline of the channel. Dynamometer readings indicate that for a given speed, the tension is 40 lb in cable AB and 60 lb in cable AE. Determine the drag force exerted on the hull and the tension in cable AC.

SOLUTION

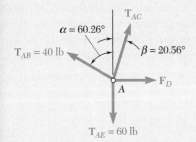

Determination of the Angles. First, the angles α and β defining the direction of cables AB and AC are determined. We write

$$\tan \alpha = \frac{7 \text{ ft}}{4 \text{ ft}} = 1.75 \qquad \tan \beta = \frac{1.5 \text{ ft}}{4 \text{ ft}} = 0.375$$

$$\alpha = 60.26° \qquad\qquad \beta = 20.56°$$

Free-Body Diagram. Choosing the hull as a free body, we draw the free-body diagram shown. It includes the forces exerted by the three cables on the hull, as well as the drag force $\mathbf{F}_D$ exerted by the flow.

Equilibrium Condition. We express that the hull is in equilibrium by writing that the resultant of all forces is zero:

$$\mathbf{R} = \mathbf{T}_{AB} + \mathbf{T}_{AC} + \mathbf{T}_{AE} + \mathbf{F}_D = 0 \qquad (1)$$

Since more than three forces are involved, we resolve the forces into x and y components:

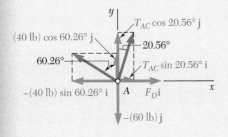

$$\mathbf{T}_{AB} = -(40 \text{ lb}) \sin 60.26°\mathbf{i} + (40 \text{ lb}) \cos 60.26°\mathbf{j}$$
$$= -(34.73 \text{ lb})\mathbf{i} + (19.84 \text{ lb})\mathbf{j}$$
$$\mathbf{T}_{AC} = T_{AC} \sin 20.56°\mathbf{i} + T_{AC} \cos 20.56°\mathbf{j}$$
$$= 0.3512T_{AC}\mathbf{i} + 0.9363T_{AC}\mathbf{j}$$
$$\mathbf{T}_{AE} = -(60 \text{ lb})\mathbf{j}$$
$$\mathbf{F}_D = F_D\mathbf{i}$$

Substituting the expressions obtained into Eq. (1) and factoring the unit vectors $\mathbf{i}$ and $\mathbf{j}$, we have

$$(-34.73 \text{ lb} + 0.3512T_{AC} + F_D)\mathbf{i} + (19.84 \text{ lb} + 0.9363T_{AC} - 60 \text{ lb})\mathbf{j} = 0$$

This equation will be satisfied if, and only if, the coefficients of $\mathbf{i}$ and $\mathbf{j}$ are equal to zero. We thus obtain the following two equilibrium equations, which express, respectively, that the sum of the x components and the sum of the y components of the given forces must be zero.

$$(\Sigma F_x = 0:) \qquad -34.73 \text{ lb} + 0.3512T_{AC} + F_D = 0 \qquad (2)$$
$$(\Sigma F_y = 0:) \qquad 19.84 \text{ lb} + 0.9363T_{AC} - 60 \text{ lb} = 0 \qquad (3)$$

From Eq. (3) we find $\qquad\qquad\qquad\qquad\qquad T_{AC} = +42.9 \text{ lb} \quad \blacktriangleleft$
and, substituting this value into Eq. (2), $\qquad\qquad F_D = +19.66 \text{ lb} \quad \blacktriangleleft$

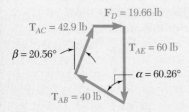

In drawing the free-body diagram, we assumed a sense for each unknown force. A positive sign in the answer indicates that the assumed sense is correct. The complete force polygon may be drawn to check the results.

SOLVING PROBLEMS ON YOUR OWN

When a particle is in *equilibrium,* the resultant of the forces acting on the particle must be zero. Expressing this fact in the case of a particle under *coplanar forces* will provide you with two relations among these forces. As you saw in the preceding sample problems, these relations may be used to determine two unknowns—such as the magnitude and direction of one force or the magnitudes of two forces.

Drawing a free-body diagram is the first step in the solution of a problem involving the equilibrium of a particle. This diagram shows the particle and all the forces acting on it. Indicate in your free-body diagram the magnitudes of known forces, as well as any angle or dimensions that define the direction of a force. Any unknown magnitude or angle should be denoted by an appropriate symbol. Nothing else should be included in the free-body diagram.

Drawing a clear and accurate free-body diagram is a must in the solution of any equilibrium problem. Skipping this step might save you pencil and paper, but is very likely to lead you to a wrong solution.

Case 1. If only three forces are involved in the free-body diagram, the rest of the solution is best carried out by drawing these forces in tip-to-tail fashion to form a *force triangle.* This triangle can be solved graphically or by trigonometry for no more than two unknowns [Sample Probs. 2.4 and 2.5].

Case 2. If more than three forces are involved, it is to your advantage to use an *analytic solution.* You select x and y axes and resolve each of the forces shown in the free-body diagram into x and y components. Expressing that the sum of the x components and the sum of the y components of all the forces are both zero, you will obtain two equations which you can solve for no more than two unknowns [Sample Prob. 2.6].

It is strongly recommended that when using an analytic solution the equations of equilibrium be written in the same form as Eqs. (2) and (3) of Sample Prob. 2.6. The practice adopted by some students of initially placing the unknowns on the left side of the equation and the known quantities on the right side may lead to confusion in assigning the appropriate sign to each term.

We have noted that regardless of the method used to solve a two-dimensional equilibrium problem we can determine at most two unknowns. If a two-dimensional problem involves more than two unknowns, one or more additional relations must be obtained from the information contained in the statement of the problem.

PROBLEMS

2.43 Two cables are tied together at C and are loaded as shown. Knowing that $\alpha = 20°$, determine the tension (*a*) in cable AC, (*b*) in cable BC.

2.44 Two cables are tied together at C and are loaded as shown. Determine the tension (*a*) in cable AC, (*b*) in cable BC.

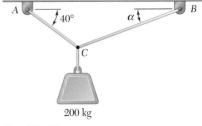

Fig. P2.43

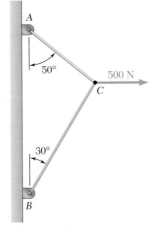

Fig. P2.44

2.45 Two cables are tied together at C and are loaded as shown. Knowing that $\mathbf{P} = 500$ N and $\alpha = 60°$, determine the tension in (*a*) in cable AC, (*b*) in cable BC.

2.46 Two cables are tied together at C and are loaded as shown. Determine the tension (*a*) in cable AC, (*b*) in cable BC.

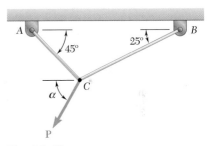

Fig. P2.45

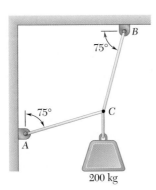

Fig. P2.46

41

2.47 Knowing that $\alpha = 20°$, determine the tension (*a*) in cable *AC*, (*b*) in rope *BC*.

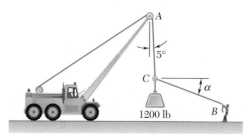

Fig. P2.47

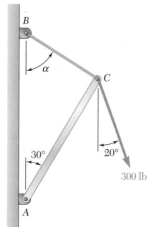

Fig. P2.48

2.48 Knowing that $\alpha = 55°$ and that boom *AC* exerts on pin *C* a force directed along line *AC*, determine (*a*) the magnitude of that force, (*b*) the tension in cable *BC*.

2.49 Two forces **P** and **Q** are applied as shown to an aircraft connection. Knowing that the connection is in equilibrium and that $P = 500$ lb and $Q = 650$ lb, determine the magnitudes of the forces exerted on the rods *A* and *B*.

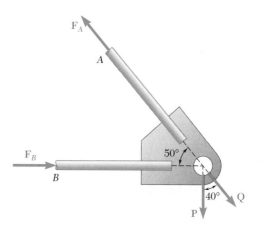

Fig. P2.49 and P2.50

2.50 Two forces **P** and **Q** are applied as shown to an aircraft connection. Knowing that the connection is in equilibrium and that the magnitudes of the forces exerted on rods *A* and *B* are $F_A = 750$ lb and $F_B = 400$ lb, determine the magnitudes of **P** and **Q**.

2.51 A welded connection is in equilibrium under the action of the four forces shown. Knowing that $F_A = 8$ kN and $F_B = 16$ kN, determine the magnitudes of the other two forces.

2.52 A welded connection is in equilibrium under the action of the four forces shown. Knowing that $F_A = 5$ kN and $F_D = 6$ kN, determine the magnitudes of the other two forces.

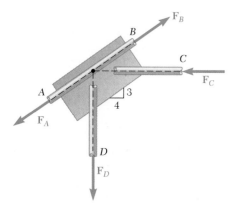

Fig. P2.51 and P2.52

2.53 Two cables tied together at C are loaded as shown. Knowing that $Q = 60$ lb, determine the tension (a) in cable AC, (b) in cable BC.

2.54 Two cables tied together at C are loaded as shown. Determine the range of values of Q for which the tension will not exceed 60 lb in either cable.

2.55 A sailor is being rescued using a boatswain's chair that is suspended from a pulley that can roll freely on the support cable ACB and is pulled at a constant speed by cable CD. Knowing that $\alpha = 30°$ and $\beta = 10°$ and that the combined weight of the boatswain's chair and the sailor is 900 N, determine the tension (a) in the support cable ACB, (b) in the traction cable CD.

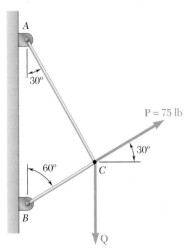

Fig. P2.53 and P2.54

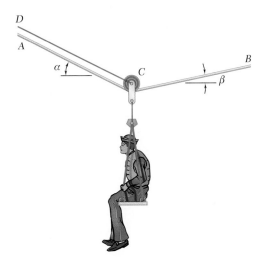

Fig. P2.55 and P2.56

2.56 A sailor is being rescued using a boatswain's chair that is suspended from a pulley that can roll freely on the support cable ACB and is pulled at a constant speed by cable CD. Knowing that $\alpha = 25°$ and $\beta = 15°$ and that the tension in cable CD is 80 N, determine (a) the combined weight of the boatswain's chair and the sailor, (b) the tension in the support cable ACB.

2.57 For the cables of Prob. 2.45, it is known that the maximum allowable tension is 600 N in cable AC and 750 N in cable BC. Determine (a) the maximum force P that can be applied at C, (b) the corresponding value of α.

2.58 For the situation described in Fig. P2.47, determine (a) the value of α for which the tension in rope BC is as small as possible, (b) the corresponding value of the tension.

2.59 For the structure and loading of Prob. 2.48, determine (a) the value of α for which the tension in cable BC is as small as possible, (b) the corresponding value of the tension.

2.60 Knowing that portions AC and BC of cable ACB must be equal, determine the shortest length of cable that can be used to support the load shown if the tension in the cable is not to exceed 870 N.

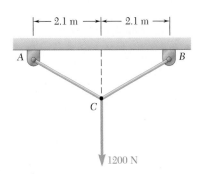

Fig. P2.60

2.61 Two cables tied together at C are loaded as shown. Knowing that the maximum allowable tension in each cable is 800 N, determine (a) the magnitude of the largest force **P** that can be applied at C, (b) the corresponding value of α.

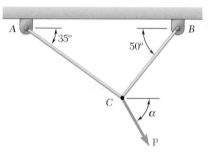

Fig. P2.61 and P2.62

2.62 Two cables tied together at C are loaded as shown. Knowing that the maximum allowable tension is 1200 N in cable AC and 600 N in cable BC, determine (a) the magnitude of the largest force **P** that can be applied at C, (b) the corresponding value of α.

2.63 Collar A is connected as shown to a 50-lb load and can slide on a frictionless horizontal rod. Determine the magnitude of the force **P** required to maintain the equilibrium of the collar when (a) $x = 4.5$ in., (b) $x = 15$ in.

2.64 Collar A is connected as shown to a 50-lb load and can slide on a frictionless horizontal rod. Determine the distance x for which the collar is in equilibrium when $P = 48$ lb.

2.65 A 160-kg load is supported by the rope-and-pulley arrangement shown. Knowing that $\beta = 20°$, determine the magnitude and direction of the force **P** that must be exerted on the free end of the rope to maintain equilibrium. (*Hint:* The tension in the rope is the same on each side of a simple pulley. This can be proved by the methods of Chap. 4.)

2.66 A 160-kg load is supported by the rope-and-pulley arrangement shown. Knowing that $\alpha = 40°$, determine (a) the angle β, (b) the magnitude of the force **P** that must be exerted on the free end of the rope to maintain equilibrium. (See the hint for Prob. 2.65.)

2.67 A 600-lb crate is supported by several rope-and-pulley arrangements as shown. Determine for each arrangement the tension in the rope. (See the hint for Prob. 2.65.)

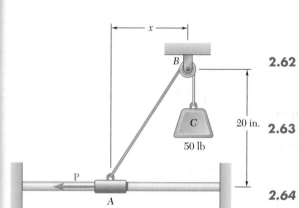

Fig. P2.63 and P2.64

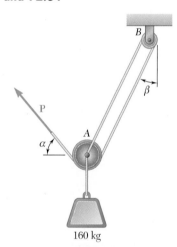

Fig. P2.65 and P2.66

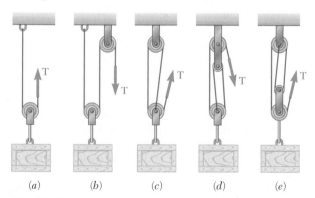

Fig. P2.67

2.68 Solve parts b and d of Prob. 2.67, assuming that the free end of the rope is attached to the crate.

2.69 A load **Q** is applied to the pulley C, which can roll on the cable ACB. The pulley is held in the position shown by a second cable CAD, which passes over the pulley A and supports a load **P**. Knowing that $P = 750$ N, determine (a) the tension in cable ACB, (b) the magnitude of load **Q**.

2.70 An 1800-N load **Q** is applied to the pulley C, which can roll on the cable ACB. The pulley is held in the position shown by a second cable CAD, which passes over the pulley A and supports a load **P**. Determine (a) the tension in cable ACB, (b) the magnitude of load **P**.

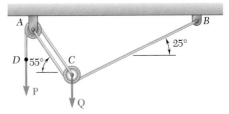

Fig. P2.69 and P2.70

FORCES IN SPACE

2.12 RECTANGULAR COMPONENTS OF A FORCE IN SPACE

The problems considered in the first part of this chapter involved only two dimensions; they could be formulated and solved in a single plane. In this section and in the remaining sections of the chapter, we will discuss problems involving the three dimensions of space.

Consider a force **F** acting at the origin O of the system of rectangular coordinates x, y, z. To define the direction of **F**, we draw the vertical plane $OBAC$ containing **F** (Fig. 2.30a). This plane passes through the vertical y axis; its orientation is defined by the angle ϕ it forms with the xy plane. The direction of **F** within the plane is defined by the angle θ_y that **F** forms with the y axis. The force **F** may be resolved into a vertical component $\mathbf{F}_y$ and a horizontal component $\mathbf{F}_h$; this operation, shown in Fig. 2.30b, is carried out in plane $OBAC$ according to the rules developed in the first part of the chapter. The corresponding scalar components are

$$F_y = F \cos \theta_y \qquad F_h = F \sin \theta_y \qquad (2.16)$$

But $\mathbf{F}_h$ may be resolved into two rectangular components $\mathbf{F}_x$ and $\mathbf{F}_z$ along the x and z axes, respectively. This operation, shown in Fig. 2.30c, is carried out in the xz plane. We obtain the following expressions for the corresponding scalar components:

$$F_x = F_h \cos \phi = F \sin \theta_y \cos \phi$$
$$F_z = F_h \sin \phi = F \sin \theta_y \sin \phi \qquad (2.17)$$

The given force **F** has thus been resolved into three rectangular vector components $\mathbf{F}_x$, $\mathbf{F}_y$, $\mathbf{F}_z$, which are directed along the three coordinate axes.

Applying the Pythagorean theorem to the triangles OAB and OCD of Fig. 2.30, we write

$$F^2 = (OA)^2 = (OB)^2 + (BA)^2 = F_y^2 + F_h^2$$
$$F_h^2 = (OC)^2 = (OD)^2 + (DC)^2 = F_x^2 + F_z^2$$

Eliminating F_h^2 from these two equations and solving for F, we obtain the following relation between the magnitude of **F** and its rectangular scalar components:

$$F = \sqrt{F_x^2 + F_y^2 + F_z^2} \qquad (2.18)$$

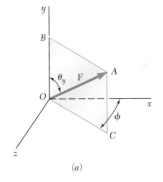

(a)

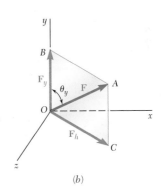

(b)

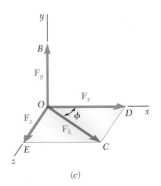

(c)

Fig. 2.30

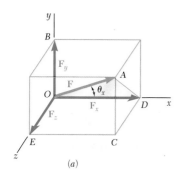

(a)

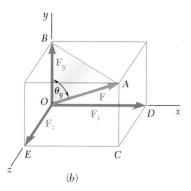

(b)

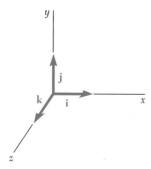

(c)

Fig. 2.31

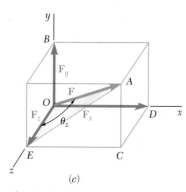

Fig. 2.32

The relationship existing between the force **F** and its three components F_x, F_y, F_z is more easily visualized if a "box" having F_x, F_y, F_z for edges is drawn as shown in Fig. 2.31. The force **F** is then represented by the diagonal OA of this box. Figure 2.31*b* shows the right triangle OAB used to derive the first of the formulas (2.16): $F_y = F \cos \theta_y$. In Fig. 2.31*a* and *c*, two other right triangles have also been drawn: OAD and OAE. These triangles are seen to occupy in the box positions comparable with that of triangle OAB. Denoting by θ_x and θ_z, respectively, the angles that **F** forms with the x and z axes, we can derive two formulas similar to $F_y = F \cos \theta_y$. We thus write

$$F_x = F \cos \theta_x \qquad F_y = F \cos \theta_y \qquad F_z = F \cos \theta_z \quad (2.19)$$

The three angles θ_x, θ_y, θ_z define the direction of the force **F**; they are more commonly used for this purpose than the angles θ_y and ϕ introduced at the beginning of this section. The cosines of θ_x, θ_y, θ_z are known as the *direction cosines* of the force **F**.

Introducing the unit vectors **i**, **j**, and **k**, directed respectively along the x, y, and z axes (Fig. 2.32), we can express **F** in the form

$$\mathbf{F} = F_x\mathbf{i} + F_y\mathbf{j} + F_z\mathbf{k} \quad (2.20)$$

where the scalar components F_x, F_y, F_z are defined by the relations (2.19).

EXAMPLE 1. A force of 500 N forms angles of 60°, 45°, and 120°, respectively, with the x, y, and z axes. Find the components F_x, F_y, and F_z of the force.

Substituting $F = 500$ N, $\theta_x = 60°$, $\theta_y = 45°$, $\theta_z = 120°$ into formulas (2.19), we write

$$F_x = (500 \text{ N}) \cos 60° = +250 \text{ N}$$
$$F_y = (500 \text{ N}) \cos 45° = +354 \text{ N}$$
$$F_z = (500 \text{ N}) \cos 120° = -250 \text{ N}$$

Carrying into Eq. (2.20) the values obtained for the scalar components of **F**, we have

$$\mathbf{F} = (250 \text{ N})\mathbf{i} + (354 \text{ N})\mathbf{j} - (250 \text{ N})\mathbf{k}$$

As in the case of two-dimensional problems, a plus sign indicates that the component has the same sense as the corresponding axis, and a minus sign indicates that it has the opposite sense. ■

The angle a force **F** forms with an axis should be measured from the positive side of the axis and will always be between 0 and 180°. An angle θ_x smaller than 90° (acute) indicates that **F** (assumed attached to O) is on the same side of the yz plane as the positive x axis; $\cos \theta_x$ and F_x will then be positive. An angle θ_x larger than 90° (obtuse) indicates that **F** is on the other side of the yz plane; $\cos \theta_x$ and F_x will then be negative. In Example 1 the angles θ_x and θ_y are acute, while θ_z is obtuse; consequently, F_x and F_y are positive, while F_z is negative.

Substituting into (2.20) the expressions obtained for F_x, F_y, F_z in (2.19), we write

$$\mathbf{F} = F(\cos\theta_x\mathbf{i} + \cos\theta_y\mathbf{j} + \cos\theta_z\mathbf{k}) \qquad (2.21)$$

which shows that the force $\mathbf{F}$ can be expressed as the product of the scalar F and the vector

$$\boldsymbol{\lambda} = \cos\theta_x\mathbf{i} + \cos\theta_y\mathbf{j} + \cos\theta_z\mathbf{k} \qquad (2.22)$$

Clearly, the vector $\boldsymbol{\lambda}$ is a vector whose magnitude is equal to 1 and whose direction is the same as that of $\mathbf{F}$ (Fig. 2.33). The vector $\boldsymbol{\lambda}$ is referred to as the *unit vector* along the line of action of $\mathbf{F}$. It follows from (2.22) that the components of the unit vector $\boldsymbol{\lambda}$ are respectively equal to the direction cosines of the line of action of $\mathbf{F}$:

$$\lambda_x = \cos\theta_x \qquad \lambda_y = \cos\theta_y \qquad \lambda_z = \cos\theta_z \qquad (2.23)$$

We should observe that the values of the three angles θ_x, θ_y, θ_z are not independent. Recalling that the sum of the squares of the components of a vector is equal to the square of its magnitude, we write

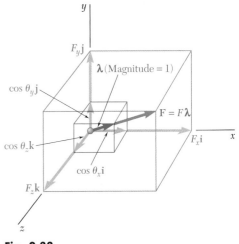

Fig. 2.33

$$\lambda_x^2 + \lambda_y^2 + \lambda_z^2 = 1$$

or, substituting for λ_x, λ_y, λ_z from (2.23),

$$\cos^2\theta_x + \cos^2\theta_y + \cos^2\theta_z = 1 \qquad (2.24)$$

In Example 1, for instance, once the values $\theta_x = 60°$ and $\theta_y = 45°$ have been selected, the value of θ_z *must* be equal to $60°$ or $120°$ in order to satisfy identity (2.24).

When the components F_x, F_y, F_z of a force $\mathbf{F}$ are given, the magnitude F of the force is obtained from (2.18).† The relations (2.19) can then be solved for the direction cosines,

$$\cos\theta_x = \frac{F_x}{F} \qquad \cos\theta_y = \frac{F_y}{F} \qquad \cos\theta_z = \frac{F_z}{F} \qquad (2.25)$$

and the angles θ_x, θ_y, θ_z characterizing the direction of $\mathbf{F}$ can be found.

EXAMPLE 2. A force $\mathbf{F}$ has the components $F_x = 20$ lb, $F_y = -30$ lb, $F_z = 60$ lb. Determine its magnitude F and the angles θ_x, θ_y, θ_z it forms with the coordinate axes.

From formula (2.18) we obtain†

$$\begin{aligned}
F &= \sqrt{F_x^2 + F_y^2 + F_z^2} \\
&= \sqrt{(20\text{ lb})^2 + (-30\text{ lb})^2 + (60\text{ lb})^2} \\
&= \sqrt{4900}\text{ lb} = 70\text{ lb}
\end{aligned}$$

†With a calculator programmed to convert rectangular coordinates into polar coordinates, the following procedure will be found more expeditious for computing F: First determine F_h from its two rectangular components F_x and F_z (Fig. 2.30c), then determine F from its two rectangular components F_h and F_y (Fig. 2.30b). The actual order in which the three components F_x, F_y, F_z are entered is immaterial.

Substituting the values of the components and magnitude of **F** into Eqs. (2.25), we write

$$\cos \theta_x = \frac{F_x}{F} = \frac{20 \text{ lb}}{70 \text{ lb}} \qquad \cos \theta_y = \frac{F_y}{F} = \frac{-30 \text{ lb}}{70 \text{ lb}} \qquad \cos \theta_z = \frac{F_z}{F} = \frac{60 \text{ lb}}{70 \text{ lb}}$$

Calculating successively each quotient and its arc cosine, we obtain

$$\theta_x = 73.4° \qquad \theta_y = 115.4° \qquad \theta_z = 31.0°$$

These computations can be carried out easily with a calculator. ▪

2.13 FORCE DEFINED BY ITS MAGNITUDE AND TWO POINTS ON ITS LINE OF ACTION

In many applications, the direction of a force **F** is defined by the coordinates of two points, $M(x_1, y_1, z_1)$ and $N(x_2, y_2, z_2)$, located on its line of action (Fig. 2.34). Consider the vector $\overrightarrow{MN}$ joining M and N

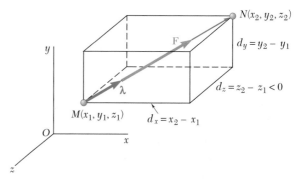

Fig. 2.34

and of the same sense as **F**. Denoting its scalar components by d_x, d_y, d_z, respectively, we write

$$\overrightarrow{MN} = d_x\mathbf{i} + d_y\mathbf{j} + d_z\mathbf{k} \tag{2.26}$$

The unit vector $\boldsymbol{\lambda}$ along the line of action of **F** (i.e., along the line MN) may be obtained by dividing the vector $\overrightarrow{MN}$ by its magnitude MN. Substituting for $\overrightarrow{MN}$ from (2.26) and observing that MN is equal to the distance d from M to N, we write

$$\boldsymbol{\lambda} = \frac{\overrightarrow{MN}}{MN} = \frac{1}{d}(d_x\mathbf{i} + d_y\mathbf{j} + d_z\mathbf{k}) \tag{2.27}$$

Recalling that **F** is equal to the product of F and λ, we have

$$\mathbf{F} = F\boldsymbol{\lambda} = \frac{F}{d}(d_x\mathbf{i} + d_y\mathbf{j} + d_z\mathbf{k}) \tag{2.28}$$

from which it follows that the scalar components of **F** are, respectively,

$$F_x = \frac{Fd_x}{d} \qquad F_y = \frac{Fd_y}{d} \qquad F_z = \frac{Fd_z}{d} \tag{2.29}$$

The relations (2.29) considerably simplify the determination of the components of a force **F** of given magnitude F when the line of action of **F** is defined by two points M and N. Subtracting the coordinates of M from those of N, we first determine the components of the vector $\overrightarrow{MN}$ and the distance d from M to N:

$$d_x = x_2 - x_1 \qquad d_y = y_2 - y_1 \qquad d_z = z_2 - z_1$$
$$d = \sqrt{d_x^2 + d_y^2 + d_z^2}$$

Substituting for F and for d_x, d_y, d_z, and d into the relations (2.29), we obtain the components F_x, F_y, F_z of the force.

The angles θ_x, θ_y, θ_z that **F** forms with the coordinate axes can then be obtained from Eqs. (2.25). Comparing Eqs. (2.22) and (2.27), we can also write

$$\cos \theta_x = \frac{d_x}{d} \qquad \cos \theta_y = \frac{d_y}{d} \qquad \cos \theta_z = \frac{d_z}{d} \qquad (2.30)$$

and determine the angles θ_x, θ_y, θ_z directly from the components and magnitude of the vector $\overrightarrow{MN}$.

2.14 ADDITION OF CONCURRENT FORCES IN SPACE

The resultant **R** of two or more forces in space will be determined by summing their rectangular components. Graphical or trigonometric methods are generally not practical in the case of forces in space.

The method followed here is similar to that used in Sec. 2.8 with coplanar forces. Setting

$$\mathbf{R} = \Sigma \mathbf{F}$$

we resolve each force into its rectangular components and write

$$R_x\mathbf{i} + R_y\mathbf{j} + R_z\mathbf{k} = \Sigma(F_x\mathbf{i} + F_y\mathbf{j} + F_z\mathbf{k})$$
$$= (\Sigma F_x)\mathbf{i} + (\Sigma F_y)\mathbf{j} + (\Sigma F_z)\mathbf{k}$$

from which it follows that

$$R_x = \Sigma F_x \qquad R_y = \Sigma F_y \qquad R_z = \Sigma F_z \qquad (2.31)$$

The magnitude of the resultant and the angles θ_x, θ_y, θ_z that the resultant forms with the coordinate axes are obtained using the method discussed in Sec. 2.12. We write

$$R = \sqrt{R_x^2 + R_y^2 + R_z^2} \qquad (2.32)$$

$$\cos \theta_x = \frac{R_x}{R} \qquad \cos \theta_y = \frac{R_y}{R} \qquad \cos \theta_z = \frac{R_z}{R} \qquad (2.33)$$

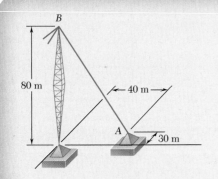

SAMPLE PROBLEM 2.7

A tower guy wire is anchored by means of a bolt at A. The tension in the wire is 2500 N. Determine (a) the components F_x, F_y, F_z of the force acting on the bolt, (b) the angles θ_x, θ_y, θ_z defining the direction of the force.

SOLUTION

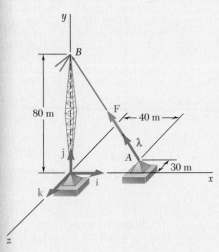

a. Components of the Force. The line of action of the force acting on the bolt passes through A and B, and the force is directed from A to B. The components of the vector $\overrightarrow{AB}$, which has the same direction as the force, are

$$d_x = -40 \text{ m} \qquad d_y = +80 \text{ m} \qquad d_z = +30 \text{ m}$$

The total distance from A to B is

$$AB = d = \sqrt{d_x^2 + d_y^2 + d_z^2} = 94.3 \text{ m}$$

Denoting by $\mathbf{i}, \mathbf{j}, \mathbf{k}$ the unit vectors along the coordinate axes, we have

$$\overrightarrow{AB} = -(40 \text{ m})\mathbf{i} + (80 \text{ m})\mathbf{j} + (30 \text{ m})\mathbf{k}$$

Introducing the unit vector $\boldsymbol{\lambda} = \overrightarrow{AB}/AB$, we write

$$\mathbf{F} = F\boldsymbol{\lambda} = F\frac{\overrightarrow{AB}}{AB} = \frac{2500 \text{ N}}{94.3 \text{ m}}\overrightarrow{AB}$$

Substituting the expression found for $\overrightarrow{AB}$, we obtain

$$\mathbf{F} = \frac{2500 \text{ N}}{94.3 \text{ m}}[-(40 \text{ m})\mathbf{i} + (80 \text{ m})\mathbf{j} + (30 \text{ m})\mathbf{k}]$$
$$\mathbf{F} = -(1060 \text{ N})\mathbf{i} + (2120 \text{ N})\mathbf{j} + (795 \text{ N})\mathbf{k}$$

The components of $\mathbf{F}$, therefore, are

$$F_x = -1060 \text{ N} \qquad F_y = +2120 \text{ N} \qquad F_z = +795 \text{ N} \quad \blacktriangleleft$$

b. Direction of the Force. Using Eqs. (2.25), we write

$$\cos \theta_x = \frac{F_x}{F} = \frac{-1060 \text{ N}}{2500 \text{ N}} \qquad \cos \theta_y = \frac{F_y}{F} = \frac{+2120 \text{ N}}{2500 \text{ N}}$$

$$\cos \theta_z = \frac{F_z}{F} = \frac{+795 \text{ N}}{2500 \text{ N}}$$

Calculating successively each quotient and its arc cosine, we obtain

$$\theta_x = 115.1° \qquad \theta_y = 32.0° \qquad \theta_z = 71.5° \quad \blacktriangleleft$$

(*Note.* This result could have been obtained by using the components and magnitude of the vector $\overrightarrow{AB}$ rather than those of the force $\mathbf{F}$.)

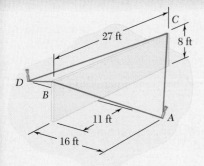

SAMPLE PROBLEM 2.8

A wall section of precast concrete is temporarily held by the cables shown. Knowing that the tension is 840 lb in cable AB and 1200 lb in cable AC, determine the magnitude and direction of the resultant of the forces exerted by cables AB and AC on stake A.

SOLUTION

Components of the Forces. The force exerted by each cable on stake A will be resolved into x, y, and z components. We first determine the components and magnitude of the vectors $\overrightarrow{AB}$ and $\overrightarrow{AC}$, measuring them from A toward the wall section. Denoting by $\mathbf{i}$, $\mathbf{j}$, $\mathbf{k}$ the unit vectors along the coordinate axes, we write

$$\overrightarrow{AB} = -(16\text{ ft})\mathbf{i} + (8\text{ ft})\mathbf{j} + (11\text{ ft})\mathbf{k} \qquad AB = 21\text{ ft}$$
$$\overrightarrow{AC} = -(16\text{ ft})\mathbf{i} + (8\text{ ft})\mathbf{j} - (16\text{ ft})\mathbf{k} \qquad AC = 24\text{ ft}$$

Denoting by $\boldsymbol{\lambda}_{AB}$ the unit vector along AB, we have

$$\mathbf{T}_{AB} = T_{AB}\boldsymbol{\lambda}_{AB} = T_{AB}\frac{\overrightarrow{AB}}{AB} = \frac{840\text{ lb}}{21\text{ ft}}\overrightarrow{AB}$$

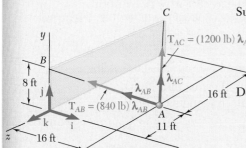

Substituting the expression found for $\overrightarrow{AB}$, we obtain

$$\mathbf{T}_{AB} = \frac{840\text{ lb}}{21\text{ ft}}[-(16\text{ ft})\mathbf{i} + (8\text{ ft})\mathbf{j} + (11\text{ ft})\mathbf{k}]$$
$$\mathbf{T}_{AB} = -(640\text{ lb})\mathbf{i} + (320\text{ lb})\mathbf{j} + (440\text{ lb})\mathbf{k}$$

Denoting by $\boldsymbol{\lambda}_{AC}$ the unit vector along AC, we obtain in a similar way

$$\mathbf{T}_{AC} = T_{AC}\boldsymbol{\lambda}_{AC} = T_{AC}\frac{\overrightarrow{AC}}{AC} = \frac{1200\text{ lb}}{24\text{ ft}}\overrightarrow{AC}$$
$$\mathbf{T}_{AC} = -(800\text{ lb})\mathbf{i} + (400\text{ lb})\mathbf{j} - (800\text{ lb})\mathbf{k}$$

Resultant of the Forces. The resultant $\mathbf{R}$ of the forces exerted by the two cables is

$$\mathbf{R} = \mathbf{T}_{AB} + \mathbf{T}_{AC} = -(1440\text{ lb})\mathbf{i} + (720\text{ lb})\mathbf{j} - (360\text{ lb})\mathbf{k}$$

The magnitude and direction of the resultant are now determined:

$$R = \sqrt{R_x^2 + R_y^2 + R_z^2} = \sqrt{(-1440)^2 + (720)^2 + (-360)^2}$$
$$R = 1650\text{ lb} \quad \blacktriangleleft$$

From Eqs. (2.33) we obtain

$$\cos\theta_x = \frac{R_x}{R} = \frac{-1440\text{ lb}}{1650\text{ lb}} \qquad \cos\theta_y = \frac{R_y}{R} = \frac{+720\text{ lb}}{1650\text{ lb}}$$
$$\cos\theta_z = \frac{R_z}{R} = \frac{-360\text{ lb}}{1650\text{ lb}}$$

Calculating successively each quotient and its arc cosine, we have

$$\theta_x = 150.8° \qquad \theta_y = 64.1° \qquad \theta_z = 102.6° \quad \blacktriangleleft$$

SOLVING PROBLEMS
ON YOUR OWN

In this lesson we saw that *forces in space* may be defined by their magnitude and direction or by the three rectangular components F_x, F_y, and F_z.

A. When a force is defined by its magnitude and direction, its rectangular components F_x, F_y, and F_z may be found as follows:

Case 1. If the direction of the force **F** is defined by the angles θ_y and ϕ shown in Fig. 2.30, projections of **F** through these angles or their complements will yield the components of **F** [Eqs. (2.17)]. Note that the x and z components of **F** are found by first projecting **F** onto the horizontal plane; the projection $\mathbf{F}_h$ obtained in this way is then resolved into the components $\mathbf{F}_x$ and $\mathbf{F}_z$ (Fig. 2.30c).

Case 2. If the direction of the force **F** is defined by the angles θ_x, θ_y, θ_z that **F** forms with the coordinate axes, each component can be obtained by multiplying the magnitude F of the force by the cosine of the corresponding angle [Example 1]:

$$F_x = F \cos \theta_x \qquad F_y = F \cos \theta_y \qquad F_z = F \cos \theta_z$$

Case 3. If the drection of the force **F** is defined by two points M and N located on its line of action (Fig. 2.34), you will first express the vector $\overrightarrow{MN}$ drawn from M to N in terms of its components d_x, d_y, d_z and the unit vectors **i**, **j**, **k**:

$$\overrightarrow{MN} = d_x\mathbf{i} + d_y\mathbf{j} + d_z\mathbf{k}$$

Next, you will determine the unit vector $\boldsymbol{\lambda}$ along the line of action of **F** by dividing the vector $\overrightarrow{MN}$ by its magnitude MN. Multiplying $\boldsymbol{\lambda}$ by the magnitude of **F**, you will obtain the desired expression for **F** in terms of its rectangular components [Sample Prob. 2.7]:

$$\mathbf{F} = F\boldsymbol{\lambda} = \frac{F}{d}(d_x\mathbf{i} + d_y\mathbf{j} + d_z\mathbf{k})$$

It is advantageous to use a consistent and meaningful system of notation when determining the rectangular components of a force. The method used in this text is illustrated in Sample Prob. 2.8 where, for example, the force $\mathbf{T}_{AB}$ acts from stake A toward point B. Note that the subscripts have been ordered to agree with the direction of the force. It is recommended that you adopt the same notation, as it will help you identify point 1 (the first subscript) and point 2 (the second subscript).

When forming the vector defining the line of action of a force, you may think of its scalar components as the number of steps you must take in each coordinate direction to go from point 1 to point 2. It is essential that you always remember to assign the correct sign to each of the components.

B. When a force is defined by its rectangular components F_x, F_y, F_z, you can obtain its magnitude F by writing

$$F = \sqrt{F_x^2 + F_y^2 + F_z^2}$$

You can determine the direction cosines of the line of action of **F** by dividing the components of the force by F:

$$\cos\theta_x = \frac{F_x}{F} \quad \cos\theta_y = \frac{F_y}{F} \quad \cos\theta_z = \frac{F_z}{F}$$

From the direction cosines you can obtain the angles θ_x, θ_y, θ_z that **F** forms with the coordinate axes [Example 2].

C. To determine the resultant R **of two or more forces** in three-dimensional space, first determine the rectangular components of each force by one of the procedures described above. Adding these components will yield the components R_x, R_y, R_z of the resultant. The magnitude and direction of the resultant may then be obtained as indicated above for a force **F** [Sample Prob. 2.8].

PROBLEMS

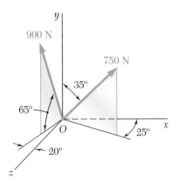

Fig. P2.71 and P2.72

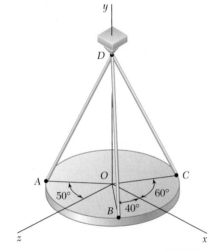

Fig. P2.73, P2.74, P2.75, and P2.76

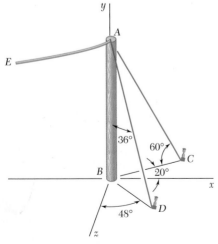

Fig. P2.77 and P2.78

2.71 Determine (*a*) the *x*, *y*, and *z* components of the 750-N force, (*b*) the angles θ_x, θ_y, and θ_z that the force forms with the coordinate axes.

2.72 Determine (*a*) the *x*, *y*, and *z* components of the 900-N force, (*b*) the angles θ_x, θ_y, and θ_z that the force forms with the coordinate axes.

2.73 A horizontal circular plate is suspended as shown from three wires that are attached to a support at *D* and form 30° angles with the vertical. Knowing that the *x* component of the force exerted by wire *AD* on the plate is 110.3 N, determine (*a*) the tension in wire *AD*, (*b*) the angles θ_x, θ_y, and θ_z that the force exerted at *A* forms with the coordinate axes.

2.74 A horizontal circular plate is suspended as shown from three wires that are attached to a support at *D* and form 30° angles with the vertical. Knowing that the *z* component of the force exerted by wire *BD* on the plate is −32.14 N, determine (*a*) the tension in wire *BD*, (*b*) the angles θ_x, θ_y, and θ_z that the force exerted at *B* forms with the coordinate axes.

2.75 A horizontal circular plate is suspended as shown from three wires that are attached to a support at *D* and form 30° angles with the vertical. Knowing that the tension in wire *CD* is 60 lb, determine (*a*) the components of the force exerted by this wire on the plate, (*b*) the angles θ_x, θ_y, and θ_z that the force forms with the coordinate axes.

2.76 A horizontal circular plate is suspended as shown from three wires that are attached to a support at *D* and form 30° angles with the vertical. Knowing that the *x* component of the force exerted by wire *CD* on the plate is −20 lb, determine (*a*) the tension in wire *CD*, (*b*) the angles θ_x, θ_y, and θ_z that the force exerted at *C* forms with the coordinate axes.

2.77 The end of the coaxial cable *AE* is attached to the pole *AB*, which is strengthened by the guy wires *AC* and *AD*. Knowing that the tension in wire *AC* is 120 lb, determine (*a*) the components of the force exerted by this wire on the pole, (*b*) the angles θ_x, θ_y, and θ_z that the force forms with the coordinate axes.

2.78 The end of the coaxial cable *AE* is attached to the pole *AB*, which is strengthened by the guy wires *AC* and *AD*. Knowing that the tension in wire *AD* is 85 lb, determine (*a*) the components of the force exerted by this wire on the pole, (*b*) the angles θ_x, θ_y, and θ_z that the force forms with the coordinate axes.

2.79 Determine the magnitude and direction of the force $\mathbf{F} = (320 \text{ N})\mathbf{i} + (400 \text{ N})\mathbf{j} - (250 \text{ N})\mathbf{k}$.

2.80 Determine the magnitude and direction of the force $\mathbf{F} = (240 \text{ N})\mathbf{i} - (270 \text{ N})\mathbf{j} + (680 \text{ N})\mathbf{k}$.

2.81 A force acts at the origin of a coordinate system in a direction defined by the angles $\theta_x = 70.9°$ and $\theta_y = 144.9°$. Knowing that the z component of the force is -52 lb, determine (*a*) the angle θ_z, (*b*) the other components and the magnitude of the force.

2.82 A force acts at the origin of a coordinate system in a direction defined by the angles $\theta_y = 55°$ and $\theta_z = 45°$. Knowing that the x component of the force is -500 lb, determine (*a*) the angle θ_x, (*b*) the other components and the magnitude of the force.

2.83 A force $\mathbf{F}$ of magnitude 210 N acts at the origin of a coordinate system. Knowing that $F_x = 80$ N, $\theta_z = 151.2°$, and $F_y < 0$, determine (*a*) the components F_y and F_z, (*b*) the angles θ_x and θ_y.

2.84 A force $\mathbf{F}$ of magnitude 230 N acts at the origin of a coordinate system. Knowing that $\theta_x = 32.5°$, $F_y = -60$ N, and $F_z > 0$, determine (*a*) the components F_x and F_z, (*b*) the angles θ_y and θ_z.

2.85 A transmission tower is held by three guy wires anchored by bolts at B, C, and D. If the tension in wire AB is 525 lb, determine the components of the force exerted by the wire on the bolt at B.

2.86 A transmission tower is held by three guy wires anchored by bolts at B, C, and D. If the tension in wire AD is 315 lb, determine the components of the force exerted by the wire on the bolt at D.

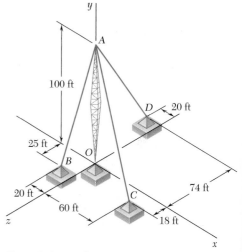

Fig. P2.85 and P2.86

2.87 A frame ABC is supported in part by cable DBE that passes through a frictionless ring at B. Knowing that the tension in the cable is 385 N, determine the components of the force exerted by the cable on the support at D.

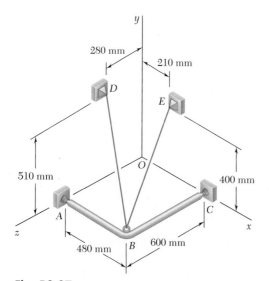

Fig. P2.87

2.88 For the frame and cable of Prob. 2.87, determine the components of the force exerted by the cable on the support at *E*.

2.89 Knowing that the tension in cable *AB* is 1425 N, determine the components of the force exerted on the plate at *B*.

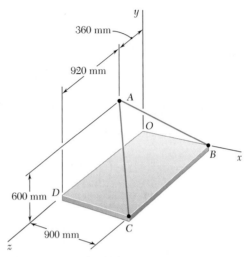

Fig. P2.89 and P2.90

2.90 Knowing that the tension in cable *AC* is 2130 N, determine the components of the force exerted on the plate at *C*.

2.91 Find the magnitude and direction of the resultant of the two forces shown knowing that $P = 300$ N and $Q = 400$ N.

2.92 Find the magnitude and direction of the resultant of the two forces shown knowing that $P = 400$ N and $Q = 300$ N.

2.93 Knowing that the tension is 425 lb in cable *AB* and 510 lb in cable *AC*, determine the magnitude and direction of the resultant of the forces exerted at *A* by the two cables.

2.94 Knowing that the tension is 510 lb in cable *AB* and 425 lb in cable *AC*, determine the magnitude and direction of the resultant of the forces exerted at *A* by the two cables.

2.95 For the frame of Prob. 2.87, determine the magnitude and direction of the resultant of the forces exerted by the cable at *B* knowing that the tension in the cable is 385 N.

2.96 For the cables of Prob. 2.89, knowing that the tension is 1425 N in cable *AB* and 2130 N in cable *AC*, determine the magnitude and direction of the resultant of the forces exerted at *A* by the two cables.

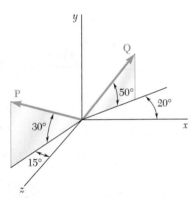

Fig. P2.91 and P2.92

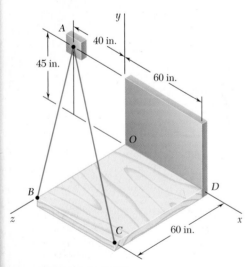

Fig. P2.93 and P2.94

2.97 The end of the coaxial cable AE is attached to the pole AB, which is strengthened by the guy wires AC and AD. Knowing that the tension in AC is 150 lb and that the resultant of the forces exerted at A by wires AC and AD must be contained in the xy plane, determine (a) the tension in AD, (b) the magnitude and direction of the resultant of the two forces.

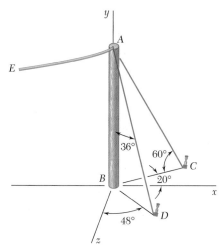

Fig. P2.97 and P2.98

2.98 The end of the coaxial cable AE is attached to the pole AB, which is strengthened by the guy wires AC and AD. Knowing that the tension in AD is 125 lb and that the resultant of the forces exerted at A by wires AC and AD must be contained in the xy plane, determine (a) the tension in AC, (b) the magnitude and direction of the resultant of the two forces.

2.15 EQUILIBRIUM OF A PARTICLE IN SPACE

According to the definition given in Sec. 2.9, a particle A is in equilibrium if the resultant of all the forces acting on A is zero. The components R_x, R_y, R_z of the resultant are given by the relations (2.31); expressing that the components of the resultant are zero, we write

$$\Sigma F_x = 0 \qquad \Sigma F_y = 0 \qquad \Sigma F_z = 0 \qquad (2.34)$$

Equations (2.34) represent the necessary and sufficient conditions for the equilibrium of a particle in space. They can be used to solve problems dealing with the equilibrium of a particle involving no more than three unknowns.

To solve such problems, you first should draw a free-body diagram showing the particle in equilibrium and *all* the forces acting on it. You can then write the equations of equilibrium (2.34) and solve them for three unknowns. In the more common types of problems, these unknowns will represent (1) the three components of a single force or (2) the magnitude of three forces, each of known direction.

Photo 2.2 While the tension in the *four* cables supporting the car cannot be found using the *three* equations of (2.34), a relation between the tensions can be obtained by considering the equilibrium of the hook.

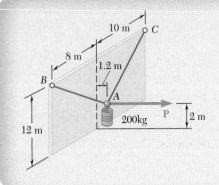

SAMPLE PROBLEM 2.9

A 200-kg cylinder is hung by means of two cables AB and AC, which are attached to the top of a vertical wall. A horizontal force $\mathbf{P}$ perpendicular to the wall holds the cylinder in the position shown. Determine the magnitude of $\mathbf{P}$ and the tension in each cable.

SOLUTION

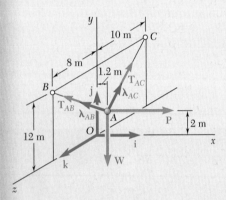

Free-body Diagram. Point A is chosen as a free body; this point is subjected to four forces, three of which are of unknown magnitude.

Introducing the unit vectors $\mathbf{i}$, $\mathbf{j}$, $\mathbf{k}$, we resolve each force into rectangular components.

$$\mathbf{P} = P\mathbf{i}$$
$$\mathbf{W} = -mg\mathbf{j} = -(200 \text{ kg})(9.81 \text{ m/s}^2)\mathbf{j} = -(1962 \text{ N})\mathbf{j} \qquad (1)$$

In the case of $\mathbf{T}_{AB}$ and $\mathbf{T}_{AC}$, it is necessary first to determine the components and magnitudes of the vectors $\overrightarrow{AB}$ and $\overrightarrow{AC}$. Denoting by $\boldsymbol{\lambda}_{AB}$ the unit vector along AB, we write

$$\overrightarrow{AB} = -(1.2 \text{ m})\mathbf{i} + (10 \text{ m})\mathbf{j} + (8 \text{ m})\mathbf{k} \qquad AB = 12.862 \text{ m}$$
$$\boldsymbol{\lambda}_{AB} = \frac{\overrightarrow{AB}}{12.862 \text{ m}} = -0.09330\mathbf{i} + 0.7775\mathbf{j} + 0.6220\mathbf{k}$$
$$\mathbf{T}_{AB} = T_{AB}\boldsymbol{\lambda}_{AB} = -0.09330T_{AB}\mathbf{i} + 0.7775T_{AB}\mathbf{j} + 0.6220T_{AB}\mathbf{k} \qquad (2)$$

Denoting by $\boldsymbol{\lambda}_{AC}$ the unit vector along AC, we write in a similar way

$$\overrightarrow{AC} = -(1.2 \text{ m})\mathbf{i} + (10 \text{ m})\mathbf{j} - (10 \text{ m})\mathbf{k} \qquad AC = 14.193 \text{ m}$$
$$\boldsymbol{\lambda}_{AC} = \frac{\overrightarrow{AC}}{14.193 \text{ m}} = -0.08455\mathbf{i} + 0.7046\mathbf{j} - 0.7046\mathbf{k}$$
$$\mathbf{T}_{AC} = T_{AC}\boldsymbol{\lambda}_{AC} = -0.08455T_{AC}\mathbf{i} + 0.7046T_{AC}\mathbf{j} - 0.7046T_{AC}\mathbf{k} \qquad (3)$$

Equilibrium Condition. Since A is in equilibrium, we must have

$$\Sigma\mathbf{F} = 0: \qquad \mathbf{T}_{AB} + \mathbf{T}_{AC} + \mathbf{P} + \mathbf{W} = 0$$

or, substituting from (1), (2), (3) for the forces and factoring $\mathbf{i}$, $\mathbf{j}$, $\mathbf{k}$,

$$(-0.09330T_{AB} - 0.08455T_{AC} + P)\mathbf{i}$$
$$+ (0.7775T_{AB} + 0.7046T_{AC} - 1962 \text{ N})\mathbf{j}$$
$$+ (0.6220T_{AB} - 0.7046T_{AC})\mathbf{k} = 0$$

Setting the coefficients of $\mathbf{i}$, $\mathbf{j}$, $\mathbf{k}$ equal to zero, we write three scalar equations, which express that the sums of the x, y, and z components of the forces are respectively equal to zero.

$$(\Sigma F_x = 0:) \qquad -0.09330T_{AB} - 0.08455T_{AC} + P = 0$$
$$(\Sigma F_y = 0:) \qquad +0.7775T_{AB} + 0.7046T_{AC} - 1962 \text{ N} = 0$$
$$(\Sigma F_z = 0:) \qquad +0.6220T_{AB} - 0.7046T_{AC} = 0$$

Solving these equations, we obtain

$$P = 235 \text{ N} \qquad T_{AB} = 1402 \text{ N} \qquad T_{AC} = 1238 \text{ N} \quad \blacktriangleleft$$

SOLVING PROBLEMS ON YOUR OWN

We saw earlier that when a particle is in *equilibrium*, the resultant of the forces acting on the particle must be zero. Expressing this fact in the case of the equilibrium of a *particle in three-dimensional space* will provide you with three relations among the forces acting on the particle. These relations may be used to determine three unknowns—usually the magnitudes of three forces.

Your solution will consist of the following steps:

1. Draw a free-body diagram of the particle. This diagram shows the particle and all the forces acting on it. Indicate on the diagram the magnitudes of known forces, as well as any angles or dimensions that define the direction of a force. Any unknown magnitude or angle should be denoted by an appropriate symbol. Nothing else should be included in your free-body diagram.

2. Resolve each of the forces into rectangular components. Following the method used in the preceding lesson, you will determine for each force **F** the unit vector $\boldsymbol{\lambda}$ defining the direction of that force and express **F** as the product of its magnitude F and the unit vector $\boldsymbol{\lambda}$. You will obtain an expression of the form

$$\mathbf{F} = F\boldsymbol{\lambda} = \frac{F}{d}\,(d_x\mathbf{i} + d_y\mathbf{j} + d_z\mathbf{k})$$

where d, d_x, d_y, and d_z are dimensions obtained from the free-body diagram of the particle. If a force is known in magnitude as well as in direction, then F is known and the expression obtained for **F** is well defined; otherwise F is one of the three unknowns that should be determined.

3. Set the resultant, or sum, of the forces exerted on the particle equal to zero. You will obtain a vectorial equation consisting of terms containing the unit vectors **i**, **j**, or **k**. You will group the terms containing the same unit vector and factor that vector. For the vectorial equation to be satisfied, the coefficient of each of the unit vectors must be set equal to zero. This will yield three scalar equations that you can solve for no more than three unknowns [Sample Prob. 2.9].

PROBLEMS

2.99 Three cables are used to tether a balloon as shown. Determine the vertical force **P** exerted by the balloon at A knowing that the tension in cable AB is 259 N.

2.100 Three cables are used to tether a balloon as shown. Determine the vertical force **P** exerted by the balloon at A knowing that the tension in cable AC is 444 N.

2.101 Three cables are used to tether a balloon as shown. Determine the vertical force **P** exerted by the balloon at A knowing that the tension in cable AD is 481 N.

2.102 Three cables are used to tether a balloon as shown. Knowing that the balloon exerts an 800-N vertical force at A, determine the tension in each cable.

2.103 A crate is supported by three cables as shown. Determine the weight of the crate knowing that the tension in cable AB is 750 lb.

2.104 A crate is supported by three cables as shown. Determine the weight of the crate knowing that the tension in cable AD is 616 lb.

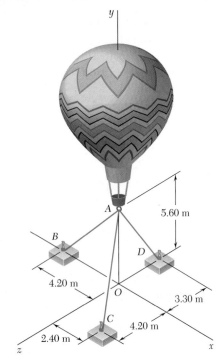

Fig. P2.99, P2.100, P2.101, and P2.102

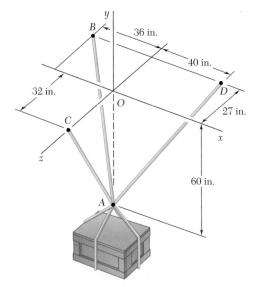

Fig. P2.103, P2.104, P2.105, and P2.106

2.105 A crate is supported by three cables as shown. Determine the weight of the crate knowing that the tension in cable AC is 544 lb.

2.106 A 1600-lb crate is supported by three cables as shown. Determine the tension in each cable.

2.107 Three cables are connected at *A*, where the forces **P** and **Q** are applied as shown. Knowing that *Q* = 0, find the value of *P* for which the tension in cable *AD* is 305 N.

2.108 Three cables are connected at *A*, where the forces **P** and **Q** are applied as shown. Knowing that *P* = 1200 N, determine the values of *Q* for which cable *AD* is taut.

2.109 A transmission tower is held by three guy wires attached to a pin at *A* and anchored by bolts at *B*, *C*, and *D*. If the tension in wire *AB* is 630 lb, determine the vertical force **P** exerted by the tower on the pin at *A*.

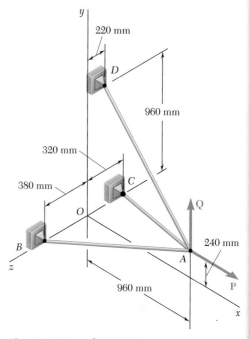

Fig. P2.107 and P2.108

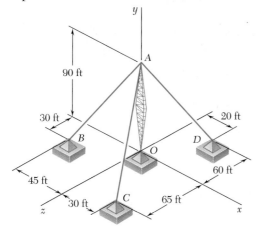

Fig. P2.109, and *P2.110*

2.110 A transmission tower is held by three guy wires attached to a pin at *A* and anchored by bolts at *B*, *C*, and *D*. If the tension in wire *AC* is 920 lb, determine the vertical force **P** exerted by the tower on the pin at *A*.

2.111 A rectangular plate is supported by three cables as shown. Knowing that the tension in cable *AC* is 60 N, determine the weight of the plate.

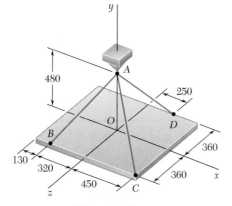

Dimensions in mm

Fig. P2.111 and P2.112

2.112 A rectangular plate is supported by three cables as shown. Knowing that the tension in cable *AD* is 520 N, determine the weight of the plate.

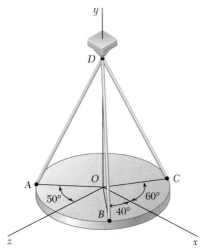

Fig. P2.114

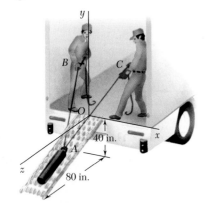

Fig. P2.119

2.113 For the transmission tower of Probs. 2.109 and 2.110, determine the tension in each guy wire knowing that the tower exerts on the pin at A an upward vertical force of 2100 lb.

2.114 A horizontal circular plate weighing 60 lb is suspended as shown from three wires that are attached to a support at D and form 30° angles with the vertical. Determine the tension in each wire.

2.115 For the rectangular plate of Probs. 2.111 and 2.112, determine the tension in each of the three cables knowing that the weight of the plate is 792 N.

2.116 For the cable system of Probs. 2.107 and 2.108, determine the tension in each cable knowing that $P = 2880$ N and $Q = 0$.

2.117 For the cable system of Probs. 2.107 and 2.108, determine the tension in each cable knowing that $P = 2880$ N and $Q = 576$ N.

2.118 For the cable system of Probs. 2.107 and 2.108, determine the tension in each cable knowing that $P = 2880$ N and $Q = -576$ N (Q is directed downward).

2.119 Using two ropes and a roller chute, two workers are unloading a 200-lb cast-iron counterweight from a truck. Knowing that at the instant shown the counterweight is kept from moving and that the positions of points A, B, and C are, respectively, $A(0, -20$ in., 40 in.), $B(-40$ in., 50 in., 0), and $C(45$ in., 40 in., 0), and assuming that no friction exists between the counterweight and the chute, determine the tension in each rope. (*Hint:* Since there is no friction, the force exerted by the chute on the counterweight must be perpendicular to the chute.)

2.120 Solve Prob. 2.119 assuming that a third worker is exerting a force $\mathbf{P} = -(40$ lb)$\mathbf{i}$ on the counterweight.

2.121 A container of weight W is suspended from ring A. Cable BAC passes through the ring and is attached to fixed supports at B and C. Two forces $\mathbf{P} = P\mathbf{i}$ and $\mathbf{Q} = Q\mathbf{k}$ are applied to the ring to maintain the container in the position shown. Knowing that $W = 376$ N, determine P and Q. (*Hint:* The tension is the same in both portions of cable BAC.)

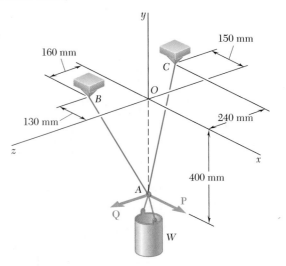

Fig. P2.121

2.122 For the system of Prob. 2.121, determine W and Q knowing that $P = 164$ N.

2.123 A container of weight W is suspended from ring A, to which cables AC and AE are attached. A force **P** is applied to the end F of a third cable that passes over a pulley at B and through ring A and that is attached to a support at D. Knowing that $W = 1000$ N, determine the magnitude of **P**. (*Hint:* The tension is the same in all portions of cable *FBAD*.)

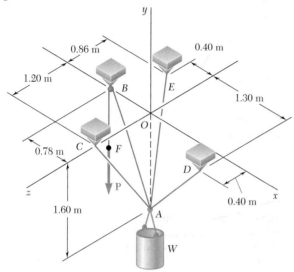

Fig. P2.123

2.124 Knowing that the tension in cable AC of the system described in Prob. 2.123 is 150 N, determine (*a*) the magnitude of the force **P**, (*b*) the weight W of the container.

2.125 Collars A and B are connected by a 25-in.-long wire and can slide freely on frictionless rods. If a 60-lb force **Q** is applied to collar B as shown, determine (*a*) the tension in the wire when $x = 9$ in., (*b*) the corresponding magnitude of the force **P** required to maintain the equilibrium of the system.

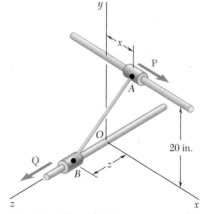

Fig. P2.125 and P2.126

2.126 Collars A and B are connected by a 25-in.-long wire and can slide freely on frictionless rods. Determine the distances x and z for which the equilibrium of the system is maintained when $P = 120$ lb and $Q = 60$ lb.

REVIEW AND SUMMARY

In this chapter we have studied the effect of forces on particles, i.e., on bodies of such shape and size that all forces acting on them may be assumed applied at the same point.

Resultant of two forces

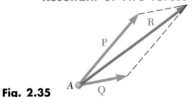

Fig. 2.35

Forces are *vector quantities*; they are characterized by a *point of application*, a *magnitude*, and a *direction*, and they add according to the *parallelogram law* (Fig. 2.35). The magnitude and direction of the resultant **R** of two forces **P** and **Q** can be determined either graphically or by trigonometry, using successively the law of cosines and the law of sines [Sample Prob. 2.1].

Components of a force

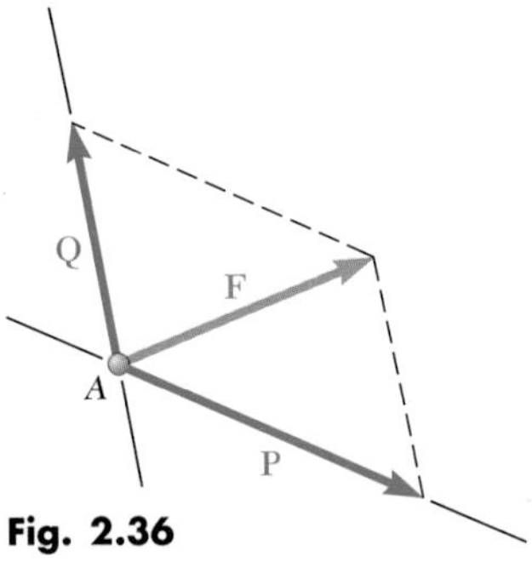

Any given force acting on a particle can be resolved into two or more *components*, i.e., it can be replaced by two or more forces which have the same effect on the particle. A force **F** can be resolved into two components **P** and **Q** by drawing a parallelogram which has **F** for its diagonal; the components **P** and **Q** are then represented by the two adjacent sides of the parallelogram (Fig. 2.36) and can be determined either graphically or by trigonometry [Sec. 2.6].

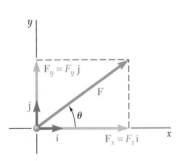

Fig. 2.36

Rectangular components
Unit vectors

A force **F** is said to have been resolved into two *rectangular components* if its components F_x and F_y are perpendicular to each other and are directed along the coordinate axes (Fig. 2.37). Introducing the *unit vectors* **i** and **j** along the x and y axes, respectively, we write [Sec. 2.7]

$$F_x = F_x\mathbf{i} \qquad F_y = F_y\mathbf{j} \qquad (2.6)$$

and

$$\mathbf{F} = F_x\mathbf{i} + F_y\mathbf{j} \qquad (2.7)$$

where F_x and F_y are the *scalar components* of **F**. These components, which can be positive or negative, are defined by the relations

$$F_x = F \cos\theta \qquad F_y = F \sin\theta \qquad (2.8)$$

When the rectangular components F_x and F_y of a force **F** are given, the angle θ defining the direction of the force can be obtained by writing

$$\tan\theta = \frac{F_y}{F_x} \qquad (2.9)$$

The magnitude F of the force can then be obtained by solving one of the equations (2.8) for F or by applying the Pythagorean theorem and writing

$$F = \sqrt{F_x^2 + F_y^2} \qquad (2.10)$$

Fig. 2.37

When *three or more coplanar forces* act on a particle, the rectangular components of their resultant **R** can be obtained by adding algebraically the corresponding components of the given forces [Sec. 2.8]. We have

$$R_x = \Sigma F_x \qquad R_y = \Sigma F_y \qquad (2.13)$$

The magnitude and direction of **R** can then be determined from relations similar to Eqs. (2.9) and (2.10) [Sample Prob. 2.3].

A force **F** in *three-dimensional space* can be resolved into rectangular components F_x, F_y, and F_z [Sec. 2.12]. Denoting by θ_x, θ_y, and θ_z, respectively, the angles that **F** forms with the x, y, and z axes (Fig. 2.38), we have

Forces in space

$$F_x = F \cos \theta_x \qquad F_y = F \cos \theta_y \qquad F_z = F \cos \theta_z \qquad (2.19)$$

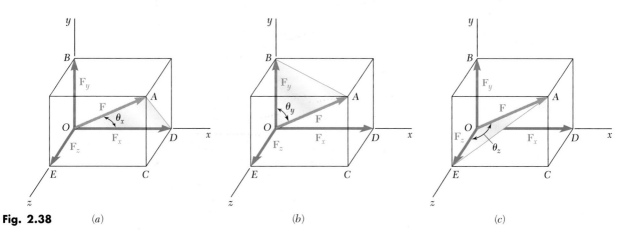

Fig. 2.38   (*a*)   (*b*)   (*c*)

The cosines of θ_x, θ_y, θ_z are known as the *direction cosines* of the force **F**. Introducing the unit vectors **i**, **j**, **k** along the coordinate axes, we write

Direction cosines

$$\mathbf{F} = F_x\mathbf{i} + F_y\mathbf{j} + F_z\mathbf{k} \qquad (2.20)$$

or

$$\mathbf{F} = F(\cos \theta_x\mathbf{i} + \cos \theta_y\mathbf{j} + \cos \theta_z\mathbf{k}) \qquad (2.21)$$

which shows (Fig. 2.39) that **F** is the product of its magnitude F and the unit vector

$$\boldsymbol{\lambda} = \cos \theta_x\mathbf{i} + \cos \theta_y\mathbf{j} + \cos \theta_z\mathbf{k}$$

Since the magnitude of $\boldsymbol{\lambda}$ is equal to unity, we must have

$$\cos^2 \theta_x + \cos^2 \theta_y + \cos^2 \theta_z = 1 \qquad (2.24)$$

When the rectangular components F_x, F_y, F_z of a force **F** are given, the magnitude F of the force is found by writing

$$F = \sqrt{F_x^2 + F_y^2 + F_z^2} \qquad (2.18)$$

and the direction cosines of **F** are obtained from Eqs. (2.19). We have

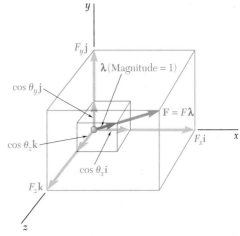

Fig. 2.39

$$\cos \theta_x = \frac{F_x}{F} \qquad \cos \theta_y = \frac{F_y}{F} \qquad \cos \theta_z = \frac{F_z}{F} \qquad (2.25)$$

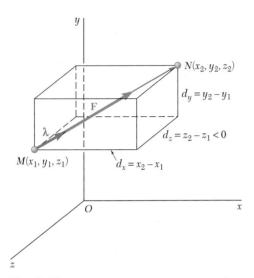

Fig. 2.40

When a force **F** is defined in three-dimensional space by its magnitude F and two points M and N on its line of action [Sec. 2.13], its rectangular components can be obtained as follows. We first express the vector $\overrightarrow{MN}$ joining points M and N in terms of its components d_x, d_y, and d_z (Fig. 2.40); we write

$$\overrightarrow{MN} = d_x\mathbf{i} + d_y\mathbf{j} + d_z\mathbf{k} \qquad (2.26)$$

We next determine the unit vector $\boldsymbol{\lambda}$ along the line of action of **F** by dividing $\overrightarrow{MN}$ by its magnitude $MN = d$:

$$\boldsymbol{\lambda} = \frac{\overrightarrow{MN}}{MN} = \frac{1}{d}(d_x\mathbf{i} + d_y\mathbf{j} + d_z\mathbf{k}) \qquad (2.27)$$

Recalling that **F** is equal to the product of F and $\boldsymbol{\lambda}$, we have

$$\mathbf{F} = F\boldsymbol{\lambda} = \frac{F}{d}(d_x\mathbf{i} + d_y\mathbf{j} + d_z\mathbf{k}) \qquad (2.28)$$

from which it follows [Sample Probs. 2.7 and 2.8] that the scalar components of **F** are, respectively,

$$F_x = \frac{Fd_x}{d} \qquad F_y = \frac{Fd_y}{d} \qquad F_z = \frac{Fd_z}{d} \qquad (2.29)$$

Resultant of forces in space

When *two or more forces* act on a particle in *three-dimensional space,* the rectangular components of their resultant **R** can be obtained by adding algebraically the corresponding components of the given forces [Sec. 2.14]. We have

$$R_x = \Sigma F_x \qquad R_y = \Sigma F_y \qquad R_z = \Sigma F_z \qquad (2.31)$$

The magnitude and direction of **R** can then be determined from relations similar to Eqs. (2.18) and (2.25) [Sample Prob. 2.8].

Equilibrium of a particle

A particle is said to be in *equilibrium* when the resultant of all the forces acting on it is zero [Sec. 2.9]. The particle will then remain at rest (if originally at rest) or move with constant speed in a straight line (if originally in motion) [Sec. 2.10].

Free-body diagram

To solve a problem involving a particle in equilibrium, one first should draw a *free-body diagram* of the particle showing all the forces acting on it [Sec. 2.11]. If *only three coplanar forces* act on the particle, a *force triangle* may be drawn to express that the particle is in equilibrium. Using graphical methods of trigonometry, this triangle can be solved for no more than two unknowns [Sample Prob. 2.4]. If *more than three coplanar forces* are involved, the equations of equilibrium

$$\Sigma F_x = 0 \qquad \Sigma F_y = 0 \qquad (2.15)$$

should be used. These equations can be solved for no more than two unknowns [Sample Prob. 2.6].

Equilibrium in space

When a particle is in *equilibrium in three-dimensional space* [Sec. 2.15], the three equations of equilibrium

$$\Sigma F_x = 0 \qquad \Sigma F_y = 0 \qquad \Sigma F_z = 0 \qquad (2.34)$$

should be used. These equations can be solved for no more than three unknowns [Sample Prob. 2.9].

REVIEW PROBLEMS

2.127 The direction of the 75-lb forces may vary, but the angle between the forces is always 50°. Determine the value of α for which the resultant of the forces acting at A is directed horizontally to the left.

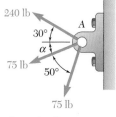

Fig. P2.127

2.128 A stake is being pulled out of the ground by means of two ropes as shown. Knowing the magnitude and direction of the force exerted on one rope, determine the magnitude and direction of the force **P** that should be exerted on the other rope if the resultant of these two forces is to be a 40-lb vertical force.

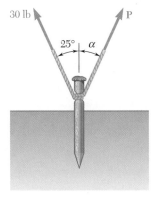

Fig. P2.128

2.129 Member BD exerts on member ABC a force **P** directed along line BD. Knowing that **P** must have a 240-lb vertical component, determine (a) the magnitude of the force **P**, (b) its horizontal component.

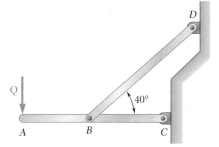

Fig. P2.129

2.130 Two cables are tied together at C and loaded as shown. Determine the tension (a) in cable AC, (b) in cable BC.

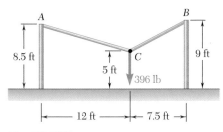

Fig. P2.130

2.131 Two cables are tied together at C and loaded as shown. Knowing that $P = 360$ N, determine the tension (a) in cable AC, (b) in cable BC.

2.132 Two cables are tied together at C and loaded as shown. Determine the range of values of P for which both cables remain taut.

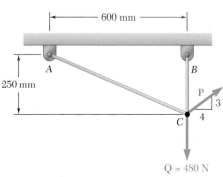

Fig. P2.131 and P2.132

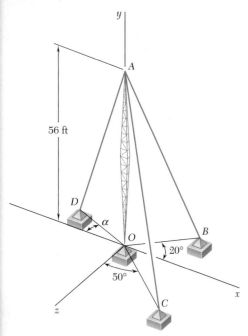

Fig. P2.134

2.133 A force acts at the origin of a coordinate system in a direction defined by the angles $\theta_x = 69.3°$ and $\theta_z = 57.9°$. Knowing that the y component of the force is -174 lb, determine (a) the angle θ_y, (b) the other components and the magnitude of the force.

2.134 Cable AB is 65 ft long, and the tension in that cable is 3900 lb. Determine (a) the x, y, and z components of the force exerted by the cable on the anchor B, (b) the angles θ_x, θ_y, and θ_z defining the direction of that force.

2.135 In order to move a wrecked truck, two cables are attached at A and pulled by winches B and C as shown. Knowing that the tension is 10 kN in cable AB and 7.5 kN in cable AC, determine the magnitude and direction of the resultant of the forces exerted at A by the two cables.

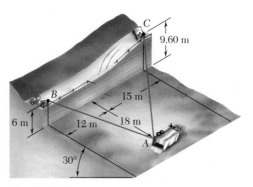

Fig. P2.135

2.136 A container of weight $W = 1165$ N is supported by three cables as shown. Determine the tension in each cable.

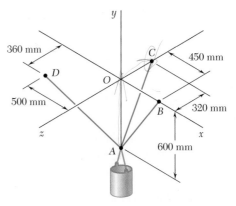

Fig. P2.136

2.137 Collars A and B are connected by a 525-mm-long wire and can slide freely on frictionless rods. If a force $\mathbf{P} = (341\ \text{N})\mathbf{j}$ is applied to collar A, determine (*a*) the tension in the wire when $y = 155$ mm, (*b*) the magnitude of the force $\mathbf{Q}$ required to maintain the equilibrium of the system.

Fig. P2.137

2.138 Solve Prob. 2.137 assuming that $y = 275$ mm.

COMPUTER PROBLEMS

2.C1 Using computational software, determine the magnitude and direction of the resultant of n coplanar forces applied at a point A. Use this program to solve Probs. 2.32, 2.33, 2.35, and 2.38.

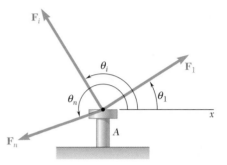

Fig. P2.C1

2.C2 A load **P** is supported by two cables as shown. Using computational software, determine the tension in each cable for any given value of P and for values of θ ranging from $\theta_1 = \beta - 90°$ to $\theta_2 = 90° - \alpha$, using given increments $\Delta\theta$. Use this program to determine for the following three sets of numerical values (a) the tension in each cable for values of θ ranging from θ_1 to θ_2, (b) the value of θ for which the tension in the two cables is as small as possible, (c) the corresponding value of the tension:

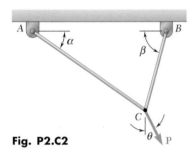

Fig. P2.C2

(1) $\alpha = 35°$, $\beta = 75°$, $P = 400$ lb, $\Delta\theta = 5°$
(2) $\alpha = 50°$, $\beta = 30°$, $P = 600$ lb, $\Delta\theta = 10°$
(3) $\alpha = 40°$, $\beta = 60°$, $P = 250$ lb, $\Delta\theta = 5°$

2.C3 An acrobat is walking on a tightrope of length $L = 20.1$ m attached to supports A and B at a distance of 20.0 m from each other. The combined weight of the acrobat and his balancing pole is 800 N, and the friction between his shoes and the rope is large enough to prevent him from slipping. Neglecting the weight of the rope and any elastic deformation, use computational software to calculate the deflection y and the tension in portions AC and BC of the rope for values of x from 0.5 m to 10.0 m using 0.5-m increments. From the data obtained, determine (a) the maximum deflection of the rope, (b) the maximum tension in the rope, (c) the smallest values of the tension in portions AC and BC of the rope.

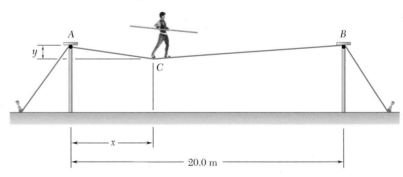

Fig. P2.C3

2.C4 Write a computer program that can be used to determine the magnitude and direction of the resultant of n forces $\mathbf{F}_i$, where $i = 1, 2, \ldots, n$, that are applied at point A_0 of coordinates x_0, y_0, and z_0, knowing that the line of action of $\mathbf{F}_i$ passes through point A_i of coordinates x_i, y_i, and z_i. Use this program to solve Probs. 2.93, 2.94, 2.95, and 2.135.

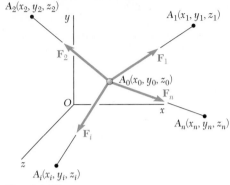

Fig. P2.C4

2.C5 Three cables are attached at points A_1, A_2, and A_3, respectively, and are connected at point A_0, to which a given load $\mathbf{P}$ is applied as shown. Write a computer program that can be used to determine the tension in each of the cables. Use this program to solve Probs. 2.102, 2.106, 2.107, and 2.115.

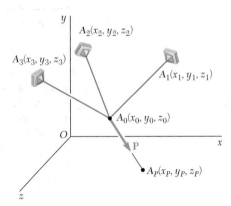

Fig. P2.C5

The battleship USS *New Jersey* is maneuvered by four tugboats at Bremerton Naval Shipyard. It will be shown in this chapter that the forces exerted on the ship by the tugboats could be replaced by an equivalent force exerted by a single, more powerful, tugboat.

Rigid Bodies:
Equivalent Systems of Forces

3.1 INTRODUCTION

In the preceding chapter it was assumed that each of the bodies considered could be treated as a single particle. Such a view, however, is not always possible, and a body, in general, should be treated as a combination of a large number of particles. The size of the body will have to be taken into consideration, as well as the fact that forces will act on different particles and thus will have different points of application.

Most of the bodies considered in elementary mechanics are assumed to be *rigid*, a *rigid body* being defined as one which does not deform. Actual structures and machines, however, are never absolutely rigid and deform under the loads to which they are subjected. But these deformations are usually small and do not appreciably affect the conditions of equilibrium or motion of the structure under consideration. They are important, though, as far as the resistance of the structure to failure is concerned and are considered in the study of mechanics of materials.

In this chapter you will study the effect of forces exerted on a rigid body, and you will learn how to replace a given system of forces by a simpler equivalent system. This analysis will rest on the fundamental assumption that the effect of a given force on a rigid body remains unchanged if that force is moved along its line of action (*principle of transmissibility*). It follows that forces acting on a rigid body can be represented by *sliding vectors*, as indicated earlier in Sec. 2.3.

Two important concepts associated with the effect of a force on a rigid body are the *moment of a force about a point* (Sec. 3.6) and the *moment of a force about an axis* (Sec. 3.11). Since the determination of these quantities involves the computation of vector products and scalar products of two vectors, the fundamentals of vector algebra will be introduced in this chapter and applied to the solution of problems involving forces acting on rigid bodies.

Another concept introduced in this chapter is that of a *couple*, i.e., the combination of two forces which have the same magnitude, parallel lines of action, and opposite sense (Sec. 3.12). As you will see, any system of forces acting on a rigid body can be replaced by an equivalent system consisting of one force acting at a given point and one couple. This basic system is called a *force-couple system*. In the case of concurrent, coplanar, or parallel forces, the equivalent force-couple system can be further reduced to a single force, called the *resultant* of the system, or to a single couple, called the *resultant couple* of the system.

3.2 EXTERNAL AND INTERNAL FORCES

Forces acting on rigid bodies can be separated into two groups: (1) *external forces* and (2) *internal forces*.

1. The *external forces* represent the action of other bodies on the rigid body under consideration. They are entirely responsible for the external behavior of the rigid body. They will either cause it to move or ensure that it remains at rest. We shall be concerned only with external forces in this chapter and in Chaps. 4 and 5.

2. The *internal forces* are the forces which hold together the particles forming the rigid body. If the rigid body is structurally composed of several parts, the forces holding the component parts together are also defined as internal forces. Internal forces will be considered in Chaps. 6 and 7.

As an example of external forces, let us consider the forces acting on a disabled truck that three people are pulling forward by means of a rope attached to the front bumper (Fig. 3.1). The external forces acting on the truck are shown in a *free-body diagram* (Fig. 3.2). Let us first consider the *weight* of the truck. Although it embodies the effect of the earth's pull on each of the particles forming the truck, the weight can be represented by the single force **W**. The *point of application* of this force, i.e., the point at which the force acts, is defined as the *center of gravity* of the truck. It will be seen in Chap. 5 how centers of gravity can be determined. The weight **W** tends to make the truck move vertically downward. In fact, it would actually cause the truck to move downward, i.e., to fall, if it were not for the presence of the ground. The ground opposes the downward motion of the truck by means of the reactions **R**₁ and **R**₂. These forces are exerted *by* the ground *on* the truck and must therefore be included among the external forces acting on the truck.

Fig. 3.1

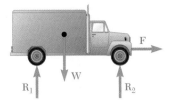

Fig. 3.2

The people pulling on the rope exert the force **F**. The point of application of **F** is on the front bumper. The force **F** tends to make the truck move forward in a straight line and does actually make it move, since no external force opposes this motion. (Rolling resistance has been neglected here for simplicity.) This forward motion of the truck, during which each straight line keeps its original orientation (the floor of the truck remains horizontal, and the walls remain vertical), is known as a *translation*. Other forces might cause the truck to move differently. For example, the force exerted by a jack placed under the front axle would cause the truck to pivot about its rear axle. Such a motion is a *rotation*. It can be concluded, therefore, that each of the *external forces* acting on a *rigid body* can, if unopposed, impart to the rigid body a motion of translation or rotation, or both.

3.3 PRINCIPLE OF TRANSMISSIBILITY. EQUIVALENT FORCES

The *principle of transmissibility* states that the conditions of equilibrium or motion of a rigid body will remain unchanged if a force **F** acting at a given point of the rigid body is replaced by a force **F**′ of the same magnitude and same direction, but acting at a different point, *provided that the two forces have the same line of action* (Fig. 3.3). The two forces **F** and **F**′ have the same effect on the rigid body and are said to be *equivalent*. This principle, which states that the action of a force may be *transmitted* along its line of action, is based on experimental evidence. It *cannot* be derived from the properties established so far in this text and must therefore be accepted as an experimental law. However, as you will see in Sec. 16.5, the principle of transmissibility can be derived from the study of the dynamics of rigid bodies, but this study requires the introduction of Newton's

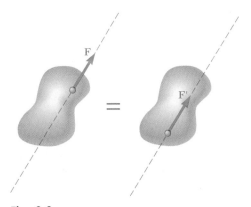

Fig. 3.3

second and third laws and of a number of other concepts as well. Therefore, our study of the statics of rigid bodies will be based on the three principles introduced so far, i.e., the parallelogram law of addition, Newton's first law, and the principle of transmissibility.

It was indicated in Chap. 2 that the forces acting on a particle could be represented by vectors. These vectors had a well-defined point of application, namely, the particle itself, and were therefore fixed, or bound, vectors. In the case of forces acting on a rigid body, however, the point of application of the force does not matter, as long as the line of action remains unchanged. Thus, forces acting on a rigid body must be represented by a different kind of vector, known as a *sliding vector*, since forces may be allowed to slide along their lines of action. We should note that all the properties which will be derived in the following sections for the forces acting on a rigid body will be valid more generally for any system of sliding vectors. In order to keep our presentation more intuitive, however, we will carry it out in terms of physical forces rather than in terms of mathematical sliding vectors.

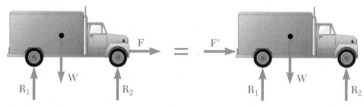

Fig. 3.4

Returning to the example of the truck, we first observe that the line of action of the force **F** is a horizontal line passing through both the front and the rear bumpers of the truck (Fig. 3.4). Using the principle of transmissibility, we can therefore replace **F** by an *equivalent force* **F′** acting on the rear bumper. In other words, the conditions of motion are unaffected, and all the other external forces acting on the truck (**W**, $\mathbf{R}_1$, $\mathbf{R}_2$) remain unchanged if the people push on the rear bumper instead of pulling on the front bumper.

The principle of transmissibility and the concept of equivalent forces have limitations, however. Consider, for example, a short bar AB acted upon by equal and opposite axial forces $\mathbf{P}_1$ and $\mathbf{P}_2$, as shown in Fig. 3.5a. According to the principle of transmissibility, the force $\mathbf{P}_2$ can be replaced by a force $\mathbf{P}_2'$ having the same magnitude, the same direction, and the same line of action but acting at A instead of B (Fig. 3.5b). The forces $\mathbf{P}_1$ and $\mathbf{P}_2'$ acting on the same particle

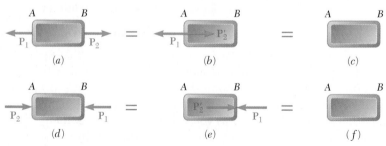

Fig. 3.5

can be added according to the rules of Chap. 2, and, as these forces are equal and opposite, their sum is equal to zero. Thus, in terms of the external behavior of the bar, the original system of forces shown in Fig. 3.5a is equivalent to no force at all (Fig. 3.5c).

Consider now the two equal and opposite forces $\mathbf{P}_1$ and $\mathbf{P}_2$ acting on the bar AB as shown in Fig. 3.5d. The force $\mathbf{P}_2$ can be replaced by a force $\mathbf{P}_2'$ having the same magnitude, the same direction, and the same line of action but acting at B instead of at A (Fig. 3.5e). The forces $\mathbf{P}_1$ and $\mathbf{P}_2'$ can then be added, and their sum is again zero (Fig. 3.5f). From the point of view of the mechanics of rigid bodies, the systems shown in Fig. 3.5a and d are thus equivalent. But the *internal forces* and *deformations* produced by the two systems are clearly different. The bar of Fig. 3.5a is in *tension* and, if not absolutely rigid, will increase in length slightly; the bar of Fig. 3.5d is in *compression* and, if not absolutely rigid, will decrease in length slightly. Thus, while the principle of transmissibility may be used freely to determine the conditions of motion or equilibrium of rigid bodies and to compute the external forces acting on these bodies, it should be avoided, or at least used with care, in determining internal forces and deformations.

3.4 VECTOR PRODUCT OF TWO VECTORS

In order to gain a better understanding of the effect of a force on a rigid body, a new concept, the concept of *a moment of a force about a point,* will be introduced at this time. This concept will be more clearly understood, and applied more effectively, if we first add to the mathematical tools at our disposal the *vector product* of two vectors.

The vector product of two vectors $\mathbf{P}$ and $\mathbf{Q}$ is defined as the vector $\mathbf{V}$ which satisfies the following conditions.

1. The line of action of $\mathbf{V}$ is perpendicular to the plane containing $\mathbf{P}$ and $\mathbf{Q}$ (Fig. 3.6a).
2. The magnitude of $\mathbf{V}$ is the product of the magnitudes of $\mathbf{P}$ and $\mathbf{Q}$ and of the sine of the angle θ formed by $\mathbf{P}$ and $\mathbf{Q}$ (the measure of which will always be 180° or less); we thus have

$$V = PQ \sin \theta \tag{3.1}$$

3. The direction of $\mathbf{V}$ is obtained from the *right-hand rule.* Close your right hand and hold it so that your fingers are curled in the same sense as the rotation through θ which brings the vector $\mathbf{P}$ in line with the vector $\mathbf{Q}$; your thumb will then indicate the direction of the vector $\mathbf{V}$ (Fig. 3.6b). Note that if $\mathbf{P}$ and $\mathbf{Q}$ do not have a common point of application, they should first be redrawn from the same point. The three vectors $\mathbf{P}$, $\mathbf{Q}$, and $\mathbf{V}$—taken in that order—are said to form a *right-handed triad.*†

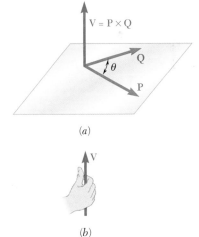

(a)

(b)

Fig. 3.6

†We should note that the x, y, and z axes used in Chap. 2 form a right-handed system of orthogonal axes and that the unit vectors $\mathbf{i}$, $\mathbf{j}$, $\mathbf{k}$ defined in Sec. 2.12 form a right-handed orthogonal triad.

As stated above, the vector **V** satisfying these three conditions (which define it uniquely) is referred to as the vector product of **P** and **Q**; it is represented by the mathematical expression

$$\mathbf{V} = \mathbf{P} \times \mathbf{Q} \tag{3.2}$$

Because of the notation used, the vector product of two vectors **P** and **Q** is also referred to as the *cross product* of **P** and **Q**.

It follows from Eq. (3.1) that, when two vectors **P** and **Q** have either the same direction or opposite directions, their vector product is zero. In the general case when the angle θ formed by the two vectors is neither 0° nor 180°, Eq. (3.1) can be given a simple geometric interpretation: The magnitude V of the vector product of **P** and **Q** is equal to the area of the parallelogram which has **P** and **Q** for sides (Fig. 3.7). The vector product **P** × **Q** will therefore remain unchanged if we replace **Q** by a vector **Q′** which is coplanar with **P** and **Q** and such that the line joining the tips of **Q** and **Q′** is parallel to **P**. We write

$$\mathbf{V} = \mathbf{P} \times \mathbf{Q} = \mathbf{P} \times \mathbf{Q}' \tag{3.3}$$

From the third condition used to define the vector product **V** of **P** and **Q**, namely, the condition stating that **P**, **Q**, and **V** must form a right-handed triad, it follows that vector products *are not commutative*, i.e., **Q** × **P** is not equal to **P** × **Q**. Indeed, we can easily check that **Q** × **P** is represented by the vector −**V**, which is equal and opposite to **V**. We thus write

$$\mathbf{Q} \times \mathbf{P} = -(\mathbf{P} \times \mathbf{Q}) \tag{3.4}$$

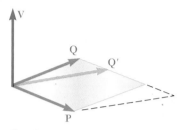

Fig. 3.7

EXAMPLE   Let us compute the vector product **V** = **P** × **Q** where the vector **P** is of magnitude 6 and lies in the zx plane at an angle of 30° with the x axis, and where the vector **Q** is of magnitude 4 and lies along the x axis (Fig. 3.8).

It follows immediately from the definition of the vector product that the vector **V** must lie along the y axis, have the magnitude

$$V = PQ \sin \theta = (6)(4) \sin 30° = 12$$

and be directed upward. ■

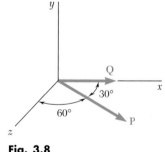

Fig. 3.8

We saw that the commutative property does not apply to vector products. We may wonder whether the *distributive* property holds, i.e., whether the relation

$$\mathbf{P} \times (\mathbf{Q}_1 + \mathbf{Q}_2) = \mathbf{P} \times \mathbf{Q}_1 + \mathbf{P} \times \mathbf{Q}_2 \tag{3.5}$$

is valid. The answer is *yes*. Many readers are probably willing to accept without formal proof an answer which they intuitively feel is correct. However, since the entire structure of both vector algebra and statics depends upon the relation (3.5), we should take time out to derive it.

We can, without any loss of generality, assume that **P** is directed along the y axis (Fig. 3.9a). Denoting by **Q** the sum of **Q**$_1$ and **Q**$_2$, we drop perpendiculars from the tips of **Q**, **Q**$_1$, and **Q**$_2$ onto the zx plane, defining in this way the vectors **Q′**, **Q′**$_1$, and **Q′**$_2$. These vectors will be referred to, respectively, as the *projections* of **Q**, **Q**$_1$, and **Q**$_2$ on the zx plane. Recalling the property expressed by Eq. (3.3), we note that the left-hand member of Eq. (3.5) can be replaced by $\mathbf{P} \times \mathbf{Q}'$ and that, similarly, the vector products $\mathbf{P} \times \mathbf{Q}_1$ and $\mathbf{P} \times \mathbf{Q}_2$ can respectively be replaced by $\mathbf{P} \times \mathbf{Q}_1'$ and $\mathbf{P} \times \mathbf{Q}_2'$. Thus, the relation to be proved can be written in the form

$$\mathbf{P} \times \mathbf{Q}' = \mathbf{P} \times \mathbf{Q}_1' + \mathbf{P} \times \mathbf{Q}_2' \qquad (3.5')$$

We now observe that $\mathbf{P} \times \mathbf{Q}'$ can be obtained from $\mathbf{Q}'$ by multiplying this vector by the scalar P and rotating it counterclockwise through $90°$ in the zx plane (Fig. 3.9b); the other two vector

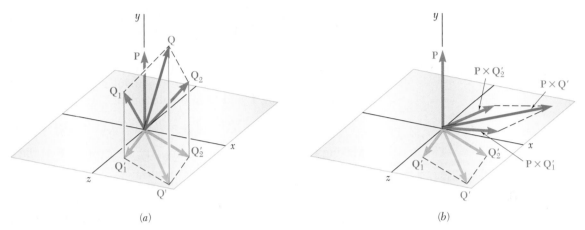

(a)   (b)

Fig. 3.9

products in (3.5$'$) can be obtained in the same manner from $\mathbf{Q}_1'$ and $\mathbf{Q}_2'$, respectively. Now, since the projection of a parallelogram onto an arbitrary plane is a parallelogram, the projection $\mathbf{Q}'$ of the sum $\mathbf{Q}$ of $\mathbf{Q}_1$ and $\mathbf{Q}_2$ must be the sum of the projections $\mathbf{Q}_1'$ and $\mathbf{Q}_2'$ of $\mathbf{Q}_1$ and $\mathbf{Q}_2$ on the same plane (Fig. 3.9a). This relation between the vectors $\mathbf{Q}'$, $\mathbf{Q}_1'$, and $\mathbf{Q}_2'$ will still hold after the three vectors have been multiplied by the scalar P and rotated through $90°$ (Fig. 3.9b). Thus, the relation (3.5$'$) has been proved, and we can now be sure that the distributive property holds for vector products.

A third property, the associative property, does not apply to vector products; we have in general

$$(\mathbf{P} \times \mathbf{Q}) \times \mathbf{S} \neq \mathbf{P} \times (\mathbf{Q} \times \mathbf{S}) \qquad (3.6)$$

3.5 VECTOR PRODUCTS EXPRESSED IN TERMS OF RECTANGULAR COMPONENTS

Let us now determine the vector product of any two of the unit vectors $\mathbf{i}, \mathbf{j}$, and $\mathbf{k}$, which were defined in Chap. 2. Consider first the product $\mathbf{i} \times \mathbf{j}$ (Fig. 3.10a). Since both vectors have a magnitude equal to 1 and since they are at a right angle to each other, their vector product will also be a unit vector. This unit vector must be $\mathbf{k}$, since the vectors $\mathbf{i}, \mathbf{j}$, and $\mathbf{k}$ are mutually perpendicular and form a right-handed triad. On the other hand, it follows from the right-hand rule given on page 77 that the product $\mathbf{j} \times \mathbf{i}$ will be equal to $-\mathbf{k}$ (Fig. 3.10b). Finally, it should be observed that the vector product

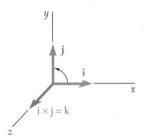

(a)

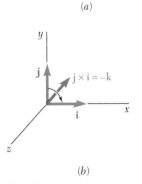

(b)

Fig. 3.10

of a unit vector with itself, such as $\mathbf{i} \times \mathbf{i}$, is equal to zero, since both vectors have the same direction. The vector products of the various possible pairs of unit vectors are

$$
\begin{array}{lll}
\mathbf{i} \times \mathbf{i} = \mathbf{0} & \mathbf{j} \times \mathbf{i} = -\mathbf{k} & \mathbf{k} \times \mathbf{i} = \mathbf{j} \\
\mathbf{i} \times \mathbf{j} = \mathbf{k} & \mathbf{j} \times \mathbf{j} = \mathbf{0} & \mathbf{k} \times \mathbf{j} = -\mathbf{i} \\
\mathbf{i} \times \mathbf{k} = -\mathbf{j} & \mathbf{j} \times \mathbf{k} = \mathbf{i} & \mathbf{k} \times \mathbf{k} = \mathbf{0}
\end{array}
\quad (3.7)
$$

Fig. 3.11

By arranging in a circle and in counterclockwise order the three letters representing the unit vectors (Fig. 3.11), we can simplify the determination of the sign of the vector product of two unit vectors: The product of two unit vectors will be positive if they follow each other in counterclockwise order and will be negative if they follow each other in clockwise order.

We can now easily express the vector product $\mathbf{V}$ of two given vectors $\mathbf{P}$ and $\mathbf{Q}$ in terms of the rectangular components of these vectors. Resolving $\mathbf{P}$ and $\mathbf{Q}$ into components, we first write

$$\mathbf{V} = \mathbf{P} \times \mathbf{Q} = (P_x\mathbf{i} + P_y\mathbf{j} + P_z\mathbf{k}) \times (Q_x\mathbf{i} + Q_y\mathbf{j} + Q_z\mathbf{k})$$

Making use of the distributive property, we express $\mathbf{V}$ as the sum of vector products, such as $P_x\mathbf{i} \times Q_y\mathbf{j}$. Observing that each of the expressions obtained is equal to the vector product of two unit vectors, such as $\mathbf{i} \times \mathbf{j}$, multiplied by the product of two scalars, such as P_xQ_y, and recalling the identities (3.7), we obtain, after factoring out $\mathbf{i}$, $\mathbf{j}$, and $\mathbf{k}$,

$$\mathbf{V} = (P_yQ_z - P_zQ_y)\mathbf{i} + (P_zQ_x - P_xQ_z)\mathbf{j} + (P_xQ_y - P_yQ_x)\mathbf{k} \quad (3.8)$$

The rectangular components of the vector product $\mathbf{V}$ are thus found to be

$$
\begin{aligned}
V_x &= P_yQ_z - P_zQ_y \\
V_y &= P_zQ_x - P_xQ_z \\
V_z &= P_xQ_y - P_yQ_x
\end{aligned}
\quad (3.9)
$$

Returning to Eq. (3.8), we observe that its right-hand member represents the expansion of a determinant. The vector product $\mathbf{V}$ can thus be expressed in the following form, which is more easily memorized:†

$$
\mathbf{V} = \begin{vmatrix} \mathbf{i} & \mathbf{j} & \mathbf{k} \\ P_x & P_y & P_z \\ Q_x & Q_y & Q_z \end{vmatrix}
\quad (3.10)
$$

---

†Any determinant consisting of three rows and three columns can be evaluated by repeating the first and second columns and forming products along each diagonal line. The sum of the products obtained along the red lines is then subtracted from the sum of the products obtained along the black lines.

3.6 MOMENT OF A FORCE ABOUT A POINT

Let us now consider a force **F** acting on a rigid body (Fig. 3.12*a*). As we know, the force **F** is represented by a vector which defines its magnitude and direction. However, the effect of the force on the rigid body depends also upon its point of application *A*. The position of *A* can be conveniently defined by the vector **r** which joins the fixed reference point *O* with *A*; this vector is known as the *position vector* of *A*.† The position vector **r** and the force **F** define the plane shown in Fig. 3.12*a*.

We will define the *moment of* **F** *about O* as the vector product of **r** and **F**:

$$\mathbf{M}_O = \mathbf{r} \times \mathbf{F} \tag{3.11}$$

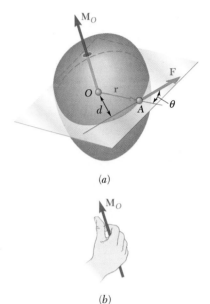

(a)

(b)

Fig. 3.12

According to the definition of the vector product given in Sec. 3.4, the moment $\mathbf{M}_O$ must be perpendicular to the plane containing *O* and the force **F**. The sense of $\mathbf{M}_O$ is defined by the sense of the rotation which will bring the vector **r** in line with the vector **F**; this rotation will be observed as *counterclockwise* by an observer located at the tip of $\mathbf{M}_O$. Another way of defining the sense of $\mathbf{M}_O$ is furnished by a variation of the right-hand rule: Close your right hand and hold it so that your fingers are curled in the sense of the rotation that **F** would impart to the rigid body about a fixed axis directed along the line of action of $\mathbf{M}_O$; your thumb will indicate the sense of the moment $\mathbf{M}_O$ (Fig. 3.12*b*).

Finally, denoting by θ the angle between the lines of action of the position vector **r** and the force **F**, we find that the magnitude of the moment of **F** about *O* is

$$M_O = rF \sin \theta = Fd \tag{3.12}$$

where *d* represents the perpendicular distance from *O* to the line of action of **F**. Since the tendency of a force **F** to make a rigid body rotate about a fixed axis perpendicular to the force depends upon the distance of **F** from that axis as well as upon the magnitude of **F**, we note that *the magnitude of* $\mathbf{M}_O$ *measures the tendency of the force* **F** *to make the rigid body rotate about a fixed axis directed along* $\mathbf{M}_O$.

In the SI system of units, where a force is expressed in newtons (N) and a distance in meters (m), the moment of a force is expressed in newton-meters (N · m). In the U.S. customary system of units, where a force is expressed in pounds and a distance in feet or inches, the moment of a force is expressed in lb · ft or lb · in.

We can observe that although the moment $\mathbf{M}_O$ of a force about a point depends upon the magnitude, the line of action, and the sense of the force, it does *not* depend upon the actual position of the point of application of the force along its line of action. Conversely, the moment $\mathbf{M}_O$ of a force **F** does not characterize the position of the point of application of **F**.

---

†We can easily verify that position vectors obey the law of vector addition and, thus, are truly vectors. Consider, for example, the position vectors **r** and **r**′ of *A* with respect to two reference points *O* and *O*′ and the position vector **s** of *O* with respect to *O*′ (Fig. 3.40*a*, Sec. 3.16). We verify that the position vector **r**′ = $\overrightarrow{O'A}$ can be obtained from the position vectors s = $\overrightarrow{O'O}$ and **r** = $\overrightarrow{OA}$ by applying the triangle rule for the addition of vectors.

However, as it will be seen presently, the moment $\mathbf{M}_O$ of a force $\mathbf{F}$ of given magnitude and direction *completely defines the line of action of* $\mathbf{F}$. Indeed, the line of action of $\mathbf{F}$ must lie in a plane through O perpendicular to the moment $\mathbf{M}_O$; its distance d from O must be equal to the quotient M_O/F of the magnitudes of $\mathbf{M}_O$ and $\mathbf{F}$; and the sense of $\mathbf{M}_O$ determines whether the line of action of $\mathbf{F}$ is to be drawn on one side or the other of the point O.

We recall from Sec. 3.3 that the principle of transmissibility states that two forces $\mathbf{F}$ and $\mathbf{F}'$ are equivalent (i.e., have the same effect on a rigid body) if they have the same magnitude, same direction, and same line of action. This principle can now be restated as follows: *Two forces $\mathbf{F}$ and $\mathbf{F}'$ are equivalent if, and only if, they are equal* (i.e., have the same magnitude and same direction) *and have equal moments about a given point O.* The necessary and sufficient conditions for two forces $\mathbf{F}$ and $\mathbf{F}'$ to be equivalent are thus

$$\mathbf{F} = \mathbf{F}' \qquad \text{and} \qquad \mathbf{M}_O = \mathbf{M}'_O \tag{3.13}$$

We should observe that it follows from this statement that if the relations (3.13) hold for a given point O, they will hold for any other point.

Problems Involving Only Two Dimensions.   Many applications deal with two-dimensional structures, i.e., structures which have length and breadth but only negligible depth and which are subjected to forces contained in the plane of the structure. Two-dimensional structures and the forces acting on them can be readily represented on a sheet of paper or on a blackboard. Their analysis is therefore considerably simpler than that of three-dimensional structures and forces.

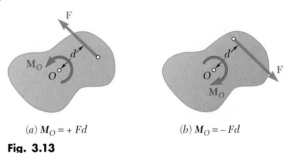

(a) $\mathbf{M}_O = + Fd$ (b) $\mathbf{M}_O = -Fd$

Fig. 3.13

Consider, for example, a rigid slab acted upon by a force $\mathbf{F}$ (Fig. 3.13). The moment of $\mathbf{F}$ about a point O chosen in the plane of the figure is represented by a vector $\mathbf{M}_O$ perpendicular to that plane and of magnitude Fd. In the case of Fig. 3.13a the vector $\mathbf{M}_O$ points *out of* the paper, while in the case of Fig. 3.13b it points *into* the paper. As we look at the figure, we observe in the first case that $\mathbf{F}$ tends to rotate the slab counterclockwise and in the second case that it tends to rotate the slab clockwise. Therefore, it is natural to refer to the sense of the moment of $\mathbf{F}$ about O in Fig. 3.13a as counterclockwise ↺, and in Fig. 3.13b as clockwise ↻.

Since the moment of a force $\mathbf{F}$ acting in the plane of the figure must be perpendicular to that plane, we need only specify the *magnitude* and the *sense* of the moment of $\mathbf{F}$ about O. This can be done by assigning to the magnitude M_O of the moment a positive or negative sign according to whether the vector $\mathbf{M}_O$ points out of or into the paper.

3.7 VARIGNON'S THEOREM

The distributive property of vector products can be used to determine the moment of the resultant of several *concurrent forces*. If several forces $\mathbf{F}_1$, $\mathbf{F}_2$, . . . are applied at the same point A (Fig. 3.14), and if we denote by $\mathbf{r}$ the position vector of A, it follows immediately from Eq. (3.5) of Sec. 3.4 that

$$\mathbf{r} \times (\mathbf{F}_1 + \mathbf{F}_2 + \cdots) = \mathbf{r} \times \mathbf{F}_1 + \mathbf{r} \times \mathbf{F}_2 + \cdots \quad (3.14)$$

In words, *the moment about a given point O of the resultant of several concurrent forces is equal to the sum of the moments of the various forces about the same point O.* This property, which was originally established by the French mathematician Varignon (1654–1722) long before the introduction of vector algebra, is known as *Varignon's theorem.*

The relation (3.14) makes it possible to replace the direct determination of the moment of a force $\mathbf{F}$ by the determination of the moments of two or more component forces. As you will see in the next section, $\mathbf{F}$ will generally be resolved into components parallel to the coordinate axes. However, it may be more expeditious in some instances to resolve $\mathbf{F}$ into components which are not parallel to the coordinate axes (see Sample Prob. 3.3).

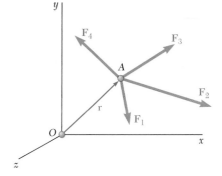

Fig. 3.14

3.8 RECTANGULAR COMPONENTS OF THE MOMENT OF A FORCE

In general, the determination of the moment of a force in space will be considerably simplified if the force and the position vector of its point of application are resolved into rectangular x, y, and z components. Consider, for example, the moment $\mathbf{M}_O$ about O of a force $\mathbf{F}$ whose components are F_x, F_y, and F_z and which is applied at a point A of coordinates x, y, and z (Fig. 3.15). Observing that the components of the position vector $\mathbf{r}$ are respectively equal to the coordinates x, y, and z of the point A, we write

$$\mathbf{r} = x\mathbf{i} + y\mathbf{j} + z\mathbf{k} \quad (3.15)$$
$$\mathbf{F} = F_x\mathbf{i} + F_y\mathbf{j} + F_z\mathbf{k} \quad (3.16)$$

Substituting for $\mathbf{r}$ and $\mathbf{F}$ from (3.15) and (3.16) into

$$\mathbf{M}_O = \mathbf{r} \times \mathbf{F} \quad (3.11)$$

and recalling the results obtained in Sec. 3.5, we write the moment $\mathbf{M}_O$ of $\mathbf{F}$ about O in the form

$$\mathbf{M}_O = M_x\mathbf{i} + M_y\mathbf{j} + M_z\mathbf{k} \quad (3.17)$$

where the components M_x, M_y, and M_z are defined by the relations

$$
\begin{aligned}
M_x &= yF_z - zF_y \\
M_y &= zF_x - xF_z \\
M_z &= xF_y - yF_x
\end{aligned}
\quad (3.18)
$$

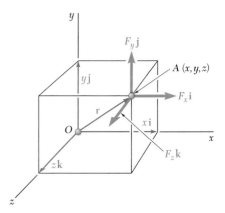

Fig. 3.15

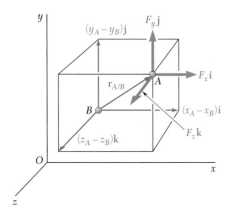

Fig. 3.16

As you will see in Sec. 3.11, the scalar components M_x, M_y, and M_z of the moment $\mathbf{M}_O$ measure the tendency of the force $\mathbf{F}$ to impart to a rigid body a motion of rotation about the x, y, and z axes, respectively. Substituting from (3.18) into (3.17), we can also write $\mathbf{M}_O$ in the form of the determinant

$$\mathbf{M}_O = \begin{vmatrix} \mathbf{i} & \mathbf{j} & \mathbf{k} \\ x & y & z \\ F_x & F_y & F_z \end{vmatrix} \tag{3.19}$$

To compute the moment $\mathbf{M}_B$ about an arbitrary point B of a force $\mathbf{F}$ applied at A (Fig. 3.16), we must replace the position vector $\mathbf{r}$ in Eq. (3.11) by a vector drawn from B to A. This vector is the *position vector of A relative to B* and will be denoted by $\mathbf{r}_{A/B}$. Observing that $\mathbf{r}_{A/B}$ can be obtained by subtracting $\mathbf{r}_B$ from $\mathbf{r}_A$, we write

$$\mathbf{M}_B = \mathbf{r}_{A/B} \times \mathbf{F} = (\mathbf{r}_A - \mathbf{r}_B) \times \mathbf{F} \tag{3.20}$$

or, using the determinant form,

$$\mathbf{M}_B = \begin{vmatrix} \mathbf{i} & \mathbf{j} & \mathbf{k} \\ x_{A/B} & y_{A/B} & z_{A/B} \\ F_x & F_y & F_z \end{vmatrix} \tag{3.21}$$

where $x_{A/B}$, $y_{A/B}$, and $z_{A/B}$ denote the components of the vector $\mathbf{r}_{A/B}$:

$$x_{A/B} = x_A - x_B \qquad y_{A/B} = y_A - y_B \qquad z_{A/B} = z_A - z_B$$

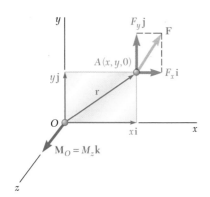

Fig. 3.17

In the case of *problems involving only two dimensions*, the force $\mathbf{F}$ can be assumed to lie in the xy plane (Fig. 3.17). Setting $z = 0$ and $F_z = 0$ in Eq. (3.19), we obtain

$$\mathbf{M}_O = (xF_y - yF_x)\mathbf{k}$$

We verify that the moment of $\mathbf{F}$ about O is perpendicular to the plane of the figure and that it is completely defined by the scalar

$$M_O = M_z = xF_y - yF_x \tag{3.22}$$

As noted earlier, a positive value for M_O indicates that the vector $\mathbf{M}_O$ points out of the paper (the force $\mathbf{F}$ tends to rotate the body counterclockwise about O), and a negative value indicates that the vector $\mathbf{M}_O$ points into the paper (the force $\mathbf{F}$ tends to rotate the body clockwise about O).

To compute the moment about $B(x_B, y_B)$ of a force lying in the xy plane and applied at $A(x_A, y_A)$ (Fig. 3.18), we set $z_{A/B} = 0$ and $F_z = 0$ in the relations (3.21) and note that the vector $\mathbf{M}_B$ is perpendicular to the xy plane and is defined in magnitude and sense by the scalar

$$M_B = (x_A - x_B)F_y - (y_A - y_B)F_x \tag{3.23}$$

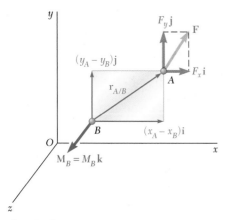

Fig. 3.18

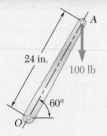

SAMPLE PROBLEM 3.1

A 100-lb vertical force is applied to the end of a lever which is attached to a shaft at O. Determine (a) the moment of the 100-lb force about O; (b) the horizontal force applied at A which creates the same moment about O; (c) the smallest force applied at A which creates the same moment about O; (d) how far from the shaft a 240-lb vertical force must act to create the same moment about O; (e) whether any one of the forces obtained in parts b, c, and d is equivalent to the original force.

SOLUTION

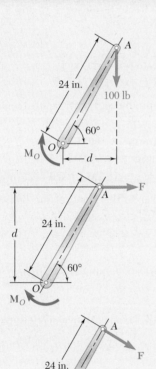

a. Moment about O.   The perpendicular distance from O to the line of action of the 100-lb force is

$$d = (24 \text{ in.}) \cos 60° = 12 \text{ in.}$$

The magnitude of the moment about O of the 100-lb force is

$$M_O = Fd = (100 \text{ lb})(12 \text{ in.}) = 1200 \text{ lb} \cdot \text{in.}$$

Since the force tends to rotate the lever clockwise about O, the moment will be represented by a vector $\mathbf{M}_O$ perpendicular to the plane of the figure and pointing *into* the paper. We express this fact by writing

$$\mathbf{M}_O = 1200 \text{ lb} \cdot \text{in.} \; \downarrow \quad \blacktriangleleft$$

b. Horizontal Force.   In this case, we have

$$d = (24 \text{ in.}) \sin 60° = 20.8 \text{ in.}$$

Since the moment about O must be 1200 lb · in., we write

$$M_O = Fd$$
$$1200 \text{ lb} \cdot \text{in.} = F(20.8 \text{ in.})$$
$$F = 57.7 \text{ lb} \qquad \mathbf{F} = 57.7 \text{ lb} \rightarrow \quad \blacktriangleleft$$

c. Smallest Force.   Since $M_O = Fd$, the smallest value of F occurs when d is maximum. We choose the force perpendicular to OA and note that $d = 24$ in.; thus

$$M_O = Fd$$
$$1200 \text{ lb} \cdot \text{in.} = F(24 \text{ in.})$$
$$F = 50 \text{ lb} \qquad \mathbf{F} = 50 \text{ lb} \; \diagdown 30° \quad \blacktriangleleft$$

d. 240-lb Vertical Force.   In this case $M_O = Fd$ yields

$$1200 \text{ lb} \cdot \text{in.} = (240 \text{ lb})d \qquad d = 5 \text{ in.}$$
but
$$OB \cos 60° = d \qquad\qquad OB = 10 \text{ in.} \quad \blacktriangleleft$$

e. None of the forces considered in parts b, c, and d is equivalent to the original 100-lb force. Although they have the same moment about O, they have different x and y components. In other words, although each force tends to rotate the shaft in the same manner, each causes the lever to pull on the shaft in a different way.

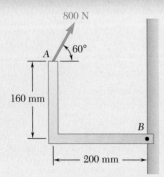

SAMPLE PROBLEM 3.2

A force of 800 N acts on a bracket as shown. Determine the moment of the force about B.

SOLUTION

The moment $\mathbf{M}_B$ of the force $\mathbf{F}$ about B is obtained by forming the vector product

$$\mathbf{M}_B = \mathbf{r}_{A/B} \times \mathbf{F}$$

where $\mathbf{r}_{A/B}$ is the vector drawn from B to A. Resolving $\mathbf{r}_{A/B}$ and $\mathbf{F}$ into rectangular components, we have

$$\mathbf{r}_{A/B} = -(0.2\ \text{m})\mathbf{i} + (0.16\ \text{m})\mathbf{j}$$
$$\mathbf{F} = (800\ \text{N}) \cos 60°\mathbf{i} + (800\ \text{N}) \sin 60°\mathbf{j}$$
$$= (400\ \text{N})\mathbf{i} + (693\ \text{N})\mathbf{j}$$

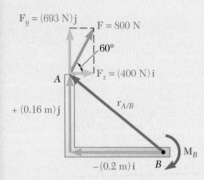

Recalling the relations (3.7) for the cross products of unit vectors (Sec. 3.5), we obtain

$$\mathbf{M}_B = \mathbf{r}_{A/B} \times \mathbf{F} = [-(0.2\ \text{m})\mathbf{i} + (0.16\ \text{m})\mathbf{j}] \times [(400\ \text{N})\mathbf{i} + (693\ \text{N})\mathbf{j}]$$
$$= -(138.6\ \text{N} \cdot \text{m})\mathbf{k} - (64.0\ \text{N} \cdot \text{m})\mathbf{k}$$
$$= -(202.6\ \text{N} \cdot \text{m})\mathbf{k} \qquad \mathbf{M}_B = 203\ \text{N} \cdot \text{m} \downarrow \blacktriangleleft$$

The moment $\mathbf{M}_B$ is a vector perpendicular to the plane of the figure and pointing *into* the paper.

SAMPLE PROBLEM 3.3

A 30-lb force acts on the end of the 3-ft lever as shown. Determine the moment of the force about O.

SOLUTION

The force is replaced by two components, one component $\mathbf{P}$ in the direction of OA and one component $\mathbf{Q}$ perpendicular to OA. Since O is on the line of action of $\mathbf{P}$, the moment of $\mathbf{P}$ about O is zero and the moment of the 30-lb force reduces to the moment of $\mathbf{Q}$, which is clockwise and, thus, is represented by a negative scalar.

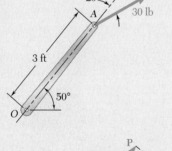

$$Q = (30\ \text{lb}) \sin 20° = 10.26\ \text{lb}$$
$$M_O = -Q(3\ \text{ft}) = -(10.26\ \text{lb})(3\ \text{ft}) = -30.8\ \text{lb} \cdot \text{ft}$$

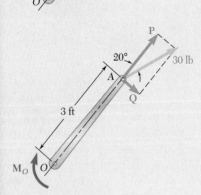

Since the value obtained for the scalar M_O is negative, the moment $\mathbf{M}_O$ points *into* the paper. We write

$$\mathbf{M}_O = 30.8\ \text{lb} \cdot \text{ft} \downarrow \blacktriangleleft$$

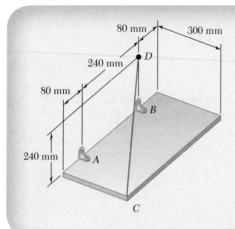

SAMPLE PROBLEM 3.4

A rectangular plate is supported by brackets at A and B and by a wire CD. Knowing that the tension in the wire is 200 N, determine the moment about A of the force exerted by the wire on point C.

SOLUTION

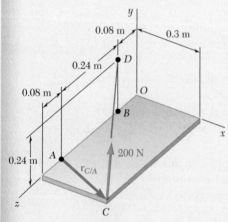

The moment $\mathbf{M}_A$ about A of the force $\mathbf{F}$ exerted by the wire on point C is obtained by forming the vector product

$$\mathbf{M}_A = \mathbf{r}_{C/A} \times \mathbf{F} \tag{1}$$

where $\mathbf{r}_{C/A}$ is the vector drawn from A to C,

$$\mathbf{r}_{C/A} = \overrightarrow{AC} = (0.3 \text{ m})\mathbf{i} + (0.08 \text{ m})\mathbf{k} \tag{2}$$

and $\mathbf{F}$ is the 200-N force directed along CD. Introducing the unit vector $\boldsymbol{\lambda} = \overrightarrow{CD}/CD$, we write

$$\mathbf{F} = F\boldsymbol{\lambda} = (200\,\text{N}) \frac{\overrightarrow{CD}}{CD} \tag{3}$$

Resolving the vector $\overrightarrow{CD}$ into rectangular components, we have

$$\overrightarrow{CD} = -(0.3 \text{ m})\mathbf{i} + (0.24 \text{ m})\mathbf{j} - (0.32 \text{ m})\mathbf{k} \qquad CD = 0.50 \text{ m}$$

Substituting into (3), we obtain

$$\mathbf{F} = \frac{200\,\text{N}}{0.50\,\text{m}} [-(0.3 \text{ m})\mathbf{i} + (0.24 \text{ m})\mathbf{j} - (0.32 \text{ m})\mathbf{k}]$$
$$= -(120 \text{ N})\mathbf{i} + (96 \text{ N})\mathbf{j} - (128 \text{ N})\mathbf{k} \tag{4}$$

Substituting for $\mathbf{r}_{C/A}$ and $\mathbf{F}$ from (2) and (4) into (1) and recalling the relations (3.7) of Sec. 3.5, we obtain

$$\mathbf{M}_A = \mathbf{r}_{C/A} \times \mathbf{F} = (0.3\mathbf{i} + 0.08\mathbf{k}) \times (-120\mathbf{i} + 96\mathbf{j} - 128\mathbf{k})$$
$$= (0.3)(96)\mathbf{k} + (0.3)(-128)(-\mathbf{j}) + (0.08)(-120)\mathbf{j} + (0.08)(96)(-\mathbf{i})$$
$$\mathbf{M}_A = -(7.68 \text{ N} \cdot \text{m})\mathbf{i} + (28.8 \text{ N} \cdot \text{m})\mathbf{j} + (28.8 \text{ N} \cdot \text{m})\mathbf{k} \blacktriangleleft$$

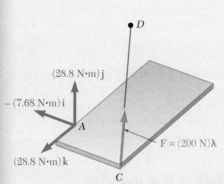

Alternative Solution. As indicated in Sec. 3.8, the moment $\mathbf{M}_A$ can be expressed in the form of a determinant:

$$\mathbf{M}_A = \begin{vmatrix} \mathbf{i} & \mathbf{j} & \mathbf{k} \\ x_C - x_A & y_C - y_A & z_C - z_A \\ F_x & F_y & F_z \end{vmatrix} = \begin{vmatrix} \mathbf{i} & \mathbf{j} & \mathbf{k} \\ 0.3 & 0 & 0.08 \\ -120 & 96 & -128 \end{vmatrix}$$

$$\mathbf{M}_A = -(7.68 \text{ N} \cdot \text{m})\mathbf{i} + (28.8 \text{ N} \cdot \text{m})\mathbf{j} + (28.8 \text{ N} \cdot \text{m})\mathbf{k} \blacktriangleleft$$

SOLVING PROBLEMS ON YOUR OWN

In this lesson we introduced the *vector product* or *cross product* of two vectors. In the following problems, you may want to use the vector product to compute the *moment of a force about a point* and also to determine the *perpendicular distance* from a point to a line.

We defined the moment of the force **F** about the point O of a rigid body as

$$\mathbf{M}_O = \mathbf{r} \times \mathbf{F} \tag{3.11}$$

where **r** is the position vector *from O to any point* on the line of action of **F**. Since the vector product is not commutative, it is absolutely necessary when computing such a product that you place the vectors in the proper order and that each vector have the correct sense. The moment $\mathbf{M}_O$ is important because its magnitude is a measure of the tendency of the force **F** to cause the rigid body to rotate about an axis directed along $\mathbf{M}_O$.

1. Computing the moment M_O of a force in two dimensions. You can use one of the following procedures:

a. Use Eq. (3.12), $M_O = Fd$, which expresses the magnitude of the moment as the product of the magnitude of **F** and the *perpendicular distance d* from O to the line of action of **F** (Sample Prob. 3.1).

b. Express **r** and **F** in component form and formally evaluate the vector product $\mathbf{M}_O = \mathbf{r} \times \mathbf{F}$ [Sample Prob. 3.2].

c. Resolve **F** into components respectively parallel and perpendicular to the position vector **r**. Only the perpendicular component contributes to the moment of **F** [Sample Prob. 3.3].

d. Use Eq. (3.22), $M_O = M_z = xF_y - yF_x$. When applying this method, the simplest approach is to treat the scalar components of **r** and **F** as positive and then to assign, by observation, the proper sign to the moment produced by each force component. For example, applying this method to solve Sample Prob. 3.2, we observe that both force components tend to produce a clockwise rotation about B. Therefore, the moment of each force about B should be represented by a negative scalar. We then have for the total moment

$$M_B = -(0.16\ \text{m})(400\ \text{N}) - (0.20\ \text{m})(693\ \text{N}) = -202.6\ \text{N} \cdot \text{m}$$

2. Computing the moment M_O of a force F in three dimensions. Following the method of Sample Prob. 3.4, the first step in the process is to select the most convenient (simplest) position vector **r**. You should next express **F** in terms of its rectangular components. The final step is to evaluate the vector product $\mathbf{r} \times \mathbf{F}$ to determine the moment. In most three-dimensional problems you will find it easiest to calculate the vector product using a determinant.

3. Determining the perpendicular distance d from a point A to a given line. First assume that a force **F** of known magnitude F lies along the given line. Next determine its moment about A by forming the vector product $\mathbf{M}_A = \mathbf{r} \times \mathbf{F}$, and calculate this product as indicated above. Then compute its magnitude M_A. Finally, substitute the values of F and M_A into the equation $M_A = Fd$ and solve for d.

PROBLEMS

3.1 A foot valve for a pneumatic system is hinged at B. Knowing that $\alpha = 28°$, determine the moment of the 16-N force about point B by resolving the force into horizontal and vertical components.

3.2 A foot valve for a pneumatic system is hinged at B. Knowing that $\alpha = 28°$, determine the moment of the 16-N force about point B by resolving the force into components along ABC and in a direction perpendicular to ABC.

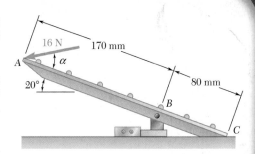

Fig. P3.1 and P3.2

3.3 A 300-N force is applied at A as shown. Determine (*a*) the moment of the 300-N force about D, (*b*) the smallest force applied at B that creates the same moment about D.

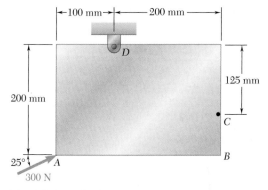

Fig. P3.3 and P3.4

3.4 A 300-N force is applied at A as shown. Determine (*a*) the moment of the 300-N force about D, (*b*) the magnitude and sense of the horizontal force applied at C that creates the same moment about D, (*c*) the smallest force applied at C that creates the same moment about D.

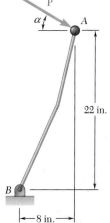

Fig. P3.5, P3.6, and P3.7

3.5 An 8-lb force $\mathbf{P}$ is applied to a shift lever. Determine the moment of $\mathbf{P}$ about B when α is equal to $25°$.

3.6 For the shift lever shown, determine the magnitude and the direction of the smallest force $\mathbf{P}$ that has a 210-lb · in. clockwise moment about B.

3.7 An 11-lb force $\mathbf{P}$ is applied to a shift lever. The moment of $\mathbf{P}$ about B is clockwise and has a magnitude of 250 lb · in. Determine the value of α.

3.8 It is known that a vertical force of 200 lb is required to remove the nail at C from the board. As the nail first starts moving, determine (*a*) the moment about B of the force exerted on the nail, (*b*) the magnitude of the force $\mathbf{P}$ that creates the same moment about B if $\alpha = 10°$, (*c*) the smallest force $\mathbf{P}$ that creates the same moment about B.

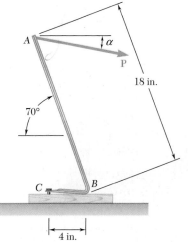

Fig. P3.8

3.9 A winch puller AB is used to straighten a fence post. Knowing that the tension in cable BC is 1040 N and length d is 1.90 m, determine the moment about D of the force exerted by the cable at C by resolving that force into horizontal and vertical components applied (a) at point C, (b) at point E.

3.10 It is known that a force with a moment of 960 N · m about D is required to straighten the fence post CD. If $d = 2.80$ m, determine the tension that must be developed in the cable of winch puller AB to create the required moment about point D.

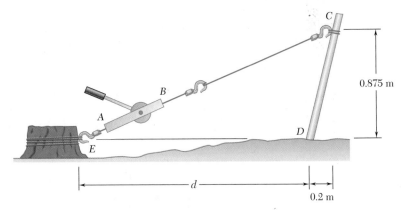

Fig. P3.9, P3.10, and *P3.11*

3.11 It is known that a force with a moment of 960 N · m about D is required to straighten the fence post CD. If the capacity of winch puller AB is 2400 N, determine the minimum value of distance d to create the specified moment about point D.

3.12 and 3.13 The tailgate of a car is supported by the hydraulic lift BC. If the lift exerts a 125-lb force directed along its centerline on the ball and socket at B, determine the moment of the force about A.

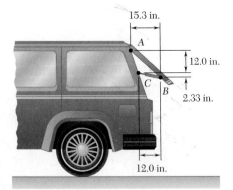

Fig. P3.12

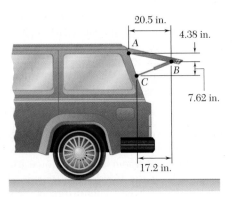

Fig. P3.13

3.14 A mechanic uses a piece of pipe AB as a lever when tightening an alternator belt. When he pushes down at A, a force of 485 N is exerted on the alternator at B. Determine the moment of that force about bolt C if its line of action passes through O.

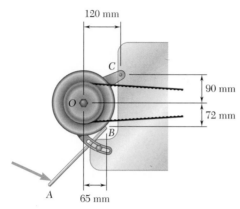

120 mm

90 mm

72 mm

65 mm

Fig. P3.14

3.15 Form the vector products $\mathbf{B} \times \mathbf{C}$ and $\mathbf{B}' \times \mathbf{C}$, where $B = B'$, and use the results obtained to prove the identity

$$\sin \alpha \cos \beta = \tfrac{1}{2} \sin (\alpha + \beta) + \tfrac{1}{2} \sin (\alpha - \beta).$$

3.16 A line passes through the points (20 m, 16 m) and (−1 m, −4 m). Determine the perpendicular distance d from the line to the origin O of the system of coordinates.

3.17 The vectors $\mathbf{P}$ and $\mathbf{Q}$ are two adjacent sides of a parallelogram. Determine the area of the parallelogram when (a) $\mathbf{P} = -7\mathbf{i} + 3\mathbf{j} - 3\mathbf{k}$ and $\mathbf{Q} = 2\mathbf{i} + 2\mathbf{j} + 5\mathbf{k}$, (b) $\mathbf{P} = 6\mathbf{i} - 5\mathbf{j} - 2\mathbf{k}$ and $\mathbf{Q} = -2\mathbf{i} + 5\mathbf{j} - \mathbf{k}$.

3.18 A plane contains the vectors $\mathbf{A}$ and $\mathbf{B}$. Determine the unit vector normal to the plane when $\mathbf{A}$ and $\mathbf{B}$ are equal to, respectively, (a) $\mathbf{i} + 2\mathbf{j} - 5\mathbf{k}$ and $4\mathbf{i} - 7\mathbf{j} - 5\mathbf{k}$, (b) $3\mathbf{i} - 3\mathbf{j} + 2\mathbf{k}$ and $-2\mathbf{i} + 6\mathbf{j} - 4\mathbf{k}$.

3.19 Determine the moment about the origin O of the force $\mathbf{F} = 4\mathbf{i} + 5\mathbf{j} - 3\mathbf{k}$ that acts at a point A. Assume that the position vector of A is (a) $\mathbf{r} = 2\mathbf{i} - 3\mathbf{j} + 4\mathbf{k}$, (b) $\mathbf{r} = 2\mathbf{i} + 2.5\mathbf{j} - 1.5\mathbf{k}$, (c) $\mathbf{r} = 2\mathbf{i} + 5\mathbf{j} + 6\mathbf{k}$.

3.20 Determine the moment about the origin O of the force $\mathbf{F} = -2\mathbf{i} + 3\mathbf{j} + 5\mathbf{k}$ that acts at a point A. Assume that the position vector of A is (a) $\mathbf{r} = \mathbf{i} + \mathbf{j} + \mathbf{k}$, (b) $\mathbf{r} = 2\mathbf{i} + 3\mathbf{j} - 5\mathbf{k}$, (c) $\mathbf{r} = -4\mathbf{i} + 6\mathbf{j} + 10\mathbf{k}$.

3.21 A 200-N force is applied as shown to the bracket ABC. Determine the moment of the force about A.

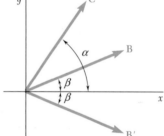

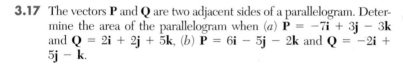

Fig. P3.15

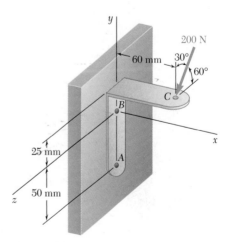

200 N

60 mm

30°

60°

25 mm

50 mm

Fig. P3.21

3.22 Before the trunk of a large tree is felled, cables *AB* and *BC* are attached as shown. Knowing that the tensions in cables *AB* and *BC* are 555 N and 660 N, respectively, determine the moment about *O* of the resultant force exerted on the tree by the cables at *B*.

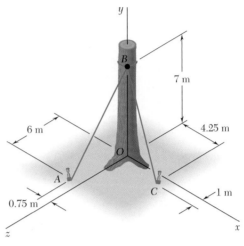

Fig. P3.22

3.23 The 6-m boom *AB* has a fixed end *A*. A steel cable is stretched from the free end *B* of the boom to a point *C* located on the vertical wall. If the tension in the cable is 2.5 kN, determine the moment about *A* of the force exerted by the cable at *B*.

3.24 A wooden board *AB*, which is used as a temporary prop to support a small roof, exerts at point *A* of the roof a 57-lb force directed along *BA*. Determine the moment about *C* of that force.

3.25 The ramp *ABCD* is supported by cables at corners *C* and *D*. The tension in each of the cables is 810 N. Determine the moment about *A* of the force exerted by (*a*) the cable at *D*, (*b*) the cable at *C*.

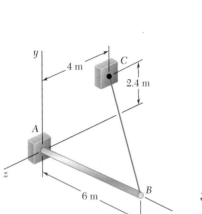

Fig. P3.23

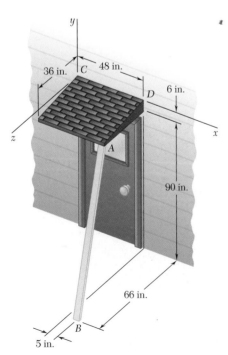

Fig. P3.24

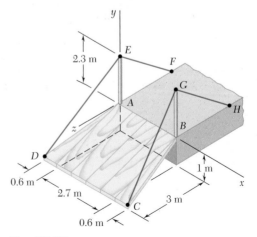

Fig. P3.25

3.26 A small boat hangs from two davits, one of which is shown in the figure. The tension in line *ABAD* is 82 lb. Determine the moment about *C* of the resultant force $\mathbf{R}_A$ exerted on the davit at *A*.

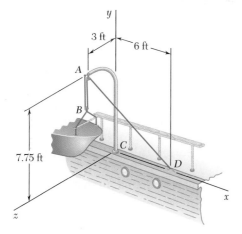

Fig. P3.26

3.27 In Prob. 3.22, determine the perpendicular distance from point *O* to cable *AB*.

3.28 In Prob. 3.22, determine the perpendicular distance from point *O* to cable *BC*.

3.29 In Prob. 3.24, determine the perpendicular distance from point *D* to a line drawn through points *A* and *B*.

3.30 In Prob. 3.24, determine the perpendicular distance from point *C* to a line drawn through points *A* and *B*.

3.31 In Prob. 3.25, determine the perpendicular distance from point *A* to portion *DE* of cable *DEF*.

3.32 In Prob. 3.25, determine the perpendicular distance from point *A* to a line drawn through points *C* and *G*.

3.33 In Prob. 3.26, determine the perpendicular distance from point *C* to portion *AD* of the line *ABAD*.

3.34 Determine the value of *a* that minimizes the perpendicular distance from point *C* to a section of pipeline that passes through points *A* and *B*.

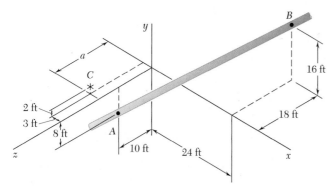

Fig. *P3.34*

3.9 SCALAR PRODUCT OF TWO VECTORS

Fig. 3.19

The *scalar product* of two vectors **P** and **Q** is defined as the product of the magnitudes of **P** and **Q** and of the cosine of the angle θ formed by **P** and **Q** (Fig. 3.19). The scalar product of **P** and **Q** is denoted by **P** · **Q**. We write therefore

$$\mathbf{P} \cdot \mathbf{Q} = PQ \cos \theta \qquad (3.24)$$

Note that the expression just defined is not a vector but a *scalar*, which explains the name *scalar product*; because of the notation used, **P** · **Q** is also referred to as the *dot product* of the vectors **P** and **Q**.

It follows from its very definition that the scalar product of two vectors is *commutative*, i.e., that

$$\mathbf{P} \cdot \mathbf{Q} = \mathbf{Q} \cdot \mathbf{P} \qquad (3.25)$$

To prove that the scalar product is also *distributive*, we must prove the relation

$$\mathbf{P} \cdot (\mathbf{Q}_1 + \mathbf{Q}_2) = \mathbf{P} \cdot \mathbf{Q}_1 + \mathbf{P} \cdot \mathbf{Q}_2 \qquad (3.26)$$

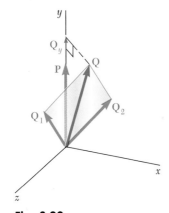

Fig. 3.20

We can, without any loss of generality, assume that **P** is directed along the y axis (Fig. 3.20). Denoting by **Q** the sum of $\mathbf{Q}_1$ and $\mathbf{Q}_2$ and by θ_y the angle **Q** forms with the y axis, we express the left-hand member of (3.26) as follows:

$$\mathbf{P} \cdot (\mathbf{Q}_1 + \mathbf{Q}_2) = \mathbf{P} \cdot \mathbf{Q} = PQ \cos \theta_y = PQ_y \qquad (3.27)$$

where Q_y is the y component of **Q**. We can, in a similar way, express the right-hand member of (3.26) as

$$\mathbf{P} \cdot \mathbf{Q}_1 + \mathbf{P} \cdot \mathbf{Q}_2 = P(Q_1)_y + P(Q_2)_y \qquad (3.28)$$

Since **Q** is the sum of $\mathbf{Q}_1$ and $\mathbf{Q}_2$, its y component must be equal to the sum of the y components of $\mathbf{Q}_1$ and $\mathbf{Q}_2$. Thus, the expressions obtained in (3.27) and (3.28) are equal, and the relation (3.26) has been proved.

As far as the third property—the associative property—is concerned, we note that this property cannot apply to scalar products. Indeed, $(\mathbf{P} \cdot \mathbf{Q}) \cdot \mathbf{S}$ has no meaning, since **P** · **Q** is not a vector but a scalar.

The scalar product of two vectors **P** and **Q** can be expressed in terms of their rectangular components. Resolving **P** and **Q** into components, we first write

$$\mathbf{P} \cdot \mathbf{Q} = (P_x\mathbf{i} + P_y\mathbf{j} + P_z\mathbf{k}) \cdot (Q_x\mathbf{i} + Q_y\mathbf{j} + Q_z\mathbf{k})$$

Making use of the distributive property, we express **P** · **Q** as the sum of scalar products, such as $P_x\mathbf{i} \cdot Q_x\mathbf{i}$ and $P_x\mathbf{i} \cdot Q_y\mathbf{j}$. However, from the definition of the scalar product it follows that the scalar products of the unit vectors are either zero or one.

$$\begin{matrix} \mathbf{i} \cdot \mathbf{i} = 1 & \mathbf{j} \cdot \mathbf{j} = 1 & \mathbf{k} \cdot \mathbf{k} = 1 \\ \mathbf{i} \cdot \mathbf{j} = 0 & \mathbf{j} \cdot \mathbf{k} = 0 & \mathbf{k} \cdot \mathbf{i} = 0 \end{matrix} \qquad (3.29)$$

Thus, the expression obtained for $\mathbf{P} \cdot \mathbf{Q}$ reduces to

$$\mathbf{P} \cdot \mathbf{Q} = P_x Q_x + P_y Q_y + P_z Q_z \qquad (3.30)$$

In the particular case when $\mathbf{P}$ and $\mathbf{Q}$ are equal, we note that

$$\mathbf{P} \cdot \mathbf{P} = P_x^2 + P_y^2 + P_z^2 = P^2 \qquad (3.31)$$

Applications

1. *Angle formed by two given vectors.* Let two vectors be given in terms of their components:

$$\mathbf{P} = P_x \mathbf{i} + P_y \mathbf{j} + P_z \mathbf{k}$$
$$\mathbf{Q} = Q_x \mathbf{i} + Q_y \mathbf{j} + Q_z \mathbf{k}$$

To determine the angle formed by the two vectors, we equate the expressions obtained in (3.24) and (3.30) for their scalar product and write

$$PQ \cos \theta = P_x Q_x + P_y Q_y + P_z Q_z$$

Solving for $\cos \theta$, we have

$$\cos \theta = \frac{P_x Q_x + P_y Q_y + P_z Q_z}{PQ} \qquad (3.32)$$

2. *Projection of a vector on a given axis.* Consider a vector $\mathbf{P}$ forming an angle θ with an axis, or directed line, OL (Fig. 3.21). The *projection of $\mathbf{P}$ on the axis OL* is defined as the scalar

$$P_{OL} = P \cos \theta \qquad (3.33)$$

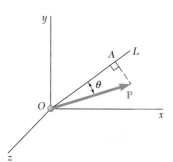

Fig. 3.21

We note that the projection P_{OL} is equal in absolute value to the length of the segment OA; it will be positive if OA has the same sense as the axis OL, that is, if θ is acute, and negative otherwise. If $\mathbf{P}$ and OL are at a right angle, the projection of $\mathbf{P}$ on OL is zero.

Consider now a vector $\mathbf{Q}$ directed along OL and of the same sense as OL (Fig. 3.22). The scalar product of $\mathbf{P}$ and $\mathbf{Q}$ can be expressed as

$$\mathbf{P} \cdot \mathbf{Q} = PQ \cos \theta = P_{OL} Q \qquad (3.34)$$

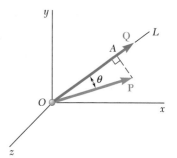

Fig. 3.22

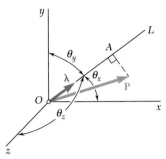

Fig. 3.23

from which it follows that

$$P_{OL} = \frac{\mathbf{P} \cdot \mathbf{Q}}{Q} = \frac{P_x Q_x + P_y Q_y + P_z Q_z}{Q} \qquad (3.35)$$

In the particular case when the vector selected along OL is the unit vector $\boldsymbol{\lambda}$ (Fig. 3.23), we write

$$P_{OL} = \mathbf{P} \cdot \boldsymbol{\lambda} \qquad (3.36)$$

Resolving $\mathbf{P}$ and $\boldsymbol{\lambda}$ into rectangular components and recalling from Sec. 2.12 that the components of $\boldsymbol{\lambda}$ along the coordinate axes are respectively equal to the direction cosines of OL, we express the projection of $\mathbf{P}$ on OL as

$$P_{OL} = P_x \cos \theta_x + P_y \cos \theta_y + P_z \cos \theta_z \qquad (3.37)$$

where θ_x, θ_y, and θ_z denote the angles that the axis OL forms with the coordinate axes.

3.10 MIXED TRIPLE PRODUCT OF THREE VECTORS

We define the *mixed triple product* of the three vectors $\mathbf{S}$, $\mathbf{P}$, and $\mathbf{Q}$ as the scalar expression

$$\mathbf{S} \cdot (\mathbf{P} \times \mathbf{Q}) \qquad (3.38)$$

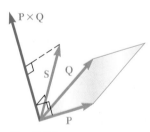

Fig. 3.24

obtained by forming the scalar product of $\mathbf{S}$ with the vector product of $\mathbf{P}$ and $\mathbf{Q}$.†

A simple geometrical interpretation can be given for the mixed triple product of $\mathbf{S}$, $\mathbf{P}$, and $\mathbf{Q}$ (Fig. 3.24). We first recall from Sec. 3.4 that the vector $\mathbf{P} \times \mathbf{Q}$ is perpendicular to the plane containing $\mathbf{P}$ and $\mathbf{Q}$ and that its magnitude is equal to the area of the parallelogram which has $\mathbf{P}$ and $\mathbf{Q}$ for sides. On the other hand, Eq. (3.34) indicates that the scalar product of $\mathbf{S}$ and $\mathbf{P} \times \mathbf{Q}$ can be obtained by multiplying the magnitude of $\mathbf{P} \times \mathbf{Q}$ (i.e., the area of the parallelogram defined by $\mathbf{P}$ and $\mathbf{Q}$) by the projection of $\mathbf{S}$ on the vector $\mathbf{P} \times \mathbf{Q}$ (i.e., by the projection of $\mathbf{S}$ on the normal to the plane containing the parallelogram). The mixed triple product is thus equal, in absolute value, to the volume of the parallelepiped having the vectors $\mathbf{S}$, $\mathbf{P}$, and $\mathbf{Q}$ for sides (Fig. 3.25). We note that the sign of the mixed triple product will be positive if $\mathbf{S}$, $\mathbf{P}$, and $\mathbf{Q}$ form a right-handed triad and negative if they form a left-handed triad [that is, $\mathbf{S} \cdot (\mathbf{P} \times \mathbf{Q})$ will be negative if the rotation which brings $\mathbf{P}$ into line with $\mathbf{Q}$ is observed as clockwise from the

Fig. 3.25

---

†Another kind of triple product will be introduced later (Chap. 15): the *vector triple product* $\mathbf{S} \times (\mathbf{P} \times \mathbf{Q})$.

tip of **S**]. The mixed triple product will be zero if **S**, **P**, and **Q** are coplanar.

Since the parallelepiped defined in the preceding paragraph is independent of the order in which the three vectors are taken, the six mixed triple products which can be formed with **S**, **P**, and **Q** will all have the same absolute value, although not the same sign. It is easily shown that

$$\begin{aligned}\mathbf{S}\cdot(\mathbf{P}\times\mathbf{Q}) &= \mathbf{P}\cdot(\mathbf{Q}\times\mathbf{S}) = \mathbf{Q}\cdot(\mathbf{S}\times\mathbf{P})\\ &= -\mathbf{S}\cdot(\mathbf{Q}\times\mathbf{P}) = -\mathbf{P}\cdot(\mathbf{S}\times\mathbf{Q}) = -\mathbf{Q}\cdot(\mathbf{P}\times\mathbf{S})\end{aligned} \tag{3.39}$$

Fig. 3.26

Arranging in a circle and in counterclockwise order the letters representing the three vectors (Fig. 3.26), we observe that the sign of the mixed triple product remains unchanged if the vectors are permuted in such a way that they are still read in counterclockwise order. Such a permutation is said to be a *circular permutation*. It also follows from Eq. (3.39) and from the commutative property of scalar products that the mixed triple product of **S**, **P**, and **Q** can be defined equally well as $\mathbf{S}\cdot(\mathbf{P}\times\mathbf{Q})$ or $(\mathbf{S}\times\mathbf{P})\cdot\mathbf{Q}$.

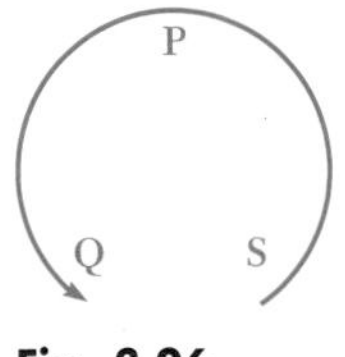

The mixed triple product of the vectors **S**, **P**, and **Q** can be expressed in terms of the rectangular components of these vectors. Denoting $\mathbf{P}\times\mathbf{Q}$ by **V** and using formula (3.30) to express the scalar product of **S** and **V**, we write

$$\mathbf{S}\cdot(\mathbf{P}\times\mathbf{Q}) = \mathbf{S}\cdot\mathbf{V} = S_xV_x + S_yV_y + S_zV_z$$

Substituting from the relations (3.9) for the components of **V**, we obtain

$$\begin{aligned}\mathbf{S}\cdot(\mathbf{P}\times\mathbf{Q}) = S_x(P_yQ_z - P_zQ_y) + S_y(P_zQ_x - P_xQ_z)\\ + S_z(P_xQ_y - P_yQ_x)\end{aligned} \tag{3.40}$$

This expression can be written in a more compact form if we observe that it represents the expansion of a determinant:

$$\mathbf{S}\cdot(\mathbf{P}\times\mathbf{Q}) = \begin{vmatrix} S_x & S_y & S_z \\ P_x & P_y & P_z \\ Q_x & Q_y & Q_z \end{vmatrix} \tag{3.41}$$

By applying the rules governing the permutation of rows in a determinant, we could easily verify the relations (3.39) which were derived earlier from geometrical considerations.

Fig. 3.27

3.11 MOMENT OF A FORCE ABOUT A GIVEN AXIS

Now that we have further increased our knowledge of vector algebra, we can introduce a new concept, the concept of *moment of a force about an axis*. Consider again a force **F** acting on a rigid body and the moment $\mathbf{M}_O$ of that force about O (Fig. 3.27). Let OL be

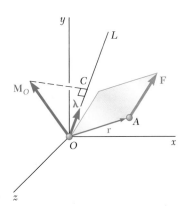

an axis through O; *we define the moment M_{OL} of $\mathbf{F}$ about OL as the projection OC of the moment $\mathbf{M}_O$ onto the axis OL.* Denoting by $\boldsymbol{\lambda}$ the unit vector along OL and recalling from Secs. 3.9 and 3.6, respectively, the expressions (3.36) and (3.11) obtained for the projection of a vector on a given axis and for the moment $\mathbf{M}_O$ of a force $\mathbf{F}$, we write

$$M_{OL} = \boldsymbol{\lambda} \cdot \mathbf{M}_O = \boldsymbol{\lambda} \cdot (\mathbf{r} \times \mathbf{F}) \tag{3.42}$$

which shows that the moment M_{OL} of $\mathbf{F}$ about the axis OL is the scalar obtained by forming the mixed triple product of $\boldsymbol{\lambda}$, $\mathbf{r}$, and $\mathbf{F}$. Expressing M_{OL} in the form of a determinant, we write

$$M_{OL} = \begin{vmatrix} \lambda_x & \lambda_y & \lambda_z \\ x & y & z \\ F_x & F_y & F_z \end{vmatrix} \tag{3.43}$$

where $\lambda x,\ \lambda y,\ \lambda z$ = direction cosines of axis OL
$\qquad\quad\ x,\ y,\ z$ = coordinates of point of application of $\mathbf{F}$
$\qquad F_x,\ F_y,\ F_z$ = components of force $\mathbf{F}$

The physical significance of the moment M_{OL} of a force $\mathbf{F}$ about a fixed axis OL becomes more apparent if we resolve $\mathbf{F}$ into two rectangular components $\mathbf{F}_1$ and $\mathbf{F}_2$, with $\mathbf{F}_1$ parallel to OL and $\mathbf{F}_2$ lying in a plane P perpendicular to OL (Fig. 3.28). Resolving $\mathbf{r}$ similarly into two components $\mathbf{r}_1$ and $\mathbf{r}_2$ and substituting for $\mathbf{F}$ and $\mathbf{r}$ into (3.42), we write

$$\begin{aligned} M_{OL} &= \boldsymbol{\lambda} \cdot [(\mathbf{r}_1 + \mathbf{r}_2) \times (\mathbf{F}_1 + \mathbf{F}_2)] \\ &= \boldsymbol{\lambda} \cdot (\mathbf{r}_1 \times \mathbf{F}_1) + \boldsymbol{\lambda} \cdot (\mathbf{r}_1 \times \mathbf{F}_2) + \boldsymbol{\lambda} \cdot (\mathbf{r}_2 \times \mathbf{F}_1) + \boldsymbol{\lambda} \cdot (\mathbf{r}_2 \times \mathbf{F}_2) \end{aligned}$$

Noting that all of the mixed triple products except the last one are equal to zero, since they involve vectors which are coplanar when drawn from a common origin (Sec. 3.10), we have

$$M_{OL} = \boldsymbol{\lambda} \cdot (\mathbf{r}_2 \times \mathbf{F}_2) \tag{3.44}$$

The vector product $\mathbf{r}_2 \times \mathbf{F}_2$ is perpendicular to the plane P and represents the moment of the component $\mathbf{F}_2$ of $\mathbf{F}$ about the point Q where OL intersects P. Therefore, the scalar M_{OL}, which will be positive if $\mathbf{r}_2 \times \mathbf{F}_2$ and OL have the same sense and negative otherwise, measures the tendency of $\mathbf{F}_2$ to make the rigid body rotate about the fixed axis OL. Since the other component $\mathbf{F}_1$ of $\mathbf{F}$ does not tend to make the body rotate about OL, we conclude that *the moment M_{OL} of $\mathbf{F}$ about OL measures the tendency of the force $\mathbf{F}$ to impart to the rigid body a motion of rotation about the fixed axis OL.*

It follows from the definition of the moment of a force about an axis that the moment of $\mathbf{F}$ about a coordinate axis is equal to the component of $\mathbf{M}_O$ along that axis. Substituting successively each

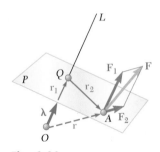

Fig. 3.28

of the unit vectors **i**, **j**, and **k** for $\boldsymbol{\lambda}$ in (3.42), we observe that the expressions thus obtained for the *moments of* **F** *about the coordinate axes* are respectively equal to the expressions obtained in Sec. 3.8 for the components of the moment $\mathbf{M}_O$ of **F** about O:

$$
\begin{aligned}
M_x &= yF_z - zF_y \\
M_y &= zF_x - xF_z \\
M_z &= xF_y - yF_x
\end{aligned}
\tag{3.18}
$$

We observe that just as the components F_x, F_y, and F_z of a force **F** acting on a rigid body measure, respectively, the tendency of **F** to move the rigid body in the x, y, and z directions, the moments M_x, M_y, and M_z of **F** about the coordinate axes measure the tendency of **F** to impart to the rigid body a motion of rotation about the x, y, and z axes, respectively.

More generally, the moment of a force **F** applied at A about an axis which does not pass through the origin is obtained by choosing an arbitrary point B on the axis (Fig. 3.29) and determining the projection on the axis BL of the moment $\mathbf{M}_B$ of **F** about B. We write

$$
M_{BL} = \boldsymbol{\lambda} \cdot \mathbf{M}_B = \boldsymbol{\lambda} \cdot (\mathbf{r}_{A/B} \times \mathbf{F})
\tag{3.45}
$$

where $\mathbf{r}_{A/B} = \mathbf{r}_A - \mathbf{r}_B$ represents the vector drawn from B to A. Expressing M_{BL} in the form of a determinant, we have

$$
M_{BL} = \begin{vmatrix}
\lambda_x & \lambda_y & \lambda_z \\
x_{A/B} & y_{A/B} & z_{A/B} \\
F_x & F_y & F_z
\end{vmatrix}
\tag{3.46}
$$

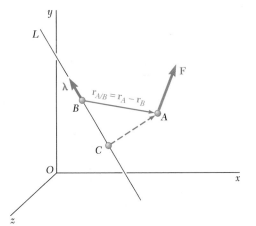

Fig. 3.29

where $\lambda_x, \lambda_y, \lambda_z$ = direction cosines of axis BL
$\qquad x_{A/B} = x_A - x_B \qquad y_{A/B} = y_A - y_B \qquad z_{A/B} = z_A - z_B$
$\quad F_x, F_y, F_z$ = components of force **F**

It should be noted that the result obtained is independent of the choice of the point B on the given axis. Indeed, denoting by M_{CL} the result obtained with a different point C, we have

$$
\begin{aligned}
M_{CL} &= \boldsymbol{\lambda} \cdot [(\mathbf{r}_A - \mathbf{r}_C) \times \mathbf{F}] \\
&= \boldsymbol{\lambda} \cdot [(\mathbf{r}_A - \mathbf{r}_B) \times \mathbf{F}] + \boldsymbol{\lambda} \cdot [(\mathbf{r}_B - \mathbf{r}_C) \times \mathbf{F}]
\end{aligned}
$$

But, since the vectors $\boldsymbol{\lambda}$ and $\mathbf{r}_B - \mathbf{r}_C$ lie in the same line, the volume of the parallelepiped having the vectors $\boldsymbol{\lambda}$, $\mathbf{r}_B - \mathbf{r}_C$, and **F** for sides is zero, as is the mixed triple product of these three vectors (Sec. 3.10). The expression obtained for M_{CL} thus reduces to its first term, which is the expression used earlier to define M_{BL}. In addition, it follows from Sec. 3.6 that, when computing the moment of **F** about the given axis, A can be any point on the line of action of **F**.

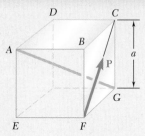

SAMPLE PROBLEM 3.5

A cube of side a is acted upon by a force $\mathbf{P}$ as shown. Determine the moment of $\mathbf{P}$ (a) about A, (b) about the edge AB, (c) about the diagonal AG of the cube, (d). Using the result of part c, determine the perpendicular distance between AG and FC.

SOLUTION

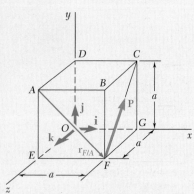

a. Moment about A. Choosing x, y, and z axes as shown, we resolve into rectangular components the force $\mathbf{P}$ and the vector $\mathbf{r}_{F/A} = \overrightarrow{AF}$ drawn from A to the point of application F of $\mathbf{P}$.

$$\mathbf{r}_{F/A} = a\mathbf{i} - a\mathbf{j} = a(\mathbf{i} - \mathbf{j})$$
$$\mathbf{P} = (P/\sqrt{2})\mathbf{j} - (P/\sqrt{2})\mathbf{k} = (P/\sqrt{2})(\mathbf{j} - \mathbf{k})$$

The moment of $\mathbf{P}$ about A is

$$\mathbf{M}_A = \mathbf{r}_{F/A} \times \mathbf{P} = a(\mathbf{i} - \mathbf{j}) \times (P/\sqrt{2})(\mathbf{j} - \mathbf{k})$$
$$\mathbf{M}_A = (aP/\sqrt{2})(\mathbf{i} + \mathbf{j} + \mathbf{k}) \quad \blacktriangleleft$$

b. Moment about AB. Projecting $\mathbf{M}_A$ on AB, we write

$$M_{AB} = \mathbf{i} \cdot \mathbf{M}_A = \mathbf{i} \cdot (aP/\sqrt{2})(\mathbf{i} + \mathbf{j} + \mathbf{k})$$
$$M_{AB} = aP/\sqrt{2} \quad \blacktriangleleft$$

We verify that, since AB is parallel to the x axis, M_{AB} is also the x component of the moment $\mathbf{M}_A$.

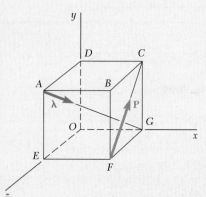

c. Moment about Diagonal AG. The moment of $\mathbf{P}$ about AG is obtained by projecting $\mathbf{M}_A$ on AG. Denoting by $\boldsymbol{\lambda}$ the unit vector along AG, we have

$$\boldsymbol{\lambda} = \frac{\overrightarrow{AG}}{AG} = \frac{a\mathbf{i} - a\mathbf{j} - a\mathbf{k}}{a\sqrt{3}} = (1/\sqrt{3})(\mathbf{i} - \mathbf{j} - \mathbf{k})$$
$$M_{AG} = \boldsymbol{\lambda} \cdot \mathbf{M}_A = (1/\sqrt{3})(\mathbf{i} - \mathbf{j} - \mathbf{k}) \cdot (aP/\sqrt{2})(\mathbf{i} + \mathbf{j} + \mathbf{k})$$
$$M_{AG} = (aP/\sqrt{6})(1 - 1 - 1) \quad M_{AG} = -aP/\sqrt{6} \quad \blacktriangleleft$$

Alternative Method. The moment of $\mathbf{P}$ about AG can also be expressed in the form of a determinant:

$$M_{AG} = \begin{vmatrix} \lambda_x & \lambda_y & \lambda_z \\ x_{F/A} & y_{F/A} & z_{F/A} \\ F_x & F_y & F_z \end{vmatrix} = \begin{vmatrix} 1/\sqrt{3} & -1/\sqrt{3} & -1/\sqrt{3} \\ a & -a & 0 \\ 0 & P/\sqrt{2} & -P/\sqrt{2} \end{vmatrix} = -aP/\sqrt{6}$$

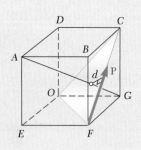

d. Perpendicular Distance between AG and FC. We first observe that $\mathbf{P}$ is perpendicular to the diagonal AG. This can be checked by forming the scalar product $\mathbf{P} \cdot \boldsymbol{\lambda}$ and verifying that it is zero:

$$\mathbf{P} \cdot \boldsymbol{\lambda} = (P/\sqrt{2})(\mathbf{j} - \mathbf{k}) \cdot (1/\sqrt{3})(\mathbf{i} - \mathbf{j} - \mathbf{k}) = (P\sqrt{6})(0 - 1 + 1) = 0$$

The moment M_{AG} can then be expressed as $-Pd$, where d is the perpendicular distance from AG to FC. (The negative sign is used since the rotation imparted to the cube by $\mathbf{P}$ appears as clockwise to an observer at G.) Recalling the value found for M_{AG} in part c,

$$M_{AG} = -Pd = -aP/\sqrt{6} \qquad d = a/\sqrt{6} \quad \blacktriangleleft$$

SOLVING PROBLEMS ON YOUR OWN

In the problems for this lesson you will apply the *scalar product* or *dot product* of two vectors to determine the *angle formed by two given vectors* and the *projection of a force on a given axis*. You will also use the *mixed triple product* of three vectors to find the *moment of a force about a given axis* and the *perpendicular distance between two lines*.

1. Calculating the angle formed by two given vectors. First express the vectors in terms of their components and determine the magnitudes of the two vectors. The cosine of the desired angle is then obtained by dividing the scalar product of the two vectors by the product of their magnitudes [Eq. (3.32)].

2. Computing the projection of a vector P on a given axis OL. In general, begin by expressing $\mathbf{P}$ and the unit vector $\boldsymbol{\lambda}$, that defines the direction of the axis, in component form. Take care that $\boldsymbol{\lambda}$ has the correct sense (that is, $\boldsymbol{\lambda}$ is directed from O to L). The required projection is then equal to the scalar product $\mathbf{P} \cdot \boldsymbol{\lambda}$. However, if you know the angle θ formed by $\mathbf{P}$ and $\boldsymbol{\lambda}$, the projection is also given by $P \cos \theta$.

3. Determining the moment M_{OL} of a force about a given axis OL. We defined M_{OL} as

$$M_{OL} = \boldsymbol{\lambda} \cdot \mathbf{M}_O = \boldsymbol{\lambda} \cdot (\mathbf{r} \times \mathbf{F}) \tag{3.42}$$

where $\boldsymbol{\lambda}$ is the unit vector along OL and $\mathbf{r}$ is a position vector *from any point* on the line OL *to any point* on the line of action of $\mathbf{F}$. As was the case for the moment of a force about a point, choosing the most convenient position vector will simplify your calculations. Also, recall the warning of the previous lesson: the vectors $\mathbf{r}$ and $\mathbf{F}$ must have the correct sense, and they must be placed in the proper order. The procedure you should follow when computing the moment of a force about an axis is illustrated in part c of Sample Prob. 3.5. The two essential steps in this procedure are to first express $\boldsymbol{\lambda}$, $\mathbf{r}$, and $\mathbf{F}$ in terms of their rectangular components and to then evaluate the mixed triple product $\boldsymbol{\lambda} \cdot (\mathbf{r} \times \mathbf{F})$ to determine the moment about the axis. In most three-dimensional problems the most convenient way to compute the mixed triple product is by using a determinant.

As noted in the text, when $\boldsymbol{\lambda}$ is directed along one of the coordinate axes, M_{OL} is equal to the scalar component of $\mathbf{M}_O$ along that axis.

(continued)

4. Determining the perpendicular distance between two lines. You should remember that it is the perpendicular component $\mathbf{F}_2$ of the force $\mathbf{F}$ that tends to make a body rotate about a given axis OL (Fig. 3.28). It then follows that

$$M_{OL} = F_2 d$$

where M_{OL} is the moment of $\mathbf{F}$ about axis OL and d is the perpendicular distance between OL and the line of action of $\mathbf{F}$. This last equation gives us a simple technique for determining d. First assume that a force $\mathbf{F}$ of known magnitude F lies along one of the given lines and that the unit vector $\boldsymbol{\lambda}$ lies along the other line. Next compute the moment M_{OL} of the force $\mathbf{F}$ about the second line using the method discussed above. The magnitude of the parallel component, F_1, of $\mathbf{F}$ is obtained using the scalar product:

$$F_1 = \mathbf{F} \cdot \boldsymbol{\lambda}$$

The value of F_2 is then determined from

$$F_2 = \sqrt{F^2 - F_1^2}$$

Finally, substitute the values of M_{OL} and F_2 into the equation $M_{OL} = F_2 d$ and solve for d.

You should now realize that the calculation of the perpendicular distance in part d of Sample Prob. 3.5 was simplified by $\mathbf{P}$ being perpendicular to the diagonal AG. In general, the two given lines will not be perpendicular, so that the technique just outlined will have to be used when determining the perpendicular distance between them.

PROBLEMS

3.35 Given the vectors $\mathbf{P} = 3\mathbf{i} - \mathbf{j} + 2\mathbf{k}$, $\mathbf{Q} = 4\mathbf{i} + 5\mathbf{j} - 3\mathbf{k}$, and $\mathbf{S} = -2\mathbf{i} + 3\mathbf{j} - \mathbf{k}$, compute the scalar products $\mathbf{P} \cdot \mathbf{Q}$, $\mathbf{P} \cdot \mathbf{S}$, and $\mathbf{Q} \cdot \mathbf{S}$.

3.36 Form the scalar products $\mathbf{B} \cdot \mathbf{C}$ and $\mathbf{B'} \cdot \mathbf{C}$, where $B = B'$, and use the results obtained to prove the identity

$$\cos \alpha \cos \beta = \tfrac{1}{2}\cos(\alpha + \beta) + \tfrac{1}{2}\cos(\alpha - \beta).$$

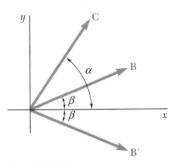

Fig. P3.36

3.37 Section AB of a pipeline lies in the yz plane and forms an angle of 37° with the z axis. Branch lines CD and EF join AB as shown. Determine the angle formed by pipes AB and CD.

3.38 Section AB of a pipeline lies in the yz plane and forms an angle of 37° with the z axis. Branch lines CD and EF join AB as shown. Determine the angle formed by pipes AB and EF.

3.39 Consider the volleyball net shown. Determine the angle formed by guy wires AB and AC.

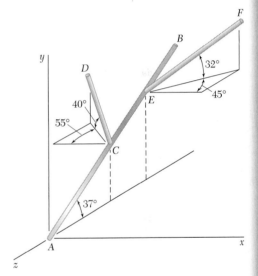

Fig. P3.37 and P3.38

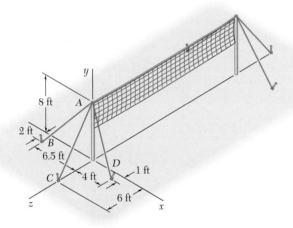

Fig. P3.39 and P3.40

3.40 Consider the volleyball net shown. Determine the angle formed by guy wires AC and AD.

3.41 Knowing that the tension in cable AC is 1260 N, determine (a) the angle between cable AC and the boom AB, (b) the projection on AB of the force exerted by cable AC at point A.

3.42 Knowing that the tension in cable AD is 405 N, determine (a) the angle between cable AD and the boom AB, (b) the projection on AB of the force exerted by cable AD at point A.

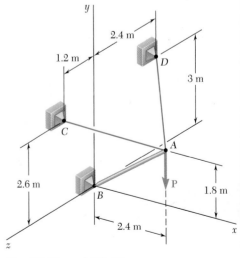

Fig. P3.41 and P3.42

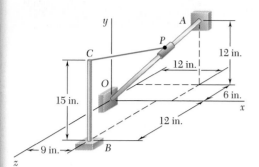

Fig. P3.43 and P3.44

3.43 Slider P can move along rod OA. An elastic cord PC is attached to the slider and to the vertical member BC. Knowing that the distance from O to P is 6 in. and that the tension in the cord is 3 lb, determine (*a*) the angle between the elastic cord and the rod OA, (*b*) the projection on OA of the force exerted by cord PC at point P.

3.44 Slider P can move along rod OA. An elastic cord PC is attached to the slider and to the vertical member BC. Determine the distance from O to P for which cord PC and rod OA are perpendicular.

3.45 Determine the volume of the parallelepiped of Fig. 3.25 when (*a*) $\mathbf{P} = 4\mathbf{i} - 3\mathbf{j} + 2\mathbf{k}$, $\mathbf{Q} = -2\mathbf{i} - 5\mathbf{j} + \mathbf{k}$, and $\mathbf{S} = 7\mathbf{i} + \mathbf{j} - \mathbf{k}$, (*b*) $\mathbf{P} = 5\mathbf{i} - \mathbf{j} + 6\mathbf{k}$, $\mathbf{Q} = 2\mathbf{i} + 3\mathbf{j} + \mathbf{k}$, and $\mathbf{S} = -3\mathbf{i} - 2\mathbf{j} + 4\mathbf{k}$.

3.46 Given the vectors $\mathbf{P} = 4\mathbf{i} - 2\mathbf{j} + 3\mathbf{k}$, $\mathbf{Q} = 2\mathbf{i} + 4\mathbf{j} - 5\mathbf{k}$, and $\mathbf{S} = S_x\mathbf{i} - \mathbf{j} + 2\mathbf{k}$, determine the value of S_x for which the three vectors are coplanar.

3.47 The 0.61×1.00-m lid $ABCD$ of a storage bin is hinged along side AB and is held open by looping cord DEC over a frictionless hook at E. If the tension in the cord is 66 N, determine the moment about each of the coordinate axes of the force exerted by the cord at D.

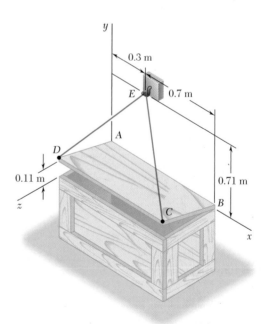

Fig. P3.47 and P3.48

3.48 The 0.61×1.00-m lid $ABCD$ of a storage bin is hinged along side AB and is held open by looping cord DEC over a frictionless hook at E. If the tension in the cord is 66 N, determine the moment about each of the coordinate axes of the force exerted by the cord at C.

3.49 To lift a heavy crate, a man uses a block and tackle attached to the bottom of an I-beam at hook *B*. Knowing that the moments about the *y* and the *z* axes of the force exerted at *B* by portion *AB* of the rope are, respectively, 120 N · m and −460 N · m, determine the distance *a*.

3.50 To lift a heavy crate, a man uses a block and tackle attached to the bottom of an I-beam at hook *B*. Knowing that the man applies a 195-N force to end A of the rope and that the moment of that force about the *y* axis is 132 N · m, determine the distance *a*.

3.51 A small boat hangs from two davits, one of which is shown in the figure. It is known that the moment about the *z* axis of the resultant force $\mathbf{R}_A$ exerted on the davit at *A* must not exceed 279 lb · ft in absolute value. Determine the largest allowable tension in line *ABAD* when *x* = 6 ft.

3.52 For the davit of Prob. 3.51, determine the largest allowable distance *x* when the tension in line *ABAD* is 60 lb.

3.53 To loosen a frozen valve, a force **F** of magnitude 70 lb is applied to the handle of the valve. Knowing that $\theta = 25°$, $M_x = -61$ lb · ft, and $M_z = -43$ lb · ft, determine ϕ and *d*.

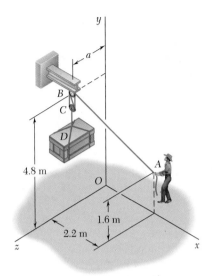

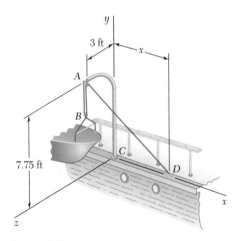

Fig. P3.49 and P3.50

Fig. P3.51

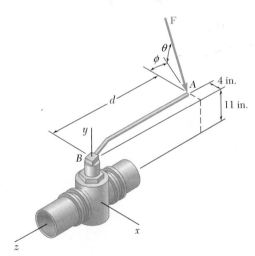

Fig. P3.53 and P3.54

3.54 When a force **F** is applied to the handle of the valve shown, its moments about the *x* and *z* axes are, respectively, $M_x = -77$ lb · ft and $M_z = -81$ lb · ft. For *d* = 27 in., determine the moment M_y of **F** about the *y* axis.

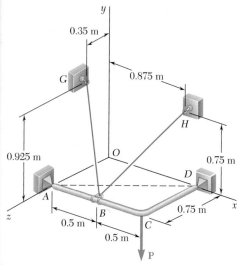

Fig. P3.55

3.55 The frame *ACD* is hinged at *A* and *D* and is supported by a cable that passes through a ring at *B* and is attached to hooks at *G* and *H*. Knowing that the tension in the cable is 450 N, determine the moment about the diagonal *AD* of the force exerted on the frame by portion *BH* of the cable.

3.56 In Prob. 3.55, determine the moment about the diagonal *AD* of the force exerted on the frame by portion *BG* of the cable.

3.57 The triangular plate *ABC* is supported by ball-and-socket joints at *B* and *D* and is held in the position shown by cables *AE* and *CF*. If the force exerted by cable *AE* at *A* is 55 N, determine the moment of that force about the line joining points *D* and *B*.

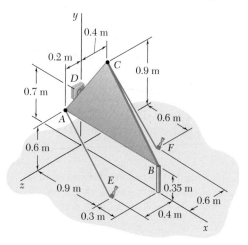

Fig. P3.57 and P3.58

3.58 The triangular plate *ABC* is supported by ball-and-socket joints at *B* and *D* and is held in the position shown by cables *AE* and *CF*. If the force exerted by cable *CF* at *C* is 33 N, determine the moment of that force about the line joining points *D* and *B*.

3.59 A regular tetrahedron has six edges of length *a*. A force **P** is directed as shown along edge BC. Determine the moment of **P** about edge *OA*.

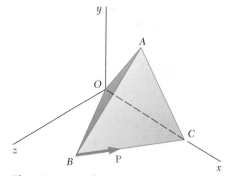

Fig. P3.59 and P3.60

3.60 A regular tetrahedron has six edges of length *a*. (*a*) Show that two opposite edges, such as *OA* and *BC*, are perpendicular to each other. (*b*) Use this property and the result obtained in Prob. 3.59 to determine the perpendicular distance between edges *OA* and *BC*.

3.61 A sign erected on uneven ground is guyed by cables *EF* and *EG*. If the force exerted by cable *EF* at *E* is 46 lb, determine the moment of that force about the line joining points *A* and *D*.

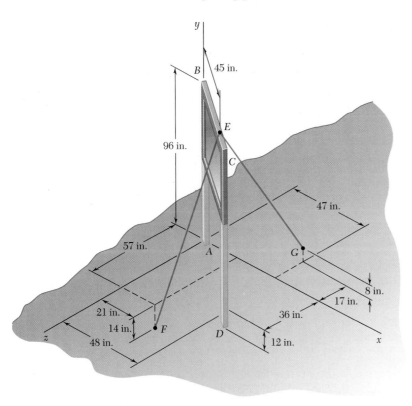

Fig. P3.61 and P3.62

3.62 A sign erected on uneven ground is guyed by cables *EF* and *EG*. If the force exerted by cable *EG* at *E* is 54 lb, determine the moment of that force about the line joining points *A* and *D*.

3.63 Two forces $\mathbf{F}_1$ and $\mathbf{F}_2$ in space have the same magnitude *F*. Prove that the moment of $\mathbf{F}_1$ about the line of action of $\mathbf{F}_2$ is equal to the moment of $\mathbf{F}_2$ about the line of action of $\mathbf{F}_1$.

*3.64 In Prob. 3.55, determine the perpendicular distance between portion *BH* of the cable and the diagonal *AD*.

*3.65 In Prob. 3.56, determine the perpendicular distance between portion *BG* of the cable and the diagonal *AD*.

*3.66 In Prob. 3.57, determine the perpendicular distance between cable *AE* and the line joining points *D* and *B*.

*3.67 In Prob. 3.58, determine the perpendicular distance between cable *CF* and the line joining points *D* and *B*.

*3.68 In Prob. 3.61, determine the perpendicular distance between cable *EF* and the line joining points *A* and *D*.

*3.69 In Prob. 3.62, determine the perpendicular distance between cable *EG* and the line joining points *A* and *D*.

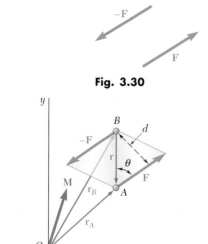

Fig. 3.30

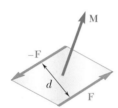

Fig. 3.31

Fig. 3.32

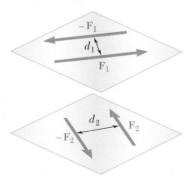

Photo 3.1 The parallel upward and downward forces of equal magnitude exerted on the arms of the lug nut wrench are an example of a couple.

3.12 MOMENT OF A COUPLE

*Two forces **F** and **−F** having the same magnitude, parallel lines of action, and opposite sense are said to form a* couple (Fig. 3.30). Clearly, the sum of the components of the two forces in any direction is zero. The sum of the moments of the two forces about a given point, however, is not zero. While the two forces will not translate the body on which they act, they will tend to make it rotate.

Denoting by $\mathbf{r}_A$ and $\mathbf{r}_B$, respectively, the position vectors of the points of application of **F** and **−F** (Fig. 3.31), we find that the sum of the moments of the two forces about O is

$$\mathbf{r}_A \times \mathbf{F} + \mathbf{r}_B \times (-\mathbf{F}) = (\mathbf{r}_A - \mathbf{r}_B) \times \mathbf{F}$$

Setting $\mathbf{r}_A - \mathbf{r}_B = \mathbf{r}$, where **r** is the vector joining the points of application of the two forces, we conclude that the sum of the moments of **F** and **−F** about O is represented by the vector

$$\mathbf{M} = \mathbf{r} \times \mathbf{F} \tag{3.47}$$

The vector **M** is called the *moment of the couple;* it is a vector perpendicular to the plane containing the two forces, and its magnitude is

$$M = rF \sin \theta = Fd \tag{3.48}$$

where d is the perpendicular distance between the lines of action of **F** and **−F**. The sense of **M** is defined by the right-hand rule.

Since the vector **r** in (3.47) is independent of the choice of the origin O of the coordinate axes, we note that the same result would have been obtained if the moments of **F** and **−F** had been computed about a different point O'. Thus, the moment **M** of a couple is a *free vector* (Sec. 2.3) which can be applied at any point (Fig. 3.32).

From the definition of the moment of a couple, it also follows that two couples, one consisting of the forces $\mathbf{F}_1$ and $-\mathbf{F}_1$, the other of the forces $\mathbf{F}_2$ and $-\mathbf{F}_2$ (Fig. 3.33), will have equal moments if

$$F_1 d_1 = F_2 d_2 \tag{3.49}$$

and if the two couples lie in parallel planes (or in the same plane) and have the same sense.

Fig. 3.33

3.13 EQUIVALENT COUPLES

Figure 3.34 shows three couples which act successively on the same rectangular box. As seen in the preceding section, the only motion a couple can impart to a rigid body is a rotation. Since each of the three couples shown has the same moment **M** (same direction and same magnitude $M = 120$ lb · in.), we can expect the three couples to have the same effect on the box.

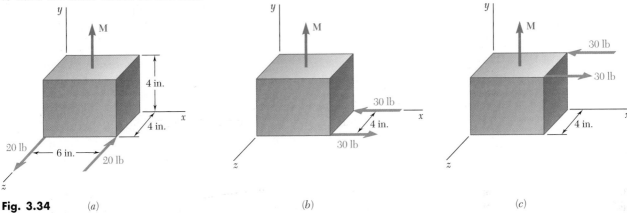

Fig. 3.34   (a)   (b)   (c)

As reasonable as this conclusion appears, we should not accept it hastily. While intuitive feeling is of great help in the study of mechanics, it should not be accepted as a substitute for logical reasoning. Before stating that two systems (or groups) of forces have the same effect on a rigid body, we should prove that fact on the basis of the experimental evidence introduced so far. This evidence consists of the parallelogram law for the addition of two forces (Sec. 2.2) and the principle of transmissibility (Sec. 3.3). Therefore, we will state that *two systems of forces are equivalent* (i.e., they have the same effect on a rigid body) *if we can transform one of them into the other by means of one or several of the following operations*: (1) replacing two forces acting on the same particle by their resultant; (2) resolving a force into two components; (3) canceling two equal and opposite forces acting on the same particle; (4) attaching to the same particle two equal and opposite forces; (5) moving a force along its line of action. Each of these operations is easily justified on the basis of the parallelogram law or the principle of transmissibility.

Let us now prove that *two couples having the same moment* **M** *are equivalent*. First consider two couples contained in the same plane, and assume that this plane coincides with the plane of the figure (Fig. 3.35). The first couple consists of the forces $\mathbf{F}_1$ and $-\mathbf{F}_1$ of magnitude F_1, which are located at a distance d_1 from each other (Fig. 3.35a), and the second couple consists of the forces $\mathbf{F}_2$ and $-\mathbf{F}_2$ of magnitude F_2, which are located at a distance d_2 from each other (Fig. 3.35d). Since the two couples have the same moment **M**, which is perpendicular to the plane of the figure, they must have the same sense (assumed here to be counterclockwise), and the relation

$$F_1 d_1 = F_2 d_2 \qquad (3.49)$$

must be satisfied. To prove that they are equivalent, we shall show that the first couple can be transformed into the second by means of the operations listed above.

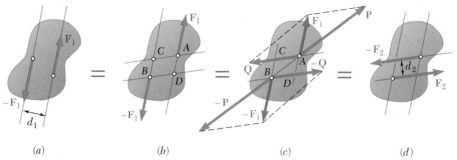

(a)   (b)   (c)   (d)

Fig. 3.35

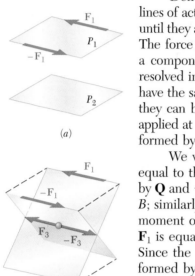

(a)

(b)

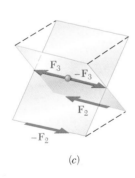

(c)

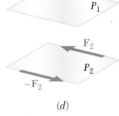

(d)

Fig. 3.36

Denoting by A, B, C, and D the points of intersection of the lines of action of the two couples, we first slide the forces $\mathbf{F}_1$ and $-\mathbf{F}_1$ until they are attached, respectively, at A and B, as shown in Fig. 3.35b. The force $\mathbf{F}_1$ is then resolved into a component $\mathbf{P}$ along line AB and a component $\mathbf{Q}$ along AC (Fig. 3.35c); similarly, the force $-\mathbf{F}_1$ is resolved into $-\mathbf{P}$ along AB and $-\mathbf{Q}$ along BD. The forces $\mathbf{P}$ and $-\mathbf{P}$ have the same magnitude, the same line of action, and opposite sense; they can be moved along their common line of action until they are applied at the same point and may then be canceled. Thus the couple formed by $\mathbf{F}_1$ and $-\mathbf{F}_1$ reduces to a couple consisting of $\mathbf{Q}$ and $-\mathbf{Q}$.

We will now show that the forces $\mathbf{Q}$ and $-\mathbf{Q}$ are respectively equal to the forces $-\mathbf{F}_2$ and $\mathbf{F}_2$. The moment of the couple formed by $\mathbf{Q}$ and $-\mathbf{Q}$ can be obtained by computing the moment of $\mathbf{Q}$ about B; similarly, the moment of the couple formed by $\mathbf{F}_1$ and $-\mathbf{F}_1$ is the moment of $\mathbf{F}_1$ about B. But, by Varignon's theorem, the moment of $\mathbf{F}_1$ is equal to the sum of the moments of its components $\mathbf{P}$ and $\mathbf{Q}$. Since the moment of $\mathbf{P}$ about B is zero, the moment of the couple formed by $\mathbf{Q}$ and $-\mathbf{Q}$ must be equal to the moment of the couple formed by $\mathbf{F}_1$ and $-\mathbf{F}_1$. Recalling (3.49), we write

$$Qd_2 = F_1d_1 = F_2d_2 \qquad \text{and} \qquad Q = F_2$$

Thus the forces $\mathbf{Q}$ and $-\mathbf{Q}$ are respectively equal to the forces $-\mathbf{F}_2$ and $\mathbf{F}_2$, and the couple of Fig. 3.35a is equivalent to the couple of Fig. 3.35d.

Next consider two couples contained in parallel planes P_1 and P_2; we will prove that they are equivalent if they have the same moment. In view of the foregoing, we can assume that the couples consist of forces of the same magnitude F acting along parallel lines (Fig. 3.36a and d). We propose to show that the couple contained in plane P_1 can be transformed into the couple contained in plane P_2 by means of the standard operations listed above.

Let us consider the two planes defined respectively by the lines of action of $\mathbf{F}_1$ and $-\mathbf{F}_2$ and by those of $-\mathbf{F}_1$ and $\mathbf{F}_2$ (Fig. 3.36b). At a point on their line of intersection we attach two forces $\mathbf{F}_3$ and $-\mathbf{F}_3$, respectively equal to $\mathbf{F}_1$ and $-\mathbf{F}_1$. The couple formed by $\mathbf{F}_1$ and $-\mathbf{F}_3$ can be replaced by a couple consisting of $\mathbf{F}_3$ and $-\mathbf{F}_2$ (Fig. 3.36c), since both couples clearly have the same moment and are contained in the same plane. Similarly, the couple formed by $-\mathbf{F}_1$ and $\mathbf{F}_3$ can be replaced by a couple consisting of $-\mathbf{F}_3$ and $\mathbf{F}_2$. Canceling the two equal and opposite forces $\mathbf{F}_3$ and $-\mathbf{F}_3$, we obtain the desired couple in plane P_2 (Fig. 3.36d). Thus, we conclude that two couples having the same moment **M** are equivalent, whether they are contained in the same plane or in parallel planes.

The property we have just established is very important for the correct understanding of the mechanics of rigid bodies. It indicates that when a couple acts on a rigid body, it does not matter where the two forces forming the couple act or what magnitude and direction they have. The only thing which counts is the *moment* of the couple (magnitude and direction). Couples with the same moment will have the same effect on the rigid body.

3.14   ADDITION OF COUPLES

Consider two intersecting planes P_1 and P_2 and two couples acting respectively in P_1 and P_2. We can, without any loss of generality, assume that the couple in P_1 consists of two forces $\mathbf{F}_1$ and $-\mathbf{F}_1$ perpendicular to the line of intersection of the two planes and acting respectively at A and B (Fig. 3.37a). Similarly, we assume that the couple in P_2 consists of two forces $\mathbf{F}_2$ and $-\mathbf{F}_2$ perpendicular to AB and acting respectively at A and B. It is clear that the resultant $\mathbf{R}$ of $\mathbf{F}_1$ and $\mathbf{F}_2$ and the resultant $-\mathbf{R}$ of $-\mathbf{F}_1$ and $-\mathbf{F}_2$ form a couple. Denoting by $\mathbf{r}$ the vector joining B to A and recalling the definition of the moment of a couple (Sec. 3.12), we express the moment $\mathbf{M}$ of the resulting couple as follows:

$$\mathbf{M} = \mathbf{r} \times \mathbf{R} = \mathbf{r} \times (\mathbf{F}_1 + \mathbf{F}_2)$$

and, by Varignon's theorem,

$$\mathbf{M} = \mathbf{r} \times \mathbf{F}_1 + \mathbf{r} \times \mathbf{F}_2$$

But the first term in the expression obtained represents the moment $\mathbf{M}_1$ of the couple in P_1, and the second term represents the moment $\mathbf{M}_2$ of the couple in P_2. We have

$$\mathbf{M} = \mathbf{M}_1 + \mathbf{M}_2 \qquad (3.50)$$

and we conclude that the sum of two couples of moments $\mathbf{M}_1$ and $\mathbf{M}_2$ is a couple of moment $\mathbf{M}$ equal to the vector sum of $\mathbf{M}_1$ and $\mathbf{M}_2$ (Fig. 3.37b).

3.15   COUPLES CAN BE REPRESENTED BY VECTORS

As we saw in Sec. 3.13, couples which have the same moment, whether they act in the same plane or in parallel planes, are equivalent. There is therefore no need to draw the actual forces forming a given couple in order to define its effect on a rigid body (Fig. 3.38a). It is sufficient to draw an arrow equal in magnitude and direction to the moment **M** of the couple (Fig. 3.38b). On the other hand, we saw in Sec. 3.14 that the sum of two couples is itself a couple and that the moment **M** of the resultant couple can be obtained by forming the vector sum of the moments $\mathbf{M}_1$ and $\mathbf{M}_2$ of the given couples. Thus, couples obey the law of addition of vectors, and the arrow used in Fig. 3.38b to represent the couple defined in Fig. 3.38a can truly be considered a vector.

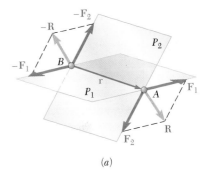

(a)

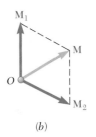

(b)

Fig. 3.37

The vector representing a couple is called a *couple vector*. Note that, in Fig. 3.38, a red arrow is used to distinguish the couple vector, *which represents the couple itself*, from the *moment* of the couple, which was represented by a green arrow in earlier figures. Also note that the symbol ↰ is added to this red arrow to avoid any confusion with vectors representing forces. A couple vector, like the moment of a couple, is a free vector. Its point of application, therefore, can be chosen at the origin of the system of coordinates, if so desired (Fig. 3.38c). Furthermore, the couple vector **M** can be resolved into component vectors $\mathbf{M}_x$, $\mathbf{M}_y$, and $\mathbf{M}_z$, which are directed along the coordinate axes (Fig. 3.38d). These component vectors represent couples acting, respectively, in the yz, zx, and xy planes.

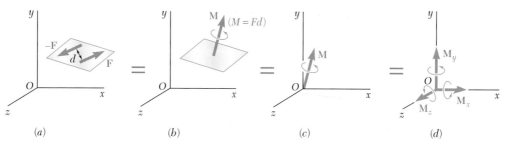

(a)   (b)   (c)   (d)

Fig. 3.38

3.16 RESOLUTION OF A GIVEN FORCE INTO A FORCE AT O AND A COUPLE

Consider a force **F** acting on a rigid body at a point A defined by the position vector **r** (Fig. 3.39a). Suppose that for some reason we would rather have the force act at point O. While we can move **F** along its line of action (principle of transmissibility), we cannot move it to a point O which does not lie on the original line of action without modifying the action of **F** on the rigid body.

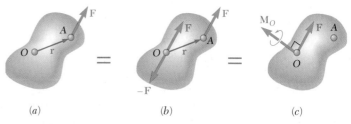

(a)   (b)   (c)

Fig. 3.39

We can, however, attach two forces at point O, one equal to **F** and the other equal to −**F**, without modifying the action of the original force on the rigid body (Fig. 3.39b). As a result of this transformation, a force **F** is now applied at O; the other two forces form a couple of moment $\mathbf{M}_O = \mathbf{r} \times \mathbf{F}$. Thus, *any force **F** acting on a rigid body can be moved to an arbitrary point O provided that a couple is added whose moment is equal to the moment of **F** about O*. The couple tends to impart to the rigid body the same rotational motion about O that the force $\mathbf{F}$ tended to produce before it was transferred to O. The couple is represented by a couple vector $\mathbf{M}_O$ perpendicular to the plane containing $\mathbf{r}$ and $\mathbf{F}$. Since $\mathbf{M}_O$ is a free vector, it may be applied anywhere; for convenience, however, the couple vector is usually attached at O, together with $\mathbf{F}$, and the combination obtained is referred to as a *force-couple system* (Fig. 3.39c).

If the force $\mathbf{F}$ had been moved from A to a different point O' (Fig. 3.40a and c), the moment $\mathbf{M}_{O'} = \mathbf{r}' \times \mathbf{F}$ of $\mathbf{F}$ about O' should have been computed, and a new force-couple system, consisting of $\mathbf{F}$ and of the couple vector $\mathbf{M}_{O'}$, would have been attached at O'. The relation existing between the moments of $\mathbf{F}$ about O and O' is obtained by writing

$$\mathbf{M}_{O'} = \mathbf{r}' \times \mathbf{F} = (\mathbf{r} + \mathbf{s}) \times \mathbf{F} = \mathbf{r} \times \mathbf{F} + \mathbf{s} \times \mathbf{F}$$

$$\mathbf{M}_{O'} = \mathbf{M}_O + \mathbf{s} \times \mathbf{F} \tag{3.51}$$

where $\mathbf{s}$ is the vector joining O' to O. Thus, the moment $\mathbf{M}_{O'}$ of $\mathbf{F}$ about O' is obtained by adding to the moment $\mathbf{M}_O$ of $\mathbf{F}$ about O the vector product $\mathbf{s} \times \mathbf{F}$ representing the moment about O' of the force $\mathbf{F}$ applied at O.

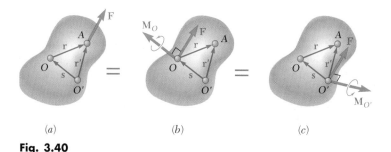

(a) (b) (c)

Fig. 3.40

This result could also have been established by observing that, in order to transfer to O' the force-couple system attached at O (Fig. 3.40b and c), the couple vector $\mathbf{M}_O$ can be freely moved to O'; to move the force $\mathbf{F}$ from O to O', however, it is necessary to add to $\mathbf{F}$ a couple vector whose moment is equal to the moment about O' of the force $\mathbf{F}$ applied at O. Thus, the couple vector $\mathbf{M}_{O'}$ must be the sum of $\mathbf{M}_O$ and the vector $\mathbf{s} \times \mathbf{F}$.

As noted above, the force-couple system obtained by transferring a force $\mathbf{F}$ from a point A to a point O consists of $\mathbf{F}$ and a couple vector $\mathbf{M}_O$ perpendicular to $\mathbf{F}$. Conversely, any force-couple system consisting of a force $\mathbf{F}$ and a couple vector $\mathbf{M}_O$ which are *mutually perpendicular* can be replaced by a single equivalent force. This is done by moving the force $\mathbf{F}$ in the plane perpendicular to $\mathbf{M}_O$ until its moment about O is equal to the moment of the couple to be eliminated.

Photo 3.2 The force exerted by each hand on the wrench could be replaced with an equivalent force-couple system acting on the nut.

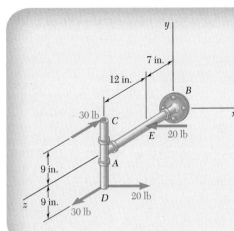

SAMPLE PROBLEM 3.6

Determine the components of the single couple equivalent to the two couples shown.

SOLUTION

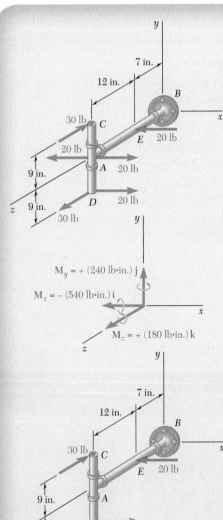

Our computations will be simplified if we attach two equal and opposite 20-lb forces at A. This enables us to replace the original 20-lb-force couple by two new 20-lb-force couples, one of which lies in the zx plane and the other in a plane parallel to the xy plane. The three couples shown in the adjoining sketch can be represented by three couple vectors $\mathbf{M}_x$, $\mathbf{M}_y$, and $\mathbf{M}_z$ directed along the coordinate axes. The corresponding moments are

$$M_x = -(30 \text{ lb})(18 \text{ in.}) = -540 \text{ lb} \cdot \text{in.}$$
$$M_y = +(20 \text{ lb})(12 \text{ in.}) = +240 \text{ lb} \cdot \text{in.}$$
$$M_z = +(20 \text{ lb})(9 \text{ in.}) = +180 \text{ lb} \cdot \text{in.}$$

These three moments represent the components of the single couple $\mathbf{M}$ equivalent to the two given couples. We write

$$\mathbf{M} = -(540 \text{ lb} \cdot \text{in.})\mathbf{i} + (240 \text{ lb} \cdot \text{in.})\mathbf{j} + (180 \text{ lb} \cdot \text{in.})\mathbf{k} \quad \blacktriangleleft$$

Alternative Solution. The components of the equivalent single couple $\mathbf{M}$ can also be obtained by computing the sum of the moments of the four given forces about an arbitrary point. Selecting point D, we write

$$\mathbf{M} = \mathbf{M}_D = (18 \text{ in.})\mathbf{j} \times (-30 \text{ lb})\mathbf{k} + [(9 \text{ in.})\mathbf{j} - (12 \text{ in.})\mathbf{k}] \times (-20 \text{ lb})\mathbf{i}$$

and, after computing the various cross products,

$$\mathbf{M} = -(540 \text{ lb} \cdot \text{in.})\mathbf{i} + (240 \text{ lb} \cdot \text{in.})\mathbf{j} + (180 \text{ lb} \cdot \text{in.})\mathbf{k} \quad \blacktriangleleft$$

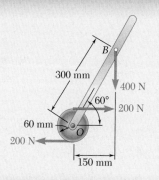

SAMPLE PROBLEM 3.7

Replace the couple and force shown by an equivalent single force applied to the lever. Determine the distance from the shaft to the point of application of this equivalent force.

SOLUTION

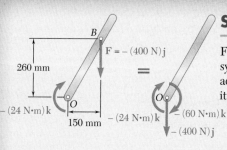

First the given force and couple are replaced by an equivalent force-couple system at O. We move the force $\mathbf{F} = -(400\text{ N})\mathbf{j}$ to O and at the same time add a couple of moment $\mathbf{M}_O$ equal to the moment about O of the force in its original position.

$$\mathbf{M}_O = \overrightarrow{OB} \times \mathbf{F} = [(0.150\text{ m})\mathbf{i} + (0.260\text{ m})\mathbf{j}] \times (-400\text{ N})\mathbf{j}$$
$$= -(60\text{ N} \cdot \text{m})\mathbf{k}$$

This couple is added to the couple of moment $-(24\text{ N} \cdot \text{m})\mathbf{k}$ formed by the two 200-N forces, and a couple of moment $-(84\text{ N} \cdot \text{m})\mathbf{k}$ is obtained. This last couple can be eliminated by applying $\mathbf{F}$ at a point C chosen in such a way that

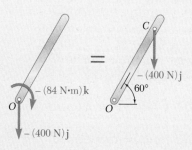

$$-(84\text{ N} \cdot \text{m})\mathbf{k} = \overrightarrow{OC} \times \mathbf{F}$$
$$= [(OC)\cos 60°\mathbf{i} + (OC)\sin 60°\mathbf{j}] \times (-400\text{ N})\mathbf{j}$$
$$= -(OC)\cos 60°(400\text{ N})\mathbf{k}$$

We conclude that

$$(OC)\cos 60° = 0.210\text{ m} = 210\text{ mm} \qquad OC = 420\text{ mm} \quad \blacktriangleleft$$

Alternative Solution. Since the effect of a couple does not depend on its location, the couple of moment $-(24\text{ N} \cdot \text{m})\mathbf{k}$ can be moved to B; we thus obtain a force-couple system at B. The couple can now be eliminated by applying $\mathbf{F}$ at a point C chosen in such a way that

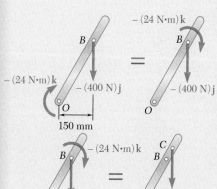

$$-(24\text{ N} \cdot \text{m})\mathbf{k} = \overrightarrow{BC} \times \mathbf{F}$$
$$= -(BC)\cos 60°(400\text{ N})\mathbf{k}$$

We conclude that

$$(BC)\cos 60° = 0.060\text{ m} = 60\text{ mm} \qquad BC = 120\text{ mm}$$
$$OC = OB + BC = 300\text{ mm} + 120\text{ mm} \qquad OC = 420\text{ mm} \quad \blacktriangleleft$$

SOLVING PROBLEMS
ON YOUR OWN

In this lesson we discussed the properties of *couples*. To solve the problems which follow, you will need to remember that the net effect of a couple is to produce a moment **M**. Since this moment is independent of the point about which it is computed, **M** is a *free vector* and thus remains unchanged as it is moved from point to point. Also, two couples are *equivalent* (that is, they have the same effect on a given rigid body) if they produce the same moment.

When determining the moment of a couple, all previous techniques for computing moments apply. Also, since the moment of a couple is a free vector, it should be computed relative to the most convenient point.

Because the only effect of a couple is to produce a moment, it is possible to represent a couple with a vector, the *couple vector,* which is equal to the moment of the couple. The couple vector is a free vector and will be represented by a special symbol, ↗, to distinguish it from force vectors.

In solving the problems in this lesson, you will be called upon to perform the following operations:

1. Adding two or more couples. This results in a new couple, the moment of which is obtained by adding vectorially the moments of the given couples [Sample Prob. 3.6].

2. Replacing a force with an equivalent force-couple system at a specified point. As explained in Sec. 3.16, the force of the force-couple system is equal to the original force, while the required couple vector is equal to the moment of the original force about the given point. In addition, it is important to observe that the force and the couple vector are perpendicular to each other. Conversely, it follows that a force-couple system can be reduced to a single force only if the force and couple vector are mutually perpendicular (see the next paragraph).

3. Replacing a force-couple system (with F perpendicular to M) with a single equivalent force. Note that the requirement that **F** and **M** be mutually perpendicular will be satisfied in all two-dimensional problems. The single equivalent force is equal to **F** and is applied in such a way that its moment about the original point of application is equal to **M** [Sample Prob. 3.7].

PROBLEMS

3.70 Two parallel 60-N forces are applied to a lever as shown. Determine the moment of the couple formed by the two forces (*a*) by resolving each force into horizontal and vertical components and adding the moments of the two resulting couples, (*b*) by using the perpendicular distance between the two forces, (*c*) by summing the moments of the two forces about point *A*.

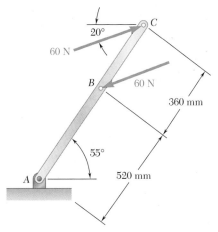

Fig. P3.70

3.71 A plate in the shape of a parallelogram is acted upon by two couples. Determine (*a*) the moment of the couple formed by the two 21-lb forces, (*b*) the perpendicular distance between the 12-lb forces if the resultant of the two couples is zero, (*c*) the value of α if the resultant couple is 72 lb · in. clockwise and *d* is 42 in.

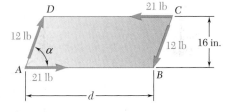

Fig. P3.71

3.72 A couple **M** of magnitude 18 N · m is applied to the handle of a screwdriver to tighten a screw into a block of wood. Determine the magnitudes of the two smallest horizontal forces that are equivalent to **M** if they are applied (*a*) at corners *A* and *D*, (*b*) at corners *B* and *C*, (*c*) anywhere on the block.

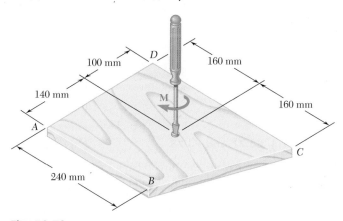

Fig. P3.72

117

3.73 Four 1-in.-diameter pegs are attached to a board as shown. Two strings are passed around the pegs and pulled with the forces indicated. (*a*) Determine the resultant couple acting on the board. (*b*) If only one string is used, around which pegs should it pass and in what directions should it be pulled to create the same couple with the minimum tension in the string? (*c*) What is the value of that minimum tension?

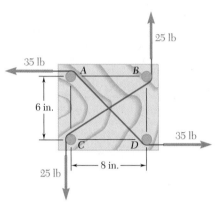

Fig. *P3.73* and *P3.74*

3.74 Four pegs of the same diameter are attached to a board as shown. Two strings are passed around the pegs and pulled with the forces indicated. Determine the diameter of the pegs knowing that the resultant couple applied to the board is 485 lb · in. counterclockwise.

3.75 The shafts of an angle drive are acted upon by the two couples shown. Replace the two couples with a single equivalent couple, specifying its magnitude and the direction of its axis.

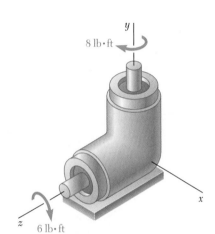

Fig. P3.75

3.76 and 3.77 If *P* = 0, replace the two remaining couples with a single equivalent couple, specifying its magnitude and the direction of its axis.

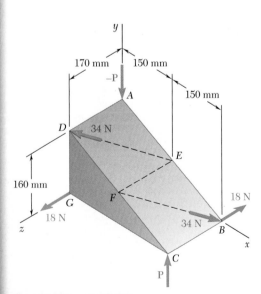

Fig. P3.76 and P3.79

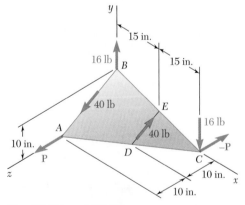

Fig. *P3.77* and *P3.78*

3.78 If *P* = 20 lb, replace the three couples with a single equivalent couple, specifying its magnitude and the direction of its axis.

3.79 If *P* = 20 N, replace the three couples with a single equivalent couple, specifying its magnitude and the direction of its axis.

3.80 Shafts A and B connect the gear box to the wheel assemblies of a tractor, and shaft C connects it to the engine. Shafts A and B lie in the vertical yz plane, while shaft C is directed along the x axis. Replace the couples applied to the shafts with a single equivalent couple, specifying its magnitude and the direction of its axis.

3.81 The tension in the cable attached to the end C of an adjustable boom ABC is 560 lb. Replace the force exerted by the cable at C with an equivalent force-couple system (a) at A, (b) at B.

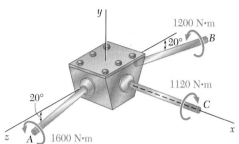

Fig. P3.80

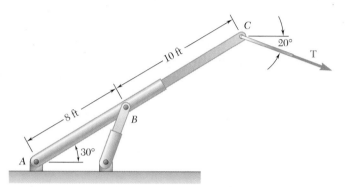

Fig. P3.81

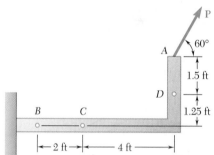

Fig. P3.82

3.82 A 160-lb force **P** is applied at point A of a structural member. Replace **P** with (a) an equivalent force-couple system at C, (b) an equivalent system consisting of a vertical force at B and a second force at D.

3.83 The 80-N horizontal force **P** acts on a bell crank as shown. (a) Replace **P** with an equivalent force-couple system at B. (b) Find the two vertical forces at C and D that are equivalent to the couple found in part a.

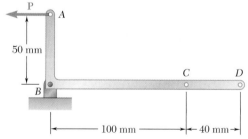

Fig. P3.83

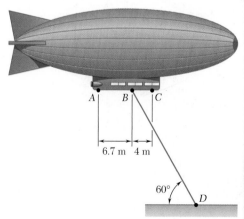

Fig. P3.84

3.84 A dirigible is tethered by a cable attached to its cabin at B. If the tension in the cable is 1040 N, replace the force exerted by the cable at B with an equivalent system formed by two parallel forces applied at A and C.

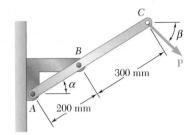

Fig. P3.85

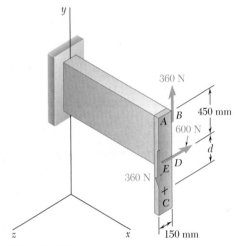

Fig. P3.87

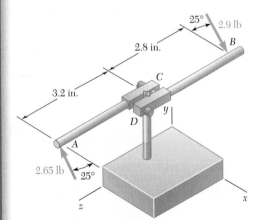

Fig. P3.89

3.85 The force **P** has a magnitude of 250 N and is applied at the end C of a 500-mm rod AC attached to a bracket at A and B. Assuming α = 30° and β = 60°, replace **P** with (a) an equivalent force-couple system at B, (b) an equivalent system formed by two parallel forces applied at A and B.

3.86 Solve Prob. 3.85, assuming α = β = 25°.

3.87 A force and a couple are applied as shown to the end of a cantilever beam. (a) Replace this system with a single force **F** applied at point C, and determine the distance d from C to a line drawn through points D and E. (b) Solve part a if the directions of the two 360-N forces are reversed.

3.88 The shearing forces exerted on the cross section of a steel channel can be represented by a 900-N vertical force and two 250-N horizontal forces as shown. Replace this force and couple with a single force **F** applied at point C, and determine the distance x from C to line BD. (Point C is defined as the *shear center* of the section.)

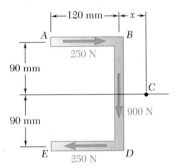

Fig. P3.88

3.89 While tapping a hole, a machinist applies the horizontal forces shown to the handle of the tap wrench. Show that these forces are equivalent to a single force, and specify, if possible, the point of application of the single force on the handle.

3.90 Three control rods attached to a lever ABC exert on it the forces shown. (a) Replace the three forces with an equivalent force-couple system at B. (b) Determine the single force that is equivalent to the force-couple system obtained in part a, and specify its point of application on the lever.

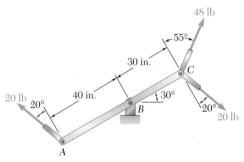

Fig. P3.90

3.91 A hexagonal plate is acted upon by the force **P** and the couple shown. Determine the magnitude and the direction of the smallest force **P** for which this system can be replaced with a single force at *E*.

3.92 A rectangular plate is acted upon by the force and couple shown. This system is to be replaced with a single equivalent force. (*a*) For $\alpha = 40°$, specify the magnitude and the line of action of the equivalent force. (*b*) Specify the value of α if the line of action of the equivalent force is to intersect line *CD* 300 mm to the right of *D*.

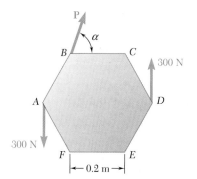

Fig. P3.91

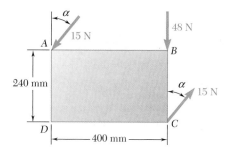

Fig. P3.92

3.93 An eccentric, compressive 1220-N force **P** is applied to the end of a cantilever beam. Replace **P** with an equivalent force-couple system at *G*.

3.94 To keep a door closed, a wooden stick is wedged between the floor and the doorknob. The stick exerts at *B* a 175-N force directed along line *AB*. Replace that force with an equivalent force-couple system at *C*.

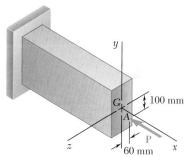

Fig. P3.93

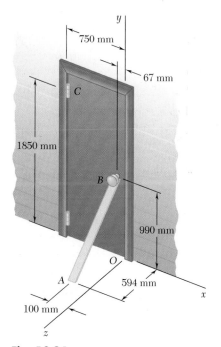

Fig. P3.94

3.95 An antenna is guyed by three cables as shown. Knowing that the tension in cable *AB* is 288 lb, replace the force exerted at *A* by cable *AB* with an equivalent force-couple system at the center *O* of the base of the antenna.

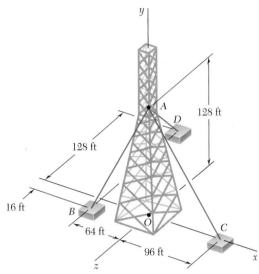

Fig. P3.95 and P3.96

3.96 An antenna is guyed by three cables as shown. Knowing that the tension in cable *AD* is 270 lb, replace the force exerted at *A* by cable *AD* with an equivalent force-couple system at the center *O* of the base of the antenna.

3.97 Replace the 150-N force with an equivalent force-couple system at *A*.

3.98 A 77-N force $\mathbf{F}_1$ and a 31-N · m couple $\mathbf{M}_1$ are applied to corner *E* of the bent plate shown. If $\mathbf{F}_1$ and $\mathbf{M}_1$ are to be replaced with an equivalent force-couple system $(\mathbf{F}_2, \mathbf{M}_2)$ at corner *B* and if $(M_2)_z = 0$, determine (*a*) the distance *d*, (*b*) $\mathbf{F}_2$ and $\mathbf{M}_2$.

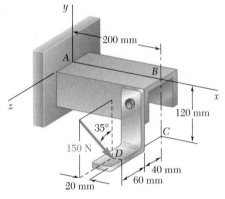

Fig. P3.97

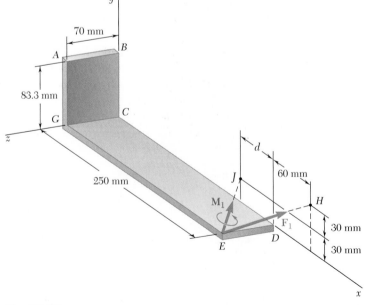

Fig. P3.98

3.99 A 46-lb force **F** and a 2120-lb · in. couple **M** are applied to corner
A of the block shown. Replace the given force-couple system with
an equivalent force-couple system at corner *H*.

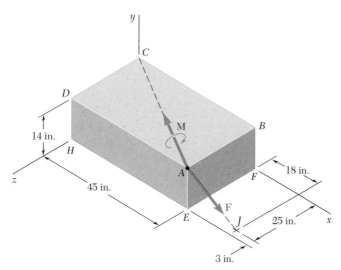

Fig. P3.99

3.100 The handpiece for a miniature industrial grinder weighs 0.6 lb,
and its center of gravity is located on the *y* axis. The head of the
handpiece is offset in the *xz* plane in such a way that line *BC*
forms an angle of 25° with the *x* direction. Show that the weight
of the handpiece and the two couples **M**$_1$ and **M**$_2$ can be replaced
with a single equivalent force. Further, assuming that $M_1 = 0.68$
lb · in. and $M_2 = 0.65$ lb · in., determine (*a*) the magnitude and
the direction of the equivalent force, (*b*) the point where its line
of action intersects the *xz* plane.

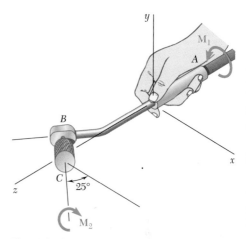

Fig. P3.100

3.17 REDUCTION OF A SYSTEM OF FORCES TO ONE FORCE AND ONE COUPLE

Consider a system of forces **F**$_1$, **F**$_2$, **F**$_3$, . . . , acting on a rigid body at
the points A_1, A_2, A_3, . . . , *defined by the position vectors* **r**$_1$, **r**$_2$, **r**$_3$,
etc. (Fig. 3.41*a*). As seen in the preceding section, **F**$_1$ can be moved
from A_1 to a given point *O* if a couple of moment **M**$_1$ equal to the
moment **r**$_1$ × **F**$_1$ of **F**$_1$ about *O* is added to the original system of
forces. Repeating this procedure with **F**$_2$, **F**$_3$, . . . , we obtain the

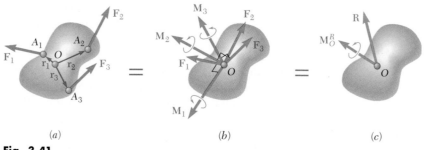

(*a*)   (*b*)   (*c*)

Fig. 3.41

system shown in Fig. 3.41*b*, which consists of the original forces, now acting at O, and the added couple vectors. Since the forces are now concurrent, they can be added vectorially and replaced by their resultant **R**. Similarly, the couple vectors $\mathbf{M}_1$, $\mathbf{M}_2$, $\mathbf{M}_3$, . . . , can be added vectorially and replaced by a single couple vector $\mathbf{M}_O^R$. Any system of forces, however complex, can thus be reduced to an *equivalent force-couple system acting at a given point O* (Fig. 3.41*c*). We should note that while each of the couple vectors $\mathbf{M}_1$, $\mathbf{M}_2$, $\mathbf{M}_3$, . . . , in Fig. 3.41*b* is perpendicular to its corresponding force, the resultant force **R** and the resultant couple vector $\mathbf{M}_O^R$ in Fig. 3.41*c* will not, in general, be perpendicular to each other.

The equivalent force-couple system is defined by the equations

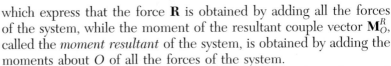

$$\mathbf{R} = \Sigma \mathbf{F} \qquad \mathbf{M}_O^R = \Sigma \mathbf{M}_O = \Sigma(\mathbf{r} \times \mathbf{F}) \qquad (3.52)$$

which express that the force **R** is obtained by adding all the forces of the system, while the moment of the resultant couple vector $\mathbf{M}_O^R$, called the *moment resultant* of the system, is obtained by adding the moments about O of all the forces of the system.

Once a given system of forces has been reduced to a force and a couple at a point O, it can easily be reduced to a force and a couple at another point O'. While the resultant force **R** will remain unchanged, the new moment resultant $\mathbf{M}_{O'}^R$ will be equal to the sum of $\mathbf{M}_O^R$ and the moment about O' of the force **R** attached at O (Fig. 3.42). We have

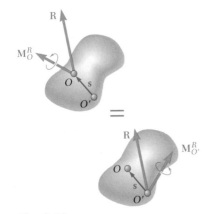

Fig. 3.42

$$\mathbf{M}_{O'}^R = \mathbf{M}_O^R + \mathbf{s} \times \mathbf{R} \qquad (3.53)$$

In practice, the reduction of a given system of forces to a single force **R** at O and a couple vector $\mathbf{M}_O^R$ will be carried out in terms of components. Resolving each position vector **r** and each force **F** of the system into rectangular components, we write

$$\mathbf{r} = x\mathbf{i} + y\mathbf{j} + z\mathbf{k} \qquad (3.54)$$
$$\mathbf{F} = F_x\mathbf{i} + F_y\mathbf{j} + F_z\mathbf{k} \qquad (3.55)$$

Substituting for **r** and **F** in (3.52) and factoring out the unit vectors **i**, **j**, **k**, we obtain **R** and $\mathbf{M}_O^R$ in the form

$$\mathbf{R} = R_x\mathbf{i} + R_y\mathbf{j} + R_z\mathbf{k} \qquad \mathbf{M}_O^R = M_x^R\mathbf{i} + M_y^R\mathbf{j} + M_z^R\mathbf{k} \quad (3.56)$$

The components R_x, R_y, R_z represent, respectively, the sums of the x, y, and z components of the given forces and measure the tendency of the system to impart to the rigid body a motion of translation in the x, y, or z direction. Similarly, the components M_x^R, M_y^R, M_z^R represent, respectively, the sum of the moments of the given forces about the x, y, and z axes and measure the tendency of the system to impart to the rigid body a motion of rotation about the x, y, or z axis.

If the magnitude and direction of the force **R** are desired, they can be obtained from the components R_x, R_y, R_z by means of the relations (2.18) and (2.19) of Sec. 2.12; similar computations will yield the magnitude and direction of the couple vector $\mathbf{M}_O^R$.

3.18 EQUIVALENT SYSTEMS OF FORCES

We saw in the preceding section that any system of forces acting on a rigid body can be reduced to a force-couple system at a given point O. This equivalent force-couple system characterizes completely the effect of the given force system on the rigid body. *Two systems of forces are equivalent, therefore, if they can be reduced to the same force-couple system at a given point O.* Recalling that the force-couple system at O is defined by the relations (3.52), we state that *two systems of forces, $\mathbf{F}_1$, $\mathbf{F}_2$, $\mathbf{F}_3$, . . . , and $\mathbf{F}'_1$, $\mathbf{F}'_2$, $\mathbf{F}'_3$, . . . , which act on the same rigid body are equivalent if, and only if, the sums of the forces and the sums of the moments about a given point O of the forces of the two systems are, respectively, equal.* Expressed mathematically, the necessary and sufficient conditions for the two systems of forces to be equivalent are

$$\Sigma \mathbf{F} = \Sigma \mathbf{F}' \quad \text{and} \quad \Sigma \mathbf{M}_O = \Sigma \mathbf{M}'_O \tag{3.57}$$

Photo 3.3 The forces exerted by the children upon the wagon can be replaced with an equivalent force-couple system when analyzing the motion of the wagon.

Note that to prove that two systems of forces are equivalent, the second of the relations (3.57) must be established with respect to *only one point O*. It will hold, however, with respect to *any point* if the two systems are equivalent.

Resolving the forces and moments in (3.57) into their rectangular components, we can express the necessary and sufficient conditions for the equivalence of two systems of forces acting on a rigid body as follows:

$$\begin{array}{ccc} \Sigma F_x = \Sigma F'_x & \Sigma F_y = \Sigma F'_y & \Sigma F_z = \Sigma F'_z \\ \Sigma M_x = \Sigma M'_x & \Sigma M_y = \Sigma M'_y & \Sigma M_z = \Sigma M'_z \end{array} \tag{3.58}$$

These equations have a simple physical significance. They express that two systems of forces are equivalent if they tend to impart to the rigid body (1) the same translation in the x, y, and z directions, respectively, and (2) the same rotation about the x, y, and z axes, respectively.

3.19 EQUIPOLLENT SYSTEMS OF VECTORS

In general, when two systems of vectors satisfy Eqs. (3.57) or (3.58), i.e., when their resultants and their moment resultants about an arbitrary point O are respectively equal, the two systems are said to be *equipollent*. The result established in the preceding section can thus be restated as follows: *If two systems of forces acting on a rigid body are equipollent, they are also equivalent.*

It is important to note that this statement does not apply to *any* system of vectors. Consider, for example, a system of forces acting on a set of independent particles which do *not* form a rigid body. A different system of forces acting on the same particles may happen to be equipollent to the first one; i.e., it may have the same resultant and the same moment resultant. Yet, since different forces will now act on the various particles, their effects on these particles will be different; the two systems of forces, while equipollent, are *not equivalent*.

3.20 FURTHER REDUCTION OF A SYSTEM OF FORCES

We saw in Sec. 3.17 that any given system of forces acting on a rigid body can be reduced to an equivalent force-couple system at O consisting of a force $\mathbf{R}$ equal to the sum of the forces of the system and a couple vector $\mathbf{M}_O^R$ of moment equal to the moment resultant of the system.

When $\mathbf{R} = 0$, the force-couple system reduces to the couple vector $\mathbf{M}_O^R$. The given system of forces can then be reduced to a single couple, called the *resultant couple* of the system.

Let us now investigate the conditions under which a given system of forces can be reduced to a single force. It follows from Sec. 3.16 that the force-couple system at O can be replaced by a single force $\mathbf{R}$ acting along a new line of action if $\mathbf{R}$ and $\mathbf{M}_O^R$ are mutually perpendicular. The systems of forces which can be reduced to a single force, or *resultant*, are therefore the systems for which the force $\mathbf{R}$ and the couple vector $\mathbf{M}_O^R$ are mutually perpendicular. While this condition *is generally not satisfied* by systems of forces in space, it *will be satisfied* by systems consisting of (1) concurrent forces, (2) coplanar forces, or (3) parallel forces. These three cases will be discussed separately.

1. *Concurrent forces* are applied at the same point and can therefore be added directly to obtain their resultant $\mathbf{R}$. Thus, they always reduce to a single force. Concurrent forces were discussed in detail in Chap. 2.

2. *Coplanar forces* act in the same plane, which may be assumed to be the plane of the figure (Fig. 3.43a). The sum $\mathbf{R}$ of the forces of the system will also lie in the plane of the figure, while the moment of each force about O, and thus the moment resultant $\mathbf{M}_O^R$, will be perpendicular to that plane. The force-couple system at O consists, therefore, of a force $\mathbf{R}$ and a couple vector $\mathbf{M}_O^R$ which are mutually perpendicular (Fig. 3.43b).† They can be reduced to a single force $\mathbf{R}$ by moving $\mathbf{R}$ in the plane of the figure until its moment about O becomes equal to $\mathbf{M}_O^R$. The distance from O to the line of action of $\mathbf{R}$ is $d = M_O^R/R$ (Fig. 3.43c).

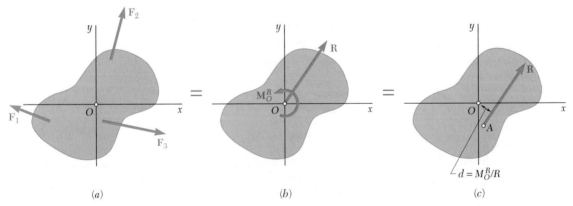

(a)　　　　　(b)　　　　　(c)

Fig. 3.43

---

†Since the couple vector $\mathbf{M}_O^R$ is perpendicular to the plane of the figure, it has been represented by the symbol ⌐. A counterclockwise couple ⌐ represents a vector pointing out of the paper, and a clockwise couple ⌐ represents a vector pointing into the paper.

As noted in Sec. 3.17, the reduction of a system of forces is considerably simplified if the forces are resolved into rectangular components. The force-couple system at O is then characterized by the components (Fig. 3.44a)

$$R_x = \Sigma F_x \qquad R_y = \Sigma F_y \qquad M_z^R = M_O^R = \Sigma M_O \qquad (3.59)$$

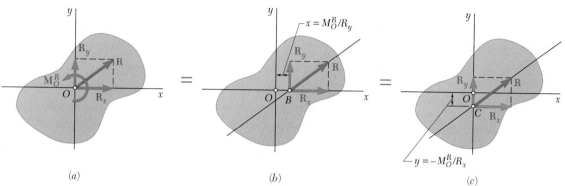

Fig. 3.44

To reduce the system to a single force $\mathbf{R}$, we express that the moment of $\mathbf{R}$ about O must be equal to $\mathbf{M}_O^R$. Denoting by x and y the coordinates of the point of application of the resultant and recalling formula (3.22) of Sec. 3.8, we write

$$xR_y - yR_x = M_O^R$$

which represents the equation of the line of action of $\mathbf{R}$. We can also determine directly the x and y intercepts of the line of action of the resultant by noting that $\mathbf{M}_O^R$ must be equal to the moment about O of the y component of $\mathbf{R}$ when $\mathbf{R}$ is attached at B (Fig. 3.44b) and to the moment of its x component when $\mathbf{R}$ is attached at C (Fig. 3.44c).

3. *Parallel forces* have parallel lines of action and may or may not have the same sense. Assuming here that the forces are parallel to the y axis (Fig. 3.45a), we note that their sum $\mathbf{R}$ will also be parallel to the y axis. On the other hand, since the moment of a given force must be perpendicular to that force, the moment about O of each force of the system, and thus the moment resultant $\mathbf{M}_O^R$, will lie in the zx plane. The force-couple system at O consists, therefore,

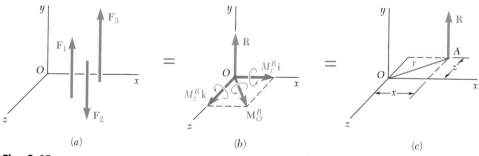

Fig. 3.45

Photo 3.4 The parallel wind forces acting on the highway signs can be reduced to a single equivalent force. Determining this force can simplify the calculation of the forces acting on the supports of the frame to which the signs are attached.

of a force $\mathbf{R}$ and a couple vector $\mathbf{M}_O^R$ which are mutually perpendicular (Fig. 3.45*b*). They can be reduced to a single force $\mathbf{R}$ (Fig. 3.45*c*) or, if $\mathbf{R} = 0$, to a single couple of moment $\mathbf{M}_O^R$.

In practice, the force-couple system at O will be characterized by the components

$$R_y = \Sigma F_y \qquad M_x^R = \Sigma M_x \qquad M_z^R = \Sigma M_z \qquad (3.60)$$

The reduction of the system to a single force can be carried out by moving $\mathbf{R}$ to a new point of application $A(x, 0, z)$ chosen so that the moment of $\mathbf{R}$ about O is equal to $\mathbf{M}_O^R$. We write

$$\mathbf{r} \times \mathbf{R} = \mathbf{M}_O^R$$
$$(x\mathbf{i} + z\mathbf{k}) \times R_y\mathbf{j} = M_x^R\mathbf{i} + M_z^R\mathbf{k}$$

By computing the vector products and equating the coefficients of the corresponding unit vectors in both members of the equation, we obtain two scalar equations which define the coordinates of A:

$$-zR_y = M_x^R \qquad xR_y = M_z^R$$

These equations express that the moments of $\mathbf{R}$ about the x and z axes must, respectively, be equal to M_x^R and M_z^R.

*3.21 REDUCTION OF A SYSTEM OF FORCES TO A WRENCH

In the general case of a system of forces in space, the equivalent force-couple system at O consists of a force $\mathbf{R}$ and a couple vector $\mathbf{M}_O^R$ which are not perpendicular, and neither of which is zero (Fig. 3.46*a*). Thus, the system of forces *cannot* be reduced to a single force or to a single couple. The couple vector, however, can be replaced by two other couple vectors obtained by resolving $\mathbf{M}_O^R$ into a component $\mathbf{M}_1$ along $\mathbf{R}$ and a component $\mathbf{M}_2$ in a plane perpendicular to $\mathbf{R}$ (Fig. 3.46*b*). The couple vector $\mathbf{M}_2$ and the force $\mathbf{R}$ can then be replaced by a single force $\mathbf{R}$ acting along a new line of action. The original system of forces thus reduces to $\mathbf{R}$ and to the couple vector $\mathbf{M}_1$ (Fig. 3.46*c*), i.e., to $\mathbf{R}$ and a couple acting in the plane perpendicular to $\mathbf{R}$. This particular force-couple system is called a *wrench* because the resulting combination of push and twist is the same as that which would be caused by an actual wrench. The line of action of $\mathbf{R}$ is known as the *axis of the wrench*, and the ratio $p = M_1/R$ is called the *pitch*

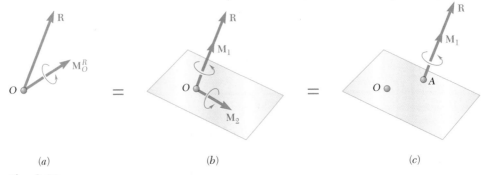

(a) $\qquad\qquad$ (b) $\qquad\qquad$ (c)

Fig. 3.46

of the wrench. A wrench, therefore, consists of two collinear vectors, namely, a force $\mathbf{R}$ and a couple vector

$$\mathbf{M}_1 = p\mathbf{R} \tag{3.61}$$

Recalling the expression (3.35) obtained in Sec. 3.9 for the projection of a vector on the line of action of another vector, we note that the projection of $\mathbf{M}_O^R$ on the line of action of $\mathbf{R}$ is

$$M_1 = \frac{\mathbf{R} \cdot \mathbf{M}_O^R}{R}$$

Thus, the pitch of the wrench can be expressed as†

$$p = \frac{M_1}{R} = \frac{\mathbf{R} \cdot \mathbf{M}_O^R}{R^2} \tag{3.62}$$

To define the axis of the wrench, we can write a relation involving the position vector $\mathbf{r}$ of an arbitrary point P located on that axis. Attaching the resultant force $\mathbf{R}$ and couple vector $\mathbf{M}_1$ at P (Fig. 3.47) and expressing that the moment about O of this force-couple system is equal to the moment resultant $\mathbf{M}_O^R$ of the original force system, we write

$$\mathbf{M}_1 + \mathbf{r} \times \mathbf{R} = \mathbf{M}_O^R \tag{3.63}$$

or, recalling Eq. (3.61),

$$p\mathbf{R} + \mathbf{r} \times \mathbf{R} = \mathbf{M}_O^R \tag{3.64}$$

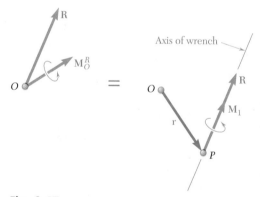

Fig. 3.47

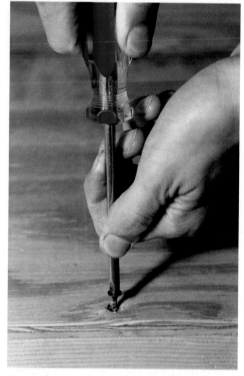

Photo 3.5 The pushing-turning action associated with the tightening of a screw illustrates the collinear lines of action of the force and couple vector that constitute a wrench.

†The expressions obtained for the projection of the couple vector on the line of action of $\mathbf{R}$ and for the pitch of the wrench are independent of the choice of point O. Using the relation (3.53) of Sec. 3.17, we note that if a different point O' had been used, the numerator in (3.62) would have been

$$\mathbf{R} \cdot \mathbf{M}_{O'}^R = \mathbf{R} \cdot (\mathbf{M}_O^R + \mathbf{s} \times \mathbf{R}) = \mathbf{R} \cdot \mathbf{M}_O^R + \mathbf{R} \cdot (\mathbf{s} \times \mathbf{R})$$

Since the mixed triple product $\mathbf{R} \cdot (\mathbf{s} \times \mathbf{R})$ is identically equal to zero, we have

$$\mathbf{R} \cdot \mathbf{M}_{O'}^R = \mathbf{R} \cdot \mathbf{M}_O^R$$

Thus, the scalar product $\mathbf{R} \cdot \mathbf{M}_O^R$ is independent of the choice of point O.

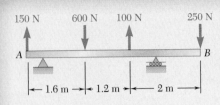

A 4.80-m-long beam is subjected to the forces shown. Reduce the given system of forces to (*a*) an equivalent force-couple system at *A*, (*b*) an equivalent force-couple system at *B*, (*c*) a single force or resultant.

Note. Since the reactions at the supports are not included in the given system of forces, the given system will not maintain the beam in equilibrium.

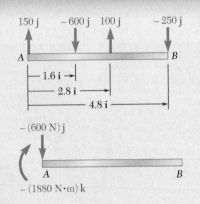

SOLUTION

a. Force-Couple System at A. The force-couple system at *A* equivalent to the given system of forces consists of a force **R** and a couple $\mathbf{M}_A^R$ defined as follows:

$$\mathbf{R} = \Sigma\mathbf{F}$$
$$= (150 \text{ N})\mathbf{j} - (600 \text{ N})\mathbf{j} + (100 \text{ N})\mathbf{j} - (250 \text{ N})\mathbf{j} = -(600 \text{ N})\mathbf{j}$$
$$\mathbf{M}_A^R = \Sigma(\mathbf{r} \times \mathbf{F})$$
$$= (1.6\mathbf{i}) \times (-600\mathbf{j}) + (2.8\mathbf{i}) \times (100\mathbf{j}) + (4.8\mathbf{i}) \times (-250\mathbf{j})$$
$$= -(1880 \text{ N} \cdot \text{m})\mathbf{k}$$

The equivalent force-couple system at *A* is thus

$$\mathbf{R} = 600 \text{ N} \downarrow \qquad \mathbf{M}_A^R = 1880 \text{ N} \cdot \text{m} \downarrow \quad \blacktriangleleft$$

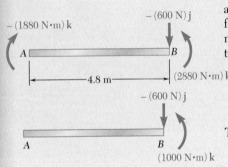

b. Force-Couple System at B. We propose to find a force-couple system at *B* equivalent to the force-couple system at *A* determined in part *a*. The force **R** is unchanged, but a new couple $\mathbf{M}_B^R$ must be determined, the moment of which is equal to the moment about *B* of the force-couple system determined in part *a*. Thus, we have

$$\mathbf{M}_B^R = \mathbf{M}_A^R + \overrightarrow{BA} \times \mathbf{R}$$
$$= -(1880 \text{ N} \cdot \text{m})\mathbf{k} + (-4.8 \text{ m})\mathbf{i} \times (-600 \text{ N})\mathbf{j}$$
$$= -(1880 \text{ N} \cdot \text{m})\mathbf{k} + (2880 \text{ N} \cdot \text{m})\mathbf{k} = +(1000 \text{ N} \cdot \text{m})\mathbf{k}$$

The equivalent force-couple system at *B* is thus

$$\mathbf{R} = 600 \text{ N} \downarrow \qquad \mathbf{M}_B^R = 1000 \text{ N} \cdot \text{m} \uparrow \quad \blacktriangleleft$$

c. Single Force or Resultant. The resultant of the given system of forces is equal to **R**, and its point of application must be such that the moment of **R** about *A* is equal to $\mathbf{M}_A^R$. We write

$$\mathbf{r} \times \mathbf{R} = \mathbf{M}_A^R$$
$$x\mathbf{i} \times (-600 \text{ N})\mathbf{j} = -(1880 \text{ N} \cdot \text{m})\mathbf{k}$$
$$-x(600 \text{ N})\mathbf{k} = -(1880 \text{ N} \cdot \text{m})\mathbf{k}$$

and conclude that $x = 3.13$ m. Thus, the single force equivalent to the given system is defined as

$$\mathbf{R} = 600 \text{ N} \downarrow \qquad x = 3.13 \text{ m} \quad \blacktriangleleft$$

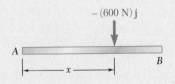

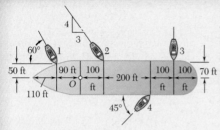

SAMPLE PROBLEM 3.9

Four tugboats are used to bring an ocean liner to its pier. Each tugboat exerts a 5000-lb force in the direction shown. Determine (*a*) the equivalent force-couple system at the foremast *O*, (*b*) the point on the hull where a single, more powerful tugboat should push to produce the same effect as the original four tugboats.

SOLUTION

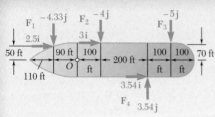

a. Force-Couple System at O. Each of the given forces is resolved into components in the diagram shown (kip units are used). The force-couple system at *O* equivalent to the given system of forces consists of a force **R** and a couple $\mathbf{M}_O^R$ defined as follows:

$$\mathbf{R} = \Sigma \mathbf{F}$$
$$= (2.50\mathbf{i} - 4.33\mathbf{j}) + (3.00\mathbf{i} - 4.00\mathbf{j}) + (-5.00\mathbf{j}) + (3.54\mathbf{i} + 3.54\mathbf{j})$$
$$= 9.04\mathbf{i} - 9.79\mathbf{j}$$

$$\mathbf{M}_O^R = \Sigma(\mathbf{r} \times \mathbf{F})$$
$$= (-90\mathbf{i} + 50\mathbf{j}) \times (2.50\mathbf{i} - 4.33\mathbf{j})$$
$$+ (100\mathbf{i} + 70\mathbf{j}) \times (3.00\mathbf{i} - 4.00\mathbf{j})$$
$$+ (400\mathbf{i} + 70\mathbf{j}) \times (-5.00\mathbf{j})$$
$$+ (300\mathbf{i} - 70\mathbf{j}) \times (3.54\mathbf{i} + 3.54\mathbf{j})$$
$$= (390 - 125 - 400 - 210 - 2000 + 1062 + 248)\mathbf{k}$$
$$= -1035\mathbf{k}$$

The equivalent force-couple system at *O* is thus

$$\mathbf{R} = (9.04 \text{ kips})\mathbf{i} - (9.79 \text{ kips})\mathbf{j} \qquad \mathbf{M}_O^R = -(1035 \text{ kip} \cdot \text{ft})\mathbf{k}$$

or $\qquad \mathbf{R} = 13.33 \text{ kips} \, \diagdown 47.3° \qquad \mathbf{M}_O^R = 1035 \text{ kip} \cdot \text{ft} \, \downarrow$ ◄

Remark. Since all the forces are contained in the plane of the figure, we could have expected the sum of their moments to be perpendicular to that plane. Note that the moment of each force component could have been obtained directly from the diagram by first forming the product of its magnitude and perpendicular distance to *O* and then assigning to this product a positive or a negative sign depending upon the sense of the moment.

b. Single Tugboat. The force exerted by a single tugboat must be equal to **R**, and its point of application *A* must be such that the moment of **R** about *O* is equal to $\mathbf{M}_O^R$. Observing that the position vector of *A* is

$$\mathbf{r} = x\mathbf{i} + 70\mathbf{j}$$

we write

$$\mathbf{r} \times \mathbf{R} = \mathbf{M}_O^R$$
$$(x\mathbf{i} + 70\mathbf{j}) \times (9.04\mathbf{i} - 9.79\mathbf{j}) = -1035\mathbf{k}$$
$$-x(9.79)\mathbf{k} - 633\mathbf{k} = -1035\mathbf{k} \qquad x = 41.1 \text{ ft} \quad ◄$$

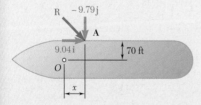

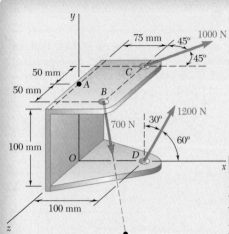

E(150 mm, –50 mm, 100 mm)

SAMPLE PROBLEM 3.10

Three cables are attached to a bracket as shown. Replace the forces exerted by the cables with an equivalent force-couple system at A.

SOLUTION

We first determine the relative position vectors drawn from point A to the points of application of the various forces and resolve the forces into rectangular components. Observing that $\mathbf{F}_B = (700\ \text{N})\boldsymbol{\lambda}_{BE}$ where

$$\boldsymbol{\lambda}_{BE} = \frac{\overrightarrow{BE}}{BE} = \frac{75\mathbf{i} - 150\mathbf{j} + 50\mathbf{k}}{175}$$

we have, using meters and newtons,

$$\mathbf{r}_{B/A} = \overrightarrow{AB} = 0.075\mathbf{i} + 0.050\mathbf{k} \qquad \mathbf{F}_B = 300\mathbf{i} - 600\mathbf{j} + 200\mathbf{k}$$
$$\mathbf{r}_{C/A} = \overrightarrow{AC} = 0.075\mathbf{i} - 0.050\mathbf{k} \qquad \mathbf{F}_C = 707\mathbf{i} \qquad\quad - 707\mathbf{k}$$
$$\mathbf{r}_{D/A} = \overrightarrow{AD} = 0.100\mathbf{i} - 0.100\mathbf{j} \qquad \mathbf{F}_D = 600\mathbf{i} + 1039\mathbf{j}$$

The force-couple system at A equivalent to the given forces consists of a force $\mathbf{R} = \Sigma\mathbf{F}$ and a couple $\mathbf{M}_A^R = \Sigma(\mathbf{r} \times \mathbf{F})$. The force $\mathbf{R}$ is readily obtained by adding respectively the x, y, and z components of the forces:

$$\mathbf{R} = \Sigma\mathbf{F} = (1607\ \text{N})\mathbf{i} + (439\ \text{N})\mathbf{j} - (507\ \text{N})\mathbf{k} \quad \blacktriangleleft$$

The computation of $\mathbf{M}_A^R$ will be facilitated if we express the moments of the forces in the form of determinants (Sec. 3.8):

$$\mathbf{r}_{B/A} \times \mathbf{F}_B = \begin{vmatrix} \mathbf{i} & \mathbf{j} & \mathbf{k} \\ 0.075 & 0 & 0.050 \\ 300 & -600 & 200 \end{vmatrix} = 30\mathbf{i} \qquad\qquad -45\mathbf{k}$$

$$\mathbf{r}_{C/A} \times \mathbf{F}_C = \begin{vmatrix} \mathbf{i} & \mathbf{j} & \mathbf{k} \\ 0.075 & 0 & -0.050 \\ 707 & 0 & -707 \end{vmatrix} = \qquad 17.68\mathbf{j}$$

$$\mathbf{r}_{D/A} \times \mathbf{F}_D = \begin{vmatrix} \mathbf{i} & \mathbf{j} & \mathbf{k} \\ 0.100 & -0.100 & 0 \\ 600 & 1039 & 0 \end{vmatrix} = \qquad\qquad 163.9\mathbf{k}$$

Adding the expressions obtained, we have

$$\mathbf{M}_A^R = \Sigma(\mathbf{r} \times \mathbf{F}) = (30\ \text{N}\cdot\text{m})\mathbf{i} + (17.68\ \text{N}\cdot\text{m})\mathbf{j} + (118.9\ \text{N}\cdot\text{m})\mathbf{k} \quad \blacktriangleleft$$

The rectangular components of the force $\mathbf{R}$ and the couple $\mathbf{M}_A^R$ are shown in the adjoining sketch.

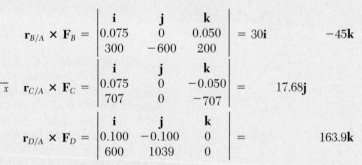

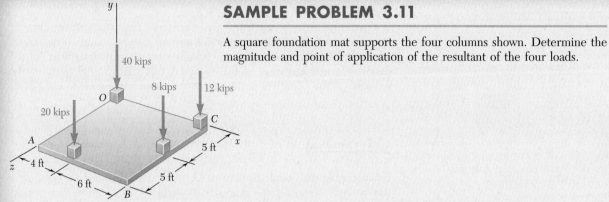

SAMPLE PROBLEM 3.11

A square foundation mat supports the four columns shown. Determine the magnitude and point of application of the resultant of the four loads.

SOLUTION

We first reduce the given system of forces to a force-couple system at the origin O of the coordinate system. This force-couple system consists of a force $\mathbf{R}$ and a couple vector $\mathbf{M}_O^R$ defined as follows:

$$\mathbf{R} = \Sigma \mathbf{F} \qquad \mathbf{M}_O^R = \Sigma(\mathbf{r} \times \mathbf{F})$$

The position vectors of the points of application of the various forces are determined, and the computations are arranged in tabular form.

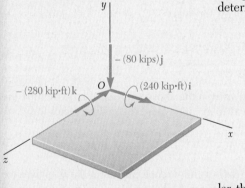

r, ft	F, kips	r × F, kip · ft
0	$-40\mathbf{j}$	0
$10\mathbf{i}$	$-12\mathbf{j}$	$-120\mathbf{k}$
$10\mathbf{i} + 5\mathbf{k}$	$-8\mathbf{j}$	$40\mathbf{i} - 80\mathbf{k}$
$4\mathbf{i} + 10\mathbf{k}$	$-20\mathbf{j}$	$200\mathbf{i} - 80\mathbf{k}$
	$\mathbf{R} = -80\mathbf{j}$	$\mathbf{M}_O^R = 240\mathbf{i} - 280\mathbf{k}$

Since the force $\mathbf{R}$ and the couple vector $\mathbf{M}_O^R$ are mutually perpendicular, the force-couple system obtained can be reduced further to a single force $\mathbf{R}$. The new point of application of $\mathbf{R}$ will be selected in the plane of the mat and in such a way that the moment of $\mathbf{R}$ about O will be equal to $\mathbf{M}_O^R$. Denoting by $\mathbf{r}$ the position vector of the desired point of application, and by x and z its coordinates, we write

$$\mathbf{r} \times \mathbf{R} = \mathbf{M}_O^R$$
$$(x\mathbf{i} + z\mathbf{k}) \times (-80\mathbf{j}) = 240\mathbf{i} - 280\mathbf{k}$$
$$-80x\mathbf{k} + 80z\mathbf{i} = 240\mathbf{i} - 280\mathbf{k}$$

from which it follows that

$$-80x = -280 \qquad 80z = 240$$
$$x = 3.50 \text{ ft} \qquad z = 3.00 \text{ ft}$$

We conclude that the resultant of the given system of forces is

$$\mathbf{R} = 80 \text{ kips} \downarrow \qquad \text{at } x = 3.50 \text{ ft}, z = 3.00 \text{ ft} \quad \blacktriangleleft$$

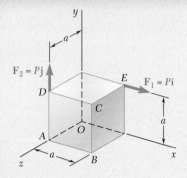

SAMPLE PROBLEM 3.12

Two forces of the same magnitude P act on a cube of side a as shown. Replace the two forces by an equivalent wrench, and determine (a) the magnitude and direction of the resultant force $\mathbf{R}$, (b) the pitch of the wrench, (c) the point where the axis of the wrench intersects the yz plane.

SOLUTION

Equivalent Force-Couple System at O. We first determine the equivalent force-couple system at the origin O. We observe that the position vectors of the points of application E and D of the two given forces are $\mathbf{r}_E = a\mathbf{i} + a\mathbf{j}$ and $\mathbf{r}_D = a\mathbf{j} + a\mathbf{k}$. The resultant $\mathbf{R}$ of the two forces and their moment resultant $\mathbf{M}_O^R$ about O are

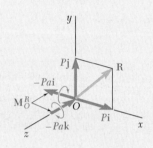

$$\mathbf{R} = \mathbf{F}_1 + \mathbf{F}_2 = P\mathbf{i} + P\mathbf{j} = P(\mathbf{i} + \mathbf{j}) \qquad (1)$$
$$\mathbf{M}_O^R = \mathbf{r}_E \times \mathbf{F}_1 + \mathbf{r}_D \times \mathbf{F}_2 = (a\mathbf{i} + a\mathbf{j}) \times P\mathbf{i} + (a\mathbf{j} + a\mathbf{k}) \times P\mathbf{j}$$
$$= -Pa\mathbf{k} - Pa\mathbf{i} = -Pa(\mathbf{i} + \mathbf{k}) \qquad (2)$$

a. Resultant Force R. It follows from Eq. (1) and the adjoining sketch that the resultant force $\mathbf{R}$ has the magnitude $R = P\sqrt{2}$, lies in the xy plane, and forms angles of $45°$ with the x and y axes. Thus

$$R = P\sqrt{2} \qquad \theta_x = \theta_y = 45° \qquad \theta_z = 90° \quad \blacktriangleleft$$

b. Pitch of Wrench. Recalling formula (3.62) of Sec. 3.21 and Eqs. (1) and (2) above, we write

$$p = \frac{\mathbf{R} \cdot \mathbf{M}_O^R}{R^2} = \frac{P(\mathbf{i} + \mathbf{j}) \cdot (-Pa)(\mathbf{i} + \mathbf{k})}{(P\sqrt{2})^2} = \frac{-P^2a(1 + 0 + 0)}{2P^2} \qquad p = -\frac{a}{2} \quad \blacktriangleleft$$

c. Axis of Wrench. It follows from the above and from Eq. (3.61) that the wrench consists of the force $\mathbf{R}$ found in (1) and the couple vector

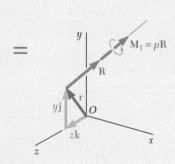

$$\mathbf{M}_1 = p\mathbf{R} = -\frac{a}{2}P(\mathbf{i} + \mathbf{j}) = -\frac{Pa}{2}(\mathbf{i} + \mathbf{j}) \qquad (3)$$

To find the point where the axis of the wrench intersects the yz plane, we express that the moment of the wrench about O is equal to the moment resultant $\mathbf{M}_O^R$ of the original system:

$$\mathbf{M}_1 + \mathbf{r} \times \mathbf{R} = \mathbf{M}_O^R$$

or, noting that $\mathbf{r} = y\mathbf{j} + z\mathbf{k}$ and substituting for $\mathbf{R}$, $\mathbf{M}_O^R$, and $\mathbf{M}_1$ from Eqs. (1), (2), and (3),

$$-\frac{Pa}{2}(\mathbf{i} + \mathbf{j}) + (y\mathbf{j} + z\mathbf{k}) \times P(\mathbf{i} + \mathbf{j}) = -Pa(\mathbf{i} + \mathbf{k})$$

$$-\frac{Pa}{2}\mathbf{i} - \frac{Pa}{2}\mathbf{j} - Py\mathbf{k} + Pz\mathbf{j} - Pz\mathbf{i} = -Pa\mathbf{i} - Pa\mathbf{k}$$

Equating the coefficients of $\mathbf{k}$, and then the coefficients of $\mathbf{j}$, we find

$$y = a \qquad z = a/2 \quad \blacktriangleleft$$

SOLVING PROBLEMS
ON YOUR OWN

This lesson was devoted to the reduction and simplification of force systems. In solving the problems which follow, you will be asked to perform the operations discussed below.

1. Reducing a force system to a force and a couple at a given point A. The force is the *resultant* **R** of the system and is obtained by adding the various forces; the moment of the couple is the *moment resultant* of the system and is obtained by adding the moments about A of the various forces. We have

$$\mathbf{R} = \Sigma\mathbf{F} \qquad \mathbf{M}_A^R = \Sigma(\mathbf{r} \times \mathbf{F})$$

where the position vector **r** is drawn from A to *any point* on the line of action of **F**.

2. Moving a force-couple system from point A to point B. If you wish to reduce a given force system to a force-couple system at point B after you have reduced it to a force-couple system at point A, you need not recompute the moments of the forces about B. The resultant **R** remains unchanged, and the new moment resultant $\mathbf{M}_B^R$ can be obtained by adding to $\mathbf{M}_A^R$ the moment about B of the force **R** applied at A [Sample Prob. 3.8]. Denoting by **s** the vector drawn from B to A, you can write

$$\mathbf{M}_B^R = \mathbf{M}_A^R + \mathbf{s} \times \mathbf{R}$$

3. Checking whether two force systems are equivalent. First reduce each force system to a force-couple system *at the same, but arbitrary, point A* (as explained in paragraph 1). The two systems are equivalent (that is, they have the same effect on the given rigid body) if the two force-couple systems you have obtained are identical, that is, if

$$\Sigma\mathbf{F} = \Sigma\mathbf{F}' \qquad \text{and} \qquad \Sigma\mathbf{M}_A = \Sigma\mathbf{M}_A'$$

You should recognize that if the first of these equations is not satisfied, that is, if the two systems do not have the same resultant **R**, the two systems cannot be equivalent and there is then no need to check whether or not the second equation is satisfied.

4. Reducing a given force system to a single force. First reduce the given system to a force-couple system consisting of the resultant **R** and the couple vector $\mathbf{M}_A^R$ at some convenient point A (as explained in paragraph 1). You will recall from the previous lesson that further reduction to a single force is possible *only if the*

(continued)

force **R** *and the couple vector* $\mathbf{M}_A^R$ *are mutually perpendicular*. This will certainly be the case for systems of forces which are either *concurrent*, *coplanar*, or *parallel*. The required single force can then be obtained by moving **R** until its moment about A is equal to $\mathbf{M}_A^R$, as you did in several problems of the preceding lesson. More formally, you can write that the position vector **r** drawn from A to any point on the line of action of the single force **R** must satisfy the equation

$$\mathbf{r} \times \mathbf{R} = \mathbf{M}_A^R$$

This procedure was used in Sample Probs. 3.8, 3.9, and 3.11.

5. Reducing a given force system to a wrench. If the given system is comprised of forces which are not concurrent, coplanar, or parallel, the equivalent force-couple system at a point A will consist of a force **R** and a couple vector $\mathbf{M}_A^R$ which, in general, *are not mutually perpendicular*. (To check whether **R** and $\mathbf{M}_A^R$ are mutually perpendicular, form their scalar product. If this product is zero, they are mutually perpendicular; otherwise, they are not.) If **R** and $\mathbf{M}_A^R$ are not mutually perpendicular, the force-couple system (and thus the given system of forces) *cannot be reduced to a single force*. However, the system can be reduced to a *wrench*—the combination of a force **R** and a couple vector $\mathbf{M}_1$ directed along a common line of action called the *axis of the wrench* (Fig. 3.47). The ratio $p = M_1/R$ is called the *pitch* of the wrench.

To reduce a given force system to a wrench, you should follow these steps:

   a. Reduce the given system to an equivalent force-couple system $(\mathbf{R}, \mathbf{M}_O^R)$, typically located at the origin O.
   b. Determine the pitch p from Eq. (3.62)

$$p = \frac{M_1}{R} = \frac{\mathbf{R} \cdot \mathbf{M}_O^R}{R^2} \tag{3.62}$$

and the couple vector from $\mathbf{M}_1 = p\mathbf{R}$.
   c. Express that the moment about O of the wrench is equal to the moment resultant $\mathbf{M}_O^R$ of the force-couple system at O:

$$\mathbf{M}_1 + \mathbf{r} \times \mathbf{R} = \mathbf{M}_O^R \tag{3.63}$$

This equation allows you to determine the point where the line of action of the wrench intersects a specified plane, since the position vector **r** is directed from O to that point.

These steps are illustrated in Sample Prob. 3.12. Although the determination of a wrench and the point where its axis intersects a plane may appear difficult, the process is simply the application of several of the ideas and techniques developed in this chapter. Thus, once you have mastered the wrench, you can feel confident that you understand much of Chap. 3.

PROBLEMS

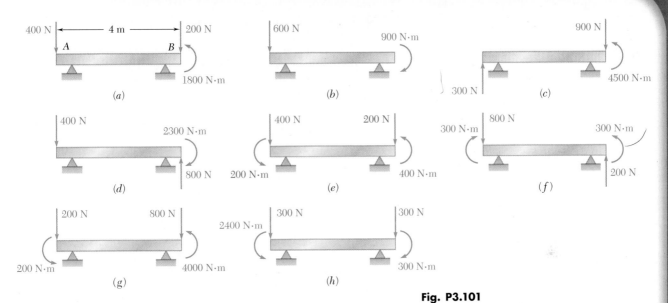

Fig. P3.101

3.101 A 4-m-long beam is subjected to a variety of loadings. (*a*) Replace each loading with an equivalent force-couple system at end *A* of the beam. (*b*) Which of the loadings are equivalent?

3.102 A 4-m-long beam is loaded as shown. Determine the loading of Prob. 3.101 which is equivalent to this loading.

3.103 Determine the single equivalent force and the distance from point *A* to its line of action for the beam and loading of (*a*) Prob. 3.101*b*, (*b*) Prob. 3.101*d*, (*c*) Prob. 3.101*e*.

3.104 Five separate force-couple systems act at the corners of a piece of sheet metal, which has been bent into the shape shown. Determine which of these systems is equivalent to a force **F** = (10 lb)**i** and a couple of moment **M** = (15 lb · ft)**j** + (15 lb · ft)**k** located at the origin.

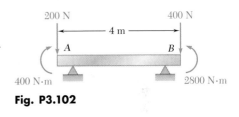

Fig. P3.102

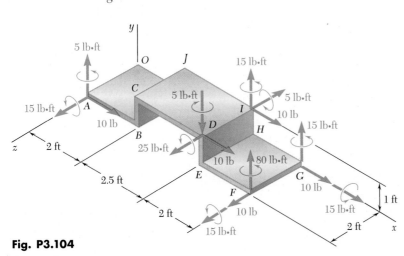

Fig. P3.104

137

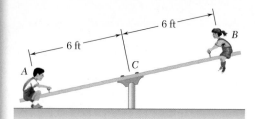

Fig. P3.105

3.105 The weights of two children sitting at ends A and B of a seesaw are 84 lb and 64 lb, respectively. Where should a third child sit so that the resultant of the weights of the three children will pass through C if she weighs (*a*) 60 lb, (*b*) 52 lb.

3.106 Three stage lights are mounted on a pipe as shown. The lights at A and B each weigh 4.1 lb, while the one at C weighs 3.5 lb. (*a*) If $d = 25$ in., determine the distance from D to the line of action of the resultant of the weights of the three lights. (*b*) Determine the value of d so that the resultant of the weights passes through the midpoint of the pipe.

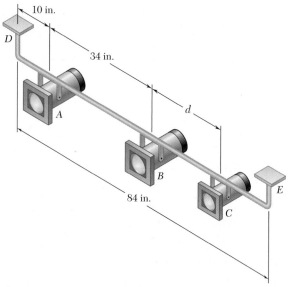

Fig. P3.106

3.107 A beam supports three loads of given magnitude and a fourth load whose magnitude is a function of position. If $b = 1.5$ m and the loads are to be replaced with a single equivalent force, determine (*a*) the value of a so that the distance from support A to the line of action of the equivalent force is maximum, (*b*) the magnitude of the equivalent force and its point of application on the beam.

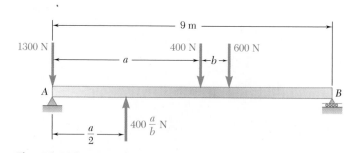

Fig. *P3.107*

3.108 Gear C is rigidly attached to arm AB. If the forces and couple shown can be reduced to a single equivalent force at A, determine the equivalent force and the magnitude of the couple **M**.

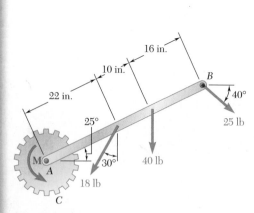

Fig. P3.108

3.109 A couple of magnitude $M = 54$ lb · in. and the three forces shown are applied to an angle bracket. (a) Find the resultant of this system of forces. (b) Locate the points where the line of action of the resultant intersects line AB and line BC.

3.110 A couple **M** and the three forces shown are applied to an angle bracket. Find the moment of the couple if the line of action of the resultant of the force system is to pass through (a) point A, (b) point B, (c) point C.

3.111 Four forces act on a 700×375-mm plate as shown. (a) Find the resultant of these forces. (b) Locate the two points where the line of action of the resultant intersects the edge of the plate.

3.112 Solve Prob. 3.111, assuming that the 760-N force is directed to the right.

3.113 A truss supports the loading shown. Determine the equivalent force acting on the truss and the point of intersection of its line of action with a line drawn through points A and G.

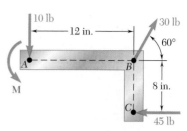

Fig. P3.109 and P3.110

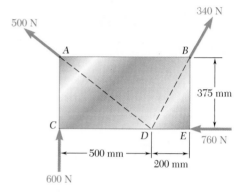

Fig. P3.111

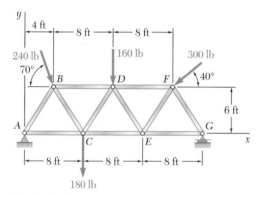

Fig. P3.113

3.114 Pulleys A and B are mounted on bracket $CDEF$. The tension on each side of the two belts is as shown. Replace the four forces with a single equivalent force, and determine where its line of action intersects the bottom edge of the bracket.

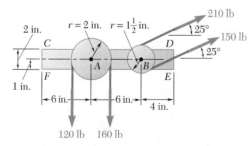

Fig. P3.114

3.115 A machine component is subjected to the forces and couples shown. The component is to be held in place by a single rivet that can resist a force but not a couple. For $P = 0$, determine the location of the rivet hole if it is to be located (a) on line FG, (b) on line GH.

3.116 Solve Prob. 3.115, assuming that $P = 60$ N.

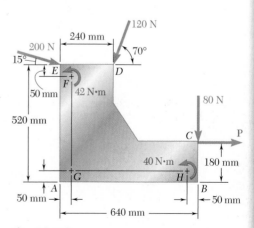

Fig. P3.115

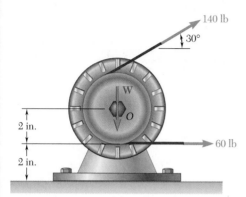

Fig. P3.117

3.117 A 32-lb motor is mounted on the floor. Find the resultant of the weight and the forces exerted on the belt, and determine where the line of action of the resultant intersects the floor.

3.118 As follower AB rolls along the surface of member C, it exerts a constant force $\mathbf{F}$ perpendicular to the surface. (*a*) Replace $\mathbf{F}$ with an equivalent force-couple system at the point D obtained by drawing the perpendicular from the point of contact to the x axis. (*b*) For $a = 1$ m and $b = 2$ m, determine the value of x for which the moment of the equivalent force-couple system at D is maximum.

3.119 Four forces are applied to the machine component $ABDE$ as shown. Replace these forces by an equivalent force-couple system at A.

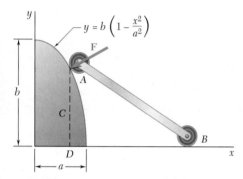

Fig. P3.118

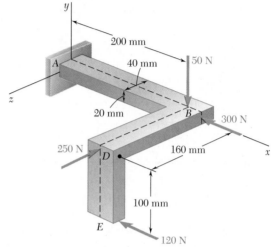

Fig. P3.119

3.120 Two 150-mm-diameter pulleys are mounted on line shaft AD. The belts at B and C lie in vertical planes parallel to the yz plane. Replace the belt forces shown with an equivalent force-couple system at A.

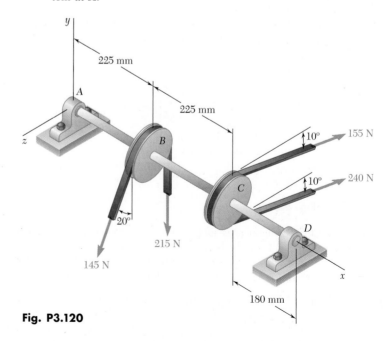

Fig. P3.120

3.121 While using a pencil sharpener, a student applies the forces and couple shown. (*a*) Determine the forces exerted at *B* and *C* knowing that these forces and the couple are equivalent to a force-couple system at *A* consisting of the force $\mathbf{R} = (2.6 \text{ lb})\mathbf{i} + R_y\mathbf{j} - (0.7 \text{ lb})\mathbf{k}$ and the couple $\mathbf{M}_A^R = M_x\mathbf{i} + (1.0 \text{ lb} \cdot \text{ft})\mathbf{j} - (0.72 \text{ lb} \cdot \text{ft})\mathbf{k}$. (*b*) Find the corresponding values of R_y and M_x.

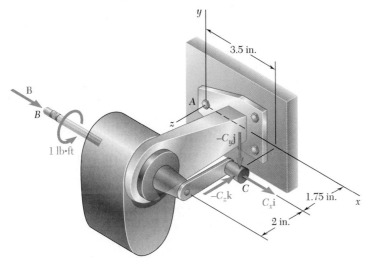

Fig. P3.121

3.122 A mechanic uses a crowfoot wrench to loosen a bolt at *C*. The mechanic holds the socket wrench handle at points *A* and *B* and applies forces at these points. Knowing that these forces are equivalent to a force-couple system at *C* consisting of the force $\mathbf{C} = -(8 \text{ lb})\mathbf{i} + (4 \text{ lb})\mathbf{k}$ and the couple $\mathbf{M}_C = (360 \text{ lb} \cdot \text{in.})\mathbf{i}$, determine the forces applied at *A* and at *B* when $A_z = 2$ lb.

3.123 As an adjustable brace *BC* is used to bring a wall into plumb, the force-couple system shown is exerted on the wall. Replace this force-couple system with an equivalent force-couple system at *A* if $R = 21.2$ lb and $M = 13.25$ lb $\cdot$ ft.

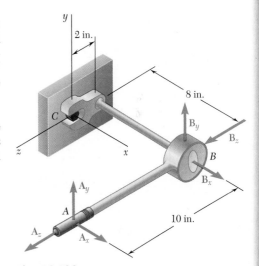

Fig. P3.122

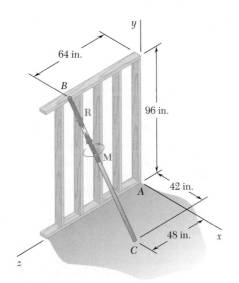

Fig. P3.123

3.124 A mechanic replaces a car's exhaust system by firmly clamping the catalytic converter *FG* to its mounting brackets *H* and *I* and then loosely assembling the mufflers and the exhaust pipes. To position the tailpipe *AB*, he pushes in and up at *A* while pulling down at *B*. (*a*) Replace the given force system with an equivalent force-couple system at *D*. (*b*) Determine whether pipe *CD* tends to rotate clockwise or counterclockwise relative to muffler *DE*, as viewed by the mechanic.

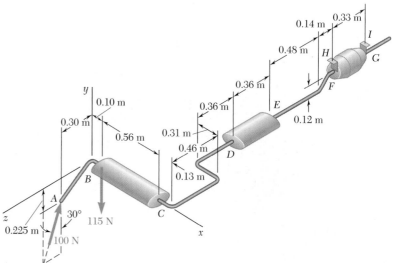

Fig. P3.124

3.125 For the exhaust system of Prob. 3.124, (*a*) replace the given force system with an equivalent force-couple system at *F*, where the exhaust pipe is connected to the catalytic converter, (*b*) determine whether pipe *EF* tends to rotate clockwise or counterclockwise, as viewed by the mechanic.

3.126 The head-and-motor assembly of a radial drill press was originally positioned with arm *AB* parallel to the *z* axis and the axis of the chuck and bit parallel to the *y* axis. The assembly was then rotated 25° about the *y* axis and 20° about the centerline of the horizontal arm *AB*, bringing it into the position shown. The drilling process was started by switching on the motor and rotating the handle to bring the bit into contact with the workpiece. Replace the force and couple exerted by the drill press with an equivalent force-couple system at the center *O* of the base of the vertical column.

3.127 Three children are standing on a 5 × 5-m raft. If the weights of the children at points *A*, *B*, and *C* are 375 N, 260 N, and 400 N, respectively, determine the magnitude and the point of application of the resultant of the three weights.

3.128 Three children are standing on a 5 × 5-m raft. The weights of the children at points *A*, *B*, and *C* are 375 N, 260 N, and 400 N, respectively. If a fourth child of weight 425 N climbs onto the raft, determine where she should stand if the other children remain in the positions shown and the line of action of the resultant of the four weights is to pass through the center of the raft.

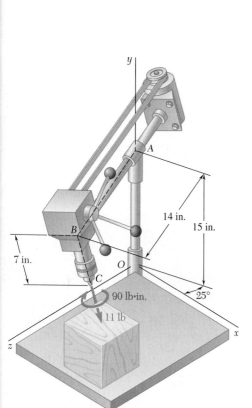

Fig. P3.126

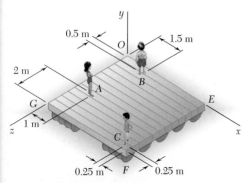

Fig. P3.127 and P3.128

3.129 Four signs are mounted on a frame spanning a highway, and the magnitudes of the horizontal wind forces acting on the signs are as shown. Determine the magnitude and the point of application of the resultant of the four wind forces when $a = 1$ ft and $b = 12$ ft.

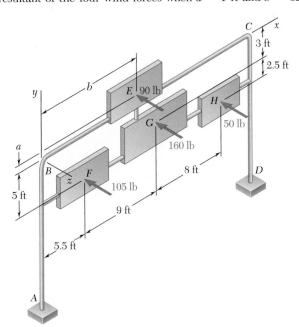

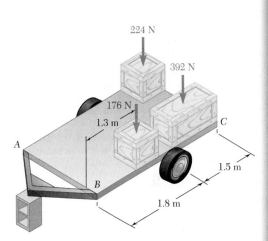

Fig. P3.131

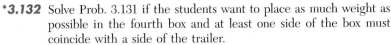

Fig. P3.129 and P3.130

3.130 Four signs are mounted on a frame spanning a highway, and the magnitudes of the horizontal wind forces acting on the signs are as shown. Determine a and b so that the point of application of the resultant of the four forces is at G.

*3.131 A group of students loads a 2×3.3-m flatbed trailer with two $0.66 \times 0.66 \times 0.66$-m boxes and one $0.66 \times 0.66 \times 1.2$-m box. Each of the boxes at the rear of the trailer is positioned so that it is aligned with both the back and a side of the trailer. Determine the smallest load the students should place in a second $0.66 \times 0.66 \times 1.2$-m box and where on the trailer they should secure it, without any part of the box overhanging the sides of the trailer, if each box is uniformly loaded and the line of action of the resultant of the weights of the four boxes is to pass through the point of intersection of the centerlines of the trailer and the axle. (*Hint:* Keep in mind that the box may be placed either on its side or on its end.)

*3.132 Solve Prob. 3.131 if the students want to place as much weight as possible in the fourth box and at least one side of the box must coincide with a side of the trailer.

*3.133 Three forces of the same magnitude P act on a cube of side a as shown. Replace the three forces by an equivalent wrench and determine (*a*) the magnitude and direction of the resultant force **R**, (*b*) the pitch of the wrench, (*c*) the axis of the wrench.

*3.134 A piece of sheet metal is bent into the shape shown and is acted upon by three forces. If the forces have the same magnitude P, replace them with an equivalent wrench and determine (*a*) the magnitude and the direction of the resultant force **R**, (*b*) the pitch of the wrench, (*c*) the axis of the wrench.

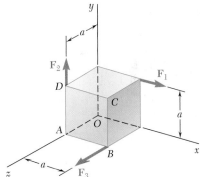

Fig. P3.133

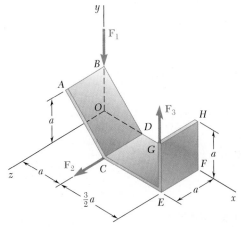

Fig. P3.134

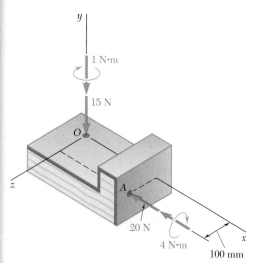

Fig. P3.135

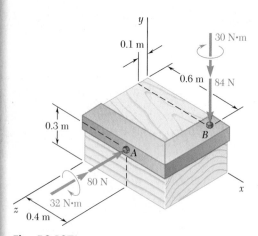

Fig. P3.137

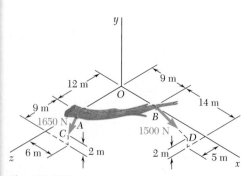

Fig. P3.139

*3.135 and *3.136 The forces and couples shown are applied to two screws as a piece of sheet metal is fastened to a block of wood. Reduce the forces and the couples to an equivalent wrench and determine (a) the resultant force **R**, (b) the pitch of the wrench, (c) the point where the axis of the wrench intersects the xz plane.

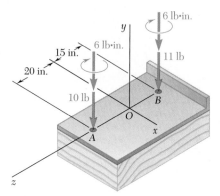

Fig. P3.136

*3.137 and *3.138 Two bolts at A and B are tightened by applying the forces and couples shown. Replace the two wrenches with a single equivalent wrench and determine (a) the resultant **R**, (b the pitch of the single equivalent wrench, (c) the point where the axis of the wrench intersects the xz plane.

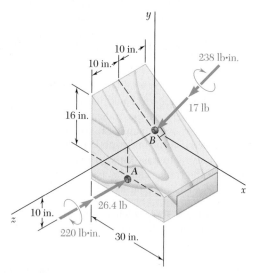

Fig. P3.138

*3.139 Two ropes attached at A and B are used to move the trunk of a fallen tree. Replace the forces exerted by the ropes with an equivalent wrench and determine (a) the resultant force **R**, (b) the pitch of the wrench, (c) the point where the axis of the wrench intersects the yz plane.

*3.140 A flagpole is guyed by three cables. If the tensions in the cables have the same magnitude P, replace the forces exerted on the pole with an equivalent wrench and determine (*a*) the resultant force **R**, (*b*) the pitch of the wrench, (*c*) the point where the axis of the wrench intersects the xz plane.

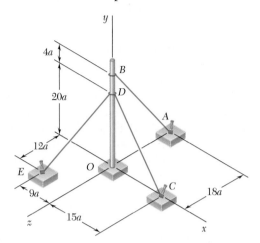

Fig. P3.140

*3.141 and *3.142 Determine whether the force-and-couple system shown can be reduced to a single equivalent force **R**. If it can, determine **R** and the point where the line of action of **R** intersects the yz plane. If it cannot be so reduced, replace the given system with an equivalent wrench and determine its resultant, its pitch, and the point where its axis intersects the yz plane.

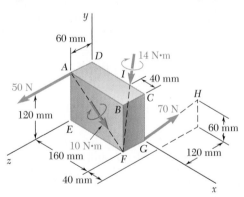

Fig. P3.141

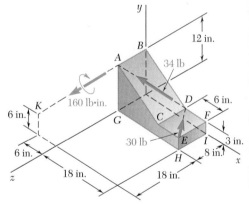

Fig. P3.142

*3.143 Replace the wrench shown with an equivalent system consisting of two forces perpendicular to the y axis and applied respectively at A and B.

*3.144 Show that, in general, a wrench can be replaced with two forces chosen in such a way that one force passes through a given point while the other force lies in a given plane.

*3.145 Show that a wrench can be replaced with two perpendicular forces, one of which is applied at a given point.

*3.146 Show that a wrench can be replaced with two forces, one of which has a prescribed line of action.

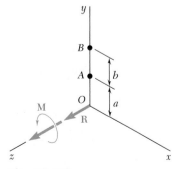

Fig. P3.143

REVIEW AND SUMMARY

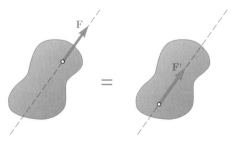

Fig. 3.48

In this chapter we studied the effect of forces exerted on a rigid body. We first learned to distinguish between *external* and *internal* forces [Sec. 3.2] and saw that, according to the *principle of transmissibility*, the effect of an external force on a rigid body remains unchanged if that force is moved along its line of action [Sec. 3.3]. In other words, two forces **F** and **F′** acting on a rigid body at two different points have the same effect on that body if they have the same magnitude, same direction, and same one of action (Fig. 3.48). Two such forces are said to be *equivalent*.

Before proceeding with the discussion of *equivalent systems of forces,* we introduced the concept of the *vector product of two vectors* [Sec. 3.4]. The vector product

Vector product of two vectors

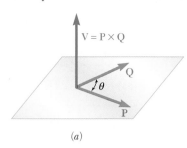

(a)

(b)

Fig. 3.49

$$\mathbf{V} = \mathbf{P} \times \mathbf{Q}$$

of the vectors **P** and **Q** was defined as a vector perpendicular to the plane containing **P** and **Q** (Fig. 3.49), of magnitude

$$V = PQ \sin \theta \tag{3.1}$$

and directed in such a way that a person located at the tip of **V** will observe as counterclockwise the rotation through θ which brings the vector **P** in line with the vector **Q**. The three vectors **P**, **Q**, and **V**—taken in that order—are said to form a *right-handed triad*. It follows that the vector products **Q** × **P** and **P** × **Q** are represented by equal and opposite vectors. We have

$$\mathbf{Q} \times \mathbf{P} = -(\mathbf{P} \times \mathbf{Q}) \tag{3.4}$$

Fig. 3.50

It also follows from the definition of the vector product of two vectors that the vector products of the unit vectors **i**, **j**, and **k** are

$$\mathbf{i} \times \mathbf{i} = 0 \qquad \mathbf{i} \times \mathbf{j} = \mathbf{k} \qquad \mathbf{j} \times \mathbf{i} = -\mathbf{k}$$

and so on. The sign of the vector product of two unit vectors can be obtained by arranging in a circle and in counterclockwise order the three letters representing the unit vectors (Fig. 3.50): The vector product of two unit vectors will be positive if they follow each other in counterclockwise order and negative if they follow each other in clockwise order.

Rectangular components of vector product

The *rectangular components of the vector product* **V** of two vectors **P** and **Q** were expressed [Sec. 3.5] as

$$\begin{aligned} V_x &= P_y Q_z - P_z Q_y \\ V_y &= P_z Q_x - P_x Q_z \\ V_z &= P_x Q_y - P_y Q_x \end{aligned} \tag{3.9}$$

Using a determinant, we also wrote

$$V = \begin{vmatrix} i & j & k \\ P_x & P_y & P_z \\ Q_x & Q_y & Q_z \end{vmatrix} \quad (3.10)$$

The *moment of a force* **F** *about a point O* was defined [Sec. 3.6] as the vector product

$$M_O = r \times F \quad (3.11)$$

where **r** is the *position vector* drawn from O to the point of application A of the force **F** (Fig. 3.51). Denoting by θ the angle between the lines of action of **r** and **F**, we found that the magnitude of the moment of **F** about O can be expressed as

$$M_O = rF \sin \theta = Fd \quad (3.12)$$

where d represents the perpendicular distance from O to the line of action of **F**.

The *rectangular components of the moment* M_O of a force **F** were expressed [Sec. 3.8] as

$$\begin{aligned} M_x &= yF_z - zF_y \\ M_y &= zF_x - xF_z \\ M_z &= xF_y - yF_x \end{aligned} \quad (3.18)$$

where x, y, z are the components of the position vector **r** (Fig. 3.52). Using a determinant form, we also wrote

$$M_O = \begin{vmatrix} i & j & k \\ x & y & z \\ F_x & F_y & F_z \end{vmatrix} \quad (3.19)$$

In the more general case of the moment about an arbitrary point B of a force **F** applied at A, we had

$$M_B = \begin{vmatrix} i & j & k \\ x_{A/B} & y_{A/B} & z_{A/B} \\ F_x & F_y & F_z \end{vmatrix} \quad (3.21)$$

where $x_{A/B}$, $y_{A/B}$, and $z_{A/B}$ denote the components of the vector $r_{A/B}$:

$$x_{A/B} = x_A - x_B \qquad y_{A/B} = y_A - y_B \qquad z_{A/B} = z_A - z_B$$

In the case of *problems involving only two dimensions*, the force **F** can be assumed to lie in the xy plane. Its moment M_B about a point B in the same plane is perpendicular to that plane (Fig. 3.53) and is completely defined by the scalar

$$M_B = (x_A - x_B)F_y - (y_A - y_B)F_x \quad (3.23)$$

Various methods for the computation of the moment of a force about a point were illustrated in Sample Probs. 3.1 through 3.4.

The *scalar product* of two vectors **P** and **Q** [Sec. 3.9] was denoted by $P \cdot Q$ and was defined as the scalar quantity

$$P \cdot Q = PQ \cos \theta \quad (3.24)$$

Moment of a force about a point

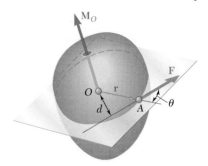

Fig. 3.51

Rectangular components of moment

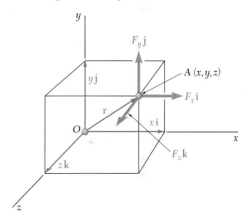

Fig. 3.52

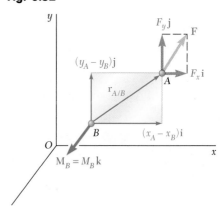

Fig. 3.53

Scalar product of two vectors

where θ is the angle between $\mathbf{P}$ and $\mathbf{Q}$ (Fig. 3.54). By expressing the scalar product of $\mathbf{P}$ and $\mathbf{Q}$ in terms of the rectangular components of the two vectors, we determined that

$$\mathbf{P} \cdot \mathbf{Q} = P_x Q_x + P_y Q_y + P_z Q_z \qquad (3.30)$$

Fig. 3.54

Projection of a vector on an axis

The *projection of a vector* $\mathbf{P}$ *on an axis OL* (Fig. 3.55) can be obtained by forming the scalar product of $\mathbf{P}$ and the unit vector $\boldsymbol{\lambda}$ along OL. We have

$$P_{OL} = \mathbf{P} \cdot \boldsymbol{\lambda} \qquad (3.36)$$

or, using rectangular components,

$$P_{OL} = P_x \cos \theta_x + P_y \cos \theta_y + P_z \cos \theta_z \qquad (3.37)$$

where θ_x, θ_y, and θ_z denote the angles that the axis OL forms with the coordinate axes.

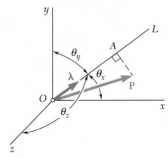

Fig. 3.55

Mixed triple product of three vectors

The *mixed triple product* of the three vectors $\mathbf{S}$, $\mathbf{P}$, and $\mathbf{Q}$ was defined as the scalar expression

$$\mathbf{S} \cdot (\mathbf{P} \times \mathbf{Q}) \qquad (3.38)$$

obtained by forming the scalar product of $\mathbf{S}$ with the vector product of $\mathbf{P}$ and $\mathbf{Q}$ [Sec. 3.10]. It was shown that

$$\mathbf{S} \cdot (\mathbf{P} \times \mathbf{Q}) = \begin{vmatrix} S_x & S_y & S_z \\ P_x & P_y & P_z \\ Q_x & Q_y & Q_z \end{vmatrix} \qquad (3.41)$$

where the elements of the determinant are the rectangular components of the three vectors.

Moment of a force about an axis

The *moment of a force* $\mathbf{F}$ *about an axis OL* [Sec. 3.11] was defined as the projection OC on OL of the moment $\mathbf{M}_O$ of the force $\mathbf{F}$ (Fig. 3.56), i.e., as the mixed triple product of the unit vector $\boldsymbol{\lambda}$, the position vector $\mathbf{r}$, and the force $\mathbf{F}$:

$$M_{OL} = \boldsymbol{\lambda} \cdot \mathbf{M}_O = \boldsymbol{\lambda} \cdot (\mathbf{r} \times \mathbf{F}) \qquad (3.42)$$

Using the determinant form for the mixed triple product, we have

$$M_{OL} = \begin{vmatrix} \lambda_x & \lambda_y & \lambda_z \\ x & y & z \\ F_x & F_y & F_z \end{vmatrix} \qquad (3.43)$$

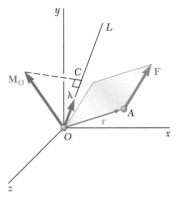

Fig. 3.56

where $\lambda_x, \lambda_y, \lambda_z$ = direction cosines of axis OL
x, y, z = components of $\mathbf{r}$
F_x, F_y, F_z = components of $\mathbf{F}$

An example of the determination of the moment of a force about a skew axis was given in Sample Prob. 3.5.

Two forces **F** and **−F** having the same magnitude, parallel lines of action, and opposite sense are said to form a couple [Sec. 3.12]. It was shown that the moment of a couple is independent of the point about which it is computed; it is a vector **M** perpendicular to the plane of the couple and equal in magnitude to the product of the common magnitude F of the forces and the perpendicular distance d between their lines of action (Fig. 3.57).

Couples

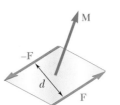

Fig. 3.57

Two couples having the same moment **M** are *equivalent*, i.e., they have the same effect on a given rigid body [Sec. 3.13]. The sum of two couples is itself a couple [Sec. 3.14], and the moment **M** of the resultant couple can be obtained by adding vectorially the moments **M₁** and **M₂** of the original couples [Sample Prob. 3.6]. It follows that a couple can be represented by a vector, called a *couple vector*, equal in magnitude and direction to the moment **M** of the couple [Sec. 3.15]. A couple vector is a *free vector* which can be attached to the origin O if so desired and resolved into components (Fig. 3.58).

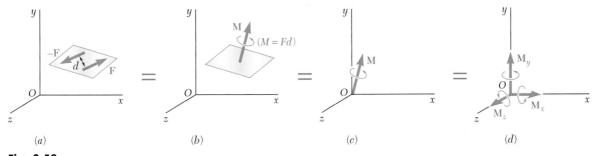

(a) (b) (c) (d)

Fig. 3.58

Any force **F** acting at a point A of a rigid body can be replaced by a *force-couple system* at an arbitrary point O, consisting of the force **F** applied at O and a couple of moment **M**$_O$ equal to the moment about O of the force **F** in its original position [Sec. 3.16]; it should be noted that the force **F** and the couple vector **M**$_O$ are always perpendicular to each other (Fig. 3.59).

Force-couple system

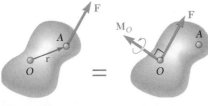

Fig. 3.59

It follows [Sec. 3.17] that *any system of forces can be reduced to a force-couple system at a given point O* by first replacing each of the forces of the system by an equivalent force-couple system at O

Reduction of a system of forces to a force-couple system

(Fig. 3.60) and then adding all the forces and all the couples determined in this manner to obtain a resultant force $\mathbf{R}$ and a resultant couple vector $\mathbf{M}_O^R$ [Sample Probs. 3.8 through 3.11]. Note that, in general, the resultant $\mathbf{R}$ and the couple vector $\mathbf{M}_O^R$ will not be perpendicular to each other.

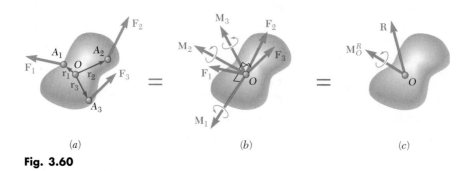

(a)   (b)   (c)

Fig. 3.60

Equivalent systems of forces   We concluded from the above [Sec. 3.18] that, as far as rigid bodies are concerned, *two systems of forces, $\mathbf{F}_1$, $\mathbf{F}_2$, $\mathbf{F}_3$, . . . and $\mathbf{F}_1'$, $\mathbf{F}_2'$, $\mathbf{F}_3'$, . . . , are equivalent if, and only if,*

$$\Sigma\mathbf{F} = \Sigma\mathbf{F}' \qquad \text{and} \qquad \Sigma\mathbf{M}_O = \Sigma\mathbf{M}_O' \qquad (3.57)$$

Further reduction of a system of forces   If the resultant force $\mathbf{R}$ and the resultant couple vector $\mathbf{M}_O^R$ are perpendicular to each other, the force-couple system at O can be further reduced to a single resultant force [Sec. 3.20]. This will be the case for systems consisting either of (a) concurrent forces (cf. Chap. 2), (b) coplanar forces [Sample Probs. 3.8 and 3.9], or (c) parallel forces [Sample Prob. 3.11]. If the resultant $\mathbf{R}$ and the couple vector $\mathbf{M}_O^R$ are *not* perpendicular to each other, the system *cannot* be reduced to a single force. It can, however, be reduced to a special type of force-couple system called a *wrench,* consisting of the resultant $\mathbf{R}$ and a couple vector $\mathbf{M}_1$ directed along $\mathbf{R}$ [Sec. 3.21 and Sample Prob. 3.12].

REVIEW PROBLEMS

3.147 A crate of mass 80 kg is held in the position shown. Determine (*a*) the moment produced by the weight **W** of the crate about *E*, (*b*) the smallest force applied at *B* that creates a moment of equal magnitude and opposite sense about *E*.

3.148 It is known that the connecting rod *AB* exerts on the crank *BC* a 1.5-kN force directed down and to the left along the centerline of *AB*. Determine the moment of the force about *C*.

3.149 A 6-ft-long fishing rod *AB* is securely anchored in the sand of a beach. After a fish takes the bait, the resulting force in the line is 6 lb. Determine the moment about *A* of the force exerted by the line at *B*.

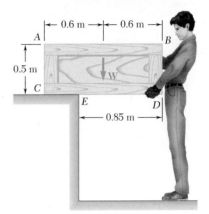

Fig. P3.147

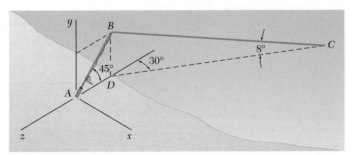

Fig. P3.149

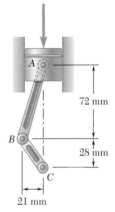

Fig. P3.148

3.150 Ropes *AB* and *BC* are two of the ropes used to support a tent. The two ropes are attached to a stake at *B*. If the tension in rope *AB* is 540 N, determine (*a*) the angle between rope *AB* and the stake, (*b*) the projection on the stake of the force exerted by rope *AB* at point *B*.

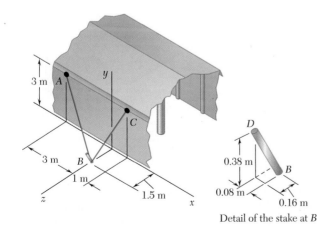

Detail of the stake at *B*

Fig. P3.150

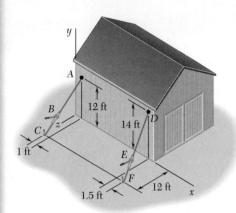

Fig. P3.151

3.151 A farmer uses cables and winch pullers B and E to plumb one side of a small barn. If it is known that the sum of the moments about the x axis of the forces exerted by the cables on the barn at points A and D is equal to 4728 lb · ft, determine the magnitude of $\mathbf{T}_{DE}$ when $T_{AB} = 255$ lb.

3.152 Solve Prob. 3.151 when the tension in cable AB is 306 lb.

3.153 A wiring harness is made by routing either two or three wires around 2-in.-diameter pegs mounted on a sheet of plywood. If the force in each wire is 3 lb, determine the resultant couple acting on the plywood when $a = 18$ in. and (*a*) only wires AB and CD are in place, (*b*) all three wires are in place.

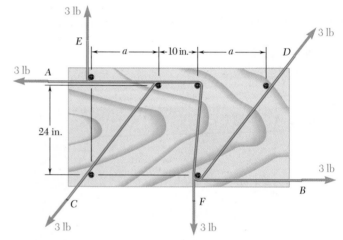

Fig. P3.153

3.154 A worker tries to move a rock by applying a 360-N force to a steel bar as shown. (*a*) Replace that force with an equivalent force-couple system at D. (*b*) Two workers attempt to move the same rock by applying a vertical force at A and another force at D. Determine these two forces if they are to be equivalent to the single force of part *a*.

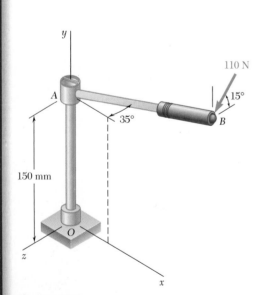

Fig. P3.155

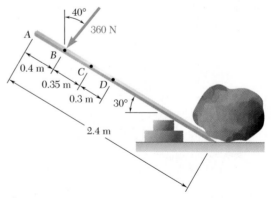

Fig. *P3.154*

3.155 A 110-N force acting in a vertical plane parallel to the yz plane is applied to the 220-mm-long horizontal handle AB of a socket wrench. Replace the force with an equivalent force-couple system at the origin O of the coordinate system.

3.156 Four ropes are attached to a crate and exert the forces shown. If the forces are to be replaced with a single equivalent force applied at a point on line *AB*, determine (*a*) the equivalent force and the distance from *A* to the point of application of the force when $\alpha = 30°$, (*b*) the value of α so that the single equivalent force is applied at point *B*.

3.157 A blade held in a brace is used to tighten a screw at *A*. (*a*) Determine the forces exerted at *B* and *C*, knowing that these forces are equivalent to a force-couple system at *A* consisting of $\mathbf{R} = -(30 \text{ N})\mathbf{i} + R_y\mathbf{j} + R_z\mathbf{k}$ and $\mathbf{M}_A^R = -(12 \text{ N} \cdot \text{m})\mathbf{i}$. (*b*) Find the corresponding values of R_y and R_z. (*c*) What is the orientation of the slot in the head of the screw for which the blade is least likely to slip when the brace is in the position shown?

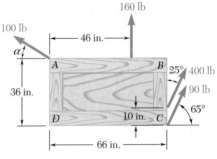

Fig. P3.156

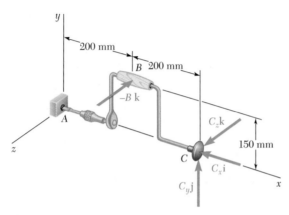

Fig. P3.157

3.158 A concrete foundation mat in the shape of a regular hexagon of side 12 ft supports four column loads as shown. Determine the magnitudes of the additional loads that must be applied at *B* and *F* if the resultant of all six loads is to pass through the center of the mat.

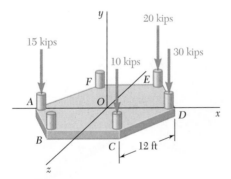

Fig. P3.158

COMPUTER PROBLEMS

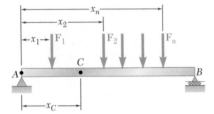

Fig. P3.C1

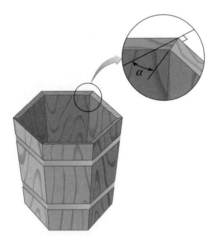

Fig. P3.C3

3.C1 A beam AB is subjected to several vertical forces as shown. Using computational software, determine the magnitude of the resultant of the forces and the distance x_C to point C, the point where the line of action of the resultant intersects AB. Use this program to solve (*a*) Sample Prob. 3.8*c*, (*b*) Prob. 3.106*a*.

3.C2 Using computational software, determine the magnitude and the point of application of the resultant of the vertical forces $\mathbf{P}_1$, $\mathbf{P}_2$, . . . , $\mathbf{P}_n$ that act at points $\mathbf{A}_1$, $\mathbf{A}_2$, . . . , $\mathbf{A}_n$ that are located in the xz plane. Use this program to solve (*a*) Sample Prob. 3.11, (*b*) Prob. 3.127, (*c*) Prob. 3.129.

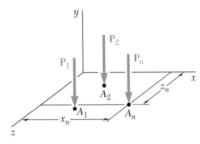

Fig. P3.C2

3.C3 A friend asks for your help in designing flower planter boxes. The boxes are to have 4, 5, 6, or 8 sides, which are to tilt outward at 10°, 20°, or 30°. Using computational software, determine the bevel angle α for each of the twelve planter designs. (*Hint:* The bevel angle is equal to one-half of the angle formed by the inward normals of two adjacent sides.)

3.C4 The manufacturer of a spool for hoses wants to determine the moment of the force $\mathbf{F}$ about the axis AA'. The magnitude of the force, in newtons, is defined by the relation $F = 300(1 - x/L)$, where x is the length of hose wound on the 0.6-m-diameter drum and L is the total length of the hose. Using computational software, calculate the required moment for a hose 30 m long and 50 mm in diameter. Beginning with $x = 0$, compute the moment after every revolution of the drum until the hose is wound on the drum.

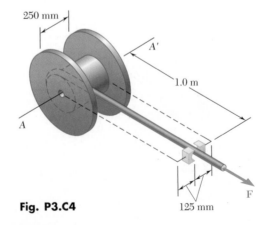

Fig. P3.C4

3.C5 A body is acted upon by a system of n forces. Using computational software, calculate the equivalent force-couple system at the origin of the coordinate axes and to determine, if the equivalent force and the equivalent couple are orthogonal, the magnitude and the point of application in the xz plane of the resultant of the original force system. Use this program to solve (a) Prob. 3.113, (b) Prob. 3.120, (c) Prob. 3.127.

3.C6 Two cylindrical ducts, AB and CD, enter a room through two parallel walls. The centerlines of the ducts are parallel to each other but are not perpendicular to the walls. The ducts are to be connected by two flexible elbows and a straight center portion. Using computational software, determine the lengths of AB and CD that minimize the distance between the axis of the straight portion and a thermometer mounted on the wall at E. Assume that the elbows are of negligible length and that AB and CD have centerlines defined by $\lambda_{AB} = (7\mathbf{i} - 4\mathbf{j} + 4\mathbf{k})/9$ and $\lambda_{CD} = (-7\mathbf{i} + 4\mathbf{j} - 4\mathbf{k})/9$ and can vary in length from 9 in. to 36 in.

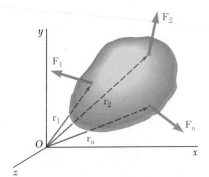

Fig. P3.C5

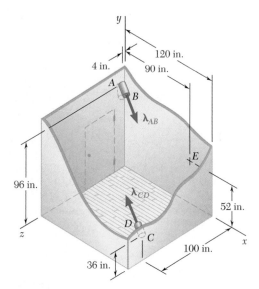

Fig. P3.C6

This telecommunications tower, constructed in the heart of the Barcelona Olympic complex to broadcast the 1992 games, was designed to remain in equilibrium under the vertical force of gravity and the lateral forces exerted by wind.

CHAPTER 4

Equilibrium of Rigid Bodies

Chapter 4 Equilibrium of Rigid Bodies

4.1 INTRODUCTION

We saw in the preceding chapter that the external forces acting on a rigid body can be reduced to a force-couple system at some arbitrary point O. When the force and the couple are both equal to zero, the external forces form a system equivalent to zero, and the rigid body is said to be in *equilibrium.*

The necessary and sufficient conditions for the equilibrium of a rigid body, therefore, can be obtained by setting $\mathbf{R}$ and $\mathbf{M}_O^R$ equal to zero in the relations (3.52) of Sec. 3.17:

$$\Sigma\mathbf{F} = 0 \qquad \Sigma\mathbf{M}_O = \Sigma(\mathbf{r} \times \mathbf{F}) = 0 \tag{4.1}$$

Resolving each force and each moment into its rectangular components, we can express the necessary and sufficient conditions for the equilibrium of a rigid body with the following six scalar equations:

$$\Sigma F_x = 0 \qquad \Sigma F_y = 0 \qquad \Sigma F_z = 0 \tag{4.2}$$
$$\Sigma M_x = 0 \qquad \Sigma M_y = 0 \qquad \Sigma M_z = 0 \tag{4.3}$$

The equations obtained can be used to determine unknown forces applied to the rigid body or unknown reactions exerted on it by its supports. We note that Eqs. (4.2) express the fact that the components of the external forces in the x, y, and z directions are balanced; Eqs. (4.3) express the fact that the moments of the external forces about the x, y, and z axes are balanced. Therefore, for a rigid body in equilibrium, the system of the external forces will impart no translational or rotational motion to the body considered.

In order to write the equations of equilibrium for a rigid body, it is essential to first identify all of the forces acting on that body and then to draw the corresponding *free-body diagram.* In this chapter we first consider the equilibrium of *two-dimensional structures* subjected to forces contained in their planes and learn how to draw their free-body diagrams. In addition to the forces *applied* to a structure, the *reactions* exerted on the structure by its supports will be considered. A specific reaction will be associated with each type of support. You will learn how to determine whether the structure is properly supported, so that you can know in advance whether the equations of equilibrium can be solved for the unknown forces and reactions.

Later in the chapter, the equilibrium of three-dimensional structures will be considered, and the same kind of analysis will be given to these structures and their supports.

4.2 FREE-BODY DIAGRAM

In solving a problem concerning the equilibrium of a rigid body, it is essential to consider *all* of the forces acting on the body; it is equally important to exclude any force which is not directly applied to the body. Omitting a force or adding an extraneous one would destroy the conditions of equilibrium. Therefore, the first step in the solution of the problem should be to draw a *free-body diagram* of the rigid body under consideration. Free-body diagrams have already been used on many occasions in Chap. 2. However, in view of their importance to the solution of equilibrium problems, we summarize here the various steps which must be followed in drawing a free-body diagram.

1. A clear decision should be made regarding the choice of the free body to be used. This body is then detached from the ground and is separated from all other bodies. The contour of the body thus isolated is sketched.

2. All external forces should be indicated on the free-body diagram. These forces represent the actions exerted *on* the free body *by* the ground and *by* the bodies which have been detached; they should be applied at the various points where the free body was supported by the ground or was connected to the other bodies. The *weight* of the free body should also be included among the external forces, since it represents the attraction exerted by the earth on the various particles forming the free body. As will be seen in Chap. 5, the weight should be applied at the center of gravity of the body. When the free body is made of several parts, the forces the various parts exert on each other should *not* be included among the external forces. These forces are internal forces as far as the free body is concerned.

3. The magnitudes and directions of the *known external forces* should be clearly marked on the free-body diagram. When indicating the directions of these forces, it must be remembered that the forces shown on the free-body diagram must be those which are exerted *on*, and not *by*, the free body. Known external forces generally include the *weight* of the free body and *forces applied* for a given purpose.

4. *Unknown external forces* usually consist of the *reactions*, through which the ground and other bodies oppose a possible motion of the free body. The reactions constrain the free body to remain in the same position, and, for that reason, are sometimes called *constraining forces*. Reactions are exerted at the points where the free body is *supported by* or *connected to* other bodies and should be clearly indicated. Reactions are discussed in detail in Secs. 4.3 and 4.8.

5. The free-body diagram should also include dimensions, since these may be needed in the computation of moments of forces. Any other detail, however, should be omitted.

Photo 4.1 A free-body diagram of the tractor shown would include all of the external forces acting on the tractor: the weight of the tractor, the weight of the load in the bucket, and the forces exerted by the ground on the tires.

Photo 4.2 In Chap. 6, we will discuss how to determine the internal forces in structures made of several connected pieces, such as the forces in the members that support the bucket of the tractor of Photo 4.1.

Photo 4.3 As the link of the awning window opening mechanism is extended, the force it exerts on the slider results in a normal force being applied to the rod, which causes the window to open.

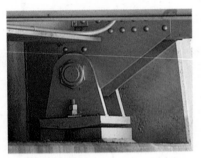

Photo 4.4 The abutment-mounted rocker bearing shown is used to support the roadway of a bridge.

Photo 4.5 Shown is the rocker expansion bearing of a plate girder bridge. The convex surface of the rocker allows the support of the girder to move horizontally.

EQUILIBRIUM IN TWO DIMENSIONS

4.3 REACTIONS AT SUPPORTS AND CONNECTIONS FOR A TWO-DIMENSIONAL STRUCTURE

In the first part of this chapter, the equilibrium of a two-dimensional structure is considered; i.e., it is assumed that the structure being analyzed and the forces applied to it are contained in the same plane. Clearly, the reactions needed to maintain the structure in the same position will also be contained in this plane.

The reactions exerted on a two-dimensional structure can be divided into three groups corresponding to three types of *supports*, or *connections:*

1. *Reactions Equivalent to a Force with Known Line of Action.* Supports and connections causing reactions of this type include *rollers, rockers, frictionless surfaces, short links and cables, collars on frictionless rods,* and *frictionless pins in slots.* Each of these supports and connections can prevent motion in one direction only. They are shown in Fig. 4.1, together with the reactions they produce. Each of these reactions involves *one unknown,* namely, the magnitude of the reaction; this magnitude should be denoted by an appropriate letter. The line of action of the reaction is known and should be indicated clearly in the free-body diagram. The sense of the reaction must be as shown in Fig. 4.1 for the cases of a frictionless surface (toward the free body) or a cable (away from the free body). The reaction can be directed either way in the case of double-track rollers, links, collars on rods, and pins in slots. Single-track rollers and rockers are generally assumed to be reversible, and thus the corresponding reactions can also be directed either way.

2. *Reactions Equivalent to a Force of Unknown Direction and Magnitude.* Supports and connections causing reactions of this type include *frictionless pins in fitted holes, hinges,* and *rough surfaces.* They can prevent translation of the free body in all directions, but they cannot prevent the body from rotating about the connection. Reactions of this group involve *two unknowns* and are usually represented by their x and y components. In the case of a rough surface, the component normal to the surface must be directed away from the surface.

3. *Reactions Equivalent to a Force and a Couple.* These reactions are caused by *fixed supports,* which oppose any motion of the free body and thus constrain it completely. Fixed supports actually produce forces over the entire surface of contact; these forces, however, form a system which can be reduced to a force and a couple. Reactions of this group involve *three unknowns,* consisting usually of the two components of the force and the moment of the couple.

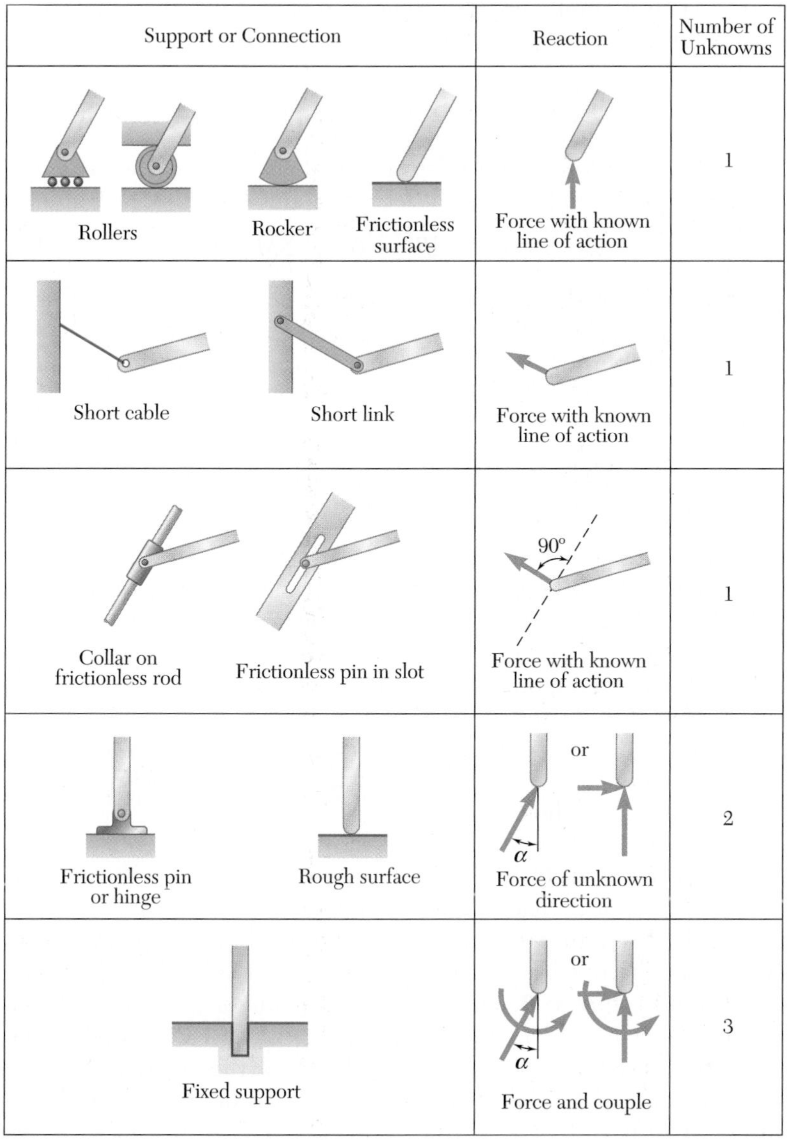

Support or Connection				Reaction	Number of Unknowns
Rollers	Rocker	Frictionless surface		Force with known line of action	1
Short cable		Short link		Force with known line of action	1
Collar on frictionless rod		Frictionless pin in slot		90° Force with known line of action	1
Frictionless pin or hinge		Rough surface		or α Force of unknown direction	2
Fixed support				or α Force and couple	3

Fig. 4.1 Reactions at supports and connections.

When the sense of an unknown force or couple is not readily apparent, no attempt should be made to determine it. Instead, the sense of the force or couple should be arbitrarily assumed; the sign of the answer obtained will indicate whether the assumption is correct or not.

4.4 EQUILIBRIUM OF A RIGID BODY IN TWO DIMENSIONS

The conditions stated in Sec. 4.1 for the equilibrium of a rigid body become considerably simpler for the case of a two-dimensional structure. Choosing the x and y axes to be in the plane of the structure, we have

$$F_z = 0 \qquad M_x = M_y = 0 \qquad M_z = M_O$$

for each of the forces applied to the structure. Thus, the six equations of equilibrium derived in Sec. 4.1 reduce to

$$\Sigma F_x = 0 \qquad \Sigma F_y = 0 \qquad \Sigma M_O = 0 \qquad (4.4)$$

and to three trivial identities, $0 = 0$. Since $\Sigma M_O = 0$ must be satisfied regardless of the choice of the origin O, we can write the equations of equilibrium for a two-dimensional structure in the more general form

$$\Sigma F_x = 0 \qquad \Sigma F_y = 0 \qquad \Sigma M_A = 0 \qquad (4.5)$$

where A is any point in the plane of the structure. The three equations obtained can be solved for no more than *three unknowns*.

We saw in the preceding section that unknown forces include reactions and that the number of unknowns corresponding to a given reaction depends upon the type of support or connection causing that reaction. Referring to Sec. 4.3, we observe that the equilibrium equations (4.5) can be used to determine the reactions associated with two rollers and one cable, one fixed support, or one roller and one pin in a fitted hole, etc.

Consider Fig. 4.2*a*, in which the truss shown is subjected to the given forces **P**, **Q**, and **S**. The truss is held in place by a pin at A and a roller at B. The pin prevents point A from moving by exerting on the truss a force which can be resolved into the components $\mathbf{A}_x$ and $\mathbf{A}_y$; the roller keeps the truss from rotating about A by exerting the vertical force **B**. The free-body diagram of the truss is shown in Fig. 4.2*b*; it includes the reactions $\mathbf{A}_x$, $\mathbf{A}_y$, and **B** as well as the applied forces **P**, **Q**, **S** and the weight **W** of the truss. Expressing that the sum of the moments about A of all of the forces shown in Fig. 4.2*b* is zero, we write the equation $\Sigma M_A = 0$, which can be used to determine the magnitude B since it does not contain A_x or A_y. Next, expressing that the sum of the x components and the sum of the y components of the forces are zero, we write the equations $\Sigma F_x = 0$ and $\Sigma F_y = 0$, from which we can obtain the components A_x and A_y, respectively.

An additional equation could be obtained by expressing that the sum of the moments of the external forces about a point other than A is zero. We could write, for instance, $\Sigma M_B = 0$. Such a statement, however, does not contain any new information, since it has already been established that the system of the forces shown in Fig. 4.2*b* is equivalent to zero. The additional equation *is not independent* and cannot be used to determine a fourth unknown. It will be useful,

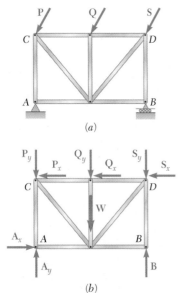

(a)

(b)

Fig. 4.2

however, for checking the solution obtained from the original three equations of equilibrium.

While the three equations of equilibrium cannot be *augmented* by additional equations, any of them can be *replaced* by another equation. Therefore, an alternative system of equations of equilibrium is

$$\Sigma F_x = 0 \qquad \Sigma M_A = 0 \qquad \Sigma M_B = 0 \tag{4.6}$$

where the second point about which the moments are summed (in this case, point B) cannot lie on the line parallel to the y axis that passes through point A (Fig. 4.2b). These equations are sufficient conditions for the equilibrium of the truss. The first two equations indicate that the external forces must reduce to a single vertical force at A. Since the third equation requires that the moment of this force be zero about a point B which is not on its line of action, the force must be zero, and the rigid body is in equilibrium.

A third possible set of equations of equilibrium is

$$\Sigma M_A = 0 \qquad \Sigma M_B = 0 \qquad \Sigma M_C = 0 \tag{4.7}$$

where the points A, B, and C do not lie in a straight line (Fig. 4.2b). The first equation requires that the external forces reduce to a single force at A; the second equation requires that this force pass through B; and the third equation requires that it pass through C. Since the points A, B, C do not lie in a straight line, the force must be zero, and the rigid body is in equilibrium.

The equation $\Sigma M_A = 0$, which expresses that the sum of the moments of the forces about pin A is zero, possesses a more definite physical meaning than either of the other two equations (4.7). These two equations express a similar idea of balance, but with respect to points about which the rigid body is not actually hinged. They are, however, as useful as the first equation, and our choice of equilibrium equations should not be unduly influenced by the physical meaning of these equations. Indeed, it will be desirable in practice to choose equations of equilibrium containing only one unknown, since this eliminates the necessity of solving simultaneous equations. Equations containing only one unknown can be obtained by summing moments about the point of intersection of the lines of action of two unknown forces or, if these forces are parallel, by summing components in a direction perpendicular to their common direction. For example, in Fig. 4.3, in which the truss shown is held by rollers at A and B and a short link at D, the reactions at A and B can be eliminated by summing x components. The reactions at A and D will be eliminated by summing moments about C, and the reactions at B and D by summing moments about D. The equations obtained are

$$\Sigma F_x = 0 \qquad \Sigma M_C = 0 \qquad \Sigma M_D = 0$$

Each of these equations contains only one unknown.

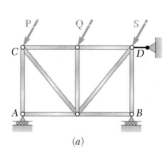

(a)

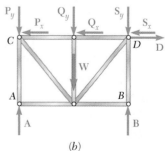

(b)

Fig. 4.3

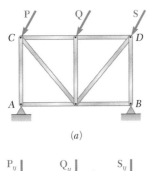

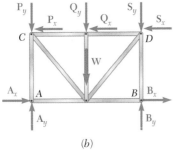

Fig. 4.4 Statically indeterminate reactions.

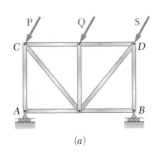

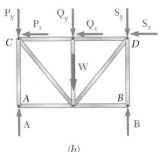

Fig. 4.5 Partial constraints.

4.5 STATICALLY INDETERMINATE REACTIONS. PARTIAL CONSTRAINTS

In the two examples considered in the preceding section (Figs. 4.2 and 4.3), the types of supports used were such that the rigid body could not possibly move under the given loads or under any other loading conditions. In such cases, the rigid body is said to be *completely constrained*. We also recall that the reactions corresponding to these supports involved *three unknowns* and could be determined by solving the three equations of equilibrium. When such a situation exists, the reactions are said to be *statically determinate*.

Consider Fig. 4.4a, in which the truss shown is held by pins at A and B. These supports provide more constraints than are necessary to keep the truss from moving under the given loads or under any other loading conditions. We also note from the free-body diagram of Fig. 4.4b that the corresponding reactions involve *four unknowns*. Since, as was pointed out in Sec. 4.4, only three independent equilibrium equations are available, there are *more unknowns than equations;* thus, all of the unknowns cannot be determined. While the equations $\Sigma M_A = 0$ and $\Sigma M_B = 0$ yield the vertical components B_y and A_y, respectively, the equation $\Sigma F_x = 0$ gives only the sum $A_x + B_x$ of the horizontal components of the reactions at A and B. The components A_x and B_x are said to be *statically indeterminate*. They could be determined by considering the deformations produced in the truss by the given loading, but this method is beyond the scope of statics and belongs to the study of mechanics of materials.

The supports used to hold the truss shown in Fig. 4.5a consist of rollers at A and B. Clearly, the constraints provided by these supports are not sufficient to keep the truss from moving. While any vertical motion is prevented, the truss is free to move horizontally. The truss is said to be *partially constrained*.† Turning our attention to Fig. 4.5b, we note that the reactions at A and B involve only *two unknowns*. Since three equations of equilibrium must still be satisfied, there are *fewer unknowns than equations,* and, in general, one of the equilibrium equations will not be satisfied. While the equations $\Sigma M_A = 0$ and $\Sigma M_B = 0$ can be satisfied by a proper choice of reactions at A and B, the equation $\Sigma F_x = 0$ will not be satisfied unless the sum of the horizontal components of the applied forces happens to be zero. We thus observe that the equlibrium of the truss of Fig. 4.5 cannot be maintained under general loading conditions.

It appears from the above that if a rigid body is to be completely constrained and if the reactions at its supports are to be statically determinate, *there must be as many unknowns as there are equations of equilibrium.* When this condition is *not* satisfied, we can be certain that either the rigid body is not completely constrained or that the reactions at its supports are not statically determinate; it is also possible that the rigid body is not completely constrained *and* that the reactions are statically indeterminate.

We should note, however, that, while *necessary*, the above condition is *not sufficient.* In other words, the fact that the number of

---

†Partially constrained bodies are often referred to as *unstable.* However, to avoid confusion between this type of instability, due to insufficient constraints, and the type of instability considered in Chap. 10, which relates to the behavior of a rigid body when its equilibrium is disturbed, we shall restrict the use of the words *stable* and *unstable* to the latter case.

unknowns is equal to the number of equations is no guarantee that the body is completely constrained or that the reactions at its supports are statically determinate. Consider Fig. 4.6*a*, in which the truss shown is held by rollers at *A*, *B*, and *E*. While there are three unknown reactions, **A**, **B**, and **E** (Fig. 4.6*b*), the equation $\Sigma F_x = 0$ will not be satisfied unless the sum of the horizontal components of the applied forces happens to be zero. Although there are a sufficient number of constraints, these constraints are not properly arranged, and the truss is free to move horizontally. We say that the truss is *improperly constrained*. Since only two equilibrium equations are left for determining three unknowns, the reactions will be statically indeterminate. Thus, improper constraints also produce static indeterminacy.

Another example of improper constraints—and of static indeterminacy—is provided by the truss shown in Fig. 4.7. This truss is held by a pin at *A* and by rollers at *B* and *C*, which altogether involve four unknowns. Since only three independent equilibrium equations are available, the reactions at the supports are statically indeterminate. On the other hand, we note that the equation $\Sigma M_A = 0$ cannot be satisfied under general loading conditions, since the lines of action of the reactions **B** and **C** pass through *A*. We conclude that the truss can rotate about *A* and that it is improperly constrained.†

The examples of Figs. 4.6 and 4.7 lead us to conclude that *a rigid body is improperly constrained whenever the supports*, even though they may provide a sufficient number of reactions, *are arranged in such a way that the reactions must be either concurrent or parallel.*‡

In summary, to be sure that a two-dimensional rigid body is completely constrained and that the reactions at its supports are statically determinate, we should verify that the reactions involve three—and only three—unknowns and that the supports are arranged in such a way that they do not require the reactions to be either concurrent or parallel.

Supports involving statically indeterminate reactions should be used with care in the *design* of structures and only with a full knowledge of the problems they may cause. On the other hand, the *analysis* of structures possessing statically indeterminate reactions often can be partially carried out by the methods of statics. In the case of the truss of Fig. 4.4, for example, the vertical components of the reactions at *A* and *B* were obtained from the equilibrium equations.

For obvious reasons, supports producing partial or improper constraints should be avoided in the design of stationary structures. However, a partially or improperly constrained structure will not necessarily collapse; under particular loading conditions, equilibrium can be maintained. For example, the trusses of Figs. 4.5 and 4.6 will be in equilibrium if the applied forces **P**, **Q**, and **S** are vertical. Besides, structures which are designed to move *should* be only partially constrained. A railroad car, for instance, would be of little use if it were completely constrained by having its brakes applied permanently.

---

†Rotation of the truss about *A* requires some "play" in the supports at *B* and *C*. In practice such play will always exist. In addition, we note that if the play is kept small, the displacements of the rollers *B* and *C* and, thus, the distances from *A* to the lines of action of the reactions **B** and **C** will also be small. The equation $\Sigma M_A = 0$ then requires that **B** and **C** be very large, a situation which can result in the failure of the supports at *B* and *C*.

‡Because this situation arises from an inadequate arrangement or *geometry* of the supports, it is often referred to as *geometric instability*.

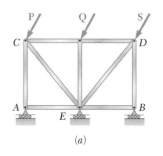

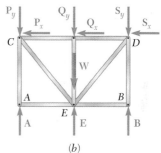

Fig. 4.6 Improper constraints.

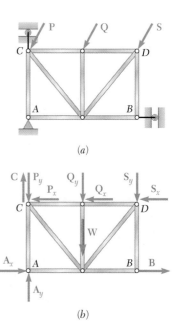

Fig. 4.7 Improper constraints.

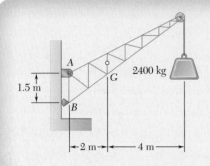

SAMPLE PROBLEM 4.1

A fixed crane has a mass of 1000 kg and is used to lift a 2400-kg crate. It is held in place by a pin at A and a rocker at B. The center of gravity of the crane is located at G. Determine the components of the reactions at A and B.

SOLUTION

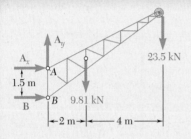

Free-Body Diagram. A free-body diagram of the crane is drawn. By multiplying the masses of the crane and of the crate by $g = 9.81$ m/s^2, we obtain the corresponding weights, that is, 9810 N or 9.81 kN, and 23 500 N or 23.5 kN. The reaction at pin A is a force of unknown direction; it is represented by its components $\mathbf{A}_x$ and $\mathbf{A}_y$. The reaction at the rocker B is perpendicular to the rocker surface; thus, it is horizontal. We assume that $\mathbf{A}_x$, $\mathbf{A}_y$, and $\mathbf{B}$ act in the directions shown.

Determination of B. We express that the sum of the moments of all external forces about point A is zero. The equation obtained will contain neither A_x nor A_y, since the moments of $\mathbf{A}_x$ and $\mathbf{A}_y$ about A are zero. Multiplying the magnitude of each force by its perpendicular distance from A, we write

$$+\curvearrowleft \Sigma M_A = 0: \quad +B(1.5 \text{ m}) - (9.81 \text{ kN})(2 \text{ m}) - (23.5 \text{ kN})(6 \text{ m}) = 0$$
$$B = +107.1 \text{ kN} \qquad \mathbf{B} = 107.1 \text{ kN} \rightarrow \quad \blacktriangleleft$$

Since the result is positive, the reaction is directed as assumed.

Determination of A_x. The magnitude of $\mathbf{A}_x$ is determined by expressing that the sum of the horizontal components of all external forces is zero.

$$\xrightarrow{+} \Sigma F_x = 0: \quad A_x + B = 0$$
$$A_x + 107.1 \text{ kN} = 0$$
$$A_x = -107.1 \text{ kN} \qquad \mathbf{A}_x = 107.1 \text{ kN} \leftarrow \quad \blacktriangleleft$$

Since the result is negative, the sense of $\mathbf{A}_x$ is opposite to that assumed originally.

Determination of A_y. The sum of the vertical components must also equal zero.

$$+\uparrow \Sigma F_y = 0: \quad A_y - 9.81 \text{ kN} - 23.5 \text{ kN} = 0$$
$$A_y = +33.3 \text{ kN} \qquad \mathbf{A}_y = 33.3 \text{ kN} \uparrow \quad \blacktriangleleft$$

Adding vectorially the components $\mathbf{A}_x$ and $\mathbf{A}_y$, we find that the reaction at A is 112.2 kN $\measuredangle 17.3°$.

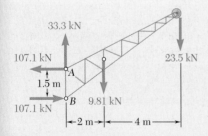

Check. The values obtained for the reactions can be checked by recalling that the sum of the moments of all of the external forces about any point must be zero. For example, considering point B, we write

$$+\curvearrowleft \Sigma M_B = -(9.81 \text{ kN})(2 \text{ m}) - (23.5 \text{ kN})(6 \text{ m}) + (107.1 \text{ kN})(1.5 \text{ m}) = 0$$

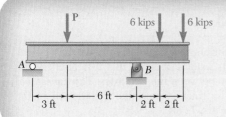

SAMPLE PROBLEM 4.2

Three loads are applied to a beam as shown. The beam is supported by a roller at A and by a pin at B. Neglecting the weight of the beam, determine the reactions at A and B when $P = 15$ kips.

SOLUTION

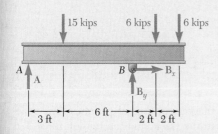

Free-Body Diagram. A free-body diagram of the beam is drawn. The reaction at A is vertical and is denoted by **A**. The reaction at B is represented by components $\mathbf{B}_x$ and $\mathbf{B}_y$. Each component is assumed to act in the direction shown.

Equilibrium Equations. We write the following three equilibrium equations and solve for the reactions indicated:

$$\xrightarrow{+}\Sigma F_x = 0: \qquad\qquad B_x = 0 \qquad\qquad \mathbf{B}_x = 0 \quad \blacktriangleleft$$

$$+\curvearrowleft\Sigma M_A = 0:$$
$$-(15 \text{ kips})(3 \text{ ft}) + B_y(9 \text{ ft}) - (6 \text{ kips})(11 \text{ ft}) - (6 \text{ kips})(13 \text{ ft}) = 0$$
$$B_y = +21.0 \text{ kips} \qquad \mathbf{B}_y = 21.0 \text{ kips} \uparrow \quad \blacktriangleleft$$

$$+\curvearrowleft\Sigma M_B = 0:$$
$$-A(9 \text{ ft}) + (15 \text{ kips})(6 \text{ ft}) - (6 \text{ kips})(2 \text{ ft}) - (6 \text{ kips})(4 \text{ ft}) = 0$$
$$A = +6.00 \text{ kips} \qquad \mathbf{A} = 6.00 \text{ kips} \uparrow \quad \blacktriangleleft$$

Check. The results are checked by adding the vertical components of all of the external forces:

$$+\uparrow\Sigma F_y = +6.00 \text{ kips} - 15 \text{ kips} + 21.0 \text{ kips} - 6 \text{ kips} - 6 \text{ kips} = 0$$

Remark. In this problem the reactions at both A and B are vertical; however, these reactions are vertical for different reasons. At A, the beam is supported by a roller; hence the reaction cannot have any horizontal component. At B, the horizontal component of the reaction is zero because it must satisfy the equilibrium equation $\Sigma F_x = 0$ and because none of the other forces acting on the beam has a horizontal component.

We could have noticed at first glance that the reaction at B was vertical and dispensed with the horizontal component $\mathbf{B}_x$. This, however, is a bad practice. In following it, we would run the risk of forgetting the component $\mathbf{B}_x$ when the loading conditions require such a component (i.e., when a horizontal load is included). Also, the component $\mathbf{B}_x$ was found to be zero by using and solving an equilibrium equation, $\Sigma F_x = 0$. By setting $\mathbf{B}_x$ equal to zero immediately, we might not realize that we actually make use of this equation and thus might lose track of the number of equations available for solving the problem.

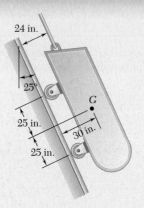

SAMPLE PROBLEM 4.3

A loading car is at rest on a track forming an angle of 25° with the vertical. The gross weight of the car and its load is 5500 lb, and it is applied at a point 30 in. from the track, halfway between the two axles. The car is held by a cable attached 24 in. from the track. Determine the tension in the cable and the reaction at each pair of wheels.

SOLUTION

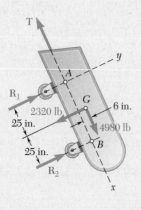

Free-Body Diagram. A free-body diagram of the car is drawn. The reaction at each wheel is perpendicular to the track, and the tension force **T** is parallel to the track. For convenience, we choose the x axis parallel to the track and the y axis perpendicular to the track. The 5500-lb weight is then resolved into x and y components.

$$W_x = +(5500 \text{ lb}) \cos 25° = +4980 \text{ lb}$$
$$W_y = -(5500 \text{ lb}) \sin 25° = -2320 \text{ lb}$$

Equilibrium Equations. We take moments about A to eliminate **T** and $\mathbf{R}_1$ from the computation.

$+\curvearrowleft\Sigma M_A = 0$: $-(2320 \text{ lb})(25 \text{ in.}) - (4980 \text{ lb})(6 \text{ in.}) + R_2(50 \text{ in.}) = 0$
$R_2 = +1758 \text{ lb}$ $\mathbf{R}_2 = 1758 \text{ lb} \nearrow$ ◀

Now, taking moments about B to eliminate **T** and $\mathbf{R}_2$ from the computation, we write

$+\curvearrowleft\Sigma M_B = 0$: $(2320 \text{ lb})(25 \text{ in.}) - (4980 \text{ lb})(6 \text{ in.}) - R_1(50 \text{ in.}) = 0$
$R_1 = +562 \text{ lb}$ $\mathbf{R}_1 = +562 \text{ lb} \nearrow$ ◀

The value of T is found by writing

$\searrow+\Sigma F_x = 0$: $+4980 \text{ lb} - T = 0$
$T = +4980 \text{ lb}$ $\mathbf{T} = 4980 \text{ lb} \nwarrow$ ◀

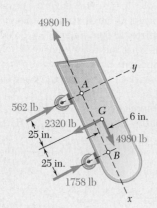

The computed values of the reactions are shown in the adjacent sketch.

Check. The computations are verified by writing

$$\nearrow+\Sigma F_y = +562 \text{ lb} + 1758 \text{ lb} - 2320 \text{ lb} = 0$$

The solution could also have been checked by computing moments about any point other than A or B.

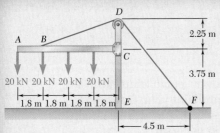

SAMPLE PROBLEM 4.4

The frame shown supports part of the roof of a small building. Knowing that the tension in the cable is 150 kN, determine the reaction at the fixed end E.

SOLUTION

Free-Body Diagram. A free-body diagram of the frame and of the cable BDF is drawn. The reaction at the fixed end E is represented by the force components $\mathbf{E}_x$ and $\mathbf{E}_y$ and the couple $\mathbf{M}_E$. The other forces acting on the free body are the four 20-kN loads and the 150-kN force exerted at end F of the cable.

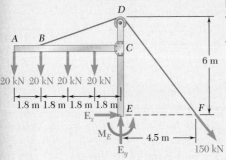

Equilibrium Equations. Noting that $DF = \sqrt{(4.5 \text{ m})^2 + (6 \text{ m})^2} = 7.5$ m, we write

$$\xrightarrow{+}\Sigma F_x = 0: \qquad E_x + \frac{4.5}{7.5}(150 \text{ kN}) = 0$$

$$E_x = -90.0 \text{ kN} \qquad \mathbf{E}_x = 90.0 \text{ kN} \leftarrow \blacktriangleleft$$

$$+\uparrow\Sigma F_y = 0: \qquad E_y - 4(20 \text{ kN}) - \frac{6}{7.5}(150 \text{ kN}) = 0$$

$$E_y = +200 \text{ kN} \qquad \mathbf{E}_y = 200 \text{ kN} \uparrow \blacktriangleleft$$

$$+\curvearrowleft\Sigma M_E = 0: \quad (20 \text{ kN})(7.2 \text{ m}) + (20 \text{ kN})(5.4 \text{ m}) + (20 \text{ kN})(3.6 \text{ m})$$

$$+ (20 \text{ kN})(1.8 \text{ m}) - \frac{6}{7.5}(150 \text{ kN})(4.5 \text{ m}) + M_E = 0$$

$$M_E = +180.0 \text{ kN} \cdot \text{m} \qquad \mathbf{M}_E = 180.0 \text{ kN} \cdot \text{m} \curvearrowleft \blacktriangleleft$$

SAMPLE PROBLEM 4.5

A 400-lb weight is attached at A to the lever shown. The constant of the spring BC is $k = 250$ lb/in., and the spring is unstretched when $\theta = 0$. Determine the position of equilibrium.

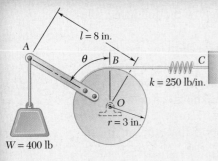

SOLUTION

Free-Body Diagram. We draw a free-body diagram of the lever and cylinder. Denoting by s the deflection of the spring from its undeformed position, and noting that $s = r\theta$, we have $F = ks = kr\theta$.

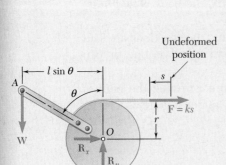

Equilibrium Equation. Summing the moments of $\mathbf{W}$ and $\mathbf{F}$ about O, we write

$$+\curvearrowleft\Sigma M_O = 0: \qquad Wl \sin\theta - r(kr\theta) = 0 \qquad \sin\theta = \frac{kr^2}{Wl}\theta$$

Substituting the given data, we obtain

$$\sin\theta = \frac{(250 \text{ lb/in.})(3 \text{ in.})^2}{(400 \text{ lb})(8 \text{ in.})}\theta \qquad \sin\theta = 0.703\,\theta$$

Solving by trial and error, we find $\qquad \theta = 0 \qquad \theta = 80.3° \blacktriangleleft$

SOLVING PROBLEMS
ON YOUR OWN

You saw that the external forces acting on a rigid body in equilibrium form a system equivalent to zero. To solve an equilibrium problem your first task is to draw a neat, reasonably large *free-body diagram* on which you will show all external forces. Both known and unknown forces must be included.

For a two-dimensional rigid body, the reactions at the supports can involve one, two, or three unknowns depending on the type of support (Fig. 4.1). For the successful solution of a problem, a correct free-body diagram is essential. Never proceed with the solution of a problem until you are sure that your free-body diagram includes all loads, all reactions, and the weight of the body (if appropriate).

1. You can write three equilibrium equations and solve them for *three unknowns.* The three equations might be

$$\Sigma F_x = 0 \qquad \Sigma F_y = 0 \qquad \Sigma M_O = 0$$

However, there are usually several sets of equations that you can write, such as

$$\Sigma F_x = 0 \qquad \Sigma M_A = 0 \qquad \Sigma M_B = 0$$

where point B is chosen in such a way that the line AB is not parallel to the y axis, or

$$\Sigma M_A = 0 \qquad \Sigma M_B = 0 \qquad \Sigma M_C = 0$$

where the points A, B, and C do not lie in a straight line.

2. To simplify your solution, it may be helpful to use one of the following solution techniques if applicable.

 a. By summing moments about the point of intersection of the lines of action of two unknown forces, you will obtain an equation in a single unknown.

 b. By summing components in a direction perpendicular to two unknown parallel forces, you will obtain an equation in a single unknown.

3. After drawing your free-body diagram, you may find that one of the following special situations exists.

 a. The reactions involve fewer than three unknowns; the body is said to be *partially constrained* and motion of the body is possible.

 b. The reactions involve more than three unknowns; the reactions are said to be *statically indeterminate.* While you may be able to calculate one or two reactions, you cannot determine all of the reactions.

 c. The reactions pass through a single point or are parallel; the body is said to be *improperly constrained* and motion can occur under a general loading condition.

PROBLEMS

4.1 A 2100-lb tractor is used to lift 900 lb of gravel. Determine the reaction at each of the two (*a*) rear wheels *A*, (*b*) front wheels *B*.

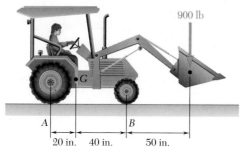

900 lb

A   *G*   *B*

20 in.   40 in.   50 in.

Fig. P4.1

4.2 A gardener uses a 60-N wheelbarrow to transport a 250-N bag of fertilizer. What force must she exert on each handle?

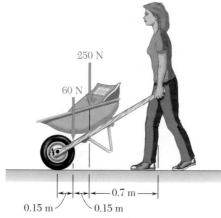

250 N

60 N

0.7 m

0.15 m   0.15 m

Fig. P4.2

4.3 The gardener of Prob. 4.2 wishes to transport a second 250-N bag of fertilizer at the same time as the first one. Determine the maximum allowable horizontal distance from the axle *A* of the wheelbarrow to the center of gravity of the second bag if she can hold only 75 N with each arm.

4.4 For the beam and loading shown, determine (*a*) the reaction at *A*, (*b*) the tension in cable *BC*.

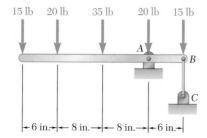

15 lb   20 lb   35 lb   20 lb   15 lb

A

B

C

6 in. → ← 8 in. → ← 8 in. → ← 6 in.

Fig. P4.4

4.5 Two crates, each of mass 350 kg, are placed as shown in the bed of a 1400-kg pickup truck. Determine the reactions at each of the two (*a*) rear wheels *A*, (*b*) front wheels *B*.

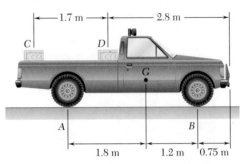

Fig. P4.5

4.6 Solve Prob. 4.5, assuming that crate *D* is removed and that the position of crate *C* is unchanged.

4.7 A T-shaped bracket supports the four loads shown. Determine the reactions at *A* and *B* (*a*) if *a* = 10 in., (*b*) if *a* = 7 in.

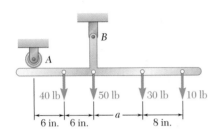

Fig. P4.7

4.8 For the bracket and loading of Prob. 4.7, determine the smallest distance *a* if the bracket is not to move.

4.9 The maximum allowable value of each of the reactions is 180 N. Neglecting the weight of the beam, determine the range of the distance *d* for which the beam is safe.

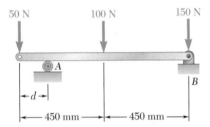

Fig. P4.9

4.10 Solve Prob. 4.9 if the 50-N load is replaced by an 80-N load.

4.11 For the beam of Sample Prob. 4.2, determine the range of values of *P* for which the beam will be safe, knowing that the maximum allowable value of each of the reactions is 30 kips and that the reaction at *A* must be directed upward.

4.12 The 10-m beam *AB* rests upon, but is not attached to, supports at *C* and *D*. Neglecting the weight of the beam, determine the range of values of *P* for which the beam will remain in equilibrium.

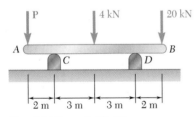

Fig. P4.12 and P4.13

4.13 The maximum allowable value of each of the reactions is 50 kN, and each reaction must be directed upward. Neglecting the weight of the beam, determine the range of values of *P* for which the beam is safe.

4.14 For the beam and loading shown, determine the range of the distance *a* for which the reaction at *B* does not exceed 100 lb downward or 200 lb upward.

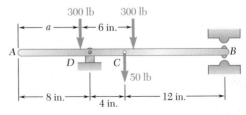

Fig. P4.14

4.15 Two links *AB* and *DE* are connected by a bell crank as shown. Knowing that the tension in link *AB* is 720 N, determine (*a*) the tension in link *DE*, (*b*) the reaction at *C*.

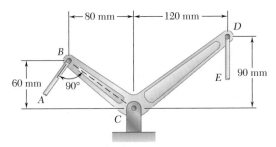

Fig. P4.15 and P4.16

4.16 Two links *AB* and *DE* are connected by a bell crank as shown. Determine the maximum force that can be safely exerted by link *AB* on the bell crank if the maximum allowable value for the reaction at *C* is 1600 N.

4.17 The required tension in cable *AB* is 200 lb. Determine (*a*) the vertical force **P** that must be applied to the pedal, (*b*) the corresponding reaction at *C*.

4.18 Determine the maximum tension that can be developed in cable *AB* if the maximum allowable value of the reaction at *C* is 250 lb.

4.19 The bracket *BCD* is hinged at *C* and attached to a control cable at *B*. For the loading shown, determine (*a*) the tension in the cable, (*b*) the reaction at *C*.

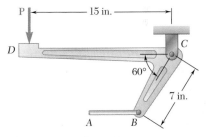

Fig. P4.17 and P4.18

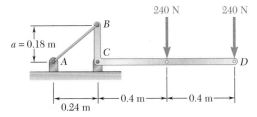

Fig. P4.19

4.20 Solve Prob. 4.19, assuming that *a* = 0.32 m.

4.21 Determine the reactions at *A* and *B* when (*a*) *h* = 0, (*b*) *h* = 200 mm.

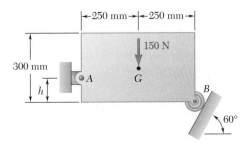

Fig. P4.21

4.22 For the frame and loading shown, determine the reactions at *A* and *E* when (*a*) α = 30°, (*b*) α = 45°.

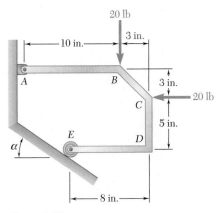

Fig. P4.22

4.23 and 4.24 For each of the plates and loadings shown, determine the reactions at A and B.

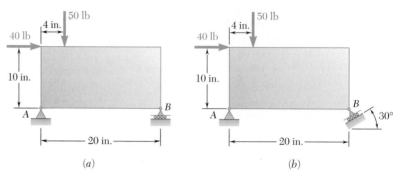

(a)   (b)

Fig. P4.23

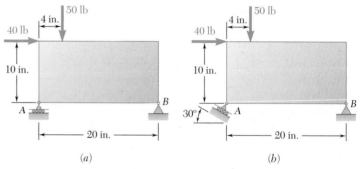

(a)   (b)

Fig. P4.24

4.25 Determine the reactions at A and B when (a) $\alpha = 0$, (b) $\alpha = 90°$, (c) $\alpha = 30°$.

4.26 A rod AB, hinged at A and attached at B to cable BD, supports the loads shown. Knowing that $d = 200$ mm, determine (a) the tension in cable BD, (b) the reaction at A.

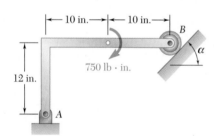

Fig. P4.25

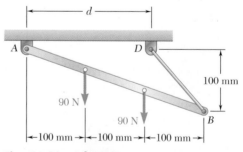

Fig. P4.26 and P4.27

4.27 A rod AB, hinged at A and attached at B to cable BD, supports the loads shown. Knowing that $d = 150$ mm, determine (a) the tension in cable BD, (b) the reaction at A.

4.28 A lever AB is hinged at C and attached to a control cable at A. If the lever is subjected to a 500-N horizontal force at B, determine (a) the tension in the cable, (b) the reaction at C.

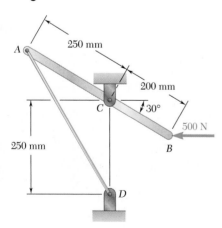

Fig. P4.28

4.29 A force **P** of magnitude 280 lb is applied to member *ABCD*, which is supported by a frictionless pin at *A* and by the cable *CED*. Since the cable passes over a small pulley at *E*, the tension may be assumed to be the same in portions *CE* and *ED* of the cable. For the case when *a* = 3 in., determine (*a*) the tension in the cable, (*b*) the reaction at *A*.

4.30 Neglecting friction, determine the tension in cable *ABD* and the reaction at support *C*.

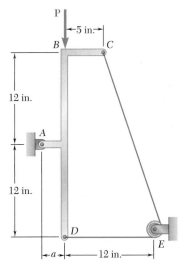

Fig. P4.29

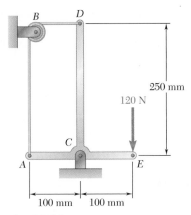

Fig. P4.30

4.31 Rod *ABC* is bent in the shape of an arc of circle of radius *R*. Knowing that θ = 30°, determine the reaction (*a*) at *B*, (*b*) at *C*.

4.32 Rod *ABC* is bent in the shape of an arc of circle of radius *R*. Knowing that θ = 60°, determine the reaction (*a*) at *B*, (*b*) at *C*.

4.33 Neglecting friction, determine the tension in cable *ABD* and the reaction at *C* when θ = 60°.

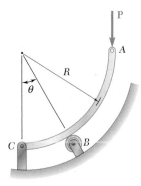

Fig. P4.31 and P4.32

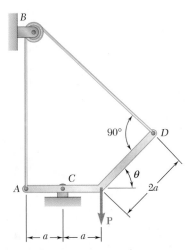

Fig. P4.33 and P4.34

4.34 Neglecting friction, determine the tension in cable *ABD* and the reaction at *C* when θ = 45°.

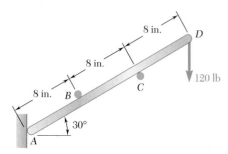

Fig. P4.35

4.35 A light rod AD is supported by frictionless pegs at B and C and rests against a frictionless wall at A. A vertical 120-lb force is applied at D. Determine the reactions at A, B, and C.

4.36 A light bar AD is suspended from a cable BE and supports a 50-lb block at C. The ends A and D of the bar are in contact with frictionless vertical walls. Determine the tension in cable BE and the reactions at A and D.

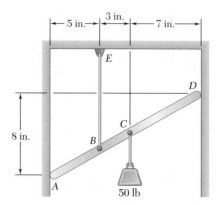

Fig. P4.36

4.37 Bar AC supports two 400-N loads as shown. Rollers at A and C rest against frictionless surfaces and a cable BD is attached at B. Determine (a) the tension in cable BD, (b) the reaction at A, (c) the reaction at C.

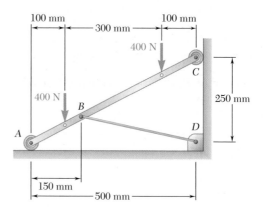

Fig. P4.37

4.38 Determine the tension in each cable and the reaction at D.

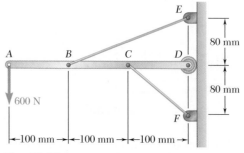

Fig. P4.38

4.39 Two slots have been cut in plate *DEF*, and the plate has been placed so that the slots fit two fixed, frictionless pins *A* and *B*. Knowing that $P = 15$ lb, determine (*a*) the force each pin exerts on the plate, (*b*) the reaction at *F*.

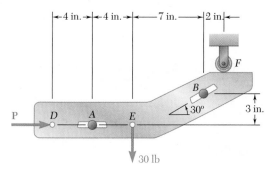

Fig. P4.39

4.40 For the plate of Prob. 4.39 the reaction at *F* must be directed downward, and its maximum allowable value is 20 lb. Neglecting friction at the pins, determine the required range of values of *P*.

4.41 Bar *AD* is attached at *A* and *C* to collars that can move freely on the rods shown. If the cord *BE* is vertical ($\alpha = 0$), determine the tension in the cord and the reactions at *A* and *C*.

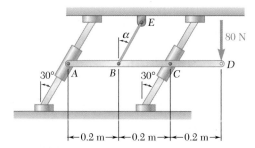

Fig. P4.41

4.42 Solve Prob. 4.41 if the cord *BE* is parallel to the rods ($\alpha = 30°$).

4.43 An 8-kg mass can be supported in the three different ways shown. Knowing that the pulleys have a 100-mm radius, determine the reaction at *A* in each case.

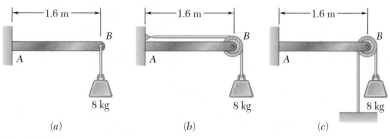

Fig. P4.43

4.44 A tension of 5 lb is maintained in a tape as it passes through the support system shown. Knowing that the radius of each pulley is 0.4 in., determine the reaction at C.

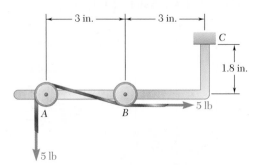

Fig. P4.44

4.45 Solve Prob. 4.44, assuming that 0.6-in.-radius pulleys are used.

4.46 A 6-m telephone pole weighing 1600 N is used to support the ends of two wires. The wires form the angles shown with the horizontal and the tensions in the wires are, respectively, $T_1 = 600$ N and $T_2 = 375$ N. Determine the reaction at the fixed end A.

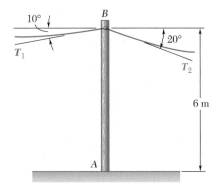

Fig. P4.46

4.47 Beam AD carries the two 40-lb loads shown. The beam is held by a fixed support at D and by the cable BE that is attached to the counterweight W. Determine the reaction at D when (a) $W = 100$ lb, (b) $W = 90$ lb.

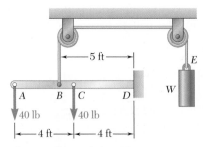

Fig. P4.47 and P4.48

4.48 For the beam and loading shown, determine the range of values of W for which the magnitude of the couple at D does not exceed 40 lb · ft.

4.49 Knowing that the tension in wire BD is 1300 N, determine the reaction at the fixed support C of the frame shown.

4.50 Determine the range of allowable values of the tension in wire BD if the magnitude of the couple at the fixed support C is not to exceed 100 N · m.

4.51 A vertical load **P** is applied at end B of rod BC. (*a*) Neglecting the weight of the rod, express the angle θ corresponding to the equilibrium position in terms of P, l, and the counterweight W. (*b*) Determine the value of θ corresponding to equilibrium if $P = 2W$.

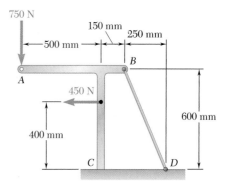

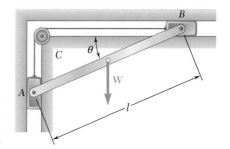

Fig. P4.49 and P4.50

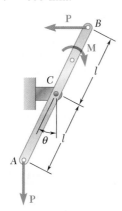

Fig. P4.51

4.52 A slender rod AB, of weight W, is attached to blocks A and B, which move freely in the guides shown. The blocks are connected by an elastic cord that passes over a pulley at C. (*a*) Express the tension in the cord in terms of W and θ. (*b*) Determine the value of θ for which the tension in the cord is equal to $3W$.

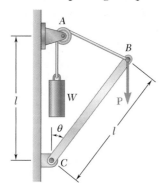

Fig. P4.52

4.53 Rod AB is acted upon by a couple **M** and two forces, each of magnitude P. (*a*) Derive an equation in θ, P, M, and l that must be satisfied when the rod is in equilibrium. (*b*) Determine the value of θ corresponding to equilibrium when $M = 150$ N · m, $P = 200$ N, and $l = 600$ mm.

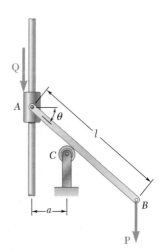

Fig. P4.53

4.54 Rod AB is attached to a collar at A and rests against a small roller at C. (*a*) Neglecting the weight of rod AB, derive an equation in P, Q, a, l, and θ that must be satisfied when the rod is in equilibrium. (*b*) Determine the value of θ corresponding to equilibrium when $P = 16$ lb, $Q = 12$ lb, $l = 20$ in., and $a = 5$ in.

Fig. P4.54

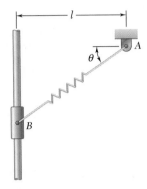

Fig. P4.55

4.55 A collar B of weight W can move freely along the vertical rod shown. The constant of the spring is k, and the spring is unstretched when $\theta = 0$. (a) Derive an equation in θ, W, k, and l that must be satisfied when the collar is in equilibrium. (b) Knowing that $W = 300$ N, $l = 500$ mm, and $k = 800$ N/m, determine the value of θ corresponding to equilibrium.

4.56 A vertical load $\mathbf{P}$ is applied at end B of rod BC. The constant of the spring is k, and the spring is unstretched when $\theta = 90°$. (a) Neglecting the weight of the rod, express the angle θ corresponding to equilibrium in terms of P, k, and l. (b) Determine the value of θ corresponding to equilibrium when $P = \frac{1}{4}kl$.

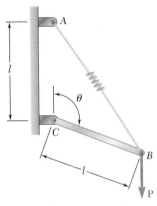

Fig. P4.56

4.57 Solve Sample Prob. 4.5, assuming that the spring is unstretched when $\theta = 90°$.

4.58 A slender rod AB, of weight W, is attached to blocks A and B that move freely in the guides shown. The constant of the spring is k, and the spring is unstretched when $\theta = 0$. (a) Neglecting the weight of the blocks, derive an equation in W, k, l, and θ that must be satisfied when the rod is in equilibrium. (b) Determine the value of θ when $W = 75$ lb, $l = 30$ in., and $k = 3$ lb/in.

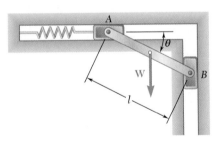

Fig. P4.58

4.59 Eight identical 500×750-mm rectangular plates, each of mass $m = 40$ kg, are held in a vertical plane as shown. All connections consist of frictionless pins, rollers, or short links. In each case, determine whether (a) the plate is completely, partially, or improperly constrained, (b) the reactions are statically determinate or indeterminate, (c) the equilibrium of the plate is maintained in the position shown. Also, wherever possible, compute the reactions.

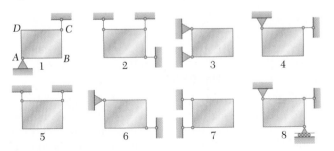

Fig. P4.59

4.60 The bracket *ABC* can be supported in the eight different ways shown. All connections consist of smooth pins, rollers, or short links. For each case, answer the questions listed in Prob. 4.59, and, wherever possible, compute the reactions, assuming that the magnitude of the force **P** is 100 lb.

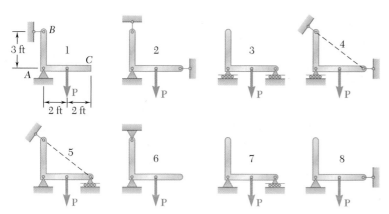

Fig. P4.60

4.6 EQUILIBRIUM OF A TWO-FORCE BODY

A particular case of equilibrium which is of considerable interest is that of a rigid body subjected to two forces. Such a body is commonly called a *two-force body*. It will be shown that *if a two-force body is in equilibrium, the two forces must have the same magnitude, the same line of action, and opposite sense.*

Consider a corner plate subjected to two forces **F**₁ and **F**₂ acting at *A* and *B*, respectively (Fig. 4.8*a*). If the plate is to be in equilibrium, the sum of the moments of **F**₁ and **F**₂ about any axis must be zero. First, we sum moments about *A*. Since the moment of **F**₁ is obviously zero, the moment of **F**₂ must also be zero and the line of action of **F**₂ must pass through *A* (Fig. 4.8*b*). Summing moments about *B*, we prove similarly that the line of action of **F**₁ must pass through *B* (Fig. 4.8*c*). Therefore, both forces have the same line of action (line *AB*). From either of the equations $\Sigma F_x = 0$ and $\Sigma F_y = 0$ it is seen that they must also have the same magnitude but opposite sense.

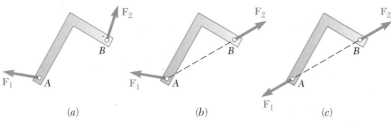

Fig. 4.8

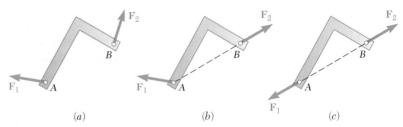

Fig. 4.8 *(repeated)*

If several forces act at two points *A* and *B*, the forces acting at *A* can be replaced by their resultant $\mathbf{F}_1$ and those acting at *B* can be replaced by their resultant $\mathbf{F}_2$. Thus a two-force body can be more generally defined as *a rigid body subjected to forces acting at only two points*. The resultants $\mathbf{F}_1$ and $\mathbf{F}_2$ then must have the same line of action, the same magnitude, and opposite sense (Fig. 4.8).

In the study of structures, frames, and machines, you will see how the recognition of two-force bodies simplifies the solution of certain problems.

4.7 EQUILIBRIUM OF A THREE-FORCE BODY

Another case of equilibrium that is of great interest is that of a *three-force body*, i.e., a rigid body subjected to three forces or, more generally, *a rigid body subjected to forces acting at only three points*. Consider a rigid body subjected to a system of forces which can be reduced to three forces $\mathbf{F}_1$, $\mathbf{F}_2$, and $\mathbf{F}_3$ acting at *A*, *B*, and *C*, respectively (Fig. 4.9a). It will be shown that if the body is in equilibrium, *the lines of action of the three forces must be either concurrent or parallel.*

Since the rigid body is in equilibrium, the sum of the moments of $\mathbf{F}_1$, $\mathbf{F}_2$, and $\mathbf{F}_3$ about any axis must be zero. Assuming that the lines of action of $\mathbf{F}_1$ and $\mathbf{F}_2$ intersect and denoting their point of intersection by *D*, we sum moments about *D* (Fig. 4.9b). Since the moments of $\mathbf{F}_1$ and $\mathbf{F}_2$ about *D* are zero, the moment of $\mathbf{F}_3$ about *D* must also be zero, and the line of action of $\mathbf{F}_3$ must pass through *D* (Fig. 4.9c). Therefore, the three lines of action are concurrent. The only exception occurs when none of the lines intersect; the lines of action are then parallel.

Although problems concerning three-force bodies can be solved by the general methods of Secs. 4.3 to 4.5, the property just established can be used to solve them either graphically or mathematically from simple trigonometric or geometric relations.

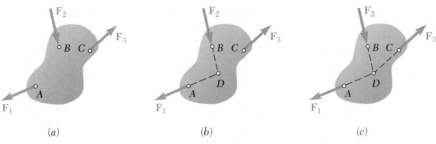

Fig. 4.9

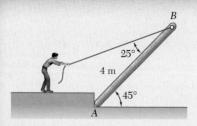

SAMPLE PROBLEM 4.6

A man raises a 10-kg joist, of length 4 m, by pulling on a rope. Find the tension T in the rope and the reaction at A.

SOLUTION

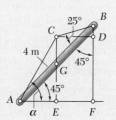

Free-Body Diagram. The joist is a three-force body, since it is acted upon by three forces: its weight **W**, the force **T** exerted by the rope, and the reaction **R** of the ground at A. We note that

$$W = mg = (10 \text{ kg})(9.81 \text{ m/s}^2) = 98.1 \text{ N}$$

Three-Force Body. Since the joist is a three-force body, the forces acting on it must be concurrent. The reaction **R**, therefore, will pass through the point of intersection C of the lines of action of the weight **W** and the tension force **T**. This fact will be used to determine the angle α that **R** forms with the horizontal.

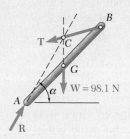

Drawing the vertical BF through B and the horizontal CD through C, we note that

$$
\begin{aligned}
AF &= BF = (AB) \cos 45° = (4 \text{ m}) \cos 45° = 2.828 \text{ m}\\
CD &= EF = AE = \tfrac{1}{2}(AF) = 1.414 \text{ m}\\
BD &= (CD) \cot (45° + 25°) = (1.414 \text{ m}) \tan 20° = 0.515 \text{ m}\\
CE &= DF = BF - BD = 2.828 \text{ m} - 0.515 \text{ m} = 2.313 \text{ m}
\end{aligned}
$$

We write

$$\tan \alpha = \frac{CE}{AE} = \frac{2.313 \text{ m}}{1.414 \text{ m}} = 1.636$$

$$\alpha = 58.6° \quad \blacktriangleleft$$

We now know the direction of all the forces acting on the joist.

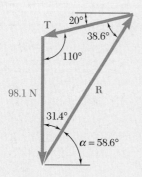

Force Triangle. A force triangle is drawn as shown, and its interior angles are computed from the known directions of the forces. Using the law of sines, we write

$$\frac{T}{\sin 31.4°} = \frac{R}{\sin 110°} = \frac{98.1 \text{ N}}{\sin 38.6°}$$

$$T = 81.9 \text{ N} \quad \blacktriangleleft$$
$$R = 147.8 \text{ N} \ \measuredangle 58.6° \quad \blacktriangleleft$$

SOLVING PROBLEMS ON YOUR OWN

The preceding sections covered two particular cases of equilibrium of a rigid body.

1. A two-force body is a body subjected to forces at only two points. The resultants of the forces acting at each of these points must have the *same magnitude, the same line of action, and opposite sense*. This property will allow you to simplify the solutions of some problems by replacing the two unknown components of a reaction by a single force of unknown magnitude but of *known direction*.

2. A three-force body is subjected to forces at only three points. The resultants of the forces acting at each of these points must be *concurrent or parallel*. To solve a problem involving a three-force body with concurrent forces, draw your free-body diagram showing that these three forces pass through the same point. The use of simple geometry may then allow you to complete the solution by using a force triangle [Sample Prob. 4.6].

Although the principle noted above for the solution of problems involving three-force bodies is easily understood, it can be difficult to sketch the needed geometric constructions. If you encounter difficulty, first draw a reasonably large free-body diagram and then seek a relation between known or easily calculated lengths and a dimension that involves an unknown. This was done in Sample Prob. 4.6, where the easily calculated dimensions AE and CE were used to determine the angle α.

PROBLEMS

4.61 Determine the reactions at A and B when $a = 180$ mm.

4.62 For the bracket and loading shown, determine the range of values of the distance a for which the magnitude of the reaction at B does not exceed 600 N.

4.63 Using the method of Sec. 4.7, solve Prob. 4.17.

4.64 Using the method of Sec. 4.7, solve Prob. 4.18.

4.65 The spanner shown is used to rotate a shaft. A pin fits in a hole at A, while a flat, frictionless surface rests against the shaft at B. If a 60-lb force $\mathbf{P}$ is exerted on the spanner at D, find the reactions at A and B.

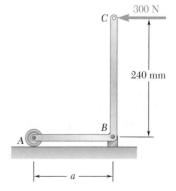

Fig. P4.61 and P4.62

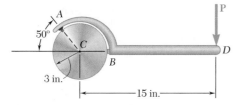

Fig. P4.65

4.66 Determine the reactions at B and D when $b = 60$ mm.

4.67 Determine the reactions at B and D when $b = 120$ mm.

4.68 Determine the reactions at B and C when $a = 1.5$ in.

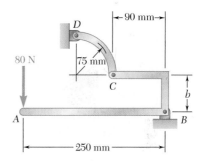

Fig. P4.66 and P4.67

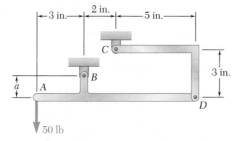

Fig. P4.68

4.69 A 50-kg crate is attached to the trolley-beam system shown. Knowing that $a = 1.5$ m, determine (*a*) the tension in cable CD, (*b*) the reaction at B.

4.70 Solve Prob. 4.69, assuming that $a = 3$ m.

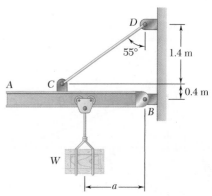

Fig. P4.69

185

4.71 One end of rod AB rests in the corner A and the other end is attached to cord BD. If the rod supports a 40-lb load at its midpoint C, find the reaction at A and the tension in the cord.

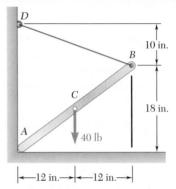

Fig. P4.71

4.72 Determine the reactions at A and D when $\beta = 30°$.

4.73 Determine the reactions at A and D when $\beta = 60°$.

4.74 A 40-lb roller, of diameter 8 in., which is to be used on a tile floor, is resting directly on the subflooring as shown. Knowing that the thickness of each tile is 0.3 in., determine the force **P** required to move the roller onto the tiles if the roller is (*a*) pushed to the left, (*b*) pulled to the right.

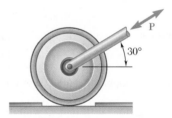

Fig. P4.74

4.75 and 4.76 Member ABC is supported by a pin and bracket at B and by an inextensible cord attached at A and C and passing over a frictionless pulley at D. The tension may be assumed to be the same in portions AD and CD of the cord. For the loading shown and neglecting the size of the pulley, determine the tension in the cord and the reaction at B.

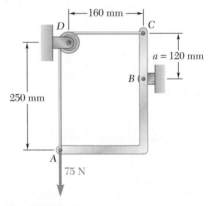

Fig. P4.76

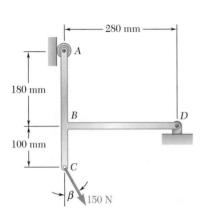

Fig. P4.72 and P4.73

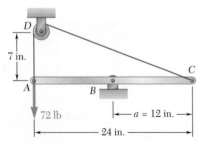

Fig. P4.75

4.77 Rod *AB* is supported by a pin and bracket at *A* and rests against a frictionless peg at *C*. Determine the reactions at *A* and *C* when a 170-N vertical force is applied at *B*.

4.78 Solve Prob. 4.77, assuming that the 170-N force applied at *B* is horizontal and directed to the left.

4.79 Using the method of Sec. 4.7, solve Prob. 4.21.

4.80 Using the method of Sec. 4.7, solve Prob. 4.28.

4.81 Knowing that $\theta = 30°$, determine the reaction (*a*) at *B*, (*b*) at *C*.

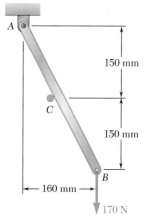

Fig. P4.77

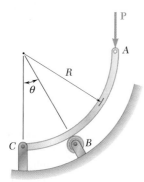

Fig. P4.81 and P4.82

4.82 Knowing that $\theta = 60°$, determine the reaction (*a*) at *B*, (*b*) at *C*.

4.83 Rod *AB* is bent into the shape of an arc of circle and is lodged between two pegs *D* and *E*. It supports a load **P** at end *B*. Neglecting friction and the weight of the rod, determine the distance *c* corresponding to equilibrium when $a = 20$ mm and $R = 100$ mm.

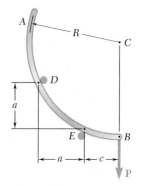

Fig. P4.83

4.84 A slender rod of length *L* is attached to collars that can slide freely along the guides shown. Knowing that the rod is in equilibrium, derive an expression for the angle θ in terms of the angle β.

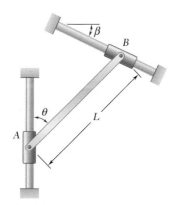

Fig. P4.84 and P4.85

4.85 An 8-kg slender rod of length *L* is attached to collars that can slide freely along the guides shown. Knowing that the rod is in equilibrium and that $\beta = 30°$, determine (*a*) the angle θ that the rod forms with the vertical, (*b*) the reactions at *A* and *B*.

4.86 A slender uniform rod of length L is held in equilibrium as shown, with one end against a frictionless wall and the other end attached to a cord of length S. Derive an expression for the distance h in terms of L and S. Show that this position of equilibrium does not exist if $S > 2L$.

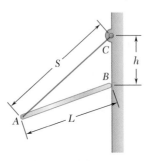

Fig. P4.86 and P4.87

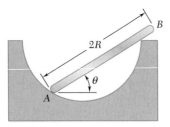

Fig. P4.88

4.87 A slender uniform rod of length $L = 20$ in. is held in equilibrium as shown, with one end against a frictionless wall and the other end attached to a cord of length $S = 30$ in. Knowing that the weight of the rod is 10 lb, determine (*a*) the distance h, (*b*) the tension in the cord, (*c*) the reaction at B.

4.88 A uniform rod AB of length $2R$ rests inside a hemispherical bowl of radius R as shown. Neglecting friction, determine the angle θ corresponding to equilibrium.

4.89 A slender rod of length L and weight W is attached to a collar at A and is fitted with a small wheel at B. Knowing that the wheel rolls freely along a cylindrical surface of radius R, and neglecting friction, derive an equation in θ, L, and R that must be satisfied when the rod is in equilibrium.

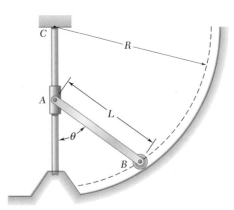

Fig. P4.89

4.90 Knowing that for the rod of Prob. 4.89, $L = 15$ in., $R = 20$ in., and $W = 10$ lb, determine (*a*) the angle θ corresponding to equilibrium, (*b*) the reactions at A and B.

4.8 EQUILIBRIUM OF A RIGID BODY IN THREE DIMENSIONS

We saw in Sec. 4.1 that six scalar equations are required to express the conditions for the equilibrium of a rigid body in the general three-dimensional case:

$$\Sigma F_x = 0 \qquad \Sigma F_y = 0 \qquad \Sigma F_z = 0 \qquad (4.2)$$
$$\Sigma M_x = 0 \qquad \Sigma M_y = 0 \qquad \Sigma M_z = 0 \qquad (4.3)$$

These equations can be solved for no more than *six unknowns,* which generally will represent reactions at supports or connections.

In most problems the scalar equations (4.2) and (4.3) will be more conveniently obtained if we first express in vector form the conditions for the equilibrium of the rigid body considered. We write

$$\Sigma \mathbf{F} = 0 \qquad \Sigma \mathbf{M}_O = \Sigma(\mathbf{r} \times \mathbf{F}) = 0 \qquad (4.1)$$

and express the forces $\mathbf{F}$ and position vectors $\mathbf{r}$ in terms of scalar components and unit vectors. Next, we compute all vector products, either by direct calculation or by means of determinants (see Sec. 3.8). We observe that as many as three unknown reaction components may be eliminated from these computations through a judicious choice of the point O. By equating to zero the coefficients of the unit vectors in each of the two relations (4.1), we obtain the desired scalar equations.†

4.9 REACTIONS AT SUPPORTS AND CONNECTIONS FOR A THREE-DIMENSIONAL STRUCTURE

The reactions on a three-dimensional structure range from the single force of known direction exerted by a frictionless surface to the force-couple system exerted by a fixed support. Consequently, in problems involving the equilibrium of a three-dimensional structure, there can be between one and six unknowns associated with the reaction at each support or connection. Various types of supports and

---

†In some problems, it will be found convenient to eliminate the reactions at two points A and B from the solution by writing the equilibrium equation $\Sigma M_{AB} = 0$, which involves the determination of the moments of the forces about the axis AB joining points A and B (see Sample Prob. 4.10).

Photo 4.6 Universal joints, easily seen on the drive shafts of rear-wheel-drive cars and trucks, allow rotational motion to be transferred between two noncollinear shafts.

Photo 4.7 The pillow block bearing shown supports the shaft of a fan used in an industrial facility.

connections are shown in Fig. 4.10 with their corresponding reactions. A simple way of determining the type of reaction corresponding to a given support or connection and the number of unknowns involved is to find which of the six fundamental motions (translation in the x, y, and z directions, rotation about the x, y, and z axes) are allowed and which motions are prevented.

Ball supports, frictionless surfaces, and cables, for example, prevent translation in one direction only and thus exert a single force whose line of action is known; each of these supports involves one unknown, namely, the magnitude of the reaction. Rollers on rough surfaces and wheels on rails prevent translation in two directions; the corresponding reactions consist of two unknown force components. Rough surfaces in direct contact and ball-and-socket supports prevent translation in three directions; these supports involve three unknown force components.

Some supports and connections can prevent rotation as well as translation; the corresponding reactions include couples as well as forces. For example, the reaction at a fixed support, which prevents any motion (rotation as well as translation), consists of three unknown forces and three unknown couples. A universal joint, which is designed to allow rotation about two axes, will exert a reaction consisting of three unknown force components and one unknown couple.

Other supports and connections are primarily intended to prevent translation; their design, however, is such that they also prevent some rotations. The corresponding reactions consist essentially of force components but *may* also include couples. One group of supports of this type includes hinges and bearings designed to support radial loads only (for example, journal bearings, roller bearings). The corresponding reactions consist of two force components but may also include two couples. Another group includes pin-and-bracket supports, hinges, and bearings designed to support an axial thrust as well as a radial load (for example, ball bearings). The corresponding reactions consist of three force components but may include two couples. However, these supports will not exert any appreciable couples under normal conditions of use. Therefore, *only* force components should be included in their analysis *unless* it is found that couples are necessary to maintain the equilibrium of the rigid body, or unless the support is known to have been specifically designed to exert a couple (see Probs. 4.119 through 4.122).

If the reactions involve more than six unknowns, there are more unknowns than equations, and some of the reactions are *statically indeterminate*. If the reactions involve fewer than six unknowns, there are more equations than unknowns, and some of the equations of equilibrium cannot be satisfied under general loading conditions; the rigid body is only *partially constrained*. Under the particular loading conditions corresponding to a given problem, however, the extra equations often reduce to trivial identities, such as $0 = 0$, and can be disregarded; although only partially constrained, the rigid body remains in equilibrium (see Sample Probs. 4.7 and 4.8). Even with six or more unknowns, it is possible that some equations of equilibrium will not be satisfied. This can occur when the reactions associated with the given supports either are parallel or intersect the same line; the rigid body is then *improperly constrained*.

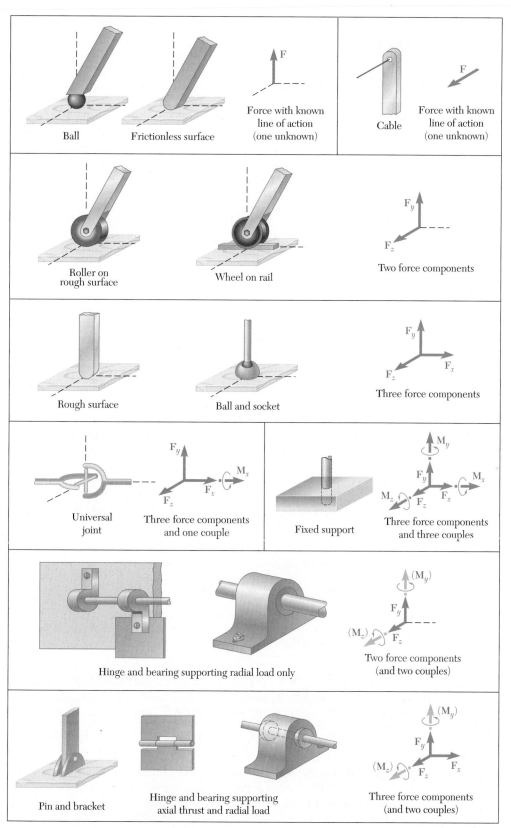

Fig. 4.10 Reactions at supports and connections.

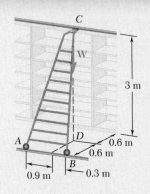

SAMPLE PROBLEM 4.7

A 20-kg ladder used to reach high shelves in a storeroom is supported by two flanged wheels A and B mounted on a rail and by an unflanged wheel C resting against a rail fixed to the wall. An 80-kg man stands on the ladder and leans to the right. The line of action of the combined weight $\mathbf{W}$ of the man and ladder intersects the floor at point D. Determine the reactions at A, B, and C.

SOLUTION

Free-Body Diagram. A free-body diagram of the ladder is drawn. The forces involved are the combined weight of the man and ladder,

$$\mathbf{W} = -mg\mathbf{j} = -(80 \text{ kg} + 20 \text{ kg})(9.81 \text{ m/s}^2)\mathbf{j} = -(981 \text{ N})\mathbf{j}$$

and five unknown reaction components, two at each flanged wheel and one at the unflanged wheel. The ladder is thus only partially constrained; it is free to roll along the rails. It is, however, in equilibrium under the given load since the equation $\Sigma F_x = 0$ is satisfied.

Equilibrium Equations. We express that the forces acting on the ladder form a system equivalent to zero:

$$\Sigma\mathbf{F} = 0: \quad A_y\mathbf{j} + A_z\mathbf{k} + B_y\mathbf{j} + B_z\mathbf{k} - (981 \text{ N})\mathbf{j} + C\mathbf{k} = 0$$
$$(A_y + B_y - 981 \text{ N})\mathbf{j} + (A_z + B_z + C)\mathbf{k} = 0 \quad (1)$$
$$\Sigma\mathbf{M}_A = \Sigma(\mathbf{r} \times \mathbf{F}) = 0: \quad 1.2\mathbf{i} \times (B_y\mathbf{j} + B_z\mathbf{k}) + (0.9\mathbf{i} - 0.6\mathbf{k}) \times (-981\mathbf{j})$$
$$+ (0.6\mathbf{i} + 3\mathbf{j} - 1.2\mathbf{k}) \times C\mathbf{k} = 0$$

Computing the vector products, we have†

$$1.2B_y\mathbf{k} - 1.2B_z\mathbf{j} - 882.9\mathbf{k} - 588.6\mathbf{i} - 0.6C\mathbf{j} + 3C\mathbf{i} = 0$$
$$(3C - 588.6)\mathbf{i} - (1.2B_z + 0.6C)\mathbf{j} + (1.2B_y - 882.9)\mathbf{k} = 0 \quad (2)$$

Setting the coefficients of $\mathbf{i}$, $\mathbf{j}$, $\mathbf{k}$ equal to zero in Eq. (2), we obtain the following three scalar equations, which express that the sum of the moments about each coordinate axis must be zero:

$$3C - 588.6 = 0 \qquad C = +196.2 \text{ N}$$
$$1.2B_z + 0.6C = 0 \qquad B_z = -98.1 \text{ N}$$
$$1.2B_y - 882.9 = 0 \qquad B_y = +736 \text{ N}$$

The reactions at B and C are therefore

$$\mathbf{B} = +(736 \text{ N})\mathbf{j} - (98.1 \text{ N})\mathbf{k} \qquad \mathbf{C} = +(196.2 \text{ N})\mathbf{k} \quad \blacktriangleleft$$

Setting the coefficients of $\mathbf{j}$ and $\mathbf{k}$ equal to zero in Eq. (1), we obtain two scalar equations expressing that the sums of the components in the y and z directions are zero. Substituting for B_y, B_z, and C the values obtained above, we write

$$A_y + B_y - 981 = 0 \qquad A_y + 736 - 981 = 0 \qquad A_y = +245 \text{ N}$$
$$A_z + B_z + C = 0 \qquad A_z - 98.1 + 196.2 = 0 \qquad A_z = -98.1 \text{ N}$$

We conclude that the reaction at A is $\quad \mathbf{A} = +(245 \text{ N})\mathbf{j} - (98.1 \text{ N})\mathbf{k} \quad \blacktriangleleft$

†The moments in this sample problem and in Sample Probs. 4.8 and 4.9 can also be expressed in the form of determinants (see Sample Prob. 3.10).

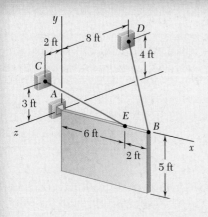

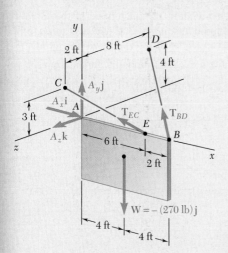

A 5×8-ft sign of uniform density weighs 270 lb and is supported by a ball-and-socket joint at A and by two cables. Determine the tension in each cable and the reaction at A.

SOLUTION

Free-Body Diagram. A free-body diagram of the sign is drawn. The forces acting on the free body are the weight $\mathbf{W} = -(270 \text{ lb})\mathbf{j}$ and the reactions at A, B, and E. The reaction at A is a force of unknown direction and is represented by three unknown components. Since the directions of the forces exerted by the cables are known, these forces involve only one unknown each, namely, the magnitudes T_{BD} and T_{EC}. Since there are only five unknowns, the sign is partially constrained. It can rotate freely about the x axis; it is, however, in equilibrium under the given loading, since the equation $\Sigma M_x = 0$ is satisfied.

The components of the forces $\mathbf{T}_{BD}$ and $\mathbf{T}_{EC}$ can be expressed in terms of the unknown magnitudes T_{BD} and T_{EC} by writing

$$\overrightarrow{BD} = -(8 \text{ ft})\mathbf{i} + (4 \text{ ft})\mathbf{j} - (8 \text{ ft})\mathbf{k} \qquad BD = 12 \text{ ft}$$
$$\overrightarrow{EC} = -(6 \text{ ft})\mathbf{i} + (3 \text{ ft})\mathbf{j} + (2 \text{ ft})\mathbf{k} \qquad EC = 7 \text{ ft}$$
$$\mathbf{T}_{BD} = T_{BD}\left(\frac{\overrightarrow{BD}}{BD}\right) = T_{BD}(-\tfrac{2}{3}\mathbf{i} + \tfrac{1}{3}\mathbf{j} - \tfrac{2}{3}\mathbf{k})$$
$$\mathbf{T}_{EC} = T_{EC}\left(\frac{\overrightarrow{EC}}{EC}\right) = T_{EC}(-\tfrac{6}{7}\mathbf{i} + \tfrac{3}{7}\mathbf{j} - \tfrac{2}{7}\mathbf{k})$$

Equilibrium Equations. We express that the forces acting on the sign form a system equivalent to zero:

$$\Sigma \mathbf{F} = 0: \qquad A_x\mathbf{i} + A_y\mathbf{j} + A_z\mathbf{k} + \mathbf{T}_{BD} + \mathbf{T}_{EC} - (270 \text{ lb})\mathbf{j} = 0$$
$$(A_x - \tfrac{2}{3}T_{BD} - \tfrac{6}{7}T_{EC})\mathbf{i} + (A_y + \tfrac{1}{3}T_{BD} + \tfrac{3}{7}T_{EC} - 270 \text{ lb})\mathbf{j}$$
$$+ (A_z - \tfrac{2}{3}T_{BD} + \tfrac{2}{7}T_{EC})\mathbf{k} = 0 \quad (1)$$

$$\Sigma \mathbf{M}_A = \Sigma(\mathbf{r} \times \mathbf{F}) = 0:$$
$$(8 \text{ ft})\mathbf{i} \times T_{BD}(-\tfrac{2}{3}\mathbf{i} + \tfrac{1}{3}\mathbf{j} - \tfrac{2}{3}\mathbf{k}) + (6 \text{ ft})\mathbf{i} \times T_{EC}(-\tfrac{6}{7}\mathbf{i} + \tfrac{3}{7}\mathbf{j} + \tfrac{2}{7}\mathbf{k})$$
$$+ (4 \text{ ft})\mathbf{i} \times (-270 \text{ lb})\mathbf{j} = 0$$
$$(2.667T_{BD} + 2.571T_{EC} - 1080 \text{ lb})\mathbf{k} + (5.333T_{BD} - 1.714T_{EC})\mathbf{j} = 0 \quad (2)$$

Setting the coefficients of $\mathbf{j}$ and $\mathbf{k}$ equal to zero in Eq. (2), we obtain two scalar equations which can be solved for T_{BD} and T_{EC}:

$$T_{BD} = 101.3 \text{ lb} \qquad T_{EC} = 315 \text{ lb} \quad \blacktriangleleft$$

Setting the coefficients of $\mathbf{i}$, $\mathbf{j}$, and $\mathbf{k}$ equal to zero in Eq. (1), we obtain three more equations, which yield the components of $\mathbf{A}$. We have

$$\mathbf{A} = +(338 \text{ lb})\mathbf{i} + (101.2 \text{ lb})\mathbf{j} - (22.5 \text{ lb})\mathbf{k} \quad \blacktriangleleft$$

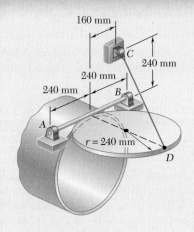

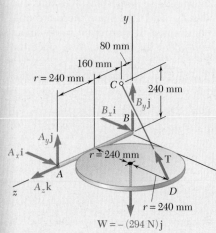

SAMPLE PROBLEM 4.9

A uniform pipe cover of radius $r = 240$ mm and mass 30 kg is held in a horizontal position by the cable CD. Assuming that the bearing at B does not exert any axial thrust, determine the tension in the cable and the reactions at A and B.

SOLUTION

Free-Body Diagram. A free-body diagram is drawn with the coordinate axes shown. The forces acting on the free body are the weight of the cover,

$$\mathbf{W} = -mg\mathbf{j} = -(30 \text{ kg})(9.81 \text{ m/s}^2)\mathbf{j} = -(294 \text{ N})\mathbf{j}$$

and reactions involving six unknowns, namely, the magnitude of the force $\mathbf{T}$ exerted by the cable, three force components at hinge A, and two at hinge B. The components of $\mathbf{T}$ are expressed in terms of the unknown magnitude T by resolving the vector $\overrightarrow{DC}$ into rectangular components and writing

$$\overrightarrow{DC} = -(480 \text{ mm})\mathbf{i} + (240 \text{ mm})\mathbf{j} - (160 \text{ mm})\mathbf{k} \qquad DC = 560 \text{ mm}$$

$$\mathbf{T} = T\frac{\overrightarrow{DC}}{DC} = -\tfrac{6}{7}T\mathbf{i} + \tfrac{3}{7}T\mathbf{j} - \tfrac{2}{7}T\mathbf{k}$$

Equilibrium Equations. We express that the forces acting on the pipe cover form a system equivalent to zero:

$$\Sigma\mathbf{F} = 0: \qquad A_x\mathbf{i} + A_y\mathbf{j} + A_z\mathbf{k} + B_x\mathbf{i} + B_y\mathbf{j} + \mathbf{T} - (294 \text{ N})\mathbf{j} = 0$$
$$(A_x + B_x - \tfrac{6}{7}T)\mathbf{i} + (A_y + B_y + \tfrac{3}{7}T - 294 \text{ N})\mathbf{j} + (A_z - \tfrac{2}{7}T)\mathbf{k} = 0 \quad (1)$$

$$\Sigma\mathbf{M}_B = \Sigma(\mathbf{r} \times \mathbf{F}) = 0:$$
$$2r\mathbf{k} \times (A_x\mathbf{i} + A_y\mathbf{j} + A_z\mathbf{k})$$
$$+ (2r\mathbf{i} + r\mathbf{k}) \times (-\tfrac{6}{7}T\mathbf{i} + \tfrac{3}{7}T\mathbf{j} - \tfrac{2}{7}T\mathbf{k})$$
$$+ (r\mathbf{i} + r\mathbf{k}) \times (-294 \text{ N})\mathbf{j} = 0$$
$$(-2A_y - \tfrac{3}{7}T + 294 \text{ N})r\mathbf{i} + (2A_x - \tfrac{2}{7}T)r\mathbf{j} + (\tfrac{6}{7}T - 294 \text{ N})r\mathbf{k} = 0 \quad (2)$$

Setting the coefficients of the unit vectors equal to zero in Eq. (2), we write three scalar equations, which yield

$$A_x = +49.0 \text{ N} \qquad A_y = +73.5 \text{ N} \qquad T = 343 \text{ N} \quad \blacktriangleleft$$

Setting the coefficients of the unit vectors equal to zero in Eq. (1), we obtain three more scalar equations. After substituting the values of T, A_x, and A_y into these equations, we obtain

$$A_z = +98.0 \text{ N} \qquad B_x = +245 \text{ N} \qquad B_y = +73.5 \text{ N}$$

The reactions at A and B are therefore

$$\mathbf{A} = +(49.0 \text{ N})\mathbf{i} + (73.5 \text{ N})\mathbf{j} + (98.0 \text{ N})\mathbf{k} \quad \blacktriangleleft$$
$$\mathbf{B} = +(245 \text{ N})\mathbf{i} + (73.5 \text{ N})\mathbf{j} \quad \blacktriangleleft$$

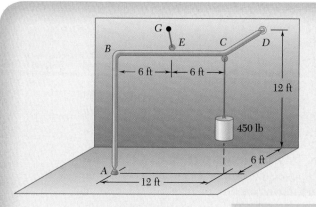

SAMPLE PROBLEM 4.10

A 450-lb load hangs from the corner C of a rigid piece of pipe $ABCD$ which has been bent as shown. The pipe is supported by the ball-and-socket joints A and D, which are fastened, respectively, to the floor and to a vertical wall, and by a cable attached at the midpoint E of the portion BC of the pipe and at a point G on the wall. Determine (*a*) where G should be located if the tension in the cable is to be minimum, (*b*) the corresponding minimum value of the tension.

SOLUTION

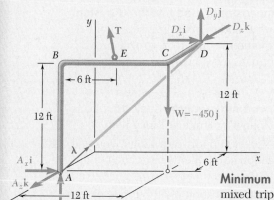

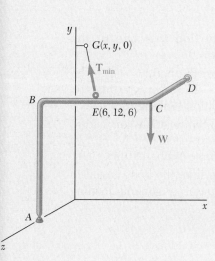

Free-Body Diagram. The free-body diagram of the pipe includes the load $\mathbf{W} = (-450 \text{ lb})\mathbf{j}$, the reactions at A and D, and the force $\mathbf{T}$ exerted by the cable. To eliminate the reactions at A and D from the computations, we express that the sum of the moments of the forces about AD is zero. Denoting by $\boldsymbol{\lambda}$ the unit vector along AD, we write

$$\Sigma M_{AD} = 0: \quad \boldsymbol{\lambda} \cdot (\overrightarrow{AE} \times \mathbf{T}) + \boldsymbol{\lambda} \cdot (\overrightarrow{AC} \times \mathbf{W}) = 0 \quad (1)$$

The second term in Eq. (1) can be computed as follows:

$$\overrightarrow{AC} \times \mathbf{W} = (12\mathbf{i} + 12\mathbf{j}) \times (-450\mathbf{j}) = -5400\mathbf{k}$$

$$\boldsymbol{\lambda} = \frac{\overrightarrow{AD}}{AD} = \frac{12\mathbf{i} + 12\mathbf{j} - 6\mathbf{k}}{18} = \tfrac{2}{3}\mathbf{i} + \tfrac{2}{3}\mathbf{j} - \tfrac{1}{3}\mathbf{k}$$

$$\boldsymbol{\lambda} \cdot (\overrightarrow{AC} \times \mathbf{W}) = (\tfrac{2}{3}\mathbf{i} + \tfrac{2}{3}\mathbf{j} - \tfrac{1}{3}\mathbf{k}) \cdot (-5400\mathbf{k}) = +1800$$

Substituting the value obtained into Eq. (1), we write

$$\boldsymbol{\lambda} \cdot (\overrightarrow{AE} \times \mathbf{T}) = -1800 \text{ lb} \cdot \text{ft} \quad (2)$$

Minimum Value of Tension. Recalling the commutative property for mixed triple products, we rewrite Eq. (2) in the form

$$\mathbf{T} \cdot (\boldsymbol{\lambda} \times \overrightarrow{AE}) = -1800 \text{ lb} \cdot \text{ft} \quad (3)$$

which shows that the projection of $\mathbf{T}$ on the vector $\boldsymbol{\lambda} \times \overrightarrow{AE}$ is a constant. It follows that $\mathbf{T}$ is minimum when parallel to the vector

$$\boldsymbol{\lambda} \times \overrightarrow{AE} = (\tfrac{2}{3}\mathbf{i} + \tfrac{2}{3}\mathbf{j} - \tfrac{1}{3}\mathbf{k}) \times (6\mathbf{i} + 12\mathbf{j}) = 4\mathbf{i} - 2\mathbf{j} + 4\mathbf{k}$$

Since the corresponding unit vector is $\tfrac{2}{3}\mathbf{i} - \tfrac{1}{3}\mathbf{j} + \tfrac{2}{3}\mathbf{k}$, we write

$$\mathbf{T}_{\min} = T(\tfrac{2}{3}\mathbf{i} - \tfrac{1}{3}\mathbf{j} + \tfrac{2}{3}\mathbf{k}) \quad (4)$$

Substituting for $\mathbf{T}$ and $\boldsymbol{\lambda} \times \overrightarrow{AE}$ in Eq. (3) and computing the dot products, we obtain $6T = -1800$ and, thus, $T = -300$. Carrying this value into (4), we obtain

$$\mathbf{T}_{\min} = -200\mathbf{i} + 100\mathbf{j} - 200\mathbf{k} \qquad T_{\min} = 300 \text{ lb} \quad \blacktriangleleft$$

Location of G. Since the vector $\overrightarrow{EG}$ and the force $\mathbf{T}_{\min}$ have the same direction, their components must be proportional. Denoting the coordinates of G by x, y, 0, we write

$$\frac{x - 6}{-200} = \frac{y - 12}{+100} = \frac{0 - 6}{-200} \qquad x = 0 \qquad y = 15 \text{ ft} \quad \blacktriangleleft$$

195

SOLVING PROBLEMS ON YOUR OWN

The equilibrium of a *three-dimensional body* was considered in the sections you just completed. It is again most important that you draw a complete *free-body diagram* as the first step of your solution.

1. As you draw the free-body diagram, pay particular attention to the reactions at the supports. The number of unknowns at a support can range from one to six (Fig. 4.10). To decide whether an unknown reaction or reaction component exists at a support, ask yourself whether the support prevents motion of the body in a certain direction or about a certain axis.

    a. If motion is prevented in a certain direction, include in your free-body diagram an unknown *reaction* or *reaction component* that acts in the *same direction.*

    b. If a support prevents rotation about a certain axis, include in your free-body diagram a *couple* of unknown magnitude that acts about the *same axis.*

2. The external forces acting on a three-dimensional body form a system equivalent to zero. Writing $\Sigma \mathbf{F} = 0$ and $\Sigma \mathbf{M}_A = 0$ about an appropriate point A, and setting the coefficients of $\mathbf{i}$, $\mathbf{j}$, $\mathbf{k}$ in both equations equal to zero will provide you with six scalar equations. In general, these equations will contain six unknowns and may be solved for these unknowns.

3. After completing your free-body diagram, you may want to seek equations involving as few unknowns as possible. The following strategies may help you.

    a. By summing moments about a ball-and-socket support or a hinge, you will obtain equations from which three unknown reaction components have been eliminated [Sample Probs. 4.8 and 4.9].

    b. If you can draw an axis through the points of application of all but one of the unknown reactions, summing moments about that axis will yield an equation in a single unknown [Sample Prob. 4.10].

4. After drawing your free-body diagram, you may find that one of the following situations exists.

    a. The reactions involve fewer than six unknowns; the body is said to be *partially constrained* and motion of the body is possible. However, you may be able to determine the reactions for a given loading condition [Sample Prob. 4.7].

    b. The reactions involve more than six unknowns; the reactions are said to be *statically indeterminate.* Although you may be able to calculate one or two reactions, you cannot determine all of the reactions [Sample Prob. 4.10].

    c. The reactions are parallel or intersect the same line; the body is said to be *improperly constrained*, and motion can occur under a general loading condition.

4.91 A 4 × 8-ft sheet of plywood weighing 34 lb has been temporarily placed among three pipe supports. The lower edge of the sheet rests on small collars at A and B and its upper edge leans against pipe C. Neglecting friction at all surfaces, determine the reactions at A, B, and C.

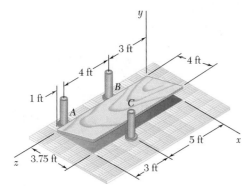

Fig. P4.91

4.92 Two tape spools are attached to an axle supported by bearings at A and D. The radius of spool B is 30 mm and the radius of spool C is 40 mm. Knowing that $T_B = 80$ N and that the system rotates at a constant rate, determine the reactions at A and D. Assume that the bearing at A does not exert any axial thrust and neglect the weights of the spools and axle.

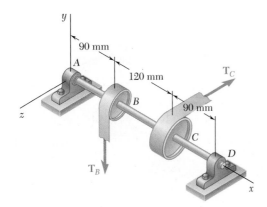

Fig. P4.92

4.93 Solve Prob. 4.92, assuming that the spool C is replaced by a spool of radius 50 mm.

4.94 Two transmission belts pass over sheaves welded to an axle supported by bearings at B and D. The sheave at A has a radius of 2.5 in., and the sheave at C has a radius of 2 in. Knowing that the system rotates at a constant rate, determine (a) the tension T, (b) the reactions at B and D. Assume that the bearing at D does not exert any axial thrust and neglect the weights of the sheaves and axle.

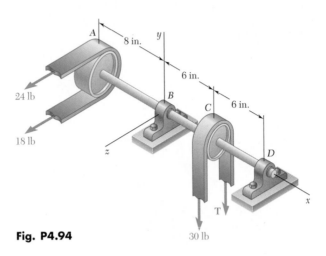

Fig. P4.94

4.95 A 200-mm lever and a 240-mm-diameter pulley are welded to the axle BE that is supported by bearings at C and D. If a 720-N vertical load is applied at A when the lever is horizontal, determine (a) the tension in the cord, (b) the reactions at C and D. Assume that the bearing at D does not exert any axial thrust.

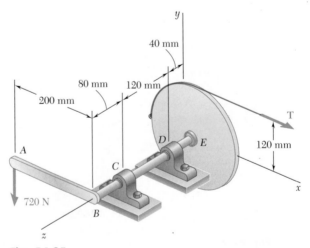

Fig. P4.95

4.96 Solve Prob. 4.95, assuming that the axle has been rotated clockwise in its bearings by 30° and that the 720-N load remains vertical.

4.97 An opening in a floor is covered by a 1 × 1.2-m sheet of plywood of mass 18 kg. The sheet is hinged at A and B and is maintained in a position slightly above the floor by a small block C. Determine the vertical component of the reaction (*a*) at A, (*b*) at B, (*c*) at C.

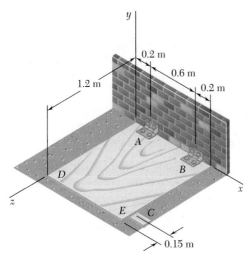

Fig. P4.97

4.98 Solve Prob. 4.97, assuming that the small block C is moved and placed under edge DE at a point 0.15 m from corner E.

4.99 The rectangular plate shown weighs 80 lb and is supported by three vertical wires. Determine the tension in each wire.

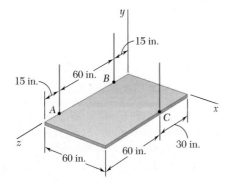

Fig. P4.99 and P4.100

4.100 The rectangular plate shown weighs 80 lb and is supported by three vertical wires. Determine the weight and location of the lightest block that should be placed on the plate if the tensions in the three wires are to be equal.

4.101 Two steel pipes AB and BC, each having a mass per unit length of 8 kg/m, are welded together at B and supported by three wires. Knowing that $a = 0.4$ m, determine the tension in each wire.

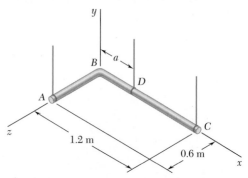

Fig. P4.101

4.102 For the pipe assembly of Prob. 4.101, determine (*a*) the largest permissible value of a if the assembly is not to tip, (*b*) the corresponding tension in each wire.

4.103 The 24-lb square plate shown is supported by three vertical wires. Determine (*a*) the tension in each wire when $a = 10$ in., (*b*) the value of a for which the tension in each wire is 8 lb.

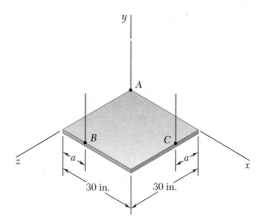

Fig. P4.103

4.104 The table shown weighs 30 lb and has a diameter of 4 ft. It is supported by three legs equally spaced around the edge. A vertical load **P** of magnitude 100 lb is applied to the top of the table at D. Determine the maximum value of a if the table is not to tip over. Show, on a sketch, the area of the table over which **P** can act without tipping the table.

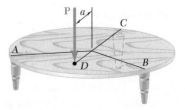

Fig. P4.104

4.105 A 10-ft boom is acted upon by the 840-lb force shown. Determine the tension in each cable and the reaction at the ball-and-socket joint at A.

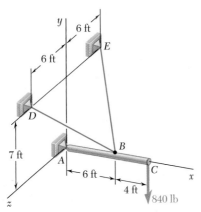

Fig. P4.105

4.106 A 2.4-m boom is held by a ball-and-socket joint at C and by two cables AD and AE. Determine the tension in each cable and the reaction at C.

4.107 Solve Prob. 4.106, assuming that the 3.6-kN load is applied at point A.

4.108 A 600-lb crate hangs from a cable that passes over a pulley B and is attached to a support at H. The 200-lb boom AB is supported by a ball-and-socket joint at A and by two cables DE and DF. The center of gravity of the boom is located at G. Determine (a) the tension in cables DE and DF, (b) the reaction at A.

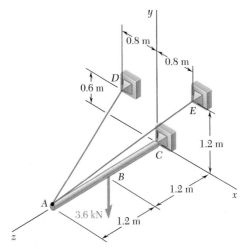

Fig. P4.106

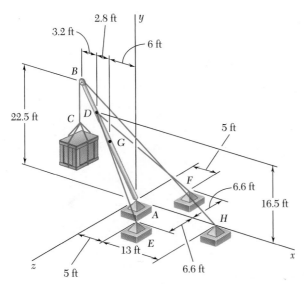

Fig. P4.108

4.109 A 3-m pole is supported by a ball-and-socket joint at A and by the cables CD and CE. Knowing that the 5-kN force acts vertically downward ($\phi = 0$), determine (a) the tension in cables CD and CE, (b) the reaction at A.

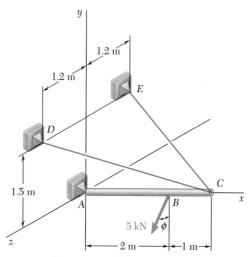

Fig. P4.109 and P4.110

4.110 A 3-m pole is supported by a ball-and-socket joint at A and by the cables CD and CE. Knowing that the line of action of the 5-kN force forms an angle $\phi = 30°$ with the vertical xy plane, determine (a) the tension in cables CD and CE, (b) the reaction at A.

4.111 A 48-in. boom is held by a ball-and-socket joint at C and by two cables BF and DAE; cable DAE passes around a frictionless pulley at A. For the loading shown, determine the tension in each cable and the reaction at C.

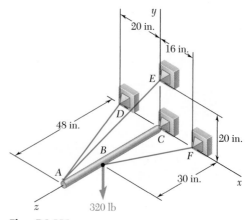

Fig. P4.111

4.112 Solve Prob. 4.111, assuming that the 320-lb load is applied at *A*.

4.113 A 20-kg cover for a roof opening is hinged at corners *A* and *B*. The roof forms an angle of 30° with the horizontal, and the cover is maintained in a horizontal position by the brace *CE*. Determine (*a*) the magnitude of the force exerted by the brace, (*b*) the reactions at the hinges. Assume that the hinge at *A* does not exert any axial thrust.

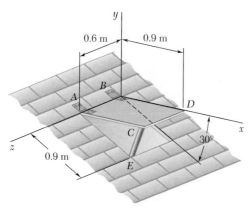

Fig. P4.113

4.114 The bent rod *ABEF* is supported by bearings at *C* and *D* and by wire *AH*. Knowing that portion *AB* of the rod is 250 mm long, determine (*a*) the tension in wire *AH*, (*b*) the reactions at *C* and *D*. Assume that the bearing at *D* does not exert any axial thrust.

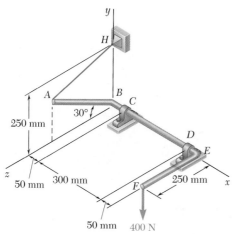

Fig. P4.114

4.115 A 100-kg uniform rectangular plate is supported in the position shown by hinges A and B and by cable DCE that passes over a frictionless hook at C. Assuming that the tension is the same in both parts of the cable, determine (a) the tension in the cable, (b) the reactions at A and B. Assume that the hinge at B does not exert any axial thrust.

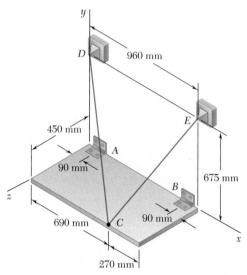

Fig. P4.115

4.116 Solve Prob. 4.115, assuming that cable DCE is replaced by a cable attached to point E and hook C.

4.117 The rectangular plate shown weighs 75 lb and is held in the position shown by hinges at A and B and by cable EF. Assuming that the hinge at B does not exert any axial thrust, determine (a) the tension in the cable, (b) the reactions at A and B.

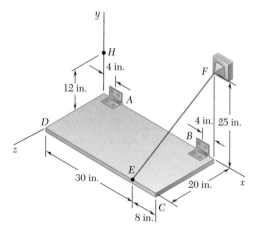

Fig. P4.117

4.118 Solve Prob. 4.117, assuming that cable EF is replaced by a cable attached at points E and H.

4.119 Solve Prob. 4.114, assuming that the bearing at D is removed and that the bearing at C can exert couples about axes parallel to the y and z axes.

4.120 Solve Prob. 4.117, assuming that the hinge at B is removed and that the hinge at A can exert couples about axes parallel to the y and z axes.

4.121 The assembly shown is used to control the tension T in a tape that passes around a frictionless spool at E. Collar C is welded to rods ABC and CDE. It can rotate about shaft FG but its motion along the shaft is prevented by a washer S. For the loading shown, determine (a) the tension T in the tape, (b) the reaction at C.

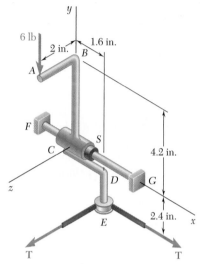

Fig. P4.121

4.122 The assembly shown is welded to collar A that fits on the vertical pin shown. The pin can exert couples about the x and z axes but does not prevent motion about or along the y axis. For the loading shown, determine the tension in each cable and the reaction at A.

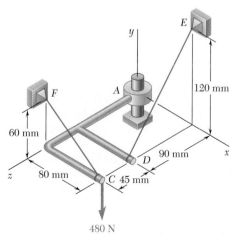

Fig. P4.122

4.123 The rigid L-shaped member *ABC* is supported by a ball-and-socket joint at *A* and by three cables. If a 450-lb load is applied at *F*, determine the tension in each cable.

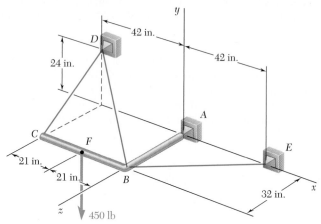

Fig. P4.123

4.124 Solve Prob. 4.123, assuming that the 450-lb load is applied at *C*.

4.125 Frame *ABCD* is supported by a ball-and-socket joint at *A* and by three cables. For $a = 150$ mm, determine the tension in each cable and the reaction at *A*.

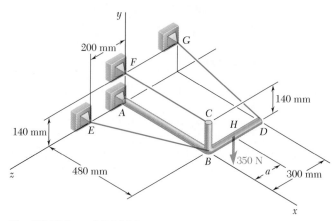

Fig. P4.125 and P4.126

4.126 Frame *ABCD* is supported by a ball-and-socket joint at *A* and by three cables. Knowing that the 350-N load is applied at *D* ($a = 300$ mm), determine the tension in each cable and the reaction at *A*.

4.127 Three rods are welded together to form a "corner" that is supported by three eyebolts. Neglecting friction, determine the reactions at *A*, *B*, and *C* when $P = 240$ lb, $a = 12$ in., $b = 8$ in., and $c = 10$ in.

4.128 Solve Prob. 4.127, assuming that the force **P** is removed and is replaced by a couple $\mathbf{M} = +(600 \text{ lb} \cdot \text{in.})\mathbf{j}$ acting at *B*.

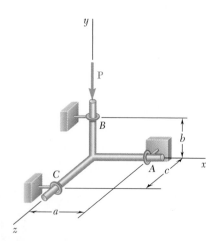

Fig. P4.127

4.129 In order to clean the clogged drainpipe AE, a plumber has disconnected both ends of the pipe and inserted a power snake through the opening at A. The cutting head of the snake is connected by a heavy cable to an electric motor that rotates at a constant speed as the plumber forces the cable into the pipe. The forces exerted by the plumber and the motor on the end of the cable can be represented by the wrench $\mathbf{F} = -(48 \text{ N})\mathbf{k}$, $\mathbf{M} = -(90 \text{ N} \cdot \text{m})\mathbf{k}$. Determine the additional reactions at B, C, and D caused by the cleaning operation. Assume that the reaction at each support consists of two force components perpendicular to the pipe.

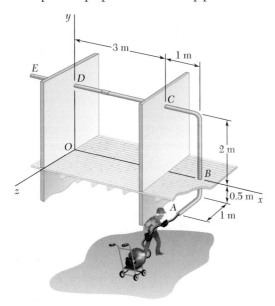

Fig. P4.129

4.130 Solve Prob. 4.129, assuming that the plumber exerts a force $\mathbf{F} = -(48 \text{ N})\mathbf{k}$ and that the motor is turned off ($\mathbf{M} = 0$).

4.131 The assembly shown consists of an 80-mm rod AF that is welded to a cross consisting of four 200-mm arms. The assembly is supported by a ball-and-socket joint at F and by three short links, each of which forms an angle of $45°$ with the vertical. For the loading shown, determine (a) the tension in each link, (b) the reaction at F.

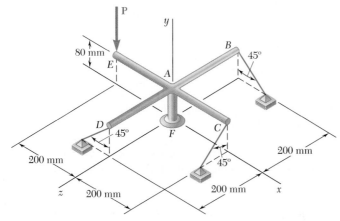

Fig. P4.131

4.132 The uniform 10-kg rod AB is supported by a ball-and-socket joint at A and by the cord CG that is attached to the midpoint G of the rod. Knowing that the rod leans against a frictionless vertical wall at B, determine (a) the tension in the cord, (b) the reactions at A and B.

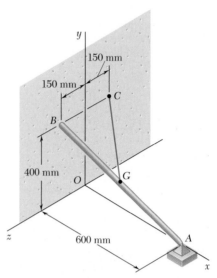

Fig. P4.132

4.133 The bent rod $ABDE$ is supported by ball-and-socket joints at A and E and by the cable DF. If a 60-lb load is applied at C as shown, determine the tension in the cable.

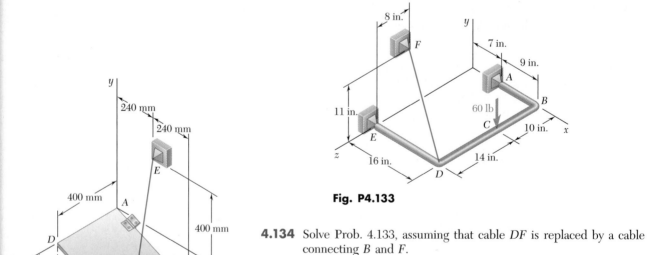

Fig. P4.135

Fig. P4.133

4.134 Solve Prob. 4.133, assuming that cable DF is replaced by a cable connecting B and F.

4.135 The 50-kg plate $ABCD$ is supported by hinges along edge AB and by wire CE. Knowing that the plate is uniform, determine the tension in the wire.

4.136 Solve Prob. 4.135, assuming that wire CE is replaced by a wire connecting E and D.

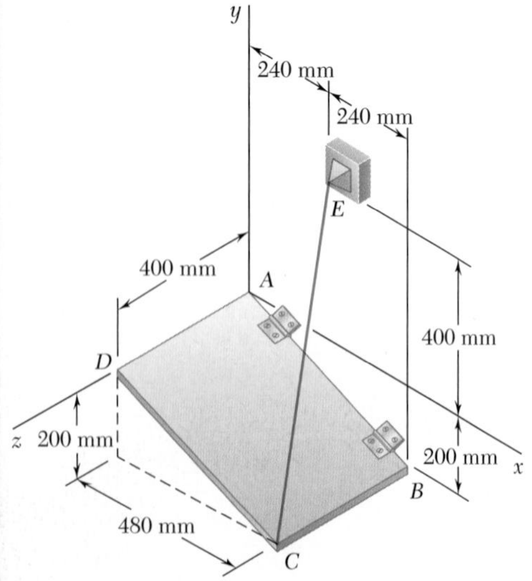

4.137 Two rectangular plates are welded together to form the assembly shown. The assembly is supported by ball-and-socket joints at B and D and by a ball on a horizontal surface at C. For the loading shown, determine the reaction at C.

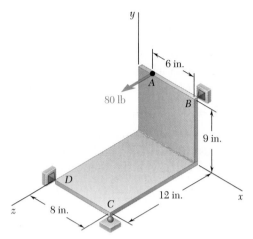

Fig. P4.137

4.138 Two 2×4-ft plywood panels, each of weight 12 lb, are nailed together as shown. The panels are supported by ball-and-socket joints at A and F and by the wire BH. Determine (*a*) the location of H in the xy plane if the tension in the wire is to be minimum, (*b*) the corresponding minimum tension.

4.139 Solve Prob. 4.138, subject to the restriction that H must lie on the y axis.

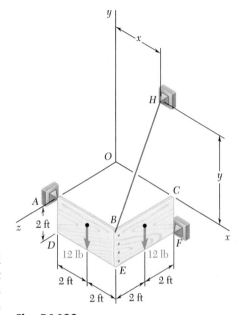

Fig. P4.138

4.140 The pipe $ACDE$ is supported by ball-and-socket joints at A and E and by the wire DF. Determine the tension in the wire when a 640-N load is applied at B as shown.

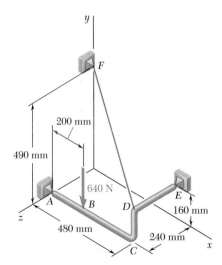

Fig. P4.140

4.141 Solve Prob. 4.140, assuming that wire DF is replaced by a wire connecting C and F.

REVIEW AND SUMMARY

Equilibrium equations

This chapter was devoted to the study of the *equilibrium of rigid bodies*, i.e., to the situation when the external forces acting on a rigid body *form a system equivalent to zero* [Sec. 4.1]. We then have

$$\Sigma \mathbf{F} = 0 \qquad \Sigma \mathbf{M}_O = \Sigma(\mathbf{r} \times \mathbf{F}) = 0 \qquad (4.1)$$

Resolving each force and each moment into its rectangular components, we can express the necessary and sufficient conditions for the equilibrium of a rigid body with the following six scalar equations:

$$\Sigma F_x = 0 \qquad \Sigma F_y = 0 \qquad \Sigma F_z = 0 \qquad (4.2)$$
$$\Sigma M_x = 0 \qquad \Sigma M_y = 0 \qquad \Sigma M_z = 0 \qquad (4.3)$$

These equations can be used to determine unknown forces applied to the rigid body or unknown reactions exerted by its supports.

Free-body diagram

When solving a problem involving the equilibrium of a rigid body, it is essential to consider *all* of the forces acting on the body. Therefore, the first step in the solution of the problem should be to draw a *free-body diagram* showing the body under consideration and all of the unknown as well as known forces acting on it [Sec. 4.2].

Equilibrium of a two-dimensional structure

In the first part of the chapter, we considered the *equilibrium of a two-dimensional structure;* i.e., we assumed that the structure considered and the forces applied to it were contained in the same plane. We saw that each of the reactions exerted on the structure by its supports could involve one, two, or three unknowns, depending upon the type of support [Sec. 4.3].

In the case of a two-dimensional structure, Eqs. (4.1), or Eqs. (4.2) and (4.3), reduce to *three equilibrium equations,* namely

$$\Sigma F_x = 0 \qquad \Sigma F_y = 0 \qquad \Sigma M_A = 0 \qquad (4.5)$$

where A is an arbitrary point in the plane of the structure [Sec. 4.4]. These equations can be used to solve for three unknowns. While the three equilibrium equations (4.5) cannot be *augmented* with additional equations, any of them can be *replaced* by another equation. Therefore, we can write alternative sets of equilibrium equations, such as

$$\Sigma F_x = 0 \qquad \Sigma M_A = 0 \qquad \Sigma M_B = 0 \qquad (4.6)$$

where point B is chosen in such a way that the line AB is not parallel to the y axis, or

$$\Sigma M_A = 0 \qquad \Sigma M_B = 0 \qquad \Sigma M_C = 0 \qquad (4.7)$$

where the points A, B, and C do not lie in a straight line.

Since any set of equilibrium equations can be solved for only three unknowns, the reactions at the supports of a rigid two-dimensional structure cannot be completely determined if they involve *more than three unknowns;* they are said to be *statically indeterminate* [Sec. 4.5]. On the other hand, if the reactions involve *fewer than three unknowns,* equilibrium will not be maintained under general loading conditions; the structure is said to be *partially constrained.* The fact that the reactions involve exactly three unknowns is no guarantee that the equilibrium equations can be solved for all three unknowns. If the supports are arranged in such a way that the reactions are *either concurrent or parallel,* the reactions are statically indeterminate, and the structure is said to be *improperly constrained.*

Statical indeterminacy

Partial constraints

Improper constraints

Two particular cases of equilibrium of a rigid body were given special attention. In Sec. 4.6, a *two-force body* was defined as a rigid body subjected to forces at only two points, and it was shown that the resultants $\mathbf{F}_1$ and $\mathbf{F}_2$ of these forces must have the *same magnitude, the same line of action, and opposite sense* (Fig. 4.11), a property which will simplify the solution of certain problems in later chapters. In Sec. 4.7, a *three-force body* was defined as a rigid body subjected to forces at only three points, and it was shown that the resultants $\mathbf{F}_1$, $\mathbf{F}_2$, and $\mathbf{F}_3$ of these forces must be *either concurrent* (Fig. 4.12) *or parallel.* This property provides us with an alternative approach to the solution of problems involving a three-force body [Sample Prob. 4.6].

Two-force body

Three-force body

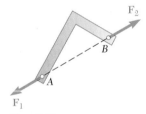

Fig. 4.11

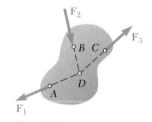

Fig. 4.12

In the second part of the chapter, we considered the *equilibrium of a three-dimensional body* and saw that each of the reactions exerted on the body by its supports could involve between one and six unknowns, depending upon the type of support [Sec. 4.8].

Equilibrium of a three-dimensional body

In the general case of the equilibrium of a three-dimensional body, all of the six scalar equilibrium equations (4.2) and (4.3) listed at the beginning of this review should be used and solved for *six unknowns* [Sec. 4.9]. In most problems, however, these equations will be more conveniently obtained if we first write

$$\Sigma \mathbf{F} = 0 \qquad \Sigma \mathbf{M}_O = \Sigma(\mathbf{r} \times \mathbf{F}) = 0 \qquad (4.1)$$

and express the forces $\mathbf{F}$ and position vectors $\mathbf{r}$ in terms of scalar components and unit vectors. The vector products can then be computed either directly or by means of determinants, and the desired scalar equations obtained by equating to zero the coefficients of the unit vectors [Sample Probs. 4.7 through 4.9].

We noted that as many as three unknown reaction components may be eliminated from the computation of $\Sigma\mathbf{M}_O$ in the second of the relations (4.1) through a judicious choice of point O. Also, the reactions at two points A and B can be eliminated from the solution of some problems by writing the equation $\Sigma M_{AB} = 0$, which involves the computation of the moments of the forces about an axis AB joining points A and B [Sample Prob. 4.10].

If the reactions involve more than six unknowns, some of the reactions are *statically indeterminate;* if they involve fewer than six unknowns, the rigid body is only *partially constrained.* Even with six or more unknowns, the rigid body will be *improperly constrained* if the reactions associated with the given supports either are parallel or intersect the same line.

REVIEW PROBLEMS

4.142 A hand truck is used to move two kegs, each of mass 40 kg. Neglecting the mass of the hand truck, determine (a) the vertical force **P** that should be applied to the handle to maintain equilibrium when $\alpha = 35°$, (b) the corresponding reaction at each of the two wheels.

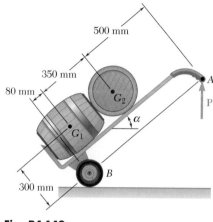

Fig. P4.142

4.143 Determine the reactions at A and C when (a) $\alpha = 0$, (b) $\alpha = 30°$.

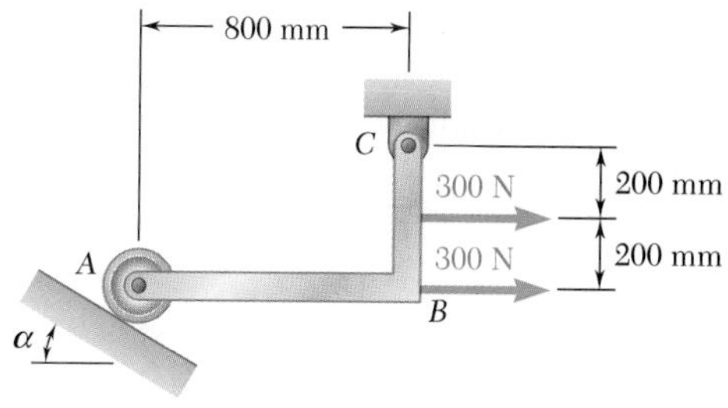

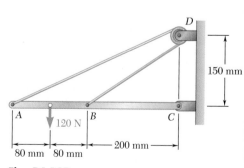

Fig. P4.143

4.144 A lever AB is hinged at C and attached to a control cable at A. If the lever is subjected to a 75-lb vertical force at B, determine (a) the tension in the cable, (b) the reaction at C.

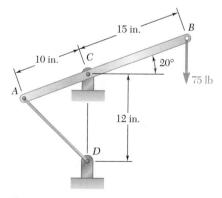

Fig. P4.144

4.145 Neglecting friction and the radius of the pulley, determine (a) the tension in cable ADB, (b) the reaction at C.

Fig. P4.145

213

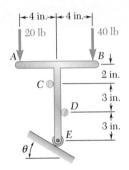

**Fig. P4.146
and P4.147**

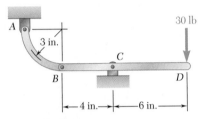

Fig. P4.148

4.146 The T-shaped bracket shown is supported by a small wheel at E and pegs at C and D. Neglecting the effect of friction, determine the reactions at C, D, and E when $\theta = 30°$.

4.147 The T-shaped bracket shown is supported by a small wheel at E and pegs at C and D. Neglecting the effect of friction, determine (a) the smallest value of θ for which the equilibrium of the bracket is maintained, (b) the corresponding reactions at C, D, and E.

4.148 For the frame and loading shown, determine the reactions at A and C.

4.149 Determine the reactions at A and B when $\beta = 50°$.

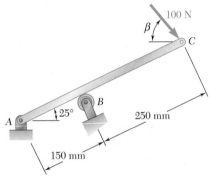

Fig. P4.149

4.150 The 6-m pole ABC is acted upon by a 455-N force as shown. The pole is held by a ball-and-socket joint at A and by two cables BD and BE. For $a = 3$ m, determine the tension in each cable and the reaction at A.

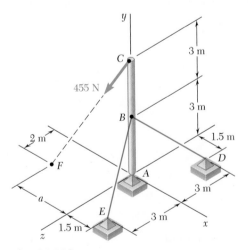

Fig. P4.150

4.151 Solve Prob. 4.150 for $a = 1.5$ m.

4.152 The rigid L-shaped member *ABF* is supported by a ball-and-socket joint at *A* and by three cables. For the loading shown, determine the tension in each cable and the reaction at *A*.

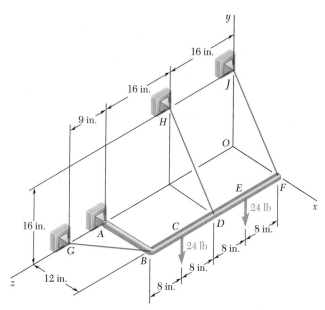

Fig. P4.152

4.153 A force **P** is applied to a bent rod *ABC*, which may be supported in four different ways as shown. In each case, if possible, determine the reactions at the supports.

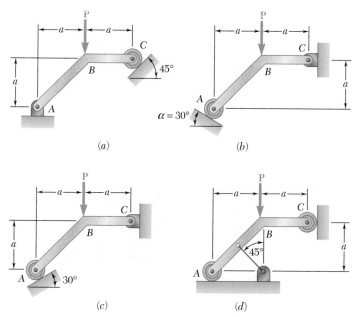

Fig. P4.153

COMPUTER PROBLEMS

4.C1 The position of the L-shaped rod shown is controlled by a cable attached at B. Knowing that the rod supports a load of magnitude $P = 50$ lb, use computational software to calculate the tension T in the cable for values of θ from 0 to 120° using 10° increments. Using appropriate smaller increments, calculate the maximum tension T and the corresponding value of θ.

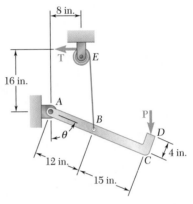

Fig. P4.C1

4.C2 The position of the 10-kg rod AB is controlled by the block shown, which is slowly moved to the left by the force **P**. Neglecting the effect of friction, use computational software to calculate the magnitude P of the force for values of x decreasing from 750 mm to 0 using 50-mm increments. Using appropriate smaller increments, determine the maximum value of P and the corresponding value of x.

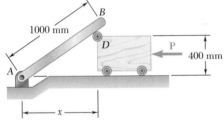

Fig. P4.C2

4.C3 and 4.C4 The constant of spring AB is k, and the spring is unstretched when $\theta = 0$. Knowing that $R = 10$ in., $a = 20$ in., and $k = 5$ lb/in., use computational software to calculate the weight W corresponding to equilibrium for values of θ from 0 to 90° using 10° increments. Using appropriate smaller increments, determine the value of θ corresponding to equilibrium when $W = 5$ lb.

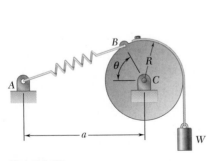

Fig. P4.C3

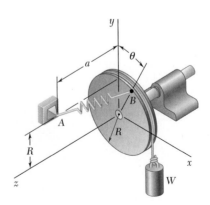

Fig. P4.C4

4.C5 A 200 × 250-mm panel of mass 20 kg is supported by hinges along edge *AB*. Cable *CDE* is attached to the panel at *C*, passes over a small pulley at *D*, and supports a cylinder of mass *m*. Neglecting the effect of friction, use computational software to calculate the mass of the cylinder corresponding to equilibrium for values of θ from 0 to 90° using 10° increments. Using appropriate smaller increments, determine the value of θ corresponding to $m = 10$ kg.

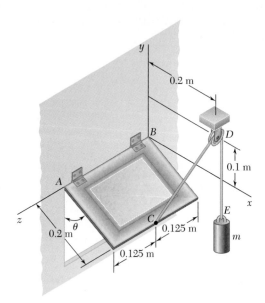

Fig. P4.C5

4.C6 The derrick shown supports a 2000-kg crate. It is held by a ball-and-socket joint at *A* and by two cables attached at *D* and *E*. Knowing that the derrick stands in a vertical plane forming an angle ϕ with the *xy* plane, use computational software to calculate the tension in each cable for values of ϕ from 0 to 60° using 5° increments. Using appropriate smaller increments, determine the value of ϕ for which the tension in cable *BE* is maximum.

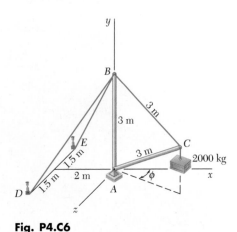

Fig. P4.C6

The Revelstoke Dam, located on the Columbia River in British Columbia, is subjected to three different kinds of distributed forces: the weights of its constituent elements, the pressure forces exerted by the water of its submerged face, and the pressure forces exerted by the ground on its base.

CHAPTER 5

Distributed Forces: Centroids and Centers of Gravity

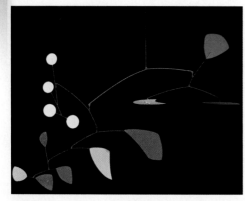

Photo 5.1 The precise balancing of the components of a mobile requires an understanding of centers of gravity and centroids, the main topics of this chapter.

5.1 INTRODUCTION

We have assumed so far that the attraction exerted by the earth on a rigid body could be represented by a single force **W**. This force, called the force of gravity or the weight of the body, was to be applied at the *center of gravity* of the body (Sec. 3.2). Actually, the earth exerts a force on each of the particles forming the body. The action of the earth on a rigid body should thus be represented by a large number of small forces distributed over the entire body. You will learn in this chapter, however, that all of these small forces can be replaced by a single equivalent force **W**. You will also learn how to determine the center of gravity, i.e., the point of application of the resultant **W**, for bodies of various shapes.

In the first part of the chapter, two-dimensional bodies, such as flat plates and wires contained in a given plane, are considered. Two concepts closely associated with the determination of the center of gravity of a plate or a wire are introduced: the concept of the *centroid* of an area or a line and the concept of the *first moment* of an area or a line with respect to a given axis.

You will also learn that the computation of the area of a surface of revolution or of the volume of a body of revolution is directly related to the determination of the centroid of the line or area used to generate that surface or body of revolution (Theorems of Pappus-Guldinus). And, as is shown in Secs. 5.8 and 5.9, the determination of the centroid of an area simplifies the analysis of beams subjected to distributed loads and the computation of the forces exerted on submerged rectangular surfaces, such as hydraulic gates and portions of dams.

In the last part of the chapter, you will learn how to determine the center of gravity of a three-dimensional body as well as the centroid of a volume and the first moments of that volume with respect to the coordinate planes.

AREAS AND LINES

5.2 CENTER OF GRAVITY OF A TWO-DIMENSIONAL BODY

Let us first consider a flat horizontal plate (Fig. 5.1). We can divide the plate into n small elements. The coordinates of the first element

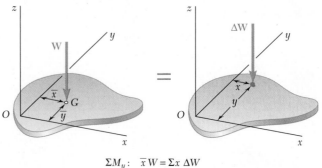

$$\Sigma M_y: \quad \bar{x} W = \Sigma x\, \Delta W$$
$$\Sigma M_x: \quad \bar{y} W = \Sigma y\, \Delta W$$

Fig. 5.1 Center of gravity of a plate.

are denoted by x_1 and y_1, those of the second element by x_2 and y_2, etc. The forces exerted by the earth on the elements of plate will be denoted, respectively, by $\Delta\mathbf{W}_1$, $\Delta\mathbf{W}_2$, ... , $\Delta\mathbf{W}_n$. These forces or weights are directed toward the center of the earth; however, for all practical purposes they can be assumed to be parallel. Their resultant is therefore a single force in the same direction. The magnitude W of this force is obtained by adding the magnitudes of the elemental weights.

$$\Sigma F_z: \qquad W = \Delta W_1 + \Delta W_2 + \cdots + \Delta W_n$$

To obtain the coordinates $\bar{x}$ and $\bar{y}$ of the point G where the resultant $\mathbf{W}$ should be applied, we write that the moments of $\mathbf{W}$ about the y and x axes are equal to the sum of the corresponding moments of the elemental weights,

$$\Sigma M_y: \qquad \bar{x}W = x_1\,\Delta W_1 + x_2\,\Delta W_2 + \cdots + x_n\,\Delta W_n$$
$$\Sigma M_x: \qquad \bar{y}W = y_1\,\Delta W_1 + y_2\,\Delta W_2 + \cdots + y_n\,\Delta W_n \qquad (5.1)$$

If we now increase the number of elements into which the plate is divided and simultaneously decrease the size of each element, we obtain in the limit the following expressions:

$$W = \int dW \qquad \bar{x}\,W = \int x\,dW \qquad \bar{y}\,W = \int y\,dW \qquad (5.2)$$

These equations define the weight $\mathbf{W}$ and the coordinates $\bar{x}$ and $\bar{y}$ of the center of gravity G of a flat plate. The same equations can be derived for a wire lying in the xy plane (Fig. 5.2). We note that the center of gravity G of a wire is usually not located on the wire.

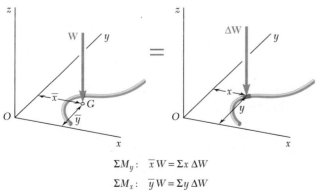

$$\Sigma M_y: \quad \bar{x}\,W = \Sigma x\,\Delta W$$
$$\Sigma M_x: \quad \bar{y}\,W = \Sigma y\,\Delta W$$

Fig. 5.2 Center of gravity of a wire.

5.3 CENTROIDS OF AREAS AND LINES

In the case of a flat homogeneous plate of uniform thickness, the magnitude ΔW of the weight of an element of the plate can be expressed as

$$\Delta W = \gamma t \, \Delta A$$

where γ = specific weight (weight per unit volume) of the material
t = thickness of the plate
ΔA = area of the element

Similarly, we can express the magnitude W of the weight of the entire plate as

$$W = \gamma t A$$

where A is the total area of the plate.

If U.S. customary units are used, the specific weight γ should be expressed in lb/ft^3, the thickness t in feet, and the areas ΔA and A in square feet. We observe that ΔW and W will then be expressed in pounds. If SI units are used, γ should be expressed in N/m^3, t in meters, and the areas ΔA and A in square meters; the weights ΔW and W will then be expressed in newtons.†

Substituting for ΔW and W in the moment equations (5.1) and dividing throughout by γt, we obtain

$$\Sigma M_y: \quad \bar{x}A = x_1 \, \Delta A_1 + x_2 \, \Delta A_2 + \cdots + x_n \, \Delta A_n$$
$$\Sigma M_x: \quad \bar{y}A = y_1 \, \Delta A_1 + y_2 \, \Delta A_2 + \cdots + y_n \, \Delta A_n$$

If we increase the number of elements into which the area A is divided and simultaneously decrease the size of each element, we obtain in the limit

$$\bar{x}A = \int x \, dA \qquad \bar{y}A = \int y \, dA \qquad (5.3)$$

These equations define the coordinates $\bar{x}$ and $\bar{y}$ of the center of gravity of a homogeneous plate. The point whose coordinates are $\bar{x}$ and $\bar{y}$ is also known as the *centroid C of the area A* of the plate (Fig. 5.3). If the plate is not homogeneous, these equations cannot be used to determine the center of gravity of the plate; they still define, however, the centroid of the area.

In the case of a homogeneous wire of uniform cross section, the magnitude ΔW of the weight of an element of wire can be expressed as

$$\Delta W = \gamma a \, \Delta L$$

where γ = specific weight of the material
a = cross-sectional area of the wire
ΔL = length of the element

---

†It should be noted that in the SI system of units a given material is generally characterized by its density ρ (mass per unit volume) rather than by its specific weight γ. The specific weight of the material can then be obtained from the relation

$$\gamma = \rho g$$

where g = 9.81 m/s^2. Since ρ is expressed in kg/m^3, we observe that γ will be expressed in (kg/m^3)(m/s^2), that is, in N/m^3.

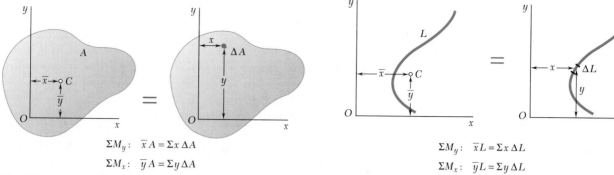

$$\Sigma M_y: \quad \bar{x}A = \Sigma x\,\Delta A$$
$$\Sigma M_x: \quad \bar{y}A = \Sigma y\,\Delta A$$

Fig. 5.3 Centroid of an area.

$$\Sigma M_y: \quad \bar{x}L = \Sigma x\,\Delta L$$
$$\Sigma M_x: \quad \bar{y}L = \Sigma y\,\Delta L$$

Fig. 5.4 Centroid of a line.

The center of gravity of the wire then coincides with the *centroid C of the line L* defining the shape of the wire (Fig. 5.4). The coordinates $\bar{x}$ and $\bar{y}$ of the centroid of the line L are obtained from the equations

$$\bar{x}L = \int x\,dL \qquad \bar{y}L = \int y\,dL \qquad (5.4)$$

5.4 FIRST MOMENTS OF AREAS AND LINES

The integral $\int x\,dA$ in Eqs. (5.3) of the preceding section is known as the *first moment of the area A with respect to the y axis* and is denoted by Q_y. Similarly, the integral $\int y\,dA$ defines the *first moment of A with respect to the x axis* and is denoted by Q_x. We write

$$Q_y = \int x\,dA \qquad Q_x = \int y\,dA \qquad (5.5)$$

Comparing Eqs. (5.3) with Eqs. (5.5), we note that the first moments of the area A can be expressed as the products of the area and the coordinates of its centroid:

$$Q_y = \bar{x}A \qquad Q_x = \bar{y}A \qquad (5.6)$$

It follows from Eqs. (5.6) that the coordinates of the centroid of an area can be obtained by dividing the first moments of that area by the area itself. The first moments of the area are also useful in mechanics of materials for determining the shearing stresses in beams under transverse loadings. Finally, we observe from Eqs. (5.6) that if the centroid of an area is located on a coordinate axis, the first moment of the area with respect to that axis is zero. Conversely, if the first moment of an area with respect to a coordinate axis is zero, then the centroid of the area is located on that axis.

Relations similar to Eqs. (5.5) and (5.6) can be used to define the first moments of a line with respect to the coordinate axes and

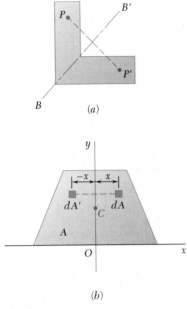

Fig. 5.5

to express these moments as the products of the length L of the line and the coordinates $\bar{x}$ and $\bar{y}$ of its centroid.

An area A is said to be *symmetric with respect to an axis BB'* if for every point P of the area there exists a point P' of the same area such that the line PP' is perpendicular to BB' and is divided into two equal parts by that axis (Fig. 5.5a). A line L is said to be symmetric with respect to an axis BB' if it satisfies similar conditions. When an area A or a line L possesses an axis of symmetry BB', its first moment with respect to BB' is zero, and its centroid is located on that axis. For example, in the case of the area A of Fig. 5.5b, which is symmetric with respect to the y axis, we observe that for every element of area dA of abscissa x there exists an element dA' of equal area and with abscissa $-x$. It follows that the integral in the first of Eqs. (5.5) is zero and, thus, that $Q_y = 0$. It also follows from the first of the relations (5.3) that $\bar{x} = 0$. Thus, if an area A or a line L possesses an axis of symmetry, its centroid C is located on that axis.

We further note that if an area or line possesses two axes of symmetry, its centroid C must be located at the intersection of the two axes (Fig. 5.6). This property enables us to determine immediately the centroid of areas such as circles, ellipses, squares, rectangles, equilateral triangles, or other symmetric figures as well as the centroid of lines in the shape of the circumference of a circle, the perimeter of a square, etc.

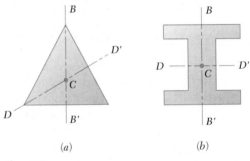

(a)   (b)

Fig. 5.6

An area A is said to be *symmetric with respect to a center O* if for every element of area dA of coordinates x and y there exists an element dA' of equal area with coordinates $-x$ and $-y$ (Fig. 5.7). It then follows that the integrals in Eqs. (5.5) are both zero and that $Q_x = Q_y = 0$. It also follows from Eqs. (5.3) that $\bar{x} = \bar{y} = 0$, that is, that the centroid of the area coincides with its center of symmetry O. Similarly, if a line possesses a center of symmetry O, the centroid of the line will coincide with the center O.

It should be noted that a figure possessing a center of symmetry does not necessarily possess an axis of symmetry (Fig. 5.7), while a figure possessing two axes of symmetry does not necessarily possess a center of symmetry (Fig. 5.6a). However, if a figure possesses two axes of symmetry at a right angle to each other, the point of intersection of these axes is a center of symmetry (Fig. 5.6b).

Determining the centroids of unsymmetrical areas and lines and of areas and lines possessing only one axis of symmetry will be discussed in Secs. 5.6 and 5.7. Centroids of common shapes of areas and lines are shown in Fig. 5.8A and B.

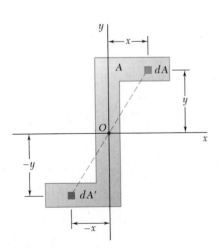

Fig. 5.7

Shape		$\bar{x}$	$\bar{y}$	Area
Triangular area	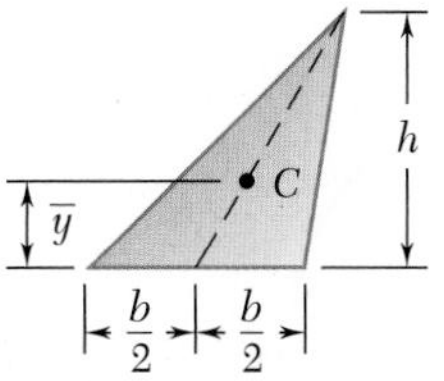		$\dfrac{h}{3}$	$\dfrac{bh}{2}$
Quarter-circular area	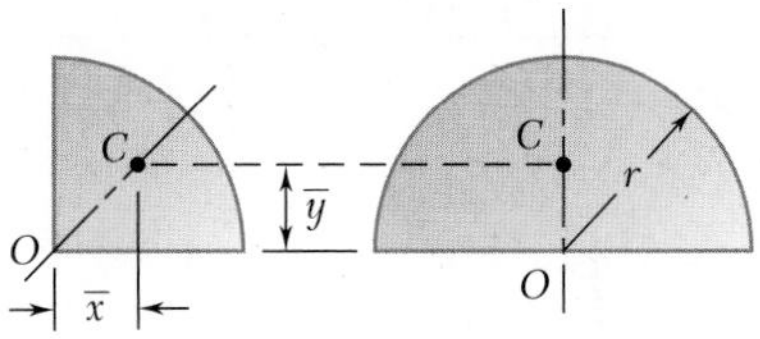	$\dfrac{4r}{3\pi}$	$\dfrac{4r}{3\pi}$	$\dfrac{\pi r^2}{4}$
Semicircular area		0	$\dfrac{4r}{3\pi}$	$\dfrac{\pi r^2}{2}$
Quarter-elliptical area	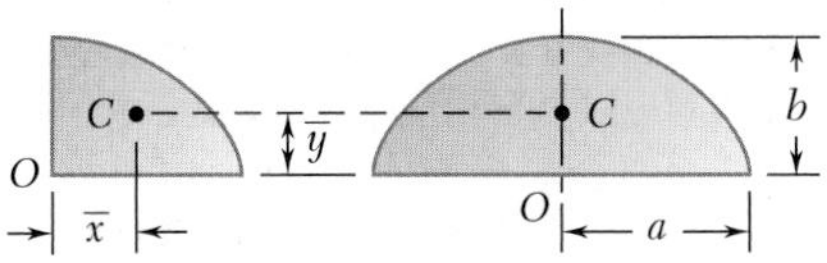	$\dfrac{4a}{3\pi}$	$\dfrac{4b}{3\pi}$	$\dfrac{\pi ab}{4}$
Semielliptical area		0	$\dfrac{4b}{3\pi}$	$\dfrac{\pi ab}{2}$
Semiparabolic area	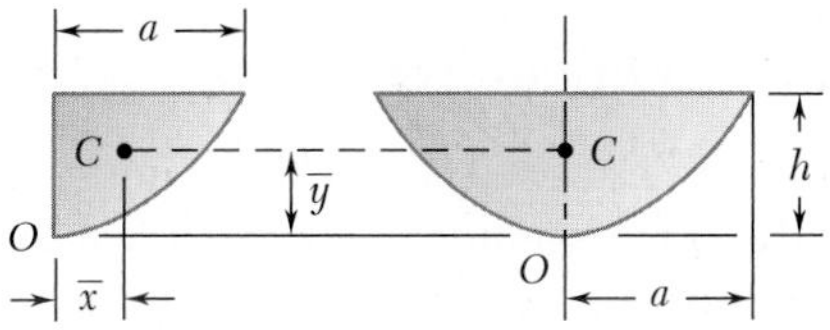	$\dfrac{3a}{8}$	$\dfrac{3h}{5}$	$\dfrac{2ah}{3}$
Parabolic area		0	$\dfrac{3h}{5}$	$\dfrac{4ah}{3}$
Parabolic spandrel	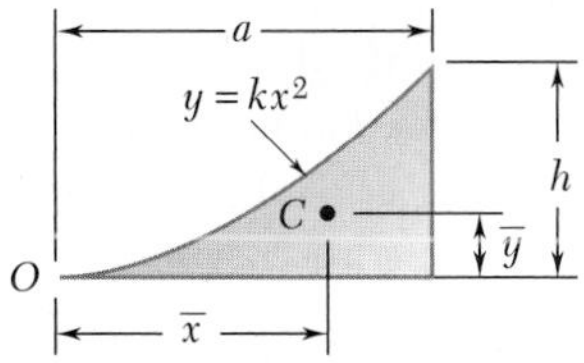	$\dfrac{3a}{4}$	$\dfrac{3h}{10}$	$\dfrac{ah}{3}$
General spandrel	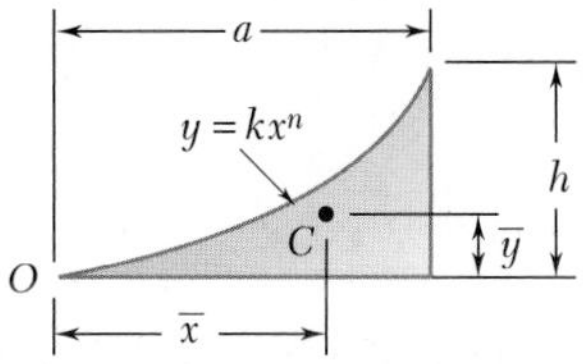	$\dfrac{n+1}{n+2}a$	$\dfrac{n+1}{4n+2}h$	$\dfrac{ah}{n+1}$
Circular sector	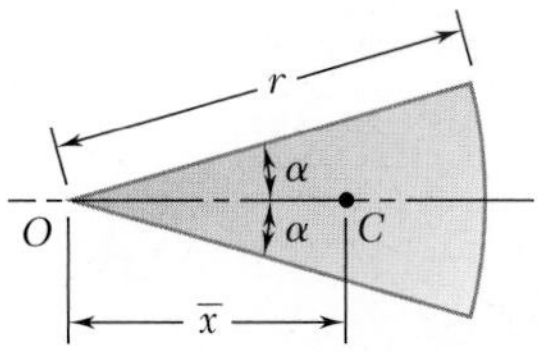	$\dfrac{2r\sin\alpha}{3\alpha}$	0	αr^2

Fig. 5.8A Centroids of common shapes of areas.

Shape		$\bar{x}$	$\bar{y}$	Length
Quarter-circular arc	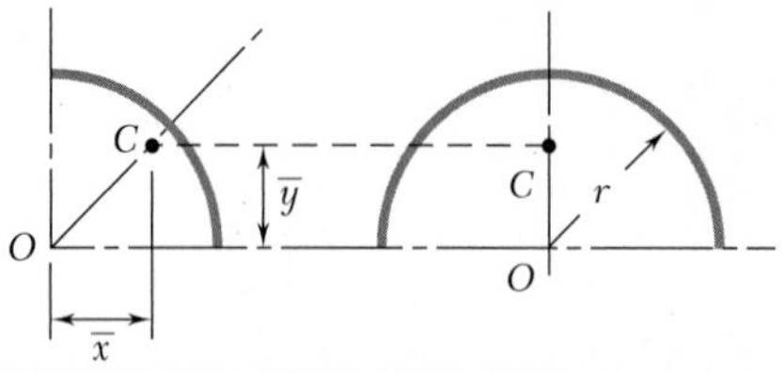	$\dfrac{2r}{\pi}$	$\dfrac{2r}{\pi}$	$\dfrac{\pi r}{2}$
Semicircular arc		0	$\dfrac{2r}{\pi}$	πr
Arc of circle	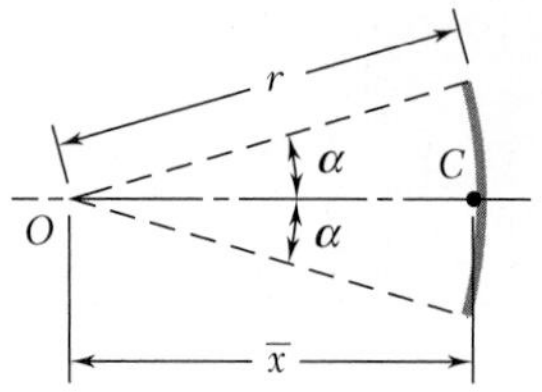	$\dfrac{r\sin\alpha}{\alpha}$	0	$2\alpha r$

Fig. 5.8B Centroids of common shapes of lines.

5.5 COMPOSITE PLATES AND WIRES

In many instances, a flat plate can be divided into rectangles, triangles, or the other common shapes shown in Fig. 5.8A. The abscissa $\overline{X}$ of its center of gravity G can be determined from the abscissas $\bar{x}_1, \bar{x}_2, \ldots, \bar{x}_n$ of the centers of gravity of the various parts by expressing that the moment of the weight of the whole plate about the y axis is equal to the sum of the moments of the weights of the various parts about the same axis (Fig. 5.9). The ordinate $\overline{Y}$ of the center of gravity of the plate is found in a similar way by equating moments about the x axis. We write

$$\Sigma M_y: \quad \overline{X}(W_1 + W_2 + \cdots + W_n) = \bar{x}_1 W_1 + \bar{x}_2 W_2 + \cdots + \bar{x}_n W_n$$
$$\Sigma M_x: \quad \overline{Y}(W_1 + W_2 + \cdots + W_n) = \bar{y}_1 W_1 + \bar{y}_2 W_2 + \cdots + \bar{y}_n W_n$$

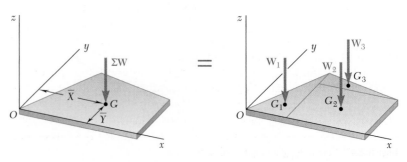

$$\Sigma M_y: \quad \overline{X}\,\Sigma W = \Sigma\,\bar{x}\,W$$
$$\Sigma M_x: \quad \overline{Y}\,\Sigma W = \Sigma\,\bar{y}\,W$$

Fig. 5.9 Center of gravity of a composite plate.

or, for short,

$$\overline{X}\Sigma W = \Sigma \overline{x}W \qquad \overline{Y}\Sigma W = \Sigma \overline{y}W \qquad (5.7)$$

These equations can be solved for the coordinates $\overline{X}$ and $\overline{Y}$ of the center of gravity of the plate.

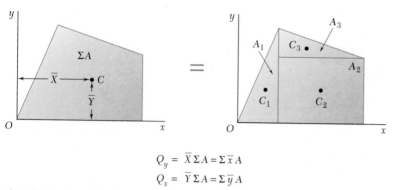

$$Q_y = \overline{X}\Sigma A = \Sigma \overline{x}A$$
$$Q_x = \overline{Y}\Sigma A = \Sigma \overline{y}A$$

Fig. 5.10 Centroid of a composite area.

If the plate is homogeneous and of uniform thickness, the center of gravity coincides with the centroid C of its area. The abscissa $\overline{X}$ of the centroid of the area can be determined by noting that the first moment Q_y of the composite area with respect to the y axis can be expressed both as the product of $\overline{X}$ and the total area and as the sum of the first moments of the elementary areas with respect to the y axis (Fig. 5.10). The ordinate $\overline{Y}$ of the centroid is found in a similar way by considering the first moment Q_x of the composite area. We have

$$Q_y = \overline{X}(A_1 + A_2 + \cdots + A_n) = \overline{x}_1 A_1 + \overline{x}_2 A_2 + \cdots + \overline{x}_n A_n$$
$$Q_x = \overline{Y}(A_1 + A_2 + \cdots + A_n) = \overline{y}_1 A_1 + \overline{y}_2 A_2 + \cdots + \overline{y}_n A_n$$

or, for short,

$$Q_y = \overline{X}\Sigma A = \Sigma \overline{x}A \qquad Q_x = \overline{Y}\Sigma A = \Sigma \overline{y}A \qquad (5.8)$$

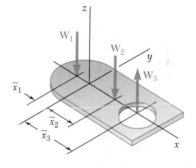

These equations yield the first moments of the composite area, or they can be used to obtain the coordinates $\overline{X}$ and $\overline{Y}$ of its centroid.

Care should be taken to assign the appropriate sign to the moment of each area. First moments of areas, like moments of forces, can be positive or negative. For example, an area whose centroid is located to the left of the y axis will have a negative first moment with respect to that axis. Also, the area of a hole should be assigned a negative sign (Fig. 5.11).

Similarly, it is possible in many cases to determine the center of gravity of a composite wire or the centroid of a composite line by dividing the wire or line into simpler elements (see Sample Prob. 5.2).

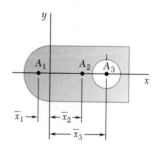

	$\overline{x}$	A	$\overline{x}A$
A_1 Semicircle	$-$	$+$	$-$
A_2 Full rectangle	$+$	$+$	$+$
A_3 Circular hole	$+$	$-$	$-$

Fig. 5.11

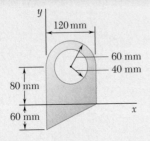

SAMPLE PROBLEM 5.1

For the plane area shown, determine (*a*) the first moments with respect to the *x* and *y* axes, (*b*) the location of the centroid.

SOLUTION

Components of Area. The area is obtained by adding a rectangle, a triangle, and a semicircle and by then subtracting a circle. Using the coordinate axes shown, the area and the coordinates of the centroid of each of the component areas are determined and entered in the table below. The area of the circle is indicated as negative, since it is to be subtracted from the other areas. We note that the coordinate $\bar{y}$ of the centroid of the triangle is negative for the axes shown. The first moments of the component areas with respect to the coordinate axes are computed and entered in the table.

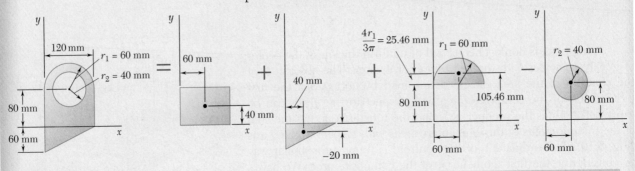

Component	A, mm^2	$\bar{x}$, mm	$\bar{y}$, mm	$\bar{x}A$, mm^3	$\bar{y}A$, mm^3
Rectangle	$(120)(80) = 9.6 \times 10^3$	60	40	$+576 \times 10^3$	$+384 \times 10^3$
Triangle	$\frac{1}{2}(120)(60) = 3.6 \times 10^3$	40	-20	$+144 \times 10^3$	-72×10^3
Semicircle	$\frac{1}{2}\pi(60)^2 = 5.655 \times 10^3$	60	105.46	$+339.3 \times 10^3$	$+596.4 \times 10^3$
Circle	$-\pi(40)^2 = -5.027 \times 10^3$	60	80	-301.6×10^3	-402.2×10^3
	$\Sigma A = 13.828 \times 10^3$			$\Sigma \bar{x}A = +757.7 \times 10^3$	$\Sigma \bar{y}A = +506.2 \times 10^3$

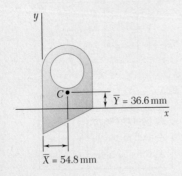

a. First Moments of the Area. Using Eqs. (5.8), we write

$$Q_x = \Sigma \bar{y}A = 506.2 \times 10^3 \text{ mm}^3 \qquad Q_x = 506 \times 10^3 \text{ mm}^3 \blacktriangleleft$$
$$Q_y = \Sigma \bar{x}A = 757.7 \times 10^3 \text{ mm}^3 \qquad Q_y = 758 \times 10^3 \text{ mm}^3 \blacktriangleleft$$

b. Location of Centroid. Substituting the values given in the table into the equations defining the centroid of a composite area, we obtain

$$\bar{X}\Sigma A = \Sigma \bar{x}A: \quad \bar{X}(13.828 \times 10^3 \text{ mm}^2) = 757.7 \times 10^3 \text{ mm}^3$$
$$\bar{X} = 54.8 \text{ mm} \blacktriangleleft$$

$$\bar{Y}\Sigma A = \Sigma \bar{y}A: \quad \bar{Y}(13.828 \times 10^3 \text{ mm}^2) = 506.2 \times 10^3 \text{ mm}^3$$
$$\bar{Y} = 36.6 \text{ mm} \blacktriangleleft$$

228

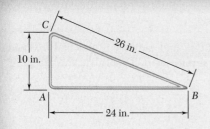

SAMPLE PROBLEM 5.2

The figure shown is made from a piece of thin, homogeneous wire. Determine the location of its center of gravity.

SOLUTION

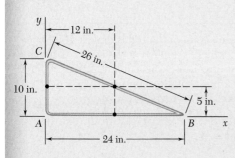

Since the figure is formed of homogeneous wire, its center of gravity coincides with the centroid of the corresponding line. Therefore, that centroid will be determined. Choosing the coordinate axes shown, with origin at A, we determine the coordinates of the centroid of each line segment and compute the first moments with respect to the coordinate axes.

Segment	L, in.	$\bar{x}$, in.	$\bar{y}$, in.	$\bar{x}L$, in^2	$\bar{y}L$, in^2
AB	24	12	0	288	0
BC	26	12	5	312	130
CA	10	0	5	0	50
	$\Sigma L = 60$			$\Sigma \bar{x}L = 600$	$\Sigma \bar{y}L = 180$

Substituting the values obtained from the table into the equations defining the centroid of a composite line, we obtain

$$\overline{X}\Sigma L = \Sigma \bar{x}L: \qquad \overline{X}(60 \text{ in.}) = 600 \text{ in}^2 \qquad \overline{X} = 10 \text{ in.} \blacktriangleleft$$
$$\overline{Y}\Sigma L = \Sigma \bar{y}L: \qquad \overline{Y}(60 \text{ in.}) = 180 \text{ in}^2 \qquad \overline{Y} = 3 \text{ in.} \blacktriangleleft$$

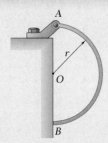

SAMPLE PROBLEM 5.3

A uniform semicircular rod of weight W and radius r is attached to a pin at A and rests against a frictionless surface at B. Determine the reactions at A and B.

SOLUTION

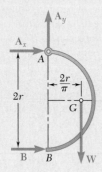

Free-Body Diagram. A free-body diagram of the rod is drawn. The forces acting on the rod are its weight $\mathbf{W}$, which is applied at the center of gravity G (whose position is obtained from Fig. 5.8B); a reaction at A, represented by its components $\mathbf{A}_x$ and $\mathbf{A}_y$; and a horizontal reaction at B.

Equilibrium Equations

$$+\!\uparrow \Sigma M_A = 0: \qquad B(2r) - W\!\left(\frac{2r}{\pi}\right) = 0$$

$$B = +\frac{W}{\pi} \qquad\qquad\qquad \mathbf{B} = \frac{W}{\pi} \rightarrow \quad \blacktriangleleft$$

$$\xrightarrow{+} \Sigma F_x = 0: \qquad A_x + B = 0$$

$$A_x = -B = -\frac{W}{\pi} \qquad \mathbf{A}_x = \frac{W}{\pi} \leftarrow$$

$$+\!\uparrow \Sigma F_y = 0: \qquad A_y - W = 0 \qquad \mathbf{A}_y = W \uparrow$$

Adding the two components of the reaction at A:

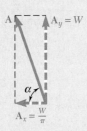

$$A = \left[W^2 + \left(\frac{W}{\pi}\right)^2\right]^{1/2} \qquad\qquad A = W\left(1 + \frac{1}{\pi^2}\right)^{1/2} \quad \blacktriangleleft$$

$$\tan \alpha = \frac{W}{W/\pi} = \pi \qquad\qquad\qquad \alpha = \tan^{-1}\pi \quad \blacktriangleleft$$

The answers can also be expressed as follows:

$$\mathbf{A} = 1.049W \,\measuredangle 72.3° \qquad \mathbf{B} = 0.318W \rightarrow \quad \blacktriangleleft$$

SOLVING PROBLEMS
ON YOUR OWN

In this lesson we developed the general equations for locating the centers of gravity of two-dimensional bodies and wires [Eqs. (5.2)] and the centroids of plane areas [Eqs. (5.3)] and lines [Eqs. (5.4)]. In the following problems, you will have to locate the centroids of composite areas and lines or determine the first moments of the area for composite plates [Eqs. (5.8)].

1. Locating the centroids of composite areas and lines. Sample Problems 5.1 and 5.2 illustrate the procedure you should follow when solving problems of this type. There are, however, several points that should be emphasized.

a. The first step in your solution should be to decide how to construct the given area or line from the common shapes of Fig. 5.8. You should recognize that for plane areas it is often possible to construct a particular shape in more than one way. Also, showing the different components (as is done in Sample Prob. 5.1) will help you to correctly establish their centroids and areas or lengths. Do not forget that you can subtract areas as well as add them to obtain a desired shape.

b. We strongly recommend that for each problem you construct a table containing the areas or lengths and the respective coordinates of the centroids. It is essential for you to remember that areas which are "removed" (for example, holes) are treated as negative. Also, the sign of negative coordinates must be included. Therefore, you should always carefully note the location of the origin of the coordinate axes.

c. When possible, use symmetry [Sec. 5.4] to help you determine the location of a centroid.

d. In the formulas for the circular sector and for the arc of a circle in Fig. 5.8, the angle α must always be expressed in radians.

2. Calculating the first moments of an area. The procedures for locating the centroid of an area and for determining the first moments of an area are similar; however, for the latter it is not necessary to compute the total area. Also, as noted in Sec. 5.4, you should recognize that the first moment of an area relative to a centroidal axis is zero.

3. Solving problems involving the center of gravity. The bodies considered in the following problems are homogeneous; thus, their centers of gravity and centroids coincide. In addition, when a body that is suspended from a single pin is in equilibrium, the pin and the body's center of gravity must lie on the same vertical line.

It may appear that many of the problems in this lesson have little to do with the study of mechanics. However, being able to locate the centroid of composite shapes will be essential in several topics that you will soon encounter.

PROBLEMS

5.1 through 5.9 Locate the centroid of the plane area shown.

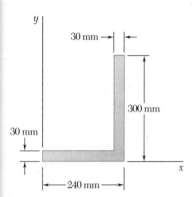

Fig. P5.1

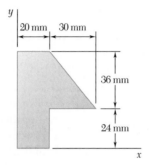

Fig. P5.2

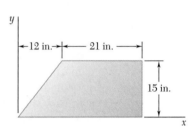

Fig. P5.3

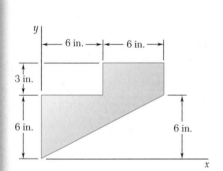

Fig. P5.4

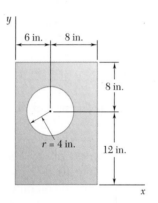

Fig. P5.5

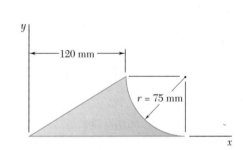

Fig. P5.6

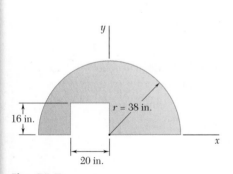

Fig. *P5.7*

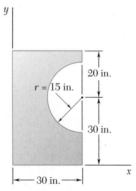

Fig. *P5.8*

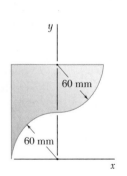

Fig. P5.9

5.10 through 5.15 Locate the centroid of the plane area shown.

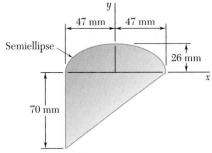

Fig. P5.10

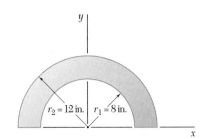

Fig. P5.11

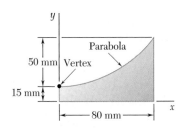

Fig. P5.12

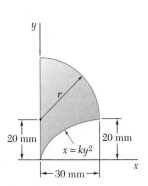

Fig. *P5.13*

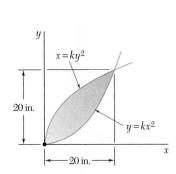

Fig. P5.14

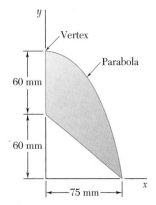

Fig. *P5.15*

5.16 Determine the y coordinate of the centroid of the shaded area in terms of r_1, r_2, and α.

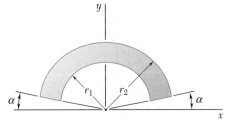

Fig. P5.16 and P5.17

5.17 Show that as r_1 approaches r_2, the location of the centroid approaches that for an arc of circle of radius $(r_1 + r_2)/2$.

5.18 For the area shown, determine the ratio a/b for which $\bar{x} = \bar{y}$.

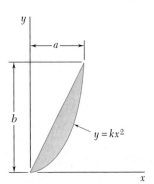

Fig. P5.18

5.19 For the semiannular area of Prob. 5.11, determine the ratio r_2/r_1 so that $\bar{y} = 3r_1/4$.

5.20 A composite beam is constructed by bolting four plates to four $60 \times 60 \times 12$-mm angles as shown. The bolts are equally spaced along the beam, and the beam supports a vertical load. As proved in mechanics of materials, the shearing forces exerted on the bolts at A and B are proportional to the first moments with respect to the centroidal x axis of the red shaded areas shown, respectively, in parts a and b of the figure. Knowing that the force exerted on the bolt at A is 280 N, determine the force exerted on the bolt at B.

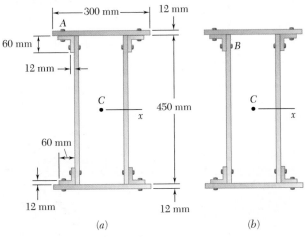

Fig. P5.20

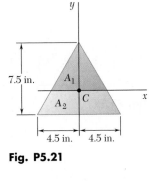

Fig. P5.21

5.21 and 5.22 The horizontal x axis is drawn through the centroid C of the area shown, and it divides the area into two component areas A_1 and A_2. Determine the first moment of each component area with respect to the x axis, and explain the results obtained.

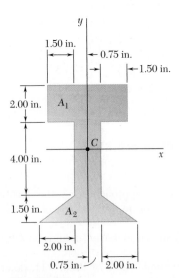

Fig. P5.22

5.23 The first moment of the shaded area with respect to the x axis is denoted by Q_x. (*a*) Express Q_x in terms of b, c, and the distance y from the base of the shaded area to the x axis. (*b*) For what value of y is Q_x maximum, and what is that maximum value?

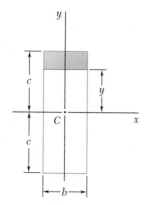

Fig. P5.23

5.24 through 5.27 A thin, homogeneous wire is bent to form the perimeter of the figure indicated. Locate the center of gravity of the wire figure thus formed.

    5.24   Fig. P5.1.
    5.25   Fig. P5.2.
    5.26   Fig. P5.3.
    5.27   Fig. P5.7.

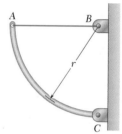

5.28 A uniform circular rod of weight 8 lb and radius 10 in. is attached to a pin at C and to the cable AB. Determine (*a*) the tension in the cable, (*b*) the reaction at C.

Fig. P5.28

5.29 Member $ABCDE$ is a component of a mobile and is formed from a single piece of aluminum tubing. Knowing that the member is supported at C and that $l = 2$ m, determine the distance d so that portion BCD of the member is horizontal.

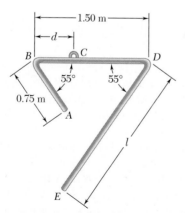

Fig. P5.29 and P5.30

5.30 Member $ABCDE$ is a component of a mobile and is formed from a single piece of aluminum tubing. Knowing that the member is supported at C and that d is 0.50 m, determine the length l of arm DE so that this portion of the member is horizontal.

5.31 The homogeneous wire ABC is bent into a semicircular arc and a
straight section as shown and is attached to a hinge at A. Determine the value of θ for which the wire is in equilibrium for the
indicated position.

5.32 Determine the distance h for which the centroid of the shaded
area is as far above line BB' as possible when (a) $k = 0.10$,
(b) $k = 0.80$.

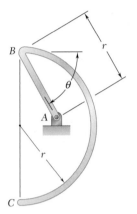

Fig. P5.31

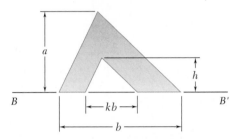

Fig. P5.32 and P5.33

5.33 Knowing that the distance h has been selected to maximize the
distance $\bar{y}$ from line BB' to the centroid of the shaded area, show
that $\bar{y} = 2h/3$.

5.6 DETERMINATION OF CENTROIDS BY INTEGRATION

The centroid of an area bounded by analytical curves (i.e., curves
defined by algebraic equations) is usually determined by evaluating
the integrals in Eqs. (5.3) of Sec. 5.3:

$$\bar{x}A = \int x \, dA \qquad \bar{y}A = \int y \, dA \qquad (5.3)$$

If the element of area dA is a small rectangle of sides dx and dy,
the evaluation of each of these integrals requires a *double integration* with respect to x and y. A double integration is also necessary
if polar coordinates are used for which dA is a small element of
sides dr and $r \, d\theta$.

In most cases, however, it is possible to determine the coordinates of the centroid of an area by performing a single integration.
This is achieved by choosing dA to be a thin rectangle or strip or a
thin sector or pie-shaped element (Fig. 5.12); the centroid of the
thin rectangle is located at its center, and the centroid of the thin
sector is located at a distance $\frac{2}{3}r$ from its vertex (as it is for a
triangle). The coordinates of the centroid of the area under consideration are
then obtained by expressing that the first moment of the entire area
with respect to each of the coordinate axes is equal to the sum (or
integral) of the corresponding moments of the elements of area.

Denoting by $\bar{x}_{el}$ and $\bar{y}_{el}$ the coordinates of the centroid of the element dA, we write

$$Q_y = \bar{x}A = \int \bar{x}_{el}\, dA$$

$$Q_x = \bar{y}A = \int \bar{y}_{el}\, dA$$

(5.9)

If the area A is not already known, it can also be computed from these elements.

The coordinates $\bar{x}_{el}$ and $\bar{y}_{el}$ of the centroid of the element of area dA should be expressed in terms of the coordinates of a point located on the curve bounding the area under consideration. Also, the area of the element dA should be expressed in terms of the coordinates of that point and the appropriate differentials. This has been done in Fig. 5.12 for three common types of elements; the pie-shaped element of part c should be used when the equation of the curve bounding the area is given in polar coordinates. The appropriate expressions should be substituted into formulas (5.9), and the equation of the bounding curve should be used to express one of the coordinates in terms of the other. The integration is thus reduced to a single integration. Once the area has been determined and the integrals in Eqs. (5.9) have been evaluated, these equations can be solved for the coordinates $\bar{x}$ and $\bar{y}$ of the centroid of the area.

When a line is defined by an algebraic equation, its centroid can be determined by evaluating the integrals in Eqs. (5.4) of Sec. 5.3:

$$\bar{x}L = \int x\, dL \qquad \bar{y}L = \int y\, dL \qquad (5.4)$$

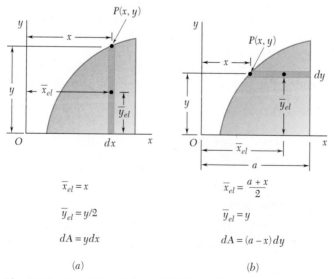

$\bar{x}_{el} = x$

$\bar{y}_{el} = y/2$

$dA = y\,dx$

(a)

$\bar{x}_{el} = \dfrac{a + x}{2}$

$\bar{y}_{el} = y$

$dA = (a - x)\,dy$

(b)

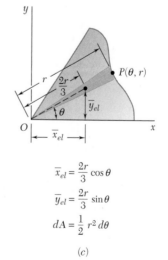

$\bar{x}_{el} = \dfrac{2r}{3}\cos\theta$

$\bar{y}_{el} = \dfrac{2r}{3}\sin\theta$

$dA = \dfrac{1}{2}r^2\,d\theta$

(c)

Fig. 5.12 Centroids and areas of differential elements.

The differential length dL should be replaced by one of the following expressions, depending upon which coordinate, x, y, or θ, is chosen as the independent variable in the equation used to define the line (these expressions can be derived using the Pythagorean theorem):

$$dL = \sqrt{1 + \left(\frac{dy}{dx}\right)^2}\, dx \qquad dL = \sqrt{1 + \left(\frac{dx}{dy}\right)^2}\, dy$$

$$dL = \sqrt{r^2 + \left(\frac{dr}{d\theta}\right)^2}\, d\theta$$

After the equation of the line has been used to express one of the coordinates in terms of the other, the integration can be performed, and Eqs. (5.4) can be solved for the coordinates $\bar{x}$ and $\bar{y}$ of the centroid of the line.

5.7 THEOREMS OF PAPPUS-GULDINUS

These theorems, which were first formulated by the Greek geometer Pappus during the third century A.D. and later restated by the Swiss mathematician Guldinus, or Guldin, (1577–1643) deal with surfaces and bodies of revolution.

A *surface of revolution* is a surface which can be generated by rotating a plane curve about a fixed axis. For example (Fig. 5.13), the

Photo 5.2 The storage tanks shown are all bodies of revolution. Thus, their surface areas and volumes can be determined using the theorems of Pappus-Guldinus.

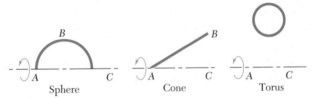

Fig. 5.13

surface of a sphere can be obtained by rotating a semicircular arc ABC about the diameter AC, the surface of a cone can be produced by rotating a straight line AB about an axis AC, and the surface of a torus or ring can be generated by rotating the circumference of a circle about a nonintersecting axis. A *body of revolution* is a body which can be generated by rotating a plane area about a fixed axis. As shown in Fig. 5.14, a sphere, a cone, and a torus can each be generated by rotating the appropriate shape about the indicated axis.

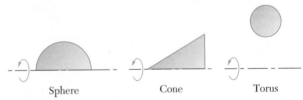

Fig. 5.14

THEOREM I. *The area of a surface of revolution is equal to the length of the generating curve times the distance traveled by the centroid of the curve while the surface is being generated.*

Proof. Consider an element dL of the line L (Fig. 5.15), which is revolved about the x axis. The area dA generated by the element

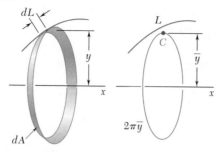

Fig. 5.15

dL is equal to $2\pi y\, dL$. Thus, the entire area generated by L is $A = \int 2\pi y\, dL$. Recalling that we found in Sec. 5.3 that the integral $\int y\, dL$ is equal to $\bar{y}L$, we therefore have

$$A = 2\pi\bar{y}L \tag{5.10}$$

where $2\pi\bar{y}$ is the distance traveled by the centroid of L (Fig. 5.15). It should be noted that the generating curve must not cross the axis about which it is rotated; if it did, the two sections on either side of the axis would generate areas having opposite signs, and the theorem would not apply.

THEOREM II. *The volume of a body of revolution is equal to the generating area times the distance traveled by the centroid of the area while the body is being generated.*

Proof. Consider an element dA of the area A which is revolved about the x axis (Fig. 5.16). The volume dV generated by the element dA is equal to $2\pi y\, dA$. Thus, the entire volume generated by A is $V = \int 2\pi y\, dA$, and since the integral $\int y\, dA$ is equal to $\bar{y}A$ (Sec. 5.3), we have

$$V = 2\pi\bar{y}A \tag{5.11}$$

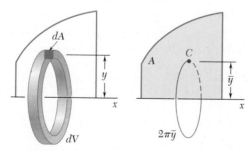

Fig. 5.16

where $2\pi\bar{y}$ is the distance traveled by the centroid of A. Again, it should be noted that the theorem does not apply if the axis of rotation intersects the generating area.

The theorems of Pappus-Guldinus offer a simple way to compute the areas of surfaces of revolution and the volumes of bodies of revolution. Conversely, they can also be used to determine the centroid of a plane curve when the area of the surface generated by the curve is known or to determine the centroid of a plane area when the volume of the body generated by the area is known (see Sample Prob. 5.8).

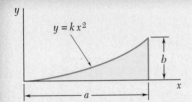

SAMPLE PROBLEM 5.4

Determine by direct integration the location of the centroid of a parabolic spandrel.

SOLUTION

Determination of the Constant k. The value of k is determined by substituting $x = a$ and $y = b$ into the given equation. We have $b = ka^2$ or $k = b/a^2$. The equation of the curve is thus

$$y = \frac{b}{a^2} x^2 \qquad \text{or} \qquad x = \frac{a}{b^{1/2}} y^{1/2}$$

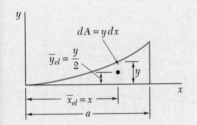

Vertical Differential Element. We choose the differential element shown and find the total area of the figure.

$$A = \int dA = \int y \, dx = \int_0^a \frac{b}{a^2} x^2 \, dx = \left[\frac{b}{a^2} \frac{x^3}{3} \right]_0^a = \frac{ab}{3}$$

The first moment of the differential element with respect to the y axis is $\bar{x}_{el} \, dA$; hence, the first moment of the entire area with respect to this axis is

$$Q_y = \int \bar{x}_{el} \, dA = \int xy \, dx = \int_0^a x \left(\frac{b}{a^2} x^2 \right) dx = \left[\frac{b}{a^2} \frac{x^4}{4} \right]_0^a = \frac{a^2 b}{4}$$

Since $Q_y = \bar{x}A$, we have

$$\bar{x}A = \int \bar{x}_{el} \, dA \qquad \bar{x}\frac{ab}{3} = \frac{a^2 b}{4} \qquad \bar{x} = \tfrac{3}{4}a \quad \blacktriangleleft$$

Likewise, the first moment of the differential element with respect to the x axis is $\bar{y}_{el} \, dA$, and the first moment of the entire area is

$$Q_x = \int \bar{y}_{el} \, dA = \int \frac{y}{2} y \, dx = \int_0^a \frac{1}{2} \left(\frac{b}{a^2} x^2 \right)^2 dx = \left[\frac{b^2}{2a^4} \frac{x^5}{5} \right]_0^a = \frac{ab^2}{10}$$

Since $Q_x = \bar{y}A$, we have

$$\bar{y}A = \int \bar{y}_{el} \, dA \qquad \bar{y}\frac{ab}{3} = \frac{ab^2}{10} \qquad \bar{y} = \tfrac{3}{10}b \quad \blacktriangleleft$$

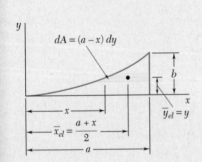

Horizontal Differential Element. The same results can be obtained by considering a horizontal element. The first moments of the area are

$$Q_y = \int \bar{x}_{el} \, dA = \int \frac{a + x}{2}(a - x) \, dy = \int_0^b \frac{a^2 - x^2}{2} dy$$

$$= \frac{1}{2} \int_0^b \left(a^2 - \frac{a^2}{b} y \right) dy = \frac{a^2 b}{4}$$

$$Q_x = \int \bar{y}_{el} \, dA = \int y(a - x) \, dy = \int y \left(a - \frac{a}{b^{1/2}} y^{1/2} \right) dy$$

$$= \int_0^b \left(ay - \frac{a}{b^{1/2}} y^{3/2} \right) dy = \frac{ab^2}{10}$$

To determine $\bar{x}$ and $\bar{y}$, the expressions obtained are again substituted into the equations defining the centroid of the area.

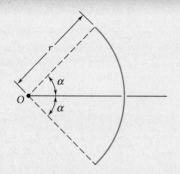

SAMPLE PROBLEM 5.5

Determine the location of the centroid of the arc of circle shown.

SOLUTION

Since the arc is symmetrical with respect to the x axis, $\bar{y} = 0$. A differential element is chosen as shown, and the length of the arc is determined by integration.

$$L = \int dL = \int_{-\alpha}^{\alpha} r\, d\theta = r \int_{-\alpha}^{\alpha} d\theta = 2r\alpha$$

The first moment of the arc with respect to the y axis is

$$Q_y = \int x\, dL = \int_{-\alpha}^{\alpha} (r\cos\theta)(r\, d\theta) = r^2 \int_{-\alpha}^{\alpha} \cos\theta\, d\theta$$
$$= r^2 [\sin\theta]_{-\alpha}^{\alpha} = 2r^2 \sin\alpha$$

Since $Q_y = \bar{x}L$, we write

$$\bar{x}(2r\alpha) = 2r^2 \sin\alpha \qquad \bar{x} = \frac{r\sin\alpha}{\alpha} \quad \blacktriangleleft$$

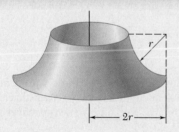

SAMPLE PROBLEM 5.6

Determine the area of the surface of revolution shown, which is obtained by rotating a quarter-circular arc about a vertical axis.

SOLUTION

According to Theorem I of Pappus-Guldinus, the area generated is equal to the product of the length of the arc and the distance traveled by its centroid. Referring to Fig. 5.8B, we have

$$\bar{x} = 2r - \frac{2r}{\pi} = 2r\left(1 - \frac{1}{\pi}\right)$$
$$A = 2\pi\bar{x}L = 2\pi\left[2r\left(1 - \frac{1}{\pi}\right)\right]\left(\frac{\pi r}{2}\right)$$
$$A = 2\pi r^2(\pi - 1) \quad \blacktriangleleft$$

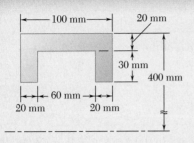

SAMPLE PROBLEM 5.7

The outside diameter of a pulley is 0.8 m, and the cross section of its rim is as shown. Knowing that the pulley is made of steel and that the density of steel is $\rho = 7.85 \times 10^3$ kg/m^3, determine the mass and the weight of the rim.

SOLUTION

The volume of the rim can be found by applying Theorem II of Pappus-Guldinus, which states that the volume equals the product of the given cross-sectional area and the distance traveled by its centroid in one complete revolution. However, the volume can be more easily determined if we observe that the cross section can be formed from rectangle I, whose area is positive, and rectangle II, whose area is negative.

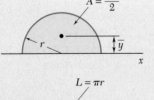

	Area, mm^2	$\bar{y}$, mm	Distance Traveled by C, mm	Volume, mm^3
I	+5000	375	$2\pi(375) = 2356$	$(5000)(2356) = 11.78 \times 10^6$
II	−1800	365	$2\pi(365) = 2293$	$(-1800)(2293) = -4.13 \times 10^6$
				Volume of rim $= 7.65 \times 10^6$

Since 1 mm $= 10^{-3}$ m, we have 1 mm$^3 = (10^{-3} \text{ m})^3 = 10^{-9}$ m^3, and we obtain $V = 7.65 \times 10^6$ mm$^3 = (7.65 \times 10^6)(10^{-9} \text{ m}^3) = 7.65 \times 10^{-3}$ m^3.

$$m = \rho V = (7.85 \times 10^3 \text{ kg/m}^3)(7.65 \times 10^{-3} \text{ m}^3) \qquad m = 60.0 \text{ kg} \blacktriangleleft$$
$$W = mg = (60.0 \text{ kg})(9.81 \text{ m/s}^2) = 589 \text{ kg} \cdot \text{m/s}^2 \qquad W = 589 \text{ N} \blacktriangleleft$$

SAMPLE PROBLEM 5.8

Using the theorems of Pappus-Guldinus, determine (a) the centroid of a semicircular area, (b) the centroid of a semicircular arc. We recall that the volume and the surface area of a sphere are $\frac{4}{3}\pi r^3$ and $4\pi r^2$, respectively.

SOLUTION

The volume of a sphere is equal to the product of the area of a semicircle and the distance traveled by the centroid of the semicircle in one revolution about the x axis.

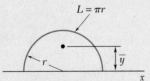

$$V = 2\pi\bar{y}A \qquad \tfrac{4}{3}\pi r^3 = 2\pi\bar{y}(\tfrac{1}{2}\pi r^2) \qquad \bar{y} = \frac{4r}{3\pi} \blacktriangleleft$$

Likewise, the area of a sphere is equal to the product of the length of the generating semicircle and the distance traveled by its centroid in one revolution.

$$A = 2\pi\bar{y}L \qquad 4\pi r^2 = 2\pi\bar{y}(\pi r) \qquad \bar{y} = \frac{2r}{\pi} \blacktriangleleft$$

SOLVING PROBLEMS ON YOUR OWN

In the problems for this lesson, you will use the equations

$$\bar{x}A = \int x \, dA \qquad \bar{y}A = \int y \, dA \qquad (5.3)$$

$$\bar{x}L = \int x \, dL \qquad \bar{y}L = \int y \, dL \qquad (5.4)$$

to locate the centroids of plane areas and lines, respectively. You will also apply the theorems of Pappus-Guldinus (Sec. 5.7) to determine the areas of surfaces of revolution and the volumes of bodies of revolution.

1. Determining by direct integration the centroids of areas and lines. When solving problems of this type, you should follow the method of solution shown in Sample Probs. 5.4 and 5.5: compute A or L, determine the first moments of the area or the line, and solve Eqs. (5.3) or (5.4) for the coordinates of the centroid. In addition, you should pay particular attention to the following points.

a. Begin your solution by carefully defining or determining each term in the applicable integral formulas. We strongly encourage you to show on your sketch of the given area or line your choice for dA or dL and the distances to its centroid.

b. As explained in Sec. 5.6, the x and the y in the above equations represent the *coordinates of the centroid* of the differential elements dA and dL. It is important to recognize that the coordinates of the centroid of dA are not equal to the coordinates of a point located on the curve bounding the area under consideration. You should carefully study Fig. 5.12 until you fully understand this important point.

c. To possibly simplify or minimize your computations, always examine the shape of the given area or line before defining the differential element that you will use. For example, sometimes it may be preferable to use horizontal rectangular elements instead of vertical ones. Also, it will usually be advantageous to use polar coordinates when a line or an area has circular symmetry.

d. Although most of the integrations in this lesson are straightforward, at times it may be necessary to use more advanced techniques, such as trigonometric substitution or integration by parts. Of course, using a table of integrals is the fastest method to evaluate difficult integrals.

2. Applying the theorems of Pappus-Guldinus. As shown in Sample Probs. 5.6 through 5.8, these simple, yet very useful theorems allow you to apply your knowledge of centroids to the computation of areas and volumes. Although the theorems refer to the distance traveled by the centroid and to the length of the generating curve or to the generating area, the resulting equations [Eqs. (5.10) and (5.11)] contain the products of these quantities, which are simply the first moments of a line ($\bar{y}L$) and an area ($\bar{y}A$), respectively. Thus, for those problems for which the generating line or area consists of more than one common shape, you need only determine $\bar{y}L$ or $\bar{y}A$; you do not have to calculate the length of the generating curve or the generating area.

PROBLEMS

5.34 through 5.36 Determine by direct integration the centroid of the area shown. Express your answer in terms of a and h.

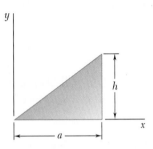

Fig. P5.34

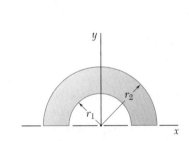

Fig. P5.35

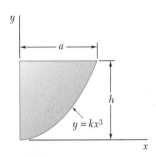

Fig. P5.36

5.37 through 5.39 Determine by direct integration the centroid of the area shown.

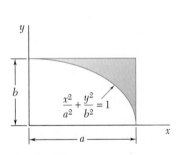

Fig. P5.37

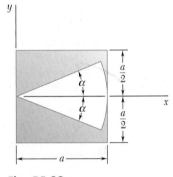

Fig. P5.38

Fig. P5.39

5.40 and 5.41 Determine by direct integration the centroid of the area shown. Express your answer in terms of a and b.

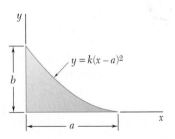

Fig. P5.40

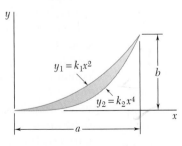

Fig. P5.41

5.42 Determine by direct integration the centroid of the area shown.

5.43 and 5.44 Determine by direct integration the centroid of the area shown. Express your answer in terms of a and b.

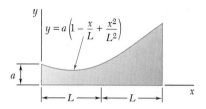

Fig. P5.42

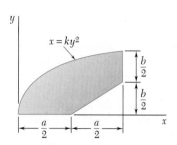

Fig. P5.43

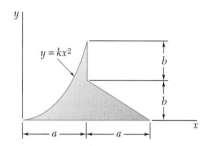

Fig. P5.44

5.45 and 5.46 A homogeneous wire is bent into the shape shown. Determine by direct integration the x coordinate of its centroid.

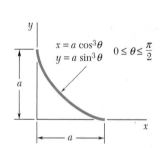

Fig. P5.45

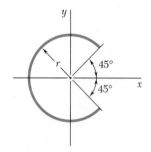

Fig. P5.46

***5.47** A homogeneous wire is bent into the shape shown. Determine by direct integration the x coordinate of its centroid. Express your answer in terms of a.

***5.48 and *5.49** Determine by direct integration the centroid of the area shown.

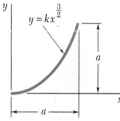

Fig. P5.47

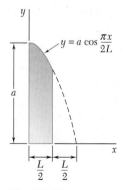

Fig. P5.48

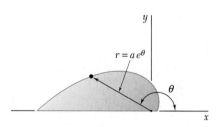

Fig. P5.49

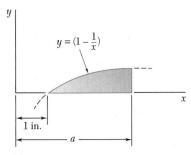

$y = (1 - \frac{1}{x})$

1 in.

a

Fig. P5.50 and P5.51

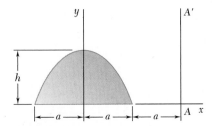

Fig. P5.55

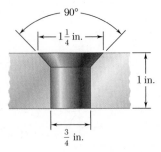

90°

$1\frac{1}{4}$ in.

1 in.

$\frac{3}{4}$ in.

Fig. P5.58

5.50 Determine the centroid of the area shown when $a = 2$ in.

5.51 Determine the value of a for which the ratio $\bar{x}/\bar{y}$ is 9.

5.52 Determine the volume and the surface area of the solid obtained by rotating the area of Prob. 5.1 about (*a*) the line $x = 240$ mm, (*b*) the *y* axis.

5.53 Determine the volume and the surface area of the solid obtained by rotating the area of Prob. 5.2 about (*a*) the line $y = 60$ mm, (*b*) the *y* axis.

5.54 Determine the volume and the surface area of the solid obtained by rotating the area of Prob. 5.8 about (*a*) the *x* axis, (*b*) the *y* axis.

5.55 Determine the volume of the solid generated by rotating the parabolic area shown about (*a*) the *x* axis, (*b*) the axis AA'.

5.56 Determine the volume and the surface area of the chain link shown, which is made from a 6-mm-diameter bar, if $R = 10$ mm and $L = 30$ mm.

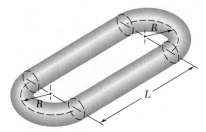

Fig. P5.56

5.57 Verify that the expressions for the volumes of the first four shapes in Fig. 5.21 on page 260 are correct.

5.58 A $\frac{3}{4}$-in.-diameter hole is drilled in a piece of 1-in.-thick steel; the hole is then countersunk as shown. Determine the volume of steel removed during the countersinking process.

5.59 Determine the capacity, in liters, of the punch bowl shown if $R = 250$ mm.

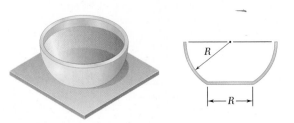

R

R

Fig. P5.59

5.60 Three different drive belt profiles are to be studied. If at any given time each belt makes contact with one-half of the circumference of its pulley, determine the *contact area* between the belt and the pulley for each design.

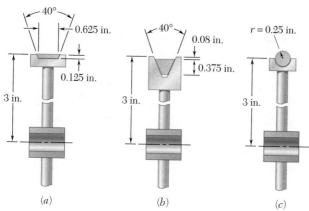

(a)   (b)   (c)

Fig. P5.60

5.61 The aluminum shade for the small high-intensity lamp shown has a uniform thickness of 1 mm. Knowing that the density of aluminum is 2800 kg/m^3, determine the mass of the shade.

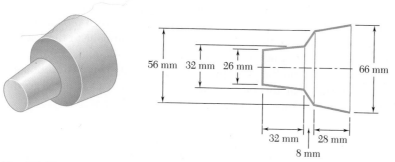

Fig. P5.61

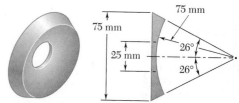

Fig. P5.62

5.62 The escutcheon (a decorative plate placed on a pipe where the pipe exits from a wall) shown is cast from brass. Knowing that the density of brass is 8470 kg/m^3, determine the mass of the escutcheon.

5.63 A manufacturer is planning to produce 20,000 wooden pegs having the shape shown. Determine how many gallons of paint should be ordered, knowing that each peg will be given two coats of paint and that one gallon of paint covers 100 ft^2.

5.64 The wooden peg shown is turned from a dowel 1 in. in diameter and 4 in. long. Determine the percentage of the initial volume of the dowel that becomes waste.

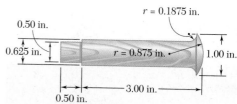

Fig. P5.63 and P5.64

*5.65 The shade for a wall-mounted light is formed from a thin sheet of translucent plastic. Determine the surface area of the outside of the shade, knowing that it has the parabolic cross section shown.

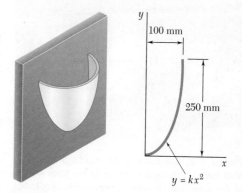

Fig. P5.65

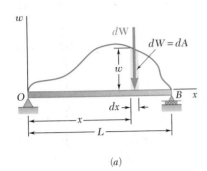

(a)

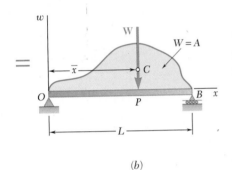

(b)

Fig. 5.17

Photo 5.3 The roofs of the buildings shown
must be able to support not only the total weight
of the snow but also the nonsymmetric distributed
loads resulting from drifting of the snow.

*5.8 DISTRIBUTED LOADS ON BEAMS

The concept of the centroid of an area can be used to solve other
problems besides those dealing with the weights of flat plates. Consider, for example, a beam supporting a *distributed load*; this load may
consist of the weight of materials supported directly or indirectly by
the beam, or it may be caused by wind or hydrostatic pressure. The
distributed load can be represented by plotting the load w supported
per unit length (Fig. 5.17); this load is expressed in N/m or in lb/ft.
The magnitude of the force exerted on an element of beam of length
dx is $dW = w\ dx$, and the total load supported by the beam is

$$W = \int_0^L w\ dx$$

We observe that the product $w\ dx$ is equal in magnitude to the element of area dA shown in Fig. 5.17a. The load W is thus equal in
magnitude to the total area A under the load curve:

$$W = \int dA = A$$

We now determine where a *single concentrated load* $\mathbf{W}$, of the
same magnitude W as the total distributed load, should be applied
on the beam if it is to produce the same reactions at the supports
(Fig. 5.17b). However, this concentrated load $\mathbf{W}$, which represents the
resultant of the given distributed loading, is equivalent to the loading
only when considering the free-body diagram of the entire beam. The
point of application P of the equivalent concentrated load $\mathbf{W}$ is obtained
by expressing that the moment of $\mathbf{W}$ about point O is equal to the
sum of the moments of the elemental loads $d\mathbf{W}$ about O:

$$(OP)W = \int x\ dW$$

or, since $dW = w\ dx = dA$ and $W = A$,

$$(OP)A = \int_0^L x\ dA \qquad (5.12)$$

Since the integral represents the first moment with respect to the w
axis of the area under the load curve, it can be replaced by the
product $\bar{x}A$. We therefore have $OP = \bar{x}$, where $\bar{x}$ is the distance
from the w axis to the centroid C of the area A (this is *not* the centroid of the beam).

A *distributed load on a beam can thus be replaced by a concentrated load; the magnitude of this single load is equal to the area
under the load curve, and its line of action passes through the centroid of that area.* It should be noted, however, that the concentrated
load is equivalent to the given loading only as far as external forces
are concerned. It can be used to determine reactions but should not
be used to compute internal forces and deflections.

*5.9 FORCES ON SUBMERGED SURFACES

The approach used in the preceding section can be used to determine the resultant of the hydrostatic pressure forces exerted on a *rectangular surface* submerged in a liquid. Consider the rectangular plate shown in Fig. 5.18, which is of length L and width b, where b is measured perpendicular to the plane of the figure. As noted in Sec. 5.8, the load exerted on an element of the plate of length dx is $w\, dx$, where w is the load per unit length. However, this load can also be expressed as $p\, dA = pb\, dx$, where p is the gage pressure in the liquid† and b is the width of the plate; thus, $w = bp$. Since the gage pressure in a liquid is $p = \gamma h$, where γ is the specific weight of the liquid and h is the vertical distance from the free surface, it follows that

$$w = bp = b\gamma h \qquad (5.13)$$

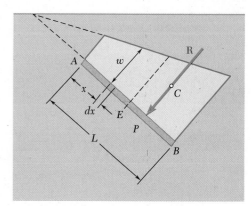

Fig. 5.18

which shows that the load per unit length w is proportional to h and, thus, varies linearly with x.

Recalling the results of Sec. 5.8, we observe that the resultant **R** of the hydrostatic forces exerted on one side of the plate is equal in magnitude to the trapezoidal area under the load curve and that its line of action passes through the centroid C of that area. The point P of the plate where **R** is applied is known as the *center of pressure*.‡

Next, we consider the forces exerted by a liquid on a curved surface of constant width (Fig. 5.19a). Since the determination of the resultant **R** of these forces by direct integration would not be easy, we consider the free body obtained by detaching the volume of liquid ABD bounded by the curved surface AB and by the two plane surfaces AD and DB shown in Fig. 5.19b. The forces acting on the free body ABD are the weight **W** of the detached volume of liquid, the resultant **R**$_1$ of the forces exerted on AD, the resultant **R**$_2$ of the forces exerted on BD, and the resultant $-$**R** of the forces exerted *by the curved surface on the liquid*. The resultant $-$**R** is equal and opposite to, and has the same line of action as, the resultant **R** of the forces exerted *by the liquid on the curved surface*. The forces **W**, **R**$_1$, and **R**$_2$ can be determined by standard methods; after their values have been found, the force $-$**R** is obtained by solving the equations of equilibrium for the free body of Fig. 5.19b. The resultant **R** of the hydrostatic forces exerted on the curved surface is then obtained by reversing the sense of $-$**R**.

The methods outlined in this section can be used to determine the resultant of the hydrostatic forces exerted on the surfaces of dams and rectangular gates and vanes. The resultants of forces on submerged surfaces of variable width will be determined in Chap. 9.

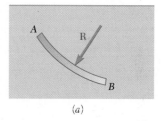

(a)

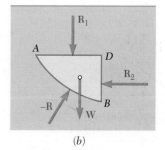

(b)

Fig. 5.19

---

†The pressure p, which represents a load per unit area, is expressed in N/m^2 or in lb/ft^2. The derived SI unit N/m^2 is called a *pascal* (Pa).

‡Noting that the area under the load curve is equal to $w_E L$, where w_E is the load per unit length at the center E of the plate, and recalling Eq. (5.13), we can write

$$R = w_E L = (bp_E)L = p_E(bL) = p_E A$$

where A denotes the area of the *plate*. Thus, the magnitude of **R** can be obtained by multiplying the area of the plate by the pressure at its center E. The resultant **R**, however, *should be applied at P, not at E*.

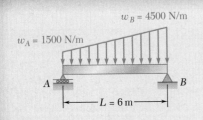

$w_B = 4500$ N/m

$w_A = 1500$ N/m

A B

$L = 6$ m

SAMPLE PROBLEM 5.9

A beam supports a distributed load as shown. (*a*) Determine the equivalent concentrated load. (*b*) Determine the reactions at the supports.

SOLUTION

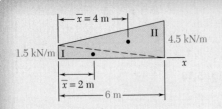

$\bar{x} = 4$ m

II 4.5 kN/m

1.5 kN/m I

x

$\bar{x} = 2$ m

6 m

a. Equivalent Concentrated Load.
The magnitude of the resultant of the load is equal to the area under the load curve, and the line of action of the resultant passes through the centroid of the same area. We divide the area under the load curve into two triangles and construct the table below. To simplify the computations and tabulation, the given loads per unit length have been converted into kN/m.

Component	A, kN	$\bar{x}$, m	$\bar{x}A$, kN · m
Triangle I	4.5	2	9
Triangle II	13.5	4	54
	$\Sigma A = 18.0$		$\Sigma \bar{x}A = 63$

Thus, $\bar{X}\Sigma A = \Sigma \bar{x}A$: $\bar{X}(18$ kN$) = 63$ kN · m $\bar{X} = 3.5$ m

The equivalent concentrated load is

$$\mathbf{W} = 18 \text{ kN} \downarrow \quad \blacktriangleleft$$

and its line of action is located at a distance

$$\bar{X} = 3.5 \text{ m to the right of } A \quad \blacktriangleleft$$

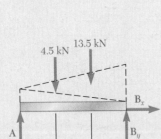

18 kN

$\bar{X} = 3.5$ m

A B

b. Reactions.
The reaction at A is vertical and is denoted by $\mathbf{A}$; the reaction at B is represented by its components $\mathbf{B}_x$ and $\mathbf{B}_y$. The given load can be considered to be the sum of two triangular loads as shown. The resultant of each triangular load is equal to the area of the triangle and acts at its centroid. We write the following equilibrium equations for the free body shown:

4.5 kN 13.5 kN

B_x

A B_y

2 m

4 m

6 m

$\xrightarrow{+} \Sigma F_x = 0$: $\mathbf{B}_x = 0 \quad \blacktriangleleft$

$+\uparrow \Sigma M_A = 0$: $-(4.5$ kN$)(2$ m$) - (13.5$ kN$)(4$ m$) + B_y(6$ m$) = 0$

$\mathbf{B}_y = 10.5$ kN $\uparrow \quad \blacktriangleleft$

$+\uparrow \Sigma M_B = 0$: $+(4.5$ kN$)(4$ m$) + (13.5$ kN$)(2$ m$) - A(6$ m$) = 0$

$\mathbf{A} = 7.5$ kN $\uparrow \quad \blacktriangleleft$

Alternative Solution. The given distributed load can be replaced by its resultant, which was found in part *a*. The reactions can be determined by writing the equilibrium equations $\Sigma F_x = 0$, $\Sigma M_A = 0$, and $\Sigma M_B = 0$. We again obtain

$$\mathbf{B}_x = 0 \quad \mathbf{B}_y = 10.5 \text{ kN} \uparrow \quad \mathbf{A} = 7.5 \text{ kN} \uparrow \quad \blacktriangleleft$$

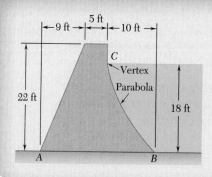

SAMPLE PROBLEM 5.10

The cross section of a concrete dam is as shown. Consider a 1-ft-thick section of the dam, and determine (a) the resultant of the reaction forces exerted by the ground on the base AB of the dam, (b) the resultant of the pressure forces exerted by the water on the face BC of the dam. The specific weights of concrete and water are 150 lb/ft³ and 62.4 lb/ft³, respectively.

SOLUTION

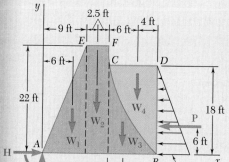

a. Ground Reaction. We choose as a free body the 1-ft-thick section AEFCDB of the dam and water. The reaction forces exerted by the ground on the base AB are represented by an equivalent force-couple system at A. Other forces acting on the free body are the weight of the dam, represented by the weights of its components $\mathbf{W}_1$, $\mathbf{W}_2$, and $\mathbf{W}_3$; the weight of the water $\mathbf{W}_4$; and the resultant $\mathbf{P}$ of the pressure forces exerted on section BD by the water to the right of section BD. We have

$$W_1 = \tfrac{1}{2}(9\text{ ft})(22\text{ ft})(1\text{ ft})(150\text{ lb/ft}^3) = 14{,}850\text{ lb}$$
$$W_2 = (5\text{ ft})(22\text{ ft})(1\text{ ft})(150\text{ lb/ft}^3) = 16{,}500\text{ lb}$$
$$W_3 = \tfrac{1}{3}(10\text{ ft})(18\text{ ft})(1\text{ ft})(150\text{ lb/ft}^3) = 9000\text{ lb}$$
$$W_4 = \tfrac{2}{3}(10\text{ ft})(18\text{ ft})(1\text{ ft})(62.4\text{ lb/ft}^3) = 7488\text{ lb}$$
$$P = \tfrac{1}{2}(18\text{ ft})(1\text{ ft})(18\text{ ft})(62.4\text{ lb/ft}^3) = 10{,}109\text{ lb}$$

Equilibrium Equations

$$\xrightarrow{+}\Sigma F_x = 0: \qquad H - 10{,}109\text{ lb} = 0 \qquad\qquad \mathbf{H} = 10{,}110\text{ lb} \rightarrow \quad \blacktriangleleft$$

$$+\uparrow \Sigma F_y = 0: \qquad V - 14{,}850\text{ lb} - 16{,}500\text{ lb} - 9000\text{ lb} - 7488\text{ lb} = 0$$
$$\mathbf{V} = 47{,}840\text{ lb} \uparrow \quad \blacktriangleleft$$

$$+\!\!\uparrow \Sigma M_A = 0: \quad -(14{,}850\text{ lb})(6\text{ ft}) - (16{,}500\text{ lb})(11.5\text{ ft})$$
$$- (9000\text{ lb})(17\text{ ft}) - (7488\text{ lb})(20\text{ ft}) + (10{,}109\text{ lb})(6\text{ ft}) + M = 0$$

$$\mathbf{M} = 520{,}960\text{ lb} \cdot \text{ft} \uparrow \quad \blacktriangleleft$$

We can replace the force-couple system obtained by a single force acting at a distance d to the right of A, where

$$d = \frac{520{,}960\text{ lb} \cdot \text{ft}}{47{,}840\text{ lb}} = 10.89\text{ ft}$$

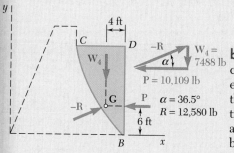

b. Resultant R of Water Forces. The parabolic section of water BCD is chosen as a free body. The forces involved are the resultant $-\mathbf{R}$ of the forces exerted by the dam on the water, the weight $\mathbf{W}_4$, and the force $\mathbf{P}$. Since these forces must be concurrent, $-\mathbf{R}$ passes through the point of intersection G of $\mathbf{W}_4$ and $\mathbf{P}$. A force triangle is drawn from which the magnitude and direction of $-\mathbf{R}$ are determined. The resultant $\mathbf{R}$ of the forces exerted by the water on the face BC is equal and opposite:

$$\mathbf{R} = 12{,}580\text{ lb} \measuredangle 36.5° \quad \blacktriangleleft$$

SOLVING PROBLEMS
ON YOUR OWN

The problems in this lesson involve two common and very important types of loading: distributed loads on beams and forces on submerged surfaces of constant width. As we discussed in Secs. 5.8 and 5.9 and illustrated in Sample Probs. 5.9 and 5.10, determining the single equivalent force for each of these loadings requires a knowledge of centroids.

1. Analyzing beams subjected to distributed loads. In Sec. 5.8, we showed that a distributed load on a beam can be replaced by a single equivalent force. The magnitude of this force is equal to the area under the distributed load curve and its line of action passes through the centroid of that area. Thus, you should begin your solution by replacing the various distributed loads on a given beam by their respective single equivalent forces. The reactions at the supports of the beam can then be determined by using the methods of Chap. 4.

When possible, complex distributed loads should be divided into the common-shape areas shown in Fig. 5.8A [Sample Prob. 5.9]. Each of these areas can then be replaced by a single equivalent force. If required, the system of equivalent forces can be reduced further to a single equivalent force. As you study Sample Prob. 5.9, note how we have used the analogy between force and area and the techniques for locating the centroid of a composite area to analyze a beam subjected to a distributed load.

2. Solving problems involving forces on submerged bodies. The following points and techniques should be remembered when solving problems of this type.

a. The pressure p at a depth h below the free surface of a liquid is equal to γh or $\rho g h$, where γ and ρ are the specific weight and the density of the liquid, respectively. The load per unit length w acting on a submerged surface of constant width b is then

$$w = bp = b\gamma h = b\rho g h$$

b. The line of action of the resultant force **R** acting on a submerged plane surface is perpendicular to the surface.

c. For a vertical or inclined plane rectangular surface of width b, the loading on the surface can be represented by a linearly distributed load which is trapezoidal in shape (Fig. 5.18). Further, the magnitude of **R** is given by

$$R = \gamma h_E A$$

where h_E is the vertical distance to the center of the surface and A is the area of the surface.

d. The load curve will be triangular (rather than trapezoidal) when the top edge of a plane rectangular surface coincides with the free surface of the liquid, since the pressure of the liquid at the free surface is zero. For this case, the line of action of **R** is easily determined, for it passes through the centroid of a *triangular* distributed load.

e. For the general case, rather than analyzing a trapezoid, we suggest that you use the method indicated in part *b* of Sample Prob. 5.9. First divide the trapezoidal distributed load into two triangles, and then compute the magnitude of the resultant of each triangular load. (The magnitude is equal to the area of the triangle times the width of the plate.) Note that the line of action of each resultant force passes through the centroid of the corresponding triangle and that the sum of these forces is equivalent to **R**. Thus, rather than using **R**, you can use the two equivalent resultant forces, whose points of application are easily calculated. Of course, the equation given for R in paragraph *c* should be used when only the magnitude of **R** is needed.

f. When the submerged surface of constant width is curved, the resultant force acting on the surface is obtained by considering the equilibrium of the volume of liquid bounded by the curved surface and by horizontal and vertical planes (Fig. 5.19). Observe that the force $\mathbf{R}_1$ of Fig. 5.19 is equal to the weight of the liquid lying above the plane *AD*. The method of solution for problems involving curved surfaces is shown in part *b* of Sample Prob. 5.10.

In subsequent mechanics courses (in particular, mechanics of materials and fluid mechanics), you will have ample opportunity to use the ideas introduced in this lesson.

PROBLEMS

5.66 and 5.67 For the beam and loading shown, determine (*a*) the magnitude and location of the resultant of the distributed load, (*b*) the reactions at the beam supports.

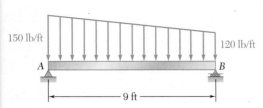

Fig. P5.66

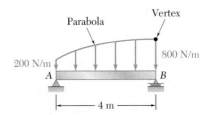

Fig. P5.67

5.68 through 5.73 Determine the reactions at the beam supports for the given loading.

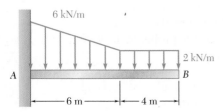

Fig. P5.68

Fig. P5.69

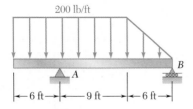

Fig. P5.70

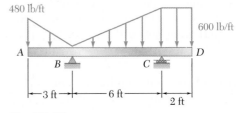

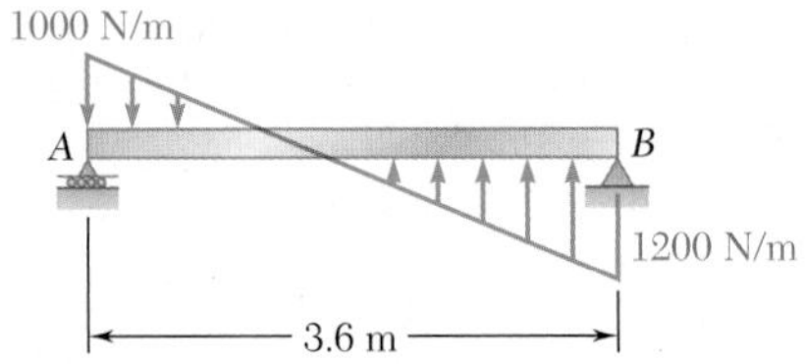

Fig. P5.71

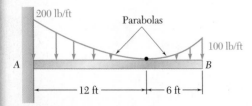

Fig. P5.72

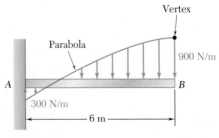

Fig. P5.73

5.74 Determine (a) the distance *a* so that the vertical reactions at supports *A* and *B* are equal, (b) the corresponding reactions at the supports.

5.75 Determine (a) the distance *a* so that the reaction at support *B* is minimum, (b) the corresponding reactions at the supports.

5.76 Determine the reactions at the beam supports for the given loading when $w_0 = 150$ lb/ft.

5.77 Determine (a) the distributed load w_0 at the end *D* of the beam *ABCD* for which the reaction at *B* is zero, (b) the corresponding reaction at *C*.

5.78 The beam *AB* supports two concentrated loads and rests on soil that exerts a linearly distributed upward load as shown. Determine the values of w_A and w_B corresponding to equilibrium.

5.79 For the beam and loading of Prob. 5.78, determine (a) the distance *a* for which $w_A = 20$ kN/m, (b) the corresponding value of w_B.

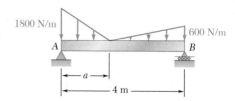

Fig. P5.74 and P5.75

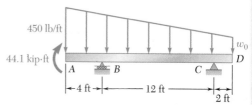

Fig. P5.76 and P5.77

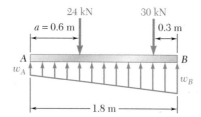

Fig. P5.78

In the following problems, use $\gamma = 62.4$ lb/ft³ for the specific weight of fresh water and $\gamma_c = 150$ lb/ft³ for the specific weight of concrete if U.S. customary units are used. With SI units, use $\rho = 10^3$ kg/m³ for the density of fresh water and $\rho_c = 2.40 \times 10^3$ kg/m³ for the density of concrete. (See the footnote on page 222 for how to determine the specific weight of a material given its density.)

5.80 The cross section of a concrete dam is as shown. For a 1-m-wide dam section determine (a) the resultant of the reaction forces exerted by the ground on the base *AB* of the dam, (b) the point of application of the resultant of part *a*, (c) the resultant of the pressure forces exerted by the water on the face *BC* of the dam.

5.81 The cross section of a concrete dam is as shown. For a 1-ft-wide dam section determine (a) the resultant of the reaction forces exerted by the ground on the base *AB* of the dam, (b) the point of application of the resultant of part *a*, (c) the resultant of the pressure forces exerted by the water on the face *BC* of the dam.

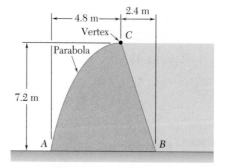

Fig. P5.80

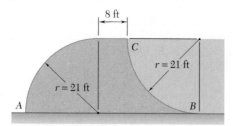

Fig. P5.81

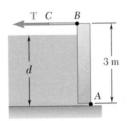

Fig. P5.82 and P5.83

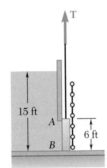

Fig. P5.84

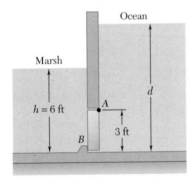

Fig. P5.85

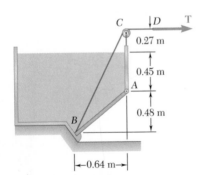

Fig. P5.88 and P5.89

5.82 The 3 × 4-m side AB of a tank is hinged at its bottom A and is held in place by a thin rod BC. The maximum tensile force the rod can withstand without breaking is 200 kN, and the design specifications require the force in the rod not to exceed 20 percent of this value. If the tank is slowly filled with water, determine the maximum allowable depth of water d in the tank.

5.83 The 3 × 4-m side of an open tank is hinged at its bottom A and is held in place by a thin rod BC. The tank is to be filled with glycerine, whose density is 1263 kg/m³. Determine the force **T** in the rod and the reactions at the hinge after the tank is filled to a depth of 2.9 m.

5.84 The friction force between a 6 × 6-ft square sluice gate AB and its guides is equal to 10 percent of the resultant of the pressure forces exerted by the water on the face of the gate. Determine the initial force needed to lift the gate if it weighs 1000 lb.

5.85 A freshwater marsh is drained to the ocean through an automatic tide gate that is 4 ft wide and 3 ft high. The gate is held by hinges located along its top edge at A and bears on a sill at B. If the water level in the marsh is h = 6 ft, determine the ocean level d for which the gate will open. (Specific weight of salt water = 64 lb/ft³.)

5.86 The dam for a lake is designed to withstand the additional force caused by silt that has settled on the lake bottom. Assuming that silt is equivalent to a liquid of density $\rho_s = 1.76 \times 10^3$ kg/m³ and considering a 1-m-wide section of dam, determine the percentage increase in the force acting on the dam face for a silt accumulation of depth 2 m.

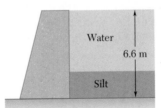

Fig. P5.86 and P5.87

5.87 The base of a dam for a lake is designed to resist up to 120 percent of the horizontal force of the water. After construction, it is found that silt (that is equivalent to a liquid of density $\rho_s = 1.76 \times 10^3$ kg/m³) is settling on the lake bottom at the rate of 12 mm/year. Considering a 1-m-wide section of dam, determine the number of years until the dam becomes unsafe.

5.88 A 0.5 × 0.8-m gate AB is located at the bottom of a tank filled with water. The gate is hinged along its top edge A and rests on a frictionless stop at B. Determine the reactions at A and B when cable BCD is slack.

5.89 A 0.5 × 0.8-m gate AB is located at the bottom of a tank filled with water. The gate is hinged along its top edge A and rests on a frictionless stop at B. Determine the minimum tension required in cable BCD to open the gate.

5.90 A long trough is supported by a continuous hinge along its lower edge and by a series of horizontal cables attached to its upper edge. Determine the tension in each of the cables, at a time when the trough is completely full of water.

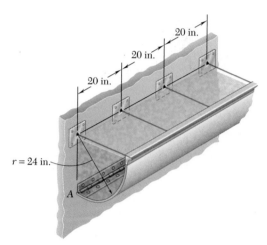

Fig. P5.90

5.91 A 4 × 2-ft gate is hinged at A and is held in position by rod CD. End D rests against a spring whose constant is 828 lb/ft. The spring is undeformed when the gate is vertical. Assuming that the force exerted by rod CD on the gate remains horizontal, determine the minimum depth of water d for which the bottom B of the gate will move to the end of the cylindrical portion of the floor.

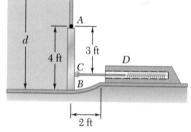

Fig. P5.91

5.92 Solve Prob. 5.91 if the gate weighs 1000 lb.

5.93 A prismatically shaped gate placed at the end of a freshwater channel is supported by a pin and bracket at A and rests on a frictionless support at B. The pin is located at a distance $h = 0.10$ m below the center of gravity C of the gate. Determine the depth of water d for which the gate will open.

5.94 A prismatically shaped gate placed at the end of a freshwater channel is supported by a pin and bracket at A and rests on a frictionless support at B. Determine the distance h if the gate is to open when $d = 0.75$ m.

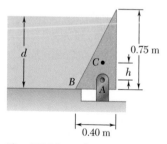

Fig. P5.93 and P5.94

5.95 A 55-gallon 23-in.-diameter drum is placed on its side to act as a dam in a 30-in.-wide freshwater channel. Knowing that the drum is anchored to the sides of the channel, determine the resultant of the pressure forces acting on the drum.

Fig. P5.95

Photo 5.4 To predict the flight characteristics
of the modified Boeing 747 when used to
transport a space shuttle, the center of gravity of
each craft had to be determined.

VOLUMES

5.10 CENTER OF GRAVITY OF A THREE-DIMENSIONAL BODY. CENTROID OF A VOLUME

The *center of gravity* G of a three-dimensional body is obtained by
dividing the body into small elements and by then expressing that
the weight **W** of the body acting at G is equivalent to the system of
distributed forces **ΔW** representing the weights of the small elements. Choosing the y axis to be vertical with positive sense upward
(Fig. 5.20) and denoting by **r̄** the position vector of G, we write that

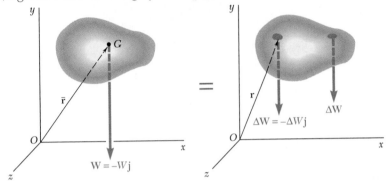

Fig. 5.20

W is equal to the sum of the elemental weights **ΔW** and that its
moment about O is equal to the sum of the moments about O of
the elemental weights:

$$\Sigma \mathbf{F}: \qquad -W\mathbf{j} = \Sigma(-\Delta W\mathbf{j})$$
$$\Sigma \mathbf{M}_O: \qquad \mathbf{\bar{r}} \times (-W\mathbf{j}) = \Sigma[\mathbf{r} \times (-\Delta W\mathbf{j})] \qquad (5.14)$$

Rewriting the last equation in the form

$$\mathbf{\bar{r}}W \times (-\mathbf{j}) = (\Sigma\mathbf{r} \, \Delta W) \times (-\mathbf{j}) \qquad (5.15)$$

we observe that the weight **W** of the body is equivalent to the system
of the elemental weights **ΔW** if the following conditions are satisfied:

$$W = \Sigma \, \Delta W \qquad \mathbf{\bar{r}}W = \Sigma\mathbf{r} \, \Delta W$$

Increasing the number of elements and simultaneously decreasing
the size of each element, we obtain in the limit

$$W = \int dW \qquad \mathbf{\bar{r}}W = \int \mathbf{r} \, dW \qquad (5.16)$$

We note that the relations obtained are independent of the orientation of the body. For example, if the body and the coordinate axes
were rotated so that the z axis pointed upward, the unit vector $-\mathbf{j}$
would be replaced by $-\mathbf{k}$ in Eqs. (5.14) and (5.15), but the relations
(5.16) would remain unchanged. Resolving the vectors **r̄** and **r** into
rectangular components, we note that the second of the relations
(5.16) is equivalent to the three scalar equations

$$\bar{x}W = \int x \, dW \qquad \bar{y}W = \int y \, dW \qquad \bar{z}W = \int z \, dW \qquad (5.17)$$

If the body is made of a homogeneous material of specific weight γ, the magnitude dW of the weight of an infinitesimal element can be expressed in terms of the volume dV of the element, and the magnitude W of the total weight can be expressed in terms of the total volume V. We write

$$dW = \gamma\, dV \qquad W = \gamma V$$

Substituting for dW and W in the second of the relations (5.16), we write

$$\bar{\mathbf{r}}V = \int \mathbf{r}\, dV \tag{5.18}$$

or, in scalar form,

$$\bar{x}V = \int x\, dV \qquad \bar{y}V = \int y\, dV \qquad \bar{z}V = \int z\, dV \tag{5.19}$$

The point whose coordinates are $\bar{x}, \bar{y}, \bar{z}$ is also known as the *centroid C of the volume V* of the body. If the body is not homogeneous, Eqs. (5.19) cannot be used to determine the center of gravity of the body; however, Eqs. (5.19) still define the centroid of the volume.

The integral $\int x\, dV$ is known as the *first moment of the volume with respect to the yz plane*. Similarly, the integrals $\int y\, dV$ and $\int z\, dV$ define the first moments of the volume with respect to the zx plane and the xy plane, respectively. It is seen from Eqs. (5.19) that if the centroid of a volume is located in a coordinate plane, the first moment of the volume with respect to that plane is zero.

A volume is said to be symmetrical with respect to a given plane if for every point P of the volume there exists a point P' of the same volume, such that the line PP' is perpendicular to the given plane and is bisected by that plane. The plane is said to be a *plane of symmetry* for the given volume. When a volume V possesses a plane of symmetry, the first moment of V with respect to that plane is zero, and the centroid of the volume is located in the plane of symmetry. When a volume possesses two planes of symmetry, the centroid of the volume is located on the line of intersection of the two planes. Finally, when a volume possesses three planes of symmetry which intersect at a well-defined point (i.e., not along a common line), the point of intersection of the three planes coincides with the centroid of the volume. This property enables us to determine immediately the locations of the centroids of spheres, ellipsoids, cubes, rectangular parallelepipeds, etc.

The centroids of unsymmetrical volumes or of volumes possessing only one or two planes of symmetry should be determined by integration (Sec. 5.12). The centroids of several common volumes are shown in Fig. 5.21. It should be observed that in general the centroid of a volume of revolution *does not coincide* with the centroid of its cross section. Thus, the centroid of a hemisphere is different from that of a semicircular area, and the centroid of a cone is different from that of a triangle.

Shape		$\overline{x}$	Volume
Hemisphere	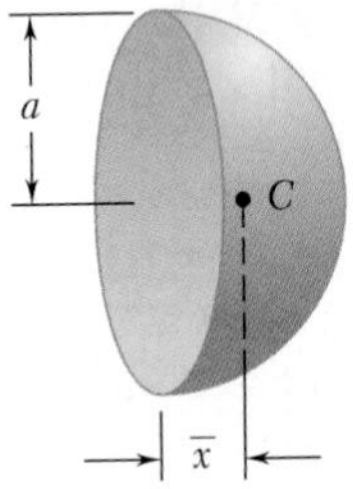	$\dfrac{3a}{8}$	$\dfrac{2}{3}\pi a^3$
Semiellipsoid of revolution	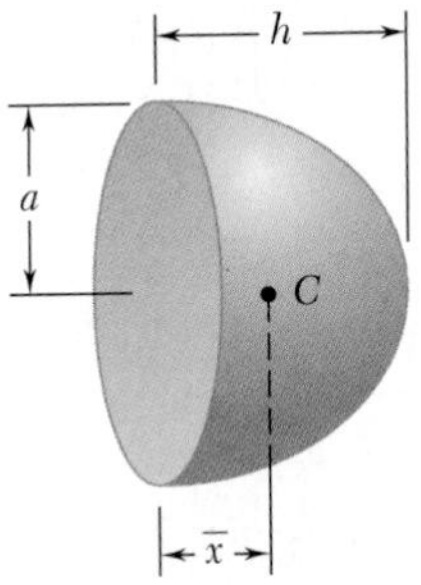	$\dfrac{3h}{8}$	$\dfrac{2}{3}\pi a^2 h$
Paraboloid of revolution	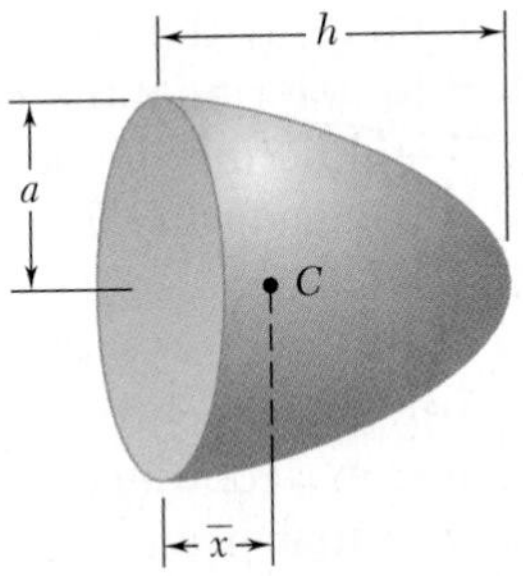	$\dfrac{h}{3}$	$\dfrac{1}{2}\pi a^2 h$
Cone	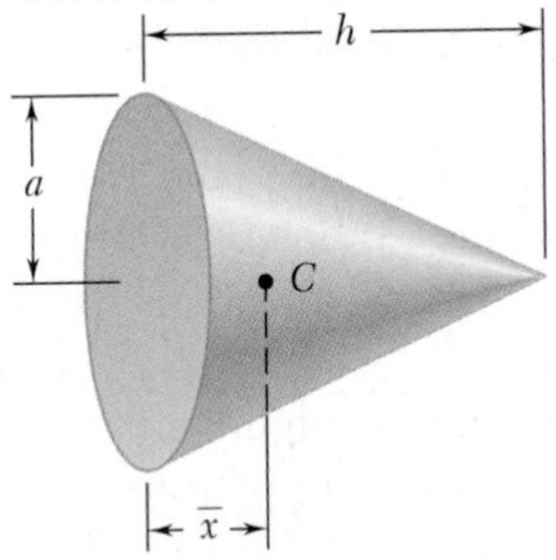	$\dfrac{h}{4}$	$\dfrac{1}{3}\pi a^2 h$
Pyramid	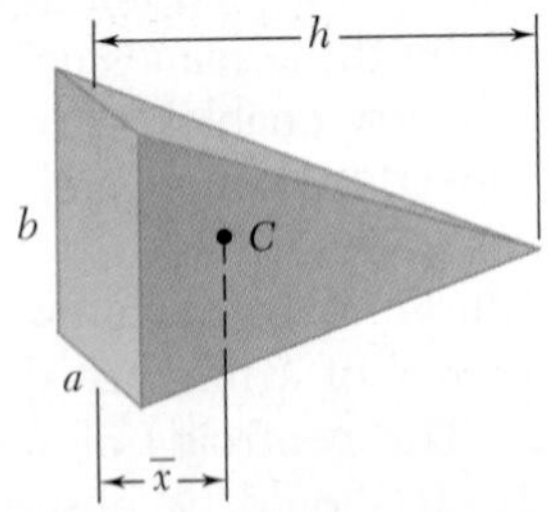	$\dfrac{h}{4}$	$\dfrac{1}{3}abh$

Fig. 5.21 Centroids of common shapes and volumes.

5.100 For the stop bracket shown, locate the x coordinate of the center of gravity.

5.101 For the stop bracket shown, locate the z coordinate of the center of gravity.

5.102 and 5.103 For the machine element shown, locate the y coordinate of the center of gravity.

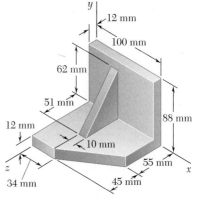

Fig. P5.100 and P5.101

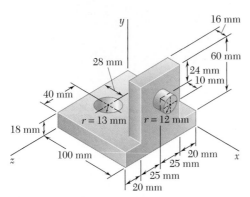

Fig. *P5.102* and *P5.105*

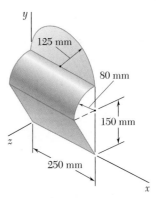

Fig. P5.103 and P5.104

5.104 For the machine element shown, locate the z coordinate of the center of gravity.

5.105 For the machine element shown, locate the x coordinate of the center of gravity.

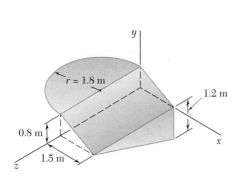

Fig. P5.106

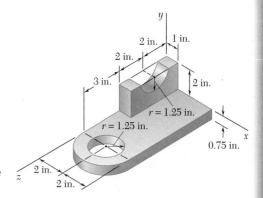

Fig. P5.107

5.106 and 5.107 Locate the center of gravity of the sheet-metal form shown.

5.108 A wastebasket, designed to fit in the corner of a room, is 16 in.
high and has a base in the shape of a quarter circle of radius 10 in.
Locate the center of gravity of the wastebasket, knowing that it is
made of sheet metal of uniform thickness.

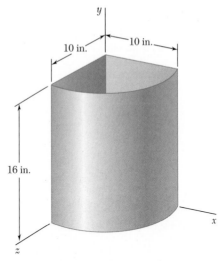

Fig. P5.108

5.109 A mounting bracket for electronic components is formed from
sheet metal of uniform thickness. Locate the center of gravity of
the bracket.

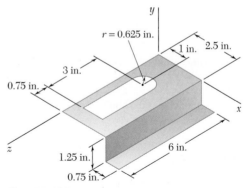

Fig. P5.109

5.110 A thin sheet of plastic of uniform thickness is bent to form a desk
organizer. Locate the center of gravity of the organizer.

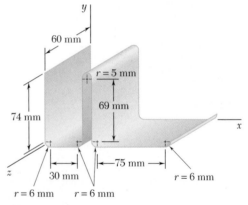

Fig. P5.110

5.111 A window awning is fabricated from sheet metal of uniform thickness. Locate the center of gravity of the awning.

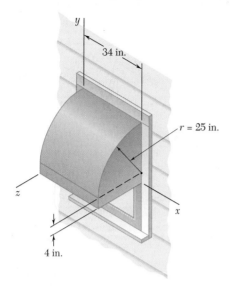

Fig. P5.111

5.112 An elbow for the duct of a ventilating system is made of sheet metal of uniform thickness. Locate the center of gravity of the elbow.

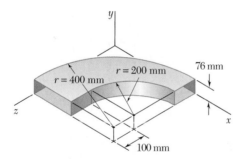

Fig. P5.112

5.113 An 8-in.-diameter cylindrical duct and a 4 × 8-in. rectangular duct are to be joined as indicated. Knowing that the ducts were fabricated from the same sheet metal, which is of uniform thickness, locate the center of gravity of the assembly.

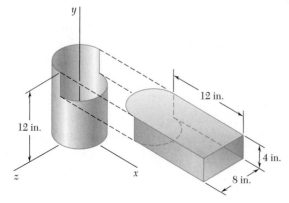

Fig. P5.113

5.114 A thin steel wire of uniform cross section is bent into the shape shown. Locate its center of gravity.

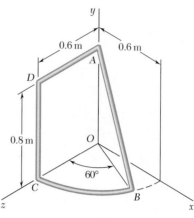

Fig. P5.114

5.115 and 5.116 Locate the center of gravity of the figure shown, knowing that it is made of thin brass rods of uniform diameter.

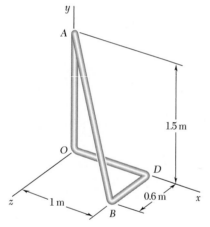

Fig. P5.115

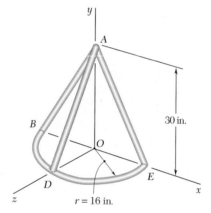

Fig. P5.116

5.117 The frame of a greenhouse is constructed from uniform aluminum channels. Locate the center of gravity of the portion of the frame shown.

5.118 A scratch awl has a plastic handle and a steel blade and shank. Knowing that the density of plastic is 1030 kg/m^3 and of steel is 7860 kg/m^3, locate the center of gravity of the awl.

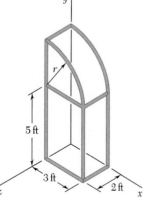

Fig. P5.117

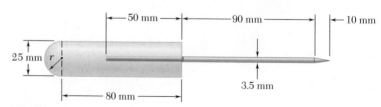

Fig. P5.118

5.119 A bronze bushing is mounted inside a steel sleeve. Knowing that the specific weight of bronze is 0.318 lb/in^3 and of steel is 0.284 lb/in^3, determine the location of the center of gravity of the assembly.

5.120 A brass collar, of length 2.5 in., is mounted on an aluminum rod of length 4 in. Locate the center of gravity of the composite body. (Specific weights: brass = 0.306 lb/in^3, aluminum = 0.101 lb/in^3.)

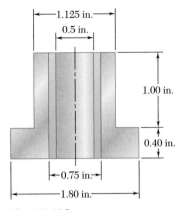

Fig. P5.119

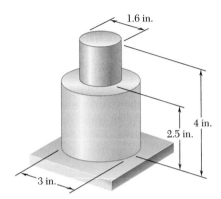

Fig. P5.120

5.121 The three legs of a small glass-topped table are equally spaced and are made of steel tubing, which has an outside diameter of 24 mm and a cross-sectional area of 150 mm^2. The diameter and the thickness of the table top are 600 mm and 10 mm, respectively. Knowing that the density of steel is 7860 kg/m^3 and of glass is 2190 kg/m^3, locate the center of gravity of the table.

5.122 through 5.124 Determine by direct integration the values of $\bar{x}$ for the two volumes obtained by passing a vertical cutting plane through the given shape of Fig. 5.21. The cutting plane is parallel to the base of the given shape and divides the shape into two volumes of equal height.

    5.122 A hemisphere

    5.123 A semiellipsoid of revolution

    5.124 A paraboloid of revolution.

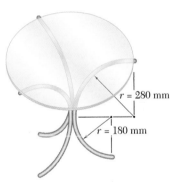

Fig. P5.121

5.125 and 5.126 Locate the centroid of the volume obtained by rotating the shaded area about the x axis.

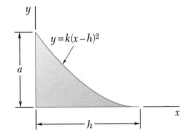

Fig. P5.125

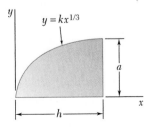

Fig. P5.126

5.127 Locate the centroid of the volume obtained by rotating the shaded area about the line $x = h$.

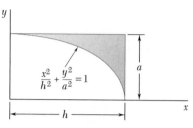

$$\frac{x^2}{h^2} + \frac{y^2}{a^2} = 1$$

Fig. P5.127

*5.128 Locate the centroid of the volume generated by revolving the portion of the sine curve shown about the x axis.

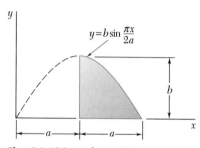

$$y = b \sin \frac{\pi x}{2a}$$

Fig. P5.128 and P5.129

*5.129 Locate the centroid of the volume generated by revolving the portion of the sine curve shown about the y axis. (*Hint:* Use a thin cylindrical shell of radius r and thickness dr as the element of volume.)

*5.130 Show that for a regular pyramid of height h and n sides ($n =$ 3, 4, . . .) the centroid of the volume of the pyramid is located at a distance $h/4$ above the base.

5.131 Determine by direct integration the location of the centroid of one-half of a thin, uniform hemispherical shell of radius R.

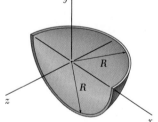

Fig. P5.131

5.132 The sides and the base of a punch bowl are of uniform thickness t. If $t \ll R$ and $R = 250$ mm, determine the location of the center of gravity of (*a*) the bowl, (*b*) the punch.

Fig. P5.132

5.133 After grading a lot, a builder places four stakes to designate the corners of the slab for a house. To provide a firm, level base for the slab, the builder places a minimum of 3 in. of gravel beneath the slab. Determine the volume of gravel needed and the x coordinate of the centroid of the volume of the gravel. (*Hint:* The bottom surface of the gravel is an oblique plane, which can be represented by the equation $y = a + bx + cz$.)

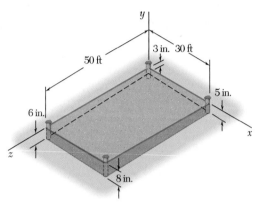

Fig. P5.133

5.134 Determine by direct integration the location of the centroid of the volume between the xz plane and the portion shown of the surface $y = 16h(ax - x^2)(bz - z^2)/a^2b^2$.

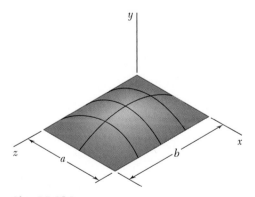

Fig. P5.134

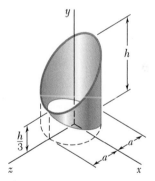

Fig. P5.135

5.135 Locate the centroid of the section shown, which was cut from a thin circular pipe by two oblique planes.

*5.136 Locate the centroid of the section shown, which was cut from an elliptical cylinder by an oblique plane.

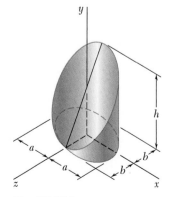

Fig. P5.136

REVIEW AND SUMMARY

This chapter was devoted chiefly to the determination of the *center of gravity* of a rigid body, i.e., to the determination of the point G where a single force **W**, called the *weight* of the body, can be applied to represent the effect of the earth's attraction on the body.

Center of gravity of a two-dimensional body

In the first part of the chapter, we considered *two-dimensional bodies*, such as flat plates and wires contained in the xy plane. By adding force components in the vertical z direction and moments about the horizontal y and x axes [Sec. 5.2], we derived the relations

$$W = \int dW \qquad \bar{x}W = \int x\, dW \qquad \bar{y}W = \int y\, dW \qquad (5.2)$$

which define the weight of the body and the coordinates $\bar{x}$ and $\bar{y}$ of its center of gravity.

Centroid of an area or line

In the case of a *homogeneous flat plate of uniform thickness* [Sec. 5.3], the center of gravity G of the plate coincides with the *centroid C of the area A* of the plate, the coordinates of which are defined by the relations

$$\bar{x}A = \int x\, dA \qquad \bar{y}A = \int y\, dA \qquad (5.3)$$

Similarly, the determination of the center of gravity of a *homogeneous wire of uniform cross section* contained in a plane reduces to the determination of the *centroid C of the line L* representing the wire; we have

$$\bar{x}L = \int x\, dL \qquad \bar{y}L = \int y\, dL \qquad (5.4)$$

First moments

The integrals in Eqs. (5.3) are referred to as the *first moments* of the area A with respect to the y and x axes and are denoted by Q_y and Q_x, respectively [Sec. 5.4]. We have

$$Q_y = \bar{x}A \qquad Q_x = \bar{y}A \qquad (5.6)$$

The first moments of a line can be defined in a similar way.

Properties of symmetry

The determination of the centroid C of an area or line is simplified when the area or line possesses certain *properties of symmetry*. If the area or line is symmetric with respect to an axis, its centroid C

lies on that axis; if it is symmetric with respect to two axes, C is located at the intersection of the two axes; if it is symmetric with respect to a center O, C coincides with O.

The *areas and the centroids of various common shapes* are tabulated in Fig. 5.8. When a flat plate can be divided into several of these shapes, the coordinates $\overline{X}$ and $\overline{Y}$ of its center of gravity G can be determined from the coordinates $\overline{x}_1, \overline{x}_2, \ldots$ and $\overline{y}_1, \overline{y}_2, \ldots$ of the centers of gravity $G_1, G_2, \ldots$ of the various parts [Sec. 5.5]. Equating moments about the y and x axes, respectively (Fig. 5.24), we have

Center of gravity of a composite body

$$\overline{X}\Sigma W = \Sigma \overline{x}W \qquad \overline{Y}\Sigma W = \Sigma \overline{y}W \qquad (5.7)$$

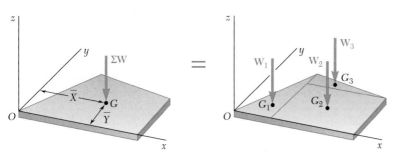

Fig. 5.24

If the plate is homogeneous and of uniform thickness, its center of gravity coincides with the centroid C of the area of the plate, and Eqs. (5.7) reduce to

$$Q_y = \overline{X}\Sigma A = \Sigma \overline{x}A \qquad Q_x = \overline{Y}\Sigma A = \Sigma \overline{y}A \qquad (5.8)$$

These equations yield the first moments of the composite area, or they can be solved for the coordinates $\overline{X}$ and $\overline{Y}$ of its centroid [Sample Prob. 5.1]. The determination of the center of gravity of a composite wire is carried out in a similar fashion [Sample Prob. 5.2].

When an area is bounded by analytical curves, the coordinates of its centroid can be determined by *integration* [Sec. 5.6]. This can be done by evaluating either the double integrals in Eqs. (5.3) or a *single integral* which uses one of the thin rectangular or pie-shaped elements of area shown in Fig. 5.12. Denoting by $\overline{x}_{el}$ and $\overline{y}_{el}$ the coordinates of the centroid of the element dA, we have

Determination of centroid by integration

$$Q_y = \overline{x}A = \int \overline{x}_{el}\,dA \qquad Q_x = \overline{y}A = \int \overline{y}_{el}\,dA \qquad (5.9)$$

It is advantageous to use the same element of area to compute both of the first moments Q_y and Q_x; the same element can also be used to determine the area A [Sample Prob. 5.4].

Theorems of Pappus-Guldinus

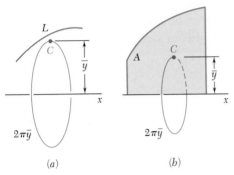

$2\pi\bar{y}$

(a)

$2\pi\bar{y}$

(b)

Fig. 5.25

Distributed loads

The *theorems of Pappus-Guldinus* relate the determination of the area of a surface of revolution or the volume of a body of revolution to the determination of the centroid of the generating curve or area [Sec. 5.7]. The area A of the surface generated by rotating a curve of length L about a fixed axis (Fig. 5.25a) is

$$A = 2\pi\bar{y}L \tag{5.10}$$

where $\bar{y}$ represents the distance from the centroid C of the curve to the fixed axis. Similarly, the volume V of the body generated by rotating an area A about a fixed axis (Fig. 5.25b) is

$$V = 2\pi\bar{y}A \tag{5.11}$$

where $\bar{y}$ represents the distance from the centroid C of the area to the fixed axis.

The concept of centroid of an area can also be used to solve problems other than those dealing with the weight of flat plates. For example, to determine the reactions at the supports of a beam [Sec. 5.8], we can replace a *distributed load* w by a concentrated load $\mathbf{W}$ equal in magnitude to the area A under the load curve and passing through the centroid C of that area (Fig. 5.26). The same approach can be used to determine the resultant of the hydrostatic forces exerted on a *rectangular plate submerged in a liquid* [Sec. 5.9].

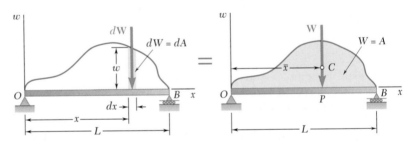

Fig. 5.26

Center of gravity of a three-dimensional body

The last part of the chapter was devoted to the determination of the *center of gravity* G *of a three-dimensional body*. The coordinates $\bar{x}$, $\bar{y}$, $\bar{z}$ of G were defined by the relations

$$\bar{x}W = \int x\,dW \qquad \bar{y}W = \int y\,dW \qquad \bar{z}W = \int z\,dW \tag{5.17}$$

Centroid of a volume

In the case of a *homogeneous body*, the center of gravity G coincides with the *centroid* C *of the volume* V of the body; the coordinates of C are defined by the relations

$$\bar{x}V = \int x\,dV \qquad \bar{y}V = \int y\,dV \qquad \bar{z}V = \int z\,dV \tag{5.19}$$

If the volume possesses a *plane of symmetry*, its centroid C will lie in that plane; if it possesses two planes of symmetry, C will be located on the line of intersection of the two planes; if it possesses three planes of symmetry which intersect at only one point, C will coincide with that point [Sec. 5.10].

The *volumes and centroids of various common three-dimensional shapes* are tabulated in Fig. 5.21. When a body can be divided into several of these shapes, the coordinates $\overline{X}$, $\overline{Y}$, $\overline{Z}$ of its center of gravity G can be determined from the corresponding coordinates of the centers of gravity of its various parts [Sec. 5.11]. We have

$$\overline{X}\Sigma W = \Sigma\overline{x}\,W \qquad \overline{Y}\Sigma W = \Sigma\overline{y}\,W \qquad \overline{Z}\Sigma W = \Sigma\overline{z}\,W \qquad (5.20)$$

If the body is made of a homogeneous material, its center of gravity coincides with the centroid C of its volume, and we write [Sample Probs. 5.11 and 5.12]

$$\overline{X}\Sigma V = \Sigma\overline{x}\,V \qquad \overline{Y}\Sigma V = \Sigma\overline{y}\,V \qquad \overline{Z}\Sigma V = \Sigma\overline{z}\,V \qquad (5.21)$$

When a volume is bounded by analytical surfaces, the coordinates of its centroid can be determined by *integration* [Sec. 5.12]. To avoid the computation of the triple integrals in Eqs. (5.19), we can use elements of volume in the shape of thin filaments, as shown in Fig. 5.27.

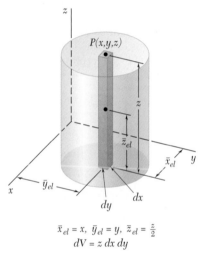

$$\overline{x}_{el} = x, \; \overline{y}_{el} = y, \; \overline{z}_{el} = \tfrac{z}{2}$$
$$dV = z\,dx\,dy$$

Fig. 5.27

Denoting by $\overline{x}_{el}$, $\overline{y}_{el}$, and $\overline{z}_{el}$ the coordinates of the centroid of the element dV, we rewrite Eqs. (5.19) as

$$\overline{x}V = \int \overline{x}_{el}\,dV \qquad \overline{y}V = \int \overline{y}_{el}\,dV \qquad \overline{z}V = \int \overline{z}_{el}\,dV \qquad (5.23)$$

which involve only double integrals. If the volume possesses *two planes of symmetry*, its centroid C is located on their line of intersection. Choosing the x axis to lie along that line and dividing the volume into thin slabs parallel to the yz plane, we can determine C from the relation

$$\overline{x}V = \int \overline{x}_{el}\,dV \qquad (5.24)$$

with a *single integration* [Sample Prob. 5.13]. For a body of revolution, these slabs are circular and their volume is given in Fig. 5.28.

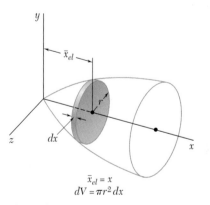

$$\overline{x}_{el} = x$$
$$dV = \pi r^2\,dx$$

Fig. 5.28

REVIEW PROBLEMS

5.137 and 5.138 Locate the centroid of the plane area shown.

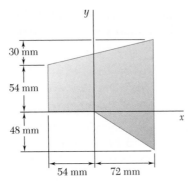

Fig. P5.137

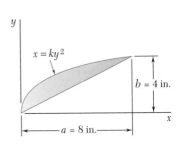

Fig. P5.138

5.139 The frame for a sign is fabricated from thin, flat steel bar stock of mass per unit length 4.73 kg/m. The frame is supported by a pin at C and by a cable AB. Determine (a) the tension in the cable, (b) the reaction at C.

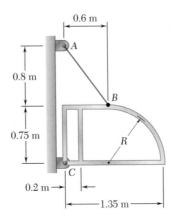

Fig. P5.139

5.140 Determine by direct integration the centroid of the area shown. Express your answer in terms of a and h.

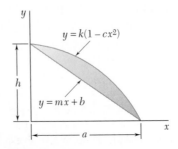

Fig. P5.140

5.141 Determine by direct integration the centroid of the area shown. Express your answer in terms of a and b.

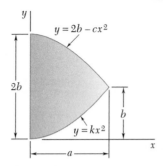

Fig. P5.141

5.142 Knowing that two equal caps have been removed from a 10-in.-diameter wooden sphere, determine the total surface area of the remaining portion.

Fig. P5.142

5.143 Determine the reactions at the beam supports for the given loading.

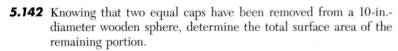

Fig. P5.143

5.144 A beam is subjected to a linearly distributed downward load and rests on two wide supports BC and DE, which exert uniformly distributed upward loads as shown. Determine the values of w_{BC} and w_{DE} corresponding to equilibrium when $w_A = 600$ N/m.

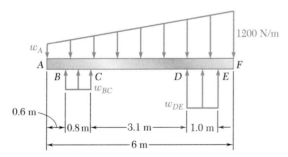

Fig. P5.144

5.145 The square gate AB is held in the position shown by hinges along its top edge A and by a shear pin at B. For a depth of water $d = 3.5$ ft, determine the force exerted on the gate by the shear pin.

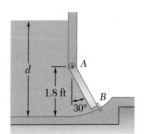

Fig. P5.145

5.146 Consider the composite body shown. Determine (*a*) the value of $\bar{x}$ when $h = L/2$, (*b*) the ratio h/L for which $\bar{x} = L$.

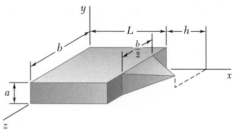

Fig. P5.146

5.147 Locate the center of gravity of the sheet-metal form shown.

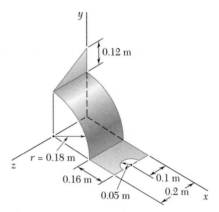

Fig. P5.147

5.148 Locate the centroid of the volume obtained by rotating the shaded area about the *x* axis.

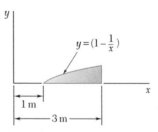

Fig. P5.148

COMPUTER PROBLEMS

5.C1 A beam is to carry a series of uniform and uniformly varying distributed loads as shown in part *a* of the figure. Divide the area under each portion of the load curve into two triangles (see Sample Prob. 5.9), and then use computational software to calculate the reactions at *A* and *B*. Use this program to calculate the reactions at the supports for the beams shown in parts *b* and *c* of the figure.

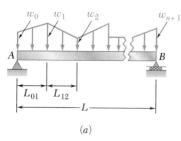

(a)

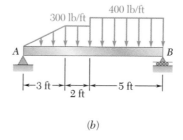

(b)

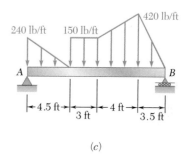

(c)

Fig. P5.C1

5.C2 The three-dimensional structure shown is fabricated from five thin steel rods of equal diameter. Using computational software, calculate the coordinates of the center of gravity of the structure. Use this program to locate the center of gravity when (*a*) $h = 12$ m, $R = 5$ m, $\alpha = 90°$; (*b*) $h = 570$ mm, $R = 760$ mm, $\alpha = 30°$; (*c*) $h = 21$ m, $R = 20$ m, $\alpha = 135°$.

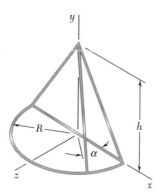

Fig. P5.C2

5.C3 An open tank is to be slowly filled with water. (The density of water is 10^3 kg/m^3.) Using computational software, determine the resultant of the pressure forces exerted by the water on a 1-m-wide section of side *ABC* of the tank. Determine the resultant of the pressure forces for values of *d* from 0 to 3 m using 0.25-m increments.

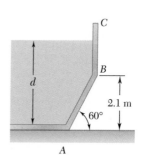

Fig. P5.C3

5.C4 Approximate the curve shown using 10 straight-line segments, and then use computational software, to determine the location of the centroid of the line. Use this program to determine the location of the centroid when (*a*) *a* = 1 in., *L* = 11 in., *h* = 2 in.; (*b*) *a* = 2 in., *L* = 17 in., *h* = 4 in.; (*c*) *a* = 5 in., *L* = 12 in., *h* = 1 in.

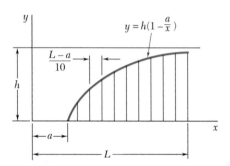

Fig. P5.C4

5.C5 Approximate the general spandrel shown using a series of *n* rectangles, each of width Δ*a* and of the form *bcc'b'*, and then use computational software to calculate the coordinates of the centroid of the area. Use this program to locate the centroid when (*a*) *m* = 2, *a* = 80 mm, *h* = 80 mm; (*b*) *m* = 2, *a* = 80 mm, *h* = 500 mm; (*c*) *m* = 5, *a* = 80 mm, *h* = 80 mm; (*d*) *m* = 5, *a* = 80 mm, *h* = 500 mm. In each case, compare the answers obtained to the exact values of $\bar{x}$ and $\bar{y}$ computed from the formulas given in Fig. 5.8A and determine the percentage error.

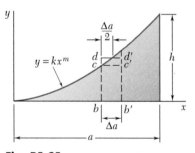

Fig. P5.C5

5.C6 Solve Prob. 5.C5, using rectangles of the form *bdd'b'*.

*5.C7 A farmer asks a group of engineering students to determine the volume of water in a small pond. Using cord, the students first establish a 2 × 2-ft grid across the pond and then record the depth of the water, in feet, at each intersection point of the grid (see the accompanying table). Using computational software, determine (*a*) the volume of water in the pond, (*b*) the location of the center of gravity of the water. Approximate the depth of each 2 × 2-ft element of water using the average of the water depths at the four corners of the element.

	Cord									
	1	2	3	4	5	6	7	8	9	10
1	…	…	…	…	0	0	0	…	…	…
2	…	…	0	0	0	1	0	0	0	…
3	…	0	0	1	3	3	3	1	0	0
4	0	0	1	3	6	6	6	3	1	0
5	0	1	3	6	8	8	6	3	1	0
6	0	1	3	6	8	7	7	3	0	0
7	0	3	4	6	6	6	4	1	0	…
8	0	3	3	3	3	3	1	0	0	…
9	0	0	0	1	1	0	0	0	…	…
10	…	…	0	0	0	0	…	…	…	…

The leftmost column (rows 1–10) is labeled **Cord**.

Trusses, such as this Pratt-style cantilever arch bridge in New York State, provide both a practical and an economical solution to many engineering problems.

284

CHAPTER 6

Analysis of Structures

Chapter 6 Analysis of Structures

6.1 INTRODUCTION

The problems considered in the preceding chapters concerned the equilibrium of a single rigid body, and all forces involved were external to the rigid body. We now consider problems dealing with the equilibrium of structures made of several connected parts. These problems call for the determination not only of the external forces acting on the structure but also of the forces which hold together the various parts of the structure. From the point of view of the structure as a whole, these forces are *internal forces*.

Consider, for example, the crane shown in Fig. 6.1*a*, which carries a load *W*. The crane consists of three beams *AD*, *CF*, and *BE* connected by frictionless pins; it is supported by a pin at *A* and by a cable *DG*. The free-body diagram of the crane has been drawn in Fig. 6.1*b*. The external forces, which are shown in the diagram, include the weight **W**, the two components $\mathbf{A}_x$ and $\mathbf{A}_y$ of the reaction at *A*, and the force **T** exerted by the cable at *D*. The internal forces holding the various parts of the crane together do not appear in the diagram. If, however, the crane is dismembered and if a free-body diagram is drawn for each of its component parts, the forces holding the three beams together will also be represented, since these forces are external forces from the point of view of each component part (Fig. 6.1*c*).

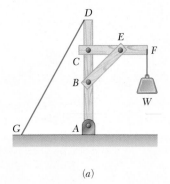

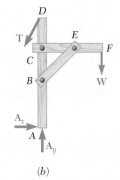

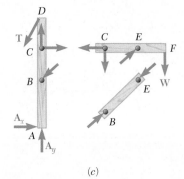

(a)

(b)

(c)

Fig. 6.1

It will be noted that the force exerted at *B* by member *BE* on member *AD* has been represented as equal and opposite to the force exerted at the same point by member *AD* on member *BE*; the force exerted at *E* by *BE* on *CF* is shown equal and opposite to the force exerted by *CF* on *BE*; and the components of the force exerted at *C* by *CF* on *AD* are shown equal and opposite to the components of the force exerted by *AD* on *CF*. This is in conformity with Newton's third law, which states that *the forces of action and reaction between bodies in contact have the same magnitude, same line of action, and opposite sense.* As pointed out in Chap. 1, this law, which is based on experimental evidence, is one of the six fundamental principles of elementary mechanics, and its application is essential to the solution of problems involving connected bodies.

In this chapter, three broad categories of engineering structures will be considered:

1. *Trusses,* which are designed to support loads and are usually stationary, fully constrained structures. Trusses consist exclusively of straight members connected at joints located at the ends of each member. Members of a truss, therefore, are *two-force members,* i.e., members acted upon by two equal and opposite forces directed along the member.
2. *Frames,* which are also designed to support loads and are also usually stationary, fully constrained structures. However, like the crane of Fig. 6.1, frames always contain at least one *multiforce member,* i.e., a member acted upon by three or more forces which, in general, are not directed along the member.
3. *Machines,* which are designed to transmit and modify forces and are structures containing moving parts. Machines, like frames, always contain at least one multiforce member.

Photo 6.1 Shown is a pin-jointed connection on the approach span to the San Francisco–Oakland Bay Bridge.

TRUSSES

6.2 DEFINITION OF A TRUSS

The truss is one of the major types of engineering structures. It provides both a practical and an economical solution to many engineering situations, especially in the design of bridges and buildings. A typical truss is shown in Fig. 6.2*a*. A truss consists of straight members connected at joints. Truss members are connected at their extremities only; thus no member is continuous through a joint. In Fig. 6.2*a*, for example, there is no member *AB*; there are instead two distinct members *AD* and *DB*. Most actual structures are made of several trusses joined together to form a space framework. Each truss is designed to carry those loads which act in its plane and thus may be treated as a two-dimensional structure.

In general, the members of a truss are slender and can support little lateral load; all loads, therefore, must be applied to the various joints, and not to the members themselves. When a concentrated load is to be applied between two joints, or when a distributed load is to be supported by the truss, as in the case of a bridge truss, a floor system must be provided which, through the use of stringers and floor beams, transmits the load to the joints (Fig. 6.3).

The weights of the members of the truss are also assumed to be applied to the joints, half of the weight of each member being applied to each of the two joints the member connects. Although the members are actually joined together by means of welded, bolted, or riveted connections, it is customary to assume that the members are pinned together; therefore, the forces acting at each end of a member reduce to a single force and no couple. Thus, the only forces assumed to be applied to a truss member are a single

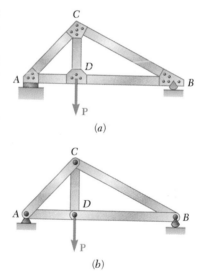

Fig. 6.2

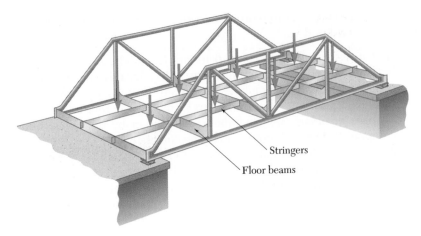

Stringers

Floor beams

Fig. 6.3

(*a*)   (*b*)

Fig. 6.4

force at each end of the member. Each member can then be treated as a two-force member, and the entire truss can be considered as a group of pins and two-force members (Fig. 6.2*b*). An individual member can be acted upon as shown in either of the two sketches of Fig. 6.4. In Fig. 6.4*a*, the forces tend to pull the member apart, and the member is in tension; in Fig. 6.4*b*, the forces tend to compress the member, and the member is in compression. A number of typical trusses are shown in Fig. 6.5.

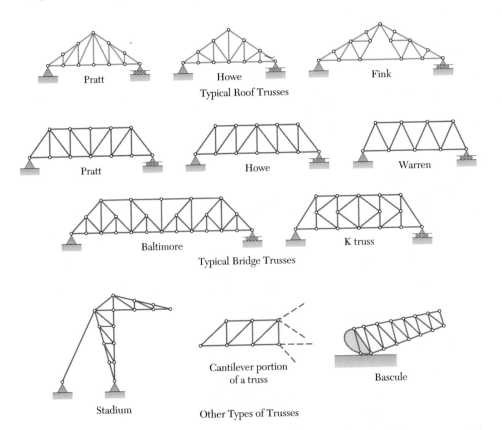

Pratt   Howe   Fink

Typical Roof Trusses

Pratt   Howe   Warren

Baltimore   K truss

Typical Bridge Trusses

Stadium   Cantilever portion of a truss   Bascule

Other Types of Trusses

Fig. 6.5

6.3 SIMPLE TRUSSES

Consider the truss of Fig. 6.6a, which is made of four members connected by pins at A, B, C, and D. If a load is applied at B, the truss will greatly deform, completely losing its original shape. In contrast, the truss of Fig. 6.6b, which is made of three members connected by pins at A, B, and C, will deform only slightly under a load applied at B. The only possible deformation for this truss is one involving small changes in the length of its members. The truss of Fig. 6.6b is said to be a *rigid truss*, the term rigid being used here to indicate that the truss *will not collapse*.

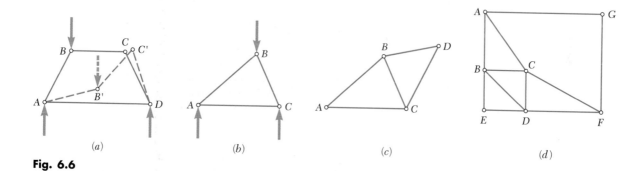

(a)　　(b)　　(c)　　(d)

Fig. 6.6

As shown in Fig. 6.6c, a larger rigid truss can be obtained by adding two members BD and CD to the basic triangular truss of Fig. 6.6b. This procedure can be repeated as many times as desired, and the resulting truss will be rigid if each time two new members are added, they are attached to two existing joints and connected at a new joint.† A truss which can be constructed in this manner is called a *simple truss*.

It should be noted that a simple truss is not necessarily made only of triangles. The truss of Fig. 6.6d, for example, is a simple truss which was constructed from triangle ABC by adding successively the joints D, E, F, and G. On the other hand, rigid trusses are not always simple trusses, even when they appear to be made of triangles. The Fink and Baltimore trusses shown in Fig. 6.5, for instance, are not simple trusses, since they cannot be constructed from a single triangle in the manner described above. All the other trusses shown in Fig. 6.5 are simple trusses, as may be easily checked. (For the K truss, start with one of the central triangles.)

Returning to Fig. 6.6, we note that the basic triangular truss of Fig. 6.6b has three members and three joints. The truss of Fig. 6.6c has two more members and one more joint, i.e., five members and four joints altogether. Observing that every time two new members are added, the number of joints is increased by one, we find that in a simple truss the total number of members is $m = 2n - 3$, where n is the total number of joints.

Photo 6.2 Two K-trusses were used as the main components of the movable bridge shown which moved above a large stockpile of ore. The bucket below the trusses picked up ore and redeposited it until the ore was thoroughly mixed. The ore was then sent to the mill for processing into steel.

†The three joints must not be in a straight line.

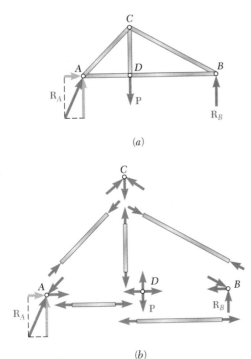

(a)

(b)

Fig. 6.7

Photo 6.3 Because roof trusses, such as those shown, require support only at their ends, it is possible to construct buildings with large, unobstructed floor areas.

6.4 ANALYSIS OF TRUSSES BY THE METHOD OF JOINTS

We saw in Sec. 6.2 that a truss can be considered as a group of pins and two-force members. The truss of Fig. 6.2, whose free-body diagram is shown in Fig. 6.7a, can thus be dismembered, and a free-body diagram can be drawn for each pin and each member (Fig. 6.7b). Each member is acted upon by two forces, one at each end; these forces have the same magnitude, same line of action, and opposite sense (Sec. 4.6). Furthermore, Newton's third law indicates that the forces of action and reaction between a member and a pin are equal and opposite. Therefore, the forces exerted by a member on the two pins it connects must be directed along that member and be equal and opposite. The common magnitude of the forces exerted by a member on the two pins it connects is commonly referred to as the *force in the member* considered, even though this quantity is actually a scalar. Since the lines of action of all the internal forces in a truss are known, the analysis of a truss reduces to computing the forces in its various members and to determining whether each of its members is in tension or in compression.

Since the entire truss is in equilibrium, each pin must be in equilibrium. The fact that a pin is in equilibrium can be expressed by drawing its free-body diagram and writing two equilibrium equations (Sec. 2.9). If the truss contains n pins, there will, therefore, be $2n$ equations available, which can be solved for $2n$ unknowns. In the case of a simple truss, we have $m = 2n - 3$, that is, $2n = m + 3$, and the number of unknowns which can be determined from the free-body diagrams of the pins is thus $m + 3$. This means that the forces in all the members, the two components of the reaction $\mathbf{R}_A$, and the reaction $\mathbf{R}_B$ can be found by considering the free-body diagrams of the pins.

The fact that the entire truss is a rigid body in equilibrium can be used to write three more equations involving the forces shown in the free-body diagram of Fig. 6.7a. Since they do not contain any new information, these equations are not independent of the equations associated with the free-body diagrams of the pins. Nevertheless, they can be used to determine the components of the reactions at the supports. The arrangement of pins and members in a simple truss is such that it will then always be possible to find a joint involving only two unknown forces. These forces can be determined by the methods of Sec. 2.11 and their values transferred to the adjacent joints and treated as known quantities at these joints. This procedure can be repeated until all unknown forces have been determined.

As an example, the truss of Fig. 6.7 will be analyzed by considering the equilibrium of each pin successively, starting with a joint at which only two forces are unknown. In the truss considered, all pins are subjected to at least three unknown forces. Therefore, the reactions at the supports must first be determined by considering the entire truss as a free body and using the equations of equilibrium of a rigid body. We find in this way that $\mathbf{R}_A$ is vertical and determine the magnitudes of $\mathbf{R}_A$ and $\mathbf{R}_B$.

The number of unknown forces at joint A is thus reduced to two, and these forces can be determined by considering the equilibrium of pin A. The reaction $\mathbf{R}_A$ and the forces $\mathbf{F}_{AC}$ and $\mathbf{F}_{AD}$ exerted on pin A by members AC and AD, respectively, must form a force triangle. First we draw $\mathbf{R}_A$ (Fig. 6.8); noting that $\mathbf{F}_{AC}$ and $\mathbf{F}_{AD}$ are directed along AC and AD, respectively, we complete the triangle and determine the magnitude and sense of $\mathbf{F}_{AC}$ and $\mathbf{F}_{AD}$. The magnitudes F_{AC} and F_{AD} represent the forces in members AC and AD. Since $\mathbf{F}_{AC}$ is directed down and to the left, that is, *toward* joint A, member AC pushes on pin A and is in compression. Since $\mathbf{F}_{AD}$ is directed *away* from joint A, member AD pulls on pin A and is in tension.

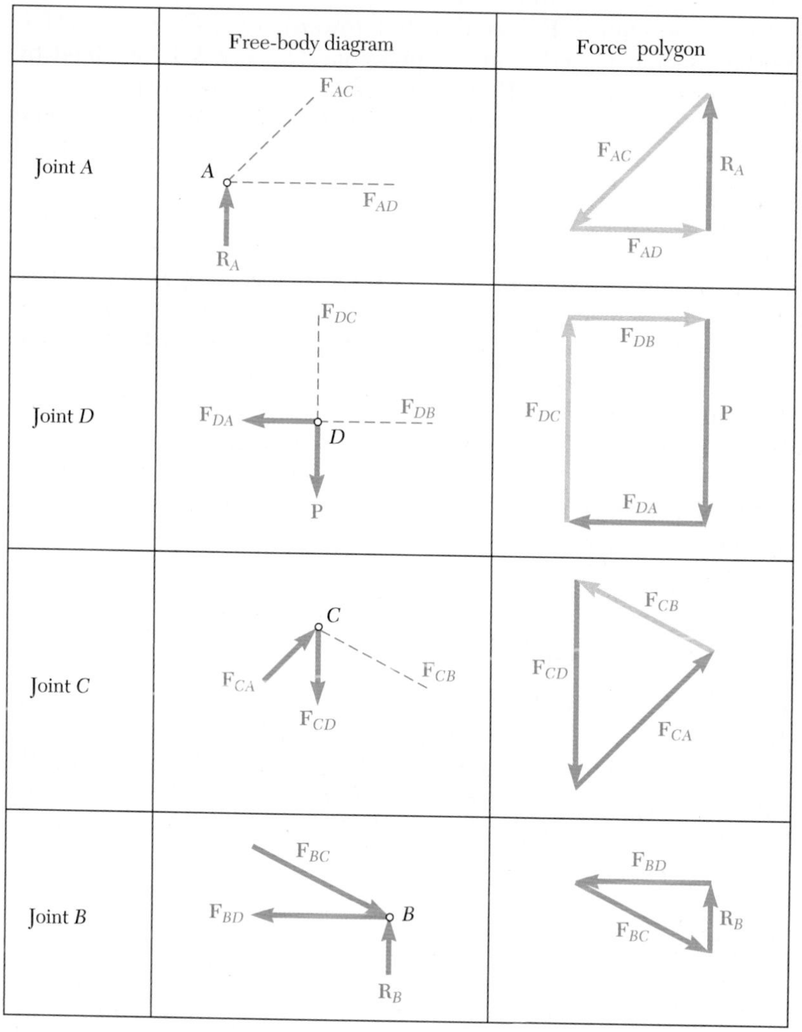

Fig. 6.8

We can now proceed to joint D, where only two forces, $\mathbf{F}_{DC}$ and $\mathbf{F}_{DB}$, are still unknown. The other forces are the load $\mathbf{P}$, which is given, and the force $\mathbf{F}_{DA}$ exerted on the pin by member AD. As indicated above, this force is equal and opposite to the force $\mathbf{F}_{AD}$ exerted by the same member on pin A. We can draw the force polygon corresponding to joint D, as shown in Fig. 6.8, and determine the forces

$\mathbf{F}_{DC}$ and $\mathbf{F}_{DB}$ from that polygon. However, when more than three forces are involved, it is usually more convenient to solve the equations of equilibrium $\Sigma F_x = 0$ and $\Sigma F_y = 0$ for the two unknown forces. Since both of these forces are found to be directed away from joint D, members DC and DB pull on the pin and are in tension.

Next, joint C is considered; its free-body diagram is shown in Fig. 6.8. It is noted that both $\mathbf{F}_{CD}$ and $\mathbf{F}_{CA}$ are known from the analysis of the preceding joints and that only $\mathbf{F}_{CB}$ is unknown. Since the equilibrium of each pin provides sufficient information to determine two unknowns, a check of our analysis is obtained at this joint. The force triangle is drawn, and the magnitude and sense of $\mathbf{F}_{CB}$ are determined. Since $\mathbf{F}_{CB}$ is directed toward joint C, member CB pushes on pin C and is in compression. The check is obtained by verifying that the force $\mathbf{F}_{CB}$ and member CB are parallel.

At joint B, all of the forces are known. Since the corresponding pin is in equilibrium, the force triangle must close and an additional check of the analysis is obtained.

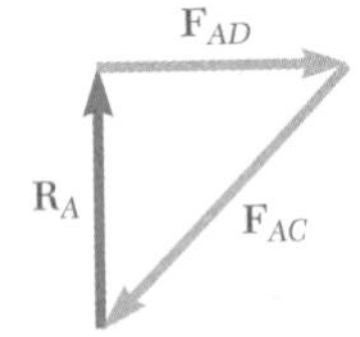

It should be noted that the force polygons shown in Fig. 6.8 are not unique. Each of them could be replaced by an alternative configuration. For example, the force triangle corresponding to joint A could be drawn as shown in Fig. 6.9. The triangle actually shown in Fig. 6.8 was obtained by drawing the three forces $\mathbf{R}_A$, $\mathbf{F}_{AC}$, and $\mathbf{F}_{AD}$ in tip-to-tail fashion in the order in which their lines of action are encountered when moving clockwise around joint A. The other force polygons in Fig. 6.8, having been drawn in the same way, can be made to fit into a single diagram, as shown in Fig. 6.10. Such a diagram, known as *Maxwell's diagram*, greatly facilitates the *graphical analysis* of truss problems.

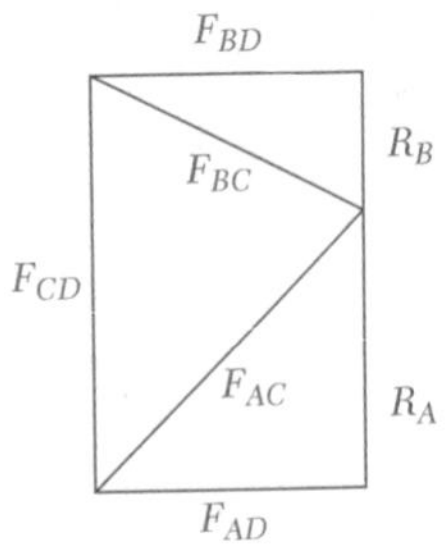

Fig. 6.9

Fig. 6.10

*6.5 JOINTS UNDER SPECIAL LOADING CONDITIONS

Consider Fig. 6.11*a*, in which the joint shown connects four members lying in two intersecting straight lines. The free-body diagram of Fig. 6.11*b* shows that pin A is subjected to two pairs of directly opposite forces. The corresponding force polygon, therefore, must be a parallelogram (Fig. 6.11*c*), and *the forces in opposite members must be equal.*

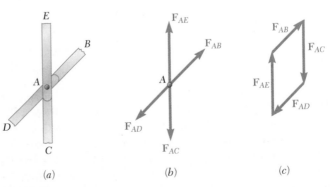

(a)   (b)   (c)

Fig. 6.11

Consider next Fig. 6.12*a*, in which the joint shown connects three members and supports a load **P**. Two of the members lie in the same line, and the load **P** acts along the third member. The free-body diagram of pin *A* and the corresponding force polygon will be as shown in Fig. 6.11*b* and *c*, with $\mathbf{F}_{AE}$ replaced by the load **P**. Thus, *the forces in the two opposite members must be equal, and the force in the other member must equal P.* A particular case of special interest is shown in Fig. 6.12*b*. Since, in this case, no external load is applied to the joint, we have $P = 0$, and the force in member *AC* is zero. Member *AC* is said to be a *zero-force member*.

Consider now a joint connecting two members only. From Sec. 2.9, we know that a particle which is acted upon by two forces will be in equilibrium if the two forces have the same magnitude, same line of action, and opposite sense. In the case of the joint of Fig. 6.13*a*, which connects two members *AB* and *AD* lying in the same line, *the forces in the two members must be equal* for pin *A* to be in equilibrium. In the case of the joint of Fig. 6.13*b*, pin *A* cannot be in equilibrium unless the forces in both members are zero. Members connected as shown in Fig. 6.13*b*, therefore, must be *zero-force members*.

Spotting the joints which are under the special loading conditions listed above will expedite the analysis of a truss. Consider, for example, a Howe truss loaded as shown in Fig. 6.14. All of the members represented by green lines will be recognized as zero-force members. Joint *C* connects three members, two of which lie in the same line, and is not subjected to any external load; member *BC* is thus a zero-force member. Applying the same reasoning to joint *K*, we find that member *JK* is also a zero-force member. But joint *J* is now in the same situation as joints *C* and *K*, and member *IJ* must be a zero-force member. The examination of joints *C*, *J*, and *K* also shows that the forces in members *AC* and *CE* are equal, that the forces in members *HJ* and *JL* are equal, and that the forces in members *IK* and *KL* are equal. Turning our attention to joint *I*, where the 20-kN load and member *HI* are collinear, we note that the force in member *HI* is 20 kN (tension) and that the forces in members *GI* and *IK* are equal. Hence, the forces in members *GI*, *IK*, and *KL* are equal.

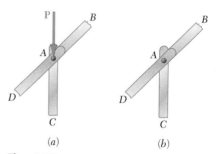

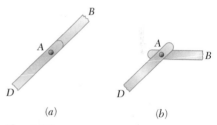

Fig. 6.12

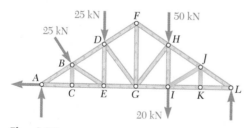

Fig. 6.14

Note that the conditions described above do not apply to joints *B* and *D* in Fig. 6.14, and it would be wrong to assume that the force in member *DE* is 25 kN or that the forces in members *AB* and *BD* are equal. The forces in these members and in all remaining members should be found by carrying out the analysis of joints *A*, *B*, *D*, *E*, *F*, *G*, *H*, and *L* in the usual manner. Thus, until you have become thoroughly familiar with the conditions under which the rules established in this

Fig. 6.13

Photo 6.4 Three-dimensional or space trusses are used for broadcast and power transmission line towers, roof framing, and spacecraft applications, such as components of the *International Space Station*.

section can be applied, you should draw the free-body diagrams of all pins and write the corresponding equilibrium equations (or draw the corresponding force polygons) whether or not the joints being considered are under one of the special loading conditions described above.

A final remark concerning zero-force members: These members are not useless. For example, although the zero-force members of Fig. 6.14 do not carry any loads under the loading conditions shown, the same members would probably carry loads if the loading conditions were changed. Besides, even in the case considered, these members are needed to support the weight of the truss and to maintain the truss in the desired shape.

*6.6 SPACE TRUSSES

When several straight members are joined together at their extremities to form a three-dimensional configuration, the structure obtained is called a *space truss*.

We recall from Sec. 6.3 that the most elementary two-dimensional rigid truss consisted of three members joined at their extremities to form the sides of a triangle; by adding two members at a time to this basic configuration, and connecting them at a new joint, it was possible to obtain a larger rigid structure which was defined as a simple truss. Similarly, the most elementary rigid space truss consists of six members joined at their extremities to form the edges of a tetrahedron *ABCD* (Fig. 6.15*a*). By adding three members at a time to this basic configuration, such as *AE*, *BE*, and *CE*, attaching them to three existing joints, and connecting them at a new joint,† we can obtain a larger rigid structure which is defined as a *simple space truss* (Fig. 6.15*b*). Observing that the basic tetrahedron has six members and four joints and that every time three members are added, the number of joints is increased by one, we conclude that in a simple space truss the total number of members is $m = 3n - 6$, where n is the total number of joints.

If a space truss is to be completely constrained and if the reactions at its supports are to be statically determinate, the supports should consist of a combination of balls, rollers, and balls and sockets which provides six unknown reactions (see Sec. 4.9). These unknown reactions may be readily determined by solving the six equations expressing that the three-dimensional truss is in equilibrium.

Although the members of a space truss are actually joined together by means of bolted or welded connections, it is assumed that each joint consists of a ball-and-socket connection. Thus, no couple will be applied to the members of the truss, and each member can be treated as a two-force member. The conditions of equilibrium for each joint will be expressed by the three equations $\Sigma F_x = 0$, $\Sigma F_y = 0$, and $\Sigma F_z = 0$. In the case of a simple space truss containing n joints, writing the conditions of equilibrium for each joint will thus yield $3n$ equations. Since $m = 3n - 6$, these equations suffice to determine all unknown forces (forces in m members and six reactions at the supports). However, to avoid the necessity of solving simultaneous equations, care should be taken to select joints in such an order that no selected joint will involve more than three unknown forces.

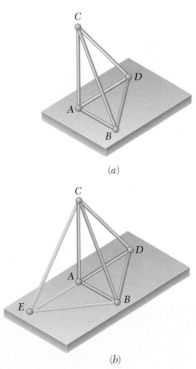

(a)

(b)

Fig. 6.15

---

†The four joints must not lie in a plane.

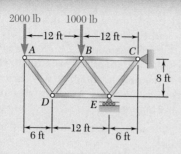

SAMPLE PROBLEM 6.1

Using the method of joints, determine the force in each member of the truss shown.

SOLUTION

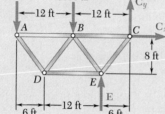

Free-Body: Entire Truss. A free-body diagram of the entire truss is drawn; external forces acting on this free body consist of the applied loads and the reactions at C and E. We write the following equilibrium equations.

$+\uparrow\Sigma M_C = 0$: $\quad$ (2000 lb)(24 ft) + (1000 lb)(12 ft) − E(6 ft) = 0

$\qquad\qquad\qquad E = +10,000$ lb $\qquad\qquad\qquad$ **E** = 10,000 lb↑

$\xrightarrow{+}\Sigma F_x = 0$: $\qquad\qquad\qquad\qquad\qquad\qquad\qquad\qquad$ **C**$_x$ = 0

$+\uparrow\Sigma F_y = 0$: $\quad$ −2000 lb − 1000 lb + 10,000 lb + C_y = 0

$\qquad\qquad\qquad C_y = -7000$ lb $\qquad\qquad\qquad$ **C**$_y$ = 7000 lb↓

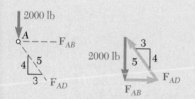

Free-Body: Joint A. This joint is subjected to only two unknown forces, namely, the forces exerted by members AB and AD. A force triangle is used to determine $\mathbf{F}_{AB}$ and $\mathbf{F}_{AD}$. We note that member AB pulls on the joint and thus is in tension and that member AD pushes on the joint and thus is in compression. The magnitudes of the two forces are obtained from the proportion

$$\frac{2000\ \text{lb}}{4} = \frac{F_{AB}}{3} = \frac{F_{AD}}{5}$$

$$F_{AB} = 1500\ \text{lb}\ T \quad \blacktriangleleft$$
$$F_{AD} = 2500\ \text{lb}\ C \quad \blacktriangleleft$$

Free-Body: Joint D. Since the force exerted by member AD has been determined, only two unknown forces are now involved at this joint. Again, a force triangle is used to determine the unknown forces in members DB and DE.

$$F_{DB} = F_{DA} \qquad\qquad F_{DB} = 2500\ \text{lb}\ T \quad \blacktriangleleft$$
$$F_{DE} = 2(\tfrac{3}{5})F_{DA} \qquad F_{DE} = 3000\ \text{lb}\ C \quad \blacktriangleleft$$

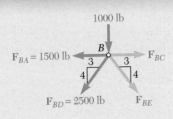

Free-Body: Joint B. Since more than three forces act at this joint, we determine the two unknown forces $\mathbf{F}_{BC}$ and $\mathbf{F}_{BE}$ by solving the equilibrium equations $\Sigma F_x = 0$ and $\Sigma F_y = 0$. We arbitrarily assume that both unknown forces act away from the joint, i.e., that the members are in tension. The positive value obtained for F_{BC} indicates that our assumption was correct; member BC is in tension. The negative value of F_{BE} indicates that our assumption was wrong; member BE is in compression.

$$+\uparrow\Sigma F_y = 0: \quad -1000 - \tfrac{4}{5}(2500) - \tfrac{4}{5}F_{BE} = 0$$
$$F_{BE} = -3750 \text{ lb} \qquad F_{BE} = 3750 \text{ lb } C \quad \blacktriangleleft$$

$$\xrightarrow{+}\Sigma F_x = 0: \quad F_{BC} - 1500 - \tfrac{3}{5}(2500) - \tfrac{3}{5}(3750) = 0$$
$$F_{BC} = +5250 \text{ lb} \qquad F_{BC} = 5250 \text{ lb } T \quad \blacktriangleleft$$

Free-Body: Joint E. The unknown force $\mathbf{F}_{EC}$ is assumed to act away from the joint. Summing x components, we write

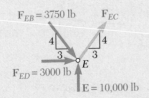

$$\xrightarrow{+}\Sigma F_x = 0: \quad \tfrac{3}{5}F_{EC} + 3000 + \tfrac{3}{5}(3750) = 0$$
$$F_{EC} = -8750 \text{ lb} \qquad F_{EC} = 8750 \text{ lb } C \quad \blacktriangleleft$$

Summing y components, we obtain a check of our computations:

$$+\uparrow\Sigma F_y = 10{,}000 - \tfrac{4}{5}(3750) - \tfrac{4}{5}(8750)$$
$$= 10{,}000 - 3000 - 7000 = 0 \qquad \text{(checks)}$$

Free-Body: Joint C. Using the computed values of $\mathbf{F}_{CB}$ and $\mathbf{F}_{CE}$, we can determine the reactions $\mathbf{C}_x$ and $\mathbf{C}_y$ by considering the equilibrium of this joint. Since these reactions have already been determined from the equilibrium of the entire truss, we will obtain two checks of our computations. We can also simply use the computed values of all forces acting on the joint (forces in members and reactions) and check that the joint is in equilibrium:

$$\xrightarrow{+}\Sigma F_x = -5250 + \tfrac{3}{5}(8750) = -5250 + 5250 = 0 \qquad \text{(checks)}$$
$$+\uparrow\Sigma F_y = -7000 + \tfrac{4}{5}(8750) = -7000 + 7000 = 0 \qquad \text{(checks)}$$

SOLVING PROBLEMS
ON YOUR OWN

In this lesson you learned to use the *method of joints* to determine the forces in the members of a *simple truss*, that is, a truss that can be constructed from a basic triangular truss by adding to it two new members at a time and connecting them at a new joint.

Your solution will consist of the following steps:

1. Draw a free-body diagram of the entire truss, and use this diagram to determine the reactions at the supports.

2. Locate a joint connecting only two members, and draw the free-body diagram of its pin. Use this free-body diagram to determine the unknown force in each of the two members. If only three forces are involved (the two unknown forces and a known one), you will probably find it more convenient to draw and solve the corresponding force triangle. If more than three forces are involved, you should write and solve the equilibrium equations for the pin, $\Sigma F_x = 0$ and $\Sigma F_y = 0$, assuming that the members are in tension. A positive answer means that the member is in tension, a negative answer that the member is in compression. Once the forces have been found, enter their values on a sketch of the truss, with T for tension and C for compression.

3. Next, locate a joint where the forces in only two of the connected members are still unknown. Draw the free-body diagram of the pin and use it as indicated above to determine the two unknown forces.

4. Repeat this procedure until the forces in all the members of the truss have been found. Since you previously used the three equilibrium equations associated with the free-body diagram of the entire truss to determine the reactions at the supports, you will end up with three extra equations. These equations can be used to check your computations.

5. Note that the choice of the first joint is not unique. Once you have determined the reactions at the supports of the truss, you can choose either of two joints as a starting point for your analysis. In Sample Prob. 6.1, we started at joint A and proceeded through joints D, B, E, and C, but we could also have started at joint C and proceeded through joints E, B, D, and A. On the other hand, having selected a first joint, you may in some cases reach a point in your analysis beyond which you cannot proceed. You must then start again from another joint to complete your solution.

Keep in mind that the analysis of a *simple truss* can always be carried out by the method of joints. Also remember that it is helpful to outline your solution *before* starting any computations.

PROBLEMS

6.1 through 6.8   Using the method of joints, determine the force in each member of the truss shown. State whether each member is in tension or compression.

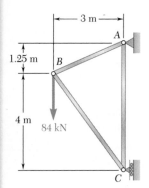

Fig. P6.1

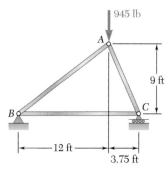

Fig. P6.2

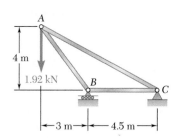

Fig. P6.3

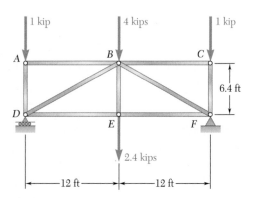

Fig. *P6.4*

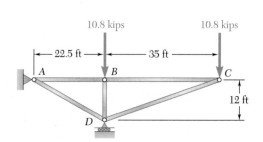

Fig. P6.5

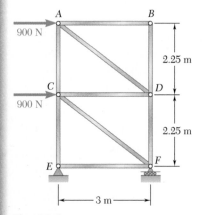

Fig. P6.6

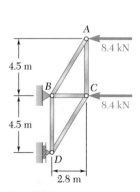

Fig. P6.7

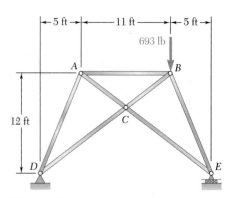

Fig. *P6.8*

6.9 Determine the force in each member of the Pratt roof truss shown. State whether each member is in tension or compression.

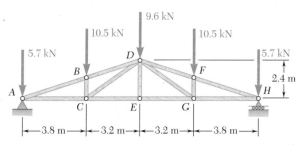

Fig. P6.9

6.10 Determine the force in each member of the fan roof truss shown. State whether each member is in tension or compression.

6.11 Determine the force in each member of the Howe roof truss shown. State whether each member is in tension or compression.

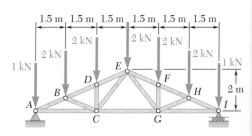

Fig. P6.10

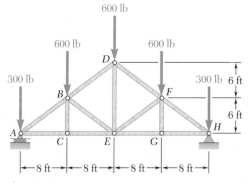

Fig. P6.11

6.12 Determine the force in each member of the Gambrel roof truss shown. State whether each member is in tension or compression.

6.13 Determine the force in each member of the truss shown.

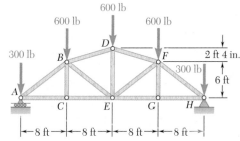

Fig. P6.12

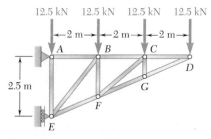

Fig. P6.13

6.14 Determine the force in each member of the roof truss shown. State whether each member is in tension or compression.

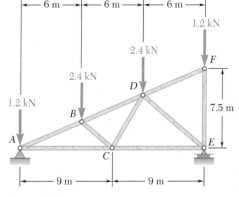

Fig. P6.14

6.15 Determine the force in each member of the Warren bridge truss shown. State whether each member is in tension or compression.

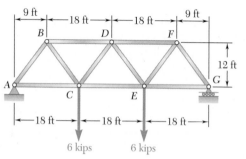

Fig. P6.15

6.16 Solve Prob. 6.15 assuming that the load applied at E has been removed.

6.17 Determine the force in member DE and in each of the members located to the left of DE for the inverted Howe roof truss shown. State whether each member is in tension or compression.

6.18 Determine the force in each of the members located to the right of DE for the inverted Howe roof truss shown. State whether each member is in tension or compression.

6.19 Determine the force in each of the members located to the left of FG for the scissors roof truss shown. State whether each member is in tension or compression.

6.20 Determine the force in member FG and in each of the members located to the right of FG for the scissors roof truss shown. State whether each member is in tension or compression.

6.21 Determine the force in each of the members located to the left of line FGH for the studio roof truss shown. State whether each member is in tension or compression.

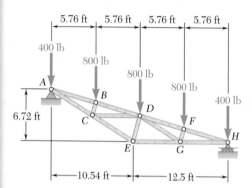

Fig. P6.17 and P6.18

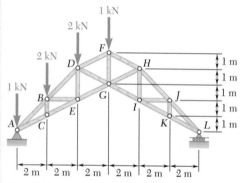

Fig. P6.19 and P6.20

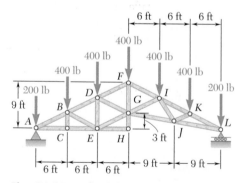

Fig. P6.21 and P6.22

6.22 Determine the force in member FG and in each of the members located to the right of FG for the studio roof truss shown. State whether each member is in tension or compression.

6.23 Determine the force in each of the members connecting joints A through F of the vaulted roof truss shown. State whether each member is in tension or compression.

6.24 The portion of truss shown represents the upper part of a power transmission line tower. For the given loading, determine the force in each of the members located above HJ. State whether each member is in tension or compression.

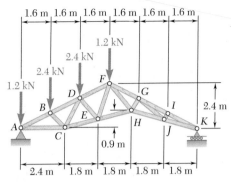

Fig. P6.23

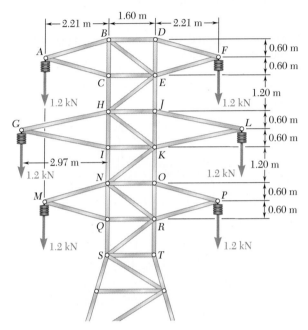

Fig. P6.24

6.25 For the tower and loading of Prob. 6.24 and knowing that $F_{CH} = F_{EJ} = 1.2$ kN C and $F_{EH} = 0$, determine the force in member HJ and in each of the members located between HJ and NO. State whether each member is in tension or compression.

6.26 Solve Prob. 6.24 assuming that the cables hanging from the right side of the tower have fallen to the ground.

6.27 Determine the force in each member of the truss shown. State whether each member is in tension or compression.

6.28 Determine the force in each member of the truss shown. State whether each member is in tension or compression.

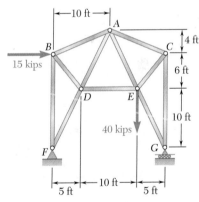

Fig. P6.27

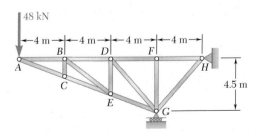

Fig. P6.28

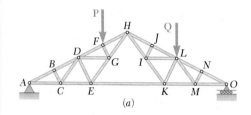

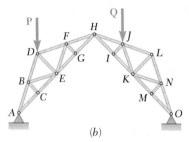

(a)

(b)

Fig. P6.31

6.29 Determine whether the trusses of Probs. 6.31*a*, 6.32*a*, and 6.33*a* are simple trusses.

6.30 Determine whether the trusses of Probs. 6.31*b*, 6.32*b*, and 6.33*b* are simple trusses.

6.31 For the given loading, determine the zero-force members in each of the two trusses shown.

6.32 For the given loading, determine the zero-force members in each of the two trusses shown.

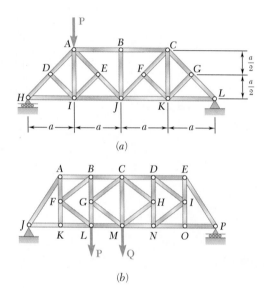

(a)

(b)

Fig. P6.32

6.33 For the given loading, determine the zero-force members in each of the two trusses shown.

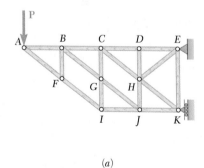

(a)

Fig. P6.33

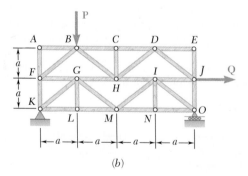

(b)

6.34 Determine the zero-force members in the truss of (*a*) Prob. 6.23, (*b*) Prob. 6.28.

*6.35 The truss shown consists of six members and is supported by a short link at A, two short links at B, and a ball and socket at D. Determine the force in each of the members for the given loading.

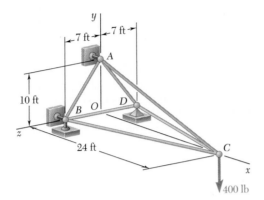

Fig. P6.35

*6.36 The truss shown consists of six members and is supported by a ball and socket at B, a short link at C, and two short links at D. Determine the force in each of the members for $\mathbf{P} = (-2184\ N)\mathbf{j}$ and $\mathbf{Q} = 0$.

*6.37 The truss shown consists of six members and is supported by a ball and socket at B, a short link at C, and two short links at D. Determine the force in each of the members for $\mathbf{P} = 0$ and $\mathbf{Q} = (2968\ N)\mathbf{i}$.

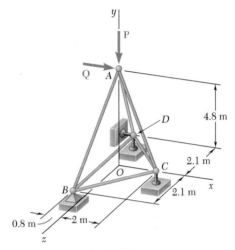

Fig. P6.36 and P6.37

*6.38 The truss shown consists of nine members and is supported by a ball and socket at A, two short links at B, and a short link at C. Determine the force in each of the members for the given loading.

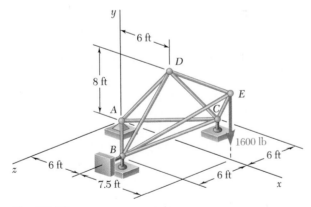

Fig. P6.38

*6.39 The truss shown consists of nine members and is supported by a ball and socket at B, a short link at C, and two short links at D. (a) Check that this truss is a simple truss, that it is completely constrained, and that the reactions at its supports are statically determinate. (b) Determine the force in each member for $\mathbf{P} = (-1200\ N)\mathbf{j}$ and $\mathbf{Q} = 0$.

*6.40 Solve Prob. 6.39 for $\mathbf{P} = 0$ and $\mathbf{Q} = (-900\ N)\mathbf{k}$.

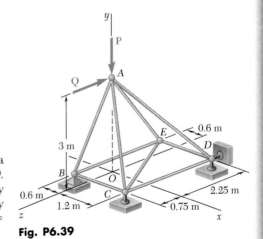

Fig. P6.39

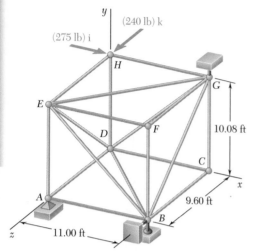

(240 lb) k

(275 lb) i

y

H

G

E

D

F

10.08 ft

C

x

A

9.60 ft

B

z

11.00 ft

Fig. P6.41 and P6.42

*6.41 The truss shown consists of 18 members and is supported by a ball and socket at A, two short links at B, and one short link at G. (a) Check that this truss is a simple truss, that it is completely constrained, and that the reactions at its supports are statically determinate. (b) For the given loading, determine the force in each of the six members joined at E.

*6.42 The truss shown consists of 18 members and is supported by a ball and socket at A, two short links at B, and one short link at G. (a) Check that this truss is a simple truss, that it is completely constrained, and that the reactions at its supports are statically determinate. (b) For the given loading, determine the force in each of the six members joined at G.

6.7 ANALYSIS OF TRUSSES BY THE METHOD OF SECTIONS

The method of joints is most effective when the forces in all the members of a truss are to be determined. If, however, the force in only one member or the forces in a very few members are desired, another method, the method of sections, is more efficient.

Assume, for example, that we want to determine the force in member BD of the truss shown in Fig. 6.16a. To do this, we must determine the force with which member BD acts on either joint B or joint D. If we were to use the method of joints, we would choose either joint B or joint D as a free body. However, we can also choose as a free body a larger portion of the truss, composed of several joints and members, provided that the desired force is one of the external forces acting on that portion. If, in addition, the portion of the truss is chosen so that there is a total of only three unknown forces acting upon it, the desired force can be obtained by solving the equations of equilibrium for this portion of the truss. In practice, the portion of the truss to be utilized is obtained by *passing a section* through three members of the truss, one of which is the desired member, i.e., by drawing a line which divides the truss into two completely separate parts but does not intersect more than three members. Either of the two portions of the truss obtained after the intersected members have been removed can then be used as a free body.†

In Fig. 6.16a, the section nn has been passed through members BD, BE, and CE, and the portion ABC of the truss is chosen as the free body (Fig. 6.16b). The forces acting on the free body are the loads $\mathbf{P}_1$ and $\mathbf{P}_2$ at points A and B and the three unknown forces $\mathbf{F}_{BD}$, $\mathbf{F}_{BE}$, and $\mathbf{F}_{CE}$. Since it is not known whether the members removed were in tension or compression, the three forces have been arbitrarily drawn away from the free body as if the members were in tension.

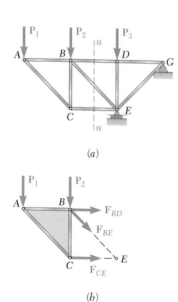

P_1 P_2 P_3

A $\quad$ B $\quad$ D $\quad$ G

C $\quad$ E

n

n

(a)

P_1 P_2

A $\quad$ B

F_{BD}

F_{BE}

C $\quad$ F_{CE} $\quad$ E

(b)

Fig. 6.16

†In the analysis of certain trusses, sections are passed which intersect more than three members; the forces in one, or possibly two, of the intersected members may be obtained if equilibrium equations can be found, each of which involves only one unknown (see Probs. 6.61 through 6.64).

The fact that the rigid body *ABC* is in equilibrium can be expressed by writing three equations which can be solved for the three unknown forces. If only the force $\mathbf{F}_{BD}$ is desired, we need write only one equation, provided that the equation does not contain the other unknowns. Thus the equation $\Sigma M_E = 0$ yields the value of the magnitude F_{BD} of the force $\mathbf{F}_{BD}$ (Fig. 6.16*b*). A positive sign in the answer will indicate that our original assumption regarding the sense of $\mathbf{F}_{BD}$ was correct and that member *BD* is in tension; a negative sign will indicate that our assumption was incorrect and that *BD* is in compression.

On the other hand, if only the force $\mathbf{F}_{CE}$ is desired, an equation which does not involve $\mathbf{F}_{BD}$ or $\mathbf{F}_{BE}$ should be written; the appropriate equation is $\Sigma M_B = 0$. Again a positive sign for the magnitude F_{CE} of the desired force indicates a correct assumption, that is, tension; and a negative sign indicates an incorrect assumption, that is, compression.

If only the force $\mathbf{F}_{BE}$ is desired, the appropriate equation is $\Sigma F_y = 0$. Whether the member is in tension or compression is again determined from the sign of the answer.

When the force in only one member is determined, no independent check of the computation is available. However, when all the unknown forces acting on the free body are determined, the computations can be checked by writing an additional equation. For instance, if $\mathbf{F}_{BD}$, $\mathbf{F}_{BE}$, and $\mathbf{F}_{CE}$ are determined as indicated above, the computation can be checked by verifying that $\Sigma F_x = 0$.

*6.8 TRUSSES MADE OF SEVERAL SIMPLE TRUSSES

Consider two simple trusses *ABC* and *DEF*. If they are connected by three bars *BD*, *BE*, and *CE* as shown in Fig. 6.17*a*, they will form together a rigid truss *ABDF*. The trusses *ABC* and *DEF* can also be combined into a single rigid truss by joining joints *B* and *D* into a single joint *B* and by connecting joints *C* and *E* by a bar *CE* (Fig. 6.17*b*). The truss thus obtained is known as a *Fink truss*. It should be noted that the trusses of Fig. 6.17*a* and *b* are *not* simple trusses; they cannot be constructed from a triangular truss by adding successive pairs of members as prescribed in Sec. 6.3. They are rigid trusses, however, as we can check by comparing the systems of connections used to hold the simple trusses *ABC* and *DEF* together (three bars in Fig. 6.17*a*, one pin and one bar in Fig. 6.17*b*) with the systems of supports discussed in Secs. 4.4 and 4.5. Trusses made of several simple trusses rigidly connected are known as *compound trusses*.

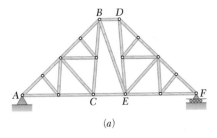

(a)

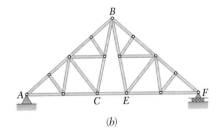

(b)

Fig. 6.17

In a compound truss the number of members m and the number of joints n are still related by the formula $m = 2n - 3$. This can be verified by observing that, if a compound truss is supported by a frictionless pin and a roller (involving three unknown reactions), the total number of unknowns is $m + 3$, and this number must be equal to the number $2n$ of equations obtained by expressing that the n pins are in equilibrium; it follows that $m = 2n - 3$. Compound trusses supported by a pin and a roller, or by an equivalent system of supports, are *statically determinate, rigid,* and *completely constrained.* This means that all of the unknown reactions and the forces in all the members can be determined by the methods of statics, and that the truss will neither collapse nor move. The forces in the members, however, cannot all be determined by the method of joints, except by solving a large number of simultaneous equations. In the case of the compound truss of Fig. 6.17a, for example, it is more efficient to pass a section through members BD, BE, and CE to determine the forces in these members.

Suppose, now, that the simple trusses ABC and DEF are connected by *four* bars BD, BE, CD, or CE (Fig. 6.18). The number of members m is now larger than $2n - 3$; the truss obtained is *overrigid,* and one of the four members BD, BE, CD, or CE is said to be *redundant.* If the truss is supported by a pin at A and a roller at F, the total number of unknowns is $m + 3$. Since $m > 2n - 3$, the number $m + 3$ of unknowns is now larger than the number $2n$ of available independent equations; the truss is *statically indeterminate.*

Finally, let us assume that the two simple trusses ABC and DEF are joined by a pin as shown in Fig. 6.19a. The number of members m is smaller than $2n - 3$. If the truss is supported by a pin at A and a roller at F, the total number of unknowns is $m + 3$. Since $m < 2n - 3$, the number $m + 3$ of unknowns is now smaller than the number $2n$ of equilibrium equations which should be satisfied; the truss is *non-rigid* and will collapse under its own weight. However, if two pins are used to support it, the truss becomes *rigid* and will not collapse (Fig. 6.19b). We note that the total number of unknowns is now $m + 4$ and is equal to the number $2n$ of equations. More generally, if the reactions at the supports involve r unknowns, the condition for a compound truss to be statically determinate, rigid, and completely constrained is $m + r = 2n$. However, while necessary this condition is not sufficient for the equilibrium of a structure which ceases to be rigid when detached from its supports (see Sec. 6.11).

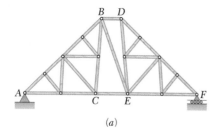

Fig. 6.17   (repeated)

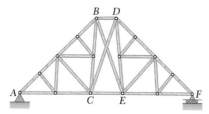

Fig. 6.18

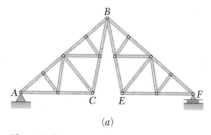

(a)

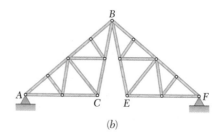

(b)

Fig. 6.19

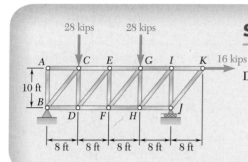

SAMPLE PROBLEM 6.2

Determine the force in members EF and GI of the truss shown.

SOLUTION

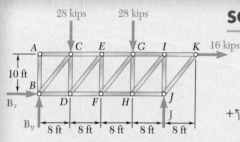

Free-Body: Entire Truss. A free-body diagram of the entire truss is drawn; external forces acting on this free body consist of the applied loads and the reactions at B and J. We write the following equilibrium equations.

$+\gamma\Sigma M_B = 0:$

$-(28 \text{ kips})(8 \text{ ft}) - (28 \text{ kips})(24 \text{ ft}) - (16 \text{ kips})(10 \text{ ft}) + J(32 \text{ ft}) = 0$

$J = +33 \text{ kips} \qquad \mathbf{J} = 33 \text{ kips}\uparrow$

$\xrightarrow{+}\Sigma F_x = 0: \qquad B_x + 16 \text{ kips} = 0$

$B_x = -16 \text{ kips} \qquad \mathbf{B}_x = 16 \text{ kips}\leftarrow$

$+\gamma\Sigma M_J = 0:$

$(28 \text{ kips})(24 \text{ ft}) + (28 \text{ kips})(8 \text{ ft}) - (16 \text{ kips})(10 \text{ ft}) - B_y(32 \text{ ft}) = 0$

$B_y = +23 \text{ kips} \qquad \mathbf{B}_y = 23 \text{ kips}\uparrow$

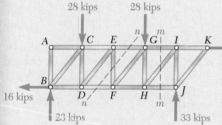

Force in Member EF. Section nn is passed through the truss so that it intersects member EF and only two additional members. After the intersected members have been removed, the left-hand portion of the truss is chosen as a free body. Three unknowns are involved; to eliminate the two horizontal forces, we write

$+\uparrow\Sigma F_y = 0: \qquad +23 \text{ kips} - 28 \text{ kips} - F_{EF} = 0$

$F_{EF} = -5 \text{ kips}$

The sense of $\mathbf{F}_{EF}$ was chosen assuming member EF to be in tension; the negative sign obtained indicates that the member is in compression.

$$F_{EF} = 5 \text{ kips } C \quad \blacktriangleleft$$

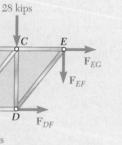

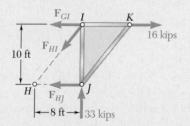

Force in Member GI. Section mm is passed through the truss so that it intersects member GI and only two additional members. After the intersected members have been removed, we choose the right-hand portion of the truss as a free body. Three unknown forces are again involved; to eliminate the two forces passing through point H, we write

$+\gamma\Sigma M_H = 0: \qquad (33 \text{ kips})(8 \text{ ft}) - (16 \text{ kips})(10 \text{ ft}) + F_{GI}(10 \text{ ft}) = 0$

$F_{GI} = -10.4 \text{ kips} \qquad F_{GI} = 10.4 \text{ kips } C \quad \blacktriangleleft$

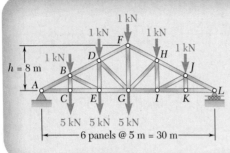

1 kN
1 kN
1 kN
F
1 kN
D
H
1 kN
h = 8 m
B
J
A
C E G I K L
5 kN 5 kN 5 kN
6 panels @ 5 m = 30 m

SAMPLE PROBLEM 6.3

Determine the force in members FH, GH, and GI of the roof truss shown.

SOLUTION

Free Body: Entire Truss. From the free-body diagram of the entire truss, we find the reactions at A and L:

$$\mathbf{A} = 12.50 \text{ kN} \uparrow \qquad \mathbf{L} = 7.50 \text{ kN} \uparrow$$

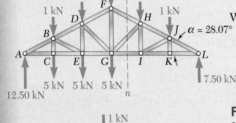

We note that

$$\tan \alpha = \frac{FG}{GL} = \frac{8 \text{ m}}{15 \text{ m}} = 0.5333 \qquad \alpha = 28.07°$$

Force in Member GI. Section nn is passed through the truss as shown. Using the portion HLI of the truss as a free body, the value of F_{GI} is obtained by writing

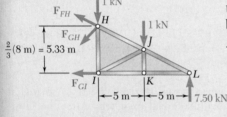

$$+\circlearrowright\Sigma M_H = 0: \qquad (7.50 \text{ kN})(10 \text{ m}) - (1 \text{ kN})(5 \text{ m}) - F_{GI}(5.33 \text{ m}) = 0$$
$$F_{GI} = +13.13 \text{ kN} \qquad F_{GI} = 13.13 \text{ kN } T \quad \blacktriangleleft$$

Force in Member FH. The value of F_{FH} is obtained from the equation $\Sigma M_G = 0$. We move $\mathbf{F}_{FH}$ along its line of action until it acts at point F, where it is resolved into its x and y components. The moment of $\mathbf{F}_{FH}$ with respect to point G is now equal to $(F_{FH} \cos \alpha)(8 \text{ m})$.

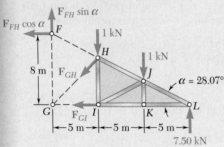

$$+\circlearrowright\Sigma M_G = 0:$$
$$(7.50 \text{ kN})(15 \text{ m}) - (1 \text{ kN})(10 \text{ m}) - (1 \text{ kN})(5 \text{ m}) + (F_{FH} \cos \alpha)(8 \text{ m}) = 0$$
$$F_{FH} = -13.81 \text{ kN} \qquad F_{FH} = 13.81 \text{ kN } C \quad \blacktriangleleft$$

Force in Member GH. We first note that

$$\tan \beta = \frac{GI}{HI} = \frac{5 \text{ m}}{\frac{2}{3}(8 \text{ m})} = 0.9375 \qquad \beta = 43.15°$$

The value of F_{GH} is then determined by resolving the force $\mathbf{F}_{GH}$ into x and y components at point G and solving the equation $\Sigma M_L = 0$.

$$+\circlearrowright\Sigma M_L = 0: \qquad (1 \text{ kN})(10 \text{ m}) + (1 \text{ kN})(5 \text{ m}) + (F_{GH} \cos \beta)(15 \text{ m}) = 0$$
$$F_{GH} = -1.371 \text{ kN} \qquad F_{GH} = 1.371 \text{ kN } C \quad \blacktriangleleft$$

SOLVING PROBLEMS ON YOUR OWN

The *method of joints* that you studied earlier is usually the best method to use when the forces *in all the members* of a simple truss are to be found. However, the method of sections, which was covered in this lesson, is more effective when the force *in only one member* or the forces *in a very few members* of a simple truss are desired. The method of sections must also be used when the truss *is not a simple truss.*

A. To determine the force in a given truss member by the method of sections, you should follow these steps:

1. Draw a free-body diagram of the entire truss, and use this diagram to determine the reactions at the supports.

2. Pass a section through three members of the truss, one of which is the desired member. After you have removed these members, you will obtain two separate portions of truss.

3. Select one of the two portions of truss you have obtained, and draw its free-body diagram. This diagram should include the external forces applied to the selected portion as well as the forces exerted on it by the intersected members before these members were removed.

4. You can now write three equilibrium equations which can be solved for the forces in the three intersected members.

5. An alternative approach is to write a single equation, which can be solved for the force in the desired member. To do so, first observe whether the forces exerted by the other two members on the free body are parallel or whether their lines of action intersect.

   a. If these forces are parallel, they can be eliminated by writing an equilibrium equation involving *components in a direction perpendicular* to these two forces.

   b. If their lines of action intersect at a point H, they can be eliminated by writing an equilibrium equation involving *moments about H.*

6. Keep in mind that the section you use must intersect three members only. This is because the equilibrium equations in step 4 can be solved for three unknowns only. However, you can pass a section through more than three members to find the force in one of those members if you can write an equilibrium equation containing only that force as an unknown. Such special situations are found in Probs. 6.61 through 6.64.

(continued)

B. About completely constrained and determinate trusses:

1. First note that any simple truss which is simply supported is a completely constrained and determinate truss.

2. To determine whether any other truss is or is not completely constrained and determinate, you first count the number m of its members, the number n of its joints, and the number r of the reaction components at its supports. You then compare the sum $m + r$ representing the number of unknowns and the product $2n$ representing the number of available independent equilibrium equations.

    a. If $m + r < 2n$, there are fewer unknowns than equations. Thus, some of the equations cannot be satisfied; the truss is only *partially constrained.*

    b. If $m + r > 2n$, there are more unknowns than equations. Thus, some of the unknowns cannot be determined; the truss is *indeterminate.*

    c. If $m + r = 2n$, there are as many unknowns as there are equations. This, however, does not mean that all the unknowns can be determined and that all the equations can be satisfied. To find out whether the truss is *completely* or *improperly constrained,* you should try to determine the reactions at its supports and the forces in its members. If all can be found, the truss is *completely constrained and determinate.*

PROBLEMS

6.43 A Warren bridge truss is loaded as shown. Determine the force in members *CE*, *DE*, and *DF*.

6.44 A Warren bridge truss is loaded as shown. Determine the force in members *EG*, *FG*, and *FH*.

6.45 Determine the force in members *BD* and *DE* of the truss shown.

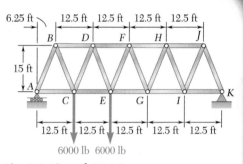

Fig. P6.43 and P6.44

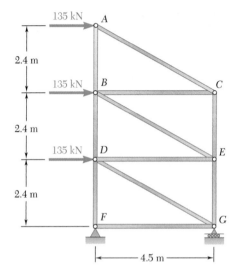

Fig. P6.45 and P6.46

6.46 Determine the force in members *DG* and *EG* of the truss shown.

6.47 A floor truss is loaded as shown. Determine the force in members *CF*, *EF*, and *EG*.

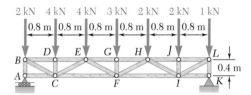

Fig. P6.47 and P6.48

6.48 A floor truss is loaded as shown. Determine the force in members *FI*, *HI*, and *HJ*.

6.49 A pitched flat roof truss is loaded as shown. Determine the force in members *CE*, *DE*, and *DF*.

6.50 A pitched flat roof truss is loaded as shown. Determine the force in members *EG*, *GH*, and *HJ*.

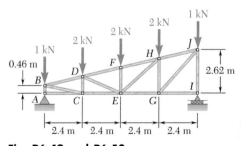

Fig. P6.49 and P6.50

6.51 A Howe scissors roof truss is loaded as shown. Determine the force in members *DF*, *DG*, and *EG*.

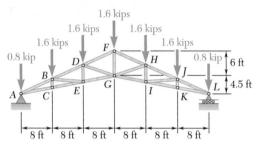

Fig. P6.51 and P6.52

6.52 A Howe scissors roof truss is loaded as shown. Determine the force in members *GI*, *HI*, and *HJ*.

6.53 A Pratt roof truss is loaded as shown. Determine the force in members *CE*, *DE*, and *DF*.

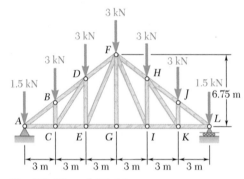

Fig. P6.53 and P6.54

6.54 A Pratt roof truss is loaded as shown. Determine the force in members *FH*, *FI*, and *GI*.

6.55 Determine the force in members *AD*, *CD*, and *CE* of the truss shown.

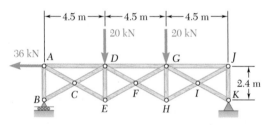

Fig. P6.55 and P6.56

6.56 Determine the force in members *DG*, *FG*, and *FH* of the truss shown.

6.57 A stadium roof truss is loaded as shown. Determine the force in members *AB*, *AG*, and *FG*.

6.58 A stadium roof truss is loaded as shown. Determine the force in members *AE*, *EF*, and *FJ*.

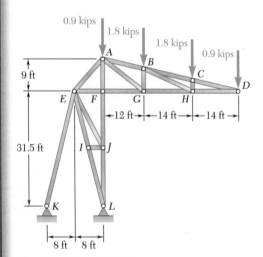

Fig. P6.57 and P6.58

6.59 A Polynesian, or duopitch, roof truss is loaded as shown. Determine the force in members *DF*, *EF*, and *EG*.

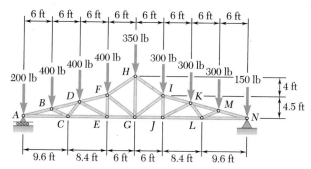

Fig. P6.59 and P6.60

6.60 A Polynesian, or duopitch, roof truss is loaded as shown. Determine the force in members *HI*, *GI*, and *GJ*.

6.61 Determine the force in members *AF* and *EJ* of the truss shown when *P* = *Q* = 1.2 kN. (*Hint:* Use section *aa*.)

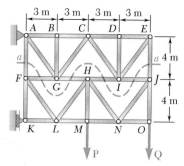

Fig. P6.61 and P6.62

6.62 Determine the force in members *AF* and *EJ* of the truss shown when *P* = 1.2 kN and *Q* = 0. (*Hint:* Use section *aa*.)

6.63 Determine the force in members *EH* and *GI* of the truss shown. (*Hint:* Use section *aa*.)

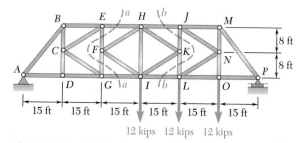

Fig. P6.63 and P6.64

6.64 Determine the force in members *HJ* and *IL* of the truss shown. (*Hint:* Use section *bb*.)

6.65 and 6.66 The diagonal members in the center panels of the power transmission line tower shown are very slender and can act only in tension; such members are known as *counters*. For the given loading, determine (*a*) which of the two counters listed below is acting, (*b*) the force in that counter.

6.65 Counters *CJ* and *HE*.

6.66 Counters *IO* and *KN*.

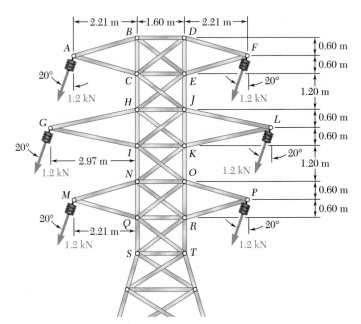

Fig. P6.65 and P6.66

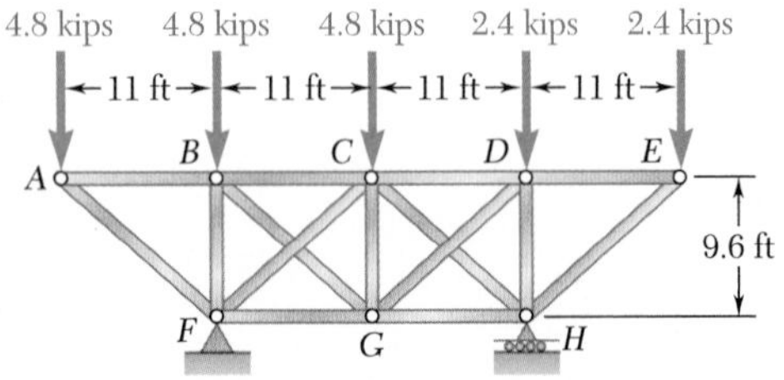

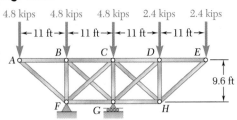

Fig. P6.67

Fig. P6.68

6.67 and 6.68 The diagonal members in the center panels of the truss shown are very slender and can act only in tension; such members are known as *counters*. Determine the forces in the counters that are acting under the given loading.

6.69 Classify each of the structures shown as completely, partially, or improperly constrained; if completely constrained, further classify as determinate or indeterminate. (All members can act both in tension and in compression.)

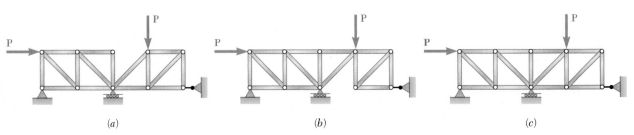

(*a*)   (*b*)   (*c*)

Fig. P6.69

6.70 through 6.74 Classify each of the structures shown as completely, partially, or improperly constrained; if completely constrained, further classify as determinate or indeterminate. (All members can act both in tension and in compression.)

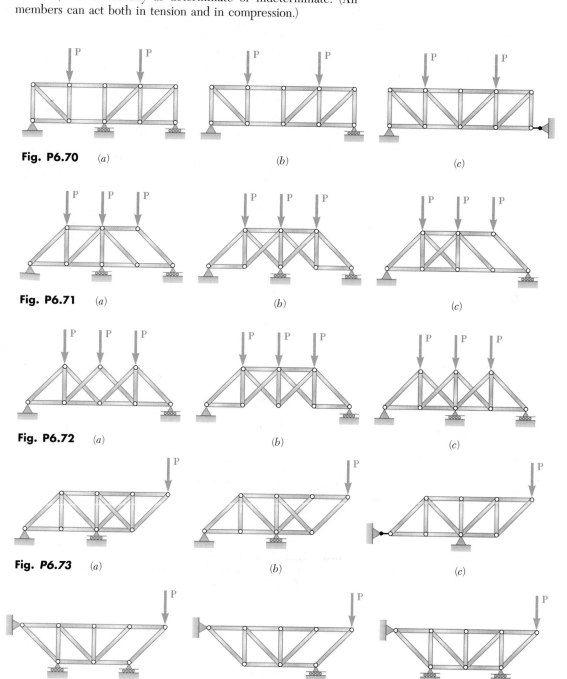

Fig. P6.70   (*a*)   (*b*)   (*c*)

Fig. P6.71   (*a*)   (*b*)   (*c*)

Fig. P6.72   (*a*)   (*b*)   (*c*)

Fig. P6.73   (*a*)   (*b*)   (*c*)

Fig. P6.74   (*a*)   (*b*)   (*c*)

6.9 STRUCTURES CONTAINING MULTIFORCE MEMBERS

Under trusses, we have considered structures consisting entirely of pins and straight two-force members. The forces acting on the two-force members were known to be directed along the members themselves. We now consider structures in which at least one of the members is a *multiforce* member, i.e., a member acted upon by three or more forces. These forces will generally not be directed along the members on which they act; their direction is unknown, and they should be represented therefore by two unknown components.

Frames and machines are structures containing multiforce members. *Frames* are designed to support loads and are usually stationary, fully constrained structures. *Machines* are designed to transmit and modify forces; they may or may not be stationary and will always contain moving parts.

6.10 ANALYSIS OF A FRAME

As a first example of analysis of a frame, the crane described in Sec. 6.1, which carries a given load W (Fig. 6.20a), will again be considered. The free-body diagram of the entire frame is shown in Fig. 6.20b. This diagram can be used to determine the external forces acting on the frame. Summing moments about A, we first determine the force **T** exerted by the cable; summing x and y components, we then determine the components $\mathbf{A}_x$ and $\mathbf{A}_y$ of the reaction at the pin A.

In order to determine the internal forces holding the various parts of a frame together, we must dismember the frame and draw a free-body diagram for each of its component parts (Fig. 6.20c). First, the two-force members should be considered. In this frame, member BE is the only two-force member. The forces acting at each end of this member must have the same magnitude, same line of action, and opposite sense (Sec. 4.6). They are therefore directed along BE and will be denoted, respectively, by $\mathbf{F}_{BE}$ and $-\mathbf{F}_{BE}$. Their sense will be arbitrarily assumed as shown in Fig. 6.20c; later the sign obtained for the common magnitude F_{BE} of the two forces will confirm or deny this assumption.

Next, we consider the multiforce members, i.e., the members which are acted upon by three or more forces. According to Newton's third law, the force exerted at B by member BE on member AD must be equal and opposite to the force $\mathbf{F}_{BE}$ exerted by AD on BE. Similarly, the force exerted at E by member BE on member CF must be equal and opposite to the force $-\mathbf{F}_{BE}$ exerted by CF on BE. Thus the forces that the two-force member BE exerts on AD and CF are, respectively, equal to $-\mathbf{F}_{BE}$ and $\mathbf{F}_{BE}$; they have the same magnitude F_{BE} and opposite sense, and should be directed as shown in Fig. 6.20c.

At C two multiforce members are connected. Since neither the direction nor the magnitude of the forces acting at C is known, these forces will be represented by their x and y components. The components $\mathbf{C}_x$ and $\mathbf{C}_y$ of the force acting on member AD will be

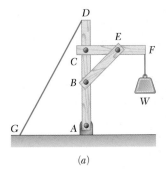

(a)

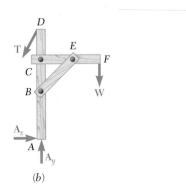

(b)

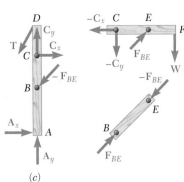

(c)

Fig. 6.20

arbitrarily directed to the right and upward. Since, according to Newton's third law, the forces exerted by member CF on AD and by member AD on CF are equal and opposite, the components of the force acting on member CF *must* be directed to the left and downward; they will be denoted, respectively, by $-\mathbf{C}_x$ and $-\mathbf{C}_y$. Whether the force $\mathbf{C}_x$ is actually directed to the right and the force $-\mathbf{C}_x$ is actually directed to the left will be determined later from the sign of their common magnitude C_x, a plus sign indicating that the assumption made was correct, and a minus sign that it was wrong. The free-body diagrams of the multiforce members are completed by showing the external forces acting at A, D, and F.†

The internal forces can now be determined by considering the free-body diagram of either of the two multiforce members. Choosing the free-body diagram of CF, for example, we write the equations $\Sigma M_C = 0$, $\Sigma M_E = 0$, and $\Sigma F_x = 0$, which yield the values of the magnitudes F_{BE}, C_y, and C_x, respectively. These values can be checked by verifying that member AD is also in equilibrium.

It should be noted that the pins in Fig. 6.20 were assumed to form an integral part of one of the two members they connected and so it was not necessary to show their free-body diagram. This assumption can always be used to simplify the analysis of frames and machines. When a pin connects three or more members, however, or when a pin connects a support and two or more members, or when a load is applied to a pin, a clear decision must be made in choosing the member to which the pin will be assumed to belong. (If multiforce members are involved, the pin should be attached to one of these members.) The various forces exerted on the pin should then be clearly identified. This is illustrated in Sample Prob. 6.6.

6.11 FRAMES WHICH CEASE TO BE RIGID WHEN DETACHED FROM THEIR SUPPORTS

The crane analyzed in Sec. 6.10 was so constructed that it could keep the same shape without the help of its supports; it was therefore considered as a rigid body. Many frames, however, will collapse if detached from their supports; such frames cannot be considered as rigid bodies. Consider, for example, the frame shown in Fig. 6.21*a*, which consists of two members AC and CB carrying loads $\mathbf{P}$ and $\mathbf{Q}$ at their midpoints; the members are supported by pins at A and B and are connected by a pin at C. If detached from its supports, this frame will not maintain its shape; it should therefore be considered as made of *two distinct rigid parts AC and CB.*

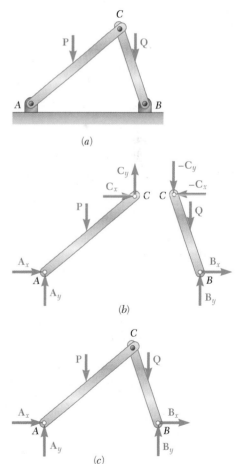

Fig. 6.21

---

†It is not strictly necessary to use a minus sign to distinguish the force exerted by one member on another from the equal and opposite force exerted by the second member on the first, since the two forces belong to different free-body diagrams and thus cannot easily be confused. In the Sample Problems, the same symbol is used to represent equal and opposite forces which are applied to different free bodies. It should be noted that, under these conditions, the sign obtained for a given force component will not directly relate the sense of that component to the sense of the corresponding coordinate axis. Rather, a positive sign will indicate that *the sense assumed for that component in the free-body diagram* is correct, and a negative sign will indicate that it is wrong.

The equations $\Sigma F_x = 0$, $\Sigma F_y = 0$, $\Sigma M = 0$ (about any given point) express the conditions for the *equilibrium of a rigid body* (Chap. 4); we should use them, therefore, in connection with the free-body diagrams of rigid bodies, namely, the free-body diagrams of members AC and CB (Fig. 6.21b). Since these members are multiforce members, and since pins are used at the supports and at the connection, the reactions at A and B and the forces at C will each be represented by two components. In accordance with Newton's third law, the components of the force exerted by CB on AC and the components of the force exerted by AC on CB will be represented by vectors of the same magnitude and opposite sense; thus, if the first pair of components consists of $\mathbf{C}_x$ and $\mathbf{C}_y$, the second pair will be represented by $-\mathbf{C}_x$ and $-\mathbf{C}_y$. We note that four unknown force components act on free body AC, while only three independent equations can be used to express that the body is in equilibrium; similarly, four unknowns, but only three equations, are associated with CB. However, only six different unknowns are involved in the analysis of the two members, and altogether six equations are available to express that the members are in equilibrium. Writing $\Sigma M_A = 0$ for free body AC and $\Sigma M_B = 0$ for CB, we obtain two simultaneous equations which may be solved for the common magnitude C_x of the components $\mathbf{C}_x$ and $-\mathbf{C}_x$, and for the common magnitude C_y of the components $\mathbf{C}_y$ and $-\mathbf{C}_y$. We then write $\Sigma F_x = 0$ and $\Sigma F_y = 0$ for each of the two free bodies, obtaining, successively, the magnitudes A_x, A_y, B_x, and B_y.

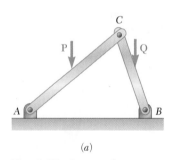

(a)

Fig. 6.21 (repeated)

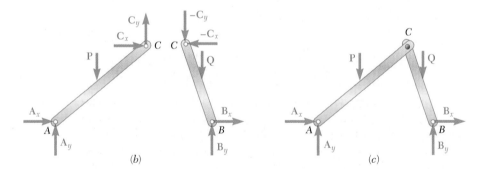

(b)

(c)

It can now be observed that since the equations of equilibrium $\Sigma F_x = 0$, $\Sigma F_y = 0$, and $\Sigma M = 0$ (about any given point) are satisfied by the forces acting on free body AC, and since they are also satisfied by the forces acting on free body CB, they must be satisfied when the forces acting on the two free bodies are considered simultaneously. Since the internal forces at C cancel each other, we find that the equations of equilibrium must be satisfied by the external forces shown on the free-body diagram of the frame ACB itself (Fig. 6.21c), although the frame is not a rigid body. These equations can be used to determine some of the components of the reactions at A and B. We will also find, however, that *the reactions cannot be completely determined from the free-body diagram of the whole frame*. It is thus necessary to

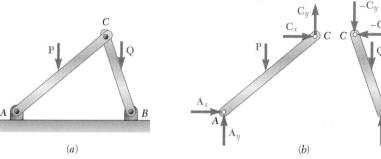
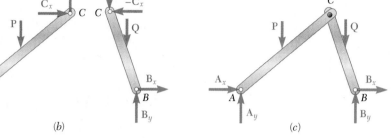

(a)   (b)   (c)

Fig. 6.21 *(repeated)*

dismember the frame and to consider the free-body diagrams of
its component parts (Fig. 6.21*b*), even when we are interested in
determining external reactions only. This is because the equilibrium
equations obtained for free body *ACB are necessary conditions* for
the equilibrium of a nonrigid structure, *but are not sufficient
conditions*.

The method of solution outlined in the second paragraph of
this section involved simultaneous equations. A more efficient method
is now presented, which utilizes the free body *ACB* as well as the
free bodies *AC* and *CB*. Writing $\Sigma M_A = 0$ and $\Sigma M_B = 0$ for free
body *ACB*, we obtain B_y and A_y. Writing $\Sigma M_C = 0$, $\Sigma F_x = 0$, and
$\Sigma F_y = 0$ for free body *AC*, we obtain, successively, A_x, C_x, and C_y.
Finally, writing $\Sigma F_x = 0$ for *ACB*, we obtain B_x.

We noted above that the analysis of the frame of Fig. 6.21
involves six unknown force components and six independent equilibrium equations. (The equilibrium equations for the whole frame
were obtained from the original six equations and, therefore, are not
independent.) Moreover, we checked that all unknowns could be
actually determined and that all equations could be satisfied. The
frame considered is *statically determinate and rigid*.† In general, to
determine whether a structure is statically determinate and rigid, we
should draw a free-body diagram for each of its component parts and
count the reactions and internal forces involved. We should also
determine the number of independent equilibrium equations (exclud-
ing equations expressing the equilibrium of the whole structure or
of groups of component parts already analyzed). If there are more
unknowns than equations, the structure is *statically indeterminate*.
If there are fewer unknowns than equations, the structure is *nonrigid*. If there are as many unknowns as equations, *and if all unknowns
can be determined and all equations satisfied* under general loading
conditions, the structure is *statically determinate and rigid*. If, however, due to an *improper arrangement* of members and supports, all
unknowns cannot be determined and all equations cannot be satisfied, the structure is *statically indeterminate and nonrigid*.

---

†The word "rigid" is used here to indicate that the frame will maintain its shape as long
as it remains attached to its supports.

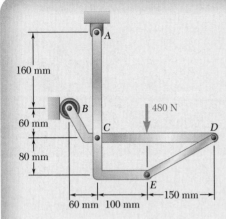

SAMPLE PROBLEM 6.4

In the frame shown, members *ACE* and *BCD* are connected by a pin at *C* and by the link *DE*. For the loading shown, determine the force in link *DE* and the components of the force exerted at *C* on member *BCD*.

SOLUTION

Free Body: Entire Frame. Since the external reactions involve only three unknowns, we compute the reactions by considering the free-body diagram of the entire frame.

$+\uparrow\Sigma F_y = 0$: $A_y - 480 \text{ N} = 0$ $A_y = +480 \text{ N}$ $\mathbf{A}_y = 480 \text{ N}\uparrow$

$+\gamma\Sigma M_A = 0$: $-(480 \text{ N})(100 \text{ mm}) + B(160 \text{ mm}) = 0$

$B = +300 \text{ N}$ $\mathbf{B} = 300 \text{ N}\rightarrow$

$\xrightarrow{+}\Sigma F_x = 0$: $B + A_x = 0$

$300 \text{ N} + A_x = 0$ $A_x = -300 \text{ N}$ $\mathbf{A}_x = 300 \text{ N}\leftarrow$

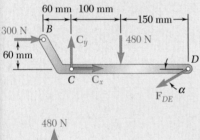

Members. We now dismember the frame. Since only two members are connected at *C*, the components of the unknown forces acting on *ACE* and *BCD* are, respectively, equal and opposite and are assumed directed as shown. We assume that link *DE* is in tension and exerts equal and opposite forces at *D* and *E*, directed as shown.

α = tan⁻¹ $\frac{80}{150}$ = 28.07°

Free Body: Member BCD. Using the free body *BCD*, we write

$+\gamma\Sigma M_C = 0$:

$(F_{DE} \sin \alpha)(250 \text{ mm}) + (300 \text{ N})(80 \text{ mm}) + (480 \text{ N})(100 \text{ mm}) = 0$

$F_{DE} = -561 \text{ N}$ $F_{DE} = 561 \text{ N } C$ ◀

$\xrightarrow{+}\Sigma F_x = 0$: $C_x - F_{DE} \cos \alpha + 300 \text{ N} = 0$

$C_x - (-561 \text{ N}) \cos 28.07° + 300 \text{ N} = 0$ $C_x = -795 \text{ N}$

$+\uparrow\Sigma F_y = 0$: $C_y - F_{DE} \sin \alpha - 480 \text{ N} = 0$

$C_y - (-561 \text{ N}) \sin 28.07° - 480 \text{ N} = 0$ $C_y = +216 \text{ N}$

From the signs obtained for C_x and C_y we conclude that the force components $\mathbf{C}_x$ and $\mathbf{C}_y$ exerted on member *BCD* are directed, respectively, to the left and up. We have

$\mathbf{C}_x = 795 \text{ N}\leftarrow, C_y = \underline{216 \text{ N}\uparrow}$ ◀

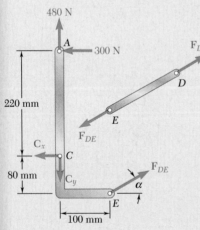

Free Body: Member ACE (Check). The computations are checked by considering the free body *ACE*. For example,

$+\gamma\Sigma M_A = (F_{DE} \cos \alpha)(300 \text{ mm}) + (F_{DE} \sin \alpha)(100 \text{ mm}) - C_x(220 \text{ mm})$
$= (-561 \cos \alpha)(300) + (-561 \sin \alpha)(100) - (-795)(220) = 0$

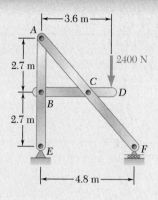

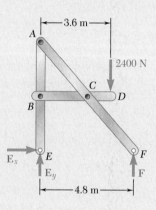

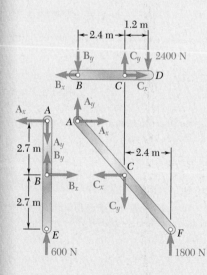

Determine the components of the forces acting on each member of the frame shown.

SOLUTION

Free Body: Entire Frame. Since the external reactions involve only three unknowns, we compute the reactions by considering the free-body diagram of the entire frame.

$$+\curvearrowleft\Sigma M_E = 0: \qquad -(2400\text{ N})(3.6\text{ m}) + F(4.8\text{ m}) = 0$$
$$F = +1800\text{ N} \qquad\qquad\qquad \mathbf{F} = 1800\text{ N}\uparrow \quad \blacktriangleleft$$
$$+\uparrow\Sigma F_y = 0: \qquad -2400\text{ N} + 1800\text{ N} + E_y = 0$$
$$E_y = +600\text{ N} \qquad\qquad\qquad \mathbf{E}_y = 600\text{ N}\uparrow \quad \blacktriangleleft$$
$$\xrightarrow{+}\Sigma F_x = 0: \qquad\qquad\qquad\qquad\qquad\qquad\qquad \mathbf{E}_x = 0 \quad \blacktriangleleft$$

Members. The frame is now dismembered; since only two members are connected at each joint, equal and opposite components are shown on each member at each joint.

Free Body: Member BCD

$$+\curvearrowleft\Sigma M_B = 0: \quad -(2400\text{ N})(3.6\text{ m}) + C_y(2.4\text{ m}) = 0 \quad C_y = +3600\text{ N} \quad \blacktriangleleft$$
$$+\curvearrowleft\Sigma M_C = 0: \quad -(2400\text{ N})(1.2\text{ m}) + B_y(2.4\text{ m}) = 0 \quad B_y = +1200\text{ N} \quad \blacktriangleleft$$
$$\xrightarrow{+}\Sigma F_x = 0: \quad -B_x + C_x = 0$$

We note that neither B_x nor C_x can be obtained by considering only member *BCD*. The positive values obtained for B_y and C_y indicate that the force components $\mathbf{B}_y$ and $\mathbf{C}_y$ are directed as assumed.

Free Body: Member ABE

$$+\curvearrowleft\Sigma M_A = 0: \qquad B_x(2.7\text{ m}) = 0 \qquad\qquad\qquad\qquad B_x = 0 \quad \blacktriangleleft$$
$$\xrightarrow{+}\Sigma F_x = 0: \qquad +B_x - A_x = 0 \qquad\qquad\qquad\qquad A_x = 0 \quad \blacktriangleleft$$
$$+\uparrow\Sigma F_y = 0: \qquad -A_y + B_y + 600\text{ N} = 0$$
$$-A_y + 1200\text{ N} + 600\text{ N} = 0 \qquad A_y = +1800\text{ N} \quad \blacktriangleleft$$

Free Body: Member BCD. Returning now to member *BCD*, we write

$$\xrightarrow{+}\Sigma F_x = 0: \qquad -B_x + C_x = 0 \qquad 0 + C_x = 0 \qquad\qquad C_x = 0 \quad \blacktriangleleft$$

Free Body: Member ACF (Check). All unknown components have now been found; to check the results, we verify that member *ACF* is in equilibrium.

$$+\curvearrowleft\Sigma M_C = (1800\text{ N})(2.4\text{ m}) - A_y(2.4\text{ m}) - A_x(2.7\text{ m})$$
$$= (1800\text{ N})(2.4\text{ m}) - (1800\text{ N})(2.4\text{ m}) - 0 = 0 \qquad \text{(checks)}$$

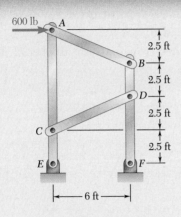

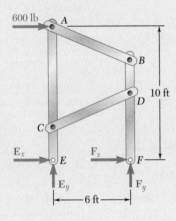

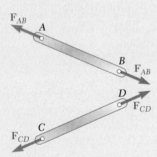

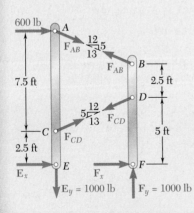

SAMPLE PROBLEM 6.6

A 600-lb horizontal force is applied to pin A of the frame shown. Determine the forces acting on the two vertical members of the frame.

SOLUTION

Free Body: Entire Frame. The entire frame is chosen as a free body; although the reactions involve four unknowns, $\mathbf{E}_y$ and $\mathbf{F}_y$ may be determined by writing

$$+\!\!\curvearrowleft\Sigma M_E = 0: \qquad -(600\text{ lb})(10\text{ ft}) + F_y(6\text{ ft}) = 0$$
$$F_y = +1000\text{ lb} \qquad\qquad \mathbf{F}_y = 1000\text{ lb}\uparrow \quad\blacktriangleleft$$
$$+\!\uparrow\Sigma F_y = 0: \qquad E_y + F_y = 0$$
$$E_y = -1000\text{ lb} \qquad\qquad \mathbf{E}_y = 1000\text{ lb}\downarrow \quad\blacktriangleleft$$

Members. The equations of equilibrium of the entire frame are not sufficient to determine $\mathbf{E}_x$ and $\mathbf{F}_x$. The free-body diagrams of the various members must now be considered in order to proceed with the solution. In dismembering the frame we will assume that pin A is attached to the multiforce member ACE and, thus, that the 600-lb force is applied to that member. We also note that AB and CD are two-force members.

Free Body: Member ACE

$$+\!\uparrow\Sigma F_y = 0: \qquad -\tfrac{5}{13}F_{AB} + \tfrac{5}{13}F_{CD} - 1000\text{ lb} = 0$$
$$+\!\!\curvearrowleft\Sigma M_E = 0: \qquad -(600\text{ lb})(10\text{ ft}) - (\tfrac{12}{13}F_{AB})(10\text{ ft}) - (\tfrac{12}{13}F_{CD})(2.5\text{ ft}) = 0$$

Solving these equations simultaneously, we find

$$F_{AB} = -1040\text{ lb} \qquad F_{CD} = +1560\text{ lb} \quad\blacktriangleleft$$

The signs obtained indicate that the sense assumed for F_{CD} was correct and the sense for F_{AB} incorrect. Summing now x components,

$$\xrightarrow{+}\Sigma F_x = 0: \qquad 600\text{ lb} + \tfrac{12}{13}(-1040\text{ lb}) + \tfrac{12}{13}(+1560\text{ lb}) + E_x = 0$$
$$E_x = -1080\text{ lb} \qquad\qquad \mathbf{E}_x = 1080\text{ lb}\leftarrow \quad\blacktriangleleft$$

Free Body: Entire Frame. Since $\mathbf{E}_x$ has been determined, we can return to the free-body diagram of the entire frame and write

$$\xrightarrow{+}\Sigma F_x = 0: \qquad 600\text{ lb} - 1080\text{ lb} + F_x = 0$$
$$F_x = +480\text{ lb} \qquad\qquad \mathbf{F}_x = 480\text{ lb}\rightarrow \quad\blacktriangleleft$$

Free Body: Member BDF (Check). We can check our computations by verifying that the equation $\Sigma M_B = 0$ is satisfied by the forces acting on member BDF.

$$+\!\!\curvearrowleft\Sigma M_B = -\left(\tfrac{12}{13}F_{CD}\right)(2.5\text{ ft}) + (F_x)(7.5\text{ ft})$$
$$= -\tfrac{12}{13}(1560\text{ lb})(2.5\text{ ft}) + (480\text{ lb})(7.5\text{ ft})$$
$$= -3600\text{ lb}\cdot\text{ft} + 3600\text{ lb}\cdot\text{ft} = 0 \qquad\text{(checks)}$$

SOLVING PROBLEMS ON YOUR OWN

In this lesson you learned to analyze *frames containing one or more multiforce members.* In the problems that follow you will be asked to determine the external reactions exerted on the frame and the internal forces that hold together the members of the frame.

In solving problems involving frames containing one or more multiforce members, follow these steps:

1. Draw a free-body diagram of the entire frame. Use this free-body diagram to calculate, to the extent possible, the reactions at the supports. (In Sample Prob. 6.6 only two of the four reaction components could be found from the free body of the entire frame.)

2. Dismember the frame, and draw a free-body diagram of each member.

3. Considering first the two-force members, apply equal and opposite forces to each two-force member at the points where it is connected to another member. If the two-force member is a straight member, these forces will be directed along the axis of the member. If you cannot tell at this point whether the member is in tension or compression, just *assume* that the member is in tension and *direct both of the forces away from the member.* Since these forces have the same unknown magnitude, give them both the *same name* and, to avoid any confusion later, *do not use a plus sign or a minus sign.*

4. Next, consider the multiforce members. For each of these members, show all the forces acting on the member, including *applied loads, reactions, and internal forces at connections.* The magnitude and direction of any reaction or reaction component found earlier from the free-body diagram of the entire frame should be clearly indicated.

 a. Where a multiforce member is connected to a two-force member, apply to the multiforce member a force *equal and opposite* to the force drawn on the free-body diagram of the two-force member, *giving it the same name.*

 b. Where a multiforce member is connected to another multiforce member, use *horizontal and vertical components* to represent the internal forces at that point, since neither the direction nor the magnitude of these forces is known. The direction you choose for each of the two force components exerted on the first multiforce member is arbitrary, but *you must apply equal and opposite force components of the same name* to the other multiforce member. Again, *do not use a plus sign or a minus sign.*

(continued)

5. The internal forces may now be determined, as well as any *reactions* that you have not already found.

a. The free-body diagram of each of the multiforce members can provide you with *three equilibrium equations*.

b. To simplify your solution, you should seek a way to write an equation involving a single unknown. If you can locate *a point where all but one of the unknown force components intersect*, you will obtain an equation in a single unknown by summing moments about that point. *If all unknown forces except one are parallel*, you will obtain an equation in a single unknown by summing force components in a direction perpendicular to the parallel forces.

c. Since you arbitrarily chose the direction of each of the unknown forces, you cannot determine until the solution is completed whether your guess was correct. To do that, consider the *sign* of the value found for each of the unknowns: a *positive* sign means that the direction you selected was *correct*; a *negative* sign means that the direction is *opposite* to the direction you assumed.

6. To be more effective and efficient as you proceed through your solution, observe the following rules:

a. If an equation involving only one unknown can be found, write that equation and *solve it for that unknown*. Immediately *replace* that unknown wherever it appears on other free-body diagrams *by the value you have found*. Repeat this process by seeking equilibrium equations involving only one unknown until you have found all of the internal forces and unknown reactions.

b. If an equation involving only one unknown cannot be found, you may have to *solve a pair of simultaneous equations*. Before doing so, check that you have shown the values of all of the reactions that were obtained from the free-body diagram of the entire frame.

c. The total number of equations of equilibrium for the entire frame and for the individual members *will be larger than the number of unknown forces and reactions*. After you have found all the reactions and all the internal forces, you can use the remaining equations to check the accuracy of your computations.

PROBLEMS

6.75 For the frame and loading shown, determine the force acting on member *ABC* (*a*) at *B*, (*b*) at *C*.

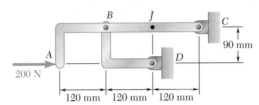

Fig. P6.75

6.76 Determine the force in member *BD* and the components of the reaction at *C*.

6.77 Rod *CD* is fitted with a collar at *D* that can be moved along rod *AB*, which is bent in the shape of an arc of circle. For the position when $\theta = 30°$, determine (*a*) the force in rod *CD*, (*b*) the reaction at *B*.

6.78 Solve Prob. 6.77 when $\theta = 150°$.

6.79 Determine the components of all forces acting on member *ABCD* when $\theta = 0$.

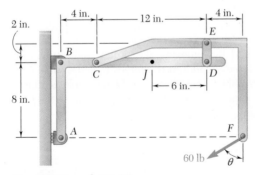

Fig. P6.79 and P6.80

6.80 Determine the components of all forces acting on member *ABCD* when $\theta = 90°$.

6.81 For the frame and loading shown, determine the components of all forces acting on member *ABC*.

6.82 Solve Prob. 6.81 assuming that the 18-kN load is replaced by a clockwise couple of magnitude 72 kN · m applied to member *CDEF* at point *D*.

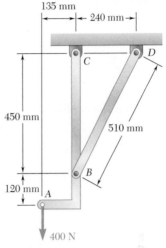

Fig. P6.76

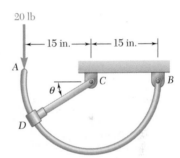

Fig. P6.77

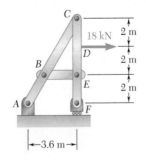

Fig. P6.81

325

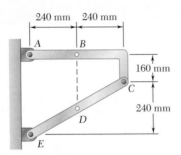

240 mm   240 mm

A   B

160 mm

C

240 mm

D

E

Fig. P6.83 and P6.85

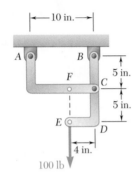

10 in.

A   B

F

5 in.

C

5 in.

E

D

4 in.

100 lb

Fig. P6.87

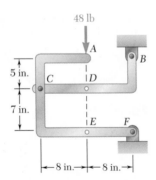

48 lb

A

B

5 in.

C   D

7 in.

E   F

8 in.   8 in.

Fig. P6.88 and P6.89

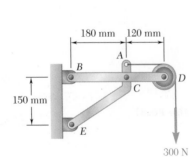

180 mm   120 mm

A

B

C

D

150 mm

E

300 N

Fig. P6.91

6.83 and 6.84 Determine the components of the reactions at A and E if a 750-N force directed vertically downward is applied (a) at B, (b) at D.

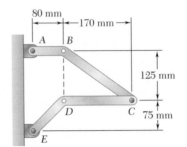

80 mm

170 mm

A   B

125 mm

D   C   75 mm

E

Fig. P6.84 and P6.86

6.85 and 6.86 Determine the components of the reactions at A and E if the frame is loaded by a clockwise couple of magnitude 36 N · m applied (a) at B, (b) at D.

6.87 Determine the components of the reactions at A and B, (a) if the 500-N load is applied as shown, (b) if the 500-N load is moved along its line of action and is applied at point F.

6.88 The 48-lb load can be moved along the line of action shown and applied at A, D, or E. Determine the components of the reactions at B and F if the 48-lb load is applied (a) at A, (b) at D, (c) at E.

6.89 The 48-lb load is removed and a 288-lb · in. clockwise couple is applied successively at A, D, and E. Determine the components of the reactions at B and F if the couple is applied (a) at A, (b) at D, (c) at E.

6.90 (a) Show that when a frame supports a pulley at A, an equivalent loading of the frame and of each of its component parts can be obtained by removing the pulley and applying at A two forces equal and parallel to the forces that the cable exerted on the pulley. (b) Show that if one end of the cable is attached to the frame at a point B, a force of magnitude equal to the tension in the cable should also be applied at B.

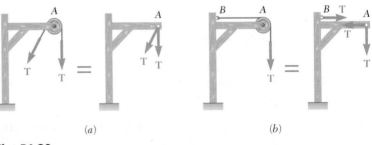

(a)   (b)

Fig. P6.90

6.91 Knowing that the pulley has a radius of 50 mm, determine the components of the reactions at B and E.

6.92 Knowing that each pulley has a radius of 250 mm, determine the components of the reactions at D and E.

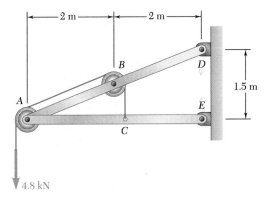

Fig. P6.92

6.93 Two 9-in.-diameter pipes (pipe *1* and pipe *2*) are supported every 7.5 ft by a small frame like that shown. Knowing that the combined weight of each pipe and its contents is 30 lb/ft and assuming frictionless surfaces, determine the components of the reactions at A and G.

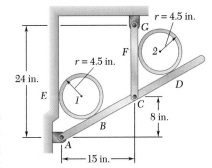

Fig. P6.93

6.94 Solve Prob. 6.93 assuming that pipe *1* is removed and that only pipe *2* is supported by the frames.

6.95 A trailer weighing 2400 lb is attached to a 2900-lb pickup truck by a ball-and-socket truck hitch at D. Determine (*a*) the reactions at each of the six wheels when the truck and trailer are at rest, (*b*) the additional load on each of the truck wheels due to the trailer.

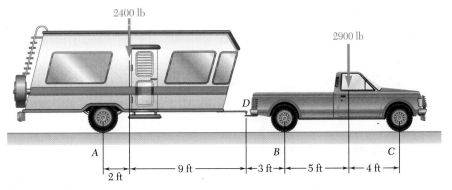

Fig. P6.95

6.96 In order to obtain a better weight distribution over the four wheels of the pickup truck of Prob. 6.95, a compensating hitch of the type shown is used to attach the trailer to the truck. The hitch consists of two bar springs (only one is shown in the figure) that fit into bearings inside a support rigidly attached to the truck. The springs are also connected by chains to the trailer frame, and specially designed hooks make it possible to place both chains in tension. (*a*) Determine the tension T required in each of the two chains if the additional load due to the trailer is to be evenly distributed over the four wheels of the truck. (*b*) What are the resulting reactions at each of the six wheels of the trailer-truck combination?

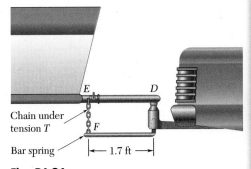

Fig. P6.96

6.97 The cab and motor units of the front-end loader shown are connected by a vertical pin located 2 m behind the cab wheels. The distance from C to D is 1 m. The center of gravity of the 300-kN motor unit is located at G_m, while the centers of gravity of the 100-kN cab and 75-kN load are located, respectively, at G_c and G_l. Knowing that the machine is at rest with its brakes released, determine (a) the reactions at each of the four wheels, (b) the forces exerted on the motor unit at C and D.

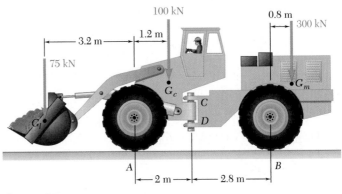

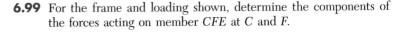

Fig. P6.97

6.98 Solve Prob. 6.97 assuming that the 75-kN load has been removed.

6.99 For the frame and loading shown, determine the components of the forces acting on member CFE at C and F.

6.100 For the frame and loading shown, determine the components of the forces acting on member CDE at C and D.

6.101 and 6.102 For the frame and loading shown, determine the components of all forces acting on member ABE.

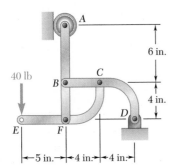

Fig. P6.99

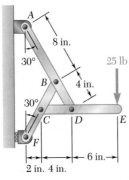

Fig. P6.100

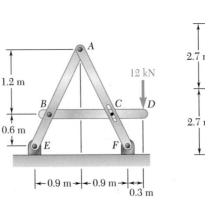

Fig. P6.101

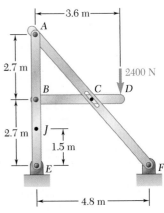

Fig. P6.102

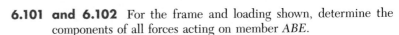

6.103 Knowing that $P = 15$ lb and $Q = 65$ lb, determine the components of the forces exerted (*a*) on member *BCDF* at *C* and *D*, (*b*) on member *ACEG* at *E*.

6.104 Knowing that $P = 25$ lb and $Q = 55$ lb, determine the components of the forces exerted (*a*) on member *BCDF* at *C* and *D*, (*b*) on member *ACEG* at *E*.

6.105 For the frame and loading shown, determine the components of the forces acting on member *DABC* at *B* and *D*.

6.106 Solve Prob. 6.105 assuming that the 6-kN load has been removed.

6.107 The axis of the three-hinge arch *ABC* is a parabola with vertex at *B*. Knowing that $P = 112$ kN and $Q = 140$ kN, determine (*a*) the components of the reaction at *A*, (*b*) the components of the force exerted at *B* on segment *AB*.

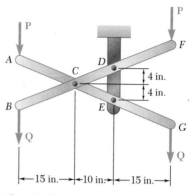

Fig. P6.103 and P6.104

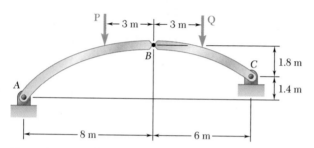

Fig. P6.107 and P6.108

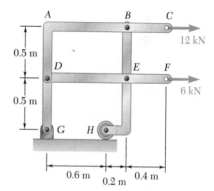

Fig. P6.105

6.108 The axis of the three-hinge arch *ABC* is a parabola with vertex at *B*. Knowing that $P = 140$ kN and $Q = 112$ kN, determine (*a*) the components of the reaction at *A*, (*b*) the components of the force exerted at *B* on segment *AB*.

6.109 Knowing that the surfaces at *A* and *D* are frictionless, determine the forces exerted at *B* and *C* on member *BCE*.

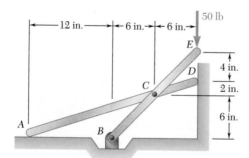

Fig. P6.109

6.110 For the frame and loading shown, determine (*a*) the reaction at *C*, (*b*) the force in member *AD*.

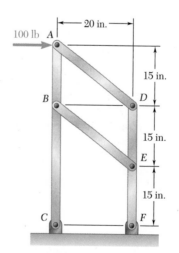

Fig. P6.110

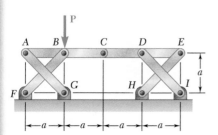

Fig. P6.111

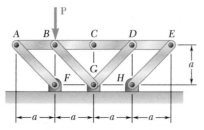

Fig. P6.112

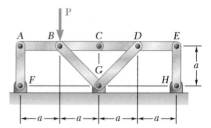

Fig. P6.113

6.111, 6.112, and 6.113 Members *ABC* and *CDE* are pin-connected at *C* and supported by four links. For the loading shown, determine the force in each link.

6.114 Members *ABC* and *CDE* are pin-connected at *C* and supported by the four links *AF*, *BG*, *DG*, and *EH*. For the loading shown, determine the force in each link.

6.115 Solve Prob. 6.113 assuming that the force **P** is replaced by a clockwise couple of moment M_0 applied to member *CDE* at *D*.

6.116 Solve Prob. 6.114 assuming that the force **P** is replaced by a clockwise couple of moment M_0 applied to member *CDE* at *D*.

6.117 Four beams, each of length 3*a*, are held together by single nails at *A*, *B*, *C*, and *D*. Each beam is attached to a support located at a distance *a* from an end of the beam as shown. Assuming that only vertical forces are exerted at the connections, determine the vertical reactions at *E*, *F*, *G*, and *H*.

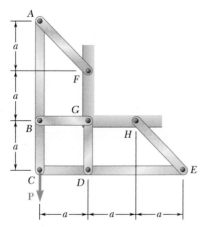

Fig. P6.114

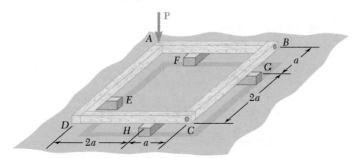

Fig. P6.117

6.118 Four beams, each of length 2*a*, are nailed together at their midpoints to form the support system shown. Assuming that only vertical forces are exerted at the connections, determine the vertical reactions at *A*, *D*, *E*, and *H*.

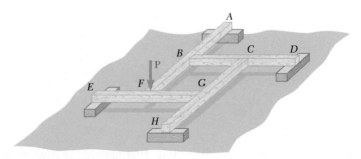

Fig. P6.118

6.119 through 6.121 Each of the frames shown consists of two L-shaped members connected by two rigid links. For each frame, determine the reactions at the supports and indicate whether the frame is rigid.

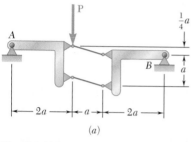

(a)

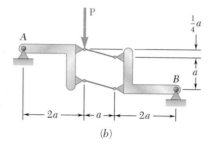

(b)

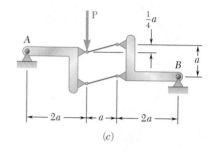

(c)

Fig. P6.119

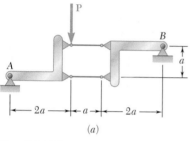

(a)

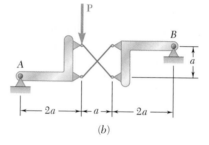

(b)

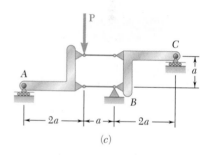

(c)

Fig. P6.120

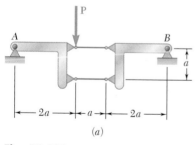

(a)

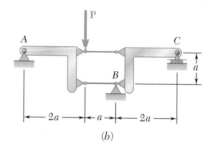

(b)

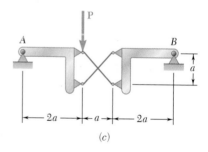

(c)

Fig. P6.121

6.12 MACHINES

Machines are structures designed to transmit and modify forces. Whether they are simple tools or include complicated mechanisms, their main purpose is to transform *input forces* into *output forces*. Consider, for example, a pair of cutting pliers used to cut a wire (Fig. 6.22*a*). If we apply two equal and opposite forces **P** and −**P** on their handles, they will exert two equal and opposite forces **Q** and −**Q** on the wire (Fig. 6.22*b*).

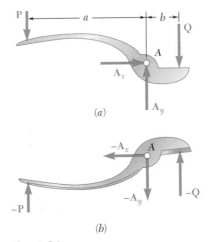

(a)   (b)

Fig. 6.22

Photo 6.5 The lamp shown can be placed in many positions. By considering various free bodies, the force in the springs and the internal forces at the joints can be determined.

To determine the magnitude Q of the output forces when the magnitude P of the input forces is known (or, conversely, to determine P when Q is known), we draw a free-body diagram of the pliers *alone,* showing the input forces $\mathbf{P}$ and $-\mathbf{P}$ and the *reactions* $-\mathbf{Q}$ and $\mathbf{Q}$ that the wire exerts on the pliers (Fig. 6.23). However, since a pair of pliers forms a nonrigid structure, we must use one of the component parts as a free body in order to determine the unknown forces. Considering Fig. 6.24a, for example, and taking moments about A, we obtain the relation $Pa = Qb$, which defines the magnitude Q in terms of P or P in terms of Q. The same free-body diagram can be used to determine the components of the internal force at A; we find $A_x = 0$ and $A_y = P + Q$.

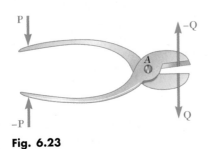

Fig. 6.23

(a)

(b)

Fig. 6.24

In the case of more complicated machines, it generally will be necessary to use several free-body diagrams and, possibly, to solve simultaneous equations involving various internal forces. The free bodies should be chosen to include the input forces and the reactions to the output forces, and the total number of unknown force components involved should not exceed the number of available independent equations. It is advisable, before attempting to solve a problem, to determine whether the structure considered is determinate. There is no point, however, in discussing the rigidity of a machine, since a machine includes moving parts and thus *must* be nonrigid.

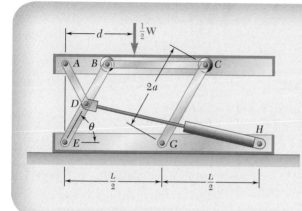

SAMPLE PROBLEM 6.7

A hydraulic-lift table is used to raise a 1000-kg crate. It consists of a platform and two identical linkages on which hydraulic cylinders exert equal forces. (Only one linkage and one cylinder are shown.) Members EDB and CG are each of length $2a$, and member AD is pinned to the midpoint of EDB. If the crate is placed on the table, so that half of its weight is supported by the system shown, determine the force exerted by each cylinder in raising the crate for $\theta = 60°$, $a = 0.70$ m, and $L = 3.20$ m. Show that the result obtained is independent of the distance d.

SOLUTION

The machine considered consists of the platform and of the linkage. Its free-body diagram includes an input force $\mathbf{F}_{DH}$ exerted by the cylinder, the weight $\frac{1}{2}\mathbf{W}$, equal and opposite to the output force, and reactions at E and G that we assume to be directed as shown. Since more than three unknowns are involved, this diagram will not be used. The mechanism is dismembered and a free-body diagram is drawn for each of its component parts. We note that AD, BC, and CG are two-force members. We already assumed member CG to be in compression; we now assume that AD and BC are in tension and direct as shown the forces exerted on them. Equal and opposite vectors will be used to represent the forces exerted by the two-force members on the platform, on member BDE, and on roller C.

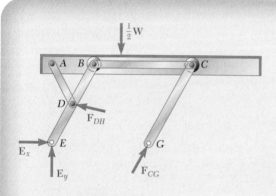

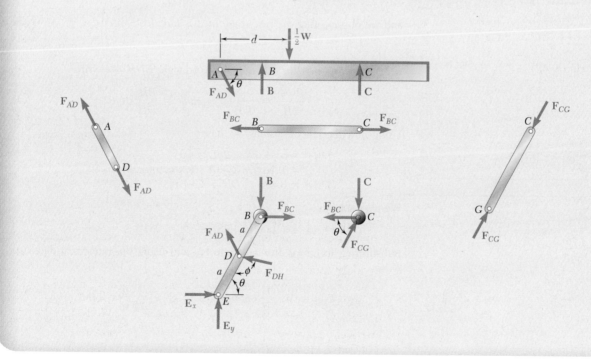

333

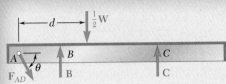

Free Body: Platform ABC.

$$\xrightarrow{+}\Sigma F_x = 0: \qquad F_{AD}\cos\theta = 0 \qquad F_{AD} = 0$$
$$+\uparrow\Sigma F_y = 0: \qquad B + C - \tfrac{1}{2}W = 0 \qquad B + C = \tfrac{1}{2}W \tag{1}$$

Free Body: Roller C. We draw a force triangle and obtain $F_{BC} = C\cot\theta$.

 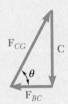

Free Body: Member BDE. Recalling that $F_{AD} = 0$,

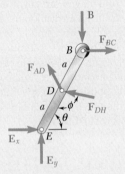

$$+\!\!\curvearrowleft\Sigma M_E = 0: \quad F_{DH}\cos(\phi - 90°)a - B(2a\cos\theta) - F_{BC}(2a\sin\theta) = 0$$
$$F_{DH}a\sin\phi - B(2a\cos\theta) - (C\cot\theta)(2a\sin\theta) = 0$$
$$F_{DH}\sin\phi - 2(B + C)\cos\theta = 0$$

Recalling Eq. (1), we have

$$F_{DH} = W\frac{\cos\theta}{\sin\phi} \tag{2}$$

and we observe that *the result obtained is independent of d.* ◀

Applying first the law of sines to triangle *EDH*, we write

$$\frac{\sin\phi}{EH} = \frac{\sin\theta}{DH} \qquad \sin\phi = \frac{EH}{DH}\sin\theta \tag{3}$$

Using now the law of cosines, we have

$$(DH)^2 = a^2 + L^2 - 2aL\cos\theta$$
$$= (0.70)^2 + (3.20)^2 - 2(0.70)(3.20)\cos 60°$$
$$(DH)^2 = 8.49 \qquad DH = 2.91\text{ m}$$

We also note that

$$W = mg = (1000\text{ kg})(9.81\text{ m/s}^2) = 9810\text{ N} = 9.81\text{ kN}$$

Substituting for $\sin\phi$ from (3) into (2) and using the numerical data, we write

$$F_{DH} = W\frac{DH}{EH}\cot\theta = (9.81\text{ kN})\frac{2.91\text{ m}}{3.20\text{ m}}\cot 60°$$
$$F_{DH} = 5.15\text{ kN} \quad ◀$$

SOLVING PROBLEMS ON YOUR OWN

This lesson was devoted to the analysis of *machines.* Since machines are designed to transmit or modify forces, they always contain moving parts. However, the machines considered here will always be at rest, and you will be working with the set of *forces required to maintain the equilibrium of the machine.*

Known forces that act on a machine are called *input forces.* A *machine transforms the input forces into output forces,* such as the cutting forces applied by the pliers of Fig. 6.22. You will determine the output forces by finding the forces equal and opposite to the output forces that should be applied to the machine to maintain its equilibrium.

In the preceding lesson you analyzed frames; you will now use almost the same procedure to analyze machines:

1. Draw a free-body diagram of the whole machine, and use it to determine as many as possible of the unknown forces exerted on the machine.

2. Dismember the machine, and draw a free-body diagram of each member.

3. Considering first the two-force members, apply equal and opposite forces to each two-force member at the points where it is connected to another member. If you cannot tell at this point whether the member is in tension or in compression just *assume* that the member is in tension and *direct both of the forces away from the member.* Since these forces have the same unknown magnitude, *give them both the same name.*

4. Next consider the multiforce members. For each of these members, show all the forces acting on the member, including applied loads and forces, reactions, and internal forces at connections.

    a. Where a multiforce member is connected to a two-force member, apply to the multiforce member a force *equal and opposite* to the force drawn on the free-body diagram of the two-force member, *giving it the same name.*

    b. Where a multiforce member is connected to another multiforce member, use *horizontal and vertical components* to represent the internal forces at that point. The directions you choose for each of the two force components exerted on the first multiforce member are arbitrary, but *you must apply equal and opposite force components of the same name* to the other multiforce member.

5. Equilibrium equations can be written after you have completed the various free-body diagrams.

    a. To simplify your solution, you should, whenever possible, write and solve equilibrium equations involving single unknowns.

    b. Since you arbitrarily chose the direction of each of the unknown forces, you must determine at the end of the solution whether your guess was correct. To that effect, *consider the sign* of the value found for each of the unknowns. A *positive* sign indicates that your guess was correct, and a *negative* sign indicates that it was not.

6. Finally, you should check your solution by substituting the results obtained into an equilibrium equation that you have not previously used.

PROBLEMS

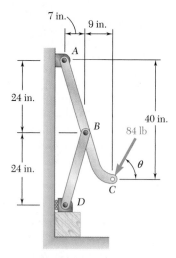

Fig. P6.122

6.122 An 84-lb force is applied to the toggle vise at *C*. Knowing that $\theta = 90°$, determine (*a*) the vertical force exerted on the block at *D*, (*b*) the force exerted on member *ABC* at *B*.

6.123 Solve Prob. 6.122 when $\theta = 0$.

6.124 The control rod *CE* passes through a horizontal hole in the body of the toggle system shown. Knowing that link *BD* is 250 mm long, determine the force **Q** required to hold the system in equilibrium when $\beta = 20°$.

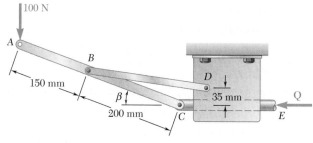

Fig. P6.124

6.125 Solve Prob. 6.124 when (*a*) $\beta = 0$, (*b*) $\beta = 6°$.

6.126 The press shown is used to emboss a small seal at *E*. Knowing that $P = 250$ N, determine (*a*) the vertical component of the force exerted on the seal, (*b*) the reaction at *A*.

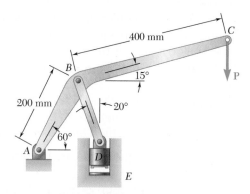

Fig. P6.126 and P6.127

6.127 The press shown is used to emboss a small seal at *E*. Knowing that the vertical component of the force exerted on the seal must be 900 N, determine (*a*) the required vertical force **P**, (*b*) the corresponding reaction at *A*.

6.128 Water pressure in the supply system exerts a downward force of 135 N on the vertical plug at *A*. Determine the tension in the fusible link *DE* and the force exerted on member *BCE* at *B*.

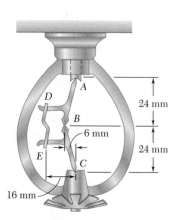

Fig. P6.128

6.129 A couple **M** of magnitude 1.5 kN · m is applied to the crank of the engine system shown. For each of the two positions shown, determine the force **P** required to hold the system in equilibrium.

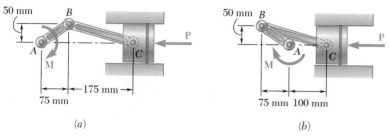

(a)   (b)

Fig. P6.129 and P6.130

6.130 A force **P** of magnitude 16 kN is applied to the piston of the engine system shown. For each of the two positions shown, determine the couple **M** required to hold the system in equilibrium.

6.131 The pin at B is attached to member ABC and can slide freely along the slot cut in the fixed plate. Neglecting the effect of friction, determine the couple **M** required to hold the system in equilibrium when $\theta = 30°$.

6.132 The pin at B is attached to member ABC and can slide freely along the slot cut in the fixed plate. Neglecting the effect of friction, determine the couple **M** required to hold the system in equilibrium when $\theta = 60°$.

6.133 Arm ABC is connected by pins to a collar at B and to crank CD at C. Neglecting the effect of friction, determine the couple **M** required to hold the system in equilibrium when $\theta = 0$.

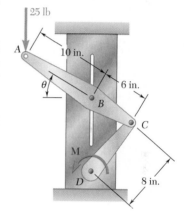

Fig. P6.131 and P6.132

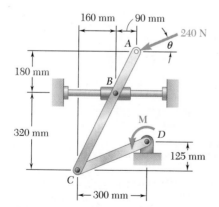

Fig. P6.133 and P6.134

6.134 Arm ABC is connected by pins to a collar at B and to crank CD at C. Neglecting the effect of friction, determine the couple **M** required to hold the system in equilibrium when $\theta = 90°$.

6.135 and 6.136 Two rods are connected by a slider block as shown. Neglecting the effect of friction, determine the couple M_A required to hold the system in equilibrium.

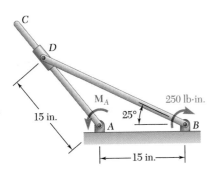

Fig. P6.135

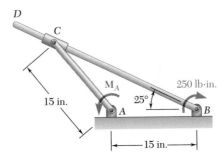

Fig. P6.136

6.137 and 6.138 Rod CD is attached to the collar D and passes through a collar welded to end B of lever AB. Neglecting the effect of friction, determine the couple M required to hold the system in equilibrium when $\theta = 30°$.

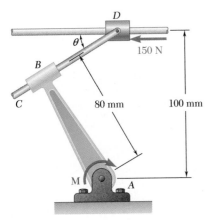

Fig. P6.138

Fig. P6.137

6.139 Two hydraulic cylinders control the position of the robotic arm ABC. Knowing that in the position shown the cylinders are parallel, determine the force exerted by each cylinder when $P = 160$ N and $Q = 80$ N.

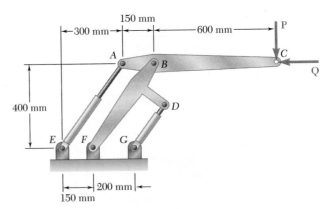

Fig. P6.139 and P6.140

6.140 Two hydraulic cylinders control the position of the robotic arm ABC. In the position shown, the cylinders are parallel and both are in tension. Knowing that $F_{AE} = 600$ N and $F_{DG} = 50$ N, determine the forces P and Q applied at C to arm ABC.

6.141 A log weighing 800 lb is lifted by a pair of tongs as shown. Determine the forces exerted at E and F on tong DEF.

6.142 A 39-ft length of railroad rail of weight 44 lb/ft is lifted by the tongs shown. Determine the forces exerted at D and F on tong BDF.

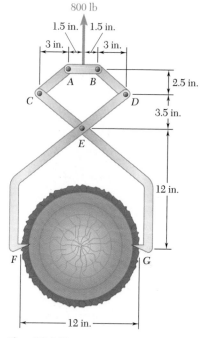

Fig. P6.141

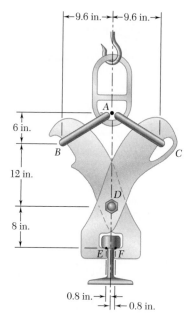

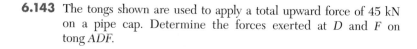

Fig. P6.142

6.143 The tongs shown are used to apply a total upward force of 45 kN on a pipe cap. Determine the forces exerted at D and F on tong ADF.

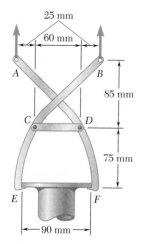

Fig. P6.143

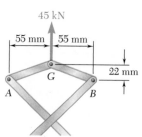

Fig. P6.144

6.144 If the toggle shown is added to the tongs of Prob. 6.143 and a single vertical force is applied at G, determine the forces exerted at D and F on tong ADF.

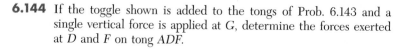

6.145 The pliers shown are used to grip a 0.3-in.-diameter rod. Knowing that two 60-lb forces are applied to the handles, determine (a) the magnitude of the forces exerted on the rod, (b) the force exerted by the pin at A on portion AB of the pliers.

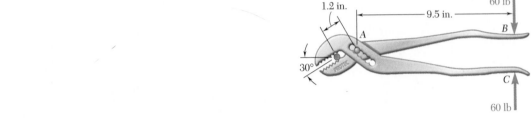

Fig. P6.145

6.146 In using the bolt cutter shown, a worker applies two 300-N forces to the handles. Determine the magnitude of the forces exerted by the cutter on the bolt.

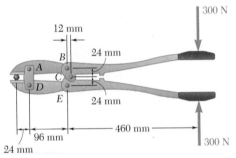

Fig. P6.146

6.147 Determine the magnitude of the gripping forces exerted along line aa on the nut when two 50-lb forces are applied to the handles as shown. Assume that pins A and D slide freely in slots cut in the jaws.

6.148 Determine the magnitude of the gripping forces produced when two 300-N forces are applied as shown.

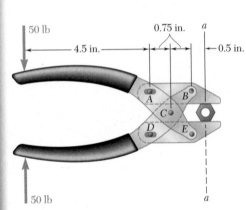

Fig. P6.147

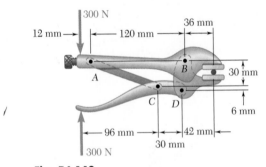

Fig. P6.148

6.149 Knowing that the frame shown has a sag at B of a = 1 in., determine the force **P** required to maintain equilibrium in the position shown.

6.150 Knowing that the frame shown has a sag at B of a = 0.5 in., determine the force **P** required to maintain equilibrium in the position shown.

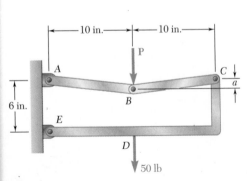

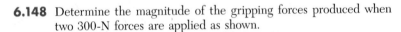

Fig. P6.149 and P6.150

6.151 The garden shears shown consist of two blades and two handles. The two handles are connected by pin C and the two blades are connected by pin D. The left blade and the right handle are connected by pin A; the right blade and the left handle are connected by pin B. Determine the magnitude of the forces exerted on the small branch at E when two 80-N forces are applied to the handles as shown.

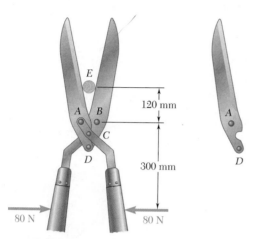

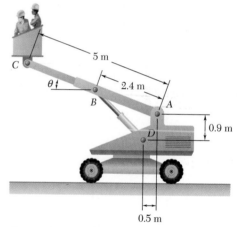

Fig. P6.151

6.152 The telescoping arm ABC is used to provide an elevated platform for construction workers. The workers and the platform together have a mass of 200 kg and have a combined center of gravity located directly above C. For the position when $\theta = 20°$, determine (a) the force exerted at B by the single hydraulic cylinder BD, (b) the force exerted on the supporting carriage at A.

6.153 The telescoping arm ABC can be lowered until end C is close to the ground, so that workers can easily board the platform. For the position when $\theta = -20°$, determine (a) the force exerted at B by the single hydraulic cylinder BD, (b) the force exerted on the supporting carriage at A.

Fig. P6.152 and P6.153

6.154 The position of member ABC is controlled by the hydraulic cylinder CD. Knowing that $\theta = 30°$, determine for the loading shown (a) the force exerted by the hydraulic cylinder on pin C, (b) the reaction at B.

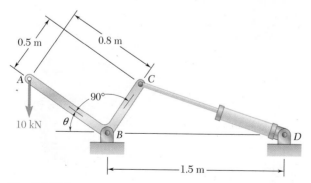

Fig. P6.154

6.155 The motion of the bucket of the front-end loader shown is controlled by two arms and a linkage that are pin-connected at *D*. The arms are located symmetrically with respect to the central, vertical, and longitudinal plane of the loader; one arm *AFJ* and its control cylinder *EF* are shown. The single linkage *GHDB* and its control cylinder *BC* are located in the plane of symmetry. For the position and loading shown, determine the force exerted (*a*) by cylinder *BC*, (*b*) by cylinder *EF*.

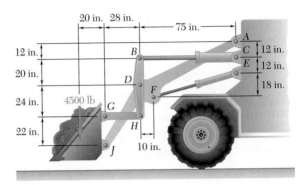

Fig. P6.155

6.156 The bucket of the front-end loader shown carries a 3200-lb load. The motion of the bucket is controlled by two identical mechanisms, only one of which is shown. Knowing that the mechanism shown supports one-half of the 3200-lb load, determine the force exerted (*a*) by cylinder *CD*, (*b*) by cylinder *FH*.

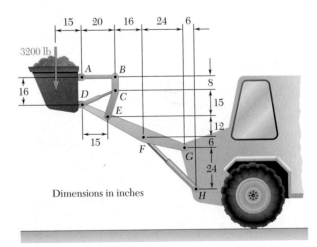

Dimensions in inches

Fig. P6.156

6.157 The motion of the backhoe bucket shown is controlled by the hydraulic cylinders *AD*, *CG*, and *EF*. As a result of an attempt to dislodge a portion of a slab, a 2-kip force **P** is exerted on the bucket teeth at *J*. Knowing that $\theta = 45°$, determine the force exerted by each cylinder.

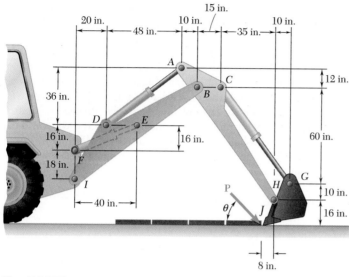

Fig. P6.157

6.158 Solve Prob. 6.157 assuming that the 2-kip force **P** acts horizontally to the right ($\theta = 0$).

6.159 The gears *D* and *G* are rigidly attached to shafts that are held by frictionless bearings. If $r_D = 90$ mm and $r_G = 30$ mm, determine (*a*) the couple M_0 that must be applied for equilibrium, (*b*) the reactions at *A* and *B*.

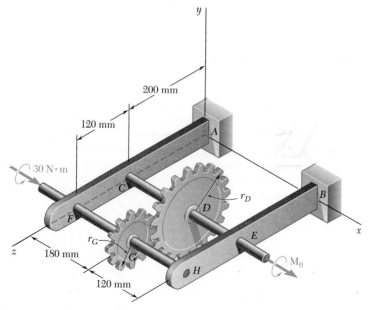

Fig. P6.159

Fig. P6.160

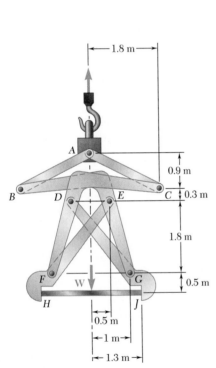

Fig. P6.163

6.160 In the planetary gear system shown, the radius of the central gear A is $a = 18$ mm, the radius of each planetary gear is b, and the radius of the outer gear E is $(a + 2b)$. A clockwise couple of magnitude $M_A = 10$ N · m is applied to the central gear A and a counterclockwise couple of magnitude $M_S = 50$ N · m is applied to the spider BCD. If the system is to be in equilibrium, determine (a) the required radius b of the planetary gears, (b) the magnitude M_E of the couple that must be applied to the outer gear E.

*6.161 Two shafts AC and CF, which lie in the vertical xy plane, are connected by a universal joint at C. The bearings at B and D do not exert any axial force. A couple of magnitude 500 lb · in. (clockwise when viewed from the positive x axis) is applied to shaft CF at F. At a time when the arm of the crosspiece attached to shaft CF is horizontal, determine (a) the magnitude of the couple that must be applied to shaft AC at A to maintain equilibrium, (b) the reactions at B, D, and E. (*Hint:* The sum of the couples exerted on the crosspiece must be zero.)

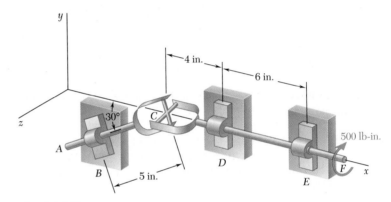

Fig. P6.161

*6.162 Solve Prob. 6.161 assuming that the arm of the crosspiece attached to shaft CF is vertical.

*6.163 The large mechanical tongs shown are used to grab and lift a thick 7500-kg steel slab HJ. Knowing that slipping does not occur between the tong grips and the slab at H and J, determine the components of all forces acting on member EFH. (*Hint:* Consider the symmetry of the tongs to establish relationships between the components of the force acting at E on EFH and the components of the force acting at D on CDF.)

In this chapter you learned to determine the *internal forces* holding together the various parts of a structure.

Analysis of trusses

The first half of the chapter was devoted to the analysis of *trusses,* i.e., to the analysis of structures consisting of *straight members connected at their extremities only.* The members being slender and unable to support lateral loads, all the loads must be applied at the joints; a truss may thus be assumed to consist of *pins and two-force members* [Sec. 6.2].

Simple trusses

A truss is said to be *rigid* if it is designed in such a way that it will not greatly deform or collapse under a small load. A triangular truss consisting of three members connected at three joints is clearly a rigid truss (Fig. 6.25a) and so will be the truss obtained by adding two new members to the first one and connecting them at a new joint (Fig. 6.25b). Trusses obtained by repeating this procedure are called *simple trusses.* We may check that in a simple truss the total number of members is $m = 2n - 3$, where n is the total number of joints [Sec. 6.3].

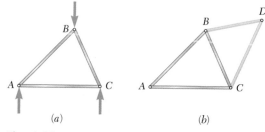

(a)   (b)

Fig. 6.25

Method of joints

The forces in the various members of a simple truss can be determined by the *method of joints* [Sec. 6.4]. First, the reactions at the supports can be obtained by considering the entire truss as a free body. The free-body diagram of each pin is then drawn, showing the forces exerted on the pin by the members or supports it connects. Since the members are straight two-force members, the force exerted by a member on the pin is directed along that member, and only the magnitude of the force is unknown. It is always possible in the case of a simple truss to draw the free-body diagrams of the pins in such an order that only two unknown forces are included in each diagram. These forces can be obtained from the corresponding two equilibrium equations or—if only three forces are involved—from the corresponding force triangle. If the force exerted by a member on a pin is directed toward that pin, the member is in *compression;*

if it is directed away from the pin, the member is in *tension* [Sample Prob. 6.1]. The analysis of a truss is sometimes expedited by first recognizing *joints under special loading conditions* [Sec. 6.5]. The method of joints can also be extended to the analysis of three-dimensional or *space trusses* [Sec. 6.6].

Method of sections   The *method of sections* is usually preferred to the method of joints when the force in only one member—or very few members—of a truss is desired [Sec. 6.7]. To determine the force in member *BD* of the truss of Fig. 6.26*a*, for example, we *pass a section* through members *BD*, *BE*, and *CE*, remove these members, and use the portion *ABC* of the truss as a free body (Fig. 6.26*b*). Writing $\Sigma M_E = 0$, we determine the magnitude of the force $\mathbf{F}_{BD}$, which represents the force in member *BD*. A positive sign indicates that the member is in *tension*; a negative sign indicates that it is in *compression* [Sample Probs. 6.2 and 6.3].

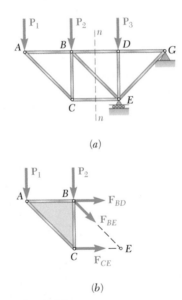

Fig. 6.26

Compound trusses   The method of sections is particularly useful in the analysis of *compound trusses*, i.e., trusses which cannot be constructed from the basic triangular truss of Fig. 6.25*a* but which can be obtained by rigidly connecting several simple trusses [Sec. 6.8]. If the component trusses have been properly connected (e.g., one pin and one link, or three nonconcurrent and nonparallel links) and if the resulting structure is properly supported (e.g., one pin and one roller), the compound truss is *statically determinate, rigid, and completely constrained*. The following necessary—but not sufficient—condition is then satisfied: $m + r = 2n$, where m is the number of members, r is the number of unknowns representing the reactions at the supports, and n is the number of joints.

The second part of the chapter was devoted to the analysis of *frames and machines*. Frames and machines are structures which contain *multiforce members,* i.e., members acted upon by three or more forces. Frames are designed to support loads and are usually stationary, fully constrained structures. Machines are designed to transmit or modify forces and always contain moving parts [Sec. 6.9].

Frames and machines

To *analyze a frame,* we first consider the *entire frame as a free body* and write three equilibrium equations [Sec. 6.10]. If the frame remains rigid when detached from its supports, the reactions involve only three unknowns and may be determined from these equations [Sample Probs. 6.4 and 6.5]. On the other hand, if the frame ceases to be rigid when detached from its supports, the reactions involve more than three unknowns and cannot be completely determined from the equilibrium equations of the frame [Sec. 6.11; Sample Prob. 6.6].

Analysis of a frame

We then *dismember the frame* and identify the various members as either two-force members or multiforce members; pins are assumed to form an integral part of one of the members they connect. We draw the free-body diagram of each of the multiforce members, noting that when two multiforce members are connected to the same two-force member, they are acted upon by that member with *equal and opposite forces of unknown magnitude but known direction.* When two multiforce members are connected by a pin, they exert on each other *equal and opposite forces of unknown direction,* which should be represented by *two unknown components.* The equilibrium equations obtained from the free-body diagrams of the multiforce members can then be solved for the various internal forces [Sample Probs. 6.4 and 6.5]. The equilibrium equations can also be used to complete the determination of the reactions at the supports [Sample Prob. 6.6]. Actually, if the frame is *statically determinate and rigid,* the free-body diagrams of the multiforce members could provide as many equations as there are unknown forces (including the reactions) [Sec. 6.11]. However, as suggested above, it is advisable to first consider the free-body diagram of the entire frame to minimize the number of equations that must be solved simultaneously.

Multiforce members

To *analyze a machine,* we dismember it and, following the same procedure as for a frame, draw the free-body diagram of each of the multiforce members. The corresponding equilibrium equations yield the *output forces* exerted by the machine in terms of the *input forces* applied to it, as well as the *internal forces* at the various connections [Sec. 6.12; Sample Prob. 6.7].

Analysis of a machine

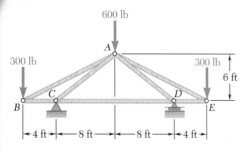

Fig. P6.164

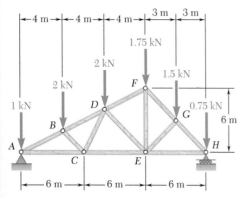

Fig. P6.165

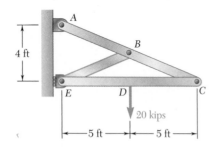

Fig. P6.168

6.164 Using the method of joints, determine the force in each member of the truss shown. State whether each member is in tension or compression.

6.165 Using the method of joints, determine the force in each member of the double-pitch roof truss shown. State whether each member is in tension or compression.

6.166 The truss shown was designed to support the roof of a food market. For the given loading, determine the force in members *FG*, *EG*, and *EH*.

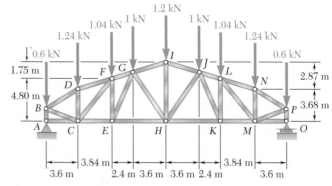

Fig. P6.166 and P6.167

6.167 The truss shown was designed to support the roof of a food market. For the given loading, determine the force in members *KM*, *LM*, and *LN*.

6.168 For the frame and loading shown, determine the components of all forces acting on member *ABC*.

6.169 Solve Prob. 6.168 assuming that the 20-kip load is replaced by a clockwise couple of magnitude 100 kip · ft applied to member *EDC* at point *D*.

6.170 Knowing that the pulley has a radius of 0.5 m, determine the components of the reactions at *A* and *E*.

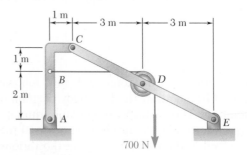

Fig. P6.170

6.171 For the frame and loading shown, determine the reactions at A, B, D, and E. Assume that the surface at each support is frictionless.

6.172 For the system and loading shown, determine (a) the force **P** required for equilibrium, (b) the corresponding force in member BD, (c) the corresponding reaction at C.

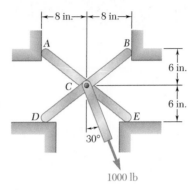

Fig. P6.171

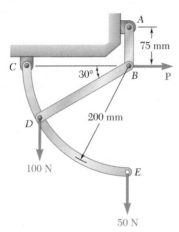

Fig. P6.172

6.173 A small barrel weighing 60 lb is lifted by a pair of tongs as shown. Knowing that $a = 5$ in., determine the forces exerted at B and D on tong ABD.

6.174 A 20-kg shelf is held horizontally by a self-locking brace that consists of two parts EDC and CDB hinged at C and bearing against each other at D. Determine the force **P** required to release the brace.

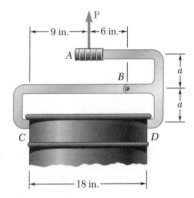

Fig. P6.173

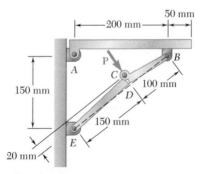

Fig. P6.174

6.175 The specialized plumbing wrench shown is used in confined areas (e.g., under a basin or sink). It consists essentially of a jaw BC pinned at B to a long rod. Knowing that the forces exerted on the nut are equivalent to a clockwise (when viewed from above) couple of magnitude 135 lb · in., determine (a) the magnitude of the force exerted by pin B on jaw BC, (b) the couple **M**₀ that is applied to the wrench.

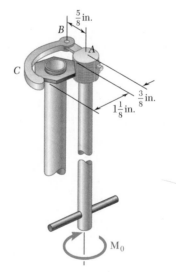

Fig. P6.175

COMPUTER PROBLEMS

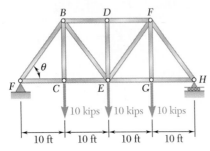

Fig. P6.C1

6.C1 A Pratt steel truss is to be designed to support three 10-kip loads as shown. The length of the truss is to be 40 ft. The height of the truss and thus the angle θ, as well as the cross-sectional areas of the various members, are to be selected to obtain the most economical design. Specifically, the cross-sectional area of each member is to be chosen so that the stress (force divided by area) in that member is equal to 20 kips/in², the allowable stress for the steel used; the total weight of the steel, and thus its cost, must be as small as possible. (*a*) Knowing that the specific weight of the steel used is 0.284 lb/in³, use computational software to calculate the weight of the truss and the cross-sectional area of each load-bearing member located to the left of *DE* for values of θ from 20° to 80° using 5° increments. (*b*) Using appropriate smaller increments, determine the optimum value of θ and the corresponding values of the weight of the truss and of the cross-sectional areas of the various members. Ignore the weight of any zero-force member in your computations.

6.C2 The floor of a bridge will rest on stringers that will be simply supported by transverse floor beams, as in Fig. 6.3. The ends of the beams will be connected to the upper joints of two trusses, one of which is shown in Fig. P6.C2. As part of the design of the bridge, it is desired to simulate the effect on this truss of driving a 12-kN truck over the bridge. Knowing that the distance between the truck's axles is $b = 2.25$ m and assuming that the weight of the truck is equally distributed over its four wheels, use computational software to calculate the forces created by the truck in members *BH* and *GH* for values of *x* from 0 to 17.25 m using 0.75-m increments. From the results obtained, determine (*a*) the maximum tensile force in *BH*, (*b*) the maximum compressive force in *BH*, (*c*) the maximum tensile force in *GH*. Indicate in each case the corresponding value of *x*. (*Note:* The increments have been selected so that the desired values are among those that will be tabulated.)

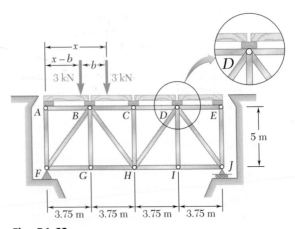

Fig. P6.C2

6.C3 In the mechanism shown the position of boom AC is controlled by arm BD. For the loading shown, use computational software to determine the couple **M** required to hold the system in equilibrium for values of θ from $-30°$ to $90°$ using $10°$ increments. Also, for the same values of θ, determine the reaction at A. As a part of the design process of the mechanism, use appropriate smaller increments and determine (a) the value of θ for which M is maximum and the corresponding value of M, (b) the value of θ for which the reaction at A is maximum and the corresponding magnitude of this reaction.

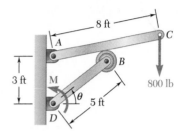

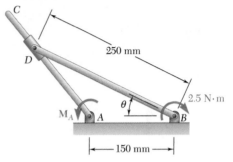

Fig. P6.C3

6.C4 The design of a robotic system calls for the two-rod mechanism shown. Rods AC and BD are connected by a slider block D as shown. Neglecting the effect of friction, use computational software to determine the couple $\mathbf{M}_A$ required to hold the rods in equilibrium for values of θ from 0 to $120°$ using $10°$ increments. For the same values of θ, determine the magnitude of the force **F** exerted by rod AC on the slider block.

6.C5 The compound-lever pruning shears shown can be adjusted by placing pin A at various ratchet positions on blade ACE. Knowing that the length AB is 0.85 in., use computational software to determine the magnitude of the vertical forces applied to the small branch for values of d from 0.4 in. to 0.6 in. using 0.025 in. increments. As a part of the design of the shears, use appropriate smaller increments and determine the smallest allowable value of d if the force in link AB is not to exceed 500 lb.

Fig. P6.C4

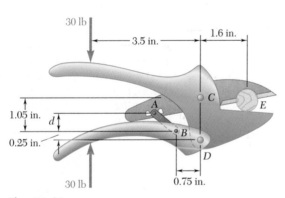

Fig. P6.C5

6.C6 Rod CD is attached to collar D and passes through a collar welded to end B of lever AB. As an initial step in the design of lever AB, use computational software to calculate the magnitude M of the couple required to hold the system in equilibrium for values of θ from $15°$ to $90°$ using $5°$ increments. Using appropriate smaller increments, determine the value of θ for which M is minimum and the corresponding value of M.

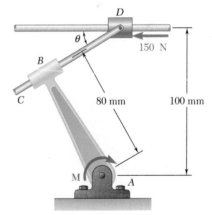

Fig. P6.C6

The George Washington Bridge connects Manhattan, New York, and Fort Lee, New Jersey. This suspension bridge carries traffic on two levels over roadways that are supported by a system of beams. Trusses are used both to connect these roadways to complete the overall bridge span as well as to form the towers. The bridge span itself is supported by the cable system.

CHAPTER 7

Forces in Beams and Cables

*7.1 INTRODUCTION

In preceding chapters, two basic problems involving structures were considered: (1) determining the external forces acting on a structure (Chap. 4) and (2) determining the forces which hold together the various members forming a structure (Chap. 6). The problem of determining the internal forces which hold together the various parts of a given member will now be considered.

We will first analyze the internal forces in the members of a frame, such as the crane considered in Secs. 6.1 and 6.10, noting that whereas the internal forces in a straight two-force member can produce only *tension* or *compression* in that member, the internal forces in any other type of member usually produce *shear* and *bending* as well.

Most of this chapter will be devoted to the analysis of the internal forces in two important types of engineering structures, namely,

1. *Beams,* which are usually long, straight prismatic members designed to support loads applied at various points along the member.
2. *Cables,* which are flexible members capable of withstanding only tension, designed to support either concentrated or distributed loads. Cables are used in many engineering applications, such as suspension bridges and transmission lines.

*7.2 INTERNAL FORCES IN MEMBERS

Let us first consider a *straight two-force member AB* (Fig. 7.1a). From Sec. 4.6, we know that the forces $\mathbf{F}$ and $-\mathbf{F}$ acting at A and B, respectively, must be directed along AB in opposite sense and have the same magnitude F. Now, let us cut the member at C. To maintain the equilibrium of the free bodies AC and CB thus obtained, we must apply to AC a force $-\mathbf{F}$ equal and opposite to $\mathbf{F}$, and to CB a force $\mathbf{F}$ equal and opposite to $-\mathbf{F}$ (Fig. 7.1b). These new forces are directed along AB in opposite sense and have the same magnitude F. Since the two parts AC and CB were in equilibrium before the member was cut, *internal forces* equivalent to these new forces must have existed in the member itself. We conclude that in the case of a straight two-force member, the internal forces that the two portions of the member exert on each other are equivalent to *axial forces*. The common magnitude F of these forces does not depend upon the location of the section C and is referred to as the *force in member AB*. In the case considered, the member is in tension and will elongate under the action of the internal forces. In the case represented in Fig. 7.2, the member is in compression and will decrease in length under the action of the internal forces.

Next, let us consider a *multiforce member*. Take, for instance, member AD of the crane analyzed in Sec. 6.10. This crane is shown again in Fig. 7.3a, and the free-body diagram of member AD is drawn in Fig. 7.3b. We now cut member AD at J and draw a free-body diagram for each of the portions JD and AJ of the member

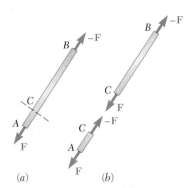

Fig. 7.1

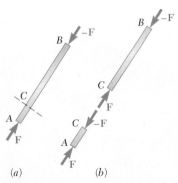

Fig. 7.2

354

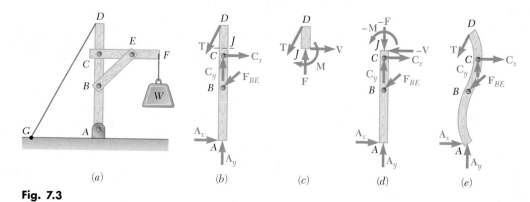

Fig. 7.3

(Fig. 7.3c and d). Considering the free body *JD*, we find that its equilibrium will be maintained if we apply at *J* a force **F** to balance the vertical component of **T**, a force **V** to balance the horizontal component of **T**, and a couple **M** to balance the moment of **T** about *J*. Again we conclude that internal forces must have existed at *J* before member *AD* was cut. The internal forces acting on the portion *JD* of member *AD* are equivalent to the force-couple system shown in Fig. 7.3c. According to Newton's third law, the internal forces acting on *AJ* must be equivalent to an equal and opposite force-couple system, as shown in Fig. 7.3d. It is clear that the action of the internal forces in member *AD* *is not limited to producing tension or compression* as in the case of straight two-force members; the internal forces *also produce shear and bending.* The force **F** is an *axial force;* the force **V** is called a *shearing force;* and the moment **M** of the couple is known as the *bending moment at J.* We note that when determining internal forces in a member, we should clearly indicate on which portion of the member the forces are supposed to act. The deformation which will occur in member *AD* is sketched in Fig. 7.3e. The actual analysis of such a deformation is part of the study of mechanics of materials.

It should be noted that in a *two-force member which is not straight,* the internal forces are also equivalent to a force-couple system. This is shown in Fig. 7.4, where the two-force member *ABC* has been cut at *D*.

Photo 7.1 The design of the shaft of a circular saw must account for the internal forces resulting from the forces applied to the teeth of the blade. At a given point in the shaft, these internal forces are equivalent to a force-couple system consisting of axial and shearing forces and a couple representing the bending and torsional moments.

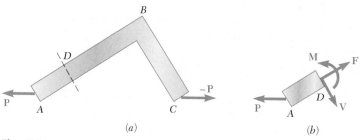

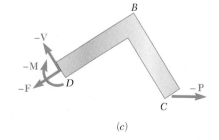

Fig. 7.4

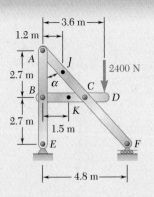

SAMPLE PROBLEM 7.1

In the frame shown, determine the internal forces (*a*) in member *ACF* at point *J*, (*b*) in member *BCD* at point *K*. This frame has been previously considered in Sample Prob. 6.5.

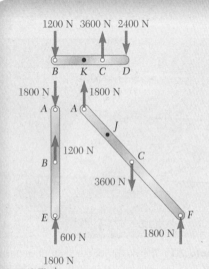

SOLUTION

Reactions and Forces at Connections. The reactions and the forces acting on each member of the frame are determined; this has been previously done in Sample Prob. 6.5, and the results are repeated here.

a. Internal Forces at J. Member *ACF* is cut at point *J*, and the two parts shown are obtained. The internal forces at *J* are represented by an equivalent force-couple system and can be determined by considering the equilibrium of either part. Considering the *free body AJ*, we write

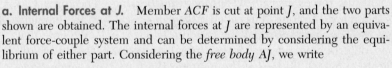

$+\curvearrowleft \Sigma M_J = 0:$ $\quad -(1800 \text{ N})(1.2 \text{ m}) + M = 0$

$\quad\quad M = +2160 \text{ N} \cdot \text{m}$ $\quad\quad \mathbf{M} = 2160 \text{ N} \cdot \text{m} \curvearrowleft$ ◀

$+\searrow \Sigma F_x = 0:$ $\quad F - (1800 \text{ N}) \cos 41.7° = 0$

$\quad\quad F = +1344 \text{ N}$ $\quad\quad \mathbf{F} = 1344 \text{ N} \searrow$ ◀

$+\nearrow \Sigma F_y = 0:$ $\quad -V + (1800 \text{ N}) \sin 41.7° = 0$

$\quad\quad V = +1197 \text{ N}$ $\quad\quad \mathbf{V} = 1197 \text{ N} \swarrow$ ◀

The internal forces at *J* are therefore equivalent to a couple **M**, an axial force **F**, and a shearing force **V**. The internal force-couple system acting on part *JCF* is equal and opposite.

b. Internal Forces at K. We cut member *BCD* at *K* and obtain the two parts shown. Considering the *free body BK*, we write

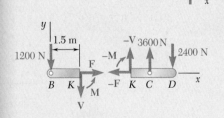

$+\curvearrowleft \Sigma M_K = 0:$ $\quad (1200 \text{ N})(1.5 \text{ m}) + M = 0$

$\quad\quad M = -1800 \text{ N} \cdot \text{m}$ $\quad\quad \mathbf{M} = 1800 \text{ N} \cdot \text{m} \curvearrowright$ ◀

$\xrightarrow{+} \Sigma F_x = 0:$ $\quad F = 0$ $\quad\quad \mathbf{F} = 0$ ◀

$+\uparrow \Sigma F_y = 0:$ $\quad -1200 \text{ N} - V = 0$

$\quad\quad V = -1200 \text{ N}$ $\quad\quad \mathbf{V} = 1200 \text{ N} \uparrow$ ◀

SOLVING PROBLEMS ON YOUR OWN

In this lesson you learned to determine the internal forces in the member of a frame. The internal forces at a given point in a *straight two-force member* reduce to an axial force, but in all other cases, they are equivalent to a *force-couple system* consisting of an *axial force* **F**, a *shearing force* **V**, and a couple **M** representing the *bending moment* at that point.

To determine the internal forces at a given point *J* of the member of a frame, you should take the following steps.

1. Draw a free-body diagram of the entire frame, and use it to determine as many of the reactions at the supports as you can.

2. Dismember the frame, and draw a free-body diagram of each of its members. Write as many equilibrium equations as are necessary to find all the forces acting on the member on which point *J* is located.

3. Cut the member at point J, and draw a free-body diagram of each of the two portions of the member that you have obtained, applying to each portion at point *J* the force components and couple representing the internal forces exerted by the other portion. Note that these force components and couples are equal in magnitude and opposite in sense.

4. Select one of the two free-body diagrams you have drawn and use it to write three equilibrium equations for the corresponding portion of member.

    a. Summing moments about J and equating them to zero will yield the bending moment at point *J*.

    b. Summing components in directions parallel and perpendicular to the member at *J* and equating them to zero will yield, respectively, the axial and shearing force.

5. When recording your answers, be sure to specify the portion of the member you have used, since the forces and couples acting on the two portions have opposite senses.

Since the solutions of the problems in this lesson require the determination of the forces exerted on each other by the various members of a frame, be sure to review the methods used in Chap. 6 to solve this type of problem. When frames involve pulleys and cables, for instance, remember that the forces exerted by a pulley on the member of the frame to which it is attached have the same magnitude and direction as the forces exerted by the cable on the pulley [Prob. 6.90].

PROBLEMS

7.1 and 7.2 Determine the internal forces (axial force, shearing force, and bending moment) at point *J* of the structure indicated.

    7.1 Frame and loading of Prob. 6.79

    7.2 Frame and loading of Prob. 6.80

7.3 Determine the internal forces at point *J* when $\alpha = 90°$.

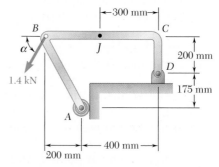

Fig. P7.3 and P7.4

7.4 Determine the internal forces at point *J* when $\alpha = 0$.

7.5 Determine the internal forces at point *J* of the structure shown.

7.6 Determine the internal forces at point *K* of the structure shown.

7.7 A semicircular rod is loaded as shown. Determine the internal forces at point *J*.

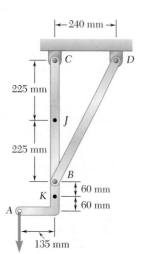

Fig. P7.5 and P7.6

Fig. P7.7 and P7.8

7.8 A semicircular rod is loaded as shown. Determine the internal forces at point *K*.

7.9 An archer aiming at a target is pulling with a 45-lb force on the bowstring. Assuming that the shape of the bow can be approximated by a parabola, determine the internal forces at point *J*.

7.10 For the bow of Prob. 7.9, determine the magnitude and location of the maximum (*a*) axial force, (*b*) shearing force, (*c*) bending moment.

7.11 Two members, each consisting of a straight and a quarter-circular portion of rod, are connected as shown and support a 75-lb load at *A*. Determine the internal forces at point *J*.

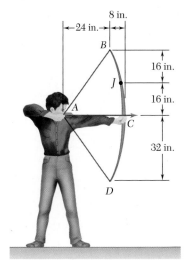

Fig. P7.9

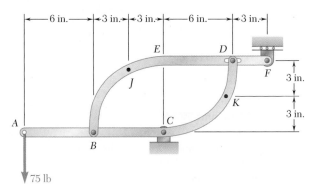

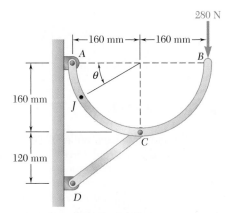

Fig. *P7.11* and *P7.12*

7.12 Two members, each consisting of a straight and a quarter-circular portion of rod, are connected as shown and support a 75-lb load at *A*. Determine the internal forces at point *K*.

7.13 A semicircular rod is loaded as shown. Determine the internal forces at point *J* knowing that $\theta = 30°$.

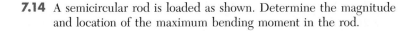

Fig. P7.13 and P7.14

7.14 A semicircular rod is loaded as shown. Determine the magnitude and location of the maximum bending moment in the rod.

7.15 Knowing that the radius of each pulley is 150 mm, that $\alpha = 20°$, and neglecting friction, determine the internal forces at (a) point J, (b) point K.

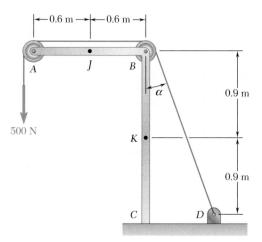

Fig. P7.15 and P7.16

7.16 Knowing that the radius of each pulley is 150 mm, that $\alpha = 30°$, and neglecting friction, determine the internal forces at (a) point J, (b) point K.

7.17 Knowing that the radius of each pulley is 200 mm and neglecting friction, determine the internal forces at point J of the frame shown.

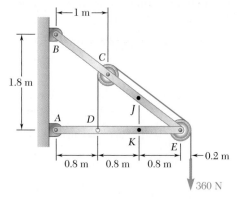

Fig. P7.17 and P7.18

7.18 Knowing that the radius of each pulley is 200 mm and neglecting friction, determine the internal forces at point K of the frame shown.

7.19 A 5-in.-diameter pipe is supported every 9 ft by a small frame consisting of two members as shown. Knowing that the combined weight of the pipe and its contents is 10 lb/ft and neglecting the effect of friction, determine the magnitude and location of the maximum bending moment in member AC.

7.20 For the frame of Prob. 7.19, determine the magnitude and location of the maximum bending moment in member BC.

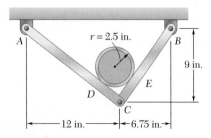

Fig. P7.19

7.21 and 7.22 A force **P** is applied to a bent rod that is supported by a roller and a pin and bracket. For each of the three cases shown, determine the internal forces at point *J*.

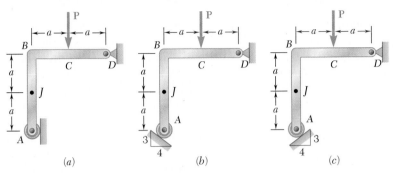

(a)   (b)   (c)

Fig. P7.21

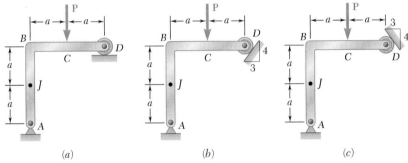

(a)   (b)   (c)

Fig. P7.22

7.23 A semicircular rod of weight W and uniform cross section is supported as shown. Determine the bending moment at point J when $\theta = 60°$.

7.24 A semicircular rod of weight W and uniform cross section is supported as shown. Determine the bending moment at point J when $\theta = 150°$.

7.25 and 7.26 A quarter-circular rod of weight W and uniform cross section is supported as shown. Determine the bending moment at point J when $\theta = 30°$.

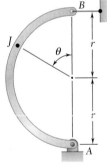

Fig. P7.23 and P7.24

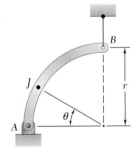

Fig. P7.25

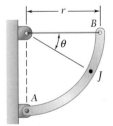

Fig. P7.26

7.27 For the rod of Prob. 7.25, determine the magnitude and location of the maximum bending moment.

7.28 For the rod of Prob. 7.26, determine the magnitude and location of the maximum bending moment.

BEAMS

*7.3 VARIOUS TYPES OF LOADING AND SUPPORT

A structural member designed to support loads applied at various points along the member is known as a *beam*. In most cases, the loads are perpendicular to the axis of the beam and will cause only shear and bending in the beam. When the loads are not at a right angle to the beam, they will also produce axial forces in the beam.

Beams are usually long, straight prismatic bars. Designing a beam for the most effective support of the applied loads is a two-part process: (1) determining the shearing forces and bending moments produced by the loads and (2) selecting the cross section best suited to resist the shearing forces and bending moments determined in the first part. Here we are concerned with the first part of the problem of beam design. The second part belongs to the study of mechanics of materials.

A beam can be subjected to *concentrated loads* $\mathbf{P}_1$, $\mathbf{P}_2$, . . ., expressed in newtons, pounds, or their multiples kilonewtons and kips (Fig. 7.5*a*), to a *distributed load* w, expressed in N/m, kN/m, lb/ft, or kips/ft (Fig. 7.5*b*), or to a combination of both. When the load w per unit length has a constant value over part of the beam (as between A and B in Fig. 7.5*b*), the load is said to be *uniformly distributed* over that part of the beam. The determination of the reactions at the supports is considerably simplified if distributed loads are replaced by equivalent concentrated loads, as explained in Sec. 5.8. This substitution, however, should not be performed, or at least should be performed with care, when internal forces are being computed (see Sample Prob. 7.3).

Beams are classified according to the way in which they are supported. Several types of beams frequently used are shown in Fig. 7.6. The distance L between supports is called the *span*. It should be noted that the reactions will be determinate if the supports involve only three unknowns. If more unknowns are involved, the

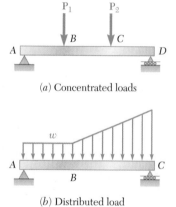

(*a*) Concentrated loads

(*b*) Distributed load

Fig. 7.5

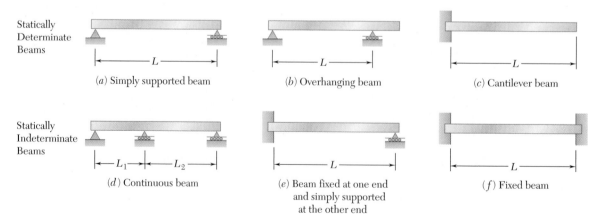

Statically Determinate Beams

(*a*) Simply supported beam

(*b*) Overhanging beam

(*c*) Cantilever beam

Statically Indeterminate Beams

(*d*) Continuous beam

(*e*) Beam fixed at one end and simply supported at the other end

(*f*) Fixed beam

Fig. 7.6

reactions will be statically indeterminate and the methods of statics will not be sufficient to determine the reactions; the properties of the beam with regard to its resistance to bending must then be taken into consideration. Beams supported by two rollers are not shown here; they are only partially constrained and will move under certain loadings.

Sometimes two or more beams are connected by hinges to form a single continuous structure. Two examples of beams hinged at a point H are shown in Fig. 7.7. It will be noted that the reactions at the supports involve four unknowns and cannot be determined from the free-body diagram of the two-beam system. They can be determined, however, by considering the free-body diagram of each beam separately; six unknowns are involved (including two force components at the hinge), and six equations are available.

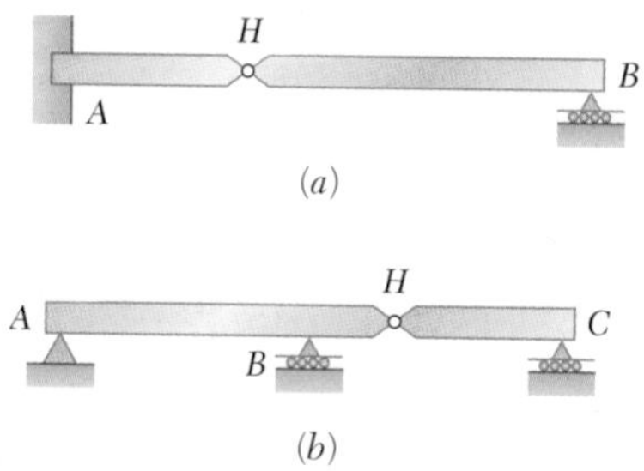

Fig. 7.7

*7.4   SHEAR AND BENDING MOMENT IN A BEAM

Consider a beam AB subjected to various concentrated and distributed loads (Fig. 7.8a). We propose to determine the shearing force and bending moment at any point of the beam. In the example considered here, the beam is simply supported, but the method used could be applied to any type of statically determinate beam.

First we determine the reactions at A and B by choosing the entire beam as a free body (Fig. 7.8b); writing $\Sigma M_A = 0$ and $\Sigma M_B = 0$, we obtain, respectively, $\mathbf{R}_B$ and $\mathbf{R}_A$.

To determine the internal forces at C, we cut the beam at C and draw the free-body diagrams of the portions AC and CB of the

Photo 7.2   The internal forces in the beams of the overpass shown vary as the truck crosses the overpass.

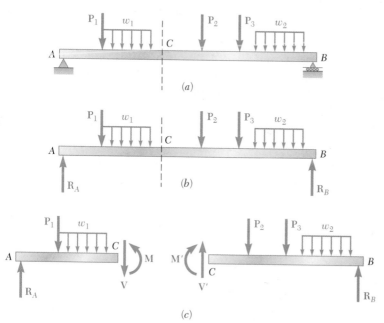

Fig. 7.8

beam (Fig. 7.8c). Using the free-body diagram of AC, we can determine the shearing force **V** at C by equating to zero the sum of the vertical components of all forces acting on AC. Similarly, the bending moment **M** at C can be found by equating to zero the sum of the moments about C of all forces and couples acting on AC. Alternatively, we could use the free-body diagram of CB† and determine the shearing force **V'** and the bending moment **M'** by equating to zero the sum of the vertical components and the sum of the moments about C of all forces and couples acting on CB. While this choice of free bodies may facilitate the computation of the numerical values of the shearing force and bending moment, it makes it necessary to indicate on which portion of the beam the internal forces considered are acting. If the shearing force and bending moment are to be computed at every point of the beam and efficiently recorded, we must find a way to avoid having to specify every time which portion of the beam is used as a free body. We shall adopt, therefore, the following conventions:

In determining the shearing force in a beam, *it will always be assumed* that the internal forces **V** and **V'** are directed as shown in Fig. 7.8c. A positive value obtained for their common magnitude V will indicate that this assumption was correct and that the shearing forces are actually directed as shown. A negative value obtained for V will indicate that the assumption was wrong and that the shearing forces are directed in the opposite way. Thus, only the magnitude V, together with a plus or minus sign, needs to be recorded to define completely the shearing forces at a given point of the beam. The scalar V is commonly referred to as the *shear* at the given point of the beam.

Similarly, *it will always be assumed* that the internal couples **M** and **M'** are directed as shown in Fig. 7.8c. A positive value obtained for their magnitude M, commonly referred to as the bending moment, will indicate that this assumption was correct, and a negative value will indicate that it was wrong. Summarizing the sign conventions we have presented, we state:

The shear V and the bending moment M at a given point of a beam are said to be positive when the internal forces and couples acting on each portion of the beam are directed as shown in Fig. 7.9a.

These conventions can be more easily remembered if we note that:

1. *The shear at C is positive when the **external** forces (loads and reactions) acting on the beam tend to shear off the beam at C as indicated in Fig. 7.9b.*
2. *The bending moment at C is positive when the **external** forces acting on the beam tend to bend the beam at C as indicated in Fig. 7.9c.*

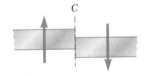

(a) Internal forces at section
(positive shear and positive bending moment)

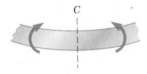

(b) Effect of external forces
(positive shear)

(c) Effect of external forces
(positive bending moment)

Fig. 7.9

---

†The force and couple representing the internal forces acting on CB will now be denoted by **V'** and **M'**, rather than by −**V** and −**M** as done earlier, in order to avoid confusion when applying the sign convention which we are about to introduce.

It may also help to note that the situation described in Fig. 7.9, in which the values of the shear and of the bending moment are positive, is precisely the situation which occurs in the left half of a simply supported beam carrying a single concentrated load at its midpoint. This particular example is fully discussed in the following section.

*7.5 SHEAR AND BENDING-MOMENT DIAGRAMS

Now that shear and bending moment have been clearly defined in sense as well as in magnitude, we can easily record their values at any point of a beam by plotting these values against the distance x measured from one end of the beam. The graphs obtained in this way are called, respectively, the *shear diagram* and the *bending-moment diagram*. As an example, consider a simply supported beam AB of span L subjected to a single concentrated load $\mathbf{P}$ applied at its midpoint D (Fig. 7.10a). We first determine the reactions at the supports from the free-body diagram of the entire beam (Fig. 7.10b); we find that the magnitude of each reaction is equal to $P/2$.

Next we cut the beam at a point C between A and D and draw the free-body diagrams of AC and CB (Fig. 7.10c). *Assuming that shear and bending moment are positive*, we direct the internal forces $\mathbf{V}$ and $\mathbf{V}'$ and the internal couples $\mathbf{M}$ and $\mathbf{M}'$ as indicated in Fig. 7.9a. Considering the free body AC and writing that the sum of the vertical components and the sum of the moments about C of the forces acting on the free body are zero, we find $V = +P/2$ and $M = +Px/2$. Both shear and bending moment are therefore positive; this can be checked by observing that the reaction at A tends to shear off and to bend the beam at C as indicated in Fig. 7.9b and c. We can plot V and M between A and D (Fig. 7.10e and f); the shear has a constant value $V = P/2$, while the bending moment increases linearly from $M = 0$ at $x = 0$ to $M = PL/4$ at $x = L/2$.

Cutting, now, the beam at a point E between D and B and considering the free body EB (Fig. 7.10d), we write that the sum of the vertical components and the sum of the moments about E of the forces acting on the free body are zero. We obtain $V = -P/2$ and $M = P(L - x)/2$. The shear is therefore negative and the bending moment positive; this can be checked by observing that the reaction at B bends the beam at E as indicated in Fig. 7.9c but tends to shear it off in a manner opposite to that shown in Fig. 7.9b. We can complete, now, the shear and bending-moment diagrams of Fig. 7.10e and f; the shear has a constant value $V = -P/2$ between D and B, while the bending moment decreases linearly from $M = PL/4$ at $x = L/2$ to $M = 0$ at $x = L$.

It should be noted that when a beam is subjected to concentrated loads only, the shear is of constant value between loads and the bending moment varies linearly between loads, but when a beam is subjected to distributed loads, the shear and bending moment vary quite differently (see Sample Prob. 7.3).

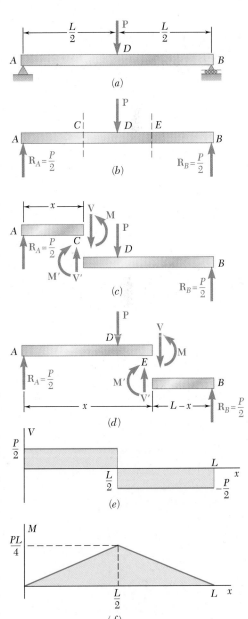

Fig. 7.10

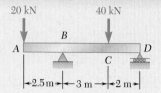

20 kN   40 kN

B

A   D

$\leftarrow$2.5m$\rightarrow$$\leftarrow$3 m$\rightarrow$$\leftarrow$2 m$\rightarrow$

SAMPLE PROBLEM 7.2

Draw the shear and bending-moment diagrams for the beam and loading shown.

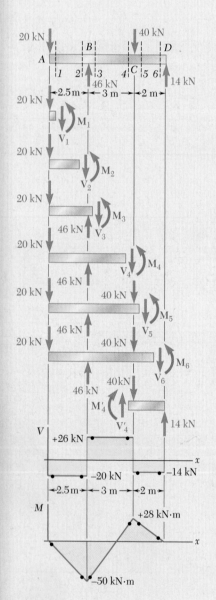

SOLUTION

Free-Body: Entire Beam.   From the free-body diagram of the entire beam, we find the reactions at B and D:

$$\mathbf{R}_B = 46 \text{ kN} \uparrow \qquad \mathbf{R}_D = 14 \text{ kN} \uparrow$$

Shear and Bending Moment.   We first determine the internal forces just to the right of the 20-kN load at A. Considering the stub of beam to the left of section 1 as a free body and assuming V and M to be positive (according to the standard convention), we write

$+\uparrow\Sigma F_y = 0$: $\qquad -20 \text{ kN} - V_1 = 0$ $\qquad\qquad\qquad V_1 = -20 \text{ kN}$
$+\gamma\ \Sigma M_1 = 0$: $\qquad (20 \text{ kN})(0 \text{ m}) + M_1 = 0$ $\qquad\qquad M_1 = 0$

We next consider as a free body the portion of the beam to the left of section 2 and write

$+\uparrow\Sigma F_y = 0$: $\qquad -20 \text{ kN} - V_2 = 0$ $\qquad\qquad\qquad V_2 = -20 \text{ kN}$
$+\gamma\ \Sigma M_2 = 0$: $\qquad (20 \text{ kN})(2.5 \text{ m}) + M_2 = 0$ $\qquad M_2 = -50 \text{ kN} \cdot \text{m}$

The shear and bending moment at sections 3, 4, 5, and 6 are determined in a similar way from the free-body diagrams shown. We obtain

$$
\begin{aligned}
V_3 &= +26 \text{ kN} & M_3 &= -50 \text{ kN} \cdot \text{m} \\
V_4 &= +26 \text{ kN} & M_4 &= +28 \text{ kN} \cdot \text{m} \\
V_5 &= -14 \text{ kN} & M_5 &= +28 \text{ kN} \cdot \text{m} \\
V_6 &= -14 \text{ kN} & M_6 &= 0
\end{aligned}
$$

For several of the latter sections, the results are more easily obtained by considering as a free body the portion of the beam to the right of the section. For example, considering the portion of the beam to the right of section 4, we write

$+\uparrow\Sigma F_y = 0$: $\qquad V_4 - 40 \text{ kN} + 14 \text{ kN} = 0$ $\qquad V_4 = +26 \text{ kN}$
$+\gamma\ \Sigma M_4 = 0$: $\qquad -M_4 + (14 \text{ kN})(2 \text{ m}) = 0$ $\qquad M_4 = +28 \text{ kN} \cdot \text{m}$

Shear and Bending-Moment Diagrams.   We can now plot the six points shown on the shear and bending-moment diagrams. As indicated in Sec. 7.5, the shear is of constant value between concentrated loads, and the bending moment varies linearly; we therefore obtain the shear and bending-moment diagrams shown.

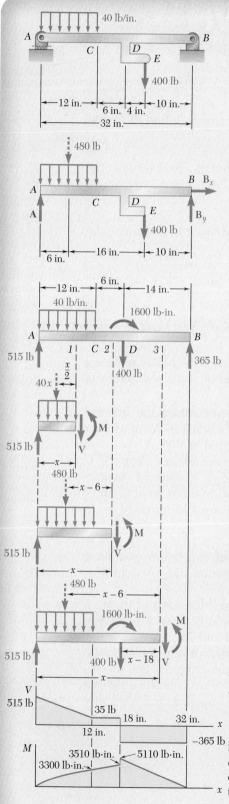

SAMPLE PROBLEM 7.3

Draw the shear and bending-moment diagrams for the beam AB. The distributed load of 40 lb/in. extends over 12 in. of the beam, from A to C, and the 400-lb load is applied at E.

SOLUTION

Free-Body: Entire Beam. The reactions are determined by considering the entire beam as a free body.

$+\uparrow \Sigma M_A = 0$: $B_y(32 \text{ in.}) - (480 \text{ lb})(6 \text{ in.}) - (400 \text{ lb})(22 \text{ in.}) = 0$
$B_y = +365 \text{ lb}$ $\mathbf{B}_y = 365 \text{ lb} \uparrow$
$+\uparrow \Sigma M_B = 0$: $(480 \text{ lb})(26 \text{ in.}) + (400 \text{ lb})(10 \text{ in.}) - A(32 \text{ in.}) = 0$
$A = +515 \text{ lb}$ $\mathbf{A} = 515 \text{ lb} \uparrow$
$\xrightarrow{+} \Sigma F_x = 0$: $B_x = 0$ $\mathbf{B}_x = 0$

The 400-lb load is now replaced by an equivalent force-couple system acting on the beam at point D.

Shear and Bending Moment. *From A to C.* We determine the internal forces at a distance x from point A by considering the portion of the beam to the left of section 1. That part of the distributed load acting on the free body is replaced by its resultant, and we write

$+\uparrow \Sigma F_y = 0$: $515 - 40x - V = 0$ $V = 515 - 40x$
$+\uparrow \Sigma M_1 = 0$: $-515x + 40x(\tfrac{1}{2}x) + M = 0$ $M = 515x - 20x^2$

Since the free-body diagram shown can be used for all values of x smaller than 12 in., the expressions obtained for V and M are valid throughout the region $0 < x < 12$ in.

From C to D. Considering the portion of the beam to the left of section 2 and again replacing the distributed load by its resultant, we obtain

$+\uparrow \Sigma F_y = 0$: $515 - 480 - V = 0$ $V = 35 \text{ lb}$
$+\uparrow \Sigma M_2 = 0$: $-515x + 480(x - 6) + M = 0$ $M = (2880 + 35x) \text{ lb} \cdot \text{in.}$

These expressions are valid in the region 12 in. $< x < 18$ in.

From D to B. Using the portion of the beam to the left of section 3, we obtain for the region 18 in. $< x < 32$ in.

$+\uparrow \Sigma F_y = 0$: $515 - 480 - 400 - V = 0$ $V = -365 \text{ lb}$
$+\uparrow \Sigma M_3 = 0$: $-515x + 480(x - 6) - 1600 + 400(x - 18) + M = 0$
$M = (11{,}680 - 365x) \text{ lb} \cdot \text{in.}$

Shear and Bending-Moment Diagrams. The shear and bending-moment diagrams for the entire beam can now be plotted. We note that the couple of moment 1600 lb · in. applied at point D introduces a discontinuity into the bending-moment diagram.

SOLVING PROBLEMS ON YOUR OWN

In this lesson you learned to determine the shear V and the *bending moment* M at any point in a beam. You also learned to draw the *shear diagram* and the *bending-moment diagram* for the beam by plotting, respectively, V and M against the distance x measured along the beam.

A. Determining the shear and bending moment in a beam. To determine the shear V and the bending moment M at a given point C of a beam, you should take the following steps.

1. Draw a free-body diagram of the entire beam, and use it to determine the reactions at the beam supports.

2. Cut the beam at point C, and, using the original loading, select one of the two portions of the beam you have obtained.

3. Draw the free-body diagram of the portion of the beam you have selected, showing:

 a. The loads and the reaction exerted on that portion of the beam, replacing each distributed load by an equivalent concentrated load as explained earlier in Sec. 5.8.

 b. The shearing force and the bending couple representing the internal forces at C. To facilitate recording the shear V and the bending moment M after they have been determined, follow the convention indicated in Figs. 7.8 and 7.9. Thus, if you are using the portion of the beam located to the *left of C*, apply at C a *shearing force* **V** *directed downward* and a *bending couple* **M** *directed counterclockwise*. If you are using the portion of the beam located to the *right of C*, apply at C a *shearing force* **V′** *directed upward* and a *bending couple* **M′** *directed clockwise* [Sample Prob. 7.2].

4. Write the equilibrium equations for the portion of the beam you have selected. Solve the equation $\Sigma F_y = 0$ for V and the equation $\Sigma M_C = 0$ for M.

5. Record the values of V and M with the sign obtained for each of them. A positive sign for V means that the shearing forces exerted at C on each of the two portions of the beam are directed as shown in Figs. 7.8 and 7.9; a negative sign means that they have the opposite sense. Similarly, a positive sign for M means that the bending couples at C are directed as shown in these figures, and a negative sign means that they have the opposite sense. In addition, a positive sign for M means that the concavity of the beam at C is directed upward, and a negative sign means that it is directed downward.

B. Drawing the shear and bending-moment diagrams for a beam. These diagrams are obtained by plotting, respectively, V and M against the distance x measured along the beam. However, in most cases the values of V and M need to be computed only at a few points.

1. For a beam supporting only concentrated loads, we note [Sample Prob. 7.2] that

a. The shear diagram consists of segments of horizontal lines. Thus, to draw the shear diagram of the beam you will need to compute V only just to the left or just to the right of the points where the loads or the reactions are applied.

b. The bending-moment diagram consists of segments of oblique straight lines. Thus, to draw the bending-moment diagram of the beam you will need to compute M only at the points where the loads or the reactions are applied.

2. For a beam supporting uniformly distributed loads, we note [Sample Prob. 7.3] that under each of the distributed loads:

a. The shear diagram consists of a segment of an oblique straight line. Thus, you will need to compute V only where the distributed load begins and where it ends.

b. The bending-moment diagram consists of an arc of parabola. In most cases you will need to compute M only where the distributed load begins and where it ends.

3. For a beam with a more complicated loading, it is necessary to consider the free-body diagram of a portion of the beam of arbitrary length x and determine V and M as functions of x. This procedure may have to be repeated several times, since V and M are often represented by different functions in various parts of the beam [Sample Prob. 7.3].

4. When a couple is applied to a beam, the shear has the same value on both sides of the point of application of the couple, but the bending-moment diagram will show a discontinuity at that point, rising or falling by an amount equal to the magnitude of the couple. Note that a couple can either be applied directly to the beam, or result from the application of a load on a curved member rigidly attached to the beam [Sample Prob. 7.3].

PROBLEMS

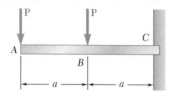

Fig. P7.29

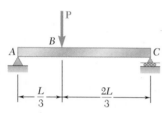

Fig. P7.30

7.29 through 7.32 For the beam and loading shown, (*a*) draw the shear and bending-moment diagrams, (*b*) determine the maximum absolute values of the shear and bending moment.

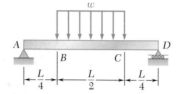

Fig. P7.31

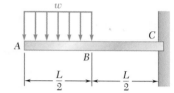

Fig. P7.32

7.33 and 7.34 For the beam and loading shown, (*a*) draw the shear and bending-moment diagrams, (*b*) determine the maximum absolute values of the shear and bending moment.

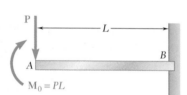

Fig. *P7.33*

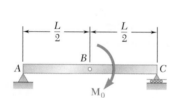

Fig. *P7.34*

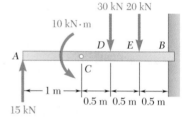

Fig. P7.35

7.35 and 7.36 For the beam and loading shown, (*a*) draw the shear and bending-moment diagrams, (*b*) determine the maximum absolute values of the shear and bending moment.

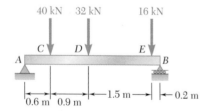

Fig. P7.36

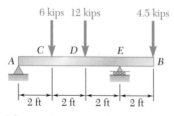

Fig. *P7.37*

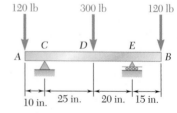

Fig. *P7.38*

7.37 and 7.38 For the beam and loading shown, (*a*) draw the shear and bending-moment diagrams, (*b*) determine the maximum absolute values of the shear and bending moment.

7.39 through 7.42 For the beam and loading shown, (a) draw the shear and bending-moment diagrams, (b) determine the maximum absolute values of the shear and bending moment.

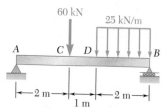

Fig. P7.39

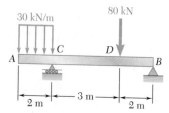

Fig. P7.40

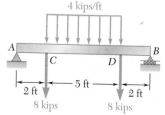

Fig. P7.41

7.43 Assuming the upward reaction of the ground on beam AB to be uniformly distributed and knowing that $a = 0.3$ m, (a) draw the shear and bending-moment diagrams, (b) determine the maximum absolute values of the shear and bending moment.

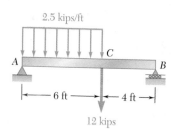

Fig. P7.42

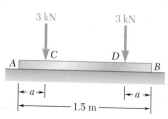

Fig. P7.43

7.44 Solve Prob. 7.43 knowing that $a = 0.5$ m.

7.45 and 7.46 Assuming the upward reaction of the ground on beam AB to be uniformly distributed, (a) draw the shear and bending-moment diagrams, (b) determine the maximum absolute values of the shear and bending moment.

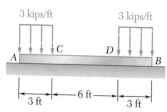

Fig. P7.45

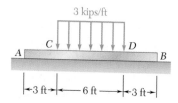

Fig. P7.46

7.47 Assuming the upward reaction of the ground on beam AB to be uniformly distributed and knowing that $P = wa$, (a) draw the shear and bending-moment diagrams, (b) determine the maximum absolute values of the shear and bending moment.

7.48 Solve Prob. 7.47 knowing that $P = 3wa$.

7.49 Draw the shear and bending-moment diagrams for the beam AB, and determine the shear and bending moment (a) just to the left of C, (b) just to the right of C.

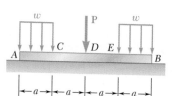

Fig. P7.47

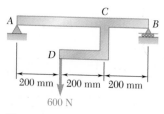

Fig. P7.49

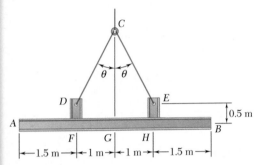

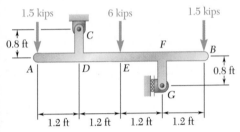

Fig. P7.50

Fig. P7.52

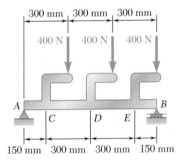

Fig. P7.54

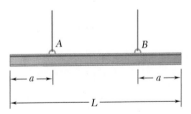

Fig. P7.58

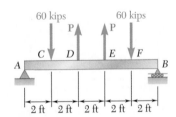

Fig. P7.59

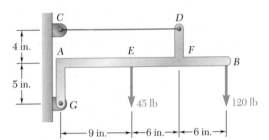

Fig. P7.53

7.50 Two small channel sections *DF* and *EH* have been welded to the uniform beam *AB* of weight *W* = 3 kN to form the rigid structural member shown. This member is being lifted by two cables attached at *D* and *E*. Knowing that θ = 30° and neglecting the weight of the channel sections, (*a*) draw the shear and bending-moment diagrams for beam *AB*, (*b*) determine the maximum absolute values of the shear and bending moment in the beam.

7.51 Solve Prob. 7.50 when θ = 60°.

7.52 through 7.54 Draw the shear and bending-moment diagrams for the beam *AB*, and determine the maximum absolute values of the shear and bending moment.

7.55 For the structural member of Prob. 7.50, determine (*a*) the angle θ for which the maximum absolute value of the bending moment in beam *AB* is as small as possible, (*b*) the corresponding value of $|M|_{max}$. (*Hint:* Draw the bending-moment diagram and then equate the absolute values of the largest positive and negative bending moments obtained.)

7.56 For the beam of Prob. 7.43, determine (*a*) the distance *a* for which the maximum absolute value of the bending moment in the beam is as small as possible, (*b*) the corresponding value of $|M|_{max}$. (See hint for Prob. 7.55.)

7.57 For the beam of Prob. 7.47, determine (*a*) the ratio *k* = *P/wa* for which the maximum absolute value of the bending moment in the beam is as small as possible, (*b*) the corresponding value of $|M|_{max}$. (See hint for Prob. 7.55.)

7.58 A uniform beam is to be picked up by crane cables attached at *A* and *B*. Determine the distance *a* from the ends of the beam to the points where the cables should be attached if the maximum absolute value of the bending moment in the beam is to be as small as possible. (*Hint:* Draw the bending-moment diagram in terms of *a*, *L*, and the weight *w* per unit length, and then equate the absolute values of the largest positive and negative bending moments obtained.)

7.59 For the beam shown, determine (*a*) the magnitude *P* of the two upward forces for which the maximum absolute value of the bending moment in the beam is as small as possible, (*b*) the corresponding value of $|M|_{max}$. (See hint for Prob. 7.55.)

7.60 Knowing that $P = Q = 150$ lb, determine (a) the distance a for which the maximum absolute value of the bending moment in beam AB is as small as possible, (b) the corresponding value of $|M|_{max}$. (See hint for Prob. 7.55.)

7.61 Solve Prob. 7.60 assuming that $P = 300$ lb and $Q = 150$ lb.

*7.62 In order to reduce the bending moment in the cantilever beam AB, a cable and counterweight are permanently attached at end B. Determine the magnitude of the counterweight for which the maximum absolute value of the bending moment in the beam is as small as possible and the corresponding value of $|M|_{max}$. Consider (a) the case when the distributed load is permanently applied to the beam, (b) the more general case when the distributed load may either be applied or removed.

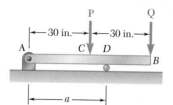

Fig. P7.60

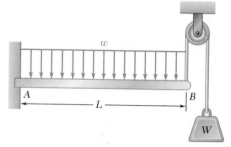

Fig. P7.62

*7.6 RELATIONS AMONG LOAD, SHEAR, AND BENDING MOMENT

When a beam carries more than two or three concentrated loads, or when it carries distributed loads, the method outlined in Sec. 7.5 for plotting shear and bending moment is likely to be quite cumbersome. The construction of the shear diagram and, especially, of the bending-moment diagram will be greatly facilitated if certain relations existing among load, shear, and bending moment are taken into consideration.

Let us consider a simply supported beam AB carrying a distributed load w per unit length (Fig. 7.11a), and let C and C' be two points of the beam at a distance Δx from each other. The shear and bending moment at C will be denoted by V and M, respectively, and will be assumed positive; the shear and bending moment at C' will be denoted by $V + \Delta V$ and $M + \Delta M$.

Let us now detach the portion of beam CC' and draw its free-body diagram (Fig. 7.11b). The forces exerted on the free body include a load of magnitude $w \, \Delta x$ and internal forces and couples at C and C'. Since shear and bending moment have been assumed positive, the forces and couples will be directed as shown in the figure.

Relations between Load and Shear. We write that the sum of the vertical components of the forces acting on the free body CC' is zero:

$$V - (V + \Delta V) - w \, \Delta x = 0$$
$$\Delta V = -w \, \Delta x$$

Dividing both members of the equation by Δx and then letting Δx approach zero, we obtain

$$\frac{dV}{dx} = -w \qquad (7.1)$$

Formula (7.1) indicates that for a beam loaded as shown in Fig. 7.11a, the slope dV/dx of the shear curve is negative; the numerical value of the slope at any point is equal to the load per unit length at that point.

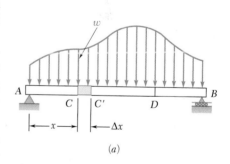

(a)

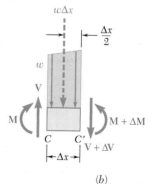

(b)

Fig. 7.11

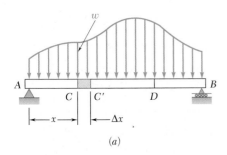

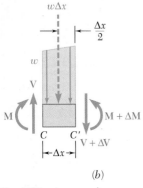

Fig. 7.11 (repeated)

Integrating (7.1) between points C and D, we obtain

$$V_D - V_C = -\int_{x_C}^{x_D} w \, dx \qquad (7.2)$$

$$V_D - V_C = -(\text{area under load curve between } C \text{ and } D) \qquad (7.2')$$

Note that this result could also have been obtained by considering the equilibrium of the portion of beam CD, since the area under the load curve represents the total load applied between C and D.

It should be observed that formula (7.1) *is not valid* at a point where a concentrated load is applied; the shear curve is discontinuous at such a point, as seen in Sec. 7.5. Similarly, formulas (7.2) and (7.2') cease to be valid when concentrated loads are applied between C and D, since they do not take into account the sudden change in shear caused by a concentrated load. Formulas (7.2) and (7.2'), therefore, should be applied only between successive concentrated loads.

Relations between Shear and Bending Moment. Returning to the free-body diagram of Fig. 7.11*b*, and writing now that the sum of the moments about C' is zero, we obtain

$$(M + \Delta M) - M - V \, \Delta x + w \, \Delta x \frac{\Delta x}{2} = 0$$
$$\Delta M = V \, \Delta x - \tfrac{1}{2} w (\Delta x)^2$$

Dividing both members of the equation by Δx and then letting Δx approach zero, we obtain

$$\frac{dM}{dx} = V \qquad (7.3)$$

Formula (7.3) indicates that the slope dM/dx of the bending-moment curve is equal to the value of the shear. This is true at any point where the shear has a well-defined value, i.e., at any point where no concentrated load is applied. Formula (7.3) also shows that the shear is zero at points where the bending moment is maximum. This property facilitates the determination of the points where the beam is likely to fail under bending.

Integrating (7.3) between points C and D, we obtain

$$M_D - M_C = \int_{x_C}^{x_D} V \, dx \qquad (7.4)$$

$$M_D - M_C = \text{area under shear curve between } C \text{ and } D \qquad (7.4')$$

Note that the area under the shear curve should be considered positive where the shear is positive and negative where the shear is negative. Formulas (7.4) and (7.4') are valid even when concentrated loads are applied between C and D, as long as the shear curve has been correctly drawn. The formulas cease to be valid, however, if a *couple* is applied at a point between C and D, since they do not take into account the sudden change in bending moment caused by a couple (see Sample Prob. 7.7).

EXAMPLE   Let us consider a simply supported beam AB of span L carrying a uniformly distributed load w (Fig. 7.12a). From the free-body diagram of the entire beam we determine the magnitude of the reactions at the supports: $R_A = R_B = wL/2$ (Fig. 7.12b). Next, we draw the shear diagram. Close to the end A of the beam, the shear is equal to R_A, that is, to $wL/2$, as we can check by considering a very small portion of the beam as a free body. Using formula (7.2), we can then determine the shear V at any distance x from A. We write

$$V - V_A = -\int_0^x w\, dx = -wx$$

$$V = V_A - wx = \frac{wL}{2} - wx = w\left(\frac{L}{2} - x\right)$$

The shear curve is thus an oblique straight line which crosses the x axis at $x = L/2$ (Fig. 7.12c). Considering, now, the bending moment, we first observe that $M_A = 0$. The value M of the bending moment at any distance x from A can then be obtained from formula (7.4); we have

$$M - M_A = \int_0^x V\, dx$$

$$M = \int_0^x w\left(\frac{L}{2} - x\right) dx = \frac{w}{2}(Lx - x^2)$$

The bending-moment curve is a parabola. The maximum value of the bending moment occurs when $x = L/2$, since V (and thus dM/dx) is zero for that value of x. Substituting $x = L/2$ in the last equation, we obtain $M_{\max} = wL^2/8$. ∎

In most engineering applications, the value of the bending moment needs to be known only at a few specific points. Once the shear diagram has been drawn, and after M has been determined at one of the ends of the beam, the value of the bending moment can then be obtained at any given point by computing the area under the shear curve and using formula (7.4$'$). For instance, since $M_A = 0$ for the beam of Fig. 7.12, the maximum value of the bending moment for that beam can be obtained simply by measuring the area of the shaded triangle in the shear diagram:

$$M_{\max} = \frac{1}{2}\frac{L}{2}\frac{wL}{2} = \frac{wL^2}{8}$$

In this example, the load curve is a horizontal straight line, the shear curve is an oblique straight line, and the bending-moment curve is a parabola. If the load curve had been an oblique straight line (first degree), the shear curve would have been a parabola (second degree), and the bending-moment curve would have been a cubic (third degree). The shear and bending-moment curves will always be, respectively, one and two degrees higher than the load curve. Thus, once a few values of the shear and bending moment have been computed, we should be able to sketch the shear and bending-moment diagrams without actually determining the functions $V(x)$ and $M(x)$. The sketches obtained will be more accurate if we make use of the fact that at any point where the curves are continuous, the slope of the shear curve is equal to $-w$ and the slope of the bending-moment curve is equal to V.

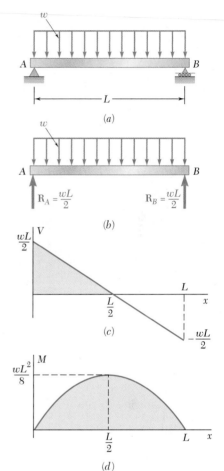

Fig. 7.12

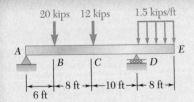

Draw the shear and bending-moment diagrams for the beam and loading shown.

SOLUTION

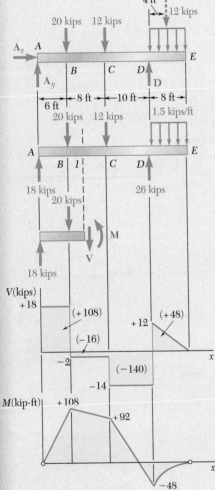

Free-Body: Entire Beam. Considering the entire beam as a free body, we determine the reactions:

$+\Sigma\uparrow M_A = 0$:
$$D(24 \text{ ft}) - (20 \text{ kips})(6 \text{ ft}) - (12 \text{ kips})(14 \text{ ft}) - (12 \text{ kips})(28 \text{ ft}) = 0$$
$$D = +26 \text{ kips} \qquad \mathbf{D} = 26 \text{ kips} \uparrow$$

$+\uparrow\Sigma F_y = 0$: $\quad A_y - 20 \text{ kips} - 12 \text{ kips} + 26 \text{ kips} - 12 \text{ kips} = 0$
$$A_y = +18 \text{ kips} \qquad \mathbf{A}_y = 18 \text{ kips} \uparrow$$

$\xrightarrow{+}\Sigma F_x = 0$: $\quad A_x = 0 \qquad\qquad\qquad\qquad \mathbf{A}_x = 0$

We also note that at both A and E the bending moment is zero; thus two points (indicated by small circles) are obtained on the bending-moment diagram.

Shear Diagram. Since $dV/dx = -w$, we find that between concentrated loads and reactions the slope of the shear diagram is zero (i.e., the shear is constant). The shear at any point is determined by dividing the beam into two parts and considering either part as a free body. For example, using the portion of beam to the left of section 1, we obtain the shear between B and C:

$+\uparrow\Sigma F_y = 0$: $\quad +18 \text{ kips} - 20 \text{ kips} - V = 0 \qquad V = -2 \text{ kips}$

We also find that the shear is $+12$ kips just to the right of D and zero at end E. Since the slope $dV/dx = -w$ is constant between D and E, the shear diagram between these two points is a straight line.

Bending-Moment Diagram. We recall that the area under the shear curve between two points is equal to the change in bending moment between the same two points. For convenience, the area of each portion of the shear diagram is computed and is indicated on the diagram. Since the bending moment M_A at the left end is known to be zero, we write

$$
\begin{array}{ll}
M_B - M_A = +108 & M_B = +108 \text{ kip} \cdot \text{ft} \\
M_C - M_B = -16 & M_C = +92 \text{ kip} \cdot \text{ft} \\
M_D - M_C = -140 & M_D = -48 \text{ kip} \cdot \text{ft} \\
M_E - M_D = +48 & M_E = 0
\end{array}
$$

Since M_E is known to be zero, a check of the computations is obtained.

Between the concentrated loads and reactions the shear is constant; thus the slope dM/dx is constant, and the bending-moment diagram is drawn by connecting the known points with straight lines. Between D and E, where the shear diagram is an oblique straight line, the bending-moment diagram is a parabola.

From the V and M diagrams we note that $V_{\max} = 18$ kips and $M_{\max} = 108$ kip $\cdot$ ft.

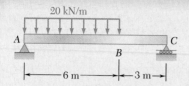

SAMPLE PROBLEM 7.5

Draw the shear and bending-moment diagrams for the beam and loading shown and determine the location and magnitude of the maximum bending moment.

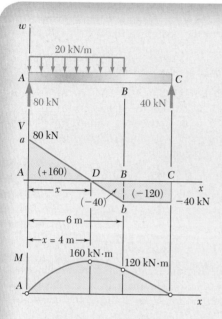

SOLUTION

Free-Body: Entire Beam. Considering the entire beam as a free body, we obtain the reactions

$$\mathbf{R}_A = 80 \text{ kN} \uparrow \qquad \mathbf{R}_C = 40 \text{ kN} \uparrow$$

Shear Diagram. The shear just to the right of A is $V_A = +80$ kN. Since the change in shear between two points is equal to *minus* the area under the load curve between the same two points, we obtain V_B by writing

$$V_B - V_A = -(20 \text{ kN/m})(6 \text{ m}) = -120 \text{ kN}$$
$$V_B = -120 + V_A = -120 + 80 = -40 \text{ kN}$$

Since the slope $dV/dx = -w$ is constant between A and B, the shear diagram between these two points is represented by a straight line. Between B and C, the area under the load curve is zero; therefore,

$$V_C - V_B = 0 \qquad V_C = V_B = -40 \text{ kN}$$

and the shear is constant between B and C.

Bending-Moment Diagram. We note that the bending moment at each end of the beam is zero. In order to determine the maximum bending moment, we locate the section D of the beam where $V = 0$. We write

$$V_D - V_A = -wx$$
$$0 - 80 \text{ kN} = -(20 \text{ kN/m})x$$

and, solving for x: $\qquad\qquad\qquad\qquad\qquad\qquad\qquad x = 4 \text{ m} \quad \blacktriangleleft$

The maximum bending moment occurs at point D, where we have $dM/dx = V = 0$. The areas of the various portions of the shear diagram are computed and are given (in parentheses) on the diagram. Since the area of the shear diagram between two points is equal to the change in bending moment between the same two points, we write

$$
\begin{aligned}
M_D - M_A &= +160 \text{ kN} \cdot \text{m} & M_D &= +160 \text{ kN} \cdot \text{m} \\
M_B - M_D &= -40 \text{ kN} \cdot \text{m} & M_B &= +120 \text{ kN} \cdot \text{m} \\
M_C - M_B &= -120 \text{ kN} \cdot \text{m} & M_C &= 0
\end{aligned}
$$

The bending-moment diagram consists of an arc of parabola followed by a segment of straight line; the slope of the parabola at A is equal to the value of V at that point.

The maximum bending moment is

$$M_{\text{max}} = M_D = +160 \text{ kN} \cdot \text{m} \quad \blacktriangleleft$$

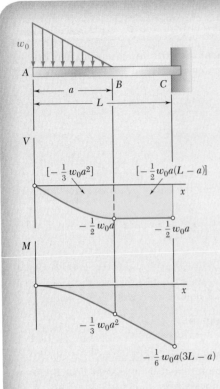

SAMPLE PROBLEM 7.6

Sketch the shear and bending-moment diagrams for the cantilever beam shown.

SOLUTION

Shear Diagram. At the free end of the beam, we find $V_A = 0$. Between A and B, the area under the load curve is $\frac{1}{2}w_0 a$; we find V_B by writing

$$V_B - V_A = -\tfrac{1}{2}w_0 a \qquad V_B = -\tfrac{1}{2}w_0 a$$

Between B and C, the beam is not loaded; thus $V_C = V_B$. At A, we have $w = w_0$, and, according to Eq. (7.1), the slope of the shear curve is $dV/dx = -w_0$, while at B the slope is $dV/dx = 0$. Between A and B, the loading decreases linearly, and the shear diagram is parabolic. Between B and C, $w = 0$, and the shear diagram is a horizontal line.

Bending-Moment Diagram. We note that $M_A = 0$ at the free end of the beam. We compute the area under the shear curve and write

$$M_B - M_A = -\tfrac{1}{3}w_0 a^2 \qquad M_B = -\tfrac{1}{3}w_0 a^2$$
$$M_C - M_B = -\tfrac{1}{2}w_0 a(L - a)$$
$$M_C = -\tfrac{1}{6}w_0 a(3L - a)$$

The sketch of the bending-moment diagram is completed by recalling that $dM/dx = V$. We find that between A and B the diagram is represented by a cubic curve with zero slope at A, and between B and C the diagram is represented by a straight line.

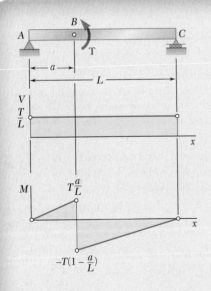

SAMPLE PROBLEM 7.7

The simple beam AC is loaded by a couple of magnitude T applied at point B. Draw the shear and bending-moment diagrams for the beam.

SOLUTION

Free Body: Entire Beam. The entire beam is taken as a free body, and we obtain

$$\mathbf{R}_A = \frac{T}{L}\uparrow \qquad \mathbf{R}_C = \frac{T}{L}\downarrow$$

Shear and Bending-Moment Diagrams. The shear at any section is constant and equal to T/L. Since a couple is applied at B, the bending-moment diagram is discontinuous at B; the bending moment decreases suddenly by an amount equal to T.

SOLVING PROBLEMS ON YOUR OWN

$\mathbf{I}$n this lesson you learned how to use the relations existing among load, shear, and bending moment to simplify the drawing of the shear and bending-moment diagrams. These relations are

$$\frac{dV}{dx} = -w \tag{7.1}$$

$$\frac{dM}{dx} = V \tag{7.3}$$

$$V_D - V_C = -(\text{area under load curve between } C \text{ and } D) \tag{7.2'}$$
$$M_D - M_C = (\text{area under shear curve between } C \text{ and } D) \tag{7.4'}$$

Taking into account these relations, you can use the following procedure to draw the shear and bending-moment diagrams for a beam.

1. Draw a free-body diagram of the entire beam, and use it to determine the reactions at the beam supports.

2. Draw the shear diagram. This can be done as in the preceding lesson by cutting the beam at various points and considering the free-body diagram of one of the two portions of the beam that you have obtained [Sample Prob. 7.3]. You can, however, consider one of the following alternative procedures.

    a. The shear V at any point of the beam is the sum of the reactions and loads to the left of that point; an upward force is counted as positive, and a downward force is counted as negative.

    b. For a beam carrying a distributed load, you can start from a point where you know V and use Eq. (7.2') repeatedly to find V at all the other points of interest.

3. Draw the bending-moment diagram, using the following procedure.

    a. Compute the area under each portion of the shear curve, assigning a positive sign to areas located above the x axis and a negative sign to areas located below the x axis.

    b. Apply Eq. (7.4') repeatedly [Sample Probs. 7.4 and 7.5], starting from the left end of the beam, where $M = 0$ (except if a couple is applied at that end, or if the beam is a cantilever beam with a fixed left end).

    c. Where a couple is applied to the beam, be careful to show a discontinuity in the bending-moment diagram by *increasing* the value of M at that point by an amount equal to the magnitude of the couple if the couple is *clockwise*, or *decreasing* the value of M by that amount if the couple is *counterclockwise* [Sample Prob. 7.7].

(*continued*)

4. Determine the location and magnitude of $|M|_{max}$. The maximum absolute value of the bending moment occurs at one of the points where $dM/dx = 0$, that is, according to Eq. (7.3), at a point where V is equal to zero or changes sign. You should, therefore:

a. Determine from the shear diagram the value of $|M|$ where V changes sign; this will occur under the concentrated loads [Sample Prob. 7.4].

b. Determine the points where $V = 0$ and the corresponding values of $|M|$; this will occur under a distributed load. To find the distance x between point C, where the distributed load starts, and point D, where the shear is zero, use Eq. (7.2′); for V_C use the known value of the shear at point C, for V_D use zero, and express the area under the load curve as a function of x [Sample Prob. 7.5].

5. You can improve the quality of your drawings by keeping in mind that at any given point, according to Eqs. (7.1) and (7.3), the slope of the V curve is equal to $-w$ and the slope of the M curve is equal to V.

6. Finally, for beams supporting a distributed load expressed as a function $w(x)$, remember that the shear V can be obtained by integrating the function $-w(x)$, and the bending moment M can be obtained by integrating $V(x)$ [Eqs. (7.3) and (7.4)].

PROBLEMS

7.63 Using the method of Sec. 7.6, solve Prob. 7.29.

7.64 Using the method of Sec. 7.6, solve Prob. 7.30.

7.65 Using the method of Sec. 7.6, solve Prob. 7.31.

7.66 Using the method of Sec. 7.6, solve Prob. 7.32.

7.67 Using the method of Sec. 7.6, solve Prob. 7.33.

7.68 Using the method of Sec. 7.6, solve Prob. 7.34.

7.69 and 7.70 For the beam and loading shown, (*a*) draw the shear and bending-moment diagrams, (*b*) determine the maximum absolute values of the shear and bending moment.

7.71 Using the method of Sec. 7.6, solve Prob. 7.39.

7.72 Using the method of Sec. 7.6, solve Prob. 7.40.

7.73 Using the method of Sec. 7.6, solve Prob. 7.41.

7.74 Using the method of Sec. 7.6, solve Prob. 7.42.

7.75 and 7.76 For the beam and loading shown, (*a*) draw the shear and bending-moment diagrams, (*b*) determine the maximum absolute values of the shear and bending moment.

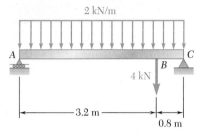

Fig. P7.69

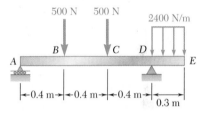

Fig. P7.70

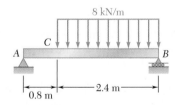

Fig. *P7.75*

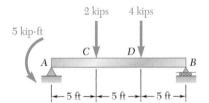

Fig. *P7.76*

7.77 and 7.78 For the beam and loading shown, (*a*) draw the shear and bending-moment diagrams, (*b*) determine the magnitude and location of the maximum bending moment.

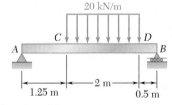

Fig. P7.77

Fig. P7.78

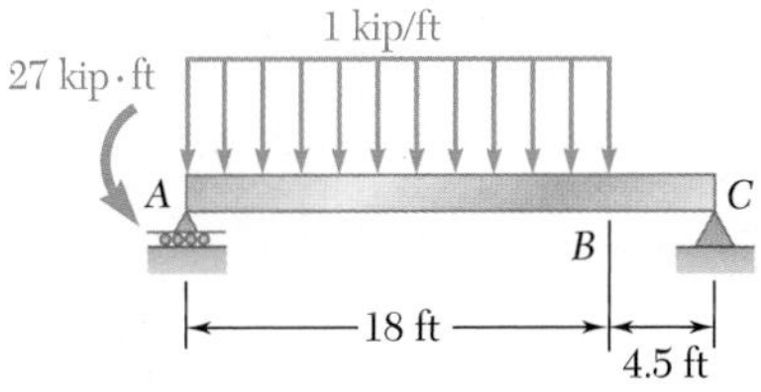

7.79 and 7.80 For the beam and loading shown, (*a*) draw the shear and bending-moment diagrams, (*b*) determine the magnitude and location of the maximum absolute value of the bending moment.

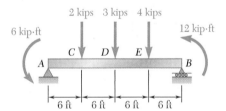

Fig. P7.79

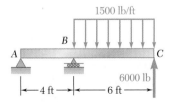

Fig. P7.80

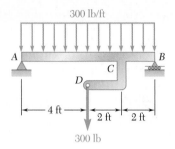

300 lb/ft

300 lb

4 ft

2 ft

2 ft

Fig. P7.81

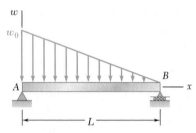

w

w_0

A

B

x

L

Fig. P7.85

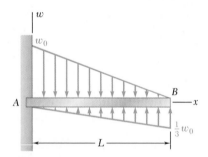

w

w_0

A

B

x

$\frac{1}{3}w_0$

L

Fig. P7.86

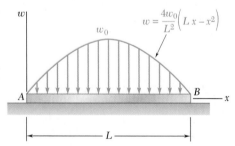

w

w_0

$w = \frac{4w_0}{L^2}\left(L\,x - x^2\right)$

A

B

x

L

Fig. P7.88

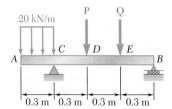

20 kN/m

P

Q

A

C

D

E

B

0.3 m 0.3 m 0.3 m 0.3 m

Fig. P7.89

7.81 (a) Draw the shear and bending-moment diagrams for beam AB, (b) determine the magnitude and location of the maximum absolute value of the bending moment.

7.82 Solve Prob. 7.81 assuming that the 300-lb force applied at D is directed upward.

7.83 For the beam and loading shown, (a) draw the shear and bending-moment diagrams, (b) determine the magnitude and location of the maximum absolute value of the bending moment.

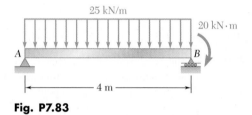

25 kN/m

20 kN·m

A

B

4 m

Fig. P7.83

7.84 Solve Prob. 7.83 assuming that the 20-kN · m couple applied at B is counterclockwise.

7.85 and 7.86 For the beam and loading shown, (a) write the equations of the shear and bending-moment curves, (b) determine the magnitude and location of the maximum bending moment.

7.87 For the beam and loading shown, (a) write the equations of the shear and bending-moment curves, (b) determine the magnitude and location of the maximum bending moment.

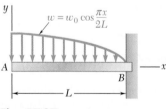

y

$w = w_0 \cos\dfrac{\pi x}{2L}$

A

B

x

L

Fig. P7.87

7.88 The beam AB, which lies on the ground, supports the parabolic load shown. Assuming the upward reaction of the ground to be uniformly distributed, (a) write the equations of the shear and bending-moment curves, (b) determine the maximum bending moment.

7.89 The beam AB is subjected to the uniformly distributed load shown and to two unknown forces $\mathbf{P}$ and $\mathbf{Q}$. Knowing that it has been experimentally determined that the bending moment is +800 N · m at D and +1300 N · m at E, (a) determine $\mathbf{P}$ and $\mathbf{Q}$, (b) draw the shear and bending-moment diagrams for the beam.

7.90 Solve Prob. 7.89 assuming that the bending moment was found to be +650 N · m at D and +1450 N · m at E.

*7.91 The beam AB is subjected to the uniformly distributed load shown and to two unknown forces **P** and **Q**. Knowing that it has been experimentally determined that the bending moment is $+6.10$ kip · ft at D and $+5.50$ kip · ft at E, (a) determine **P** and **Q**, (b) draw the shear and bending-moment diagrams for the beam.

*7.92 Solve Prob. 7.91 assuming that the bending moment was found to be $+5.96$ kip · ft at D and $+6.84$ kip · ft at E.

Fig. P7.91

CABLES

*7.7 CABLES WITH CONCENTRATED LOADS

Cables are used in many engineering applications, such as suspension bridges, transmission lines, aerial tramways, guy wires for high towers, etc. Cables may be divided into two categories, according to their loading: (1) cables supporting concentrated loads, (2) cables supporting distributed loads. In this section, cables of the first category are examined.

Consider a cable attached to two fixed points A and B and supporting n vertical concentrated loads $\mathbf{P}_1, \mathbf{P}_2, \ldots, \mathbf{P}_n$ (Fig. 7.13a). We assume that the cable is *flexible*, i.e., that its resistance to bending is small and can be neglected. We further assume that the *weight of the cable is negligible* compared with the loads supported by the cable. Any portion of cable between successive loads can therefore be considered as a two-force member, and the internal forces at any point in the cable reduce to a *force of tension directed along the cable*.

We assume that each of the loads lies in a given vertical line, i.e., that the horizontal distance from support A to each of the loads is known; we also assume that the horizontal and vertical distances between the supports are known. We propose to determine the shape of the cable, i.e., the vertical distance from support A to each of the points $C_1, C_2, \ldots, C_n$, and also the tension T in each portion of the cable.

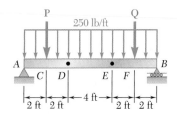

Photo 7.3 Since the weight of the cable of the chairlift shown is negligible compared to the weights of the chairs and skiers, the methods of this section can be used to determine the force at any point in the cable.

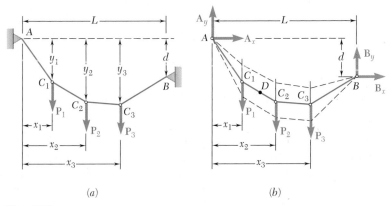

(a)   (b)

Fig. 7.13

We first draw the free-body diagram of the entire cable (Fig. 7.13b). Since the slope of the portions of cable attached at A and B is not known, the reactions at A and B must be represented by two components each. Thus, four unknowns are involved, and the three equations of equilibrium are not sufficient to determine the reactions at A and B.† We must

†Clearly, the cable is not a rigid body; the equilibrium equations represent, therefore, *necessary but not sufficient* conditions (see Sec. 6.11).

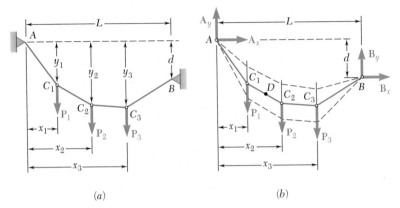

Fig. 7.13 (repeated)

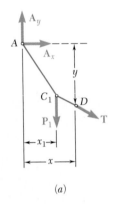

(a)

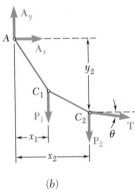

(b)

Fig. 7.14

therefore obtain an additional equation by considering the equilibrium of a portion of the cable. This is possible if we know the coordinates x and y of a point D of the cable. Drawing the free-body diagram of the portion of cable AD (Fig. 7.14a) and writing $\Sigma M_D = 0$, we obtain an additional relation between the scalar components A_x and A_y and can determine the reactions at A and B. The problem would remain indeterminate, however, if we did not know the coordinates of D, unless some other relation between A_x and A_y (or between B_x and B_y) were given. The cable might hang in any of various possible ways, as indicated by the dashed lines in Fig. 7.13b.

Once A_x and A_y have been determined, the vertical distance from A to any point of the cable can easily be found. Considering point C_2, for example, we draw the free-body diagram of the portion of cable AC_2 (Fig. 7.14b). Writing $\Sigma M_{C_2} = 0$, we obtain an equation which can be solved for y_2. Writing $\Sigma F_x = 0$ and $\Sigma F_y = 0$, we obtain the components of the force $\mathbf{T}$ representing the tension in the portion of cable to the right of C_2. We observe that $T \cos \theta = -A_x$; *the horizontal component of the tension force is the same at any point of the cable.* It follows that the tension T is maximum when $\cos \theta$ is minimum, i.e., in the portion of cable which has the largest angle of inclination θ. Clearly, this portion of cable must be adjacent to one of the two supports of the cable.

*7.8 CABLES WITH DISTRIBUTED LOADS

Consider a cable attached to two fixed points A and B and carrying a *distributed load* (Fig. 7.15a). We saw in the preceding section that for a cable supporting concentrated loads, the internal force at any point is a force of tension directed along the cable. In the case of a cable carrying a distributed load, the cable hangs in the shape of a curve, and the internal force at a point D is a force of tension $\mathbf{T}$ *directed along the tangent to the curve.* In this section, you will learn to determine the tension at any point of a cable supporting a given distributed load. In the following sections, the shape of the cable will be determined for two particular types of distributed loads.

Considering the most general case of distributed load, we draw the free-body diagram of the portion of cable extending from the lowest point C to a given point D of the cable (Fig. 7.15b). The

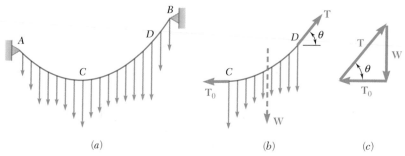

(a)　　　　　　　　　　(b)　　　　　　　　(c)

Fig. 7.15

forces acting on the free body are the tension force $\mathbf{T}_0$ at C, which is horizontal, the tension force $\mathbf{T}$ at D, directed along the tangent to the cable at D, and the resultant $\mathbf{W}$ of the distributed load supported by the portion of cable CD. Drawing the corresponding force triangle (Fig. 7.15c), we obtain the following relations:

$$T \cos \theta = T_0 \qquad\qquad T \sin \theta = W \qquad (7.5)$$

$$T = \sqrt{T_0^2 + W^2} \qquad \tan \theta = \frac{W}{T_0} \qquad (7.6)$$

From the relations (7.5), it appears that the horizontal component of the tension force $\mathbf{T}$ is the same at any point and that the vertical component of $\mathbf{T}$ is equal to the magnitude W of the load measured from the lowest point. Relations (7.6) show that the tension T is minimum at the lowest point and maximum at one of the two points of support.

*7.9 PARABOLIC CABLE

Let us assume, now, that the cable AB carries a load *uniformly distributed along the horizontal* (Fig. 7.16a). Cables of suspension bridges may be assumed loaded in this way, since the weight of the cables is small compared with the weight of the roadway. We denote by w the load per unit length (*measured horizontally*) and express it in N/m or in lb/ft. Choosing coordinate axes with origin at the lowest point C of the cable, we find that the magnitude W of the total load carried by the portion of cable extending from C to the point D of coordinates x and y is $W = wx$. The relations (7.6) defining the magnitude and direction of the tension force at D become

$$T = \sqrt{T_0^2 + w^2 x^2} \qquad \tan \theta = \frac{wx}{T_0} \qquad (7.7)$$

Moreover, the distance from D to the line of action of the resultant $\mathbf{W}$ is equal to half the horizontal distance from C to D (Fig. 7.16b). Summing moments about D, we write

$$+\!\uparrow \Sigma M_D = 0: \qquad wx\frac{x}{2} - T_0 y = 0$$

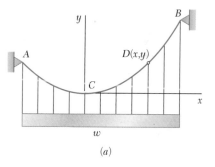

(a)

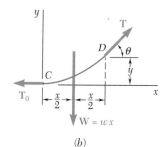

(b)

Fig. 7.16

and, solving for y,

$$y = \frac{wx^2}{2T_0} \qquad (7.8)$$

This is the equation of a *parabola* with a vertical axis and its vertex at the origin of coordinates. The curve formed by cables loaded uniformly along the horizontal is thus a parabola.†

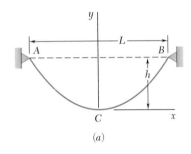

When the supports A and B of the cable have the same elevation, the distance L between the supports is called the *span* of the cable and the vertical distance h from the supports to the lowest point is called the *sag* of the cable (Fig. 7.17*a*). If the span and sag of a cable are known, and if the load w per unit horizontal length is given, the minimum tension T_0 may be found by substituting $x = L/2$ and $y = h$ in Eq. (7.8). Equations (7.7) will then yield the tension and the slope at any point of the cable and Eq. (7.8) will define the shape of the cable.

(a)

When the supports have different elevations, the position of the lowest point of the cable is not known and the coordinates x_A, y_A and x_B, y_B of the supports must be determined. To this effect, we express that the coordinates of A and B satisfy Eq. (7.8) and that $x_B - x_A = L$ and $y_B - y_A = d$, where L and d denote, respectively, the horizontal and vertical distances between the two supports (Fig. 7.17*b* and *c*).

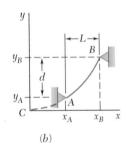

The length of the cable from its lowest point C to its support B can be obtained from the formula

(b)

$$s_B = \int_0^{x_B} \sqrt{1 + \left(\frac{dy}{dx}\right)^2}\, dx \qquad (7.9)$$

Differentiating (7.8), we obtain the derivative $dy/dx = wx/T_0$; substituting into (7.9) and using the binomial theorem to expand the radical in an infinite series, we have

$$s_B = \int_0^{x_B} \sqrt{1 + \frac{w^2 x^2}{T_0^2}}\, dx = \int_0^{x_B}\left(1 + \frac{w^2 x^2}{2T_0^2} - \frac{w^4 x^4}{8T_0^4} + \cdots\right) dx$$

$$s_B = x_B\left(1 + \frac{w^2 x_B^2}{6T_0^2} - \frac{w^4 x_B^4}{40T_0^4} + \cdots\right)$$

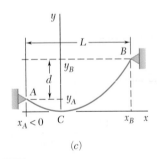

(c)

Fig. 7.17

and, since $wx_B^2/2T_0 = y_B$,

$$s_B = x_B\left[1 + \frac{2}{3}\left(\frac{y_B}{x_B}\right)^2 - \frac{2}{5}\left(\frac{y_B}{x_B}\right)^4 + \cdots\right] \qquad (7.10)$$

The series converges for values of the ratio y_B/x_B less than 0.5; in most cases, this ratio is much smaller, and only the first two terms of the series need be computed.

---

†Cables hanging under their own weight are not loaded uniformly along the horizontal, and they do not form a parabola. The error introduced by assuming a parabolic shape for cables hanging under their weight, however, is small when the cable is sufficiently taut. A complete discussion of cables hanging under their own weight is given in the next section.

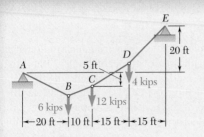

SAMPLE PROBLEM 7.8

The cable AE supports three vertical loads from the points indicated. If point C is 5 ft below the left support, determine (a) the elevation of points B and D, (b) the maximum slope and the maximum tension in the cable.

SOLUTION

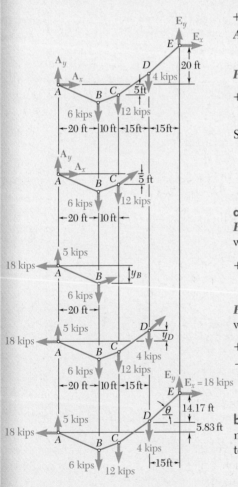

Reactions at Supports. The reaction components $\mathbf{A}_x$ and $\mathbf{A}_y$ are determined as follows:

Free Body: Entire Cable

$+\circlearrowleft \Sigma M_E = 0$:
$$A_x(20 \text{ ft}) - A_y(60 \text{ ft}) + (6 \text{ kips})(40 \text{ ft}) + (12 \text{ kips})(30 \text{ ft}) + (4 \text{ kips})(15 \text{ ft}) = 0$$
$$20A_x - 60A_y + 660 = 0$$

Free Body: ABC

$+\circlearrowleft \Sigma M_C = 0$: $-A_x(5 \text{ ft}) - A_y(30 \text{ ft}) + (6 \text{ kips})(10 \text{ ft}) = 0$
$$-5A_x - 30A_y + 60 = 0$$

Solving the two equations simultaneously, we obtain

$$A_x = -18 \text{ kips} \qquad \mathbf{A}_x = 18 \text{ kips} \leftarrow$$
$$A_y = +5 \text{ kips} \qquad \mathbf{A}_y = 5 \text{ kips} \uparrow$$

a. Elevation of Points *B* and *D*.
Free Body: AB   Considering the portion of cable AB as a free body, we write

$+\circlearrowleft \Sigma M_B = 0$: $(18 \text{ kips})y_B - (5 \text{ kips})(20 \text{ ft}) = 0$
$$y_B = 5.56 \text{ ft below } A \quad \blacktriangleleft$$

Free Body: ABCD   Using the portion of cable $ABCD$ as a free body, we write

$+\circlearrowleft \Sigma M_D = 0$:
$$-(18 \text{ kips})y_D - (5 \text{ kips})(45 \text{ ft}) + (6 \text{ kips})(25 \text{ ft}) + (12 \text{ kips})(15 \text{ ft}) = 0$$
$$y_D = 5.83 \text{ ft above } A \quad \blacktriangleleft$$

b. Maximum Slope and Maximum Tension.
We observe that the maximum slope occurs in portion DE. Since the horizontal component of the tension is constant and equal to 18 kips, we write

$$\tan \theta = \frac{14.17}{15 \text{ ft}} \qquad\qquad \theta = 43.4° \quad \blacktriangleleft$$

$$T_{max} = \frac{18 \text{ kips}}{\cos \theta} \qquad\qquad T_{max} = 24.8 \text{ kips} \quad \blacktriangleleft$$

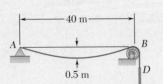

SAMPLE PROBLEM 7.9

A light cable is attached to a support at A, passes over a small pulley at B, and supports a load **P**. Knowing that the sag of the cable is 0.5 m and that the mass per unit length of the cable is 0.75 kg/m, determine (a) the magnitude of the load **P**, (b) the slope of the cable at B, (c) the total length of the cable from A to B. Since the ratio of the sag to the span is small, assume the cable to be parabolic. Also, neglect the weight of the portion of cable from B to D.

SOLUTION

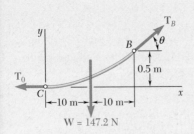

a. Load P. We denote by C the lowest point of the cable and draw the free-body diagram of the portion CB of cable. Assuming the load to be uniformly distributed along the horizontal, we write

$$w = (0.75 \text{ kg/m})(9.81 \text{ m/s}^2) = 7.36 \text{ N/m}$$

The total load for the portion CB of cable is

$$W = wx_B = (7.36 \text{ N/m})(20 \text{ m}) = 147.2 \text{ N}$$

and is applied halfway between C and B. Summing moments about B, we write

$$+\gamma \ \Sigma M_B = 0: \quad (147.2 \text{ N})(10 \text{ m}) - T_0(0.5 \text{ m}) = 0 \qquad T_0 = 2944 \text{ N}$$

From the force triangle we obtain

$$T_B = \sqrt{T_0^2 + W^2}$$
$$= \sqrt{(2944 \text{ N})^2 + (147.2 \text{ N})^2} = 2948 \text{ N}$$

Since the tension on each side of the pulley is the same, we find

$$P = T_B = 2948 \text{ N} \ \blacktriangleleft$$

b. Slope of Cable at B. We also obtain from the force triangle

$$\tan \theta = \frac{W}{T_0} = \frac{147.2 \text{ N}}{2944 \text{ N}} = 0.05$$

$$\theta = 2.9° \ \blacktriangleleft$$

c. Length of Cable. Applying Eq. (7.10) between C and B, we write

$$s_B = x_B \left[1 + \frac{2}{3}\left(\frac{y_B}{x_B}\right)^2 + \cdots \right]$$

$$= (20 \text{ m})\left[1 + \frac{2}{3}\left(\frac{0.5 \text{ m}}{20 \text{ m}}\right)^2 + \cdots \right] = 20.00833 \text{ m}$$

The total length of the cable between A and B is twice this value,

$$\text{Length} = 2s_B = 40.0167 \text{ m} \ \blacktriangleleft$$

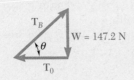

SOLVING PROBLEMS ON YOUR OWN

In the problems of this section you will apply the equations of equilibrium to *cables that lie in a vertical plane*. We assume that a cable cannot resist bending, so that the force of tension in the cable is always directed along the cable.

A. In the first part of this lesson we considered cables subjected to concentrated loads. Since the weight of the cable is neglected, the cable is straight between loads.

Your solution will consist of the following steps:

1. Draw a free-body diagram of the entire cable showing the loads and the horizontal and vertical components of the reaction at each support. Use this free-body diagram to write the corresponding equilibrium equations.

2. You will be confronted with four unknown components and only three equations of equilibrium (see Fig. 7.13). You must therefore find an additional piece of information, such as the *position* of a point on the cable or the *slope* of the cable at a given point.

3. After you have identified the point of the cable where the additional information exists, cut the cable at that point, and draw a free-body diagram of one of the two portions of the cable you have obtained.

   a. If you know the position of the point where you have cut the cable, writing $\Sigma M = 0$ about that point for the new free body will yield the additional equation required to solve for the four unknown components of the reactions. [Sample Prob. 7.8].

   b. If you know the slope of the portion of the cable you have cut, writing $\Sigma F_x = 0$ and $\Sigma F_y = 0$ for the new free body will yield two equilibrium equations which, together with the original three, can be solved for the four reaction components and for the tension in the cable where it has been cut.

4. To find the elevation of a given point of the cable and the slope and tension at that point once the reactions at the supports have been found, you should cut the cable at that point and draw a free-body diagram of one of the two portions of the cable you have obtained. Writing $\Sigma M = 0$ about the given point yields its elevation. Writing $\Sigma F_x = 0$ and $\Sigma F_y = 0$ yields the components of the tension force, from which its magnitude and direction can easily be found.

(continued)

5. For a cable supporting vertical loads only, you will observe that *the horizontal component of the tension force is the same at any point*. It follows that, for such a cable, the *maximum tension occurs in the steepest portion of the cable*.

B. In the second portion of this lesson we considered cables carrying a load uniformly distributed along the horizontal. The shape of the cable is then parabolic.

Your solution will use one or more of the following concepts:

1. Placing the origin of coordinates at the lowest point of the cable and directing the x and y axes to the right and upward, respectively, we find that *the equation of the parabola* is

$$y = \frac{wx^2}{2T_0} \tag{7.8}$$

The minimum cable tension occurs at the origin, where the cable is horizontal, and the maximum tension is at the support where the slope is maximum.

2. If the supports of the cable have the same elevation, the sag h of the cable is the vertical distance from the lowest point of the cable to the horizontal line joining the supports. To solve a problem involving such a parabolic cable, you should write Eq. (7.8) for one of the supports; this equation can be solved for one unknown.

3. If the supports of the cable have different elevations, you will have to write Eq. (7.8) for each of the supports (see Fig. 7.17).

4. To find the length of the cable from the lowest point to one of the supports, you can use Eq. (7.10). In most cases, you will need to compute only the first two terms of the series.

PROBLEMS

7.93 Two loads are suspended as shown from the cable *ABCD*. Knowing that $h_B = 1.8$ m, determine (*a*) the distance h_C, (*b*) the components of the reaction at *D*, (*c*) the maximum tension in the cable.

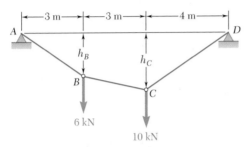

Fig. P7.93 and P7.94

7.94 Knowing that the maximum tension in cable *ABCD* is 15 kN, determine (*a*) the distance h_B, (*b*) the distance h_C.

7.95 If $d_C = 8$ ft, determine (*a*) the reaction at *A*, (*b*) the reaction at *E*.

7.96 If $d_C = 4.5$ ft, determine (*a*) the reaction at *A*, (*b*) the reaction at *E*.

7.97 Knowing that $d_C = 3$ m, determine (*a*) the distances d_B and d_D, (*b*) the reaction at *E*.

7.98 Determine (*a*) distance d_C for which portion *DE* of the cable is horizontal, (*b*) the corresponding reactions at *A* and *E*.

7.99 If $d_C = 15$ ft, determine (*a*) the distances d_B and d_D, (*b*) the maximum tension in the cable.

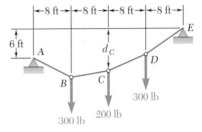

Fig. P7.95 and P7.96

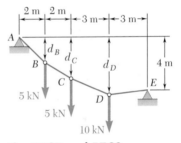

Fig. P7.97 and P7.98

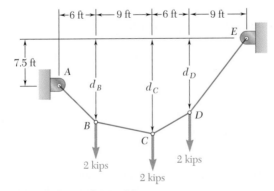

Fig. P7.99 and P7.100

7.100 Determine (*a*) the distance d_C for which portion *BC* of the cable is horizontal, (*b*) the corresponding components of the reaction at *E*.

391

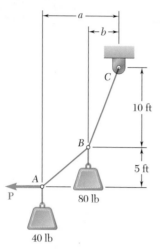

Fig. P7.101 and P7.102

7.101 Cable ABC supports two loads as shown. Knowing that $b = 4$ ft, determine (*a*) the required magnitude of the horizontal force **P**, (*b*) the corresponding distance a.

7.102 Cable ABC supports two loads as shown. Determine the distances a and b when a horizontal force **P** of magnitude 60 lb is applied at A.

7.103 Knowing that $m_B = 70$ kg and $m_C = 25$ kg, determine the magnitude of the force **P** required to maintain equilibrium.

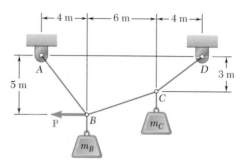

Fig. P7.103 and P7.104

7.104 Knowing that $m_B = 18$ kg and $m_C = 10$ kg, determine the magnitude of the force **P** required to maintain equilibrium.

7.105 If $a = 3$ m, determine the magnitudes of **P** and **Q** required to maintain the cable in the shape shown.

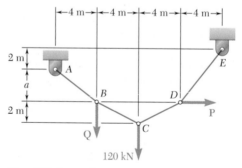

Fig. P7.105 and P7.106

7.106 If $a = 4$ m, determine the magnitudes of **P** and **Q** required to maintain the cable in the shape shown.

7.107 A wire having a mass per unit length of 0.65 kg/m is suspended from two supports at the same elevation that are 120 m apart. If the sag is 30 m, determine (*a*) the total length of the wire, (*b*) the maximum tension in the wire.

7.108 Two cables of the same gauge are attached to a transmission tower at B. Since the tower is slender, the horizontal component of the resultant of the forces exerted by the cables at B is to be zero. Knowing that the mass per unit length of the cables is 0.4 kg/m, determine (*a*) the required sag h, (*b*) the maximum tension in each cable.

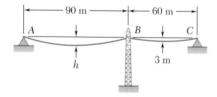

Fig. P7.108

7.109 Each cable of the Golden Gate Bridge supports a load $w =$ 11.1 kips/ft along the horizontal. Knowing that the span L is 4150 ft and that the sag h is 464 ft, determine (a) the maximum tension in each cable, (b) the length of each cable.

7.110 The center span of the George Washington Bridge, as originally constructed, consisted of a uniform roadway suspended from four cables. The uniform load supported by each cable was $w =$ 9.75 kips/ft along the horizontal. Knowing that the span L is 3500 ft and that the sag h is 316 ft, determine for the original configuration (a) the maximum tension in each cable, (b) the length of each cable.

7.111 The total mass of cable AC is 25 kg. Assuming that the mass of the cable is distributed uniformly along the horizontal, determine the sag h and the slope of the cable at A and C.

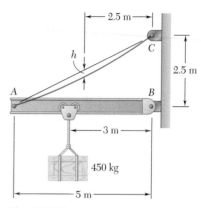

Fig. P7.111

7.112 A 50.5-m length of wire having a mass per unit length of 0.75 kg/m is used to span a horizontal distance of 50 m. Determine (a) the approximate sag of the wire, (b) the maximum tension in the wire. [*Hint:* Use only the first two terms of Eq. (7.10).]

7.113 A cable of length $L + \Delta$ is suspended between two points that are at the same elevation and a distance L apart. (a) Assuming that Δ is small compared to L and that the cable is parabolic, determine the approximate sag in terms of L and Δ. (b) If $L =$ 100 ft and $\Delta =$ 4 ft, determine the approximate sag. [*Hint:* Use only the first two terms of Eq. (7.10).]

7.114 The center span of the Verrazano-Narrows Bridge consists of two uniform roadways suspended from four cables. The design of the bridge allows for the effect of extreme temperature changes that cause the sag of the center span to vary from $h_w =$ 386 ft in winter to $h_s =$ 394 ft in summer. Knowing that the span is $L =$ 4260 ft, determine the change in length of the cables due to extreme temperature changes.

7.115 Each cable of the side spans of the Golden Gate Bridge supports a load $w =$ 10.2 kips/ft along the horizontal. Knowing that for the side spans the maximum vertical distance h from each cable to the chord AB is 30 ft and occurs at midspan, determine (a) the maximum tension in each cable, (b) the slope at B.

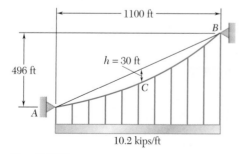

Fig. P7.115

7.116 A steam pipe weighing 45 lb/ft that passes between two buildings 40 ft apart is supported by a system of cables as shown. Assuming that the weight of the cable system is equivalent to a uniformly distributed loading of 5 lb/ft, determine (a) the location of the lowest point C of the cable, (b) the maximum tension in the cable.

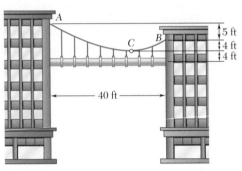

Fig. P7.116

7.117 Cable AB supports a load uniformly distributed along the horizontal as shown. Knowing that at B the cable forms an angle $\theta_B = 35°$ with the horizontal, determine (a) the maximum tension in the cable, (b) the vertical distance a from A to the lowest point of the cable.

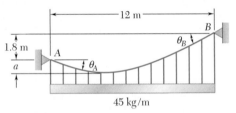

Fig. P7.117 and P7.118

7.118 Cable AB supports a load uniformly distributed along the horizontal as shown. Knowing that the lowest point of the cable is located at a distance $a = 0.6$ m below A, determine (a) the maximum tension in the cable, (b) the angle θ_B that the cable forms with the horizontal at B.

*7.119 A cable AB of span L and a simple beam $A'B'$ of the same span are subjected to identical vertical loadings as shown. Show that the magnitude of the bending moment at a point C' in the beam is equal to the product T_0h, where T_0 is the magnitude of the horizontal component of the tension force in the cable and h is the vertical distance between point C and the chord joining the points of support A and B.

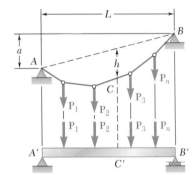

Fig. P7.119

7.120 through 7.123 Making use of the property established in Prob. 7.119, solve the problem indicated by first solving the corresponding beam problem.

    7.120   Prob. 7.94a.
    7.121   Prob. 7.97a.
    7.122   Prob. 7.99a.
    7.123   Prob. 7.100a.

*7.124 Show that the curve assumed by a cable that carries a distributed load $w(x)$ is defined by the differential equation $d^2y/dx^2 = w(x)/T_0$, where T_0 is the tension at the lowest point.

*7.125 Using the property indicated in Prob. 7.124, determine the curve assumed by a cable of span L and sag h carrying a distributed load $w = w_0 \cos(\pi x/L)$, where x is measured from mid-span. Also determine the maximum and minimum values of the tension in the cable.

*7.126 If the weight per unit length of the cable AB is $w_0/\cos^2 \theta$, prove that the curve formed by the cable is a circular arc. (*Hint:* Use the property indicated in Prob. 7.124.)

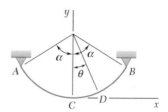

Fig. P7.126

*7.10 CATENARY

Let us now consider a cable AB carrying a load *uniformly distributed along the cable itself* (Fig. 7.18a). Cables hanging under their own weight are loaded in this way. We denote by w the load per unit length (*measured along the cable*) and express it in N/m or in lb/ft. The magnitude W of the total load carried by a portion of cable of length s extending from the lowest point C to a point D is $W = ws$. Substituting this value for W in formula (7.6), we obtain the tension at D:

$$T = \sqrt{T_0^2 + w^2 s^2}$$

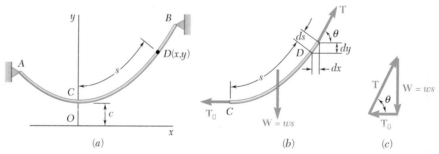

Fig. 7.18

In order to simplify the subsequent computations, we introduce the constant $c = T_0/w$. We thus write

$$T_0 = wc \qquad W = ws \qquad T = w\sqrt{c^2 + s^2} \qquad (7.11)$$

The free-body diagram of the portion of cable CD is shown in Fig. 7.18b. This diagram, however, cannot be used to obtain directly the equation of the curve assumed by the cable, since we do not know the horizontal distance from D to the line of action of the resultant $\mathbf{W}$ of the load. To obtain this equation, we first write that the horizontal projection of a small element of cable of length ds is

Photo 7.4 The forces on the supports and the internal forces in the cables of the power line shown are discussed in this section.

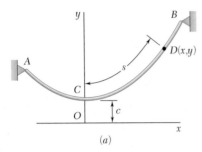

(a)

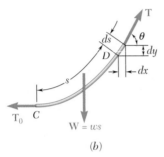

(b)

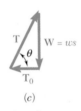

(c)

Fig. 7.18 *(continued)*

$dx = ds \cos \theta$. Observing from Fig. 7.18c that $\cos \theta = T_0/T$ and using (7.11), we write

$$dx = ds \cos \theta = \frac{T_0}{T} ds = \frac{wc\, ds}{w\sqrt{c^2 + s^2}} = \frac{ds}{\sqrt{1 + s^2/c^2}}$$

Selecting the origin O of the coordinates at a distance c directly below C (Fig. 7.18a) and integrating from $C(0, c)$ to $D(x, y)$, we obtain†

$$x = \int_0^s \frac{ds}{\sqrt{1 + s^2/c^2}} = c\left[\sinh^{-1} \frac{s}{c} \right]_0^s = c \sinh^{-1} \frac{s}{c}$$

This equation, which relates the length s of the portion of cable CD and the horizontal distance x, can be written in the form

$$s = c \sinh \frac{x}{c} \tag{7.15}$$

The relation between the coordinates x and y can now be obtained by writing $dy = dx \tan \theta$. Observing from Fig. 7.18c that $\tan \theta = W/T_0$ and using (7.11) and (7.15), we write

$$dy = dx \tan \theta = \frac{W}{T_0} dx = \frac{s}{c} dx = \sinh \frac{x}{c} dx$$

Integrating from $C(0, c)$ to $D(x, y)$ and using (7.12) and (7.13), we obtain

$$y - c = \int_0^x \sinh \frac{x}{c} dx = c\left[\cosh \frac{x}{c} \right]_0^x = c\left(\cosh \frac{x}{c} - 1 \right)$$

$$y - c = c \cosh \frac{x}{c} - c$$

---

†This integral can be found in all standard integral tables. The function

$$z = \sinh^{-1} u$$

(read "arc hyperbolic sine u") is the *inverse* of the function $u = \sinh z$ (read "hyperbolic sine z"). This function and the function $v = \cosh z$ (read "hyperbolic cosine z") are defined as follows:

$$u = \sinh z = \tfrac{1}{2}(e^z - e^{-z}) \qquad v = \cosh z = \tfrac{1}{2}(e^z + e^{-z})$$

Numerical values of the functions $\sinh z$ and $\cosh z$ are found in *tables of hyperbolic functions*. They may also be computed on most calculators either directly or from the above definitions. The student is referred to any calculus text for a complete description of the properties of these functions. In this section, we use only the following properties, which are easily derived from the above definitions:

$$\frac{d \sinh z}{dz} = \cosh z \qquad \frac{d \cosh z}{dz} = \sinh z \tag{7.12}$$

$$\sinh 0 = 0 \qquad \cosh 0 = 1 \tag{7.13}$$

$$\cosh^2 z - \sinh^2 z = 1 \tag{7.14}$$

$$y = c \cosh \frac{x}{c} \qquad (7.16)$$

This is the equation of a *catenary* with vertical axis. The ordinate c of the lowest point C is called the *parameter* of the catenary. Squaring both sides of Eqs. (7.15) and (7.16), subtracting, and taking (7.14) into account, we obtain the following relation between y and s:

$$y^2 - s^2 = c^2 \qquad (7.17)$$

Solving (7.17) for s^2 and carrying into the last of the relations (7.11), we write these relations as follows:

$$T_0 = wc \qquad W = ws \qquad T = wy \qquad (7.18)$$

The last relation indicates that the tension at any point D of the cable is proportional to the vertical distance from D to the horizontal line representing the x axis.

When the supports A and B of the cable have the same elevation, the distance L between the supports is called the *span* of the cable and the vertical distance h from the supports to the lowest point C is called the *sag* of the cable. These definitions are the same as those given in the case of parabolic cables, but it should be noted that because of our choice of coordinate axes, the sag h is now

$$h = y_A - c \qquad (7.19)$$

It should also be observed that certain catenary problems involve transcendental equations which must be solved by successive approximations (see Sample Prob. 7.10). When the cable is fairly taut, however, the load can be assumed uniformly distributed *along the horizontal* and the catenary can be replaced by a parabola. This greatly simplifies the solution of the problem, and the error introduced is small.

When the supports A and B have different elevations, the position of the lowest point of the cable is not known. The problem can then be solved in a manner similar to that indicated for parabolic cables, by expressing that the cable must pass through the supports and that $x_B - x_A = L$ and $y_B - y_A = d$, where L and d denote, respectively, the horizontal and vertical distances between the two supports.

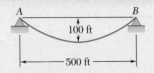

SAMPLE PROBLEM 7.10

A uniform cable weighing 3 lb/ft is suspended between two points A and B as shown. Determine (a) the maximum and minimum values of the tension in the cable, (b) the length of the cable.

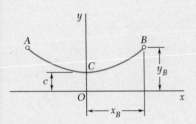

SOLUTION

Equation of Cable. The origin of coordinates is placed at a distance c below the lowest point of the cable. The equation of the cable is given by Eq. (7.16),

$$y = c \cosh \frac{x}{c}$$

The coordinates of point B are

$$x_B = 250 \text{ ft} \qquad y_B = 100 + c$$

Substituting these coordinates into the equation of the cable, we obtain

$$100 + c = c \cosh \frac{250}{c}$$

$$\frac{100}{c} + 1 = \cosh \frac{250}{c}$$

The value of c is determined by assuming successive trial values, as shown in the following table:

c	$\dfrac{250}{c}$	$\dfrac{100}{c}$	$\dfrac{100}{c} + 1$	$\cosh \dfrac{250}{c}$
300	0.833	0.333	1.333	1.367
350	0.714	0.286	1.286	1.266
330	0.758	0.303	1.303	1.301
328	0.762	0.305	1.305	1.305

Taking $c = 328$, we have

$$y_B = 100 + c = 428 \text{ ft}$$

a. Maximum and Minimum Values of the Tension. Using Eqs. (7.18), we obtain

$$T_{\min} = T_0 = wc = (3 \text{ lb/ft})(328 \text{ ft}) \qquad T_{\min} = 984 \text{ lb} \blacktriangleleft$$
$$T_{\max} = T_B = wy_B = (3 \text{ lb/ft})(428 \text{ ft}) \qquad T_{\max} = 1284 \text{ lb} \blacktriangleleft$$

b. Length of Cable. One-half the length of the cable is found by solving Eq. (7.17):

$$y_B^2 - s_{CB}^2 = c^2 \qquad s_{CB}^2 = y_B^2 - c^2 = (428)^2 - (328)^2 \qquad s_{CB} = 275 \text{ ft}$$

The total length of the cable is therefore

$$s_{AB} = 2s_{CB} = 2(275 \text{ ft}) \qquad s_{AB} = 550 \text{ ft} \blacktriangleleft$$

SOLVING PROBLEMS
ON YOUR OWN

In the last section of this chapter you learned to solve problems involving a *cable carrying a load uniformly distributed along the cable*. The shape assumed by the cable is a catenary and is defined by the equation:

$$y = c \cosh \frac{x}{c} \qquad (7.16)$$

1. You should keep in mind that the origin of coordinates for a catenary is located at a distance c directly below the lowest point of the catenary. The length of the cable from the origin to any point is expressed as

$$s = c \sinh \frac{x}{c} \qquad (7.15)$$

2. You should first identify all of the known and unknown quantities. Then consider each of the equations listed in the text (Eqs. 7.15 through 7.19), and solve an equation that contains only one unknown. Substitute the value found into another equation, and solve that equation for another unknown.

3. If the sag h is given, use Eq. (7.19) to replace y by $h + c$ in Eq. (7.16) if x is known [Sample Prob. 7.10], or in Eq. (7.17) if s is known, and solve the equation obtained for the constant c.

4. Many of the problems that you will encounter will involve the solution by trial and error of an equation involving a hyperbolic sine or cosine. You can make your work easier by keeping track of your calculations in a table, as in Sample Prob. 7.10, or by applying a numerical methods approach using a computer or calculator.

PROBLEMS

7.127 A 30-m cable is strung as shown between two buildings. The maximum tension is found to be 500 N, and the lowest point of the cable is observed to be 4 m above the ground. Determine (*a*) the horizontal distance between the buildings, (*b*) the total mass of the cable.

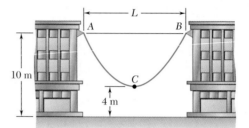

Fig. P7.127

7.128 A 200-ft steel surveying tape weighs 4 lb. If the tape is stretched between two points at the same elevation and pulled until the tension at each end is 16 lb, determine the horizontal distance between the ends of the tape. Neglect the elongation of the tape due to the tension.

7.129 A 200-m-long aerial tramway cable having a mass per unit length of 3.5 kg/m is suspended between two points at the same elevation. Knowing that the sag is 50 m, find (*a*) the horizontal distance between the supports, (*b*) the maximum tension in the cable.

7.130 An electric transmission cable of length 400 ft weighing 2.5 lb/ft is suspended between two points at the same elevation. Knowing that the sag is 100 ft, determine the horizontal distance between the supports and the maximum tension.

7.131 A 20-m length of wire having a mass per unit length of 0.2 kg/m is attached to a fixed support at A and to a collar at B. Neglecting the effect of friction, determine (*a*) the force **P** for which $h = 8$ m, (*b*) the corresponding span L.

7.132 A 20-m length of wire having a mass per unit length of 0.2 kg/m is attached to a fixed support at A and to a collar at B. Knowing that the magnitude of the horizontal force applied to the collar is $P = 20$ N, determine (*a*) the sag h, (*b*) the span L.

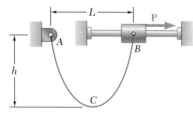

Fig. P7.131, P7.132, and P7.133

7.133 A 20-m length of wire having a mass per unit length of 0.2 kg/m is attached to a fixed support at A and to a collar at B. Neglecting the effect of friction, determine (*a*) the sag h for which $L = 15$ m, (*b*) the corresponding force **P**.

7.134 Determine the sag of a 30-ft chain that is attached to two points at the same elevation that are 20 ft apart.

7.135 A 90-m wire is suspended between two points at the same elevation that are 60 m apart. Knowing that the maximum tension is 300 N, determine (*a*) the sag of the wire, (*b*) the total mass of the wire.

7.136 A counterweight *D* is attached to a cable that passes over a small pulley at *A* and is attached to a support at *B*. Knowing that $L = 45$ ft and $h = 15$ ft, determine (*a*) the length of the cable from *A* to *B*, (*b*) the weight per unit length of the cable. Neglect the weight of the cable from *A* to *D*.

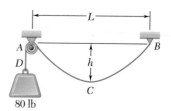

Fig. P7.136

7.137 A uniform cord 50 in. long passes over a pulley at *B* and is attached to a pin support at *A*. Knowing that $L = 20$ in. and neglecting the effect of friction, determine the smaller of the two values of *h* for which the cord is in equilibrium.

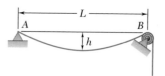

7.138 A cable weighing 2 lb/ft is suspended between two points at the same elevation that are 160 ft apart. Determine the smallest allowable sag of the cable if the maximum tension is not to exceed 400 lb.

Fig. P7.137

7.139 A motor *M* is used to slowly reel in the cable shown. Knowing that the mass per unit length of the cable is 0.4 kg/m, determine the maximum tension in the cable when $h = 5$ m.

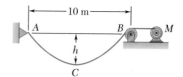

7.140 A motor *M* is used to slowly reel in the cable shown. Knowing that the mass per unit length of the cable is 0.4 kg/m, determine the maximum tension in the cable when $h = 3$ m.

Fig. P7.139 and P7.140

7.141 A uniform cable weighing 3 lb/ft is held in the position shown by a horizontal force **P** applied at *B*. Knowing that $P = 180$ lb and $\theta_A = 60°$, determine (*a*) the location of point *B*, (*b*) the length of the cable.

7.142 A uniform cable weighing 3 lb/ft is held in the position shown by a horizontal force **P** applied at *B*. Knowing that $P = 150$ lb and $\theta_A = 60°$, determine (*a*) the location of point *B*, (*b*) the length of the cable.

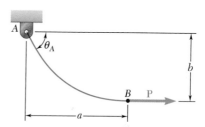

Fig. P7.141 and P7.142

7.143 To the left of point *B* the long cable *ABDE* rests on the rough horizontal surface shown. Knowing that the mass per unit length of the cable is 2 kg/m, determine the force **F** when $a = 3.6$ m.

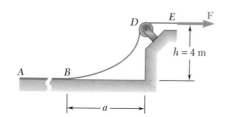

Fig. P7.143 and P7.144

7.144 To the left of point *B* the long cable *ABDE* rests on the rough horizontal surface shown. Knowing that the mass per unit length of the cable is 2 kg/m, determine the force **F** when $a = 6$ m.

7.145 The cable ACB has a mass per unit length of 0.45 kg/m. Knowing that the lowest point of the cable is located at a distance $a = 0.6$ m below the support A, determine (a) the location of the lowest point C, (b) the maximum tension in the cable.

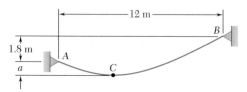

Fig. P7.145 and P7.146

7.146 The cable ACB has a mass per unit length of 0.45 kg/m. Knowing that the lowest point of the cable is located at a distance $a = 2$ m below the support A, determine (a) the location of the lowest point C, (b) the maximum tension in the cable.

*7.147 The 10-ft cable AB is attached to two collars as shown. The collar at A can slide freely along the rod; a stop attached to the rod prevents the collar at B from moving on the rod. Neglecting the effect of friction and the weight of the collars, determine the distance a.

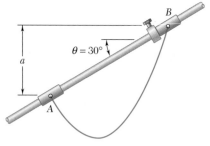

Fig. P7.147

*7.148 Solve Prob. 7.147 assuming that the angle θ formed by the rod and the horizontal is 45°.

7.149 Denoting by θ the angle formed by a uniform cable and the horizontal, show that at any point (a) $s = c \tan \theta$, (b) $y = c \sec \theta$.

*7.150 (a) Determine the maximum allowable horizontal span for a uniform cable of weight w per unit length if the tension in the cable is not to exceed a given value T_m. (b) Using the result of part a, determine the maximum span of a steel wire for which $w = 0.25$ lb/ft and $T_m = 8000$ lb.

*7.151 A cable has a mass per unit length of 3 kg/m and is supported as shown. Knowing that the span L is 6 m, determine the *two* values of the sag h for which the maximum tension is 350 N.

Fig. P7.151, P7.152, and P7.153

*7.152 Determine the sag-to-span ratio for which the maximum tension in the cable is equal to the total weight of the entire cable AB.

*7.153 A cable of weight w per unit length is suspended between two points at the same elevation that are a distance L apart. Determine (a) the sag-to-span ratio for which the maximum tension is as small as possible, (b) the corresponding values of θ_B and T_m.

REVIEW AND SUMMARY

In this chapter you learned to determine the internal forces which hold together the various parts of a given member in a structure.

Considering first a *straight two-force member AB* [Sec. 7.2], we recall that such a member is subjected at A and B to equal and opposite forces $\mathbf{F}$ and $-\mathbf{F}$ directed along AB (Fig. 7.19a). Cutting member AB at C and drawing the free-body diagram of portion AC, we conclude that the internal forces which existed at C in member AB are equivalent to an *axial force* $-\mathbf{F}$ equal and opposite to $\mathbf{F}$ (Fig. 7.19b). We note that in the case of a two-force member which is not straight, the internal forces reduce to a force-couple system and not to a single force.

Forces in straight two-force members

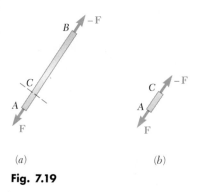

(a)   (b)

Fig. 7.19

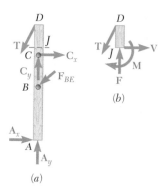

(a)

Fig. 7.20

Considering next a *multiforce member AD* (Fig. 7.20a), cutting it at J, and drawing the free-body diagram of portion JD, we conclude that the internal forces at J are equivalent to a force-couple system consisting of the *axial force* $\mathbf{F}$, the *shearing force* $\mathbf{V}$, and a couple $\mathbf{M}$ (Fig. 7.20b). The magnitude of the shearing force measures the *shear* at point J, and the moment of the couple is referred to as the *bending moment* at J. Since an equal and opposite force-couple system would have been obtained by considering the free-body diagram of portion AJ, it is necessary to specify which portion of member AD was used when recording the answers [Sample Prob. 7.1].

Forces in multiforce members

Most of the chapter was devoted to the analysis of the internal forces in two important types of engineering structures: *beams* and *cables*. *Beams* are usually long, straight prismatic members designed to support loads applied at various points along the member. In general the loads are perpendicular to the axis of the beam and produce only *shear and bending* in the beam. The loads may be either *concentrated*

Forces in beams

at specific points, or *distributed* along the entire length or a portion of the beam. The beam itself may be supported in various ways; since only statically determinate beams are considered in this text, we limited our analysis to that of *simply supported beams, overhanging beams,* and *cantilever beams* [Sec. 7.3].

Shear and bending moment in a beam

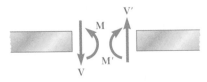

Internal forces at section
(positive shear and positive bending moment)

Fig. 7.21

To obtain the *shear V* and *bending moment M* at a given point *C* of a beam, we first determine the reactions at the supports by considering the entire beam as a free body. We then cut the beam at *C* and use the free-body diagram of one of the two portions obtained in this fashion to determine *V* and *M*. In order to avoid any confusion regarding the sense of the shearing force **V** and couple **M** (which act in opposite directions on the two portions of the beam), the sign convention illustrated in Fig. 7.21 was adopted [Sec. 7.4]. Once the values of the shear and bending moment have been determined at a few selected points of the beam, it is usually possible to draw a *shear diagram* and a *bending-moment diagram* representing, respectively, the shear and bending moment at any point of the beam [Sec. 7.5]. When a beam is subjected to concentrated loads only, the shear is of constant value between loads and the bending moment varies linearly between loads [Sample Prob. 7.2]. On the other hand, when a beam is subjected to distributed loads, the shear and bending moment vary quite differently [Sample Prob. 7.3].

Relations among load, shear, and bending moment

The construction of the shear and bending-moment diagrams is facilitated if the following relations are taken into account. Denoting by w the distributed load per unit length (assumed positive if directed downward), we have [Sec. 7.5]:

$$\frac{dV}{dx} = -w \tag{7.1}$$

$$\frac{dM}{dx} = V \tag{7.3}$$

or, in integrated form,

$$V_D - V_C = -(\text{area under load curve between } C \text{ and } D) \tag{7.2'}$$
$$M_D - M_C = \text{area under shear curve between } C \text{ and } D \tag{7.4'}$$

Equation (7.2′) makes it possible to draw the shear diagram of a beam from the curve representing the distributed load on that beam and the value of V at one end of the beam. Similarly, Eq. (7.4′) makes it possible to draw the bending-moment diagram from the shear diagram and the value of M at one end of the beam. However, concentrated loads introduce discontinuities in the shear diagram and concentrated couples in the bending-moment diagram, none of which are accounted for in these equations [Sample Probs. 7.4 and 7.7]. Finally, we note from Eq. (7.3) that the points of the beam where the bending moment is maximum or minimum are also the points where the shear is zero [Sample Prob. 7.5].

Cables with concentrated loads

The second half of the chapter was devoted to the analysis of *flexible cables.* We first considered a cable of negligible weight supporting *concentrated loads* [Sec. 7.7]. Using the entire cable *AB* as a free body (Fig. 7.22), we noted that the three available equilibrium equations were not sufficient to determine the four unknowns representing the reactions at the supports A and B. However, if the coordinates of a point D of the cable are known, an additional equation can be obtained by considering the free-body diagram of the portion AD or DB of the cable. Once the reactions at the supports have been determined, the elevation of any point of the cable and the tension in any portion of the cable can be found from the appropriate free-body diagram [Sample Prob. 7.8]. It was noted that the horizontal component of the force $\mathbf{T}$ representing the tension is the same at any point of the cable.

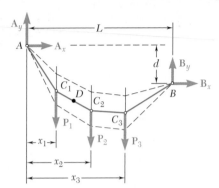

Fig. 7.22

Cables with distributed loads

We next considered cables carrying *distributed loads* [Sec. 7.8]. Using as a free body a portion of cable CD extending from the lowest point C to an arbitrary point D of the cable (Fig. 7.23), we observed that the horizontal component of the tension force $\mathbf{T}$ at D is constant and equal to the tension T_0 at C, while its vertical component is equal to the weight W of the portion of cable CD. The magnitude and direction of $\mathbf{T}$ were obtained from the force triangle:

$$T = \sqrt{T_0^2 + W^2} \qquad \tan \theta = \frac{W}{T_0} \qquad (7.6)$$

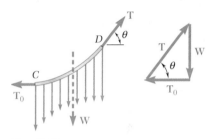

Fig. 7.23

Parabolic cable

In the case of a load *uniformly distributed along the horizontal*—as in a suspension bridge (Fig. 7.24)—the load supported by portion CD is $W = wx$, where w is the constant load per unit horizontal length [Sec. 7.9]. We also found that the curve formed by the cable is a *parabola* of equation

$$y = \frac{wx^2}{2T_0} \qquad (7.8)$$

and that the length of the cable can be found by using the expansion in series given in Eq. (7.10) [Sample Prob. 7.9].

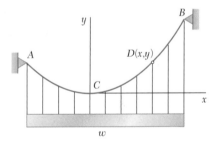

Fig. 7.24

Catenary

In the case of a load *uniformly distributed along the cable itself*—e.g., a cable hanging under its own weight (Fig. 7.25)—the load supported by portion CD is $W = ws$, where s is the length measured along the cable and w is the constant load per unit length [Sec. 7.10]. Choosing the origin O of the coordinate axes at a distance $c = T_0/w$ below C, we derived the relations

$$s = c \sinh \frac{x}{c} \qquad (7.15)$$

$$y = c \cosh \frac{x}{c} \qquad (7.16)$$

$$y^2 - s^2 = c^2 \qquad (7.17)$$

$$T_0 = wc \qquad W = ws \qquad T = wy \qquad (7.18)$$

which can be used to solve problems involving cables hanging under their own weight [Sample Prob. 7.10]. Equation (7.16), which defines the shape of the cable, is the equation of a *catenary*.

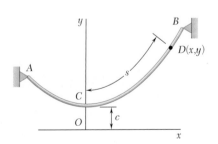

Fig. 7.25

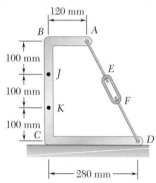

7.154 It has been experimentally determined that the bending moment at point K of the frame shown is 300 N · m. Determine (a) the tension in rods AE and FD, (b) the corresponding internal forces at point J.

7.155 Knowing that the radius of each pulley is 200 mm and neglecting friction, determine the internal forces at point J of the frame shown.

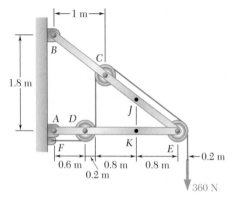

Fig. P7.155

7.156 A steel channel of weight per unit length $w = 20$ lb/ft forms one side of a flight of stairs. Determine the internal forces at the center C of the channel due to its own weight for each of the support conditions shown.

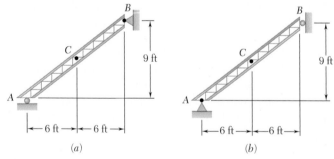

Fig. P7.156

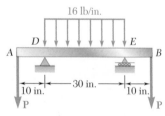

Fig. P7.157 and P7.158

7.157 For the beam shown, determine (a) the magnitude P of the two concentrated loads for which the maximum absolute value of the bending moment is as small as possible, (b) the corresponding value of $|M|_{\text{max}}$.

7.158 Knowing that the magnitude of the concentrated loads **P** is 75 lb, (a) draw the shear and bending-moment diagrams for beam AB, (b) determine the maximum absolute values of the shear and bending moment.

7.159 For the beam and loading shown, (a) draw the shear and bending-moment diagrams, (b) determine the maximum absolute values of the shear and bending moment.

7.160 For the beam shown, draw the shear and bending-moment diagrams, and determine the magnitude and location of the maximum absolute value of the bending moment, knowing that (a) $P = 6$ kips, (b) $P = 3$ kips.

7.161 For the beam and loading shown, (a) write the equations of the shear and bending-moment curves, (b) determine the maximum bending moment.

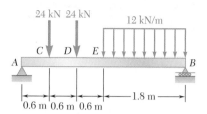

Fig. P7.159

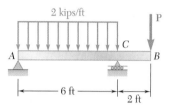

Fig. P7.160

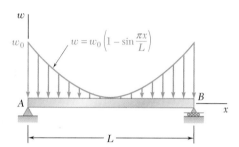

Fig. P7.161

7.162 An oil pipeline is supported at 6-ft intervals by vertical hangers attached to the cable shown. Due to the combined weight of the pipe and its contents the tension in each hanger is 400 lb. Knowing that $d_C = 12$ ft, determine (a) the maximum tension in the cable, (b) the distance d_D.

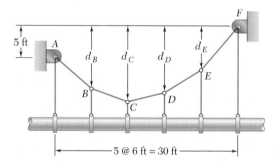

Fig. P7.162

7.163 Solve Prob. 7.162 assuming that $d_C = 9$ ft.

7.164 A transmission cable having a mass per unit length of 0.8 kg/m is strung between two insulators at the same elevation that are 75 m apart. Knowing that the sag of the cable is 2 m, determine (a) the maximum tension in the cable, (b) the length of the cable.

7.165 Cable *ACB* supports a load uniformly distributed along the horizontal as shown. The lowest point *C* is located 9 m to the right of *A*. Determine (a) the vertical distance *a*, (b) the length of the cable, (c) the components of the reaction at *A*.

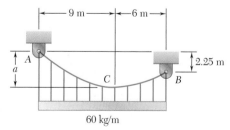

Fig. P7.165

COMPUTER PROBLEMS

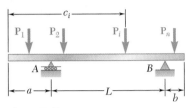

Fig. P7.C1

7.C1 An overhanging beam is to be designed to support several concentrated loads. One of the first steps in the design of the beam is to determine the values of the bending moment that can be expected at the supports A and B and under each of the concentrated loads. Using computational software, calculate those values for the arbitrary beam and loading shown. Use this program for the beam and loading of (*a*) Prob. 7.36, (*b*) Prob. 7.37, (*c*) Prob. 7.38.

7.C2 Several concentrated loads and a uniformly distributed load are to be applied to a simply supported beam AB. As a first step in the design of the beam, use computational software to calculate the shear and bending moment in the beam for the arbitrary loading shown using given increments Δx. Use this program for the beam of (*a*) Prob. 7.39, with $\Delta x = 0.25$ m; (*b*) Prob. 7.41, with $\Delta x = 0.5$ ft; (*c*) Prob. 7.42, with $\Delta x = 0.5$ ft.

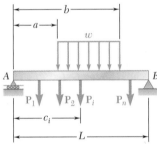

Fig. P7.C2

7.C3 A beam AB hinged at B and supported by a roller at D is to be designed to carry a load uniformly distributed from its end A to its midpoint C with maximum efficiency. As part of the design process, use computational software to determine the distance a from end A to the point D where the roller should be placed to minimize the absolute value of the bending moment M in the beam. (*Note:* A short preliminary analysis will show that the roller should be placed under the load and that the largest negative value of M will occur at D, while its largest positive value will occur somewhere between D and C. Also see the hint for Prob. 7.55.)

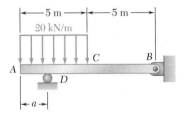

Fig. P7.C3

7.C4 The floor of a bridge will consist of narrow planks resting on two simply supported beams, one of which is shown in the figure. As part of the design of the bridge, it is desired to simulate the effect that driving a 3000-lb truck over the bridge will have on this beam. The distance between the truck's axles is 6 ft, and it is assumed that the weight of the truck is equally distributed over its four wheels. (*a*) Using computational software, calculate the magnitude and location of the maximum bending moment in the beam for values of x from -3 ft to 10 ft using 0.5-ft increments. (*b*) Using smaller increments if necessary, determine the largest value of the bending moment that occurs in the beam as the truck is driven over the bridge and determine the corresponding value of x.

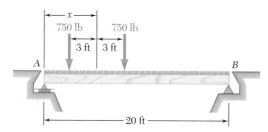

Fig. P7.C4

*7.C5 Using computational software, plot the shear and bending-moment diagrams for the beam of Prob. 7.C1. Using this program and a plotting increment $\Delta x \leq L/100$, plot the V and M diagrams for the beam and loading of (*a*) Prob. 7.36, (*b*) Prob. 7.37, (*c*) Prob. 7.38.

*7.C6 Using computational software, plot the shear and bending-moment diagrams for the beam of Prob. 7.C2. Using this program and a plotting increment $\Delta x \leq L/100$, plot the V and M diagrams for the beam and loading of (*a*) Prob. 7.39, (*b*) Prob. 7.41, (*c*) Prob. 7.42.

7.C7 Using computational software, design cable supports to calculate the horizontal and vertical components of the reaction at the support A_n from values of the loads P_1, P_2, . . ., P_{n-1}, the horizontal distances d_1, d_2, . . ., d_n, and the two vertical distances h_0 and h_k. Use this program to solve Probs. 7.95*b*, 7.96*b*, and 7.97*b*.

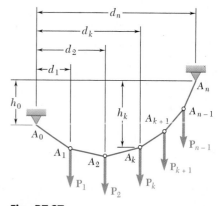

Fig. P7.C7

7.C8 A typical transmission-line installation consists of a cable of length s_{AB} and weight w per unit length suspended as shown between two points at the same elevation. Using computational software, develop a table that can be used in the design of future installations. The table should present the dimensionless quantities h/L, s_{AB}/L, T_0/wL, and T_{max}/wL for values of c/L from 0.2 to 0.5 using 0.025 increments and from 0.5 to 4 using 0.5 increments.

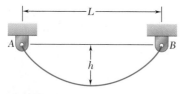

Fig. P7.C8

7.C9 Using computational software, solve Prob. 7.132 for values of P from 0 to 50 N using 5-N increments.

The tractive force that a railroad locomotive can develop depends upon the frictional resistance between the drive wheels and the rails. When the potential exists for wheel slip to occur, such as when a train travels upgrade over wet rails, sand is deposited on top of the railhead to increase this friction.

CHAPTER

8

Friction

411

8.1 INTRODUCTION

In the preceding chapters, it was assumed that surfaces in contact were either *frictionless* or *rough*. If they were frictionless, the force each surface exerted on the other was normal to the surfaces and the two surfaces could move freely with respect to each other. If they were rough, it was assumed that tangential forces could develop to prevent the motion of one surface with respect to the other.

This view was a simplified one. Actually, no perfectly frictionless surface exists. When two surfaces are in contact, tangential forces, called *friction forces,* will always develop if one attempts to move one surface with respect to the other. On the other hand, these friction forces are limited in magnitude and will not prevent motion if sufficiently large forces are applied. The distinction between frictionless and rough surfaces is thus a matter of degree. This will be seen more clearly in the present chapter, which is devoted to the study of friction and of its applications to common engineering situations.

There are two types of friction: *dry friction,* sometimes called *Coulomb friction,* and *fluid friction.* Fluid friction develops between layers of fluid moving at different velocities. Fluid friction is of great importance in problems involving the flow of fluids through pipes and orifices or dealing with bodies immersed in moving fluids. It is also basic in the analysis of the motion of *lubricated mechanisms.* Such problems are considered in texts on fluid mechanics. The present study is limited to dry friction, i.e., to problems involving rigid bodies which are in contact along *nonlubricated* surfaces.

In the first part of this chapter, the equilibrium of various rigid bodies and structures, assuming dry friction at the surfaces of contact, is analyzed. Later a number of specific engineering applications where dry friction plays an important role are considered: wedges, square-threaded screws, journal bearings, thrust bearings, rolling resistance, and belt friction.

8.2 THE LAWS OF DRY FRICTION. COEFFICIENTS OF FRICTION

The laws of dry friction are exemplified by the following experiment. A block of weight **W** is placed on a horizontal plane surface (Fig. 8.1*a*). The forces acting on the block are its weight **W** and the reaction of the surface. Since the weight has no horizontal component, the reaction of the surface also has no horizontal component; the reaction is therefore *normal* to the surface and is represented by **N** in Fig. 8.1*a*. Suppose, now, that a horizontal force **P** is applied to the block (Fig. 8.1*b*). If **P** is small, the block will not move; some other horizontal force must therefore exist, which balances **P**. This other force is the *static-friction force* **F**, which is actually the resultant of a great number of forces acting over the entire surface of contact between the block and the plane. The nature of these forces is not known exactly, but it is generally assumed that these forces are due to the irregularities of the surfaces in contact and, to a certain extent, to molecular attraction.

If the force **P** is increased, the friction force **F** also increases, continuing to oppose **P**, until its magnitude reaches a certain *maximum value* F_m (Fig. 8.1c). If **P** is further increased, the friction force

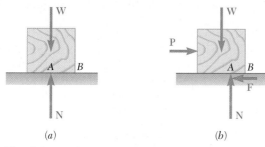

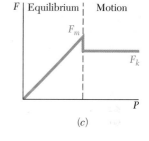

(a)   (b)   (c)

Fig. 8.1

cannot balance it any more and the block starts sliding.† As soon as the block has been set in motion, the magnitude of **F** drops from F_m to a lower value F_k. This is because there is less interpenetration between the irregularities of the surfaces in contact when these surfaces move with respect to each other. From then on, the block keeps sliding with increasing velocity while the friction force, denoted by $\mathbf{F}_k$ and called the *kinetic-friction force*, remains approximately constant.

Experimental evidence shows that the maximum value F_m of the static-friction force is proportional to the normal component N of the reaction of the surface. We have

$$F_m = \mu_s N \qquad (8.1)$$

where μ_s is a constant called the *coefficient of static friction*. Similarly, the magnitude F_k of the kinetic-friction force may be put in the form

$$F_k = \mu_k N \qquad (8.2)$$

where μ_k is a constant called the *coefficient of kinetic friction*. The coefficients of friction μ_s and μ_k do not depend upon the area of

---

†It should be noted that, as the magnitude F of the friction force increases from 0 to F_m, the point of application A of the resultant **N** of the normal forces of contact moves to the right, so that the couples formed, respectively, by **P** and **F** and by **W** and **N** remain balanced. If **N** reaches B before F reaches its maximum value F_m, the block will tip about B before it can start sliding (see Probs. 8.15 and 8.16).

the surfaces in contact. Both coefficients, however, depend strongly on the *nature* of the surfaces in contact. Since they also depend upon the exact condition of the surfaces, their value is seldom known with an accuracy greater than 5 percent. Approximate values of coefficients of static friction for various dry surfaces are given in Table 8.1. The corresponding values of the coefficient of kinetic friction would be about 25 percent smaller. Since coefficients of friction are dimensionless quantities, the values given in Table 8.1 can be used with both SI units and U.S. customary units.

TABLE 8.1   Approximate Values of Coefficient of Static Friction for Dry Surfaces

Metal on metal	0.15–0.60
Metal on wood	0.20–0.60
Metal on stone	0.30–0.70
Metal on leather	0.30–0.60
Wood on wood	0.25–0.50
Wood on leather	0.25–0.50
Stone on stone	0.40–0.70
Earth on earth	0.20–1.00
Rubber on concrete	0.60–0.90

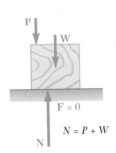

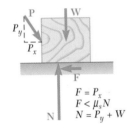

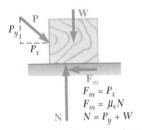

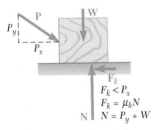

(a) No friction $(P_x = 0)$

$F = 0$
$N = P + W$

(b) No motion $(P_x < F_m)$

$F = P_x$
$F < \mu_s N$
$N = P_y + W$

(c) Motion impending $\longrightarrow (P_x = F_m)$

$F_m = P_x$
$F_m = \mu_s N$
$N = P_y + W$

(d) Motion $\longrightarrow (P_x > F_m)$

$F_k < P_x$
$F_k = \mu_k N$
$N = P_y + W$

Fig. 8.2

From the description given above, it appears that four different situations can occur when a rigid body is in contact with a horizontal surface:

1. The forces applied to the body do not tend to move it along the surface of contact; there is no friction force (Fig. 8.2*a*).
2. The applied forces tend to move the body along the surface of contact but are not large enough to set it in motion. The friction force **F** which has developed can be found by solving the equations of equilibrium for the body. Since there is no evidence that **F** has reached its maximum value, the equation $F_m = \mu_s N$ *cannot be used* to determine the friction force (Fig. 8.2*b*).
3. The applied forces are such that the body is just about to slide. We say that *motion is impending*. The friction force **F** has reached its maximum value F_m and, together with the normal force **N**, balances the applied forces. Both the equations of equilibrium and the equation $F_m = \mu_s N$ *can be used*. We also note that the friction force has a sense opposite to the sense of impending motion (Fig. 8.2*c*).
4. The body is sliding under the action of the applied forces, and the equations of equilibrium do not apply any more. However, **F** is now equal to F_k and the equation $F_k = \mu_k N$ may be used. The sense of F_k is opposite to the sense of motion (Fig. 8.2*d*).

8.3 ANGLES OF FRICTION

It is sometimes convenient to replace the normal force **N** and the friction force **F** by their resultant **R**. Let us consider again a block of weight **W** resting on a horizontal plane surface. If no horizontal force is applied to the block, the resultant **R** reduces to the normal force **N** (Fig. 8.3a). However, if the applied force **P** has a horizontal component $\mathbf{P}_x$ which tends to move the block, the force **R** will have a horizontal component **F** and, thus, will form an angle ϕ with the normal to the surface (Fig. 8.3b). If $\mathbf{P}_x$ is increased until motion becomes impending, the angle between **R** and the vertical grows and reaches a maximum value (Fig. 8.3c). This value is called the *angle of static friction* and is denoted by ϕ_s. From the geometry of Fig. 8.3c, we note that

$$\tan \phi_s = \frac{F_m}{N} = \frac{\mu_s N}{N}$$

$$\tan \phi_s = \mu_s \qquad (8.3)$$

If motion actually takes place, the magnitude of the friction force drops to F_k; similarly, the angle ϕ between **R** and **N** drops to a lower value ϕ_k, called the *angle of kinetic friction* (Fig. 8.3d). From the geometry of Fig. 8.3d, we write

$$\tan \phi_k = \frac{F_k}{N} = \frac{\mu_k N}{N}$$

$$\tan \phi_k = \mu_k \qquad (8.4)$$

Another example will show how the angle of friction can be used to advantage in the analysis of certain types of problems. Consider a block resting on a board and subjected to no other force than its weight **W** and the reaction **R** of the board. The board can be given any desired inclination. If the board is horizontal, the force **R** exerted by the board on the block is perpendicular to the board and balances the weight **W** (Fig. 8.4a). If the board is given a small angle of inclination θ, the force **R** will deviate from the perpendicular to the board by the angle θ and will keep balancing **W** (Fig. 8.4b); it will then have a normal component **N** of magnitude $N = W \cos \theta$ and a tangential component **F** of magnitude $F = W \sin \theta$.

If we keep increasing the angle of inclination, motion will soon become impending. At that time, the angle between **R** and the normal will have reached its maximum value ϕ_s (Fig. 8.4c). The value of the angle of inclination corresponding to impending motion is called the *angle of repose*. Clearly, the angle of repose is equal to the angle of static friction ϕ_s. If the angle of inclination θ is further increased, motion starts and the angle between **R** and the normal drops to the lower value ϕ_k (Fig. 8.4d). The reaction **R** is not vertical any more, and the forces acting on the block are unbalanced.

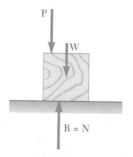

(a) No friction

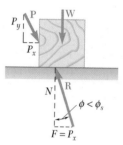

(b) No motion

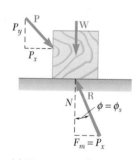

(c) Motion impending ⟶

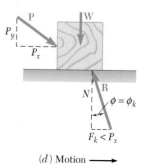

(d) Motion ⟶

Fig. 8.3

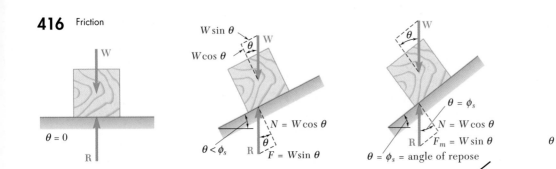

(a) No friction (b) No motion (c) Motion impending (d) Motion

Fig. 8.4

Photo 8.1 The coefficient of static friction between a package and the inclined conveyer belt must be sufficiently large to enable the package to be transported without slipping.

8.4 PROBLEMS INVOLVING DRY FRICTION

Problems involving dry friction are found in many engineering applications. Some deal with simple situations such as the block sliding on a plane described in the preceding sections. Others involve more complicated situations as in Sample Prob. 8.3; many deal with the stability of rigid bodies in accelerated motion and will be studied in dynamics. Also, a number of common machines and mechanisms can be analyzed by applying the laws of dry friction. These include wedges, screws, journal and thrust bearings, and belt transmissions. They will be studied in the following sections.

The *methods* which should be used to solve problems involving dry friction are the same that were used in the preceding chapters. If a problem involves only a motion of translation, with no possible rotation, the body under consideration can usually be treated as a particle, and the methods of Chap. 2 used. If the problem involves a possible rotation, the body must be considered as a rigid body, and the methods of Chap. 4 should be used. If the structure considered is made of several parts, the principle of action and reaction must be used as was done in Chap. 6.

If the body considered is acted upon by more than three forces (including the reactions at the surfaces of contact), the reaction at each surface will be represented by its components N and F and the problem will be solved from the equations of equilibrium. If only three forces act on the body under consideration, it may be more convenient to represent each reaction by the single force R and to solve the problem by drawing a force triangle.

Most problems involving friction fall into one of the following *three groups*: In the *first group* of problems, all applied forces are given and the coefficients of friction are known; we are to determine whether the body considered will remain at rest or slide. The friction force F *required to maintain equilibrium* is unknown (its magnitude is *not* equal to $\mu_s N$) and should be determined, together with the normal force N, by drawing a free-body diagram and *solving the equations of equilibrium* (Fig. 8.5a). The value found for the magnitude F of the friction force is then compared with the maximum value $F_m = \mu_s N$. If F is smaller than or equal to F_m, the body remains at rest. If the value found for F is larger than F_m, equilibrium cannot be maintained and motion takes place; the actual magnitude of the friction force is then $F_k = \mu_k N$.

In problems of the *second group,* all applied forces are given and the motion is known to be impending; we are to determine the value of the coefficient of static friction. Here again, we determine the friction force and the normal force by drawing a free-body diagram and solving the equations of equilibrium (Fig. 8.5b). Since we know that the value found for F is the maximum value F_m, the coefficient of friction may be found by writing and solving the equation $F_m = \mu_s N$.

In problems of the *third group,* the coefficient of static friction is given, and it is known that the motion is impending in a given direction; we are to determine the magnitude or the direction of one of the applied forces. The friction force should be shown in the free-body diagram with a *sense opposite to that of the impending motion* and with a magnitude $F_m = \mu_s N$ (Fig. 8.5c). The equations of equilibrium can then be written, and the desired force determined.

As noted above, when only three forces are involved it may be more convenient to represent the reaction of the surface by a single force **R** and to solve the problem by drawing a force triangle. Such a solution is used in Sample Prob. 8.2.

When two bodies A and B are in contact (Fig. 8.6a), the forces of friction exerted, respectively, by A on B and by B on A are equal and opposite (Newton's third law). In drawing the free-body diagram of one of the bodies, it is important to include the appropriate friction force with its correct sense. The following rule should then be observed: *The sense of the friction force acting on A is opposite to that of the motion (or impending motion) of A as observed from B* (Fig. 8.6b).† The sense of the friction force acting on B is determined in a similar way (Fig. 8.6c). Note that the motion of A as observed from B is a *relative motion.* For example, if body A is fixed and body B moves, body A will have a relative motion with respect to B. Also, if both B and A are moving down but B is moving faster than A, body A will be observed, from B, to be moving up.

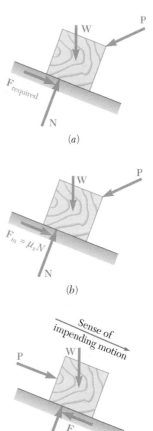

(a)

(b)

(c)

Fig. 8.5

†It is therefore *the same as that of the motion of B as observed from A.*

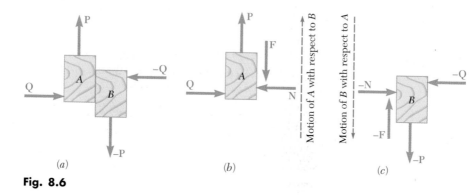

(a)   (b)   (c)

Fig. 8.6

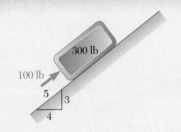

SAMPLE PROBLEM 8.1

A 100-lb force acts as shown on a 300-lb block placed on an inclined plane. The coefficients of friction between the block and the plane are $\mu_s = 0.25$ and $\mu_k = 0.20$. Determine whether the block is in equilibrium, and find the value of the friction force.

SOLUTION

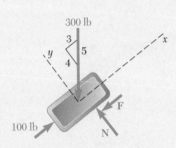

Force Required for Equilibrium. We first determine the value of the friction force *required to maintain equilibrium*. Assuming that $\mathbf{F}$ is directed down and to the left, we draw the free-body diagram of the block and write

$$+\nearrow \Sigma F_x = 0: \qquad 100 \text{ lb} - \tfrac{3}{5}(300 \text{ lb}) - F = 0$$
$$F = -80 \text{ lb} \qquad \mathbf{F} = 80 \text{ lb} \nearrow$$

$$+\nwarrow \Sigma F_y = 0: \qquad N - \tfrac{4}{5}(300 \text{ lb}) = 0$$
$$N = +240 \text{ lb} \qquad \mathbf{N} = 240 \text{ lb} \nwarrow$$

The force $\mathbf{F}$ required to maintain equilibrium is an 80-lb force directed up and to the right; the tendency of the block is thus to move down the plane.

Maximum Friction Force. The magnitude of the maximum friction force which may be developed is

$$F_m = \mu_s N \qquad F_m = 0.25(240 \text{ lb}) = 60 \text{ lb}$$

Since the value of the force required to maintain equilibrium (80 lb) is larger than the maximum value which may be obtained (60 lb), equilibrium will not be maintained and *the block will slide down the plane*.

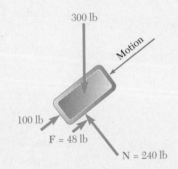

Actual Value of Friction Force. The magnitude of the actual friction force is obtained as follows:

$$F_{\text{actual}} = F_k = \mu_k N$$
$$= 0.20(240 \text{ lb}) = 48 \text{ lb}$$

The sense of this force is opposite to the sense of motion; the force is thus directed up and to the right:

$$\mathbf{F}_{\text{actual}} = 48 \text{ lb} \nearrow \qquad \blacktriangleleft$$

It should be noted that the forces acting on the block are not balanced; the resultant is

$$\tfrac{3}{5}(300 \text{ lb}) - 100 \text{ lb} - 48 \text{ lb} = 32 \text{ lb} \swarrow$$

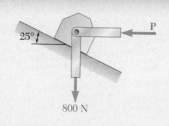

800 N

SAMPLE PROBLEM 8.2

A support block is acted upon by two forces as shown. Knowing that the coefficients of friction between the block and the incline are $\mu_s = 0.35$ and $\mu_k = 0.25$, determine the force **P** required (*a*) to start the block moving up the incline, (*b*) to keep it moving up, (*c*) to prevent it from sliding down.

SOLUTION

Free-Body Diagram. For each part of the problem we draw a free-body diagram of the block and a force triangle including the 800-N vertical force, the horizontal force **P**, and the force **R** exerted on the block by the incline. The direction of **R** must be determined in each separate case. We note that since **P** is perpendicular to the 800-N force, the force triangle is a right triangle, which can easily be solved for **P**. In most other problems, however, the force triangle will be an oblique triangle and should be solved by applying the law of sines.

a. Force *P* to Start Block Moving Up

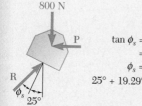

$$\tan \phi_s = \mu_s$$
$$= 0.35$$
$$\phi_s = 19.29°$$
$$25° + 19.29° = 44.29°$$

$$P = (800 \text{ N}) \tan 44.29° \qquad \mathbf{P} = 780 \text{ N} \leftarrow \blacktriangleleft$$

b. Force *P* to Keep Block Moving Up

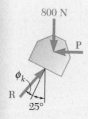

$$\tan \phi_k = \mu_k$$
$$= 0.25$$
$$\phi_k = 14.04°$$
$$25° + 14.04° = 39.04°$$

$$P = (800 \text{ N}) \tan 39.04° \qquad \mathbf{P} = 649 \text{ N} \leftarrow \blacktriangleleft$$

c. Force *P* to Prevent Block from Sliding Down

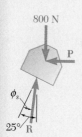

$$\phi_s = 19.29°$$
$$25° - 19.29° = 5.71°$$

$$P = (800 \text{ N}) \tan 5.71° \qquad \mathbf{P} = 80.0 \text{ N} \leftarrow \blacktriangleleft$$

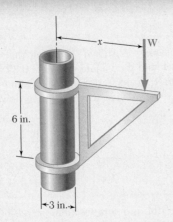

SAMPLE PROBLEM 8.3

The movable bracket shown may be placed at any height on the 3-in.-diameter pipe. If the coefficient of static friction between the pipe and bracket is 0.25, determine the minimum distance x at which the load **W** can be supported. Neglect the weight of the bracket.

SOLUTION

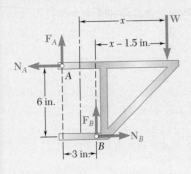

Free-Body Diagram. We draw the free-body diagram of the bracket. When **W** is placed at the minimum distance x from the axis of the pipe, the bracket is just about to slip, and the forces of friction at A and B have reached their maximum values:

$$F_A = \mu_s N_A = 0.25 \, N_A$$
$$F_B = \mu_s N_B = 0.25 \, N_B$$

Equilibrium Equations

$\xrightarrow{+} \Sigma F_x = 0: \qquad N_B - N_A = 0$
$$N_B = N_A$$

$+\uparrow \Sigma F_y = 0: \qquad F_A + F_B - W = 0$
$$0.25 N_A + 0.25 N_B = W$$

And, since N_B has been found equal to N_A,

$$0.50 N_A = W$$
$$N_A = 2W$$

$+\uparrow \Sigma M_B = 0: \qquad N_A(6 \text{ in.}) - F_A(3 \text{ in.}) - W(x - 1.5 \text{ in.}) = 0$
$$6N_A - 3(0.25 N_A) - Wx + 1.5W = 0$$
$$6(2W) - 0.75(2W) - Wx + 1.5W = 0$$

Dividing through by W and solving for x,

$$x = 12 \text{ in.} \quad \blacktriangleleft$$

SOLVING PROBLEMS
ON YOUR OWN

In this lesson you studied and applied the *laws of dry friction*. Previously you had encountered only (*a*) frictionless surfaces that could move freely with respect to each other, (*b*) rough surfaces that allowed no motion relative to each other.

A. In solving problems involving dry friction, you should keep the following in mind.

1. The reaction R exerted by a surface on a free body can be resolved into a component **N** and a tangential component **F**. The tangential component is known as the *friction force*. When a body is in contact with a fixed surface the direction of the friction force **F** is opposite to that of the actual or impending motion of the body.

    a. No motion will occur as long as F does not exceed the maximum value $F_m = \mu_s N$, where μ_s is the *coefficient of static friction*.

    b. Motion will occur if a value of F larger than F_m is required to maintain equilibrium. As motion takes place, the actual value of F drops to $F_k = \mu_k N$, where μ_k is the *coefficient of kinetic friction* [Sample Prob. 8.1].

2. When only three forces are involved an alternative approach to the analysis of friction may be preferred [Sample Prob. 8.2]. The reaction **R** is defined by its magnitude R and the angle ϕ it forms with the normal to the surface. No motion will occur as long as ϕ does not exceed the maximum value ϕ_s, where $\tan \phi_s = \mu_s$. Motion will occur if a value of ϕ larger than ϕ_s is required to maintain equilibrium, and the actual value of ϕ will drop to ϕ_k, where $\tan \phi_k = \mu_k$.

3. When two bodies are in contact the sense of the actual or impending relative motion at the point of contact must be determined. On each of the two bodies a friction force **F** should be shown in a direction opposite to that of the actual or impending motion of the body as seen from the other body.

(*continued*)

B. Methods of solution. The first step in your solution is to *draw a free-body diagram* of the body under consideration, resolving the force exerted on each surface where friction exists into a normal component **N** and a friction force **F**. If several bodies are involved, draw a free-body diagram of each of them, labeling and directing the forces at each surface of contact as you learned to do when analyzing frames in Chap. 6.

The problem you have to solve may fall in one of the following three categories:

1. All the applied forces and the coefficients of friction are known, and you must determine whether equilibrium is maintained. Note that in this situation the friction force is unknown and *cannot be assumed to be equal* to $\mu_s N$.

    a. Write the equations of equilibrium to determine N and F.

    b. Calculate the maximum allowable friction force, $F_m = \mu_s N$. If $F \leq F_m$, equilibrium is maintained. If $F > F_m$, motion occurs, and the magnitude of the friction force is $F_k = \mu_k N$ [Sample Prob. 8.1].

2. All the applied forces are known, and you must find the smallest allowable value of μ_s for which equilibrium is maintained. You will assume that motion is impending and determine the corresponding value of μ_s.

    a. Write the equations of equilibrium to determine N and F.

    b. Since motion is impending, $F = F_m$. Substitute the values found for N and F into the equation $F_m = \mu_s N$ and solve for μ_s.

3. The motion of the body is impending and μ_s is known; you must find some unknown quantity, such as a distance, an angle, the magnitude of a force, or the direction of a force.

    a. Assume a possible motion of the body and, on the free-body diagram, draw the friction force in a direction opposite to that of the assumed motion.

    b. Since motion is impending, $F = F_m = \mu_s N$. Substituting for μ_s its known value, you can express F in terms of N on the free-body diagram, thus eliminating one unknown.

    c. Write and solve the equilibrium equations for the unknown you seek [Sample Prob. 8.3].

PROBLEMS

8.1 Determine whether the block shown is in equilibrium and find the magnitude and direction of the friction force when $\theta = 25°$ and $P = 150$ lb.

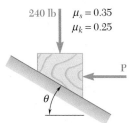

240 lb $\mu_s = 0.35$
         $\mu_k = 0.25$

P

θ

Fig. P8.1 and P8.2

8.2 Determine whether the block shown is in equilibrium and find the magnitude and direction of the friction force when $\theta = 30°$ and $P = 30$ lb.

8.3 Determine whether the block shown is in equilibrium and find the magnitude and direction of the friction force when $\theta = 40°$ and $P = 400$ N.

8.4 Determine whether the block shown is in equilibrium and find the magnitude and direction of the friction force when $\theta = 35°$ and $P = 200$ N.

8.5 Knowing that $\theta = 45°$, determine the range of values of P for which equilibrium is maintained.

8.6 Determine the range of values of P for which equilibrium of the block shown is maintained.

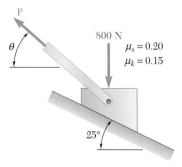

P
800 N $\mu_s = 0.20$
         $\mu_k = 0.15$
θ
25°

Fig. P8.3, P8.4, and P8.5

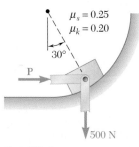

$\mu_s = 0.25$
$\mu_k = 0.20$
30°
P
500 N

Fig. P8.6

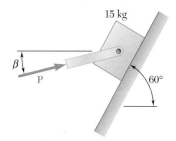

15 kg
β
P
60°

Fig. P8.7

8.7 Knowing that the coefficient of friction between the 15-kg block and the incline is $\mu_s = 0.25$, determine (a) the smallest value of P required to maintain the block in equilibrium, (b) the corresponding value of β.

8.8 Considering only values of θ less than 90°, determine the smallest value of θ required to start the block moving to the right when (a) $W = 75$ lb, (b) $W = 100$ lb.

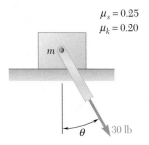

$\mu_s = 0.25$
$\mu_k = 0.20$
m
θ 30 lb

Fig. P8.8

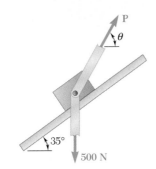

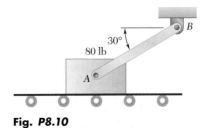

Fig. P8.9

8.9 The coefficients of friction between the block and the rail are $\mu_s = 0.30$ and $\mu_k = 0.25$. Knowing that $\theta = 65°$, determine the smallest value of P required (a) to start the block moving up the rail, (b) to keep it from moving down.

8.10 The 80-lb block is attached to link AB and rests on a moving belt. Knowing that $\mu_s = 0.25$ and $\mu_k = 0.20$, determine the magnitude of the horizontal force $\mathbf{P}$ that should be applied to the belt to maintain its motion (a) to the right, (b) to the left.

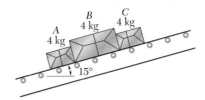

Fig. P8.10

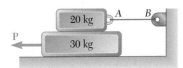

Fig. P8.11

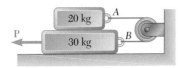

Fig. P8.12

8.11 and 8.12 The coefficients of friction are $\mu_s = 0.40$ and $\mu_k = 0.30$ between all surfaces of contact. Determine the smallest force P required to start the 30-kg block moving if cable AB (a) is attached as shown, (b) is removed.

8.13 Three 4-kg packages A, B, and C are placed on a conveyor belt that is at rest. Between the belt and both packages A and C the coefficients of friction are $\mu_s = 0.30$ and $\mu_k = 0.20$; between package B and the belt the coefficients are $\mu_s = 0.10$ and $\mu_k = 0.08$. The packages are placed on the belt so that they are in contact with each other and at rest. Determine which, if any, of the packages will move and the friction force acting on each package.

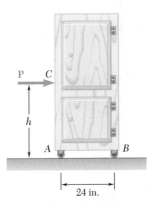

8.14 Solve Prob. 8.13 assuming that package B is placed to the right of both packages A and C.

8.15 A 120-lb cabinet is mounted on casters that can be locked to prevent their rotation. The coefficient of static friction between the floor and each caster is 0.30. If $h = 32$ in., determine the magnitude of the force $\mathbf{P}$ required to move the cabinet to the right (a) if all casters are locked, (b) if the casters at B are locked and the casters at A are free to rotate, (c) if the casters at A are locked and the casters at B are free to rotate.

8.16 A 120-lb cabinet is mounted on casters that can be locked to prevent their rotation. The coefficient of static friction between the floor and each caster is 0.30. Assuming that the casters at both A and B are locked, determine (a) the force $\mathbf{P}$ required to move the cabinet to the right, (b) the largest allowable value of h if the cabinet is not to tip over.

Fig. P8.15 and P8.16

8.17 The cylinder shown is of weight W and radius r, and the coefficient of static friction μ_s is the same at A and B. Determine the magnitude of the largest couple **M** that can be applied to the cylinder if it is not to rotate.

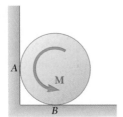

Fig. P8.17 and P8.18

8.18 The cylinder shown is of weight W and radius r. Express in terms W and r the magnitude of the largest couple **M** that can be applied to the cylinder if it is not to rotate, assuming the coefficient of static friction to be (*a*) zero at A and 0.30 at B, (*b*) 0.25 at A and 0.30 at B.

8.19 The hydraulic cylinder shown exerts a force of 3 kN directed to the right on point B and to the left on point E. Determine the magnitude of the couple **M** required to rotate the drum clockwise at a constant speed.

8.20 A couple **M** of magnitude 100 N · m is applied to the drum as shown. Determine the smallest force that must be exerted by the hydraulic cylinder on joints B and E if the drum is not to rotate.

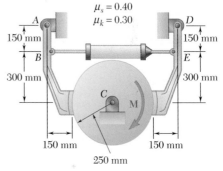

Fig. P8.19 and P8.20

8.21 A 6.5-m ladder AB leans against a wall as shown. Assuming that the coefficient of static friction μ_s is zero at B, determine the smallest value of μ_s at A for which equilibrium is maintained.

8.22 A 6.5-m ladder AB leans against a wall as shown. Assuming that the coefficient of static friction μ_s is the same at A and B, determine the smallest value of μ_s for which equilibrium is maintained.

8.23 and 8.24 End A of a slender, uniform rod of length L and weight W bears on a surface as shown, while end B is supported by a cord BC. Knowing that the coefficients of friction are $\mu_s = 0.40$ and $\mu_k = 0.30$, determine (*a*) the largest value of θ for which motion is impending, (*b*) the corresponding value of the tension in the cord.

Fig. P8.21 and *P8.22*

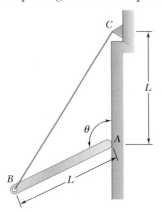

Fig. P8.23

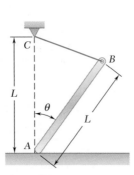

Fig. *P8.24*

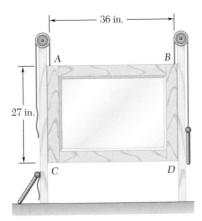

36 in.

A B

27 in.

C D

Fig. P8.25

8.25 A window sash weighing 10 lb is normally supported by two 5-lb sash weights. Knowing that the window remains open after one sash cord has broken, determine the smallest possible value of the coefficient of static friction. (Assume that the sash is slightly smaller than the frame and will bind only at points A and D.)

8.26 A 500-N concrete block is to be lifted by the pair of tongs shown. Determine the smallest allowable value of the coefficient of static friction between the block and the tongs at F and G.

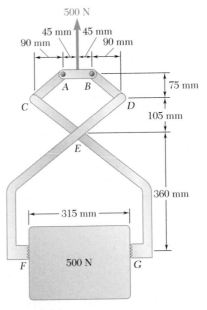

500 N

45 mm   45 mm

90 mm   90 mm

A B

C D

75 mm

105 mm

E

360 mm

315 mm

500 N

F G

Fig. P8.26

8.27 The press shown is used to emboss a small seal at E. Knowing that the coefficient of static friction between the vertical guide and the embossing die D is 0.30, determine the force exerted by the die on the seal.

8.28 The 100-mm-radius cam shown is used to control the motion of the plate CD. Knowing that the coefficient of static friction between the cam and the plate is 0.45 and neglecting friction at the roller supports, determine (a) the force **P** required to maintain the motion of the plate, knowing that the plate is 20 mm thick, (b) the largest thickness of the plate for which the mechanism is self locking (i.e., for which the plate cannot be moved however large the force **P** may be).

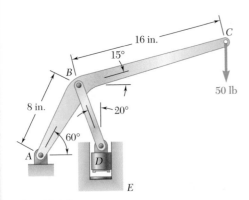

16 in.

15°

B

C

50 lb

8 in.

20°

60°

A

D

E

Fig. P8.27

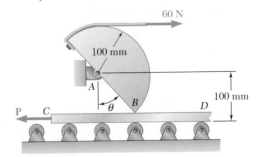

60 N

100 mm

A

100 mm

P   C

θ   B   D

Fig. P8.28

8.29 A slender rod of length L is lodged between peg C and the vertical wall and supports a load **P** at end A. Knowing that the coefficient of static friction is 0.20 at both B and C, find the range of values of the ratio L/a for which equilibrium is maintained.

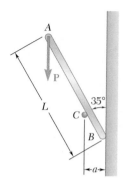

Fig. P8.29

8.30 The 50-lb plate $ABCD$ is attached at A and D to collars that can slide on the vertical rod. Knowing that the coefficient of static friction is 0.40 between both collars and the rod, determine whether the plate is in equilibrium in the position shown when the magnitude of the vertical force applied at E is (a) $P = 0$, (b) $P = 20$ lb.

8.31 In Prob. 8.30, determine the range of values of the magnitude P of the vertical force applied at E for which the plate will move downward.

8.32 A pipe of diameter 60 mm is gripped by the stillson wrench shown. Portions AB and DE of the wrench are rigidly attached to each other, and portion CF is connected by a pin at D. If the wrench is to grip the pipe and be self-locking, determine the required minimum coefficients of friction at A and C.

8.33 Solve Prob. 8.32 assuming that the diameter of the pipe is 30 mm.

8.34 A 10-ft beam, weighing 1200 lb, is to be moved to the left onto the platform. A horizontal force **P** is applied to the dolly, which is mounted on frictionless wheels. The coefficients of friction between all surfaces are $\mu_s = 0.30$ and $\mu_k = 0.25$, and initially $x = 2$ ft. Knowing that the top surface of the dolly is slightly higher than the platform, determine the force **P** required to start moving the beam. (*Hint:* The beam is supported at A and D.)

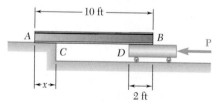

Fig. P8.34

8.35 (a) Show that the beam of Prob. 8.34 *cannot* be moved if the top surface of the dolly is slightly *lower* than the platform. (b) Show that the beam *can* be moved if two 175-lb workers stand on the beam at B and determine how far to the left the beam can be moved.

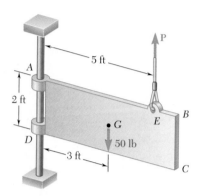

Fig. P8.30

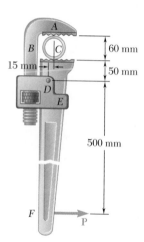

Fig. P8.32

8.36 Knowing that the coefficient of static friction between the collar and the rod is 0.35, determine the range of values of P for which equilibrium is maintained when $\theta = 50°$ and $M = 20$ N · m.

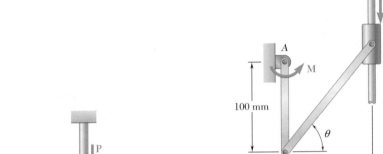

Fig. P8.36 and P8.37

8.37 Knowing that the coefficient of static friction between the collar and the rod is 0.40, determine the range of values of M for which equilibrium is maintained when $\theta = 60°$ and $P = 200$ N.

8.38 The slender rod AB of length $l = 600$ mm is attached to a collar at B and rests on a small wheel located at a horizontal distance $a = 80$ mm from the vertical rod on which the collar slides. Knowing that the coefficient of static friction between the collar and the vertical rod is 0.25 and neglecting the radius of the wheel, determine the range of values of P for which equilibrium is maintained when $Q = 100$ N and $\theta = 30°$.

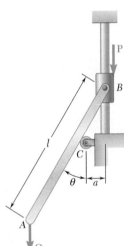

Fig. P8.38

8.39 Two 10-lb blocks A and B are connected by a slender rod of negligible weight. The coefficient of static friction is 0.30 between all surfaces of contact, and the rod forms an angle $\theta = 30°$ with the vertical. (*a*) Show that the system is in equilibrium when $P = 0$. (*b*) Determine the largest value of P for which equilibrium is maintained.

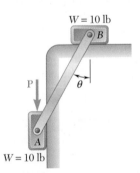

Fig. P8.39

8.40 Two identical uniform boards, each of weight 40 lb, are temporarily leaned against each other as shown. Knowing that the coefficient of static friction between all surfaces is 0.40, determine (*a*) the largest magnitude of the force P for which equilibrium will be maintained, (*b*) the surface at which motion will impend.

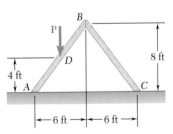

Fig. P8.40

8.41 Two identical 5-ft-long rods connected by a pin at *B* are placed between two walls and a horizontal surface as shown. Denoting by μ_s the coefficient of static friction at *A*, *B*, and *C*, determine the smallest value of μ_s for which equilibrium is maintained.

8.42 Two 8-kg blocks *A* and *B* resting on shelves are connected by a rod of negligible mass. Knowing that the magnitude of a horizontal force **P** applied at *C* is slowly increased from zero, determine the value of *P* for which motion occurs, and what that motion is, when the coefficient of static friction between all surfaces is (*a*) $\mu_s =$ 0.40, (*b*) $\mu_s = 0.50$.

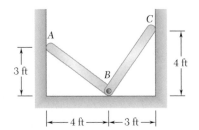

Fig. P8.41

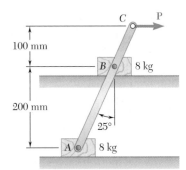

Fig. P8.42

8.43 A slender steel rod of length 225 mm is placed inside a pipe as shown. Knowing that the coefficient of static friction between the rod and the pipe is 0.20, determine the largest value of θ for which the rod will not fall into the pipe.

8.44 In Prob. 8.43, determine the smallest value of θ for which the rod will not fall out the pipe.

8.45 Two slender rods of negligible weight are pin-connected at *C* and attached to blocks *A* and *B*, each of weight *W*. Knowing that $\theta =$ 80° and that the coefficient of static friction between the blocks and the horizontal surface is 0.30, determine the largest value of *P* for which equilibrium is maintained.

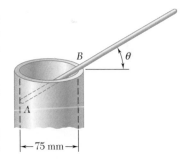

Fig. P8.43

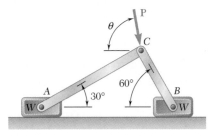

Fig. P8.45

8.5 WEDGES

Wedges are simple machines used to raise large stone blocks and other heavy loads. These loads can be raised by applying to the wedge a force usually considerably smaller than the weight of the load. In addition, because of the friction between the surfaces in contact, a properly shaped wedge will remain in place after being forced under the load. Wedges can thus be used advantageously to make small adjustments in the position of heavy pieces of machinery.

Consider the block A shown in Fig. 8.7a. This block rests against a vertical wall B and is to be raised slightly by forcing a wedge C between block A and a second wedge D. We want to find the minimum value of the force $\mathbf{P}$ which must be applied to the wedge C to move the block. It will be assumed that the weight $\mathbf{W}$ of the block is known, either given in pounds or determined in newtons from the mass of the block expressed in kilograms.

The free-body diagrams of block A and of wedge C have been drawn in Fig. 8.7b and c. The forces acting on the block include its weight and the normal and friction forces at the surfaces of contact with wall B and wedge C. The magnitudes of the friction forces $\mathbf{F}_1$ and $\mathbf{F}_2$ are equal, respectively, to $\mu_s N_1$ and $\mu_s N_2$ since the motion of the block must be started. It is important to show the friction forces with their correct sense. Since the block will move upward, the force $\mathbf{F}_1$ exerted by the wall on the block must be directed downward. On the other hand, since the wedge C moves to the right, the relative motion of A with respect to C is to the left and the force $\mathbf{F}_2$ exerted by C on A must be directed to the right.

Considering now the free body C in Fig. 8.7c, we note that the forces acting on C include the applied force $\mathbf{P}$ and the normal and friction forces at the surfaces of contact with A and D. The weight of the wedge is small compared with the other forces involved and can be neglected. The forces exerted by A on C are equal and opposite to the forces $\mathbf{N}_2$ and $\mathbf{F}_2$ exerted by C on A and are denoted, respectively, by $-\mathbf{N}_2$ and $-\mathbf{F}_2$; the friction force $-\mathbf{F}_2$ must therefore be directed to the left. We check that the force $\mathbf{F}_3$ exerted by D is also directed to the left.

The total number of unknowns involved in the two free-body diagrams can be reduced to four if the friction forces are expressed in terms of the normal forces. Expressing that block A and wedge C are in equilibrium will provide four equations which can be solved to obtain the magnitude of $\mathbf{P}$. It should be noted that in the example considered here, it will be more convenient to replace each pair of normal and friction forces by their resultant. Each free body is then subjected to only three forces, and the problem can be solved by drawing the corresponding force triangles (see Sample Prob. 8.4).

8.6 SQUARE-THREADED SCREWS

Square-threaded screws are frequently used in jacks, presses, and other mechanisms. Their analysis is similar to the analysis of a block sliding along an inclined plane.

Consider the jack shown in Fig. 8.8. The screw carries a load $\mathbf{W}$ and is supported by the base of the jack. Contact between screw and base takes place along a portion of their threads. By applying a force $\mathbf{P}$ on the handle, the screw can be made to turn and to raise the load $\mathbf{W}$.

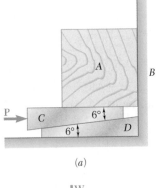

(a)

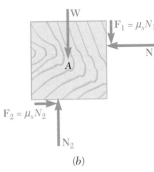

(b)

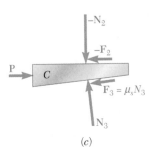

(c)

Fig. 8.7

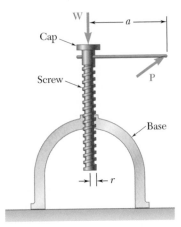

Fig. 8.8

The thread of the base has been unwrapped and shown as a straight line in Fig. 8.9a. The correct slope was obtained by plotting horizontally the product $2\pi r$, where r is the mean radius of the thread, and vertically the *lead L* of the screw, i.e., the distance through which the screw advances in one turn. The angle θ this line forms with the horizontal is the *lead angle*. Since the force of friction between two surfaces in contact does not depend upon the area of contact, a much smaller than actual area of contact between the two threads can be assumed, and the screw can be represented by the block shown in Fig. 8.9a. It should be noted, however, that in this analysis of the jack, the friction between cap and screw is neglected.

The free-body diagram of the block should include the load $\mathbf{W}$, the reaction $\mathbf{R}$ of the base thread, and a horizontal force $\mathbf{Q}$ having the same effect as the force $\mathbf{P}$ exerted on the handle. The force $\mathbf{Q}$ should have the same moment as $\mathbf{P}$ about the axis of the screw and its magnitude should thus be $Q = Pa/r$. The force $\mathbf{Q}$, and thus the force $\mathbf{P}$ required to raise the load $\mathbf{W}$, can be obtained from the free-body diagram shown in Fig. 8.9a. The friction angle is taken equal to ϕ_s since the load will presumably be raised through a succession of short strokes. In mechanisms providing for the continuous rotation of a screw, it may be desirable to distinguish between the force required to start motion (using ϕ_s) and that required to maintain motion (using ϕ_k).

Photo 8.2 Wedges are used as shown to split tree trunks because the normal forces exerted by the wedges on the wood are much larger than the forces required to insert the wedges.

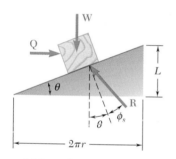

(*a*) Impending motion upward

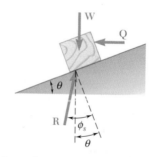

(*b*) Impending motion downward with $\phi_s > \theta$

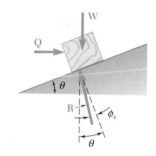

(*c*) Impending motion downward with $\phi_s < \theta$

Fig. 8.9   Block-and-incline analysis of a screw.

If the friction angle ϕ_s is larger than the lead angle θ, the screw is said to be *self-locking*; it will remain in place under the load. To lower the load, we must then apply the force shown in Fig. 8.9b. If ϕ_s is smaller than θ, the screw will unwind under the load; it is then necessary to apply the force shown in Fig. 8.9c to maintain equilibrium.

The lead of a screw should not be confused with its *pitch*. The lead was defined as the distance through which the screw advances in one turn; the pitch is the distance measured between two consecutive threads. While lead and pitch are equal in the case of *single-threaded* screws, they are different in the case of *multiple-threaded* screws, i.e., screws having several independent threads. It is easily verified that for double-threaded screws, the lead is twice as large as the pitch; for triple-threaded screws, it is three times as large as the pitch; etc.

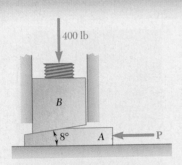

400 lb

B

8° A ← P

SAMPLE PROBLEM 8.4

The position of the machine block B is adjusted by moving the wedge A. Knowing that the coefficient of static friction is 0.35 between all surfaces of contact, determine the force $\mathbf{P}$ required (a) to raise block B, (b) to lower block B.

SOLUTION

For each part, the free-body diagrams of block B and wedge A are drawn, together with the corresponding force triangles, and the law of sines is used to find the desired forces. We note that since $\mu_s = 0.35$, the angle of friction is

$$\phi_s = \tan^{-1} 0.35 = 19.3°$$

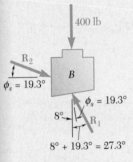

400 lb

R_2

$\phi_s = 19.3°$ B

$\phi_s = 19.3°$

8° R_1

8° + 19.3° = 27.3°

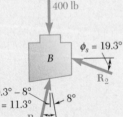

27.3°

$R_1 = 549$ lb

A ← P

R_3 19.3°

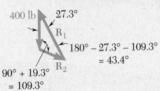

400 lb 27.3°

R_1

180° − 27.3° − 109.3°
= 43.4°

R_2

90° + 19.3°
= 109.3°

a. Force P to Raise Block

Free Body: Block B

$$\frac{R_1}{\sin 109.3°} = \frac{400 \text{ lb}}{\sin 43.4°}$$

$$R_1 = 549 \text{ lb}$$

90° − 19.3° = 70.7°

P

19.3°

27.3° R_3

549 lb

27.3° + 19.3°
= 46.6°

Free Body: Wedge A

$$\frac{P}{\sin 46.6°} = \frac{549 \text{ lb}}{\sin 70.7°}$$

$$P = 423 \text{ lb} \qquad \mathbf{P} = 423 \text{ lb} \leftarrow \quad \blacktriangleleft$$

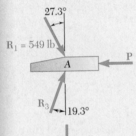

400 lb

B $\phi_s = 19.3°$

R_2

19.3° − 8°
= 11.3° 8°

R_1

$\phi_s = 19.3°$

90° − 19.3° = 70.7°

R_2

180° − 70.7° − 11.3°
= 98.0°

400 lb R_1

11.3°

b. Force P to Lower Block

Free Body: Block B

$$\frac{R_1}{\sin 70.7°} = \frac{400 \text{ lb}}{\sin 98.0°}$$

$$R_1 = 381 \text{ lb}$$

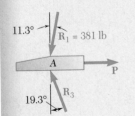

11.3°

$R_1 = 381$ lb

A

P

19.3° R_3

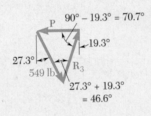

90° − 19.3° = 70.7°

P

11.3°

19.3° 381 lb

R_3 19.3° + 11.3°
= 30.6°

Free Body: Wedge A

$$\frac{P}{\sin 30.6°} = \frac{381 \text{ lb}}{\sin 70.7°}$$

$$P = 206 \text{ lb} \qquad \mathbf{P} = 206 \text{ lb} \rightarrow \quad \blacktriangleleft$$

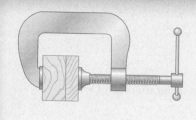

SAMPLE PROBLEM 8.5

A clamp is used to hold two pieces of wood together as shown. The clamp has a double square thread of mean diameter equal to 10 mm with a pitch of 2 mm. The coefficient of friction between threads is $\mu_s = 0.30$. If a maximum couple of 40 N · m is applied in tightening the clamp, determine (a) the force exerted on the pieces of wood, (b) the couple required to loosen the clamp.

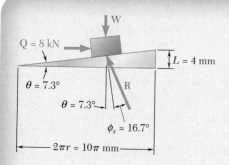

SOLUTION

a. Force Exerted by Clamp. The mean radius of the screw is $r = 5$ mm. Since the screw is double-threaded, the lead L is equal to twice the pitch: $L = 2(2 \text{ mm}) = 4$ mm. The lead angle θ and the friction angle ϕ_s are obtained by writing

$$\tan \theta = \frac{L}{2\pi r} = \frac{4 \text{ mm}}{10\pi \text{ mm}} = 0.1273 \qquad \theta = 7.3°$$

$$\tan \phi_s = \mu_s = 0.30 \qquad\qquad\qquad \phi_s = 16.7°$$

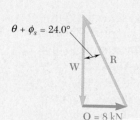

The force **Q** which should be applied to the block representing the screw is obtained by expressing that its moment Qr about the axis of the screw is equal to the applied couple.

$$Q(5 \text{ mm}) = 40 \text{ N} \cdot \text{m}$$

$$Q = \frac{40 \text{ N} \cdot \text{m}}{5 \text{ mm}} = \frac{40 \text{ N} \cdot \text{m}}{5 \times 10^{-3} \text{ m}} = 8000 \text{ N} = 8 \text{ kN}$$

The free-body diagram and the corresponding force triangle can now be drawn for the block; the magnitude of the force **W** exerted on the pieces of wood is obtained by solving the triangle.

$$W = \frac{Q}{\tan(\theta + \phi_s)} = \frac{8 \text{ kN}}{\tan 24.0°}$$

$$W = 17.97 \text{ kN} \quad \blacktriangleleft$$

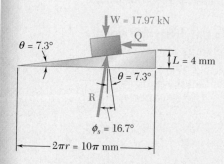

b. Couple Required to Loosen Clamp. The force **Q** required to loosen the clamp and the corresponding couple are obtained from the free-body diagram and force triangle shown.

$$Q = W \tan(\phi_s - \theta) = (17.97 \text{ kN}) \tan 9.4°$$
$$= 2.975 \text{ kN}$$

$$\text{Couple} = Qr = (2.975 \text{ kN})(5 \text{ mm})$$
$$= (2.975 \times 10^3 \text{ N})(5 \times 10^{-3} \text{ m}) = 14.87 \text{ N} \cdot \text{m}$$

$$\text{Couple} = 14.87 \text{ N} \cdot \text{m} \quad \blacktriangleleft$$

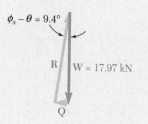

SOLVING PROBLEMS
ON YOUR OWN

In this lesson you learned to apply the laws of friction to the solution of problems involving *wedges* and *square-threaded screws*.

1. Wedges. Keep the following in mind when solving a problem involving a wedge:

a. First draw a free-body diagram of the wedge and of all the other bodies involved. Carefully note the sense of the relative motion of all surfaces of contact and show each friction force acting in *a direction opposite* to the direction of that relative motion.

b. Show the maximum static friction force F_m at each surface if the wedge is to be inserted or removed, *since motion will be impending in each of these cases.*

c. The reaction R and the angle of friction, rather than the normal force and the friction force, can be used in many applications. You can then draw one or more force triangles and determine the unknown quantities either graphically or by trigonometry [Sample Prob. 8.4].

2. Square-Threaded Screws. The analysis of a square-threaded screw is equivalent to the analysis of a block sliding on an incline. To draw the appropriate incline, you should unwrap the thread of the screw and represent it by a straight line [Sample Prob. 8.5]. When solving a problem involving a square-threaded screw, keep the following in mind:

a. Do not confuse the pitch of a screw with the lead of a screw. The *pitch* of a screw is the distance between two consecutive threads, while the *lead* of a screw is the distance the screw advances in one full turn. The lead and the pitch are equal only in single-threaded screws. In a double-threaded screw, the lead is twice the pitch.

b. The couple required to tighten a screw is different from the couple required to loosen it. Also, screws used in jacks and clamps are usually *self-locking;* that is, the screw will remain stationary as long as no couple is applied to it, and a couple must be applied to the screw to loosen it [Sample Prob. 8.5].

PROBLEMS

8.46 The machine part *ABC* is supported by a frictionless hinge at *B* and a 10° wedge at *C*. Knowing that the coefficient of static friction is 0.20 at both surfaces of the wedge, determine (*a*) the force **P** required to move the wedge to the left, (*b*) the components of the corresponding reaction at *B*.

8.47 Solve Prob. 8.46 assuming that the wedge is to be moved to the right.

8.48 and **8.49** Two 8° wedges of negligible weight are used to move and position the 800-kg block. Knowing that the coefficient of static friction is 0.30 at all surfaces of contact, determine the smallest force **P** that should be applied as shown to one of the wedges.

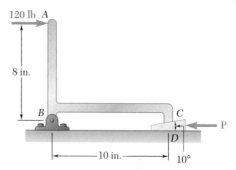

Fig. P8.46

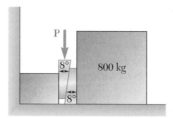

Fig. P8.48

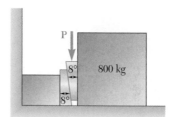

Fig. P8.49

8.50 and **8.51** The elevation of the end of the steel beam supported by a concrete floor is adjusted by means of the steel wedges *E* and *F*. The base plate *CD* has been welded to the lower flange of the beam, and the end reaction of the beam is known to be 100 kN. The coefficient of static friction is 0.30 between two steel surfaces and 0.60 between steel and concrete. If the horizontal motion of the beam is prevented by the force **Q**, determine (*a*) the force **P** required to raise the beam, (*b*) the corresponding force **Q**.

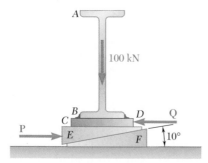

Fig. P8.50

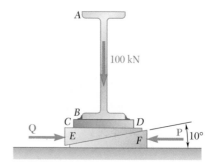

Fig. P8.51

8.52 A wedge A of negligible weight is to be driven between two 100-lb plates B and C. The coefficient of static friction between all surfaces of contact is 0.35. Determine the magnitude of the force **P** required to start moving the wedge (*a*) if the plates are equally free to move, (*b*) if plate C is securely bolted to the surface.

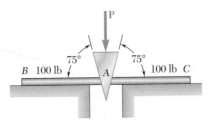

Fig. P8.52

8.53 Block A supports a pipe column and rests as shown on wedge B. Knowing that the coefficient of static friction at all surfaces of contact is 0.25 and that $\theta = 45°$, determine the smallest force **P** required to raise block A.

8.54 Block A supports a pipe column and rests as shown on wedge B. Knowing that the coefficient of static friction at all surfaces of contact is 0.25 and that $\theta = 45°$, determine the smallest force **P** for which equilibrium is maintained.

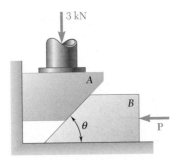

Fig. P8.53, P8.54, and P8.55

8.55 Block A supports a pipe column and rests as shown on wedge B. The coefficient of static friction at all surfaces of contact is 0.25. If **P** = 0, determine (*a*) the angle θ for which sliding is impending, (*b*) the corresponding force exerted on the block by the vertical wall.

8.56 A 12° wedge is used to spread a split ring. The coefficient of static friction between the wedge and the ring is 0.30. Knowing that a force **P** of magnitude 25 lb was required to insert the wedge, determine the magnitude of the forces exerted on the ring by the wedge after insertion.

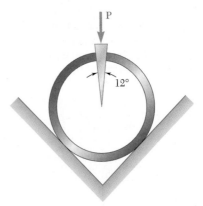

Fig. P8.56

8.57 A 10° wedge is to be forced under end B of the 5-kg rod AB. Knowing that the coefficient of static friction is 0.40 between the wedge and the rod and 0.20 between the wedge and the floor, determine the smallest force **P** required to raise end B of the rod.

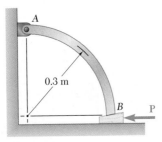

Fig. P8.57

8.58 A 10° wedge is used to split a section of a log. The coefficient of static friction between the wedge and the log is 0.35. Knowing that a force **P** of magnitude 600 lb was required to insert the wedge, determine the magnitude of the forces exerted on the wood by the wedge after insertion.

8.59 A conical wedge is placed between two horizontal plates that are then slowly moved toward each other. Indicate what will happen to the wedge (*a*) if $\mu_s = 0.20$, (*b*) if $\mu_s = 0.30$.

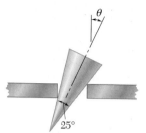

Fig. P8.59

Fig. P8.58

8.60 A 15° wedge is forced under a 50-kg pipe as shown. The coefficient of static friction at all surfaces is 0.20. (*a*) Show that slipping will occur between the pipe and the vertical wall. (*b*) Determine the force **P** required to move the wedge.

8.61 A 15° wedge is forced under a 50-kg pipe as shown. Knowing that the coefficient of static friction at both surfaces of the wedge is 0.20, determine the largest coefficient of static friction between the pipe and the vertical wall for which slipping will occur at *A*.

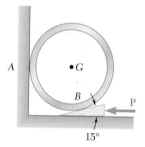

Fig. P8.60 and P8.61

8.62 An 8° wedge is to be forced under a machine base at *B*. Knowing that the coefficient of static friction at all surfaces of contact is 0.15, (*a*) determine the force **P** required to move the wedge, (*b*) indicate whether the machine base will slide on the floor.

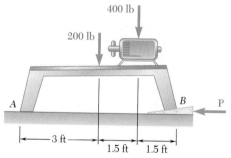

Fig. P8.62

8.63 Solve Prob. 8.62 assuming that the wedge is to be forced under the machine base at *A* instead of *B*.

*__*8.64** A 200-N block rests as shown on a wedge of negligible weight. The coefficient of static friction μ_s is the same at both surfaces of the wedge, and friction between the block and the vertical wall may be neglected. For $P = 100$ N, determine the value of μ_s for which motion is impending. (*Hint:* Solve the equation obtained by trial and error.)

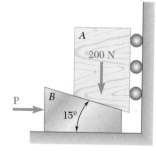

Fig. P8.64

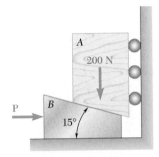

***8.65** Solve Prob. 8.64 assuming that the rollers are removed and that μ_s is the coefficient of friction at all surfaces of contact.

8.66 Derive the following formulas relating the load **W** and the force **P** exerted on the handle of the jack discussed in Sec. 8.6. (*a*) $P = (Wr/a) \tan (\theta + \phi_s)$, to raise the load; (*b*) $P = (Wr/a) \tan (\phi_s - \theta)$, to lower the load if the screw is self-locking; (*c*) $P = (Wr/a) \tan (\theta - \phi_s)$, to hold the load if the screw is not self-locking.

8.67 The square-threaded worm gear shown has a mean radius of 1.5 in. and a lead of 0.375 in. The large gear is subjected to a constant clockwise couple of 7.2 kip · in. Knowing that the coefficient of static friction between the two gears is 0.12, determine the couple that must be applied to shaft AB in order to rotate the large gear counterclockwise. Neglect friction in the bearings at A, B, and C.

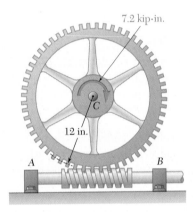

Fig. P8.67

8.68 In Prob. 8.67, determine the couple that must be applied to shaft AB in order to rotate the large gear clockwise.

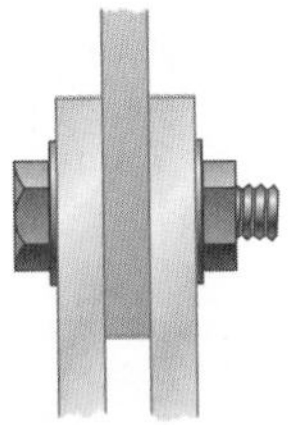

8.69 High-strength bolts are used in the construction of many steel structures. For a 24-mm-nominal-diameter bolt the required minimum bolt tension is 210 kN. Assuming the coefficient of friction to be 0.40, determine the required couple that should be applied to the bolt and nut. The mean diameter of the thread is 22.6 mm, and the lead is 3 mm. Neglect friction between the nut and washer, and assume the bolt to be square-threaded.

Fig. P8.69

8.70 The ends of two fixed rods A and B are each made in the form of a single-threaded screw of mean radius 6 mm and pitch 2 mm. Rod A has a right-handed thread and rod B has a left-handed thread. The coefficient of static friction between the rods and the threaded sleeve is 0.12. Determine the magnitude of the couple that must be applied to the sleeve in order to draw the rods closer together.

Fig. P8.70

8.71 Assuming that in Prob. 8.70 a right-handed thread is used on *both* rods *A* and *B*, determine the magnitude of the couple that must be applied to the sleeve in order to rotate it.

8.72 In the machinist's vise shown, the movable jaw *D* is rigidly attached to the tongue *AB* that fits loosely into the fixed body of the vise. The screw is single-threaded into the fixed base and has a mean diameter of 0.75 in. and a pitch of 0.25 in. The coefficient of static friction is 0.25 between the threads and also between the tongue and the body. Neglecting bearing friction between the screw and the movable head, determine the couple that must be applied to the handle in order to produce a clamping force of 1 kip.

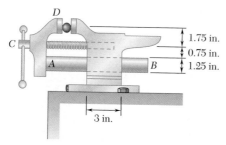

1.75 in.
0.75 in.
1.25 in.

3 in.

Fig. P8.72

8.73 In Prob. 8.72, a clamping force of 1 kip was obtained by tightening the vise. Determine the couple that must be applied to the screw to loosen the vise.

8.74 In the gear-pulling assembly shown the square-threaded screw *AB* has a mean radius of 15 mm and a lead of 4 mm. Knowing that the coefficient of static friction is 0.10, determine the couple that must be applied to the screw in order to produce a force of 3 kN on the gear. Neglect friction at end *A* of the screw.

Fig. P8.74

*8.7 JOURNAL BEARINGS. AXLE FRICTION

Journal bearings are used to provide lateral support to rotating shafts and axles. Thrust bearings, which will be studied in the next section, are used to provide axial support to shafts and axles. If the journal bearing is fully lubricated, the frictional resistance depends upon the speed of rotation, the clearance between axle and bearing, and the viscosity of the lubricant. As indicated in Sec. 8.1, such problems are studied in fluid mechanics. The methods of this chapter, however, can be applied to the study of axle friction when the bearing is not lubricated or only partially lubricated. It can then be assumed that the axle and the bearing are in direct contact along a single straight line.

Consider two wheels, each of weight **W**, rigidly mounted on an axle supported symmetrically by two journal bearings (Fig. 8.10*a*). If the wheels rotate, we find that to keep them rotating at constant speed, it is necessary to apply to each of them a couple **M**. The free-body

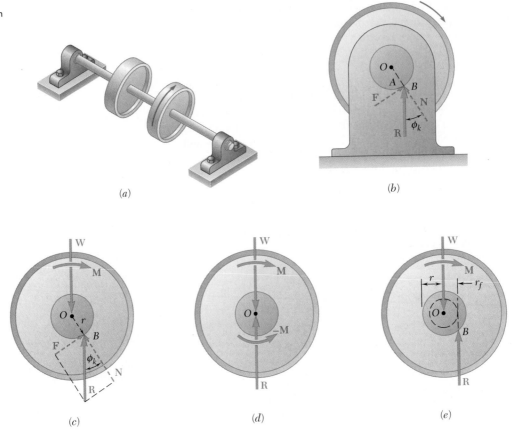

(a)

(b)

(c)

(d)

(e)

Fig. 8.10

diagram in Fig. 8.10*c* represents one of the wheels and the corresponding half axle in projection on a plane perpendicular to the axle. The forces acting on the free body include the weight **W** of the wheel, the couple **M** required to maintain its motion, and a force **R** representing the reaction of the bearing. This force is vertical, equal, and opposite to **W** but does not pass through the center *O* of the axle; **R** is located to the right of *O* at a distance such that its moment about *O* balances the moment **M** of the couple. Therefore, contact between the axle and bearing does not take place at the lowest point *A* when the axle rotates. It takes place at point *B* (Fig. 8.10*b*) or, rather, along a straight line intersecting the plane of the figure at *B*. Physically, this is explained by the fact that when the wheels are set in motion, the axle "climbs" in the bearings until slippage occurs. After sliding back slightly, the axle settles more or less in the position shown. This position is such that the angle between the reaction **R** and the normal to the surface of the bearing is equal to the angle of kinetic friction ϕ_k. The distance from *O* to the line of action of **R** is thus $r \sin \phi_k$, where r is the radius of the axle. Writing that $\Sigma M_O = 0$ for the forces acting on the free body considered, we obtain the magnitude of the couple **M** required to overcome the frictional resistance of one of the bearings:

$$M = Rr \sin \phi_k \qquad (8.5)$$

Observing that, for small values of the angle of friction, $\sin \phi_k$ can be replaced by $\tan \phi_k$, that is, by μ_k, we write the approximate formula

$$M \approx Rr\mu_k \qquad (8.6)$$

In the solution of certain problems, it may be more convenient to let the line of action of **R** pass through O, as it does when the axle does not rotate. A couple $-\mathbf{M}$ of the same magnitude as the couple **M** but of opposite sense must then be added to the reaction **R** (Fig. 8.10d). This couple represents the frictional resistance of the bearing.

In case a graphical solution is preferred, the line of action of **R** can be readily drawn (Fig. 8.10e) if we note that it must be tangent to a circle centered at O and of radius

$$r_f = r \sin \phi_k \approx r\mu_k \qquad (8.7)$$

This circle is called the *circle of friction* of the axle and bearing and is independent of the loading conditions of the axle.

*8.8 THRUST BEARINGS. DISK FRICTION

Two types of thrust bearings are used to provide axial support to rotating shafts and axles: (1) *end bearings* and (2) *collar bearings* (Fig. 8.11). In the case of collar bearings, friction forces develop between the two ring-shaped areas which are in contact. In the case of end bearings, friction takes place over full circular areas, or over ring-shaped areas when the end of the shaft is hollow. Friction between circular areas, called *disk friction,* also occurs in other mechanisms, such as *disk clutches*.

(a) End bearing   (b) Collar bearing

Fig. 8.11   Thrust bearings.

To obtain a formula which is valid in the most general case of disk friction, let us consider a rotating hollow shaft. A couple **M** keeps the shaft rotating at constant speed while a force **P** maintains it in contact with a fixed bearing (Fig. 8.12). Contact between the shaft and

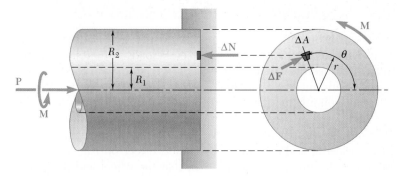

Fig. 8.12

the bearing takes place over a ring-shaped area of inner radius R_1 and outer radius R_2. Assuming that the pressure between the two surfaces in contact is uniform, we find that the magnitude of the normal force $\Delta \mathbf{N}$ exerted on an element of area ΔA is $\Delta N = P\, \Delta A / A$, where $A = \pi(R_2^2 - R_1^2)$, and that the magnitude of the friction force $\Delta \mathbf{F}$ acting on ΔA is $\Delta F = \mu_k\, \Delta N$. Denoting by r the distance from the axis of the shaft to the element of area ΔA, we express the magnitude ΔM of the moment of $\Delta \mathbf{F}$ about the axis of the shaft as follows:

$$\Delta M = r\, \Delta F = \frac{r\mu_k P\, \Delta A}{\pi(R_2^2 - R_1^2)}$$

The equilibrium of the shaft requires that the moment $\mathbf{M}$ of the couple applied to the shaft be equal in magnitude to the sum of the moments of the friction forces $\Delta \mathbf{F}$. Replacing ΔA by the infinitesimal element $dA = r\, d\theta\, dr$ used with polar coordinates, and integrating over the area of contact, we thus obtain the following expression for the magnitude of the couple $\mathbf{M}$ required to overcome the frictional resistance of the bearing:

$$M = \frac{\mu_k P}{\pi(R_2^2 - R_1^2)} \int_0^{2\pi} \int_{R_1}^{R_2} r^2\, dr\, d\theta$$

$$= \frac{\mu_k P}{\pi(R_2^2 - R_1^2)} \int_0^{2\pi} \tfrac{1}{3}(R_2^3 - R_1^3)\, d\theta$$

$$M = \tfrac{2}{3}\mu_k P \frac{R_2^3 - R_1^3}{R_2^2 - R_1^2} \qquad (8.8)$$

When contact takes place over a full circle of radius R, formula (8.8) reduces to

$$M = \tfrac{2}{3}\mu_k PR \qquad (8.9)$$

The value of M is then the same as would be obtained if contact between shaft and bearing took place at a single point located at a distance $2R/3$ from the axis of the shaft.

The largest couple which can be transmitted by a disk clutch without causing slippage is given by a formula similar to (8.9), where μ_k has been replaced by the coefficient of static friction μ_s.

*8.9 WHEEL FRICTION. ROLLING RESISTANCE

The wheel is one of the most important inventions of our civilization. Its use makes it possible to move heavy loads with relatively little effort. Because the point of the wheel in contact with the ground at any given instant has no relative motion with respect to the ground, the wheel eliminates the large friction forces which would arise if the load were in direct contact with the ground. However, some resistance to the wheel's motion exists. This resistance has two distinct causes. It is due (1) to a combined effect of axle friction and friction at the rim and (2) to the fact that the wheel and the ground deform, with the result that contact between wheel and ground takes place over a certain area, rather than at a single point.

To understand better the first cause of resistance to the motion of a wheel, let us consider a railroad car supported by eight wheels mounted on axles and bearings. The car is assumed to be moving to the right at constant speed along a straight horizontal track. The free-body diagram of one of the wheels is shown in Fig. 8.13*a*. The forces acting on the free body include the load **W** supported by the wheel and the normal reaction **N** of the track. Since **W** is drawn through the center *O* of the axle, the frictional resistance of the bearing should be represented by a counterclockwise couple **M** (see Sec. 8.7). To keep the free body in equilibrium, we must add two equal and oppo-site forces **P** and **F**, forming a clockwise couple of moment −**M**. The force **F** is the friction force exerted by the track on the wheel, and **P** represents the force which should be applied to the wheel to keep it rolling at constant speed. Note that the forces **P** and **F** would not exist if there were no friction between wheel and track. The couple **M** representing the axle friction would then be zero; the wheel would slide on the track without turning in its bearing.

The couple **M** and the forces **P** and **F** also reduce to zero when there is no axle friction. For example, a wheel which is not held in bearings and rolls freely and at constant speed on horizontal ground (Fig. 8.13*b*) will be subjected to only two forces: its own weight **W** and the normal reaction **N** of the ground. Regardless of the value of the coefficient of friction between wheel and ground no friction force will act on the wheel. A wheel rolling freely on horizontal ground should thus keep rolling indefinitely.

Experience, however, indicates that the wheel will slow down and eventually come to rest. This is due to the second type of resis-tance mentioned at the beginning of this section, known as the *roll-ing resistance*. Under the load **W**, both the wheel and the ground deform slightly, causing the contact between wheel and ground to take place over a certain area. Experimental evidence shows that the resultant of the forces exerted by the ground on the wheel over this area is a force **R** applied at a point *B*, which is not located directly under the center *O* of the wheel, but slightly in front of it (Fig. 8.13*c*). To balance the moment of **W** about *B* and to keep the wheel rolling at constant speed, it is necessary to apply a horizontal force **P** at the center of the wheel. Writing $\Sigma M_B = 0$, we obtain

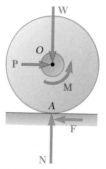

(*a*) Effect of axle friction

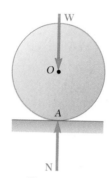

(*b*) Free wheel

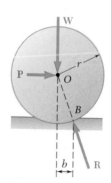

(*c*) Rolling resistance

Fig. 8.13

$$Pr = Wb \tag{8.10}$$

where r = radius of wheel
 b = horizontal distance between O and B

The distance b is commonly called the *coefficient of rolling resis-tance*. It should be noted that b is not a dimensionless coefficient since it represents a length; b is usually expressed in inches or in millimeters. The value of b depends upon several parameters in a manner which has not yet been clearly established. Values of the coefficient of rolling resistance vary from about 0.01 in. or 0.25 mm for a steel wheel on a steel rail to 5.0 in. or 125 mm for the same wheel on soft ground.

SAMPLE PROBLEM 8.6

A pulley of diameter 4 in. can rotate about a fixed shaft of diameter 2 in. The coefficient of static friction between the pulley and shaft is 0.20. Determine (a) the smallest vertical force **P** required to start raising a 500-lb load, (b) the smallest vertical force **P** required to hold the load, (c) the smallest horizontal force **P** required to start raising the same load.

SOLUTION

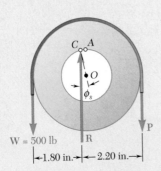

a. Vertical Force P Required to Start Raising the Load. When the forces in both parts of the rope are equal, contact between the pulley and shaft takes place at A. When **P** is increased, the pulley rolls around the shaft slightly and contact takes place at B. The free-body diagram of the pulley when motion is impending is drawn. The perpendicular distance from the center O of the pulley to the line of action of **R** is

$$r_f = r \sin \phi_s \approx r\mu_s \qquad r_f \approx (1 \text{ in.})0.20 = 0.20 \text{ in.}$$

Summing moments about B, we write

$$+\hspace{-0.3em}\uparrow \ \Sigma M_B = 0: \qquad (2.20 \text{ in.})(500 \text{ lb}) - (1.80 \text{ in.})P = 0$$
$$P = 611 \text{ lb} \qquad\qquad\qquad \mathbf{P = 611 \text{ lb}} \downarrow \ \blacktriangleleft$$

b. Vertical Force P to Hold the Load. As the force **P** is decreased, the pulley rolls around the shaft and contact takes place at C. Considering the pulley as a free body and summing moments about C, we write

$$+\hspace{-0.3em}\uparrow \ \Sigma M_C = 0: \qquad (1.80 \text{ in.})(500 \text{ lb}) - (2.20 \text{ in.})P = 0$$
$$P = 409 \text{ lb} \qquad\qquad\qquad \mathbf{P = 409 \text{ lb}} \downarrow \ \blacktriangleleft$$

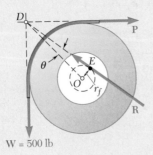

c. Horizontal Force P to Start Raising the Load. Since the three forces **W**, **P**, and **R** are not parallel, they must be concurrent. The direction of **R** is thus determined from the fact that its line of action must pass through the point of intersection D of **W** and **P**, and must be tangent to the circle of friction. Recalling that the radius of the circle of friction is $r_f = 0.20$ in., we write

$$\sin \theta = \frac{OE}{OD} = \frac{0.20 \text{ in.}}{(2 \text{ in.})\sqrt{2}} = 0.0707 \qquad \theta = 4.1°$$

From the force triangle, we obtain

$$P = W \cot (45° - \theta) = (500 \text{ lb}) \cot 40.9°$$
$$= 577 \text{ lb} \qquad\qquad\qquad \mathbf{P = 577 \text{ lb}} \rightarrow \ \blacktriangleleft$$

SOLVING PROBLEMS
ON YOUR OWN

In this lesson you learned about several additional engineering applications of the laws of friction.

1. Journal bearings and axle friction. In journal bearings, the *reaction does not pass through the center of the shaft or axle* which is being supported. The distance from the center of the shaft or axle to the line of action of the reaction (Fig. 8.10) is defined by the equation.

$$r_f = r \sin \phi_k \approx r\mu_k$$

if motion is actually taking place, and by the equation

$$r_f = r \sin \phi_s \approx r\mu_s$$

if the motion is impending.

Once you have determined the line of action of the reaction, you can draw a *free-body diagram* and use the corresponding equations of equilibrium to complete your solution [Sample Prob. 8.6]. In some problems, it is useful to observe that the line of action of the reaction must be tangent to a circle of radius $r_f \approx r\mu_k$, or $r_f \approx r\mu_s$, known as the *circle of friction* [Sample Prob. 8.6, part c].

2. Thrust bearings and disk friction. In a *thrust bearing* the magnitude of the couple required to overcome frictional resistance is equal to the sum of the moments of the *kinetic friction forces* exerted on the elements of the end of the shaft [Eqs. (8.8) and (8.9)].

An example of disk friction is the *disk clutch*. It is analyzed in the same way as a thrust bearing, except that to determine the largest couple that can be transmitted, you must compute the sum of the moments of the *maximum static friction forces* exerted on the disk.

3. Wheel friction and rolling resistance. You saw that the rolling resistance of a wheel is caused by deformations of both the wheel and the ground. The line of action of the reaction **R** of the ground on the wheel intersects the ground at a horizontal distance b from the center of the wheel. The distance b is known as the *coefficient of rolling resistance* and is expressed in inches or millimeters.

4. In problems involving both rolling resistance and axle friction, your free-body diagram should show that the line of action of the reaction **R** of the ground on the wheel is tangent to the friction circle of the axle and intersects the ground at a horizontal distance from the center of the wheel equal to the coefficient of rolling resistance.

PROBLEMS

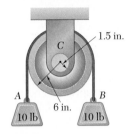

Fig. P8.75

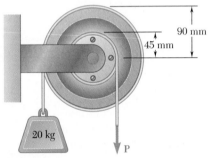

Fig. P8.76 and P8.78

8.75 A 6-in.-radius pulley of weight 5 lb is attached to a 1.5-in.-radius shaft that fits loosely in a fixed bearing. It is observed that the pulley will just start rotating if a 0.5-lb weight is added to block *A*. Determine the coefficient of static friction between the shaft and the bearing.

8.76 and 8.77 The double pulley shown is attached to a 10-mm-radius shaft that fits loosely in a fixed bearing. Knowing that the coefficient of static friction between the shaft and the poorly lubricated bearing is 0.40, determine the magnitude of the force **P** required to start raising the load.

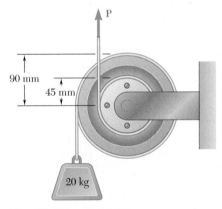

Fig. P8.77 and P8.79

8.78 and 8.79 The double pulley shown is attached to a 10-mm-radius shaft that fits loosely in a fixed bearing. Knowing that the coefficient of static friction between the shaft and the poorly lubricated bearing is 0.40, determine the magnitude of the smallest force **P** required to maintain equilibrium.

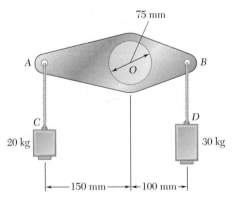

Fig. P8.80

8.80 A lever of negligible weight is loosely fitted onto a 75-mm-diameter fixed shaft. It is observed that the lever will just start rotating if a 3-kg mass is added at *C*. Determine the coefficient of static friction between the shaft and the lever.

8.81 The block and tackle shown are used to raise a 150-lb load. Each of the 3-in.-diameter pulleys rotates on a 0.5-in.-diameter axle. Knowing that the coefficient of static friction is 0.20, determine the tension in each portion of the rope as the load is slowly raised.

8.82 The block and tackle shown are used to lower a 150-lb load. Each of the 3-in.-diameter pulleys rotates on a 0.5-in.-diameter axle. Knowing that the coefficient of static friction is 0.20, determine the tension in each portion of the rope as the load is slowly lowered.

8.83 A loaded railroad car has a mass of 30 Mg and is supported by eight 800-mm-diameter wheels with 125-mm-diameter axles. Knowing that the coefficients of friction are $\mu_s = 0.020$ and $\mu_k = 0.015$, determine the horizontal force required (*a*) to start the car moving, (*b*) to keep the car moving at a constant speed. Neglect rolling resistance between the wheels and the track.

8.84 and 8.85 A lever *AB* of negligible weight is loosely fitted onto a 2.5-in.-diameter fixed shaft. Knowing that the coefficient of static friction between the fixed shaft and the lever is 0.15, determine the force **P** required to start the lever rotating counterclockwise.

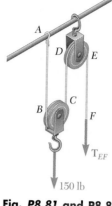

Fig. P8.81 and P8.82

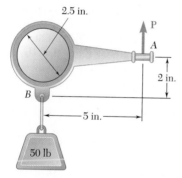

Fig. P8.84 and P8.86

8.86 and 8.87 A lever *AB* of negligible weight is loosely fitted onto a 2.5-in.-diameter fixed shaft. Knowing that the coefficient of static friction between the fixed shaft and the lever is 0.15, determine the force **P** required to start the lever rotating clockwise.

8.88 The link arrangement shown is frequently used in highway bridge construction to allow for expansion due to changes in temperature. At each of the 60-mm-diameter pins *A* and *B* the coefficient of static friction is 0.20. Knowing that the vertical component of the force exerted by *BC* on the link is 200 kN, determine (*a*) the horizontal force that should be exerted on beam *BC* to just move the link, (*b*) the angle that the resulting force exerted by beam *BC* on the link will form with the vertical.

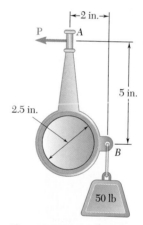

Fig. P8.85 and P8.87

Fig. P8.88

8.89 A scooter is to be designed to roll down a 2 percent slope at a constant speed. Assuming that the coefficient of kinetic friction between the 25-mm-diameter axles and the bearings is 0.10, determine the required diameter of the wheels. Neglect the rolling resistance between the wheels and the ground.

8.90 A 50-lb electric floor polisher is operated on a surface for which the coefficient of kinetic friction is 0.25. Assuming that the normal force per unit area between the disk and the floor is uniformly distributed, determine the magnitude Q of the horizontal forces required to prevent motion of the machine.

Fig. P8.90

8.91 Knowing that a couple of magnitude 30 N · m is required to start the vertical shaft rotating, determine the coefficient of static friction between the annular surfaces of contact.

*8.92 The frictional resistance of a thrust bearing decreases as the shaft and bearing surfaces wear out. It is generally assumed that the wear is directly proportional to the distance traveled by any given point of the shaft and thus to the distance r from the point to the axis of the shaft. Assuming, then, that the normal force per unit area is inversely proportional to r, show that the magnitude M of the couple required to overcome the frictional resistance of a worn-out end bearing (with contact over the full circular area) is equal to 75 percent of the value given by Eq. (8.9) for a new bearing.

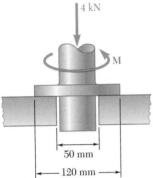

Fig. P8.91

*8.93 Assuming that bearings wear out as indicated in Prob. 8.92, show that the magnitude M of the couple required to overcome the frictional resistance of a worn-out collar bearing is

$$M = \tfrac{1}{2}\mu_k P(R_1 + R_2)$$

where P = magnitude of the total axial force
R_1, R_2 = inner and outer radii of collar

*8.94 Assuming that the pressure between the surfaces of contact is uniform, show that the magnitude M of the couple required to overcome frictional resistance for the conical bearing shown is

$$M = \frac{2}{3}\frac{\mu_k P}{\sin\theta}\frac{R_2^3 - R_1^3}{R_2^2 - R_1^2}$$

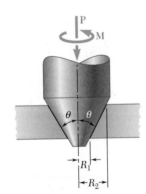

Fig. P8.94

8.95 Solve Prob. 8.90 assuming that the normal force per unit area between the disk and the floor varies linearly from a maximum at the center to zero at the circumference of the disk.

8.96 A 900-kg machine base is rolled along a concrete floor using a series of steel pipes with outside diameters of 100 mm. Knowing that the coefficient of rolling resistance is 0.5 mm between the pipes and the base and 1.25 mm between the pipes and the concrete floor, determine the magnitude of the force **P** required to slowly move the base along the floor.

Fig. P8.96

8.97 Knowing that a 6-in.-diameter disk rolls at a constant velocity down a 2 percent incline, determine the coefficient of rolling resistance between the disk and the incline.

8.98 Determine the horizontal force required to move a 2500-lb automobile with 23-in.-diameter tires along a horizontal road at a constant speed. Neglect all forms of friction except rolling resistance, and assume the coefficient of rolling resistance to be 0.05 in.

8.99 Solve Prob. 8.83 including the effect of a coefficient of rolling resistance of 0.5 mm.

8.100 Solve Prob. 8.89 including the effect of a coefficient of rolling resistance of 1.75 mm.

8.10 BELT FRICTION

Consider a flat belt passing over a fixed cylindrical drum (Fig. 8.14a). We propose to determine the relation existing between the values T_1 and T_2 of the tension in the two parts of the belt when the belt is just about to slide toward the right.

Let us detach from the belt a small element PP' subtending an angle $\Delta\theta$. Denoting by T the tension at P and by $T + \Delta T$ the tension at P', we draw the free-body diagram of the element of the belt (Fig. 8.14b). Besides the two forces of tension, the forces acting on the free body are the normal component $\Delta\mathbf{N}$ of the reaction of the drum and the friction force $\Delta\mathbf{F}$. Since motion is assumed to be impending, we have $\Delta F = \mu_s \Delta N$. It should be noted that if $\Delta\theta$ is made to approach zero, the magnitudes ΔN and ΔF, and the *difference* ΔT between the tension at P and the tension at P', will also approach zero; the value T of the tension at P, however, will remain unchanged. This observation helps in understanding our choice of notations.

Choosing the coordinate axes shown in Fig. 8.14b, we write the equations of equilibrium for the element PP':

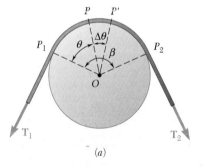
(a)

$$\Sigma F_x = 0: \quad (T + \Delta T) \cos\frac{\Delta\theta}{2} - T \cos\frac{\Delta\theta}{2} - \mu_s \Delta N = 0 \quad (8.11)$$

$$\Sigma F_y = 0: \quad \Delta N - (T + \Delta T) \sin\frac{\Delta\theta}{2} - T \sin\frac{\Delta\theta}{2} = 0 \quad (8.12)$$

Solving Eq. (8.12) for ΔN and substituting into (8.11), we obtain after reductions

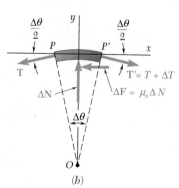
(b)

$$\Delta T \cos\frac{\Delta\theta}{2} - \mu_s(2T + \Delta T) \sin\frac{\Delta\theta}{2} = 0$$

Both terms are now divided by $\Delta\theta$. For the first term, this is done simply by dividing ΔT by $\Delta\theta$. The division of the second term is

Fig. 8.14

carried out by dividing the terms in the parentheses by 2 and the sine by $\Delta\theta/2$. We write

$$\frac{\Delta T}{\Delta\theta}\cos\frac{\Delta\theta}{2} - \mu_s\left(T + \frac{\Delta T}{2}\right)\frac{\sin(\Delta\theta/2)}{\Delta\theta/2} = 0$$

If we now let $\Delta\theta$ approach 0, the cosine approaches 1 and $\Delta T/2$ approaches zero, as noted above. The quotient of $\sin(\Delta\theta/2)$ over $\Delta\theta/2$ approaches 1, according to a lemma derived in all calculus textbooks. Since the limit of $\Delta T/\Delta\theta$ is by definition equal to the derivative $dT/d\theta$, we write

$$\frac{dT}{d\theta} - \mu_s T = 0 \qquad \frac{dT}{T} = \mu_s d\theta$$

Both members of the last equation (Fig. 8.14a) will now be integrated from P_1 to P_2. At P_1, we have $\theta = 0$ and $T = T_1$; at P_2, we have $\theta = \beta$ and $T = T_2$. Integrating between these limits, we write

$$\int_{T_1}^{T_2}\frac{dT}{T} = \int_0^\beta \mu_s d\theta$$

$$\ln T_2 - \ln T_1 = \mu_s\beta$$

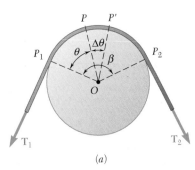

Fig. 8.14a (repeated)

or, noting that the left-hand member is equal to the natural logarithm of the quotient of T_2 and T_1,

$$\ln\frac{T_2}{T_1} = \mu_s\beta \qquad (8.13)$$

This relation can also be written in the form

$$\frac{T_2}{T_1} = e^{\mu_s\beta} \qquad (8.14)$$

Photo 8.3 By wrapping the rope around the bollard, the force exerted by the worker to control the rope is much smaller than the tension in the taut portion of the rope.

The formulas we have derived apply equally well to problems involving flat belts passing over fixed cylindrical drums and to problems involving ropes wrapped around a post or capstan. They can also be used to solve problems involving band brakes. In such problems, it is the drum which is about to rotate, while the band remains fixed. The formulas can also be applied to problems involving belt drives. In these problems, both the pulley and the belt rotate; our concern is then to find whether the belt will slip, i.e., whether it will move *with respect* to the pulley.

Formulas (8.13) and (8.14) should be used only if the belt, rope, or brake is *about to slip*. Formula (8.14) will be used if T_1 or T_2 is desired; formula (8.13) will be preferred if either μ_s or the angle of contact β is desired. We should note that T_2 is always larger than T_1; T_2 therefore represents the tension in that part of the belt or rope which *pulls*, while T_1 is the tension in the part which *resists*. We should also observe that the angle of contact β must be expressed in *radians*. The angle β may be larger than 2π; for example, if a rope is wrapped n times around a post, β is equal to $2\pi n$.

If the belt, rope, or brake is actually slipping, formulas similar to (8.13) and (8.14), but involving the coefficient of kinetic friction μ_k, should be used. If the belt, rope, or brake is not slipping and is not about to slip, none of these formulas can be used.

The belts used in belt drives are often V-shaped. In the V belt shown in Fig. 8.15*a* contact between belt and pulley takes place

(a)

Fig. 8.15

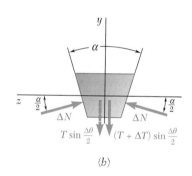

(b)

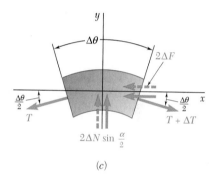

(c)

along the sides of the groove. The relation existing between the values T_1 and T_2 of the tension in the two parts of the belt when the belt is just about to slip can again be obtained by drawing the free-body diagram of an element of belt (Fig. 8.15*b* and *c*). Equations similar to (8.11) and (8.12) are derived, but the magnitude of the total friction force acting on the element is now $2\,\Delta F$, and the sum of the y components of the normal forces is $2\,\Delta N \sin(\alpha/2)$. Proceeding as above, we obtain

$$\ln \frac{T_2}{T_1} = \frac{\mu_s \beta}{\sin(\alpha/2)} \tag{8.15}$$

or,

$$\frac{T_2}{T_1} = e^{\mu_s \beta / \sin(\alpha/2)} \tag{8.16}$$

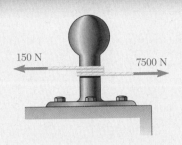

150 N   7500 N

SAMPLE PROBLEM 8.7

A hawser thrown from a ship to a pier is wrapped two full turns around a bollard. The tension in the hawser is 7500 N; by exerting a force of 150 N on its free end, a dockworker can just keep the hawser from slipping. (*a*) Determine the coefficient of friction between the hawser and the bollard. (*b*) Determine the tension in the hawser that could be resisted by the 150-N force if the hawser were wrapped three full turns around the bollard.

SOLUTION

a. Coefficient of Friction. Since slipping of the hawser is impending, we use Eq. (8.13):

$$\ln \frac{T_2}{T_1} = \mu_s \beta$$

Since the hawser is wrapped two full turns around the bollard, we have

$$\beta = 2(2\pi \text{ rad}) = 12.57 \text{ rad}$$
$$T_1 = 150 \text{ N} \qquad T_2 = 7500 \text{ N}$$

Therefore,

$$\mu_s \beta = \ln \frac{T_2}{T_1}$$

$$\mu_s(12.57 \text{ rad}) = \ln \frac{7500 \text{ N}}{150 \text{ N}} = \ln 50 = 3.91$$

$$\mu_s = 0.311 \qquad\qquad\qquad \mu_s = 0.311 \quad \blacktriangleleft$$

b. Hawser Wrapped Three Turns around Bollard. Using the value of μ_s obtained in part *a*, we now have

$$\beta = 3(2\pi \text{ rad}) = 18.85 \text{ rad}$$
$$T_1 = 150 \text{ N} \qquad \mu_s = 0.311$$

Substituting these values into Eq. (8.14), we obtain

$$\frac{T_2}{T_1} = e^{\mu_s \beta}$$

$$\frac{T_2}{150 \text{ N}} = e^{(0.311)(18.85)} = e^{5.862} = 351.5$$

$$T_2 = 52\ 725 \text{ N}$$

$$T_2 = 52.7 \text{ kN} \quad \blacktriangleleft$$

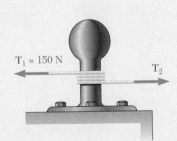

$T_1 = 150 \text{ N}$ T_2

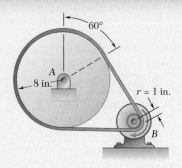

SAMPLE PROBLEM 8.8

A flat belt connects pulley A, which drives a machine tool, to pulley B, which is attached to the shaft of an electric motor. The coefficients of friction are $\mu_s = 0.25$ and $\mu_k = 0.20$ between both pulleys and the belt. Knowing that the maximum allowable tension in the belt is 600 lb, determine the largest torque which can be exerted by the belt on pulley A.

SOLUTION

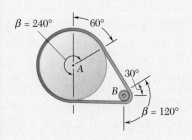

Since the resistance to slippage depends upon the angle of contact β between pulley and belt, as well as upon the coefficient of static friction μ_s, and since μ_s is the same for both pulleys, slippage will occur first on pulley B, for which β is smaller.

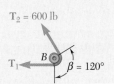

Pulley B. Using Eq. (8.14) with $T_2 = 600$ lb, $\mu_s = 0.25$, and $\beta = 120° = 2\pi/3$ rad, we write

$$\frac{T_2}{T_1} = e^{\mu_s\beta} \qquad \frac{600 \text{ lb}}{T_1} = e^{0.25(2\pi/3)} = 1.688$$

$$T_1 = \frac{600 \text{ lb}}{1.688} = 355.4 \text{ lb}$$

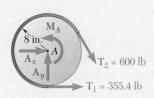

Pulley A. We draw the free-body diagram of pulley A. The couple $\mathbf{M}_A$ is applied to the pulley by the machine tool to which it is attached and is equal and opposite to the torque exerted by the belt. We write

$$+\!\uparrow\!\!\curvearrowleft \Sigma M_A = 0: \quad M_A - (600 \text{ lb})(8 \text{ in.}) + (355.4 \text{ lb})(8 \text{ in.}) = 0$$
$$M_A = 1957 \text{ lb} \cdot \text{in.} \qquad\qquad M_A = 163.1 \text{ lb} \cdot \text{ft} \quad \blacktriangleleft$$

Note. We may check that the belt does not slip on pulley A by computing the value of μ_s required to prevent slipping at A and verifying that it is smaller than the actual value of μ_s. From Eq. (8.13) we have

$$\mu_s\beta = \ln\frac{T_2}{T_1} = \ln\frac{600 \text{ lb}}{355.4 \text{ lb}} = 0.524$$

and, since $\beta = 240° = 4\pi/3$ rad,

$$\frac{4\pi}{3}\mu_s = 0.524 \qquad \mu_s = 0.125 < 0.25$$

SOLVING PROBLEMS
ON YOUR OWN

In the preceding section you learned about *belt friction*. The problems you will have to solve include belts passing over fixed drums, band brakes in which the drum rotates while the band remains fixed, and belt drives.

1. Problems involving belt friction fall into one of the following two categories:

a. Problems in which slipping is impending. One of the following formulas, involving the *coefficient of static friction* μ_s, may then be used,

$$\ln\frac{T_2}{T_1} = \mu_s\beta \tag{8.13}$$

or

$$\frac{T_2}{T_1} = e^{\mu_s\beta} \tag{8.14}$$

b. Problems in which slipping is occurring. The formulas to be used can be obtained from Eqs. (8.13) and (8.14) by replacing μ_s with the *coefficient of kinetic friction* μ_k.

2. As you start solving a belt-friction problem, be sure to remember the following:

a. The angle β must be expressed in radians. In a belt-and-drum problem, this is the angle subtending the arc of the drum on which the belt is wrapped.

b. The larger tension is always denoted by T_2 and the *smaller tension is denoted by T_1*.

c. The larger tension occurs at the end of the belt which is in the direction of the motion, or impending motion, of the belt relative to the drum.

3. In each of the problems you will be asked to solve, three of the four quantities T_1, T_2, β, and μ_s (or μ_k) will either be given or readily found, and you will then solve the appropriate equation for the fourth quantity. Here are two kinds of problems that you will encounter:

a. Find μ_s between belt and drum, knowing that slipping is impending. From the given data, determine T_1, T_2, and β; substitute these values into Eq. (8.13) and solve for μ_s [Sample Prob. 8.7, part *a*]. Follow the same procedure to find the *smallest value* of μ_s for which slipping will not occur.

b. Find the magnitude of a force or couple applied to the belt or drum, knowing that slipping is impending. The given data should include μ_s and β. If it also includes T_1 or T_2, use Eq. (8.14) to find the other tension. If neither T_1 nor T_2 is known but some other data is given, use the free-body diagram of the belt-drum system to write an equilibrium equation that you will solve simultaneously with Eq. (8.14) for T_1 and T_2. You will then be able to find the magnitude of the specified force or couple from the free-body diagram of the system. Follow the same procedure to determine the *largest value* of a force or couple which can be applied to the belt or drum if no slipping is to occur [Sample Prob. 8.8].

PROBLEMS

8.101 A hawser is wrapped two full turns around a bollard. By exerting an 80-lb force on the free end of the hawser, a dockworker can resist a force of 5000 lb on the other end of the hawser. Determine (*a*) the coefficient of static friction between the hawser and the bollard, (*b*) the number of times the hawser should be wrapped around the bollard if a 20,000-lb force is to be resisted by the same 80-lb force.

8.102 A rope *ABCD* is looped over two pipes as shown. Knowing that the coefficient of static friction is 0.25, determine (*a*) the smallest value of the mass *m* for which equilibrium is possible, (*b*) the corresponding tension in portion *BC* of the rope.

8.103 A rope *ABCD* is looped over two pipes as shown. Knowing that the coefficient of static friction is 0.25, determine (*a*) the largest value of the mass *m* for which equilibrium is possible, (*b*) the corresponding tension in portion *BC* of the rope.

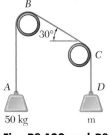

Fig. P8.102 and P8.103

8.104 A 300-lb block is supported by a rope that is wrapped $1\frac{1}{2}$ times around a horizontal rod. Knowing that the coefficient of static friction between the rope and the rod is 0.15, determine the range of values of *P* for which equilibrium is maintained.

8.105 The coefficient of static friction between block *B* and the horizontal surface and between the rope and support *C* is 0.40. Knowing that $m_A = 12$ kg, determine the smallest mass of block *B* for which equilibrium is maintained.

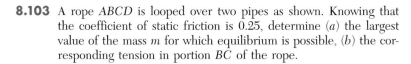

Fig. P8.104

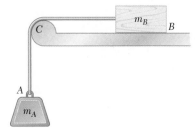

Fig. P8.105 and P8.106

8.106 The coefficient of static friction μ_s is the same between block *B* and the horizontal surface and between the rope and support *C*. Knowing that $m_A = m_B$, determine the smallest value of μ_s for which equilibrium is maintained.

8.107 A flat belt is used to transmit a couple from drum *B* to drum *A*. Knowing that the coefficient of static friction is 0.40 and that the allowable belt tension is 450 N, determine the largest couple that can be exerted on drum *A*.

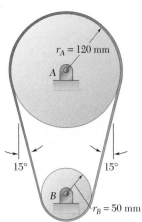

Fig. P8.107

455

8.108 A flat belt is used to transmit a couple from pulley A to pulley B. The radius of each pulley is 60 mm, and a force of magnitude $P = 900$ N is applied as shown to the axle of pulley A. Knowing that the coefficient of static friction is 0.35, determine (a) the largest couple that can be transmitted, (b) the corresponding maximum value of the tension in the belt.

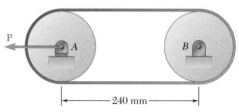

Fig. P8.108

8.109 Solve Prob. 8.108 assuming that the belt is looped around the pulleys in a figure eight.

8.110 In the pivoted motor mount shown the weight **W** of the 175-lb motor is used to maintain tension in the drive belt. Knowing that the coefficient of static friction between the flat belt and drums A and B is 0.40, and neglecting the weight of platform CD, determine the largest couple that can be transmitted to drum B when the drive drum A is rotating clockwise.

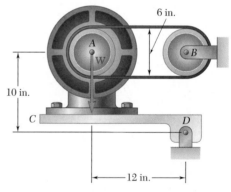

Fig. P8.110

8.111 Solve Prob. 8.110 assuming that the drive drum A is rotating counterclockwise.

8.112 A band brake is used to control the speed of a flywheel as shown. The coefficients of friction are $\mu_s = 0.30$ and $\mu_k = 0.25$. Determine the magnitude of the couple being applied to the flywheel, knowing that $P = 45$ N and that the flywheel is rotating counterclockwise at a constant speed.

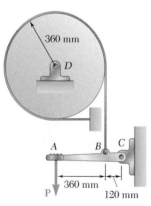

Fig. P8.112

8.113 The speed of the brake drum shown is controlled by a belt attached to the control bar *AD*. A force **P** of magnitude 25 lb is applied to the control bar at *A*. Determine the magnitude of the couple being applied to the drum, knowing that the coefficient of kinetic friction between the belt and the drum is 0.25, that $a = 4$ in., and that the drum is rotating at a constant speed (*a*) counterclockwise, (*b*) clockwise.

8.114 Knowing that $a = 4$ in., determine the maximum value of the coefficient of static friction for which the brake is not self-locking when the drum rotates counterclockwise.

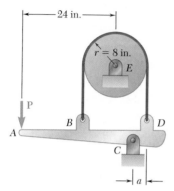

Fig. P8.113, P8.114, and P8.115

8.115 Knowing that the coefficient of static friction is 0.30 and that the brake drum is rotating counterclockwise, determine the minimum value of *a* for which the brake is not self-locking.

8.116 Bucket *A* and block *C* are connected by a cable that passes over drum *B*. Knowing that drum *B* rotates slowly counterclockwise and that the coefficients of friction at all surfaces are $\mu_s = 0.35$ and $\mu_k = 0.25$, determine the smallest combined mass *m* of the bucket and its contents for which block *C* will (*a*) remain at rest, (*b*) start moving up the incline, (*c*) continue moving up the incline at a constant speed.

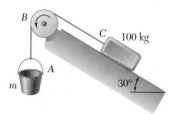

Fig. P8.116

8.117 Solve Prob. 8.116 assuming that drum *B* is frozen and cannot rotate.

8.118 and 8.120 A cable is placed around three parallel pipes. Knowing that the coefficients of friction are $\mu_s = 0.25$ and $\mu_k = 0.20$, determine (a) the smallest weight W for which equilibrium is maintained, (b) the largest weight W that can be raised if pipe B is slowly rotated counterclockwise while pipes A and C remain fixed.

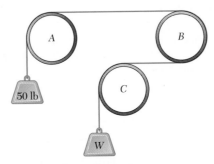

Fig. P8.120 and P8.121

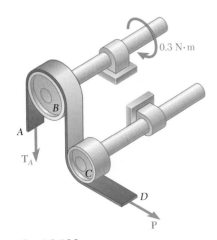

Fig. P8.118 and P8.119

8.119 and 8.121 A cable is placed around three parallel pipes. Two of the pipes are fixed and do not rotate; the third pipe is slowly rotated. Knowing that the coefficients of friction are $\mu_s = 0.25$ and $\mu_k = 0.20$, determine the largest weight W that can be raised (a) if only pipe A is rotated counterclockwise, (b) if only pipe C is rotated clockwise.

8.122 A recording tape passes over the 20-mm-radius drive drum B and under the idler drum C. Knowing that the coefficients of friction between the tape and the drums are $\mu_s = 0.40$ and $\mu_k = 0.30$ and that drum C is free to rotate, determine the smallest allowable value of P if slipping of the tape on drum B is not to occur.

8.123 Solve Prob. 8.122 assuming that the idler drum C is frozen and cannot rotate.

8.124 The 10-lb bar AE is suspended by a cable that passes over a 5-in.-radius drum. Vertical motion of end E of the bar is prevented by the two stops shown. Knowing that $\mu_s = 0.30$ between the cable and the drum, determine (a) the largest counterclockwise couple $\mathbf{M}_0$ that can be applied to the drum if slipping is not to occur, (b) the corresponding force exerted on end E of the bar.

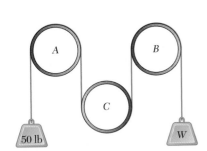

Fig. P8.122

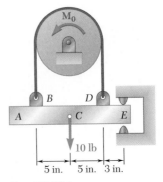

Fig. P8.124

8.125 Solve Prob. 8.124 assuming that a clockwise couple $\mathbf{M}_0$ is applied to the drum.

8.126 The strap wrench shown is used to grip the pipe firmly without marring the external surface of the pipe. Knowing that the coefficient of static friction is the same for all surfaces of contact, determine the smallest value of μ_s for which the wrench will be self-locking when $a = 200$ mm, $r = 30$ mm, and $\theta = 65°$.

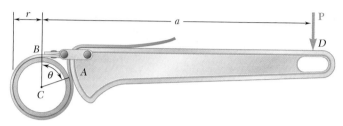

Fig. P8.126

8.127 Solve Prob. 8.126 assuming that $\theta = 75°$.

8.128 Prove that Eqs. (8.13) and (8.14) are valid for any shape of surface provided that the coefficient of friction is the same at all points of contact.

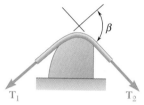

Fig. P8.128

8.129 Complete the derivation of Eq. (8.15), which relates the tension in both parts of a V belt.

8.130 Solve Prob. 8.107 assuming that the flat belt and drums are replaced by a V belt and V pulleys with $\alpha = 36°$. (The angle α is as shown in Fig. 8.15a.)

8.131 Solve Prob. 8.108 assuming that the flat belt and pulleys are replaced by a V belt and V pulleys with $\alpha = 36°$. (The angle α is as shown in Fig. 8.15a.)

REVIEW AND SUMMARY

This chapter was devoted to the study of *dry friction*, i.e., to problems involving rigid bodies which are in contact along *nonlubricated surfaces*.

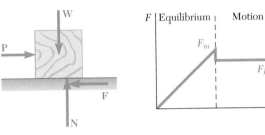

Fig. 8.16

Static and kinetic friction

Applying a horizontal force **P** to a block resting on a horizontal surface [Sec. 8.2], we note that the block at first does not move. This shows that a *friction force* **F** must have developed to balance **P** (Fig. 8.16). As the magnitude of **P** is increased, the magnitude of **F** also increases until it reaches a maximum value F_m. If **P** is further increased, the block starts sliding and the magnitude of **F** drops from F_m to a lower value F_k. Experimental evidence shows that F_m and F_k are proportional to the normal component N of the reaction of the surface. We have

$$F_m = \mu_s N \qquad F_k = \mu_k N \qquad (8.1, 8.2)$$

where μ_s and μ_k are called, respectively, the *coefficient of static friction* and the *coefficient of kinetic friction*. These coefficients depend on the nature and the condition of the surfaces in contact. Approximate values of the coefficients of static friction were given in Table 8.1.

Angles of friction

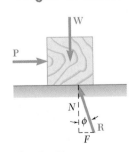

Fig. 8.17

It is sometimes convenient to replace the normal force **N** and the friction force **F** by their resultant **R** (Fig. 8.17). As the friction force increases and reaches its maximum value $F_m = \mu_s N$, the angle ϕ that **R** forms with the normal to the surface increases and reaches a maximum value ϕ_s, called the *angle of static friction*. If motion actually takes place, the magnitude of **F** drops to F_k; similarly the angle ϕ drops to a lower value ϕ_k, called the *angle of kinetic friction*. As shown in Sec. 8.3, we have

$$\tan \phi_s = \mu_s \qquad \tan \phi_k = \mu_k \qquad (8.3, 8.4)$$

When solving equilibrium problems involving friction, we should keep in mind that the magnitude F of the friction force is equal to $F_m = \mu_s N$ only *if the body is about to slide* [Sec. 8.4]. *If motion is not impending,* F and N should be considered as *independent unknowns* to be determined from the equilibrium equations (Fig. 8.18a). We

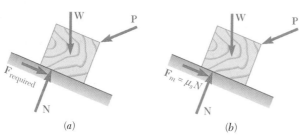

Fig. 8.18

should also check that the value of F required to maintain equilibrium is not larger than F_m; if it were, the body would move and the magnitude of the friction force would be $F_k = \mu_k N$ [Sample Prob. 8.1]. On the other hand, *if motion is known to be impending,* F has reached its maximum value $F_m = \mu_s N$ (Fig. 8.18b), and this expression may be substituted for F in the equilibrium equations [Sample Prob. 8.3]. When only three forces are involved in a free-body diagram, including the reaction **R** of the surface in contact with the body, it is usually more convenient to solve the problem by drawing a force triangle [Sample Prob. 8.2].

When a problem involves the analysis of the forces exerted on each other by *two bodies A and B*, it is important to show the friction forces with their correct sense. The correct sense for the friction force exerted by B on A, for instance, is opposite to that of the *relative motion* (or impending motion) of A with respect to B [Fig. 8.6].

In the second part of the chapter we considered a number of specific engineering applications where dry friction plays an important role. In the case of *wedges,* which are simple machines used to raise heavy loads [Sec. 8.5], two or more free-body diagrams were drawn and care was taken to show each friction force with its correct sense [Sample Prob. 8.4]. The analysis of *square-threaded screws,* which are frequently used in jacks, presses, and other mechanisms, was reduced to the analysis of a block sliding on an incline by unwrapping the thread of the screw and showing it as a straight line [Sec. 8.6]. This is done again in Fig. 8.19, where r denotes the *mean radius* of the thread, L is the *lead* of the screw, i.e., the distance through which the screw advances in one turn, **W** is the load, and Qr is equal to the couple exerted on the screw. It was noted that in the case of multiple-threaded screws the lead L of the screw is *not* equal to its pitch, which is the distance measured between two consecutive threads.

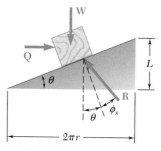

Fig. 8.19

Other engineering applications considered in this chapter were *journal bearings* and *axle friction* [Sec. 8.7], *thrust bearings* and *disk friction* [Sec. 8.8], *wheel friction* and *rolling resistance* [Sec. 8.9], and *belt friction* [Sec. 8.10].

Belt friction

In solving a problem involving a *flat belt* passing over a fixed cylinder, it is important to first determine the direction in which the belt slips or is about to slip. If the drum is rotating, the motion or impending motion of the belt should be determined *relative* to the rotating drum. For instance, if the belt shown in Fig. 8.20 is about to slip to

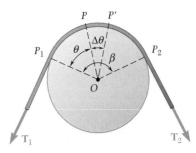

Fig. 8.20

the right relative to the drum, the friction forces exerted by the drum on the belt will be directed to the left and the tension will be larger in the right-hand portion of the belt than in the left-hand portion. Denoting the larger tension by T_2, the smaller tension by T_1, the coefficient of static friction by μ_s, and the angle (in radians) subtended by the belt by β, we derived in Sec. 8.10 the formulas

$$\ln \frac{T_2}{T_1} = \mu_s \beta \tag{8.13}$$

$$\frac{T_2}{T_1} = e^{\mu_s \beta} \tag{8.14}$$

which were used in solving Sample Probs. 8.7 and 8.8. If the belt actually slips on the drum, the coefficient of static friction μ_s should be replaced by the coefficient of kinetic friction μ_k in both of these formulas.

8.132 Knowing that the coefficient of friction between the 25-kg block and the incline is $\mu_s = 0.25$, determine (a) the smallest value of P required to start the block moving up the incline, (b) the corresponding value of β.

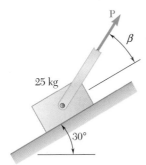

Fig. P8.132

8.133 The 20-lb block A and the 30-lb block B are supported by an incline that is held in the position shown. Knowing that the coefficient of static friction is 0.15 between all surfaces of contact, determine the value of θ for which motion is impending.

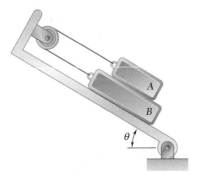

Fig. P8.133

8.134 A worker slowly moves a 50-kg crate to the left along a loading dock by applying a force **P** at corner B as shown. Knowing that the crate starts to tip about the edge E of the loading dock when $a = 200$ mm, determine (a) the coefficient of kinetic friction between the crate and the loading dock, (b) the corresponding magnitude P of the force.

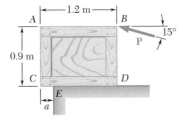

Fig. P8.134

8.135 A slender rod of length L is lodged between peg C and the vertical wall and supports a load **P** at end A. Knowing that the coefficient of static friction between the peg and the rod is 0.15 and neglecting friction at the roller, determine the range of values of the ratio L/a for which equilibrium is maintained.

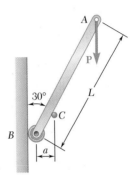

Fig. P8.135

8.136 A safety device used by workers climbing ladders fixed to high structures consists of a rail attached to the ladder and a sleeve that can slide on the flange of the rail. A chain connects the worker's belt to the end of an eccentric cam that can be rotated about an axle attached to the sleeve at C. Determine the smallest allowable common value of the coefficient of static friction between the flange of the rail, the pins at A and B, and the eccentric cam if the sleeve is not to slide down when the chain is pulled vertically downward.

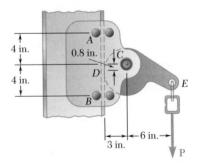

Fig. P8.136

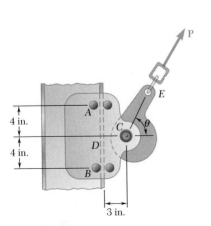

Fig. P8.137

8.137 To be of practical use, the safety sleeve described in the preceding problem must be free to slide along the rail when pulled upward. Determine the largest allowable value of the coefficient of static friction between the flange of the rail and the pins at A and B if the sleeve is to be free to slide when pulled as shown in the figure, assuming (a) $\theta = 60°$, (b) $\theta = 50°$, (c) $\theta = 40°$.

8.138 Bar *AB* is attached to collars that can slide on the inclined rods shown. A force **P** is applied at point *D* located at a distance *a* from end *A*. Knowing that the coefficient of static friction μ_s between each collar and the rod upon which it slides is 0.30 and neglecting the weights of the bar and of the collars, determine the smallest value of the ratio *a/L* for which equilibrium is maintained.

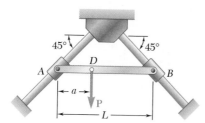

Fig. P8.138

8.139 The machine part *ABC* is supported by a frictionless hinge at *B* and a 10° wedge at *C*. Knowing that the coefficient of static friction at both surfaces of the wedge is 0.20, determine (*a*) the force **P** required to move the wedge, (*b*) the components of the corresponding reaction at *B*.

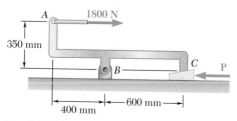

Fig. P8.139

8.140 A wedge *A* of negligible weight is to be driven between two 100-lb blocks *B* and *C* resting on a horizontal surface. Knowing that the coefficient of static friction at all surfaces of contact is 0.35, determine the smallest force **P** required to start moving the wedge (*a*) if the blocks are equally free to move, (*b*) if block *C* is securely bolted to the horizontal surface.

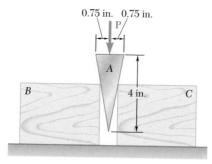

Fig. P8.140

8.141 The position of the automobile jack shown is controlled by a screw *ABC* that is single-threaded at each end (right-handed thread at *A*, left-handed thread at *C*). Each thread has a pitch of 0.1 in. and a mean diameter of 0.375 in. If the coefficient of static friction is 0.15, determine the magnitude of the couple **M** that must be applied to raise the automobile.

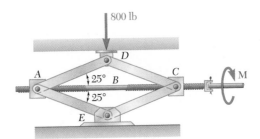

Fig. P8.141

8.142 A lever of negligible weight is loosely fitted onto a 30-mm-radius fixed shaft as shown. Knowing that a force **P** of magnitude 275 N will just start the lever rotating clockwise, determine (*a*) the coefficient of static friction between the shaft and the lever, (*b*) the smallest force **P** for which the lever does not start rotating counterclockwise.

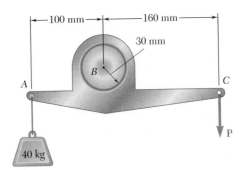

Fig. P8.142

8.143 A couple $\mathbf{M}_B$ is applied to the drive drum *B* to maintain a constant speed in the polishing belt shown. Knowing that $\mu_k = 0.45$ between the belt and the 15-kg block being polished and $\mu_s = 0.30$ between the belt and the drive drum *B*, determine (*a*) the couple $\mathbf{M}_B$, (*b*) the minimum tension in the lower portion of the belt if no slipping is to occur between the belt and the drive drum.

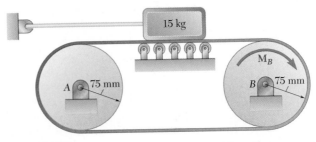

Fig. P8.143

COMPUTER PROBLEMS

8.C1 The position of the 10-kg rod AB is controlled by the 2-kg block shown, which is slowly moved to the left by the force **P**. Knowing that the coefficient of kinetic friction between all surfaces of contact is 0.25, use computational software to calculate the magnitude P of the force for values of x from 900 to 100 mm, using 50-mm decrements. Using appropriate smaller decrements, determine the maximum value of P and the corresponding value of x.

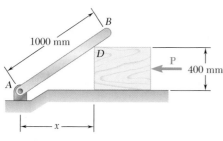

Fig. P8.C1

8.C2 Blocks A and B are supported by an incline that is held in the position shown. Knowing that block A weighs 20 lb and that the coefficient of static friction between all surfaces of contact is 0.15, use computational software to calculate the value of θ for which motion is impending for weights of block B from 0 to 100 lb, using 10-lb increments.

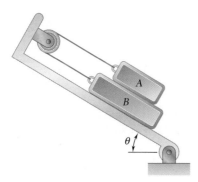

Fig. P8.C2

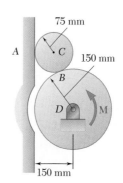

Fig. P8.C3

8.C3 A 300-g cylinder C rests on cylinder D as shown. Knowing that the coefficient of static friction μ_s is the same at A and B, use computational software to determine, for values of μ_s from 0 to 0.40 and using 0.05 increments, the largest counterclockwise couple **M** that can be applied to cylinder D if it is not to rotate.

8.C4 Two rods are connected by a slider block D and are held in equilibrium by the couple $\mathbf{M}_A$ as shown. Knowing that the coefficient of static friction between rod AC and the slider block is 0.40, use computational software to determine, for values of θ from 0 to 120° and using 10° increments, the range of values of M_A for which equilibrium is maintained.

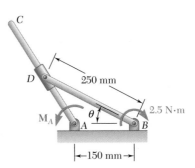

Fig. P8.C4

8.C5 The 10-lb block A is slowly moved up the circular cylindrical surface by a cable that passes over a small fixed cylindrical drum at B. The coefficient of kinetic friction is known to be 0.30 between the block and the surface and between the cable and the drum. Using computational software, calculate the force $\mathbf{P}$ required to maintain the motion for values of θ from 0 to 90°, using 10° increments. For the same values of θ calculate the magnitude of the reaction between the block and the surface. [Note that the angle of contact between the cable and the fixed drum is $\beta = \pi - (\theta/2)$.]

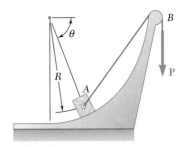

Fig. P8.C5

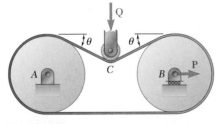

Fig. P8.C6

8.C6 A flat belt is used to transmit a couple from drum A to drum B. The radius of each drum is 80 mm, and the system is fitted with an idler wheel C that is used to increase the contact between the belt and the drums. The allowable belt tension is 200 N, and the coefficient of static friction between the belt and the drums is 0.30. Using computational software, calculate the largest couple that can be transmitted for values of θ from 0 to 30°, using 5° increments.

8.C7 Two collars A and B that slide on vertical rods with negligible friction are connected by a 30-in. cord that passes over a fixed shaft at C. The coefficient of static friction between the cord and the fixed shaft is 0.30. Knowing that the weight of collar B is 8 lb, use computational software to determine, for values of θ from 0 to 60° and using 10° increments, the largest and smallest weight of collar A for which equilibrium is maintained.

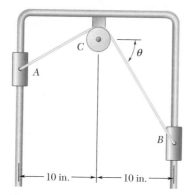

— 10 in. —|— 10 in. —

Fig. P8.C7

8.C8 The end B of a uniform beam of length L is being pulled by a stationary crane. Initially the beam lies on the ground with end A directly below pulley C. As the cable is slowly pulled in, the beam first slides to the left with $\theta = 0$ until it has moved through a distance x_0. In a second phase, end B is raised, while end A keeps sliding to the left until x reaches its maximum value x_m and θ the corresponding value θ_1. The beam then rotates about A' while θ keeps increasing. As θ reaches the value θ_2, end A starts sliding to the right and keeps sliding in an irregular manner until B reaches C. Knowing that the coefficients of friction between the beam and the ground are $\mu_s = 0.50$ and $\mu_k = 0.40$, (a) use computational software to compute x for any value of θ while the beam is sliding to the left and use this program to determine x_0, x_m, and θ_1, (b) modify the program to compute for any θ the value of x for which sliding would be impending to the right and use this new program to determine the value θ_2 of θ corresponding to $x = x_m$.

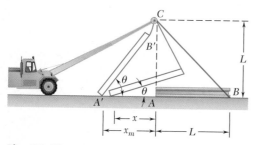

Fig. P8.C8

The strength of structural members used in the construction of buildings depends to a large extent on the properties of their cross sections. This includes the second moments of area, or moments of inertia, of these cross sections.

CHAPTER

9

Distributed Forces:
Moments of Inertia

9.1 INTRODUCTION

In Chap. 5, we analyzed various systems of forces distributed over an area or volume. The three main types of forces considered were (1) weights of homogeneous plates of uniform thickness (Secs. 5.3 through 5.6), (2) distributed loads on beams (Sec. 5.8) and hydrostatic forces (Sec. 5.9), and (3) weights of homogeneous three-dimensional bodies (Secs. 5.10 and 5.11). In the case of homogeneous plates, the magnitude ΔW of the weight of an element of a plate was proportional to the area ΔA of the element. For distributed loads on beams, the magnitude ΔW of each elemental weight was represented by an element of area $\Delta A = \Delta W$ under the load curve; in the case of hydrostatic forces on submerged rectangular surfaces, a similar procedure was followed. In the case of homogeneous three-dimensional bodies, the magnitude ΔW of the weight of an element of the body was proportional to the volume ΔV of the element. Thus, in all cases considered in Chap. 5, the distributed forces were proportional to the elemental areas or volumes associated with them. The resultant of these forces, therefore, could be obtained by summing the corresponding areas or volumes, and the moment of the resultant about any given axis could be determined by computing the first moments of the areas or volumes about that axis.

In the first part of this chapter, we consider distributed forces $\Delta \mathbf{F}$ whose magnitudes depend not only upon the elements of area ΔA on which these forces act but also upon the distance from ΔA to some given axis. More precisely, the magnitude of the force per unit area $\Delta F/\Delta A$ is assumed to vary linearly with the distance to the axis. As indicated in the next section, forces of this type are found in the study of the bending of beams and in problems involving submerged non-rectangular surfaces. Assuming that the elemental forces involved are distributed over an area A and vary linearly with the distance y to the x axis, it will be shown that while the magnitude of their resultant $\mathbf{R}$ depends upon the first moment $Q_x = \int y \, dA$ of the area A, the location of the point where $\mathbf{R}$ is applied depends upon the *second moment*, or *moment of inertia*, $I_x = \int y^2 \, dA$ of the same area with respect to the x axis. You will learn to compute the moments of inertia of various areas with respect to given x and y axes. Also introduced in the first part of this chapter is the *polar moment of inertia* $J_O = \int r^2 \, dA$ of an area, where r is the distance from the element of area dA to the point O. To facilitate your computations, a relation will be established between the moment of inertia I_x of an area A with respect to a given x axis and the moment of inertia $I_{x'}$ of the same area with respect to the parallel centroidal x' axis (parallel-axis theorem). You will also study the transformation of the moments of inertia of a given area when the coordinate axes are rotated (Secs. 9.9 and 9.10).

In the second part of the chapter, you will learn how to determine the moments of inertia of various *masses* with respect to a given axis. As you will see in Sec. 9.11, the moment of inertia of a given mass about an axis AA' is defined as $I = \int r^2 \, dm$, where r is the distance from the axis AA' to the element of mass dm. Moments of inertia of masses are encountered in dynamics in problems involving the rotation of a rigid body about an axis. To facilitate the computation of mass moments of inertia, the parallel-axis theorem will be introduced (Sec. 9.12). Finally, you will learn to analyze the transformation of moments of inertia of masses when the coordinate axes are rotated (Secs. 9.16 through 9.18).

MOMENTS OF INERTIA OF AREAS

9.2 SECOND MOMENT, OR MOMENT OF INERTIA, OF AN AREA

In the first part of this chapter, we consider distributed forces $\Delta\mathbf{F}$ whose magnitudes ΔF are proportional to the elements of area ΔA on which the forces act and at the same time vary linearly with the distance from ΔA to a given axis.

Consider, for example, a beam of uniform cross section which is subjected to two equal and opposite couples applied at each end of the beam. Such a beam is said to be in *pure bending*, and it is shown in mechanics of materials that the internal forces in any section of the beam are distributed forces whose magnitudes $\Delta F = ky\,\Delta A$ vary linearly with the distance y between the element of area ΔA and an axis passing through the centroid of the section. This axis, represented by the x axis in Fig. 9.1, is known as the *neutral axis* of the section. The forces on one side of the neutral axis are forces of compression, while those on the other side are forces of tension; on the neutral axis itself the forces are zero.

The magnitude of the resultant $\mathbf{R}$ of the elemental forces $\Delta\mathbf{F}$ which act over the entire section is

$$R = \int ky\,dA = k\int y\,dA$$

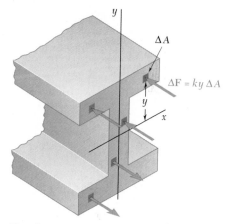

Fig. 9.1

The last integral obtained is recognized as the *first moment* Q_x of the section about the x axis; it is equal to $\bar{y}A$ and is thus equal to zero, since the centroid of the section is located on the x axis. The system of the forces $\Delta\mathbf{F}$ thus reduces to a couple. The magnitude M of this couple (bending moment) must be equal to the sum of the moments $\Delta M_x = y\,\Delta F = ky^2\,\Delta A$ of the elemental forces. Integrating over the entire section, we obtain

$$M = \int ky^2\,dA = k\int y^2\,dA$$

The last integral is known as the *second moment*, or *moment of inertia*,[†] of the beam section with respect to the x axis and is denoted by I_x. It is obtained by multiplying each element of area dA by the *square of its distance* from the x axis and integrating over the beam section. Since each product $y^2\,dA$ is positive, regardless of the sign of y, or zero (if y is zero), the integral I_x will always be positive.

Another example of a second moment, or moment of inertia, of an area is provided by the following problem from hydrostatics: A

[†]The term *second moment* is more proper than the term moment of inertia, since, logically, the latter should be used only to denote integrals of mass (see Sec. 9.11). In engineering practice, however, moment of inertia is used in connection with areas as well as masses.

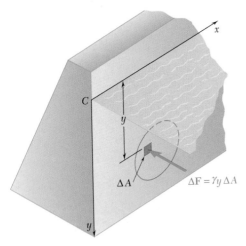

Fig. 9.2

vertical circular gate used to close the outlet of a large reservoir is submerged under water as shown in Fig. 9.2. What is the resultant of the forces exerted by the water on the gate, and what is the moment of the resultant about the line of intersection of the plane of the gate and the water surface (x axis)?

If the gate were rectangular, the resultant of the forces of pressure could be determined from the pressure curve, as was done in Sec. 5.9. Since the gate is circular, however, a more general method must be used. Denoting by y the depth of an element of area ΔA and by γ the specific weight of water, the pressure at the element is $p = \gamma y$, and the magnitude of the elemental force exerted on ΔA is $\Delta F = p\,\Delta A = \gamma y\,\Delta A$. The magnitude of the resultant of the elemental forces is thus

$$R = \int \gamma y\,dA = \gamma \int y\,dA$$

and can be obtained by computing the first moment $Q_x = \int y\,dA$ of the area of the gate with respect to the x axis. The moment M_x of the resultant must be equal to the sum of the moments $\Delta M_x = y\,\Delta F = \gamma y^2\,\Delta A$ of the elemental forces. Integrating over the area of the gate, we have

$$M_x = \int \gamma y^2\,dA = \gamma \int y^2\,dA$$

Here again, the integral obtained represents the second moment, or moment of inertia, I_x of the area with respect to the x axis.

9.3 DETERMINATION OF THE MOMENT OF INERTIA OF AN AREA BY INTEGRATION

We defined in the preceding section the second moment, or moment of inertia, of an area A with respect to the x axis. Defining in a similar way the moment of inertia I_y of the area A with respect to the y axis, we write (Fig. 9.3a)

$$I_x = \int y^2\,dA \qquad I_y = \int x^2\,dA \tag{9.1}$$

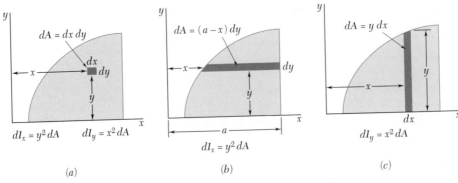

Fig. 9.3

These integrals, known as the *rectangular moments of inertia* of the area A, can be more easily evaluated if we choose dA to be a thin strip parallel to one of the coordinate axes. To compute I_x, the strip is chosen parallel to the x axis, so that all of the points of the strip are at the same distance y from the x axis (Fig. 9.3b); the moment of inertia dI_x of the strip is then obtained by multiplying the area dA of the strip by y^2. To compute I_y, the strip is chosen parallel to the y axis so that all of the points of the strip are at the same distance x from the y axis (Fig. 9.3c); the moment of inertia dI_y of the strip is $x^2\,dA$.

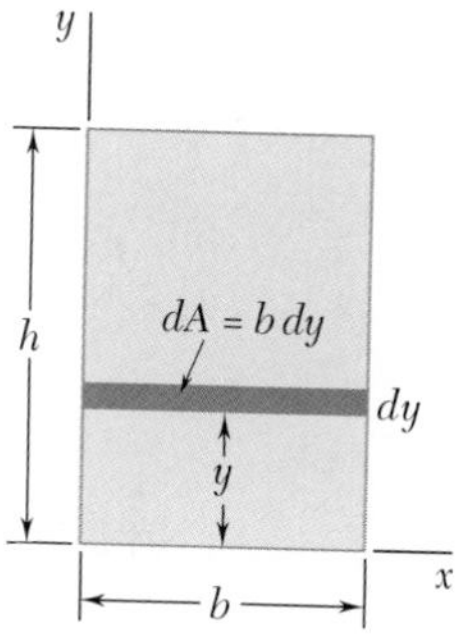

Moment of Inertia of a Rectangular Area. As an example, let us determine the moment of inertia of a rectangle with respect to its base (Fig. 9.4). Dividing the rectangle into strips parallel to the x axis, we obtain

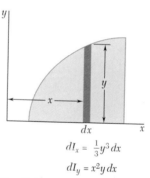

Fig. 9.4

$$dA = b\,dy \qquad dI_x = y^2 b\,dy$$

$$I_x = \int_0^h by^2\,dy = \tfrac{1}{3}bh^3 \tag{9.2}$$

Computing I_x and I_y Using the Same Elemental Strips. The formula just derived can be used to determine the moment of inertia dI_x with respect to the x axis of a rectangular strip which is parallel to the y axis, such as the strip shown in Fig. 9.3c. Setting $b = dx$ and $h = y$ in formula (9.2), we write

$$dI_x = \tfrac{1}{3}y^3\,dx$$

On the other hand, we have

$$dI_y = x^2\,dA = x^2 y\,dx$$

The same element can thus be used to compute the moments of inertia I_x and I_y of a given area (Fig. 9.5).

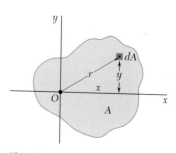

$$dI_x = \tfrac{1}{3}y^3\,dx$$
$$dI_y = x^2 y\,dx$$

Fig. 9.5

9.4 POLAR MOMENT OF INERTIA

An integral of great importance in problems concerning the torsion of cylindrical shafts and in problems dealing with the rotation of slabs is

$$J_O = \int r^2\,dA \tag{9.3}$$

where r is the distance from O to the element of area dA (Fig. 9.6). This integral is the *polar moment of inertia* of the area A with respect to the "pole" O.

The polar moment of inertia of a given area can be computed from the rectangular moments of inertia I_x and I_y of the area if these quantities are already known. Indeed, noting that $r^2 = x^2 + y^2$, we write

$$J_O = \int r^2\,dA = \int (x^2 + y^2)\,dA = \int y^2\,dA + \int x^2\,dA$$

Fig. 9.6

that is,

$$J_O = I_x + I_y \tag{9.4}$$

9.5 RADIUS OF GYRATION OF AN AREA

Consider an area A which has a moment of inertia I_x with respect to the x axis (Fig. 9.7a). Let us imagine that we concentrate this area into a thin strip parallel to the x axis (Fig. 9.7b). If the area A, thus concentrated, is to have the same moment of inertia with respect to the x axis, the strip should be placed at a distance k_x from the x axis, where k_x is defined by the relation

$$I_x = k_x^2 A$$

Solving for k_x, we write

$$k_x = \sqrt{\frac{I_x}{A}} \tag{9.5}$$

The distance k_x is referred to as the *radius of gyration* of the area with respect to the x axis. In a similar way, we can define the radii of gyration k_y and k_O (Fig. 9.7c and d); we write

$$I_y = k_y^2 A \qquad k_y = \sqrt{\frac{I_y}{A}} \tag{9.6}$$

$$J_O = k_O^2 A \qquad k_O = \sqrt{\frac{J_O}{A}} \tag{9.7}$$

If we rewrite Eq. (9.4) in terms of the radii of gyration, we find that

$$k_O^2 = k_x^2 + k_y^2 \tag{9.8}$$

EXAMPLE For the rectangle shown in Fig. 9.8, let us compute the radius of gyration k_x with respect to its base. Using formulas (9.5) and (9.2), we write

$$k_x^2 = \frac{I_x}{A} = \frac{\frac{1}{3}bh^3}{bh} = \frac{h^2}{3} \qquad k_x = \frac{h}{\sqrt{3}}$$

The radius of gyration k_x of the rectangle is shown in Fig. 9.8. It should not be confused with the ordinate $\bar{y} = h/2$ of the centroid of the area. While k_x depends upon the *second moment*, or moment of inertia, of the area, the ordinate $\bar{y}$ is related to the *first moment* of the area. ∎

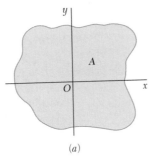

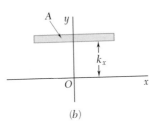

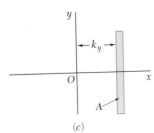

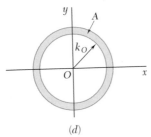

Fig. 9.7

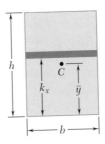

Fig. 9.8

SAMPLE PROBLEM 9.1

Determine the moment of inertia of a triangle with respect to its base.

SOLUTION

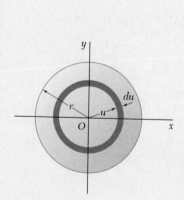

A triangle of base b and height h is drawn; the x axis is chosen to coincide with the base. A differential strip parallel to the x axis is chosen to be dA. Since all portions of the strip are at the same distance from the x axis, we write

$$dI_x = y^2\, dA \qquad dA = l\, dy$$

Using similar triangles, we have

$$\frac{l}{b} = \frac{h-y}{h} \qquad l = b\frac{h-y}{h} \qquad dA = b\frac{h-y}{h}\,dy$$

Integrating dI_x from $y = 0$ to $y = h$, we obtain

$$I_x = \int y^2\, dA = \int_0^h y^2 b\frac{h-y}{h}\,dy = \frac{b}{h}\int_0^h (hy^2 - y^3)\,dy$$

$$= \frac{b}{h}\left[h\frac{y^3}{3} - \frac{y^4}{4} \right]_0^h \qquad\qquad I_x = \frac{bh^3}{12} \quad \blacktriangleleft$$

SAMPLE PROBLEM 9.2

(a) Determine the centroidal polar moment of inertia of a circular area by direct integration. (b) Using the result of part a, determine the moment of inertia of a circular area with respect to a diameter.

SOLUTION

a. Polar Moment of Inertia. An annular differential element of area is chosen to be dA. Since all portions of the differential area are at the same distance from the origin, we write

$$dJ_O = u^2\, dA \qquad dA = 2\pi u\, du$$

$$J_O = \int dJ_O = \int_0^r u^2 (2\pi u\, du) = 2\pi \int_0^r u^3\, du$$

$$J_O = \frac{\pi}{2} r^4 \quad \blacktriangleleft$$

b. Moment of Inertia with Respect to a Diameter. Because of the symmetry of the circular area, we have $I_x = I_y$. We then write

$$J_O = I_x + I_y = 2I_x \qquad \frac{\pi}{2} r^4 = 2I_x \qquad I_{\text{diameter}} = I_x = \frac{\pi}{4} r^4 \quad \blacktriangleleft$$

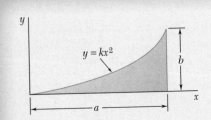

SAMPLE PROBLEM 9.3

(a) Determine the moment of inertia of the shaded area shown with respect to each of the coordinate axes. (Properties of this area were considered in Sample Prob. 5.4.) (b) Using the results of part a, determine the radius of gyration of the shaded area with respect to each of the coordinate axes.

SOLUTION

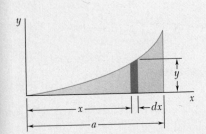

Referring to Sample Prob. 5.4, we obtain the following expressions for the equation of the curve and the total area:

$$y = \frac{b}{a^2}x^2 \qquad A = \tfrac{1}{3}ab$$

Moment of Inertia I_x. A vertical differential element of area is chosen to be dA. Since all portions of this element are *not* at the same distance from the x axis, we must treat the element as a thin rectangle. The moment of inertia of the element with respect to the x axis is then

$$dI_x = \tfrac{1}{3}y^3\,dx = \frac{1}{3}\left(\frac{b}{a^2}x^2\right)^3 dx = \frac{1}{3}\frac{b^3}{a^6}x^6\,dx$$

$$I_x = \int dI_x = \int_0^a \frac{1}{3}\frac{b^3}{a^6}x^6\,dx = \left[\frac{1}{3}\frac{b^3}{a^6}\frac{x^7}{7}\right]_0^a$$

$$I_x = \frac{ab^3}{21} \quad \blacktriangleleft$$

Moment of Inertia I_y. The same vertical differential element of area is used. Since all portions of the element are at the same distance from the y axis, we write

$$dI_y = x^2\,dA = x^2(y\,dx) = x^2\left(\frac{b}{a^2}x^2\right)dx = \frac{b}{a^2}x^4\,dx$$

$$I_y = \int dI_y = \int_0^a \frac{b}{a^2}x^4\,dx = \left[\frac{b}{a^2}\frac{x^5}{5}\right]_0^a$$

$$I_y = \frac{a^3b}{5} \quad \blacktriangleleft$$

Radii of Gyration k_x and k_y. We have, by definition,

$$k_x^2 = \frac{I_x}{A} = \frac{ab^3/21}{ab/3} = \frac{b^2}{7} \qquad k_x = \sqrt{\tfrac{1}{7}}\,b \quad \blacktriangleleft$$

and

$$k_y^2 = \frac{I_y}{A} = \frac{a^3b/5}{ab/3} = \tfrac{3}{5}a^2 \qquad k_y = \sqrt{\tfrac{3}{5}}\,a \quad \blacktriangleleft$$

SOLVING PROBLEMS
ON YOUR OWN

The purpose of this lesson was to introduce the *rectangular and polar moments of inertia of areas* and the corresponding *radii of gyration*. Although the problems you are about to solve may appear to be more appropriate for a calculus class than for one in mechanics, we hope that our introductory comments have convinced you of the relevance of the moments of inertia to your study of a variety of engineering topics.

1. Calculating the rectangular moments of inertia I_x and I_y. We defined these quantities as

$$I_x = \int y^2 \, dA \qquad I_y = \int x^2 \, dA \qquad (9.1)$$

where dA is a differential element of area $dx \, dy$. The moments of inertia are *the second moments of the area*; it is for that reason that I_x, for example, depends on the perpendicular distance y to the area dA. As you study Sec. 9.3, you should recognize the importance of carefully defining the shape and the orientation of dA. Further, you should note the following points.

 a. The moments of inertia of most areas can be obtained by means of a single integration. The expressions given in Figs. 9.3*b* and *c* and Fig. 9.5 can be used to calculate I_x and I_y. Regardless of whether you use a single or a double integration, be sure to show on your sketch the element dA that you have chosen.

 b. The moment of inertia of an area is always positive, regardless of the location of the area with respect to the coordinate axes. This is because it is obtained by integrating the product of dA and the *square* of distance. (Note how this differs from the results for the first moment of the area.) Only when an area is *removed* (as in the case for a hole) will its moment of inertia be entered in your computations with a minus sign.

 c. As a partial check of your work, observe that the moments of inertia are equal to an area times the square of a length. Thus, every term in an expression for a moment of inertia must be a *length to the fourth power*.

2. Computing the polar moment of inertia J_O. We defined J_O as

$$J_O = \int r^2 \, dA \qquad (9.3)$$

where $r^2 = x^2 + y^2$. If the given area has circular symmetry (as in Sample Prob. 9.2), it is possible to express dA as a function of r and to compute J_O with a single integration. When the area lacks circular symmetry, it is usually easier first to calculate I_x and I_y and then to determine J_O from

$$J_O = I_x + I_y \qquad (9.4)$$

Lastly, if the equation of the curve that bounds the given area is expressed in polar coordinates, then $dA = r \, dr \, d\theta$ and a double integration is required to compute the integral for J_O [see Prob. 9.27].

3. Determining the radii of gyration k_x and k_y and the polar radius of gyration k_O. These quantities were defined in Sec. 9.5, and you should realize that they can be determined only after the area and the appropriate moments of inertia have been computed. It is important to remember that k_x is measured in the y direction, while k_y is measured in the x direction; you should carefully study Sec. 9.5 until you understand this point.

PROBLEMS

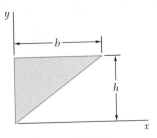

Fig. P9.1 and *P9.5*

9.1 through 9.4 Determine by direct integration the moment of inertia of the shaded area with respect to the y axis.

9.5 through 9.8 Determine by direct integration the moment of inertia of the shaded area with respect to the x axis.

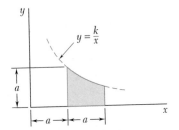

Fig. P9.2 and P9.6

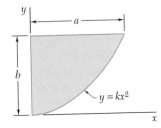

Fig. P9.3 and P9.7

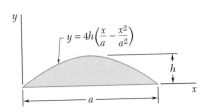

Fig. P9.4 and *P9.8*

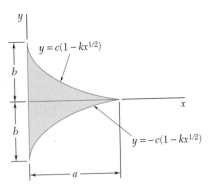

Fig. P9.9 and P9.12

9.9 through 9.11 Determine by direct integration the moment of inertia of the shaded area with respect to the x axis.

9.12 through 9.14 Determine by direct integration the moment of inertia of the shaded area with respect to the y axis.

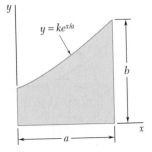

Fig. P9.10 and *P9.13*

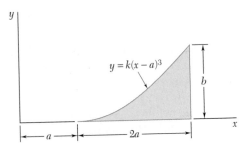

Fig. P9.11 and *P9.14*

9.15 and 9.16 Determine the moment of inertia and the radius of gyration of the shaded area shown with respect to the x axis.

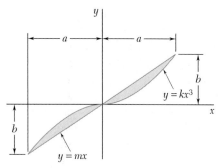

Fig. P9.15 and P9.17

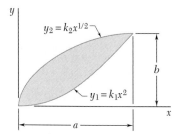

Fig. P9.16 and P9.18

9.17 and 9.18 Determine the moment of inertia and the radius of gyration of the shaded area shown with respect to the y axis.

9.19 Determine the moment of inertia and the radius of gyration of the shaded area shown with respect to the x axis.

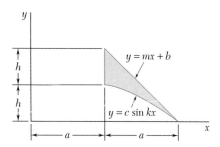

Fig. *P9.19* and *P9.20*

9.20 Determine the moment of inertia and the radius of gyration of the shaded area shown with respect to the y axis.

9.21 and 9.22 Determine the polar moment of inertia and the polar radius of gyration of the shaded area shown with respect to point P.

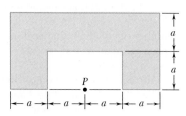

Fig. P9.21

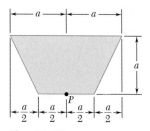

Fig. P9.22

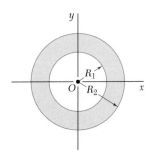

Fig. P9.23 and P9.24

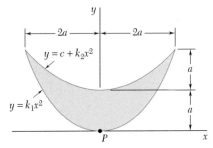

Fig. P9.25

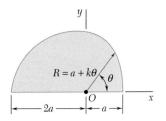

Fig. P9.27

9.23 (a) Determine by direct integration the polar moment of inertia of the annular area shown with respect to point O. (b) Using the result of part a, determine the moment of inertia of the given area with respect to the x axis.

9.24 (a) Show that the polar radius of gyration k_O of the annular area shown is approximately equal to the mean radius $R_m = (R_1 + R_2)/2$ for small values of the thickness $t = R_2 - R_1$. (b) Determine the percentage error introduced by using R_m in place of k_O for the following values of t/R_m: 1, $\frac{1}{2}$, and $\frac{1}{10}$.

9.25 and 9.26 Determine the polar moment of inertia and the polar radius of gyration of the shaded area shown with respect to point P.

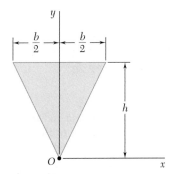

Fig. P9.26

9.27 Determine the polar moment of inertia and the polar radius of gyration of the shaded area shown with respect to point O.

9.28 Determine the polar moment of inertia and the polar radius of gyration of the isosceles triangle shown with respect to point O.

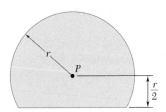

Fig. P9.28

*9.29 Using the polar moment of inertia of the isosceles triangle of Prob. 9.28, show that the centroidal polar moment of inertia of a circular area of radius r is $\pi r^4/2$. (*Hint:* As a circular area is divided into an increasing number of equal circular sectors, what is the approximate shape of each circular sector?)

*9.30 Prove that the centroidal polar moment of inertia of a given area A cannot be smaller than $A^2/2\pi$. (*Hint:* Compare the moment of inertia of the given area with the moment of inertia of a circle that has the same area and the same centroid.)

9.6 PARALLEL-AXIS THEOREM

Consider the moment of inertia I of an area A with respect to an axis AA' (Fig. 9.9). Denoting by y the distance from an element of area dA to AA', we write

$$I = \int y^2 \, dA$$

Let us now draw through the centroid C of the area an axis BB' parallel to AA'; this axis is called a *centroidal axis*. Denoting by y'

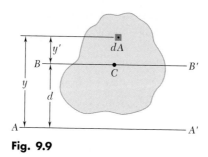

Fig. 9.9

the distance from the element dA to BB', we write $y = y' + d$, where d is the distance between the axes AA' and BB'. Substituting for y in the above integral, we write

$$I = \int y^2 \, dA = \int (y' + d)^2 \, dA$$

$$= \int y'^2 \, dA + 2d \int y' \, dA + d^2 \int dA$$

The first integral represents the moment of inertia $\bar{I}$ of the area with respect to the centroidal axis BB'. The second integral represents the first moment of the area with respect to BB'; since the centroid C of the area is located on that axis, the second integral must be zero. Finally, we observe that the last integral is equal to the total area A. Therefore, we have

$$I = \bar{I} + Ad^2 \qquad (9.9)$$

This formula expresses that the moment of inertia I of an area with respect to any given axis AA' is equal to the moment of inertia $\bar{I}$ of the area with respect to a centroidal axis BB' parallel to AA' *plus* the product of the area A and the square of the distance d between the two axes. This theorem is known as the *parallel-axis theorem*. Substituting k^2A for I and $\bar{k}^2 A$ for $\bar{I}$, the theorem can also be expressed as

$$k^2 = \bar{k}^2 + d^2 \qquad (9.10)$$

A similar theorem can be used to relate the polar moment of inertia J_O of an area about a point O to the polar moment of inertia $\bar{J}_C$ of the same area about its centroid C. Denoting by d the distance between O and C, we write

$$J_O = \bar{J}_C + Ad^2 \qquad \text{or} \qquad k_O^2 = \bar{k}_C^2 + d^2 \qquad (9.11)$$

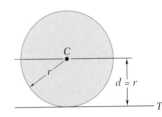

Fig. 9.10

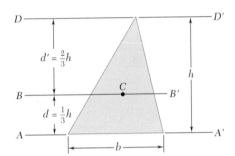

Fig. 9.11

Photo 9.1 Figure 9.13 tabulates data for a small sample of the rolled-steel shapes that are readily available. Shown above are two examples of wide-flange shapes that are commonly used in the construction of buildings.

EXAMPLE 1 As an application of the parallel-axis theorem, let us determine the moment of inertia I_T of a circular area with respect to a line tangent to the circle (Fig. 9.10). We found in Sample Prob. 9.2 that the moment of inertia of a circular area about a centroidal axis is $\bar{I} = \frac{1}{4}\pi r^4$. We can write, therefore,

$$I_T = \bar{I} + Ad^2 = \frac{1}{4}\pi r^4 + (\pi r^2)r^2 = \frac{5}{4}\pi r^4 \quad \blacksquare$$

EXAMPLE 2 The parallel-axis theorem can also be used to determine the centroidal moment of inertia of an area when the moment of inertia of the area with respect to a parallel axis is known. Consider, for instance, a triangular area (Fig. 9.11). We found in Sample Prob. 9.1 that the moment of inertia of a triangle with respect to its base AA' is equal to $\frac{1}{12}bh^3$. Using the parallel-axis theorem, we write

$$I_{AA'} = \bar{I}_{BB'} + Ad^2$$
$$\bar{I}_{BB'} = I_{AA'} - Ad^2 = \frac{1}{12}bh^3 - \frac{1}{2}bh(\frac{1}{3}h)^2 = \frac{1}{36}bh^3$$

It should be observed that the product Ad^2 was *subtracted* from the given moment of inertia in order to obtain the centroidal moment of inertia of the triangle. Note that this product is *added* when transferring *from* a centroidal axis to a parallel axis, but it should be *subtracted* when transferring *to* a centroidal axis. In other words, the moment of inertia of an area is always smaller with respect to a centroidal axis than with respect to any parallel axis.

Returning to Fig. 9.11, we observe that the moment of inertia of the triangle with respect to the line DD' (which is drawn through a vertex) can be obtained by writing

$$I_{DD'} = \bar{I}_{BB'} + Ad'^2 = \frac{1}{36}bh^3 + \frac{1}{2}bh(\frac{2}{3}h)^2 = \frac{1}{4}bh^3$$

Note that $I_{DD'}$ could not have been obtained directly from $I_{AA'}$. The parallel-axis theorem can be applied only if one of the two parallel axes passes through the centroid of the area. $\blacksquare$

9.7 MOMENTS OF INERTIA OF COMPOSITE AREAS

Consider a composite area A made of several component areas A_1, A_2, A_3, ... Since the integral representing the moment of inertia of A can be subdivided into integrals evaluated over A_1, A_2, A_3, ..., the moment of inertia of A with respect to a given axis is obtained by adding the moments of inertia of the areas A_1, A_2, A_3, ..., with respect to the same axis. The moment of inertia of an area consisting of several of the common shapes shown in Fig. 9.12 can thus be obtained by using the formulas given in that figure. Before adding the moments of inertia of the component areas, however, the parallel-axis theorem may have to be used to transfer each moment of inertia to the desired axis. This is shown in Sample Probs. 9.4 and 9.5.

The properties of the cross sections of various structural shapes are given in Fig. 9.13. As noted in Sec. 9.2, the moment of inertia of a beam section about its neutral axis is closely related to the computation of the bending moment in that section of the beam. The

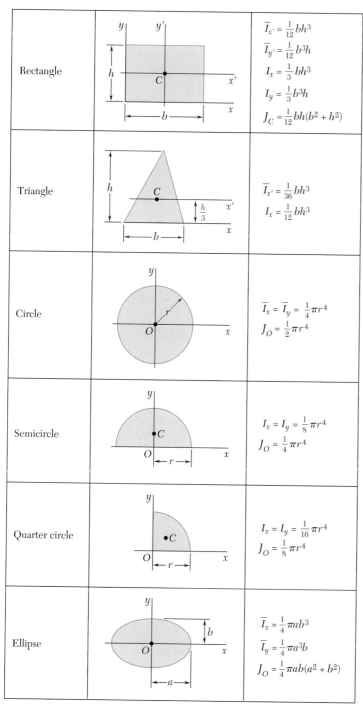

Rectangle		$\overline{I}_{x'} = \frac{1}{12}bh^3$ $\overline{I}_{y'} = \frac{1}{12}b^3h$ $I_x = \frac{1}{3}bh^3$ $I_y = \frac{1}{3}b^3h$ $J_C = \frac{1}{12}bh(b^2 + h^2)$
Triangle		$\overline{I}_{x'} = \frac{1}{36}bh^3$ $I_x = \frac{1}{12}bh^3$
Circle		$\overline{I}_x = \overline{I}_y = \frac{1}{4}\pi r^4$ $J_O = \frac{1}{2}\pi r^4$
Semicircle		$I_x = I_y = \frac{1}{8}\pi r^4$ $J_O = \frac{1}{4}\pi r^4$
Quarter circle		$I_x = I_y = \frac{1}{16}\pi r^4$ $J_O = \frac{1}{8}\pi r^4$
Ellipse		$\overline{I}_x = \frac{1}{4}\pi ab^3$ $\overline{I}_y = \frac{1}{4}\pi a^3b$ $J_O = \frac{1}{4}\pi ab(a^2 + b^2)$

Fig. 9.12 Moments of inertia of common geometric shapes.

determination of moments of inertia is thus a prerequisite to the analysis and design of structural members.

It should be noted that the radius of gyration of a composite area is *not* equal to the sum of the radii of gyration of the component areas. In order to determine the radius of gyration of a composite area, it is first necessary to compute the moment of inertia of the area.

	Designation	Area in^2	Depth in.	Width in.	Axis X-X			Axis Y-Y		
					$\overline{I}_x$, in^4	$\overline{k}_x$, in.	$\overline{y}$, in.	$\overline{I}_y$, in^4	$\overline{k}_y$, in.	$\overline{x}$, in.
W Shapes (Wide-Flange Shapes)	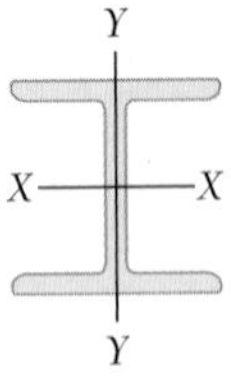 W18 × 76†	22.3	18.2	11.0	1330	7.73		152	2.61	
	W16 × 57	16.8	16.4	7.12	758	6.72		43.1	1.60	
	W14 × 38	11.2	14.1	6.77	385	5.87		26.7	1.55	
	W8 × 31	9.12	8.00	8.00	110	3.47		37.1	2.02	
S Shapes (American Standard Shapes)	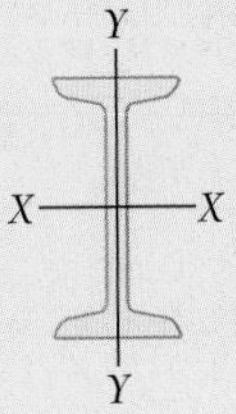 S18 × 54.7†	16.0	18.0	6.00	801	7.07		20.7	1.14	
	S12 × 31.8	9.31	12.0	5.00	217	4.83		9.33	1.00	
	S10 × 25.4	7.45	10.0	4.66	123	4.07		6.73	0.950	
	S6 × 12.5	3.66	6.00	3.33	22.0	2.45		1.80	0.702	
C Shapes (American Standard Channels)	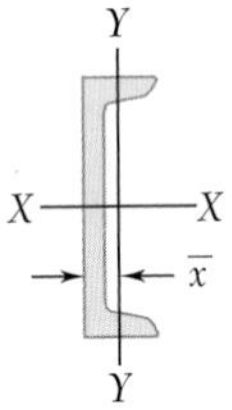 C12 × 20.7†	6.08	12.0	2.94	129	4.61		3.86	0.797	0.698
	C10 × 15.3	4.48	10.0	2.60	67.3	3.87		2.27	0.711	0.634
	C8 × 11.5	3.37	8.00	2.26	32.5	3.11		1.31	0.623	0.572
	C6 × 8.2	2.39	6.00	1.92	13.1	2.34		0.687	0.536	0.512
Angles	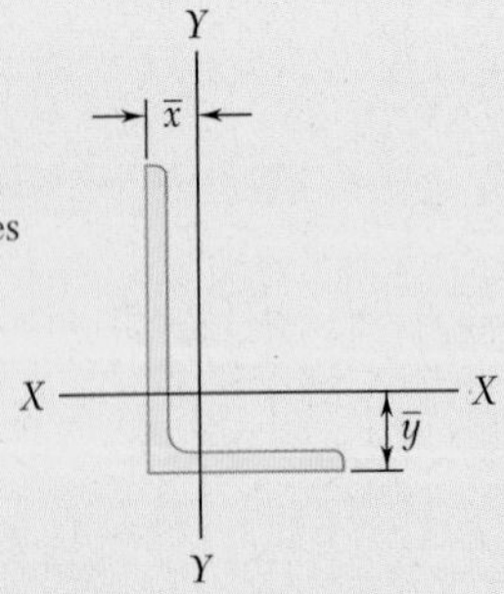 L6 × 6 × 1‡	11.0			35.4	1.79	1.86	35.4	1.79	1.86
	L4 × 4 × $\frac{1}{2}$	3.75			5.52	1.21	1.18	5.52	1.21	1.18
	L3 × 3 × $\frac{1}{4}$	1.44			1.23	0.926	0.836	1.23	0.926	0.836
	L6 × 4 × $\frac{1}{2}$	4.75			17.3	1.91	1.98	6.22	1.14	0.981
	L5 × 3 × $\frac{1}{2}$	3.75			9.43	1.58	1.74	2.55	0.824	0.746
	L3 × 2 × $\frac{1}{4}$	1.19			1.09	0.953	0.980	0.390	0.569	0.487

Fig. 9.13A Properties of rolled-steel shapes (U.S. customary units).*

*Courtesy of the American Institute of Steel Construction, Chicago, Illinois
†Nominal depth in inches and weight in pounds per foot
‡Depth, width, and thickness in inches

	Designation	Area mm^2	Depth mm	Width mm	Axis X-X			Axis Y-Y		
					$\bar{I}_x$ $10^6\ mm^4$	$\bar{k}_x$ mm	$\bar{y}$ mm	$\bar{I}_y$ $10^6\ mm^4$	$\bar{k}_y$ mm	$\bar{x}$ mm
W Shapes (Wide-Flange Shapes) 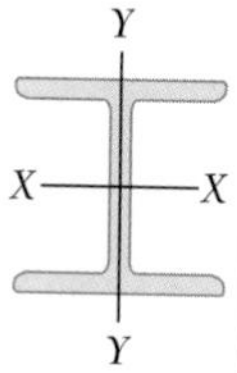	W460 × 113†	14400	462	279	554	196		63.3	66.3	
	W410 × 85	10800	417	181	316	171		17.9	40.6	
	W360 × 57.8	7230	358	172	160	149		11.1	39.4	
	W200 × 46.1	5880	203	203	45.8	88.1		15.4	51.3	
S Shapes (American Standard Shapes) 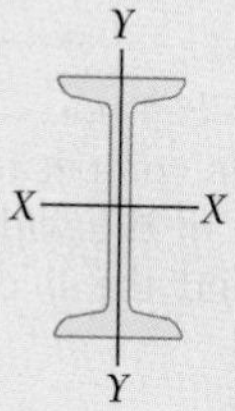	S460 × 81.4†	10300	457	152	333	180		8.62	29.0	
	S310 × 47.3	6010	305	127	90.3	123		3.88	25.4	
	S250 × 37.8	4810	254	118	51.2	103		2.80	24.1	
	S150 × 18.6	2360	152	84.6	9.16	62.2		0.749	17.8	
C Shapes (American Standard Channels) 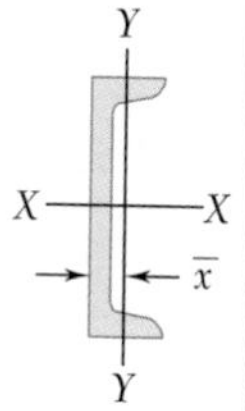	C310 × 30.8†	3920	305	74.7	53.7	117		1.61	20.2	17.7
	C250 × 22.8	2890	254	66.0	28.0	98.3		0.945	18.1	16.1
	C200 × 17.1	2170	203	57.4	13.5	79.0		0.545	15.8	14.5
	C150 × 12.2	1540	152	48.8	5.45	59.4		0.286	13.6	13.0
Angles 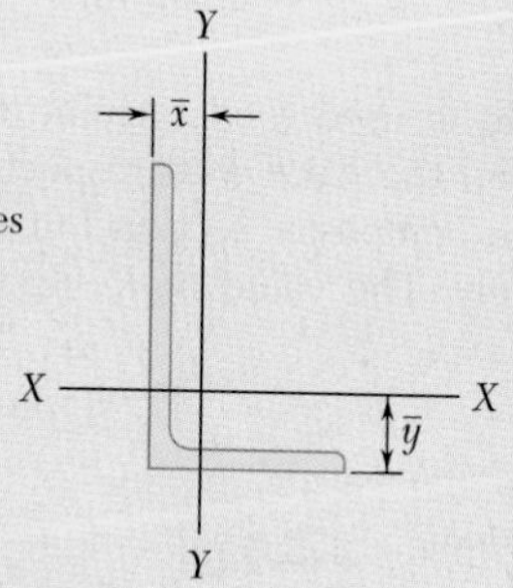	L152 × 152 × 25.4‡	7100			14.7	45.5	47.2	14.7	45.5	47.2
	L102 × 102 × 12.7	2420			2.30	30.7	30.0	2.30	30.7	30.0
	L76 × 76 × 6.4	929			0.512	23.5	21.2	0.512	23.5	21.2
	L152 × 102 × 12.7	3060			7.20	48.5	50.3	2.59	29.0	24.9
	L127 × 76 × 12.7	2420			3.93	40.1	44.2	1.06	20.9	18.9
	L76 × 51 × 6.4	768			0.454	24.2	24.9	0.162	14.5	12.4

Fig. 9.13B Properties of rolled-steel shapes (SI units).

†Nominal depth in millimeters and mass in kilograms per meter
‡Depth, width, and thickness in millimeters

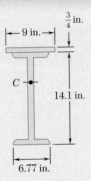

SAMPLE PROBLEM 9.4

The strength of a W14 × 38 rolled-steel beam is increased by attaching a $9 \times \frac{3}{4}$-in. plate to its upper flange as shown. Determine the moment of inertia and the radius of gyration of the composite section with respect to an axis which is parallel to the plate and passes through the centroid C of the section.

SOLUTION

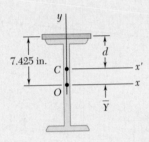

7.425 in.

C d x'

O x

$\overline{Y}$

The origin O of the coordinates is placed at the centroid of the wide-flange shape, and the distance $\overline{Y}$ to the centroid of the composite section is computed using the methods of Chap. 5. The area of the wide-flange shape is found by referring to Fig. 9.13A. The area and the y coordinate of the centroid of the plate are

$$A = (9 \text{ in.})(0.75 \text{ in.}) = 6.75 \text{ in}^2$$
$$\overline{y} = \tfrac{1}{2}(14.1 \text{ in.}) + \tfrac{1}{2}(0.75 \text{ in.}) = 7.425 \text{ in.}$$

Section	Area, in²	$\overline{y}$, in.	$\overline{y}A$, in³
Plate	6.75	7.425	50.12
Wide-flange shape	11.2	0	0
	$\Sigma A = 17.95$		$\Sigma \overline{y}A = 50.12$

$$\overline{Y}\Sigma A = \Sigma \overline{y}A \qquad \overline{Y}(17.95) = 50.12 \qquad \overline{Y} = 2.792 \text{ in.}$$

Moment of Inertia. The parallel-axis theorem is used to determine the moments of inertia of the wide-flange shape and the plate with respect to the x' axis. This axis is a centroidal axis for the composite section but *not* for either of the elements considered separately. The value of $\overline{I}_x$ for the wide-flange shape is obtained from Fig. 9.13A.

For the wide-flange shape,

$$I_{x'} = \overline{I}_x + A\overline{Y}^2 = 385 + (11.2)(2.792)^2 = 472.3 \text{ in}^4$$

For the plate,

$$I_{x'} = \overline{I}_x + Ad^2 = (\tfrac{1}{12})(9)(\tfrac{3}{4})^3 + (6.75)(7.425 - 2.792)^2 = 145.2 \text{ in}^4$$

For the composite area,

$$I_{x'} = 472.3 + 145.2 = 617.5 \text{ in}^4 \qquad I_{x'} = 618 \text{ in}^4 \blacktriangleleft$$

Radius of Gyration. We have

$$k_{x'}^2 = \frac{I_{x'}}{A} = \frac{617.5 \text{ in}^4}{17.95 \text{ in}^2} \qquad k_{x'} = 5.87 \text{ in.} \blacktriangleleft$$

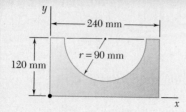

SAMPLE PROBLEM 9.5

Determine the moment of inertia of the shaded area with respect to the x axis.

SOLUTION

The given area can be obtained by subtracting a half circle from a rectangle. The moments of inertia of the rectangle and the half circle will be computed separately.

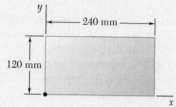

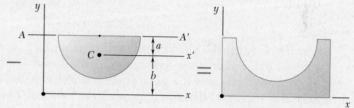

Moment of Inertia of Rectangle. Referring to Fig. 9.12, we obtain
$$I_x = \tfrac{1}{3}bh^3 = \tfrac{1}{3}(240 \text{ mm})(120 \text{ mm})^3 = 138.2 \times 10^6 \text{ mm}^4$$

Moment of Inertia of Half Circle. Referring to Fig. 5.8, we determine the location of the centroid C of the half circle with respect to diameter AA'.

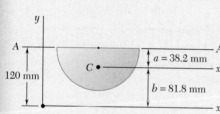

$$a = \frac{4r}{3\pi} = \frac{(4)(90 \text{ mm})}{3\pi} = 38.2 \text{ mm}$$

The distance b from the centroid C to the x axis is
$$b = 120 \text{ mm} - a = 120 \text{ mm} - 38.2 \text{ mm} = 81.8 \text{ mm}$$

Referring now to Fig. 9.12, we compute the moment of inertia of the half circle with respect to diameter AA'; we also compute the area of the half circle.
$$I_{AA'} = \tfrac{1}{8}\pi r^4 = \tfrac{1}{8}\pi(90 \text{ mm})^4 = 25.76 \times 10^6 \text{ mm}^4$$
$$A = \tfrac{1}{2}\pi r^2 = \tfrac{1}{2}\pi(90 \text{ mm})^2 = 12.72 \times 10^3 \text{ mm}^2$$

Using the parallel-axis theorem, we obtain the value of $\bar{I}_{x'}$:
$$I_{AA'} = \bar{I}_{x'} + Aa^2$$
$$25.76 \times 10^6 \text{ mm}^4 = \bar{I}_{x'} + (12.72 \times 10^3 \text{ mm}^2)(38.2 \text{ mm})^2$$
$$\bar{I}_{x'} = 7.20 \times 10^6 \text{ mm}^4$$

Again using the parallel-axis theorem, we obtain the value of I_x:
$$I_x = \bar{I}_{x'} + Ab^2 = 7.20 \times 10^6 \text{ mm}^4 + (12.72 \times 10^3 \text{ mm}^2)(81.8 \text{ mm})^2$$
$$= 92.3 \times 10^6 \text{ mm}^4$$

Moment of Inertia of Given Area. Subtracting the moment of inertia of the half circle from that of the rectangle, we obtain
$$I_x = 138.2 \times 10^6 \text{ mm}^4 - 92.3 \times 10^6 \text{ mm}^4$$
$$I_x = 45.9 \times 10^6 \text{ mm}^4 \quad \blacktriangleleft$$

SOLVING PROBLEMS
ON YOUR OWN

In this lesson we introduced the *parallel-axis theorem* and illustrated how it can be used to simplify the computation of moments and polar moments of inertia of composite areas. The areas that you will consider in the following problems will consist of common shapes and rolled-steel shapes. You will also use the parallel-axis theorem to locate the point of application (the center of pressure) of the resultant of the hydrostatic forces acting on a submerged plane area.

1. Applying the parallel-axis theorem. In Sec. 9.6 we derived the parallel-axis theorem

$$I = \bar{I} + Ad^2 \qquad\qquad (9.9)$$

which states that the moment of inertia I of an area A with respect to a given axis is equal to the sum of the moment of inertia $\bar{I}$ of that area with respect to a *parallel centroidal axis* and the product Ad^2, where d is the distance between the two axes. It is important that you remember the following points as you use the parallel-axis theorem.

a. The centroidal moment of inertia $\bar{I}$ of an area A can be obtained by subtracting the product Ad^2 from the moment of inertia I of the area with respect to a parallel axis. It follows that the moment of inertia $\bar{I}$ is *smaller* than the moment of inertia I of the same area with respect to any parallel axis.

b. The parallel-axis theorem can be applied only if one of the two axes involved is a centroidal axis. Therefore, as we noted in Example 2, to compute the moment of inertia of an area with respect to a *noncentroidal axis* when the moment of inertia of the area is known with respect to *another noncentroidal axis*, it is necessary to *first compute* the moment of inertia of the area with respect to a *centroidal axis parallel to the two given axes*.

2. Computing the moments and polar moments of inertia of composite areas. Sample Probs. 9.4 and 9.5 illustrate the steps you should follow to solve problems of this type. As with all composite-area problems, you should show on your sketch the common shapes or rolled-steel shapes that constitute the various elements of the given area, as well as the distances between the centroidal axes of the elements and the axes about which the moments of inertia are to be computed. In addition, it is important that the following points be noted.

a. The moment of inertia of an area is always positive, regardless of the location of the axis with respect to which it is computed. As pointed out in the comments for the preceding lesson, it is only when an area is *removed* (as in the case of a hole) that its moment of inertia should be entered in your computations with a minus sign.

b. The moments of inertia of a semiellipse and a quarter ellipse can be determined by dividing the moment of inertia of an ellipse by 2 and 4, respectively. It should be noted, however, that the moments of inertia obtained in this manner are *with respect to the axes of symmetry of the ellipse*. To obtain the *centroidal* moments of inertia of these shapes, the parallel-axis theorem should be used. Note that this remark also applies to a semicircle and to a quarter circle and that the expressions given for these shapes in Fig. 9.12 are *not* centroidal moments of inertia.

c. To calculate the polar moment of inertia of a composite area, you can use either the expressions given in Fig. 9.12 for J_O or the relationship

$$J_O = I_x + I_y \tag{9.4}$$

depending on the shape of the given area.

d. Before computing the centroidal moments of inertia of a given area, you may find it necessary to first locate the centroid of the area using the methods of Chapter 5.

3. Locating the point of application of the resultant of a system of hydrostatic forces. In Sec. 9.2 we found that

$$R = \gamma \int y \, dA = \gamma \bar{y} A$$

$$M_x = \gamma \int y^2 \, dA = \gamma I_x$$

where $\bar{y}$ is the distance from the x axis to the centroid of the submerged plane area. Since **R** is equivalent to the system of elemental hydrostatic forces, it follows that

$$\Sigma M_x: \qquad y_P R = M_x$$

where y_P is the depth of the point of application of **R**. Then

$$y_P(\gamma \bar{y} A) = \gamma I_x \qquad \text{or} \qquad y_P = \frac{I_x}{\bar{y} A}$$

In closing, we encourage you to carefully study the notation used in Fig. 9.13 for the rolled-steel shapes, as you will likely encounter it again in subsequent engineering courses.

9.31 and 9.32 Determine the moment of inertia and the radius of gyration of the shaded area with respect to the x axis.

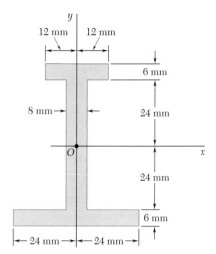

Fig. P9.31 and P9.33

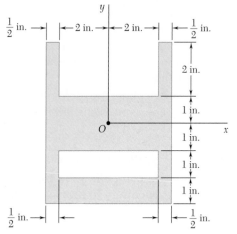

Fig. P9.32 and P9.34

9.33 and 9.34 Determine the moment of inertia and the radius of gyration of the shaded area with respect to the y axis.

9.35 and 9.36 Determine the moments of inertia of the shaded area shown with respect to the x and y axes when $a = 20$ mm.

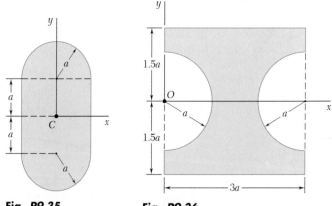

Fig. P9.35   **Fig. P9.36**

9.37 For the 4000-mm^2 shaded area shown, determine the distance d_2 and the moment of inertia with respect to the centroidal axis parallel to AA' knowing that the moments of inertia with respect to AA' and BB' are 12×10^6 mm^4 and 23.9×10^6 mm^4, respectively, and that $d_1 = 25$ mm.

9.38 Determine for the shaded region the area and the moment of inertia with respect to the centroidal axis parallel to BB', knowing that $d_1 = 25$ mm and $d_2 = 15$ mm and that the moments of inertia with respect to AA' and BB' are 7.84×10^6 mm^4 and 5.20×10^6 mm^4, respectively.

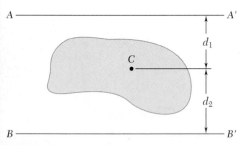

Fig. P9.37 and P9.38

9.39 The shaded area is equal to 50 in². Determine its centroidal moments of inertia $\bar{I}_x$ and $\bar{I}_y$, knowing that $\bar{I}_y = 2\bar{I}_x$ and that the polar moment of inertia of the area about point A is $J_A = 2250$ in⁴.

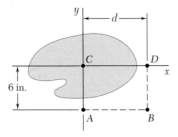

Fig. P9.39 and P9.40

9.40 The polar moments of inertia of the shaded area with respect to points A, B, and D are, respectively, $J_A = 2880$ in⁴, $J_B = 6720$ in⁴, and $J_D = 4560$ in⁴. Determine the shaded area, its centroidal moment of inertia $\bar{J}_C$, and the distance d from C to D.

9.41 through 9.44 Determine the moments of inertia $\bar{I}_x$ and $\bar{I}_y$ of the area shown with respect to centroidal axes respectively parallel and perpendicular to side AB.

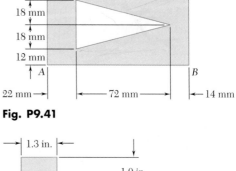

Fig. P9.41

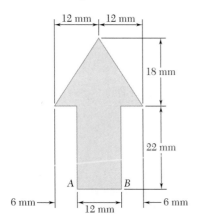

Fig. P9.42

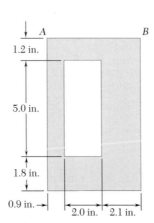

Fig. P9.43

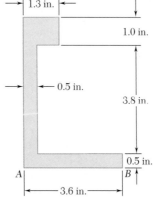

Fig. P9.44

9.45 and 9.46 Determine the polar moment of inertia of the area shown with respect to (a) point O, (b) the centroid of the area.

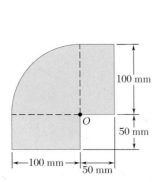

Fig. P9.45

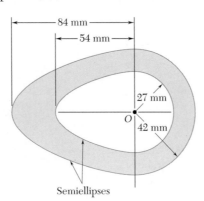

Fig. P9.46

9.47 and 9.48 Determine the polar moment of inertia of the area shown with respect to (a) point O, (b) the centroid of the area.

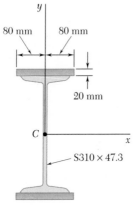

Fig. **P9.47**

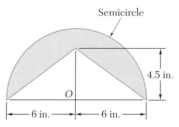

Semicircle

4.5 in.

O

6 in. 6 in.

Fig. **P9.48**

9.49 Two 20-mm steel plates are welded to a rolled S section as shown. Determine the moments of inertia and the radii of gyration of the combined section with respect to the centroidal x and y axes.

9.50 Two channels are welded to a rolled W section as shown. Determine the moments of inertia and the radii of gyration of the combined section with respect to the centroidal x and y axes.

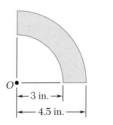

80 mm   80 mm

20 mm

C

x

S310 × 47.3

Fig. **P9.49**

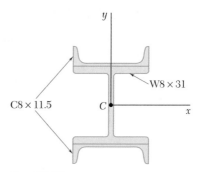

W8 × 31

C8 × 11.5   C x

Fig. **P9.50**

9.51 To form a reinforced box section, two rolled W sections and two plates are welded together. Determine the moments of inertia and the radii of gyration of the combined section with respect to the centroidal axes shown.

9.52 Two channels are welded to a $d \times 12$-in. steel plate as shown. Determine the width d for which the ratio $\bar{I}_x/\bar{I}_y$ of the centroidal moments of inertia of the section is 16.

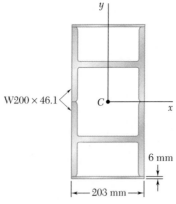

W200 × 46.1   C x

6 mm

203 mm

Fig. **P9.51**

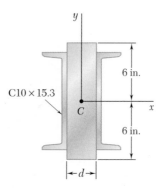

C10 × 15.3

C

6 in.

6 in.

x

d

Fig. **P9.52**

9.53 Two L76 × 76 × 6.4-mm angles are welded to a C250 × 22.8 channel. Determine the moments of inertia of the combined section with respect to centroidal axes respectively parallel and perpendicular to the web of the channel.

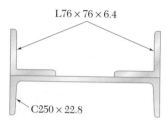

L76 × 76 × 6.4

C250 × 22.8

Fig. P9.53

9.54 Two L4 × 4 × $\frac{1}{2}$-in. angles are welded to a steel plate as shown. Determine the moments of inertia of the combined section with respect to centroidal axes respectively parallel and perpendicular to the plate.

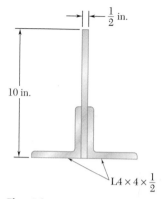

$\frac{1}{2}$ in.

10 in.

L4 × 4 × $\frac{1}{2}$

Fig. P9.54

9.55 The strength of the rolled W section shown is increased by welding a channel to its upper flange. Determine the moments of inertia of the combined section with respect to its centroidal x and y axes.

9.56 Two L5 × 3 × $\frac{1}{2}$-in. angles are welded to a $\frac{1}{2}$-in. steel plate. Determine the distance b and the centroidal moments of inertia $\bar{I}_x$ and $\bar{I}_y$ of the combined section, knowing that $\bar{I}_y = 4\bar{I}_x$.

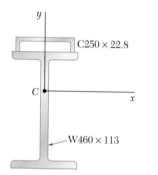

y

C250 × 22.8

C

x

W460 × 113

Fig. P9.55

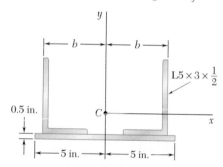

y

b   b

L5 × 3 × $\frac{1}{2}$

0.5 in.

C   x

5 in.   5 in.

Fig. P9.56

9.57 and 9.58 The panel shown forms the end of a trough that is filled with water to the line AA'. Referring to Sec. 9.2, determine the depth of the point of application of the resultant of the hydrostatic forces acting on the panel (the center of pressure).

9.59 and *9.60 The panel shown forms the end of a trough that is filled with water to the line AA'. Referring to Sec. 9.2, determine the depth of the point of application of the resultant of the hydrostatic forces acting on the panel (the center of pressure).

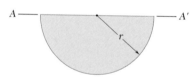

A   A'

r

Fig. P9.57

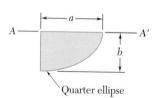

a

A   A'

b

Quarter ellipse

Fig. P9.58

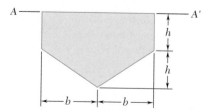

A   A'

h

h

b   b

Fig. P9.59

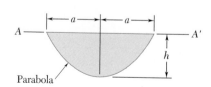

a   a

A   A'

h

Parabola

Fig. P9.60

9.61 The cover for a 0.5-m-diameter access hole in a water storage tank is attached to the tank with four equally spaced bolts as shown. Determine the additional force on each bolt due to the water pressure when the center of the cover is located 1.4 m below the water surface.

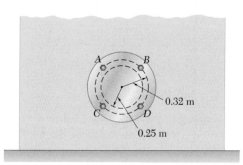

Fig. P9.61

9.62 A vertical trapezoidal gate that is used as an automatic valve is held shut by two springs attached to hinges located along edge AB. Knowing that each spring exerts a couple of magnitude 1470 N · m, determine the depth d of water for which the gate will open.

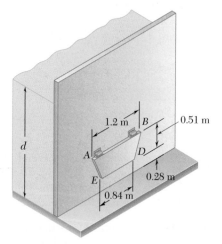

Fig. P9.63

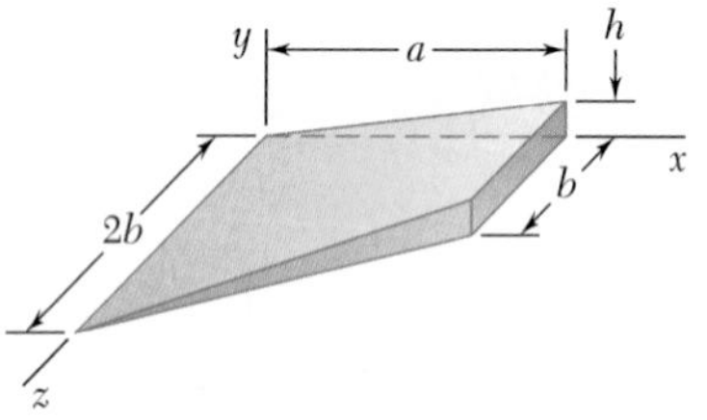

Fig. P9.62

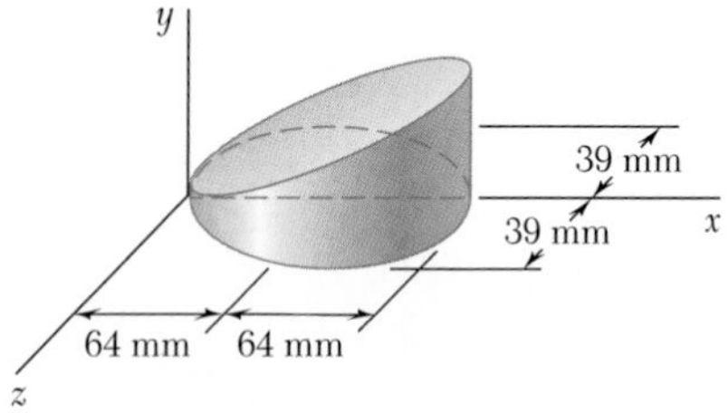

Fig. P9.64

*9.63 Determine the x coordinate of the centroid of the volume shown. (*Hint:* The height y of the volume is proportional to the x coordinate; consider an analogy between this height and the water pressure on a submerged surface.)

*9.64 Determine the x coordinate of the centroid of the volume shown; this volume was obtained by intersecting an elliptic cylinder with an oblique plane. (See hint of Prob. 9.63.)

*9.65 Show that the system of hydrostatic forces acting on a submerged plane area A can be reduced to a force **P** at the centroid C of the area and two couples. The force **P** is perpendicular to the area and is of magnitude $P = \gamma A \bar{y} \sin \theta$, where γ is the specific weight of the liquid, and the couples are $\mathbf{M}_{x'} = (\gamma \bar{I}_{x'} \sin \theta)\mathbf{i}$ and $\mathbf{M}_{y'} = (\gamma \bar{I}_{x'y'} \sin \theta)\mathbf{j}$, where $\bar{I}_{x'y'} = \int x'y' \, dA$ (see Sec. 9.8). Note that the couples are independent of the depth at which the area is submerged.

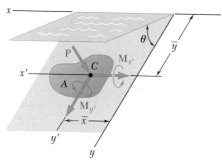

Fig. P9.65

*9.66 Show that the resultant of the hydrostatic forces acting on a submerged plane area A is a force **P** perpendicular to the area and of magnitude $P = \gamma A \bar{y} \sin \theta = \bar{p}A$, where γ is the specific weight of the liquid and $\bar{p}$ is the pressure at the centroid C of the area. Show that **P** is applied at a point C_P, called the center of pressure, whose coordinates are $x_P = I_{xy}/A\bar{y}$ and $y_P = I_x/A\bar{y}$, where $I_{xy} = \int xy \, dA$ (see Sec. 9.8). Show also that the difference of ordinates $y_P - \bar{y}$ is equal to $\bar{k}_{x'}^2/\bar{y}$ and thus depends upon the depth at which the area is submerged.

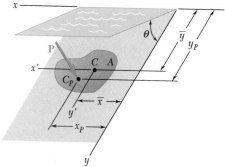

Fig. P9.66

*9.8 PRODUCT OF INERTIA

The integral

$$I_{xy} = \int xy \, dA \qquad (9.12)$$

which is obtained by multiplying each element dA of an area A by its coordinates x and y and integrating over the area (Fig. 9.14), is known as the *product of inertia* of the area A with respect to the x and y axes. Unlike the moments of inertia I_x and I_y, the product of inertia I_{xy} can be positive, negative, or zero.

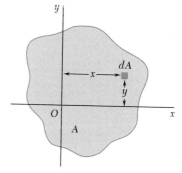

Fig. 9.14

When one or both of the x and y axes are axes of symmetry for the area A, the product of inertia I_{xy} is zero. Consider, for example, the channel section shown in Fig. 9.15. Since this section is symmetrical with respect to the x axis, we can associate with each element dA of coordinates x and y an element dA' of coordinates x and $-y$. Clearly, the contributions to I_{xy} of any pair of elements chosen in this way cancel out, and the integral (9.12) reduces to zero.

A parallel-axis theorem similar to the one established in Sec. 9.6 for moments of inertia can be derived for products of inertia. Consider an area A and a system of rectangular coordinates x and y

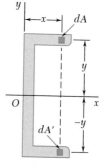

Fig. 9.15

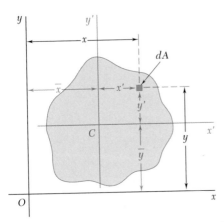

Fig. 9.16

(Fig. 9.16). Through the centroid C of the area, of coordinates $\bar{x}$ and $\bar{y}$, we draw two *centroidal axes* x' and y' which are parallel, respectively, to the x and y axes. Denoting by x and y the coordinates of an element of area dA with respect to the original axes, and by x' and y' the coordinates of the same element with respect to the centroidal axes, we write $x = x' + \bar{x}$ and $y = y' + \bar{y}$. Substituting into (9.12), we obtain the following expression for the product of inertia I_{xy}:

$$I_{xy} = \int xy \, dA = \int (x' + \bar{x})(y' + \bar{y}) \, dA$$

$$= \int x'y' \, dA + \bar{y} \int x' \, dA + \bar{x} \int y' \, dA + \bar{x}\bar{y} \int dA$$

The first integral represents the product of inertia $\bar{I}_{x'y'}$ of the area A with respect to the centroidal axes x' and y'. The next two integrals represent first moments of the area with respect to the centroidal axes; they reduce to zero, since the centroid C is located on these axes. Finally, we observe that the last integral is equal to the total area A. Therefore, we have

$$I_{xy} = \bar{I}_{x'y'} + \bar{x}\bar{y}A \tag{9.13}$$

*9.9 PRINCIPAL AXES AND PRINCIPAL MOMENTS OF INERTIA

Consider the area A and the coordinate axes x and y (Fig. 9.17). Assuming that the moments and product of inertia

$$I_x = \int y^2 \, dA \qquad I_y = \int x^2 \, dA \qquad I_{xy} = \int xy \, dA \tag{9.14}$$

of the area A are known, we propose to determine the moments and product of inertia $I_{x'}$, $I_{y'}$, and $I_{x'y'}$ of A with respect to new axes x' and y' which are obtained by rotating the original axes about the origin through an angle θ.

We first note the following relations between the coordinates x', y' and x, y of an element of area dA:

$$x' = x \cos \theta + y \sin \theta \qquad y' = y \cos \theta - x \sin \theta$$

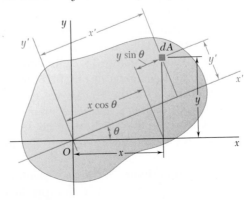

Fig. 9.17

Substituting for y' in the expression for $I_{x'}$, we write

$$I_{x'} = \int (y')^2 \, dA = \int (y \cos \theta - x \sin \theta)^2 \, dA$$

$$= \cos^2 \theta \int y^2 \, dA - 2 \sin \theta \cos \theta \int xy \, dA + \sin^2 \theta \int x^2 \, dA$$

Using the relations (9.14), we write

$$I_{x'} = I_x \cos^2 \theta - 2I_{xy} \sin \theta \cos \theta + I_y \sin^2 \theta \qquad (9.15)$$

Similarly, we obtain for $I_{y'}$ and $I_{x'y'}$ the expressions

$$I_{y'} = I_x \sin^2 \theta + 2I_{xy} \sin \theta \cos \theta + I_y \cos^2 \theta \qquad (9.16)$$
$$I_{x'y'} = (I_x - I_y) \sin \theta \cos \theta + I_{xy}(\cos^2 \theta - \sin^2 \theta) \qquad (9.17)$$

Recalling the trigonometric relations

$$\sin 2\theta = 2 \sin \theta \cos \theta \qquad \cos 2\theta = \cos^2 \theta - \sin^2 \theta$$

and

$$\cos^2 \theta = \frac{1 + \cos 2\theta}{2} \qquad \sin^2 \theta = \frac{1 - \cos 2\theta}{2}$$

we can write (9.15), (9.16), and (9.17) as follows:

$$I_{x'} = \frac{I_x + I_y}{2} + \frac{I_x - I_y}{2} \cos 2\theta - I_{xy} \sin 2\theta \qquad (9.18)$$

$$I_{y'} = \frac{I_x + I_y}{2} - \frac{I_x - I_y}{2} \cos 2\theta + I_{xy} \sin 2\theta \qquad (9.19)$$

$$I_{x'y'} = \frac{I_x - I_y}{2} \sin 2\theta + I_{xy} \cos 2\theta \qquad (9.20)$$

Adding (9.18) and (9.19) we observe that

$$I_{x'} + I_{y'} = I_x + I_y \qquad (9.21)$$

This result could have been anticipated, since both members of (9.21) are equal to the polar moment of inertia J_O.

Equations (9.18) and (9.20) are the parametric equations of a circle. This means that if we choose a set of rectangular axes and plot a point M of abscissa $I_{x'}$ and ordinate $I_{x'y'}$ for any given value of the parameter θ, all of the points thus obtained will lie on a circle. To establish this property, we eliminate θ from Eqs. (9.18) and (9.20); this is done by transposing $(I_x + I_y)/2$ in Eq. (9.18), squaring both members of Eqs. (9.18) and (9.20), and adding. We write

$$\left(I_{x'} - \frac{I_x + I_y}{2}\right)^2 + I_{x'y'}^2 = \left(\frac{I_x - I_y}{2}\right)^2 + I_{xy}^2 \qquad (9.22)$$

Setting

$$I_{ave} = \frac{I_x + I_y}{2} \qquad \text{and} \qquad R = \sqrt{\left(\frac{I_x - I_y}{2}\right)^2 + I_{xy}^2} \qquad (9.23)$$

we write the identity (9.22) in the form

$$(I_{x'} - I_{ave})^2 + I_{x'y'}^2 = R^2 \qquad (9.24)$$

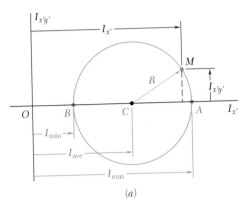

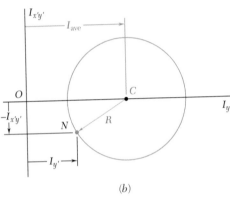

Fig. 9.18

which is the equation of a circle of radius R centered at the point C whose x and y coordinates are I_{ave} and 0, respectively (Fig. 9.18a). We observe that Eqs. (9.19) and (9.20) are the parametric equations of the same circle. Furthermore, because of the symmetry of the circle about the horizontal axis, the same result would have been obtained if instead of plotting M, we had plotted a point N of coordinates $I_{y'}$ and $-I_{x'y'}$ (Fig. 9.18b). This property will be used in Sec. 9.10.

The two points A and B where the above circle intersects the horizontal axis (Fig. 9.18a) are of special interest: Point A corresponds to the maximum value of the moment of inertia $I_{x'}$, while point B corresponds to its minimum value. In addition, both points correspond to a zero value of the product of inertia $I_{x'y'}$. Thus, the values θ_m of the parameter θ which correspond to the points A and B can be obtained by setting $I_{x'y'} = 0$ in Eq. (9.20). We obtain†

$$\tan 2\theta_m = -\frac{2I_{xy}}{I_x - I_y} \tag{9.25}$$

This equation defines two values $2\theta_m$ which are 180° apart and thus two values θ_m which are 90° apart. One of these values corresponds to point A in Fig. 9.18a and to an axis through O in Fig. 9.17 with respect to which the moment of inertia of the given area is maximum; the other value corresponds to point B and to an axis through O with respect to which the moment of inertia of the area is minimum. The two axes thus defined, which are perpendicular to each other, are called the *principal axes of the area about O*, and the corresponding values I_{max} and I_{min} of the moment of inertia are called the *principal moments of inertia of the area about O*. Since the two values θ_m defined by Eq. (9.25) were obtained by setting $I_{x'y'} = 0$ in Eq. (9.20), it is clear that the product of inertia of the given area with respect to its principal axes is zero.

We observe from Fig. 9.18a that

$$I_{max} = I_{ave} + R \qquad I_{min} = I_{ave} - R \tag{9.26}$$

Using the values for I_{ave} and R from formulas (9.23), we write

$$I_{max,min} = \frac{I_x + I_y}{2} \pm \sqrt{\left(\frac{I_x - I_y}{2}\right)^2 + I_{xy}^2} \tag{9.27}$$

Unless it is possible to tell by inspection which of the two principal axes corresponds to I_{max} and which corresponds to I_{min}, it is necessary to substitute one of the values of θ_m into Eq. (9.18) in order to determine which of the two corresponds to the maximum value of the moment of inertia of the area about O.

Referring to Sec. 9.8, we note that if an area possesses an axis of symmetry through a point O, this axis must be a principal axis of the area about O. On the other hand, a principal axis does not need to be an axis of symmetry; whether or not an area possesses any axes of symmetry, it will have two principal axes of inertia about any point O.

The properties we have established hold for any point O located inside or outside the given area. If the point O is chosen to coincide with the centroid of the area, any axis through O is a centroidal axis; the two principal axes of the area about its centroid are referred to as the *principal centroidal axes of the area*.

---

†This relation can also be obtained by differentiating $I_{x'}$ in Eq. (9.18) and setting $dI_{x'}/d\theta = 0$.

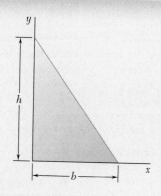

SAMPLE PROBLEM 9.6

Determine the product of inertia of the right triangle shown (a) with respect to the x and y axes and (b) with respect to centroidal axes parallel to the x and y axes.

SOLUTION

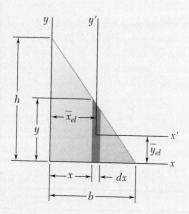

a. Product of Inertia I_{xy}.
A vertical rectangular strip is chosen as the differential element of area. Using the parallel-axis theorem, we write

$$dI_{xy} = dI_{x'y'} + \bar{x}_{el}\bar{y}_{el}\, dA$$

Since the element is symmetrical with respect to the x' and y' axes, we note that $dI_{x'y'} = 0$. From the geometry of the triangle, we obtain

$$y = h\left(1 - \frac{x}{b}\right) \qquad dA = y\, dx = h\left(1 - \frac{x}{b}\right) dx$$

$$\bar{x}_{el} = x \qquad \bar{y}_{el} = \tfrac{1}{2}y = \tfrac{1}{2}h\left(1 - \frac{x}{b}\right)$$

Integrating dI_{xy} from $x = 0$ to $x = b$, we obtain

$$I_{xy} = \int dI_{xy} = \int \bar{x}_{el}\bar{y}_{el}\, dA = \int_0^b x(\tfrac{1}{2})h^2\left(1 - \frac{x}{b}\right)^2 dx$$

$$= h^2\int_0^b\left(\frac{x}{2} - \frac{x^2}{b} + \frac{x^3}{2b^2}\right) dx = h^2\left[\frac{x^2}{4} - \frac{x^3}{3b} + \frac{x^4}{8b^2}\right]_0^b$$

$$I_{xy} = \tfrac{1}{24}b^2h^2 \qquad \blacktriangleleft$$

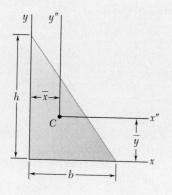

b. Product of Inertia $\bar{I}_{x''y''}$.
The coordinates of the centroid of the triangle relative to the x and y axes are

$$\bar{x} = \tfrac{1}{3}b \qquad \bar{y} = \tfrac{1}{3}h$$

Using the expression for I_{xy} obtained in part a, we apply the parallel-axis theorem and write

$$I_{xy} = \bar{I}_{x''y''} + \bar{x}\,\bar{y}A$$
$$\tfrac{1}{24}b^2h^2 = \bar{I}_{x''y''} + (\tfrac{1}{3}b)(\tfrac{1}{3}h)(\tfrac{1}{2}bh)$$
$$\bar{I}_{x''y''} = \tfrac{1}{24}b^2h^2 - \tfrac{1}{18}b^2h^2$$

$$\bar{I}_{x''y''} = -\tfrac{1}{72}b^2h^2 \qquad \blacktriangleleft$$

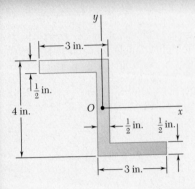

SAMPLE PROBLEM 9.7

For the section shown, the moments of inertia with respect to the x and y axes have been computed and are known to be

$$I_x = 10.38 \text{ in}^4 \qquad I_y = 6.97 \text{ in}^4$$

Determine (a) the orientation of the principal axes of the section about O, (b) the values of the principal moments of inertia of the section about O.

SOLUTION

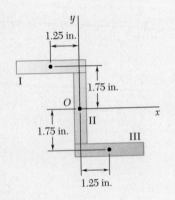

We first compute the product of inertia with respect to the x and y axes. The area is divided into three rectangles as shown. We note that the product of inertia $\bar{I}_{x'y'}$ with respect to centroidal axes parallel to the x and y axes is zero for each rectangle. Using the parallel-axis theorem $I_{xy} = \bar{I}_{x'y'} + \bar{x}\,\bar{y}A$, we find that I_{xy} reduces to $\bar{x}\,\bar{y}A$ for each rectangle.

Rectangle	Area, in²	$\bar{x}$, in.	$\bar{y}$, in.	$\bar{x}\bar{y}A$, in⁴
I	1.5	−1.25	+1.75	−3.28
II	1.5	0	0	0
III	1.5	+1.25	−1.75	−3.28
				$\Sigma\bar{x}\bar{y}A = -6.56$

$$I_{xy} = \Sigma\bar{x}\,\bar{y}A = -6.56 \text{ in}^4$$

a. Principal Axes. Since the magnitudes of I_x, I_y, and I_{xy} are known, Eq. (9.25) is used to determine the values of θ_m:

$$\tan 2\theta_m = -\frac{2I_{xy}}{I_x - I_y} = -\frac{2(-6.56)}{10.38 - 6.97} = +3.85$$

$$2\theta_m = 75.4° \text{ and } 255.4°$$

$$\theta_m = 37.7° \quad \text{and} \quad \theta_m = 127.7° \quad \blacktriangleleft$$

b. Principal Moments of Inertia. Using Eq. (9.27), we write

$$I_{\text{max,min}} = \frac{I_x + I_y}{2} \pm \sqrt{\left(\frac{I_x - I_y}{2}\right)^2 + I_{xy}^2}$$

$$= \frac{10.38 + 6.97}{2} \pm \sqrt{\left(\frac{10.38 - 6.97}{2}\right)^2 + (-6.56)^2}$$

$$I_{\text{max}} = 15.45 \text{ in}^4 \qquad I_{\text{min}} = 1.897 \text{ in}^4 \quad \blacktriangleleft$$

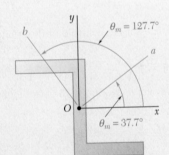

Noting that the elements of the area of the section are more closely distributed about the b axis than about the a axis, we conclude that $I_a = I_{\text{max}} = 15.45 \text{ in}^4$ and $I_b = I_{\text{min}} = 1.897 \text{ in}^4$. This conclusion can be verified by substituting $\theta = 37.7°$ into Eqs. (9.18) and (9.19).

SOLVING PROBLEMS
ON YOUR OWN

In the problems for this lesson, you will continue your work with *moments of inertia* and will utilize various techniques for computing *products of inertia*. Although the problems are generally straightforward, several items are worth noting.

1. **Calculating the product of inertia I_{xy} by integration.** We defined this quantity as

$$I_{xy} = \int xy \, dA \qquad (9.12)$$

and stated that its value can be positive, negative, or zero. The product of inertia can be computed directly from the above equation using double integration, or it can be determined using single integration as shown in Sample Prob. 9.6. When applying the latter technique and using the parallel-axis theorem, it is important to remember that $\bar{x}_{el}$ and $\bar{y}_{el}$ in the equation

$$dI_{xy} = dI_{x'y'} + \bar{x}_{el}\bar{y}_{el} \, dA$$

are the coordinates of the centroid of the element of area dA. Thus, if dA is not in the first quadrant, one or both of these coordinates will be negative.

2. **Calculating the products of inertia of composite areas.** They can easily be computed from the products of inertia of their component parts by using the parallel-axis theorem

$$I_{xy} = \bar{I}_{x'y'} + \bar{x}\bar{y}A \qquad (9.13)$$

The proper technique to use for problems of this type is illustrated in Sample Probs. 9.6 and 9.7. In addition to the usual rules for composite-area problems, it is essential that you remember the following points.

    a. If either of the centroidal axes of a component area is an axis of symmetry for that area, the product of inertia $\bar{I}_{x'y'}$ for that area is zero. Thus, $\bar{I}_{x'y'}$ is zero for component areas such as circles, semicircles, rectangles, and isosceles triangles which possess an axis of symmetry parallel to one of the coordinate axes.

    b. Pay careful attention to the signs of the coordinates $\bar{x}$ and $\bar{y}$ of each component area when you use the parallel-axis theorem [Sample Prob. 9.7].

3. **Determining the moments of inertia and the product of inertia for rotated coordinate axes.** In Sec. 9.9 we derived Eqs. (9.18), (9.19), and (9.20), from which the moments of inertia and the product of inertia can be computed for coordinate axes which have been rotated about the origin O. To apply these equations, you must know a set of values I_x, I_y, and I_{xy} for a given orientation of the axes, and you must remember that θ is positive for counterclockwise rotations of the axes and negative for clockwise rotations of the axes.

4. **Computing the principal moments of inertia.** We showed in Sec. 9.9 that there is a particular orientation of the coordinate axes for which the moments of inertia attain their maximum and minimum values, I_{max} and I_{min}, and for which the product of inertia is zero. Equation (9.27) can be used to compute these values, known as the *principal moments of inertia* of the area about O. The corresponding axes are referred to as the *principal axes* of the area about O, and their orientation is defined by Eq. (9.25). *To determine which of the principal axes corresponds to I_{max} and which corresponds to I_{min},* you can either follow the procedure outlined in the text after Eq. (9.27) or observe about which of the two principal axes the area is more closely distributed; that axis corresponds to I_{min} [Sample Prob. 9.7].

PROBLEMS

9.67 through 9.70 Determine by direct integration the product of inertia of the given area with respect to the x and y axes.

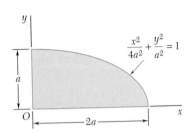

Fig. P9.67

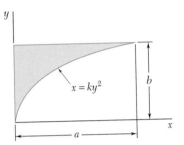

Fig. P9.68

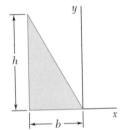

Fig. P9.69

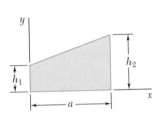

Fig. P9.70

9.71 through 9.74 Using the parallel-axis theorem, determine the product of inertia of the area shown with respect to the centroidal x and y axes.

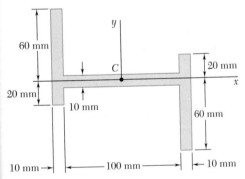

Fig. P9.71

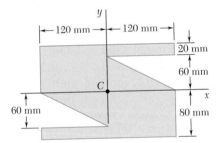

Fig. P9.72

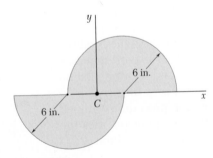

Fig. P9.73

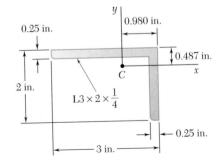

Fig. P9.74

9.75 through 9.78 Using the parallel-axis theorem, determine the product of inertia of the area shown with respect to the centroidal x and y axes.

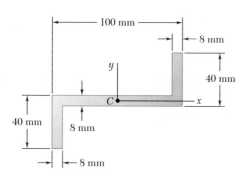

Fig. P9.75

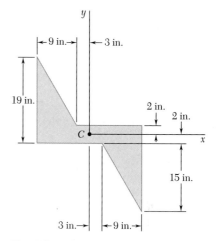

Fig. P9.76

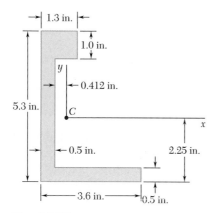

Fig. P9.77

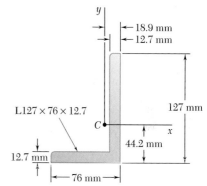

Fig. P9.78

9.79 Determine for the quarter ellipse of Prob. 9.67 the moments of inertia and the product of inertia with respect to new axes obtained by rotating the x and y axes about O (a) through 45° counterclockwise, (b) through 30° clockwise.

9.80 Determine the moments of inertia and the product of inertia of the area of Prob. 9.72 with respect to new centroidal axes obtained by rotating the x and y axes 30° counterclockwise.

9.81 Determine the moments of inertia and the product of inertia of the area of Prob. 9.73 with respect to new centroidal axes obtained by rotating the x and y axes 60° counterclockwise.

9.82 Determine the moments of inertia and the product of inertia of the area of Prob. 9.75 with respect to new centroidal axes obtained by rotating the x and y axes 45° clockwise.

9.83 Determine the moments of inertia and the product of inertia of the L3 × 2 × $\frac{1}{4}$-in. angle cross section of Prob. 9.74 with respect to new centroidal axes obtained by rotating the x and y axes 30° clockwise.

9.84 Determine the moments of inertia and the product of inertia of the L127 × 76 × 12.7-mm angle cross section of Prob. 9.78 with respect to new centroidal axes obtained by rotating the x and y axes 45° counterclockwise.

9.85 For the quarter ellipse of Prob. 9.67, determine the orientation of the principal axes at the origin and the corresponding values of the moments of inertia.

9.86 through 9.88 For the area indicated, determine the orientation of the principal axes at the origin and the corresponding values of the moments of inertia.

    9.86 Area of Prob. 9.72
    9.87 Area of Prob. 9.73
    9.88 Area of Prob. 9.75

9.89 and 9.90 For the angle cross section indicated, determine the orientation of the principal axes at the origin and the corresponding values of the moments of inertia.

    9.89 The L3 × 2 × $\frac{1}{4}$-in. angle cross section of Prob. 9.74
    9.90 The L127 × 76 × 12.7-mm angle cross section of Prob. 9.78

*9.10 MOHR'S CIRCLE FOR MOMENTS AND PRODUCTS OF INERTIA

The circle used in the preceding section to illustrate the relations existing between the moments and products of inertia of a given area with respect to axes passing through a fixed point O was first introduced by the German engineer Otto Mohr (1835–1918) and is known as *Mohr's circle*. It will be shown that if the moments and product of inertia of an area A are known with respect to two rectangular x and y axes which pass through a point O, Mohr's circle can be used to graphically determine (a) the principal axes and principal moments of inertia of the area about O and (b) the moments and product of inertia of the area with respect to any other pair of rectangular axes x' and y' through O.

Consider a given area A and two rectangular coordinate axes x and y (Fig. 9.19a). Assuming that the moments of inertia I_x and I_y and the product of inertia I_{xy} are known, we will represent them on a diagram by plotting a point X of coordinates I_x and I_{xy} and a point Y of coordinates I_y and $-I_{xy}$ (Fig. 9.19b). If I_{xy} is positive, as assumed in Fig. 9.19a, point X is located above the horizontal axis and point Y is located below, as shown in Fig. 9.19b. If I_{xy} is negative, X is located below the horizontal axis and Y is located above. Joining X and Y with a straight line, we denote by C the point of intersection of line XY with the horizontal axis and draw the circle of center C and diameter XY. Noting that the abscissa of C and the radius of the circle are respectively equal to the quantities I_{ave} and R defined by the formula (9.23), we conclude that the circle obtained is Mohr's circle for the given area about point O. Thus, the abscissas of the points A and B where the circle intersects the horizontal axis represent respectively the principal moments of inertia I_{max} and I_{min} of the area.

We also note that, since $\tan (XCA) = 2I_{xy}/(I_x - I_y)$, the angle XCA is equal in magnitude to one of the angles $2\theta_m$ which satisfy Eq. (9.25);

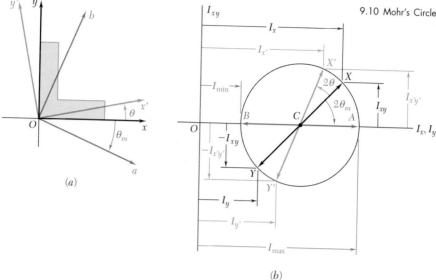

(a)

(b)

Fig. 9.19

thus, the angle θ_m, which defines in Fig. 9.19a the principal axis Oa corresponding to point A in Fig. 9.19b, is equal to half of the angle XCA of Mohr's circle. We further observe that if $I_x > I_y$ and $I_{xy} > 0$, as in the case considered here, the rotation which brings CX into CA is clockwise. Also, under these conditions, the angle θ_m obtained from Eq. (9.25), which defines the principal axis Oa in Fig. 9.19a, is negative; thus, the rotation which brings Ox into Oa is also clockwise. We conclude that the senses of rotation in both parts of Fig. 9.19 are the same. If a clockwise rotation through $2\theta_m$ is required to bring CX into CA on Mohr's circle, a clockwise rotation through θ_m will bring Ox into the corresponding principal axis Oa in Fig. 9.19a.

Since Mohr's circle is uniquely defined, the same circle can be obtained by considering the moments and product of inertia of the area A with respect to the rectangular axes x' and y' (Fig. 9.19a). The point X' of coordinates $I_{x'}$ and $I_{x'y'}$ and the point Y' of coordinates $I_{y'}$ and $-I_{x'y'}$ are thus located on Mohr's circle, and the angle $X'CA$ in Fig. 9.19b must be equal to twice the angle $x'Oa$ in Fig. 9.19a. Since, as noted above, the angle XCA is twice the angle xOa, it follows that the angle XCX' in Fig. 9.19b is twice the angle xOx' in Fig. 9.19a. The diameter $X'Y'$, which defines the moments and product of inertia $I_{x'}$, $I_{y'}$, and $I_{x'y'}$ of the given area with respect to rectangular axes x' and y' forming an angle θ with the x and y axes can be obtained by rotating through an angle 2θ the diameter XY which corresponds to the moments and product of inertia I_x, I_y, and I_{xy}. We note that the rotation which brings the diameter XY into the diameter $X'Y'$ in Fig. 9.19b has the same sense as the rotation which brings the x and y axes into the x' and y' axes in Fig. 9.19a.

It should be noted that the use of Mohr's circle is not limited to graphical solutions, i.e., to solutions based on the careful drawing and measuring of the various parameters involved. By merely sketching Mohr's circle and using trigonometry, one can easily derive the various relations required for a numerical solution of a given problem (see Sample Prob. 9.8).

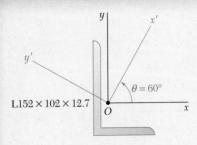

L152 × 102 × 12.7

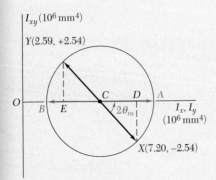

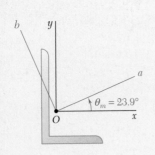

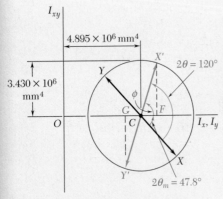

SAMPLE PROBLEM 9.8

For the section shown, the moments and product of inertia with respect to the x and y axes are known to be

$$I_x = 7.20 \times 10^6 \text{ mm}^4 \qquad I_y = 2.59 \times 10^6 \text{ mm}^4 \qquad I_{xy} = -2.54 \times 10^6 \text{ mm}^4$$

Using Mohr's circle, determine (a) the principal axes of the section about O, (b) the values of the principal moments of inertia of the section about O, (c) the moments and product of inertia of the section with respect to the x' and y' axes which form an angle of 60° with the x and y axes.

SOLUTION

Drawing Mohr's Circle. We first plot point X of coordinates $I_x = 7.20$, $I_{xy} = -2.54$, and point Y of coordinates $I_y = 2.59$, $-I_{xy} = +2.54$. Joining X and Y with a straight line, we define the center C of Mohr's circle. The abscissa of C, which represents I_{ave}, and the radius R of the circle can be measured directly or calculated as follows:

$$I_{ave} = OC = \tfrac{1}{2}(I_x + I_y) = \tfrac{1}{2}(7.20 \times 10^6 + 2.59 \times 10^6) = 4.895 \times 10^6 \text{ mm}^4$$
$$CD = \tfrac{1}{2}(I_x - I_y) = \tfrac{1}{2}(7.20 \times 10^6 - 2.59 \times 10^6) = 2.305 \times 10^6 \text{ mm}^4$$
$$R = \sqrt{(CD)^2 + (DX)^2} = \sqrt{(2.305 \times 10^6)^2 + (2.54 \times 10^6)^2}$$
$$= 3.430 \times 10^6 \text{ mm}^4$$

a. Principal Axes. The principal axes of the section correspond to points A and B on Mohr's circle, and the angle through which we should rotate CX to bring it into CA defines $2\theta_m$. We have

$$\tan 2\theta_m = \frac{DX}{CD} = \frac{2.54}{2.305} = 1.102 \qquad 2\theta_m = 47.8° \text{↰} \qquad \theta_m = 23.9° \text{↰} \quad \blacktriangleleft$$

Thus, the principal axis Oa corresponding to the maximum value of the moment of inertia is obtained by rotating the x axis through 23.9° counterclockwise; the principal axis Ob corresponding to the minimum value of the moment of inertia can be obtained by rotating the y axis through the same angle.

b. Principal Moments of Inertia. The principal moments of inertia are represented by the abscissas of A and B. We have

$$I_{max} = OA = OC + CA = I_{ave} + R = (4.895 + 3.430)10^6 \text{ mm}^4$$
$$I_{max} = 8.33 \times 10^6 \text{ mm}^4 \quad \blacktriangleleft$$
$$I_{min} = OB = OC - BC = I_{ave} - R = (4.895 - 3.430)10^6 \text{ mm}^4$$
$$I_{min} = 1.47 \times 10^6 \text{ mm}^4 \quad \blacktriangleleft$$

c. Moments and Product of Inertia with Respect to the x' and y' Axes. On Mohr's circle, the points X' and Y', which correspond to the x' and y' axes, are obtained by rotating CX and CY through an angle $2\theta = 2(60°) = 120°$ counterclockwise. The coordinates of X' and Y' yield the desired moments and product of inertia. Noting that the angle that CX' forms with the horizontal axis is $\phi = 120° - 47.8° = 72.2°$, we write

$$I_{x'} = OF = OC + CF = 4.895 \times 10^6 \text{ mm}^4 + (3.430 \times 10^6 \text{ mm}^4) \cos 72.2°$$
$$I_{x'} = 5.94 \times 10^6 \text{ mm}^4 \quad \blacktriangleleft$$
$$I_{y'} = OG = OC - GC = 4.895 \times 10^6 \text{ mm}^4 - (3.430 \times 10^6 \text{ mm}^4) \cos 72.2°$$
$$I_{y'} = 3.85 \times 10^6 \text{ mm}^4 \quad \blacktriangleleft$$
$$I_{x'y'} = FX' = (3.430 \times 10^6 \text{ mm}^4) \sin 72.2°$$
$$I_{x'y'} = 3.27 \times 10^6 \text{ mm}^4 \quad \blacktriangleleft$$

SOLVING PROBLEMS
ON YOUR OWN

In the problems for this lesson, you will use *Mohr's circle* to determine the moments and products of inertia of a given area for different orientations of the coordinate axes. Although in some cases using Mohr's circle may not be as direct as substituting into the appropriate equations [Eqs. (9.18) through (9.20)], this method of solution has the advantage of providing a visual representation of the relationships among the various variables. Further, Mohr's circle shows all of the values of the moments and products of inertia which are possible for a given problem.

Using Mohr's circle. The underlying theory was presented in Sec. 9.9, and we discussed the application of this method in Sec. 9.10 and in Sample Prob. 9.8. In the same problem, we presented the steps you should follow to determine the *principal axes,* the *principal moments of inertia,* and the *moments and product of inertia with respect to a specified orientation of the coordinates axes.* When you use Mohr's circle to solve problems, it is important that you remember the following points.

a. Mohr's circle is completely defined by the quantities R and I_{ave}, which represent, respectively, the radius of the circle and the distance from the origin O to the center C of the circle. These quantities can be obtained from Eqs. (9.23) if the moments and product of inertia are known for a given orientation of the axes. However, Mohr's circle can be defined by other combinations of known values [Probs. 9.103, 9.106, and 9.107]. For these cases, it may be necessary to first make one or more assumptions, such as choosing an arbitrary location for the center when I_{ave} is unknown, assigning relative magnitudes to the moments of inertia (for example, $I_x > I_y$), or selecting the sign of the product of inertia.

b. Point X of coordinates (I_x, I_{xy}) and point Y of coordinates $(I_y, -I_{xy})$ are both located on Mohr's circle and are diametrically opposite.

c. Since moments of inertia must be positive, the entire Mohr's circle must lie to the right of the I_{xy} axis; it follows that $I_{ave} > R$ for all cases.

d. As the coordinate axes are rotated through an angle θ, the associated rotation of the diameter of Mohr's circle is equal to 2θ and is in the same sense (clockwise or counterclockwise). We strongly suggest that the known points on the circumference of the circle be labeled with the appropriate capital letter, as was done in Fig. 9.19b and for the Mohr circles of Sample Prob. 9.8. This will enable you to determine, for each value of θ, the sign of the corresponding product of inertia and to determine which moment of inertia is associated with each of the coordinate axes [Sample Prob. 9.8, parts *a* and *c*].

Although we have introduced Mohr's circle within the specific context of the study of moments and products of inertia, the Mohr circle technique is also applicable to the solution of analogous but physically different problems in mechanics of materials. This multiple use of a specific technique is not unique, and as you pursue your engineering studies, you will encounter several methods of solution which can be applied to a variety of problems.

PROBLEMS

9.91 Using Mohr's circle, determine for the quarter ellipse of Prob. 9.67 the moments of inertia and the product of inertia with respect to new axes obtained by rotating the x and y axes about O (a) through 45° counterclockwise, (b) through 30° clockwise.

9.92 Using Mohr's circle, determine the moments of inertia and the product of inertia of the area of Prob. 9.72 with respect to new centroidal axes obtained by rotating the x and y axes 30° counterclockwise.

9.93 Using Mohr's circle, determine the moments of inertia and the product of inertia of the area of Prob. 9.73 with respect to new centroidal axes obtained by rotating the x and y axes 60° counterclockwise.

9.94 Using Mohr's circle, determine the moments of inertia and the product of inertia of the area of Prob. 9.75 with respect to new centroidal axes obtained by rotating the x and y axes 45° clockwise.

9.95 Using Mohr's circle, determine the moments of inertia and the product of inertia of the L3 × 2 × $\frac{1}{4}$-in. angle cross section of Prob. 9.74 with respect to new centroidal axes obtained by rotating the x and y axes 30° clockwise.

9.96 Using Mohr's circle, determine the moments of inertia and the product of inertia of the L127 × 76 × 12.7-mm angle cross section of Prob. 9.78 with respect to new centroidal axes obtained by rotating the x and y axes 45° counterclockwise.

9.97 For the quarter ellipse of Prob. 9.67, use Mohr's circle to determine the orientation of the principal axes at the origin and the corresponding values of the moments of inertia.

9.98 through 9.102 Using Mohr's circle, determine for the area indicated the orientation of the principal centroidal axes and the corresponding values of the moments of inertia.
   9.98 Area of Prob. 9.72
   9.99 Area of Prob. 9.76
   9.100 Area of Prob. 9.73
   9.101 Area of Prob. 9.74
   9.102 Area of Prob. 9.77
(The moments of inertia $\bar{I}_x$ and $\bar{I}_y$ of the area of Prob. 9.102 were determined in Prob. 9.44.)

9.103 The moments and product of inertia of an L4 × 3 × $\frac{1}{4}$-in. angle cross section with respect to two rectangular axes x and y through C are, respectively, $\bar{I}_x = 1.33$ in⁴, $\bar{I}_y = 2.75$ in⁴, and $\bar{I}_{xy} < 0$, with the minimum value of the moment of inertia of the area with respect to any axis through C being $\bar{I}_{min} = 0.692$ in⁴. Using Mohr's circle, determine (a) the product of inertia $\bar{I}_{xy}$ of the area, (b) the orientation of the principal axes, (c) the value of $\bar{I}_{max}$.

9.104 and 9.105 Using Mohr's circle, determine for the cross section of the rolled-steel angle shown the orientation of the principal centroidal axes and the corresponding values of the moments of inertia. (Properties of the cross sections are given in Fig. 9.13.)

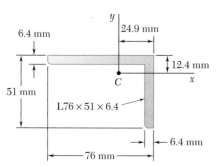

Fig. P9.104

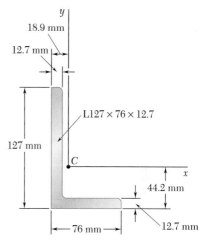

Fig. P9.105

*9.106 For a given area the moments of inertia with respect to two rectangular centroidal x and y axes are $\bar{I}_x = 1200$ in^4 and $\bar{I}_y = 300$ in^4, respectively. Knowing that after rotating the x and y axes about the centroid $30°$ counterclockwise, the moment of inertia relative to the rotated x axis is 1450 in^4, use Mohr's circle to determine (*a*) the orientation of the principal axes, (*b*) the principal centroidal moments of inertia.

9.107 It is known that for a given area $\bar{I}_y = 48 \times 10^6$ mm^4 and $\bar{I}_{xy} = -20 \times 10^6$ mm^4, where the x and y axes are rectangular centroidal axes. If the axis corresponding to the maximum product of inertia is obtained by rotating the x axis $67.5°$ counterclockwise about C, use Mohr's circle to determine (*a*) the moment of inertia $\bar{I}_x$ of the area, (*b*) the principal centroidal moments of inertia.

9.108 Using Mohr's circle, show that for any regular polygon (such as a pentagon) (*a*) the moment of inertia with respect to every axis through the centroid is the same, (*b*) the product of inertia with respect to every pair of rectangular axes through the centroid is zero.

9.109 Using Mohr's circle, prove that the expression $I_{x'}I_{y'} - I_{x'y'}^2$ is independent of the orientation of the x' and y' axes, where $I_{x'}$, $I_{y'}$, and $I_{x'y'}$ represent the moments and product of inertia, respectively, of a given area with respect to a pair of rectangular axes x' and y' through a given point O. Also show that the given expression is equal to the square of the length of the tangent drawn from the origin of the coordinate system to Mohr's circle.

9.110 Using the invariance property established in the preceding problem, express the product of inertia I_{xy} of an area A with respect to a pair of rectangular axes through O in terms of the moments of inertia I_x and I_y of A and the principal moments of inertia $I_{\min}$ and $I_{\max}$ of A about O. Use the formula obtained to calculate the product of inertia I_{xy} of the L3 $\times$ 2 $\times$ $\frac{1}{4}$-in. angle cross section shown in Fig. 9.13A, knowing that its maximum moment of inertia is 1.257 in^4.

MOMENTS OF INERTIA OF MASSES

9.11 MOMENT OF INERTIA OF A MASS

Consider a small mass Δm mounted on a rod of negligible mass which can rotate freely about an axis AA' (Fig. 9.20a). If a couple is applied to the system, the rod and mass, assumed to be initially at rest, will start rotating about AA'. The details of this motion will be studied later in dynamics. At present, we wish only to indicate that the time required for the system to reach a given speed of rotation is proportional to the mass Δm and to the square of the distance r. The product $r^2\,\Delta m$ provides, therefore, a measure of the *inertia* of the system, i.e., a measure of the resistance the system offers when we try to set it in motion. For this reason, the product $r^2\,\Delta m$ is called the *moment of inertia* of the mass Δm with respect to the axis AA'.

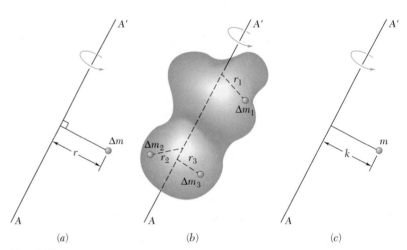

Fig. 9.20

Consider now a body of mass m which is to be rotated about an axis AA' (Fig. 9.20b). Dividing the body into elements of mass Δm_1, Δm_2, etc., we find that the body's resistance to being rotated is measured by the sum $r_1^2\,\Delta m_1 + r_2^2\,\Delta m_2 + \cdots$. This sum defines, therefore, the moment of inertia of the body with respect to the axis AA'. Increasing the number of elements, we find that the moment of inertia is equal, in the limit, to the integral

$$I = \int r^2\,dm \tag{9.28}$$

The *radius of gyration* k of the body with respect to the axis AA' is defined by the relation

$$I = k^2 m \qquad \text{or} \qquad k = \sqrt{\frac{I}{m}} \qquad (9.29)$$

The radius of gyration k represents, therefore, the distance at which the entire mass of the body should be concentrated if its moment of inertia with respect to AA' is to remain unchanged (Fig. 9.20c). Whether it is kept in its original shape (Fig. 9.20b) or whether it is concentrated as shown in Fig. 9.20c, the mass m will react in the same way to a rotation, or *gyration*, about AA'.

If SI units are used, the radius of gyration k is expressed in meters and the mass m in kilograms, and thus the unit used for the moment of inertia of a mass is $\text{kg} \cdot \text{m}^2$. If U.S. customary units are used, the radius of gyration is expressed in feet and the mass in slugs (i.e., in $\text{lb} \cdot \text{s}^2/\text{ft}$), and thus the derived unit used for the moment of inertia of a mass is $\text{lb} \cdot \text{ft} \cdot \text{s}^2$.†

The moment of inertia of a body with respect to a coordinate axis can easily be expressed in terms of the coordinates x, y, z of the element of mass dm (Fig. 9.21). Noting, for example, that the square of the distance r from the element dm to the y axis is $z^2 + x^2$, we express the moment of inertia of the body with respect to the y axis as

$$I_y = \int r^2 \, dm = \int (z^2 + x^2) \, dm$$

Similar expressions can be obtained for the moments of inertia with respect to the x and z axes. We write

$$I_x = \int (y^2 + z^2) \, dm$$

$$I_y = \int (z^2 + x^2) \, dm \qquad (9.30)$$

$$I_z = \int (x^2 + y^2) \, dm$$

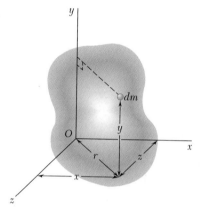

Fig. 9.21

Photo 9.2 As you will discuss in your dynamics course, the rotational behavior of the camshaft shown is dependent upon the mass moment of inertia of the camshaft with respect to its axis of rotation.

†It should be kept in mind when converting the moment of inertia of a mass from U.S. customary units to SI units that the base unit *pound* used in the derived unit $\text{lb} \cdot \text{ft} \cdot \text{s}^2$ is a unit of force (*not* of mass) and should therefore be converted into newtons. We have

$$1 \text{ lb} \cdot \text{ft} \cdot \text{s}^2 = (4.45 \text{ N})(0.3048 \text{ m})(1 \text{ s})^2 = 1.356 \text{ N} \cdot \text{m} \cdot \text{s}^2$$

or, since $1 \text{ N} = 1 \text{ kg} \cdot \text{m/s}^2$,

$$1 \text{ lb} \cdot \text{ft} \cdot \text{s}^2 = 1.356 \text{ kg} \cdot \text{m}^2$$

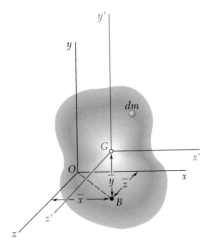

Fig. 9.22

9.12 PARALLEL-AXIS THEOREM

Consider a body of mass m. Let $Oxyz$ be a system of rectangular coordinates whose origin is at the arbitrary point O, and $Gx'y'z'$ a system of parallel *centroidal axes*, i.e., a system whose origin is at the center of gravity G of the body† and whose axes x', y', z' are parallel to the $x, y,$ and z axes, respectively (Fig. 9.22). Denoting by $\bar{x}, \bar{y}, \bar{z}$ the coordinates of G with respect to $Oxyz$, we write the following relations between the coordinates x, y, z of the element dm with respect to $Oxyz$ and its coordinates x', y', z' with respect to the centroidal axes $Gx'y'z'$:

$$x = x' + \bar{x} \qquad y = y' + \bar{y} \qquad z = z' + \bar{z} \tag{9.31}$$

Referring to Eqs. (9.30), we can express the moment of inertia of the body with respect to the x axis as follows:

$$I_x = \int (y^2 + z^2)\, dm = \int [(y' + \bar{y})^2 + (z' + \bar{z})^2]\, dm$$
$$= \int (y'^2 + z'^2)\, dm + 2\bar{y}\int y'\, dm + 2\bar{z}\int z'\, dm + (\bar{y}^2 + \bar{z}^2)\int dm$$

The first integral in this expression represents the moment of inertia $\bar{I}_{x'}$ of the body with respect to the centroidal axis x'; the second and third integrals represent the first moment of the body with respect to the $z'x'$ and $x'y'$ planes, respectively, and, since both planes contain G, the two integrals are zero; the last integral is equal to the total mass m of the body. We write, therefore,

$$I_x = \bar{I}_{x'} + m(\bar{y}^2 + \bar{z}^2) \tag{9.32}$$

and, similarly,

$$I_y = \bar{I}_{y'} + m(\bar{z}^2 + \bar{x}^2) \qquad I_z = \bar{I}_{z'} + m(\bar{x}^2 + \bar{y}^2) \tag{9.32'}$$

We easily verify from Fig. 9.22 that the sum $\bar{z}^2 + \bar{x}^2$ represents the square of the distance OB between the y and y' axes. Similarly, $\bar{y}^2 + \bar{z}^2$ and $\bar{x}^2 + \bar{y}^2$ represent the squares of the distance between the x and x' axes and the z and z' axes, respectively. Denoting by d the distance between an arbitrary axis AA' and a parallel centroidal axis BB' (Fig. 9.23), we can, therefore, write the following general relation between the moment of inertia I of the body with respect to AA' and its moment of inertia $\bar{I}$ with respect to BB':

$$I = \bar{I} + md^2 \tag{9.33}$$

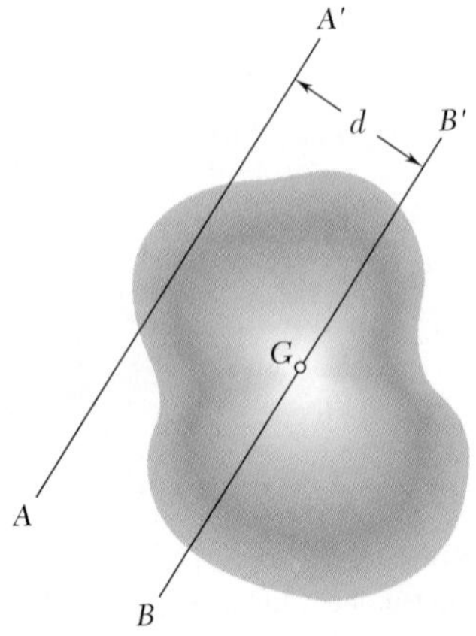

Expressing the moments of inertia in terms of the corresponding radii of gyration, we can also write

$$k^2 = \bar{k}^2 + d^2 \tag{9.34}$$

where k and $\bar{k}$ represent the radii of gyration of the body about AA' and BB', respectively.

Fig. 9.23

†Note that the term *centroidal* is used here to define an axis passing through the center of gravity G of the body, whether or not G coincides with the centroid of the volume of the body.

9.13 MOMENTS OF INERTIA OF THIN PLATES

Consider a thin plate of uniform thickness t, which is made of a homogeneous material of density ρ (density = mass per unit volume). The mass moment of inertia of the plate with respect to an axis AA' *contained in the plane* of the plate (Fig. 9.24a) is

$$I_{AA', \text{mass}} = \int r^2 \, dm$$

Since $dm = \rho t \, dA$, we write

$$I_{AA', \text{mass}} = \rho t \int r^2 \, dA$$

But r represents the distance of the element of area dA to the axis

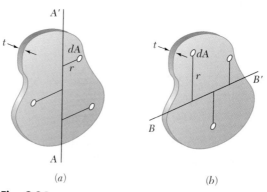

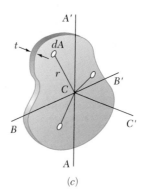

(a) (b) (c)

Fig. 9.24

AA'; the integral is therefore equal to the moment of inertia of the area of the plate with respect to AA'. We have

$$I_{AA',\text{mass}} = \rho t I_{AA',\text{area}} \tag{9.35}$$

Similarly, for an axis BB' which is contained in the plane of the plate and is perpendicular to AA' (Fig. 9.24b), we have

$$I_{BB',\text{mass}} = \rho t I_{BB',\text{area}} \tag{9.36}$$

Considering now the axis CC' which is *perpendicular* to the plate and passes through the point of intersection C of AA' and BB' (Fig. 9.24c), we write

$$I_{CC',\text{mass}} = \rho t J_{C,\text{area}} \tag{9.37}$$

where J_C is the *polar* moment of inertia of the area of the plate with respect to point C.

Recalling the relation $J_C = I_{AA'} + I_{BB'}$ which exists between polar and rectangular moments of inertia of an area, we write the following relation between the mass moments of inertia of a thin plate:

$$I_{CC'} = I_{AA'} + I_{BB'} \tag{9.38}$$

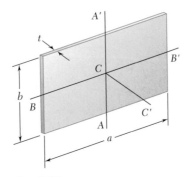

Fig. 9.25

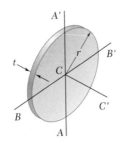

Fig. 9.26

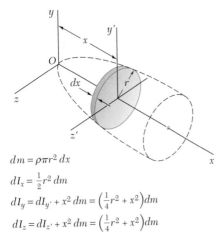

$dm = \rho\pi r^2\, dx$

$dI_x = \frac{1}{2}r^2\, dm$

$dI_y = dI_{y'} + x^2\, dm = \left(\frac{1}{4}r^2 + x^2\right)dm$

$dI_z = dI_{z'} + x^2\, dm = \left(\frac{1}{4}r^2 + x^2\right)dm$

Fig. 9.27 Determination of the moment of inertia of a body of revolution.

Rectangular Plate. In the case of a rectangular plate of sides a and b (Fig. 9.25), we obtain the following mass moments of inertia with respect to axes through the center of gravity of the plate:

$$I_{AA',\text{mass}} = \rho t I_{AA',\text{area}} = \rho t (\tfrac{1}{12}a^3 b)$$
$$I_{BB',\text{mass}} = \rho t I_{BB',\text{area}} = \rho t (\tfrac{1}{12}ab^3)$$

Observing that the product ρabt is equal to the mass m of the plate, we write the mass moments of inertia of a thin rectangular plate as follows:

$$I_{AA'} = \tfrac{1}{12}ma^2 \qquad I_{BB'} = \tfrac{1}{12}mb^2 \tag{9.39}$$
$$I_{CC'} = I_{AA'} + I_{BB'} = \tfrac{1}{12}m(a^2 + b^2) \tag{9.40}$$

Circular Plate. In the case of a circular plate, or disk, of radius r (Fig. 9.26), we write

$$I_{AA',\text{mass}} = \rho t I_{AA',\text{area}} = \rho t (\tfrac{1}{4}\pi r^4)$$

Observing that the product $\rho\pi r^2 t$ is equal to the mass m of the plate and that $I_{AA'} = I_{BB'}$, we write the mass moments of inertia of a circular plate as follows:

$$I_{AA'} = I_{BB'} = \tfrac{1}{4}mr^2 \tag{9.41}$$
$$I_{CC'} = I_{AA'} + I_{BB'} = \tfrac{1}{2}mr^2 \tag{9.42}$$

9.14 DETERMINATION OF THE MOMENT OF INERTIA OF A THREE-DIMENSIONAL BODY BY INTEGRATION

The moment of inertia of a three-dimensional body is obtained by evaluating the integral $I = \int r^2\, dm$. If the body is made of a homogeneous material of density ρ, the element of mass dm is equal to $\rho\, dV$ and we can write $I = \rho \int r^2\, dV$. This integral depends only upon the shape of the body. Thus, in order to compute the moment of inertia of a three-dimensional body, it will generally be necessary to perform a triple, or at least a double, integration.

However, if the body possesses two planes of symmetry, it is usually possible to determine the body's moment of inertia with a single integration by choosing as the element of mass dm a thin slab which is perpendicular to the planes of symmetry. In the case of bodies of revolution, for example, the element of mass would be a thin disk (Fig. 9.27). Using formula (9.42), the moment of inertia of the disk with respect to the axis of revolution can be expressed as indicated in Fig. 9.27. Its moment of inertia with respect to each of the other two coordinate axes is obtained by using formula (9.41) and the parallel-axis theorem. Integration of the expression obtained yields the desired moment of inertia of the body.

9.15 MOMENTS OF INERTIA OF COMPOSITE BODIES

The moments of inertia of a few common shapes are shown in Fig. 9.28. For a body consisting of several of these simple shapes, the moment of inertia of the body with respect to a given axis can be obtained by first computing the moments of inertia of its component parts about the desired axis and then adding them together. As was the case for areas, the radius of gyration of a composite body *cannot* be obtained by adding the radii of gyration of its componet parts.

Slender rod	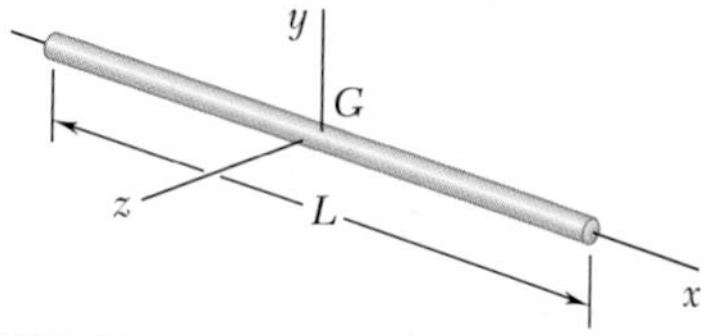	$I_y = I_z = \frac{1}{12} mL^2$
Thin rectangular plate	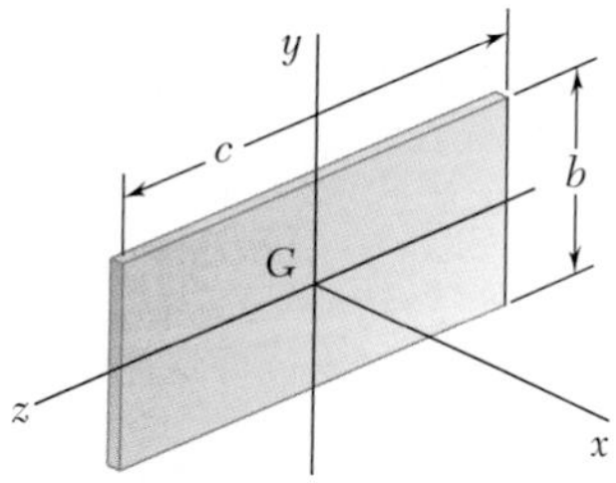	$I_x = \frac{1}{12} m(b^2 + c^2)$ $I_y = \frac{1}{12} mc^2$ $I_z = \frac{1}{12} mb^2$
Rectangular prism	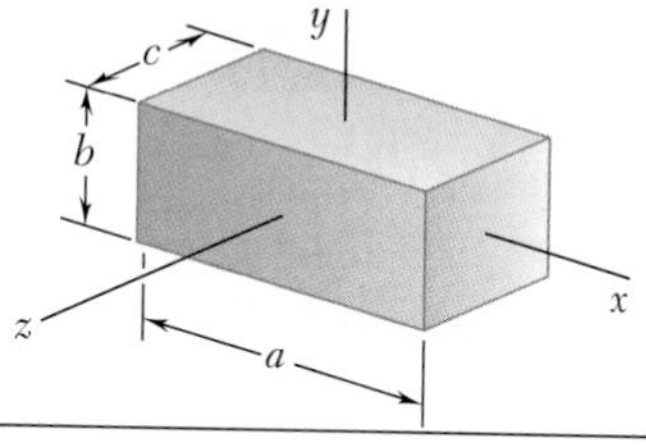	$I_x = \frac{1}{12} m(b^2 + c^2)$ $I_y = \frac{1}{12} m(c^2 + a^2)$ $I_z = \frac{1}{12} m(a^2 + b^2)$
Thin disk	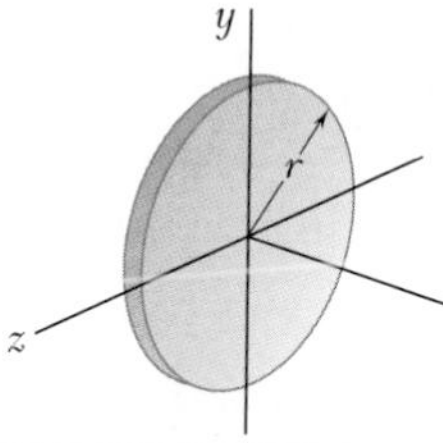	$I_x = \frac{1}{2} mr^2$ $I_y = I_z = \frac{1}{4} mr^2$
Circular cylinder	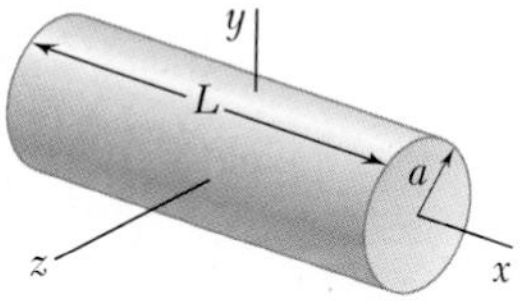	$I_x = \frac{1}{2} ma^2$ $I_y = I_z = \frac{1}{12} m(3a^2 + L^2)$
Circular cone	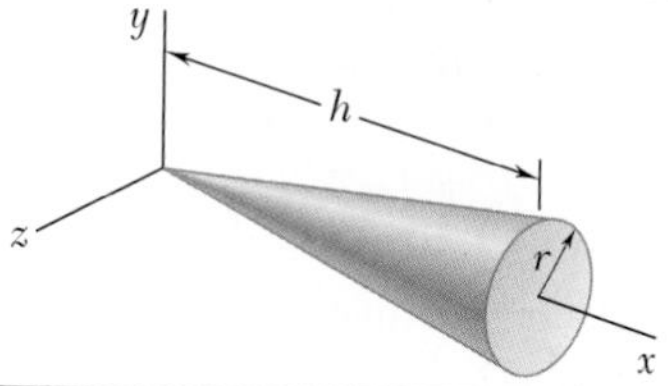	$I_x = \frac{3}{10} ma^2$ $I_y = I_z = \frac{3}{5} m(\frac{1}{4} a^2 + h^2)$
Sphere	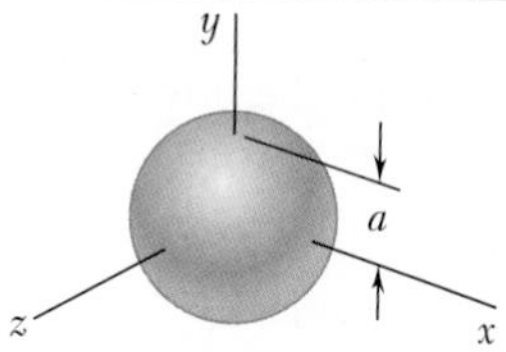	$I_x = I_y = I_z = \frac{2}{5} ma^2$

Fig. 9.28 Mass moments of inertia of common geometric shapes.

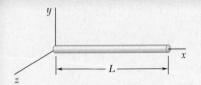

SAMPLE PROBLEM 9.9

Determine the moment of inertia of a slender rod of length L and mass m with respect to an axis which is perpendicular to the rod and passes through one end of the rod.

SOLUTION

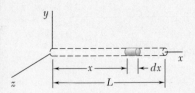

Choosing the differential element of mass shown, we write

$$dm = \frac{m}{L}dx$$

$$I_y = \int x^2 \, dm = \int_0^L x^2 \frac{m}{L}dx = \left[\frac{m}{L}\frac{x^3}{3}\right]_0^L \qquad I_y = \tfrac{1}{3}mL^2 \blacktriangleleft$$

SAMPLE PROBLEM 9.10

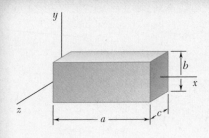

For the homogeneous rectangular prism shown, determine the moment of inertia with respect to the z axis.

SOLUTION

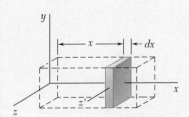

We choose as the differential element of mass the thin slab shown; thus

$$dm = \rho bc \, dx$$

Referring to Sec. 9.13, we find that the moment of inertia of the element with respect to the z' axis is

$$dI_{z'} = \tfrac{1}{12}b^2 \, dm$$

Applying the parallel-axis theorem, we obtain the mass moment of inertia of the slab with respect to the z axis.

$$dI_z = dI_{z'} + x^2 \, dm = \tfrac{1}{12}b^2 \, dm + x^2 \, dm = (\tfrac{1}{12}b^2 + x^2)\rho bc \, dx$$

Integrating from $x = 0$ to $x = a$, we obtain

$$I_z = \int dI_z = \int_0^a (\tfrac{1}{12}b^2 + x^2)\rho bc \, dx = \rho abc(\tfrac{1}{12}b^2 + \tfrac{1}{3}a^2)$$

Since the total mass of the prism is $m = \rho abc$, we can write

$$I_z = m(\tfrac{1}{12}b^2 + \tfrac{1}{3}a^2) \qquad I_z = \tfrac{1}{12}m(4a^2 + b^2) \blacktriangleleft$$

We note that if the prism is thin, b is small compared to a, and the expression for I_z reduces to $\tfrac{1}{3}ma^2$, which is the result obtained in Sample Prob. 9.9 when $L = a$.

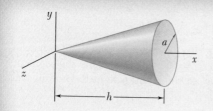

SAMPLE PROBLEM 9.11

Determine the moment of inertia of a right circular cone with respect to (a) its longitudinal axis, (b) an axis through the apex of the cone and perpendicular to its longitudinal axis, (c) an axis through the centroid of the cone and perpendicular to its longitudinal axis.

SOLUTION

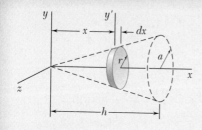

We choose the differential element of mass shown.

$$r = a\frac{x}{h} \qquad dm = \rho\pi r^2\,dx = \rho\pi\frac{a^2}{h^2}x^2\,dx$$

a. Moment of Inertia I_x. Using the expression derived in Sec. 9.13 for a thin disk, we compute the mass moment of inertia of the differential element with respect to the x axis.

$$dI_x = \tfrac{1}{2}r^2\,dm = \tfrac{1}{2}\left(a\frac{x}{h}\right)^2\left(\rho\pi\frac{a^2}{h^2}x^2\,dx\right) = \tfrac{1}{2}\rho\pi\frac{a^4}{h^4}x^4\,dx$$

Integrating from $x = 0$ to $x = h$, we obtain

$$I_x = \int dI_x = \int_0^h \tfrac{1}{2}\rho\pi\frac{a^4}{h^4}x^4\,dx = \tfrac{1}{2}\rho\pi\frac{a^4}{h^4}\frac{h^5}{5} = \tfrac{1}{10}\rho\pi a^4 h$$

Since the total mass of the cone is $m = \tfrac{1}{3}\rho\pi a^2 h$, we can write

$$I_x = \tfrac{1}{10}\rho\pi a^4 h = \tfrac{3}{10}a^2(\tfrac{1}{3}\rho\pi a^2 h) = \tfrac{3}{10}ma^2 \qquad I_x = \tfrac{3}{10}ma^2 \quad \blacktriangleleft$$

b. Moment of Inertia I_y. The same differential element is used. Applying the parallel-axis theorem and using the expression derived in Sec. 9.13 for a thin disk, we write

$$dI_y = dI_{y'} + x^2\,dm = \tfrac{1}{4}r^2\,dm + x^2\,dm = (\tfrac{1}{4}r^2 + x^2)\,dm$$

Substituting the expressions for r and dm into the equation, we obtain

$$dI_y = \left(\frac{1}{4}\frac{a^2}{h^2}x^2 + x^2\right)\left(\rho\pi\frac{a^2}{h^2}x^2\,dx\right) = \rho\pi\frac{a^2}{h^2}\left(\frac{a^2}{4h^2} + 1\right)x^4\,dx$$

$$I_y = \int dI_y = \int_0^h \rho\pi\frac{a^2}{h^2}\left(\frac{a^2}{4h^2} + 1\right)x^4\,dx = \rho\pi\frac{a^2}{h^2}\left(\frac{a^2}{4h^2} + 1\right)\frac{h^5}{5}$$

Introducing the total mass of the cone m, we rewrite I_y as follows:

$$I_y = \tfrac{3}{5}(\tfrac{1}{4}a^2 + h^2)\tfrac{1}{3}\rho\pi a^2 h \qquad I_y = \tfrac{3}{5}m(\tfrac{1}{4}a^2 + h^2) \quad \blacktriangleleft$$

c. Moment of Inertia $I_{y'}$. We apply the parallel-axis theorem and write

$$I_y = \bar{I}_{y''} + m\bar{x}^2$$

Solving for $\bar{I}_{y''}$ and recalling that $\bar{x} = \tfrac{3}{4}h$, we have

$$\bar{I}_{y''} = I_y - m\bar{x}^2 = \tfrac{3}{5}m(\tfrac{1}{4}a^2 + h^2) - m(\tfrac{3}{4}h)^2$$

$$\bar{I}_{y''} = \tfrac{3}{20}m(a^2 + \tfrac{1}{4}h^2) \quad \blacktriangleleft$$

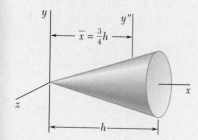

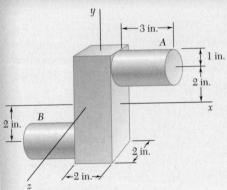

SAMPLE PROBLEM 9.12

A steel forging consists of a 6 × 2 × 2-in. rectangular prism and two cylinders of diameter 2 in. and length 3 in. as shown. Determine the moments of inertia of the forging with respect to the coordinate axes, knowing that the specific weight of steel is 490 lb/ft³.

SOLUTION

Computation of Masses

Prism

$$V = (2 \text{ in.})(2 \text{ in.})(6 \text{ in.}) = 24 \text{ in}^3$$

$$W = \frac{(24 \text{ in}^3)(490 \text{ lb/ft}^3)}{1728 \text{ in}^3/\text{ft}^3} = 6.81 \text{ lb}$$

$$m = \frac{6.81 \text{ lb}}{32.2 \text{ ft/s}^2} = 0.211 \text{ lb} \cdot \text{s}^2/\text{ft}$$

Each Cylinder

$$V = \pi(1 \text{ in.})^2(3 \text{ in.}) = 9.42 \text{ in}^3$$

$$W = \frac{(9.42 \text{ in}^3)(490 \text{ lb/ft}^3)}{1728 \text{ in}^3/\text{ft}^3} = 2.67 \text{ lb}$$

$$m = \frac{2.67 \text{ lb}}{32.2 \text{ ft/s}^2} = 0.0829 \text{ lb} \cdot \text{s}^2/\text{ft}$$

Moments of Inertia. The moments of inertia of each component are computed from Fig. 9.28, using the parallel-axis theorem when necessary. Note that all lengths should be expressed in feet.

Prism

$$I_x = I_z = \tfrac{1}{12}(0.211 \text{ lb} \cdot \text{s}^2/\text{ft})[(\tfrac{6}{12} \text{ ft})^2 + (\tfrac{2}{12} \text{ ft})^2] = 4.88 \times 10^{-3} \text{ lb} \cdot \text{ft} \cdot \text{s}^2$$

$$I_y = \tfrac{1}{12}(0.211 \text{ lb} \cdot \text{s}^2/\text{ft})[(\tfrac{2}{12} \text{ ft})^2 + (\tfrac{2}{12} \text{ ft})^2] = 0.977 \times 10^{-3} \text{ lb} \cdot \text{ft} \cdot \text{s}^2$$

Each Cylinder

$$I_x = \tfrac{1}{2}ma^2 + m\overline{y}^2 = \tfrac{1}{2}(0.0829 \text{ lb} \cdot \text{s}^2/\text{ft})(\tfrac{1}{12} \text{ ft})^2$$
$$+ (0.0829 \text{ lb} \cdot \text{s}^2/\text{ft})(\tfrac{2}{12} \text{ ft})^2 = 2.59 \times 10^{-3} \text{ lb} \cdot \text{ft} \cdot \text{s}^2$$

$$I_y = \tfrac{1}{12}m(3a^2 + L^2) = m\overline{x}^2 = \tfrac{1}{12}(0.0829 \text{ lb} \cdot \text{s}^2/\text{ft})[3(\tfrac{1}{12} \text{ ft})^2 + (\tfrac{3}{12} \text{ ft})^2]$$
$$+ (0.0829 \text{ lb} \cdot \text{s}^2/\text{ft})(\tfrac{2.5}{12} \text{ ft})^2 = 4.17 \times 10^{-3} \text{ lb} \cdot \text{ft} \cdot \text{s}^2$$

$$I_z = \tfrac{1}{12}m(3a^2 + L^2) + m(\overline{x}^2 + \overline{y}^2) = \tfrac{1}{12}(0.0829 \text{ lb} \cdot \text{s}^2/\text{ft})[3(\tfrac{1}{12} \text{ ft})^2 + (\tfrac{3}{12} \text{ ft})^2]$$
$$+ (0.0829 \text{ lb} \cdot \text{s}^2/\text{ft})[(\tfrac{2.5}{12} \text{ ft})^2 + (\tfrac{2}{12} \text{ ft})^2] = 6.48 \times 10^{-3} \text{ lb} \cdot \text{ft} \cdot \text{s}^2$$

Entire Body. Adding the values obtained,

$$I_x = 4.88 \times 10^{-3} + 2(2.59 \times 10^{-3}) \qquad I_x = 10.06 \times 10^{-3} \text{ lb} \cdot \text{ft} \cdot \text{s}^2 \quad \blacktriangleleft$$

$$I_y = 0.977 \times 10^{-3} + 2(4.17 \times 10^{-3}) \qquad I_y = 9.32 \times 10^{-3} \text{ lb} \cdot \text{ft} \cdot \text{s}^2 \quad \blacktriangleleft$$

$$I_z = 4.88 \times 10^{-3} + 2(6.48 \times 10^{-3}) \qquad I_z = 17.84 \times 10^{-3} \text{ lb} \cdot \text{ft} \cdot \text{s}^2 \quad \blacktriangleleft$$

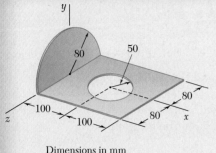

Dimensions in mm

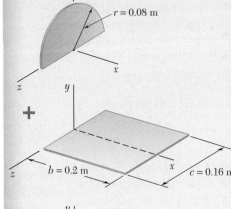

+

−

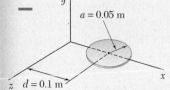

SAMPLE PROBLEM 9.13

A thin steel plate which is 4 mm thick is cut and bent to form the machine part shown. Knowing that the density of steel is 7850 kg/m³, determine the moments of inertia of the machine part with respect to the coordinate axes.

SOLUTION

We observe that the machine part consists of a semicircular plate and a rectangular plate from which a circular plate has been removed.

Computation of Masses. *Semicircular Plate*

$$V_1 = \tfrac{1}{2}\pi r^2 t = \tfrac{1}{2}\pi(0.08 \text{ m})^2(0.004 \text{ m}) = 40.21 \times 10^{-6} \text{ m}^3$$
$$m_1 = \rho V_1 = (7.85 \times 10^3 \text{ kg/m}^3)(40.21 \times 10^{-6} \text{ m}^3) = 0.3156 \text{ kg}$$

Rectangular Plate

$$V_2 = (0.200 \text{ m})(0.160 \text{ m})(0.004 \text{ m}) = 128 \times 10^{-6} \text{ m}^3$$
$$m_2 = \rho V_2 = (7.85 \times 10^3 \text{ kg/m}^3)(128 \times 10^{-6} \text{ m}^3) = 1.005 \text{ kg}$$

Circular Plate

$$V_3 = \pi a^2 t = \pi(0.050 \text{ m})^2(0.004 \text{ m}) = 31.42 \times 10^{-6} \text{ m}^3$$
$$m_3 = \rho V_3 = (7.85 \times 10^3 \text{ kg/m}^3)(31.42 \times 10^{-6} \text{ m}^3) = 0.2466 \text{ kg}$$

Moments of Inertia. Using the method presented in Sec. 9.13, we compute the moments of inertia of each component.

Semicircular Plate. From Fig. 9.28, we observe that for a circular plate of mass m and radius r

$$I_x = \tfrac{1}{2}mr^2 \qquad I_y = I_z = \tfrac{1}{4}mr^2$$

Because of symmetry, we note that for a semicircular plate

$$I_x = \tfrac{1}{2}(\tfrac{1}{2}mr^2) \qquad I_y = I_z = \tfrac{1}{2}(\tfrac{1}{4}mr^2)$$

Since the mass of the semicircular plate is $m_1 = \tfrac{1}{2}m$, we have

$$I_x = \tfrac{1}{2}m_1 r^2 = \tfrac{1}{2}(0.3156 \text{ kg})(0.08 \text{ m})^2 = 1.010 \times 10^{-3} \text{ kg} \cdot \text{m}^2$$
$$I_y = I_z = \tfrac{1}{4}(\tfrac{1}{2}mr^2) = \tfrac{1}{4}m_1 r^2 = \tfrac{1}{4}(0.3156 \text{ kg})(0.08 \text{ m})^2 = 0.505 \times 10^{-3} \text{ kg} \cdot \text{m}^2$$

Rectangular Plate

$$I_x = \tfrac{1}{12}m_2 c^2 = \tfrac{1}{12}(1.005 \text{ kg})(0.16 \text{ m})^2 = 2.144 \times 10^{-3} \text{ kg} \cdot \text{m}^2$$
$$I_z = \tfrac{1}{3}m_2 b^2 = \tfrac{1}{3}(1.005 \text{ kg})(0.2 \text{ m})^2 = 13.400 \times 10^{-3} \text{ kg} \cdot \text{m}^2$$
$$I_y = I_x + I_z = (2.144 + 13.400)(10^{-3}) = 15.544 \times 10^{-3} \text{ kg} \cdot \text{m}^2$$

Circular Plate

$$I_x = \tfrac{1}{4}m_3 a^2 = \tfrac{1}{4}(0.2466 \text{ kg})(0.05 \text{ m})^2 = 0.154 \times 10^{-3} \text{ kg} \cdot \text{m}^2$$
$$I_y = \tfrac{1}{2}m_3 a^2 + m_3 d^2$$
$$= \tfrac{1}{2}(0.2466 \text{ kg})(0.05 \text{ m})^2 + (0.2466 \text{ kg})(0.1 \text{ m})^2 = 2.774 \times 10^{-3} \text{ kg} \cdot \text{m}^2$$
$$I_z = \tfrac{1}{4}m_3 a^2 + m_3 d^2 = \tfrac{1}{4}(0.2466 \text{ kg})(0.05 \text{ m})^2 + (0.2466 \text{ kg})(0.1 \text{ m})^2$$
$$= 2.620 \times 10^{-3} \text{ kg} \cdot \text{m}^2$$

Entire Machine Part

$$I_x = (1.010 + 2.144 - 0.154)(10^{-3}) \text{ kg} \cdot \text{m}^2 \qquad I_x = 3.00 \times 10^{-3} \text{ kg} \cdot \text{m}^2 \quad \blacktriangleleft$$
$$I_y = (0.505 + 15.544 - 2.774)(10^{-3}) \text{ kg} \cdot \text{m}^2 \qquad I_y = 13.28 \times 10^{-3} \text{ kg} \cdot \text{m}^2 \quad \blacktriangleleft$$
$$I_z = (0.505 + 13.400 - 2.620)(10^{-3}) \text{ kg} \cdot \text{m}^2 \qquad I_z = 11.29 \times 10^{-3} \text{ kg} \cdot \text{m}^2 \quad \blacktriangleleft$$

SOLVING PROBLEMS
ON YOUR OWN

In this lesson we introduced the *mass moment of inertia* and the *radius of gyration* of a three-dimensional body with respect to a given axis [Eqs. (9.28) and (9.29)]. We also derived a *parallel-axis theorem* for use with mass moments of inertia and discussed the computation of the mass moments of inertia of thin plates and three-dimensional bodies.

1. Computing mass moments of inertia. The mass moment of inertia I of a body with respect to a given axis can be calculated directly from the definition given in Eq. (9.28) for simple shapes [Sample Prob. 9.9]. In most cases, however, it is necessary to divide the body into thin slabs, compute the moment of inertia of a typical slab with respect to the given axis—using the parallel-axis theorem if necessary—and integrate the expression obtained.

2. Applying the parallel-axis theorem. In Sec. 9.12 we derived the parallel-axis theorem for mass moments of inertia

$$I = \bar{I} + md^2 \tag{9.33}$$

which states that the moment of inertia I of a body of mass m with respect to a given axis is equal to the sum of the moment of inertia $\bar{I}$ of that body with respect to a *parallel centroidal axis* and the product md^2, where d is the distance between the two axes. When the moment of inertia of a three-dimensional body is calculated with respect to one of the coordinate axes, d^2 can be replaced by the sum of the squares of distances measured along the other two coordinate axes [Eqs. (9.32) and (9.32′)].

3. Avoiding unit-related errors. To avoid errors, it is essential that you be consistent in your use of units. Thus, all lengths should be expressed in meters or feet, as appropriate, and for problems using U.S. customary units, masses should be given in lb · s^2/ft. In addition, we strongly recommend that you include units as you perform your calculations [Sample Probs. 9.12 and 9.13].

4. Calculating the mass moment of inertia of thin plates. We showed in Sec. 9.13 that the mass moment of inertia of a thin plate with respect to a given axis can be obtained by multiplying the corresponding moment of inertia of the area of the plate by the density ρ and the thickness t of the plate [Eqs. (9.35) through (9.37)]. Note that since the axis CC' in Fig. 9.24c is *perpendicular to the plate*, $I_{CC',\text{mass}}$ is associated with the *polar* moment of inertia $J_{C,\text{area}}$.

Instead of calculating directly the moment of inertia of a thin plate with respect to a specified axis, you may sometimes find it convenient to first compute its moment of inertia with respect to an axis parallel to the specified axis and then apply the parallel-axis theorem. Further, to determine the moment of inertia of a thin plate with respect to an axis perpendicular to the plate, you may wish to first determine its moments of inertia with respect to two perpendicular in-plane axes and then use Eq. (9.38). Finally, remember that the mass of a plate of area A, thickness t, and density ρ is $m = \rho tA$.

5. Determining the moment of inertia of a body by direct single integration. We discussed in Sec. 9.14 and illustrated in Sample Probs. 9.10 and 9.11 how single integration can be used to compute the moment of inertia of a body that can be divided into a series of thin, parallel slabs. For such cases, you will often need to express the mass of the body in terms of the body's density and dimensions. Assuming that the body has been divided, as in the sample problems, into thin slabs perpendicular to the x axis, you will need to express the dimensions of each slab as functions of the variable x.

   a. In the special case of a body of revolution, the elemental slab is a thin disk, and the equations given in Fig. 9.27 should be used to determine the moments of inertia of the body [Sample Prob. 9.11].

   b. In the general case, when the body is not of revolution, the differential element is not a disk, but a thin slab of a different shape, and the equations of Fig. 9.27 cannot be used. See, for example, Sample Prob. 9.10, where the element was a thin, rectangular slab. For more complex configurations, you may want to use one or more of the following equations, which are based on Eqs. (9.32) and (9.32′) of Sec. 9.12.

$$dI_x = dI_{x'} + (\overline{y}_{el}^2 + \overline{z}_{el}^2)\, dm$$
$$dI_y = dI_{y'} + (\overline{z}_{el}^2 + \overline{x}_{el}^2)\, dm$$
$$dI_z = dI_{z'} + (\overline{x}_{el}^2 + \overline{y}_{el}^2)\, dm$$

where the primes denote the centroidal axes of each elemental slab, and where $\overline{x}_{el}$, $\overline{y}_{el}$, and $\overline{z}_{el}$ represent the coordinates of its centroid. The centroidal moments of inertia of the slab are determined in the manner described earlier for a thin plate: Referring to Fig. 9.12 on page 485, calculate the corresponding moments of inertia of the area of the slab and multiply the result by the density ρ and the thickness t of the slab. Also, assuming that the body has been divided into thin slabs perpendicular to the x axis, remember that you can obtain $dI_{x'}$ by adding $dI_{y'}$ and $dI_{z'}$ instead of computing it directly. Finally, using the geometry of the body, express the result obtained in terms of the single variable x and integrate in x.

6. Computing the moment of inertia of a composite body. As stated in Sec. 9.15, the moment of inertia of a composite body with respect to a specified axis is equal to the sum of the moments of its components with respect to that axis. Sample Probs. 9.12 and 9.13 illustrate the appropriate method of solution. You must also remember that the moment of inertia of a component will be negative only if the component is *removed* (as in the case of a hole).

Although the composite-body problems in this lesson are relatively straightforward, you will have to work carefully to avoid computational errors. In addition, if some of the moments of inertia that you need are not given in Fig. 9.28, you will have to derive your own formulas, using the techniques of this lesson.

PROBLEMS

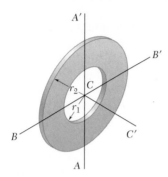

Fig. P9.111

9.111 Determine the mass moment of inertia of a ring of mass m, cut from a thin uniform plate, with respect to (*a*) the axis AA', (*b*) the centroidal axis CC' that is perpendicular to the plane of the ring.

9.112 A thin semicircular plate has a radius a and a mass m. Determine the mass moment of inertia of the plate with respect to (*a*) the centroidal axis BB', (*b*) the centroidal axis CC' that is perpendicular to the plate.

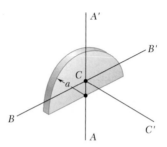

Fig. P9.112

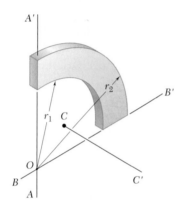

Fig. P9.113

9.113 The quarter ring shown has a mass m and was cut from a thin, uniform plate. Knowing that $r_1 = \frac{3}{4}r_2$, determine the mass moment of inertia of the quarter ring with respect to (*a*) the axis AA', (*b*) the centroidal axis CC' that is perpendicular to the plane of the quarter ring.

9.114 The parabolic spandrel shown was cut from a thin, uniform plate. Denoting the mass of the spandrel by m, determine its mass moment of inertia with respect to (*a*) the axis BB', (*b*) the axis DD' that is perpendicular to the spandrel. (*Hint:* See Sample Prob. 9.3.)

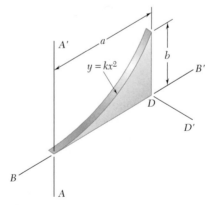

Fig. P9.114

9.115 A thin plate of mass m was cut in the shape of a parallelogram as shown. Determine the mass moment of inertia of the plate with respect to (a) the x axis, (b) the axis BB', which is perpendicular to the plate.

9.116 A thin plate of mass m was cut in the shape of a parallelogram as shown. Determine the mass moment of inertia of the plate with respect to (a) the y axis, (b) the axis AA', which is perpendicular to the plate.

9.117 A thin plate of mass m has the trapezoidal shape shown. Determine the mass moment of inertia of the plate with respect to (a) the x axis, (b) the y axis.

9.118 A thin plate of mass m has the trapezoidal shape shown. Determine the mass moment of inertia of the plate with respect to (a) the centroidal axis CC' that is perpendicular to the plate, (b) the axis AA' that is parallel to the x axis and is located at a distance $1.5a$ from the plate.

9.119 The area shown is revolved about the x axis to form a homogeneous solid of revolution of mass m. Using direct integration, express the mass moment of inertia of the solid with respect to the x axis in terms of m and h.

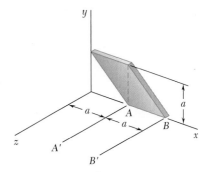

Fig. P9.115 and P9.116

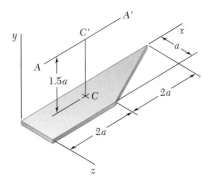

Fig. P9.117 and P9.118

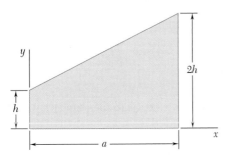

Fig. P9.119

9.120 Determine by direct integration the mass moment of inertia with respect to the y axis of the right circular cylinder shown, assuming that it has a uniform density and a mass m.

9.121 The area shown is revolved about the x axis to form a homogeneous solid of revolution of mass m. Determine by direct integration the mass moment of inertia of the solid with respect to (a) the x axis, (b) the y axis. Express your answers in terms of m and the dimensions of the solid.

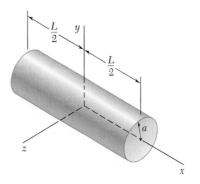

Fig. P9.120

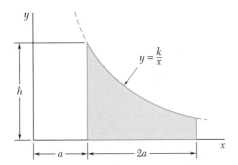

Fig. P9.121

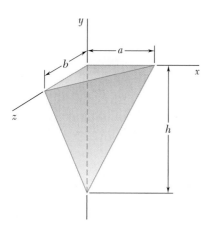

Fig. P9.122 and P9.123

9.122 Determine by direct integration the mass moment of inertia with respect to the x axis of the tetrahedron shown, assuming that it has a uniform density and a mass m.

9.123 Determine by direct integration the mass moment of inertia with respect to the y axis of the tetrahedron shown, assuming that it has a uniform density and a mass m.

*9.124 Determine by direct integration the mass moment of inertia with respect to the z axis of the semiellipsoid shown, assuming that it has a uniform density and a mass m.

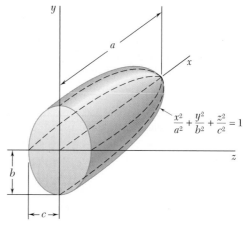

$$\frac{x^2}{a^2} + \frac{y^2}{b^2} + \frac{z^2}{c^2} = 1$$

Fig. P9.124

*9.125 A thin steel wire is bent into the shape shown. Denoting the mass per unit length of the wire by m', determine by direct integration the mass moment of inertia of the wire with respect to each of the coordinate axes.

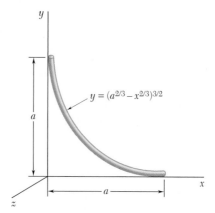

$$y = (a^{2/3} - x^{2/3})^{3/2}$$

Fig. P9.125

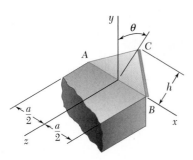

Fig. P9.126

9.126 A thin triangular plate of mass m is welded along its base AB to a block as shown. Knowing that the plate forms an angle θ with the y axis, determine by direct integration the mass moment of inertia of the plate with respect to (a) the x axis, (b) the y axis, (c) the z axis.

9.127 Shown is the cross section of a molded flat-belt pulley. Determine its mass moment of inertia and its radius of gyration with respect to the axis AA'. (The density of brass is 8650 kg/m^3 and the density of the fiber-reinforced polycarbonate used is 1250 kg/m^3.)

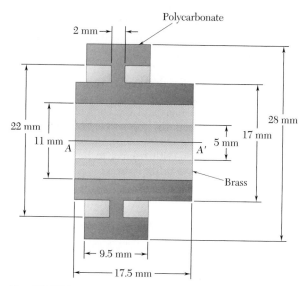

Fig. P9.127

9.128 Shown is the cross section of an idler roller. Determine its mass moment of inertia and its radius of gyration with respect to the axis AA'. (The specific weight of bronze is 0.310 lb/in^3; of aluminum, 0.100 lb/in^3; and of neoprene, 0.0452 lb/in^3.)

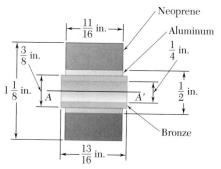

Fig. P9.128

9.129 Knowing that the thin cylindrical shell shown is of mass m, thickness t, and height h, determine the mass moment of inertia of the shell with respect to the x axis. (*Hint:* Consider the shell as formed by removing a cylinder of radius a and height h from a cylinder of radius $a + t$ and height h; then neglect terms containing t^2 and t^3 and keep those terms containing t.)

9.130 The machine part shown is formed by machining a conical surface into a circular cylinder. For $b = \frac{1}{2}h$, determine the mass moment of inertia and the radius of gyration of the machine part with respect to the y axis.

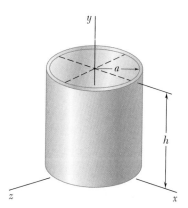

Fig. P9.129

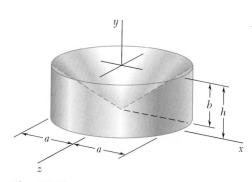

Fig. P9.130

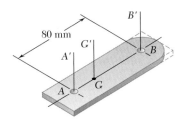

80 mm

Fig. P9.131

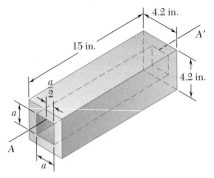

0.4 in.

2.4 in.

1.2 in.

1.6 in.

Fig. P9.132

9.131 After a period of use, one of the blades of a shredder has been worn to the shape shown and is of mass 0.18 kg. Knowing that the mass moments of inertia of the blade with respect to the AA' and BB' axes are $0.320 \text{ g} \cdot \text{m}^2$ and $0.680 \text{ g} \cdot \text{m}^2$, respectively, determine (a) the location of the centroidal axis GG', (b) the radius of gyration with respect to axis GG'.

9.132 Determine the mass moment of inertia of the 0.9-lb machine component shown with respect to the axis AA'.

9.133 A square hole is centered in and extends through the aluminum machine component shown. Determine (a) the value of a for which the mass moment of inertia of the component with respect to the axis AA', which bisects the top surface of the hole, is maximum, (b) the corresponding values of the mass moment of inertia and the radius of gyration with respect to the axis AA'. (The specific weight of aluminum is 0.100 lb/in^3.)

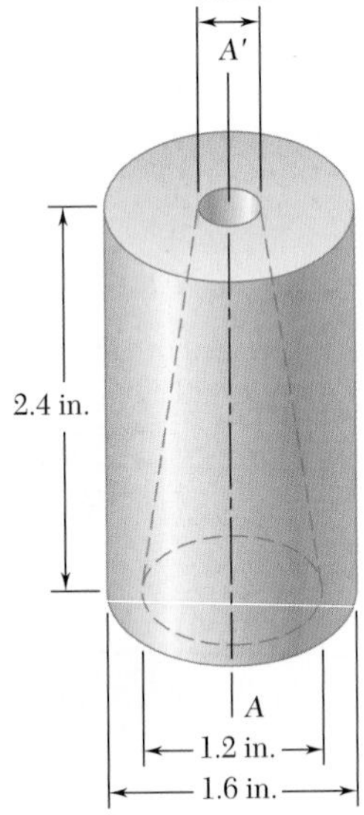

15 in.

4.2 in.

4.2 in.

$\frac{a}{2}$

a

a

Fig. P9.133

9.134 The cups and the arms of an anemometer are fabricated from a material of density ρ. Knowing that the mass moment of inertia of a thin, hemispherical shell of mass m and thickness t with respect to its centroidal axis GG' is $5ma^2/12$, determine (a) the mass moment of inertia of the anemometer with respect to the axis AA', (b) the ratio of a to l for which the centroidal moment of inertia of the cups is equal to 1 percent of the moment of inertia of the cups with respect to the axis AA'.

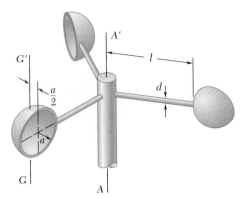

l

d

$\frac{a}{2}$

a

Fig. P9.134

9.135 and 9.136 A 2-mm thick piece of sheet steel is cut and bent into the machine component shown. Knowing that the density of steel is 7850 kg/m³, determine the mass moment of inertia of the component with respect to each of the coordinate axes.

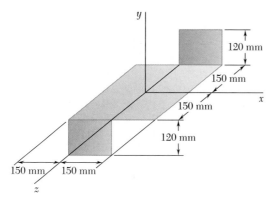

Fig. P9.135

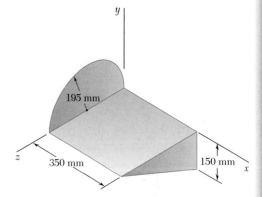

Fig. P9.136

9.137 The cover for an electronic device is formed from sheet aluminum that is 0.05 in. thick. Determine the mass moment of inertia of the cover with respect to each of the coordinate axes. (The specific weight of aluminum is 0.100 lb/in³.)

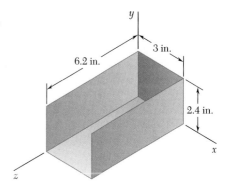

Fig. P9.137

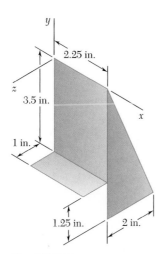

Fig. P9.138

9.138 A framing anchor is formed of 0.05-in.-thick galvanized steel. Determine the mass moment of inertia of the anchor with respect to each of the coordinate axes. (The specific weight of galvanized steel is 470 lb/ft³.)

9.139 A subassembly for a model airplane is fabricated from three pieces of 1.5-mm plywood. Neglecting the mass of the adhesive used to assemble the three pieces, determine the mass moment of inertia of the subassembly with respect to each of the coordinate axes. (The density of the plywood is 780 kg/m³.)

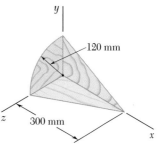

Fig. P9.139

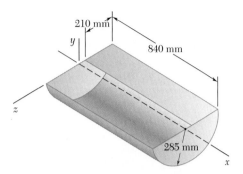

Fig. P9.140

*9.140 A farmer constructs a trough by welding a rectangular piece of 2-mm-thick sheet steel to half of a steel drum. Knowing that the density of steel is 7850 kg/m³ and that the thickness of the walls of the drum is 1.8 mm, determine the mass moment of inertia of the trough with respect to each of the coordinate axes. Neglect the mass of the welds.

9.141 The machine element shown is fabricated from steel. Determine the mass moment of inertia of the assembly with respect to (a) the x axis, (b) the y axis, (c) the z axis. (The density of steel is 7850 kg/m³.)

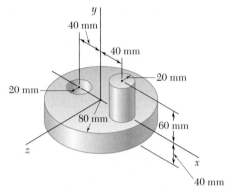

Fig. P9.141

9.142 Determine the mass moment of inertia of the steel machine element shown with respect to the y axis. (The specific weight of steel is 490 lb/ft³.)

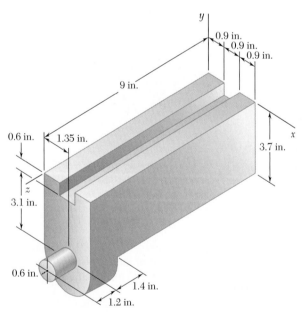

Fig. P9.142 and P9.143

9.143 Determine the mass moment of inertia of the steel machine element shown with respect to the z axis. (The specific weight of steel is 490 lb/ft³.)

9.144 Determine the mass moment of inertia and the radius of gyration of the steel machine element shown with respect to the x axis. (The density of steel is 7850 kg/m³.)

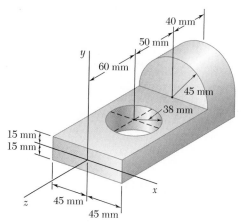

Fig. P9.144

9.145 Determine the mass moment of inertia of the steel fixture shown with respect to (*a*) the x axis, (*b*) the y axis, (*c*) the z axis. (The density of steel is 7850 kg/m³.)

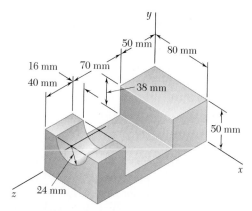

Fig. P9.145

9.146 Aluminum wire with a weight per unit length of 0.033 lb/ft is used to form the circle and the straight members of the figure shown. Determine the mass moment of inertia of the assembly with respect to each of the coordinate axes.

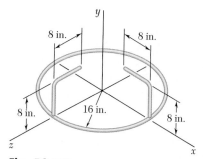

Fig. P9.146

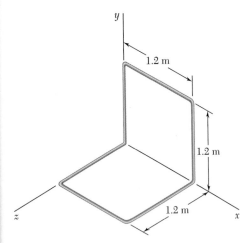

1.2 m

1.2 m

1.2 m

Fig. P9.148

9.147 The figure shown is formed of $\frac{1}{8}$-in.-diameter steel wire. Knowing that the specific weight of the steel is 490 lb/ft^3, determine the mass moment of inertia of the wire with respect to each of the coordinate axes.

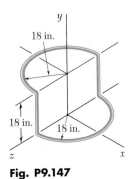

18 in.

18 in.

18 in.

Fig. P9.147

9.148 A homogeneous wire with a mass per unit length of 0.056 kg/m is used to form the figure shown. Determine the mass moment of inertia of the wire with respect to each of the coordinate axes.

*9.16 MOMENT OF INERTIA OF A BODY WITH RESPECT TO AN ARBITRARY AXIS THROUGH O. MASS PRODUCTS OF INERTIA

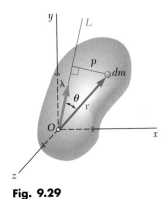

Fig. 9.29

In this section you will see how the moment of inertia of a body can be determined with respect to an arbitrary axis OL through the origin (Fig. 9.29) if its moments of inertia with respect to the three coordinate axes, as well as certain other quantities to be defined below, have already been determined.

The moment of inertia I_{OL} of the body with respect to OL is equal to $\int p^2 dm$, where p denotes the perpendicular distance from the element of mass dm to the axis OL. If we denote by $\boldsymbol{\lambda}$ the unit vector along OL and by $\mathbf{r}$ the position vector of the element dm, we observe that the perpendicular distance p is equal to $r \sin \theta$, which is the magnitude of the vector product $\boldsymbol{\lambda} \times \mathbf{r}$. We therefore write

$$I_{OL} = \int p^2\, dm = \int |\boldsymbol{\lambda} \times \mathbf{r}|^2\, dm \qquad (9.43)$$

Expressing $|\boldsymbol{\lambda} \times \mathbf{r}|^2$ in terms of the rectangular components of the vector product, we have

$$I_{OL} = \int [(\lambda_x y - \lambda_y x)^2 + (\lambda_y z - \lambda_z y)^2 + (\lambda_z x - \lambda_x z)^2]\, dm$$

where the components λ_x, λ_y, λ_z of the unit vector $\boldsymbol{\lambda}$ represent the direction cosines of the axis OL and the components x, y, z of $\mathbf{r}$ represent the coordinates of the element of mass dm. Expanding the squares and rearranging the terms, we write

$$I_{OL} = \lambda_x^2 \int (y^2 + z^2)\, dm + \lambda_y^2 \int (z^2 + x^2)\, dm + \lambda_z^2 \int (x^2 + y^2)\, dm$$

$$- 2\lambda_x\lambda_y \int xy\, dm - 2\lambda_y\lambda_z \int yz\, dm - 2\lambda_z\lambda_x \int zx\, dm \qquad (9.44)$$

Referring to Eqs. (9.30), we note that the first three integrals in (9.44) represent, respectively, the moments of inertia I_x, I_y, and I_z of the body with respect to the coordinate axes. The last three integrals in (9.44), which involve products of coordinates, are called the *products of inertia* of the body with respect to the x and y axes, the y and z axes, and the z and x axes, respectively. We write

$$I_{xy} = \int xy \, dm \qquad I_{yz} = \int yz \, dm \qquad I_{zx} = \int zx \, dm \qquad (9.45)$$

Rewriting Eq. (9.44) in terms of the integrals defined in Eqs. (9.30) and (9.45), we have

$$I_{OL} = I_x\lambda_x^2 + I_y\lambda_y^2 + I_z\lambda_z^2 - 2I_{xy}\lambda_x\lambda_y - 2I_{yz}\lambda_y\lambda_z - 2I_{zx}\lambda_z\lambda_x \qquad (9.46)$$

We note that the definition of the products of inertia of a mass given in Eqs. (9.45) is an extension of the definition of the product of inertia of an area (Sec. 9.8). Mass products of inertia reduce to zero under the same conditions of symmetry as do products of inertia of areas, and the parallel-axis theorem for mass products of inertia is expressed by relations similar to the formula derived for the product of inertia of an area. Substituting the expressions for x, y, and z given in Eqs. (9.31) into Eqs. (9.45), we find that

$$\begin{aligned} I_{xy} &= \bar{I}_{x'y'} + m\bar{x}\,\bar{y} \\ I_{yz} &= \bar{I}_{y'z'} + m\bar{y}\,\bar{z} \\ I_{zx} &= \bar{I}_{z'x'} + m\bar{z}\,\bar{x} \end{aligned} \qquad (9.47)$$

where $\bar{x}, \bar{y}, \bar{z}$ are the coordinates of the center of gravity G of the body and $\bar{I}_{x'y'}, \bar{I}_{y'z'}, \bar{I}_{z'x'}$ denote the products of inertia of the body with respect to the centroidal axes x', y', z' (Fig. 9.22).

*9.17 ELLIPSOID OF INERTIA. PRINCIPAL AXES OF INERTIA

Let us assume that the moment of inertia of the body considered in the preceding section has been determined with respect to a large number of axes OL through the fixed point O and that a point Q has been plotted on each axis OL at a distance $OQ = 1/\sqrt{I_{OL}}$ from O. The locus of the points Q thus obtained forms a surface (Fig. 9.30). The equation of that surface can be obtained by substituting $1/(OQ)^2$ for I_{OL} in (9.46) and then multiplying both sides of the equation by $(OQ)^2$. Observing that

$$(OQ)\lambda_x = x \qquad (OQ)\lambda_y = y \qquad (OQ)\lambda_z = z$$

where x, y, z denote the rectangular coordinates of Q, we write

$$I_x x^2 + I_y y^2 + I_z z^2 - 2I_{xy}xy - 2I_{yz}yz - 2I_{zx}zx = 1 \qquad (9.48)$$

The equation obtained is the equation of a *quadric surface*. Since the moment of inertia I_{OL} is different from zero for every axis OL, no point Q can be at an infinite distance from O. Thus, the quadric surface obtained is an *ellipsoid*. This ellipsoid, which defines the

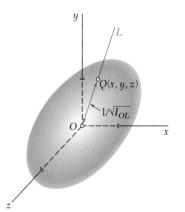

Fig. 9.30

moment of inertia of the body with respect to any axis through O, is known as the *ellipsoid of inertia* of the body at O.

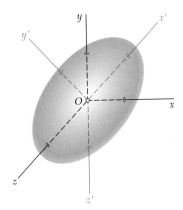

Fig. 9.31

We observe that if the axes in Fig. 9.30 are rotated, the coefficients of the equation defining the ellipsoid change, since they are equal to the moments and products of inertia of the body with respect to the rotated coordinate axes. However, the *ellipsoid itself remains unaffected*, since its shape depends only upon the distribution of mass in the given body. Suppose that we choose as coordinate axes the principal axes x', y', z' of the ellipsoid of inertia (Fig. 9.31). The equation of the ellipsoid with respect to these coordinate axes is known to be of the form

$$I_{x'}x'^2 + I_{y'}y'^2 + I_{z'}z'^2 = 1 \tag{9.49}$$

which does not contain any products of the coordinates. Comparing Eqs. (9.48) and (9.49), we observe that the products of inertia of the body with respect to the x', y', z' axes must be zero. The x', y', z' axes are known as the *principal axes of inertia* of the body at O, and the coefficients $I_{x'}$, $I_{y'}$, $I_{z'}$ are referred to as the *principal moments of inertia* of the body at O. Note that, given a body of arbitrary shape and a point O, it is always possible to find axes which are the principal axes of inertia of the body at O, that is, axes with respect to which the products of inertia of the body are zero. Indeed, whatever the shape of the body, the moments and products of inertia of the body with respect to x, y, and z axes through O will define an ellipsoid, and this ellipsoid will have principal axes which, by definition, are the principal axes of inertia of the body at O.

If the principal axes of inertia x', y', z' are used as coordinate axes, the expression obtained in Eq. (9.46) for the moment of inertia of a body with respect to an arbitrary axis through O reduces to

$$I_{OL} = I_{x'}\lambda_{x'}^2 + I_{y'}\lambda_{y'}^2 + I_{z'}\lambda_{z'}^2 \tag{9.50}$$

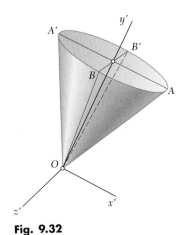

Fig. 9.32

The determination of the principal axes of inertia of a body of arbitrary shape is somewhat involved and will be discussed in the next section. There are many cases, however, where these axes can be spotted immediately. Consider, for instance, the homogeneous cone of elliptical base shown in Fig. 9.32; this cone possesses two mutually perpendicular planes of symmetry OAA' and OBB'. From the definition (9.45), we observe that if the $x'y'$ and $y'z'$ planes are chosen to coincide with the two planes of symmetry, all of the products of inertia are zero. The x', y', and z' axes thus selected are therefore the principal axes of inertia of the cone at O. In the case of the homogeneous regular tetrahedron $OABC$ shown in Fig. 9.33, the line joining the corner O to the center D of the opposite face is a principal axis of inertia at O, and any line through O perpendicular to OD is also a principal axis of inertia at O. This property is apparent if we observe that rotating the tetrahedron through 120° about OD leaves its shape and mass distribution unchanged. It follows that the ellipsoid of inertia at O also remains unchanged under this rotation. The ellipsoid, therefore, is a body of revolution whose axis of revolution is OD, and the line OD, as well as any perpendicular line through O, must be a principal axis of the ellipsoid.

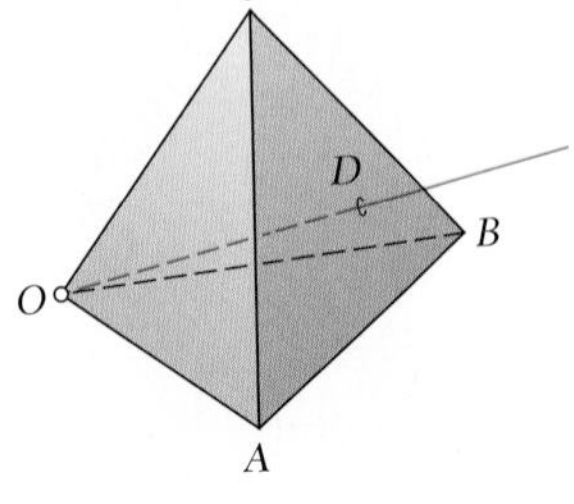

Fig. 9.33

*9.18 DETERMINATION OF THE PRINCIPAL AXES AND PRINCIPAL MOMENTS OF INERTIA OF A BODY OF ARBITRARY SHAPE

The method of analysis described in this section should be used when the body under consideration has no obvious property of symmetry.

Consider the ellipsoid of inertia of the body at a given point O (Fig. 9.34); let $\mathbf{r}$ be the radius vector of a point P on the surface of the ellipsoid and let $\mathbf{n}$ be the unit vector along the normal to that surface at P. We observe that the only points where $\mathbf{r}$ and $\mathbf{n}$ are collinear are the points P_1, P_2, and P_3, where the principal axes intersect the visible portion of the surface of the ellipsoid, and the corresponding points on the other side of the ellipsoid.

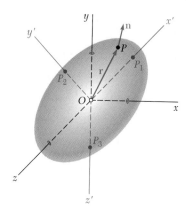

Fig. 9.34

We now recall from calculus that the direction of the normal to a surface of equation $f(x, y, z) = 0$ at a point $P(x, y, z)$ is defined by the gradient ∇f of the function f at that point. To obtain the points where the principal axes intersect the surface of the ellipsoid of inertia, we must therefore write that $\mathbf{r}$ and ∇f are collinear,

$$\nabla f = (2K)\mathbf{r} \tag{9.51}$$

where K is a constant, $\mathbf{r} = x\mathbf{i} + y\mathbf{j} + z\mathbf{k}$, and

$$\nabla f = \frac{\partial f}{\partial x}\mathbf{i} + \frac{\partial f}{\partial y}\mathbf{j} + \frac{\partial f}{\partial x}\mathbf{k}$$

Recalling Eq. (9.48), we note that the function $f(x, y, z)$ corresponding to the ellipsoid of inertia is

$$f(x, y, z) = I_x x^2 + I_y y^2 + I_z z^2 - 2I_{xy}xy - 2I_{yz}yz - 2I_{zx}zx - 1$$

Substituting for $\mathbf{r}$ and ∇f into Eq. (9.51) and equating the coefficients of the unit vectors, we write

$$\begin{aligned}
I_x x &- I_{xy}y - I_{zx}z = Kx \\
-I_{xy}x &+ I_y y - I_{yz}z = Ky \\
-I_{zx}x &- I_{yz}y + I_z z = Kz
\end{aligned} \tag{9.52}$$

Dividing each term by the distance r from O to P, we obtain similar equations involving the direction cosines λ_x, λ_y, and λ_z:

$$\begin{aligned} I_x\lambda_x - I_{xy}\lambda_y - I_{zx}\lambda_z &= K\lambda_x \\ -I_{xy}\lambda_x + I_y\lambda_y - I_{yz}\lambda_z &= K\lambda_y \\ -I_{zx}\lambda_x - I_{yz}\lambda_y + I_z\lambda_z &= K\lambda_z \end{aligned} \tag{9.53}$$

Transposing the right-hand members leads to the following homogeneous linear equations:

$$\begin{aligned} (I_x - K)\lambda_x - I_{xy}\lambda_y - I_{zx}\lambda_z &= 0 \\ -I_{xy}\lambda_x + (I_y - K)\lambda_y - I_{yz}\lambda_z &= 0 \\ -I_{zx}\lambda_x - I_{yz}\lambda_y + (I_z - K)\lambda_z &= 0 \end{aligned} \tag{9.54}$$

For this system of equations to have a solution different from $\lambda_x = \lambda_y = \lambda_z = 0$, its discriminant must be zero:

$$\begin{vmatrix} I_x - K & -I_{xy} & -I_{zx} \\ -I_{xy} & I_y - K & -I_{yz} \\ -I_{zx} & -I_{yz} & I_z - K \end{vmatrix} = 0 \tag{9.55}$$

Expanding this determinant and changing signs, we write

$$K^3 - (I_x + I_y + I_z)K^2 + (I_xI_y + I_yI_z + I_zI_x - I_{xy}^2 - I_{yz}^2 - I_{zx}^2)K \\ - (I_xI_yI_z - I_xI_{yz}^2 - I_yI_{zx}^2 - I_zI_{xy}^2 - 2I_{xy}I_{yz}I_{zx}) = 0 \tag{9.56}$$

This is a cubic equation in K, which yields three real, positive roots K_1, K_2, and K_3.

To obtain the direction cosines of the principal axis corresponding to the root K_1 we substitute K_1 for K in Eqs. (9.54). Since these equations are now linearly dependent, only two of them may be used to determine λ_x, λ_y, and λ_z. An additional equation may be obtained, however, by recalling from Sec. 2.12 that the direction cosines must satisfy the relation

$$\lambda_x^2 + \lambda_y^2 + \lambda_z^2 = 1 \tag{9.57}$$

Repeating this procedure with K_2 and K_3, we obtain the direction cosines of the other two principal axes.

We will now show that *the roots K_1, K_2, and K_3 of Eq. (9.56) are the principal moments of inertia of the given body.* Let us substitute for K in Eqs. (9.53) the root K_1, and for λ_x, λ_y, and λ_z the corresponding values $(\lambda_x)_1$, $(\lambda_y)_1$, and $(\lambda_z)_1$ of the direction cosines; the three equations will be satisfied. We now multiply by $(\lambda_x)_1$, $(\lambda_y)_1$, and $(\lambda_z)_1$, respectively, each term in the first, second, and third equation and add the equations obtained in this way. We write

$$I_x^2(\lambda_x)_1^2 + I_y^2(\lambda_y)_1^2 + I_z^2(\lambda_z)_1^2 - 2I_{xy}(\lambda_x)_1(\lambda_y)_1 \\ - 2I_{yz}(\lambda_y)_1(\lambda_z)_1 - 2I_{zx}(\lambda_z)_1(\lambda_x)_1 = K_1[(\lambda_x)_1^2 + (\lambda_y)_1^2 + (\lambda_z)_1^2]$$

Recalling Eq. (9.46), we observe that the left-hand member of this equation represents the moment of inertia of the body with respect to the principal axis corresponding to K_1; it is thus the principal moment of inertia corresponding to that root. On the other hand, recalling Eq. (9.57), we note that the right-hand member reduces to K_1. Thus K_1 itself is the principal moment of inertia. We can show in the same fashion that K_2 and K_3 are the other two principal moments of inertia of the body.

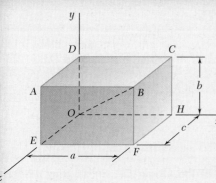

SAMPLE PROBLEM 9.14

Consider a rectangular prism of mass m and sides a, b, c. Determine (a) the moments and products of inertia of the prism with respect to the coordinate axes shown, (b) its moment of inertia with respect to the diagonal OB.

SOLUTION

a. Moments and Products of Inertia with Respect to the Coordinate Axes. *Moments of Inertia.* Introducing the centroidal axes x', y', z', with respect to which the moments of inertia are given in Fig. 9.28, we apply the parallel-axis theorem:

$$I_x = \bar{I}_{x'} + m(\bar{y}^2 + \bar{z}^2) = \tfrac{1}{12}m(b^2 + c^2) + m(\tfrac{1}{4}b^2 + \tfrac{1}{4}c^2)$$
$$I_x = \tfrac{1}{3}m(b^2 + c^2) \quad \blacktriangleleft$$

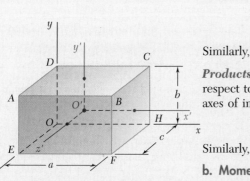

Similarly, $\qquad I_y = \tfrac{1}{3}m(c^2 + a^2) \qquad I_z = \tfrac{1}{3}m(a^2 + b^2) \quad \blacktriangleleft$

Products of Inertia. Because of symmetry, the products of inertia with respect to the centroidal axes x', y', z' are zero, and these axes are principal axes of inertia. Using the parallel-axis theorem, we have

$$I_{xy} = \bar{I}_{x'y'} + m\bar{x}\,\bar{y} = 0 + m(\tfrac{1}{2}a)(\tfrac{1}{2}b) \qquad I_{xy} = \tfrac{1}{4}mab \quad \blacktriangleleft$$

Similarly, $\qquad\qquad\qquad\qquad I_{yz} = \tfrac{1}{4}mbc \qquad I_{zx} = \tfrac{1}{4}mca \quad \blacktriangleleft$

b. Moment of Inertia with Respect to OB. We recall Eq. (9.46):

$$I_{OB} = I_x\lambda_x^2 + I_y\lambda_y^2 + I_z\lambda_z^2 - 2I_{xy}\lambda_x\lambda_y - 2I_{yz}\lambda_y\lambda_z - 2I_{zx}\lambda_z\lambda_x$$

where the direction cosines of OB are

$$\lambda_x = \cos\theta_x = \frac{OH}{OB} = \frac{a}{(a^2 + b^2 + c^2)^{1/2}}$$

$$\lambda_y = \frac{b}{(a^2 + b^2 + c^2)^{1/2}} \qquad \lambda_z = \frac{c}{(a^2 + b^2 + c^2)^{1/2}}$$

Substituting the values obtained for the moments and products of inertia and for the direction cosines into the equation for I_{OB}, we have

$$I_{OB} = \frac{1}{a^2 + b^2 + c^2}\left[\tfrac{1}{3}m(b^2 + c^2)a^2 + \tfrac{1}{3}m(c^2 + a^2)b^2 + \tfrac{1}{3}m(a^2 + b^2)c^2\right.$$
$$\left. - \tfrac{1}{2}ma^2b^2 - \tfrac{1}{2}mb^2c^2 - \tfrac{1}{2}mc^2a^2\right]$$

$$I_{OB} = \frac{m}{6}\frac{a^2b^2 + b^2c^2 + c^2a^2}{a^2 + b^2 + c^2} \quad \blacktriangleleft$$

Alternative Solution. The moment of inertia I_{OB} can be obtained directly from the principal moments of inertia $\bar{I}_{x'}$, $\bar{I}_{y'}$, $\bar{I}_{z'}$, since the line OB passes through the centroid O'. Since the x', y', z' axes are principal axes of inertia, we use Eq. (9.50) to write

$$I_{OB} = \bar{I}_{x'}\lambda_x^2 + \bar{I}_{y'}\lambda_y^2 + \bar{I}_{z'}\lambda_z^2$$
$$= \frac{1}{a^2 + b^2 + c^2}\left[\frac{m}{12}(b^2 + c^2)a^2 + \frac{m}{12}(c^2 + a^2)b^2 + \frac{m}{12}(a^2 + b^2)c^2\right]$$

$$I_{OB} = \frac{m}{6}\frac{a^2b^2 + b^2c^2 + c^2a^2}{a^2 + b^2 + c^2} \quad \blacktriangleleft$$

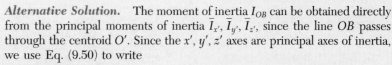

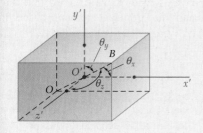

SAMPLE PROBLEM 9.15

If $a = 3c$ and $b = 2c$ for the rectangular prism of Sample Prob. 9.14, determine (a) the principal moments of inertia at the origin O, (b) the principal axes of inertia at O.

SOLUTION

a. Principal Moments of Inertia at the Origin O. Substituting $a = 3c$ and $b = 2c$ into the solution to Sample Prob. 9.14, we have

$$I_x = \tfrac{5}{3}mc^2 \qquad I_y = \tfrac{10}{3}mc^2 \qquad I_z = \tfrac{13}{3}mc^2$$
$$I_{xy} = \tfrac{3}{2}mc^2 \qquad I_{yz} = \tfrac{1}{2}mc^2 \qquad I_{zx} = \tfrac{3}{4}mc^2$$

Substituting the values of the moments and products of inertia into Eq. (9.56) and collecting terms yields

$$K^3 - (\tfrac{28}{3}mc^2)K^2 + (\tfrac{3479}{144}m^2c^4)K - \tfrac{589}{54}m^3c^6 = 0$$

We then solve for the roots of this equation; from the discussion in Sec. 9.18, it follows that these roots are the principal moments of inertia of the body at the origin.

$$K_1 = 0.568867mc^2 \qquad K_2 = 4.20885mc^2 \qquad K_3 = 4.55562mc^2$$
$$K_1 = 0.569mc^2 \qquad K_2 = 4.21mc^2 \qquad K_3 = 4.56mc^2 \qquad \blacktriangleleft$$

b. Principal Axes of Inertia at O. To determine the direction of a principal axis of inertia, we first substitute the corresponding value of K into two of the equations (9.54); the resulting equations together with Eq. (9.57) constitute a system of three equations from which the direction cosines of the corresponding principal axis can be determined. Thus, we have for the first principal moment of inertia K_1:

$$(\tfrac{5}{3} - 0.568867)mc^2(\lambda_x)_1 - \tfrac{3}{2}mc^2(\lambda_y)_1 - \tfrac{3}{4}mc^2(\lambda_z)_1 = 0$$
$$-\tfrac{3}{2}mc^2(\lambda_x)_1 + (\tfrac{10}{3} - 0.568867)mc^2(\lambda_y)_1 - \tfrac{1}{2}mc^2(\lambda_z)_1 = 0$$
$$(\lambda_x)_1^2 + (\lambda_y)_1^2 + (\lambda_z)_1^2 = 1$$

Solving yields

$$(\lambda_x)_1 = 0.836600 \qquad (\lambda_y)_1 = 0.496001 \qquad (\lambda_z)_1 = 0.232557$$

The angles that the first principal axis of inertia forms with the coordinate axes are then

$$(\theta_x)_1 = 33.2° \qquad (\theta_y)_1 = 60.3° \qquad (\theta_z)_1 = 76.6° \qquad \blacktriangleleft$$

Using the same set of equations successively with K_2 and K_3, we find that the angles associated with the second and third principal moments of inertia at the origin are, respectively,

$$(\theta_x)_2 = 57.8° \qquad (\theta_y)_2 = 146.6° \qquad (\theta_z)_2 = 98.0° \qquad \blacktriangleleft$$

and

$$(\theta_x)_3 = 82.8° \qquad (\theta_y)_3 = 76.1° \qquad (\theta_z)_3 = 164.3° \qquad \blacktriangleleft$$

SOLVING PROBLEMS ON YOUR OWN

In this lesson we defined the *mass products of inertia* I_{xy}, I_{yz}, and I_{zx} of a body and showed you how to determine the moments of inertia of that body with respect to an arbitrary axis passing through the origin O. You also learned how to determine at the origin O the *principal axes of inertia* of a body and the corresponding *principal moments of inertia*.

1. Determining the mass products of inertia of a composite body. The mass products of inertia of a composite body with respect to the coordinate axes can be expressed as the sums of the products of inertia of its component parts with respect to those axes. For each component part, we can use the parallel-axis theorem and write Eqs. (9.47)

$$I_{xy} = \bar{I}_{x'y'} + m\bar{x}\bar{y} \qquad I_{yz} = \bar{I}_{y'z'} + m\bar{y}\bar{z} \qquad I_{zx} = \bar{I}_{z'x'} + m\bar{z}\bar{x}$$

where the primes denote the centroidal axes of each component part and where $\bar{x}$, $\bar{y}$, and $\bar{z}$ represent the coordinates of its center of gravity. Keep in mind that the mass products of inertia can be positive, negative, or zero, and be sure to take into account the signs of $\bar{x}$, $\bar{y}$, and $\bar{z}$.

    a. From the properties of symmetry of a component part, you can deduce that two or all three of its centroidal mass products of inertia are zero. For instance, you can verify that for a thin plate parallel to the xy plane; a wire lying in a plane parallel to the xy plane; a body with a plane of symmetry parallel to the xy plane; and a body with an axis of symmetry parallel to the z axis, *the products of inertia $\bar{I}_{y'z'}$ and $\bar{I}_{z'x'}$ are zero.*

    For rectangular, circular, or semicircular plates with axes of symmetry parallel to the coordinate axes; straight wires parallel to a coordinate axis; circular and semicircular wires with axes of symmetry parallel to the coordinate axes; and rectangular prisms with axes of symmetry parallel to the coordinate axes, *the products of inertia $\bar{I}_{x'y'}$, $\bar{I}_{y'z'}$, and $\bar{I}_{z'x'}$ are all zero.*

    b. Mass products of inertia which are different from zero can be computed from Eqs. (9.45). Although, in general, a triple integration is required to determine a mass product of inertia, a single integration can be used if the given body can be divided into a series of thin, parallel slabs. The computations are then similar to those discussed in the previous lesson for moments of inertia.

(continued)

2. Computing the moment of inertia of a body with respect to an arbitrary axis OL. An expression for the moment of inertia I_{OL} was derived in Sec. 9.16 and is given in Eq. (9.46). Before computing I_{OL}, you must first determine the mass moments and products of inertia of the body with respect to the given coordinate axes as well as the direction cosines of the unit vector $\boldsymbol{\lambda}$ along OL.

3. Calculating the principal moments of inertia of a body and determining its principal axes of inertia. You saw in Sec. 9.17 that it is always possible to find an orientation of the coordinate axes for which the mass products of inertia are zero. These axes are referred to as the *principal axes of inertia* and the corresponding moments of inertia are known as the *principal moments of inertia* of the body. In many cases, the principal axes of inertia of a body can be determined from its properties of symmetry. The procedure required to determine the principal moments and principal axes of inertia of a body with no obvious property of symmetry was discussed in Sec. 9.18 and was illustrated in Sample Prob. 9.15. It consists of the following steps.

   a. Expand the determinant in Eq. (9.55) and solve the resulting cubic equation. The solution can be obtained by trial and error or, preferably, with an advanced scientific calculator or with the appropriate computer software. The roots K_1, K_2, and K_3 of this equation are the principal moments of inertia of the body.

   b. To determine the direction of the principal axis corresponding to K_1, substitute this value for K in two of the equations (9.54) and solve these equations together with Eq. (9.57) for the direction cosines of the principal axis corresponding to K_1.

   c. Repeat this procedure with K_2 and K_3 to determine the directions of the other two principal axes. As a check of your computations, you may wish to verify that the scalar product of any two of the unit vectors along the three axes you have obtained is zero and, thus, that these axes are perpendicular to each other.

PROBLEMS

9.149 Determine the mass products of inertia I_{xy}, I_{yz}, and I_{zx} of the steel fixture shown. (The density of steel is 7850 kg/m³.)

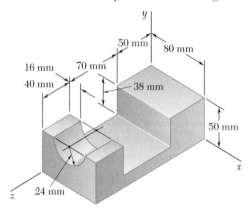

Fig. P9.149

9.150 Determine the mass products of inertia I_{xy}, I_{yz}, and I_{zx} of the steel machine element shown. (The density of steel is 7850 kg/m³.)

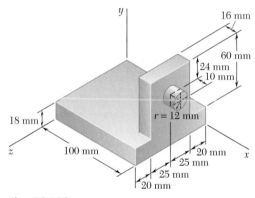

Fig. P9.150

9.151 and 9.152 Determine the mass products of inertia I_{xy}, I_{yz}, and I_{zx} of the cast aluminum machine component shown. (The specific weight of aluminum is 0.100 lb/in.³)

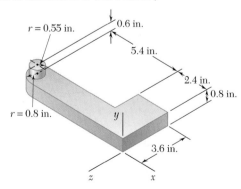

Fig. P9.151

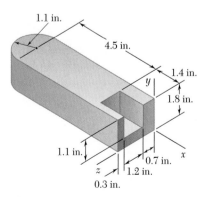

Fig. P9.152

9.153 through 9.156 A section of sheet steel 2 mm thick is cut and bent into the machine component shown. Knowing that the density of steel is 7850 kg/m³, determine the mass products of inertia I_{xy}, I_{yz}, and I_{zx} of the component.

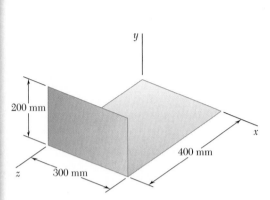

Fig. P9.153

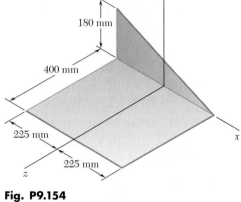

Fig. P9.154

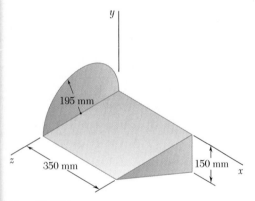

Fig. P9.155

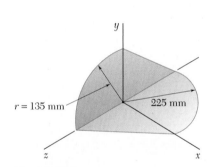

Fig. P9.156

9.157 and 9.158 Brass wire with a weight per unit length w is used to form the figure shown. Determine the mass products of inertia I_{xy}, I_{yz}, and I_{zx} of the wire figure.

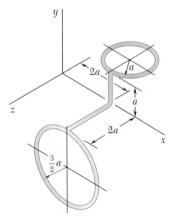

Fig. P9.157

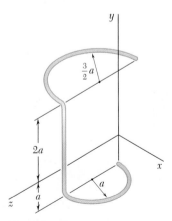

Fig. P9.158

9.159 The figure shown is formed of 1.5-mm-diameter aluminum wire. Knowing that the density of aluminum is 2800 kg/m³, determine the mass products of inertia I_{xy}, I_{yz}, and I_{zx} of the wire figure.

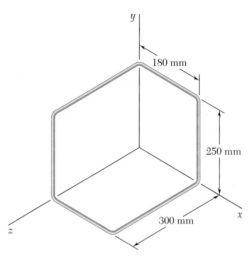

Fig. P9.159

9.160 Thin aluminum wire of uniform diameter is used to form the figure shown. Denoting by m' the mass per unit length of the wire, determine the mass products of inertia I_{xy}, I_{yz}, and I_{zx} of the wire figure.

9.161 Complete the derivation of Eqs. (9.47), which express the parallel-axis theorem for mass products of inertia.

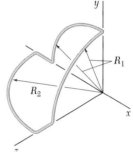

Fig. P9.160

9.162 For the homogeneous tetrahedron of mass m shown, (a) determine by direct integration the mass product of inertia I_{zx}, (b) deduce I_{yz} and I_{xy} from the result obtained in part a.

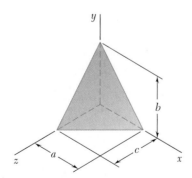

Fig. P9.162

9.163 The homogeneous circular cylinder shown has a mass m. Determine the mass moment of inertia of the cylinder with respect to the line joining the origin O and point A that is located on the perimeter of the top surface of the cylinder.

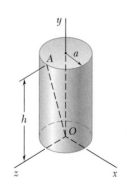

Fig. P9.163

9.164 The homogeneous circular cone shown has a mass m. Determine the mass moment of inertia of the cone with respect to the line joining the origin O and point A.

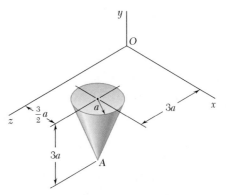

Fig. P9.164

9.165 Shown is the machine element of Prob. 9.141. Determine its mass moment of inertia with respect to the line joining the origin O and point A.

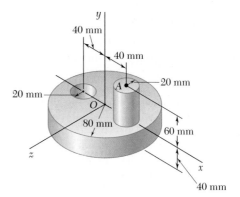

Fig. P9.165

9.166 Determine the mass moment of inertia of the steel fixture of Probs. 9.145 and 9.149 with respect to the axis through the origin that forms equal angles with the x, y, and z axes.

9.167 The thin bent plate shown is of uniform density and weight W. Determine its mass moment of inertia with respect to the line joining the origin O and point A.

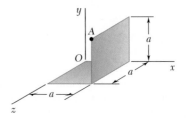

Fig. P9.167

9.168 A piece of sheet steel of thickness t and specific weight γ is cut and bent into the machine component shown. Determine the mass moment of inertia of the component with respect to the line joining the origin O and point A.

9.169 Determine the mass moment of inertia of the machine component of Probs. 9.136 and 9.155 with respect to the axis through the origin characterized by the unit vector $\boldsymbol{\lambda} = (-4\mathbf{i} + 8\mathbf{j} + \mathbf{k})/9$.

9.170 through 9.172 For the wire figure of the problem indicated, determine the mass moment of inertia of the figure with respect to the axis through the origin characterized by the unit vector $\boldsymbol{\lambda} = (-3\mathbf{i} - 6\mathbf{j} + 2\mathbf{k})/7$.

    9.170 Prob. 9.148
    9.171 Prob. 9.147
    9.172 Prob. 9.146

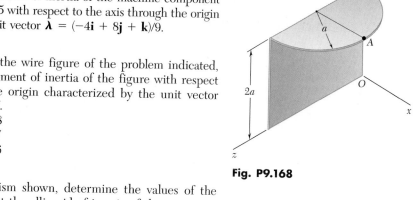

Fig. P9.168

9.173 For the rectangular prism shown, determine the values of the ratios b/a and c/a so that the ellipsoid of inertia of the prism is a sphere when computed (a) at point A, (b) at point B.

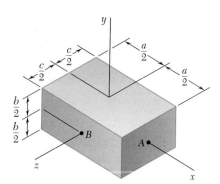

Fig. P9.173

9.174 For the right circular cone of Sample Prob. 9.11, determine the value of the ratio a/h for which the ellipsoid of inertia of the cone is a sphere when computed (a) at the apex of the cone, (b) at the center of the base of the cone.

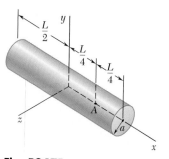

9.175 For the homogeneous circular cylinder shown, of radius a and length L, determine the value of the ratio a/L for which the ellipsoid of inertia of the cylinder is a sphere when computed (a) at the centroid of the cylinder, (b) at point A.

Fig. P9.175

9.176 Given an arbitrary body and three rectangular axes x, y, and z, prove that the mass moment of inertia of the body with respect to any one of the three axes cannot be larger than the sum of the mass moments of inertia of the body with respect to the other two axes. That is, prove that the inequality $I_x \leq I_y + I_z$ and the two similar inequalities are satisfied. Further, prove that $I_y \geq \frac{1}{2}I_x$ if the body is a homogeneous solid of revolution, where x is the axis of revolution and y is a transverse axis.

9.177 Consider a cube of mass m and side a. (a) Show that the ellipsoid of inertia at the center of the cube is a sphere, and use this property to determine the moment of inertia of the cube with respect to one of its diagonals. (b) Show that the ellipsoid of inertia at one of the corners of the cube is an ellipsoid of revolution, and determine the principal moments of inertia of the cube at that point.

9.178 Given a homogeneous body of mass m and of arbitrary shape and three rectangular axes x, y, and z with origin at O, prove that the sum $I_x + I_y + I_z$ of the mass moments of inertia of the body cannot be smaller than the similar sum computed for a sphere of the same mass and the same material centered at O. Further, using the result of Prob. 9.176, prove that if the body is a solid of revolution, where x is the axis of revolution, its mass moment of inertia I_y about a transverse axis y cannot be smaller than $3ma^2/10$, where a is the radius of the sphere of the same mass and the same material.

*9.179 The homogeneous circular cylinder shown has a mass m, and the diameter OB of its top surface forms 45° angles with the x and z axes. (a) Determine the principal mass moments of inertia of the cylinder at the origin O. (b) Compute the angles that the principal axes of inertia at O form with the coordinate axes. (c) Sketch the cylinder, and show the orientation of the principal axes of inertia relative to the x, y, and z axes.

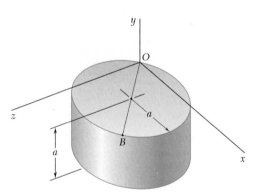

Fig. P9.179

9.180 through 9.184 For the component described in the problem indicated, determine (a) the principal mass moments of inertia at the origin, (b) the principal axes of inertia at the origin. Sketch the body and show the orientation of the principal axes of inertia relative to the x, y, and z axes.

    *9.180 Prob. 9.165
    *9.181 Probs. 9.145 and 9.149
    *9.182 Prob. 9.167
    *9.183 Prob. 9.168
    *9.184 Probs. 9.148 and 9.170

REVIEW AND SUMMARY

In the first half of this chapter, we discussed the determination of the resultant $\mathbf{R}$ of forces $\Delta\mathbf{F}$ distributed over a plane area A when the magnitudes of these forces are proportional to both the areas ΔA of the elements on which they act and the distances y from these elements to a given x axis; we thus had $\Delta F = ky\ \Delta A$. We found that the magnitude of the resultant $\mathbf{R}$ is proportional to the first moment $Q_x = \int y\ dA$ of the area A, while the moment of $\mathbf{R}$ about the x axis is proportional to the *second moment*, or *moment of inertia*, $I_x = \int y^2\ dA$ of A with respect to the same axis [Sec. 9.2].

The *rectangular moments of inertia I_x and I_y of an area* [Sec. 9.3] were obtained by evaluating the integrals

Rectangular moments of inertia

$$I_x = \int y^2\ dA \qquad I_y = \int x^2\ dA \qquad (9.1)$$

These computations can be reduced to single integrations by choosing dA to be a thin strip parallel to one of the coordinate axes. We also recall that it is possible to compute I_x and I_y from the same elemental strip (Fig. 9.35) using the formula for the moment of inertia of a rectangular area [Sample Prob. 9.3].

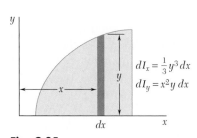

$$dI_x = \frac{1}{3}y^3\ dx$$
$$dI_y = x^2 y\ dx$$

Fig. 9.35

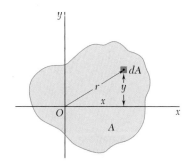

Fig. 9.36

The *polar moment of inertia of an area A with respect to the pole O* [Sec. 9.4] was defined as

Polar moment of inertia

$$J_O = \int r^2\ dA \qquad (9.3)$$

where r is the distance from O to the element of area dA (Fig. 9.36). Observing that $r^2 = x^2 + y^2$, we established the relation

$$J_O = I_x + I_y \qquad (9.4)$$

547

Radius of gyration

The *radius of gyration of an area A* with respect to the x axis [Sec. 9.5] was defined as the distance k_x, where $I_x = K_x^2 A$. With similar definitions for the radii of gyration of A with respect to the y axis and with respect to O, we had

$$k_x = \sqrt{\frac{I_x}{A}} \qquad k_y = \sqrt{\frac{I_y}{A}} \qquad k_O = \sqrt{\frac{J_O}{A}} \qquad (9.5\text{--}9.7)$$

Parallel-axis theorem

The parallel-axis theorem was presented in Sec. 9.6. It states that the moment of inertia I of an area with respect to any given axis AA' (Fig. 9.37) is equal to the moment of inertia $\bar{I}$ of the area with respect to the centroidal axis BB' that is parallel to AA' *plus* the product of the area A and the square of the distance d between the two axes:

$$I = \bar{I} + Ad^2 \qquad (9.9)$$

This formula can also be used to determine the moment of inertia $\bar{I}$ of an area with respect to a centroidal axis BB' when its moment of inertia I with respect to a parallel axis AA' is known. In this case, however, the product Ad^2 should be *subtracted* from the known moment of inertia I.

A similar relation holds between the polar moment of inertia J_O of an area about a point O and the polar moment of inertia $\bar{J}_C$ of the same area about its centroid C. Letting d be the distance between O and C, we have

$$J_O = \bar{J}_C + Ad^2 \qquad (9.11)$$

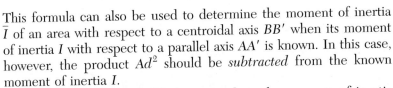

Fig. 9.37

Composite areas

The parallel-axis theorem can be used very effectively to compute the *moment of inertia of a composite area* with respect to a given axis [Sec. 9.7]. Considering each component area separately, we first compute the moment of inertia of each area with respect to its centroidal axis, using the data provided in Figs. 9.12 and 9.13 whenever possible. The parallel-axis theorem is then applied to determine the moment of inertia of each component area with respect to the desired axis, and the various values obtained are added [Sample Probs. 9.4 and 9.5].

Product of inertia

Sections 9.8 through 9.10 were devoted to the transformation of the moments of inertia of an area *under a rotation of the coordinate axes*. First, we defined the *product of inertia of an area A* as

$$I_{xy} = \int xy \, dA \qquad (9.12)$$

and showed that $I_{xy} = 0$ if the area A is symmetrical with respect to either or both of the coordinate axes. We also derived the *parallel-axis theorem for products of inertia*. We had

$$I_{xy} = \bar{I}_{x'y'} + \bar{x}\,\bar{y}\,A \qquad (9.13)$$

where $\bar{I}_{x'y'}$ is the product of inertia of the area with respect to the centroidal axes x' and y' which are parallel to the x and y axis and $\bar{x}$ and $\bar{y}$ are the coordinates of the centroid of the area [Sec. 9.8].

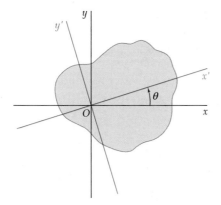

Fig. 9.38

In Sec. 9.9 we determined the moments and product of inertia $I_{x'}$, $I_{y'}$, and $I_{x'y'}$ of an area with respect to x' and y' axes obtained by rotating the original x and y coordinate axes through an angle θ counterclockwise (Fig. 9.38). We expressed $I_{x'}$, $I_{y'}$, and $I_{x'y'}$ in terms of the moments and product of inertia I_x, I_y, and I_{xy} computed with respect to the original x and y axes. We had

Rotation of axes

$$I_{x'} = \frac{I_x + I_y}{2} + \frac{I_x - I_y}{2} \cos 2\theta - I_{xy} \sin 2\theta \qquad (9.18)$$

$$I_{y'} = \frac{I_x + I_y}{2} - \frac{I_x - I_y}{2} \cos 2\theta + I_{xy} \sin 2\theta \qquad (9.19)$$

$$I_{x'y'} = \frac{I_x - I_y}{2} \sin 2\theta + I_{xy} \cos 2\theta \qquad (9.20)$$

The *principal axes of the area about O* were defined as the two axes perpendicular to each other, with respect to which the moments of inertia of the area are maximum and minimum. The corresponding values of θ, denoted by θ_m, were obtained from the formula

Principal axes

$$\tan 2\theta_m = -\frac{2I_{xy}}{I_x - I_y} \qquad (9.25)$$

The corresponding maximum and minimum values of I are called the *principal moments of inertia* of the area about O; we had

Principal moments of inertia

$$I_{\max,\min} = \frac{I_x + I_y}{2} \pm \sqrt{\left(\frac{I_x - I_y}{2}\right)^2 + I_{xy}^2} \qquad (9.27)$$

We also noted that the corresponding value of the product of inertia is zero.

The transformation of the moments and product of inertia of an area under a rotation of axes can be represented graphically by drawing *Mohr's circle* [Sec. 9.10]. Given the moments and product of inertia I_x, I_y, and I_{xy} of the area with respect to the x and y coordinate axes, we

Mohr's circle

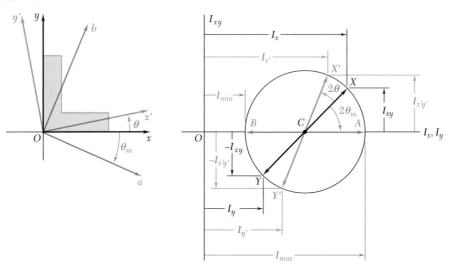

Fig. 9.39

plot points X (I_x, I_{xy}) and Y $(I_y, -I_{xy})$ and draw the line joining these two points (Fig. 9.39). This line is a diameter of Mohr's circle and thus defines this circle. As the coordinate axes are rotated through θ, the diameter rotates through *twice that angle*, and the coordinates of X' and Y' yield the new values $I_{x'}$, $I_{y'}$, and $I_{x'y'}$ of the moments and product of inertia of the area. Also, the angle θ_m and the coordinates of points A and B define the principal axes a and b and the principal moments of inertia of the area [Sample Prob. 9.8].

Moments of inertia of masses The second half of the chapter was devoted to the determination of *moments of inertia of masses*, which are encountered in dynamics in problems involving the rotation of a rigid body about an axis. The mass moment of inertia of a body with respect to an axis AA' (Fig. 9.40) was defined as

$$I = \int r^2 \, dm \tag{9.28}$$

where r is the distance from AA' to the element of mass [Sec. 9.11]. The *radius of gyration* of the body was defined as

$$k = \sqrt{\frac{I}{m}} \tag{9.29}$$

The moments of inertia of a body with respect to the coordinates axes were expressed as

$$I_x = \int (y^2 + z^2) \, dm$$

$$I_y = \int (z^2 + x^2) \, dm \tag{9.30}$$

$$I_z = \int (x^2 + y^2) \, dm$$

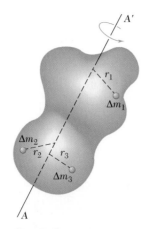

Fig. 9.40

We saw that the *parallel-axis theorem* also applies to mass moments of inertia [Sec. 9.12]. Thus, the moment of inertia I of a body with respect to an arbitrary axis AA' (Fig. 9.41) can be expressed as

$$I = \bar{I} + md^2 \tag{9.33}$$

where $\bar{I}$ is the moment of inertia of the body with respect to the centroidal axis BB' which is parallel to the axis AA', m is the mass of the body, and d is the distance between the two axes.

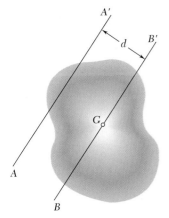

Fig. 9.41

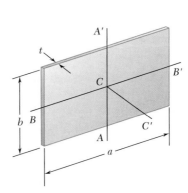

Fig. 9.42

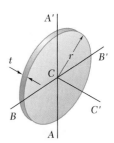

Fig. 9.43

The moments of inertia of *thin plates* can be readily obtained from the moments of inertia of their areas [Sec. 9.13]. We found that for a *rectangular plate* the moments of inertia with respect to the axes shown (Fig. 9.42) are

$$I_{AA'} = \tfrac{1}{12}ma^2 \qquad I_{BB'} = \tfrac{1}{12}mb^2 \tag{9.39}$$
$$I_{CC'} = I_{AA'} + I_{BB'} = \tfrac{1}{12}m(a^2 + b^2) \tag{9.40}$$

while for a *circular plate* (Fig. 9.43) they are

$$I_{AA'} = I_{BB'} = \tfrac{1}{4}mr^2 \tag{9.41}$$
$$I_{CC'} = I_{AA'} + I_{BB'} = \tfrac{1}{2}mr^2 \tag{9.42}$$

When a body possesses *two planes of symmetry*, it is usually possible to use a single integration to determine its moment of inertia with respect to a given axis by selecting the element of mass dm to be a thin plate [Sample Probs. 9.10 and 9.11]. On the other hand, when a body consists of *several common geometric shapes*, its moment of inertia with respect to a given axis can be obtained by using the formulas given in Fig. 9.28 together with the parallel-axis theorem [Sample Probs. 9.12 and 9.13].

In the last portion of the chapter, we learned to determine the moment of inertia of a body *with respect to an arbitrary axis OL* which is drawn through the origin O [Sec. 9.16]. Denoting by λx, λ_y,

λ_z the components of the unit vector $\boldsymbol{\lambda}$ along OL (Fig. 9.44) and introducing the *products of inertia*

$$I_{xy} = \int xy \, dm \qquad I_{yz} = \int yz \, dm \qquad I_{zx} = \int zx \, dm \qquad (9.45)$$

we found that the moment of inertia of the body with respect to OL could be expressed as

$$I_{OL} = I_x\lambda_x^2 + I_y\lambda_y^2 + I_z\lambda_z^2 - 2I_{xy}\lambda_x\lambda_y - 2I_{yz}\lambda_y\lambda_z - 2I_{zx}\lambda_z\lambda_x \qquad (9.46)$$

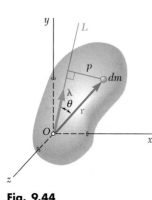

Fig. 9.44

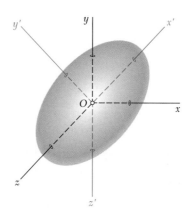

Fig. 9.45

Ellipsoid of inertia

Principal axes of inertia
Principal moments of inertia

By plotting a point Q along each axis OL at a distance $OQ = 1\sqrt{I_{OL}}$ from O [Sec. 9.17], we obtained the surface of an ellipsoid, known as the *ellipsoid of inertia* of the body at point O. The principal axes x', y', z' of this ellipsoid (Fig. 9.45) are the *principal axes of inertia* of the body; that is, the products of inertia $I_{x'y'}$, $I_{y'z'}$, $I_{z'x'}$ of the body with respect to these axes are all zero. There are many situations when the principal axes of inertia of a body can be deduced from properties of symmetry of the body. Choosing these axes to be the coordinate axes, we can then express I_{OL} as

$$I_{OL} = I_{x'}\lambda_{x'}^2 + I_{y'}\lambda_{y'}^2 + I_{z'}\lambda_{z'}^2 \qquad (9.50)$$

where $I_{x'}$, $I_{y'}$, $I_{z'}$ are the *principal moments of inertia* of the body at O.

When the principal axes of inertia cannot be obtained by observation [Sec. 9.17], it is necessary to solve the cubic equation

$$K^3 - (I_x + I_y + I_z)K^2 + (I_xI_y + I_yI_z + I_zI_x - I_{xy}^2 - I_{yz}^2 - I_{zx}^2)K$$
$$- (I_xI_yI_z - I_xI_{yz}^2 - I_yI_{zx}^2 - I_zI_{xy}^2 - 2I_{xy}I_{yz}I_{zx}) = 0 \qquad (9.56)$$

We found [Sec. 9.18] that the roots K_1, K_2, and K_3 of this equation are the principal moments of inertia of the given body. The direction cosines $(\lambda_x)_1$, $(\lambda_y)_1$, and $(\lambda_z)_1$ of the principal axis corresponding to the principal moment of inertia K_1 are then determined by substituting K_1 into Eqs. (9.54) and solving two of these equations and Eq. (9.57) simultaneously. The same procedure is then repeated using K_2 and K_3 to determine the direction cosines of the other two principal axes [Sample Prob. 9.15].

REVIEW PROBLEMS

9.185 Determine by direct integration the moments of inertia of the shaded area with respect to the x and y axes.

9.186 Determine the moments of inertia and the radii of gyration of the shaded area shown with respect to the x and y axes.

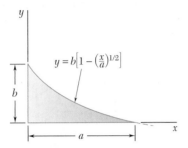

Fig. P9.186

9.187 Determine the moment of inertia and the radius of gyration of the shaded area shown with respect to the y axis.

9.188 Determine the moments of inertia of the shaded area shown with respect to the x and y axes.

9.189 Determine the polar moment of inertia of the area shown with respect to (a) point O, (b) the centroid of the area.

9.190 To form an unsymmetrical girder, two L76 × 76 × 6.4-mm angles and two L152 × 102 × 12.7-mm angles are welded to a 16-mm steel plate as shown. Determine the moments of inertia of the combined section with respect to its centroidal x and y axes.

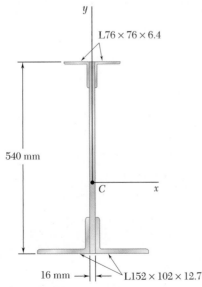

Fig. P9.190

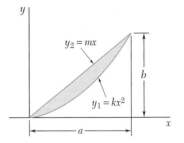

Fig. P9.185

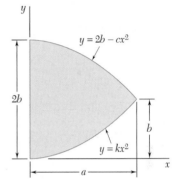

Fig. P9.187

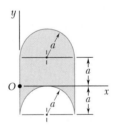

Fig. P9.188

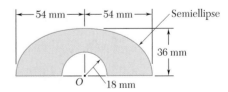

Fig. P9.189

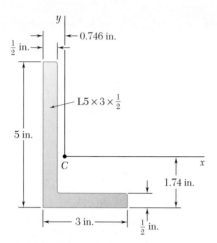

$\frac{1}{2}$ in. →

← 0.746 in.

L5 × 3 × $\frac{1}{2}$

5 in.

C

1.74 in.

← 3 in. →

$\frac{1}{2}$ in.

Fig. P9.191 and P9.192

9.191 Using the parallel-axis theorem, determine the product of inertia of the L5 × 3 × $\frac{1}{2}$-in. angle cross section shown with respect to the centroidal x and y axes.

9.192 For the L5 × 3 × $\frac{1}{2}$-in. angle cross section shown, use Mohr's circle to determine (*a*) the moments of inertia and the product of inertia with respect to new centroidal axes obtained by rotating the x and y axes 30° clockwise, (*b*) the orientation of the principal axes through the centroid and the corresponding values of the moments of inertia.

9.193 A piece of thin, uniform sheet metal is cut to form the machine component shown. Denoting the mass of the component by m, determine its mass moment of inertia with respect to (*a*) the x axis, (*b*) the y axis.

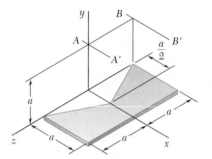

Fig. P9.193 and P9.194

9.194 A piece of thin, uniform sheet metal is cut to form the machine component shown. Denoting the mass of the component by m, determine its mass moment of inertia with respect to (*a*) the axis AA', (*b*) the axis BB', where the AA' and BB' axes are parallel to the x axis and lie in a plane parallel to and at a distance a above the xz plane.

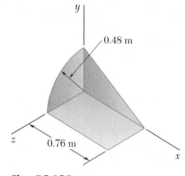

0.48 m

0.76 m

Fig. P9.195

9.195 A 2-mm thick piece of sheet steel is cut and bent into the machine component shown. Knowing that the density of steel is 7850 kg/m³, determine the mass moment of inertia of the component with respect to each of the coordinate axes.

9.196 Determine the mass moments of inertia and the radii of gyration of the steel machine element shown with respect to the x and y axes. (The density of steel is 7850 kg/m³.)

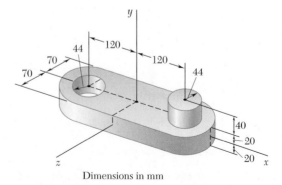

Dimensions in mm

Fig. P9.196

COMPUTER PROBLEMS

9.C1 Use computational software that, for an area with known moments and product of inertia I_x, I_y, and I_{xy}, can be used to calculate the moments and product of inertia $I_{x'}$, $I_{y'}$, and $I_{x'y'}$ of the area with respect to axes x' and y' obtained by rotating the original axes counterclockwise through an angle θ. Use this program to compute $I_{x'}$, $I_{y'}$, and $I_{x'y'}$ for the section of Sample Prob. 9.7 for values of θ from 0 to 90° using 5° increments.

9.C2 Use computational software that, for an area with known moments and product of inertia I_x, I_y, and I_{xy}, can be used to calculate the orientation of the principal axes of the area and the corresponding values of the principal moments of inertia. Use this program to solve (*a*) Prob. 9.89, (*b*) Sample Prob. 9.7.

9.C3 Many cross sections can be approximated by a series of rectangles as shown. Using computational software, calculate the moments of inertia and the radii of gyration of cross sections of this type with respect to horizontal and vertical centroidal axes. Apply this program to the cross sections shown in (*a*) Figs. P9.31 and P9.33, (*b*) Figs. P9.32 and P9.34, (*c*) Fig. P9.43, (*d*) Fig. P9.44.

9.C4 Many cross sections can be approximated by a series of rectangles as shown. Using computational software, calculate the products of inertia of cross sections of this type with respect to horizontal and vertical centroidal axes. Use this program to solve (*a*) Prob. P9.71, (*b*) Prob. P9.75, (*c*) Prob. 9.77.

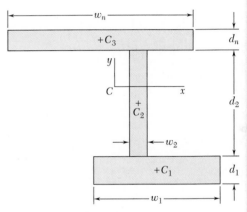

Fig. P9.C3 and P9.C4

9.C5 The area shown is revolved about the x axis to form a homogeneous solid of mass m. Approximate the area using a series of 400 rectangles of the form $bcc'b'$, each of width Δl, and then use computational software to determine the mass moment of inertia of the solid with respect to the x axis. Use this program to solve part a of (*a*) Sample Prob. 9.11, (*b*) Prob. 9.121, assuming that in these problems $m = 2$ kg, $a = 100$ mm, and $h = 400$ mm.

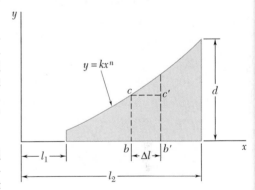

Fig. P9.C5

9.C6 A homogeneous wire with a weight per unit length of 0.04 lb/ft is used to form the figure shown. Approximate the figure using 10 straight line segments, and then use computational software to determine the mass moment of inertia I_x of the wire with respect to the x axis. Use this program to determine I_x when (*a*) $a = 1$ in., $L = 11$ in., $h = 4$ in., (*b*) $a = 2$ in., $L = 17$ in., $h = 10$ in., (*c*) $a = 5$ in., $L = 25$ in., $h = 6$ in.

*9.C7 Use computational software that, for a body with known mass moments and products of inertia I_x, I_y, I_z, I_{xy}, I_{yz}, and I_{zx}, can be used to calculate the principal mass moments of inertia K_1, K_2, and K_3 of the body at the origin. Use this program to solve part a of (*a*) Prob. 9.180, (*b*) Prob. 9.181, (*c*) Prob. 9.184.

*9.C8 Using the software from Prob. 9.C7, include the computation of the angles that the principal axes of inertia at the origin form with the coordinate axes. Use this program to solve (*a*) Prob. 9.180, (*b*) Prob. 9.181, (*c*) Prob. 9.184.

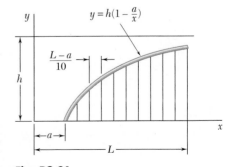

Fig. P9.C6

555

The method of virtual work is particularly effective when a simple relation can be found among the displacements of the points of application of the various forces involved. This is the case for the scissor lift platform being used by workers to gain access to a highway bridge under construction.

Method of Virtual Work

*10.1 INTRODUCTION

In the preceding chapters, problems involving the equilibrium of rigid bodies were solved by expressing that the external forces acting on the bodies were balanced. The equations of equilibrium $\Sigma F_x = 0$, $\Sigma F_y = 0$, $\Sigma M_A = 0$ were written and solved for the desired unknowns. A different method, which will prove more effective for solving certain types of equilibrium problems, will now be considered. This method is based on the *principle of virtual work* and was first formally used by the Swiss mathematician Jean Bernoulli in the eighteenth century.

As you will see in Sec. 10.3, the principle of virtual work states that if a particle or rigid body, or, more generally, a system of connected rigid bodies, which is in equilibrium under various external forces, is given an arbitrary displacement from that position of equilibrium, the total work done by the external forces during the displacement is zero. This principle is particularly effective when applied to the solution of problems involving the equilibrium of machines or mechanisms consisting of several connected members.

In the second part of the chapter, the method of virtual work will be applied in an alternative form based on the concept of *potential energy*. It will be shown in Sec. 10.8 that if a particle, rigid body, or system of rigid bodies is in equilibrium, then the derivative of its potential energy with respect to a variable defining its position must be zero.

In this chapter, you will also learn to evaluate the mechanical efficiency of a machine (Sec. 10.5) and to determine whether a given position of equilibrium is stable, unstable, or neutral (Sec. 10.9).

*10.2 WORK OF A FORCE

Let us first define the terms *displacement* and *work* as they are used in mechanics. Consider a particle which moves from a point A to a neighboring point A' (Fig. 10.1). If $\mathbf{r}$ denotes the position vector corresponding to point A, the small vector joining A and A' may be denoted by the differential $d\mathbf{r}$; the vector $d\mathbf{r}$ is called the *displacement* of the particle. Now let us assume that a force $\mathbf{F}$ is acting on the particle. The *work of the force* $\mathbf{F}$ *corresponding to the displacement* $d\mathbf{r}$ is defined as the quantity

$$dU = \mathbf{F} \cdot d\mathbf{r} \tag{10.1}$$

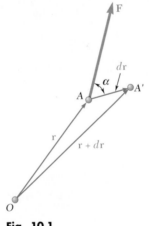

Fig. 10.1

obtained by forming the scalar product of the force $\mathbf{F}$ and the displacement $d\mathbf{r}$. Denoting respectively by F and ds the magnitudes of the force and of the displacement, and by α the angle formed by $\mathbf{F}$ and $d\mathbf{r}$, and recalling the definition of the scalar product of two vectors (Sec. 3.9), we write

$$dU = F\, ds \cos \alpha \tag{10.1'}$$

Being a *scalar quantity*, work has a magnitude and a sign, but no direction. We also note that work should be expressed in units obtained by multiplying units of length by units of force. Thus, if U.S. customary units are used, work should be expressed in ft · lb or in · lb. If SI units are used, work should be expressed in N · m. The unit of work N · m is called a *joule* (J).†

It follows from (10.1′) that the work dU is positive if the angle α is acute and negative if α is obtuse. Three particular cases are of special interest. If the force **F** has the same direction as $d\mathbf{r}$, the work dU reduces to $F\,ds$. If **F** has a direction opposite to that of $d\mathbf{r}$, the work is $dU = -F\,ds$. Finally, if **F** is perpendicular to $d\mathbf{r}$, the work dU is zero.

The work dU of a force **F** during a displacement $d\mathbf{r}$ can also be considered as the product of F and the component $ds \cos \alpha$ of the displacement $d\mathbf{r}$ along **F** (Fig. 10.2a). This view is particularly

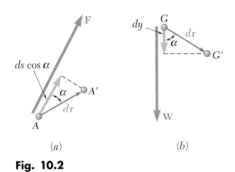

(a)   (b)

Fig. 10.2

Photo 10.1 The forces exerted by the hydraulic cylinders to position the bucket lift shown can be effectively determined using the method of virtual work since a simple relation exists among the displacements of the points of application of the forces acting on the members of the lift.

useful in the computation of the work done by the weight **W** of a body (Fig. 10.2b). The work of **W** is equal to the product of W and the vertical displacement dy of the center of gravity G of the body. If the displacement is downward, the work is positive; if it is upward, the work is negative.

A number of forces frequently encountered in statics *do no work:* forces applied to fixed points ($ds = 0$) or acting in a direction perpendicular to the displacement ($\cos \alpha = 0$). Among these forces are the reaction at a frictionless pin when the body supported rotates about the pin; the reaction at a frictionless surface when the body in contact moves along the surface; the reaction at a roller moving along its track; the weight of a body when its center of gravity moves horizontally; and the friction force acting on a wheel rolling without slipping (since at any instant the point of contact does not move). Examples of forces which *do work* are the weight of a body (except in the case considered above), the friction force acting on a body sliding on a rough surface, and most forces applied on a moving body.

†The joule is the SI unit of *energy*, whether in mechanical form (work, potential energy, kinetic energy) or in chemical, electrical, or thermal form. We should note that even though N · m = J, the moment of a force must be expressed in N · m, and not in joules, since the moment of a force is not a form of energy.

In certain cases, the sum of the work done by several forces is zero. Consider, for example, two rigid bodies *AC* and *BC* connected at *C* by a *frictionless pin* (Fig. 10.3*a*). Among the forces acting on *AC* is the force **F** exerted at *C* by *BC*. In general, the work of this

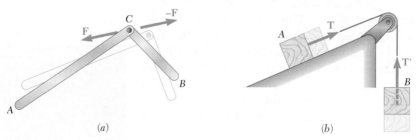

Fig. 10.3

force will not be zero, but it will be equal in magnitude and opposite in sign to the work of the force −**F** exerted by *AC* on *BC*, since these forces are equal and opposite and are applied to the same particle. Thus, when the total work done by all the forces acting on *AB* and *BC* is considered, the work of the two internal forces at *C* cancels out. A similar result is obtained if we consider a system consisting of two blocks connected by an *inextensible cord AB* (Fig. 10.3*b*). The work of the tension force **T** at *A* is equal in magnitude to the work of the tension force **T′** at *B*, since these forces have the same magnitude and the points *A* and *B* move through the same distance; but in one case the work is positive, and in the other it is negative. Thus, the work of the internal forces again cancels out.

It can be shown that the total work of the internal forces holding together the particles of a rigid body is zero. Consider two particles *A* and *B* of a rigid body and the two equal and opposite forces **F** and −**F** they exert on each other (Fig. 10.4). While, in general,

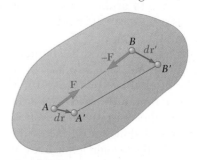

Fig. 10.4

small displacements *d***r** and *d***r′** of the two particles are different, the components of these displacements along *AB* must be equal; otherwise, the particles would not remain at the same distance from each other, and the body would not be rigid. Therefore, the work of **F** is equal in magnitude and opposite in sign to the work of −**F**, and their sum is zero.

In computing the work of the external forces acting on a rigid body, it is often convenient to determine the work of a couple without considering separately the work of each of the two forces forming the couple. Consider the two forces **F** and −**F** forming a couple of moment **M** and acting on a rigid body (Fig. 10.5). Any small displacement of the rigid body bringing A and B, respectively, into A' and B'' can be divided into two parts, one in which points A and B undergo equal displacements $d\mathbf{r}_1$, the other in which A' remains fixed while B' moves into B'' through a displacement $d\mathbf{r}_2$ of magnitude $ds_2 = r\,d\theta$. In the first part of the motion, the work of **F** is equal in magnitude and opposite in sign to the work of $-$**F**, and their sum is zero. In the second part of the motion, only force **F** works, and its work is $dU = F\,ds_2 = Fr\,d\theta$. But the product Fr is equal to the magnitude M of the moment of the couple. Thus, the work of a couple of moment **M** acting on a rigid body is

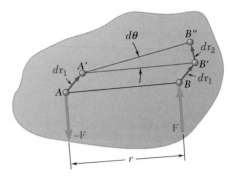

$$dU = M\,d\theta \qquad (10.2)$$

Fig. 10.5

where $d\theta$ is the small angle expressed in radians through which the body rotates. We again note that work should be expressed in units obtained by multiplying units of force by units of length.

*10.3 PRINCIPLE OF VIRTUAL WORK

Consider a particle acted upon by several forces $\mathbf{F}_1, \mathbf{F}_2, \ldots, \mathbf{F}_n$ (Fig. 10.6). We can imagine that the particle undergoes a small displacement from A to A'. This displacement is possible, but it will not necessarily take place. The forces may be balanced and the particle at rest, or the particle may move under the action of the given forces in a direction different from that of AA'. Since the displacement considered does not actually occur, it is called a *virtual displacement* and is denoted by $\delta\mathbf{r}$. The symbol $\delta\mathbf{r}$ represents a differential of the first order; it is used to distinguish the virtual displacement from the displacement $d\mathbf{r}$ which would take place under actual motion. As you will see, virtual displacements can be used to determine whether the conditions of equilibrium of a particle are satisfied.

The work of each of the forces $\mathbf{F}_1, \mathbf{F}_2, \ldots, \mathbf{F}_n$ during the virtual displacement $\delta\mathbf{r}$ is called *virtual work*. The virtual work of all the forces acting on the particle of Fig. 10.6 is

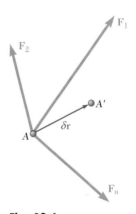

Fig. 10.6

$$\delta U = \mathbf{F}_1 \cdot \delta\mathbf{r} + \mathbf{F}_2 \cdot \delta\mathbf{r} + \cdots + \mathbf{F}_n \cdot \delta\mathbf{r}$$
$$= (\mathbf{F}_1 + \mathbf{F}_2 + \cdots + \mathbf{F}_n) \cdot \delta\mathbf{r}$$

or

$$\delta U = \mathbf{R} \cdot \delta\mathbf{r} \qquad (10.3)$$

where **R** is the resultant of the given forces. Thus, the total virtual work of the forces $\mathbf{F}_1, \mathbf{F}_2, \ldots, \mathbf{F}_n$ is equal to the virtual work of their resultant **R**.

The principle of virtual work for a particle states that *if a particle is in equilibrium, the total virtual work of the forces acting on the particle is zero for any virtual displacement of the particle.* This condition is necessary: if the particle is in equilibrium, the resultant **R** of the forces is zero, and it follows from (10.3) that the total virtual work δU is zero. The condition is also sufficient: if the total virtual work δU is zero for any virtual displacement, the scalar product $\mathbf{R} \cdot \delta\mathbf{r}$ is zero for any $\delta\mathbf{r}$, and the resultant **R** must be zero.

In the case of a rigid body, the principle of virtual work states that *if a rigid body is in equilibrium, the total virtual work of the external forces acting on the rigid body is zero for any virtual displacement of the body.* The condition is necessary: if the body is in equilibrium, all the particles forming the body are in equilibrium and the total virtual work of the forces acting on all the particles must be zero; but we have seen in the preceding section that the total work of the internal forces is zero; the total work of the external forces must therefore also be zero. The condition can also be proved to be sufficient.

The principle of virtual work can be extended to the case of a *system of connected rigid bodies.* If the system remains connected during the virtual displacement, *only the work of the forces external to the system need be considered,* since the total work of the internal forces at the various connections is zero.

*10.4 APPLICATIONS OF THE PRINCIPLE OF VIRTUAL WORK

The principle of virtual work is particularly effective when applied to the solution of problems involving machines or mechanisms consisting of several connected rigid bodies. Consider, for instance, the toggle vise *ACB* of Fig. 10.7*a*, used to compress a wooden block. We

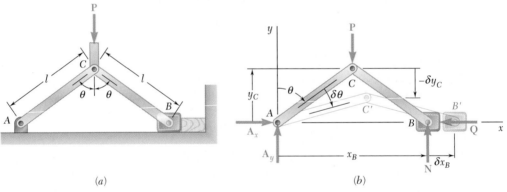

(a)   *(b)*

Fig. 10.7

wish to determine the force exerted by the vise on the block when a given force **P** is applied at *C*, assuming that there is no friction. Denoting by **Q** the reaction of the block on the vise, we draw the free-body diagram of the vise and consider the virtual displacement obtained by giving a positive increment $\delta\theta$ to the angle θ (Fig. 10.7*b*). Choosing a system of coordinate axes with origin at *A*, we note that x_B increases while y_C decreases. This is indicated in the figure, where a positive increment δx_B and a negative increment $-\delta y_C$ are shown. The reactions $\mathbf{A}_x$, $\mathbf{A}_y$, and **N** will do no work during the virtual displacement considered, and we need only compute the work of **P** and **Q**. Since **Q** and δx_B have opposite senses, the virtual work of **Q** is $\delta U_Q = -Q\,\delta x_B$. Since **P** and the increment shown $(-\delta y_C)$ have the same sense, the virtual work of **P** is $\delta U_P = +P(-\delta y_C) = -P\,\delta y_C$. The minus signs obtained could have been predicted by simply noting that the forces **Q** and **P** are directed opposite to the positive

x and y axes, respectively. Expressing the coordinates x_B and y_C in terms of the angle θ and differentiating, we obtain

$$x_B = 2l \sin \theta \qquad y_C = l \cos \theta$$
$$\delta x_B = 2l \cos \theta \, \delta\theta \qquad \delta y_C = -l \sin \theta \, \delta\theta \qquad (10.4)$$

The total virtual work of the forces $\mathbf{Q}$ and $\mathbf{P}$ is thus

$$\delta U = \delta U_Q + \delta U_P = -Q \, \delta x_B - P \, \delta y_C$$
$$= -2Ql \cos \theta \, \delta\theta + Pl \sin \theta \, \delta\theta$$

Making $\delta U = 0$, we obtain

$$2Ql \cos \theta \, \delta\theta = Pl \sin \theta \, \delta\theta \qquad (10.5)$$
$$Q = \tfrac{1}{2}P \tan \theta \qquad (10.6)$$

The superiority of the method of virtual work over the conventional equilibrium equations in the problem considered here is clear: by using the method of virtual work, we were able to eliminate all unknown reactions, while the equation $\Sigma M_A = 0$ would have eliminated only two of the unknown reactions. This property of the method of virtual work can be used in solving many problems involving machines and mechanisms. *If the virtual displacement considered is consistent with the constraints imposed by the supports and connections, all reactions and internal forces are eliminated and only the work of the loads, applied forces, and friction forces need be considered.*

The method of virtual work can also be used to solve problems involving completely constrained structures, although the virtual displacements considered will never actually take place. Consider, for example, the frame ACB shown in Fig. 10.8a. If point A is kept fixed, while B is given a horizontal virtual displacement (Fig. 10.8b), we need consider only the work of $\mathbf{P}$ and $\mathbf{B}_x$. We can thus determine

Photo 10.2 The clamping force of the toggle clamp shown can be expressed as a function of the force applied to the handle by first establishing the geometric relations among the members of the clamp and then applying the method of virtual work.

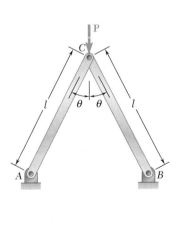

(a)

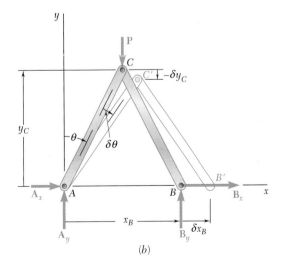

(b)

Fig. 10.8

the reaction component $\mathbf{B}_x$ in the same way as the force $\mathbf{Q}$ of the preceding example (Fig. 10.7b); we have

$$B_x = -\tfrac{1}{2}P \tan \theta$$

Keeping B fixed and giving to A a horizontal virtual displacement, we can similarly determine the reaction component $\mathbf{A}_x$. The components $\mathbf{A}_y$ and $\mathbf{B}_y$ can be determined by rotating the frame ACB as a rigid body about B and A, respectively.

The method of virtual work can also be used to determine the configuration of a system in equilibrium under given forces. For example, the value of the angle θ for which the linkage of Fig. 10.7 is in equilibrium under two given forces $\mathbf{P}$ and $\mathbf{Q}$ can be obtained by solving Eq. (10.6) for $\tan \theta$.

It should be noted, however, that the attractiveness of the method of virtual work depends to a large extent upon the existence of simple geometric relations between the various virtual displacements involved in the solution of a given problem. When no such simple relations exist, it is usually advisable to revert to the conventional method of Chap. 6.

*10.5   REAL MACHINES. MECHANICAL EFFICIENCY

In analyzing the toggle vise in the preceding section, we assumed that no friction forces were involved. Thus, the virtual work consisted only of the work of the applied force $\mathbf{P}$ and of the reaction $\mathbf{Q}$. But the work of the reaction $\mathbf{Q}$ is equal in magnitude and opposite in sign to the work of the force exerted by the vise on the block. Equation (10.5), therefore, expresses that the *output work* $2Ql \cos \theta \, \delta\theta$ is equal to the *input work* $Pl \sin \theta \, \delta\theta$. A machine in which input and output work are equal is said to be an "ideal" machine. In a "real" machine, friction forces will always do some work, and the output work will be smaller than the input work.

Consider, for example, the toggle vise of Fig. 10.7a, and assume now that a friction force $\mathbf{F}$ develops between the sliding block B and the horizontal plane (Fig. 10.9). Using the conventional methods of statics and summing moments about A, we find $N = P/2$. Denoting by μ the coefficient of friction between block B and the horizontal

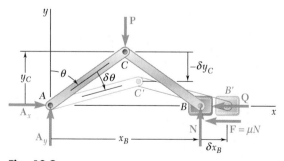

Fig. 10.9

plane, we have $F = \mu N = \mu P/2$. Recalling formulas (10.4), we find that the total virtual work of the forces **Q**, **P**, and **F** during the virtual displacement shown in Fig. 10.9 is

$$\delta U = -Q \, \delta x_B - P \, \delta y_C - F \, \delta x_B$$
$$= -2Ql \cos \theta \, \delta\theta + Pl \sin \theta \, \delta\theta - \mu Pl \cos \theta \, \delta\theta$$

Making $\delta U = 0$, we obtain

$$2Ql \cos \theta \, \delta\theta = Pl \sin \theta \, \delta\theta - \mu Pl \cos \theta \, \delta\theta \qquad (10.7)$$

which expresses that the output work is equal to the input work minus the work of the friction force. Solving for Q, we have

$$Q = \tfrac{1}{2}P(\tan \theta - \mu) \qquad (10.8)$$

We note that $Q = 0$ when $\tan \theta = \mu$, that is, when θ is equal to the angle of friction ϕ, and that $Q < 0$ when $\theta < \phi$. The toggle vise may thus be used only for values of θ larger than the angle of friction.

The *mechanical efficiency* of a machine is defined as the ratio

$$\eta = \frac{\text{output work}}{\text{input work}} \qquad (10.9)$$

Clearly, the mechanical efficiency of an ideal machine is $\eta = 1$, since input and output work are then equal, while the mechanical efficiency of a real machine will always be less than 1.

In the case of the toggle vise we have just analyzed, we write

$$\eta = \frac{\text{output work}}{\text{input work}} = \frac{2Ql \cos \theta \, \delta\theta}{Pl \sin \theta \, \delta\theta}$$

Substituting from (10.8) for Q, we obtain

$$\eta = \frac{P(\tan \theta - \mu)l \cos \theta \, \delta\theta}{Pl \sin \theta \, \delta\theta} = 1 - \mu \cot \theta \qquad (10.10)$$

We check that in the absence of friction forces, we would have $\mu = 0$ and $\eta = 1$. In the general case, when μ is different from zero, the efficiency η becomes zero for $\mu \cot \theta = 1$, that is, for $\tan \theta = \mu$, or $\theta = \tan^{-1} \mu = \phi$. We note again that the toggle vise can be used only for values of θ larger than the angle of friction ϕ.

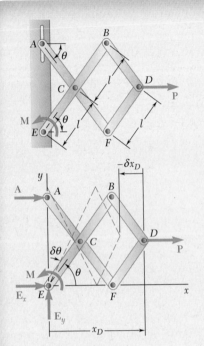

SAMPLE PROBLEM 10.1

Using the method of virtual work, determine the magnitude of the couple **M** required to maintain the equilibrium of the mechanism shown.

SOLUTION

Choosing a coordinate system with origin at E, we write

$$x_D = 3l \cos \theta \qquad \delta x_D = -3l \sin \theta \; \delta\theta$$

Principle of Virtual Work. Since the reactions **A**, $\mathbf{E}_x$, and $\mathbf{E}_y$ will do no work during the virtual displacement, the total virtual work done by **M** and **P** must be zero. Noting that **P** acts in the positive x direction and **M** acts in the positive θ direction, we write

$$\delta U = 0: \qquad +M \, \delta\theta + P \, \delta x_D = 0$$
$$+M \, \delta\theta + P(-3l \sin \theta \; \delta\theta) = 0$$

$$M = 3Pl \sin \theta \quad \blacktriangleleft$$

SAMPLE PROBLEM 10.2

Determine the expressions for θ and for the tension in the spring which correspond to the equilibrium position of the mechanism. The unstretched length of the spring is h, and the constant of the spring is k. Neglect the weight of the mechanism.

SOLUTION

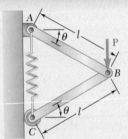

With the coordinate system shown

$$y_B = l \sin \theta \qquad y_C = 2l \sin \theta$$
$$\delta y_B = l \cos \theta \; \delta\theta \qquad \delta y_C = 2l \cos \theta \; \delta\theta$$

The elongation of the spring is $\quad s = y_C - h = 2l \sin \theta - h$

The magnitude of the force exerted at C by the spring is

$$F = ks = k(2l \sin \theta - h) \tag{1}$$

Principle of Virtual Work. Since the reactions $\mathbf{A}_x$, $\mathbf{A}_y$, and **C** do no work, the total virtual work done by **P** and **F** must be zero.

$$\delta U = 0: \qquad P \, \delta y_B - F \, \delta y_C = 0$$
$$P(l \cos \theta \; \delta\theta) - k(2l \sin \theta - h)(2l \cos \theta \; \delta\theta) = 0$$

$$\sin \theta = \frac{P + 2kh}{4kl} \quad \blacktriangleleft$$

Substituting this expression into (1), we obtain $\qquad F = \tfrac{1}{2}P \quad \blacktriangleleft$

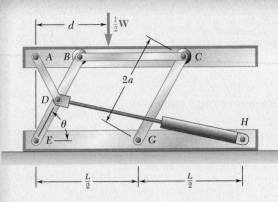

SAMPLE PROBLEM 10.3

A hydraulic-lift table is used to raise a 1000-kg crate. It consists of a platform and of two identical linkages on which hydraulic cylinders exert equal forces. (Only one linkage and one cylinder are shown.) Members EDB and CG are each of length $2a$, and member AD is pinned to the midpoint of EDB. If the crate is placed on the table, so that half of its weight is supported by the system shown, determine the force exerted by each cylinder in raising the crate for $\theta = 60°$, $a = 0.70$ m, and $L = 3.20$ m. This mechanism has been previously considered in Sample Prob. 6.7.

SOLUTION

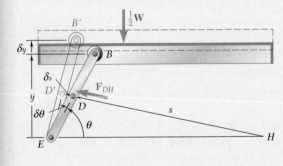

The machine considered consists of the platform and of the linkage, with an input force $\mathbf{F}_{DH}$ exerted by the cylinder and an output force equal and opposite to $\frac{1}{2}\mathbf{W}$.

Principle of Virtual Work. We first observe that the reactions at E and G do no work. Denoting by y the elevation of the platform above the base, and by s the length DH of the cylinder-and-piston assembly, we write

$$\delta U = 0: \qquad -\tfrac{1}{2}W\,\delta y + F_{DH}\,\delta s = 0 \qquad (1)$$

The vertical displacement δy of the platform is expressed in terms of the angular displacement $\delta\theta$ of EDB as follows:

$$y = (EB)\sin\theta = 2a\sin\theta$$
$$\delta y = 2a\cos\theta\,\delta\theta$$

To express δs similarly in terms of $\delta\theta$, we first note that by the law of cosines,

$$s^2 = a^2 + L^2 - 2aL\cos\theta$$

Differentiating,

$$2s\,\delta s = -2aL(-\sin\theta)\,\delta\theta$$
$$\delta s = \frac{aL\sin\theta}{s}\,\delta\theta$$

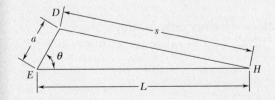

Substituting for δy and δs into (1), we write

$$(-\tfrac{1}{2}W)2a\cos\theta\,\delta\theta + F_{DH}\frac{aL\sin\theta}{s}\,\delta\theta = 0$$

$$F_{DH} = W\frac{s}{L}\cot\theta$$

With the given numerical data, we have

$$W = mg = (1000\text{ kg})(9.81\text{ m/s}^2) = 9810\text{ N} = 9.81\text{ kN}$$
$$s^2 = a^2 + L^2 - 2aL\cos\theta$$
$$= (0.70)^2 + (3.20)^2 - 2(0.70)(3.20)\cos 60° = 8.49$$
$$s = 2.91\text{ m}$$

$$F_{DH} = W\frac{s}{L}\cot\theta = (9.81\text{ kN})\frac{2.91\text{ m}}{3.20\text{ m}}\cot 60°$$

$$F_{DH} = 5.15\text{ kN} \quad \blacktriangleleft$$

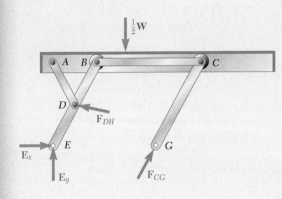

SOLVING PROBLEMS
ON YOUR OWN

In this lesson you learned to use the *method of virtual work*, which is a different way of solving problems involving the equilibrium of rigid bodies.

The work done by a force during a displacement of its point of application or by a couple during a rotation is found by using Eqs. (10.1) and (10.2), respectively:

$$dU = F \, ds \cos \alpha \qquad \qquad (10.1)$$
$$dU = M \, d\theta \qquad \qquad (10.2)$$

Principle of virtual work. In its more general and more useful form, this principle can be stated as follows: *If a system of connected rigid bodies is in equilibrium, the total virtual work of the external forces applied to the system is zero for any virtual displacement of the system.*

As you apply the principle of virtual work, keep in mind the following:

1. Virtual displacement. A machine or mechanism in equilibrium has no tendency to move. However, *we can cause, or imagine, a small displacement.* Since it does not actually occur, such a displacement is called a *virtual displacement.*

2. Virtual work. The work done by a force or couple during a virtual displacement is called *virtual work.*

3. You need consider only the forces which do work during the virtual displacement.

4. Forces which do no work during a virtual displacement that is consistent with the constraints imposed on the system are:
   a. Reactions at supports
   b. Internal forces at connections
   c. Forces exerted by inextensible cords and cables
None of these forces need be considered when you use the method of virtual work.

5. Be sure to express the various virtual displacements involved in your computations in terms of a *single virtual displacement.* This is done in each of the three preceding sample problems, where the virtual displacements are all expressed in terms of $\delta\theta$.

6. Remember that the method of virtual work is effective only in those cases where the geometry of the system makes it relatively easy to relate the displacements involved.

PROBLEMS

10.1 Determine the vertical force **P** that must be applied at C to maintain the equilibrium of the linkage.

10.2 Determine the horizontal force **P** that must be applied at A to maintain the equilibrium of the linkage.

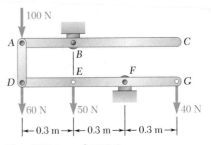

Fig. P10.1 and P10.3

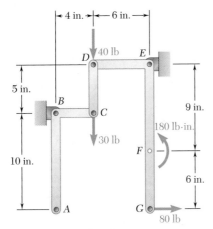

Fig. P10.2 and P10.4

10.3 and 10.4 Determine the couple **M** that must be applied to member ABC to maintain the equilibrium of the linkage.

10.5 Knowing that the maximum friction force exerted by the bottle on the cork is 60 lb, determine (*a*) the force **P** that must be applied to the corkscrew to open the bottle, (*b*) the maximum force exerted by the base of the corkscrew on the top of the bottle.

10.6 The two-bar linkage shown is supported by a pin and bracket at B and a collar at D that slides freely on a vertical rod. Determine the force **P** required to maintain the equilibrium of the linkage.

Fig. P10.5

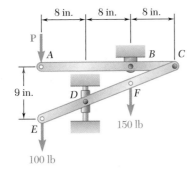

Fig. P10.6

569

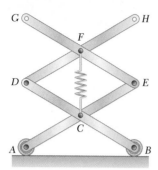

Fig. P10.7 and P10.8

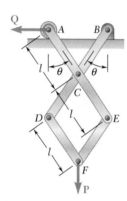

Fig. P10.11

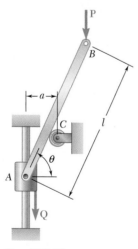

Fig. P10.12

10.7 A spring of constant 15 kN/m connects points C and F of the linkage shown. Neglecting the weight of the spring and linkage, determine the force in the spring and the vertical motion of point G when a vertical downward 120-N force is applied (*a*) at point C, (*b*) at points C and H.

10.8 A spring of constant 15 kN/m connects points C and F of the linkage shown. Neglecting the weight of the spring and linkage, determine the force in the spring and the vertical motion of point G when a vertical downward 120-N force is applied (*a*) at point E, (*b*) at points E and F.

10.9 Knowing that the line of action of the force $\mathbf{Q}$ passes through point C, derive an expression for the magnitude of $\mathbf{Q}$ required to maintain equilibrium.

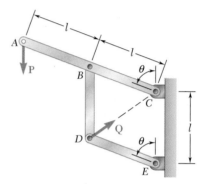

Fig. P10.9

10.10 Solve Prob. 10.9 assuming that the force $\mathbf{P}$ applied at point A acts horizontally to the left.

10.11 The mechanism shown is acted upon by the force $\mathbf{P}$; derive an expression for the magnitude of the force $\mathbf{Q}$ required to maintain equilibrium.

10.12 and 10.13 The slender rod AB is attached to a collar A and rests on a small wheel at C. Neglecting the radius of the wheel and the effect of friction, derive an expression for the magnitude of the force $\mathbf{Q}$ required to maintain the equilibrium of the rod.

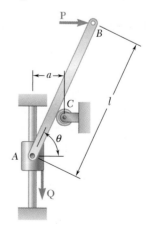

Fig. P10.13

10.14 Derive an expression for the magnitude of the force **Q** required to maintain the equilibrium of the mechanism shown.

10.15 A uniform rod *AB* of length *l* and weight *W* is suspended from two cords *AC* and *BC* of equal length. Derive an expression for the magnitude of the couple **M** required to maintain equilibrium of the rod in the position shown.

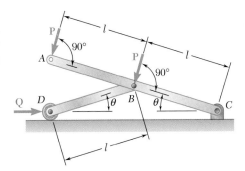

Fig. *P10.14*

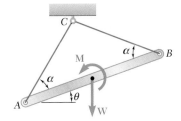

Fig. P10.15

10.16 and 10.17   Derive an expression for the magnitude of the couple **M** required to maintain the equilibrium of the linkage shown.

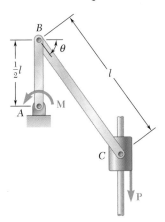

Fig. P10.16

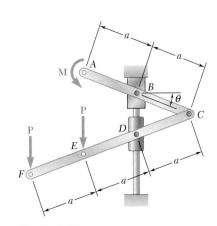

Fig. P10.17

10.18 The pin at *C* is attached to member *BCD* and can slide along a slot cut in the fixed plate shown. Neglecting the effect of friction, derive an expression for the magnitude of the couple **M** required to maintain equilibrium when the force **P** that acts at *D* is directed (*a*) as shown, (*b*) vertically downward, (*c*) horizontally to the right.

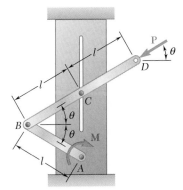

Fig. P10.18

10.19 A 4-kN force **P** is applied as shown to the piston of the engine system. Knowing that $AB = 50$ mm and $BC = 200$ mm, determine the couple **M** required to maintain the equilibrium of the system when (a) $\theta = 30°$, (b) $\theta = 150°$.

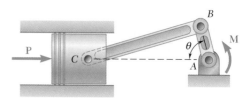

Fig. P10.19 and P10.20

10.20 A couple **M** of magnitude 100 N · m is applied as shown to the crank of the engine system. Knowing that $AB = 50$ mm and $BC = 200$ mm, determine the force **P** required to maintain the equilibrium of the system when (a) $\theta = 60°$, (b) $\theta = 120°$.

10.21 For the linkage shown, determine the couple **M** required for equilibrium when $l = 1.8$ ft, $Q = 40$ lb, and $\theta = 65°$.

10.22 For the linkage shown, determine the force **Q** required for equilibrium when $l = 18$ in., $M = 600$ lb · in., and $\theta = 70°$.

10.23 Determine the value of θ corresponding to the equilibrium position of the mechanism of Prob. 10.11 when $P = 45$ lb and $Q = 160$ lb.

10.24 Determine the value of θ corresponding to the equilibrium position of the mechanism of Prob. 10.9 when $P = 80$ N and $Q = 100$ N.

10.25 Rod AB is attached to a block at A that can slide freely in the vertical slot shown. Neglecting the effect of friction and the weights of the rods, determine the value of θ corresponding to equilibrium.

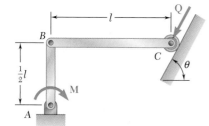

Fig. P10.21 and P10.22

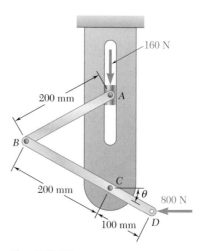

Fig. P10.25

10.26 Solve Prob. 10.25 assuming that the 800-N force is replaced by a 24-N · m clockwise couple applied at D.

10.27 Determine the value of θ corresponding to the equilibrium position of the rod of Prob. 10.12 when $l = 30$ in., $a = 5$ in., $P = 25$ lb, and $Q = 40$ lb.

10.28 Determine the values of θ corresponding to the equilibrium position of the rod of Prob. 10.13 when $l = 600$ mm, $a = 100$ mm, $P = 50$ N, and $Q = 90$ N.

10.29 Two rods AC and CE are connected by a pin at C and by a spring AE. The constant of the spring is k, and the spring is unstretched when $\theta = 30°$. For the loading shown, derive an equation in P, θ, l, and k that must be satisfied when the system is in equilibrium.

10.30 Two rods AC and CE are connected by a pin at C and by a spring AE. The constant of the spring is 1.5 lb/in., and the spring is unstretched when $\theta = 30°$. Knowing that $l = 10$ in. and neglecting the weight of the rods, determine the value of θ corresponding to equilibrium when $P = 40$ lb.

10.31 Solve Prob. 10.30 assuming that force $\mathbf{P}$ is moved to C and acts vertically downward.

10.32 Rod ABC is attached to blocks A and B that can move freely in the guides shown. The constant of the spring attached at A is $k = 3$ kN/m, and the spring is unstretched when the rod is vertical. For the loading shown, determine the value of θ corresponding to equilibrium.

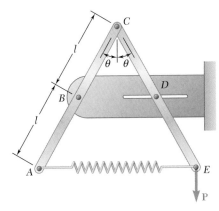

Fig. P10.29 and P10.30

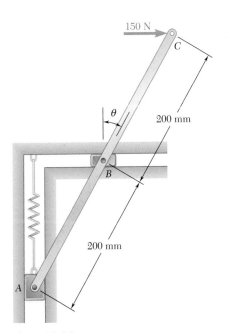

Fig. P10.32

10.33 A load **W** of magnitude 600 N is applied to the linkage at B. The constant of the spring is $k = 2.5$ kN/m, and the spring is unstretched when AB and BC are horizontal. Neglecting the weight of the linkage and knowing that $l = 300$ mm, determine the value of θ corresponding to equilibrium.

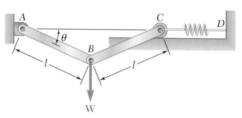

Fig. P10.33 and P10.34

10.34 A vertical load **W** is applied to the linkage at B. The constant of the spring is k, and the spring is unstretched when AB and BC are horizontal. Neglecting the weight of the linkage, derive an equation in θ, W, l, and k that must be satisfied when the linkage is in equilibrium.

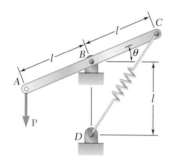

Fig. P10.35 and P10.36

10.35 and 10.36 Knowing that the constant of spring CD is k and that the spring is unstretched when rod ABC is horizontal, determine the value of θ corresponding to equilibrium for the data indicated.

    10.35 $P = 300$ N, $l = 400$ mm, $k = 5$ kN/m.
    10.36 $P = 75$ lb, $l = 15$ in., $k = 20$ lb/in.

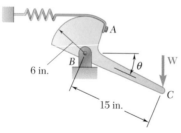

Fig. P10.37

10.37 A load **W** of magnitude 72 lb is applied to the mechanism at C. Neglecting the weight of the mechanism, determine the value of θ corresponding to equilibrium. The constant of the spring is $k = 20$ lb/in., and the spring is unstretched when $\theta = 0$.

10.38 A force **P** of magnitude 240 N is applied to end E of cable CDE, which passes under pulley D and is attached to the mechanism at C. Neglecting the weight of the mechanism and the radius of the pulley, determine the value of θ corresponding to equilibrium. The constant of the spring is $k = 4$ kN/m, and the spring is unstretched when $\theta = 90°$.

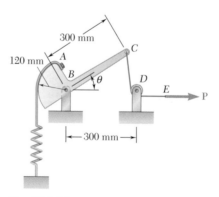

Fig. P10.38

10.39 The lever AB is attached to the horizontal shaft BC that passes through a bearing and is welded to a fixed support at C. The torsional spring constant of the shaft BC is K; that is, a couple of magnitude K is required to rotate end B through 1 rad. Knowing that the shaft is untwisted when AB is horizontal, determine the value of θ corresponding to the position of equilibrium when $P = 100$ N, $l = 250$ mm, and $K = 12.5$ N · m/rad.

10.40 Solve Prob. 10.39 assuming that $P = 350$ N, $l = 250$ mm, and $K = 12.5$ N · m/rad. Obtain answers in each of the following quadrants: $0 < \theta < 90°$, $270° < \theta < 360°$, $360° < \theta < 450°$.

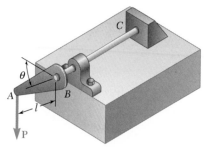

Fig. P10.39

10.41 The position of boom ABC is controlled by the hydraulic cylinder BD. For the loading shown, determine the force exerted by the hydraulic cylinder on pin B when $\theta = 65°$.

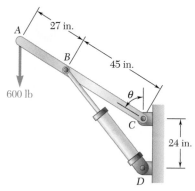

Fig. P10.41 and P10.42

10.42 The position of boom ABC is controlled by the hydraulic cylinder BD. For the loading shown, (a) express the force exerted by the hydraulic cylinder on pin B as a function of the length BD, (b) determine the smallest possible value of the angle θ if the maximum force that the cylinder can exert on pin B is 2.5 kips.

10.43 The position of member ABC is controlled by the hydraulic cylinder CD. For the loading shown, determine the force exerted by the hydraulic cylinder on pin C when $\theta = 55°$.

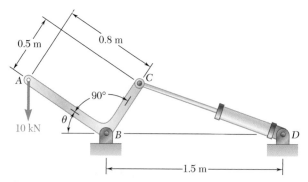

Fig. P10.43 and P10.44

10.44 The position of member ABC is controlled by the hydraulic cylinder CD. Determine the angle θ knowing that the hydraulic cylinder exerts a 15-kN force on pin C.

10.45 The telescoping arm *ABC* is used to provide an elevated platform for construction workers. The workers and the platform together weigh 500 lb and their combined center of gravity is located directly above *C*. For the position when $\theta = 20°$, determine the force exerted on pin *B* by the single hydraulic cylinder *BD*.

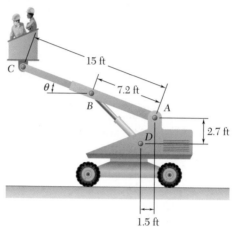

Fig. P10.45

10.46 Solve Prob. 10.45 assuming that the workers are lowered to a point near the ground so that $\theta = -20°$.

10.47 A block of weight *W* is pulled up a plane forming an angle α with the horizontal by a force **P** directed along the plane. If μ is the coefficient of friction between the block and the plane, derive an expression for the mechanical efficiency of the system. Show that the mechanical efficiency cannot exceed $\frac{1}{2}$ if the block is to remain in place when the force **P** is removed.

10.48 Denoting by μ_s the coefficient of static friction between the block attached to rod *ACE* and the horizontal surface, derive expressions in terms of *P*, μ_s, and θ for the largest and smallest magnitude of the force **Q** for which equilibrium is maintained.

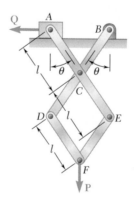

Fig. P10.48 and P10.49

10.49 Knowing that the coefficient of static friction between the block attached to rod *ACE* and the horizontal surface is 0.15, determine the magnitude of the largest and smallest force **Q** for which equilibrium is maintained when $\theta = 30°$, $l = 0.2$ m, and $P = 40$ N.

10.50 Denoting by μ_s the coefficient of static friction between collar C and the vertical rod, derive an expression for the magnitude of the largest couple **M** for which equilibrium is maintained in the position shown. Explain what happens if $\mu_s \geq \tan \theta$.

10.51 Knowing that the coefficient of static friction between collar C and the vertical rod is 0.40, determine the magnitude of the largest and smallest couple **M** for which equilibrium is maintained in the position shown, when $\theta = 35°$, $l = 600$ mm, and $P = 300$ N.

10.52 Derive an expression for the mechanical efficiency of the jack discussed in Sec. 8.6. Show that if the jack is to be self-locking, the mechanical efficiency cannot exceed $\frac{1}{2}$.

10.53 Using the method of virtual work, determine the reaction at E.

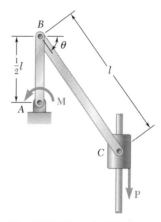

Fig. P10.50 and P10.51

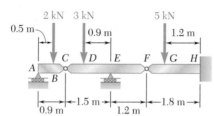

Fig. P10.53 and P10.54

10.54 Using the method of virtual work, determine separately the force and couple representing the reaction at H.

10.55 Referring to Prob. 10.43 and using the value found for the force exerted by the hydraulic cylinder CD, determine the change in the length of CD required to raise the 10-kN load by 15 mm.

10.56 Referring to Prob. 10.45 and using the value found for the force exerted by the hydraulic cylinder BD, determine the change in the length of BD required to raise the platform attached at C by 2.5 in.

10.57 Determine the vertical movement of joint D if the length of member BF is increased by 1.5 in. (*Hint:* Apply a vertical load at joint D, and, using the methods of Chap. 6, compute the force exerted by member BF on joints B and F. Then apply the method of virtual work for a virtual displacement resulting in the specified increase in length of member BF. This method should be used only for small changes in the lengths of members.)

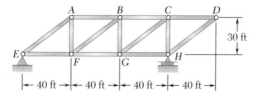

Fig. P10.57 and P10.58

10.58 Determine the horizontal movement of joint D if the length of member BF is increased by 1.5 in. (See the hint for Prob. 10.57.)

*10.6   WORK OF A FORCE DURING A FINITE DISPLACEMENT

Consider a force $\mathbf{F}$ acting on a particle. The work of $\mathbf{F}$ corresponding to an infinitesimal displacement $d\mathbf{r}$ of the particle was defined in Sec. 10.2 as

$$dU = \mathbf{F} \cdot d\mathbf{r} \tag{10.1}$$

The work of $\mathbf{F}$ corresponding to a finite displacement of the particle from A_1 to A_2 (Fig. 10.10a) is denoted by $U_{1 \rightarrow 2}$ and is obtained by integrating (10.1) along the curve described by the particle:

$$U_{1 \rightarrow 2} = \int_{A_1}^{A_2} \mathbf{F} \cdot d\mathbf{r} \tag{10.11}$$

Using the alternative expression

$$dU = F\, ds \cos \alpha \tag{10.1'}$$

given in Sec. 10.2 for the elementary work dU, we can also express the work $U_{1 \rightarrow 2}$ as

$$U_{1 \rightarrow 2} = \int_{s_1}^{s_2} (F \cos \alpha)\, ds \tag{10.11'}$$

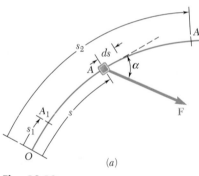

(a)

(b)

Fig. 10.10

where the variable of integration s measures the distance along the path traveled by the particle. The work $U_{1 \rightarrow 2}$ is represented by the area under the curve obtained by plotting $F \cos \alpha$ against s (Fig. 10.10b). In the case of a force $\mathbf{F}$ of constant magnitude acting in the direction of motion, formula (10.11′) yields $U_{1 \rightarrow 2} = F(s_2 - s_1)$.

Recalling from Sec. 10.2 that the work of a couple of moment $\mathbf{M}$ during an infinitesimal rotation $d\theta$ of a rigid body is

$$dU = M\, d\theta \tag{10.2}$$

we express as follows the work of the couple during a finite rotation of the body:

$$U_{1 \rightarrow 2} = \int_{\theta_1}^{\theta_2} M\, d\theta \tag{10.12}$$

In the case of a constant couple, formula (10.12) yields

$$U_{1 \rightarrow 2} = M(\theta_2 - \theta_1)$$

Work of a Weight.   It was stated in Sec. 10.2 that the work of the weight **W** of a body during an infinitesimal displacement of the body is equal to the product of W and the vertical displacement of the center of gravity of the body. With the y axis pointing upward, the work of **W** during a finite displacement of the body (Fig. 10.11) is obtained by writing

$$dU = -W \, dy$$

Integrating from A_1 to A_2, we have

$$U_{1 \to 2} = -\int_{y_1}^{y_2} W \, dy = Wy_1 - Wy_2 \qquad (10.13)$$

or

$$U_{1 \to 2} = -W(y_2 - y_1) = -W \, \Delta y \qquad (10.13')$$

where Δy is the vertical displacement from A_1 to A_2. The work of the weight **W** is thus equal to *the product of W and the vertical displacement of the center of gravity of the body.* The work is *positive* when $\Delta y < 0$, that is, *when the body moves down.*

Work of the Force Exerted by a Spring.   Consider a body A attached to a fixed point B by a spring; it is assumed that the spring is undeformed when the body is at A_0 (Fig. 10.12a). Experimental evidence shows that the magnitude of the force **F** exerted by the spring on a body A is proportional to the deflection x of the spring measured from the position A_0. We have

$$F = kx \qquad (10.14)$$

where k is the *spring constant,* expressed in N/m if SI units are used and expressed in lb/ft or lb/in. if U.S. customary units are used. The work of the force **F** exerted by the spring during a finite displacement of the body from $A_1(x = x_1)$ to $A_2(x = x_2)$ is obtained by writing

$$dU = -F \, dx = -kx \, dx$$

$$U_{1 \to 2} = -\int_{x_1}^{x_2} kx \, dx = \tfrac{1}{2}kx_1^2 - \tfrac{1}{2}kx_2^2 \qquad (10.15)$$

Care should be taken to express k and x in consistent units. For example, if U.S. customary units are used, k should be expressed in lb/ft and x expressed in feet, or k in lb/in. and x in inches; in the first case, the work is obtained in ft · lb; in the second case, in in · lb. We note that the work of the force **F** exerted by the spring on the body is *positive* when $x_2 < x_1$, that is, *when the spring is returning to its undeformed position.*

Since Eq. (10.14) is the equation of a straight line of slope k passing through the origin, the work $U_{1 \to 2}$ of **F** during the displacement from A_1 to A_2 can be obtained by evaluating the area of the trapezoid shown in Fig. 10.12b. This is done by computing the values F_1 and F_2 and multiplying the base Δx of the trapezoid by its mean height $\tfrac{1}{2}(F_1 + F_2)$. Since the work of the force **F** exerted by the spring is positive for a negative value of Δx, we write

$$U_{1 \to 2} = -\tfrac{1}{2}(F_1 + F_2) \, \Delta x \qquad (10.16)$$

Formula (10.16) is usually more convenient to use than (10.15) and affords fewer chances of confusing the units involved.

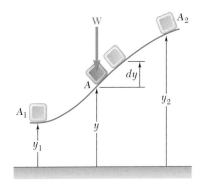

Fig. 10.11

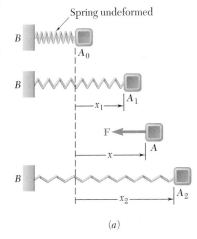

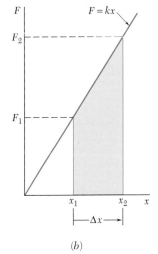

Fig. 10.12

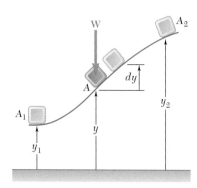

Fig. 10.11 (repeated)

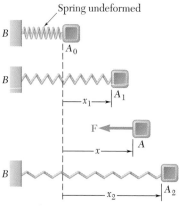

Fig. 10.12a (repeated)

*10.7 POTENTIAL ENERGY

Considering again the body of Fig. 10.11, we note from Eq. (10.13) that the work of the weight **W** during a finite displacement is obtained by subtracting the value of the function Wy corresponding to the second position of the body from its value corresponding to the first position. The work of **W** is thus independent of the actual path followed; it depends only upon the initial and final values of the function Wy. This function is called the *potential energy* of the body with respect to the *force of gravity* **W** and is denoted by V_g. We write

$$U_{1\to2} = (V_g)_1 - (V_g)_2 \qquad \text{with } V_g = Wy \qquad (10.17)$$

We note that if $(V_g)_2 > (V_g)_1$, that is, *if the potential energy increases* during the displacement (as in the case considered here), *the work $U_{1\to2}$ is negative.* If, on the other hand, the work of **W** is positive, the potential energy decreases. Therefore, the potential energy V_g of the body provides a measure of *the work which can be done* by its weight **W**. Since only the *change* in potential energy, and not the actual value of V_g, is involved in formula (10.17), an arbitrary constant can be added to the expression obtained for V_g. In other words, the level from which the elevation y is measured can be chosen arbitrarily. Note that potential energy is expressed in the same units as work, i.e., in joules (J) if SI units are used† and in ft · lb or in · lb if U.S. customary units are used.

Considering now the body of Fig. 10.12a, we note from Eq. (10.15) that the work of the elastic force **F** is obtained by subtracting the value of the function $\frac{1}{2}kx^2$ corresponding to the second position of the body from its value corresponding to the first position. This function is denoted by V_e and is called the *potential energy* of the body with respect to the *elastic force* **F**. We write

$$U_{1\to2} = (V_e)_1 - (V_e)_2 \qquad \text{with } V_e = \tfrac{1}{2}kx^2 \qquad (10.18)$$

and observe that during the displacement considered, the work of the force **F** exerted by the spring on the body is negative and the potential energy V_e increases. We should note that the expression obtained for V_e is valid only if the deflection of the spring is measured from its undeformed position.

The concept of potential energy can be used when forces other than gravity forces and elastic forces are involved. It remains valid as long as the elementary work dU of the force considered is an *exact differential.* It is then possible to find a function V, called potential energy, such that

$$dU = -dV \qquad (10.19)$$

Integrating (10.19) over a finite displacement, we obtain the general formula

$$U_{1\to2} = V_1 - V_2 \qquad (10.20)$$

which expresses that *the work of the force is independent of the path followed and is equal to minus the change in potential energy.* A force which satisfies Eq. (10.20) is said to be a *conservative force.*‡

†See footnote, page 559.

‡A detailed discussion of conservative forces is given in Sec. 13.7 of *Dynamics*.

*10.8 POTENTIAL ENERGY AND EQUILIBRIUM

The application of the principle of virtual work is considerably simplified when the potential energy of a system is known. In the case of a virtual displacement, formula (10.19) becomes $\delta U = -\delta V$. Moreover, if the position of the system is defined by a single independent variable θ, we can write $\delta V = (dV/d\theta)\, \delta\theta$. Since $\delta\theta$ must be different from zero, the condition $\delta U = 0$ for the equilibrium of the system becomes

$$\frac{dV}{d\theta} = 0 \qquad (10.21)$$

In terms of potential energy, therefore, the principle of virtual work states that *if a system is in equilibrium, the derivative of its total potential energy is zero.* If the position of the system depends upon several independent variables (the system is then said to possess *several degrees of freedom*), the partial derivatives of V with respect to each of the independent variables must be zero.

Consider, for example, a structure made of two members AC and CB and carrying a load W at C. The structure is supported by a pin at A and a roller at B, and a spring BD connects B to a fixed point D (Fig. 10.13a). The constant of the spring is k, and it is assumed that the natural length of the spring is equal to AD and thus that the spring is undeformed when B coincides with A. Neglecting the friction forces and the weight of the members, we find that the only forces which work during a displacement of the structure are the weight $\mathbf{W}$ and the force $\mathbf{F}$ exerted by the spring at point B (Fig. 10.13b). The total potential energy of the system will thus be obtained by adding the potential energy V_g corresponding to the gravity force $\mathbf{W}$ and the potential energy V_e corresponding to the elastic force $\mathbf{F}$.

Choosing a coordinate system with origin at A and noting that the deflection of the spring, measured from its undeformed position, is $AB = x_B$, we write

$$V_e = \tfrac{1}{2}kx_B^2 \qquad V_g = Wy_C$$

Expressing the coordinates x_B and y_C in terms of the angle θ, we have

$$x_B = 2l \sin \theta \qquad y_C = l \cos \theta$$
$$V_e = \tfrac{1}{2}k(2l \sin \theta)^2 \qquad V_g = W(l \cos \theta)$$
$$V = V_e + V_g = 2kl^2 \sin^2 \theta + Wl \cos \theta \qquad (10.22)$$

The positions of equilibrium of the system are obtained by equating to zero the derivative of the potential energy V. We write

$$\frac{dV}{d\theta} = 4kl^2 \sin \theta \cos \theta - Wl \sin \theta = 0$$

or, factoring $l \sin \theta$,

$$\frac{dV}{d\theta} = l \sin \theta (4kl \cos \theta - W) = 0$$

There are therefore two positions of equilibrium, corresponding to the values $\theta = 0$ and $\theta = \cos^{-1}(W/4kl)$, respectively.†

†The second position does not exist if $W > 4kl$.

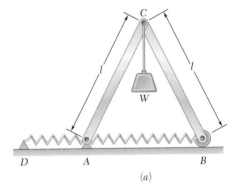

(a)

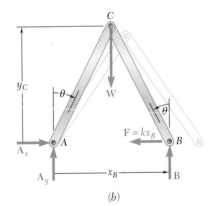

(b)

Fig. 10.13

*10.9 STABILITY OF EQUILIBRIUM

Consider the three uniform rods of length $2a$ and weight **W** shown in Fig. 10.14. While each rod is in equilibrium, there is an important difference between the three cases considered. Suppose that each rod is slightly disturbed from its position of equilibrium and then released: rod a will move back toward its original position, rod b will keep moving away from its original position, and rod c will remain in its new position. In case a, the equilibrium of the rod is said to be *stable;* in case b, it is said to be *unstable;* and, in case c, it is said to be *neutral*.

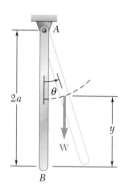

(*a*) Stable equilibrium

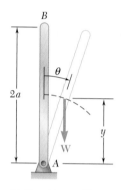

(*b*) Unstable equilibrium

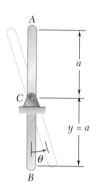

(*c*) Neutral equilibrium

Fig. 10.14

Recalling from Sec. 10.7 that the potential energy V_g with respect to gravity is equal to Wy, where y is the elevation of the point of application of **W** measured from an arbitrary level, we observe that the potential energy of rod a is minimum in the position of equilibrium considered, that the potential energy of rod b is maximum, and that the potential energy of rod c is constant. Equilibrium is thus *stable, unstable,* or *neutral* according to whether the potential energy is *minimum, maximum,* or *constant* (Fig. 10.15).

That the result obtained is quite general can be seen as follows: We first observe that a force always tends to do positive work and thus to decrease the potential energy of the system on which it is applied. Therefore, when a system is disturbed from its position of equilibrium, the forces acting on the system will tend to bring it back to its original position if V is minimum (Fig. 10.15a) and to move it farther away if V is maximum (Fig. 10.15b). If V is constant (Fig. 10.15c), the forces will not tend to move the system either way.

Recalling from calculus that a function is minimum or maximum according to whether its second derivative is positive or negative, we can summarize the conditions for the equilibrium of a system with one degree of freedom (i.e., a system the position of which is defined by a single independent variable θ) as follows:

$$\frac{dV}{d\theta} = 0 \qquad \frac{d^2V}{d\theta^2} > 0: \text{stable equilibrium}$$

$$\frac{dV}{d\theta} = 0 \qquad \frac{d^2V}{d\theta^2} < 0: \text{unstable equilibrium}$$

(10.23)

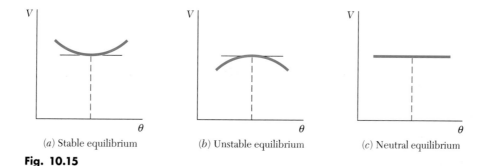

(a) Stable equilibrium   (b) Unstable equilibrium   (c) Neutral equilibrium

Fig. 10.15

If both the first and the second derivatives of V are zero, it is necessary to examine derivatives of a higher order to determine whether the equilibrium is stable, unstable, or neutral. The equilibrium will be neutral if all derivatives are zero, since the potential energy V is then a constant. The equilibrium will be stable if the first derivative found to be different from zero is of even order and positive. In all other cases the equilibrium will be unstable.

If the system considered possesses *several degrees of freedom,* the potential energy V depends upon several variables, and it is thus necessary to apply the theory of functions of several variables to determine whether V is minimum. It can be verified that a system with 2 degrees of freedom will be stable, and the corresponding potential energy $V(\theta_1, \theta_2)$ will be minimum, if the following relations are satisfied simultaneously:

$$\frac{\partial V}{\partial \theta_1} = \frac{\partial V}{\partial \theta_2} = 0$$

$$\left(\frac{\partial^2 V}{\partial \theta_1 \partial \theta_2}\right)^2 - \frac{\partial^2 V}{\partial \theta_1^2} \frac{\partial^2 V}{\partial \theta_2^2} < 0$$

(10.24)

$$\frac{\partial^2 V}{\partial \theta_1^2} > 0 \qquad \text{or} \qquad \frac{\partial^2 V}{\partial \theta_2^2} > 0$$

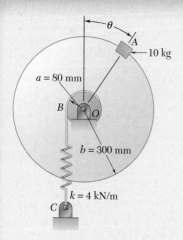

SAMPLE PROBLEM 10.4

A 10-kg block is attached to the rim of a 300-mm-radius disk as shown. Knowing that spring BC is unstretched when $\theta = 0$, determine the position or positions of equilibrium, and state in each case whether the equilibrium is stable, unstable, or neutral.

SOLUTION

Potential Energy. Denoting by s the deflection of the spring from its undeformed position and placing the origin of coordinates at O, we obtain

$$V_e = \tfrac{1}{2}ks^2 \qquad V_g = Wy = mgy$$

Measuring θ in radians, we have

$$s = a\theta \qquad y = b\cos\theta$$

Substituting for s and y in the expressions for V_e and V_g, we write

$$V_e = \tfrac{1}{2}ka^2\theta^2 \qquad V_g = mgb\cos\theta$$
$$V = V_e + V_g = \tfrac{1}{2}ka^2\theta^2 + mgb\cos\theta$$

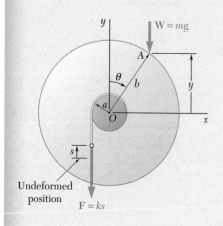

Positions of Equilibrium. Setting $dV/d\theta = 0$, we write

$$\frac{dV}{d\theta} = ka^2\theta - mgb\sin\theta = 0$$

$$\sin\theta = \frac{ka^2}{mgb}\theta$$

Substituting $a = 0.08$ m, $b = 0.3$ m, $k = 4$ kN/m, and $m = 10$ kg, we obtain

$$\sin\theta = \frac{(4 \text{ kN/m})(0.08 \text{ m})^2}{(10 \text{ kg})(9.81 \text{ m/s}^2)(0.3 \text{ m})}\theta$$
$$\sin\theta = 0.8699\,\theta$$

where θ is expressed in radians. Solving by trial and error for θ, we find

$$\theta = 0 \qquad \text{and} \qquad \theta = 0.902 \text{ rad}$$
$$\theta = 0 \qquad \text{and} \qquad \theta = 51.7° \quad \blacktriangleleft$$

Stability of Equilibrium. The second derivative of the potential energy V with respect to θ is

$$\frac{d^2V}{d\theta^2} = ka^2 - mgb\cos\theta$$
$$= (4 \text{ kN/m})(0.08 \text{ m})^2 - (10 \text{ kg})(9.81 \text{ m/s}^2)(0.3 \text{ m})\cos\theta$$
$$= 25.6 - 29.43\cos\theta$$

For $\theta = 0$: $\qquad \dfrac{d^2V}{d\theta^2} = 25.6 - 29.43\cos 0° = -3.83 < 0$

The equilibrium is unstable for $\theta = 0$ $\quad \blacktriangleleft$

For $\theta = 51.7°$: $\qquad \dfrac{d^2V}{d\theta^2} = 25.6 - 29.43\cos 51.7° = +7.36 > 0$

The equilibrium is stable for $\theta = 51.7°$ $\quad \blacktriangleleft$

SOLVING PROBLEMS
ON YOUR OWN

In this lesson we defined the *work of a force during a finite displacement* and the *potential energy* of a rigid body or a system of rigid bodies. You learned to use the concept of potential energy to determine the *equilibrium position* of a rigid body or a system of rigid bodies.

1. The potential energy V of a system is the sum of the potential energies associated with the various forces acting on the system that *do work* as the system moves. In the problems of this lesson you will determine the following:

a. Potential energy of a weight. This is the potential energy due to *gravity*, $V_g = Wy$, where y is the elevation of the weight W measured from some arbitrary reference level. Note that the potential energy V_g may be used with any vertical force **P** of constant magnitude directed downward; we write $V_g = Py$.

b. Potential energy of a spring. This is the potential energy due to the *elastic* force exerted by a spring, $V_e = \frac{1}{2}kx^2$, where k is the constant of the spring and x is the deformation of the spring *measured from its unstretched position*.

Reactions at fixed supports, internal forces at connections, forces exerted by inextensible cords and cables, and other forces which do no work do not contribute to the potential energy of the system.

2. Express all distances and angles in terms of a single variable, such as an angle θ, when computing the potential energy V of a system. This is necessary, since the determination of the equilibrium position of the system requires the computation of the derivative $dV/d\theta$.

3. When a system is in equilibrium, the first derivative of its potential energy is zero. Therefore:

a. To determine a position of equilibrium of a system, once its potential energy V has been expressed in terms of the single variable θ, compute its derivative and solve the equation $dV/d\theta = 0$ for θ.

b. To determine the force or couple required to maintain a system in a given position of equilibrium, substitute the known value of θ in the equation $dV/d\theta = 0$ and solve this equation for the desired force or couple.

4. Stability of equilibrium. The following rules generally apply:

a. Stable equilibrium occurs when the potential energy of the system is *minimum*, that is, when $dV/d\theta = 0$ and $d^2V/d\theta^2 > 0$ (Figs. 10.14*a* and 10.15*a*).

b. Unstable equilibrium occurs when the potential energy of the system is *maximum*, that is, when $dV/d\theta = 0$ and $d^2V/d\theta^2 < 0$ (Figs. 10.14*b* and 10.15*b*).

c. Neutral equilibrium occurs when the potential energy of the system is *constant*; $dV/d\theta$, $dV^2/d\theta^2$, and all the successive derivatives of V are then equal to zero (Figs. 10.14*c* and 10.15*c*).

See page 583 for a discussion of the case when $dV/d\theta$, $dV^2/d\theta^2$ but *not all* of the successive derivatives of V are equal to zero.

PROBLEMS

10.59 Using the method of Sec. 10.8, solve Prob. 10.29.

10.60 Using the method of Sec. 10.8, solve Prob. 10.30.

10.61 Using the method of Sec. 10.8, solve Prob. 10.33.

10.62 Using the method of Sec. 10.8, solve Prob. 10.34.

10.63 Using the method of Sec. 10.8, solve Prob. 10.35.

10.64 Using the method of Sec. 10.8, solve Prob. 10.36.

10.65 Using the method of Sec. 10.8, solve Prob. 10.31.

10.66 Using the method of Sec. 10.8, solve Prob. 10.38.

10.67 Show that the equilibrium is neutral in Prob. 10.1.

10.68 Show that the equilibrium is neutral in Prob. 10.6.

10.69 Two uniform rods, each of mass m and length l, are attached to drums that are connected by a belt as shown. Assuming that no slipping occurs between the belt and the drums, determine the positions of equilibrium of the system and state in each case whether the equilibrium is stable, unstable, or neutral.

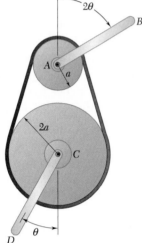

Fig. P10.69

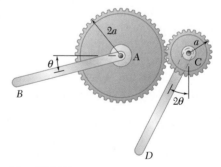

Fig. P10.70

10.70 Two uniform rods AB and CD, of the same length l, are attached to gears as shown. Knowing that rod AB weighs 3 lb and that rod CD weighs 2 lb, determine the positions of equilibrium of the system and state in each case whether the equilibrium is stable, unstable, or neutral.

10.71 Two uniform rods, each of mass m, are attached to gears of equal radii as shown. Determine the positions of equilibrium of the system and state in each case whether the equilibrium is stable, unstable, or neutral.

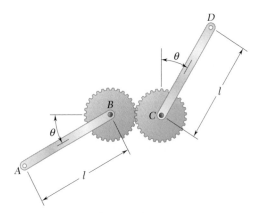

Fig. P10.71 and P10.72

10.72 Two uniform rods, AB and CD, are attached to gears of equal radii as shown. Knowing that $W_{AB} = 8$ lb and $W_{CD} = 4$ lb, determine the positions of equilibrium of the system and state in each case whether the equilibrium is stable, unstable, or neutral.

10.73 Using the method of Sec. 10.8, solve Prob. 10.39. Determine whether the equilibrium is stable, unstable, or neutral. (*Hint:* The potential energy corresponding to the couple exerted by a torsion spring is $\frac{1}{2}K\theta^2$, where K is the torsional spring constant and θ is the angle of twist.)

10.74 In Prob. 10.40, determine whether each of the positions of equilibrium is stable, unstable, or neutral. (See hint for Prob. 10.73.)

10.75 A load **W** of magnitude 100 lb is applied to the mechanism at C. Knowing that the spring is unstretched when $\theta = 15°$, determine that value of θ corresponding to equilibrium and check that the equilibrium is stable.

10.76 A load **W** of magnitude 100 lb is applied to the mechanism at C. Knowing that the spring is unstretched when $\theta = 30°$, determine that value of θ corresponding to equilibrium and check that the equilibrium is stable.

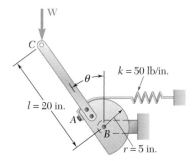

Fig. P10.75 and P10.76

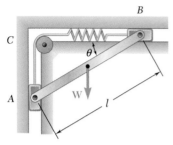

Fig. P10.77 and P10.78

10.77 A slender rod AB, of weight W, is attached to two blocks A and B that can move freely in the guides shown. The constant of the spring is k, and the spring is unstretched when AB is horizontal. Neglecting the weight of the blocks, derive an equation in θ, W, l, and k that must be satisfied when the rod is in equilibrium.

10.78 A slender rod AB, of weight W, is attached to two blocks A and B that can move freely in the guides shown. Knowing that the spring is unstretched when AB is horizontal, determine three values of θ corresponding to equilibrium when $W = 300$ lb, $l = 16$ in., and $k = 75$ lb/in. State in each case whether the equilibrium is stable, unstable, or neutral.

10.79 A slender rod AB, of weight W, is attached to two blocks A and B that can move freely in the guides shown. Knowing that the spring is unstretched when $y = 0$, determine the value of y corresponding to equilibrium when $W = 80$ N, $l = 500$ mm, and $k = 600$ N/m.

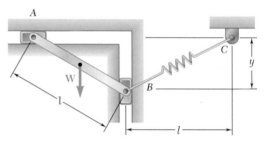

Fig. P10.79

10.80 Knowing that both springs are unstretched when $y = 0$, determine the value of y corresponding to equilibrium when $W = 80$ N, $l = 500$ mm, and $k = 600$ N/m.

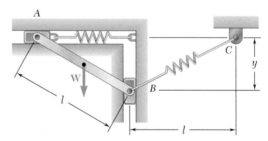

Fig. P10.80

10.81 A spring AB of constant k is attached to two identical gears as shown. Knowing that the spring is undeformed when $\theta = 0$, determine two values of the angle θ corresponding to equilibrium when $P = 30$ lb, $a = 4$ in., $b = 3$ in., $r = 6$ in., and $k = 5$ lb/in. State in each case whether the equilibrium is stable, unstable, or neutral.

10.82 A spring AB of constant k is attached to two identical gears as shown. Knowing that the spring is undeformed when $\theta = 0$, and given that $a = 60$ mm, $b = 45$ mm, $r = 90$ mm, and $k = 6$ kN/m, determine (a) the range of values of P for which a position of equilibrium exists, (b) two values of θ corresponding to equilibrium if the value of P is equal to half the upper limit of the range found in part a.

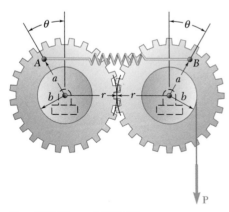

Fig. P10.81 and P10.82

10.83 A slender rod *AB* is attached to two collars *A* and *B* that can move freely along the guide rods shown. Knowing that $\beta = 30°$ and $P = Q = 400$ N, determine the value of the angle θ corresponding to equilibrium.

10.84 A slender rod *AB* is attached to two collars *A* and *B* that can move freely along the guide rods shown. Knowing that $\beta = 30°$, $P = 100$ N, and $Q = 25$ N, determine the value of the angle θ corresponding to equilibrium.

10.85 and 10.86 Collar *A* can slide freely on the semicircular rod shown. Knowing that the constant of the spring is *k* and that the unstretched length of the spring is equal to the radius *r*, determine the value of θ corresponding to equilibrium when $W = 50$ lb, $r = 9$ in., and $k = 15$ lb/in.

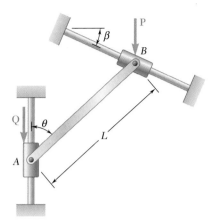

Fig. P10.83 and P10.84

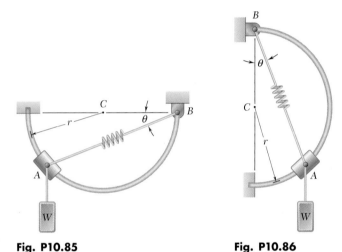

Fig. P10.85   **Fig. P10.86**

10.87 and 10.88 Cart *B*, which weighs 75 kN, rolls along a sloping track that forms an angle β with the horizontal. The spring constant is 5 kN/m, and the spring is unstretched when $x = 0$. Determine the distance *x* corresponding to equilibrium for the angle β indicated.

      10.87 Angle $\beta = 30°$
      10.88 Angle $\beta = 60°$

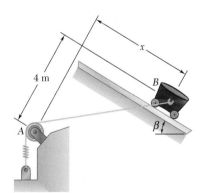

Fig. P10.87 and P10.88

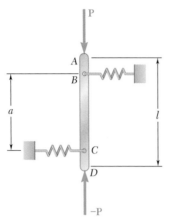

Fig. P10.89

10.89 A vertical bar AD is attached to two springs of constant k and is in equilibrium in the position shown. Determine the range of values of the magnitude P of two equal and opposite vertical forces **P** and **−P** for which the equilibrium position is stable if (a) $AB = CD$, (b) $AB = 2CD$.

10.90 Rod AB is attached to a hinge at A and to two springs, each of constant k. If $h = 25$ in., $d = 12$ in., and $W = 80$ lb, determine the range of values of k for which the equilibrium of the rod is stable in the position shown. Each spring can act in either tension or compression.

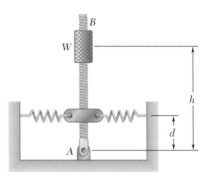

Fig. P10.90 and P10.91

10.91 Rod AB is attached to a hinge at A and to two springs, each of constant k. If $h = 45$ in., $k = 6$ lb/in., and $W = 60$ lb, determine the smallest distance d for which the equilibrium of the rod is stable in the position shown. Each spring can act in either tension or compression.

10.92 and 10.93 Two bars are attached to a single spring of constant k that is unstretched when the bars are vertical. Determine the range of values of P for which the equilibrium of the system is stable in the position shown.

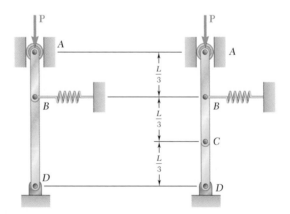

Fig. P10.92 and P10.93

10.94 Two bars AB and BC are attached to a single spring of constant k that is unstretched when the bars are vertical. Determine the range of values of P for which the equilibrium of the system is stable in the position shown.

10.95 The horizontal bar BEH is connected to three vertical bars. The collar at E can slide freely on bar DF. Determine the range of values of Q for which the equilibrium of the system is stable in the position shown when $a = 24$ in., $b = 20$ in., and $P = 150$ lb.

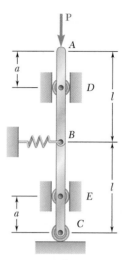

Fig. P10.94

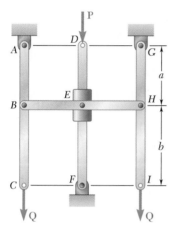

Fig. P10.95 and P10.96

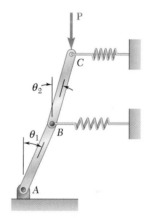

Fig. P10.97

10.96 The horizontal bar BEH is connected to three vertical bars. The collar at E can slide freely on bar DF. Determine the range of values of P for which the equilibrium of the system is stable in the position shown when $a = 150$ mm, $b = 200$ mm, and $Q = 45$ N.

*10.97 Bars AB and BC, each of length l and of negligible weight, are attached to two springs, each of constant k. The springs are undeformed, and the system is in equilibrium when $\theta_1 = \theta_2 = 0$. Determine the range of values of P for which the equilibrium position is stable.

*10.98 Solve Prob. 10.97 knowing that $l = 800$ mm and $k = 2.5$ kN/m.

*10.99 Two rods of negligible weight are attached to drums of radius r that are connected by a belt and spring of constant k. Knowing that the spring is undeformed when the rods are vertical, determine the range of values of P for which the equilibrium position $\theta_1 = \theta_2 = 0$ is stable.

*10.100 Solve Prob. 10.99 knowing that $k = 20$ lb/in., $r = 3$ in., $l = 6$ in., and (a) $W = 15$ lb, (b) $W = 60$ lb.

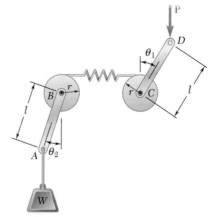

Fig. P10.99

Work of a force

The first part of this chapter was devoted to the *principle of virtual work* and to its direct application to the solution of equilibrium problems. We first defined the *work of a force* **F** *corresponding to the small displacement d***r** [Sec. 10.2] as the quantity

$$dU = \mathbf{F} \cdot d\mathbf{r} \qquad (10.1)$$

Fig. 10.16

obtained by forming the scalar product of the force **F** and the displacement d**r** (Fig. 10.16). Denoting respectively by F and ds the magnitudes of the force and of the displacement, and by α the angle formed by **F** and d**r**, we wrote

$$dU = F \, ds \cos \alpha \qquad (10.1')$$

The work dU is positive if $\alpha < 90°$, zero if $\alpha = 90°$, and negative if $\alpha > 90°$. We also found that the *work of a couple of moment* **M** acting on a rigid body is

$$dU = M \, d\theta \qquad (10.2)$$

where $d\theta$ is the small angle expressed in radians through which the body rotates.

Virtual displacement

Considering a particle located at A and acted upon by several forces $\mathbf{F}_1, \mathbf{F}_2, \ldots, \mathbf{F}_n$ [Sec. 10.3], we imagined that the particle moved to a new position A' (Fig. 10.17). Since this displacement did not actually take place, it was referred to as a *virtual displacement* and denoted by $\delta\mathbf{r}$, while the corresponding work of the forces was called *virtual work* and denoted by δU. We had

$$\delta U = \mathbf{F}_1 \cdot \delta\mathbf{r} + \mathbf{F}_2 \cdot \delta\mathbf{r} + \cdots + \mathbf{F}_n \cdot \delta\mathbf{r}$$

Principle of virtual work

The *principle of virtual work* states that *if a particle is in equilibrium, the total virtual work δU of the forces acting on the particle is zero for any virtual displacement of the particle.*

The principle of virtual work can be extended to the case of rigid bodies and systems of rigid bodies. Since it involves *only forces which do work*, its application provides a useful alternative to the use of the equilibrium equations in the solution of many engineering problems. It is particularly effective in the case of machines and mechanisms consisting of connected rigid bodies, since the work of the reactions at the supports is zero and the work of the internal forces at the pin connections cancels out [Sec. 10.4; Sample Probs. 10.1, 10.2, and 10.3].

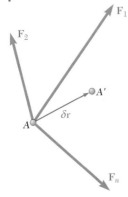

Fig. 10.17

In the case of *real machines,* however [Sec. 10.5], the work of the friction forces should be taken into account, with the result that the *output work will be less than the input work.* Defining the *mechanical efficiency* of a machine as the ratio

$$\eta = \frac{\text{output work}}{\text{input work}} \qquad (10.9)$$

we also noted that for an ideal machine (no friction) $\eta = 1$, while for a real machine $\eta < 1$.

In the second part of the chapter we considered the *work of forces corresponding to finite displacements* of their points of application. The work $U_{1 \to 2}$ of the force **F** corresponding to a displacement of the particle A from A_1 to A_2 (Fig. 10.18) was obtained by integrating the right-hand member of Eq. (10.1) or (10.1′) along the curve described by the particle [Sec. 10.6]:

or

$$U_{1 \to 2} = \int_{A_1}^{A_2} \mathbf{F} \cdot d\mathbf{r} \qquad (10.11)$$

$$U_{1 \to 2} = \int_{s_1}^{s_2} (F \cos \alpha)\, ds \qquad (10.11')$$

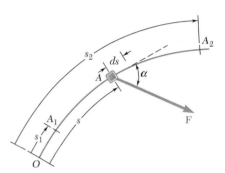

Fig. 10.18

Similarly, the work of a couple of moment **M** corresponding to a finite rotation from θ_1 to θ_2 of a rigid body was expressed as

$$U_{1 \to 2} = \int_{\theta_1}^{\theta_2} M\, d\theta \qquad (10.12)$$

The *work of the weight* **W** *of a body* as its center of gravity moves from the elevation y_1 to y_2 (Fig. 10.19) can be obtained by making $F = W$ and $\alpha = 180°$ in Eq. (10.11′):

$$U_{1 \to 2} = -\int_{y_1}^{y_2} W\, dy = W y_1 - W y_2 \qquad (10.13)$$

The work of **W** is therefore positive *when the elevation y decreases.*

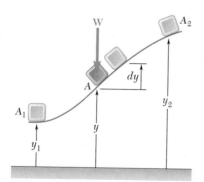

Fig. 10.19

Work of the force exerted by a spring

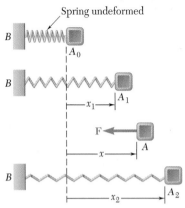

Spring undeformed

Fig. 10.20

Potential energy

Alternative expression for the principle of virtual work

Stability of equilibrium

The *work of the force* **F** *exerted by a spring* on a body A as the spring is stretched from x_1 to x_2 (Fig. 10.20) can be obtained by making $F = kx$, where k is the constant of the spring, and $\alpha = 180°$ in Eq. (10.11′):

$$U_{1 \rightarrow 2} = -\int_{x_1}^{x_2} kx \, dx = \tfrac{1}{2}kx_1^2 - \tfrac{1}{2}kx_2^2 \qquad (10.15)$$

The work of **F** is therefore positive *when the spring is returning to its undeformed position.*

When the work of a force **F** is independent of the path actually followed between A_1 and A_2, the force is said to be a *conservative force,* and its work can be expressed as

$$U_{1 \rightarrow 2} = V_1 - V_2 \qquad (10.20)$$

where V is the *potential energy* associated with **F**, and V_1 and V_2 represent the values of V at A_1 and A_2, respectively [Sec. 10.7]. The potential energies associated, respectively, with the *force of gravity* **W** and the *elastic force* **F** exerted by a spring were found to be

$$V_g = Wy \qquad \text{and} \qquad V_e = \tfrac{1}{2}kx^2 \quad (10.17,\ 10.18)$$

When the position of a mechanical system depends upon a single independent variable θ, the potential energy of the system is a function $V(\theta)$ of that variable, and it follows from Eq. (10.20) that $\delta U = -\delta V = -(dV/d\theta)\,\delta\theta$. The condition $\delta U = 0$ required by the principle of virtual work for the equilibrium of the system can thus be replaced by the condition

$$\frac{dV}{d\theta} = 0 \qquad (10.21)$$

When all the forces involved are conservative, it may be preferable to use Eq. (10.21) rather than apply the principle of virtual work directly [Sec. 10.8; Sample Prob. 10.4].

This approach presents another advantage, since it is possible to determine from the sign of the second derivative of V whether the equilibrium of the system is *stable, unstable,* or *neutral* [Sec. 10.9]. If $d^2V/d\theta^2 > 0$, V is *minimum* and the equilibrium is *stable;* if $d^2V/d\theta^2 < 0$, V is *maximum* and the equilibrium is *unstable;* if $d^2V/d\theta^2 = 0$, it is necessary to examine derivatives of a higher order.

REVIEW PROBLEMS

10.101 Determine the vertical force **P** that must be applied at G to maintain the equilibrium of the linkage.

10.102 Determine the couple **M** that must be applied to member $DEFG$ to maintain the equilibrium of the linkage.

10.103 Derive an expression for the magnitude of the couple **M** required to maintain the equilibrium of the linkage shown.

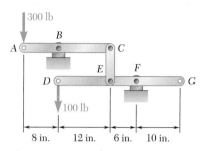

Fig. P10.101 and P10.102

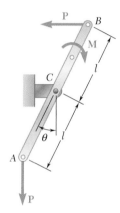

Fig. *P10.103*

10.104 Collars A and B are connected by the wire AB and can slide freely on the rods shown. Knowing that the length of the wire is 440 mm and that the weight W of collar A is 90 N, determine the magnitude of the force **P** required to maintain equilibrium of the system when (*a*) $c = 80$ mm, (*b*) $c = 280$ mm.

10.105 Collar B can slide along rod AC and is attached by a pin to a block that can slide in the vertical slot shown. Derive an expression for the magnitude of the couple **M** required to maintain equilibrium.

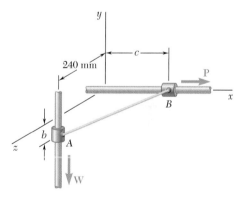

Fig. P10.104

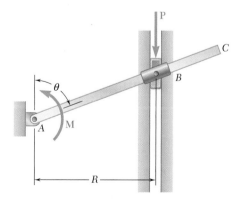

Fig. *P10.105*

595

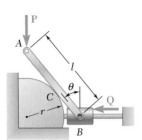

Fig. P10.106

10.106 A slender rod of length l is attached to a collar at B and rests on a portion of a circular cylinder of radius r. Neglecting the effect of friction, determine the value of θ corresponding to the equilibrium position of the mechanism when $l = 200$ mm, $r = 60$ mm, $P = 40$ N, and $Q = 80$ N.

10.107 A horizontal force **P** of magnitude 40 lb is applied to the mechanism at C. The constant of the spring is $k = 9$ lb/in., and the spring is unstretched when $\theta = 0$. Neglecting the weight of the mechanism, determine the value of θ corresponding to equilibrium.

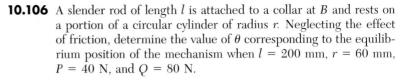
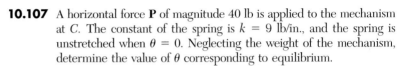
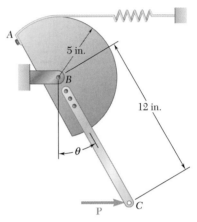

Fig. P10.107

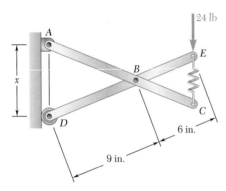

Fig. P10.108

10.108 Two identical rods ABC and DBE are connected by a pin at B and by a spring CE. Knowing that the spring is 4 in. long when unstretched and that the constant of the spring is 8 lb/in., determine the distance x corresponding to equilibrium when a 24-lb load is applied at E as shown.

10.109 Solve Prob. 10.108 assuming that the 24-lb load is applied at C instead of E.

10.110 Two uniform rods, each of mass m and length l, are attached to gears as shown. For the range $0 \le \theta \le 180°$, determine the positions of equilibrium of the system and state in each case whether the equilibrium is stable, unstable, or neutral.

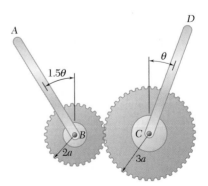

Fig. P10.110

10.111 A homogeneous hemisphere of radius r is placed on an incline as shown. Assuming that friction is sufficient to prevent slipping between the hemisphere and the incline, determine the angle θ corresponding to equilibrium when $\beta = 10°$.

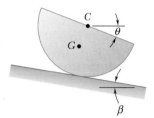

Fig. _P10.111_ and P10.112

10.112 A homogeneous hemisphere of radius r is placed on an incline as shown. Assuming that friction is sufficient to prevent slipping between the hemisphere and the incline, determine (a) the largest angle β for which a position of equilibrium exists, (b) the angle θ corresponding to equilibrium when the angle β is equal to half the value found in part _a_.

COMPUTER PROBLEMS

10.C1 A couple **M** is applied to crank AB in order to maintain the equilibrium of the engine system shown when a force **P** is applied to the piston. Knowing that $b = 2.4$ in. and $l = 7.5$ in., use computational software to calculate the ratio M/P for values of θ from 0 to 180° using 10° increments. Using appropriate smaller increments, determine the value of θ for which the ratio M/P is maximum, and the corresponding value of M/P.

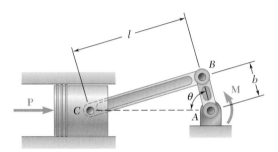

Fig. P10.C1

10.C2 Knowing that $a = 500$ mm, $b = 150$ mm, $L = 500$ mm, and $P = 100$ N, use computational software to calculate the force in member BD for values of θ from 30° to 150° using 10° increments. Using appropriate smaller increments, determine the range of values of θ for which the absolute value of the force in member BD is less than 400 N.

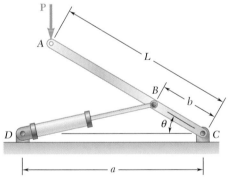

Fig. P10.C2

10.C3 Solve Prob. 10.C2 assuming that the force **P** applied at A is directed horizontally to the right.

10.C4 The constant of spring AB is k, and the spring is unstretched when $\theta = 0$. (a) Neglecting the weight of the member BCD, use computational software to calculate the potential energy of the system and its derivative $dV/d\theta$. (b) For $W = 150$ lb, $a = 10$ in., and $k = 75$ lb/in., calculate and plot the potential energy versus θ for values of θ from 0 to 165° using 15° increments. (c) Using appropriate smaller increments, determine the values of θ for which the system is in equilibrium and state in each case whether the equilibrium is stable, unstable, or neutral.

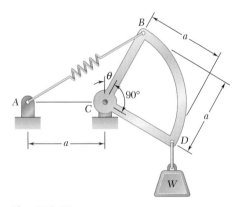

Fig. P10.C4

10.C5 Two rods, AC and DE, each of length L, are connected by a collar that is attached to rod AC at its midpoint B. (*a*) Using computational software, calculate the potential energy V of the system and its derivative $dV/d\theta$. (*b*) For $W = 75$ N, $P = 200$ N, and $L = 500$ mm, calculate V and $dV/d\theta$ for values of θ from 0 to 70° using 5° increments. (*c*) Using appropriate smaller increments, determine the values of θ for which the system is in equilibrium and state in each case whether the equilibrium is stable, unstable, or neutral.

10.C6 A slender rod ABC is attached to blocks A and B that can move freely in the guides shown. The constant of the spring is k, and the spring is unstretched when the rod is vertical. (*a*) Neglecting the weights of the rod and of the blocks, use computational software to calculate the potential energy V of the system and its derivative $dV/d\theta$. (*b*) For $P = 150$ N, $l = 200$ mm, and $k = 3$ kN/m, calculate and plot the potential energy versus θ for values of θ from 0 to 75° using 5° increments. (*c*) Using appropriate smaller increments, determine any positions of equilibrium in the range $0 \leq \theta \leq 75°$ and state in each case whether the equilibrium is stable, unstable, or neutral.

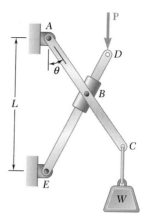

Fig. P10.C5

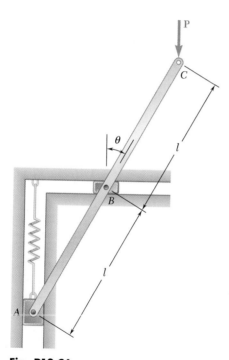

Fig. P10.C6

10.C7 Solve Prob. 10.C6 assuming that the force **P** applied at C is directed horizontally to the right.

Appendix

Fundamentals of Engineering Examination

Engineers are required to be licensed when their work directly affects the public health, safety, and welfare. The intent is to ensure that engineers have met minimum qualifications involving competence, ability, experience, and character. The licensing process involves an initial exam, called the *Fundamentals of Engineering Examination;* professional experience; and a second exam, called the *Principles and Practice of Engineering.* Those who successfully complete these requirements are licensed as a *Professional Engineer.* The exams are developed under the auspices of the *National Council of Examiners for Engineering and Surveying.*

The first exam, the *Fundamentals of Engineering Examination,* can be taken just before or after graduation from a four-year accredited engineering program. The exam stresses subject material in a typical undergraduate engineering program, including statics. The topics included in the exam cover much of the material in this book. The following is a list of the main topic areas, with references to the appropriate sections in this book. Also included are problems that can be solved to review this material.

Concurrent Force Systems (2.2–2.9; 2.12–2.14)
Problems: 2.33, 2.35, 2.36, 2.37, 2.73, 2.83, 2.92, 2.93, 2.97

Vector Forces (3.4–3.11)
Problems: 3.16, 3.18, 3.25, 3.31, 3.38, 3.40

Equilibrium in Two Dimensions (2.11; 4.1–4.7)
Problems: 4.5, 4.13, 4.14, 4.17, 4.29, 4.38, 4.66, 4.75

Equilibrium in Three Dimensions (2.15; 4.8–4.9)
Problems: 4.101, 4.104, 4.103, 4.106, 4.115, 4.117, 4.127, 4.132, 4.140

Centroid of an Area (5.2–5.7)
Problems: 5.6, 5.18, 5.29, 5.35, 5.40, 5.56, 5.58, 5.99, 5.103, 5.104, 5.125

Analysis of Trusses (6.2–6.7)
Problems: 6.3, 6.4, 6.33, 6.43, 6.44, 6.56

Equilibrium of Two-Dimensional Frames (6.9–6.11)
Problems: 6.76, 6.80, 6.87, 6.91, 6.92

Shear and Bending Moment (7.3–7.6)
Problems: 7.22, 7.25, 7.31, 7.36, 7.45, 7.49, 7.70, 7.83

Friction (8.2–8.5; 8.10)
Problems: 8.11, 8.15, 8.21, 8.30, 8.50, 8.53, 8.101, 8.104, 8.105

Moments of Inertia (9.2–9.10)
Problems: 9.5, 9.31, 9.32, 9.33, 9.77, 9.78, 9.84, 9.89, 9.101, 9.103

Photo Credits

Index

Answers to Problems

Answers to problems with a number set in straight type are given on this and the following pages. Answers to problems set in italic are not listed.

CHAPTER 2

2.1 179 N ⭦ 75.1°.
2.2 77.1 lb ⭧ 85.4°.
2.3 139.1 lb ⭧ 67.0°.
2.5 (a) 76.1°. (b) 336 lb.
2.7 (a) 37.1°. (b) 73.2 N.
2.8 (a) 44.7 N. (b) 107.1 N.
2.9 (a) 3660 N. (b) 3730 N.
2.10 2600 N ⭦ 53.5°.
2.11 (a) 392 lb. (b) 346 lb.
2.13 (a) 21.1 N ↓. (b) 45.3 N.
2.14 (a) 368 lb →. (b) 213 lb.
2.15 77.1 lb ⭧ 85.4°.
2.16 139.1 lb ⭧ 67.0°.
2.17 3.30 kN ⭦ 66.6°.
2.19 21.8 kN ⭦ 86.6°.
2.21 (800 N) 640 N, 480 N; (424 N) −224 N, −360 N; (408 N) 192.0 N, −360 N.
2.22 (29 lb) 21.0 lb, 20.0 lb; (50 lb) −14.00 lb, 48.0 lb; (51 lb) 24.0 lb, −45.0 lb.
2.23 (40 lb) 20.0 lb, −34.6 lb; (50 lb) −38.3 lb, −32.1 lb; (60 lb) 54.4 lb, 25.4 lb.
2.25 (a) 523 lb. (b) 428 lb.
2.26 (a) 2190 N. (b) 2060 N.
2.27 (a) 194.9 N. (b) 153.6 N.
2.30 (a) 610 lb. (b) 500 lb.
2.31 38.6 lb ∡ 36.6°.
2.32 251 N ⭨ 85.3°.
2.34 654 N ⭦ 21.5°.
2.35 309 N ⭧ 86.6°.
2.36 226 N ⭧ 62.3°.
2.37 203 lb ∡ 8.46°.
2.39 (a) 21.7°. (b) 229 N.
2.40 (a) 580 N. (b) 300 N.
2.42 (a) 56.3°. (b) 204 lb.
2.43 (a) 2.13 kN. (b) 1.735 kN.
2.45 (a) 305 N. (b) 514 N.
2.47 (a) 1244 lb. (b) 115.4 lb.
2.48 (a) 172.7 lb. (b) 231 lb.
2.49 F_A = 1303 lb; F_B = 420 lb.
2.51 F_C = 6.40 kN; F_D = 4.80 kN.
2.52 F_B = 15.00 kN; F_C = 8.00 kN.
2.53 (a) 52.0 lb. (b) 45.0 lb.
2.55 (a) 1213 N. (b) 166.3 N.
2.56 (a) 863 N. (b) 1216 N.
2.57 (a) 784 N. (b) 71.0°.
2.59 (a) 60.0°. (b) 230 lb.
2.60 5.80 m.
2.61 (a) 1081 N. (b) 82.5°.
2.62 (a) 1294 N. (b) 62.5°.
2.63 (a) 10.98 lb. (b) 30.0 lb.

2.65 (a) 602 N ⭨ 46.8°. (b) 1365 N ⭧ 46.8°.
2.67 (a) 300 lb. (b) 300 lb. (c) 200 lb. (d) 200 lb. (e) 150.0 lb.
2.68 (b) 200 lb. (d) 150.0 lb.
2.69 (a) 1293 N. (b) 2220 N.
2.71 (a) +390 N, +614 N, +181.8 N. (b) 58.7°, 35.0°, 76.0°.
2.72 (a) −130.1 N, +816 N, +357 N. (b) 98.3°, 25.0°, 66.6°.
2.73 (a) 288 N. (b) 67.5°, 30.0°, 108.7°.
2.74 (a) 100.0 N. (b) 112.5°, 30.0°, 108.7°.
2.76 (a) 80.0 lb. (b) 104.5°, 30.0°, 64.3°.
2.77 (a) +56.4 lb, −103.9 lb, −20.5 lb. (b) 62.0°, 150.0°, 99.8°.
2.79 F = 570 N; θ_x = 55.8°, θ_y = 45.4°, θ_z = 116.0°.
2.81 (a) 118.2°. (b) F_x = 36.0 lb, F_y = −90.0 lb; F = 110.0 lb.
2.82 (a) 114.4°. (b) F_y = 694 lb, F_z = 855 lb; F = 1209 lb.
2.84 (a) F_x = 194.0 N, F_z = 108.0 N. (b) θ_y = 105.1°, θ_z = 62.0°.
2.85 +100.0 lb, +500 lb, −125.0 lb.
2.86 +50.0 lb, +250 lb, +185.0 lb.
2.87 +240 N, −255 N, +160.0 N.
2.89 −1125 N, +750 N, +450 N.
2.91 515 N; θ_x = 70.2°, θ_y = 27.6°, θ_z = 71.5°.
2.92 515 N; θ_x = 79.8°, θ_y = 33.4°, θ_z = 58.6°.
2.94 913 lb; θ_x = 50.6°, θ_y = 117.6°, θ_z = 51.8°.
2.95 748 N; θ_x = 120.1°, θ_y = 52.5°, θ_z = 128.0°.
2.96 3120 N; θ_x = 37.4°, θ_y = 122.0°, θ_z = 72.6°.
2.97 (a) 65.2 lb. (b) 208 lb; θ_x = 61.6°, θ_y = 151.6°, θ_z = 90.0°.
2.99 1031 N ↑.
2.101 926 N ↑.
2.103 2100 lb.
2.104 1868 lb.
2.105 1049 lb.
2.107 960 N.
2.108 $0 \leq Q < 300$ N.
2.109 1572 lb.
2.111 845 N.
2.112 768 N.
2.113 T_{AB} = 842 lb; T_{AC} = 624 lb; T_{AD} = 1088 lb.
2.114 T_{AD} = 29.5 lb; T_{BD} = 10.25 lb; T_{CD} = 29.5 lb.
2.115 T_{AB} = 510 N; T_{AC} = 56.2 N; T_{AD} = 536 N.
2.116 T_{AB} = 1340 N; T_{AC} = 1025 N; T_{AD} = 915 N.
2.117 T_{AB} = 1431 N; T_{AC} = 1560 N; T_{AD} = 183.0 N.
2.118 T_{AB} = 1249 N; T_{AC} = 490 N; T_{AD} = 1647 N.
2.121 P = 131.2 N; Q = 29.6 N.
2.123 378 N.
2.125 (a) 125.0 lb. (b) 45.0 lb.
2.126 x = 13.42 in., z = 6.71 in.
2.127 37.0°.
2.130 (a) 500 lb. (b) 544 lb.
2.131 (a) 312 N. (b) 144 N.
2.133 (a) 140.3°. (b) F_x = 79.9 lb, F_z = 120.1 lb; F = 226 lb.
2.134 (a) −1861 lb, +3360 lb, +677 lb. (b) 118.5°, 30.5°, 80.0°.
2.135 15.13 kN; θ_x = 133.4°, θ_y = 43.6°, θ_z = 86.6°.
2.136 T_{AB} = 500 N; T_{AC} = 459 N; T_{AD} = 516 N.

2.137 (a) 1155 N. (b) 1012 N.
2.C2 (1) (b) 20°; (c) 244 lb. (2) (b) −10°; (c) 467 lb. (3) (b) 10°; (c) 163.2 lb.
2.C3 (a) 1.001 m. (b) 4.01 kN. (c) 1.426 kN; 1.194 kN.

CHAPTER 3

3.1 1.277 N · m ↰.
3.2 1.277 N · m ↰.
3.3 (a) 41.7 N · m ↰. (b) 147.4 N ∠ 45.0°.
3.4 (a) 41.7 N · m ↰. (b) 176.8 N ∠ 58.0°.
3.5 186.6 lb · in. ↓.
3.7 6.12° or 33.8°.
3.9 (a) 760 N · m ↰. (b) 760 N · m ↰.
3.10 1224 N.
3.12 116.2 lb · ft ↰.
3.13 128.2 lb · ft ↰.
3.16 2.21 m.
3.17 (a) 41.0. (b) 26.9.
3.19 (a) $-11\mathbf{i} + 22\mathbf{j} + 22\mathbf{k}$. (b) 0. (c) $-45\mathbf{i} + 30\mathbf{j} - 10\mathbf{k}$.
3.21 $(7.50 \text{ N} \cdot \text{m})\mathbf{i} - (6.00 \text{ N} \cdot \text{m})\mathbf{j} - (10.39 \text{ N} \cdot \text{m})\mathbf{k}$.
3.22 $(3080 \text{ N} \cdot \text{m})\mathbf{i} - (2070 \text{ N} \cdot \text{m})\mathbf{k}$.
3.24 $-(153.0 \text{ lb} \cdot \text{ft})\mathbf{i} + (63.0 \text{ lb} \cdot \text{ft})\mathbf{j} + (215 \text{ lb} \cdot \text{ft})\mathbf{k}$.
3.26 $(492 \text{ lb} \cdot \text{ft})\mathbf{i} + (144.0 \text{ lb} \cdot \text{ft})\mathbf{j} - (372 \text{ lb} \cdot \text{ft})\mathbf{k}$.
3.27 4.58 m.
3.28 3.70 m.
3.30 57.0 in.
3.31 1.564 m.
3.32 3.29 m.
3.33 4.86 ft.
3.35 $\mathbf{P} \cdot \mathbf{Q} = 1$; $\mathbf{P} \cdot \mathbf{S} = -11$; $\mathbf{Q} \cdot \mathbf{S} = 10$.
3.37 27.4°.
3.39 43.6°.
3.40 38.9°.
3.41 (a) 59.0°. (b) 648 N.
3.43 (a) 71.1°. (b) 0.973 lb.
3.44 12.00 in.
3.45 (a) 67. (b) 111.
3.46 7.
3.47 $M_x = -31.2 \text{ N} \cdot \text{m}$; $M_y = 13.20 \text{ N} \cdot \text{m}$; $M_z = -2.42 \text{ N} \cdot \text{m}$.
3.48 $M_x = -25.6 \text{ N} \cdot \text{m}$; $M_y = 10.80 \text{ N} \cdot \text{m}$; $M_z = 40.6 \text{ N} \cdot \text{m}$.
3.49 1.252 m.
3.50 1.256 m.
3.51 61.5 lb.
3.53 $\phi = 24.6°$; $d = 34.6$ in.
3.55 -90.0 N · m.
3.56 -111.0 N · m.
3.57 2.28 N · m.
3.58 -9.50 N · m.
3.59 $aP/\sqrt{2}$.
3.61 1359 lb · in.
3.65 0.249 m.
3.66 0.1198 m.
3.68 30.4 in.
3.69 43.5 in.
3.70 (a) 12.39 N · m ↓. (b) 12.39 N · m ↓. (c) 12.39 N · m ↓.
3.71 (a) 336 lb · in. ↰. (b) 28.0 in. (c) 54.0°.
3.72 (a) 75.0 N. (b) 71.2 N. (c) 45.0 N.
3.75 $M = 10.00 \text{ lb} \cdot \text{ft}$; $\theta_x = 90.0°$, $\theta_y = 143.1°$, $\theta_z = 126.9°$.
3.76 $M = 9.21 \text{ N} \cdot \text{m}$; $\theta_x = 77.9°$, $\theta_y = 12.05°$, $\theta_z = 90.0°$.
3.77 $M = 604 \text{ lb} \cdot \text{in.}$; $\theta_x = 72.8°$, $\theta_y = 27.3°$, $\theta_z = 110.5°$.
3.78 $M = 1170 \text{ lb} \cdot \text{in.}$; $\theta_x = 81.2°$, $\theta_y = 13.70°$, $\theta_z = 100.4°$.

3.79 $M = 10.92 \text{ N} \cdot \text{m}$; $\theta_x = 97.8°$, $\theta_y = 34.5°$, $\theta_z = 56.7°$.
3.80 $M = 2860 \text{ N} \cdot \text{m}$; $\theta_x = 113.0°$, $\theta_y = 92.7°$, $\theta_z = 23.2°$.
3.81 (a) $\mathbf{F} = 560 \text{ lb} \searrow 20.0°$; $\mathbf{M} = 7720 \text{ lb} \cdot \text{ft} ↓$.
(b) $\mathbf{F} = 560 \text{ lb} \searrow 20.0°$; $\mathbf{M} = 4290 \text{ lb} \cdot \text{ft} ↓$.
3.82 (a) $\mathbf{F} = 160.0 \text{ lb} \measuredangle 60.0°$; $\mathbf{M} = 334 \text{ lb} \cdot \text{ft} ↰$.
(b) $\mathbf{F}_B = 20.0 \text{ lb} ↑$; $\mathbf{F}_D = 143.0 \text{ lb} \measuredangle 56.0°$.
3.83 (a) $\mathbf{F}_B = 80.0 \text{ N} \leftarrow$; $\mathbf{M}_B = 4.00 \text{ N} \cdot \text{m} ↰$.
(b) $\mathbf{F}_C = 100.0 \text{ N} ↓$; $\mathbf{F}_D = 100.0 \text{ N} ↑$.
3.85 (a) $\mathbf{F}_B = 250 \text{ N} \searrow 60.0°$; $\mathbf{M}_B = 75.0 \text{ N} \cdot \text{m} ↓$.
(b) $\mathbf{F}_A = 375 \text{ N} \searrow 60.0°$; $\mathbf{F}_B = 625 \text{ N} \searrow 60.0°$.
3.87 (a) $\mathbf{F} = -(600 \text{ N})\mathbf{k}$; $d = 90.0$mm below ED.
(b) $\mathbf{F} = -(600 \text{ N})\mathbf{k}$; $d = 90.0$mm above ED.
3.88 $\mathbf{F} = 900 \text{ N} ↓$; $x = 50.0$ mm.
3.89 $(0.227 \text{ lb})\mathbf{i} + (0.1057 \text{ lb})\mathbf{k}$; 63.6 in. to the right of B.
3.90 (a) $\mathbf{F} = 48.0 \text{ lb} \measuredangle 65.0°$; $\mathbf{M} = 490 \text{ lb} \cdot \text{in.} ↓$.
(b) $\mathbf{F} = 48.0 \text{ lb} \measuredangle 65.0°$; 17.78 in. to the left of B.
3.93 $\mathbf{F} = -(1220 \text{ N})\mathbf{i}$; $\mathbf{M} = (73.2 \text{ N} \cdot \text{m})\mathbf{j} - (122.0 \text{ N} \cdot \text{m})\mathbf{k}$.
3.94 $\mathbf{F}_C = (5.00 \text{ N})\mathbf{i} + (150.0 \text{ N})\mathbf{j} - (90.0 \text{ N})\mathbf{k}$;
$\mathbf{M}_C = (77.4 \text{ N} \cdot \text{m})\mathbf{i} + (61.5 \text{ N} \cdot \text{m})\mathbf{j} + (106.8 \text{ N} \cdot \text{m})\mathbf{k}$.
3.95 $\mathbf{F} = -(128.0 \text{ lb})\mathbf{i} - (256 \text{ lb})\mathbf{j} + (32.0 \text{ lb})\mathbf{k}$;
$\mathbf{M} = (4.10 \text{ kip} \cdot \text{ft})\mathbf{i} + (16.38 \text{ kip} \cdot \text{ft})\mathbf{k}$.
3.97 $\mathbf{F} = -(122.9 \text{ N})\mathbf{j} - (86.0 \text{ N})\mathbf{k}$;
$\mathbf{M} = (22.6 \text{ N} \cdot \text{m})\mathbf{i} + (15.49 \text{ N} \cdot \text{m})\mathbf{j} - (22.1 \text{ N} \cdot \text{m})\mathbf{k}$.
3.98 (a) 135.0 mm. (b) $\mathbf{F}_2 = (42.0 \text{ N})\mathbf{i} + (42.0 \text{ N})\mathbf{j} - (49.0 \text{ N})\mathbf{k}$;
$\mathbf{M}_2 = -(25.9 \text{ N} \cdot \text{m})\mathbf{i} + (21.2 \text{ N} \cdot \text{m})\mathbf{j}$.
3.99 $\mathbf{F} = (36.0 \text{ lb})\mathbf{i} - (28.0 \text{ lb})\mathbf{j} - (6.00 \text{ lb})\mathbf{k}$;
$\mathbf{M} = -(157.0 \text{ lb} \cdot \text{ft})\mathbf{i} + (22.5 \text{ lb} \cdot \text{ft})\mathbf{j} - (240 \text{ lb} \cdot \text{ft})\mathbf{k}$.
3.101 (a) *Loading a*: $\mathbf{R} = 600 \text{ N} ↓$; $\mathbf{M} = 1000 \text{ N} \cdot \text{m} ↰$.
Loading b: $\mathbf{R} = 600 \text{ N} ↓$; $\mathbf{M} = 900 \text{ N} \cdot \text{m} ↓$.
Loading c: $\mathbf{R} = 600 \text{ N} ↓$; $\mathbf{M} = 900 \text{ N} \cdot \text{m} ↰$.
Loading d: $\mathbf{R} = 400 \text{ N} ↑$; $\mathbf{M} = 900 \text{ N} \cdot \text{m} ↰$.
Loading e: $\mathbf{R} = 600 \text{ N} ↓$; $\mathbf{M} = 200 \text{ N} \cdot \text{m} ↓$.
Loading f: $\mathbf{R} = 600 \text{ N} ↓$; $\mathbf{M} = 800 \text{ N} \cdot \text{m} ↰$.
Loading g: $\mathbf{R} = 1000 \text{ N} ↓$; $\mathbf{M} = 1000 \text{ N} \cdot \text{m} ↰$.
Loading h: $\mathbf{R} = 600 \text{ N} ↓$; $\mathbf{M} = 900 \text{ N} \cdot \text{m} ↰$.
(b) Loadings *c* and *h*.
3.102 Loading *f*.
3.104 Force-couple system at D.
3.105 (a) 2.00 ft to the right of C. (b) 2.31 ft to the right of C.
3.106 (a) 39.6 in. to the right of D. (b) 33.1 in.
3.108 $\mathbf{R} = 72.4 \text{ lb} \searrow 81.9°$; $\mathbf{M} = 206 \text{ lb} \cdot \text{ft}$.
3.109 (a) 34.0 lb $\searrow$ 28.0°. (b) AB: 11.64 in. to the left of B; BC: 6.20 in. below B.
3.110 (a) 48.2 lb · in. ↰. (b) 240 lb · in. ↰. (c) 0.
3.111 (a) 1562 N $\searrow$ 50.2°. (b) 250 mm to the right of C and 300 mm above C.
3.112 (a) 1308 N $\measuredangle$ 66.6°. (b) 412 mm to the right of A and 250 mm to the right of C.
3.113 773 lb $\nearrow$ 79.0°; 9.54 ft to the right of A.
3.115 (a) 0.365 m above G. (b) 0.227 m to the right of G.
3.116 (a) 0.299 m above G. (b) 0.259 m to the right of G.
3.118 (a) $\mathbf{R} = F \nearrow \tan^{-1}(a^2/2bx)$;
$\mathbf{M} = 2Fb^2(x - x^3/a^2)/\sqrt{a^4 + 4b^2x^2} ↰$. (b) 0.369 m.
3.119 $\mathbf{R} = -(420 \text{ N})\mathbf{i} - (50.0 \text{ N})\mathbf{j} - (250 \text{ N})\mathbf{k}$;
$\mathbf{M} = (30.8 \text{ N} \cdot \text{m})\mathbf{i} - (22.0 \text{ N} \cdot \text{m})\mathbf{k}$.
3.120 $\mathbf{R} = -(420 \text{ N})\mathbf{i} - (339 \text{ N})\mathbf{k}$;
$\mathbf{M} = (1.125 \text{ N} \cdot \text{m})\mathbf{i} + (163.9 \text{ N} \cdot \text{m})\mathbf{j} - (109.9 \text{ N} \cdot \text{m})\mathbf{k}$.
3.121 (a) $\mathbf{B} = (2.50 \text{ lb})\mathbf{i}$;
$\mathbf{C} = (0.1000 \text{ lb})\mathbf{i} - (2.47 \text{ lb})\mathbf{j} - (0.700 \text{ lb})\mathbf{k}$.
(b) $R_y = -2.47$ lb; $M_x = 1.360 \text{ lb} \cdot \text{ft}$.
3.122 $\mathbf{A} = (1.600 \text{ lb})\mathbf{i} - (36.0 \text{ lb})\mathbf{j} + (2.00 \text{ lb})\mathbf{k}$;
$\mathbf{B} = -(9.60 \text{ lb})\mathbf{i} + (36.0 \text{ lb})\mathbf{j} + (2.00 \text{ lb})\mathbf{k}$.

3.124 (a) $\mathbf{R} = -(28.4\ \text{N})\mathbf{j} - (50.0\ \text{N})\mathbf{k}$;
$\mathbf{M} = (8.56\ \text{N}\cdot\text{m})\mathbf{i} - (24.0\ \text{N}\cdot\text{m})\mathbf{j} + (2.13\ \text{N}\cdot\text{m})\mathbf{k}$.
(b) Counterclockwise.

3.125 (a) $\mathbf{R} = -(28.4\ \text{N})\mathbf{j} - (50.0\ \text{N})\mathbf{k}$;
$\mathbf{M} = (42.4\ \text{N}\cdot\text{m})\mathbf{i} - (24.0\ \text{N}\cdot\text{m})\mathbf{j} + (2.13\ \text{N}\cdot\text{m})\mathbf{k}$.
(b) Counterclockwise.

3.127 1035 N; 2.57 m from OG and 3.05 m from OE.

3.128 2.32 m from OG and 1.165 m from OE.

3.129 405 lb; 12.60 ft to the right of AB and 2.94 ft below BC.

3.130 $a = 0.722$ ft; $b = 20.6$ ft.

3.133 (a) $P\sqrt{3}$; $\theta_x = \theta_y = \theta_z = 54.7°$. (b) $-a$. (c) Axis of the wrench is diagonal OA.

3.134 (a) P; $\theta_x = 90.0°$, $\theta_y = 90.0°$, $\theta_z = 0$. (b) $5a/2$. (c) Axis of wrench is parallel to the z axis at $x = a$, $y = -a$.

3.136 (a) $-(21.0\ \text{lb})\mathbf{j}$. (b) 0.571 in. (c) Axis of wrench is parallel to the y axis at $x = 0$, $z = 1.667$ in.

3.137 (a) $-(84.0\ \text{N})\mathbf{j} - (80.0\ \text{N})\mathbf{k}$. (b) 0.477 m.
(c) $x = 0.526$ m, $z = -0.1857$ m.

3.140 (a) $3P(2\mathbf{i} - 20\mathbf{j} - \mathbf{k})/25$. (b) $-0.0988a$.
(c) $x = 2.00a$, $z = -1.990a$.

3.141 $\mathbf{R} = (20.0\ \text{N})\mathbf{i} + (30.0\ \text{N})\mathbf{j} - (10.00\ \text{N})\mathbf{k}$;
$y = -0.540$ m, $z = -0.420$ m.

3.143 $\mathbf{F}_A = (M/b)\mathbf{j} + R[1 + (a/b)]\mathbf{k}$; $\mathbf{F}_B = -(M/b)\mathbf{i} - (aR/b)\mathbf{k}$.

3.147 (a) 196.2 N·m ↓. (b) 199.0 N ↘ 59.5°.

3.148 42.0 N·m ↑.

3.149 $-(25.4\ \text{lb}\cdot\text{ft})\mathbf{i} - (12.60\ \text{lb}\cdot\text{ft})\mathbf{j} - (12.60\ \text{lb}\cdot\text{ft})\mathbf{k}$.

3.151 283 lb.

3.153 (a) 151.2 lb·in. ↑. (b) 67.2 lb·in. ↑.

3.155 $\mathbf{F} = -(28.5\ \text{N})\mathbf{j} + (106.3\ \text{N})\mathbf{k}$;
$\mathbf{M} = (12.35\ \text{N}\cdot\text{m})\mathbf{i} - (19.16\ \text{N}\cdot\text{m})\mathbf{j} - (5.13\ \text{N}\cdot\text{m})\mathbf{k}$.

3.156 (a) 665 lb ∡ 79.6°; 64.9 in. to the right of A. (b) 22.9°.

3.157 (a) $\mathbf{F}_B = -(80.0\ \text{N})\mathbf{k}$; $\mathbf{F}_C = -(30.0\ \text{N})\mathbf{i} + (40.0\ \text{N})\mathbf{k}$.
(b) $R_y = 0$; $R_z = -40.0$ N. (c) When the slot is vertical.

3.C3 4 sides: $\beta = 10°$, $\alpha = 44.1°$;
$\beta = 20°$, $\alpha = 41.6°$;
$\beta = 30°$, $\alpha = 37.8°$.

3.C4 $\theta = 0$ rev: $M = 97.0$ N·m;
$\theta = 6$ rev: $M = 63.3$ N·m;
$\theta = 12$ rev: $M = 9.17$ N·m.

3.C6 $d_{AB} = 36.0$ in.; $d_{CD} = 9.00$ in.; $d_{\min} = 58.3$ in.

CHAPTER 4

4.1 (a) 325 lb ↑. (b) 1175 lb ↑.

4.2 42.0 N ↑

4.3 0.264 m

4.4 (a) 245 lb. ↑. (b) 140.0 lb.

4.5 (a) 6.07 kN ↑. (b) 4.23 kN ↑.

4.6 (a) 4.89 kN ↑. (b) 3.69 kN ↑.

4.9 150.0 mm ≤ d ≤ 400 mm.

4.11 6.00 kips ≤ P ≤ 42.0 kips.

4.12 3.50 kN ≤ P ≤ 86.0 kN.

4.14 2.00 in. ≤ a ≤ 10.00 in.

4.15 (a) $F_{DE} = 600$ N. (b) $\mathbf{C} = 1253$ N ∡ 69.8°.

4.17 (a) 80.0 lb ↓. (b) 216 lb ∡ 22.0°.

4.18 232 lb.

4.19 (a) 2.00 kN. (b) 2.32 kN ∡ 46.4°.

4.21 (a) $\mathbf{A} = 150.0$ N ∡ 30.0°; $\mathbf{B} = 150.0$ N ↘ 30.0°.
(b) $\mathbf{A} = 433$ N ↖ 12.55°; $\mathbf{B} = 488$ N ↘ 30.0°.

4.23 (a) $\mathbf{A} = 44.7$ lb ↘ 26.6°; $\mathbf{B} = 30.0$ lb ↑.
(b) $\mathbf{A} = 30.2$ lb ↘ 41.4°; $\mathbf{B} = 34.6$ lb ↘ 60.0°.

4.24 (a) $\mathbf{A} = 20.0$ lb ↑; $\mathbf{B} = 50.0$ lb ↘ 36.9°.
(b) $\mathbf{A} = 23.1$ lb ∡ 60.0°; $\mathbf{B} = 59.6$ lb ↘ 30.2°.

4.26 (a) 190.9 N. (b) 142.3 N ∡ 18.43°.

4.27 (a) 324 N. (b) 270 N →.

4.28 (a) 400 N. (b) $\mathbf{C} = 458$ N ∡ 49.1°.

4.29 (a) 875 lb (b) 1584 lb ↘ 45.0°.

4.30 $T = 80.0$ N; $\mathbf{C} = 89.4$ N ∡ 26.6°.

4.33 $T = 2P/3$; $\mathbf{C} = 0.577P$ →.

4.34 $T = 0.586P$; $\mathbf{C} = 0.414P$ →.

4.35 $\mathbf{A} = 69.3$ lb →; $\mathbf{B} = 34.6$ lb ↘ 60.0°; $\mathbf{C} = 173.2$ lb ↘ 60.0°.

4.36 $T_{BE} = 50.0$ lb; $\mathbf{A} = 18.75$ lb →; $\mathbf{D} = 18.75$ lb ←.

4.37 (a) 1432 N. (b) 1100 N ↑. (c) 1400 N ←.

4.38 $T_{BE} = 3230$ N; $T_{CF} = 960$ N; $\mathbf{D} = 3750$ N ←.

4.41 $T = 80.0$ N; $\mathbf{A} = 160.0$ N ↖ 30.0°; $\mathbf{C} = 160.0$ N ↘ 30.0°.

4.42 $T = 69.3$ N; $\mathbf{A} = 140.0$ N ↖ 30.0°; $\mathbf{C} = 180.0$ N ↘ 30.0°.

4.43 (a) $\mathbf{A} = 78.5$ N; $\mathbf{M}_A = 125.6$ N·m ↑.
(b) $\mathbf{A} = 111.0$ N ∡ 45.0°; $\mathbf{M}_A = 125.6$ N·m ↑.
(c) $\mathbf{A} = 157.0$ N ↑; $\mathbf{M}_A = 251$ N·m ↑.

4.44 $\mathbf{C} = 7.07$ lb ↘ 45.0°; $\mathbf{M}_C = 43.0$ lb·in. ↓.

4.46 $\mathbf{A} = 1848$ N ∡ 82.6°; $\mathbf{M}_A = 1431$ N·m ↓.

4.47 (a) $\mathbf{D} = 20.0$ lb ↓; $\mathbf{M}_D = 20.0$ lb·ft ↑.
(b) $\mathbf{D} = 10.00$ lb ↓; $\mathbf{M}_D = 30.0$ lb·ft ↓.

4.49 $\mathbf{C} = 1951$ N ↘ 88.5°; $\mathbf{M}_C = 75.0$ N·m ↓.

4.50 1.232 kN ≤ T ≤ 1.774 kN.

4.51 (a) $\theta = 2\sin^{-1}(W/2P)$. (b) $\theta = 29.0°$.

4.52 (a) $T = \frac{1}{2}W/(1 - \tan\theta)$. (b) $\theta = 39.8°$.

4.53 (a) $\sin\theta + \cos\theta = M/Pl$. (b) 17.11° and 72.9°.

4.54 (a) $\cos^3\theta = a(P + Q)/Pl$. (b) 40.6°.

4.57 141.1°

4.58 (a) $(1 - \cos\theta)\tan\theta = W/2kl$. (b) 49.7°.

4.59 (1) completely constrained; determinate; $\mathbf{A} = \mathbf{C} = 196.2$ N ↑.
(2) completely constrained; determinate; $\mathbf{B} = 0$, $\mathbf{C} = \mathbf{D} = 196.2$ N ↑.
(3) completely constrained; indeterminate; $\mathbf{A}_x = 294$ N →; $\mathbf{D}_x = 294$ N ←.
(4) improperly constrained; indeterminate; no equilibrium.
(5) partially constrained; determinate; equilibrium; $\mathbf{C} = \mathbf{D} = 196.2$ N ↑.
(6) completely constrained; determinate; $\mathbf{B} = 294$ N →, $\mathbf{D} = 491$ N ↘ 53.1°.
(7) partially constrained; no equilibrium.
(8) completely constrained; indeterminate; $\mathbf{B} = 196.2$ N ↑, $\mathbf{D}_y = 196.2$ N ↑.

4.61 $\mathbf{A} = 400$ N ↑; $\mathbf{B} = 500$ N ↖ 53.1°.

4.62 $a \geq 138.6$ mm.

4.66 $\mathbf{B} = 888$ N ↖ 41.3°; $\mathbf{D} = 943$ N ↘ 45.0°.

4.67 $\mathbf{B} = 1001$ N ↘ 48.2°; $\mathbf{D} = 943$ N ↖ 45.0°.

4.69 (a) 499 N. (b) 457 N ↘ 26.6°.

4.70 (a) 998 N. (b) 822 N ↗ 5.72°.

4.71 $\mathbf{A} = 37.1$ lb ∡ 62.4°; $T = 18.57$ lb.

4.74 (a) 24.9 lb ↗ 30.0°. (b) 15.34 lb ∡ 30.0°.

4.75 $T = 100.0$ lb; $\mathbf{B} = 111.1$ lb ↖ 30.3°.

4.77 $\mathbf{A} = 170.0$ N ↘ 33.9°; $\mathbf{C} = 160.0$ N ∡ 28.1°.

4.80 (a) $F_{AD} = 400$ N. (b) $\mathbf{C} = 458$ N ∡ 49.1°.

4.81 (a) $2P$ ↘ 60.0°. (b) $1.239P$ ↖ 36.2°.

4.82 (a) $1.155P$ ↘ 30.0°. (b) $1.086P$ ∡ 22.9°.

4.83 60.0 mm.

4.84 $\tan\theta = 2\tan\beta$.

4.85 (a) 49.1°. (b) $\mathbf{A} = 45.3$ N ←; $\mathbf{B} = 90.6$ N ∡ 60.0°.

4.87 (a) 12.91 in. (b) 11.62 lb. (c) 5.92 lb.

4.88 32.5°.

4.90 (a) 59.4°. (b) $\mathbf{A} = 8.45$ lb →; $\mathbf{B} = 13.09$ lb ↘ 49.8°.

4.91 $\mathbf{A} = (22.9 \text{ lb})\mathbf{i} + (8.50 \text{ lb})\mathbf{j}$; $\mathbf{B} = (22.9 \text{ lb})\mathbf{i} + (25.5 \text{ lb})\mathbf{j}$; $\mathbf{C} = -(45.8 \text{ lb})\mathbf{i}$.

4.92 $\mathbf{A} = (56.0 \text{ N})\mathbf{j} + (18.00 \text{ N})\mathbf{k}$; $\mathbf{D} = (24.0 \text{ N})\mathbf{j} + (42.0 \text{ N})\mathbf{k}$.

4.93 $\mathbf{A} = (56.0 \text{ N})\mathbf{j} + (14.40 \text{ N})\mathbf{k}$; $\mathbf{D} = (24.0 \text{ N})\mathbf{j} + (33.6 \text{ N})\mathbf{k}$.

4.94 (a) 37.5 lb. (b) $\mathbf{B} = (33.8 \text{ lb})\mathbf{j} - (70.0 \text{ lb})\mathbf{k}$; $\mathbf{D} = (33.8 \text{ lb})\mathbf{j} + (28.0 \text{ lb})\mathbf{k}$.

4.97 (a) 121.9 N. (b) −46.2 N. (c) 100.9 N.

4.98 (a) 95.6 N. (b) −7.36 N. (c) 88.3 N.

4.99 $T_A = 30.0$ lb; $T_B = 10.00$ lb; $T_C = 40.0$ lb.

4.100 $(W_D)_{\min} = 40.0$ lb; $x = 0$ in.; $z = 30.0$ in.

4.101 $T_A = 23.5$ N; $T_C = 11.77$ N; $T_D = 105.9$ N.

4.102 (a) 0.480 m. (b) $T_A = 23.5$ N; $T_C = 0$; $T_D = 117.7$ N.

4.105 $T_{BD} = T_{BE} = 1100$ lb; $\mathbf{A} = (1200 \text{ lb})\mathbf{i} - (560 \text{ lb})\mathbf{j}$.

4.106 $T_{AD} = 2.60$ kN; $T_{AE} = 2.80$ kN; $\mathbf{C} = (1.800 \text{ kN})\mathbf{j} + (4.80 \text{ kN})\mathbf{k}$.

4.107 $T_{AD} = 5.20$ kN; $T_{AE} = 5.60$ kN; $\mathbf{C} = (9.60 \text{ kN})\mathbf{k}$.

4.108 (a) $T_{DE} = T_{DF} = 262$ lb. (b) $\mathbf{A} = -(801 \text{ lb})\mathbf{i} + (1544 \text{ lb})\mathbf{j}$.

4.109 (a) $T_{CD} = T_{CE} = 3.96$ kN. (b) $\mathbf{A} = (6.67 \text{ kN})\mathbf{i} + (1.667 \text{ kN})\mathbf{j}$.

4.110 (a) $T_{CD} = 0.954$ kN; $T_{CE} = 5.90$ kN. (b) $\mathbf{A} = (5.77 \text{ kN})\mathbf{i} + (1.443 \text{ kN})\mathbf{j} - (0.833 \text{ kN})\mathbf{k}$.

4.113 (a) 101.6 N. (b) $\mathbf{A} = -(26.3 \text{ N})\mathbf{i}$; $\mathbf{B} = (98.1 \text{ N})\mathbf{j}$.

4.114 (a) 462 N. (b) $\mathbf{C} = -(336 \text{ N})\mathbf{j} + (467 \text{ N})\mathbf{k}$; $\mathbf{D} = (505 \text{ N})\mathbf{j} - (66.7 \text{ N})\mathbf{k}$.

4.117 (a) 49.5 lb. (b) $\mathbf{A} = -(12.00 \text{ lb})\mathbf{i} + (22.5 \text{ lb})\mathbf{j} - (4.00 \text{ lb})\mathbf{k}$; $\mathbf{B} = (15.00 \text{ lb})\mathbf{j} + (34.0 \text{ lb})\mathbf{k}$.

4.118 (a) 118.8 lb. (b) $\mathbf{A} = (93.8 \text{ lb})\mathbf{i} + (22.5 \text{ lb})\mathbf{j} + (70.8 \text{ lb})\mathbf{k}$; $\mathbf{B} = (15.00 \text{ lb})\mathbf{j} - (8.33 \text{ lb})\mathbf{k}$.

4.119 (a) 462 N. (b) $\mathbf{C} = (169.1 \text{ N})\mathbf{j} + (400 \text{ N})\mathbf{k}$; $\mathbf{M}_C = (20.0 \text{ N} \cdot \text{m})\mathbf{j} + (151.5 \text{ N} \cdot \text{m})\mathbf{k}$.

4.120 (a) 49.5 lb. (b) $\mathbf{A} = -(12.00 \text{ lb})\mathbf{i} + (37.5 \text{ lb})\mathbf{j} + (30.0 \text{ lb})\mathbf{k}$; $\mathbf{M}_A = -(1020 \text{ lb} \cdot \text{in.})\mathbf{j} + (450 \text{ lb} \cdot \text{in.})\mathbf{k}$.

4.121 (a) 5.00 lb. (b) $\mathbf{C} = -(5.00 \text{ lb})\mathbf{i} + (6.00 \text{ lb})\mathbf{j} - (5.00 \text{ lb})\mathbf{k}$; $\mathbf{M}_C = (8.00 \text{ lb} \cdot \text{in.})\mathbf{j} - (12.00 \text{ lb} \cdot \text{in.})\mathbf{k}$.

4.122 $T_{CF} = 200$ N; $T_{DE} = 450$ N; $\mathbf{A} = (160.0 \text{ N})\mathbf{i} + (270 \text{ N})\mathbf{k}$; $\mathbf{M}_A = -(16.20 \text{ N} \cdot \text{m})\mathbf{i}$.

4.125 $T_{BE} = 975$ N; $T_{CF} = 600$ N; $T_{DG} = 625$ N; $\mathbf{A} = (2100 \text{ N})\mathbf{i} + (175.0 \text{ N})\mathbf{j} - (375 \text{ N})\mathbf{k}$.

4.126 $T_{BE} = 1950$ N; $T_{CF} = 0$; $T_{DG} = 1250$ N; $\mathbf{A} = (3000 \text{ N})\mathbf{i} - (750 \text{ N})\mathbf{k}$.

4.127 $\mathbf{A} = (120.0 \text{ lb})\mathbf{j} - (150.0 \text{ lb})\mathbf{k}$; $\mathbf{B} = (180.0 \text{ lb})\mathbf{i} + (150.0 \text{ lb})\mathbf{k}$; $\mathbf{C} = -(180.0 \text{ lb})\mathbf{i} + (120.0 \text{ lb})\mathbf{j}$.

4.128 $\mathbf{A} = (20.0 \text{ lb})\mathbf{j} + (25.0 \text{ lb})\mathbf{k}$; $\mathbf{B} = (30.0 \text{ lb})\mathbf{i} - (25.0 \text{ lb})\mathbf{k}$; $\mathbf{C} = -(30.0 \text{ lb})\mathbf{i} - (20.0 \text{ lb})\mathbf{j}$.

4.129 $\mathbf{B} = (60.0 \text{ N})\mathbf{k}$; $\mathbf{C} = (30.0 \text{ N})\mathbf{j} - (16.00 \text{ N})\mathbf{k}$; $\mathbf{D} = -(30.0 \text{ N})\mathbf{j} + (4.00 \text{ N})\mathbf{k}$.

4.130 $\mathbf{B} = (60.0 \text{ N})\mathbf{k}$; $\mathbf{C} = -(16.00 \text{ N})\mathbf{k}$; $\mathbf{D} = (4.00 \text{ N})\mathbf{k}$.

4.133 85.3 lb.

4.134 181.7 lb.

4.135 373 N

4.136 301 N

4.137 $(45.0 \text{ lb})\mathbf{j}$

4.138 (a) $x = 4.00$ ft; $y = 8.00$ ft. (b) 10.73 lb.

4.139 (a) $x = 0$ ft; $y = 16.00$ ft. (b) 11.31 lb.

4.142 (a) 37.9 N ↑. (b) 373 N ↑.

4.143 (a) $\mathbf{A} = 225$ N ↑; $\mathbf{C} = 641$ N ⟋ 20.6°. (b) $\mathbf{A} = 365$ N ⦣ 60.0°; $\mathbf{B} = 844$ N ⟋ 22.0°.

4.145 (a) 130.0 N, (b) 224 N ⟋ 2.05°.

4.146 $\mathbf{C} = 7.97$ lb →; $\mathbf{D} = 42.6$ lb ←; $\mathbf{E} = 69.3$ lb ⦣ 60.0°.

4.148 $\mathbf{A} = 63.6$ lb ⦥ 45.0°; $\mathbf{C} = 87.5$ lb ⟍ 59.0°.

4.150 $T_{BD} = 780$ N; $T_{BE} = 390$ N; $\mathbf{A} = -(195.0 \text{ N})\mathbf{i} + (1170 \text{ N})\mathbf{j} + (130.0 \text{ N})\mathbf{k}$.

4.152 $T_{FJ} = 0$; $T_{DH} = 60.0$ lb; $T_{BG} = 80.0$ lb; $\mathbf{A} = (100.0 \text{ lb})\mathbf{i} - (48.0 \text{ lb})\mathbf{k}$.

4.153 (a) $\mathbf{A} = 0.745P$ ⦣ 63.4°; $\mathbf{C} = 0.471P$ ⟍ 45.0°. (b) $\mathbf{A} = 0.812P$ ⦣ 60.0°; $\mathbf{C} = 0.503P$ ⟎ 36.2°. (c) $\mathbf{A} = 0.448P$ ⟍ 60.0°; $\mathbf{C} = 0.652P$ ⦣ 69.9°. (d) improperly constrained; no equilibrium.

4.C1 $\theta = 20°$: $T = 114.8$ lb; $\theta = 70°$: $T = 127.7$ lb; $T_{\max} = 132.2$ lb at $\theta = 50.4°$.

4.C2 $x = 600$ mm: $P = 31.4$ N; $x = 150$ mm: $P = 37.7$ N; $P_{\max} = 47.2$ N at $x = 283$ mm.

4.C3 $\theta = 30°$: $W = 9.66$ lb; $\theta = 60°$: $W = 36.6$ lb; $W = 5$ lb at $\theta = 22.9°$ [Also at $\theta = 175.7°$].

4.C4 $\theta = 30°$: $W = 0.80$ lb; $\theta = 60°$: $W = 4.57$ lb; $W = 5$ lb at $\theta = 62.6°$ [Also at $\theta = 159.6°$].

4.C5 $\theta = 30°$: $m = 7.09$ kg; $\theta = 60°$: $m = 11.02$ kg. When $m = 10$ kg, $\theta = 51.0°$.

4.C6 $\theta = 15°$: $T_{BD} = 10.30$ kN, $T_{BE} = 21.7$ kN; $\theta = 30°$: $T_{BD} = 5.69$ kN, $T_{BE} = 24.4$ kN; $T_{\max} = 26.5$ kN at $\theta = 36.9°$.

CHAPTER 5

5.1 $\overline{X} = 175.6$ mm, $\overline{Y} = 94.4$ mm.

5.2 $\overline{X} = 16.21$ mm, $\overline{Y} = 31.9$ mm.

5.3 $\overline{X} = 19.28$ in., $\overline{Y} = 6.94$ in.

5.4 $\overline{X} = 5.67$ in., $\overline{Y} = 5.17$ in.

5.5 $\overline{X} = 7.22$ in., $\overline{Y} = 9.56$ in.

5.6 $\overline{X} = 92.0$ mm, $\overline{Y} = 23.3$ mm.

5.9 $\overline{X} = -10.00$ mm, $\overline{Y} = 87.5$ mm.

5.10 $\overline{X} = -9.89$ mm, $\overline{Y} = -10.67$ mm

5.11 $\overline{X} = 0$, $\overline{Y} = 6.45$ in.

5.12 $\overline{X} = 50.5$ mm, $\overline{Y} = 19.34$ mm.

5.14 $\overline{X} = \overline{Y} = 9.00$ in.

5.16 $\overline{Y} = \dfrac{2}{3}\left(\dfrac{r_2^3 - r_1^3}{r_2^2 - r_1^2}\right)\left(\dfrac{2\cos\alpha}{\pi - 2\alpha}\right)$

5.17 $\overline{Y} = \dfrac{r_1 + r_2}{\pi - 2\alpha}\cos\alpha$

5.18 $a/b = 4/5$

5.20 459 N

5.21 $(Q_x)_1 = 25.0 \text{ in}^3$; $(Q_x)_2 = -25.0 \text{ in}^3$.

5.22 $(Q_x)_1 = 23.3 \text{ in}^3$; $(Q_x)_2 = -23.3 \text{ in}^3$.

5.24 $\overline{X} = 172.5$ mm, $\overline{Y} = 97.5$ mm

5.26 $\overline{X} = 18.45$ in., $\overline{Y} = 6.48$ in.

5.28 (a) $T = 5.09$ lb. (b) $\mathbf{C} = 9.48$ lb ⟍ 57.5°.

5.29 0.739 m

5.30 $L = 0.204$ m or 0.943 m

5.32 (a) $h = 0.513a$. (b) $h = 0.691a$.

5.34 $\overline{x} = 2/3a$, $\overline{y} = \frac{1}{3}h$.

5.35 $\overline{x} = a/2$, $\overline{y} = 2h/5$.

5.37 $\overline{x} = 2a/3(4 - \pi)$, $\overline{y} = 2b/3(4 - \pi)$

5.39 $\overline{x} = a(3 - 4\sin\alpha)/6(1 - \alpha)$, $\overline{y} = 0$.

5.40 $\overline{x} = a/4$, $\overline{y} = 3b/10$.

5.41 $\overline{x} = 5a/8$, $\overline{y} = b/3$.

5.42 $\overline{x} = 5L/4$, $\overline{y} = 33a/40$.

5.44 $\overline{x} = a$, $\overline{y} = 17b/35$.

5.45 $2/5a$

5.46 $-2\sqrt{2}r/3\pi$.

5.48 $\overline{x} = 0.236L$, $\overline{y} = 0.454a$.

5.49 $\overline{x} = -9.27a$, $\overline{y} = 3.09a$.

5.50 $\overline{x} = 1.629$ in., $\overline{y} = 0.1853$ in.

5.51 $a = 1.901$ in. or 3.74 in.

5.52 (a) $V = 6.19 \cdot 10^6$ mm^3; $A = 458 \cdot 10^3$ mm^2.
(b) $V = 16.88 \cdot 10^6$ mm^3; $A = 1.171 \cdot 10^6$ mm^2.

5.53 (a) $V = 308 \cdot 10^3$ mm^3; $A = 38.2 \cdot 10^3$ mm^2.
(b) $V = 177.2 \cdot 10^3$ mm^3; $A = 22.4 \cdot 10^3$ mm^2.

5.54 (a) $V = 169.0 \cdot 10^3$ in^3; $A = 28.4 \cdot 10^3$ in^2.
(b) $V = 88.9 \cdot 10^3$ in^3; $A = 15.48 \cdot 10^3$ in^2.

5.56 $V = 3470$ mm^3; $A = 2320$ mm^2.

5.58 $V = 0.0900$ in^3.

5.59 $V = 31.9$ liters.

5.61 $m = 0.0305$ kg.

5.63 22.0 gallons

5.64 66.5%

5.66 (a) $\mathbf{R} = 1215$ lb $\downarrow$, $\bar{x} = 4.33$ ft.
(b) $\mathbf{A} = 630$ lb $\uparrow$; $\mathbf{B} = 585$ lb $\uparrow$.

5.67 (a) $\mathbf{R} = 2400$ N $\downarrow$, 2.33 m to the right of A.
(b) $\mathbf{A} = 1000$ N $\uparrow$; $\mathbf{B} = 1400$ N $\uparrow$.

5.68 $\mathbf{A} = 32.0$ kN; $\mathbf{M}_A = 124.0$ kN $\cdot$ m $\circlearrowleft$.

5.69 $\mathbf{B} = 1360$ lb $\uparrow$; $\mathbf{C} = 2360$ lb $\uparrow$.

5.71 $\mathbf{A} = 480$ N $\uparrow$; $\mathbf{B} = 840$ N $\downarrow$.

5.73 $\mathbf{A} = 3000$ N $\uparrow$; $\mathbf{M}_A = 12.60$ kN $\cdot$ m $\circlearrowleft$.

5.74 (a) $a = 0.536$ m. (b) $\mathbf{A} = \mathbf{B} = 761$ N $\uparrow$.

5.76 $\mathbf{B} = 150.0$ lb $\uparrow$; $\mathbf{C} = 5250$ lb $\uparrow$.

5.77 (a) $w_0 = 100.0$ lb/ft. (b) $\mathbf{C} = 4950$ lb $\uparrow$.

5.78 $w_A = 10.00$ kN/m; $w_B = 50.0$ kN/m.

5.80 (a) $\mathbf{H} = 254$ kN $\rightarrow$; $\mathbf{V} = 831$ kN $\uparrow$.
(b) $x = 3.25$ m to the right of A.
(c) $\mathbf{R} = 268$ kN $\nearrow$ 18.4°.

5.81 (a) $\mathbf{H} = 13.76$ kips $\rightarrow$; $\mathbf{V} = 113.0$ kips $\uparrow$.
(b) 22.4 ft to the right of A.
(c) $\mathbf{R} = 25.6$ kips $\nearrow$ 57.5°.

5.82 $d = 2.64$ m.

5.83 $\mathbf{T} = 67.2$ kN $\leftarrow$; $\mathbf{A} = 141.2$ kN $\leftarrow$.

5.84 $\mathbf{T} = 3.70$ kips $\uparrow$.

5.85 $d = 5.88$ ft.

5.88 $\mathbf{A} = 1197$ N $\searrow$ 53.1°; $\mathbf{B} = 1511$ N $\searrow$ 53.1°.

5.89 $T = 3570$ N.

5.90 $T = 208$ lb

5.91 $d = 6.00$ ft.

5.93 $d = 0.683$ m

5.94 $h = 0.0711$ m

5.96 (a) $b/10$ to the left of base of cone.
(b) $0.01136b$ to the right of base of cone.

5.97 $\bar{Y} = -(2h^2 - 3b^2)/2(4h - 3b)$.

5.98 $\bar{Z} = -a(4h - 2b)/\pi(4h - 3b)$.

5.99 (a) $\bar{Y} = -0.402a$. (b) $h/a = 2/5$ or $2/3$.

5.100 $\bar{X} = 46.8$ mm.

5.101 $\bar{Z} = 26.2$ mm.

5.103 $\bar{Y} = -0.1403$ in.

5.104 $\bar{Z} = 3.47$ in.

5.106 $\bar{X} = 0.295$ m, $\bar{Y} = 0.423$ m, $\bar{Z} = 1.703$ m.

5.107 $\bar{X} = 125.0$ mm, $\bar{Y} = 167.0$ mm, $\bar{Z} = 33.5$ mm.

5.108 $\bar{X} = \bar{Z} = 4.21$ in., $\bar{Y} = 7.03$ in.

5.110 $\bar{X} = 46.5$ mm, $\bar{Y} = 27.2$ mm, $\bar{Z} = 30.0$ mm

5.111 $\bar{X} = 17.00$ in., $\bar{Y} = 15.68$ in., $\bar{Z} = 14.16$ in.

5.112 $\bar{X} = 180.2$ mm, $\bar{Y} = 38.0$ mm, $\bar{Z} = 193.5$ mm.

5.114 $\bar{X} = 0.1452$ m, $\bar{Y} = 0.396$ m, $\bar{Z} = 0.370$ m.

5.115 $\bar{X} = 0.410$ m, $\bar{Y} = 0.510$ m, $\bar{Z} = 0.1500$ m.

5.117 $\bar{X} = 1.750$ ft, $\bar{Y} = 4.14$ ft, $\bar{Z} = 1.355$ ft.

5.118 $\bar{X} = 61.6$ mm from the end of the handle.

5.119 $\bar{Y} = 0.526$ in. above the base.

5.121 $\bar{Y} = 421$ mm. above the floor.

5.122 $(\bar{x})_1 = 21a/88$; $(\bar{x})_2 = 27a/40$.

5.123 $(\bar{x})_1 = 21h/88$; $(\bar{x})_2 = 27h/40$.

5.124 $(\bar{x})_1 = 2h/9$; $(\bar{x})_2 = 2h/3$.

5.125 $\bar{x} = h/6$; $\bar{y} = \bar{z} = 0$.

5.128 $\bar{x} = 1.297a$, $\bar{y} = \bar{z} = 0$.

5.129 $\bar{x} = \bar{z} = 0$, $\bar{y} = 0.374b$.

5.132 (a) $\bar{x} = \bar{z} = 0$, $\bar{y} = -121.9$ mm.
(b) $\bar{x} = \bar{z} = 0$, $\bar{y} = -90.2$ mm.

5.133 $V = 688$ ft^3; $\bar{x} = 15.91$ ft.

5.134 $\bar{x} = a/2$, $\bar{y} = 8h/25$, $\bar{z} = b/2$.

5.136 $\bar{x} = 0$, $\bar{y} = 5h/16$, $\bar{z} = -b/4$.

5.137 $\bar{X} = 19.27$ mm, $\bar{Y} = 26.6$ mm.

5.138 $\bar{X} = 3.20$ in., $\bar{Y} = 2.00$ in.

5.140 $\bar{x} = a/2$, $\bar{y} = 3h/5$.

5.141 $\bar{x} = 3a/8$, $\bar{y} = b$.

5.143 $\mathbf{A} = 1300$ N $\uparrow$; $\mathbf{B} = 1850$ N $\uparrow$.

5.146 (a) $\bar{x} = 0.548L$. (b) $h/L = 2\sqrt{3}$.

5.147 $\bar{X} = 0.1402$ m, $\bar{Y} = 0.0944$ m, $\bar{Z} = 0.0959$ m.

5.148 $\bar{x} = 2.34$ m, $\bar{y} = \bar{z} = 0$.

5.C1 (b) $\mathbf{A} = 1220$ lb $\uparrow$; $\mathbf{B} = 1830$ lb $\uparrow$.
(c) $\mathbf{A} = 1265$ lb $\uparrow$; $\mathbf{B} = 1601$ lb $\uparrow$.

5.C2 (a) $\bar{X} = 0$, $\bar{Y} = 0.278$ m, $\bar{Z} = 0.0878$ m.
(b) $\bar{X} = 0.0487$ m, $\bar{Y} = 0.1265$ mm, $\bar{Z} = 0.0997$ mm.
(c) $\bar{X} = -0.0372$ m, $\bar{Y} = 0.1659$ m, $\bar{Z} = 0.1043$ m.

5.C3 $d = 1.00$ m: $\mathbf{F} = 5.66$ kN $\nwarrow$ 30°;
$d = 3.00$ m: $\mathbf{F} = 49.9$ kN $\nwarrow$ 27.7°.

5.C4 (a) $\bar{X} = 5.80$ in., $\bar{Y} = 1.492$ in. (b) $\bar{X} = 9.11$ in., $\bar{Y} = 2.78$ in.
(c) $\bar{X} = 8.49$ in., $\bar{Y} = 0.375$ in.

5.C5 With $n = 40$: (a) $\bar{X} = 60.2$ mm, $\bar{Y} = 23.4$ mm.
(b) $\bar{X} = 60.2$ mm, $\bar{Y} = 146.2$ mm.
(c) $\bar{X} = 68.7$ mm. $\bar{Y} = 20.4$ mm.
(d) $\bar{X} = 68.7$ mm, $\bar{Y} = 127.8$ mm.

5.C6 With $n = 40$: (a) $\bar{X} = 60.0$ mm, $\bar{Y} = 24.0$ mm.
(b) $\bar{X} = 60.0$ mm, $\bar{Y} = 150.0$ mm.
(c) $\bar{X} = 68.6$ mm, $\bar{Y} = 21.8$ mm.
(d) $\bar{X} = 68.6$ mm, $\bar{Y} = 136.1$ mm.

5.C7 (a) $V = 628$ ft^3.
(b) $\bar{X} = 8.65$ ft, $\bar{Y} = -4.53$ ft, $\bar{Z} = 9.27$ ft.

CHAPTER 6

6.1 $F_{AB} = 52.0$ kN T; $F_{AC} = 64.0$ kN T; $F_{BC} = 80.0$ kN C.

6.2 $F_{AB} = 375$ lb C; $F_{AC} = 780$ lb C; $F_{BC} = 300$ lb T.

6.3 $F_{AB} = 4.00$ kN C; $F_{AC} = 2.72$ kN T; $F_{BC} = 2.40$ kN C.

6.5 $F_{AB} = F_{BC} = 31.5$ kips T; $F_{AD} = 35.7$ kips C;
$F_{BD} = 10.80$ kips C; $F_{CD} = 33.3$ kips C.

6.6 $F_{AB} = F_{BD} = 0$; $F_{AC} = 675$ N T; $F_{AD} = 1125$ N C;
$F_{CD} = 900$ N T; $F_{CE} = 2025$ N T; $F_{CF} = 2250$ N C;
$F_{DF} = 675$ N C; $F_{EF} = 1800$ N T.

6.7 $F_{AB} = 15.90$ kN C; $F_{AC} = 13.50$ kN T; $F_{BC} = 16.80$ kN C;
$F_{BD} = 13.50$ kN C; $F_{CD} = 15.90$ kN T.

6.9 $F_{AB} = 47.2$ kN C; $F_{AC} = 44.6$ kN T; $F_{BC} = 10.50$ kN C;
$F_{BD} = 47.2$ kN C; $F_{CD} = 17.50$ kN T; $F_{CE} = 30.6$ kN T;
$F_{DE} = 0$.

6.10 $F_{AB} = F_{HI} = 12.31$ kN C; $F_{AC} = F_{GI} = 11.25$ kN T; $F_{BC} = F_{GH} = 2.46$ kN C; $F_{BD} = F_{DE} = F_{EF} = F_{FH} = 9.85$ kN C;
$F_{CD} = F_{FG} = 2.00$ kN C; $F_{CE} = F_{EG} = 3.75$ kN T;
$F_{CG} = 6.75$ kN T.

6.11 $F_{AB} = F_{FH} = 1500$ lb C; $F_{AC} = F_{CE} = F_{EG} = F_{GH} = 1200$ lb T; $F_{BC} = F_{FG} = 0$; $F_{BD} = F_{DF} = 1000$ lb C;
$F_{BE} = F_{EF} = 500$ lb C; $F_{DE} = 600$ lb T.

6.12 $F_{AB} = F_{FH} = 1500$ lb C; $F_{AC} = F_{CE} = F_{EG} = F_{GH} =$ 1200 lb T; $F_{BC} = F_{FG} = 0$; $F_{BD} = F_{DF} = 1200$ lb C; $F_{BE} = F_{EF} = 60.0$ lb C; $F_{DE} = 72.0$ lb T.

6.15 $F_{AB} = 7.50$ kips C; $F_{AC} = 4.50$ kips T; $F_{BC} = 7.50$ kips T; $F_{BD} = 9.00$ kips C; $F_{CD} = 0$; $F_{CE} = 9.00$ kips T.

6.16 $F_{AB} = 5.00$ kips C; $F_{AC} = 3.00$ kips T; $F_{BC} = 5.00$ kips T; $F_{BD} = 6.00$ kips C; $F_{CD} = F_{EF} = 2.50$ kips T; $F_{CE} = 4.50$ kips T; $F_{DE} = F_{FG} = 2.50$ kips C; $F_{DF} = 3.00$ kips C; $F_{EG} = 1.500$ kips T.

6.19 $F_{AB} = 9.90$ kN C; $F_{AC} = 7.83$ kN T; $F_{BC} = 0$; $F_{BD} = 7.07$ kN C; $F_{BE} = 2.00$ kN C; $F_{CE} = 7.83$ kN T; $F_{DE} = 1.000$ kN T; $F_{DF} = 5.03$ kN C; $F_{DG} = 0.559$ kN C; $F_{EG} = 5.59$ kN T.

6.20 $F_{FG} = 3.50$ kN T; $F_{FH} = 5.03$ kN C; $F_{GH} = 1.677$ kN T; $F_{GI} = F_{IK} = F_{KL} = 3.35$ kN T; $F_{HI} = F_{IJ} = F_{JK} = 0$; $F_{HJ} = F_{JL} = 4.42$ kN C.

6.21 $F_{AB} = 2240$ lb C; $F_{AC} = F_{CE} = 2000$ lb T; $F_{BC} = F_{EH} = 0$; $F_{BD} = 1789$ lb C; $F_{BE} = 447$ lb C; $F_{DE} = 600$ lb C; $F_{DF} = 2010$ lb C; $F_{DG} = 224$ lb T; $F_{EG} = 1789$ lb T.

6.22 $F_{FG} = 1400$ lb T; $F_{FI} = 2010$ lb C; $F_{GI} = 671$ lb C; $F_{GJ} = 2430$ lb T; $F_{IJ} = 361$ lb T; $F_{IK} = 2910$ lb C; $F_{JK} = 447$ lb T; $F_{JL} = 3040$ lb T; $F_{KL} = 3350$ lb C.

6.23 $F_{AB} = 9.39$ kN C; $F_{AC} = 8.40$ kN T; $F_{BC} = 2.26$ kN C; $F_{BD} = 7.60$ kN C; $F_{CD} = 0.128$ kN C; $F_{CE} = 7.07$ kN T; $F_{DE} = 2.14$ kN C; $F_{DF} = 6.10$ kN C; $F_{EF} = 2.23$ kN T.

6.24 $F_{AB} = F_{DF} = 2.29$ kN T; $F_{AC} = F_{EF} = 2.29$ kN C; $F_{BC} = F_{DE} = 0.600$ kN C; $F_{BD} = 2.21$ kN T; $F_{BE} = F_{EH} = 0$; $F_{CE} = 2.21$ kN T; $F_{CH} = F_{EJ} = 1.200$ kN C.

6.27 $F_{AB} = 31.0$ kips C; $F_{AC} = 28.3$ kips C; $F_{AD} = 15.09$ kips T; $F_{AE} = 9.50$ kips T; $F_{BD} = 21.5$ kips T; $F_{BF} = 28.0$ kips C; $F_{CE} = 41.0$ kips T; $F_{CG} = 42.0$ kips C; $F_{DE} = 22.0$ kips T; $F_{DF} = 33.5$ kips T; $F_{EG} = 0$.

6.28 $F_{AB} = 128.0$ kN T; $F_{AC} = 136.7$ kN C; $F_{BD} = F_{DF} = F_{FH} =$ 128.0 kN T; $F_{CE} = F_{EG} = 136.7$ kN C; $F_{GH} = 192.7$ kN C.

6.29 Truss of Prob. 6.33a is the only simple truss.

6.30 Truss of Prob. 6.32b is the only simple truss.

6.31 (a) BC, CD, IJ, IL, LM, MN. (b) BC, BE, DE, EF, FG, IJ, KN, MN.

6.32 (a) AI, BJ, CK, DI, EI, FK, GK. (b) FK, IO.

6.35 $F_{AB} = F_{AD} = 244$ lb C; $F_{AC} = 1040$ lb T; $F_{BC} = F_{CD} = 500$ lb C; $F_{BD} = 280$ lb T.

6.36 $F_{AB} = F_{AD} = 861$ N C; $F_{AC} = 676$ N C; $F_{BC} = F_{CD} = 162.5$ N T; $F_{BD} = 244$ N T.

6.37 $F_{AB} = F_{AD} = 2810$ N T; $F_{AC} = 5510$ N C; $F_{BC} = F_{CD} = 1325$ N T; $F_{BD} = 1908$ N C.

6.38 $F_{AB} = F_{AC} = 1061$ lb C; $F_{AD} = 2500$ lb T; $F_{BC} = 2100$ lb T; $F_{BD} = F_{CD} = 1250$ lb C; $F_{BE} = F_{CE} = 1250$ lb C; $F_{DE} = 1500$ lb T.

6.39 $F_{AB} = 840$ N C; $F_{AC} = 110.6$ N C; $F_{AD} = 394$ N C; $F_{AE} = 0$; $F_{BC} = 160.0$ N T; $F_{BE} = 200$ N T; $F_{CD} = 225$ N T; $F_{CE} = 233$ N C; $F_{DE} = 120.0$ N T.

6.40 $F_{AB} = 0$; $F_{AC} = 995$ N T; $F_{AD} = 1181$ N C; $F_{AE} = F_{BC} = 0$; $F_{BE} = 600$ N T; $F_{CD} = 375$ N T; $F_{CE} = 700$ N C; $F_{DE} = 360$ N T.

6.43 $F_{CE} = 8000$ lb T; $F_{DE} = 2600$ lb T; $F_{DF} = 9000$ lb C

6.44 $F_{EG} = 7500$ lb T; $F_{FG} = 3900$ lb C; $F_{FH} = 6000$ lb C

6.45 $F_{BD} = 216$ kN T; $F_{DE} = 270$ kN T.

6.46 $F_{DG} = 459$ kN C; $F_{EG} = 216$ kN C.

6.49 $F_{CE} = 7.20$ kN T; $F_{DE} = 1.047$ kN C; $F_{DF} = 6.39$ kN C.

6.50 $F_{EG} = 3.46$ kN T; $F_{GH} = 3.78$ kN C; $F_{HJ} = 3.55$ kN C.

6.51 $F_{DF} = 10.48$ kips C; $F_{DG} = 3.35$ kips C; $F_{EG} = 13.02$ kips T.

6.52 $F_{OI} = 13.02$ kips T; $F_{HI} = 0.800$ kips T; $F_{HJ} = 13.97$ kips C.

6.53 $F_{CE} = 8.00$ kN T; $F_{DE} = 4.50$ kN C; $F_{DF} = 10.00$ kN C.

6.54 $F_{FH} = 10.00$ kN C; $F_{FI} = 4.92$ kN T; $F_{GI} = 6.00$ kN T.

6.55 $F_{AD} = 13.5$ kN C; $F_{CD} = 0$; $F_{CE} = 56.1$ kN T.

6.56 $F_{DG} = 75.0$ kN C; $F_{FG} = 56.1$ kN T; $F_{FH} = 69.7$ kN C.

6.57 $F_{AB} = 8.20$ kips T; $F_{AG} = 4.50$ kips T; $F_{FG} = 11.60$ kips C.

6.58 $F_{AE} = 17.46$ kips T; $F_{EF} = 11.60$ kips C; $F_{FJ} = 18.45$ kips C.

6.61 $F_{AB} = 1.500$ kN T; $F_{EJ} = 0.900$ kN T.

6.62 $F_{AF} = 0.900$ kN T; $F_{EJ} = 0.300$ kN T.

6.65 (a) CJ. (b) 1.026 kN T.

6.66 (a) IO. (b) 2.05 kN T.

6.67 $F_{BG} = 5.48$ kips T; $F_{DG} = 1.825$ kips T.

6.68 $F_{CF} = 3.65$ kips T; $F_{CH} = 7.30$ kips T.

6.69 (a) improperly constrained. (b) completely constrained, determinate. (c) completely constrained, indeterminate.

6.70 (a) completely constrained, determinate. (b) partially constrained. (c) improperly constrained.

6.71 (a) completely constrained, determinate. (b) completely constrained, indeterminate. (c) improperly constrained.

6.72 (a) partially constrained. (b) completely constrained, determinate. (c) completely constrained, indeterminate.

6.75 (a) 125 N ⤿ 36.9°. (b) 125 N ⤾ 36.9°.

6.76 $F_{BD} = 255$ N C; $\mathbf{C}_x = 120.0$ N $\rightarrow$; $\mathbf{C}_y = 625$ N $\uparrow$.

6.77 (a) 80.0 lb T. (b) 72.1 lb ⤿ 16.1°.

6.78 (a) 80.0 lb T. (b) 72.1 lb ⤾ 16.1°.

6.81 $\mathbf{A}_x = 18.00$ kN $\leftarrow$; $\mathbf{A}_y = 20.0$ kN $\downarrow$; $\mathbf{B} = 9.00$ kN $\rightarrow$; $\mathbf{C}_x = 9.00$ kN $\rightarrow$, $\mathbf{C}_y = 20.0$ kN $\uparrow$.

6.82 $\mathbf{A} = 20.0$ kN $\downarrow$; $\mathbf{B} = 18.00$ kN $\leftarrow$; $\mathbf{C}_x = 18.00$ kN $\rightarrow$, $\mathbf{C}_y = 20.0$ kN $\uparrow$.

6.83 (a) $\mathbf{A}_x = 450$ N $\leftarrow$, $\mathbf{A}_y = 525$ N $\uparrow$; $\mathbf{E}_x = 450$ N $\rightarrow$, $\mathbf{E}_y = 225$ N $\uparrow$; (b) $\mathbf{A}_x = 450$ N $\leftarrow$, $\mathbf{A}_y = 150.0$ N $\uparrow$; $\mathbf{E}_x = 450$ N $\rightarrow$, $\mathbf{E}_y = 600$ N $\uparrow$.

6.84 (a) $\mathbf{A}_x = 300$ N $\leftarrow$, $\mathbf{A}_y = 660$ N $\uparrow$; $\mathbf{E}_x = 300$ N $\rightarrow$, $\mathbf{E}_y = 90.0$ N $\uparrow$. (b) $\mathbf{A}_x = 300$ N $\leftarrow$, $\mathbf{A}_y = 150.0$ N $\uparrow$; $\mathbf{E}_x = 300$ N $\rightarrow$, $\mathbf{E}_y = 600$ N $\uparrow$.

6.87 (a) $\mathbf{A}_x = 80.0$ lb $\leftarrow$, $\mathbf{A}_y = 40.0$ lb $\uparrow$; $\mathbf{B}_x = 80.0$ lb $\rightarrow$, $\mathbf{B}_y = 60.0$ lb $\uparrow$. (b) $\mathbf{A}_x = 0$, $\mathbf{A}_y = 40.0$ lb $\uparrow$; $\mathbf{B}_x = 0$, $\mathbf{B}_y = 60.0$ lb $\uparrow$.

6.88 (a) and (c) $\mathbf{B}_x = 32.0$ lb $\rightarrow$, $\mathbf{B}_y = 10.00$ lb $\uparrow$; $\mathbf{F}_x = 32.0$ lb $\leftarrow$, $\mathbf{F}_y = 38.0$ lb $\uparrow$. (b) $\mathbf{B}_x = 32.0$ lb $\rightarrow$, $\mathbf{B}_y = 34.0$ lb $\uparrow$, $\mathbf{F}_x = 32.0$ lb $\leftarrow$, $\mathbf{F}_y = 14.00$ lb $\uparrow$.

6.89 (a) and (c) $\mathbf{B}_x = 24.0$ lb $\leftarrow$, $\mathbf{B}_y = 7.50$ lb $\downarrow$; $\mathbf{F}_x = 24.0$ lb $\rightarrow$, $\mathbf{F}_y = 7.50$ lb $\uparrow$. (b) $\mathbf{B}_x = 24.0$ lb $\leftarrow$, $\mathbf{B}_y = 10.50$ lb $\uparrow$; $\mathbf{F}_x = 24.0$ lb $\rightarrow$, $\mathbf{F}_y = 10.50$ lb $\downarrow$.

6.91 $\mathbf{B}_x = 700$ N $\leftarrow$, $\mathbf{B}_y = 200$ N $\downarrow$; $\mathbf{E}_x = 700$ N $\rightarrow$, $\mathbf{E}_y = 500$ N $\uparrow$.

6.92 $\mathbf{D}_x = 13.60$ kN $\rightarrow$, $\mathbf{D}_y = 7.50$ kN $\uparrow$; $\mathbf{E}_x = 13.60$ kN $\leftarrow$, $\mathbf{E}_y = 2.70$ kN $\downarrow$

6.93 $\mathbf{A}_x = 176.3$ lb $\leftarrow$, $\mathbf{A}_y = 60.0$ lb $\downarrow$; $\mathbf{G}_x = 56.3$ lb $\rightarrow$, $\mathbf{G}_y = 510$ lb $\uparrow$.

6.94 $\mathbf{A}_x = 56.3$ lb $\leftarrow$, $\mathbf{A}_y = 157.5$ lb $\downarrow$; $\mathbf{G}_x = 56.3$ lb $\rightarrow$, $\mathbf{G}_y = 383$ lb $\uparrow$.

6.95 (a) $\mathbf{A} = 982$ lb $\uparrow$; $\mathbf{B} = 935$ lb $\uparrow$; $\mathbf{C} = 733$ lb $\uparrow$. (b) $\Delta B = +291$ lb; $\Delta C = -72.7$ lb.

6.96 (a) = 572 lb. (b) $\mathbf{A} = 1070$ lb $\uparrow$; $\mathbf{B} = 709$ lb $\uparrow$; $\mathbf{C} = 870$ lb $\uparrow$.

6.99 $\mathbf{C}_x = 78.0$ lb $\rightarrow$, $\mathbf{C}_y = 28.0$ lb $\uparrow$; $\mathbf{F}_x = 78.0$ lb $\leftarrow$, $\mathbf{F}_y = 12.00$ lb $\uparrow$.

6.100 $\mathbf{C}_x = 21.7$ lb $\rightarrow$, $\mathbf{C}_y = 37.5$ lb $\downarrow$; $\mathbf{D}_x = 21.7$ lb $\leftarrow$, $\mathbf{D}_y = 62.5$ lb $\uparrow$.

6.101 $\mathbf{A}_x = 13.00$ kN $\leftarrow$, $\mathbf{A}_y = 4.00$ kN $\downarrow$; $\mathbf{B}_x = 36.0$ kN $\rightarrow$, $\mathbf{B}_y = 6.00$ kN $\uparrow$; $\mathbf{E}_x = 23.0$ kN $\leftarrow$, $\mathbf{E}_y = 2.00$ kN $\downarrow$.

6.102 $\mathbf{A}_x = 2025$ N $\leftarrow$, $\mathbf{A}_y = 1800$ N $\downarrow$; $\mathbf{B}_x = 4050$ N $\rightarrow$, $\mathbf{B}_y = 1200$ N $\uparrow$; $\mathbf{E}_x = 2025$ N $\leftarrow$, $\mathbf{E}_y = 600$ N $\uparrow$.

6.103 (a) $\mathbf{C}_x = 100.0$ lb $\leftarrow$, $\mathbf{C}_y = 100.0$ lb $\uparrow$; $\mathbf{D}_x = 100.0$ lb $\rightarrow$, $\mathbf{D}_y = 20.0$ lb $\downarrow$. (b) $\mathbf{E}_x = 100.0$ lb $\leftarrow$, $\mathbf{E}_y = 180.0$ lb $\uparrow$.

6.104 (a) $\mathbf{C}_x = 100.0$ lb $\leftarrow$, $\mathbf{C}_y = 60.0$ lb $\uparrow$; $\mathbf{D}_x = 100.0$ lb $\rightarrow$, $\mathbf{D}_y = 20.0$ lb $\uparrow$. (b) $\mathbf{E}_x = 100.0$ lb $\leftarrow$, $\mathbf{E}_y = 140.0$ lb $\uparrow$.

6.107 (a) $\mathbf{A}_x = 200$ kN $\rightarrow$, $\mathbf{A}_y = 122$ kN $\uparrow$. (b) $\mathbf{B}_x = 200$ kN $\leftarrow$, $\mathbf{B}_y = 10.00$ kN $\downarrow$.

6.108 (a) $\mathbf{A}_x = 205$ kN $\rightarrow$, $\mathbf{A}_y = 134.5$ kN $\uparrow$. (b) $\mathbf{B}_x = 205$ kN $\leftarrow$, $\mathbf{B}_y = 5.50$ kN $\uparrow$.

6.109 $\mathbf{B} = 98.5$ lb $\measuredangle\, 24.0°$; $\mathbf{C} = 90.6$ lb $\searptail\, 6.34°$.

6.110 (a) 301 lb $\searptail\, 48.4°$. (b) 375 lb T.

6.111 $F_{AG} = \sqrt{2}\,P/6\ C$; $F_{BF} = 2\sqrt{2}\,P/3\ C$; $F_{DI} = \sqrt{2}\,P/3\ C$; $F_{EH} = \sqrt{2}\,P/6\ T$.

6.113 $F_{AF} = P/4\ C$; $F_{BG} = F_{DG} = P/\sqrt{2}\ C$; $F_{EH} = P/4\ T$.

6.115 $F_{AF} = M_0/4a\ C$; $F_{BG} = F_{DG} = M_0/\sqrt{2}a\ T$; $F_{EH} = 3M_0/4a\ C$.

6.116 $F_{AF} = \sqrt{2}\,M_0/3a\ C$; $F_{BG} = M_0/a\ T$; $F_{DG} = M_0/a\ C$; $F_{EH} = 2\sqrt{2}\,M_0/3a\ T$.

6.117 $\mathbf{E} = P/5\ \downarrow$; $\mathbf{F} = 8P/5\ \uparrow$; $\mathbf{G} = 4P/5\ \downarrow$; $\mathbf{H} = 2P/5\ \uparrow$.

6.118 $\mathbf{A} = P/15\ \uparrow$; $\mathbf{D} = 2P/15\ \uparrow$; $\mathbf{E} = 8P/15\ \uparrow$; $\mathbf{H} = 4P/15\ \uparrow$.

6.119 (a) $\mathbf{A} = 2.06P\ \measuredangle\, 14.04°$; $\mathbf{B} = 2.06P\ \searptail\, 14.04°$; frame is rigid. (b) Frame is not rigid. (c) $\mathbf{A} = 1.25P\ \searptail\, 36.9°$; $\mathbf{B} = 1.031P\ \measuredangle\, 14.04°$; frame is rigid.

6.122 (a) $(F_{BD})_y = 96.0$ lb $\downarrow$ (b) $F_{BD} = 100.0$ lb $\measuredangle\, 73.7°$.

6.123 (a) $(F_{BD})_y = 240$ lb $\downarrow$ (b) $F_{BD} = 250$ lb $\measuredangle\, 73.7°$.

6.126 (a) 746 N $\downarrow$. (b) 565 N $\searptail\, 61.3°$.

6.127 (a) 302 N $\downarrow$. (b) 682 N $\searptail\, 61.3°$.

6.128 $T_{DE} = 81.0$ N; $\mathbf{B} = 216$ N $\downarrow$.

6.129 (a) 21.0 kN $\leftarrow$. (b) 52.5 kN $\leftarrow$.

6.130 (a) 1143 N $\cdot$ m $\downarrow$. (b) 457 N $\cdot$ m $\downarrow$.

6.131 832 lb $\cdot$ in. $\uparrow$.

6.132 360 lb $\cdot$ in. $\uparrow$.

6.133 195.0 kN $\cdot$ m $\downarrow$.

6.134 40.5 kN $\cdot$ m $\uparrow$.

6.137 208 N $\cdot$ m $\downarrow$.

6.138 18.43 N $\cdot$ m $\downarrow$.

6.139 $F_{AE} = 800$ N T; $F_{DG} = 100.0$ N C.

6.140 $\mathbf{P} = 120.0$ N $\downarrow$; $\mathbf{Q} = 110.0$ N $\leftarrow$.

6.142 $\mathbf{F} = 3290$ lb $\searptail\, 15.12°$; $\mathbf{D} = 4450$ lb $\leftarrow$.

6.143 $\mathbf{D} = 30.0$ kN $\leftarrow$; $\mathbf{F} = 37.5$ kN $\searptail\, 36.9°$.

6.144 $\mathbf{D} = 150.0$ kN $\leftarrow$; $\mathbf{F} = 96.4$ kN $\searptail\, 13.50°$.

6.145 (a) 475 lb. (b) 528 lb $\searptail\, 63.3°$.

6.146 44.8 kN.

6.148 8.45 kN.

6.149 25.0 lb $\downarrow$

6.150 10.00 lb $\downarrow$.

6.151 240 N.

6.154 (a) 14.11 kN $\searptail\, 19.10°$. (b) 19.79 kN $\searptail\, 47.6°$.

6.155 (a) 4.91 kips C. (b) 10.69 kips C.

6.156 (a) 2.86 kips C. (b) 9.43 kips C.

6.159 (a) $\mathbf{M}_0 = (90.0\ \text{N} \cdot \text{m})\mathbf{i}$. (b) $\mathbf{A} = 0$; $\mathbf{B} = 0$; $\mathbf{M}_B = -(72.0\ \text{N} \cdot \text{m})\mathbf{i}$.

6.160 (a) 27.0 mm. (b) 40.0 N $\cdot$ m $\downarrow$.

6.163 $\mathbf{E}_x = 100.0$ kN $\rightarrow$, $\mathbf{E}_y = 154.9$ kN $\uparrow$; $\mathbf{F}_x = 26.5$ kN $\rightarrow$, $\mathbf{F}_y = 118.1$ kN $\downarrow$; $\mathbf{H}_x = 126.5$ kN $\leftarrow$, $\mathbf{H}_y = 36.8$ kN $\downarrow$.

6.164 $F_{AB} = F_{AE} = 671$ lb T; $F_{AC} = F_{AD} = 1000$ lb C; $F_{BC} = F_{DE} = 600$ lb C; $F_{CD} = 200$ lb T.

6.166 $F_{FG} = 5.23$ kN C; $F_{EG} = 0.1476$ kN C; $F_{EH} = 5.08$ kN T.

6.167 $F_{KM} = 5.02$ kN T; $F_{LM} = 1.963$ kN C; $F_{LN} = 3.95$ kN C.

6.168 $\mathbf{A}_x = 25.0$ kips $\leftarrow$, $\mathbf{A}_y = 20.0$ kips $\uparrow$; $\mathbf{B}_x = 25.0$ kips $\leftarrow$, $\mathbf{B}_y = 10.00$ kips $\downarrow$; $\mathbf{C}_x = 50.0$ kips $\rightarrow$, $\mathbf{C}_y = 10.00$ kips $\downarrow$.

6.170 $\mathbf{A}_x = 150.0$ N $\leftarrow$, $\mathbf{A}_y = 250$ N $\uparrow$; $\mathbf{E}_x = 150.0$ N $\rightarrow$, $\mathbf{E}_y = 450$ N $\uparrow$.

6.171 $\mathbf{A} = 327$ lb $\rightarrow$; $\mathbf{B} = 827$ lb $\leftarrow$; $\mathbf{D} = 621$ lb $\uparrow$; $\mathbf{E} = 246$ lb $\uparrow$.

6.172 (a) $\mathbf{P} = 109.8$ N $\rightarrow$. (b) 126.8 N T, (c) 139.8 N $\searptail\, 38.3°$.

6.175 (a) 312 lb. (b) 135.0 lb $\cdot$ in. $\downarrow$.

6.C1 (a) $\theta = 30°$: $W = 472$ lb, $A_{AB} = 1.500$ in^2, $A_{AC} = A_{CE} = 1.299$ in^2, $A_{BC} = A_{BE} = 0.500$ in^2, $A_{BD} = 1.732$ in^2. (b) $\theta_{\text{opt}} = 56.8°$: $W = 312$ lb, $A_{AB} = 0.896$ in^2, $A_{AC} = A_{CE} = 0.491$ in^2, $A_{BC} = 0.500$ in^2, $A_{BE} = 0.299$ in^2, $A_{BD} = 0.655$ in^2.

6.C2 (a) For $x = 9.75$ m, $F_{BH} = 3.19$ kN T. (b) For $x = 3.75$ m, $F_{BH} = 1.313$ kN C. (c) For $x = 6$ m, $F_{GH} = 3.04$ kN T.

6.C3 $\theta = 30°$: $\mathbf{M} = 5860$ lb $\cdot$ ft $\uparrow$; $\mathbf{A} = 670$ lb $\measuredangle\, 75.5°$. (a) $M_{\text{max}} = 8680$ lb $\cdot$ ft when $\theta = 65.9°$. (b) $A_{\text{max}} = 1436$ lb when $\theta = 68.5°$.

6.C4 $\theta = 30°$: $\mathbf{M}_A = 1.669$ N $\cdot$ m, $F = 11.79$ N. $\theta = 80°$: $\mathbf{M}_A = 3.21$ N $\cdot$ m $\uparrow$, $F = 11.98$ N.

6.C5 $d = 0.40$ in.: 634 lb C; $d = 0.55$ in.: 286 lb C; $d = 0.473$ in.: $F_{AB} = 500$ lb C.

6.C6 $\theta = 20°$: $M = 31.8$ N $\cdot$ m; $\theta = 75°$: $M = 12.75$ N $\cdot$ m; $\theta = 60.0°$: $M_{\text{min}} = 12.00$ N $\cdot$ m.

CHAPTER 7

7.1 $\mathbf{F} = 0$; $\mathbf{V} = 80.0$ lb $\uparrow$; $\mathbf{M} = 480$ lb $\cdot$ in. $\uparrow$.

7.2 $\mathbf{F} = 0$; $\mathbf{V} = 40.0$ lb $\uparrow$; $\mathbf{M} = 240$ lb $\cdot$ in. $\uparrow$.

7.3 $\mathbf{F} = 4.80$ kN $\leftarrow$; $\mathbf{V} = 1.400$ kN $\downarrow$; $\mathbf{M} = 1.380$ kN $\cdot$ m $\downarrow$.

7.4 $\mathbf{F} = 3.00$ kN $\leftarrow$; $\mathbf{V} = 0$; $\mathbf{M} = 0.600$ kN $\cdot$ m $\downarrow$.

7.7 (On AJ) $\mathbf{F} = 103.9$ N $\nwarrow$; $\mathbf{V} = 60.0$ N $\nearrow$; $\mathbf{M} = 18.71$ N $\cdot$ m $\downarrow$.

7.8 (On BK) $\mathbf{F} = 60.0$ N $\swarrow$; $\mathbf{V} = 103.9$ N $\searrow$; $\mathbf{M} = 10.80$ N $\cdot$ m $\uparrow$.

7.9 (On CJ) $\mathbf{F} = 23.6$ lb $\searrow$; $\mathbf{V} = 29.1$ lb $\swarrow$; $\mathbf{M} = 540$ lb $\cdot$ in. $\uparrow$.

7.10 (a) 30.0 lb at C. (b) 33.5 lb at B and D. (c) 960 lb $\cdot$ in. at C.

7.13 (On AJ) $\mathbf{F} = 194.6$ N $\searptail\, 60°$; $\mathbf{V} = 257$ N $\measuredangle\, 30°$; $\mathbf{M} = 24.7$ N $\cdot$ m $\downarrow$.

7.14 45.2 N $\cdot$ m for $\theta = 82.9°$.

7.15 (a) $\mathbf{F} = 500$ N $\leftarrow$; $\mathbf{V} = 500$ N $\uparrow$; $\mathbf{M} = 300$ N $\cdot$ m $\downarrow$. (b) $\mathbf{F} = 970$ N $\uparrow$; $\mathbf{V} = 171.0$ N $\leftarrow$; $\mathbf{M} = 446$ N $\cdot$ m $\downarrow$.

7.16 (a) $\mathbf{F} = 500$ N $\leftarrow$; $\mathbf{V} = 500$ N $\uparrow$; $\mathbf{M} = 300$ N $\cdot$ m $\downarrow$. (b) $\mathbf{F} = 933$ N $\uparrow$; $\mathbf{V} = 250$ N $\leftarrow$; $\mathbf{M} = 375$ N $\cdot$ m $\downarrow$.

7.17 (On BJ) $\mathbf{F} = 200$ N $\searrow$; $\mathbf{V} = 120.0$ N $\nearrow$; $\mathbf{M} = 120.0$ N $\cdot$ m $\uparrow$.

7.18 (On AK) $\mathbf{F} = 520$ N $\leftarrow$; $\mathbf{V} = 120.0$ N $\downarrow$; $\mathbf{M} = 96.0$ N $\cdot$ m $\downarrow$.

7.19 150.0 lb $\cdot$ in. at D.

7.20 105.0 lb $\cdot$ in. at E.

7.23 (On BJ) $0.289Wr$ $\uparrow$.

7.24 (On BJ) $0.417Wr$ $\uparrow$.

7.27 $0.1009Wr$ for $\theta = 57.3°$.

7.28 $0.357Wr$ for $\theta = 49.3°$.

7.29 (b) $|V|_{\text{max}} = 2P$; $|M|_{\text{max}} = 3Pa$.

7.30 (b) $|V|_{\text{max}} = 2P/3$; $|M|_{\text{max}} = 2PL/9$.

7.31 (b) $wL/4$; $3wL^2/32$.

7.32 (b) $wL/2$; $3wL^2/8$.

7.35 (b) $|V|_{\text{max}} = 35.0$ kN; $|M|_{\text{max}} = 12.50$ kN $\cdot$ m.

7.36 (b) $|V|_{\text{max}} = 50.5$ kN; $|M|_{\text{max}} = 39.8$ kN $\cdot$ m.

7.39 (b) $|V|_{\text{max}} = 64.0$ kN; $|M|_{\text{max}} = 92.0$ kN $\cdot$ m.

7.40 (b) $|V|_{\text{max}} = 60.0$ kN; $|M|_{\text{max}} = 72.0$ kN $\cdot$ m.

7.41 (b) $|V|_{\text{max}} = 18.00$ kips; $|M|_{\text{max}} = 48.5$ kip $\cdot$ ft.

7.42 (b) $|V|_{\text{max}} = 15.30$ kips; $|M|_{\text{max}} = 46.8$ kip $\cdot$ ft.

7.43 (b) $|V|_{\text{max}} = 1.800$ kN; $|M|_{\text{max}} = 0.225$ kN $\cdot$ m.

7.44 (b) $|V|_{\text{max}} = 2.00$ kN; $|M|_{\text{max}} = 0.500$ kN $\cdot$ m.

7.45 (a) $M \leq 0$ everywhere. (b) $|V|_{\text{max}} = 4.50$ kips; $|M|_{\text{max}} = 13.50$ kip $\cdot$ ft.

7.46 (a) $M \geq 0$ everywhere. (b) $|V|_{\text{max}} = 4.50$ kips; $|M|_{\text{max}} = 13.50$ kip $\cdot$ ft.

7.49 (a) $+400$ N; $+160.0$ N $\cdot$ m. (b) -200 N; $+40.0$ N $\cdot$ m.

7.52 $|V|_{max} = 7.50$ kips; $|M|_{max} = 7.20$ kip $\cdot$ ft.

7.53 $|V|_{max} = 165$ lb; $|M|_{max} = 1625$ lb $\cdot$ in.

7.54 $|V|_{max} = 800$ N; $|M|_{max} = 180.0$ N $\cdot$ m.

7.55 (a) $54.5°$. (b) 675 N $\cdot$ m.

7.56 (a) 0.311 m. (b) 193.0 N $\cdot$ m.

7.57 (a) 1.236. (b) $0.1180wa^2$.

7.58 $a = 0.207L$

7.59 (a) 40.0 kips, (b) 40.0 kip $\cdot$ ft.

7.62 (a) $0.414wL$; $0.0858wL^2$. (b) $0.250wL$; $0.250wL^2$.

7.63 $|V|_{max} = 2P$; $|M|_{max} = 3Pa$

7.69 $|V|_{max} = 7.20$ kN; $|M|_{max} = 5.76$ kN $\cdot$ m.

7.70 $|V|_{max} = 720$ N; $|M|_{max} = 164.0$ N $\cdot$ m.

7.72 $|V|_{max} = 60.0$ kN; $|M|_{max} = 72.0$ kN $\cdot$ m.

7.77 (b) 9.00 kN $\cdot$ m, 1.700 m from A.

7.78 (b) 26.4 kN $\cdot$ m, 2.05 m from A.

7.79 (b) 45.0 kip $\cdot$ ft, 12.00 ft from A.

7.80 (b) 12.00 kip $\cdot$ ft, 6.00 ft from A.

7.83 (b) 40.5 kN $\cdot$ m, 1.800 m from A.

7.84 (b) 60.5 kN $\cdot$ m, 2.20 m from A.

7.85 (a) $V = (w_0/6L)(3x^2 - 6Lx + 2L^2)$;
$M = (w_0/6L)(x^3 - 3Lx^2 + 2L^2x)$.
(b) $0.0642w_0L^2$, at $x = 0.423L$.

7.86 (a) $V = (w_0/3L)(2x^2 - 3Lx + L^2)$;
$M = (w_0/18L)(4x^3 - 9Lx^2 + 6L^2x - L^3)$.
(b) $w_0L^2/72$, at $x = L/2$.

7.89 (a) $\mathbf{P} = 4.00$ kN $\downarrow$; $\mathbf{Q} = 6.00$ kN $\downarrow$. (b) $M_C = -900$ N $\cdot$ m.

7.90 (a) $\mathbf{P} = 2.50$ kN $\downarrow$; $\mathbf{Q} = 7.50$ kN $\downarrow$. (b) $M_C = -900$ N $\cdot$ m.

7.91 (a) $\mathbf{P} = 1.350$ kips $\downarrow$; $\mathbf{Q} = 0.450$ kips $\downarrow$.
(b) $V_{max} = 2.70$ kips at A; $M_{max} = 6.345$ kip $\cdot$ ft,
5.40 ft from A.

7.92 (a) $\mathbf{P} = 0.540$ kips $\downarrow$; $\mathbf{Q} = 1.860$ kips $\downarrow$.
(b) $|V|_{max} = 3.14$ kips at B; $M_{max} = 6.997$ kip $\cdot$ ft,
6.88 ft from A.

7.93 (a) 2.28 m. (b) $\mathbf{D}_x = 13.67$ kN $\rightarrow$; $\mathbf{D}_y = 7.80$ kN $\uparrow$.
(c) 15.94 kN.

7.94 (a) 1.959 m. (b) 2.48 m.

7.95 (a) 838 lb $\searrow$ $17.4°$. (b) 971 lb $\measuredangle$ $34.5°$.

7.96 (a) 2670 lb $\nearrow$ $2.10°$. (b) 2810 lb $\measuredangle$ $18.6°$.

7.97 (a) $d_B = 1.733$ m; $d_D = 4.20$ m. (b) 21.5 kN $\measuredangle$ $3.81°$.

7.98 (a) 2.80 m. (b) $\mathbf{A} = 32.0$ kN $\searrow$ $38.7°$; $\mathbf{E} = 25.0$ kN $\rightarrow$.

7.101 (a) 48.0 lb. (b) 10.00 ft.

7.102 (a) 12.50 ft. (b) 5.00 ft.

7.103 196.2 N.

7.104 157.0 N.

7.107 (a) 138.1 m. (b) 602 N.

7.108 (a) 6.75 m. (b) $T_{AB} = 615$ N; $T_{BC} = 600$ N.

7.109 (a) $56,400$ kips. (b) 4280 ft.

7.110 (a) $50,200$ kips. (b) 3580 ft.

7.113 (a) $\sqrt{3L\Delta/8}$. (b) 12.25 ft.

7.114 3.75 ft.

7.115 (a) 58900 kips. (b) $29.2°$.

7.116 (a) 16.00 ft to the left of B. (b) 2000 lb.

7.117 (a) 5880 N. (b) 0.873 m.

7.118 (a) 6860 N. (b) $31.0°$.

7.125 $y = h[1 - \cos(\pi x/L)]$; $T_0 = w_0L^2/h\pi^2$;
$T_{max} = (w_0L/\pi)\sqrt{(L^2/h^2\pi^2) + 1}$.

7.127 (a) 26.7 m. (b) 70.3 kg.

7.128 199.5 ft

7.129 (a) 164.8 m. (b) 4290 N.

7.130 330 ft; 625 lb.

7.133 (a) 5.89 m. (b) 10.89 N $\rightarrow$.

7.134 10.05 ft.

7.135 (a) 30.2 m. (b) 56.6 kg.

7.136 (a) 56.3 ft. (b) 2.36 lb/ft.

7.139 31.8 N.

7.140 29.8 N.

7.141 (a) $a = 79.0$ ft; $b = 60.0$ ft. (b) 103.9 ft.

7.142 (a) $a = 65.8$ ft; $b = 50.0$ ft. (b) $= 86.6$ ft.

7.143 119.1 N $\rightarrow$.

7.144 177.6 N $\rightarrow$.

7.147 3.50 ft.

7.148 5.71 ft.

7.151 0.394 m and 10.97 m.

7.152 0.1408.

7.153 (a) 0.338. (b) $56.5°$; $0.755wL$.

7.154 (a) 1500 N. (b) (On ABJ) $\mathbf{F} = 1324$ N $\uparrow$;
$\mathbf{V} = 706$ N $\leftarrow$; $\mathbf{M} = 229$ N $\cdot$ m $\uparrow$.

7.155 (On BJ) $\mathbf{F} = 250$ N $\searrow$; $\mathbf{V} = 120.0$ N $\nearrow$; $\mathbf{M} = 120.0$ N $\cdot$ m $\uparrow$.

7.156 (a) (On AC) $\mathbf{F} = \mathbf{V} = 0$; $\mathbf{M} = 450$ lb $\cdot$ ft $\uparrow$.
(b) (On AC) $\mathbf{F} = 250$ lb $\swarrow$; $\mathbf{V} = 0$; $\mathbf{M} = 450$ lb $\cdot$ ft $\uparrow$.

7.157 (a) 90.0 lb. (b) 900 lb $\cdot$ in.

7.159 (b) 41.4 kN; 35.3 kN $\cdot$ m.

7.160 (a) 12.00 kip $\cdot$ ft, at C. (b) 6.25 kip $\cdot$ ft, 2.50 ft from A.

7.162 (a) 1229 lb. (b) 11.00 ft.

7.164 (a) 2770 N. (b) 75.14 m.

7.C1 (a) $M_D = +39.8$ kN $\cdot$ m. (b) $M_D = +14.00$ kip $\cdot$ ft.
(c) $M_D = +1800$ lb $\cdot$ in.

7.C3 $a = 1.923$ m; $M_{max} = 37.0$ kN $\cdot$ m at 4.64 m from A.

7.C4 (b) $M_{max} = 5.42$ kip $\cdot$ ft when $x = 8.5$ ft and 11.5 ft.

7.C8 $c/L = 0.300$: $h/L = 0.5225$; $s_{AB}/L = 1.532$;
$T_0/wL = 0.300$; $T_{max}/wL = 0.823$.

CHAPTER 8

8.1 Equilibrium; $\mathbf{F} = 34.5$ lb $\searrow$.

8.2 Block moves; $\mathbf{F} = 55.7$ lb $\nwarrow$.

8.3 Equilibrium; $\mathbf{F} = 48.3$ N $\nwarrow$.

8.4 Block moves; $\mathbf{F} = 103.5$ N $\nwarrow$.

8.5 225 N $\leq P \leq 479$ N.

8.6 143.0 N $\leq P \leq 483$ N.

8.7 (a) 105.8 N. (b) $46.0°$.

8.9 (a) 403 N. (b) 229 N.

8.11 (a) 353 N $\leftarrow$. (b) 196.2 N $\leftarrow$.

8.12 (a) 275 N $\leftarrow$. (b) 196.2 N $\leftarrow$.

8.15 (a) 36.0 lb $\rightarrow$. (b) 30.0 lb. (c) 12.86 lb $\rightarrow$.

8.16 (a) 36.0 lb $\rightarrow$. (b) 40.0 in.

8.17 $M = Wr\mu_s(1 + \mu_s)/(1 + \mu_s^2)$.

8.18 (a) $0.300Wr$. (b) $0.349Wr$.

8.19 151.5 N $\cdot$ m.

8.20 1.473 kN.

8.21 0.208.

8.23 (a) $136.4°$. (b) $0.928W$.

8.25 0.750.

8.26 0.860.

8.27 132.9 lb $\downarrow$.

8.28 (a) 112.5 N. (b) 8.81 mm.

8.29 $3.46 \leq \dfrac{L}{a} \leq 13.63$.

8.30 (a) Plate in equilibrium. (b) Plate moves downward.

8.31 10.00 lb $< P < 36.7$ lb.

8.34 135.0 lb.

8.36 168.4 N $\leq P \leq 308$ N.

8.37 9.38 N $\cdot$ m $\leq M \leq 15.01$ N $\cdot$ m.

8.38 -46.8 N $\leq P \leq 34.3$ N.
8.39 (b) 2.69 lb.
8.41 0.0949.
8.42 (a) System slides; $P = 62.8$ N.
(b) System rotates about B; $P = 73.2$ N.
8.43 35.8°.
8.44 20.5°.
8.45 1.225W.
8.46 (a) $\mathbf{P} = 56.6$ lb ←. (b) $\mathbf{B}_x = 82.6$ lb ←; $\mathbf{B}_y = 96.0$ lb ↓.
8.47 (a) $\mathbf{P} = 21.4$ lb →. (b) $\mathbf{B}_x = 122.2$ lb ←; $\mathbf{B}_y = 96.0$ lb ↓.
8.48 $\mathbf{P} = 2080$ N ↓.
8.49 $\mathbf{P} = 1966$ N ↓.
8.52 (a) 62.7 lb. (b) 62.7 lb.
8.53 9.86 kN ←.
8.54 913 N ←.
8.55 (a) 28.1°. (b) 728 N $\measuredangle$ 14.04°.
8.56 29.9 lb.
8.57 67.4 N.
8.60 (b) 283 N ←.
8.61 0.442.
8.62 (a) 90.0 lb. (b) Base moves.
8.63 (a) 89.4 lb. (b) Base does not move.
8.64 0.1103.
8.65 0.1013.
8.69 1068 N · m.
8.70 4.18 N · m.
8.72 169.7 lb · in.
8.73 32.7 lb · in.
8.75 0.0980.
8.76 450 N.
8.77 412 N.
8.78 344 N.
8.79 376 N.
8.80 0.226.
8.82 $T_{AB} = 77.5$ lb; $T_{CD} = 72.5$ lb; $T_{EF} = 67.8$ lb.
8.85 22.0 lb ←.
8.86 1.948 lb ↓.
8.87 18.01 lb ←.
8.88 (a) 4.80 kN. (b) 1.375°.
8.90 3.75 lb.
8.91 0.1670.
8.96 154.4 N.
8.97 0.0600 in.
8.98 10.87 lb.
8.99 (a) 1.288 kN. (b) 1.058 kN.
8.100 300 mm.
8.101 (a) 0.329. (b) 2.67 turns.
8.102 (a) 22.8 kg. (b) 291 N.
8.103 (a) 109.7 kg. (b) 828 N.
8.104 73.0 lb $\leq P \leq$ 1233 lb.
8.107 35.1 N · m
8.108 (a) 27.0 N · m (b) 675 N.
8.109 (a) 39.0 N · m. (b) 844 N.
8.110 421 lb · in.
8.111 301 lb · in.
8.112 44.9 N · m ↑.
8.115 4.49 in.
8.116 (a) 11.66 kg. (b) 38.6 kg. (c) 34.4 kg.
8.117 (a) 9.46 kg. (b) 167.2 kg. (c) 121.0 kg.
8.120 (a) 10.39 lb. (b) 58.5 lb.
8.121 (a) and (b) 28.9 lb.
8.122 5.97 N.

8.123 9.56 N.
8.124 (a) 30.3 lb · in ↑. (b) 3.78 lb ↓.
8.125 (a) 17.23 lb · in ↓. (b) 2.15 lb ↑.
8.126 0.350.
8.131 (a) 51.0 N · m. (b) 875 N.
8.132 (a) 170.5 N. (b) 14.04°.
8.133 53.5°.
8.135 $6.35 \leq L/a \leq 10.81$.
8.136 0.0533.
8.138 0.225.
8.139 (a) 620 N ←. (b) $\mathbf{B}_x = 1390$ N ←; $\mathbf{B}_y = 1050$ N ↓.
8.140 (a) and (b) 50.4 lb.
8.142 (a) 0.238. (b) 218 N ↓.
8.C1 $x = 500\ mm$: 63.3 N; $P_{max} = 67.8$ N at $x = 355$ mm.
8.C2 $W_B = 10\ lb$: $\theta = 46.4°$; $W_B = 70\ lb$: $\theta = 21.3°$.
8.C3 $\mu_A = 0.25$: $M = 0.0603$ N · m.
8.C4 $\theta = 30°$: 1.336 N · m $\leq M_A \leq 2.23$ N · m.
8.C5 $\theta = 60°$: $\mathbf{P} = 16.40$ lb ↓; $R = 5.14$ lb.
8.C6 $\theta = 20°$: 10.39 N · m.
8.C7 $\theta = 20°$: 30.3 lb; 13.25 lb.
8.C8 (a) $x_0 = 0.600L$; $x_m = 0.604L$; $\theta_1 = 5.06°$. (b) $\theta_2 = 55.4°$.

CHAPTER 9

9.1 $b^3h/12$.
9.2 $3a^4/2$.
9.3 $2a^3b/15$.
9.4 $ha^3/5$.
9.6 $a^4/8$.
9.7 $2ab^3/7$.
9.9 $ab^3/15$.
9.10 $0.1056ab^3$.
9.11 $ab^3/15$.
9.12 $2a^3b/21$.
9.15 $ab^3/10$; $b/\sqrt{5}$.
9.16 $3ab^3/35$; $b\sqrt{9/35}$.
9.17 $a^3b/6$; $a/\sqrt{3}$.
9.18 $3a^3b/35$; $a\sqrt{9/35}$.
9.21 $20a^4$; $1.826a$.
9.22 $43a^4/48$; $0.773a$.
9.23 $(\pi/2)(R_2^4 - R_1^4)$; $(\pi/4)(R_2^4 - R_1^4)$.
9.24 (b) for $t/R_m = 1$, -10.56%; for $t/R_m = \frac{1}{2}$, $-2,99\%$, for $t/R_m = \frac{1}{10}$, -0.1250%.
9.25 $64a^4/15$; $1.265a$.
9.28 $bh(12h^2 + b^2)/48$; $\sqrt{(12h^2 + b^2)/24}$.
9.31 390×10^3 mm^4; 21.9 mm.
9.32 46.0 in^4; 1.599 in.
9.33 64.3×10^3 mm^4; 8.87 mm.
9.34 46.5 in^4; 1.607 in.
9.37 $I = 9.50 \times 10^6$ mm^4; $d_2 = 60.0$ mm.
9.38 $A = 6600$ mm^2; $\bar{I} = 3.72 \times 10^6$ mm^4.
9.39 $\bar{I}_x = 150.0$ in^4; $\bar{I}_y = 300$ in^4.
9.41 $\bar{I}_x = 1.874 \times 10^6$ mm^4; $\bar{I}_y = 5.82 \times 10^6$ mm^4.
9.42 $\bar{I}_x = 48.9 \times 10^3$ mm^4; $\bar{I}_y = 8.35 \times 10^3$ mm^4.
9.43 $\bar{I}_x = 191.3$ in^4; $\bar{I}_y = 75.2$ in^4.
9.44 $\bar{I}_x = 18.13$ in^4; $\bar{I}_y = 4.51$ in^4.
9.45 (a) 80.9×10^6 mm^4. (b) 57.4×10^6 mm^4.
9.46 (a) 12.16×10^6 mm^4. (b) 9.73×10^6 mm^4.
9.49 $\bar{I}_x = 260 \times 10^6$ mm^4; $\bar{k}_x = 144.6$ mm; $\bar{I}_y = 17.53 \times 10^6$ mm^4; $\bar{k}_y = 37.6$ mm.
9.50 $\bar{I}_x = 254$ in^4; $\bar{k}_x = 4.00$ in.; $\bar{I}_y = 102.1$ in^4; $\bar{k}_y = 2.54$ in.

9.51 $\bar{I}_x = 255 \times 10^6 \text{ mm}^4$; $\bar{k}_x = 134.1 \text{ mm}$; $\bar{I}_y = 100.0 \times 10^6 \text{ mm}^4$; $\bar{k}_y = 83.9 \text{ mm}$.

9.52 1.077 in.

9.53 $\bar{I}_{x'} = 3.55 \times 10^6 \text{ mm}^4$; $\bar{I}_y = 49.8 \times 10^6 \text{ mm}^4$.

9.55 $\bar{I}_x = 745 \times 10^6 \text{ mm}^4$; $\bar{I}_y = 91.3 \times 10^6 \text{ mm}^4$.

9.57 $3\pi r/16$.

9.58 $3\pi b/16$.

9.59 $15h/14$.

9.60 $4h/7$.

9.63 $5a/8$.

9.64 80.0 mm.

9.67 $a^4/2$.

9.68 $a^2 b^2/12$.

9.69 $-b^2 h^2/8$.

9.71 $-1.760 \times 10^6 \text{ mm}^4$.

9.72 $-21.6 \times 10^6 \text{ mm}^4$.

9.74 -0.380 in^4.

9.75 $471 \times 10^3 \text{ mm}^4$.

9.76 -9010 in^4.

9.78 $1.165 \times 10^6 \text{ mm}^4$.

9.79 (a) $\bar{I}_{x'} = 0.482a^4$; $\bar{I}_{y'} = 1.482a^4$; $\bar{I}_{x'y'} = -0.589a^4$. (b) $\bar{I}_{x'} = 1.120a^4$; $\bar{I}_{y'} = 0.843a^4$; $\bar{I}_{x'y'} = 0.760a^4$.

9.80 $\bar{I}_{x'} = 103.5 \times 10^6 \text{ mm}^4$; $\bar{I}_{y'} = 97.9 \times 10^6 \text{ mm}^4$; $\bar{I}_{x'y'} = -38.3 \times 10^6 \text{ mm}^4$.

9.81 $\bar{I}_{x'} = 1033 \text{ in}^4$; $\bar{I}_{y'} = 2020 \text{ in}^4$; $\bar{I}_{x'y'} = -873 \text{ in}^4$.

9.83 $\bar{I}_{x'} = 0.236 \text{ in}^4$; $\bar{I}_{y'} = 1.244 \text{ in}^4$; $\bar{I}_{x'y'} = 0.1132 \text{ in}^4$.

9.85 $20.2°$; $1.754a^4$, $0.209a^4$.

9.86 $-17.11°$; $139.1 \times 10^6 \text{ mm}^4$, $62.3 \times 10^6 \text{ mm}^4$.

9.87 $29.7°$; 2530 in^4, 524 in^4.

9.89 $-23.7°$ and $66.3°$; 1.257 in^4, 0.224 in^4.

9.91 (a) $\bar{I}_{x'} = 0.482a^4$; $\bar{I}_{y'} = 1.482a^4$; $\bar{I}_{x'y'} = -0.589a^4$. (b) $\bar{I}_{x'} = 1.120a^4$; $\bar{I}_{y'} = 0.843a^4$; $\bar{I}_{x'y'} = 0.760a^4$.

9.92 $\bar{I}_{x'} = 103.5 \times 10^6 \text{ mm}^4$; $\bar{I}_{y'} = 97.9 \times 10^6 \text{ mm}^4$; $\bar{I}_{x'y'} = -38.3 \times 10^6 \text{ mm}^4$.

9.93 $\bar{I}_{x'} = 1033 \text{ in}^4$; $\bar{I}_{y'} = 2020 \text{ in}^4$; $\bar{I}_{x'y'} = -873 \text{ in}^4$.

9.95 $\bar{I}_{x'} = 0.236 \text{ in}^4$; $\bar{I}_{y'} = 1.244 \text{ in}^4$; $\bar{I}_{x'y'} = 0.1132 \text{ in}^4$.

9.97 $20.2°$; $1.754a^4$, $0.209a^4$.

9.98 $-17.11°$; $139.1 \times 10^6 \text{ mm}^4$, $62.3 \times 10^6 \text{ mm}^4$.

9.99 $-33.4°$; $22.1 \times 10^3 \text{ in}^4$, 2490 in^4.

9.100 $29.7°$; 2530 in^4, 524 in^4.

9.103 (a) -1.146 in^4. (b) $29.1°$ clockwise. (c) 3.39 in^4.

9.104 $23.8°$ clockwise; $0.524 \times 10^6 \text{ mm}^4$, $0.0917 \times 10^6 \text{ mm}^4$.

9.105 $19.54°$ counterclockwise; $4.34 \times 10^6 \text{ mm}^4$, $0.647 \times 10^6 \text{ mm}^4$.

9.106 (a) $25.3°$. (b) 1459 in^4, 40.5 in^4.

9.107 (a) $88.0 \times 10^6 \text{ mm}^4$. (b) $96.3 \times 10^6 \text{ mm}^4$, $39.7 \times 10^6 \text{ mm}^4$.

9.111 (a) $m(r_1^2 + r_2^2)/4$. (b) $m(r_1^2 + r_2^2)/2$.

9.112 (a) $0.0699ma^2$. (b) $0.320ma^2$.

9.113 (a) $25mr_2^2/64$. (b) $0.1522mr_2^2$.

9.114 (a) $mb^2/7$. (b) $m(7a^2 + 10b^2)/70$.

9.115 (a) $ma^2/3$. (b) $3ma^2/2$.

9.116 (a) $7ma^2/6$. (b) $ma^2/2$.

9.119 $1.329mh^2$.

9.120 $m(3a^2 + L^2)/12$.

9.121 (a) $0.241mh^2$. (b) $m(3a^2 + 0.1204h^2)$.

9.122 $m(b^2 + h^2)/10$.

9.124 $m(a^2 + b^2)/5$.

9.125 $I_x = I_y = ma^2/4$; $I_z = ma^2/2$.

9.127 $837 \times 10^{-9} \text{ kg} \cdot \text{m}^2$; 6.92 mm.

9.128 $1.160 \times 10^{-6} \text{ lb} \cdot \text{ft} \cdot \text{s}^2$; 0.341 in.

9.129 $m(3a^2 + 2h^2)/6$.

9.131 (a) 27.5 mm to the right of A. (b) 32.0 mm.

9.133 (a) 2.30 in. (b) $20.6 \times 10^{-3} \text{ lb} \cdot \text{ft} \cdot \text{s}^2$; 2.27 in.

9.134 (a) $\pi \rho l^2 \left[6a^2 t \left(\dfrac{5a^2}{3l^2} + \dfrac{2a}{l} + 1 \right) + \dfrac{d^2 l}{4} \right]$. (b) 0.1851.

9.135 $I_x = 26 \times 10^{-3} \text{ kg} \cdot \text{m}^2$; $I_y = 38.2 \times 10^{-3} \text{ kg} \cdot \text{m}^2$; $I_z = 17.55 \times 10^{-3} \text{ kg} \cdot \text{m}^2$.

9.136 $I_x = 175.5 \times 10^{-3} \text{ kg} \cdot \text{m}^2$; $I_y = 309 \times 10^{-3} \text{ kg} \cdot \text{m}^2$; $I_z = 154.4 \times 10^{-3} \text{ kg} \cdot \text{m}^2$.

9.137 $I_x = 745 \times 10^{-6} \text{ lb} \cdot \text{ft} \cdot \text{s}^2$; $I_y = 896 \times 10^{-6} \text{ lb} \cdot \text{ft} \cdot \text{s}^2$; $I_z = 304 \times 10^{-6} \text{ lb} \cdot \text{ft} \cdot \text{s}^2$.

9.138 $I_x = 344 \times 10^{-6} \text{ lb} \cdot \text{ft} \cdot \text{s}^2$; $I_y = 132.1 \times 10^{-6} \text{ lb} \cdot \text{ft} \cdot \text{s}^2$; $I_z = 453 \times 10^{-6} \text{ lb} \cdot \text{ft} \cdot \text{s}^2$.

9.141 (a) $13.99 \times 10^{-3} \text{ kg} \cdot \text{m}^2$. (b) $20.6 \times 10^{-3} \text{ kg} \cdot \text{m}^2$. (c) $14.30 \times 10^{-3} \text{ kg} \cdot \text{m}^2$.

9.142 $0.1785 \text{ lb} \cdot \text{ft} \cdot \text{s}^2$.

9.144 $I_x = 38.1 \times 10^{-3} \text{ kg} \cdot \text{m}^2$; $k_x = 110.7 \text{ mm}$.

9.145 (a) $26.4 \times 10^{-3} \text{ kg} \cdot \text{m}^2$. (b) $31.2 \times 10^{-3} \text{ kg} \cdot \text{m}^2$. (c) $8.58 \times 10^{-3} \text{ kg} \cdot \text{m}^2$.

9.147 $I_x = 0.0392 \text{ lb} \cdot \text{ft} \cdot \text{s}^2$; $I_y = 0.0363 \text{ lb} \cdot \text{ft} \cdot \text{s}^2$; $I_z = 0.0304 \text{ lb} \cdot \text{ft} \cdot \text{s}^2$.

9.148 $I_x = 0.323 \text{ kg} \cdot \text{m}^2$; $I_y = I_z = 0.419 \text{ kg} \cdot \text{m}^2$.

9.149 $I_{xy} = 2.50 \times 10^{-3} \text{ kg} \cdot \text{m}^2$; $I_{yz} = 4.06 \times 10^{-3} \text{ kg} \cdot \text{m}^2$; $I_{zx} = 8.81 \times 10^{-3} \text{ kg} \cdot \text{m}^2$.

9.150 $I_{xy} = 2.44 \times 10^{-3} \text{ kg} \cdot \text{m}^2$; $I_{yz} = 1.415 \times 10^{-3} \text{ kg} \cdot \text{m}^2$; $I_{zx} = 4.59 \times 10^{-3} \text{ kg} \cdot \text{m}^2$.

9.151 $I_{xy} = -538 \times 10^{-6} \text{ lb} \cdot \text{ft} \cdot \text{s}^2$; $I_{yz} = -171.4 \times 10^{-6} \text{ lb} \cdot \text{ft} \cdot \text{s}^2$; $I_{zx} = 1120 \times 10^{-6} \text{ lb} \cdot \text{ft} \cdot \text{s}^2$.

9.152 $I_{xy} = -1.726 \times 10^{-3} \text{ lb} \cdot \text{ft} \cdot \text{s}^2$; $I_{yz} = 0.507 \times 10^{-3} \text{ lb} \cdot \text{ft} \cdot \text{s}^2$; $I_{zx} = -2.12 \times 10^{-3} \text{ lb} \cdot \text{ft} \cdot \text{s}^2$.

9.155 $I_{xy} = -8.04 \times 10^{-3} \text{ kg} \cdot \text{m}^2$; $I_{yz} = 12.90 \times 10^{-3} \text{ kg} \cdot \text{m}^2$; $I_{zx} = 94.0 \times 10^{-3} \text{ kg} \cdot \text{m}^2$.

9.156 $I_{xy} = 0$; $I_{yz} = 48.3 \times 10^{-6} \text{ kg} \cdot \text{m}^2$; $I_{zx} = -4.43 \times 10^{-6} \text{ kg} \cdot \text{m}^2$.

9.157 $I_{xy} = wa^3(1 - 5\pi)/g$; $I_{yz} = -11\pi wa^3/g$; $I_{zx} = 4wa^3(1 + 2\pi)g$.

9.158 $I_{xy} = -11wa^3/g$; $I_{yz} = wa^3(\pi + 6)/2g$; $I_{zx} = -wa^3/4g$.

9.159 $I_{xy} = 47.9 \times 10^{-6} \text{ kg} \cdot \text{m}^2$; $I_{yz} = 102.1 \times 10^{-6} \text{ kg} \cdot \text{m}^2$; $I_{zx} = 64.1 \times 10^{-6} \text{ kg} \cdot \text{m}^2$.

9.160 $I_{xy} = -m'R_1^3/2$; $I_{yz} = m'R_1^3/2$; $I_{zx} = -m'R_2^3/2$.

9.162 (a) $mac/20$. (b) $I_{xy} = mab/20$; $I_{yz} = mbc/20$.

9.165 $18.17 \times 10^{-3} \text{ kg} \cdot \text{m}^2$.

9.166 $11.81 \times 10^{-3} \text{ kg} \cdot \text{m}^2$.

9.167 $5Wa^2/18g$.

9.168 $4.41\gamma ta^4/g$.

9.169 $281 \times 10^{-3} \text{ kg} \cdot \text{m}^2$.

9.170 $0.354 \text{ kg} \cdot \text{m}^2$.

9.173 (a) $b/a = 2$; $c/a = 2$. (b) $b/a = 1$; $c/a = 0.5$.

9.174 (a) 2. (b) $\sqrt{2/3}$.

9.175 (a) $1/\sqrt{3}$. (b) $\sqrt{7/12}$.

9.179 (a) $K_1 = 0.363ma^2$; $K_2 = 1.583ma^2$; $K_3 = 1.720ma^2$. (b) $(\theta_x)_1 = (\theta_z)_1 = 49.7°$, $(\theta_y)_1 = 113.7°$; $(\theta_x)_2 = 45.0°$, $(\theta_y)_2 = 90.0°$, $(\theta_z)_2 = 135.0°$; $(\theta_x)_3 = (\theta_z)_3 = 73.5°$, $(\theta_y)_3 = 23.7°$.

9.180 (a) $K_1 = 14.30 \times 10^{-3} \text{ kg} \cdot \text{m}^2$; $K_2 = 13.96 \times 10^{-3} \text{ kg} \cdot \text{m}^2$; $K_3 = 20.6 \times 10^{-3} \text{ kg} \cdot \text{m}^2$. (b) $(\theta_x)_1 = (\theta_y)_1 = 90.0°$, $(\theta_z)_1 = 0$; $(\theta_x)_2 = 3.42°$, $(\theta_y)_2 = 86.6°$, $(\theta_z)_2 = 90.0°$. $(\theta_x)_3 = 93.4°$, $(\theta_y)_3 = 3.43°$, $(\theta_z)_3 = 90.0°$.

9.182 (a) $K_1 = 0.1639Wa^2/g$; $K_2 = 1.054Wa^2/g$; $K_3 = 1.115Wa^2/g$. (b) $(\theta_x)_1 = 36.7°$, $(\theta_y)_1 = 71.6°$, $(\theta_z)_1 = 59.5°$; $(\theta_x)_2 = 74.9°$, $(\theta_y)_2 = 54.5°$, $(\theta_z)_2 = 140.5°$; $(\theta_x)_3 = 57.5°$, $(\theta_y)_3 = 138.8°$, $(\theta_z)_3 = 112.4°$.

9.183 (a) $K_1 = 2.26\gamma ta^4/g$; $K_2 = 17.27\gamma ta^4/g$; $K_3 = 19.08\gamma ta^4/g$.
(b) $(\theta_x)_1 = 85.0°$, $(\theta_y)_1 = 36.8°$, $(\theta_z)_1 = 53.7°$;
$(\theta_x)_2 = 81.7°$, $(\theta_y)_2 = 54.7°$, $(\theta_z)_2 = 143.4°$;
$(\theta_x)_3 = 9.70°$, $(\theta_y)_3 = 99.0°$, $(\theta_z)_3 = 86.3°$.

9.185 $I_x = ab^3/28$; $I_y = a^3b/20$.

9.187 $4a^3b/15$; $a/\sqrt{5}$.

9.188 $I_x = 4a^4$; $I_y = 16a^4/3$.

9.189 (a) 3.13×10^6 mm^4. (b) 2.41×10^6 mm^4.

9.190 $I_x = 634 \times 10^6$ mm^4; $I_y = 38.0 \times 10^6$ mm^4.

9.191 $I_{xy} = -2.81$ in^4.

9.193 (a) $7ma^2/18$. (b) $0.819ma^2$.

9.195 $I_x = 0.877$ kg $\cdot$ m^2; $I_y = 1.982$ kg $\cdot$ m^2; $I_z = 1.652$ kg $\cdot$ m^2.

9.C1 $\theta = 20°$: $I_{x'} = 14.20$ in^4, $I_{y'} = 3.15$ in^4, $I_{x'y'} = -3.93$ in^4.

9.C3 (a) $\bar{I}_{x'} = 371 \times 10^3$ mm^4, $\bar{I}_{y'} = 64.3 \times 10^3$ mm^4;
$\bar{k}_{x'} = 21.3$ mm, $\bar{k}_{y'} = 8.87$ mm. (b) $\bar{I}_{x'} = 40.4$ in^4,
$\bar{I}_{y'} = 46.5$ in^4; $\bar{k}_{x'} = 1.499$ in., $\bar{k}_{y'} = 1.607$ in.
(c) $\bar{k}_x = 2.53$ in., $\bar{k}_y = 1.583$ in. (d) $\bar{k}_x = 1.904$ in.,
$\bar{k}_y = 0.950$ in.

9.C5 (a) 5.99×10^{-3} kg $\cdot$ m^2. (b) 77.4×10^{-3} kg $\cdot$ m^2.

9.C6 (a) 74.0×10^{-6} lb $\cdot$ ft $\cdot$ s^2. (b) 645×10^{-6} lb $\cdot$ ft $\cdot$ s^2.
(c) 208×10^{-6} lb $\cdot$ ft $\cdot$ s^2.

CHAPTER 10

10.1 82.5 N $\downarrow$.

10.2 120 lb $\rightarrow$.

10.3 49.5 N $\cdot$ m $\downarrow$.

10.4 1200 lb $\cdot$ in. $\uparrow$.

10.7 (a) 60.0 N C, 8.00 mm $\downarrow$. (b) 300 N C, 40.0 mm $\downarrow$.

10.8 (a) 120.0 N C, 16.00 mm $\downarrow$. (b) 300 N C, 40.0 mm $\downarrow$.

10.9 $Q = 2P \sin\theta/\cos(\theta/2)$.

10.10 $Q = 2P \cos\theta/\cos(\theta/2)$.

10.11 $Q = (3P/2) \tan\theta$.

10.12 $Q = P[(l/a)\cos^3\theta - 1]$.

10.15 $M = \frac{1}{2}Wl \tan\alpha \sin\theta$.

10.16 $M = Pl/2 \tan\theta$.

10.17 $M = 7Pa \cos\theta$.

10.18 (a) $M = Pl \sin 2\theta$. (b) $M = 3Pl \cos\theta$. (c) $M = Pl \sin\theta$.

10.21 85.2 lb $\cdot$ ft $\downarrow$.

10.22 22.8 lb $\nearrow$ 70.0°.

10.24 36.4°.

10.25 38.7°.

10.26 68.0°.

10.28 19.81° and 51.9°.

10.30 25.0°.

10.31 39.7° and 69.0°.

10.32 52.2°.

10.33 40.2°.

10.35 22.6°.

10.36 51.1°.

10.37 52.4°.

10.38 19.40°.

10.39 59.0°.

10.40 78.7°, 324°, 379°.

10.43 12.03 kN $\searrow$.

10.44 20.4°.

10.45 2370 lb $\nwarrow$.

10.46 2550 lb $\nwarrow$.

10.47 $\eta = 1/(1 + \mu \cot\alpha)$

10.49 37.6 N, 31.6 N.

10.51 300 N $\cdot$ m, 81.8 N $\cdot$ m.

10.52 $\eta = \tan\theta/\tan(\theta + \phi_s)$.

10.53 7.75 kN $\uparrow$.

10.54 $H = 1.361$ kN $\uparrow$; $M_H = 550$ N $\cdot$ m $\uparrow$.

10.57 0.833 in. $\downarrow$.

10.58 0.625 in. $\rightarrow$.

10.66 19.40°.

10.67 Equilibrium is neutral.

10.69 $\theta = 0$ and $\theta = 180.0°$, unstable;
$\theta = 75.5°$ and $\theta = 284°$, stable.

10.70 $\theta = 90.0°$ and $\theta = 270°$ unstable;
$\theta = 22.0°$ and $\theta = 158.0°$, stable.

10.71 $\theta = -45.0°$, unstable; $\theta = 135.0°$, stable.

10.72 $\theta = -63.4°$, unstable; $\theta = 116.6°$, stable.

10.73 59.0°, stable.

10.74 78.7°, stable; 324°, unstable; 379°, stable.

10.78 9.39° and 90.0°, stable; 34.2°, unstable.

10.79 357 mm.

10.80 252 mm.

10.81 17.11°, stable; 72.9°, unstable.

10.83 49.1°.

10.85 54.8°.

10.86 37.4°.

10.88 16.88 m.

10.90 $k > 6.94$ lb/in.

10.91 15.00 in.

10.92 $P < 2kL/9$.

10.93 $P < kL/18$.

10.94 $P < k(l - a)^2/2l$.

10.96 $P < 160.0$ N.

10.98 $P < 764$ N.

10.100 (a) $P < 10.00$ lb. (b) $P < 20.0$ lb.

10.101 60.0 lb $\downarrow$.

10.102 600 lb $\cdot$ in. $\downarrow$.

10.104 (a) 20.0 N. (b) 105.0 N.

10.106 39.2°.

10.107 60.4°.

10.108 7.13 in.

10.110 (a) 0, unstable. (b) 137.8°, stable.

10.112 (a) 22.0°. (b) 30.6°.

10.C1 $\theta = 60°$: 2.42 in.; $\theta = 120°$: 1.732 in.;
$(M/P)_{max} = 2.52$ in. at $\theta = 73.7°$.

10.C2 $\theta = 60°$: 171.1 N C. For $32.5° \leq \theta \leq 134.3°$, $|F| \leq 400$ N.

10.C3 $\theta = 60°$: 296 N T. For $\theta \leq 125.7°$, $|F| \leq 400$ N.

10.C4 (b) $\theta = 60°$, datum at C: $V = -294$ in $\cdot$ lb.
(c) 34.2°, stable; 90°, unstable; 145.8°, stable

10.C5 (b) $\theta = 50°$, datum at E: $V = 100.5$ J. $dV/d\theta = 22.9$ J.
(c) $\theta = 0$, unstable; 30.4°.

10.C6 (b) $\theta = 60°$, datum at B: 30.0 J.
(c) $\theta = 0$, unstable; 41.4°, stable.

10.C7 (b) $\theta = 60°$, datum at $\theta = 0$: -37.0 J. (c) 52.2°, stable.